Financial Accounting
and Reporting

We work with leading authors to develop the strongest educational materials in business and finance, bringing cutting-edge thinking and best learning practice to a global market.

Under a range of well-known imprints, including Financial Times Prentice Hall, we craft high quality print and electronic publications which help readers to understand and apply their content, whether studying or at work.

To find out more about the complete range of our publishing please visit us on the World Wide Web at: www.pearsoneduc.com

Financial Accounting and Reporting

EIGHTH EDITION

Barry Elliott and Jamie Elliott

FT Prentice Hall
FINANCIAL TIMES

An imprint of **Pearson Education**

Harlow, England • London • New York • Boston • San Francisco • Toronto • Sydney • Singapore • Hong Kong
Tokyo • Seoul • Taipei • New Delhi • Cape Town • Madrid • Mexico City • Amsterdam • Munich • Paris • Milan

Pearson Education Limited

Edinburgh Gate
Harlow
Essex CM20 2JE
England

and Associated Companies throughout the world

Visit us on the World Wide Web at:
www.pearsoned.co.uk

First published 1993
Second edition 1996
Third edition 1999
Fourth edition 2000
Fifth edition 2001
Sixth edition 2002
Seventh edition 2003
Eighth edition 2004

© Prentice Hall International UK Limited 1993, 1999
© Pearson Education Limited 2000, 2004

The rights of Barry Elliott and Jamie Elliott to be identified as authors of this work have been asserted by them in accordance with the Copyright, Designs, and Patents Act 1988.

ISBN 0 273 68540-6

British Library Cataloguing-in-Publication Data
A catalogue record for this book is available from the British Library.

10 9 8 7 6 5 4 3 2 1
08 07 06 05 04

Typeset in 9/12pt Ehrhardt by 25.
Printed and bound in Great Britain by Bell & Bain Ltd., Glasgow

The publisher's policy is to use paper manufactured from sustainable forests.

Brief Contents

Full Contents

Preface and acknowledgements

Our objective is to provide a balanced and comprehensive framework to enable students to acquire the requisite knowledge and skills to appraise current practice critically and to evaluate proposed changes from a theoretical base. To this end, the text contains:

- current standards and exposure drafts
- illustrations from published accounts
- a range of review questions
- exercises of varying difficulty
- outline solutions to selected exercises in an appendix at the end of the book
- extensive references.

We have assumed that readers will have an understanding of financial accounting to a foundation or first-year level, although the text and exercises have been designed on the basis that a brief revision is still helpful.

Lecturers are using the text selectively to support a range of teaching programmes for 2nd and Final Year undergraduate and postgraduate programmes. We have therefore attempted to provide subject coverage of sufficient breadth and depth to assist selective use.

The text has been adopted for financial accounting, reporting and analysis modules on:

- second year undergraduate courses for Accounting, Business Studies and Combined Studies;
- final year undergraduate courses for Accounting, Business Studies and Combined Studies;
- MBA courses;
- specialist MSc courses; and
- professional courses preparing students for professional accountancy examinations.

Changes to the eighth edition

Our emphasis has been on keeping the text current and responding to constructive comments from reviewers on both the content and the order of the chapters.

The principal changes from the seventh edition are:

The past year has seen steady progress being made by regulators. The emphasis has been on the development of standards based on sound accounting principles and broad consultation but, given the political aspects, there has also had to be a measure of compromise on all sides.

- The ASB has issued Exposure Drafts based on proposed revisions to existing International Standards and fed back comments to the IASB to influence the final outcome. In some cases the ASB approach may prevail, e.g. in treatment of pensions and provisions whereas, in other cases it may have to accept an alternative approach, e.g. the banning of merger accounting and partial provisioning for deferred taxation.

- The IASB has been active in promoting dialogue with the FASB which has led to the USA considering a principles based approach and both sides taking steps to promote and maintain convergence.

The IASB is on course to produce revised IFRSs for listed companies for 2005.

In addition to the steps being taken towards the development of IFRSs that will receive broad consensus support, regulators have been active in developing further Corporate Governance requirements. These have been prompted by the accounting scandals in the USA and, more recently, in Europe and by shareholder activism fuelled by the apparent lack of any relationship between increases in directors' remuneration and company performance.

The content of financial reports continues to be subjected to discussion with a tension between preparers, stakeholders, auditors, academic accountants and standard setters; this is mirrored in the tension that exists between theory and practice.

- Preparers favour reporting transactions on a historical cost basis which is reliable but does not provide shareholders with relevant information to appraise past performance or to predict future earnings.

- Stakeholders favour forward looking reports relevant in estimating future dividend and capital growth and in understanding environmental and social impacts.

- Auditors favour reports that are verifiable so that the figures can be substantiated to avoid them being proved wrong at a later date.

- Academic accountants favour reports that reflect economic reality and are relevant in appraising management performance and in assessing the capacity of the company to adapt.

- Standard setters lean towards the academic view and favour reporting according to the commercial substance of a transaction.

In order to understand the tensions that exist, students need:

- the skill to prepare financial statements in accordance with the historical cost and current cost conventions, both of which appear in annual financial reports;

- an understanding of the main thrust of mandatory and voluntary standards;

- an understanding of the degree of flexibility available to the preparers and the impact of this on reported earnings and the balance sheet figures;

- an understanding of the limitations of these financial reports in portraying economic reality; and

- an exposure to source material and other published material in so far as time permits.

Instructor's Manual

A separate Instructor's Manual has been written to accompany this text. It contains fully worked solutions to all the exercises and is of a quality that allows them to be used as overhead transparencies. The Manual is available at no cost to lecturers on application to the publishers.

Website

An electronic version of the Manual is also available for download at www.booksites.net/ elliott_elliott.

Acknowledgements

Financial Reporting is a dynamic area and we see it as extremely important that the text should reflect this and be kept current. Assistance has been generously given by colleagues and many others in the preparation and review of the text and assessment material. This 8th edition is very much a result of the authors, colleagues, reviewers and Pearson editorial and production staff working as a team and we are grateful to all concerned for their assistance in achieving this.

We owe particular thanks to:

Sally Aisbitt of the Open University, who has updated her chapter 'International reporting and interpretation' (Chapter 28) which first appeared in the second edition.

Ron Altshul of the University of Sunderland, who has updated 'Taxation in company accounts' (Chapter 13).

Charles Batchelor of the Financial Training Company for 'Retirement benefits' (Chapter 12).

Steve Dungworth of De Montfort University, for 'Ethics for accountants' (Chapter 31) which first appeared in the third edition.

Ozer Erman of Kingston University, for 'Share capital, capital maintenance and distributable profits' (Chapter 9) and 'Reduction of share capital' (Chapter 10) which first appeared in the second edition.

Walter Hamilton, formerly of Sandwell College, for 'Foreign currency translation' (Chapter 22) which first appeared in the third edition.

Martin Howes for inputs to financial analysis.

Paul Robins of University of Wales College Newport for 'Financial Instruments' (Chapter 27) which first appeared in the seventh edition.

David Towers, formerly of Keele University, for 'Corporate Governance' (Chapter 29).

The authors are grateful for the constructive comments received from the following reviewers which have assisted us in making improvements: Iain Fleming of the University of Paisley, John Morley of the University of Brighton, John Forker of Queen's University, Belfast, Breda Sweeney of Cork University, Patricia McCourt Larres of Queen's University, Belfast and Dave Knight of Leeds Metropolitan University.

Thanks are owed to: A.T. Benedict of the South Bank University, Keith Brown of De Montfort University, Kenneth N. Field of the University of Leeds, Sue McDermott of London Guildhall University, David Murphy of Manchester Metropolitan University, Bahadur Najak of the University of Durham, Graham Sara of Coventry University, Laura

Spira of Oxford Brookes University, Ken Trunkfield, formerly of the University of Derby, and Martin Tuffy of the University of Brighton.

Thanks are also due to the following organisations: the Accounting Standards Board, the Association of Chartered Certified Accountants, the Chartered Institute of Management Accountants, the Institute of Chartered Accountants of Scotland, Chartered Institute of Public Finance and Accountancy, Chartered Institute of Bankers and the Institute of Investment Management and Research.

We would also like to thank the authors of some of the end-of-chapter exercises. Some of these exercises have been inherited from a variety of institutions with which we have been associated, and we have unfortunately lost the identities of the originators of such material with the passage of time. We are sorry that we cannot acknowledge them by name and hope that they will excuse us for using their material.

We are indebted to Paula Harris and Alison Stanford of Pearson Education for active support in keeping us largely to schedule and the attractively produced and presented text.

Finally we thank our wives, Di and Jacklin, for their continued good humoured support during the period of writing and revisions, and Giles Elliott for his critical comment at the commencement of the project. We alone remain responsible for any errors and for the thoughts and views that are expressed.

Barry and Jamie Elliott
June 2003

PART I

Income and asset value measurement systems

CHAPTER 1

Accounting and reporting on a cash flow basis

1.1 Introduction

Accountants are communicators. Accountancy is the art of communicating financial information about a business entity to users such as shareholders and managers. The communication is generally in the form of financial statements that show in money terms the economic resources under the control of the management. The art lies in selecting the information that is relevant to the user and is reliable.

Shareholders require periodic information that the managers are accounting properly for the resources under their control. This information helps the shareholders to evaluate the performance of the managers. The performance measured by the accountant shows the extent to which the economic resources of the business have grown or diminished during the year.

The shareholders also require information to **predict future performance**. At present companies are not required to publish forecast financial statements on a regular basis and the shareholders use the report of past performance when making their prediction.

Managers require information in order **to control the business and make investment decisions**.

In this chapter we will consider both categories of user, and the extent to which cash flow accounting would satisfy their information needs under the following headings:

- Shareholders
- What skills does an accountant require in respect of external reports?
- Managers
- What skills does an accountant require in respect of internal reports?
- Procedural steps when reporting to internal users
- Illustration of operating cash flows
- Illustration continued with statement of financial position
- Treatment of fixed assets in the cash flow model
- What are the characteristics of these data that make them reliable?
- Reports to external users.

1.2 Shareholders

Shareholders are external users. As such, they are unable to obtain access to the same amount of detailed historical information as the managers, e.g. total administration costs are disclosed in the published profit and loss account, but not an analysis to show how the figure is made up. Shareholders are also unable to obtain associated information, e.g. budgeted sales and costs. Even though the shareholders own a company, their entitlement to information is restricted.

The information to which shareholders are entitled is restricted to that specified by statute, e.g. the Companies Acts, or by professional regulation, e.g. Statements of Standard Accounting Practice, or by market regulations, e.g. Stock Exchange requirements. This means that there may be a tension between the **amount** of information that a shareholder would like to receive and the amount that the directors are prepared to provide. For example, shareholders might consider that forecasts of future cash flows would be helpful in predicting future dividends, but the directors might be concerned that such forecasts could help competitors or make directors open to criticism if forecasts are not met. As a result, this information is not disclosed.

There may also be a tension between the **quality** of information that shareholders would like to receive and that which directors are prepared to provide. For example, the shareholders might consider that judgements made by the directors in the valuation of long-term contracts should be fully explained, whereas the directors might prefer not to reveal this information given the high risk of error that often attaches to such estimates. In practice, companies tend to compromise: they do not reveal the judgements to the shareholders, but maintain confidence by relying on the auditor to give a clean audit report.

The financial reports presented to the shareholders are also used by other parties such as lenders and trade creditors, and they have come to be regarded as general-purpose reports. However, it may be difficult or impossible to satisfy the needs of all users. For example, users may have different time-scales – shareholders may be interested in the long-term trend of earnings over three years, whereas creditors may be interested in the likelihood of receiving cash within the next three months.

The information needs of the shareholders are regarded as the primary concern. The government perceives shareholders to be important because they provide companies with their economic resources. It is shareholders' needs that take priority in deciding on the nature and detailed content of the general-purpose reports.[1]

1.3 What skills does an accountant require in respect of external reports?

For external reporting purposes the accountant has a two-fold obligation:

- An obligation to ensure that the financial statements comply with statutory, professional and Stock Exchange requirements; this requires the accountant to possess **technical expertise**.

- An obligation to ensure that the financial statements present the substance of the commercial transactions the company has entered into; this requires the accountant to have **commercial awareness**.[2]

1.4 Managers

Managers are internal users. As such, they have access to detailed financial statements showing the current results, the extent to which these vary from the budgeted results and the future budgeted results. Examples of internal users are sole traders, partners and, in a company context, directors and managers.

There is no statutory restriction on the amount of information that an internal user may receive; the only restriction would be that imposed by the company's own policy. Frequently, companies operate a 'need to know' policy and only the directors see all the financial statements; employees, for example, would be most unlikely to receive information that would assist them in claiming a salary increase – unless, of course, it happened to be a time of recession, when information would be more freely provided by management as a means of containing claims for an increase.

1.5 What skills does an accountant require when preparing internal reports?

For the internal user, the accountant is able to tailor his or her reports. The accountant is required to produce financial statements that are specifically relevant to the user requesting them.

The accountant needs to be skilled in identifying the information that is needed and conveying its implication and meaning to the user. The user needs to be confident that the accountant understands the user's information needs and will satisfy them in a language that is understandable. The accountant must be a skilled communicator who is able to instil confidence in the user that the information is:

- relevant to the user's needs[3]
- measured objectively
- presented within a time-scale that permits decisions to be made with appropriate information
- verifiable, in that it can be confirmed that the report represents the transactions that have taken place
- reliable, in that it is as free from bias as is possible
- a complete picture of material items
- a fair representation of the business transactions and events that have occurred or are being planned.

The accountant is a trained reporter of financial information. Just as for external reporting, the accountant needs commercial awareness. It is important, therefore, that he or she should not operate in isolation.

1.5.1 Accountant's reporting role

The accountant's role is to ensure that the information provided is useful for making decisions. For external users, the accountant achieves this by providing a general-purpose financial statement that complies with statute and is reliable. For internal users, this is done by interfacing with the user and establishing exactly what financial information is relevant to the decision that is to be made.

We now consider the steps required to provide relevant information for internal users.

1.6 Procedural steps when reporting to internal users

A number of user steps and accounting action steps can be identified within a financial decision model. These are shown in Figure 1.1.

Note that, although we refer to an accountant/user interface, this is not a single occurrence because the user and accountant interface at each of the user decision steps.

At **step 1**, the accountant attempts to ensure that the decision is based on the appropriate appraisal methodology. However, the accountant is providing a service to a user and, while the accountant may give guidance, the final decision about methodology rests with the user.

At **step 2**, the accountant needs to establish the information necessary to support the decision that is to be made.

At **step 3**, the accountant needs to ensure that the user **understands** the full impact and financial implications of the accountant's report taking into account the user's level of understanding and prior knowledge. This may be overlooked by the accountant, who feels that the task has been completed when the written report has been typed.

It is important to remember in following the model that the accountant is attempting to satisfy the information needs of the individual user rather than those of a 'user group'. It is tempting to divide users into groups with apparently common information needs, without recognising that a group contains individual users with different information needs. We return to this later in the chapter, but for the moment we continue by studying a situation where the directors of a company are considering a proposed capital investment project.

Let us assume that there are three companies in the retail industry: Retail A Ltd, Retail B Ltd and Retail C Ltd. The directors of each company are considering the purchase of a warehouse. We could assume initially that, because the companies are operating in the same industry and are faced with the same investment decision, they have identical information needs. However, enquiry might establish that the directors of each company have a completely different attitude to, or perception of, the primary business objective.

For example, it might be established that Retail A Ltd is a large company and under the Fisher/Hirshleifer separation theory the directors seek to maximise profits for the benefit of the equity investors; Retail B Ltd is a medium-sized company in which the directors seek to obtain a satisfactory return for the equity shareholders; and Retail C Ltd

Figure 1.1 General financial decision model to illustrate the user/accountant interface

	USER
User step 1	Identify decision and how it is to be made
User step 2	Establish with the accountant
	the information necessary for decision-making
User step 3	Seek relevant data from the accountant
	USER/ACCOUNTANT INTERFACE
	Provide an understandable report to the user
	Prepare report for user to allow him to make decision
	Measure the relevant information
	Identify the material information needed by the user
	ACCOUNTANT

is a smaller company in which the directors seek to achieve a satisfactory return for a wider range of shareholders, including, perhaps, the employees as well as the equity shareholders.

The accountant needs to be aware that these differences may have a significant effect on the information required. Let us consider this diagrammatically in the situation where a capital investment decision is to be made, referring particularly to user step 2: 'Establish with the accountant the information necessary for decision-making'.

We can see from Figure 1.2 that the accountant has identified that:

● the relevant financial data are the same for each of the users, i.e. cash flows; but
● the appraisal methods selected, i.e. internal rate of return (IRR) and net present value (NPV), are different; and
● the appraisal criteria employed by each user, i.e. higher IRR and NPV, are different.

In practice, the user is likely to use more than one appraisal method, as each has advantages and disadvantages. However, we can see that, even when dealing with a single group of apparently homogeneous users, the accountant has first to identify the information needs of the particular user. Only then is the accountant able to identify the relevant financial data and the appropriate report. It is the **user's** needs that are predominant.

If the accountant's view of the appropriate appraisal method or criterion differs from the user's view, the accountant might decide to report from **both** views. This approach affords the opportunity to improve the user's understanding and encourages good practice.

The diagrams can be combined (Figure 1.3) to illustrate the complete process. The user is assumed to be Retail A Ltd, a company that has directors who are profit maximisers.

Figure 1.2 Impact of different user attitudes on the information needed in relation to a capital investment proposal

	USER A Directors of Retail A Ltd	USER B Directors of Retail B Ltd	USER C Directors of Retail C Ltd
User attitude	PROFIT MAXIMISER for SHAREHOLDERS	PROFIT SATISFICER for SHAREHOLDERS	PROFIT SATISFICER for SHAREHOLDERS/STAFF
Relevant data to measure	CASH FLOWS	CASH FLOWS	CASH FLOWS
Appraisal method (decided on by user)	IRR	NPV	NPV
Appraisal criterion (decided on by user)	HIGHEST IRR	NPV but only if positive	NPV possibly even if negative

Figure 1.3 User/accountant interface where the user is a profit maximiser

	General model	Specific application for Retail A Ltd
	USER	**A PROFIT MAXIMISER**
Step 1	Decision to be made	Appraise which project warrants capital investment
Step 2	Information needed	Project with the highest IRR
Step 3	Seek relevant data	Report of IRR by project
	USER/ACCOUNTANT INTERFACE	**USER/ACCOUNTANT INTERFACE**
	Provide report	Submit report of project with highest IRR per £ invested
	Prepare report	Prepare report of highest IRR
	Measure	Measure the project cash flows
	Identify information needed by the user	User decision criterion is IRR
	ACCOUNTANT	**ACCOUNTANT**

The accountant is reactive when reporting to an internal user. We observe this characteristic in the Norman example set out in section 1.8. Because the cash flows are identified as relevant to the user, it is these flows that the accountant will record, measure and appraise.

The accountant can also be proactive, by giving the user advice and guidance in areas where the accountant has specific expertise, such as the appraisal method that is most appropriate to the circumstances.

1.7 Agency costs[4]

The information in Figure 1.2 assumes that the directors have made their investment decision based on the assumed preferences of the shareholders. However, in real life, the directors might also be influenced by how the decision impinges on their own position. If, for example, their remuneration is a fixed salary, they might select not the investment with the highest IRR, but the one that maintains their security of employment. The result might be suboptimal investment and financing decisions based on risk aversion and over-retention. To the extent that the potential cash flows have been reduced, there will be an agency cost to the shareholders. This agency cost is an opportunity cost – the amount that was forgone because the decision making was suboptimal – and, as such, it will not be recorded in the books of account and will not appear in the financial statements.

1.8 Illustration of periodic financial statements prepared under the cash flow concept to disclose realised operating cash flows

In the above example of Retail A, B and C, the investment decision for the acquisition of a warehouse was based on an appraisal of cash flows. This raises the question: 'Why not continue with the cash flow concept and report the financial changes that occur after the investment has been undertaken using that same concept?'

To do this, the company will record the consequent cash flows through a number of subsequent accounting periods; report the cash flows that occur in each financial period; and produce a balance sheet at the end of each of the financial periods. For illustration we follow this procedure in paras 1.8.1 and 1.8.2 for transactions entered into by Mr S. Norman.

1.8.1 Appraisal of the initial investment decision

Mr Norman is considering whether to start up a retail business by acquiring the lease of a shop for five years at a cost of £80,000.

Our first task has been set out in Figure 1.2 above. It is to establish the information that Mr Norman needs, so that we can decide what data it will be necessary to collect and measure. Let us assume that, as a result of a discussion with Mr Norman, it has been ascertained that he is a profit satisficer who is looking to achieve at least a 10% return, which represents the time value of money. This indicates that:

- the relevant data to be measured are **cash flows**, represented by the outflow of cash invested in the lease and the inflow of cash represented by the realised operating cash flows;
- the appropriate appraisal method is **NPV**; and
- the appraisal criterion is a **positive NPV** using the discount rate of 10%.

Let us further assume that the cash to be invested in the lease is £80,000 and that the realised operating cash flows over the life of the investment in the shop are as shown in Figure 1.4. This shows that there is a forecast of £30,000 annually for five years and a final receipt of £29,000 in 20X6 when he proposes to cease trading.

We already know that Mr Norman's investment criterion is a positive NPV using a discount factor of 10%. A calculation (Figure 1.5) shows that the investment easily satisfies that criterion.

1.8.2 Preparation of periodic financial statements under the cash flow concept

Having **predicted** the realised operating cash flows for the purpose of making the investment decision, we can assume that the owner of the business will wish to obtain **feedback**

Figure 1.4 Forecast of realised operating cash flows

	Annually years 20X1–20X5	Cash in year 20X6 after shop closure
	£	£
Receipts from		
Customers	400,000	55,000
Payments for		
Trade creditors	(342,150)	(20,000)
Expense creditors	(21,600)	(3,000)
Rent	(6,250)	(3,000)
Total payments	(370,000)	(26,000)
Realised operating cash flows	30,000	29,000

Figure 1.5 NPV calculation using discount tables

	£	£
Cost of lease		(80,000)
£30,000 annually for 5 years (30,000 × 3.79)	113,700	
£29,000 received in year 6 (29,000 × 0.564)	16,356	
		130,056
Positive net present value		50,056

to evaluate the correctness of the investment decision. He does this by reviewing the actual results on a regular **timely** basis and **comparing** these with the predicted forecast. Actual results should be reported quarterly, half-yearly or annually in the same format as used when making the decision in Figure 1.4. The actual results provide management with the feedback information required to audit the initial decision; it is a technique for achieving accountability. However, frequently, companies do not provide a report of actual cash flows to compare with the forecast cash flows, and fail to carry out an audit review.

In some cases, the transactions relating to the investment cannot be readily separated from other transactions, and the information necessary for the audit review of the investment cannot be made available. In other cases, the routine accounting procedures fail to collect such cash flow information because the reporting systems have not been designed to provide financial reports on a cash flow basis; rather, they have been designed to produce reports prepared on an accrual basis.

What would financial reports look like if they were prepared on a cash flow basis?

To illustrate cash flow period accounts, we will prepare half-yearly accounts for Mr Norman. To facilitate a comparison with the forecast that underpinned the investment decision, we will redraft the forecast annual statement on a half-yearly basis. The data for the first year given in Figure 1.4 have therefore been redrafted to provide a forecast for the half-year to 30 June, as shown in Figure 1.6.

Figure 1.6 Forecast of realised operating cash flows

	Half-year to 30 June 20X1 £
Receipts from	
Customers	165,000
Payments for	
Trade creditors	(124,000)
Expense creditors	(18,000)
Rent	(6,250)
Total payments	(148,250)
Realised operating cash flows	16,750

Figure 1.7 Monthly sales, purchases and expenses for six months ended 30 June 20X1

Month	Sales invoiced £	Cash received £	Purchases invoiced £	Cash paid £	Expenses invoiced £	Cash paid £
January	15,000	7,500	16,000		3,400	3,100
February	20,000	17,500	19,000	16,000	3,500	3,400
March	35,000	27,500	29,000	19,000	3,800	3,500
April	40,000	37,500	32,000	29,000	3,900	3,800
May	40,000	40,000	33,000	32,000	3,900	3,900
June	45,000	42,500	37,000	33,000	4,000	3,900
TOTAL	195,000	172,500	166,000	129,000	22,500	21,600

Note: The following items were included under the Expenses invoiced heading:
Expense creditors – amount
Wages – £3,100 per month paid in the month
Commission – 2% of sales invoiced payable 1 month in arrears

We assume that, having applied the net present value appraisal technique to the cash flows and ascertained that the NPV was positive, Mr Norman proceeded to set up the business on 1 January 20X1. He introduced capital of £50,000, acquired a five-year lease for £80,000 and paid £6,250 in advance as rent to occupy the property to 31 December 20X1. He has decided to prepare financial statements at half-yearly intervals. The information given in Figure 1.7 concerns his trading for the half-year to 30 June 20X1.

Mr Norman was naturally eager to determine whether the business was achieving its forecast cash flows for the first six months of trading, so he produced the statement of realised operating cash flows (Figure 1.8) from the information provided in Figure 1.7. From this statement we can see that the business generated positive cash flows after the end of February. These are, of course, only the cash flows relating to the trading transactions.

The information in the 'Total' column of Figure 1.8 can be extracted to provide the financial statement for the six months ended 30 June 20X1, as shown in Figure 1.9.

The figure of £15,650 needs to be compared with the forecast cash flows used in the investment appraisal. This is a form of auditing. It allows the assumptions made on the

Figure 1.8 Monthly realised operating cash flows

	Jan £	Feb £	Mar £	Apr £	May £	Jun £	Total £
Receipts							
Debtors	7,500	17,500	27,500	37,500	40,000	42,500	172,500
Less payments							
Trade creditors		16,000	19,000	29,000	32,000	33,000	129,000
Expense creditors	3,100	3,400	3,500	3,800	3,900	3,900	21,600
Rent	6,250						6,250
Realised	−1,850	−1,900	5,000	4,700	4,100	5,600	15,650

Figure 1.9 Realised operating cash flows for the six months ended 30 June 20X1

		£
Receipts from		
Customers		172,500
Payments		
To trade creditors	(129,000)	
To expense creditors	(21,600)	
To rent	(6,250)	
		156,850
Realised operating cash flow		15,650

initial investment decision to be confirmed. The forecast/actual comparison (based on the information in Figures 1.6 and 1.9) is set out in Figure 1.10.

What are the characteristics of these data that make them relevant?

● The data are **objective**. There is no judgement involved in deciding the values to include in the financial statement, as each value or amount represents a verifiable cash transaction with a third party.

● The data are **consistent**. The statement incorporates the same cash flows within the periodic financial report of trading as the cash flows that were incorporated within the initial capital investment report. This permits a logical comparison and confirmation that the decision was realistic.

● The results have a **confirmatory** value by helping users confirm or correct their past assessments.

● The results have a **predictive** value, in that they provide a basis for revising the initial forecasts if necessary.[5]

● There is **no requirement for accounting standards** or disclosure of accounting policies that are necessary to regulate accrual accounting practices, e.g. Depreciation methods.

Figure 1.10 Forecast/actual comparison

		Actual £	Forecast £
Receipts from			
Customers		172,500	165,000
Payments			
To trade creditors	(129,000)		(124,000)
To expense creditors	(21,600)		(18,000)
To rent	(6,250)		(6,250)
Total payments		(156,850)	(148,250)
Realised operating cash flow		15,650	16,750

1.9 Illustration of preparation of balance sheet under the cash flow concept

Although the information set out in Figure 1.10 permits us to compare and evaluate the initial decision, it does not provide a sufficiently sound basis for the following:

- Assessing the stewardship over the total cash funds that have been employed within the business.
- Signalling to management whether its working capital policies are appropriate.

1.9.1 Stewardship

To assess the stewardship over the total cash funds we need to:

(a) evaluate the effectiveness of the accounting system to make certain that all transactions are recorded;

(b) extend the cash flow statement to take account of the capital cash flows; and

(c) prepare a statement of financial position or balance sheet as at 30 June 20X1.

The additional information for (b) and (c) above is set out in Figures 1.11 and 1.12 respectively.

Figure 1.11 Cash flow statement to calculate the net cash balance

	Jan £	Feb £	Mar £	Apr £	May £	Jun £	Total £
Operating cash	(1,850)	(1,900)	5,000	4,700	4,100	5,600	15,650
New capital	50,000						50,000
Lease payment	(80,000)						(80,000)
Cash balance	(31,850)	(33,750)	(28,750)	(24,050)	(19,950)	(14,350)	(14,350)

Figure 1.12 Statement of financial position

	Opening 1 Jan 20X1 £	Closing 30 Jun 20X1 £
Capital introduced	50,000	50,000
Net operating cash flow		15,650
	50,000	65,650
Lease		80,000
Net cash balance	50,000	−14,350
	50,000	65,650

The cash flow statement and statement of financial position, taken together, are a means of assessing stewardship. They identify the movement of **all** cash and derive a **net** balance figure. These statements are a normal feature of a sound system of internal control, but they have not been made available to external users.

1.9.2 Working capital policies

By 'working capital' we mean the current assets and current liabilities of the business. In addition to providing a means of making management accountable, cash flows are the raw data required by financial managers when making decisions on the management of working capital. One of the decisions would be to set the appropriate terms for credit policy. For example, Figure 1.11 shows that the business will have a £14,350 overdraft at 30 June 20X1. If this is not acceptable, management will review its working capital by reconsidering the credit given to customers, the credit taken from suppliers, stock holding levels and the timing of capital cash inflows and outflows.

If, in the example, it were possible to obtain 45 days' credit from suppliers, then the creditors at 30 June would rise from £37,000 to a new total of £53,500. This increase in trade credit of £16,500 means that half of the May purchases (£33,000/2) would not be paid for until July, which would convert the overdraft of £14,350 into a positive balance of £2,150. As a new business it might not be possible to obtain credit from all of the suppliers. In that case other steps would be considered, such as phasing the payment for the lease of the warehouse or introducing more capital.

An interesting research report[6] identified that for small firms survival and stability were the main objectives rather than profit maximisation. This, in turn, meant that cash flow indicators and managing cash flow were seen as crucial to survival. In addition, cash flow information was perceived as important to external bodies such as banks in evaluating performance.

1.10 Treatment of fixed assets in the cash flow model

The statement of financial position in Figure 1.12 does not take into account any **unrealised** cash flows. Such flows are deemed to occur as a result of any rise or fall in the realisable value of the lease. This could rise if, for example, the annual rent payable under the lease were to be substantially lower than the rate payable under a new lease entered into on 30 June 20X1. It could also fall with the passing of time, with six months having expired by 30 June 20X1. We need to consider this further and examine the possible treatment of fixed assets in the cash flow model.

Using the cash flow approach, we require an independent verification of the realisable value of the lease at 30 June 20X1. If the lease has fallen in value, the difference between the original outlay and the net realisable figure could be treated as a negative unrealised operating cash flow.

For example, if the independent estimate was that the realisable value was £74,000, then the statement of financial position would be prepared as in Figure 1.13. The fall of £6,000 in realisable value is an unrealised cash flow and, while it does not affect the calculation of the net cash balance, it does affect the statement of financial position.

The additional benefit of the statement of financial position, as revised, is that the owner is able clearly to identify the following:

Figure 1.13 Statement of financial position as at 30 June 20X1 (assuming that there were unrealised operating cash flows)

	£
Capital introduced	50,000
Net operating flow: **realised**	15,650
: unrealised	(6,000)
	59,650
Lease: **net realisable value**	74,000
Net cash balance	−14,350
	59,650

- The operating cash inflows of £15,650 that have been realised from the business operations.

- The operating cash outflow of £6,000 that has not been realised, but has arisen as a result of investing in the lease.

- The net cash balance of −£14,350.

- The statement provides a **stewardship-orientated** report: that is, it is a means of making the management accountable for the cash within its control.

1.11 What are the characteristics of these data that make them reliable?

We have already discussed some characteristics of cash flow reporting which indicate that the data in the financial statements are **relevant**, e.g. their predictive and confirmatory roles. We now introduce five more characteristics of cash flow statements which indicate that the information is also **reliable**, i.e. free from bias.[7] These are prudence, neutrality, completeness, faithful representation and freedom from material error.

1.11.1 Prudence characteristic

Revenue and profits are included in the cash flow statement only when they are realised. Realisation is deemed to occur when cash is received. In our Norman example, the £172,500 cash received from debtors represents the revenue for the half-year ended 30 June 20X1. This policy is described as prudent because it **does not anticipate** cash flows: cash flows are recorded only when they actually occur and not when they are reasonably certain of occurring. This is one of the factors that distinguishes cash flow from accrual accounting.

1.11.2 Neutrality characteristic

Financial statements are not neutral if, by their selection or presentation of information, they influence the making of a decision in order to achieve a predetermined result or outcome. With cash flow accounting, the information is not subject to management selection criteria.

Cash flow accounting avoids the tension that can arise between prudence and neutrality because, whilst neutrality involves freedom from deliberate or systematic bias, prudence is a potentially biased concept that seeks to ensure that, under conditions of uncertainty, gains and assets are not overstated and losses and liabilities are not understated.[8]

1.11.3 Completeness characteristic

The cash flows can be verified for completeness provided there are adequate internal control procedures in operation. In small and medium enterprises there can be a weakness if one person, typically the owner, has control over the accounting system and is able to under-record cash receipts.

1.11.4 Faithful representation characteristic

Cash flows can be depended upon by users to represent faithfully what they purport to represent provided, of course, that the completeness characteristic has been satisfied.

1.12 Reports to external users

1.12.1 Stewardship orientation

Cash flow accounting provides objective, consistent and prudent financial information about a business's transactions. It is stewardship orientated and offers a means of achieving accountability over cash resources and investment decisions.

1.12.2 Prediction orientation

External users are also interested in the ability of a company to pay dividends. It might be thought that the past and current cash flows are the best indicators of future cash flows and dividends. However, the cash flow might be misleading, in that a declining company might sell fixed assets and have a better **net cash position** than a growing company that buys fixed assets for future use. There is also no matching of cash inflows and outflows, in the sense that a benefit is matched with the sacrifice made to achieve it.

Consequently, it has been accepted accounting practice to view the profit and loss account prepared on the accrual accounting concept as a better predictor of future cash flows to an investor than the cash flow statements that we have illustrated in this chapter.

However, the operating cash flows arising from trading and the cash flows arising from the introduction of capital and the acquisition of fixed assets can become significant to investors, e.g. they may threaten the company's ability to survive or may indicate growth.

In the next chapter we revise the preparation of the same three statements using the **accrual accounting** model.

Summary

To review our understanding of this chapter, we should ask ourselves the following questions.

How useful is cash flow accounting for internal decision making?

Forecast cash flows are relevant for the appraisal of proposals for capital investment.

Actual cash flows are relevant for the confirmation of the decision for capital investment.

Cash flows are relevant for the management of working capital. Financial managers might have a variety of mathematical models for the efficient use of working capital, but cash flows are the raw data upon which they work.

How useful is cash flow accounting for making management accountable?

The cash flow statement is useful for confirming decisions and, together with the statement of financial position, provides a stewardship report. Lee states that 'Cash flow accounting appears to satisfy the need to supply owners and others with stewardship-orientated information as well as with decision-orientated information.'[9]
Lee further states that:

By reducing judgements in this type of financial report, management can report factually on its stewardship function, whilst at the same time disclosing data of use in the decision-making process. In other words, cash flow reporting eliminates the somewhat artificial segregation of stewardship and decision-making information.

This is exactly what we saw in our Norman example – the same realised operating cash flow information was used for both the investment decision and financial reporting. However, for stewardship purposes it was necessary to extend the cash flow to include **all** cash movements and to extend the statement of financial position to include the **unrealised** cash flows.

How useful is cash flow accounting for reporting to external users?

Cash flow information is relevant:

● as a basis for making internal management decisions in relation to both fixed assets and working capital; and
● for stewardship and accountability.

Cash flow information is reliable, being:

● objective;
● consistent;
● prudent; and
● neutral.

However, professional accounting practice requires reports to external users to be on an accrual accounting basis. This is because the accrual accounting profit figure is a better predictor for investors of the future cash flows likely to arise from the dividends paid to them by the business, and of any capital gain on disposal of their investment. It could also be argued that cash flows may not be a fair representation of the commercial substance of transactions, e.g. if a business allowed a year's credit to all its customers there would be no income recorded.

REVIEW QUESTIONS

I Explain why it is the user who should determine the information that the accountant collects, measures and reports, rather than the accountant who is the expert in financial information.

2 'Yuji Ijiri rejects decision usefulness as the main purpose of accounting and puts in its place accountability. Ijiri sees the accounting relationship as a tripartite one, involving the accountor, the accountee, and the accountant … the decision useful approach is heavily biased in favour of the accountee … with little concern for the accountor … in the central position Ijiri would put fairness.'[10] Discuss Ijiri's view in the context of cash flow accounting.

3 Discuss the extent to which you consider that accounts for a small businessperson who is carrying on business as a sole trader should be prepared on a cash flow basis.

4 Explain why your decision in question 3 might be different if the business entity were a medium-sized limited company.

5 'Realised operating cash flows are only of use for internal management purposes and are irrelevant to investors.' Discuss.

6 'While accountants may be free from bias in the measurement of economic information, they cannot be unbiased in identifying the economic information that they consider to be relevant.' Discuss.

7 Explain the effect on the statement of financial position in Figure 1.13 if the fixed asset consisted of expenditure on industry-specific machine tools rather than a lease.

8 'It is essential that the information in financial statements has a prudent characteristic if the financial statements are to be objective.' Discuss.

EXERCISES

An extract from the solution is provided in the appendix at the end of the text for exercises marked with an asterisk (*).

* Question 1

Jane Parker is going to set up a new business on 1 January 20X1. She estimates that her first six months in business will be as follows:

(i) She will put £150,000 into a bank account for the firm on 1 January 20X1.

(ii) On 1 January 20X1 she will buy machinery £30,000, motor vehicles £24,000 and premises £75,000, paying for them immediately.

(iii) All purchases will be effected on credit. She will buy £30,000 goods on 1 January and will pay for these in February. Other purchases will be: rest of January £48,000; February, March, April, May and June £60,000 each month. Other than the £30,000 worth bought in January, all other purchases will be paid for two months after purchase.

(iv) Sales (all on credit) will be £60,000 for January and £75,000 for each month after. Debtors will pay for the goods in the third month after purchase, i.e. £60,000 is received in May.

(v) She will make drawings of £1,200 per month.

(vi) Wages and salaries will be £2,250 per month and will be paid on the last day of each month.

(vii) General expenses will be £750 per month, payable in the month following that in which they are incurred.

(viii) Rates will be paid as follows: for the three months to 31 March 20X1 by cheque on 28 February 20X1; for the 12 months ended 31 March 20X2 by cheque on 31 July 20X1. Rates are £4,800 per annum.

(ix) She will introduce new capital of £82,500 on 1 April 20X1.

(x) Insurance covering the 12 months of 20X1 £2,100 will be paid for by cheque on 30 June 20X1.

(xi) All receipts and payments will be by cheque.

(xii) Stock in trade on 30 June 20X1 will be £30,000.

(xiii) The net realisable value of the vehicles is £19,200, machinery £27,000 and premises £75,000.

Required: Cash flow accounting
  (i) Draft a cash budget (includes bank) month by month for the period January to June, showing clearly the amount of bank balance or overdraft at the end of each month.
 (ii) Draft an operating cash flow statement for the six-month period.
(iii) Assuming that Jane Parker sought your advice as to whether she should actually set up in business, state what further information you would require.

* Question 2

Mr Norman set up a new business on 1 January 20X8. He invested £50,000 in the new business on that date. The following information is available.

1 Gross profit was 20% of sales. Monthly sales were as follows:

Month	Sales £	Month	Sales £
January	15,000	May	40,000
February	20,000	June	45,000
March	35,000	July	50,000
April	40,000		

2 50% of sales were for cash. Debtors (50% of sales) pay in month following sale.

3 The supplier allowed one month's credit.

4 Monthly payments were made for rent and rates £2,200 and wages £600.

5 On 1 January 20X8 the following payments were made: £80,000 for a five-year lease of business premises and £3,500 for insurances on the premises for the year. The realisable value of the lease was estimated to be £76,000 on 30 June 20X8 and £70,000 on 31 December 20X8.

6 Staff sales commission of 2% of sales was paid in the month following the sale.

Required:
(a) A purchases budget for each of the first six months.
(b) A cash flow statement for the first six months.
(c) A statement of operating cash flows and financial position as at 30 June 20X8.
(d) Write a brief letter to the bank supporting a request for an overdraft.

Question 3

Fred and Sally own a profitable business that deals in windsurfing equipment. They are the only UK agents to import 'Dryline' sails from Germany, and in addition to this they sell a variety of boards and miscellaneous equipment that they buy from other dealers in the UK.

Two years ago they diversified into custom-made boards built to individual customer requirements, each of which was supplied with a 'Dryline' sail. In order to build the boards they have had to take over larger premises, which consist of a shop front with a workshop at the rear, and employ two members of staff to help.

Demand is seasonal and Fred and Sally find that there is insufficient work during the winter months to pay rent for the increased accommodation and also wages to the extra two members of staff. The four of them could spend October to March in Lanzarote as windsurf instructors and close the UK operation down in this period. If they did, however, they would lose the 'Dryline' agency, as Dryline insists on a retail outlet in the UK for twelve months of the year. Dryline sails constitute 40% of their turnover and carry a 50% mark-up.

Trading has been static and the pattern is expected to continue as follows for 1 April 20X5 to 31 March 20X6:

Sales of boards and equipment (non-custom-built) with Dryline agency: 1 April–30 September £120,000; of this 30% was paid by credit card, which involved one month's delay in receiving cash and 4% deduction at source.

Sixty custom-built boards 1 April–30 September £60,000; of this 15% of the sales price was for the sail (a 'Dryline' 6 m² sail costs Fred and Sally £100, the average price for a sail of the same size and quality is £150 (cost to them)).

Purchasers of custom-built boards take an average of two months to pay and none pays by credit card.

Sales 1 October–31 March of boards and equipment (non-custom-built) £12,000, 30% by credit card as above.

Six custom-built boards were sold for a total of £6,000 and customers took an unexplainable average of three months to pay in the winter.

Purchases were made monthly and paid for two months in arrears.

The average mark-up on goods for resale excluding 'Dryline' sails was 25%. If they lose the agency, they expect that they will continue to sell the same number of sails, but at their average mark-up of 25%. The variable material cost of each custom-made board (excluding the sail) was £500.

Other costs were:
Wages to employees £6,000 p.a. each (gross including insurance).
Rent for premises £6,000 p.a. (six-monthly renewable lease) payable on the first day of each month.
Other miscellaneous costs:
1 April–30 September   £3,000
1 October–31 March   £900.

Bank balance on 1 April was £100.

Salary earnable over whole period in Lanzarote:
Fred and Sally £1,500 each + living accommodation
Two employees £1,500 each + living accommodation

All costs and income accruing evenly over time.

Required:
(i)   Prepare a cash budget for 1 April 20X5 to 31 March 20X6 assuming that:
      (a)   Fred and Sally close the business in the winter months.
      (b)   They stay open all year.
(ii) What additional information would you require before you advised Fred and Sally of the best course of action to take?

References

1 *Statement of Principles for Financial Reporting*, ASB, 1999, para. 1.11.
2 *Ibid.*, para. 3.12.
3 J. Arnold, T. Hope and A.J. Southworth, *Financial Accounting*, Prentice Hall, 1994, p. 64.
4 G. Whittred and I. Zimmer, *Financial Accounting Incentive Effects and Economic Consequences*, Holt, Rinehart & Winston, 1992, p. 27.
5 ASB, *op. cit.*, para. 3.3.
6 R. Jarvis, J. Kitching, J. Curran and G. Lightfoot, The financial management of small firms: an alternative perspective, ACCA Research Report No 49.
7 *Ibid.*, para. 3.8.
8 ASB, *op. cit.*, para. 3.36.
9 T.A. Lee, *Income and Value Measurement. Theory and Practice* (3rd edition) Van Nostrand Reinhold (UK), 1985, p. 173.
10 D. Solomons, *Making Accounting Policy*, Oxford University Press, 1986, p. 79.

CHAPTER 2

Accounting and reporting on an accrual accounting basis

2.1 Introduction

The Accounting Standards Board (ASB) has issued a revised draft Statement on the principles that underlie accounting and financial reporting. The intention is to specify a conceptual framework. The ASB has stated that it intends to use, wherever possible, the text issued by the International Accounting Standards Committee (IASC) entitled *Framework for the Preparation and Presentation of Financial Statements.* In this chapter, when we refer to the objectives of financial statements and the qualitative characteristics of financial information, we will be giving references to the ASB *Statement of Principles.*

In this chapter we consider the following:

- Historical cost convention
- Accrual accounting concept
- Mechanics of accrual accounting – adjusting cash receipts and payments
- Subjective judgements required in accrual accounting
  1 Adjusting cash receipts in accordance with IAS 18
  2 Adjusting cash receipts in accordance with UK accounting practice
  3 Adjusting cash payments in accordance with the matching principle
- Need for a revenue recognition standard
- Mechanics of accrual accounting – the balance sheet
- Reformatting the statement of financial position into a balance sheet
- Accounting for the sacrifice of fixed assets
- Reconciliation of cash flow and accrual accounting data

2.1.1 Objective of financial statements

The ASB has stated that the objective of financial statements is to provide information about the financial position, performance and capability of an enterprise that is useful to a wide range of users in making economic decisions.[1]

Common information needs for decision making

The ASB recognises that all the information needs of all users cannot be met by financial statements, but it takes the view that some needs are common to all users: in particular, they have some interest in the financial position, performance and adaptability of the enterprise as a whole. This leaves open the question of which user is the primary target; the ASB states that, as investors are providers of risk capital, financial statements that meet their needs would also meet the needs of other users.[2]

Stewardship role of financial statements

In addition to assisting in making economic decisions, financial statements also show the results of the stewardship of management: that is, the accountability of management for the resources entrusted to it. The ASB view[3] is that users who assess the stewardship do so in order to make economic decisions, e.g. whether to hold or sell shares in a particular company or change the management.

Decision makers need to assess ability to generate cash

The ASB considers that economic decisions also require an evaluation of an enterprise's ability to generate cash, and of the timing and certainty of its generation.[4] It believes that users are better able to make the evaluation if they are provided with information that focuses on the financial position, performance and cash flow of an enterprise.

2.1.2 Financial information to evaluate the ability to generate cash differs from financial information on actual cash flows

The ASB approach differs from the cash flow model used in Chapter 1, in that, in addition to the cash flows and statement of financial position, it includes within its definition of performance a reference to profit. It states that this information is required to assess changes in the economic resources that the enterprise is likely to control in the future. This is useful in predicting the capacity of the enterprise to generate cash flows from its existing resource base.[5]

2.1.3 Statements making up the financial statements published for external users

The ASB suggests that the financial statements published by a company for external users should consist of four primary statements:

● the profit and loss account;
● the statement of total recognised gains and losses;
● the balance sheet; and
● the cash flow statement.[6]

In this chapter we consider two of the conventions under which the profit and loss account and balance sheet are prepared: the historical cost convention; and the accrual accounting concept.

2.2 Historical cost convention

The historical cost convention results in an appropriate measure of the economic resource that has been withdrawn or replaced.

Under it, transactions are reported at the £ amount recorded at the date the transaction occurred. Financial statements produced under this convention provide a basis for determining the outcome of agency agreements with reasonable certainty and predictability because the data are relatively objective.[7]

By this we mean that various parties who deal with the enterprise, such as lenders, will know that the figures produced in any financial statements are objective and not manipulated by subjective judgements made by the directors. A typical example occurs when a lender attaches a covenant to a loan that the enterprise shall not exceed a specified level of gearing.

At an operational level, revenue and expense in the profit and loss account are stated at the £ amount that appears on the invoices. This amount is objective and verifiable. Because of this, the historical cost convention has strengths for stewardship purposes, but inflation-adjusted figures may well be more appropriate for decision usefulness.

2.3 Accrual accounting concept

The accrual concept dictates when transactions with third parties should be recognised and, in particular, determines the accounting periods in which they should be incorporated into the financial statements.[8] Under this concept the cash receipts from customers and payments to creditors are replaced by revenue and expenses respectively.

Revenue and expenses are derived by adjusting the realised operating cash flows to take account of business trading activity that has occurred during the accounting period, but has not been converted into cash receipts or payments by the end of the period.

2.3.1 Accrual accounting is a better indicator than cash flow accounting of ability to generate cash

The accounting profession generally supports the view expressed by the Financial Accounting Standards Board (FASB) in the USA that accrual accounting provides a better indication of an enterprise's present and continuing ability to generate favourable cash flows than information limited to the financial aspects of cash receipts and payments.[9]

The International Accounting Standards Committee (IASC) supported the FASB view in 1989 when it stated that financial statements prepared on an accrual basis inform users not only of past transactions involving the payment and receipt of cash, but also of obligations to pay cash in the future and of resources that represent cash to be received in the future, and that they provide the type of information about past transactions and other events that is most useful in making economic decisions.[10]

Having briefly considered why accrual accounting is more useful than cash flow accounting, we will briefly revise the preparation of financial statements under the accrual accounting convention.

2.4 Mechanics of accrual accounting – adjusting cash receipts and payments

We use the cash flows set out in Figure 1.7. The derivation of the revenue and expenses for this example is set out in Figures 2.1 and 2.2. We assume that the enterprise has incomplete records, so that the revenue is arrived at by keeping a record of unpaid invoices and adding these to the cash receipts. Clearly, if the invoices are not adequately controlled, there will be no assurance that the £22,500 figure is correct. This is a relatively straightforward process at a mechanistic level. The uncertainty is not how to adjust the cash flow figures, but when to adjust them. This decision requires managers to make subjective judgements. We now look briefly at the nature of such judgements.

Figure 2.1 Derivation of revenue

	£
Cash received	172,500
Invoices not paid (= Sales invoiced − Cash received)	22,500
Revenue = Total invoiced	195,000

Figure 2.2 Derivation of expense

	Materials £	Services £
Cash paid	129,000	21,600
Invoices not paid	37,000	900
Expense = Total invoiced	166,000	22,500

2.5 Subjective judgements required in accrual accounting 1 – adjusting cash receipts in accordance with IAS 18

In Figure 2.1 we assumed that revenue was derived simply by adding unpaid invoices to the cash receipts. In practice, however, this is influenced by the commercial facts underlying the transactions. For example, if the company is a milk producer, the point at which it should report the milk production as revenue will be influenced by the existence of a supply contract. If there is a contract with a buyer, the revenue might be recognised immediately on production.

So that financial statements are comparable, the IASC[11] has set out revenue recognition criteria in IAS 18 *Revenue* in an attempt to identify when performance was sufficient to warrant inclusion in the revenue for the period. It stated that:

In a transaction involving the sale of goods, performance should be regarded as being achieved when the following conditions have been fulfilled:
  (a) the seller of the goods has transferred to the buyer the significant risks and rewards of ownership, in that all significant acts have been completed and the seller retains no continuing managerial involvement in, or effective control of, the goods transferred to a degree usually associated with ownership; and
  (b) no significant uncertainty exists regarding:
    (i) the consideration that will be derived from the sale of the goods;
    (ii) the associated costs incurred or to be incurred in producing or purchasing the goods;
    (iii) the extent to which the goods are returned.

The criteria are simple in their intention, but difficult in their application. For instance, at what exact point in the sales cycle is there no significant uncertainty? The enterprise has to decide on the critical event that can support an assumption that revenue may be recognised.

To assist with these decisions, the standard provided an appendix with a number of examples. Figure 2.3 gives examples of critical events, but you should refer to the standard itself for further information. It is interesting to note that companies registered in other parts of the world are more explicit than UK companies. The following is an extract from the accounts of Hwa Kay Thai Holdings Ltd, a company incorporated in Bermuda and listed on the Hong Kong Stock Exchange.

Revenue of the Group for the year is recognised on the following basis:

Dividend income from investments is recognised when the shareholders' right to receive payment has been established.
Sales of goods are recognised when goods are delivered and title has passed.
Income from restaurant operations is recognised when food and beverages are sold and services rendered.
Income from property management, infrastructure and other consultancy fee income are recognised when services are rendered.
Interest income is accrued on a time basis, by reference to the principal outstanding and at the interest rate applicable.
Rental income from properties under operating leases is recognised on a straight line basis over the terms of the respective leases.

In the UK, companies disclose the accounting policy for turnover; e.g. John Laing plc, a group engaged in building homes for sale, property development and investment in infrastructure, in its 2000 annual report states:

Turnover comprises the value of work executed by construction activities, fees received on construction management, income generated in respect of services

Figure 2.3 Extracts from IAS 18 *Revenue Recognition* illustrating critical events

Transaction	Critical event
Services	
Servicing fees included in the price of the product	Where the selling price of a product includes an identifiable amount for subsequent servicing for, say, a warranty period, it will normally be appropriate to defer the relevant portion of the selling price and to recognise it as revenue over the appropriate period
Sales of goods	
Shipment made giving the buyer right of return	Recognition of revenue in such circumstances will depend on the substance of the agreement. In the case of normal retail sales (e.g. chain store offering money back if not satisfied) it may be appropriate to recognise the sale but to make a suitable provision for returns based on previous experience. In other cases the substance of the agreement may amount to a sale on consignment, in which case the revenue should not be recognised until the goods are sold to a third party

provided by our rail activities, rental income and invoiced sales after excluding intra-group transactions. In the case of private housing sales, sales are recognised at the date of legal completion, and for other property developments, sales are recognised on exchange of unconditional contract.

2.6 Subjective judgements required in accrual accounting 2 – adjusting cash receipts in accordance with UK accounting practice

The ASB differs from the IASC, in that it has not issued a standard on revenue recognition. Instead, accountants rely on established practice that recognises revenue at four points in the selling process. These are outlined below.

2.6.1 Completion of production

In the case of the milk producer, revenue might be recognised on the completion of production subject to certain provisos – there is a ready market for the milk; the price is determinable and stable; and there are no outstanding marketing costs to be incurred.

2.6.2 Time of despatch

In the case of a furniture wholesaler, when the furniture has been despatched to the retailer, the most significant uncertainties have been eliminated. The outstanding uncertainties are that the retailer will default or return the furniture as being substandard. The risk of non-payment or return can normally be estimated with reasonable certainty based on experience.

2.6.3 After despatch but before payment is received

A video wholesaler may give the retailer an agreed period of, say, thirty days to examine the goods and return them if unsatisfactory. Revenue recognition might be deferred until the end of this period; alternatively, experience might indicate that it is reasonable to recognise the revenue before the expiry of thirty days.

2.6.4 After payment

In the sale of technical equipment, such as video recorders, retailers may be permitted a warranty period of, say, a year. In this case, the revenue may be recognised but a provision is created to meet estimated future costs likely to arise under the warranty. Again, history might indicate a reasonable level of provision.

From this we can see that, although the general principles are clear, each transaction needs to be assessed on its own merits in order to ascertain whether significant uncertainties exist at the balance sheet date.

Figure 2.4 Profit and loss account for the six months ended 30 June 20X1

	Operating cash flow £	ADJUST cash flow £	Business activity £
Revenue from business activity	172,500	22,500	195,000
Less: Matching expenses			
Transactions for materials	129,000	37,000	166,000
Transactions for services	21,600	900	22,500
Transactions with landlord	6,250	(3,125)	3,125
OPERATING CASH FLOW from business activity	15,650		
Transactions NOT converted to cash or relating to a subsequent period		(12,275)	
PROFIT from business activity			3,375

2.7 Subjective judgements required in accrual accounting 3 – adjusting cash payments in accordance with the matching principle

We have seen that the enterprise needs to decide when to recognise the revenue. It then needs to decide when to include an item as an expense in the profit and loss account. This decision is based on an application of the matching principle.

The matching principle means that financial statements must include costs related to the achievement of the reported revenue. These include the internal transfers required to ensure that reductions in the assets held by a business are recorded at the same time as the revenues.[12]

The expense might be more or less than the cash paid. For example, in the Norman example, £37,000 was invoiced but not paid on materials, and £900 on services; £3,125 was prepaid on rent for the six months after June. The cash flow information therefore needs to be adjusted as in Figure 2.4.

2.8 Need for a revenue recognition standard

The ASB has recognised that it was unsatisfactory to continue without an FRS and in July 2001 it issued a Discussion Paper on revenue recognition.

Individual companies within the same sector[13] can, at present, have different accounting policies with many companies choosing a generic type of turnover policy and differing widely in their timing of income recognition. This impacts directly on the bottom line profit and provides an opportunity for companies to 'manage' earnings particularly in times of recession and profit warnings.

In order to ensure that all companies in a sector follow a uniform practice there will be a need for industry-specific guidance.[14] Following the practice introduced with the *Statement of Principles*, the ASB is seeking to establish a framework that can be used consistently to address revenue issues arising in different contexts and its Discussion Paper examines revenue recognition and measurement from first principles. Revenue is one of the key factors for investors evaluating a company's current profit and predicting any future growth. This could make it tempting for senior managers who may be under pressure to achieve sales targets to increase the turnover figure by adopting revenue recognition policies that bring future revenues into the current period, e.g. invoicing a customer at the end of an accounting period for goods that remain in stock for delivery in the following accounting period or are sent out with a possible right of return or by adopting fraudulent practices, e.g. creating fictitious invoices which inflate both turnover and trade debtors.

2.8.1 Why is revenue recognition so important?

Revenue has a multiplier impact on profits, for example, if a business has a turnover of £100,000 and a profit of £5,000 and it increases turnover by 1% (£1,000), the effect on profit is to increase it by 20%.

2.8.2 Clarifying revenue recognition policies

There is a general awareness of the recognition problem. For example, the USA and IASB are combining their research into a joint project to prepare a revised draft for IAS 18, and in the UK the ASB has issued an Exposure Draft of an Application Note to FRS 5 'Reporting the Substance of Transactions' as an interim step pending the IAS 18 replacement standard covering areas such as the correct treatment for sales that are made with the right of return. This step has been taken by the ASB because of their view[15] that it has become clear from recent reports of questionable practice in the UK market that they should not wait any longer to clarify revenue recognition principles.

2.8.3 Limiting fraudulent practices

It is very much the responsibility of the directors to adopt procedures that reduce the risk and of the auditors in carrying out tests to identify such practices.

2.9 Mechanics of accrual accounting – the balance sheet

The balance sheet or statement of financial position, as set out in Figure 1.12, needs to be amended following the change from cash flow to accrual accounting. It needs to include the £ amounts that have arisen from trading but have not been converted to cash, and the £ amounts of cash that have been received or paid but relate to a subsequent period. The adjusted statement of financial position is set out in Figure 2.5.

2.10 Reformatting the statement of financial position into a balance sheet

The item 'Net amount of activities not converted to cash, or relating to subsequent periods' is the net debtor/creditor balance. If we wished, the statement of financial position could be reframed into the customary balance sheet format, where items are classified as assets or liabilities. The ASB defines assets and liabilities in its *Statement of Principles*:

Figure 2.5 Statement of financial position adjusted to an accrual basis

	£
Capital	50,000
Net operating cash flow: **realised**	15,650
Net operating cash flow: **to be realised next period**	(12,275)
	53,375
Lease	80,000
Net cash balance (refer to Figure 1.11)	(14,350)
Net amount of activities not converted to cash, or relating to subsequent periods	(12,275)
	53,375

Figure 2.6 Balance sheet as at 30 June

		Reframed
	£	£
CAPITAL	50,000	50,000
Net operating cash flow: **realised**	15,650	
Net operating cash flow: **to be realised**	(12,275)	
NET INCOME		3,375
	53,375	53,375
FIXED ASSETS	80,000	80,000
NET CURRENT ASSETS		
Net amount of activities not converted to cash	(12,275)	
CURRENT ASSETS		
Trade debtors		22,500
Prepaid rent		3,125
CURRENT LIABILITIES		
Trade creditors		(37,000)
Expense creditors		(900)
Net cash balance	(14,350)	(14,350)
	53,375	53,375

1 An item is an asset if it possesses the following characteristic:
   a right or other access to future economic benefits controlled by an entity as a result of past transactions or events.
2 An item is a liability if it possesses the following characteristic:
   an obligation to transfer economic benefits as a result of past transactions or events.[16]

The reframed balance sheet set out in Figure 2.6 is in accordance with these definitions. Note that the same amount of £3,375 results from calculating the difference in the opening and closing net assets in the balance sheets as from calculating the residual amount in the income statement. When the amount derived from both approaches is the same, the balance sheet and income statement are said to **articulate**. The income statement provides the detailed explanation for the difference in the net assets and the amount is the same because the same concepts have been applied to both statements.

2.11 Accounting for the sacrifice of fixed assets

The income statement and balance sheet have both been prepared using verifiable data that have arisen from transactions with third parties outside the business. However, in order to determine the full sacrifice of economic resources that a business has made to achieve its revenue, it is necessary also to take account of the use made of the fixed assets during the period in which the revenue arose.

In the Norman example, the fixed asset is the lease. The extent of the sacrifice is a matter of judgement by the management. This is influenced by the prudence principle, which regulates the matching principle. The prudence principle determines the extent to which transactions that have already been included in the accounting system should be recognised in the profit and loss account.[17]

2.11.1 Treatment of fixed assets in accrual accounting

Applying the matching principle, it is necessary to estimate how much of the initial outlay should be assumed to have been revenue expenditure, i.e. used in achieving the revenue of the accounting period. The provisions of FRS 15 on **depreciation** assist by defining depreciation and stating the duty of allocation, as follows:

> Depreciation is the measure of the cost or revalued amount of the economic benefits of the tangible fixed asset that have been consumed during the period. Consumption includes the wearing out, using up or other reduction in the useful economic life of a tangible fixed asset whether arising from use, effluxion of time or obsolescence through either changes in technology or demand for the goods and services produced by the asset.[18]

> The FRS further provides that the depreciable amount of a tangible asset should be allocated on a systematic basis over its useful economic life. The depreciation method should reflect as fairly as possible the pattern in which the asset's economic benefits are consumed by the entity. The depreciation charge for each period should be recognised as an expense in the profit and loss account unless it is permitted to be included in the carrying amount of another asset.[19]

> With regard to the depreciation method FRS 15 provides that a variety of methods can be used to allocate the depreciable amount of a tangible fixed asset on a systematic basis over its useful economic life and that the method chosen should result in a depreciation charge throughout the asset's useful economic life and not just towards the end of its useful economic life or when the asset is falling in value.[20]

This sounds a rather complex requirement. It is therefore surprising, when one looks at the financial statements of a multinational company such as BP Amoco plc, to find that depreciation on tangible assets other than mineral production is simply provided on a straight line basis of an equal amount each year, calculated so as to write off the cost by equal instalments. This treatment is recognised in FRS 15 which states that where the pattern of

Figure 2.7 Income statement for the six months ending 30 June

	Operating cash flow CURRENT period £	Adjust cash flow £	Business activity CURRENT period £
Revenue from business activity	172,500	22,500	195,000
Less			
Expenditure to support this activity:			
Transactions with suppliers	129,000	37,000	166,000
Transactions with service providers	21,600	900	22,500
Transactions with landlord	6,250	3,125	3,125
OPERATING CASH FLOW from activity	15,650		
TRANSACTIONS NOT CONVERTED TO CASH		(12,275)	
INCOME from business activity			3,375
Allocation of fixed asset cost to this period			8,000
INCOME			(4,625)

Figure 2.8 Balance sheet as at 30 June

	Transaction cash flows £	Notional flows £	Reported £
CAPITAL	50,000		50,000
Net operating cash flow: **realised**	15,650		
Net operating cash flow: **to be realised**	(12,275)		
Net income before depreciation		3,375	
DEPRECIATION		(8,000)	
Net income after depreciation			(4,625)
	53,375		45,375
FIXED ASSETS	80,000	80,000	
Less depreciation		(8,000)	
Net book value			72,000
NET CURRENT ASSETS			
Net amount not converted to cash	(12,275)		
CURRENT ASSETS			
Trade debtors			22,500
Prepaid rent			3,125
CURRENT LIABILITIES			
Trade creditors			(37,000)
Expense creditors			(900)
Net cash balance	(14,350)		(14,350)
	53,375		45,375

consumption of an asset's economic benefits is uncertain, a straight line method of depreciation is usually adopted.[21] The reason is that, in accrual accounting, the depreciation charged to the income statement is a measure of the amount of the economic benefits that have been consumed, rather than a measure of the fall in realisable value. In estimating the amount of service potential expired, a business is following the **going concern concept**.

2.11.2 Going concern concept

The going concern concept assumes that the business enterprise will continue in operational existence for the foreseeable future. This assumption introduces a constraint on the prudence concept by allowing the account balances to be reported on a depreciated cost basis rather than on a net realisable value basis.[22]

It is more relevant to use the loss of service potential than the change in realisable value because there is no intention to cease trading and to sell the fixed assets at the end of the accounting period.

In our Norman example, the procedure would be to assume that, in the case of the lease, the economic resource that has been consumed can be measured by the amortisation that has occurred due to the effluxion of time. The time covered by the accounts is half a year: this means that one-tenth of the lease has expired during the half-year. As a result, £8,000 is treated as revenue expenditure in the half-year to 30 June.

This additional revenue expenditure reduces the income in the income account and the asset figure in the balance sheet. The effects are incorporated into the two statements in Figures 2.7 and 2.8. The asset amounts and the income figure in the balance sheet are also affected by the exhaustion of part of the fixed assets, as set out in Figure 2.8.

It is current accounting practice to apply the same concepts to determining the entries in both the income statement and the balance sheet. The amortisation charged in the income statement at £8,000 is the same as the amount deducted from the fixed assets in the balance sheet. As a result, the two statements articulate: the income statement explains the reason for the reduction of £4,625 in the net assets.

How decision useful to the management is the income figure that has been derived after deducting a depreciation charge?

The loss of £4,625 indicates that the distribution of any amount would further deplete the financial capital of £50,000, which was invested in the company by Mr Norman on setting up the business. This is referred to as **capital maintenance**; the particular capital maintenance concept that has been applied is the **financial capital maintenance concept**.

2.11.3 Financial capital maintenance concept

The financial capital maintenance concept recognises a profit only after the original monetary investment has been maintained. This means that, as long as the cost of the assets representing the initial monetary investment is recovered against the profit, by way of a depreciation charge, the initial monetary investment is maintained.[23]

The concept has been described in slightly different terms in the IASC *Framework for the Presentation and Preparation of Financial Statements*:

> a profit is earned only if the financial or money amount of the net assets at the end of the period exceeds the financial or money amount of the net assets at the beginning of the period, after excluding any distributions to, and contributions from, owners during the period. Financial capital maintenance can be measured in either nominal monetary units [as we are doing in this chapter] or in units of constant purchasing power [as we will be doing in Chapter 4].[24]

2.11.4 Summary of views on accrual accounting

The profit (loss) is considered to be a guide when assessing the amount, timing and uncertainty of prospective cash flows as represented by future income amounts. The IASC, FASB and ASB clearly state that the accrual accounting concept is more useful in predicting future cash flows than cash flow accounting.

Academic research provides conflicting views. In 1986 research carried out in the USA indicated that the FASB view was inconsistent with its findings and that cash flow information was a better predictor of future operating cash flows;[25] research carried out in the UK, however, indicated that accrual accounting using the historical cost convention was 'a more relevant basis for decision making than cash flow measures'.[26]

2.12 Reconciliation of cash flow and accrual accounting data

The accounting profession attempted to provide users of financial statements with the benefits of both types of data, by requiring a cash flow statement to be prepared as well as the income statement and balance sheet prepared on an accrual basis.

From the income statement prepared on an accrual basis (as in Figure 2.7) an investor is able to obtain an indication of a business's present ability to generate favourable cash flows; from the balance sheet prepared on an accrual basis (as in Figure 2.8) an investor is able to obtain an indication of a business's continuing ability to generate favourable cash flows; from the cash flow statement (as in Figure 2.9) an investor is able to reconcile the income figure with the change in net cash balance.

Figure 2.9 reconciles the information produced in Chapter 1 under the cash flow basis with the information produced under the accrual basis. It could be expanded to provide information more clearly, as in Figure 2.10. Here we are using the information from Figures 1.9 and 1.12, but within a third statement rather than the income statement and balance sheet.

Figure 2.9 Reconciliation of income figure with net cash balance

	£
Income per income statement	(4,625)
Add: unrealisable cash outflow	8,000
	3,375
Add: unrealised operating cash flows	12,275
Operating cash flow	15,650
Other sources:	
Capital	50,000
Total cash available	65,650
Applications	
Lease	(80,000)
Net cash balance	(14,350)

Figure 2.10 Cash flow statement netting amounts that have not been converted to cash

	£	£
Sales	195,000	
Debtors	(22,500)	172,500
Purchases	166,000	
Creditors	(37,000)	(129,000)
Expenses	22,500	
Creditors	(900)	(21,600)
Rent	3,125	
Prepaid	3,125	(6,250)
Net cash inflow from operating activities		15,650
Investing activities		
Lease		(80,000)
Financing		
Issue of capital		50,000
Decrease in cash		(14,350)

Figure 2.11 Cash flow statement in accordance with FRS 1 *Cash Flow Statements*

	£
Net cash inflow from operating activities	15,650
Investing activities	
Payment to acquire lease	(80,000)
Net cash outflow before financing	(64,350)
Financing	
Issue of capital	50,000
Decrease in cash	(14,350)
Reconciliation of operating loss to net cash inflow from operating activities	£
Operating profit/loss	(4,625)
Depreciation charges	8,000
Increase in debtors	(22,500)
Increase in prepayments	(3,125)
Increase in creditors	37,000
Increase in accruals	900
	15,650

2.12.1 Published cash flow statement

FRS 1 *Cash Flow Statements*[27] specifies the standard headings under which cash flows should be classified. They are:

- cash inflow or outflow from operations;
- returns on investments and servicing of finance;
- taxation;
- capital expenditure and financial investments;
- acquisitions and disposals;
- equity dividends paid;
- management of liquid resources;
- financing.

To comply with FRS 1, the cash flows from Figure 2.10 would be set out as in Figure 2.11. FRS 1 is mentioned at this stage only to illustrate that cash flows can be reconciled to the accrual accounting data. There is further discussion of FRS 1 in Chapter 24.

REVIEW QUESTIONS

1 *The Corporate Report* identified seven user groups: investors, loan creditors, business contact, analysts acting for any of these, the government, employees and the public.

(a) Explain their presumed interest with reference to the performance of the company and its financial position.

(b) Discuss which of the financial statements illustrated in Chapters 1 and 2 would be most useful to each of these seven groups if they could only receive one statement.

2 'Accrual accounting is preferable to cash flow accounting because the information is more relevant to all users of financial statements.' Discuss.

3 'Cash flow accounting and accrual accounting information are both required by a potential shareholder.' Discuss.

4 'Information contained in a profit and loss account and a balance sheet prepared under accrual accounting concepts is factual and objective.' Discuss.

5 'The asset measurement basis applied in accrual accounting can lead to financial difficulties when assets are due for replacement.' Discuss.

6 'Accountants preparing financial statements in the UK do not require a standard such as IAS 18 *Revenue*.'[28] Discuss.

7 Explain the revenue recognition principle and discuss the effect of alternative treatments on the reported results of a company.

8 'What is needed is a coherent system, such as being developed in West Africa, which starts the micro-business off with simple cash accounting, and then provides for the entity to move up the accounting ladder in stages to basic accruals and finally full IAS as it gets bigger.'[29]

Discuss the steps necessary to implement such a system and the problems that are likely to arise.

EXERCISES

An extract from the solution is provided in the appendix at the end of the text for exercises marked with an asterisk (*).

* Question 1

Jane Parker is going to set up a new business on 1 January 20X1. She estimates that her first six months in business will be as follows:

(i) She will put £150,000 into the firm on 1 January 20X1.

(ii) On 1 January 20X1 she will buy machinery £30,000, motor vehicles £24,000 and premises £75,000, paying for them immediately.

(iii) All purchases will be effected on credit. She will buy £30,000 goods on 1 January and she will pay for these in February. Other purchases will be: rest of January £48,000; February, March, April, May and June £60,000 each month. Other than the £30,000 worth bought in January, all other purchases will be paid for two months after purchase, i.e. £48,000 in March.

(iv) Sales (all on credit) will be £60,000 for January and £75,000 for each month after that. Debtors will pay for goods in the third month after purchase, i.e. £60,000 in April.

(v) Stock in trade on 30 June 20X1 will be £30,000.

(vi) Wages and salaries will be £2,250 per month and will be paid on the last day of each month.

(vii) General expenses will be £750 per month, payable in the month following that in which they are incurred.

(viii) She will introduce new capital of £75,000 on 1 June 20X1. This will be paid into the business bank account immediately.

(ix) Insurance covering the 12 months of 20X1 £26,400 will be paid for by cheque on 30 June 20X1.

(x) Rates will be paid as follows: for the three months to 31 March 20X1 by cheque on 28 February 20X2 (delay due to an oversight by Parker); for the 12 months ended 31 March 20X2 by cheque on 31 July 20X1. Rates are £8,000 per annum.

(xi) She will make drawings of £1,500 per month by cheque.

(xii) All receipts and payments are by cheque.

(xiii) Depreciate motor vehicles by 20% per annum and machinery by 10% per annum, using the straight line depreciation method.

(xiv) She has been informed by her bank manager that he is prepared to offer an overdraft facility of £30,000 for the first year.

Required:

(a) Draft a cash budget (for the firm) month by month for the period January to June, showing clearly the amount of bank balance at the end of each month.

(b) Draft the projected trading and profit and loss account for the first six months' trading, and a balance sheet as at 30 June 20X1.

(c) Advise Jane on the alternative courses of action that could be taken to cover any cash deficiency that exceeds the agreed overdraft limit.

* Question 2

Mr Norman is going to set up a new business on 1 January 20X8. He will invest £150,000 in the business on that date and has made the following estimates and policy decisions:

1 Forecast sales (in units) made at a selling price of £50 per unit are:

Month	Sales units	Month	Sales units
January	1,650	May	4,400
February	2,200	June	4,950
March	3,850	July	5,500
April	4,400		

2 50% of sales are for cash. Credit terms are payment in month following sale.

3 The units cost £40 each and the supplier is allowed one month's credit.

4 It is intended to hold stock at the end of each month sufficient to cover 25% of the following month's sales.

5 Administration £8,000 and wages £17,000 are paid monthly as they arise.

6 On 1 January 20X8, the following payments will be made: £80,000 for a five-year lease of the business premises and £350 for insurance for the year.

7 Staff sales commission of 2% of sales will be paid in the month following sale.

Required:
(a) A purchases budget for each of the first six months.
(b) A cash flow forecast for the first six months.
(c) A budgeted profit and loss account for the first six months' trading and a budgeted balance sheet as at 30 June 20X8.
(d) Advise Mr Norman on the investment of any excess cash.

Question 3

The Piano Warehouse Company Limited was established on 1 January 20X7 for the purpose of making pianos. Jeremy Holmes, the managing director, had twenty years' experience in the manufacture of pianos and was an acknowledged technical expert in the field. He had invested his life's savings of £15,000 in the company, and his decision to launch the company reflected his desire for complete independence.

Nevertheless, his commitment to the company represented a considerable financial gamble. He paid close attention to the management of its financial affairs and ensured that a careful record of all transactions was kept.

The company's activities during the year ended 31 December 20X7 were as follows:

(i) Four pianos had been built and sold for a total sum of £8,000. Holmes calculated their cost of manufacture as follows:

Materials	£2,000
Labour	£2,800
Overhead costs	£800

(ii) Two pianos were 50% completed at 31 December 20X7. Madrigal Music Limited had agreed to buy them for a total of £4,500 and had made a down-payment amounting to 20% of the agreed sale price. Holmes estimated their costs of manufacture to 31 December 20X7 as follows:

Materials	£900	
Labour	£800	
Overhead costs	£100	

(iii) Two pianos had been rebuilt and sold for a total of £3,000. Holmes paid £1,800 for them at an auction and had spent a further £400 on rebuilding them. The sale of these two pianos was made under a hire purchase agreement under which The Piano Warehouse Company received £1,000 on delivery and two payments over the next two years plus interest of 15% on the outstanding balance.

At the end of the company's first financial year, Jeremy Holmes was anxious that the company's net profit to 31 December 20X7 should be represented in the most accurate manner. There appeared to be several alternative bases on which the transactions for the year could be interpreted. It was clear to him that, in simple terms, the net profit for the year should be calculated by deducting expenses from revenues. As far as cash sales were concerned he saw no difficulty. But how should the pianos that were 50% completed be treated? Should the value of the work done up to 31 December 20X7 be included in the profit of that year, or should it be carried forward to the next year, when the work would be completed and the pianos sold? As regards the pianos sold under the hire purchase agreement, should profit be taken in 20X7 or spread over the years in which a proportion of the revenue is received?

Required:

(a) Prepare a profit and loss account for the year ended 31 December 20X7 on a basis that would reflect conventional accounting principles.

(b) Examine the problems implied in the timing of the recognition of revenues, illustrating your answer by the facts in the case of The Piano Warehouse.

(c) Discuss the significant accounting conventions that would be relevant to profit determination in this case, and discuss their limitations in this context.

(d) Advise the company on alternative accounting treatments that could increase the profit for the year.

(e) Give three reasons why managements might wish to inflate earnings.

(f) Give three examples of 'aggressive' earnings management.

(g) Give three examples of inflating earnings by fraudulent accounting.

Question 4

The following is an extract from the Financial Reporting Review Panel website (www.frrp.org.uk) relating to the Wiggins Group showing the restated financial results.

		Year					
		1995	1996	1997	1998	1999	2000
Turnover	As published	6.4	6.9	19.9	17.8	26.7	49.8
(£m)	Adjustments	(1.5)	(2.6)	(15.6)	(6.7)	(21.6)	(42.5)
	Restated	4.9	4.3	4.3	11.1	5.1	7.3
Profit/(loss)	As published	0.7	1.0	4.9	5.1	12.1	25.1
before tax	Adjustments	(1.3)	(1.9)	(10.2)	(8.5)	(17.2)	(35.0)
(£m)	Restated	(0.6)	(0.9)	(5.3)	(3.4)	(5.1)	(9.9)
Basic EPS	As published	0.14	0.20	0.66	0.64	1.21	2.87
(pence)	Adjustments	(0.26)	(0.38)	(1.67)	(1.14)	(1.91)	(4.06)
	Restated	(0.12)	(0.18)	(1.01)	(0.50)	(0.70)	(1.19)
Net assets	As published	10.2	11.4	17.5	37.5	52.2	45.8
(£m)	Adjustments	(1.3)	(3.2)	(12.0)	(19.8)	(33.8)	(35.4)
	Restated	8.9	8.2	5.5	17.7	18.4	10.4

Revenue recognition

The 1999 accounts contained an accounting policy for turnover in the following terms:

Commercial property sales are recognised at the date of exchange of contract, providing the Group is reasonably assured of the receipt of the sale proceeds.

The FRRP accepted that this wording was similar to that used by many other companies and was not on the face of it objectionable. In reviewing the company's 1999 accounts the FRRP noted that the turnover and profits recognised under this policy were not reflected in similar inflows of cash; indeed, operating cash flow was negative and the amount receivable within debtors of £46m represented more than the previous two years' turnover of £44m. As a result, the FRRP enquired into the detailed application of the policy.

Required:
Refer to the website and discuss the significance of the revenue recognition criteria on the published results.

References

1 *Statement of Principles for Financial Reporting*, ASB, 1999, para. 1.3.
2 *Ibid.*, para. 1.11.
3 *Ibid.*, para. 1.14(a).
4 *Ibid.*, para. 1.18.
5 *Ibid.*, para. 1.14(b).
6 *Ibid.*, para. 7.3.
7 M. Page, *British Accounting Review*, vol. 24(1), 1992, p. 80.
8 D. Chopping and L. Skerratt, *Applying GAAP 1997/8*, ICAEW, 1997, p. 7.
9 *Statement of Financial Accounting Concepts No. 1, Objectives of Financial Reporting by Business Enterprises*, Financial Accounting Standards Board, 1978.
10 *Framework for the Presentation and Preparation of Financial Statements*, IASC, 1989, para. 20.
11 *Revenue*, IAS 18, IASC, 1993, para. 23.
12 D. Chopping and L. Skerratt, *op. cit.*, p. 9.
13 'What do we tell the shareholders?' *Accountancy*, October 2001, pp. 102–103.
14 'We need a standard for revenue', *Accountancy*, August 2001, p. 96.
15 ASB, Pn 213, 27 February 2003.
16 ASB, 1999, *op. cit.*, Chapter 4 Principles.
17 D. Chopping and L. Skerratt, *op. cit.*, p. 10.
18 FRS 15 *Tangible Fixed Assets*, ASB, 1999, para. 2.
19 *Ibid.*, para. 77.
20 *Ibid.*, para. 81.
21 *Ibid.*, para. 81.
22 D. Chopping and L. Skerratt, *op. cit.*, p. 12.
23 J. Baillie, *Systems of Profit Measurement*, Gee & Co., 1985, p. 37.
24 *Framework for the Presentation and Preparation of Financial Statements*, IASC, 1989, para. 102.
25 R.M. Bowen, D. Burgstahler and L.A. Daley, 'Evidence on the relationships between earnings and various measures of cash flow', *Accounting Review*, October 1986, pp. 713–25.
26 J.I.G. Board and J.F.S. Day, 'The information content of cash flow figures', *Accounting and Business Research*, Winter 1989, pp. 3–11.
27 *Cash Flow Statements*, ASB 1991 Revised 1996.
28 D. Chopping and L. Skerratt, *op. cit.*, p. 55.
29 P. Walton, 'UN research into the accounting needs of SMEs', *Accounting & Business*, February 2000, pp. 34–35.

CHAPTER 3

Income and asset value measurement: an economist's approach

3.1 Introduction

This chapter discusses the need for income measurement. It compares the methods of measurement adopted by the accountant with those of the economist, the reasons for the different approaches, the relationship of income to capital and the impact of the concept of value on these measures. The prime objective is to engender an understanding of the rule of income and capital within the commercial enterprise, and to prevent misunderstanding of what initially may appear to be a conflict of method between the two disciplines. Economic value was initially perceived as an academic subject but we now see it being applied by the ASB within financial reporting, e.g. in Chapter 6 of the *Statement of Principles* (Measurement in financial statements – see section 6.9.9 below) and in FRS 11 *Impairment of Tangible Fixed Assets* where it is referred to as value in use (see section 14.10 below). In this chapter we consider the following:

- Role and objective of income measurement
- Accountant's view of income, capital and value
- Critical comment on the accountant's measure
- Economist's view of income, capital and value
- Critical comment on the economist's measure
- Income, capital and changing price levels

3.2 Role and objective of income measurement

Although accountancy has played a part in business reporting for centuries, it is only since the Companies Act 1929 that financial reporting has become income orientated. Prior to that Act an income statement was of minor importance. It was the balance sheet that mattered, providing a list of capital, assets and liabilities that revealed the financial soundness and solvency of the business.

According to some commentators,[1] this scenario may be attributed to the sources of capital funding. Until the late 1920s, as in present-day Germany, external capital finance in the UK was mainly in the hands of bankers, other lenders and trade creditors. As the main users of published financial statements, they focused on the company's ability to pay trade creditors and the interest on loans, and to meet the scheduled dates of loan repayment: they were interested in the short-term liquidity and longer-term solvency of the entity.

Thus the balance sheet was the prime document of interest. Perhaps in recognition of this, the English balance sheet, until recent times, tended to show liabilities on the left-hand side, thus making them the first part of the balance sheet read.

The gradual evolution of a sophisticated investment market, embracing a range of financial institutions, together with the growth in the number of individual investors, caused a reorientation of priorities. Investor protection and investor decision-making needs started to dominate the financial reporting scene, and the revenue statement replaced the balance sheet as the sovereign reporting document.

Consequently, attention became fixed on the income statement and on concepts of accounting for profit. Moreover, investor protection assumed a new meaning. It changed from simply protecting the **capital** that had **been invested** to protecting the **income information** used by investors when making an investment decision.

However, the sight of major companies experiencing severe liquidity problems over the past decade has revived interest in the balance sheet; while its light is perhaps not of the same intensity as that of the profit and loss account, it cannot be said to be totally subordinate to its accompanying statement of income.

The main objectives of income measurement are to provide:

- a means of control in a micro- and macroeconomic sense;
- a means of prediction;
- a basis for taxation.

We consider each of these below.

3.2.1 Income as a means of control

Assessment of stewardship performance

Managers are the stewards appointed by shareholders. Income, in the sense of net income or net profit, is the crystallisation of their accountability. Maximisation of income is seen as a major aim of the entrepreneurial entity, but the capacity of the business to pursue this aim may be subject to political and social constraints in the case of large public monopolies, and private semi-monopolies such as British Telecommunications plc.

Maximisation of net income is reflected in the earnings per share (EPS) figure, which is shown on the face of the published profit and loss account. The importance of this figure to the shareholders is evidenced by contracts that tie directors' remuneration to growth in EPS. A rising EPS may result in an increased salary or bonus for directors and upward movement in the market price of the underlying security. The effect on the market price is indicated by another extremely important statistic, which is influenced by the income statement: namely, the price/earnings (PE) ratio. The PE ratio reveals the numerical relationship between the share's current market price and the last reported EPS.

Actual performance versus predicted performance

This comparison enables the management and the investing public to use the lessons of the past to improve future performance. The public, as shareholders, may initiate a change in the company directorate if circumstances necessitate it. This may be one reason why management is generally loath to give a clear, quantified estimate of projected results – such an estimate is a potential measure of efficiency. The comparison of actual with projected results identifies apparent underachievement.

The macroeconomic concept

Good government is, of necessity, involved in managing the macroeconomic scene and as such is a user of the income measure. State policies need to be formulated concerning the allocation of economic resources and the regulation of firms and industries, as illustrated by the measures taken by Oftel and Ofwat to regulate the size of earnings by British Telecom and the water companies.

3.2.2 Income as a means of prediction

Dividend and retention policy

The payment of a dividend, its scale and that of any residual income after such dividend has been paid are influenced by the profit generated for the financial year. Other influences are also active, including the availability of cash resources within the entity, the opportunities for further internal investment, the dividend policies of capital-competing entities with comparable shares, the contemporary cost of capital and the current tempo of the capital market.

However, some question the soundness of using the profit generated for the year when making a decision to invest in an enterprise. Their view is that such a practice misunderstands the nature of income data, and that the appropriate information is the prospective cash flows. They regard the use of income figures from past periods as defective because, even if the future accrual accounting income could be forecast accurately, 'it is no more than an imperfect surrogate for future cash flows'.[2]

The counter-argument is that there is considerable resistance by both managers and accountants to the publication of future operating flows and dividend payments.[3] This means that, in the absence of relevant information, an investor needs to rely on a surrogate. The question then arises: which is the best surrogate?

In the short term, the best surrogate is the information that is currently available, i.e. income measured according to the accrual concept. In the longer term, management will be pressed by the shareholders to provide the actual forecast data on operating cash flows and dividend distribution, or to improve the surrogate information.

Suggestions for improving the surrogate information have included the provision of cash earnings per share. More fundamentally, Revsine has suggested that ideal information for investors would indicate the economic value of the business (and its assets) based on expected future cash flows. However, the Revsine suggestion itself requires information on future cash flows that it is not possible to obtain at this time.[4] Instead, he considered the use of replacement cost as a surrogate for the economic value of the business, and we return to this later in the chapter.

Future performance

While history is not a faultless indicator of future events and their financial results, it does have a role to play in assessing the level of future income. In this context, historic income is of assistance to existing investors, prospective investors and management.

Identifying maintainable profit by the analysis of matched costs

Subject to the requirement of enforced disclosure via the Companies Acts 1985 and 1989, as supplemented by *Standard Accounting Practice*, the measurement of income discloses items of income and expenditure necessarily of interest in assessing stewardship success and future prospects. In this respect, exceptional items, extraordinary items and other itemised costs and turnover are essential information.

3.2.3 Basis for taxation

The contemporary taxation philosophy, in spite of criticism from some economists, uses income measurement to measure the taxable capacity of a business entity.

However, the determination of income by the Inland Revenue is necessarily influenced by socioeconomic fiscal factors, among others, and thus accounting profit is subject to adjustment in order to achieve taxable profit. As a tax base, it has been continually eroded as the difference between accounting income and taxable income has grown.[5]

The Inland Revenue in the UK has tended to disallow expenses that are particularly susceptible to management judgement. For example, a uniform capital allowance is substituted for the subjective depreciation charge that is made by management, and certain provisions that appear as a charge in the profit and loss account are not accepted as an expense for tax purposes until the loss crystallises, e.g. a charge to increase the doubtful debts provision may not be allowed until the debt is recognised as bad.

3.3 Accountant's view of income, capital and value

Variations between accountants and economists in measuring income, capital and value are caused by their different views of these measures. In this section we introduce the accountant's view and, in the next, the economist's, in order to reconcile variations in methods of measurement.

3.3.1 The accountant's view

Income is an important part of accounting theory and practice, although until 1970, when a formal system of propagating standard accounting practice throughout the accountancy profession began, it received little attention in accountancy literature. The characteristics of measurement were basic and few, and tended to be of an intuitive, traditional nature, rather than being spelled out precisely and given mandatory status within the profession.

Accounting tradition of historical cost

The income statement is based on the actual costs of business transactions, i.e. the costs incurred in the currency and at the price levels pertaining at the time of the transactions.

Accounting income is said to be historical income, i.e. it is an *ex post* measure because it takes place after the event. The traditional profit and loss account is historical in two senses: because it concerns a past period, and because it utilises historical cost, being the cost of the transactions on which it is based. It follows that the balance sheet, being based on the residuals of transactions not yet dealt with in the profit and loss account, is also based on historical cost.

In practice, certain amendments may be made to historical cost in both profit and loss account and balance sheet, but historical cost still predominates in both statements. It is justified on a number of counts which, in principle, guard against the manipulation of data.

The main characteristics of historical cost accounting are as follows:

● **Objectivity**. It is a predominantly objective system, although it does exhibit aspects of subjectivity. Its nature is generally understood and it is invariably supported by independent documentary evidence, e.g. an invoice, statement, cheque, cheque counterfoil, receipt or voucher.

● **Factual**. As a basis of fact (with exceptions such as when amended in furtherance of revaluation), it is verifiable and to that extent is beyond dispute.

- **Profit or income concept**. Profit as a concept is generally well understood in a capital market economy, even if its precise measurement may be problematic. It constitutes the difference between revenue and expenditure or, in the economic sense, between opening and closing net assets.

Unfortunately, historical cost is not without its weaknesses. It is not always objective, owing to alternative definitions of revenue and costs and the need for estimates.

We saw in the preceding chapter that revenue could be determined according to a choice of criteria. There is also a choice of criteria for defining costs. For example, although inventories are valued at the lower of cost or net realisable value, the **cost** will differ depending upon the definition adopted, e.g. first-in-first-out, last-in-first-out or standard cost.

Estimation is needed in the case of inventory valuation, assessing possible bad debts, accruing expenses, providing for depreciation and determining the profit attributable to long-term contracts. So, although it is transaction based, there are aspects of historical cost reporting that do not result from an independently verifiable business transaction. This means that profit is not always a unique figure.

Assets are often subjected to revaluation. In an economy of changing price levels, the historical cost system has been compromised by a perceived need to restate the carrying value of those assets that comprise a large proportion of a company's capital employed; e.g. land and buildings. This practice is controversial, not least because it is said to imply that a balance sheet is a list of assets at market valuation, rather than a statement of unamortised costs not yet charged against revenue.

However, despite conventional accountancy income being partly the result of subjectivity, it is largely the product of the historical cost concept. A typical accounting policy specified in the published accounts of companies now reads as follows:

> The financial statements are prepared under the historical cost conventions as modified by the revaluation of certain fixed assets.

Nature of accounting income

Accounting income is defined in terms of the business entity. It is the excess of revenue from sales over direct and allocated indirect costs incurred in the achievement of such sales. Its measure results in a net figure. It is the numerical result of the matching and accruals concepts discussed in the preceding chapter.

We saw in the preceding chapter that accounting income is transaction based and therefore can be said to be factual, in as much as the revenue and costs have been realised and will be reflected in cash inflow and outflow, although not necessarily within the financial year.

We also saw that, under accrual accounting, the sales for a financial period are offset by the expenses incurred in generating such sales. Objectivity is a prime characteristic of accrual accounting, but the information cannot be entirely objective because of the need to break up the ongoing performance of the business entity into calendar periods or financial years for purposes of accountability reporting. The allocation of expenses between periods requires a prudent estimate of some costs, e.g. the provision for depreciation and bad debts attributable to each period.

Accounting income is presented in the form of the conventional profit and loss account or income statement. This income statement, in being based on actual transactions, is concerned with a past-defined period of time. Thus accounting profit is said to be historic income, i.e. an *ex post* measure because it is after the event.

Nature of accounting capital

The business enterprise requires the use of non-monetary assets, e.g. buildings, plant and machinery, office equipment, motor vehicles, stock of raw materials and work-in-progress. Such assets are not consumed in any one accounting period, but give service over a number of periods; therefore, the unconsumed portions of each asset are carried forward from period to period and appear in the balance sheet. This document itemises the unused asset balances at the date of the financial year-end. In addition to listing unexpired costs of non-monetary assets, the balance sheet also displays monetary assets such as debtor and cash balances, together with monetary liabilities, i.e. moneys owing to trade creditors, other creditors and lenders. Funds supplied by shareholders and retained income following the distribution of dividend are also shown. Retained profits are usually added to shareholders' capital, resulting in what is known as shareholders' funds. These represent the company's equity capital.

The net assets of the firm, i.e. that fund of unconsumed assets which exceeds moneys attributable to creditors and lenders, constitutes the company's net capital, which is the same as its equity capital. Thus the profit and loss account of a financial period can be seen as a linking statement between that period's opening and closing balance sheets: in other words, income may be linked with opening and closing capital. This linking may be expressed by formula, as follows:

$$Y_{0-1} = NA_1 - NA_0 + D_{0-1}$$

where Y_{0-1} = income for the period of time t_0 to t_1; NA_0 = net assets of the entity at point of time t_0; NA_1 = net assets of the entity at point of time t_1; D_{0-1} = dividends or distribution during period t_{0-1}.

Less formally: Y = income of financial year; NA_0 = net assets as shown in the balance sheet at beginning of financial year; NA_1 = net assets as shown in the balance sheet at end of financial year; D_{0-1} = dividends paid and proposed for the financial year. We can illustrate this as follows:

Income Y_{0-1} for the financial year t_{0-1} as compiled by the accountant was £1,200

Dividend D_{0-1} for the financial year t_{0-1} was £450

Net assets NA_0 at the beginning of the financial year were £6,000

Net assets NA_1 at the end of the financial year were £6,750.

The income account can be linked with opening and closing balance sheets, namely:

$$Y_{0-1} = NA_1 - NA_0 + D_{0-1}$$
$$= £6,750 - £6,000 + £450$$
$$= £1,200 = Y_{0-1}$$

Thus Y has been computed by using the opening and closing capitals for the period where capital equals net assets.

In practice, however, the accountant would compute income Y by compiling a profit and loss account. So, of what use is this formula? For reasons to be discussed later, the economist finds use for the formula when it is amended to take account of what we call **present values**. Computed after the end of a financial year, it is the *ex post* measure of income.

Nature of traditional accounting value

As the values of assets still in service at the end of a financial period have been based on the unconsumed costs of such assets, they are the by-product of compiling the income financial statement. These values have been fixed not by direct measurement, but simply by an assessment of costs consumed in the process of generating period turnover. We can say, then, that the balance sheet figure of net assets is a residual valuation after measuring income.

However, it is not a value in the sense of worth or market value as a buying price or selling price; it is merely a **value of unconsumed costs of assets**. This is an important point that will be encountered again later.

3.4 Critical comment on the accountant's measure

3.4.1 Virtues of the accountant's measure

As with the economist's, the accountant's measure is not without its virtues. These are invariably aspects of the historical cost concept, such as objectivity, being transaction based and being generally understood.

3.4.2 Faults of the accountant's measure

Principles of historical cost and profit realisation

The historical cost and profit realisation concepts are firmly entrenched in the transaction basis of accountancy. However, in practice, the two concepts are not free of adjustments. Because of such adjustments, some commentators argue that the system produces a heterogeneous mix of values and realised income items.[6]

For example, in the case of asset values, certain assets such as land and buildings may have a carrying figure in the balance sheet based on a revaluation to market value, while other assets such as motor vehicles may still be based on a balance of unallocated cost. The balance sheet thus pretends on the one hand to be a list of resultant costs pending allocation over future periods, and on the other hand to be a statement of current values.

Prudence concept

This concept introduces caution into the recognition of assets and income for financial reporting purposes. The cardinal rule is that income should not be recorded or recognised within the system until it is realised, but unrealised losses should be recognised immediately.

However, not all unrealised profits are excluded. For example, practice is that attributable profit on long-term contracts still in progress at the financial year-end may be taken into account. As with fixed assets, rules are not applied uniformly.

Unrealised capital profits

Capital profits are ignored as income until they are realised, when, in the accounting period of sale, they are acknowledged by the reporting system. However, all the profit is recognised in one financial period when, in truth, the surplus was generated over successive periods by gradual growth, albeit unrealised until disposal of the asset. Thus a portion of what are now realised profits applies to prior periods. Not all of this profit should be attributed to the period of sale.

Going concern

The going concern concept is fundamental to accountancy and operates on the assumption that the business entity has an indefinite life. It is used to justify basing the periodic reports of asset values on carrying forward figures that represent unallocated costs, i.e. to justify the non-recognition of the realisable or disposal values of non-monetary assets and, in so doing, the associated unrealised profits/losses. Although the life of an entity is deemed indefinite, there is uncertainty, and accountants are reluctant to predict the future. When they are matching costs with revenue for the current accounting period, they follow the prudence concept of reasonable certainty.

In the long term, economic income and accountancy income are reconciled. The unrealised profits of the economic measure are eventually realised and, at that point, they will be recognised by the accountant's measure. In the short term, however, they give different results for each period.

3.5 Economist's view of income, capital and value

Let us now consider the economist's tradition of present value and the nature of economic income.

3.5.1 Economist's tradition of present value

Present value is a technique used in valuing a future money flow, or in measuring the money value of an existing capital stock in terms of a predicted cash flow *ad infinitum*.

Present value (PV) constitutes the nature of economic capital and, indirectly, economic income. Given the choice of receiving £100 now or £100 in one year's time, the rational person will opt to receive £100 now. This behaviour exhibits an intuitive appreciation of the fact that £100 today is worth more than £100 one year hence. Thus the mind has **discounted** the value of the future sum: £100 today is worth £100; but compared with today, i.e. **compared with present value**, a similar sum receivable in twelve months' time is worth less than £100. How much less is a matter of subjective evaluation, but compensation for the time element may be found by reference to interest: a person forgoing the spending of £1 today and spending it one year later may earn interest of, say, 10% per annum in compensation for the sacrifice undergone by deferring consumption.

So £1 today invested at 10% p.a. will be worth £1.10 one year later, £1.21 two years later, £1.331 three years later, and so on. This is the concept of compound interest. It may be calculated by the formula $(1 + r)^n$, where 1 = the sum invested; r = the rate of interest; n = the number of periods of investment (in our case years). So for £1 invested at 10% p.a. for four years:

$$(1 + r)^n = (1 + 0.10)^4$$
$$= (1.1)^4$$
$$= £1.4641$$

and for five years:

$$= (1.1)^5$$
$$= £1.6105, \text{ and so on}$$

Notice how the **future value** increases because of the compound interest element – it **varies** over time – whereas the investment of £1 remains constant. So, conversely, the sum of £1.10 received at the end of year one has a PV of £1, as does £1.21 received at the end of year two and £1.331 at the end of year three.

It has been found convenient to construct tables to ease the task of calculating present values. These show the cash flow, i.e. the future values, at a constant figure of £1 and allow the investment to vary. So:

$$PV = \frac{CF}{(1+r)^n}$$

where CF = anticipated cash flow; r = the discount (i.e. interest) rate. So the PV of a cash flow of £1 receivable at the end of one year at 10% p.a. is:

$$\frac{£1}{(1+r)^1} = £0.9091$$

and £1 at the end of two years:

$$\frac{£1}{(1+r)^2} = £0.8264$$

and so on over successive years. The appropriate present values for years three, four and five would be £0.7513, £0.6830, £0.6210 respectively.

£0.9091 invested today at 10% p.a. will produce £1 at the end of one year. The PV of £1 receivable at the end of two years is £0.8264 and so on.

Tables presenting data in this way are called 'PV tables'; while the earlier method compiles tables usually referred to as 'compound interest tables'. Both types of table are compound interest tables; only the presentation of the data has changed.

To illustrate the ease of computation using PV tables, we can compute the PV of £6,152 receivable at the end of year five, given a discount rate of 10%, as being £6,152 × £0.6210 = £3,820. Thus £3,820 will total £6,152 in five years given an interest rate of 10% p.a. So the PV of that cash flow of £6,152 is £3,820, because £3,820 would generate interest of £2,332 (i.e. 6,152 − 3,820) as compensation for losing use of the principal sum for five years. Future flows must be discounted to take cognisance of the time element separating cash flows. Only then are we able to compare like with like by reducing all future flows to the comparable loss of present value.

This concept of PV has a variety of applications in accountancy and will be encountered in many different areas requiring financial measurement, comparison and decision. It originated as an economist's device within the context of economic income and economic capital models, but in accountancy it assists in the making of valid comparisons and decisions. For example, two machines may each generate an income of £10,000 over three years. However, timing of the cash flows may vary between the machines. This is illustrated in Figure 3.1.

If we simply compare the profit-generating capacity of the machines over the three-year

Figure 3.1 Dissimilar cash flows

Cash flows		
Machine A	Machine B	Receivable end of year
£	£	
1,000	5,000	1
2,000	4,000	2
7,000	1,000	3
10,000	10,000	

span, each produces a total profit of £10,000. But if we pay regard to the time element of the money flows, the machines are not so equal.

However, the technique has its faults. Future money flows are invariably the subject of **estimation** and thus the actual flow experienced may show variations from forecast. Also, the element of **interest**, which is crucial to the calculation of present values, is **subjective**. It may, for instance, be taken as the average prevailing rate operating within the economy or a rate peculiar to the firm and the element of risk involved in the particular decision. In this chapter we are concerned only with PV as a tool of the economist in evaluating economic income and economic capital.

3.5.2 Nature of economic income

Economics is concerned with the economy in general, raising questions such as: how does it function? how is wealth created? how is income generated? why is income generated? The economy as a whole is activated by income generation. The individual is motivated to generate income because of a need to satisfy personal wants by consuming goods and services. Thus the economist becomes concerned with the individual consumer's psychological state of personal **enjoyment and satisfaction**. This creates a need to treat the economy as a **behavioural entity**.

The behavioural aspect forms a substantial part of micro- and macroeconomic thought, emanating particularly from the microeconomic. We can say that the economist's version of income measurement is microeconomic orientated in contrast to the accountant's business entity orientation.

The origination of the economic measure of income commenced with Irving Fisher in 1930.[7] He saw income in terms of consumption, and consumption in terms of individual perception of personal enjoyment and satisfaction. His difficulty in formulating a standard measure of this personal psychological concept of income was overcome by equating this individual experience with the consumption of goods and services and assuming that the cost of such goods and services formed the measure.

Thus, he reasoned, consumption (C) equals income (Y); so $Y = C$. He excluded savings from income because savings were not consumed. There was no satisfaction derived from savings; enjoyment necessitated consumption, he argued. Money was worthless until spent; so growth of capital was ignored, but reductions in capital became part of income because such reductions had to be spent.

In Fisher's model, capital was a stock of wealth existing at a point in time, and as a stock it generated income. Eventually, he reconciled the value of capital with the value of income by employing the concept of present value. He assessed the PV of a future flow of income by **discounting** future flows using the discounted cash flow (DCF) technique. Fisher's model adopted the prevailing average market rate of interest as the discount factor.

Economists since Fisher have introduced savings as part of income. Sir John Hicks played a major role in this area.[8] He introduced the idea that income was the maximum consumption enjoyed by the individual without reducing the individual's capital stock, i.e. the amount a person could consume during a period of time that still left him or her with the same value of capital stock at the end of the period as at the beginning. Hicks also used the DCF technique in the valuation of capital.

If capital increases, the increase constitutes savings and grants the opportunity of consumption. The formula illustrating this was given in section 3.3, i.e. $Y_{0-1} = NA_1 - NA_0 + D_{0-1}$.

However, in the Hicksian model, $NA_1 - NA_0$, given as £6,750 and £6,000 respectively in the aforementioned example, would have been discounted to achieve present values.

The same formula may be expressed in different forms. The economist is likely to show it as $Y - C + (K_1 - K_0)$ where C = consumption, having been substituted for dividend, and K_1 and K_0 have been substituted for NA_1 and NA_0 respectively.

Hicks's income model is often spoken of as an *ex ante* model because it is usually used for the measurement of **expected** income in advance of the time period concerned. Of course, because it specifically introduces the present value concept, present values replace the balance sheet values of net assets adopted by the accountant. Measuring income **before the event** enables the individual to estimate the level of consumption that may be achieved without depleting capital stock. Before-the-event computations of income necessitate predictions of future cash flows.

Suppose that an individual proprietor of a business anticipated that his investment in the enterprise would generate earnings over the next four years, as specified in Figure 3.2. Furthermore, such earnings would be retained by the business for the financing of new equipment with a view to increasing potential output.

We will assume that the expected rate of interest on capital employed in the business is 8% p.a.

The economic value of the business at K_0 (i.e. at the beginning of year one) will be based on the discounted cash flow of the future four years. Figure 3.3 shows that K_0 is £106,853, calculated as the present value of anticipated earnings of £131,000 spread over a four-year term.

Figure 3.2 Business cash flows for four years

Years	Cash inflows £
1	26,000
2	29,000
3	35,000
4	41,000

Figure 3.3 Economic value at K_0

Year	(a) Cash flow £	(b) $DCF = \dfrac{1}{(1+r)^n}$	(c) $\dfrac{PV}{(a) \times (b)}$ £
K_1	26,000	$\dfrac{1}{(1.08)^1} = 0.9259$	24,073
K_2	29,000	$\dfrac{1}{(1.08)^2} = 0.8573$	24,862
K_3	35,000	$\dfrac{1}{(1.08)^3} = 0.7938$	27,783
K_4	41,000	$\dfrac{1}{(1.08)^4} = 0.7350$	30,135
	131,000		106,853

The economic value of the business at K_1 (i.e. at the end of year one, which is the same as saying the beginning of year two) is calculated in Figure 3.4. This shows that K_1 is £115,403 calculated as the present value of anticipated earnings of £131,000 spread over a four-year term.

From this information we are able to calculate Y for the period Y_1, as in Figure 3.5. Note that C (consumption) is nil because, in this exercise, dividends representing consumption have not been payable for Y_1. In other words, income Y_1 is entirely in the form of projected capital growth, i.e. savings.

By year-end K_1, earnings of £26,000 will have been received; in projecting the capital at K_2 such earnings will have been reinvested and at the beginning of year K_2 will have a PV of £26,000. These earnings will no longer represent a **predicted** sum because they will have been **realised** and therefore will no longer be subjected to discounting.

The income of £8,550 represents an anticipated return of 8% p.a. on the economic capital at K_0 of £106,853 (8% of £106,853 is £8,548, the difference of £2 between this figure and the figure calculated above being caused by rounding).

As long as the expectations of future cash flows and the chosen interest rate do not change, then Y_1 will equal 8% of £106,853.

What will the anticipated income for the year Y_2 amount to?

Applying the principle explained above, the anticipated income for the year Y_2 will equal 8% of the capital at the end of K_1 amounting to £115,403 = £9,233. This is proved in Figure 3.6, which shows that K_2 is £124,636 calculated as the present value of anticipated earnings of £131,000 spread over a four-year term.

Figure 3.4 Economic value at K_1

Year	(a) Cash flow £	(b) $DCF = \frac{-1}{(1+r)^n}$	(c) PV (a) × (b) £
K_1	26,000	1.0000	26,000
K_2	29,000	$\frac{1}{(1+r)^1} = 0.9259$	26,851
K_3	35,000	$\frac{1}{(1+r)^2} = 0.8573$	30,006
K_4	41,000	$\frac{1}{(1+r)^3} = 0.7938$	32,546
	131,000		115,403

Figure 3.5 Calculation of Y for the period Y_1

$Y = C + (K_1 - K_0)$
$Y = 0 + (115,403 - 106,853)$
$= 0 + 8,550$
$= £8,550$

Figure 3.6 Economic value at K_2

Year	(a) Cash flow	(b) $DCF = \dfrac{1}{(1+r)^n}$	(c) $PV = (a) \times (b)$
	£	£	£
K_1	26,000	1.08	28,080
K_2	29,000	1.0000	29,000
K_3	35,000	0.9259	32,407
K_4	41,000	0.8573	35,149
	131,000		124,636

Figure 3.7 Calculation of Y for the period Y_2

$$Y = C + (K_2 - K_1)$$
$$Y = 0 + (124,636 - 115,403)$$
$$= 0 + 9,233$$
$$= £9,233$$

From this information we are able to calculate Y for the period Y_2 as in Figure 3.7. Note that capital value attributable to the end of the year K_2 is being assessed at the beginning of K_2. This means that the £26,000 due at the end of year K_1 will have been received and reinvested, earning interest of 8% p.a. Thus by the end of year K_2 it will be worth £28,080. The sum of £29,000 will be realised at the end of year K_2 so its present value at that time will be £29,000.

If the anticipated future cash flows change, the expected capital value at the successive points in time will also change. Accordingly, the actual value of capital may vary from that forecast by the *ex ante* model.

3.6 Critical comment on the economist's measure

While the income measure enables us to formulate theories regarding the behaviour of the economy, it has inherent shortcomings not only in the economic field, but particularly in the accountancy sphere.

- The calculation of economic capital, hence economic income, is subjective in terms of the present value factor, often referred to as the DCF element. The factor may be based on any one of a number of factors, such as opportunity cost, the current return on the firm's existing capital employed, the contemporary interest payable on a short-term loan such as a bank overdraft, the average going rate of interest payable in the economy at large, or a rate considered justified on the basis of the risk attached to a particular investment.

- Investors are not of one mind or one outlook. For example, they possess different risk and time preferences and will therefore employ different discount factors.

- The model constitutes a compound of unrealised and realised flows, i.e. profits. Because of the unrealised element, it has not been used as a base for computing tax or for declaring a dividend.

- The projected income is dependent upon the success of a planned financial strategy. Investment plans may change, or fail to attain target.

- Windfall gains cannot be foreseen, so they cannot be accommodated in the *ex ante* model. Our prognostic cash flows may therefore vary from the actual flows generated, e.g. an unexpected price movement.

- It is difficult to construct a satisfactory, meaningful balance sheet detailing the unused stock of net assets by determining the present values of individual assets. Income is invariably the consequence of deploying a group of assets working in unison.

3.7 Income, capital and changing price levels

A primary concern of income measurement to both economist and accountant is the maintenance of the capital stock, i.e. the maintenance of capital values. The assumption is that income can only arise **after** the capital stock has been maintained at the same amount as at the beginning of the accounting period.

However, this raises the question of how we should define the capital that we are attempting to maintain. There are a number of possible definitions:

- **Money capital**. Should we concern ourselves with maintaining the fund of capital resources initially injected by the entrepreneur into the new enterprise? This is indeed one of the aims of traditional, transaction-based accountancy.

- **Potential consumption capital**. Is it this that should be maintained, i.e. the economist's present value philosophy expressed via the discounted cash flow technique?

- **Operating capacity capital**. Should maintenance of productive capacity be the rule, i.e. capital measured in terms of tangible or physical assets? This measure would utilise the current cost accounting system.

Revsine attempted to construct an analytical bridge between replacement cost accounting that maintains the operating capacity, and the economic concepts of **income** and **value**, by demonstrating that the distributable operating flow component of economic income is equal to the current operating component of replacement cost income, and that the unexpected income component of economic income is equal to the unrealisable cost savings of replacement cost income.[9] This will become clearer when the replacement cost model is dealt with in the next chapter.

- **Financial capital**. Should capital be maintained in terms of a fund of general purchasing power (sometimes called 'real' capital)? In essence this is the consumer purchasing power (or general purchasing power) approach, but not in a strict sense as it can be measured in a variety of ways. The basic method uses a general price index. This concept is likely to satisfy the criteria of the proprietor/shareholders of the entity. The money capital and the financial capital concepts are variations of the same theme, the former being founded on the historic cost principle and the latter applying an adjustment mechanism to take account of changing price levels.

The money capital concept has remained the foundation stone of traditional accountancy reporting, but the operating and financial capital alternatives have played a controversial secondary role over the past twenty-five years.

Potential consumption capital is peculiar to economics in terms of measurement of the business entity's aggregate capital, although, as discussed on pages 50–53, it has a major role to play as a decision-making model in financial management.

3.7.1 Why are these varying methods of concern?

The problem tackled by these devices is that plague of the economy known as 'changing price levels', particularly the upward spiralling referred to as **inflation**. Throughout this chapter we have assumed that there is a stable monetary unit and that income, capital and value changes over time have been in response to operational activity and the inter-action of supply and demand or changes in expectations.

Following the historic cost convention, capital maintenance has involved a comparison of opening and closing capital in each accounting period. It has been assumed that the purchasing power of money has remained constant over time.

If we take into account moving price levels, particularly the fall in the purchasing power of the monetary unit due to inflation, then our measure of **income** is affected if we insist upon **maintaining capital in real terms**.

3.7.2 Is it necessary to maintain capital in real terms?

Undoubtedly it is necessary if we wish to prevent an erosion of the operating capacity of the entity and thus its ability to maintain real levels of income. If we do not maintain the capacity of capital to generate the current level of profit, then the income measure, being the difference between opening and closing capitals, will be overstated or over-valued. This is because the capital measure is being understated or undervalued. In other words, there is a danger of dividends being paid out of real capital rather than out of real income. It follows that, if the need to retain profits is overlooked, the physical assets will be depleted.

In accountancy there is no theoretical difficulty in measuring the impact of changing price levels. There are, however, two practical difficulties:

- There are a number of methods, or mixes of methods, available and it has proved impossible to obtain consensus support for one method or compound of methods.

- There is a high element of subjectivity, which detracts from the objectivity of the information.

In the next chapter we deal with inflation and analyse the methods formulated, together with the difficulties that they in turn introduce into the financial reporting system.

Summary

In measuring income, capital and value, the accountant's approach varies from the sister discipline of the economist, yet both are trying to achieve similar objectives.

The accountant uses a traditional transaction-based model of computing income, capital being the residual of this model.

The economist's viewpoint is anchored in a behavioural philosophy that measures capital and deduces income to be the difference between the capital at commencement of a period and that at its end.

The objectives of income measurement are important because of the existence of a highly sophisticated capital market. These objectives involve the assessment of stewardship performance, dividend and retention policies, comparison of actual results with those predicted, assessment of future prospects, payment of taxation and disclosure of matched costs against revenue from sales.

The natures of income, capital and value must be appreciated if we are to understand and achieve measurement. The apparent conflict between the two measures can be seen as a consequence of the accountant's need for periodic reporting to shareholders. In the longer term, both methods tend to agree.

Present value as a concept is the foundation stone of the economist, while historical cost, adjusted for prudence, is that of the accountant. Present value demands a subjective discount rate and estimates that time may prove incorrect; historical cost ignores unrealised profits and in application is not always transaction based.

The economist's measure, of undoubted value in the world of micro- and macro-economics, presents difficulty in the accountancy world of annual reports. The accountant's method, with its long track record of acceptance, ignores any generated profits, which caution and the concept of the going concern deem not to exist.

The economic trauma of changing price levels is a problem that both measures can embrace, but consensus support for a particular model of measurement has proved elusive.

REVIEW QUESTIONS

1 What is the purpose of measuring income?

2 Explain the nature of economic income.

3 The historical cost concept has withstood the test of time. Specify the reasons for this success, together with any aspects of historical cost that you consider are detrimental in the sphere of financial reporting.

4 What is meant by present value? Does it take account of inflation?

5 A company contemplates purchasing a machine that will generate an income of £25,000 per year over each of the next five years. A scrap value of £2,000 is anticipated on disposal. How much would you advise the company to pay for the asset?

6 Discuss the arguments for and against revaluing fixed assets and recognising the gain or loss.

7 To an accountant, net income is essentially a historical record of the past. To an economist, net income is essentially a speculation about the future. Examine the relative merits of these two approaches for financial reporting purposes.

8 Examine and contrast the concepts of profit that you consider to be relevant to:

(a) an economist; (b) a speculator;

(c) a business executive; (d) the managing director of a company;

(e) a shareholder in a private company; (f) a shareholder in a large public company.

EXERCISES

An extract from the solution is provided in the appendix at the end of the text for exercises marked with an asterisk (*).

Question 1

(a) 'Measurement in financial statements', Chapter 6 of the ASB's *Statement of Principles,* was published in 1999. Amongst the theoretical valuation systems considered is value in use – more commonly known as economic value.

Required:
Describe the Hicksian economic model of income and value, and assess its usefulness for financial reporting.

(b) Jim Bowater purchased a parcel of 30,000 ordinary shares in New Technologies plc for £36,000 on 1 January 20X5. Jim, an Australian on a four-year contract in the UK, has it in mind to sell the shares at the end of 20X7, just before he leaves for Australia. Based on the company's forecast growth and dividend policy, his broker has advised him that his shares are likely to fetch only £35,000 then.

In its annual report for the year ended 31 December 20X4 the company had forecast annual dividend pay-outs as follows:

Year ended: 31 December 20X5, 25p per share
              31 December 20X6, 20p per share
              31 December 20X7, 20p per share

Required:
Using the Ideal Economic Model of income:
(i)   **Compute Jim's economic income for each of the three years ending on the dates indicated above.**
(ii) **Show that Jim's economic capital will be preserved at 1 January 20X5 level. Jim's cost of capital is 20%.**

* Question 2

(a) Describe briefly the theory underlying Hicks's economic model of income and capital. What are its practical limitations?

(b) Spock purchased a space invader entertainment machine at the beginning of year one for £1,000. He expects to receive at annual intervals the following receipts: at the end of year one £400; end of year two £500; end of year three £600. At the end of year three he expects to sell the machine for £400.

Spock could receive a return of 10% in the next best investment.

The present value of £1 receivable at the end of a period discounted at 10% is as follows:

End of year one   £0.909
End of year two   £0.826
End of year three   £0.751

Required:
Calculate the ideal economic income, ignoring taxation and working to the nearest £.

Your answer should show that Spock's capital is maintained throughout the period and that his income is constant.

* Question 3

Jason commenced with £135,000 cash. He acquired an established shop on 1 January 20X1. He agreed to pay £130,000 for the fixed and current assets and the goodwill. The replacement cost of the shop premises was £100,000, stock £10,000 and debtors £4,000; the balance of the purchase price was for the goodwill. He paid legal costs of £5,000. No liabilities were taken over. Jason could have resold the business immediately for £135,000. Legal costs are to be expensed in 20X1.

Jason expected to draw £25,000 per year from the business for three years and to sell the shop at the end of 20X3 for £150,000.

At 31 December 20X1 the books showed the following tangible assets and liabilities:

Cost to the business before any drawings by Jason:		He estimated that the net realisable values were:	
	£		£
Shop premises	100,000		85,000
Stock	15,500		20,000
Debtors	5,200		5,200
Cash	40,000		40,000
Creditors	5,000		5,000

Based on his experience of the first year's trading, he revised his estimates and expected to draw £35,000 per year for three years and sell the shop for £175,000 on 31 December 20X3.

Jason's opportunity cost of capital was 20%.

Required:
(a) Calculate the following income figures for 20X1:
- (i) accounting income;
- (ii) income based on net realisable values;
- (iii) economic income ex ante;
- (iv) economic income ex post.
  State any assumptions made.
(b) Evaluate each of the four income figures as indicators of performance in 20X1 and as a guide to decisions about the future.

Question 4

The following information relates to Ozone Ltd at 1 January 20X0:

Expected net receipts for 20X0	£240,000
Expected net receipts for subsequent years	£400,000 p.a.
Cost of capital	10%

Further information becomes available at 31 December 20X0:

Expected future net receipts revised to	£440,000 p.a.
Actual net receipts for 20X0	£200,000

Additionally, a decision has been taken to begin a project on 31 December 20X0 at a cost of £40,000, with estimated net receipts at £20,000 p.a. for the next four years.

Information is also available concerning the company's net assets at the start and end of 20X0:

	1 Jan 20X0 £	31 Dec 20X0 £
Net historical cost	2,920,000	2,800,000
Net replacement cost	3,800,000	2,600,000
Net realisable value	3,280,000	4,040,000

Required:

(a) Using Hicks' concept of income:
  (i) calculate the budgeted income for the year;
  (ii) calculate the actual income for the year (two versions);
  (iii) reconcile the budgeted and actual outcomes with brief narrative explanations.
(b) Briefly assess the economist's contribution to accounting measurement of income and capital.

References

1 T.A. Lee, *Income and Value Measurement: Theory and Practice* (3rd edition), Van Nostrand Reinhold (UK), 1985, p. 20.
2 D. Solomons, *Making Accounting Policy*, Oxford University Press, 1986, p. 132.
3 R.W. Scapens, *Accounting in an Inflationary Environment* (2nd edition), Macmillan, 1981, p. 125.
4 *Ibid.*, p. 127.
5 D. Solomons, *op. cit.*, p. 132.
6 T.A. Lee, *op. cit.*, pp. 52–54.
7 I. Fisher, *The Theory of Interest*, Macmillan, 1930, pp. 171–181.
8 J.R. Hicks, *Value and Capital* (2nd edition), Clarendon Press, 1946.
9 R.W. Scapens, *op. cit.*, p. 127.

Bibliography

American Institute of Certified Public Accountants, *Objectives of Financial Statements*, Report of the Study Group, 1973.
The Corporate Report, ASC, 1975, pp. 28–31.
N. Kaldor, 'The concept of income in economic theory', in R.H. Parker and G.C. Harcourt (eds), *Readings in the Concept and Measurement of Income*, Cambridge University Press, 1969.
T.A. Lee, 'The accounting entity concept, accounting standards and inflation accounting', *Accounting and Business Reseach*, Spring 1980, pp. 1–11.
J.R. Little, 'Income measurement: an introduction', *Student Newsletter*, June 1988.
D. Solomons, 'Economic and accounting concepts of income', in R.H. Parker and G.C. Harcourt, *op. cit.*
R.R. Sterling, *Theory of the Measurement of Enterprise Income*, University of Kansas Press, 1970.

CHAPTER **4**

Accounting for inflation

4.1 Introduction

In this chapter we discuss the impact of inflation on profit and capital measurement and the concepts that have been suggested to incorporate these movements into the financial reports. These concepts are still undergoing development and have not yet achieved general support among practitioners in the field. In this chapter we consider the following:

- A review of the problems of historical cost accounting (HCA)
- Inflation accounting
- The concepts in principle
- The concepts illustrated for one year's transactions – cash transations
- A critique of each model
- A comprehensive example of current cost accounts
- A critique of current cost accounting (CCA) financial statements

4.2 Review of the problems of historical cost accounting (HCA)

The transaction-based historical cost concept was unchallenged in the UK until the 1939–45 war. Then price levels started to hedge upwards at an ever-increasing pace during the 1950s and reached an annual rate of increase of 20% in the mid-1970s. The historical cost base for financial reporting witnessed growing criticism. The inherent faults of the system were discussed in Chapter 3, but inflation exacerbates the problem in the following ways:

- Profit is overstated when inflationary changes in the value of assets are ignored.
- Comparability of business entities, which is so necessary in the assessment of performance and growth, becomes distorted.
- The decision-making process, the formulation of plans and the setting of targets may be suboptimal if financial base data are out of date.
- Financial reports become confusing at best, misleading at worst, because revenue is mismatched with differing historical cost levels as the monetary unit becomes unstable.
- Unrealised profits arising in individual accounting periods are increased as a result of inflation.

In order to combat these serious defects, current value accounting became the subject of research and controversy as to the most appropriate method to use for financial reporting.

4.3 Inflation accounting

A number of versions of current value accounting (CVA) were eventually identified, but the current value postulate was said to suffer from the following disadvantages:

● It destroys the factual nature of HCA, which is transaction based: the factual characteristic is to all intents and purposes lost as transaction-based historic values are replaced by judgemental values.

● It is not as objective as HCA because it is less verifiable from auditable documentation.

● It entails recognition of unrealised profit, a practice that is anathema to the traditionalist.

● The claimed improvement in comparability between commercial entities is a myth because of the degree of subjectivity in measuring current value by each.

● The lack of a single accepted method of computing current values compounds the subjectivity aspect. One fault-laden system is being usurped by another that is also faulty.

In spite of these criticisms, the search for a system of financial reporting devoid of the defects of HCA and capable of coping with inflation has produced a number of CVA models.

4.4 The concepts in principle

Several current income and value models have been proposed to replace or operate in tandem with the historical cost convention. However, in terms of basic characteristics, they may be reduced to the following three models:

● Current purchasing power (CPP) or general purchasing power (GPP).

● Current entry cost or replacement cost (RC).

● Current exit cost or net realisable value (NRV).

We discuss each of these models below.

4.4.1 Currrent purchasing power accounting (CPPA)

The CPP model measures income and value by adopting a price index system. Movements in price levels are gauged by reference to price changes in a group of goods and services in **general** use within the economy. The aggregate price value of this **basket** of commodities-cum-services is determined at a base point in time and indexed as 100. Subsequent changes in price are compared on a regular basis with this base period price and the change recorded. For example, the price level of our chosen range of goods and services may amount to £76 on 31 March 20X1, and show changes as follows:

£76   at 31 March 20X1
£79   at 30 April 20X1
£81   at 31 May 20X1
£84   at 30 June 20X1
and so on.

The change in price may be indexed with 31 March as the base:

20X1	Calculation	Index
31 March	i.e. £76	100
30 April	i.e. $\dfrac{79}{76} \times 100$	103.9
31 May	i.e. $\dfrac{81}{76} \times 100$	106.6
30 June	i.e. $\dfrac{84}{76} \times 100$	110.5

In the UK, an index system similar in construction to this is known as the Retail Price Index (RPI). It is a barometer of fluctuating price levels covering a miscellany of goods and services as used by the average household. Thus it is a **general** price index. It is amended from time to time to take account of new commodities entering the consumer's range of choice and needs. As a model, it is unique owing to the introduction of the concept of gains and losses in **purchasing power**.

4.4.2 Current entry or replacement cost accounting (RCA)

The replacement cost (RC) model assesses income and value by reference to entry costs or current replacement costs of materials and other assets utilised within the business entity. The valuation attempts to replace like with like and thus takes account of the quality and condition of the existing assets. A motor vehicle, for instance, may have been purchased brand new for £25,000 with an expected life of five years, an anticipated residual value of nil and a straight-line depreciation policy. Its HCA carrying value in the balance sheet at the end of its first year would be £25,000 less £5,000 = £20,000. However, if a similar new replacement vehicle cost £30,000 at the end of year one, then its gross RC would be £30,000; depreciation for one year based on this sum would be £6,000 and the net RC would be £24,000. The increase of £4,000 is a holding gain and the machine with a HCA carrying value of £20,000 would be revalued at £24,000.

4.4.3 Current exit cost or net realisable value accounting (NRVA)

The net realisable value (NRV) model is based on the economist's concept of opportunity cost. It is a model that has had strong academic support, most notably in Australia from Professor Ray Chambers who referred to this approach as Continuous Contemporary Accounting (CoCoA). If an asset cost £25,000 at the beginning of year one and at the end of that year it had a NRV of £21,000 after meeting selling expenses, it would be carried in the NRV balance sheet at £21,000. This amount represents the cash forgone by holding the asset, i.e. the opportunity of possessing cash of £21,000 has been sacrificed in favour of the asset. Depreciation for the year would be £25,000 less £21,000 = £4,000.

4.5 The four models illustrated for a company with cash purchases and sales

We will illustrate the effect on the profit and net assets of Entrepreneur Ltd.

Entrepreneur Ltd commenced business on 1 January 20X1 with a capital of £3,000 to buy and sell second-hand computers. The company purchased six computers on 1 January 20X1 for £500 each and sold three of the computers on 15 January for £900 each.

The following data are available for January 20X1:

	Retail Price Index	Replacement cost per computer £	Net realisable value £
1 January	100		
15 January	112	610	
31 January	130	700	900

The profit and loss accounts and balance sheets are set out in Figure 4.1 with the detailed workings in Figure 4.2.

Figure 4.1 Trading account for the month ended 31 January 20X1

Profit and Loss Accounts for the Month ended 31 January 20X1

	HCA £		CPP CPP£		RCA £		NRVA £	
Sales	2,700	W1	3,134	W5	2,700	W1	2,700	W1
Opening stock	—		—		—		—	
Purchases	3,000	W2	3,900	W6	3,000	W2	3,000	W2
Closing stock	(1,500)	W3	(1,950)	W7	(1,500)	W3	(1,500)	W3
COSA	na		na		330	W10	na	
Cost of sales	1,500		1,950		1,830		1,500	
Holding gain	na		na		na		1,200	W15
Profit	**1,200**		**1,184**		**870**		**2,400**	

Balance Sheets as at 31 January 20X1

	£		CPP£		£		£	
Current assets								
Stock	1,500	W3	1,950	W7	2,100	W11	2,700	W14
Cash	2,700	W4	2,700		2,700		2,700	
Capital employed	**4,200**		**4,650**		**4,800**		**5,400**	
Capital	3,000		3,900	W8	3,000		3,000	
Holding gains								
On stock consumed	na		na		330	W12		
On stock in hand	na		na		600	W13		
Profit	1,200		1,184		870		2,400	
Loss on monetary items	na		(434)	W9	na		na	
	4,200		4,650		4,800		5,400	

na = not applicable

Figure 4.2 Workings (W)

HCA

WI Sales:	3 × £900 = £2,700	
W2 Purchases:	6 × £500 = £3,000	
W3 Closing stock:	3 × £500 = £1,500	
W4 Cash:	I January 20XI Capital	3,000
	I January 20XI Purchases	(3,000)
	I January 20XI Balance	nil
	15 January 20XI Sales	
	3 × £900 =	£2,700
	31 January 20XI Balance	£2,700

CPP		CPP£
W5 Sales	£2,700 × 130/112 =	3,134
W6 Purchases	£3,000 × 130/100 =	3,900
W7 Closing stock	£1,500 × 130/100 =	1,950
W8 Capital	£3,000 × 130/100 =	3,900

W9   Balance of cash was nil until 15 January when sales generated £2,700. This sum was held until 31 January during which period cash, a monetary item, lost purchasing power. The loss of purchasing power is measured by applying the general index to the cash held.

£2,700 × 130/112 − £2,700 = CPP £434.

RCA

W10   Additional replacement cost of stock consumed as at the date of sale is measured as a cost of sales adjustment (COSA). COSA is calculated as follows:

	3 × £610 =	1,830
Less:	3 × £500 =	1,500
COSA		£330

W11	Closing stock: 3 × £700 = £2,100	
W12	Holding gains on stock consumed: as for W10	= £330
W13	Stock at replacement cost	= 3 × £700 = 2,100
	Less: stock at cost	= 3 × £500 = 1,500
	Holding gains on closing stock	£600

NRVA

W14	Closing stock at net realisable value = 900 × 3 = £2,700	
W15	3 × £900 =	2,700
	3 × £500 =	1,500
	Holding gain	£1,200

4.5.1 Financial capital maintence concept

HCA and CPP are both transaction-based models that apply the financial capital main-tenance concept. This means that profit is the difference between the opening and clos-ing net assets (expressed in HC £) or the opening and closing net assets (expressed in HC £ indexed for RPI changes) adjusted for any capital introduced or withdrawn during the month.

CPP adjustments

- All historical cost values are adjusted to a common index level for the month. In theory this can be the index applicable to any day of the financial period concerned. However, in practice it has been deemed preferable to use the last day of the period; thus the financial statements show the latest price level appertaining to the period.

- The application of a general price index as an adjusting factor results in the creation of an **alien** currency of **purchasing power**, which is used in place of sterling. Note, particularly, the impact on the entity's sales and capital compared with the other models. **Actual** sales shown on **invoices** will still read £2,700.

- Note the application of the concept of gain or loss on holding monetary items. In this example there is a monetary loss of CPP £434 as shown in Working 9.

4.5.2 Operating capital maintenance concept

Under this concept capital is only maintained if sufficient income is retained to maintain the business entity's physical operating capacity, i.e. its ability to produce the existing level of goods or services. Profit is, therefore, the residual after increasing the cost of sales to the cost applicable at the date of sale.

- Basically, only two adjustments are involved: the additional replacement cost of stock consumed and holding gains on closing stocks. However, in a comprehensive exercise an adjustment will be necessary regarding fixed assets and you will also encounter a gearing adjustment.

- Notice the concept of holding gains. This model introduces, in effect, unrealised profits in respect of closing stocks. The holding gain concerning stock consumed at the time of sale has been realised and deducted from what would have been a profit of £1,200. The statement discloses profits of £870.

4.5.3 Capacity to adapt concept

The HCA, CPP and RCA models have assumed that the business will continue as a going concern and only distribute realised profits after retaining sufficient profits to maintain either the financial or operating capital.

The NRVA concept is that a business has the capacity to realise its net assets at the end of each financial period and re-invest the proceeds and that the NRV accounts provide management with this information.

- This produces the same initial profit as HCA, namely £1,200, but a peculiarity of this system is that this realised profit is supplemented by **unrealised** profit generated by holding stocks. Under RCA accounting, such gains are shown in a separate account and are not treated as part of real income.

- This simple exercise has ignored the possibility of investment in fixed assets, thus depreciation is not involved. A reduction in the NRV of fixed assets at the end of a period compared with the beginning would be treated in a similar fashion to depreciation by being charged to the revenue account, and consequently profits would be reduced. An increase in the NRV of such assets would be included as part of the profit.

4.5.4 The four models compared

Dividend distribution

We can see from Figure 4.1 that if the business were to distribute the profit reported under HCA, CPP or NRVA the physical operating capacity of the business would be reduced and it would be paying dividends out of capital:

	HCA	CPP	RCA	NRVA
Realised profit:	1,200	1,184	870	1,200
Unrealised profit	—	—	—	1,200
Profit for month	1,200	1,184	870	2,400

Shareholder orientation

The CPP model is shareholder oriented in that it shows whether shareholders' funds are keeping pace with inflation by maintaining their purchasing power. Only CPP changes the value of the share capital.

Management orientation

The RCA model is management oriented in that it identifies holding gains which represent the amounts required to be retained in order to simply maintain the operating capital.

RCA measures the impact of inflation on the individual firm, in terms of the change in price levels of its **raw materials and assets,** i.e. inflation peculiar to the company, whereas CPP measures general inflation in the economy as a whole. CPP may be meaningless in the case of an individual company. Consider a firm that carries a constant volume of stock valued at £100 in HCA terms. Now suppose that price levels double when measured by a general price index (GPI), so that its stock is restated to £200 in a CPP system. If, however, the cost of that **particular** stock has sustained a price change consisting of a five-fold increase, then under the RCA model the value of the stock should be £500.

In the mid-1970s, when the accountancy profession was debating the problem of changing price level measurement, the general price level had climbed by some 23% over a period during which petroleum-based products had risen by 500%.

4.6 Critique of each model

A critique of the various models may be formulated in terms of their characteristics and peculiarities as virtues and defects in application.

4.6.1 HCA

This model's virtues and defects have been discussed in Chapter 3 and earlier in this chapter.

4.6.2 CPP

Virtues

- It is an **objective measure** since it is still transaction based, as with HCA, and the possibility of subjectivity is constrained if a GPI is used that has been constructed by a central agency such as a government department. This applies in the UK, where the Retail Price Index is constructed by the Department of Employment.

- It is a **measure of shareholders' capital** and that capital's maintenance in terms of purchasing power units. Profit is the residual value after maintaining the money value of capital funds, taking account of changing price levels. Thus it is a measure readily understood by the shareholder/user of the accounts. It can prevent payment of a dividend out of real capital as measured by GPPA.

- It **introduces the concept of monetary items** as distinct from non-monetary items and the attendant concepts of gains and losses in holding net monetary liabilities compared with holding net monetary assets. Such gains and losses are experienced on a disturbing scale in times of inflation. They are **real** gains and losses. The **basic RCA and NRV models** do not recognise such 'surpluses' and 'deficits'.

Defects

- It is **HCA based but adjusted** to reflect general price movements. Thus it possesses the characteristics of HCA, good and bad, but with its values updated in the light of an arithmetic measure of general price changes. The major defect of becoming out of date is mitigated to a degree, but the impact of inflation on the entity's income and capital may be at variance with the rate of inflation affecting the economy in general.

- It may be **wrongly assumed that the CPP balance sheet is a current value statement**. It is not a current value document because of the defects discussed above; in particular, asset values may be subject to a different rate of inflation than that reflected by the GPI.

- It **creates an alien unit of measurement** still labelled by the £ sign. Thus we have the HCA £ and the CPP £. They are different pounds: one is the bona fide pound, the other is a synthetic unit. This may not be fully appreciated or understood by the user when faced with the financial accounts for the recent accounting period.

- Its **concept of profit is dangerous**. It pretends to cater for changing prices, but at the same time it fails to provide for the additional costs of replacing stocks sold or additional depreciation due to the escalating replacement cost of assets. The inflation encountered by the business entity will not be the same as that encountered by the whole economy. Thus the maintenance of the CPP of shareholders' capital via this concept of profit is not the maintenance of the entity's operating capital in physical terms, i.e. its capacity to produce the same volume of goods and services. The use of CPP profit as a basis for decision-making without regard to RCA profit can have disastrous consequences.

4.6.3 **RCA**

Virtues

- Its **unit of measurement** is the monetary unit and consequently it is understood and accepted by the user of accountancy reports. In contrast, the CPP system employs an artificial unit based on arithmetic relationships, which is different and thus unfamiliar.
- It **identifies and isolates holding gains** from operating income. Thus it can prevent the inadvertent distribution of dividends in excess of operating profit. It satisfies the prudence criterion of the traditional accountant and **maintains the physical operating capacity** of the entity.
- It introduces **realistic current values** of assets in the balance sheet, thus making the balance sheet a 'value' statement and consequently more meaningful to the user. This contrasts sharply with the balance sheet as a list of unallocated carrying costs in the HCA system.

Defects

- It is a **subjective measure**, in that replacement costs are often necessarily based on estimates or assessments. It does not possess the factual characteristics of HCA. It is open to manipulation within constraints. Often it is based on index numbers which themselves may be based on a compound of prices of a mixture of similar commodities used as raw material or operating assets. This subjectivity is exacerbated in circumstances where rapid technological advance and innovation are involved in the potential new replacement asset, e.g. computers, printers.
- It **assumes replacement of assets** by being based on their replacement cost. Difficulties arise if such assets are not to be replaced by similar assets. Presumably, it will then be assumed that a replacement of equivalent value to the original will be deployed, however differently, as capital within the firm.

4.6.4 **NRVA**

Virtues

- It is a concept readily understood by the user. The value of any item invariably has two measures – a buying price and a selling price – and the twain do not usually meet. However, when considering the value of an **existing** possession, the owner instinctively considers its 'value' to be that in potential sale, i.e. NRV.
- It **avoids the need to estimate depreciation** and, in consequence, the attendant problems of assessing life-span and residual values. Depreciation is treated as the arithmetic difference between the NRV at the end of a financial period and the NRV at its beginning.
- It is **based on opportunity cost** and so can be said to be more meaningful. It is the **sacrificial** cost of possessing an asset, which, it can be argued, is more authentic in terms of being a true or real cost. If the asset were not possessed, its cash equivalent would exist instead and that cash would be deployed in other opportunities. Therefore, NRV = cash = opportunity = cost.

Defects

- It is a **subjective measure** and in this respect it possesses the same major fault as RCA. It can be said to be less prudent than RCA because NRV will tend to be higher in some cases than RCA. For example, when valuing finished stocks, a profit content will be involved.

- It is **not a realistic measure** as most assets, except finished goods, are possessed in order to be utilised, not sold. Therefore, NRV is irrelevant.

- It is **not always determinable**. The assets concerned may be highly specialist and there may be no ready market by which a value can be easily assessed. Consequently, any particular value may be fictitious or erroneous, containing too high a holding gain or, indeed, too low a holding loss.

- It **violates the concept of the going concern**, which demands that the accounts are drafted on the basis that there is no intention to liquidate the entity. Admittedly, this concept was formulated with HCA in view, but the acceptance of NRV implies the possibility of a cessation of trading.

Figure 4.3 Economica plc HCA Balance Sheet

Balance Sheets as at 31 December on the basis of HCA

	20X5 £000	20X5 £000	20X4 £000	20X4 £000
Fixed assets:				
Cost	85,000		85,000	
Depreciation	34,000		25,500	
		51,000		59,500
Current assets:				
Stock	25,500		17,000	
Debtors	34,000		23,375	
Cash and bank	17,000		1,875	
	76,500		42,250	
Current liabilities:				
Trade creditors	25,500		17,000	
Corporation tax	8,500		4,250	
Dividend proposed	5,000		4,000	
	39,000		25,250	
Net current assets	37,500		17,000	
Less: 8% debentures	11,000		11,000	
		26,500		6,000
		77,500		65,500
Share capital and reserves:				
Authorised and issued £1 ordinary shares		50,000		50,000
Share premium		1,500		1,500
Profit and loss account		26,000		14,000
		77,500		65,500

4.7 Operating capital maintenance – a comprehensive example

In Figure 4.1 we considered the effect of inflation on a cash business without fixed assets, debtors or creditors. In the following example, Economica plc, we now consider the effect where there are fixed assets and credit transactions.

The HCA balance sheets as at 31 December 20X4 and 20X5 are set out in Figure 4.3 and index numbers required to restate the fixed assets, stock and monetary items in Figure 4.4.

4.7.1 Restating the opening balance sheet to current cost

The fixed assets and stock are restated to their current cost as at the date of the opening balance as shown in W1 and W2 below. The increase from HC to CC represents an unrealised holding gain which is debited to the asset account and credited to a reserve account called a current cost reserve, as in W3 below.

The calculations are as follows.

First we shall convert the HCA balance sheet in Figure 4.3, as at 31 December 20X4, to the CCA basis, using the index data in Figure 4.4.

The **non-monetary items**, comprising the fixed assets and stock, are converted and the converted amounts are taken to the CC balance sheet and the increases taken to the

Figure 4.4 Index data relating to Economica plc

1   Index numbers as prepared by the Central Statistical Office for fixed assets:

1 January 20X2	100
1 January 20X5	165
1 January 20X6	185
Average for 20X4	147
Average for 20X5	167

2   All fixed assets were acquired on 1 January 20X2. There were no further acquisitions or disposals during the four years ended 31 December 20X5.

3   Indices as prepared by the Central Statistical Office for stocks and monetary working capital adjustments were:

1 October 20X4	115
31 December 20X4	125
15 November 20X4	120
1 October 20X5	140
31 December 20X5	150
15 November 20X5	145
Average for 20X5	137.5

4   Three months' stock is carried.

5   Depreciation: historical cost based on 10% pa straight-line with residual value of nil:

	£HCA
20X4	8,500,000
20X5	8,500,000

Current cost reserve, as follows.

(W1) Fixed assets

	HCA £000	Index	CCA £000	Increase £000
Cost	85,000	$\times \frac{165}{100} =$	140,250	55,250
Depreciation	25,500	$\times \frac{165}{100} =$	42,075	16,575
	59,500		98,175	38,675

The CCA valuation at 31 December 20X4 shows a net increase in terms of numbers of pounds sterling of £38,675,000. The £59,500,000 in the HCA balance sheet will be replaced in the CCA balance sheet by £98,175,000.

(W2) Stocks

	HCA £000	Index	CCA £000	Increase £000
	17,000	$\times \frac{125}{120} =$	17,708 =	708

Note that Figure 4.4 specifies that three months' stocks are held. Thus on average they will have been purchased on 15 November 20X4, on the assumption that they have been acquired and consumed evenly throughout the calendar period. Hence the index at the time of purchase would have been 120. The £17,000,000 in the HCA balance sheet will be replaced in the CCA balance sheet by £17,708,000.

(W3) Current cost reserve

The total increase in CCA carrying values for non-monetary items is £39,383,000, which will be credited to CC reserves in the CC balance sheet. It comprises £38,675,000 on the fixed assets and £708,000 on the stock.

Note that monetary items do not change by virtue of inflation. Purchasing power will be lost or gained, but the carrying values in the CCA balance sheet will be identical to those in its HCA counterpart. We can now compile the CCA balance sheet as at 31 December 20X4 – this will show net assets of £104,883,000.

4.7.2 Adjustments that affect the profit for the year

The profit and loss account for the year ended 31 December 20X5 set out in Figure 4.5 discloses a profit before interest and tax of £26,350,000. We need to deduct realised holding gains from this profit to avoid the distribution of dividends that would reduce the operating capital. These deductions are a cost of sales adjustment (COSA), a depreciation adjustment (DA) and a monetary working capital adjustment (MWCA). The accounting treatment is to debit the profit and loss account and credit the current cost reserve.

Figure 4.5 Economica plc HCA profit and loss account

*Profit and Loss Account for the year ended
31 December 20X5, on the basis of HCA*

		20X5		20X4
		£000		£000
Turnover		42,500		38,250
Less: Cost of sales		(12,070)		(23,025)
Gross profit		30,430		15,225
Less: Distribution costs	2,460		2,210	
Less: Administrative expenses	1,620		1,540	
		(4,080)		(3,750)
Profit before interest and tax		26,350		11,475
Interest		(880)		(880)
Profit before tax		25,470		10,595
Tax		(8,470)		(4,250)
Profit after tax		17,000		6,345
Dividend		(5,000)		(4,000)
Retentions		12,000		2,345
Balance b/f		14,000		11,655
Balance c/f		26,000		14,000
EPS		34p		13p

The adjustments are calculated as follows.

(W4) Cost of sales adjustment (COSA) using the average method

We will compute the cost of sales adjustment by using the average method. The average purchase price index for 20X5 is 137.5. If price increases have moved at an even pace throughout the period, this implies that consumption occurred, on average, at 30 June, the mid-point of the financial year.

	HCA £000	*Adjustment*	*CCA* £000	*Difference* £000
Opening stock	17,000	$\times \dfrac{137.5}{120} =$	19,479 $=$	2,479
Purchases	—	—	—	—
	17,000		19,479	
Closing stock	(25,500)	$\times \dfrac{137.5}{145} =$	24,181 $=$	1,319
	(8,500)		(4,702)	3,798

The impact of price changes on the cost of sales would be an increase of £3,798,000, causing a profit decrease of like amount and a current cost reserve increase of like amount.

(W5) Depreciation adjustment: average method

As assets are consumed throughout the year, the CCA depreciation charge should be based on average current costs.

	HCA £000	Adjustment	CCA £000	Difference £000
Depreciation	8,500	$\times \quad \dfrac{167}{100} \quad =$	14,195 $\quad =$	5,695

(W6) Monetary working capital adjustment (MWCA)

The objective is to transfer from the profit and loss account to CC reserve the amount by which the need for monetary working capital (MWC) has increased due to rising price levels. The change in MWC from one balance sheet to the next will be the consequence of a combination of changes in volume and escalating price movements. Volume change may be segregated from the price change by using an average index.

	20X5 £000	20X4 £000		Change £000
Trade debtors	34,000	23,375		
Trade creditors	25,500	17,000		
MWC =	8,500	6,375	Overall change =	2,125

The MWC is now adjusted by the average index for the year.

This adjustment will reveal the change in volume.

$$\left(8,500 \times \frac{137.5}{150}\right) - \left(6,375 \times \frac{137.5}{125}\right)$$

=	7792	–	7012	= Volume change	780
So price change =					1,345

The profit before interest and tax will be reduced as follows:

	£000	£000
Profit before interest and tax		26,350
Less:		
COSA	(3,798)	
DA	(5,695)	
MWCA	(1,345)	
Current cost operating adjustments		(10,838)
Current cost operating profit		15,512

The adjustments will be credited to the current cost reserve.

4.7.3 Unrealised holding gains on non-monetary assets as at 31 December 20X5

The holding gains as at 31 December 20X4 were calculated in 4.7.1 above for fixed assets and stock. A similar calculation is required to restate these at 20X5 current costs for the closing balance sheet. The calculations are as in Working 7 below.

(W7) Non-monetary assets

(i) Holding gain on fixed assets £000
Revaluation at year-end

Fixed assets at 1 January 20X5 (as W1) at CCA revaluation	140,250
CCA value at 31 December 20X5 = $140,250 \times \dfrac{185}{165}$ =	157,250
Revaluation holding gain for 20X5 to CC reserve in W8	**17,000**

This holding gain of £17,000,000 is transferred to CC reserves.

(ii) Backlog depreciation on fixed assets

CCA aggregate depreciation at 31 December 20X5 for CC balance sheet	£000
= £HCA $34,000,000 \times \dfrac{185}{100}$ in CC balance sheet	62,900
Less: CCA aggregate depreciation at 1 January 20X5 (as per W1 and balance sheet at 1 January 20X5)	42,075
Being CCA depreciation as revealed between opening and closing balance sheets	20,825
But CCA depreciation charged in revenue accounts (i.e. £8,500,000 in £HCA plus additional depreciation of £5,695,000 per W5) =	14,195
So total backlog depreciation to CC reserve in W8	**6,630**
The CCA value of fixed assets at 31 December 20X5:	£000
Gross CCA value (above)	157,250
Depreciation (above)	62,900
Net CCA carrying value in the CC balance sheet in W8	**94,350**

This £6,630,000 is backlog depreciation for 20X5. Total backlog depreciation is not expensed (i.e. charged to revenue account) as an adjustment of HCA profit, but is charged against CCA reserves. The net effect is that the CC reserve will increase by £10,370,000 i.e. £17,000,000 − £6,630,000.

(iii) Stock valuation at year-end

CCA valuation at 31 December 20X5

£HCA000	£CCA000	£CCA000
= 25,500 × 150/145 = 26,379 = increase of		879
CCA valuation at 1 January 20X5 (per W2)		
= 17,000 × 125/120 = 17,708 = increase of		708
Stockholding gain occuring during 20X5 to W8		**171**

4.7.4 Current cost balance sheet as at 31 December 20X5

The current cost balance sheet as at 31 December 20X5 now discloses fixed assets and stock adjusted by index to their current cost and the retained profits reduced by the current cost operating adjustments. It appears as in Working 8 below.

(W8) Economica plc: CCA balance sheet as at 31 December 20X5

		20X5		20X4
Fixed assets	£000	£000	£000	£000
Cost	157,250 (W7)		140,250 (W1)	
Depreciation	62,900 (W7)		42,075 (W1)	
		94,350		98,175
Current assets				
Stock	26,379 (W7)		17,708 (W2)	
Debtors	34,000		23,375	
Cash	17,000		1,875	
	77,379		42,958	
Current liabilities				
Trade creditors	25,500		17,000	
Corporation tax	8,500		4,250	
Dividend proposed	5,000		4,000	
	39,000		25,250	
Net current assets	38,379		17,708	
Less: 8% debentures	11,000		11,000	
		27,379		6,708
		121,729		104,883
Financed by				
Share capital: authorised				
and issued £1 shares		50,000		50,000
Share premium		1,500		1,500
*CC reserve		55,067		39,383
** Retained profit		15,162		14,000
Shareholders' funds		121,729		104,883

*CC reserve	£000	£000
Opening balance		39,383 (W3)
Holding gains		
Fixed assets	17,000 (W7) (i)	
Stock	171 (W7) (iii)	
		17,171
COSA	3,798 (W4)	
MWCA	1,345 (W6)	
Less: backlog depreciation	(6,630)(W7) (ii)	(1,487)
		55,067

**Retained profit

Opening balance		14,000 (Figure 4.5)
HCA profit for 20X5	12,000	
COSA	(3,798) (W4)	
Extra depreciation	(5,695) (W5)	
MWCA	(1,345) (W6)	
		1,162
CCA profit for 20X5		15,162

4.7.5 How to take the level of borrowings into account

We have assumed that the company will need to retain £10,838,000 from the current year's earnings in order to maintain the physical operating capacity of the company. However, if the business is part financed by borrowings then part of the amount required may be assumed to come from the lenders. One of the methods advocated is to make a gearing adjustment. The gearing adjustment that we illustrate here has the effect of reducing the impact of the adjustments on the profit after interest, i.e. it is based on the realised holding gains only.

The gearing adjustment will change the carrying figures of CC reserves and retained profit, but not the shareholders' funds as the adjustment is compensating. The gearing adjustment cannot be computed before the determination of the shareholders' interest because that figure is necessary in order to complete the gearing calculation.

Gearing adjustment

The CC operating profit of the business is quantified after making such retentions from the historical profit as are required in order to maintain the physical operating capacity of the entity. However, from a shareholder standpoint, there is no need to maintain in real terms the portion of the entity financed by loans that are fixed in monetary values. Thus, in calculating profit attributable to shareholders, that part of the CC adjustments relating to the proportion of the business financed by loans can be deducted:

(W9) Gearing adjustment =

$$\frac{\text{Average net borrowings for year}}{\left(\begin{array}{c}\text{Average net borrowings}\\ \text{for year}\end{array}\right) + \left(\begin{array}{c}\text{Average shareholders'}\\ \text{funds for year}\end{array}\right)} \times \begin{array}{c}\text{Aggregate}\\ \text{adjustments}\end{array}$$

This formula is usually expressed as $\dfrac{L}{(L + S)} \times A$

where L = loans (i.e. net borrowings); S = shareholders' interest or funds; A = adjustments (i.e. extra depreciation + COSA + MWCA). Note that $L/(L + S)$ is often expressed as a percentage of A (see example below re. 6.31%).

Net borrowings

This is the sum of all liabilities less current assets, excluding items included in MWC or utilised in computing COSA. In this instance it is as follows:

	Closing balance £000	Opening balance £000
Debentures	11,000	11,000
Corporation tax	8,500	4,250
Cash	(17,000)	(1,875)
Total net borrowings, the average of which equals L	2,500	13,375

$$\text{Average net borrowings} = \frac{2,500,000 + 13,375,000}{2} = \pounds 7,937,500$$

Note: in some circumstances (e.g. new issue of debentures occurring during the year) a weighted average will be used.

Net borrowings plus shareholders' funds

	Closing balance £000	Opening balance £000
Shareholders' funds in CC £ (inclusive of proposed dividends)	126,729	108,883
Add: net borrowings	2,500	13,375
	129,229	122,258

Or, alternatively:

	£000	£000
Fixed assets	94,350	98,175
Stock	26,379	17,708
MWC	8,500	6,375
	129,229	122,258

$$\text{Avergage } L + S = \frac{129,229,000 + 122,258,000}{2}$$

$$= 125,743,500$$

$$\text{So gearing} = \frac{L}{L+S} \times A$$

$$= \frac{\pounds 7,937,500}{125,743,500} \times \begin{matrix} \text{COSA} \\ (3,798,000 \end{matrix} + \begin{matrix} \text{MWCA} \\ 1,345,000 \end{matrix} + \begin{matrix} \text{Extra depreciation} \\ 5,695,000) \end{matrix}$$

$$= 6.31\% \text{ of } \pounds 10,838,000 = \pounds 683,877, \text{ say } \pounds\textbf{684,000}$$

Thus the CC adjustment of £10,838,000 charged against historical profit may be reduced by £684,000 due to a gain being derived from net borrowings during a period of inflation as shown in Figure 4.6. The £684,000 is shown as a deduction from interest payable.

Figure 4.6 Economica plc CCA profit and loss account

Economica plc CCA Profit and Loss Account for year ended 31 December 20X5
(i.e. under the operating capital maintenance concept)

		£000
Turnover		42,500
Cost of sales		(12,070)
Gross profit		30,430
Distribution costs		(2,460)
Administrative expenses		(1,620)
Historical cost operating profit		26,350
Current cost operating adjustments		**(10,838)**
Current cost operating profit		15,512
Interest payable	(880)	
Gearing adjustment	**684**	(196)
Current profit on ordinary activities before taxation		15,316
Tax on profit on ordinary activities		(8,470)
Current cost profit for the financial year		6,846
Proposed dividends		(5,000)
Current cost profit retained		1,846
EPS		13.7p

4.7.6 The closing current cost balance sheet

The closing balance sheet with the fixed assets and stock restated at current cost and the retained profit adjusted for current cost operating adjustments as reduced by the gearing adjustment is set out in Figure 4.7.

4.7.7 Real Terms System

The Real Terms System combines both CPP and current cost concepts. This requires a calculation of total unrealised holding gains and an inflation adjustment as calculated in Workings 10 and 11 below.

(W10) Total unrealised holding gains to be used in Figure 4.8.

[Closing balance sheet at CC – Closing balance sheet at HC] – [Opening balance sheet at CC – Opening balance sheet at HC]
= (£121,729,000 – £77,500,000) – (£104,883,000 – £65,500,000) = £4,846,000
     (W8)   (Figure 4.3)   (Working 8)   (Figure 4.3)

Figure 4.7 Economica plc CCA balance sheet

Economica plc CCA Balance Sheet as at 31 December 20X5

20X4			20X5	
£000	£000	Fixed assets	£000	£000
140,250		Tangible assets	157,250	
42,075		Depreciation	62,900	
	98,175			94,350
		Current assets		
17,708		Stock	26,379	
23,375		Debtors	34,000	
1,875		Cash	17,000	
42,958			77,379	
		Creditors: amounts falling due within one year:		
17,000		Trade creditors	25,500	
		Other creditors		
4,250		— corporation tax	8,500	
4,000		— proposed dividend	5,000	
25,250			39,000	
	17,708	Net current assets		38,379
		Creditors: amounts falling due after more than one year		
	(11,000)			(11,000)
	6,708			27,379
	104,883			121,729
	£000	Capital and reserves		£000
	50,000	Called-up share capital		50,000
	1,500	Share premium account		1,500
	53,383	Total of other reserves		70,229
	104,883			121,729

Analysis of 'Total of other reserves'

	£000			£000
	14,000	Profit and loss account		15,846
	39,383	Current cost reserve		54,383
	53,383			70,229

Figure 4.7 (*cont.*)

Movements on reserves

(a) Profit and loss account: £000

  Balance at 1 January 20X5   14,000 (from Figure 4.5)

  Current cost retained profit   1,846 (from Figure 4.6)

  Balance at 31 December 20X5 15,846

(b) Current cost reserve:

	Total £000	Fixed assets £000	Stock £000	MWCA £000	Gearing £000
Balance as at 1 January 20X5	39,383	38,675	708		
Movements during the year:					
Unrealised holding gains in the year	10,541	10,370	171		
Gearing adjustment	(684)				(684)
MWCA	1,345			1,345	
COSA	3,798		3,798		
Balance as at 31 December 20X5	54,383	49,045	4,677	1,345	(684)

(W11) General price index numbers to be used to calculate the inflation adjustment in Figure 4.8

General price index at 1 January 20X5 = 317.2
General price index at 31 December 20X5 = 333.2

Opening shareholders' funds at CC × Percentage change in GPI during the year =

$$104,883,000 \times \frac{333.2 - 317.2}{317.2} = £5,290,435 \text{ say } £5,290,000$$

The GPP (or CPP) real terms financial capital

The real terms financial capital maintenance concept may be incorporated within the CCA system as in Figure 4.8 by calculating an inflation adjustment.

4.8 Critique of CCA statements

Considerable effort and expense are involved in compiling and publishing CCA statements. Does their usefulness justify the cost? CCA statements have the following uses:

1 The operating capital maintenance statement reveals CCA profit. Such profit has removed inflationary price increases in raw materials and other stocks, and thus is more realistic than the alternative HCA profit.

2 Significant increases in a company's buying and selling prices will give the HCA profit a holding gains content. That is, the reported HCA profit will include gains consequent upon holding stocks during a period when the cost of buying such stocks increases. Conversely, if specific stock prices fall, HCA profit will be reduced as it

Figure 4.8 Economica plc real terms profit and loss account

Economica plc CCA Profit and Loss Account Under the Real Terms System
for the year ended 31 December 20X5

	£000	£000
Historical cost profit after tax for the financial year		17,000
Add: Total unrealised holding gains arising during the year (see W10)	4,846	
Less: Realised holding gains previously recognised as unrealised	none	
	4,846	
Less: Inflation adjustment to CCA shareholders: funds (W11)	(5,290)	
Real holding gains		(444)
Total real gains		16,556
Deduct: proposed dividends		5,000
Amount retained		11,556

Real Terms System: Analysis of Reserves

20X4		20X5
£000		£000
53,383	Profit and loss account	64,939
—	Financial capital maintenance reserve	5,290
53,383		70,229

Movements on reserves

	Profit and loss account	Financial capital maintenance reserve
	£000	£000
Balances at 1 January 20X5	53,383	—
Amount retained	11,556	—
Inflation adjustment for year		5,290
Balances as at 31 December 20X5	64,939	5,290

takes account of losses sustained by holding stock while its price drops. Holding gains and losses are quite different from operating gains and losses. HCA profit does not distinguish between the two, whereas CCA profit does.

3 HCA profit might be adjusted to reflect the moving price level syndrome:
   (a) by use of the operating capital maintenance approach, which regards only the CCA **operating** profit as the authentic result for the period and which treats any holding gain or loss as a movement on reserves;
   (b) by adoption of the real terms **financial** capital maintenance approach, which applies a general inflation measure via the RPI, combined with CCA information regarding holding gains.

Thus the statement can reveal information to satisfy the demands of the management of the entity itself – as distinct from the shareholder/proprietor, whose awareness of inflation may centre on the RPI. In this way the concern of operating management can be accommodated with the different interest of the shareholder. The HCA profit would fail on both these counts.

4 CC profit is important because:
   (a) it quantifies cost of sales and depreciation after allowing for changing price levels; hence trading results, free of inflationary elements, grant a clear picture of entity activities and management performance;
   (b) resources are maintained, having eliminated the possibility of paying dividend out of real capital;
   (c) yardsticks for management performance are more comparable as a time series within the one entity and between entities, the distortion caused by moving prices having been alleviated.

4.9 The ASB approach

The ASB has been wary of this topic. It is only too aware that standard setters in the past have been unsuccessful in obtaining a consensus on the price level adjusting model to be used in financial statements. The chronology in Figure 4.9 illustrates the previous attempts to deal with the topic. Consequently, it has clearly decided to follow a gradualist approach and to require uniformity in the treatment of specific assets and liabilities where it is current practice to move away from historical costs.

The ASB view[1] was set out in a Discussion Paper, *The Role of Valuation in Financial Reporting*, issued in 1993. The ASB had three options when considering the existing sytem of modified historic costs:

● to remove the right to modify cost in the balance sheet;

● to introduce a coherent current value system immediately;

● to make *ad hoc* improvements to the present modified historic cost system.

4.9.1 Remove the right to modify cost in the balance sheet

This would mean pruning the system back to one rigorously based on the principles of historical costs, with current values shown by way of note.

This option has strong support from the profession not only in the UK,[2] e.g. 'in our view … the most significant advantage of historical cost over current value accounting … is that it is based on transactions which the company has undertaken and the cash flows that it has generated … this is an advantage not just in terms of reliability, but also in terms of relevance', but also in the USA,[3] e.g. 'a study showed that users were opposed to replacing the current historic cost based accounting model … because it provides them with a stable and consistent benchmark that they can rely on to establish historical trends'.

Although this would have brought UK practice into line with that of the USA and some of the EU countries, it has been rejected by the ASB. This is no doubt on the basis that the ASB wishes to see current values established in the UK in the longer term.

4.9.2 Introduce a coherent current value system immediately

This would mean developing the system into one more clearly founded on principles embracing current values. One such system, advocated by the ASB in Chapter 6 of its

Figure 4.9 Standard setters' unsuccessful attempts to replace HCA

1940s ICAEW Recommendation on Accounting Principles No. 12 *Rising Price Levels in Relation to Accounts.*

1950s ICAEW Recommendation on Accounting Principles No. 15 *Accounting for Changes in the Purchasing Power of Money.*

1974 Statement of Accounting Practice SSAP No. 7 *Accounting for Changes in the Purchasing Power of Money* advocating the CPP model.

1975 *Inflation Accounting,* Report of the Inflation Accounting Committee (The Sandilands Report) advocating current cost accounting (CCA) rather than the CPP, RCA or NRVA model. The CCA system recommended by Sandilands was based on the deprival value of an asset, i.e. the value based on the loss, direct or indirect, sustainable by an entity if it were to be deprived of the asset concerned. In effect, the CCA model became a compound of the concepts of RC, NRV and PV, with a heavy bias towards RC. The committee believed that, where RC could be estimated, it would represent the value of an asset to the business. The government, the standard setters and the accountancy profession in general accepted the report and a new committee was set up, the Morpeth Committee.

1976 The Morpeth Committee produced precise proposals for the adoption of a CCA system together with the abandonment of the HCA model of financial reporting.

1977 ED 18 was published but it failed to obtain ratification by the ICAEW in open forum because of its complexity, particularly with regard to the valuation of capital assets and stocks, its non-recognition of monetary items, and its mandatory abandonment of HCA.

1978 The standard setters produced *Interim Recommendation of the ASC* (referred to as The Hyde Guidelines). This was a holding operation until detailed proposals could be produced.

1979 ED 24, *Current cost accounting,* was issued by the ASC to be followed by a standard, SSAP 16 *Current cost accounting.*

1984 SSAP 16 *Current cost accounting* was issued by the ASC requiring listed companies to produce CCA accounts as their primary financial report. There was widespread non-compliance and a new exposure draft ED 35 was issued effectively retaining HCA accounts as their primary financial report with supplementary current cost information.

1985 SSAP 16 was withdrawn and the ASC issued *Accounting for the Effects of Changing Prices: a Handbook.* The Handbook was interesting in that it set out four valuation bases if the financial capital maintenance concept was applied and four valuation bases if the operating capital maintenance concept was applied. Its preferred options were CCA under the financial capital maintenance concept which it referred to as real terms accounting (RTA) and CCA under the operating capital maintenance concept.

Statement of Accounting Principles, is based on **value to the business**. The value to the business measurement model is eclectic in that it draws on various current value systems. The approach to establishing the value to the business of a specific asset is quite logical:

● If an asset is worth replacing, then use replacement cost (RC).

● If it is **not** worth replacing, then use:
  value in use (economic value) if it is worth keeping, **or**
  net realisable value (NRV) if it is **not** worth keeping.

However, the ASB did not see it as feasible to implement this system at that time because 'there is much work to be done to determine whether or not it is possible to devise a system that would be of economic relevance and acceptable to users and preparers of financial statements in terms of sufficient reliability without prohibitive cost'.[4]

Make *ad hoc* improvements to the present modified historical cost system

The Board favoured this option for removing anomalies, on the basis that practice should be evolutionary and should follow various ASB pronouncements (e.g. on the revaluation of properties and quoted investments) on an *ad hoc* basis. The *Statement of Accounting Principles* continues to envisage that a mixed measurement system will be used and it focuses on the mix of historical cost and current value to be adopted.[5]

It is influenced in choosing this option by the recognition that there are anxieties about the costs and benefits of moving to a full, current, value system, and by the belief that a considerable period of experimentation and learning would be needed before such a major change could be successfully introduced.[6]

Given the inability of the standard setters to implement a uniform current value system in the past, it seems a sensible, pragmatic approach for the ASB to recognise that it would fail if it made a similar attempt now.

This approach has been applied in FRS 3 with the requirement for a new primary financial statement, the statement of total recognised gains and losses (see Chapter 7 for further discussion) to report unrealised gains and losses arising from revaluation.

The historical cost based system and the current value based system have far more to commend them than the *ad hoc* option chosen by the ASB. However, as a short-term measure, it leaves the way open for the implementation in the longer term of its preferred value to the business model.

4.10 Future developments

A mixed picture emerges when we try to foresee the future of changing price levels and financial reporting. The accounting profession has been reluctant to abandon the HC concept in favour of a 'valuation accounting' approach. In the UK and Australia many companies[7] have stopped revaluing their non-current assets, with a large proportion opting instead to revert to the historical cost basis with the two main factors influencing management's decision being cost effectiveness and future reporting flexibility.

The pragmatic approach is prevailing with each class of asset and liability being considered on an individual basis, e.g. fixed assets reported at depreciated replacement cost unless this is higher than the economic value we discussed in Chapter 3; financial assets being reported at market value (exit value in the NRV model); current assets reported at lower of HC and NRV. In each case the resulting changes, both realised and unrealised, in value will find their way into the financial performance statement(s).

This means that in the future historical cost and realisation will be regarded as less relevant[8] and investors, analysts and management will need to come to terms with increased volatility in reported annual performance.

Summary

The traditional HCA system reveals disturbing inadequacies in times of changing price levels, calling into question the value of financial reports using this system. Considerable resources and energy have been expended in searching for a substitute model able to counter the distortion and confusion caused by an unstable monetary unit.

Three basic models have been developed: RCA, NRVA and CPP. Each has its merits and defects; each produces a different income value and a different capital value. However, it is important that inflation-adjusted values be computed in order to avoid a possible loss of entity resources and the collapse of the going concern.

The contemporary financial reporting scene is beset by problems such as the emergence of brand accounting, the debate on accounting for goodwill, the need for more informative revenue accounts and a sudden spate of financial scandals involving major industrial conglomerations. These have combined to raise questions regarding the adequacy of the annual accounts and the intrinsic validity of the auditors' report.

In assessing future prospects it would seem that more useful financial information is needed. This need will be met by changes in the reporting system, which are beginning to include some form of 'value accounting' as distinct from HC accounting. Such value accounting will probably embrace inflationary adjustments to enable comparability to be maintained, as far as possible, in a price-changing economic environment.

REVIEW QUESTIONS

1 (a) Explain the limitations of HCA when prices are rising.

(b) Why has the HCA model survived in spite of its shortcomings in times of inflation?

2 Explain the features of the CPP model in contrast with those of the CCA model.

3 What factors should be taken into account when designing a system of accounting for inflation?

4 To what extent are CCA statements useful to an investor?

5 Compare the operating and financial capital maintenance concepts.

6 'Historical cost accounting is the worst possible accounting convention, until one considers the alternatives.' Discuss this statement in relation to CPP, CCA and NRVA.

7 'To be relevant to investors, the profit for the year should include both realised and unrealised gains/losses.' Discuss.

8 Discuss the effect on setting performance bonuses for staff if financial performance for a period contains both realised and unrealised gains/losses.

9 'The relevant financial performance figure for an investor is the amount available for distribution at the balance sheet date.' Discuss.

10 'Financial statements should reflect realistically the performance and position of an organisation, but most of the accountant's rules conflict directly with the concept of realism.' Discuss.

11 Explain why financial reports prepared under the historical cost convention are subject to the following major limitations:
- stock on hand is undervalued
- the depreciation charge to the profit and loss account is understated
- gains and losses on net monetary assets are undisclosed
- balance sheet values are understated
- periodic comparisons are invalidated.

12 Explain how each of the limitations in question 11 could be overcome.

13 In April 2000 the G4 + 1 Group acknowledged that market exit value is generally regarded as the basis for fair value measurement of financial instruments and was discussing the use of the deprival value model for the measurement of non-financial assets or liabilities, especially in cases in which the item is highly specialised and not easily transferable in the market in its current condition. The deprival value model would require that an asset or liability be measured at its replacement cost, net realisable value, or value in use, depending on the particular circumstances.

(a) Discuss reasons why financial and non-financial assets should be measured using different bases.

(b) Explain what is meant by 'depending on the particular circumstances'.

EXERCISES

An extract from the solution is provided in the appendix at the end of the text for exercises marked with an asterisk (*).

* Question 1

Shower Ltd was incorporated towards the end of 20X2, but it did not start trading until 20X3. Its historical cost balance sheet at 1 January 20X3 was as follows:

	£
Share capital, £1 shares	2,000
Loan (interest free)	8,000
	£10,000
Fixed assets, at cost	6,000
Inventory, at cost (4,000 units)	4,000
	£10,000

A summary of Shower Limited's bank account for 20X3 is given below:

		£	£
1 Jan 20X3	Opening balance		nil
30 Jun 20X3	Sales (8,000 units)		20,000
Less			
29 Jun 20X3	Purchase (6,000 units)	9,000	
	Sundry expenses	5,000	14,000
31 Dec 20X3	Closing balance		£6,000

All the company's transactions are on a cash basis.

The fixed assets are expected to last for five years and the company intends to depreciate its fixed assets on a straight-line basis. The fixed assets had a resale value of £2,000 at 31 December 20X3.

Notes

1   The closing stock is 2,000 units and the stock is sold on a first-in-first-out basis.

2   All prices remained constant from the date of incorporation to 1 January 20X3, but thereafter, various suitable price indices moved as follows:

		Specific indices	
	General price level	*Inventory*	*Fixed assets*
1 January 20X3	100	100	100
30 June 20X3	120	150	140
31 December 20X3	240	255	200

Required:
Produce balance sheets as at December 20X3 and income statements for the year ended on that date on the basis of:
  (i)   historical cost;
 (ii)   current purchasing power (general price level);
(iii)   replacement cost;
(iv)   continuous contemporary accounting (NRVA).

Question 2

The finance director of Toy plc has been asked by a shareholder to explain items that appear in the current cost profit and loss account for the year ended 31.8.20X9 and the balance sheet as at that date:

		£	£
Historical cost profit			143,000
Cost of sales adjustment	(1)	10,000	
Additional depreciation	(2)	6,000	
Monetary working capital adjustment	(3)	2,500	18,500
Current cost operating profit before tax			124,500
Gearing adjustment	(4)		2,600
CCA Operating profit			127,100
Fixed assets at gross replacement cost		428,250	
Accumulated current cost depreciation	(5)	(95,650)	332,600
Net current assets			121,400
12% Debentures			(58,000)
			396,000
Issued share capital			250,000
Current cost reserve	(6)		75,000
Profit and Loss Account			71,000
			396,000

Required:
(a) Explain what each of the items numbered 1–6 represents and the purpose of each.
(b) What do you consider to be the benefits to users of providing current cost information?

* Question 3

The balance sheets of Parkway plc for 20X7 and 20X8 are given below, together with the profit and loss account for the year ended 30 June 20X8.

		Balance Sheet				
		20X8			20X7	
	£000	£000	£000	£000	£000	£000
Fixed assets	Cost	Depn	NBV	Cost	Depn	NBV
Freehold land	60,000	—	60,000	60,000	—	60,000
Buildings	40,000	8,000	32,000	40,000	7,200	32,800
Plant and machinery	30,000	16,000	14,000	30,000	10,000	20,000
Vehicles	40,000	20,000	20,000	40,000	12,000	28,000
	170,000	44,000	126,000	170,000	29,200	140,800

Current assets			
Stocks	80,000		70,000	
Debtors	60,000		40,000	
Short-term investments	50,000		—	
Cash at bank and in hand	5,000		5,000	
	195,000		115,000	

Creditors: amounts falling due within one year			
Trade creditors	90,000		60,000	
Bank overdraft	50,000		45,000	
Taxation	28,000		15,000	
Dividends	15,000		10,000	
	183,000		130,000	

| Net current assets | | 12,000 | | (15,000) |
| | | 138,000 | | 125,800 |

Financed by			
Ordinary share capital		80,000		80,000
Share premium		10,000		10,000
Retained profits		28,000		15,800
		118,000		105,800
Long-term loans		20,000		20,000
		138,000		125,800

Profit and Loss Account of Parkway plc for
the year ended 30 June 20X8
£000

Sales	738,000
Cost of sales	620,000
Gross profit	118,000

Notes

1 The freehold land and buildings were purchased on 1 July 20X0. The company policy is to depreciate buildings over fifty years and to provide no depreciation on land.

2 Depreciation on plant and machinery and motor vehicles is provided at the rate of 20% per annum on a straight-line basis.

3 Depreciation on buildings and plant and equipment has been included in administration expenses, while that on motor vehicles is included in distribution expenses.

4 The directors of Parkway plc have provided you with the following information relating to price rises:

	RPI	Stock	Land	Buildings	Plant	Vehicles
1 July 20X0	100	60	70	50	90	120
1 July 20X7	170	140	290	145	135	180
30 June 20X8	190	180	310	175	165	175
Average for year ending 30 June 20X8	180	160	300	163	145	177

Required:
(a) Making and stating any assumptions that are necessary, and giving reasons for those assumptions, calculate the monetary working capital adjustment for Parkway plc.
(b) Critically evaluate the usefulness of the monetary working capital adjustment.

* Question 4

Raiders plc prepares accounts annually to 31 March. The following figures, prepared on a conventional historical cost basis, are included in the company's accounts to 31 March 20X5.

1 In the profit and loss account:

	£000	£000
(i) Cost of goods sold:		
Stock at 1 April 20X4	9,600	
Purchases	39,200	
	48,800	
Stock at 31 March 20X5	11,300	37,500
(ii) Depreciation of equipment		8,640

2   In the balance sheet:

		£000	£000
(iii)	Equipment at cost	57,600	
	Less: Accumulated depreciation	16,440	41,160
(iv)	Stock		11,300

The stock held on 31 March 20X4 and 31 March 20X5 was in each case purchased evenly during the last six months of the company's accounting year.

Equipment is depreciated at a rate of 15% per annum, using the straight-line method. Equipment owned on 31 March 20X5 was purchased as follows: on 1 April 20X2 at a cost of £16 million; on 1 April 20X3 at a cost of £20 million; and on 1 April 20X4 at a cost of £21.6 million.

The following indices are available:

	Current cost of stock	Current cost of equipment	Retail Price Index
1 April 20X2	109	145	313
1 April 20X3	120	162	328
30 September 20X3	128	170	339
31 December 20X3	133	175	343
31 March/1 April 20X4	138	180	345
30 September 20X4	150	191	355
31 December 20X4	156	196	360
31 March 20X5	162	200	364

Required:

(a)   Calculate the following current cost accounting figures:
  (i)   The cost of goods sold of Raiders plc for the year ended 31 March 20X5.
  (ii)   The balance sheet value of stock at 31 March 20X5.
  (iii) The equipment depreciation charge for the year ended 31 March 20X5.
  (iv)   The net balance sheet value of equipment at 31 March 20X5.
(b)   Discuss the extent to which the figures you have calculated in (a) above (together with figures calculated on a similar basis for earlier years) provide information over and above that provided by the conventional historical cost profit and loss account and balance sheet figures.
(c)   Outline the main reasons why the standards setters have experienced so much difficulty in their attempts to develop an accounting standard on accounting for changing prices.

Question 5

The historical cost accounts of Smith plc are as follows:

Smith plc Profit and Loss Account for the year ended 31 December 20X8

	£000	£000
Sales		2,000
Cost of sales:		
Opening stock 1 January 20X8	320	
Purchases	1,680	
	2,000	
Closing stock at 31 December 20X8	280	
		1,720
Gross profit		280
Depreciation	20	
Administration expenses	100	
		120
Net profit		160

Balance Sheet of Smith plc as at 31 December 20X8

	20X7		20X8
Fixed assets	£000		£000
Land and buildings at cost	1,360		1,360
Less aggregate depreciation	(160)		(180)
	1,200		1,180
Current assets			
Stock	320	280	
Debtors	80	160	
Cash at bank	40	120	
	440	560	
Creditors	200	140	
	240		420
	1,440		1,600
Ordinary share capital	800		800
Retained profit	640		800
	1,440		1,600

Notes

1 Land and buildings were acquired in 20X0 with the buildings component costing £800,000 and depreciated over 40 years.
2 Share capital was issued in 20X0.
3 Closing stocks were acquired in the last quarter of the year.
4 RPI numbers were:

Average for 20X0	120	20X8 last quarter	232
20X7 last quarter	216	Average for 20X8	228
At 31 December 20X7	220	At 31 December 20X8	236

Required:
(i) Explain the basic concept of the CPP accounting system.
(ii) Prepare CPP accounts for Smith plc for the year ended 20X8.
   The following steps will assist in preparing the CPP accounts:
   (a) Restate the profit and loss account for the current year in terms of £CPP at the year-end.
   (b) Restate the closing balance sheet in £CPP at year-end, but excluding monetary items, i.e. debtors, creditors, cash at bank.
   (c) Restate the opening balance sheet in £CPP at year-end, but including monetary items, i.e. debtors, creditors and cash at bank, and showing equity as the balancing figure.
   (d) Compare the opening and closing equity figures derived in (b) and (c) above to arrive at the total profit/loss for the year in CPP terms. Compare this figure with the CPP profit calculated in (a) above to determine the monetary gain or monetary loss.
   (e) Reconcile monetary gains/loss in (d) with the increase/decrease in net monetary items during the year expressed in £CPP compared with the increase/decrease expressed in £HC.

* Question 6

Aspirations Ltd commenced trading as wholesale suppliers of office equipment on 1 January 20X1, issuing ordinary shares of £1 each at par in exchange for cash. The shares were fully paid on issue, the number issued being 1,500,000.

The following financial statements, based on the historical cost concept, were compiled for 20X1.

Aspirations Ltd

Trading and Profit and Loss Account for the year ended 31 December 20X1

	£	£
Sales		868,425
Purchases	520,125	
Less: Stock 31 December 20X1	24,250	
Cost of sales		495,875
Gross profit		372,550
Expenses	95,750	
Depreciation	25,250	
		121,000
Net profit		251,550

Balance Sheet as at 31 December 20X1

Fixed assets	Cost £	Depreciation £	£
Freehold property	650,000	6,500	643,500
Office equipment	375,000	18,750	356,250
	1,025,000	25,250	999,750

Current assets			
Stocks		24,250	
Debtors		253,500	
Cash		1,090,300	
		1,368,050	

Less: Creditors payable within one year		116,250	
		1,251,800	
Less: Creditors payable in more than one year		500,000	751,800
Issued share capital			1,751,550
1,500,000 £1 ordinary shares			1,500,000
Profit and loss account			251,550
			1,751,550

The year 20X1 witnessed a surge of inflation and in consequence the directors became concerned about the validity of the revenue account and balance sheet as income and capital statements. Index numbers reflecting price changes were:

Specific index numbers reflecting replacement costs	1 January 20X1	31 December 20X1	Average for 20X1
Stock	115	150	130
Freehold property	110	165	127
Office equipment	125	155	145
General price index numbers	135	170	155

Regarding current exit costs

Stock is anticipated to sell at a profit of 75% of cost.

The value of assets at 31 December 20X1 was

	£
Freehold property	640,000
Office equipment	350,000

Initial purchases of stock were effected on 1 January 20X1 amounting to £34,375; the balance of purchases was evenly spread over the twelve-month period. The fixed assets were acquired on 1 January 20X1 and, together with the initial stock, were paid for in cash on that day.

Required:

Prepare the accounts adjusted for current values using each of the three proposed models of

current value accounting: namely, the accounting methods known as replacement cost, general (or current) purchasing power and net realisable value.

References

1 *The Role of Valuation in Financial Reporting*, ASB, 1993.
2 Ernst & Young, *UK GAAP* (4th edition), 1994, p. 91.
3 *The Information Needs of Investors and Creditors*, AICPA Special Committee on Financial Reporting.
4 *The Role of Valuation in Financial Reporting*, ASB, 1993, para. 31(ii).
5 *Statement of Accounting Principles*, ASB, December 1999, para. 6.4.
6 *The Role of Valuation in Financial Reporting*, ASB, 1993, para. 33.
7 Ernst & Young, *Revaluation of Non-Current Assets*', Accounting Standard, Ernst & Young, January 2002, www.ey.com/Global/gcr.nsf/Australia.
8 A. Wilson, 'IAS: the challenge for measurement', *Accountancy*, December 2001, p. 90.

Bibliography

R.J. Chambers, *Accounting Evaluation and Economic Behaviour*, Prentice Hall, 1966.
R.J. Chambers, 'Second thoughts on continuous contemporary accounting', *Abacus*, September 1970.
R.A. Hill, 'Economic income and value: the price level problem', *ACCA Students' Newsletter*, November 1987.
T. Lee, *Income and Value Measurement, Theory and Practice* (3rd edition), Van Nostrand Reinhold (UK), 1985, Chapter 5.
'A quickfall: the elementary arithmetic of measuring real profit', *Management Accounting*, April 1980.
Accounting for Stewardship in a Period of Inflation, The Research Foundation of the ICAEW, 1968.
F. Sandilands (Chairman), *Inflation Accounting – Report of the Inflation Accounting Committee*, HMSO Cmnd 6225, 1975, pp. 139–155 and Chapter 9.
Accounting for Changes in the Purchasing Power of Money, SSAP 7, ASC, 1974.
D. Tweedie and G. Whittington, *Capital Maintenance Concepts*, ASC, 1985.
G. Whittington, 'Inflation Accounting: all the answers from Deloitte, Haskins and Sells', distinguished lecture series, Cardiff, 5 March 1981, reproduced in *Contemporary Issues in Accounting*, DHS, 1984.

CHAPTER 5

Financial reporting: statutes and standards

5.1 Introduction

In this chapter we will consider the regulatory framework applicable to financial reporting. The framework is **evolutionary** and consists of numerous regulations: some are statutory, some mandatory and others statements of best practice.

Our primary objective is to consider the dominant role of accounting standards, looking at the need for them, their nature, effectiveness and future development. We also consider the role of legislation and the continuing growth of voluntary recommended practice.

Since the mid-1960s the accountancy profession has been embroiled with a growing mass of regulations governing the measurement, presentation and disclosure of financial information. The freedom for companies to publish financial data in any format simply to tell the story the directors wished to tell has been replaced by the need to conform to universal standards. By 1991 the Financial Reporting Council was commenting on the standard setting process in its first annual report that 'This is the most promising means of devising standards that are proof against accounting innovations which are **more to do with showing a company's position in a favourable light** than with providing the clearest statement of its affairs'. There is now a recognition that, for public listed companies, financial directors report to a capital market that is both more sophisticated and more global.

The initial engine of change was probably the Stock Exchange but companies are now subject to many different regulatory bodies. In this chapter we consider each of the constituents of the framework, discussing:

- Need for mandatory regulations
- UK Standards (SSAPs and FRSs and SORPs)
- International Accounting Standards (IASs) and EU Directives
- Stock Exchange rules
- Non-mandatory Statements of Best Practice
- Operating and Financial Review (OFR)
- The Combined Code
- Interim Reports
- Financial Reporting Standard for Smaller Enterprises (FRSSE).

5.2 Statutory legislation

Until 1981 the legislative demands and constraints concerning the form and content of published accounts of limited companies were relatively slight. Then the statutory situation underwent a radical change when the UK implemented the EC Fourth Directive in its own Companies Act 1981. This was followed the Companies Act 1985 which consolidated the Acts of 1947, 1948, 1967, 1980 and 1981 and set out the general rules and formats governing the content and form of published company accounts. The primary objective of these rules is to impose a legislative standardisation of presentation with a view to facilitating inter-company comparisons. In other words, they are an attempt to assist users to understand and evaluate company progress. The 1985 Act has now been amended and supplemented by the Companies Act 1989, which gave effect to the EC Seventh Directive concerning consolidated accounts and the EC Eighth Directive concerning auditors, and also introduced regulations relating to the small company and directors.

In July 2001, The Company Law Review Steering Committee produced *Modern Company Law For a Competitive Economy: Final Report* which will lead to new company legislation expected in 2004.

5.3 Mandatory regulations

Mandatory regulations take the form of Statements of Standard Accounting Practice (SSAPs) and Financial Reporting Standards (FRSs).

5.3.1 Role of accounting numbers in defining contractual entitlements

Contracting parties frequently define the rights between themselves in terms of accounting numbers.[1] For example, the remuneration of directors and managers might be expressed in terms of a salary plus a bonus based on an agreed performance measure, e.g. growth in earnings per share. However, if there is a risk that earnings will not grow at a rate that is acceptable to the directors and managers, there could be a temptation to improve the earnings for the period by taking measures that might not be in the interest of the shareholders.

Typical measures include: **deferral of expenditure**, e.g. development expenditure; **deferral of amortisation,** e.g. capitalising development expenditure that has been incurred; and **reclassifying** deteriorating assets from current to fixed to avoid the need to recognise a loss under the lower of cost and net realisable value rule applicable to current assets.

The introduction of a mandatory standard that changes management's ability to adopt such measures will **affect wealth distribution** within the firm. For example, if managers are unable to delay the amortisation of development expenditure, then performance related bonuses will be lower and there will effectively have been a transfer of wealth from managers to shareholders.

This effect of changes in mandatory standards on wealth distribution is a major reason why standards are required, and also why it is difficult to obtain a consensus. Each party considers the economic consequence, real or imagined, on their personal position.

5.3.2 Need for mandatory standards

Mandatory standards are needed to define the way in which accounting numbers are presented in financial statements, so that presentation is less subjective. It had been thought that the accountancy profession could obtain uniformity of disclosure by persuasion but, in reality, the profession found it difficult to resist management pressures.

During the 1960s the financial sector of the UK economy lost confidence in the accountancy profession when internationally known UK-based companies were seen to have published financial data that were materially incorrect. Shareholders would normally be unaware that this had occurred and it tends only to become public knowledge in restricted circumstances, e.g. when a third party has a **vested interest** in revealing the facts such as following or during a takeover battle, or, when a company falls into the hands of an administrator, inspector or liquidator, **whose duty it is to inquire and report** on shortcomings in the management of a company.

The two scandals that we discuss (GEC/AEI and Pergamon Press)[2] were both made public in the restricted circumstances referred to above, when financial reports were prepared from the same basic information but disclosed a materially different picture.

GEC takeover of AEI in 1967

The first calamity for the profession involved GEC Ltd in its takeover bid for AEI Ltd. Each entity had compiled financial reports, but their subjectivity together with their inconsistency in the treatment of the basic information created two widely differing sets of accounts.

AEI profit forecast for 1967 as determined by the old AEI directors

AEI Ltd produced a **profit forecast of £10 million** in November 1967 and recommended its shareholders to reject the GEC bid. The forecast had the blessing of the auditors, in as much as they said that it had been prepared on a fair and reasonable basis and in a manner consistent with the principles followed in preparing the annual accounts. The investing public would normally have been quite satisfied with the forecast figure and the process by which it was produced. Clearly, AEI would not subsequently have produced other information to show that the picture was materially different from that forecast.

However, GEC was successful with its bid and as a result it was GEC's directors who had control over the preparation of the AEI accounts for 1967.

AEI profit for 1967 as determined by the new AEI directors

Under the control of the directors of GEC the accounts of AEI were produced for 1967 showing a **loss of £4.5 million**. Unfortunately, this was from basic information that was largely the same as that used by AEI when producing its profit forecast.

There can be two reasons for the difference between the figures produced. Either the facts have changed or the judgements made by the directors have changed. In this case, it seems there was a change in the facts to the extent of a post-acquisition closure of an AEI factory; this explained £5 million of the £14.5 million difference between the forecast profit and the actual loss. The remaining £9.5 million arose because of differences in judgement. For example, the new directors took a different view of the value of stock and work-in-progress.

Pergamon Press

Audited accounts were produced by Pergamon Press Ltd for 1968 showing a profit of approximately £2 million. An independent investigation by Price Waterhouse suggested that this profit should be reduced by 75% because of a number of unacceptable valuations, e.g. there had been a failure to reduce certain stock to the lower of cost and net realisable value, and there had been a change in policy on the capitalisation of printing costs of back issues of scientific journals – they were treated as a cost of closing stock in 1968, but not as a cost of opening stock in 1968.

Public view of the accounting profession following these cases

It had long been recognised that accountancy is not an exact science, but it had not been appreciated just how much latitude there was for companies to produce vastly different results based on the same transactions. Given that the auditors were perfectly happy to sign that accounts showing either a £10 million profit or a £4.5 million loss were true and fair, the public felt the need for action if investors were to have any trust in the figures that were being published.

The difficulty was that each firm of accountants tended to rely on precedents within its own firm in deciding what was true and fair. This is fine until the public becomes aware that profits depend on the particular partner who happens to be responsible for the audit. The auditors were also under pressure to agree to practices that the directors wanted because there were no professional mandatory standards.

This was the scenario that galvanised the City press and the investing public. An embarrassed, disturbed profession announced in 1969, via the ICAEW, that there was a pressing need for the introduction of Statements of Standard Accounting Practice to supplement the legislation.

5.3.3 Creation of a standard-setting body

In this section we consider the ASSC, the ASC, the Dearing Committee, the Dearing Report and the ASB.

Accounting Standards Steering Committee (ASSC)

The Accounting Standards Steering Committee was formed by the ICAEW in 1970. The committee increased its membership to include other professional accounting bodies. The objectives of the ASSC were as follows:

- **Damage limitation** by narrowing the areas of difference in accounting practice that had been bringing the profession into disrepute.
- The **development of a consensus** by encouraging wider exposure and discussion of proposals for standards. This was a vital step because failure to carry directors or the profession would lead to non-compliance or rejection, as with SSAP 7 and SSAP 16 dealing with inflation.
- To **encourage disclosure** by requiring companies to disclose the accounting policies they have adopted, e.g. depreciation policy, and also to disclose when they have not followed the accounting policy laid down in an SSAP.
- To **improve standards** by developing a continuing programme.

Accounting Standards Committee (ASC)

By 1976 the ASSC included the Institute of Chartered Accountants in England and Wales, the Institute of Chartered Accountants of Scotland, the Institute of Chartered Accountants of Ireland, the Chartered Association of Certified Accountants, the Chartered Institute of Management Accountants and the Chartered Institute of Public Finance and Accountancy. The word 'steering' was omitted and the organisation became the Accounting Standards Committee. The procedure was for the ASC to prepare a draft standard; the draft was adopted if all six professional bodies were unanimous; each of the professional accounting bodies then issued the SSAP to its own members.

By 1982 it was felt that the professional accounting bodies had too great a control over the process. Consequently, the terms of reference of the ASC were widened, e.g. to consult representatives of finance, commerce, industry and government and other persons concerned with financial reporting; the membership was reduced to twenty, including five users of financial reports who were not required to be accountants; and government officials, e.g. representatives from the Department of Trade and Industry, could be co-opted as non-voting members.

The process was also organised to give users full opportunity to make their inputs to the standard setting. The aims of the process were as follows:

- Topics that were to be the subject of a standard were made public.
- Consultation was encouraged by the issue of discussion documents.
- An exposure draft prepared by the ASC was published.
- A draft standard was prepared by the ASC, taking into account reactions to the discussion documents and exposure drafts.

The Dearing Committee[3]

Although the ASC had produced twenty-five standards by 1991, there was criticism that it was not adequately staffed, had no ground-plan and was reactive rather than proactive. However, it had operated as effectively as possible given its resources, and had indeed been ambitious in attempting to address areas where the profession was itself divided, e.g. inflation accounting.

The political climate changed in the 1980s with wider share ownership and the growing use of watchdog organisations to encourage self-regulation, e.g. Oftel in the telecommunications industry and Ofwat in the water industry. Changes in the way in which the accounting profession ensured conformity to universal standards were only to be expected.

The Dearing Committee was set up by the Consultation Committee of the Accountancy Bodies and was charged to review the standard-setting process in the light of future changes in the financial markets, i.e. recognising that financial statements are a prerequisite for a properly functioning capital market, and taking account of the current attitude of the state and public to the regulation of companies. The committee reported in 1988.

Dearing Report

The report contained a number of recommendations, including the following:

- It recommended the creation of a conceptual framework by developing work that had already taken place, e.g. FASB statements produced in the USA. The Solomons Report, which was produced with the benefit of knowing US developments, is discussed in a later section. It is a noticeable feature of the evolution of a conceptual framework that the ASB is eclectic in making use of material from a wide range of sources, e.g. the Corporate Report, the Trueblood Report or Study Group on Objectives of Financial Statements, FASB statements such as SFAC 1 and the IASC document *Framework for the Presentation and Preparation of Financial Statements*.[4]
- It recommended setting up a Financial Reporting Council with nine professional accountants, nine users, the ASB chairman and its own chairman. This Council would be responsible for giving the ASB guidance on priorities and advising the ASB on areas of public concern or controversy.

- It recommended the setting up of the Accounting Standards Board (ASB) with a salaried staff comprising accountants responsible for issuing standards. The procedure for formulating standards would be similar to that followed by the ASC. However, the ASB would found its accounting standards on stated **principles** wherever possible, to avoid the prescription of detailed, legalistic rules. In addition, the ASB would operate an Urgent Issues Task Force to make pronouncements and to amend standards if the need suddenly arose.

- It recommended setting up a Review Panel reporting to the Council to examine departures from standards by large companies. This would allow the auditor to make reference for guidance where the directors proposed to depart from a standard and where the auditor disagreed with their proposed treatment or agreed and considered that the standard needed to be amended.

Accounting Standards Board (ASB)

The ASC ceased to exist on 1 August 1990 when it was replaced by the new Accounting Standards Board (ASB). The twenty-two extant SSAPs issued by the former ASC were adopted by the new Board.

The SSAPs issued by the former ASC are mandatory on all members of the six accountancy bodies, namely, the Institute of Chartered Accountants in England and Wales, the Institute of Chartered Accountants of Scotland, the Institute of Chartered Accountants of Ireland, the Chartered Association of Certified Accountants, the Chartered Institute of Management Accountants and the Chartered Institute of Public Finance and Accountancy. This mandatory authority has been strengthened by the Companies Act 1985 Pt VII as amended by the Companies Act 1989. The SSAPs themselves are now 'accounting standards' under section 256(1) Companies Act 1985.

5.3.4 Arguments in support of standards

We discuss four arguments in support of standards based on comparability, credibility, influence and discipline.

Comparability

Financial statements should allow a user to make predictions of future cash flows, make comparisons with other companies[5] and evaluate the management's performance.

In order to be able to make valid inter-company comparisons of performance, progress and trends, investment decision makers must be supplied with relevant and reliable data that have been standardised. Such comparisons would be distorted and valueless if companies were permitted to select accounting policies at random or, even worse, with the intention of disguising changes in performance and trends.

Credibility

The accountancy profession would lose all credibility if it permitted companies experiencing similar events to produce financial reports that disclosed markedly different results simply because they could select different accounting policies. Uniformity of subjective treatment is essential if financial reports are to disclose a true and fair view. However, the explanatory foreword to the ASC standards emphasised that the standards were not intended to be a comprehensive code of rigid rules, and that they do not supersede the exercise of informed judgement in determining what constitutes a true and fair view in each circumstance.

Influence

The process of formulating standards has encouraged a constructive appraisal of the policies being proposed for individual reporting problems and has stimulated the development of a conceptual framework. For example, the standard on leasing introduced the idea in UK standards of considering the commercial substance of a transaction rather than simply the legal position.

When the ASC was set up in the 1970s there was no clear statement of accounting principles other than the four fundamental concepts of SSAP 2. The immediate task was to bring some order into accounting practice. This is illustrated by the ASC report *A Conceptual Framework for Financial Accounting and Reporting: The Possibilities for an Agreed Structure* by R. MacVe in 1981, which considered that the possibility of an agreed body of accounting principles was remote at that time.

However, the process of setting standards has stimulated accounting thought and literature to the point where, by 1994, the ASB had produced its exposure drafts of *Statement of Accounting Principles*, which appeared in final form in December 1999.

Discipline

Companies left to their own devices without the need to observe standards will eventually be disciplined by the financial market. However, in the short term, investors in such entities may suffer loss. Mandatory standards will impose systematic ongoing regulation, which should prevent serious loss to the entity and those who rely on the annual accounts when making credit, loan and investment decisions.

There is a tension between the desire that standards should not be a comprehensive code of rigid rules and the desire to regulate accounting practices that are imaginatively devised by directors and their financial advisers to create a picture that they may consider true and fair – but which others may not. Directors are under pressure to maintain and improve the market valuation of their company's securities; they will attempt to influence any financial statistic that has an impact on the market valuation, e.g. the trend in the EPS figure, the net asset backing for the shares or the gearing ratios.

The Financial Reporting Council is aware of the need to impose discipline when it stated in its annual review, November 1991, para. 2.4, that the high level of company failures in the then recession, some of which were associated with obscure financial reporting, damaged confidence in the high standard of reporting by the majority of companies.

5.3.5 ASB comments on the process of formulating standards

The ASB advises in its foreword to *Accounting Standards* 1991 paras 22–4, that:

> Topics that become the subject of FRSs are identified by the Board either from its own research or from external sources, including submissions from interested parties. An FRS is a financial reporting standard.
>
> When a topic is identified the Board commissions its staff to undertake a programme of research and consultation. This programme involves consideration of and consultation on the relevant conceptual issues, existing pronouncements and practice ... and the economic, legal and practical implications of the introduction of particular accounting requirements.
>
> When the issues have been identified and debated by the Board a discussion draft

(DD) is normally produced and circulated to parties who have registered their interest to the Board. The purpose of this draft is to form a basis for discussion with parties particularly affected by or having knowledge of the issues raised in the proposals. An exposure draft (FRED) of an FRS is then published to allow an opportunity for all interested parties to comment on the proposals and for the Board to gauge the appropriateness and level of acceptance of these proposals. A FRED is a financial reporting exposure draft.

There is a consultative process, but this should not lead us to expect that all FRSs will receive universal support.

If the experience with the ASC is a guide, then the publication of a standard will not automatically generate universal compliance. The very fact that a standard is required often indicates that the topic is contentious. The process of formulation attempts to address this, but we have seen examples where the disaffection with a standard has been so great that it has had to be revised, as with *Deferred Taxation* (SSAP 11), or withdrawn, as with the inflation standards (SSAPs 7 and 16).

The ASB has not always been unanimous when issuing an FRS. For example, a dissident view was expressed by Mr Bradfield on the issue of FRS 3 *Reporting Financial Performance* based on the fear that the FRS could frequently produce misleading measures of performance.[6]

A dissident view was also expressed by Mr Main, a Forte director and one of the ASB industry members, on the issue of FRS 7 *Fair Values in Acquisition Accounting*, based on the view that costs incurred in the immediate post-acquisition period to implement a business plan to reorganise an acquisition were an integral part of the investment appraisal process and, as such, should not be reported in the group's post-acquisition trading results. This view was supported by the chairman of the Hundred Group of Finance Directors, Mr Nigel Stapleton, who was also the chief financial officer of Reed Elsevier. Mr Stapleton's view was that the ASB had gone well beyond the accounting requirements of other countries and that the requirements of FRSs 6 and 7 would distort the profit and loss account.[7]

The ASB insisted that this complaint was without foundation and that it was determined to ensure that revenue expenses were charged to revenue.

However, the existence of dissident views reflects the differences of opinion that exist between members of the accountancy profession and management. This arises from the fact that the profession ultimately finds itself with audit responsibility, while management's primary concern is to oppose any measures that could reduce future earnings or management's flexibility to influence the year in which the profits are reported.

The ASB had a clear objective in FRS 3, FRS 6 and FRS 7: to reduce management's capacity to manipulate the reported earnings figure by enforcing the matching principle and also by requiring greater disclosure of changes occurring during the financial year. However, other issues are not quite so clear. For instance, there are disagreements as to the appropriate conceptual treatment of goodwill.

In 1995 the ASB adopted the procedure followed for a long time in the USA by the Financial Accounting Standards Board of holding public meetings as part of the consultation process.

5.3.6 Legal force of financial reporting standards

The force of reporting standards has increased. Opinions obtained in 1983 by the ASC from L. Hoffman QC and Miss Arden QC stated that compliance with accepted accounting principles was *prima facie* evidence that the accounts were true and fair. However, if there remained a strong body of professional opinion which consistently failed to apply an SSAP then the *prima facie* assumption was weakened.

We mentioned above that accounting standards have received statutory recognition in the Companies Act. In 1993 the ASB obtained another Opinion from Miss Arden QC, which strengthened its hand by stating that 'Whenever a standard is issued by the Board, then, irrespective of the lack in some quarters of support for it, the court would be bound to give special weight to the opinion of the Board in view of its status as the standard-setting body, the process of investigation, discussion and consultation that it will have undertaken before adopting the standard and the evolving nature of accounting standards.'[8]

This has given the ASB enormous confidence in dealing with controversial issues. Provided there is a process of investigation, discussion and consultation, the ASB should be able to enforce any standard that it issues. From a pragmatic point of view this should lead to greater uniformity, but it leaves unanswered the criticism that the conceptual framework is insufficiently robust to cope with really controversial issues.

It is an independent body, but the structure of standard setting in the UK provides it with additional muscle to enforce compliance with standards – over and above the ultimate sanction of looking to the courts. Figure 5.1 illustrates the structure. The ASB does not stand alone in enforcing compliance. The Urgent Issues Task Force and the Financial Reporting Review Panel have assisting roles.

The Urgent Issues Task Force

The UITF's role is to issue Abstracts where a standard is in force but is not being appropriately interpreted. Abstracts can be very specific, e.g. UITF Abstract 4 gives guidance on the disclosure of long-term debtors within current assets; or very general, e.g. UITF Abstract 7 gave guidance on the level of disclosure required when a company made use of the True and Fair Override. Abstracts that deal with specific technical disclosure might subsequently be subsumed within an FRS, e.g. UITF Abstract 2 dealing with restructuring costs was subsumed within FRS 3. If a company fails to comply with a UITF Abstract, it is required to give adequate disclosure of the fact in its financial statements.

The Financial Reporting Review Panel

The Financial Reporting Review Panel (FRRP) is completely independent of the ASB and the UITF. It has a barrister as chairman and the other members include accountants, bankers and lawyers. Its role is to review material departures from accounting standards

Figure 5.1 Structure of standard setting in the UK

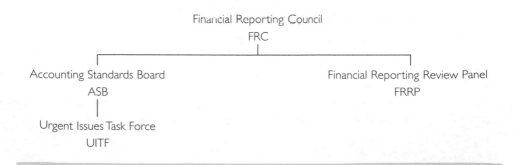

and, where financial statements are defective, to require the company to take appropriate remedial action. It operates under section 245B of the Companies Act 1985, which has given the courts power to order a company to rectify defective accounts.

The FRRP cannot create standards. If a company has used an inappropriate accounting policy that contravenes a standard, the FRRP can act. If there is no standard and a company chooses the most favourable from two or more accounting policies, the FRRP cannot act.

The FRRP is responsible for overseeing some 2,500 companies. Clearly it cannot review every set of accounts. It becomes involved as a result of a complaint by an individual, a referral from the Stock Exchange, e.g. where accounts have been qualified by an auditor for non-compliance, or following media comment.

The FRRP prefers to deal with defects by agreement, although it has threatened applying to the courts. For example, in the accounts of Trafalgar House for the year ended 30 September 1991 certain fixed assets had been reclassified from current to fixed assets – these properties were then written down in value and the reduction charged to reserves, so avoiding the profit and loss account. The FRRP disagreed with this treatment and, following an apparent reluctance by the directors of Trafalgar House to accept their opinion, informed the directors that they were 'minded to make an application to the court … requiring the directors of the company to prepare revised accounts'. The directors then agreed to make requisite changes to their 30 September 1992 accounts. As a result of the FRRP action the 1992 revised accounts saw a reported £122.5m profit turned into a £30m loss. This was clearly a significant intervention by the regulators.

The FRRP has a policing role. It obtains evidence to provide to the court to make a decision about whether accounts show a true and fair view. In practice, its opinion appears to be persuasive.

FRRP public statements

A research study[9] into companies that have been the subject of a public statement suggests that when a firm's performance comes under severe strain, even apparently well-governed firms can succumb to the pressure for creative accounting and that good governance alone is not a sufficient condition for ensuring high-quality financial reporting. The researchers compared these companies with a control group and a further interesting finding was that there were fewer Big Five auditors in the FRRP population – the researchers commented that this could be interpreted in different ways, e.g. it could be an indication that the Panel prefers to avoid confrontation with the large audit firms because of an increased risk of losing the case or a reflection of the fact that these audit firms are better at managing the politics of the investigation process and negotiating a resolution that does not lead to a public censure.

Government support

The ASB enjoys the support of the government, which has indicated that it will provide statutory backing for specific standards if necessary. This was evidenced when the Department of Trade and Industry, following an acknowledgement by the ASB[10] that it did not have the power to enforce compliance, confirmed[11] that it would legislate to adopt recommendations made by the ASB requiring companies to disclose terms of directors' share options along the lines suggested by the Cadbury Report.

5.3.7 Criticism of the FRRP for being reactive

The FRRP has since its establishment in 1988 been a reactive body responding to issues appearing in individual sets of accounts to which it is alerted by public or specific complaint. This led to the criticism that the FRRP was not addressing significant financial reporting issues and simply dealing with disclosure matters that had readily been detected. The Panel consequently commissioned a pilot study in 2000 which reviewed selected companies for non-compliance. The pilot study revealed no major incidents of non-compliance and the FRRP in November 2001 decided that a proactive approach was unnecessary.

Investor pressure for more proactive stance

However, regulatory bodies have to be responsive to a material change in investor attitudes and act if there is likely to be a loss of confidence in financial reports which could damage the capital markets. Such a loss of confidence arose following the US accounting scandals such as Enron. Regulators could no longer be simply reactive even though there had been no evidence of material non-compliance.

Proactive stance – European initiative

The Committee of European Securities Regulators (CESR),[12] at the request of the Commission, has developed proposals which would require enforcement bodies to take a proactive approach. In its *Statement of Principles: Definition and Methods of Enforcement of Accounting Standards in Europe* issued in 2002, it proposed that there should be a selection of companies and documents to be examined using a risk-based approach or a mixed model where a risk-based approach is combined with a rotation and/or a sampling approach – a pure rotation approach or a pure reactive approach would not be acceptable.

Proactive stance – UK initiative

The Coordinating Group on Accounting and Auditing Issues recommended in its Final Report[13] in 2003 that the FRRP should press ahead urgently with developing a proactive element to its work.

The FRRP response to the new requirement for a proactive approach

The Panel proposed that there should be:

- A stepped implementation with a minimum of 300 accounts being reviewed from 2004.
- The development of a risk-based approach to the selection of published accounts taking account of the risk that a particular set of accounts will not give a true and fair view of market stability and investor confidence.
- Reviews should comprise an initial desk-check of selected risk areas or whole sets of accounts followed, where appropriate, with correspondence to chairpersons.

Whilst adopting a proactive approach, the FRRP has raised concerns that stakeholders might have a false expectation that the Panel is providing a guarantee that financial statements are true and fair, stressing that no system of enforcement can or should guarantee the integrity of a financial reporting regime.

5.3.8 Arguments against standards

We have so far discussed the arguments in support of standard setting. However, there are also arguments against.

Adverse allocative effects

Adverse allocative effects could occur if standard setters did not take account of the economic consequences flowing from the standards they issued.[14] For example, additional costs could be imposed on preparers, and suboptimal managerial decisions might be taken to avoid any reduction in earnings or net assets. Furthermore, the consequences might be felt by people who did not actually use the accounts, e.g. a leasing standard might depress the leasing industry, leading to the loss of employment by staff engaged in manufacturing assets supplied under lease, or in servicing the leasing industry.

Consensus-seeking

Consensus-seeking can lead to the issuing of standards that are over-influenced by those with easiest access to the standard setters – particularly as the subject matter becomes more complex, e.g. capital instruments. It could be argued that the ASB is attempting to base its standards on the *Statement of Principles*, but there is a counter-argument that the *Statement of Principles* is too general to fulfil this role effectively.

Overload

Standard overload is not a new charge. However, it takes a number of conflicting forms, for example:

- There are too many standards.
- Standards are too detailed.
- Standards are not sufficiently detailed, so it is difficult to apply them appropriately.
- Standards are general-purpose, leaving a significant proportion of companies unassisted.
- Standards are general-purpose and fail to recognise the differences between large and small entities and interim and final accounts.
- There is more than one standard setter, e.g. statutory criteria, ASB pronouncements, UITF announcements, Financial Review Panel pronouncements, International Accounting Standards relevant to multinationals reporting in more than one country, and Stock Exchange standards. Accountants are becoming so regulated that it is difficult to exercise professional judgement.

Uncertainty of application

Uncertainty of application can take two forms. First, undisclosed interpretations of standards may be handed down by the UITF and Financial Review Panel which are not disclosed to the general body of preparers and users. This leads to a body of precedent that is clearly significant, but of which only selected parties are aware. Second, as we have already mentioned, the standard may be too general and the ASB may hope that the **spirit** of the standard will be applied.

5.3.9 Public view of accounting profession in the 21st century

In the UK, the ASB is to be congratulated on its strenuous efforts to curtail management opportunities to slant financial statements to give a biased rather than a true and fair view. The success of the ASB's approach rests to a large extent on the fact that standards are based on judgement rather than detailed rules which may take longer to formulate and are easier to circumvent. However, the collapse of the US energy company Enron has highlighted two problem areas.

The first was the inadequacy of the standards relating to the disclosure of off-balance-sheet liabilities; the second was the apparent ineffectiveness of the audit process.

With regard to standards, in the UK the transparent reporting of off-balance-sheet activities has been achieved by FRS 5 *Reporting the Substance of Transactions*; however, with regard to the effectiveness of the audit process, much needs still to be done to give users confidence that audit independence has not been weakened in those cases where the auditors receive significant amounts for non-audit services to their audit clients – often exceeding the actual audit fee.

5.4 Statements of Standard Accounting Practice (SSAPs)

Below is a list of extant standards. Breaks in the numerical sequence are a consequence of standards being withdrawn and/or renumbered on reissue. See index for further discussion.

SSAP 4 *Accounting for Government Grants*
This is a relatively non-controversial standard concerning the treatment by a company of the receipt of grants from the government.

SSAP 5 *Accounting for Value Added Tax*
This requires that Value Added Tax should be excluded from turnover and many companies refer to this in their Accounting Policies.

SSAP 9 *Stocks and Long-term Contracts*
This concerns the methods of valuing stocks and the treatment of attributable profit on long-term contracts in progress at the end of the financial year.

SSAP 13 *Accounting for Research and Development*
This insists on the expensing of expenditure to the profit and loss account unless it satisfies criteria to be classified as development expenditure when it may be carried as an asset in the balance sheet.

SSAP 17 *Accounting for Post-balance Sheet Events*
This recognises that information might become available after the end of the financial year and before the accounts are signed by the directors and auditors which may require disclosure or an adjustment to the financial statements.

SSAP 19 *Accounting for Investment Properties*
This deals with properties which have been completed and are held for investment purposes. Such properties are valued for balance sheet purposes at open market value and are not depreciated as a tangible fixed asset.

SSAP 20 *Foreign Exchange Translation*
This gives guidance on the treatment of exchange differences arising on the translation of foreign subsidiaries. In particular, it indicates whether the difference should be taken to the profit and loss account or to reserves.

SSAP 21 *Accounting for Leases and Hire Purchase Contracts*

This is a standard that addresses one aspect of off-balance-sheet finance by applying the concept of substance over form to the measurement and capitalisation of finance leases.

SSAP 25 *Segmental Reporting*

This mandates the publication of additional financial data. It is particularly important for investors following the tendency for individual companies to diversify.

FRS 1 *Cash Flow Statements*

This sets out the headings under which a cash flow should be classified.

FRS 2 *Accounting for Subsidiary Undertakings*

This defines a subsidiary undertaking and concentrates on substance rather than the technicalities which allowed off-balance-sheet finance manipulation.

FRS 3 *Reporting Financial Performance*

This concentrates on presenting an information package rather than a bottom line figure.

FRS 4 *Capital Instruments*

This deals with the accounting treatment of complex capital instruments. It requires instruments that have an obligation to transfer cash to be classified as liabilities and finance costs to be allocated to financial periods to achieve a constant rate on the net amount outstanding.

FRS 5 *Reporting the Substance of Transactions*

This requires items to be included in the accounts if they satisfy the *Statement of Principles* definition of an element, i.e. an asset, liability, ownership interest, gain, loss, contribution from owners or distribution to owners and disclosure alone is not sufficient.

FRS 6 *Acquisitions and Mergers*

This sets out the criteria for merger accounting, e.g the relative size of the combining companies is not so disparate that one company dominates by virtue of its size.

FRS 7 *Fair Values in Acquisition Accounting*

This explains how to arrive at fair values for assets and liabilities on the acquisition of a subsidiary. It takes the view that the fair value of the assets and liabilities is the value existing at the date of the acquisition.

FRS 8 *Related Party Transactions*

This explains the disclosure required when a company enters into transactions with related parties. It allows users to identify transactions that might not be at arm's length.

FRS 9 *Associates and Joint Ventures*

This provides for the first time specific guidance on dealing with joint ventures.

FRS 10 *Goodwill and Intangible Assets*

This deals with new rules for dealing with both goodwill and intangible assets.

FRS 11 *Impairment of Fixed Assets and Goodwill*
This requires any impairment to be measured and recognised on a consistent basis so that fixed assets and goodwill are not reported at more than their recoverable amount.

FRS 12 *Provisions, Contingent Liabilities and Contingent Assets*
This requires appropriate recognition criteria and measurement bases be applied and sufficient information disclosed in the notes to the financial statements to enable users to understand their nature, timing and amount.

FRS 13 *Derivatives and Other Financial Instruments: Disclosures*
The objective is to disclose information about the impact of financial instruments on the entity's risk profile, how the risks arising from financial instruments might affect the entity's performance and financial condition, and how these risks are being managed.

FRS 14 *Earnings Per Share*
This prescribes the basis for calculating and presenting the earnings per share.

FRS 15 *Tangible Fixed Assets*
This requires uniform principles to be applied to the initial measurement of tangible fixed assets, that revaluations be performed on a consistent basis, depreciation calculated in a consistent manner and sufficient information disclosed to enable users to understand the impact of accounting policies.

FRS 16 *Current Tax*
This requires current taxes be reported in a consistent and transparent manner.

FRS 17 *Retirement Benefits*
The objective is to ensure that financial statements reflect at fair value the assets and liabilities arising from an employee's retirement benefit obligations and any related funding and that the operating costs of providing retirement benefits are recognised in the accounting periods in which the benefits are earned by the employee with adequate disclosure.

FRS 18 *Accounting Policies*
The objective is to ensure that an entity adopts the accounting policies most appropriate to its particular circumstances for the purpose of giving a true and fair view, and that the policies are kept under review.

FRS 19 *Deferred Tax*
The objective is to ensure that future tax consequences of past transactions and events are recognised as liabilities or assets in the financial statements.

FRSSE *Financial Reporting Standard for Smaller Entities*
The objective is to ensure that smaller entities provide information about the financial position, performance and financial adaptability that is useful to users in assessing the stewardship of management and for making economic decisions, recognising that the balance between users' needs in respect of stewardship and economic decision-making for smaller entities is different from that for other reporting entities.

5.5 Statements of Recommended Practice (SORPs)

SORPs are produced for specialised industries or sectors to supplement accounting standards and other regulatory requirements. SORPs are issued by SORP-making bodies that have satisfied criteria laid down by the ASB and developed their SORP in accordance with the ASB's code of practice. The ASB considers a proposed SORP through one of its two advisory committees, the Financial Sector and Other Special Industries Committee and the Public Sector and Not-for-profit Committee, to check that it is not in conflict with current accounting practice, current or future FRSs and it cannot override the legal provisions, FRSs or UITF Abstracts.

Figure 5.2 Extant SORPs

SORP-making body	SORP	Issued
British Bankers' Association	Segmental Reporting	January 1993
	Contingent Liabilities	February 1996
	Derivatives	February 1996
	Advances	November 1997
Charity Commission for England and Wales	Accounting and Reporting by Charities	October 2000
Committee of Vice-Chancellors and Principals of the Universities of the United Kingdom	Accounting for Further and Higher Education	August 2000
Association of British Insurers	Accounting for Insurance Business	January 1999
Association of Investment Trust Companies	Financial Statements of Investment Trust Companies	December 1995
Finance and Leasing Association	Accounting Issues in the Asset Finance and Leasing Industry	April 2000
CIPFA	Code of Practice on Local Authority Accounting in the United Kingdom	June 2000
Oil Industry Accounting Committee	Accounting for Oil and Gas Exploration, Development, Production and Decommissioning Activities	June 2001
Pensions Research Accountants Group	Financial Reports of Pension Schemes	Revised November 2002
National Housing Federation	Accounting by Registered Social Landlords	March 1999
Investment Management Regulatory Organisation	Authorised Unit Trust Schemes	January 1997
Consultative Committee of Accountancy Bodies	Limited Liability Partnerships	May 2002

SORP-making bodies are required to satisfy the ASB that it has financial reporting problems that require ASB pronouncements to be supplemented, the body represents a major part of the industry and shares the ASB commitment to maintaining standards.

Figure 5.2 gives a list of extant SORPs which indicates why there are special industry reporting requirements.

5.6 International Accounting Standards (IASs)

The ASB makes standards to be applied to UK and Republic of Ireland group financial statements, including any overseas entities that are part of those financial statements. Accounting standards are not intended to apply to financial statements prepared overseas for local purposes.

The International Accounting Standards Committee (IASC), which came into existence in June 1973 in furtherance of an agreement by the accountancy bodies of Australia, Canada, France, Germany, Japan, Mexico, the Netherlands, the UK, Ireland and the USA, is active on the international scene. A revised agreement was signed in 1982.

The objectives of the IASC are set out in its constitution:

- To formulate and publish, in the public interest, accounting standards to be observed in the presentation of financial statements and to promote their world-wide acceptance and observance.

- To work generally for the improvement and harmonisation of regulations, accounting standards and procedures relating to the presentation of financial statements.

There is a growing closeness between the work of the IASC and national bodies such as the ASB. In formulating IASs on new subjects, the IASC 'endeavours not to make International Accounting Standards so complex that they cannot be applied effectively on a world-wide basis'. The ASB in its foreword to *Accounting Standards* states that: 'FRSs are formulated with due regard to international developments. The Board supports the IASC in its aim to harmonise international financial reporting. As part of this support an FRS contains a section explaining how it relates to the International Accounting Standard (IAS) dealing with the same topic. In most cases, compliance with an FRS automatically ensures compliance with the relevant IAS.'

At the twentieth anniversary of the IASC, the chairman of the Hundred Group of Finance Directors made the following comments:

> the purpose of an international standard must be to make access to capital markets as easy and straightforward as possible. It is not primarily to do with regulation, or prudence, or any of the various requirements that apply in individual countries for historical or cultural reasons. We should remember that there are many differences between markets, reporting and otherwise, which do not need to be harmonised, they simply need to be understood by people putting up new capital overseas.[15]

These comments emphasise that financial reports are seen by finance directors as an exercise in communication.

During the five years up to 1995 the ASB concentrated its energies on ending financial reporting abuses. It saw its role as one of enforcing national accounting treatments within the UK that were congruent with the underlying commercial nature of a transaction and represented its substance.

Following its success in attacking these abuses, the ASB became more outward-looking in 1995. In the UK, it began to work more closely with the Auditing Practices

Board and, on the international scene, it has expressed a wish to make its views known to the International Accounting Standards Committee (IASC).

As far as auditing is concerned, it is recognised that, as FRSs become more complex, it is essential to ensure that auditors can verify their application – a good example of this was the agreed approach taken to Related Party Transactions.

Why did the ASB suddenly become more interested in the IASC?

The ASB has been influenced in its international stance by the agreement reached in 1995 between the IASC and the International Organisation of Securities Commissions (IOSCO) which resulted in a core set of international standards by 1999. If International Accounting Standards (IASs) became the international language, national standard setters would be made redundant. It was as a protection against being marginalised that the ASB sought closer links with the IASC to ensure that national standards were not issued which deviated from subsequent IASC standards. Without links to the national bodies there is a risk that the IASC will become just an ivory tower.

5.6.1 IASC and IOSCO

The IASC and IOSCO have been co-operating[16] on the accounting problems of multi-national companies involved in foreign listings since 1987. In July 1995 it was agreed that if the IASC were to produce a set of core standards that were acceptable to the technical committee of IOSCO, any company would be able to use IAS financial statements to obtain listings of its securities on any foreign stock exchange. This would be particularly useful for companies seeking a listing on the US stock exchange, which currently requires companies to present financial statements in accordance with US GAAP or reconcile domestic accounts to US GAAP. The ramifications of this for preparers and users of financial statements of multinational companies are tremendous: considerable time and effort would be saved. The IASC completed its core standards in December 1998. In May 2000, IOSCO recommended that its members permit the use of IASs by multi-national issuers for cross-border offerings and listings, supplemented where necessary to address outstanding substantive issues at a national or regional level. This is clearly a major step towards the acceptance of IASs and the elimination of the necessity for multiple reporting. Nevertheless, there could still be extensive demands on preparers to provide supplementary information. The US Securities and Exchange Commission was initially seen as a stumbling block with differences between US GAAP and IAS. This has changed with the USA adopting a principle-based approach to standard setting and, following its *Concepts Release on International Accounting Standards* in February 2002, entering into constructive dialogue. The result has been sound progress with the Short-term Convergence Programme and the Memorandum of Understanding issued by both the FASB and IASB in September 2002 in which both undertook to use their best efforts (a) to make their existing financial reporting standards fully compatible as soon as is practicable and (b) to coordinate their future work programmes to ensure that once achieved, compatibility is maintained.

5.7 EU directives

The EU has undertaken the harmonisation of company law within the Union. The Council of Ministers adopts a draft directive placed before it by the EU Commission.

The member states then have a fixed time in which to incorporate the provisions of the directive into their own national legislation. Directives of particular importance to the accountancy profession have been the Fourth, Seventh and Eighth.

5.7.1 Fourth Directive

The Fourth Directive was drafted in 1971, adopted in 1978 and enacted in the UK via the Companies Act 1981 (now incorporated in the consolidating Companies Act 1985). It legalised a standard format for the profit and loss accounts and balance sheets of companies and introduced the override concept of true and fair. The true and fair concept says that, if the application of statute is likely to prejudice the true and fair view, the directors are obliged in law to waive the provisions of the Act in order to ensure that the accounts give a true and fair view. In the UK, the true and fair view has long been the dominant factor and it was given the force of law in the Companies Act 1947.

5.7.2 Seventh Directive

The Seventh Directive was issued in 1976, adopted in 1983 and enacted in the UK in the Companies Act 1989. It mainly concerns the preparation of consolidated accounts.

5.7.3 Eighth Directive

The Eighth Directive was issued in 1984 and member states had until 1988 to implement it. It concerns the regulation of auditors and was enacted in the UK in the Companies Act 1989.

Harmonisation is important. In recognition of this the IASC began its Comparability Improvement Project in 1987 with the aim of reducing or eliminating alternative accounting treatments. As a result, the IASC has revised a number of its accounting standards with effect from January 1995. For example, IAS 9 *Research and Development Costs* was revised so that the option of expensing development costs available under UK GAAP was removed, and, if development costs are eligible for deferral, they must be recognised as an asset and allocated on a systematic basis to future periods.

5.7.4 EU and IAS

In a communication from the Commission of the European Communities to the Council and the European Parliament (*EU Financial Reporting Strategy: the way forward*) in June 2000, it was proposed that all listed companies be required to prepare their consolidated financial statements in accordance with IASs from 2005 onwards. Member states will be allowed to extend the application of IASs to unlisted companies and to individual accounts. This will clearly be helpful for the increasing numbers of companies that have juggled to meet the requirements of international investors without falling foul of national regulations. The proposals follow changes in legislation in a number of member states to permit certain companies to use international standards. This could be seen as having led to a reduction in comparability as companies take different approaches. For example, in 1999, reports on Finland Stora Enso (listed in Helsinki and Stockholm) and Nokia (listed in Helsinki, Stockholm, London, Frankfurt and New York) used IASs but UPM Kymmene (listed in Helsinki and New York) used Finnish accounting practice. The proposals also reflect companies' perceptions of market demands. For example, the Danish company Berendsen changed its accounting policies on goodwill and restructuring provisions in 1999 and the annual report explains that the changes were made 'in order to come more into line with international accounting standards, thus making comparisons with foreign company accounts easier'.

However, it is important to note that the EU has not simply handed over its powers to the IASC. There is to be an endorsement mechanism in the EU, which is to ensure IASs meet the needs of EU listed companies. This may limit the number of options available to EU companies or require additional disclosures.

Why modernising the accounting provisions of the Directives is important

The Financial Services Action Plan was launched in May 1999 and due to be fully implemented by 2005. The Plan has resulted in legislative proposals[17] to achieve uniformity which have included a 2001 amendment to the Fourth and Seventh Directives to allow fair value accounting, and on 14 January 2003 the European Parliament voted to approve the proposal for a Directive amending the EU Accounting Directives to bring EU rules into line with current best practice and complement the IAS Regulation, requiring EU listed companies to use IAS for their consolidated accounts from 2005. This is particularly important in that they will apply to unlisted companies if a Member State does extend the requirement to comply with IAS to all companies.

5.7.5 UK and IAS comparison – The Convergence Handbook[18]

Following the European Commission's proposal that consolidated accounts of listed companies should be required to comply with IASs by 2005, research was carried out at the request of the ASB making a detailed comparison between UK financial reporting and International Accounting Standards. The ASB's intention was to make people aware of the differences and promote consideration as to which was the preferred treatment. This means that the outcome should result in the best quality standard being chosen rather than the UK simply adopting IASs. If this approach is replicated by other national standard setters there is the possibility of a global set of standards eventually being agreed representing the best from every jurisdiction.

5.8 The Stock Exchange

The Stock Exchange was probably the earliest promulgator of rules and regulations governing financial statements. Many of its requirements have been incorporated into statute and standards, although there are still additional demands that are not yet in the statute or standard. For example, the Stock Exchange requires interim accounts and for information to be published in the national press.

Any public company wishing to have its shares bought and sold on the Stock Exchange must first secure what is called a **quotation** or **listing** on the Exchange. Securing such a listing is not a formality. The protection of prospective shareholders is the prime objective of the Exchange and in furtherance of this objective a company wishing to be listed is subjected to a prolonged and deep investigation. The investigation looks at its history, the calibre of its management, its financial condition, its future prospects and its constitution. A successful applicant must then conform with the rules of the Stock Exchange. These rules are incorporated in the *Stock Exchange (Listing) Regulations and its Admission of Securities to Listing*.

The rules contain a section known as 'Continuing Obligations'. The objective is to control the flow of information that could be reasonably expected to have an immediate impact on the company's share price. This includes routine information such as profit and dividend announcements; and exceptional matters such as the appointment or resignation of directors. Strict observance of the obligations is a prime requisite for a fair and orderly securities market. The guiding principle is that price-sensitive information must be released in a way that ensures all users have simultaneous access to the same information.

Transfer of UK listing authority

The role of UK listing authority was transferred to the Financial Services Authority (FSA) on 1 May 2000.

5.8.1 Published accounts

The annual accounts and report must be sent to the shareholders within six months of the end of the financial year. The directors' report must contain, *inter alia*, the following information:

- significant departures from SSAPs and the reasons for them;
- explanation of material variations between actual profit and published profit forecast;
- analysis of geographical areas of turnover and contribution to trading profit from trading operations outside the UK. This is now also covered in SSAP 25;
- name of principal country in which each subsidiary operates;
- information regarding associated companies showing: principal country in which the associate operates; particulars of share and loan capitals of the associate; and the percentage of loan capital in which the listed company has an interest;
- a statement of outstanding bank loans and overdrafts and any other borrowings outstanding at the balance sheet date analysed over repayable time-spans, e.g. less than 1 year, 1–2 years;
- information regarding the capitalisation of interest; directors' shareholdings; members holding more than 5% of the issued capital; details of significant contracts; waived remuneration and waived dividends.

5.8.2 Interim information

Interim reports must be produced. These must be sent to members or inserted as advertisements in two national daily newspapers. Any preliminary profit announcement must be advertised. The ASB has issued 'best practice' Statements for both Interim Reports and Preliminary Announcements. These are discussed further in para 5.11 below.

5.8.3 Public announcements

Share-price-sensitive information must be notified to the Stock Exchange's Company Announcements Office as soon as practical. The latter also needs to be informed of matters such as proposed changes in capital structure.

5.9 Non-mandatory recommendations

The number of non-mandatory 'requirements' is growing. Initially there was only the professional bodies' guidance to their members. This has been extended with the ASB *Operating and Financial Review* document, the ASB *Interim Report* Statement and the *Combined Code*.

5.9.1 **Professional bodies**

Each of the accounting bodies issues recommendations to its members on topics of professional interest. For example, the Association of Certified Accountants issues guidance notes on technical matters relating to the presentation of financial statements, the preparation of accounts from incomplete records and the determination of realised profits and disclosure of distributable profits in the context of the Companies Acts.

5.9.2 **The Operating and Financial Review**

The *Operating and Financial Review* (OFR)[19] statement was issued by the ASB in 1993 to encourage the development of best practice. It was intended to have persuasive rather than mandatory force. The format was not prescriptive and directors were encouraged to develop the presentation of their OFR in a way that best complements the format of their annual accounts. It was not an accounting standard and was mainly for listed companies for which its use had been recommended by the Financial Reporting Council, the Hundred Group of Finance Directors and the London Stock Exchange.

The OFR was intended to provide a discussion and interpretation of the main factors and uncertainties of the business and the structure of its financing. While it was not a forecast, it should bring out those aspects of the year under review that were relevant to an assessment of future prospects, to provide a more consistent foundation for investment decisions. Companies were not required to disclose information that would allow competitors to damage their business.

Because the intention was to assist investors, the OFR should not be merely a numerical analysis. The emphasis was on providing a readily understood discussion that dealt with both good and bad aspects of the business; that commented on trends, factors and uncertainties that had affected or would affect the results; and that explained the reasons for and the effect of changes in accounting policies.

The statement also offered detailed guidance to support these general principles. For example, a discussion of factors affecting future results could include capital expenditure and the likely benefits expected from it; a discussion of uncertainties affecting future results could include scarcity of raw materials, dependence on major suppliers, skill shortages and product liability.

The financial review part of the statement was intended to explain the capital structure of the business, its treasury policy and the dynamics of its financial position – its sources of liquidity and their application, including the implications of the financing requirements arising from its capital expenditure plans.

How successful has the OFR been in encouraging companies to disclose risk?

The ASB recommended that companies identify **their principal risks** and comment on the **approach to managing these risks and, in qualitative terms, the nature of the potential impact on results**.

It is important, for example, to be aware of how a company manages financial risk. In the age of multinational accounting and economic cycles, important factors are the currencies in which borrowings are made, the use of financial instruments for hedging purposes and the current liquidity position. Risks relating to financial instruments have been the subject of FRS 13 because of the perceived high risks attached to financial instruments. The following is a brief extract from the 2001 accounts of BOC:

Management of financial risk

The board of directors sets the treasury policies and objectives of the Group which includes controls over the procedures used to manage currency, interest rate and credit risk.

Interest rate risk

In order to manage interest rate risk the Group maintains both floating rate and fixed rate debt. At 30 September 2001 there is a 30:70 ratio (2000: 49:52) between floating rate and fixed rate net debt.

How successful has the OFR been in informing investors of risk?

Although the reporting of risks attaching to financial instruments is being addressed, the reporting of business risks and how management is dealing with them has been woefully lacking. The OFR has, in general, been treated as a PR document being bland with little significant effort to highlight in advance the real sources of uncertainties that had the major impacts on returns. The previous OFR of every company that reports **unexpected** worsening of turnover, profits or liquidity should be examined to determine how these risks were presented in the annual report. Invariably there is little comment until after the event.

How could the OFR be improved?

- Make mandatory and more prescriptive

  In a research report *Operating and Financial Reviews: Views of Analysts and Institutional Investors*, some analysts believed the OFR would contain useful information, but that market forces would not be sufficient to get companies to produce high-quality reports on a voluntary basis; some believed that an entirely new set of audit skills was needed to audit an OFR properly.[20]

- Make subject to true and fair view

  The view has been put forward (Zeff)[21] that whilst 'one of the widely applauded leadership steps the ASB has taken is the recommendation that companies include an operating and financial review in their annual reports there is a need for the OFR to be made mandatory and thus subject to the true and fair view'.

- Disclose business risks more fairly to smaller investors

  At present, there is a Stock Exchange requirement that listed companies should disclose risks which are likely to have a material impact on earnings and which are unlikely to be anticipated by the general public. This does not mean that they appear in the OFR. Analysts rely instead on risk reporting by companies at company briefings and this information is not available to the smaller shareholder in a timely manner.

  This is a clear indication that it is unrealistic to expect voluntary early disclosure of significant risk without some additional external pressure. This external pressure is now coming from the ICAEW's Financial Reporting Committee which in 1997 produced a discussion paper, *Financial Reporting of Risk – Proposals for a Statement of Business Risk*.

  This paper proposes that there should be an additional report in which directors identify key risks, explain how they measure them and how they propose to deal with them. Such a report would allow investors to understand the uncertainties that their board faces, e.g. cheap foreign imports, difficulty in obtaining supplies of components and raw materials, effect of adverse publicity about products, expiry of patents for major products. There would, of course, need to be the normal relief from reporting commercially sensitive information, e.g. early negotiations to establish trading alliances where a company's major product is losing the protection of patents.

The Final Report from The Company Law Review Steering Committee issued in July 2001 proposes in para. 3.34 that there should be a New Mandatory OFR and that it should contain (para. 8.32):

- a review by the directors of the company's operations and finances modelled on current ASB guidance and best practice
- a discussion and analysis of the performance of the business and main trends and factors
  - underlying the results and financial position, and
  - likely to affect future performance.

The objective is to enable users to assess the strategies adopted by the business and the potential for successfully achieving them.

The Report further proposes that the OFR should include as mandatory items:

- A fair review of the company's business over the year, operating performance, its position at the year end and material post-year end events with details of:
  - market changes
  - new products
  - changes in market positioning, turnover and margins
  - new and discontinued products and services
  - acquisitions and disposals.
- The company's purpose, strategy and principal drivers to allow users to see:
  - the criteria by reference to which its success is evaluated
  - the source from which it derives its success
  - segmental performance against objectives
  - competitive positioning.

The Report also proposes further disclosures of material for the following:

- An account of the company's key relationships with employees, customers, suppliers and others on which its success depends, with details of:
  - employment policies and practices
  - policies on creditor payment.
- Corporate governance – values and structures, with details of:
  - the company's structures for securing an effective working relationship between members, directors and senior management.
- Dynamics of business such as trends and uncertainties which may affect future performance or investment programmes with details of risks and opportunities:
  - competition and customer/supplier dependency
  - technological change
  - financial risks
  - environmental costs and liabilities
  - investment in training, research and development, brands, intellectual property.
- Environmental policies and performance, including:
  - compliance with regulations.
- Policies and performance on community, social, ethical and reputational issues.
- Receipts from, and returns to, shareholders covering distributions and distribution policy and share repurchases.

The above appears detailed but the Report is careful to emphasise that a substantial measure of discretion has been left for directors to determine how usefully to analyse and assess their business and deliberately avoids overprescription, with the risk that involves of rigidity and a 'cookbook' approach.

The proposals appear to follow existing ASB guidelines and best practice and will be welcomed by existing and potential investors.

The Report[22] recommends that the OFR should be subject to review by the company's auditors.

The ASB[23] issued a *Revised Statement Operating and Financial Review* in January 2003 which reflected the main thrust of the Company Law Review with its added emphasis on providing information about the business objectives and strategy, the expected effect of known trends, the potential effect of risks facing the business and the key performance indicators used by management. The Statement also requires those accounting policies to be highlighted which entailed the particular exercise of judgement in their application and to which the results are most sensitive.

However, given the results of one research project[24] which analysed over 6,000 narrative disclosures in the food processing sector and revealed that only 1% were quantified and forward-looking, we do not have a great deal of confidence that companies will provide decision-useful, forward-looking and quantified disclosures without a statutory requirement to do so.

5.10 The *Combined Code*[25]

5.10.1 The Cadbury Committee Report[26]

The process started in 1991 with the setting up by the Financial Reporting Council, the London Stock Exchange and the accounting profession of the Cadbury Committee to report on the financial aspects of corporate governance. A year later the committee produced the Cadbury Committee Report, which set out a voluntary Code of Best Practice based on openness, integrity and accountability.

Although the Code was voluntary, the board of directors were responsible for applying its provisions, stating whether the accounts comply with the Code, and explaining if they did not.

The Code made proposals in four areas relating to (1) the board of directors, (2) non-executive directors, (3) executive directors and (4) controls and reporting. The general thrust of the proposals was that there should be key safeguards. These were as follows:

- The board should retain control over important decisions such as major capital expenditure programmes, bank borrowings and material loans.
- Non-executive directors should be able to exert significant influence by virtue of number and experience.
- Audit committees consisting of non-executive directors should have clear terms of reference.
- The position of chairman should be separate from that of chief executive.
- Financial reporting and auditing systems should provide full disclosure at an appropriate time to affect decisions.

The Cadbury Committee Report made its points in a general terms. For example, in the area of Board of Directors, it proposed:

1.1 The board should meet regularly, retain full and effective control over the company and monitor the executive management.

1.2 There should be a clearly accepted division of responsibilities at the head of a company, which will ensure a balance of power and authority, such that no one individual has unfettered powers of decision. Where the chairman is also the chief executive, it is essential that there should be a strong and independent element on the board, with a recognised senior member.

1.3 The board should include non-executive directors of sufficient calibre and number for their views to carry significant weight in the board's decisions.

1.4 The board should have a formal schedule of matters specifically reserved to it for decision to ensure that the direction and control of the company is firmly in its hands.

1.5 There should be an agreed procedure for directors in the furtherance of their duties to take independent professional advice if necessary, at the company's expense.

1.6 All directors should have access to the advice and services of the company secretary, who is responsible to the board for ensuring that board procedures are followed and that applicable rules and regulations are complied with. Any question of the removal of the company secretary should be a matter for the board as a whole.

The Cadbury Committee Report of 1992 was followed by the Greenbury Report in 1995 and the Hampel Report in 1998. The Combined Code is derived from the Cadbury, Greenbury and Hampel Reports.

5.10.2 The structure of the *Combined Code*

The Code has made an interesting development by separating its proposals into two parts:

- Part 1 containing *Principles of Good Governance*
- Part 2 containing *Codes of Best Practice*

Disclosure statement

The distinction between *Principles* and *Codes* is important because companies will be required to present their disclosure statement in two parts.

In the first part, the company will be required *to report on how it applies the Principles*. The *Combined Code* does not prescribe the form or content of this report and companies are encouraged to describe how they arrived at their approach.

In the second part, companies will be required *to confirm that they comply with the Code provisions* or to explain where they have not complied.

The two sections of the *Combined Code*

Part 1 and Part 2 are divided into two sections:

- Section 1 is applicable to listed companies
  - Compliance will be enforced by the London Stock Exchange (LSE)

- Section 2 is applicable to institutional shareholders with regard to their voting, dialogue with companies and evaluation of a company's governance arrangements
  - Compliance is not the responsibility of the LSE and the Committee have commended it to organisations representing institutional shareholders with the hope that at least the major institutions will voluntarily disclose to their clients and the public the extent to which they are able to give effect to these provisions.

We will consider in this chapter the Principles in Part 1 and the detailed Code Provisions in Part 2 relating to listed companies, i.e concentrating on Section 1. We will consider institutional shareholders in Chapter 29.

5.10.3 Principles of good governance relating to listed companies

The Code deals with Principles under 4 headings:

A: Directors
B: Directors' Remuneration
C: Relations with shareholders
D: Accountability and Audit

Directors, Directors' Remuneration and Accountabilty and Audit featured in the Cadbury Report but Principles for Relations with shareholders is new.

We will briefly consider the first heading A: Directors.

5.10.4 Directors

We can see from 5.10.1 above that the content of Section A: *Directors* is largely based on the Cadbury Report. However, there is now the division into Principles and detailed Code Provisions.

Directors – Principles

There are six Principles relating to directors, namely:

A1. The Board
   The Board should lead and control effectively

At the start of each year, directors will need to consider the question of how this applies to their individual company. How regularly should the board meet (this will depend on factors such as the role of subcommittees)? How much authority has been delegated? How much and how frequently should information flow to and from the board, given the degree of delegation?

At the year-end, auditors need to form an opinion on whether the company has complied with the Code. In respect to point A1, they would review the frequency of meetings, degree of delegation and adequacy of information flows. However, effective compliance with point A1 requires more than this: the auditors would assess the board's overall response to the spirit of the Code, e.g. determining whether it has appointed high-calibre non-executive directors.

A2. Chairman and CEO
   These roles should be separate with the Chairman running the Board and the CEO running the company's business

The chief executive is responsible for implementing board decisions. The chairman is responsible for seeking a balanced board, ensuring that all relevant issues are put before it and all members participate. When the roles are not separated and there is no strong independent element on the board, difficulties can arise. For example, an analysis of forty-five companies that went into receivership in 1989 and 1990 indicated that over 60 per cent of them had a combined chairman and chief executive, and in most of these cases there was evidence of a single dominant character.

The Code has been strengthened since the Cadbury Committee which accepted the situation and proposed that, where the chairman is also the chief executive, there should be a strong and independent element on the board.

A3. Board Balance
The Board should include a balance of executive and non-executive directors so that no individual or small group can dominate the Board.

The effectiveness of non-executive directors can be significantly affected by the extent to which they receive briefings and the extent to which they contribute to work on subcommittees. It is the board's responsibility as a whole to ensure that they are able to make effective inputs.

The emphasis is on bringing in strong, independent voices. A key consideration with regard to independence is that they should not be tied into the company's performance financially, e.g. by holding share options or being pensionable by the company.

A4. Supply of information
The Board should be supplied in a timely manner with information in a form and of a quality appropriate to enable it to discharge its duties.

Just as with non-executive directors, the effectiveness of executive directors can be significantly affected by the extent to which they receive briefings and the extent to which they contribute to work on subcommittees.

A5. Appointments to the Board
Appointments to the Board should be formal and transparent.

A6. Re-election
All directors should submit themselves to re-election at regular intervals and at least every three years.

Directors – Code Provisions

The Code Provisions relating to Principles A2–A6 include the following:

A2. Chairman and CEO
- Any decision to combine the roles should be publicly justified.

A3. Board Balance
- The non-executive directors should be not less than one-third of the board and of sufficient calibre that their views carry significant weight.
- The majority should be independent of management and free from any relationship that would interfere with their independent judgement.
- Shareholders should be informed as to which of the non-executive directors are independent.

A4. Supply of information

- Directors should ensure that they obtain from management all the information that they consider timely and appropriate to be able to contribute at meetings.
- They should recognise that management may not voluntarily produce all the information that they need.

A5. Appointments to the Board

- Unless the board is small there should be a nominations committee.
- The majority of its members should be non-executive directors.
- The chairman should be either the chairman of the company or a non-executive director.

A6. Re-election

- All directors should submit themselves to re-election at least every three years.
- All new director appointments should be subject to shareholder election at the first opportunity after their appointment.

We will now consider the Principle and Code Provisions relating to the board. The Combined Code sets out in Part 1 the **Principle** relating to A1 (the board) as follows:

A1. The Board
Every listed company should be headed by an effective Board which should lead and control.

The Combined Code then sets out in Part 2 the **Code Provisions** (A1.1–A1.6) relating to this Principle as follows:

A1.1 The Board should meet regularly.

At the start of each year, directors will need to consider the question of how this applies to their individual company. How regularly should the board meet (this will depend on factors such as the role of subcommittees)? How much authority has been delegated? How much and how frequently should information flow to and from the board, given the degree of delegation?

A1.2 The Board should have a formal schedule of matters specifically reserved to it for decision.

Such items typically include approval of capital projects, degree of delegated powers, corporate strategy, treasury and risk management. Many of these items also featured in the ASB's *Operating and Financial Review* requirements discussed above.

A1.3 There should be a procedure for directors to take independent professional advice if necessary.

The procedure for obtaining such advice should be set out in the director's letter of engagement.

A1.4 All directors should have access to the advice and services of the company secretary.

The procedure for obtaining such advice should be set out in the director's letter of engagement.

A1.5 All directors should bring an independent judgement to bear on issues of strategy, performance, resources (including key appointments) and standards of conduct.

This requires all directors to ensure that they are properly briefed and to recognise that they have a responsibility for each of the elements in A1.5 ranging from long-term strategy, earnings, tangible and intangible assets and the business ethics and culture of the company.

A1.6 Every director should receive appropriate training.

This was a proposal of the Hampel Committee. It is necessary given the principle that the company should be headed by an effective board which should lead and control, agree strategy, approve capital expenditure and operating budgets and be aware of when to seek professional advice.

The nature of the training will vary with circumstances. Some training may best be given on formal courses, e.g. to understand the legal liabilities of a director and to understand financial data that should be presented at board level. However, there are difficulties in that companies are of different size and subject to different risks which means that the training needs of directors are not uniform.

In a small company it may be that the company requires specialist training to supplement the formal, e.g. identifying health and safety risks is one such area. The directors may be inhibited from pursuing this training need through ignorance or cash flow concerns about the action that might be needed to reduce the risks.

In a medium-sized company there might well be established procedures in place for dealing with health and safety risks, possibly with specialists employed within the company. Its training needs may be very different, for example the dominant strategy might be to float the company in say 2 to 3 years' time. This type of training need might be satisfied by the appointment of a non-executive director with experience of floating a company to hand-hold in the period up to flotation together with the appointment of a finance director for the two years prior to flotation.

In large companies there is greater ability to delegate responsibilities for instance by appointment of internal auditors to monitor the operation of internal control procedures and also to obtain expert advice. The need for this was recognised in the Cadbury Report which stipulated that there should be an agreed procedure for directors in the furtherance of their duties to take independent professional advice if necessary, at the company's expense.

5.11 Interim reports following Cadbury

The Cadbury Committee recommended in 1992 that the ASB, in conjunction with the London Stock Exchange, should clarify the accounting principles that companies should follow in preparing Interim Reports. At the request of the ASB, the Financial Reporting Committee of the ICAEW published a consultative paper in 1993 which formed the basis for the ASB's 1996 Exposure Draft. The Exposure Draft was developed in consultation with the London Stock Exchange, The Hundred Group of Finance Directors, the Institute of Investment Management and Research, the National Association of Pension Funds, the Big Six accounting firms and the Auditing Practices Board.

There has also been significant academic research, e.g. *Financial Reporting 1993–4: A Survey of UK Reporting Practice* by Hussey and Woolfe, published by the Institute of Chartered Accountants in England and Wales.[27]

As Sir David Tweedie commented, 'Producing the ASB Statement has been very much a co-operative effort. It carries the commendation of the Financial Reporting Council, the Hundred Group and both the London and Irish Stock Exchanges. The authoritative backing of these bodies gives the Statement the best possible start in life and we greatly appreciate their support.'

In 1998 the ASB published its 'best practice' Statement on *Interim Reports*.[28] Like the Operating and Financial Review it is non-mandatory.

What is best practice?

● A shorter period for publishing.

The London Stock Exchange allowed 4 months to publish. The ASB propose that this should be reduced to 2 months.

● Use of the **discrete** method.

The ASB does not support the **integral** approach which is sometimes followed. Under this approach the interim report is merely a proportion of the estimate of the full year's results.

Instead, it favours the **discrete** method which uses the same measurement and recognition bases and accounting policies as used in the annual accounts. Consequently, the interim report should show what actually happened in the period; e.g. seasonal businesses will disclose results which differ markedly between the first half and second half of the year.

What does the ASB recommend to appear in interim reports?

The Statement recommends that interim reports should contain:

 (i) **A management commentary** to highlight and explain significant events and trends as required already by the London Stock Exchange but, in addition, to follow the end of year practice by disclosing turnover and profit by segment and the turnover and profits of discontinued operations and acquisitions.

 (ii) **A summarised profit and loss account and balance sheet** with classifications consistent with the year-end accounts and supported by a **Statement of Total Recognised Gains and Losses**.

(iii) **A summarised cash flow statement** using FRS 1 *Cash Flow Statement* headings and reconciling operating profit to operating cash flow and cash in period to movement in net debt.

The Statement was much needed. Current practice varied widely and did not always show what actually happened in the period and did not provide investors with information that was either timely or relevant. The Statement should go a long way towards securing a general improvement in consistency, comparability and quality of interim reporting. It reflects a welcome and fruitful collaborative exercise.[29]

As a result of the Statement companies are encouraged to highlight and explain the most relevant and appropriate figures in their interim reports, to give a succinct but balanced picture with an emphasis on reporting trends and the impact of events and activities since the last full annual report.

The ASB has also addressed preliminary announcements and issued a 'best practice' Statement on *Preliminary Announcements* in 1997 aimed at improving the timeliness, quality, relevance and consistency of preliminary announcements whilst complying with the need for reliability.

Will there be further developments?[30]

The US Securities and Exchange Commission requires listed companies to publish quarterly reports and UK companies with a US listing are already complying. A similar requirement will no doubt be made for UK listed companies to keep London abreast of best international practice. Although preliminary and interim results are highly price-sensitive, there has been no requirement for them to be audited or reviewed. In the USA there is a suggestion that the quarterly reports should be reviewed and, if adopted, a review by the auditors of UK companies would seem to be a natural sequel.

European proposals

Under the Financial Services Action Plan a proposed Directive on Transparency Obligations for Security Issuers has been issued for adoption in 2004 to assist in raising capital on an EU-wide basis. Prompted by the collapse of Enron, the EU have taken a view that there is a need to improve the quality, regularity and comparability of financial statements and proposed in relation to regularity that financial information should be reported on an annual, half-yearly and quarterly basis.

There is a contrary view that such quarterly reporting had not prevented Enron occurring and that it encourages short-termism, e.g. Porsche AG has refused[31] to provide quarterly reports arguing that such a requirement was a significant cause of high volatility of shares on the stock market. In the UK, however, the indications are that the Financial Services Authority will adopt the EU proposal.

Has the Cadbury Report resolved the problems of corporate governance?

Critics could argue with some justification that it is futile to rely on non-executive directors to monitor executive directors. Executive and non-executive directors are perceived to be playing musical chairs at each other's board of directors with little time or facility for any detailed role. For example, a minister of the Crown who acted as non-executive director for a company in the defence industry has gone on record that he was unaware of major business decisions made by the company. This only adds force to the view that they are engaged only for their contacts and not for any major corporate governance role. Even executive directors question whether it is feasible for part-time directors to make any valid comment on the work of the full-time professional directors, and successful entrepreneurs have been known to see them simply as a waste of money. However, there is clearly important progress being made by the ASB in developing voluntary 'best practice' statements such as *Interim Reports*.

An indication[32] that the ASB's best practice statement is taking effect is provided by a survey of interim reports comparing 1995 with 1999 which showed that 78% of companies now give cash flow information (1995: 61%) and there has been an increase in explanatory narrative sections, with 38% of companies exceeding 1,000 words (1995: 14%).

5.12 Evaluation of effectiveness of mandatory regulations

The events in the Sketchley plc takeover in 1990 suggest that mandatory regulations will not be effective.[33]

- In November 1989 Sketchley reported a fall in pre-tax profits for the half year ended 30 December 1989 from £7.2m to £5.4m.
- In February 1990 Godfrey Davis Holdings made a bid to take over Sketchley.
- In March 1990 Sketchley issued a defence document forecasting pre-tax profits for the year ended 31 March 1990 of £6m. Godfrey Davis Holdings withdrew in the light of these poor results.

● In March 1990, one week later, the Compass Group made a bid. Sketchley appointed a new management team and this second bid was defeated.

The new management team decided that the company had not made a profit of £6m for the year ended 31 March 1990 after all – they had made a loss of £2m.

This has a familiar ring. It is very like the AEI situation of 1967, almost 25 years before. The adjustments made are as follows:

Sketchley plc 1990 Preliminary results

		£000
(a)	Effect of more prudent accounting judgement (exercised by the new management team)	
	Reassessment of bad and doubtful debts	3,358
	Reassessment of stock provisions	2,770
	Write-off of fixed assets	773
		6,901
(b)	Provision for redundancy costs	554
(c)	Other items, including the effect of accounting policy changes	557
		8,012
	Profit before taxation, as forecast	6,000
	Loss before taxation, as reported	2,012

Of course, it is not too difficult to visualise the motivation of the old and new management teams. The old team would take as favourable a view as possible of the asset values in order to resist a bid. The new team would take as unfavourable a view as possible, so that their performance would appear that much better in the future. It is clear, however, that the adjustments only arose on the change of management control, and without such a change we would have been basing investment decisions on a set of accounts that showed a £6m profit rather than a £2m loss.

There is often mention of the expectation gap, whereby shareholders appear to have lost faith in financial statements. The situation just discussed does little to persuade them that they are wrong. After all, what is the point of a regulatory system that ensures that the accounts are true and fair until the very moment when such a requirement is really necessary?

The area of provisioning and the exercise of judgement has finally been addressed by the regulators with the issue in 1998 of FRS 12 *Provisions, Contingent Liabilities and Contingent Assets*.

5.13 Developments for small companies

Small firms play a major role in the UK economy and are seen to be the main job creators. Statistics published by the DTI (*Small and Medium Enterprise (SME) Statistics for the United Kingdom, 1997*, URN 98/92, July 1998) showed that in 1997 there were around 3.7 million businesses in the UK. Of these, 2.5 million were sole traders or partners without employees. There were 1.2 million companies on the Companies House register and, of these, around 12,000 (1%) were public companies (*Companies in 1997/98* (The Companies Annual Report 1997–1998) The Stationery Office) with only about 2,450 listed on the Stock Exchange. Of the companies on the register, around 7,000 had more than 250 employees, 26,000 had between 50 and 250 employees, and around 1.01 million had nine or fewer employees.

Certain companies are relieved of statutory and mandatory requirements on account of their size.

5.13.1 Statutory requirements

Every year the directors are required to submit accounts to the shareholders and file a copy with the Registrar of Companies. In recognition of the cost implications and need for different levels of privacy, there is provision for small and medium-sized companies to file abbreviated accounts.

A small company satisfies two or more of the following conditions:

● Turnover does not exceed £2.8m (proposed to increase to £4.8m).
● Assets do not exceed £1.4m (proposed to increase to £2.4m).
● Average number of employees does not exceed 50.

The company is excused from filing a profit and loss account, and the directors' report and balance sheet need only be an abbreviated version disclosing major asset and liability headings. Its privacy is protected by excusing disclosure of directors' emoluments.

A medium-sized company satisfies two or more of the following conditions:

● Turnover does not exceed £11.2m.
● Assets do not exceed £5.6m.
● Average number of employees does not exceed 250.

It is excused far less than a small company: the major concession is that it need not disclose sales turnover and cost of sales, and the profit and loss account starts with the gross profit figure. This is to protect its competitive position.

5.13.2 Mandatory requirements

The approach by the standard setters has generally been to require all companies to comply with SSAPs and FRSs. This can be justified on the grounds that compliance is necessary in order to present a true and fair view. Critics maintain that small companies might well never enter into transactions that fall within a standard, e.g. finance leasing, and that they should therefore be excused from compliance with the majority of standards. This is a weak position to take. After all, if a company actually does enter into a transaction for which a standard exists, it is difficult to see how it could be permitted to account for it in a non-standard way.

However, there is a legitimate interest in deregulation and a working party was set up by the CCAB at the request of the ASB to carry out a consultation exercise to assess whether companies should be excused from complying on the grounds of size or public interest.

From the consultations[34] there was a clear support for some relief from accounting standards to be based on size or a combination of size and public interest. The ASB accepted the recommendations of the CCAB Working Party and issued FRSSE[35] in November 1997. Recognising that there was concern as to the legality of setting different measurement and disclosure requirements, the ASB took legal advice which confirmed that smaller entities can properly be allowed exemptions or differing treatments in standards and UITFs provided such differences were justified **on rational grounds**.

How can rational grounds be established?

The test as to whether a decision is rational is based on obtaining answers to nine questions. If there are more negative responses than positive, there are rational grounds for a different treatment. The nine questions can be classified as follows:

Generic relevance

1 Is the standard essential practice for all entities?
2 Is the standard likely to be widely relevant to small entities?

Proprietary relevance

3 Would the treatment required by the standard be readily recognised by the proprietor or manager as corresponding to their understanding of the transaction?

Relevant measurement requirements

4 Is the treatment compatible with that used by the Inland Revenue in computing tax?
5 Are the measurement methods in a standard likely to be reasonably practical for small entities?
6 Is the accounting treatment the least cumbersome?

User relevance

7 Is the standard likely to meet information needs and legitimate expectations of the users of a small entity's accounts?
8 Does the standard provide disclosure likely to be meaningful and comprehensible to such a user?

Relevant to expand statutory provision

9 Do the requirements of the standard significantly augment the treatment required by statute?

How are individual standards dealt with in the FRSSE?

Standards have been dealt with in seven ways as explained in (a) to (g) below:

(a) Adopted without change
FRSSE adopted certain standards and UITFs without change, e.g. SSAP 17 *Accounting for Post Balance Sheet Events*, UITF 14 *Disclosure of Changes in Accounting Policy*, UITF 24 *Start-up-costs*.

(b) Not addressed
Certain standards were not addressed in the FRSSE, e.g. SSAP 5 *Accounting for Value Added Tax*, SSAP 25 *Segmental Reporting*, FRS 1 (Revised 1996) *Cash Flow Statements*, UITF 4 *Presentation of Long-term Debtors in Current Assets* and UITF 5, UITF 9–11, UITF 13, UITF 15–19, UITF 22, UITF 25–27, 29–30; FRS 13 *Derivatives and other Financial Instruments Disclosures*; FRS 14 *Earnings per Share*.

(c) Statements relating to groups are cross referenced

If group accounts are to be prepared the FRSSE contains the cross-references required to FRS 2 *Accounting for Subsidiary Undertakings*, FRS 6 *Acquisitions and Mergers* and FRS 7 *Fair Values in Acquisition Accounting*.

(d) Disclosure requirements removed

Certain standards apply but the disclosure requirement is removed, e.g. FRS 10 *Accounting for Goodwill*, UITF 21, *Accounting issues arising from the proposed introduction of the euro*.

(e) Disclosure requirements reduced

Certain standards apply but there is a reduced disclosure requirement, e.g.

- SSAP 9 *Stock and Long-term Contracts* applies but there is no requirement to sub-classify stock nor the disclose accounting policy.
- FRS 3 *Reporting Financial Performance* applies but:
  - no requirement to analyse the turnover, costs and results into continuing operations, acquisitions and discontinued operations;
  - no reference to the consequences of a decision to sell or terminate an operation and the provisions that may be recognised;
  - no reference to earnings per share;
  - no requirement for a note of historical cost profits and losses;
  - no requirement for a reconciliation of movements in shareholders' funds.
- FRS 16 and 19 where detailed disclosure is replaced by the requirement to disclose material components of the current tax charges.

(f) Increased requirements

Certain standards are included with certain of the requirements reduced and other of the requirements increased, e.g. under FRS 8 *Related Party Disclosure* a new paragraph has been added, clarifying that the standard requires the disclosure of directors' personal guarantees for their company's borrowings.

(g) Main requirements included

Certain standards have their main requirements included, e.g. FRS 16 *Current Tax*, FRS 18 *Accounting Policies*, FRS 19 *Deferred Tax*.

How unanimous was the response to the consultation exercise?

As one would expect, reactions were mixed with supporters both for excluding and for retaining a particular standard. For example, some commentators who represented the main users suggested that the cash flow statement should also be required from smaller entities. Their argument was that the management of cash is crucial in small, as well as large, businesses and that a cash flow statement provided a useful focus for discussions with management as well as a reference point for subsequent more detailed analysis.

The CCAB Working Party, however, accepted the arguments of those commentators who supported the exclusion of cash flow statements. Their arguments were:

- FRS 1 already exempts small entities from preparing a statement.
- For many small businesses in which transactions are straightforward, the cash flow statement adds little to what was already apparent from the balance sheet and profit and loss account.
- The gap between the period-end and the date of finalising the financial statements may be of such a length (up to ten months) as to limit the usefulness of any cash flow information.
- Managers in small businesses are well aware of the need to manage cash effectively. Their mechanisms for doing so may be informal but little would be added by a

requirement for a cash flow statement in annual accounts prepared some months after period-end.

The ASB itself, whilst recognising that cash flow statements were not mandatory under FRS 1 for smaller entities, believed that a cash flow statement is an important aid to the understanding of an entity's financial position and performance and therefore included in the FRSSE a *Voluntary Disclosures* section which recommended that smaller entities present a simplified cash flow statement using the indirect method.

Does the FRSSE improve the information provided to users?

It is interesting to note that only one of the FRSs issued by the ASB, namely FRS 8 *Related Party Disclosure*, was deemed by the CCAB and ASB to have any relevance to smaller entities. It would seem reasonable to deduce from this that the ASB exists primarily to regulate the financial reporting of the 2,000 or so companies listed on the London Stock Exchange and has had little time to consider the million other companies that prepare and file accounts.

There are two clear adverse effects of this:

● The lack of adequate research by the ASB into the information needs of the users of accounts of smaller and medium-sized companies means, according to some researchers,[36] that the FRSSE has been produced without proper regard to those needs.

● The exercise started from the wrong end of the scale, according to the Small Practitioners Association,[37] in that it started with the standards designed for large public companies and then went through the nine questions approach to decide which of these to include in the FRSSE. A more logical approach would have been to have carried out the research suggested by Dugdale, Hussey and Jarvis[38] and developed positive standards that satisfied identified user needs.

However, given the pressure to establish appropriate FRSs for listed companies and to maintain a presence in the international standard-setting scene, there seems little prospect that ASB resources could be stretched to embrace the needs of the one million non-listed companies.

One could reasonably ask questions such as:

● Why should non-listed companies require ten months to prepare and file accounts?

● Why should this be accepted by the CCAB working party as actual justification for not requiring a Cash Flow Statement?

● Is it feasible, or indeed even desirable, to expect the ASB to be concerned with non-listed company reporting given that almost 100% of the time since it was set up has been devoted to the reporting requirements of listed companies?

How will the FRSSE be kept up to date?

The ASB has set up an advisory committee, the Committee on Accounting for Smaller Entities, chaired by Professor Whittington, to assist in updating and revising the FRSSE periodically but any change in the FRSSE as a result of new standards, e.g. FRS 10, will be the subject of public consultation.

In December 2001 the ASB[39] issued FRSSE which came into effect in June 2002. Although it is revised annually it does lag behind the issue of individual FRSs. It has been suggested that one way to overcome this would be to insert a note in each new FRS as to its applicability to small enterprises.[40]

The basic principles remain unchanged:

- Smaller entities may properly be allowed exemptions or different treatment provided such differences are justified on rational grounds, as discussed in para 5.13.2 above.

- The objective of the FRSSE is to ensure that the reporting entity provides information about the financial position, performance and financial adaptability of the entity that is useful to users in assessing the stewardship of management and for making economic decisions, recognising that the balance between users' needs in respect of stewardship and economic decision-making for smaller entities is different from that for other reporting entities.

- The financial statements should present a true and fair view which takes account of the substance of any arrangement or transaction, i.e. after identifying whether the transaction has changed existing, or given rise to new, assets or liabilities.

In February 2001 the ASB published for comment a discussion paper reviewing its FRSSE. The objective of the paper was to seek respondents' views on whether, in its present form, the FRSSE best met users' needs and whether any fundamental changes should be considered to the way in which it was prepared and presented. The response was that it was widely used and generally valued by practitioners. There is the view that accounts prepared in accordance with the FRSSE can provide information that is more meaningful and understandable to owner–managers than accounts complying with Big GAAP. However, there is a contrary view[41] that whilst external accountants may consider and adopt the FRSSE, it is questionable whether directors have been involved in such consideration as they are too busy running their businesses and surviving.

Company Law Review

The Company Law Review Steering Group acknowledged that there appeared to be serious problems which required remedy arising from fact that the Companies Act:

- is structured around the needs of larger, publicly owned companies with a separation between the shareholders/investors and the directors with many provisions imposing duties on directors to provide protection for shareholders against abuses of directors' powers (Sec 5.2.3)

- is opaque and inaccessible to small business users and requires a thorough knowledge of the whole Act to understand what exemptions and adaptations are available (Sec 5.2.5)

- lays down regulatory requirements for the protection of the company's creditors that are overly burdensome and fail to serve the purposes for which they were designed (Sec 5.2.7)

- With regard to the work of the ASB, *The Strategic Framework* recognises that 'A considerable amount of piecemeal work has been done on improving approaches within the existing framework e.g. FRSSE'. It also recognises the view expressed by some directors of small companies that statutory accounts are a tiresome irrelevance but, whilst being open to consultation, reminds us that the Fourth Directive requires all limited companies to publish accounts and that any replacement of this requirement would require a change in EU law (Sec 5.2.14).

It has been interesting[42] to see the responses to the questions raised by *The Strategic Framework*. Selected questions with responses included:

Qn 9: Is it agreed that the difficulties met by small and closely-held companies in operating within the Act are serious and worthy of remedy?

Responses: The overwhelming majority supported the proposition, feeling that the present law was opaque, unwieldy, unnecessarily complex and burdensome and therefore ripe for review.

Qn 10(a): Is it agreed that it is not desirable to restrict access to limited liability?

Responses: A significant majority took the view that it was not desirable to restrict access to limited liability, arguing that limited liability status acted as a spur to entrepreneurship and innovation.

Qn 10(b): If not, then what restraints should be considered?

Responses: It was thought desirable by respondents to (b) to require a minimum capital threshold as a practical and useful measure to cause proprietors of small businesses to consider whether they needed to be incorporated.

Qn 11(a): Should the current accounting exemptions for small and medium-sized companies be removed or amended?

Responses: The vast majority took the view that some change was necessary but there was a wide divergence as to the nature of the change that was desirable. Responses ranged from complete exemption from preparing and filing accounts to replacing with alternative forms of financial information such as cash flow statements, ratios and graphical presentation, to requiring the same compliance as that required of large companies.

11(b): Do current exempt accounts provide proportionate, or any, protection to creditors, bearing in mind the cost of preparation?

Responses: The overwhelming view was that abbreviated accounts filed by small and medium-sized companies provided little or no protection to creditors.

5.13.3 How does the UK approach compare with that in the developing world?

The United Nations Conference on Trade and Development (UNCTAD) has a working group of experts on international standards of accounting and reporting (ISAR)[43] which continued to discuss the accounting needs of small and medium-sized enterprises in 2001. This is because such enterprises are regarded by governments in developing countries as important generators of employment and economic growth. Many countries have many businesses that keep no records and pay no taxes, but when they want to grow they come within regulations and are subject to additional costs and regulatory requirements.[44] As far as accounting requirements are concerned, it is suggested that a way forward would be to follow the system being developed in West Africa where the micro-business starts with simple cash accounting, and then progresses to accrual accounting and finally compliance with International Accounting Standards. In the developing world, it is felt that accounting hurdles are too high and a progressive system of accounting is required as seen in West Africa. Many small and medium-sized enterprises in the UK are halfway along the spectrum with accrual accounting and audited accounts but, as we have seen above, there are still calls in the UK for a reduction in the regulatory burden and many small enterprises are operating outside the formal system, keeping no records and paying no tax.

Summary

It is evident from cases such as AEI/GEC and the Wiggins Group (see Question 4 in Chapter 2) that management cannot be permitted to have total discretion in the way in which it presents financial information in its accounts and rules are needed to ensure uniformity in the reporting of similar commercial transactions. Decisions must then be made as to the nature of the rules and how they are to be enforced.

In the UK the standard-setting bodies have tended to lean towards rules being framed as general principles and accepting the culture of voluntary compliance.

Although there is a preference on the part of the standard setters to concentrate on general principles, there is a growing pressure from the preparers of the accounts for more detailed illustrations and explanations in how the standards are to be applied. This is apparent from FRS 4 with its Application Notes and the increasing number of Urgent Issue Task Force Abstracts.

With regard to voluntary compliance, The *Combined Code* supports the continuance of this approach but there is evidence that the government will require increasing mandatory compliance as seen with the proposal to make the OFR mandatory.

REVIEW QUESTIONS

1 Why is it necessary for financial reporting to be subject to (a) mandatory control and (b) statutory control?

2 How is it possible to make shareholders aware of the significance of the exercise of judgement by directors which can turn profits of £6m into losses of £2m?

3 Discuss the main arguments for dispensing with all SSAPs and FRSs.

4 'The effective working of the financial aspects of a market economy rests on the validity of the underlying premises of integrity in the conduct of business and reliability in the provision of information. Even though in the great majority of cases that presumption is wholly justified, there needs to be strong institutional underpinning.

'That institutional framework has been shown to be inadequate. The last two to three years have accordingly seen a series of measures by the financial and business community to strengthen it. Amongst these has been the creation of the Financial Reporting Council and the bodies which it in turn established.'[45]

Discuss the above statement with particular reference to one of the following institutions: Accounting Standards Board, Financial Reporting Review Panel, Urgent Issues Task Force. Illustrate with reference to publications or decisions from the institution you have chosen to discuss.

5 To what extent do you think FRSs should take economic consequences into account? Discuss in relation to dissident views.

6 (a) Name four UITF Abstracts and explain why they were required.

(b) 'The principles involved in decisions which the UITF give in response to an approach by directors or auditors prior to finalising the accounts should be published and should be in the public domain.' Discuss.

7 (a) Name four companies that have been the subject of FRRP pronouncements and explain the reason for FRRP involvement.

  (b) Shorter accounting standards are not a realistic option until both companies and the accountancy profession can be trusted to 'fully honour an approach limited to basic principles'. Discuss why companies and the accountancy profession cannot be so trusted.

8 Explain the main changes to interim reports following the ASB Statement of Best Practice.

9 'The most favoured way to reduce information overload was to have the company filter the available information set based on users' specifications of their needs.'[46] Discuss how this can be achieved.

10 Review a SORP and discuss the reasons why existing FRSs and UITFs need to be supplemented.

11 Quarterly reporting is essential in the interest of transparency and can, therefore, only be beneficial for investors. Discuss.

12 Every company in each European Member State should be required to prepare their financial reports in accordance with an IASSE similar in content to the UK's FRSSE. Discuss.

13 Measurement criteria are more important than disclosure requirements for small entities. Discuss.

EXERCISES

Question 1

Constructive review of the regulators.

Required:
(a) Obtain a copy of the Financial Reporting Council's Annual Review.
(b) Prepare a profile of the members of the Financial Reporting Council, the ASB, the UITF and the Financial Reporting Review Panel.
(c) Comment on the strengths and weaknesses revealed by the profile.
(d) Advise (with reasons) on changes that you consider would strengthen one or more of these bodies.

Question 2

The ASB stated in 1994 that:

> The size of its documents is a matter that the Board has constantly in mind. In essence the Board would like to publish short standards based on principle dealing with (say) 80 per cent of the issues. If many of the remaining, often peripheral and specialised, issues have to be dealt with it will disproportionately increase the length and complexity of our standards. How far the Board will be driven in that direction will depend on the willingness of the financial community to comply with the spirit of shorter standards and not to search for loopholes that will have to be plugged by the issue of further rules.

Required:
(a) Discuss how the ASB has dealt with what it describes as 'the remaining, often peripheral and specialised, issues'.
(b) Obtain an interview with the tax partner of a local firm of accountants to seek their view on following the approach recommended by the ASB (i) in relation to tax advice and (ii) in relation to financial reporting practice.

References

1 G. Whittred and I. Zimmer, *Financial Accounting Incentive Effects and Economic Consequences*, Holt, Rinehart & Winston, 1992, p. 8.

2 E.R. Farmer, *Making Sense of Company Reports*, Van Nostrand Reinhold, 1986, p. 16.

3 Dearing Report, *The Making of Accounting Standards*, CCAB, 1988.

4 *Framework for the Presentation and Preparation of Financial Statements*, IASC, 1989, para. 40.

5 *Ibid*.

6 FRS 3, *Financial Reporting Performance*, ASB, 1992.

7 *Accountancy Age*, 29 September 1994, p. 2.

8 Foreword to *Accounting Standards*, ASB, 1993, Appendix para. 10.

9 K. Peasnell, P. Pope and S. Young, 'Breaking the rules', *Accountancy International*, February 2000, p. 76.

10 UITF Abstract 10, *Disclosure of Directors' Share Options*, ASB, 1994.

11 *Accountancy Age*, 3 November 1994, p. 1.

12 CESR, *Statement of Principles: Definition and Methods of Enforcement*, CESR02–188b Principle 13, October 2002.

13 Coordinating Group on Accounting and Auditing Issues, *Final Report* para 4.22 January 2003.

14 M. Bromwich, *The Economics of Accounting Standard Setting*, Prentice Hall, 1985, p. 78.

15 *Certified Accountant*, August 1993, p. 13.

16 For further details see D. Cairns (1997) 'The future of the IASC and the implications for UK companies' in ICAEW, *Financial reporting today - current and emerging issues*, Accountancy Books, 1998 edition, pp. 115–152.

17 http://europa.eu.int/internal_market/en/finances/actionplan/annex.pdf

18 D. Cairns and C. Nobes, *The Convergence Handbook*, ICAEW, 2000.

19 *Operating and Financial Review*, ASB, 1993.

20 P. Weetman, Bill Collins and E. Davie, *Operating and Financial Review: Views of Analysts and Institutional Investors*, ICAS, 1994.

21 S. Zeff, 'Good so far but difficult decisions ahead', *Accountancy*, October 1995, p. 96.

22 *Modern Company Law for a Competitive Economy – The Final Report*, Company Law Review Steering Committee, July 2001, para. 8.63.

23 ASB, revised OFR, January 2003.

24 V. Beattie, B. McInnes and S. Fearnley, *Through the Eyes of Management: A Study of Narrative Disclosures*, Centre for Business Performance, ICAEW, June 2002.

25 *The Combined Code*, Committee on Corporate Governance, Gee, 1998.

26 Cadbury Report, 1992.

27 R. Hussey and S. Woolfe, *Interim Statements and Preliminary Profit Announcements*, ICAEW Research Board, 1994.

28 *Interim Reports*, ASB, 1998.

29 Hannah King, 'What's the latest on interim reports?' *Accountancy*, October 1997, p. 88.

30 K. Bagshaw, *Preliminary Announcements: A Guide to Best Practice and Interim Reports: A Guide to Best Practice*, Accountancy Books, 1999.

31 *The Times*, Porsche files lawsuit against Deutsche Bourse, 8 April 2003, p. 21.

32 *Progress in the Interim: Surveying Corporate Half Yearly Reporting*, Arthur Andersen, 1999.

33 *Student Financial Reporting*, ICAEW, 1991/2, p. 17.

34 A Consultative Document 'Exemptions from Standards on Grounds of Size or Public Interest', CCAB, November 1994; and A Paper 'Designed to fit – A Financial Reporting Standard for Smaller Entities', CCAB, December 1995.

35 *Financial Reporting Standard for Smaller Entities*, ASB, 1997.

36 D. Dugdale, J. Hussey and R. Jarvis, 'Can less mean more?' *Certified Accountant*, November 1997, pp. 32–33.

37 'FRSSE: OK, not perfect', *Accountancy*, December 1997, p.11.

38 D. Dugdale, *et al.*, *op. cit.*

39 FRSSE, ASB, 2001.

40 N. Sleigh-Johnson, 'In defence of the FRSSE', *Accountancy*, December 2001, p.92.

41 J. Morley, 'Who wants a FRSSE?' *Accountancy*, September 2001, p.104.

42 *Responses to the Consultation Document published by the Company Law Review Steering Group, February, 1999*, Dti, December 1999.

43 ISAR, *Accounting by SMEs*, United Nations Conference on Trade and Development (UNCTAD) 13 July 2001.

44 P. Walton, 'UN research into the accounting needs of SMEs', *Accounting and Business*, February 2000, p. 34.

45 *The State of Financial Reporting*, Financial Reporting Council Second Annual Review, November 1992.

46 V. Beattie, *Business Reporting: The Inevitable Change?* ICAS, 1999, p. 53.

CHAPTER 6

Conceptual framework

6.1 Introduction

In the previous chapter we reviewed the standard-setting process and gave an overview of the statutory and mandatory rules that govern financial reporting. In this chapter we will discuss the rationale underlying such rules or standards and consider the developments that have occurred in the search for a conceptual framework for financial reporting in the UK. In this chapter we consider the following:

A – Development of conceptual framework up to 1992

- Definition of a conceptual framework
- Historical overview of the evolution of financial accounting theory
- *The Corporate Report* – 1975
- ICAS *Making Corporate Reports Valuable* – 1988
- The Solomons Report – 1989
- IASC *Framework for the Presentation and Preparation of Financial Statements* – 1989
- AICPA *Improving Business Reporting – A Customer Focus. Meeting the Information Needs of Investors and Creditors* – 1994

B – ASB: development of conceptual framework

- ASB *Statements of Principles for Financial Reporting* 1992–1999
- FRS 18 *Accounting Policies*

A – DEVELOPMENT OF A CONCEPTUAL FRAMEWORK UP TO 1992

6.2 Definition of a conceptual framework

Standard setters in the UK have been operating in a professional environment where there has been no unique, agreed conceptual framework upon which to base new standards.

6.2.1 What exactly do we mean by a conceptual framework?

Many attempts have been made in the USA and the UK to define a conceptual framework. For example, the Financial Accounting Standards Board (FASB) in the USA stated in its *Scope and Implications of the Conceptual Framework Project* 1967 that

A conceptual framework is a constitution, a coherent system of interrelated objectives and fundamentals **that can lead to consistent standards** and that prescribes the nature, function and limits of financial accounting and financial statements.[1]

In general terms, then, it is a basic structure for organising one's thinking about what one is trying to do and how to go about it. It can answer questions such as:

● For whom and by whom are the accounts to be prepared?

● For what purposes are they wanted?

● What kind of accounting reports are suitable for these purposes?

● How do present accounts fit the bill?

● How could accounting practices be improved to make them more suitable?

In the UK, MacVe stated that a conceptual framework would 'provide **a consistent approach** for making decisions about choices of accounting practice and for setting accounting standards'.[2]

In the financial press, E. Stamp wrote in 1982 that a conceptual framework would consist of the following elements:

(a) general agreement on the overall objectives of financial reporting;

(b) general agreement on the nature and needs of the various users of financial reports;

(c) identification of a set of (ideally, mutually exclusive and collectively exhaustive) **criteria to be used in choosing between alternative solutions to standard-setting problems** and in assessing the quality and utility of financial reports.[3]

Each of these three definitions is looking for the establishment of a parameter of accounting objectives within which reference points might be fixed to give guidance in the standard-setting process. They are seeking a **mechanism to create general consistency** and avoid conflicting rules and practices. This is essential given the background, where the absence of standards allowed the preparers of financial statements to manipulate the results.

However, it would be wrong to imagine that financial reporting practices have evolved in a vacuum without any sort of accounting theory underlying them. A brief historical overview of the evolution of accounting theory will allow us to put financial reporting into context.

6.3 Historical overview of the evolution of financial accounting theory

Financial reporting constantly has to deal with problems arising from changing economic, political and commercial practices, e.g. how to take account of changing prices, changing government regulations such as grants and subsidies, and changing commercial practices such as franchising and leasing.

Because financial reporting is not a single activity carried out by one person or institution, there is the risk of inconsistency in reporting similar activities. If the annual financial reports are to be decision-useful for investors, who are regarded in the UK as the principal stakeholders, then there is a need for consistency or uniformity in reporting.

The way in which the profession has attempted to achieve consistency has varied over time. In the 1950s and 1960s it followed an **empirical inductive** approach. This resulted in the production of standards or reporting practices that were based on rationalising what happened in practice. Under this approach we saw the issue of standards such as SSAP 2, SSAP 3 and SSAP 9.

In the 1970s it followed a **deductive** approach. This resulted in the production of standards or reporting practices based on principles that had been deducted from assumptions – there was no need to refer to what actually happened in the real world. This was in part due to the fact that the deductive approach challenged established practices, e.g. the use of the historical cost model.

However, in recognition of the fact that financial reporting does occur in the real world, there has been a growing concern that theories are acceptable only if they are capable of being tested empirically, e.g. by identifying their impact on share prices, and if they satisfy cost/benefit criteria.

6.3.1 Empirical inductive approach

The empirical inductive approach looked at the practices that existed and attempted to generalise from them.

This tended to be how the technical departments of accounting firms operated. By rationalising what they did, they ensured that the firm avoided accepting different financial reporting practices for similar transactions, e.g. accepting unrealised profit appearing in the income statement of one client and not in another. The technical department's role was to advise partners and staff, i.e. it was a **defensive role** to avoid any potential charge from a user of the accounts that they had been misled.

Initially a technical circular was regarded as a private good and distribution was restricted to the firm's own staff. However, it then became recognised that it could benefit the firm if its practices were accepted as the industry benchmark, so that in the event of litigation it could rely on this fact.

When the technical advice ceased to be a private good, there was a perceived additional benefit to the firm if the nature of the practice could be changed from being a positive statement, i.e. this is how we report profits on uncompleted contracts, to a **normative** statement, i.e. this is how we report *and* this is how all other financial reporters *ought* to report.

Consequently, there has been a growing trend since the 1980s for firms to publish rationalisations for their financial reporting practices. It has been commercially prudent for them to do so. It has also been extremely helpful to academic accountants and their students.

Typical illustrations of the result of such empirical induction are the wide acceptance of the historical cost model and various concepts such as matching and realisation that we discussed in Chapter 2. In terms of standards, we have already mentioned that SSAP 2 and SSAP 9 evolved under this regime.

This approach has played an important role in the evolution of financial reporting practices and will continue to do so. After all, it is the preparers of the financial statements and their auditors who are first exposed to change, whether economic, political or commercial. They are the ones who have to think their way through each new problem that surfaces. This means that a financial reporting practice already exists by the time the problem comes to the attention of theoreticians.

The major reasons that it has been felt necessary to try other approaches are both pragmatic and theoretical.

Pragmatic reason

The main pragmatic reason is that the past procedure, whereby deduction was dependent upon generalisation from existing practice, has become untenable. The accelerating rate of economic, political and commercial change leaves too little time for effective and uniform practices to evolve.

Theoretical reasons

The theoretical reasons relate to the acceptability of the income determined under the traditional historic cost model. There are three principal reasons:

● **True income**. We have seen that economists had a view that financial reports should report a true income, which differed from the accountants' view.

● **User-defined income – public**. There is a view that there may be a number of relevant incomes depending upon differing user needs which may be regarded as public goods.

● **User-defined income – private**. There is a view that there may be a number of relevant incomes depending upon differing user needs which may be regarded as private rather than public goods.

It was thought that the limitations implicit in the empirical inductive approach could be overcome by the deductive approach.

6.3.2 Deductive approach

The deductive approach is not dependent on existing practice, which is often perceived as having been tainted because it has been determined by finance directors and auditors. However, the problem remains: from whose viewpoint is the deduction to be made?

Possible alternatives to the preparers and auditors of the accounts are economists and users. However, economists are widely perceived as promoting unrealistic models and users as having needs so diverse that they cannot be realistically satisfied in a single set of accounts. Consider the attempts made to define income. Economists have supported the concept of a true income, while users have indicated the need for a range of relevant incomes.

True income

We have already seen in Chapter 3 that there is a significant difference between the accountant's income and the economist's income applying the ideas of Fisher and Hicks.

User needs and multiple incomes

Multiple measures of income, derived from the general price level adjusted accounting model, the replacement cost accounting model and the exit price accounting model, were considered in Chapter 4. Each model provides information that is relevant for different purposes, e.g. replacement cost accounting produces an income figure that indicates how much is available for distribution while still maintaining the operating capacity of the entity.

These income figures were regarded as a public good, i.e. cost-free to the user, and were recommended in SSAP 7 and required for a trial period in SSAP 16. Latterly, it has been recognised that there is a cost implication to the production of information, i.e. that it is not a public good; that standards should be capable of being empirically tested; and that consideration should be given to the economic consequences of standards. This has resulted in a concern that standards should deal with substance rather than form, e.g. the treatment of leases introduced this concept quite specifically as part of SSAP 21.

It could be argued that the deductive approach to income, whether an economist's true income or a theoretician's multiple income, has a basic weakness in its dependence upon the viewpoint of only one user group – the investors. This weakness was recognised in the UK and the information needs of the other groups were spelt out in pronouncements such as *The Corporate Report*.[4]

The Corporate Report is discussed in greater detail below, but for all practical purposes, the rights of user groups other than investors have been 'spirited away'. In the UK it has become accepted dogma that investor needs are a surrogate for the needs of all other users. For example, Solomons, in *Guidelines for Financial Reporting Standards*, p. 32, states: 'As we have already noted that the needs of investors, creditors, employees and customers are not fundamentally different, it seems safe to look to the needs of present and potential investors as a guide ...'[5] This assumption has also been accepted by the ASB, but there is little independent evidence to support it.

Where do we stand now?

We have seen that accounting theory was initially founded on generalisations from the accounting practices followed by practitioners. Then came the deductive approach of economists and theoreticians. The latter were not perceived to be realistic and empirical testing, e.g. by examining their economic consequence on share prices, is relied on to give them credibility.

The practitioners have now staked their claim to create accounting theory or a conceptual framework through the ASB. The advantage of this is that the conceptual framework will be based on consensus. This is illustrated by Chapter 5 of the *Statement of Principles* relating to measurement, which has not attempted to make price level adjustment mandatory. Some would call this approach timid, but it is a healthy way forward. It recognises that on many issues genuine disagreements exist on what best portrays reality. What we need to encourage is experimentation.

This is the view put forward in *The Future Shape of Financial Reports*, 1989, by Arnold *et al.*:

> Change in financial reporting is bound to be evolutionary rather than revolutionary. Most of the important improvements in financial reporting in the last fifty years have had their origins in experimentation by practitioners (sometimes with ideas first developed in academic circles) rather than prescription by legislation or accounting standards; indeed legislation and accounting standards usually lag developments in practice by some years. This process has applied not only to relatively minor enhancements but also to much more fundamental changes such as the inclusion of consolidated accounts ... Most experiments would have to be outside the statutory reporting framework by way of supplementary statements ... Financial reporting practice is continually evolving and over the years many companies have been willing to experiment. We hope that this report will stimulate companies to look afresh at their reporting and initiate further experimentation based on some of our proposals.[6]

An experimentation approach is valid if companies can be relied on to produce reports that give a true and fair view. However, experience shows that this is not always the case; hence the standard setters have been compelled to issue FRSs, not to legitimise evolving practice, but to combat malpractice. Companies cannot be relied on not to cheat. Consequently the ASB has progressed from consensus to regulatory standard setting. For example, FRS 5 was issued to enforce reporting according to the substance of a transaction rather than some legalistic fiction; FRS 6 was issued to prevent companies applying merger accounting to business combinations that were clearly acquisitions in substance; FRS 7 was issued to prevent companies manipulating provisions when taking over another company with the primary object of creating higher profits in subsequent accounting periods by charging expenses of the later period against the carried forward provision.

6.4 The Corporate Report

Reports have been commissioned at various times on financial reporting. *The Corporate Report*,[4] published by the ASC in 1975, has had a continuing influence.

6.4.1 Terms of reference of *The Corporate Report*

The terms of reference under which the report was formulated claimed that the purpose of the study was to 're-examine the scope and aims of published financial reports in the light of modern needs and conditions'. It was concerned with public accountability of economic entities of all kinds, but especially business enterprises. It attempted to establish a set of working concepts as a basis for financial reporting; and to identify the persons for whom published accounts should be prepared, and the information appropriate to their interests. It considered the most suitable means of measuring and reporting the economic position, performance and prospects of undertakings for the purpose and persons identified.

6.4.2 Philosophy of *The Corporate Report*

The basic philosophy was that reports should seek to satisfy the information needs of users. It was therefore necessary to identify user needs and, from these, to arrive at the fundamental objectives of corporate reports.

In the view of the ASC there was an implied responsibility for every economic entity whose size made it significant to report publicly. By 'economic entity', it meant every type of organisation in modern economic society, i.e. central government departments, local authorities, co-operatives, limited companies, unincorporated firms and non-profit-making entities such as trade unions and charities. By 'significant', it meant an economic entity where 'the organisation commands human or material resources on such a scale that the results of its activities have significant economic implications for a community as a whole'. Economic significance was assumed if the entity was a listed company, employed more than 500 staff, and had capital employed of more than £2 million or a turnover in excess of £5 million.

6.4.3 Fundamental objective of corporate reports

The fundamental objective of corporate reports was to communicate economic measurements of, and information about, resources and performance that would be useful to those users having a right to such information. To fulfil this objective, corporate reports had to possess the following qualitative characteristics: relevance, reliability, comparability, understandability, completeness, objectivity and timeliness.

6.4.4 Who were the users recognised by *The Corporate Report*?

The Corporate Report identified seven user groups as being entitled to receive accounting information and whose information needs should be satisfied by a financial report:

● Existing and potential equity investors.

- Existing and potential loan creditors.

- Existing, potential and past employees.

- Analysts/advisers, including financial analysts, financial journalists, economists, statisticians, researchers, trade unions, stockbrokers and others such as credit rating agencies.

- The business contact group, i.e. customers, trade creditors, suppliers, competitors, business rivals and parties interested in mergers and takeovers.

- The government, i.e. the tax authorities, regulatory departments and local authorities.

- The public, i.e. taxpayers, ratepayers, consumers and community groups and special interest groups, e.g. consumer and environmental groups.

6.4.5 What are the information needs of these users?

Shareholders might wish to evaluate the entity performance in order to predict future cash flows; loan creditors to assess its stability; trade creditors its liquidity; rivals its vulnerability; employees their relative importance in the production process; the government the amount of taxes that arises.

The report considered it impractical to seek to satisfy such diverse needs by a general-purpose financial report and suggested that there should be statements in addition to the profit and loss account, balance sheet and cash flow statement. The additional statements reflected the underlying intention of the report, which was to produce statements that would be useful for improving the social as well as the economic welfare of society. It saw a company as a combination of stakeholders rather than as simply a legal vehicle for shareholders.

6.4.6 Additional statements suggested by *The Corporate Report*

The additional statements were as follows:

1 **A statement of value added** showing the amounts paid to shareholders, lenders, employees and the state, and retained for reinvestment. This statement was subsequently produced by a number of companies, but no standard has been issued and its use is decreasing.

2 **An employment report** to disclose:
   (a) a staff profile, e.g. numbers employed, reasons for change, age and sex distribution;
   (b) staff conditions, e.g. frequency of accidents, hours worked, geographical location of sites, employment costs, amounts spent on training, adequacy of the pension funds to meet future obligations, the benefits earned by employees and their contribution;
   (c) likelihood of change, e.g. material closures or acquisition of plant.

3 **A statement of money exchange with government** to disclose the flow of money between the state and the company. At various times, substantial inducements have been provided by the government in the form of tax relief, grants and subsidies. At the same time, companies have become increasingly involved in the collection of tax for the government. The statement was intended to provide a comprehensive picture of the flows of money, e.g. PAYE, VAT, business rates, corporation tax and grants.

4 **A statement of transactions in foreign currency** to disclose direct cash flows between the UK and overseas countries. Investors take into account the geographical spread of assets, liabilities and turnover when assessing the business and exchange risk. Segmental information on turnover has been required by the Stock Exchange, and

SSAP 25 *Segmental Reporting* has extended the disclosure requirements. This statement has consequently not been seen as a major improvement and is not widely used.

5 **A statement of future prospects** to show the **levels** of future profits, future employment and future investment. There are statutory requirements to disclose certain information, e.g. capital investment that has been contracted but not completed at the date of the balance sheet. Apart from such statutory requirements, there is major resistance from directors to quantifying future profits, employment or investment. This is discussed a little more fully when considering accountability.

6 **A statement of corporate objectives** to address medium–term strategic targets and show management policy. This statement gradually assumed more importance in the 1990s as companies publicised their social and environmental policies. The statement is perceived by management as a vehicle for projecting the corporate image rather than for making them accountable to users. Future developments are therefore likely to remain in the social rather than the economic area.

6.4.7 Measurement base suggested by *The Corporate Report*

The report assessed various measurement bases (e.g. historical cost, current purchasing power, replacement cost, net realisable value, value to the firm) and supported the use of current values with a general price index adjustment. As we have seen in preceding chapters, this is still undecided.

6.4.8 Short-term effect of *The Corporate Report*

The report was a comprehensive treatise that reviewed users, purposes and measurement bases for financial reporting. Unfortunately, its immediate impact was not great because many felt that it went too far in identifying user groups beyond the shareholders and creditors; too far in the demand for additional statements; and too far in wishing to discard historic cost as the measurement base.

6.4.9 Long-term effect of *The Corporate Report*

Since its issue in 1975, the report has been seen as a seminal document. Its philosophy has influenced the development of the *Statements of Principles* that the ASB has produced as the conceptual framework in the UK.

6.5 ICAS *Making Corporate Reports Valuable*

In 1988, following a major research project by its Research Committee, the Institute of Chartered Accountants of Scotland (ICAS) published *Making Corporate Reports Valuable* (MCRV).[7] The general objective was to stimulate discussion that would lead to improvements in corporate reporting. The long-term purpose was that reports should be produced that would be better able to assist the user in gauging management performance and assessing an entity's prospects; reports that were more understandable, less daunting in presentation, more readable and with as little technical jargon as possible.

In pursuit of this goal the MCRV formulated the Research Committee's views on meeting the needs of management and investors. It considered company strategy and planning, the need for clear financial statements covering such areas as entity objectives, present financial wealth, changes in financial wealth, operations, distributable wealth, cash flow and segmental information.

The report criticised historic cost accounting and supported the use of a current value system. It also advocated the publication of projected results so that the user would have available the preceding year's figures, the current year's and the subsequent year's.

To its credit, the Research Committee demonstrated that its proposals could be applied in practice by preparing the financial statements of Melody plc and obtaining feedback from the preparers of the accounts. These were published in 1990 and are perhaps a prototype of what financial statements might look like in the future.

The balance sheet was described as a statement of assets and liabilities and was a value statement. Assets, including stock, were revalued in current terms, thus breaking away from the historical cost philosophy. The net assets at the end of the period were the financial wealth generated by operations plus any increase in the realisable value of financial wealth.

The profit and loss account was described as an operations statement and, by including stock at market value, produced a residual figure called financial wealth generated by operations.

The annual report also contained a statement of cash flow, a value added statement, a chairman's review, a directors' report and a document referred to as 'Management's discussions and analysis of financial conditions and results of operations' for the year under review, supplemented by the financial plans for the following year.

The auditors' report appears as the 'Report of the independent assessors'. It is addressed to the members, creditors and employees of Melody plc and is more informative than the traditional short-form report favoured in the UK.

Another statement that makes its debut spells out 'responsibility for the financial statements'. It informs the user that the ultimate responsibility lies with the directors, and in doing so it also explains the role of the independent assessors and the nature of their report.

The MCRV is a useful addition to our experience of financial reporting and its influence will no doubt be felt as the standard setters move towards dealing with the problem of an appropriate measurement base.

It might be useful at this point to list some of the key thoughts in the MCRV report.

Representation of position

● Accounts should aim to portray economic reality.

● Substance over form is emphasised.

● The investors need the same information as the management.

Income

● It is against excessive emphasis on the bottom line with a single earnings figure.

● It emphasises the balance sheet rather than accruals-based income. Income is seen as a reconciliation between consecutive balance sheets expressed in current values.

Capital maintenance

● It takes a proprietary view in seeking to maintain the owners' purchasing power using a consumer price index.

Measurement base

● It supports the use of net realisable values.

6.6 The Solomons Report

Professor David Solomons produced *Guidelines for Financial Reporting Standards* (1989).[5] In the report he commented on the existing standard-setting process and made proposals for an explicit conceptual framework.

6.6.1 Existing standard-setting process

1 Solomons commented on the haphazard manner in which standards had developed and the fact that consistency of standards was a matter of chance. Standards created to deal with contemporary phenomena have been compiled in isolation and often conflict one with another, e.g. SSAP 2's philosophy of prudence may be said to be violated by SSAP 9's requirement to accrue for attributable profit and by SSAP 13's capitalisation of development expenditure, which also over emphasises the accrual concept.

2 He noted that, even so, there was a considerable degree of consistency, which indicated that the standard setters must have been applying an implicit framework. The Solomons Report aimed to provide the ASC with an explicit framework, or at least part of one, that would reinforce the implicit framework where it was sound and replace it where it was defective.

3 He noted that the conceptual framework in the UK differed in three respects from those operating in the USA, namely:
   (a) it saw the primary role of financial reports and statements as the assessment of enterprise and managerial performance, and regarded the balance sheet as the primary financial statement; revenues and expenditures were seen as changes in balance sheet items;
   (b) it attached great importance to representational faithfulness;
   (c) it emphasised the need to recognise adequately the pervasiveness of uncertainty in financial statements.

4 He disagreed with the provisions of some of the existing standards, e.g. SSAP 15 *Deferred Tax*, SSAP 21 *Accounting for Leases* and SSAP 24 *Accounting for Pension Costs*.

5 He took a conservative view that 'every report on a company's earnings for the past year throws light on past performance and, by doing so, helps investors to update or revise their expectations about future earnings' (*Guidelines*, p. 33).

6 He was against excessive emphasis on the bottom line with a single earnings figure (p. 19).

7 He placed emphasis on the balance sheet rather than on accruals-based income. Income was seen as a reconciliation between consecutive balance sheets expressed in current values (p. 17).

6.6.2 Proposals for an explicit conceptual framework

While Solomons supported the idea of general purpose financial statements, he addressed some of the areas that appeared in *The Corporate Report*, for example:

- **User needs** together with the functions that reports serve
- The **qualitative characteristics** of reports
- The **measurement base**

Solomons argued strongly for a move from historical cost accounting to one based on value to the business and for the maintenance of real financial capital as opposed to nominal financial capital or operating capability.

6.6.3 Reaction to the Solomons Report

The report gave rise to a number of critical responses,[8,9,10] but also received support in *The Future Shape of Financial Reports*, one objective of which was to 'demonstrate, by reference to Solomons ... that it is possible to design a revised system which allows companies to report in a way which much more closely reflects economic reality and which is related more closely to the needs of the user'.[11]

6.7 IASC *Framework for the Presentation and Preparation of Financial Statements*[12]

This Exposure Draft deals with the following:

- The objective of financial statements.
- The qualitative characteristics that determine the usefulness of information in financial statements.
- The definition, recognition and measurement of elements from which financial statements are constructed.
- The concepts of capital, capital maintenance and profit.

The **objective** of financial statements is that they should provide information about the financial position, performance and changes in financial position of an enterprise that is useful to a wide range of potential users in making economic decisions.

The **qualitative characteristics** that determine the usefulness of information are **relevance** and **reliability**. Comparability is a qualitative characteristic that interacts with both relevance and reliability. Materiality provides a threshold or cut-off point rather than being a primary qualitative characteristic. The balance between cost and benefit is a persuasive constraint rather than a qualitative characteristic.

The **definition** of an element is given in paragraph 46:

Financial statements portray the financial effects of transactions and other events by grouping the effects into broad classes according to their economic characteristics. These broad classes are termed the **elements** of financial statements. The elements directly related to the measurement of financial position in the balance sheet are assets, liabilities and equity. The elements directly related to the measurement of performance in the profit and loss account are income and expense.

The Exposure Draft defines each of the elements. For example, an asset is defined in paragraph 53: 'The future economic benefit embodied in an asset is the potential to contribute, directly or indirectly, to the flow of cash and cash equivalents to the enterprise.'

It defines when an element is to be **recognised**. For example, in paragraph 87 it states that: 'An asset is recognised in the balance sheet when it is probable that the future economic benefits will flow to the enterprise and the asset has an attribute that can be measured reliably.'

Regarding **measurement**, it comments in paragraph 99 that:

> The measurement attribute most commonly adopted by enterprises in preparing their financial statements is historical cost. This is usually combined with other measurement attributes, such as realisable value. For example, inventories are usually carried at the lower of cost and net realisable value, and marketable securities may be carried at market value, that is, their realisable value. Furthermore, many enterprises combine historical costs and current costs as a response to the inability of the historical cost model to deal with the effects of changing prices of non-monetary assets.

The document deals in a similar style with the other elements.

Finally, regarding the concepts of **capital**, **capital maintenance** and **profit**, the IASC comments that:

> At the present time, it is not the intention of the Board of the IASC to prescribe a particular measurement model (i.e. historical cost, current cost, realisable value, present value) ... This intention will, however, be reviewed in the light of world developments.

Clearly, there will be no international standard until a national standard is developed within bodies such as the ASB and until consensus is obtained.

The exposure draft is an influential document and we can trace its impact on the *Statement of Principles* issued by the ASB.

6.8 AICPA *Improving Business Reporting – A Customer Focus. Meeting the Information Needs of Investors and Creditors*

This was a study carried out by AICPA over a three-year period and published in 1994.[13] It resulted in a number of interesting recommendations to improve business reporting. A major recommendation was that standard setters should develop a comprehensive model of business reporting, focusing on factors that create longer-term value and including financial and non-financial measures to cope with rapid changes, e.g. in technology and competition.

The committee identified that users had a high interest in being able to identify:

- **trends**, e.g. from five-year summaries of key statistics, separate reporting of segments and core and non-core assets and liabilities information;
- **substance of transactions**, e.g. accounting for off-balance-sheet transactions, complex capital instruments and investments in unconsolidated entities;
- **significant risks** arising from uncertainties over the valuation of assets and liabilities.

The committee identified that the users had a lower interest in:

- variety of income theories;
- valuation of intangible assets;
- accounting for combinations.

The committee identified user interest in a number of non-financial areas:

- the corporate strategy in general terms;

- the strengths, weaknesses, opportunities and threats (SWOTs) to the company;
- performance measures that management use with an explanation of reasons for changes and trends;
- management plans and degree to which achieved;
- information about the directors, management and their remuneration package.

A review of the recommendations broadly supports the stance being taken by the ASB, with mandatory standards being introduced for the financial statements, e.g. FRS 5 *Reporting the Substance of Transactions* and voluntary disclosures for non-financial areas, e.g. *Operating and Financial Review*.

B – ASB: DEVELOPMENT OF CONCEPTUAL FRAMEWORK

6.9 ASB *Statement of Principles for Financial Reporting* 1992–1999

6.9.1 Exposure Draft – 1995

The ASB issued a draft document of a *Statement of Principles* in 1992 followed by an Exposure Draft in 1995. In its introduction to the Exposure Draft[14] the ASB stated that the purpose and status of the *Statement of Principles* was:

- to assist the Board in the development of future accounting standards and in its review of existing accounting standards;
- to assist the Board by providing a basis for reducing the number of alternative accounting treatments permitted by law and accounting standards;
- to assist preparers of financial statements in applying accounting standards and in dealing with topics that do not form the subject of an accounting standard;
- to assist auditors in forming an opinion as to whether financial statements conform with accounting standards;
- to assist users of financial statements in interpreting the information contained in financial statements prepared in conformity with accounting standards;
- to provide those who are interested in the work of the Board with information about its approach to the formulation of accounting standards.

6.9.2 ASB Progress Paper *Statement of Principles for Financial Reporting – the way ahead*[15]

The Exposure Draft was not well received and in July 1996 the ASB issued a Progress paper to clarify misunderstandings concerning the *Statement of Principles* Exposure Draft. In the Progress Paper it emphasised that:

- the *Statement* was not intended to be a mandatory accounting standard but to provide a theoretical base on which mandatory standards could be developed;
- concepts such as true and fair, accruals and going concern would remain a fundamental part of the financial reporting system; and
- a system of current cost accounting was not on the ASB agenda.

The Progress Paper explained that, in the ASB's view, many traditional accounting principles were devised for manufacturing companies and were not effective in coping with more complex financial reporting issues such as intangible assets, joint ventures and financial instruments; further, there was the risk that the ASB would not be able to participate credibly internationally unless it moved closer to the conceptual frameworks of other leading standard setters, e.g. the International Accounting Standards Committee and the US Financial Accounting Standards Board.

The ASB consequently set itself the following major objectives:

- To exclude from the balance sheet items that were neither assets nor liabilities. For example, matching would continue to be applied in the profit and loss account, but balances carried forward in the balance sheet as assets and liabilities would be subjected to a test of their authenticity, and losses could not be carried forward as assets because they do not provide future economic benefits.

- To make 'off-balance-sheet' assets and liabilities more visible by requiring their inclusion in the balance sheet wherever possible. For example, financial instruments that do not entail initial cash investments, e.g. interest rate swaps, are commonly not recorded when they are acquired. The ASB's proposals would lead to more of such transactions being recorded and brought onto the balance sheet.

- To ensure that all gains and losses are reported prominently to avoid any being overlooked: for example, as required within the statement of total recognised gains and losses. The suggestion is that gains and losses on those assets and liabilities that are held on a continuing basis, primarily in order to enable the entity's operations to be carried out, should be reported in the statement of recognised gains and losses and not in the profit and loss account, and that all other gains and losses should be reported in the profit and loss account.

- To focus performance reporting on the components of income, not just the bottom line: for example, as required within the statement of total recognised gains and losses and the layered approach of FRS 3.

- To employ current values if historical costs are inappropriate: e.g. by addressing measurement and providing a rationale for how various measures might be viewed.

It is the ASB's view that a statement of principles is designed to:

- provide a coherent frame of reference and definitions that ensure consistency of standards;
- minimise the need to reinvent fundamental concepts for every project; and
- assist preparers, auditors and others to assess alternatives when reporting treatment is not clear from statutes or standards.

The ASB also states that the main role of the *Statement of Principles* is in the standard-setting process but that it is not a mandatory standard and that there are other factors taken into account when setting standards. These other factors include:

- legal requirements
- cost/benefit considerations
- industry-specific issues
- the desirability of evolutionary change
- implementation issues.

The Statement is therefore intended to play an important role, but it is neither mandatory nor intended to frustrate evolutionary changes, e.g. the appropriate financial reporting of derivatives and other financial instruments.

As Sir David Tweedie, Chairman of the ASB commented, 'The Board has developed its *Statement of Principles* in parallel with its development of accounting standards ... It is in effect the Board's compass for when we navigate uncharted waters in the years ahead. This is essential reading for those who want to know where the Board is coming from, and where it is aiming to go.'

6.9.3 *Statement of Principles* 1999[16]

The Statement contains eight chapters dealing with key issues. Each of the chapters is commented on below.

6.9.4 Chapter 1: 'The objective of financial statements'

The *Statement of Principles* follows the IASC *Framework* in the identification of user groups. Both the ASB and IASC have followed *The Corporate Report* except for the omission of any reference to the analysts/advisers, presumably on the basis that the analysts/advisers will be acting as agents for one of the other user groups.

The statement identifies the investor group as the primary group for whom the financial statements are being prepared. It then states the information needs of each group as follows:

- **Investors**. These need information to:
  - assess the stewardship of management e.g. in safeguarding the entity's resources and using them properly, efficiently and profitably;
  - take decisions about management e.g. assessing need for new management;
  - take decisions about their investment or potential investment e.g. deciding whether to hold, buy or sell shares and assessing the ability to pay dividends.
- **Lenders**. These need information to:
  - determine whether their loans and interest will be paid on time;
  - decide whether to lend and on what terms.
- **Suppliers**. These need information to:
  - decide whether to sell to the entity;
  - determine whether they will be paid on time;
  - determine longer-term stability if the company is a major customer.
- **Employees**. These need information to:
  - assess the stability and profitability of the company;
  - assess the ability to provide remuneration, retirement benefits and employment opportunities.
- **Customers**. These need information to:
  - assess the probability of the continued existence of the company taking account of their own degree of dependence on the company e.g. for future provision of specialised replacement parts and servicing product warranties.
- **Government and other agencies**. These need information to:
  - be aware of the commercial activities of the company;

- regulate these activities;
- raise revenue;
- produce national statistics.

- **Public**. Members of the public need information to:
  - determine the effect on the local economy of the company's activities e.g. employment opportunities, use of local suppliers;
  - assess recent developments in the company's prosperity and changes in its activities.

The information needs of which group are to be dominant?

Seven groups are identified, but there is only one set of financial statements. Although they are described as general-purpose statements, a decision has to be made about which group's needs take precedence.

The *Statement of Principles* identifies the **investor group** as the defining class of user, i.e. the primary group for whom the financial statements are being prepared.

It takes the view that financial statements 'are able to focus on the common interest of users'. The common interest is described as: 'all potential users are interested, to a varying degree, in the financial performance and financial position of the entity as a whole'.

This means that it is a prerequisite that the information must be relevant to the investor group. This suggests that any need of the other groups that is not also a need of the investors will not be met by the financial statements.

The 1995 Exposure Draft stated that: 'Awarding primacy to investors does not imply that other users are to be ignored. The information prepared for investors is useful as a frame of reference for other users, against which they can evaluate more specific information that they may obtain in their dealings with the enterprise.'

It is important, therefore, for all of the other users to be aware that this is one of the principles. If they require specific disclosures that might be relevant to them, they will need to take their own steps to obtain them, particularly where there is a conflict of interest. For example, if a closure is being planned by the directors, it may be in the investors' interest for the news to be delayed as long as possible to minimise the cost to the company; employees, suppliers, customers and the public must not expect any assistance from the financial statements – their information needs are not the primary concern.

What information should be provided to satisfy the information needs?

The Statement proposes that information is required in four areas: financial performance, financial position, generation and use of cash, and financial adaptability.

Financial performance
Financial performance is defined as the return an entity obtains from the resources it controls. This return is available from the profit and loss account and provides a means to assess past management performance, how effectively resources have been utilised and the capacity to generate cash flows.

Financial position
Financial position is available from an examination of the balance sheet and includes:

- the economic resources controlled by an entity, i.e. assets and liabilities
- financial structure i.e. capital gearing indicating how profits will be divided between

the different sources of finance and the capacity for raising additional finance in the future

- liquidity and solvency i.e. current and liquid ratios
- capacity to adapt to changes – see below under **Financial adaptability**.

Generation and use of cash

Information is available from the cash flow statement which shows cash flows from operating, investment and financing activities providing a perspective that is largely free from allocation and valuation issues. This information is useful in assessing and reviewing previous assessments of cash flows.

Financial adaptability

This is an entity's ability to alter the amount and timing of its cash flows. It is desirable in order to be able to cope with difficult periods, e.g. when losses are incurred and to take advantage of unexpected investment opportunities. It is dependent on factors such as the ability, at short notice, to:

- raise new capital
- repay capital or debt
- obtain cash from disposal of assets without disrupting continuing business, i.e. realise readily marketable securities that might have been built up as a liquid reserve
- achieve a rapid improvement in net cash flows from operations.

6.9.5 Chapter 2: 'The reporting entity'

This chapter focuses on identifying when an entity should report and which activities to include in the report.

When an entity should report

The principle is that an entity should prepare and publish financial statements if:

- there is a legitimate demand for the information i.e. it is both decision-useful and benefits exceed the cost of producing the information; and
- it is a cohesive economic unit i.e. a unit under a central control that can be held accountable for its activities.

Which activities to include

The principle is that those activities should be included that are within the direct control of the entity, e.g. assets and liabilities which are reported in its own balance sheet, or indirect control, e.g. assets and liabilities of a subsidiary of the entity which are reported in the consolidated balance sheet.

Control is defined as (a) the ability to deploy the resources and (b) the ability to benefit (or to suffer) from their deployment. Indirect control by an investor can be difficult to determine. The test is not to apply a theoretical level of influence, e.g. holding $x\%$ of shares, but to review the relationship that exists between the investor and investee in practice, such as the investor having the power to veto the investee's financial and operating policies and benefit from its net assets.

6.9.6 Chapter 3: 'The qualitative characteristics of financial information'

The *Statement of Principles* is based on the IASC *Framework* and contains the same four principal qualitative characteristics relating to the content of information and how the information is presented. The two primary characteristics relating to content are the need to be relevant and reliable; the two relating to presentation are the need to be understandable and comparable. The characteristics appear diagrammatically as follows:

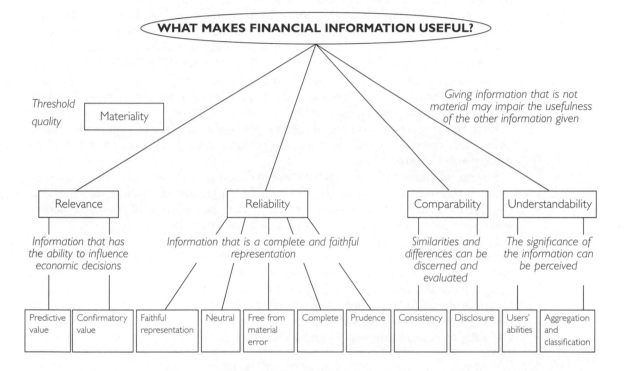

From the diagram we can see that for information content to be **relevant** it must have:

● the ability to influence the economic decisions of users;

● predictive value, i.e. help users to evaluate or assess past, present or future events; or

● confirmatory value, i.e. help users to confirm their past evaluations.

For information to be **reliable** it must be:

● free from material error, i.e. transactions have been accurately recorded and reported;

● a faithful representation, i.e. reflecting the commercial substance of transactions;

● neutral, i.e. not presented in a way to achieve a predetermined result;

● prudent, i.e. not creating hidden reserves or excessive provisions, deliberately understating assets or gains, or deliberately overstating liabilities or losses;

● complete i.e. the information is complete subject to a materiality test.

To be useful, the financial information also needs to be **comparable** over time and between companies and be **understandable**.

It satisfies the criteria for understandability if it is capable of being understood by a user with a reasonable knowledge of business activities and accounting, and a willingness to study the information with reasonable diligence. However, the trade-off between relevance and reliability comes into play with the requirement that complex information that is relevant to economic decision-making should not be omitted because some users find it too difficult to understand. There is no absolute answer where there is the possibility of a trade-off and it is recognised by the ASB that the relative importance of the characteristics in different cases is a matter of judgement.

The chapter also introduces the idea of **materiality** as a threshold quality and any item that is not material does not require to be considered further. The statement recognises that no information can be useful if it is not also material by introducing the idea of a threshold quality which it describes as follows: An item of information is material to the financial statements if its misstatement or omission might reasonably be expected to influence the economic decisions of users of those financial statements, including their assessment of management's stewardship.[17]

First, this means that it is justified not to report immaterial items which would impose unnecessary costs on preparers and impede decision-makers by obscuring material information with excessive detail.

Second, it means that the important consideration is not user expectation (e.g. they might expect turnover to be accurate to within 1%) but the effect on decision-making (e.g. there might only be an effect if turnover were to be more that 10% over- or understated, in which case only errors exceeding 10% are material).

It also states that 'Materiality depends on the size of the item or error judged in the particular circumstances of its omission or misstatement'. The need to exercise judgement means that the preparer needs to have a benchmark.

A Discussion Paper issued in January 1995 by the Financial Reporting & Auditing Group of the ICAEW entitled *Materiality in Financial Reporting FRAG 1/95* identified that there are few instances where an actual figure is given by statute or standard setters, e.g. FRS 6 para. 76 refers to a material minority and indicates that this is defined as 10%.

The Paper also referred to a rule of thumb used in the USA:

> The staff of the US Securities and Exchange Commission have an informal rule of thumb that errors of more than 10% are material, those between 5% and 10% may be material and those under 5% are usually not material. These percentages are applied to gross profit, net income, equity and any specific line in the financial statements that is potentially misstated.

The ASB has moved away from setting percentage benchmarks and there is now a need for more explicit guidance on the application of the materiality threshold.

6.9.7 Chapter 4: 'The elements of financial statements'

This chapter gives guidance on the items that *could* appear in financial statements. These are described as **elements** and have the following essential features:

- **Assets**. These are rights to future economic benefits controlled by an entity as a result of past transactions or events.
- **Liabilities**. These are obligations of an entity to transfer future economic benefits as a result of past transactions or events, i.e. ownership is not essential.
- **Ownership interest**. This is the residual amount found by deducting all liabilities from assets which belong to the owners of the entity.

- **Gains**. These are increases in ownership interest not resulting from contributions by the owners.
- **Losses**. These are decreases in ownership interest not resulting from distributions to the owners.
- **Contributions by the owners**. These are increases in ownership interest resulting from transfers from owners in their capacity as owners.
- **Distributions to owners**. These are decreases in ownership interest resulting from transfers to owners in their capacity as owners.

These definitions have been used as the basis for developing standards, e.g. FRS 5 states that the substance of a transaction means identifying whether the transaction has given rise to new assets or liabilities, defined as above.

6.9.8 Chapter 5: 'Recognition in financial statements'

The objective of financial statements is to disclose in the balance sheet and the profit and loss account the effect on the assets and liabilities of **transactions,** e.g. purchase of stock on credit and the effect of **events,** e.g. accidental destruction of a vehicle by fire. This implies that transactions are recorded under the double entry principle with an appropriate debit and credit made to the element that has been affected, e.g. the asset element (stock) and the liability element (creditors) are debited and credited to recognise stock bought on credit. Events are also recorded under the double entry principle, e.g. the asset element (vehicle) is derecognised and credited because it is no longer able to provide future economic benefits and the loss element resulting from fire damage is debited to the profit and loss account. The emphasis is on determining the effect on the assets and liabilities e.g. the increase in the asset element (stock), the increase in the liability element (creditors) and the reduction in the asset element (vehicle).

This emphasis has a particular significance for application of the matching concept in preparing the profit and loss account. The traditional approach to allocating expenditure across accounting periods has been to identify the costs that should be matched against the revenue in the profit and loss account and carry the balance into the balance sheet, i.e. the allocation is driven by the need to match costs to revenue. The *Statement of Principles* approach is different in that it identifies the amount of the expenditure to be recognised as an asset and the balance is transferred to the profit and loss account, i.e. the question is 'Should this expenditure be recognised as an asset (capitalised) and, if so, should any part of it be derecognised (written off as a loss element)?'

This means that the allocation process now requires an assessment as to whether an asset exists at the balance sheet date by applying the following test:

1 If the future economic benefits are eliminated at a single point in time, it is at that point that the loss is recognised and the expenditure derecognised, i.e. the debit balance is transferred to the profit and loss account.
2 If the future economic benefits are eliminated over several accounting periods – typically because they are being consumed over a period of time – the cost of the asset that comprises the future economic benefits will be recognised as a loss in the performance statement over those accounting periods, i.e. written off as a loss element as their future economic benefit reduces.

The result of this approach should not lead to changes in the accounts as currently prepared but it does emphasise that matching cost and revenue is not the main driver of recognition, i.e. the question is not 'How much expenditure should we match with the revenue reported in the profit and loss account?' but rather 'Are there future economic benefits arising from the expenditure to justify inclusion in the balance sheet?' and, if not, derecognise it, i.e. write it off.

Dealing with uncertainty

There is almost always some uncertainty as to when to recognise an event or transaction, e.g. when is an asset element off raw material stock to be disclosed as the asset element work-in-progress? Is it when a stock requisition is issued, when the storekeeper isolates it in the stock-to-be-issued bay, when it is issued onto the workshop floor, or when it begins to be worked on?

The *Statement of Principles* states that the principle to be applied if a transaction has created or added to an existing asset or liability is to recognise it if:

1 sufficient evidence exists that the new asset or liability has been created or that there has been an addition to an existing asset or liability; and

2 the new asset or liability or the addition to the existing asset or liability can be measured at a monetary amount with sufficient reliability.

The use of the word sufficient reflects the uncertainty that surrounds the decision when to recognise and the Statement states: 'In the business environment, uncertainty usually exists in a continuum, so the recognition process involves selecting the point on the continuum at which uncertainty becomes acceptable'.[18]

Before that point it may be appropriate to disclose by way of note to the accounts, e.g. a contingent liability that is possible (less than 50% chance of crystallising into a liability) but not probable (more than 50% chance of crystallising).

Sufficient reliability

Prudence requires more persuasive evidence of the measurement for the recognition of items that result in an increase in ownership interest than for the recognition of items that do not. However, the exercise of prudence does not allow for the omission of assets or gains where there is sufficient evidence of occurrence and reliability of measurement, or for the inclusion of liabilities or losses where there is not. This would amount to the deliberate understatement of assets or gains, or the deliberate overstatement of liabilities or losses.

Reporting gains and losses

Chapter 5 does not address the disclosure treatment of gains and losses. This is covered within specific FRSs e.g. FRS 3 *Reporting Financial Performance*. A change in assets or liabilities might arise from three classes of past event: transactions, contracts for future performance, and other events such as a change in market price.

If the change in an asset is offset by a change in liability, there will be no gain or loss. If the change in asset is not offset by a change in liability, there will be a gain or loss. If there is a gain or loss a decision is required as to whether it should be recognised in the profit and loss account or in the statement of total recognised gains and losses.

Recognition in profit and loss account

For a gain to be recognised in the profit and loss account, it must have been earned and realised. **Earned** means that no material transaction, contract or other event must occur before the change in the assets or liabilities will have occurred; **realised** means that the conversion into cash or cash equivalents must either have occurred or be reasonably assured.

Profit, as stated in the profit and loss account, is used as a prime measure of performance. Consequently, prudence requires particularly good evidence for the recognition of gains.

It is important to note that in this chapter the ASB is following a **balance sheet orientated** approach to measure gains and losses. The conventional profit and loss account approach would identify the **transactions** that had been undertaken and **allocate** these to financial accounting periods.

6.9.9 Chapter 6: 'Measurement in financial statements'

The majority of listed companies in the UK use the mixed measurement system whereby some assets and liabilities are measured using historical cost and some are measured using a current value basis. The *Statement of Principles* envisages that this will continue to be the practice and states that the aim is to select the basis that:

● Provides information about financial performance and financial position that is useful in evaluating the reporting entity's cash-generation abilities and in assessing its financial adaptability.

● The carrying values are sufficiently reliable and, if the historical cost and current value are equally reliable, the better measure is the one that is the most relevant.
  – Current values may frequently be no less reliable than historical cost figures given the level of estimation that is required in historical cost figures, e.g. determining provisions for bad debts, stock provisions, product warranties.

● Reflects what the asset and liability represents, e.g. the relevance of short-term investments to an entity will be the specific future cash flows and these are best represented by current values.

ASB view on need for a current value basis of measurement

The Statement makes the distinction[19] between return *on* capital, i.e. requiring the calculation of accounting profit, and return, *of* capital, i.e. requiring the measurement of capital and testing for capital maintenance. The Statement makes the point that the financial capital maintenance concept is not satisfactory when *significant* general or specific price changes have occurred.

ASB gradualist approach

The underlying support of the ASB for a gradualist move towards the use of current values is reflected in 'Although the objective of financial statements and the qualitative characteristics of financial information, in particular relevance and reliability may not change ... as markets develop, measurement bases that were once thought unreliable may become reliable. Similarly, as access to markets develops, so a measurement basis that was once thought insufficiently relevant may become the most relevant measure available'.[20]

Determining current value

Current value systems could be defined as replacement cost (entry value), net realisable value (exit value) or value in use (discounted present value of future cash flows). The approach of the Statement is to identify the value to the business by selecting from these three alternatives the measure that is most relevant in the circumstances. This measure is referred to as deprival value and represents the loss that the entity would suffer if it were deprived of the asset.

The value to the business is determined by considering whether the company would replace the asset. If the answer is yes, then use replacement cost; if the answer is *no* but the asset is worth keeping, then use value in use; and if *no* and the asset is not worth keeping, then use net realisable value. This can be shown diagrammatically as follows:

Will the value to the business become the accepted measurement base?

To answer this we need to look towards the IASB. At a meeting in June 2001, the IASB discussed fair value, replacement cost, net selling price, value in use and value to the business as bases for measurement, including how to define them and difficulties in applying them. Each of the bases presented problems, some of which were:

Fair value
How to measure 'real' assets such as tangible fixed assets where separate cash flows do not exist?

Replacement cost
How to find the exact replacement cost of an asset in the market as technology improves particularly accounting for capacity increases within new assets?

Net selling price
How to deal with specific tailored assets or assets where no market exists?

Value in use
Problems were seen in that future returns are incorporated; estimates were subjective and it is considered inappropriate if replacement cost is lower.

Value to the business
As this is arrived at after evaluating replacement cost, net selling price and value in use, it followed that the reservations about each method flowed through into value to the business, e.g. how to value if no active market, how to value fixed assets where separate cash flows do not exist, how to measure specialised assets.

At the meeting no preference was agreed, it being felt necessary first to resolve the overall objective of measurement. Although, therefore, the ASB has a clearly defined position within the Statement of Principles, any IASB decision awaits the outcome of a project which will take into account how assets and liabilities are currently measured under existing standards, the objective of measurement and how this will be expressed within the International Framework.

6.9.10 Chapter 7: 'Presentation of financial information'

Chapter 7 states that the objective of the presentation adopted is to communicate clearly and effectively and in as simple and straightforward manner as is possible without loss of relevance or reliability and without significantly increasing the length of the financial statements.

The point about length is well made given the length of current annual reports and accounts, e.g. Stagecoach Holdings plc extends to 69 pages, Sea Containers Ltd 76 pages and Hugo Boss 115 pages.

The Statement analyses the way in which information should be presented in financial statements to meet the objectives set out in Chapter 1. It covers the requirement for items to be aggregated and classified and outlines good presentation practices in the statement of financial performance, balance sheet, cash flow statement and accompanying information, e.g:

Statement of financial performance

Good presentation involves:

- Recognising only gains and losses.
- Classifying items by function, e.g. production, selling, administrative and nature, e.g. interest payable.
- Showing separately amounts that are affected in different ways by economic or commercial conditions, e.g. continuing, acquired and discontinued operations, segmental geographical information.
- Showing separately:
  - items unusual in amount or incidence
  - expenses that are not operating expenses, e.g. financing costs and taxation
  - expenses that relate primarily to future periods, e.g. research expenditure.

Balance sheet

Good presentation involves:

- Recognising only assets, liabilities and ownership interest.
- Classifying assets so that users can assess the nature, amounts and liquidity of available resources.
- Classifying assets and liabilities so that users can assess the nature, amounts and timing of obligations that require or may require liquid resources for settlement.
- Classifying assets by function, e.g. show fixed assets and current assets separately.

Accompanying information

Typical information includes chairman's statement, directors' report, operating and financial review, highlights and summary indicators.

The Statement states that the more complex an entity and its transactions become, the more users need an objective and comprehensive analysis and explanation of the main features underlying the entity's financial performance and financial position.

Good presentation involves discussion of:

- The main factors underlying financial performance, including the principal risks, uncertainties and trends in main business areas and how entity is responding.
- The strategies adopted for capital structure and treasury policy.

● The activities and expenditure (other than capital expenditure) that are investment in the future.

It is interesting to note the Statement view that highlights and summary indicators, such as amounts and ratios that attempt to distil key information, cannot on their own adequately describe or provide a basis for meaningful analysis or prudent decision-making. It does, however, state that, 'That having been said, well-presented highlights and summary indicators are useful to users who require only very basic information, such as the amount of sales or dividends'. The ASB will be giving further consideration to this view that there is a need for a really brief report.

6.9.11 Chapter 8: 'Accounting for interests in other entities'

Interest in other entities can have a material effect on the company's own financial performance and financial position and need to be fully reflected in the financial statements, e.g. an extract from the 1998 Annual Report and Accounts of Stagecoach plc shows:

	Company balance sheet	*Consolidated balance sheet*
Tangible fixed assets	£0.7m	£1,548.4m
Investments	£734.3m	£51.4m

In deciding whether to include the assets in the consolidated balance sheet a key factor is the degree of influence exerted over the activities and resources of the investee:

● If the degree of influence allows control of the operating and financial policies, the financial statements are aggregated.

● If the investor has joint control or significant influence, the investor's share of the gains and losses are recognised in the consolidated profit and loss account and reflected in the carrying value of the investment.

However, there is no clear agreement on the treatment of interest in other entities and further developments can be expected.

6.10 FRS 18 *Accounting Policies*[21]

6.10.1 The need for an accounting standard

The *Statement of Principles* provides us with the general principles relating to the objective of financial statements and the qualitative characteristics of financial information, the elements of financial statements together with their recognition, measurement and presentation.

However, the *Statement of Principles* does not provide a set of rules which will lead to every transaction being treated identically in the accounts. Differences in reporting may arise as follows.

At the recognition stage

Companies might have different capitalisation policies:

● on the basis of materiality e.g. in their treatment of small value expenditure on tools which may be classified as fixed assets in the balance sheet or cost of sales in the profit and loss account

- on selecting from options allowed by an FRS e.g. interest incurred in connection with the construction of fixed assets may under FRS 15 *Tangible Fixed Assets* be written off to the profit and loss account or capitalised.

In the choice of a measurement base

Companies may apply different measurement bases permitted by statute or accounting standard:

- Fixed assets, e.g. carrying at depreciated historical cost or depreciated current cost with the historical cost convention modified to include revaluation of all classes or selected classes of tangible fixed assets.
- Stock, e.g. valued at FIFO or weighted average or LIFO or current replacement cost if a company adopts the alternative accounting rules of the Companies Act 1995.
- Deferred tax, e.g. report on a discounted or undiscounted basis per FRS 19.

In the presentation in the financial statements

The Companies Act and accounting standards such as FRS 3 designate headings but a transaction might be presented differently (i.e. under different headings) because there has been a difference:

- at the recognition stage, e.g. small tools treated as a cost of sales or a fixed asset and interest treated as interest payable or as part of a fixed asset
- in management choice, e.g. certain overheads may be reported under the cost of sales heading or the administrative expenses heading.

In the formulation of estimates

Management has to make many estimates which impact on the profit and loss account and balance sheet. These include:

- fixed assets – estimating useful economic life and residual value;
- stock – estimating net realisable value when applying the lower of cost and net realisable value test;
- debtors – estimating specific and general bad debt provisions;
- creditors – estimating warranty claims and contingent outcomes.

Given that companies are permitted to report the same transaction in more than one way, there was a need for the ASB to produce an accounting standard to set out the principles to be followed in selecting accounting policies, the disclosures required to help users understand the policies that are being applied and the techniques applied when formulating estimates.

6.10.2 Accounting policies

Selecting policies

Entities are required to adopt the most appropriate accounting policies which result in similar transactions being reported in a similar way to achieve comparability and in financial statements that give a true and fair view.[22]

In making their selection of accounting policies, there are two underlying concepts which require to be taken into account. These are the going concern assumption and accruals.

The going concern basis should be applied unless there are contra-indications such as the company having ceased trading, being liquidated or the directors have significant doubts about the company's ability to continue as a going concern.[23] If the company is not a going concern then the accounts would be prepared using the NRV method explained in Chapter 4.

The accruals basis should be applied. This was often seen as a profit and loss approach but FRS 18 specifically refers to the accruals concept lying at the heart of the definitions of assets and liabilities.[24]

FRS 18 also sets out the objectives and constraints against which a company should judge the appropriateness of accounting policies to its particular circumstances. The objectives are relevance, reliability, comparability and understandability and the constraints are cost benefit and the need to balance the different objectives.[25] For example, where tension exists between relevance and reliability the choice should be the most relevant policy from those that are reliable. Where there is a tension between neutrality and prudence within reliability, then the selected policy should be the one that ensures that the deliberate and systematic understatement of assets and gains and overstatement of liabilities and losses do not occur.[26]

Estimation techniques

Entities are required to adopt the most appropriate estimation techniques which result in financial statements that give a true and fair view.[27]

Disclosures

Disclosure may be required of accounting policies, estimation techniques and changes of policy as follows.

Material policies

Accounting policies which are material and estimation techniques that are significant are required to be described.

Estimation techniques and assumptions

There is an interesting requirement that, where there is a wide range of outcomes from the choice of estimation techniques or assumptions and the use of a different amount from within the range could materially affect the view shown by the financial statements, there should be disclosure of the estimation technique and the underlying assumptions.[28] One commentator[29] has observed that this may well be a short step away from requiring the disclosure of that range so that users can assess the impact of different estimation techniques on financial statements.

Changes of policy

Details of changes from the previous year are required to be disclosed that explain the reason why the new policy is considered better and the impact on the prior and current year.[30]

Summary

Directors and accountants are constrained by a mass of rules and regulations which govern the measurement, presentation and disclosure of financial information. Regulations are derived from three major sources: the legislature in the form of statutes, the accountancy profession in the form of standards, and the Listing Rules.

There have been a number of reports relating to financial reporting in the UK and other countries. The preparation and presentation of financial statements continue to evolve. Steps are being taken to provide a conceptual framework and there is growing international agreement on the setting of standards.

User needs have been accepted as paramount; qualitative characteristics of information have been specified; the elements of financial statements have been defined precisely; the presentation of financial information has been prescribed; and comparability between companies is seen as desirable.

However, the intention remains to produce financial statements that present a true and fair view. This is not achieved by detailed rules and regulations, and the exercise of judgement will continue to be needed. This opens the way for creative accounting practices that bring financial reporting and the accounting profession into disrepute. Strenuous efforts will continue to be needed from the auditors, the ASB, the Review Panel and the Financial Reporting Council to contain the use of unacceptable practices. The regulatory bodies show that they have every intention of accepting the challenge.

The question of the measurement base that should be used has yet to be settled. Solomons suggested the use of value to the business and this has received support in *The Future Shape of Financial Reports*. The measurement question still remains a major area of financial reporting that needs to be addressed.

The *Statement of Principles* sees the objective of financial statements as providing information about the financial position, performance and financial adaptability of an enterprise that is useful to a wide range of users in making economic decisions. It recognises that they are limited because they largely show the financial effects of past events and do not necessarily show non-financial information. On the question of measurement the view has been expressed that

> historical cost has the merit of familiarity and (to some extent) objectivity; current values have the advantage of greater relevance to users of the accounts who wish to assess the current state or recent performance of the business, but they may sometimes be unreliable or too expensive to provide. It concludes that practice should develop by evolving in the direction of greater use of current values to the extent that this is consistent with the constraints of reliability, cost and acceptability to the financial community.[31]

There are critics[32] who argue that the concern with recording current asset values rather than historical costs means that

> the essential division between the ASB and its critics is one between those who are more concerned about where they want to be and those who want to be very clear about where they are now. It is a division between those who see the purpose of financial statements as taking economic decisions about the future,

and those who see it as a basis for making management accountable and for distributing the rewards among the stakeholders.

Finally, it is interesting to give some thought to extracts from two publications which indicate that there is still a long way to go in the evolution of financial reporting, and that there is little room for complacency.

The first is from *The Future Shape of Financial Reports*:

As Solomons and *Making Corporate Reports Valuable* discussed in detail, the then system of financial reporting in the UK fails to satisfy the purpose of providing information to shareholders, lenders and others to appraise past performance in order to form expectations about an organisation's future performance in five main respects:

1 ... measures of performance ... are based on original or historical costs ...
2 Much emphasis is placed on a single measure of earnings per share ...
3 ... insufficient attention is paid to changes in an enterprise's cash or liquidity position ...
4 The present system is essentially backward looking ...
5 Emphasis is often placed on the legal form rather than on the economic substance of transactions ...

We have seen that some of these five limitations are being addressed, but not all, e.g. the provision of projected figures.

The second extract is from *Making Corporate Reports Valuable*:

The present balance sheet almost defies comprehension. Assets are shown at depreciated historical cost, at amounts representing current valuations and at the results of revaluations of earlier periods (probably also depreciated); that is there is no consistency whatsoever in valuation practice. The sum total of the assets, therefore, is meaningless and combining it with the liabilities to show the entity's financial position does not in practice achieve anything worthwhile.[33]

The ASB has taken steps to deal with the frequency of revaluations but the criticism still holds in that there will continue to be financial statements produced incorporating mixed measurement bases.

The point made by some critics remains unresolved: 'Accountability and the ASB's decision usefulness are not compatible. Forward-looking decisions require forecasts of future cash flows, which in the economic model are what determines the values of assets. These values are too subjective to form the basis of accountability. The definition of assets and the recognition rules restrict assets to economic benefits the enterprise controls as a result of past events and that are measurable with sufficient reliability. But economic decision-making requires examination of all sources of future cash flows, not just a restricted sub-set of them.'[34]

The need for a conceptual framework is being addressed around the world. The UK is not alone in its search. In the USA, Australia, Canada and the IASC, the approach has been the same as that now followed by the ASB, i.e. commencing with a consideration of the objectives of financial statements, qualitative characteristics of financial information, definition of the elements, and when these are to be recognised in the financial statements. There is a general agreement on these areas.

REVIEW QUESTIONS

I (a) Name the user groups and information needs of the user groups identified by *The Corporate Report*, the IASC *Framework for the Presentation and Preparation of Financial Statements* and the ASB *Statement of Principles*.

(b) Discuss the effect of *The Corporate Report* on current financial reporting practice.

2 Compare and contrast the regulatory framework and the conceptual framework. Evaluate the ASB's attempt to find a conceptual framework.

3 Give a brief synopsis of the ICAS *Making Corporate Reports Valuable* and the Solomons Report.

4 R. MacVe in *A Conceptual Framework for Financial Accounting and Reporting: The Possibility for an Agreed Structure* suggested that the search for a conceptual framework was a political process. Discuss the effect that this thinking has had and will have on the standard setting.

5 (a) In 1999, the ASB published the *Statement of Principles*. Explain what you consider to be the purpose and status of the Statement.

(b) Chapter 4 of the Statement identifies and defines what the ASB believes to be the elements that make up financial statements. Define any four of the elements and explain how, in your opinion, the identification and definition of the elements of financial statements would enhance financial reporting.

(c) Chapter 5 of the Statement states that matching is not regarded as the driver of the recognition process. Explain what is meant by this and its probable effect in practice.

6 'The evidence suggests that the simple percentage rule has not worked ... its simplicity and rigidity leave it open to abuse!' Discuss.[35]

7 'The replacement of accrual accounting with cash flow accounting would avoid the need for a conceptual framework.' Discuss.[36]

8 Financial accounting theory has accumulated a vast literature. A cynic might be inclined to say that the vastness of the literature is in sharp contrast to its impact on practice.

(a) Describe the different approaches that have evolved in the development of accounting theory.

(b) Assess its impact on standard setting.

(c) Discuss the contribution of accounting theory to the understanding of accounting practice, and suggest contributions that it might make in the future.

EXERCISES

An extract from the solution is provided in the appendix at the end of the text for exercises marked with an asterisk (*).

* Question I

The following information is available in relation to MCRV Ltd for the year ending 31 December 20X8:

(a) Statement of assets and liabilities as at 31 December. This statement at the start of the year is assumed to contain valuations at net realisable value throughout:

(i) Fixed assets are estimated by the directors on the basis of an orderly disposal in a second-hand market.

(ii) The NRV of raw materials was assumed by the directors to be the same as their purchase price.

Statement of Assets and Liabilities as at 31 December

	20X7	20X8
	£000	£000
Fixed assets	200	270
Current assets		
Stock	50	66
Debtors	30	40
Cash	10	76
	290	452
Less:		
Current liabilities		

Creditors	35		30
Long-term loans	60		70
		95	100
		195	352

Cash Transactions during the year ended 31 December 20X8

Cash received during 20X8:	£000	£000
Credit customers		190
Long-term loans		30
		220
Cash paid during 20X8:		
Credit suppliers	85	
Fixed assets	30	
Salaries	30	
Loan interest	9	
		154
		66

---

*Journal Entries for Non-cash Transactions for the year ended
31 December 20X8*

	£	£
Debtors	200	
Sales – being credit sales		200
for 20X8		
Stock	80	
Creditors – being credit		80
purchases for 20X8		
Cost of goods sold	70	
Stock		70
Goods used for sale		
Stock	6	
Cost of goods sold – being uplift		6
in closing stock from cost to		
net realisable value		

  (iii) The NRV of finished goods was estimated as selling price less the estimated costs of disposal in the normal course of business.

(b) A summary of the cash book.

(c) The non-cash transactions during the year are as shown in the journal entries.

Required:

(a) **Prepare an operations statement for the year ended 31 December 20X8 to show wealth created by operations.**

(b) **Prepare a statement of changes in wealth, in the following format:**

        Increase in wealth due to operations

        Increase in value of fixed assets

        Decrease in value of long-term loans   _____

        Realisable increase in net assets   ========

(c) **Explain circumstances in which there can be a decrease in the value of long-term loans.**

(d) **Explain how the percentage return on capital employed, current ratio and acid test ratio based on the historical cost concept would differ from those calculated using the concept applied in the above question.**

(Adapted from extract in Melody plc annual report (ICAS))

Question 2

The following extract is from *Conceptual Framework for Financial Accounting and Reporting: Elements of Financial Statements and Their Measurement*, FASB 3, December 1976.

    The benefits of achieving agreement on a conceptual framework for financial accounting and reporting manifest themselves in several ways. Among other things, a conceptual framework can (1) guide the body responsible for establishing accounting standards, (2) provide a frame of reference for resolving accounting questions in the absence of a specific promulgated standard, (3) determine bounds for judgement in preparing financial statements, (4) increase financial statement users' understanding of and confidence in financial statements, and (5) enhance comparability.

Required:
(a) Define a conceptual framework.
(b) Critically examine why the benefits provided in the above statements are likely to flow from the development of a conceptual framework for accounting.

Question 3

The following extract is from 'Comments of Leonard Spacek', in R.T. Sprouse and M. Moonitz, *A Tentative Set of Broad Accounting Principles for Business Enterprises*, Accounting Research Study No. 3, AICPA, New York, 1962, reproduced in A. Belkaoui, *Accounting Theory*, Harcourt Brace Jovanovich.

A discussion of assets, liabilities, revenue and costs is premature and meaningless until the basic principles that will result in a fair presentation of the facts in the form of financial accounting and financial reporting are determined. This fairness of accounting and reporting must be for and to people, and these people represent the various segments of our society.

Required:
(a) Explain the term 'fair' as used in UK financial reports.
(b) Discuss the extent to which the ASB conceptual framework satisfies the above definition.

Question 4

The Financial Reporting Council's November 1991 publication *The State of Financial Reporting: A Review* had a section on the work of the Accounting Standards Board which stated that 'We have devoted much of our energies during the first year to the demanding task of developing a clear *Statement of Principles* from which our work on individual standards will derive.'

Required:
(a) Discuss why the *Statement of Principles* was not finalised until 1999 – eight years after the 1991 comment by the FRC.
(a) Summarise why the Accounting Standards Board (ASB) placed such emphasis on developing a clear *Statement of Principles*.
(b) Outline the principal matters to be dealt with in any three of the eight chapters of the *Statement of Principles* 1999.

References

1 *The Scope and Implications of the Conceptual Framework Project*, Stanford, Conn., FASB, 1967.
2 R. MacVe, *A Conceptual Framework for Financial Accounting and Reporting*, ICAEW, 1981.
3 E. Stamp, 'A conceptual framework', *Accountancy*, March 1982.
4 ASC, *The Corporate Report*, 1975.
5 D. Solomons, *Guidelines for Financial Reporting Standards*, ICAEW, 1989.
6 J. Arnold *et al.*, *The Future Shape of Financial Reports*, ICAEW, 1991.
7 ICAS, *Making Corporate Reports Valuable*, 1988.
8 T. Lee, 'In criticism of the Solomons Guidelines', *The Accountant's Magazine*, March 1989.
9 R. MacVe, 'In criticism of the Solomons Guidelines', *Accountancy*, March 1989, p. 20; *Accountancy*, April 1989, p. 26.

10 D. Solomons, 'The Solomons Guidelines: A reply to the critics', *Accountancy*, August 1989.

11 J. Arnold *et al.*, *The Future Shape of Financial Reports*, ICAEW, 1991, p. 32.

12 IASC, *Framework for the Presentation and Preparation of Financial Statements*, 1989.

13 *Improving Business Reporting – A Customer Focus. Meeting the Information Needs of Investors and Creditors*, AICPA, 1994.

14 *Statement of Principles for Financial Reporting*, ASB, 1995.

15 ASB Progress Paper *Statement of Principles for Financial Reporting – the way ahead.*

16 *Statement of Principles for Financial Reporting*, ASB, 1999.

17 *Ibid.*, para. 3.27.

18 *Ibid.*, para. 5.10.

19 *Ibid.*, para. 6.41.

20 *Ibid.*, para. 6.24.

21 FRS 18 *Accounting Policies*, ASB, 2000.

22 *Ibid.*, paras 14–17.

23 *Ibid.*, paras 21–23.

24 *Ibid.*, para. 27.

25 *Ibid.*, paras 30–31.

26 *Ibid.*, para. 43.

27 *Ibid.*, paras 50–51.

28 *Ibid.*, paras 56–57.

29 H. Lunt, 'The Fab Four's solo careers', *Accountancy*, March 2000, p. 75.

30 FRS 18 *Accounting Policies*, ASB, 2000, para. 56.

31 A. Lennard, 'The peg on which our standards hang', *Accountancy*, January 1996, p. 80.

32 S. Fearnley and M. Page, 'Why the ASB has lost its bearings', *Accountancy*, April 1996, p. 94.

33 ICAS, *Making Corporate Reports Valuable*, 1988, p. 35.

34 S. Fearnley and M. Page, *op. cit.*

35 J. Blakemore and B. Pain, 'Materiality in Accounting', *ACCA Students' Newsletter*, May 1998, pp. 34–36.

36 R. Skinner, *Accountancy*, January 1990, p. 25.

PART 2

Regulatory framework – an attempt to achieve uniformity

Published accounts of companies

7.1 Introduction

Each company sends an annual report and accounts to its shareholders. It is the means by which the directors are accountable for their stewardship of the assets and their handling of the company's affairs for the **current year**. It consists of financial data which have been audited and narrative comment which may be reviewed by the auditors to check that it does not present a picture that differs from the financial data, i.e. that the narrative is not misleading.

7.1.1 Financial data

The financial data consists of the following financial statements, namely:

- profit and loss account, segmental report, statement of total recognised gains and losses and note of historical cost profits and losses (if fixed assets have been revalued);
- balance sheet and reconciliation of movements in shareholders' funds;
- cash flow statement;
- appropriate explanatory notes.

7.1.2 Narrative reports

The narrative report from the directors satisfies two needs: (a) to explain what has been achieved in the current year and (b) to assist existing and potential investors to make their own predictions of cash flows in future years.

The current year

The narrative might appear in a number of locations such as a chairman's report, managing director's review, directors' report, finance director's review, operating and financial review, notes to the accounts. Whatever the description used, the narrative typically covers items such as:

- investor data, e.g. market conditions, share issues, share splits, buy-backs, company's share price movements (e.g. highs/lows and price relative to the market), earnings per share adjusted for selected items such as exceptional items and goodwill amortisation, dividend per share and dividend cover;

- macro-data, e.g. the economic climate, political climate and possible regulatory changes, currency fluctuations; and
- company data such as
  - key figures/financial highlights, e.g. incoming orders, turnover, earnings before interest and tax (EBIT), earnings before tax (EBT), net income, employees;
  - key ratios, e.g. sales growth, operating margins, return on equity;
  - sales performance in key markets;
  - explanations of unusual movements in financial data, e.g. why debtors have increased significantly;
  - notes to the accounts explaining treatment of acquisitions and disposals of associated and subsidiary companies.

Future cash flows

Investors need information to form their view on future cash flows which will be the basis for dividend payouts and capital gains. Directors provide selective information which they see as significant and relevant on items such as:

Fixed assets

- Capital investment programme, e.g. new facilities coming on stream.
- Research and development plans, e.g. new development agreements and alliances.
- Corporate strategy, e.g. possible divestments or acquisitions.

Financing

- Improved financial flexibility, e.g. renegotiating debt maturity profile.
- Cash flows and interest cover maintained.

Operating and finance costs

- Changes in production capacity, e.g. new facilities coming on stream, relocation to lower cost areas, cost reduction programmes.
- How to deal with any low profitability segments, divestment.
- Changes in financing.

Prognosis

- Growth, e.g. how to achieve sustainable growth.
- Targets, e.g. statements such as 'directors expect to increase sales by 5–7% in the current financial year, with even stronger growth in earnings, provided no unforeseen events occur'.

In this chapter we consider public listed companies, i.e. companies that have their shares traded on a recognised stock exchange. We use extracts from the annual reports and notes on accounts of Heidelberger Druckmaschinen AG as at 31 March 2001 and The Body Shop International plc as at 3 March 2001 and Allied Domecq plc as at 31 August 2000. We will consider the following items:

- A company's financial calendar.
- The profit and loss account:
  - Criteria for the information that is published.
  - Format of the profit and loss account required by Format 1 and Format 2.

- Classification of costs in the profit and loss account – does it matter under which heading a cost is classified provided it is not omitted?
- Treatment of discontinued operations.

● Segmental reports: effect of SSAP 25 *Segmental Reporting* on presentation.

● Other primary performance statements: rationale and format.

● FRED 22 *Revision of FRS 3 Reporting Financial Performance*:
- Statement of financial performance.
- Reconciliation of ownership interests.

● The balance sheet:
- Format of the balance sheet required by Format 1 and Format 2.
- Accounting rules for asset valuation.

● True and fair: the true and fair override.

● Additional information in annual reports:
- Directors/management reports.
- Operating and financial review.

● Accounting policies: effect of national and international standards on the analysis of the accounts.

7.2 A public company's financial calendar

The ownership and management of a public company whose shares are listed on a stock exchange are separate. The owners or shareholders are provided with regular information for stewardship accountability and to allow them to make investment decisions. Each company follows its own financial calendar. For example, the financial calendar for Heidelberger Druckmaschinen AG in 2001 is shown in Figure 7.1.

7.3 Criteria for information appearing in a published profit and loss account and balance sheet

There are three criteria that we consider:

● The format complies with the Companies Act 1985 and FRS 3.
● There are appropriate notes.
● The financial statements present a true and fair view of the profits/losses, assets and liabilities.

We comment on each of these in turn.

7.4 The prescribed formats – the profit and loss account

The Companies Act 1985 allows[1] a company choice from four formats of profit and loss account. The choices allow for the analysis of costs in different ways: according to type of expenditure, e.g. raw materials, wages and depreciation; or according to type of

Figure 7.1 Financial calendar of Heidelberger Druckmaschinen AG

31 March 2001	**End of the company's financial year**
	The income statement, balance sheet and cash flow statement are made up to this date and the auditor prepares his report for the period. The audit report was signed on 29 May 2001.
	Following the preparation of the financial statements, the supervisory board met to discuss the financial statements on 29 June 2001.
3 July 2001	**Annual press conference in Heidelberg**
	Annual analyst conference in Frankfurt
	This press conference can be used to present the results of the group to the public and the financial markets.
25 September 2001	**Annual general meeting in Heidelberg**
	A meeting at which shareholders vote for such things as:

- to approve the financial statements for the year to 31 March 2001;
- to reappoint any board members who are retiring;
- to reappoint the auditors.

26 September 2001	**Dividend distribution**
	The date on which proposed dividends are paid to shareholders.

- The above financial calendar is for a German company, and therefore at each event German legal requirements must be followed. Different countries do have different legal requirements, but the principle of issuing a financial calendar remains for companies in other countries.

- The planned programme of communication with institutional investors and analysts in recognition of the fact that the market hates surprises and share price is strengthened by regular communication. Such communication occurs in the UK also but it is interesting to see that the programme has been published.

operation, e.g. cost of sales, distribution costs and administration expenses. The formats are as follows:

- Format 1: Vertical with costs analysed according to type of operation.
- Format 2: Vertical with costs analysed according to type of expenditure.
- Format 3: Horizontal with costs analysed according to type of operation.
- Format 4: Horizontal with costs analysed according to type of expenditure.

Many companies use Format 1 with the costs analysed according to type of operation.

7.4.1 What information is required to be disclosed in Format 1 and Format 2?

An illustration of a profit and loss account using the Formats 1 and 2 is set out in Figure 7.2. Note that in both formats the same amount is disclosed for profit on ordinary activities before tax and the two statements are identical after that point.

Figure 7.2 Illustration of Formats 1 and 2

Format 1 Classification of expense by function	£000	Format 2 Classification of expense by nature	£000
Revenue	1,000	Revenue	1,000
Cost of sales	(400)		
Gross profit	600		
Other operating income	20	Other operating income	20
Distribution costs	(120)		
Administrative expenses	(70)		
		Changes in stock of finished goods and work-in-progress	20
		Work performed by enterprise and capitalised	125
		Raw materials and consumables	(140)
		Staff costs	(205)
		Depreciation and amortisation	(110)
		Other operating expenses	(280)
Profit from operations	*430*		*430*
Finance cost	*(26)*		*(26)*
Income from associates	*27*		*27*
Profit before tax	*431*		*431*
Income tax expense	*(130)*		*(130)*
Profit after tax	*301*		*301*
Extraordinary income	*0*		*0*
Extraordinary charges	*0*		*0*
Net profit for the period	*301*		*301*

Note that:

Changes in stock of finished goods and work-in-progress in this example are negative because the closing stock was less than the opening stock. The changes will be positive if the closing stock is greater than the opening stock.

The information in Format 2 is useful in predicting future cash flows and is necessary if preparing a value added statement.

7.4.2 Classification of operating expenses and other income by function as in Format 1

In order to arrive at its operating profit, a company needs to classify all of the operating expenses of the business into one of four categories:

● cost of sales;

● distribution and selling costs;

● administrative expenses; and

● other operating income.

We comment briefly on each to explain how a company might classify its trading transactions. This will also indicate how the same transaction might be classified differently by different companies and so result in a different gross profit figure. It does not affect inter-period comparisons but it is important to remember when making inter-company comparisons.

Cost of sales

Expenditure classified under cost of sales will typically include direct costs, overheads, depreciation and amortisation expense and adjustments. The items that might appear under each heading are as follows:

● Direct costs include: direct materials purchased; direct labour; other external charges that comprise production costs from external sources, e.g. equipment rental and subcontract costs.

● Overheads include: variable production overheads; fixed production overheads.

● Depreciation and amortisation include: depreciation of fixed assets used in production; impairment expense; exceptional amounts written off inventory; research costs and development costs.

● Adjustments include:
  – Change between the opening and closing stock. If closing stock is less than opening stock, the reduction must have been sold and the cost of sales will be increased by the amount that the stock has fallen. Conversely, if closing stock is more than opening stock, the amount by which it has increased will not be included as a cost of the current period's sales.
  – Capitalisation of own work as a fixed asset. Any amount of the costs listed above that have been incurred in the construction of fixed assets for retention by the company will not appear as an expense in the profit and loss account: it will be capitalised. Any amount capitalised in this way would be treated for accounting purposes as a fixed asset and depreciated.
  – Capitalisation of own work as a deferred asset. Any amount of the costs listed above that needs to be deferred to a future accounting period because the benefits of the expenditure can be reasonably matched with revenue expected in a future period, e.g. development expenditure capitalised under SSAP 13 would be treated for accounting purposes as a deferred asset and expensed by matching with the revenue as it arises in the future accounting periods. SSAP 13 is considered in detail in Chapter 16.
  – Treatment of variances from standard. Where a company uses a standard costing system, the variances can either be transferred in total to the profit and loss account or be allocated to the cost of sales and the stock. Any variance allocated to the stock will have an impact on the results of a subsequent period. (This aspect is considered in Chapter 17.)

Why cost of sales figures may not be comparable between companies

The cost of sales figure is derived under the accrual accounting concept. This means that:

(a) the cash flows have been adjusted by the management in order to arrive at the expense that management considers to be associated with the sales achieved i.e. the purchases figure will include credit purchases as discussed in Chapter 2; and

(b) additional adjustments may have been made to increase the cost of sales if the net realisable value of the closing stock is less than cost due to factors such as changes in demand, competitive pressures and obsolescence.

Clearly, when management make the additional adjustment under (b) they are estimating and it is impossible to ensure that the management of two companies faced with the same economic activity would arrive at the same assessment of net realisable value. We will now consider the following reasons for differences in calculating the cost of sales: treatment of direct costs; choice of depreciation policy; management attitudes and the accounting system capability.

Differences arising from the treatment of direct costs

Different companies may assume different physical flows when calculating the cost of direct materials used in production. This will affect the inventory valuation. One company may assume a first-in-first-out (FIFO) flow, where the cost of sales is charged for raw materials used in production as if they were issued on the basis that the first items purchased were the first items used in production. Another company may use a weighted average basis. This is illustrated for a company that started trading on 1 January 20X1 without any opening stock and sold 40,000 items on 31 March 20X1 for £4 per item as in Figure 7.3.

FIFO stock is 20,000 items at a cost of £3 per item, assuming that the purchases made on 1 January 20X1 and 1 February 20X1 were sold first. Weighted average stock is 20,000 items at a cost of £2 per item, being the total cost of £120,000 divided by the total number of items of 60,000 at the date of the sale.

The effect on the gross profit percentage would be as shown in Figure 7.4. This demonstrates that, even from a single difference in accounting treatment, the gross profit for the same transaction could be materially different in both absolute and percentage terms.

Figure 7.3 Effect on cost of sales of using FIFO and weighted average

	Items	£	FIFO £	Weighted average £
Raw materials purchased				
On 1 Jan. 20X1 at £1 per item	20,000	20,000		
On 1 Feb. 20X1 at £2 per item	20,000	40,000		
On 1 Mar. 20X1 at £3 per item	20,000	60,000		
On 1 Mar. 20X1 in stock	60,000	120,000	120,000	120,000
On 31 Mar. 20X1 in stock	20,000		60,000	40,000
Cost of sales	40,000		60,000	80,000

Figure 7.4 Effect of physical inventory flow assumptions on the percentage gross profit

	Items	FIFO £	Weighted average £	% difference in gross profit
Sales	40,000	160,000	160,000	
Cost of sales	40,000	60,000	80,000	
		100,000	80,000	
Gross profit %		62.5%	50%	25%

How can the investor determine the accounting policy and the effect of different assumptions?
Companies can select their accounting policy and disclosure is required. The policies for Heidelberger Druckmaschinen AG, British American Tobacco plc and The Body Shop International plc are as follows.

Heidelberger Druckmaschinen AG accounting policy for inventory – 2001
Inventories are carried at acquisition or manufacturing cost. Valuations are determined on the basis of the weighted average cost method. The 'last-in-first-out' (LIFO) method is applied for certain inventories. Manufacturing cost includes production-related full costs determined on the basis of normal capacity utilisation. At the individual level, the manufacturing cost of products includes directly attributable direct costs (such as production materials and wages) as well as fixed and variable production overheads (such as handling, general material and general production costs) including an appropriate proportion of depreciation charges on production plant and equipment. Particular account is taken of costs that are charged to the specific production cost centres. Costs of outside capital are not capitalised as part of the acquisition or manufacturing costs (IAS 23).

The risks of holding inventories arising from reduced saleability are accounted for by appropriate reductions in value. Lower net realisable values on the balance sheet date are applied when making the valuation. If the reasons for a lower valuation no longer apply to inventories that have formerly been reduced in value and the net sale value has therefore risen, the resultant appreciation is recorded as a reduction of material costs.

British American Tobacco plc accounting policy from the 2000 Annual Report
Stocks are valued at the lower of cost and net realisable value. The method used in calculating cost, which includes raw materials, direct labour and overheads where appropriate, is average cost.

The Body Shop International plc accounting policy from the 2001 Annual Report
Stocks are valued at the lower of cost and net realisable value. Cost is calculated as follows: raw materials – cost of purchase on first-in-last-out bases. Work in progress and finished goods – cost of raw materials and labour together with attributable overheads. Net realisable value is based on estimated selling price less further costs to completion and disposal.

Although policies are disclosed, inter-company comparison is difficult because it is not possible to assess the effect of the different policies even where there is detailed information on the costs and the method of their inclusion. Whilst we can carry out academic exercises as in Figure 7.4 and we are aware of the effect of different stock valuation policies on the level of profits, there is no way in real life that we can be certain of being able to carry out such an exercise.

Differences in cost of sales arising from the choice of depreciation policy

The charge made for depreciation might vary because of different:

- recognition policies, e.g. capitalisation or write-off of interest incurred on company constructed fixed assets;
- measurement bases, e.g. the carrying value of fixed assets might be historical cost or historical cost modified by revaluation;
- estimation techniques, e.g. straight-line or reducing balance;
- assumptions used in estimation, e.g. different assessments of the economic life of an asset and total cost to be expensed if there are different assumptions about the residual value.

Differences arising from management attitudes

Losses might be anticipated and measured at a different rate. For example, when assessing the likelihood of the net realisable value of stock falling below the cost figure, the management decision will be influenced by the optimism with which they view the future of the economy, the industry and the company. There could also be other influences, e.g. remuneration packages based on net income or preparation of the company for a buy-out by management.

Differences arising from the capability of the accounting system to provide data

Accounting systems within companies differ, e.g. costs that are collected by one company may well not be collected by another company. For example, the costs of some activities may be spread across a number of departments and different expenditure types, e.g. the cost of researching, sourcing and testing new materials for use in a production process. If it is not practicable to collect the information, consistency of presentation of this type of expenditure may not be possible. This could also affect assessment and comparison of segment performance.

Distribution costs

These are costs incurred after the production of the finished article and up to and including transfer of the goods to the customer. Expenditure classified under this heading will typically include the following:

- **Warehousing costs** – cost associated with the operation of the premises, e.g. rent, rates, insurance, utilities, depreciation, repairs and maintenance; wage costs, e.g. gross wages and pension contributions of warehouse staff.
- **Promotion costs** – advertising, trade shows.
- **Selling costs** – salaries, commissions and pension contributions of sales staff; costs associated with the premises, e.g. rent, rates; cash discounts on sales; travelling and entertainment.
- **Transport costs** – costs associated with the operation of the premises, e.g. rent, rates, insurance, utilities, depreciation, repairs, maintenance; wage costs, e.g. gross wages and pension contributions of transport staff; vehicle costs, e.g. running, maintenance, depreciation.

Administrative expenses

These are all those operating costs that have not been classified as either cost of sales or distribution costs. Expenditure classified under this heading will typically include:

- **Staff costs** – salaries, commissions and pension contributions of administration staff.
- **Establishment costs** – rent, rates.
- **Miscellaneous costs** – amounts written off the debtors that appear in the balance sheet under current assets, professional fees.

Other operating income

Under this heading a company discloses material income derived from ordinary activities of the business that have not been included in the sales turnover figure. If the amounts are not material, they would not be separately disclosed, but included within the sales turnover figure. Income classified under this heading will typically include income from:

- **Intangible assets,** e.g. royalties, commissions.
- **Third-party use of fixed tangible assets** that are surplus to the current productive needs of the company.
- **Employees,** e.g. canteen, recreation fees.

7.4.3 What costs and income are brought into account after calculating the trading profit in order to arrive at the profit on ordinary activities before tax?

We have explained the four categories of cost and other income that are taken into account when calculating the trading profit. In order to arrive at the profit on ordinary activities before tax, income from investments and loans is required to be disclosed separately and not included with the other income – unless, of course, the investment or loan income is not material and is included within the other operating income for convenience.

7.4.4 Does it really matter under which heading a cost is classified in the profit and loss account provided it is not omitted?

This depends on how readers of the accounts use the gross profit and trading profit figures. An examination of annual reports indicates that directors usually make less reference to the gross profit figure and instead draw attention to the operating profit (or trading profit) figure. Operating profit is used to calculate the return on capital employed, as illustrated by the extract from the financial highlights of the BOC Group Annual Report for 2001:

> Return on capital for 2001 was 14.5%, defined as operating profit before exceptional items as a percentage of average capital employed.

7.5 Companies Act Format improved by the FRS 3 layered approach

FRS 3 introduced changes[2] to the format required by the Companies Act 1985 in order to allow the user to make a more informed assessment of future cash flows as follows:

- Operating profit is analysed further into three components: the results of continuing operations, of newly acquired operations and of discontinued operations.
- There is further detail of three exceptional items in arriving at the profit on ordinary activities before interest, again included under the appropriate heading of continuing or discontinued.

7.5.1 Definition of discontinued operations

There could be a temptation for management to classify loss-making operations as discontinued and then reinstating them as continuing when they become profitable. It is necessary[3] therefore to satisfy all of the following conditions:

- The sale or termination is completed either in the period or before the earlier of three months after the commencement of the subsequent period and the date on which the financial statements are approved.
- If a termination, the former activities have ceased permanently.
- The sale or termination has a material effect on the nature and focus of the reporting entity's operations and represents a material reduction in its operating facilities, resulting from either its withdrawal from a particular market (whether class or business or geographical) or from a material reduction in turnover in the reporting entity's continuing markets.
- The assets, liabilities, results of operations and activities are clearly distinguishable physically, operationally and for financial reporting purposes.

The intention is that shareholders should be able to assess future cash flows on the basis of a clear change in the operation rather than merely changes made to improve the appearance of the current year's management performance. If, therefore, any of the conditions are not satisfied, the operations must be treated as continuing.

7.5.2 Critical comment on the definition of discontinued operations

Although the conditions appear straightforward, there are already uncertainties of interpretation. There is no definition of 'ceased permanently' and the meaning of 'material effect on the nature and focus' will not be obvious in all circumstances and will depend upon agreement between the auditors and the management.

There was one ASB member who dissented[4] with the requirement to provide a separate analysis of continuing and discontinued operations only down to the operating profit level because the effect of taxation and minority interest on the gain or loss on disposal is not highlighted. Taxation on the profits on a disposal of a subsidiary is based on sales proceeds and the cost of the investment which means that in the group situation the accounting and taxable profits could often be materially different where there has been a disposal. The dissenting view was that a user would benefit from the profit before tax, profit after tax, minorities and EPS being analysed into continuing and discontinued operations.

7.5.3 Accounting treatment where, at the year-end, a decision has been made to terminate

If a decision has been made to sell or terminate an operation, a provision[5] should be made to reflect:

- The direct costs of the sale or termination.
- Any operating losses of the operation to be sold or terminated after taking into account any future operating profits or profits on the sale of the assets.

Unless the operation in question qualifies as a discontinued operation in the period, the provision should be made under continuing operations. In a later period, if the operation does qualify as a discontinued operation, the provision should be used to offset the results of the operation in the discontinued category. This is to ensure that the profits from continuing operations are not massaged by making a provision under the discontinued classification when there has not actually been a discontinuance.

7.5.4 Exceptional and extraordinary items

The exceptional items to be disclosed on the face[6] of the profit and loss account are:

- Profits or losses on the sale or termination of an operation.
- Costs of a fundamental reorganisation or restructuring having a material effect on the nature and focus of the reporting entity's operations.
- Profits or losses on the disposal of fixed assets.

Other exceptional items

Other exceptional items[7] should be credited or charged in arriving at the profit or loss on ordinary activities before taxation under the statutory headings to which they relate. Exceptional items are events that fall within the ordinary activities of the business which need to be disclosed by way of note by virtue of their size or incidence.

There is an interesting proposal[8] in FRED 22 that, when exceptional items are reported in the current or prior year, there should be a note showing a breakdown and description of exceptional items for the last five years to allow users to see the make-up and pattern.

Extraordinary items

Extraordinary items are defined[9] in FRED 22 as 'material items possessing a high degree of abnormality that arise from events or transactions that fall outside the ordinary activities of the reporting entity and which are not expected to recur. They do not include exceptional items nor do they include prior period items merely because they relate to a prior period.' The ASB could not envisage any circumstances in which extraordinary items might be reported under the above definition and accordingly provided no examples. IAS 8, however, gives two examples[10] of events or transactions that generally give rise to extraordinary items, namely, the expropriation of assets or an earthquake or other natural disaster.

It is possible, however, that an item could be considered extraordinary by one enterprise but not by another. For example, a trading company might consider losses due to an earthquake as extraordinary, but an insurance company that insures against those losses would not consider payments on the policies as extraordinary. As far as the

Figure 7.5 Allied Domecq plc group profit and loss account – year to 31 August 2000

	Before goodwill and exceptional items	Goodwill and exceptional items	Total
	£m	£m	£m
Continuing operations	2,602	–	2,602
Discontinued operations	30	–	30
Less: share of turnover of joint venture			
- discontinued operation	(12)		(12)
Turnover	**2,620**	**–**	**2,620**
Operating costs – goodwill amortisation	–	(3)	(3)
– other	(2,143)	(54)	(2,197)
Continuing operations	473	(57)	416
Discontinued operations	4	–	4
Operating profit	**477**	**(57)**	**420**
Share of profits of associated undertaking			
- continuing operations	14	–	14
- discontinued operation	9	–	9
Trading profit	**500**	**(57)**	**443**
Profit on sale of business in continuing and			
discontinued operations	–	13	13
Profit/(loss) on disposal of fixed assets in			
continuing and discontinued operations	–	46	46
Profit on ordinary activities before finance			
charges	**500**	**2**	**502**

accounts format is concerned, there will still be a caption for extraordinary items, but there will rarely be anything to report against it. The effect of the ASB definition is that all expenses impact on the earnings per share figure calculated before exceptional items and they are not easily classified as extraordinary as a means of improving the EPS figure.

The FRS 3 layered format illustrated

An extract from the 2000 Annual Report of Allied Domecq plc illustrates in Figure 7.5 the layered format for continuing and discontinued operations and for exceptional items.

7.6 SSAP 25 *Segmental Reporting*

The objective of segmental reporting is to supplement the profit and loss account and assist users of accounts to evaluate the different business segments and geographical regions of a group and how they affect the overall results of that group. SSAP 25 *Segmental Reporting* sets out how these different segments should be defined and the information which should be disclosed. SSAP 25 gives guidance on the *types* of factors[11]

Figure 7.6 Allied Domecq plc Annual Report 2000 – geographical analysis

		Europe £m	Americas £m	Rest of world £m	Total £m
Turnover	– continuing operations	1,484	1,568	147	3,199
	– discontinued operations	30	–	–	30
		1,514	1,568	147	3,229
	– to group companies				(597)
	– external				2,632
Trading profit	– continuing operations	199	271	17	487
	– goodwill amortisation	–	–	(3)	(3)
	– exceptional items in continuing operations	(39)	(15)	–	(54)
	– discontinued operations	13	–	–	13
		173	256	14	443
Profit on sale of businesses in discontinued operations		13	–	–	13
Profit/(loss) on disposal of fixed assets in continuing operations		55	(9)	–	46
Profit before finance charges		**241**	**247**	**14**	**502**
Assets employed		937	739	166	1,842

that directors should take into account when determining reportable segments, e.g. the nature of the products or services, how the groups activities are organised. These factors help to determine whether a segment is distinguishable, but it must also be a significant segment to require disclosure and a significance test will measure if any of the turnover, results or assets account for more than 10% of the group's total. The geographical analysis from the Allied Domecq 2000 Annual Report is shown in Figure 7.6 (the company also published an activity analysis).

7.7 Statement of total recognised gains and losses

The profit and loss account reports realised gains and losses and users were concerned that gains and losses were sometimes masked or obscured by reserve accounting,[12] which permits items to bypass the profit and loss account. The ASB's solution in 1992 was to require a statement to reflect other changes in shareholders' equity such as un-realised surpluses on revaluation of fixed assets and trade investments (where a company adopts the historical cost convention modified by revaluation), currency differences and prior period adjustments. The result was to apply an all-inclusive approach to gains and losses.

An extract from Allied Domecq 2000 Annual Report appears in Figure 7.7.

Figure 7.7 Group statement of total recognised gains and losses for year to 31 August 2000

	£m
Profit earned for ordinary shareholders for the year	317
Currency translation differences on foreign currency net investments	7
Total recognised gains and losses for the year	324

Note: There is no unrealised surplus on revaluation because the company has adopted the historical cost convention and no prior period adjustments arose in 2000.

7.8 Statement of financial performance

The criterion used when deciding whether to report an item in the profit and loss account or statement of total recognised gains and losses (STRGL) was to report realised gains and losses in the profit and loss account and unrealised gains and losses in the STRGL. However, the ASB believes[13] that an approach to performance reporting is required that accepts that the move away from realisation as a criterion for distinguishing items of financial performance is already under way and so in FRED 22 *Revision of FRS 3 Reporting Financial Performance*, it has concluded that gains and losses should be grouped in sections of the performance statement according to their inherent nature, not whether they are realised or not.

7.8.1 FRED 22 *Revision of FRS 3 Reporting Financial Performance*

The objective[14] of the draft standard is to require reporting entities to report all gains and losses in a single performance statement as part of an information set and to highlight a range of important components. It is proposed that the statement of performance should be in three sections:

● Operating section to contain the bulk of gains and losses. There will also be an analysis into continuing, discontinuing and acquired operations.

● Financing and treasury to include interest payable and receivable, gains and losses arising on repurchase or early settlement of debt, income from investments held as part of treasury activity.

● Other gains and losses section to contain holding gains and losses on long-term items held in order to carry out the activities of the entity.

FRED 22 provides an example of a statement of financial performance based on Format 1. The layout is illustrated in Figure 7.8.

7.8.2 Reconciliation of ownership interests

A reconciliation of ownership interests[15] is required to explain the movement between the opening and closing ownership interest. The ASB consider that changes in ownership interest other than those included in the performance statement can be important in

Figure 7.8 Illustration of statement of financial performance applying FRED 22

	£m	£m
Operating		
Turnover		
Continuing operations		1,000
Acquisitions		20
		1,020
Discontinued operations		50
		1,070
Cost of sales		(750)
Gross profit		320
Net operating expenses		(180)
Operating profit		
Continuing operations	150	
Acquisitions	3	
	153	
Discontinued operations	(13)	
Operating income/profit		**140**
Financing and treasury		
Interest on debt		(62)
Financing relating to pension provision		25
Financing and treasury income/profit		**(37)**
Operating and financing income before taxation		**103**
Taxation on operating and financing income		(21)
Operating and financing income after taxation		82
Minority interest		(12)
Income from operating and financing activities for the period		**70**
Other gains and losses		
Revaluation gain on disposal of properties in continuing operations		20
Revaluation of fixed assets		15
Actuarial gain on defined benefit pension scheme		355
Profit on disposal of discontinued operations		9
Exchange translation differences on foreign currency net investments		(8)
Other gains and losses before taxation		**391**
Taxation on other gains and losses		(105)
Other gains and losses after taxation		286
Minority interests		(43)
Other gains and losses of the period		**243**
Total gains and losses of the period		**313**

Figure 7.8 (*cont.*)

Memorandum items

Earnings per share	78p
Diluted earnings per share	xxp
Dividend per share: equity	8.0p
preference	0.7p
Total dividend for the period: equity	£14.5m
preference	£2.5m

Points to note:

● The profit used as the basis for the EPS calculation is the **income from operating and financing activities for the period**.

● Currently dividends are required to be shown on the face of the profit and loss account and the ASB has approached the Department of Trade and Industry to request an amendment of the Companies Act to permit the memorandum style of presentation.

● Recycling between sections is not permitted. If a revaluation gain has been recognised in the other gains and losses section in one period, it cannot be recognised again when realised – at that point the profit is the difference between the sales proceeds and the net carrying amount.

understanding the change in financial position. The reconciliation is a primary statement but to avoid attention being diverted from the performance statement it is shown separately. An illustration is shown in Figure 7.9.

The reconciliation of ownership interests is similar in content to the current reconciliation of movements in shareholders' funds, as we can see from the extract from Allied Domecq's 2000 Annual Report in Figure 7.10.

Figure 7.9 Reconciliation of ownership interests

	£m
Recognised gains and losses relating to the period	313
Dividends	(17)
	296
New capital subscribed	30
Net addition to ownership interest	326
Opening shareholders' funds	614
Closing ownership interest	940

Figure 7.10 Group reconciliation of movements in shareholders' funds

	£m
Shareholders' funds at the beginning of the year	2,273
Total recognised gains and losses for the year	324
Ordinary dividends	(116)
Ordinary share capital issued (net of cost)	–
Capital reduction due to disposal of UK retail business	(2,294)
Preference share capital redemption	–
Goodwill written back on disposals	3
Net movement in shareholders' funds	(2,083)
Shareholders' funds at the end of the year	190

7.8.3 International view of all-inclusive performance statement

The G4 + 1 Group which comprised standard-setters from Australia, Canada, New Zealand, the UK and the USA and the IASC published a paper on the reporting of financial performance,[16] in which the approach favoured by the substantial majority of the working party was to reduce the complexity which supplementary statements may cause by proposing a single performance statement with three major components:

● operating activities;
● financing and other treasury activities;
● other gains and losses.

The contents of other gains and losses broadly corresponds to the UK statement of total recognised gains and losses which is clear confirmation that there is common support for the all-inclusive basis of reporting. The ASB has taken the lead of an internaitonal research project on leasing.

7.8.4 The rationale for a single statement of financial performance

The ASB proposed requirement for an all-inclusive statement

The ASB has favoured the idea of an 'information set' approach to the financial results and encouraged users to look further than the 'bottom line' figure. Following that philosophy it introduced the statement of total gains and losses as an additional primary statement as part of FRS 3 in 1992. It sees the proposed three-section approach as an incremental development[17] which could not be taken at the time FRS 3 was issued because it represented too great a move at one time.

In FRED 22, it comments[18] that users and preparers appear to attach different levels of confidence to gains and losses in different performance statements simply because they are reported in different statements, with the STRGL being downgraded, and so it would be preferable to require a single statement of all recognised gains and losses.

The ASB proposed solution is to require a single statement of financial performance which, in accordance with the *Statement of Principles*, recognises only gains and losses.

How conceptually sound is the proposal for a single statement and the allocation of items between the three sections?

Proposal for a single statement

The requirement for a single performance statement is not required by the *Statement of Principles* and has no conceptual basis for requiring this format. It could be argued that the ASB assumption that analysts, investors and preparers are financially so naive that the relevance of information presented in two primary statements, the profit and loss account and statement of total recognised gains and losses, is not recognised because it is presented on two pages rather than one page might be thought rather weak when in practice accounts may run to over 100 pages with detailed notes that are deemed necessary under extant Statute, FRSs and UITFs.

There also appears to be an anomaly in that, whilst the ASB question the appropriateness of the realisation concept in determining what to include in a performance statement and the relative importance attached to a single profit figure, it proposes to exclude[19] all items in the other gains and losses section when calculating the earnings per share although emphasising that the earnings per share figure can be used as a starting point to a consideration of all components of its activities.

The allocation of items to sections

Some commentators[20] argue that reporting any gains or losses on disposal of fixed assets is an indication that the depreciation charged in the operating section in previous years needed adjustment and that this should impact on the operating section not the other gains and losses section. This is contrasted with the treatment of gains and losses on the settlement of long-term debt which are dealt with appropriately in the financing section.

It is also argued that it is inappropriate to include the actuarial variations that arise from the requirement to use market values on the pension scheme in the other gains and losses section when this is basically orchestrated to avoid volatility in the profit figure used to calculate the earnings per share. This would seem to be based on expediency rather than concept.

The three-section approach is all-inclusive but only to a limited extent in that there is no uniform system of current cost that would provide comparable entries to the other gains and losses section. It could appear that the statement of total gains and losses was ignored by users and the new format in some way seeks to overcome this by presenting an information set that purports to be a statement of financial performance. Until there is a uniform system of asset and liability valuation, the all-inclusive three-section statement might be perceived to simply be a deposit for residuals of any balance sheet changes that occur without any clear conceptual rationale for either the changes or their allocation.

7.9 Prescribed formats – the balance sheet

We now explain (a) the prescribed formats for balance sheet presentation, (b) the accounting rules that govern the values at which the various assets are included in the balance sheet and (c) the explanatory notes that are required to accompany the balance sheet.

7.9.1 The prescribed format

The Companies Act specifies two formats. Format 1 is a vertical presentation of balances, while Format 2 is a horizontal presentation.

Format 1 contains the following items:

A. Called-up share capital
B. Fixed assets
   I. Intangible assets
   II. Tangible assets
   III. Investments
C. Current assets
   I. Stocks
   II. Debtors
   III. Investments
   IV. Cash at bank and in hand
D. Prepayments
E. Creditors: amounts falling due within one year
F. Net current assets
G. Total assets less current liabilities
H. Creditors: amounts falling due after more than one year
I. Provisions for liabilities and charges
J. Accruals and deferred income
K. Capital and reserves
L. Minority interests

Format 2 requires the same basic disclosure, except that it does not require the amount of the net current assets to be disclosed.

7.9.2 The accounting rules for asset valuation

The Companies Act 1985 provides two sets of accounting rules. These are the historical cost accounting rules and the alternative accounting rules.

The historical cost accounting rules are set out below, referenced to the balance sheet headings used in Format 1.

Balance sheet heading	Historical cost accounting rules
B. Fixed assets	Fixed assets are to be shown at their purchase price or production cost less depreciation.
C. Current assets	Current assets are to be stated at the lower of their net realisable value and their purchase price or production cost.

The alternative accounting rules are set out below, again referenced to the balance sheet headings used in Format 1.

Balance sheet heading	Alternative accounting rules
B. Fixed assets	Intangible fixed assets, other than goodwill, may be included at their current cost. Tangible fixed assets may be included at their market value as at the date of their last valuation or at their current cost.
C. Current assets	Stock may be included at current cost.

The Act does not define current cost and the meaning would depend on whatever accounting standard or guidance happened to be operative at the date the accounts are prepared. In practice, the majority of companies tend to use the historical cost accounting rules modified by the use of the alternative accounting rules as and when all or some of the fixed assets are revalued.

7.9.3 What are the explanatory notes that accompany a balance sheet?

We will consider four types. These are notes:

- showing the make–up of items that appear in the balance sheet;
- making it transparent where there could be conflicts of interest for management and auditors, e.g. related party transactions and audit firm's remuneration;
- providing additional information to assist shareholders assess future cash flows; and
- notes giving information of interest to other stakeholders.

Notes giving greater detail of the make-up of balance sheet figures

Each of the alpha headings may have additional detail disclosed by way of a note to the accounts e.g. fixed assets, current assets and shareholders' funds. We will illustrate the fixed asset and stock notes from The Body Shop International plc 2001 Annual Report.

Fixed assets normally have a fixed asset movements schedule as shown in Figure 7.11. From this the net book value as at 3 March 2001 is read off the total column for inclusion in the balance sheet.

Figure 7.11 The Body Shop International plc – fixed asset company movements

	Freehold property £m	Short-term leaseholds £m	Plant and equipment £m	Total £m
Cost				
At 27 February 2000	0.5	39.3	40.3	80.1
Inter-company transfers		0.3	2.8	3.1
Additions		0.3	3.3	3.6
Disposals	–	–	(0.3)	(0.3)
At 3 March 2001	0.5	39.9	46.1	86.5
Accumulated depreciation				
At 27 February 2000	0.2	12.0	28.0	40.2
Inter-company transfers	–	0.1	1.0	1.1
Charge for year	–	1.1	5.9	7.0
Accelerated depreciation	–	–	0.3	0.3
At 3 March 2001	0.2	13.2	35.2	48.6
Net book value				
At 3 March 2001	0.3	26.7	10.9	37.9
At 27 February 2000	0.3	27.3	12.3	39.9

The stock of £51.3m in The Body Shop International plc 2001 had a note as follows:

	£m
Raw materials and work-in-progress	1.0
Finished goods	50.3
	51.3

Conflicts of interest

Notes drawing attention to the existence of related party transactions
Related party relationships may mean that financial statements include transactions that have not been entered into on an arm's-length basis, which would be the normal assumption made by a user. The objective of FRS 8 *Related Party Disclosures*[21] was to ensure that disclosure drew attention to the fact that the reported financial position and results may have been affected by the existence of related parties and material transactions with them. Disclosure is required of the person controlling the reporting entity and of related party transactions such as the purchase or sale of goods, property or other assets; rendering or receiving services; agency arrangements; leasing arrangements; transfer of research and development; licence agreements; provision of finance and management contracts. As Sir David Tweedie states in the introduction to FRS 8, 'In financial matters it is not enough to look at the puppets; users need to see the strings and know who is pulling them.'

FRS 8[22] defines such a related party relationship as existing when one party has direct or indirect control of the other party, or the parties are subject to common control, or one party has such influence over the financial and operating policies of the other party that the other party might be inhibited from pursuing its own separate interests, or the parties entering into a transaction are subject to such influence from the same source that one party has subordinated its own separate interests.

Although related parties include companies in the same group and associated companies, because information has already been required, e.g. under FRS 2 and FRS 9, the principal impact will be on directors and their close families, pension funds, key management and those controlling 20% or more of the voting rights.

Notes drawing attention to how much auditors are taking out of the company
Shareholders need to form a view on the amount of work that has been undertaken and to be confident that the audit opinion is independent. Until 1989, the disclosed figure represented the amount of remuneration and expenses paid for the conduct of the audit. It did not include fees for non-audit work. By non-audit work we mean any fees paid for accounting services, such as where the client has experienced problems in producing draft accounts and needs assistance; or fees paid for tax advice or management consultancy services. In The Body Shop International plc 1999 Accounts, non-audit fees were £600,000 whilst the audit fee in the same year was £300,000. In the 2001 accounts, audit fees were £500,000 and non-audit fees were £500,000. The concern has been expressed in relation to all companies that the independence of the auditor might be perceived to be less than independent. The profession is aware of the possibility of a credibility gap and has its own rules of professional conduct in which it recognises that undue dependence of an audit client and the provision of other services are both areas of risk.

In relation to fees there is a statement[23] that 'the public's perception of a member's objectivity is likely to be in jeopardy where the fees for the audit and other recurring work paid by one client or group of connected clients exceed 15% of the gross practice income...'

In relation to the provision of other services there is an added risk of the firm being drawn into performing management functions by going beyond an advisory role. A practice, therefore, should endeavour to ensure that the recurring fee paid by one client or group of connected clients does not exceed 15% of the gross fees of the practice.

Notes providing additional information to assist shareholders assess future cash flows

These are notes intended to assist in predicting future cash flows. They give information on matters such as capital commitments that have been contracted for but not provided in the accounts, and capital commitments that have been authorised but not contracted for; future commitments, e.g. share options that have been granted; and contingent liabilities, e.g. guarantees given by the company in respect of overdraft facilities arranged by subsidiary companies or customers.

Notes giving information of interest to other stakeholders

We could place the disclosure relating to staff into this category. Directors are required to provide information on staff in categories determined by the directors, having regard to the manner in which the company's activities are organised. This information is not required to be categorised in any particular way, but it is likely that most businesses would categorise the information, possibly following the business segments and acquisitions as in the 2001 Annual Report of Anglian Water plc in Figure 7.12.

Anglian Water are expanding their operations and the business segment illustrates the growth of overseas operations.

The presentation in the Allied Domecq 2000 Annual Report was influenced by the scale of discontinued operations in 1999 as shown in Figure 7.13.

The information is useful in the context of reporting to employees. However, there is no standard form of presenting it, and it is not completely adequate for the prediction of cash flows. Staff cost information is also provided as a note but it is not analysed into the expense headings that are used in the profit and loss account and so, although the total cost is given, this is not necessarily broken down into cost of sales, distribution costs and administrative expenses.

Figure 7.12 Anglian Water plc Annual Report 2001 – employee information

	2001	2000	1999
Water and waste water services	3,799	4,041	4,305
International	3,409	2,556	739
Facilities management	417	290	241
Morrison	4,054	–	–
Other	11	12	12

Figure 7.13 Allied Domecq plc Annual Report 2001 – average number employed

	Full-Time		Part-Time		
	UK	Other	UK	Other	Total
2001 – Continuing operations	1,547	7,531	106	601	9,785
2000 – Continuing operations	1,745	8,104	90	993	10,932
1999 – Continuing operations	2,119	8,192	127	907	11,345
1999 – Discontinued operations	9,224	319	19,607	–	29,150

7.10 True and fair requirement

The Companies Act 1985 requires financial statements to give a true and fair view of the profit or loss for the financial year and the state of affairs at the end of the year via the profit and loss account and balance sheet respectively.[24]

True and fair is a legal concept and can be authoritatively decided only by a court. However the courts have never attempted to define true and fair. In the UK the Accounting Standards Committee (ASC) obtained a legal opinion which included the following statement:[25]

It is however important to observe that the application of the concept involves

- **Judgement in questions of degree**. The information contained in the accounts must be accurate and comprehensive to within acceptable limits. What is acceptable and how is this to be achieved?

- **Reasonable businessmen and accountants may differ over the degree of accuracy** or comprehensiveness which in particular cases the accounts should attain.

- Equally, there may sometimes be **room for differences over the method** to adopt in order to give a true and fair view, cases in which there may be more than one true and fair view of the same financial position.

- Again, because true and fair involves questions of degree, we think that **cost effectiveness must play a part** in deciding the amount of information which is sufficient to make accounts true and fair.

- Accounts will not be true and fair unless the information they contain is **sufficient in quantity and quality to satisfy the reasonable expectations** of the readers to whom they are addressed.

A further counsel's opinion was attained by the Accounting Standards Board (ASB) in 1991[26] and published in its foreword to *Accounting Standards*. It advised that accounting standards are an authoritative source of accounting practice and it is now the norm for financial statements to comply with them. In consequence the court may take accounting standards into consideration when forming an opinion on whether the financial statements give a true and fair view.

7.10.1 True and fair override

The ASB recognises that there may be occasions when application of an SSAP or FRS might be misleading and departure from FRS treatment is permitted. This is referred to as the true and fair override provision. If a company makes use of the override it is required to explain why compliance with IASs would be misleading and also give sufficient information to enable the user to calculate the adjustments required to comply with the standard.

The true and fair concept is familiar to the Anglo–Saxon and Netherlands accounting profession. Many countries, however, viewed the concept of the true and fair view with suspicion since it ran counter to their legal systems. In Germany the true and fair override provision has not been directly implemented and laws are interpreted according to their function and objectives. It appears that the role of true and fair in the European context is to act as a protection against over-regulation.[27] Since the wider acceptance of IASs has been occurring in recent years, the financial statements of many more companies and countries are fulfilling the principle of a true and fair view.

Examples of use of true and fair override

Taken literally, true implies that the information is accurate, i.e. in accordance with properly maintained accounting records. Fair implies that it is not misleading.

The following is an extract from the 2001 Annual Report of Severn Trent plc.

Grants and contributions received

Grants and contributions relating to infrastructure assets have been deducted from the cost of fixed assets. This is not in accordance with Schedule 4 to the Act, which requires assets to be shown at their purchase price or production cost and hence grants and contributions to be presented as deferred income. This departure from the requirements of the Act is, in the opinion of the Directors, necessary to give a true and fair view as, while a provision is made for depreciation of infrastructure assets, these assets do not have determinable finite lives and therefore no basis exists on which to recognise grants and contributions as deferred income. The effect of this departure is that the cost of fixed assets is £276.6 million lower than it would otherwise have been (2000: £236.1 million).

7.11 Additional information in the annual report

Legislation such as the Companies Act 1985 in the UK requires that additional information is included in the annual report such as a directors' report. As well as statutory information, many companies choose to give additional information with such things as operating and financial reviews, chairman's statements or business summaries. Around the world, the names and formats of the additional information does change, but the actual information included is often of a similar nature.

7.11.1 Information appearing in board or directors' reports

The typical type of information that appears in board or directors' reports might be as follows.

● Information about the business activities which includes:
  – details about principal activities during the year and any significant changes;
  – a fair review of the development of the business of the company during the year and of its position at the end of the year,[28] e.g. comment on the development of new markets, comment on any significant rationalisation involving discontinuing segments of the business, etc.;
  – likely future developments;
  – research and development activity undertaken during the year;

- significant changes in the fixed assets of the company during the year;
- any important events affecting the company which have occurred since the end of the financial year.

● Information allowing shareholders to assess asset backing which includes a note of the amount if the market value of land and buildings differs materially from the book values; this gives shareholders a view of the asset backing in determining the value of their shares.

● Information making shareholders aware of material movements in the ownership of the issued share capital which includes:
- share interests that exceed 3% of the nominal capital of the company (3% is UK disclosure guidance);
- the purchase of own shares;
- shares of the company in which directors have an interest.

● Information indicating the company's activities in the community which includes:
- political and charitable donations;
- policy in respect of applications for employment by disabled applicants;
- actions taken in respect of employee reports and consultation.

The information in the report requires a number of judgements to be made, e.g. a fair review, significant changes and any important events. Because it involves judgement and opinion (which is not easily verified), the director's report is not usually audited but may be reviewed by the auditor to ensure it does not conflict with the financial data.

7.11.2 What does a directors' report look like?

The paragraph headings from The Body Shop International plc 2001 Annual Report are set out in Figure 7.14 as an illustration of the type of information contained in a published set of accounts. The following extract indicates the culture of a company in respect

Figure 7.14 Directors' report

Principal activities	Group business review	Results and dividends
Annual general meeting	Directors	Fixed assets
Supplier payment policy	Share capital	Substantial shareholdings
Disabled employees	Employee involvement	Research and development
Donations	Auditors	Corporate governance

Note: Corporate governance is covered in a report by considering such items as:

● Board of directors and board committees
- the audit committee
- the remuneration and nominations committee
● Internal financial control
● Going concern
● Auditor's review.

of employee and commercial issues, and illustrates how the report has become almost an index for other sources of financial information:

The directors submit their report and accounts for the 52 weeks ended 3 March 2001.

Principal activities
The Group develops and sells skin and hair care products through its own shops and franchised outlets.

Group business review and future developments
A review of the Group's business during the year is contained in the chief executive's report on pages 6 to 8, and in the performance review on pages 9 to 24.

Suppliers and supply chain management
The Body Shop believes that its relationships with its suppliers should be commercially viable, mutually beneficial and based on trust and respect. As part of the social audit process, relationships with our suppliers are surveyed and reported upon. Our policy is to pay suppliers in accordance with terms that have been mutually agreed in advance.

Employees and employee involvement
The Body Shop aims to nurture a committed and motivated employee group with improving skills and knowledge. The Company's policy is for training, career development and promotion opportunities to be available to all employees. Applications for employment by disabled people are given full and fair consideration for all vacancies, taking into account their particular skills and abilities. If an employee becomes disabled while working for the Company, every effort is made to retain them.

Donations
Please see page 19 for details of charitable contributions [this described efforts to encourage employee contributions and noted that Group charitable donations totalled £0.9m in 2001 mainly via The Body Shop Foundation]. No political donations were made by the Group.

The items in Figure 7.14 have grown on an *ad hoc* basis and are a mixture of items – some that relate to the company from a business perspective such as the fair review requirement, others that appear for public policy reasons such as political and charitable donations and the employment of the disabled. The consultation document issued by The Company Law Review Steering Committee proposes that for all companies the directors' report should cease on the grounds that much of the information would be superseded by the new OFR proposed by the Committee. For companies not preparing an OFR, the existing directors' report items would be included in a new supplementary statement accompanying the accounts.[29]

7.11.3 Chief executive's report

The directors' report was supported by statements from the co-chairs and the chief executive. A brief extract from The Body Shop International plc 2001 Annual Report illustrates the type of information provided:

From the Co-Chairs

Like all journeys it has not always been easy. Over the last two years, we have been trans-forming the structure of the business to ensure that The Body Shop will continue its success as a global retailer with a unique heritage. We recognised the need to create an organisation which was more responsive to servicing our customers around the world. This has involved regionalising our management structure, reorganising our supply chain, selling our manufacturing business and concentrating our resources on our core retail business. Although we underestimated the amount of short-term disruption that this transformation would cause, we are confident that it is the right strategy for the long-term success of The Body Shop.

From the Chief Executive

Overview

We are reporting a pre-tax profit of £25.0 million (before exceptional items and restruc-turing costs) ... This is below our expectations ... However, we are confident that the strategy now in place will deliver results over the medium and long term .... Last year we did not deliver on the implementation of our strategy for three principal reasons ... We have already taken steps to address each of these issues.

Results summary

Worldwide retail sales increased by 7% to £691.4 million, with growth being achieved across all regions. Total sales growth was underpinned by 111 new store openings during the year, bringing the total to 1,841 stores by the year end. On a comparable store basis, sales were up 1% year on year, with all regions other than the UK recording positive growth.

Current year priorities

Our overall strategy for the current year is to deliver increased value for all of our stakeholders. We have set three principal objectives: to enhance The Body Shop brand through a focused product strategy and increased investment in stores; to achieve operational efficiencies in our supply chain by reducing product and inventory costs; and to reinforce our stakeholder culture.

7.11.4 Operating and financial review

The operating and financial review statement (referred to as a performance review) appearing in The Body Shop International plc 2001 Annual Report disclosed the following financial review extracts:

Retail sales

In the 53 weeks ended 3 March 2001, total retail sales across all The Body Shop outlets grew by 7% to £691.4 million, with comparable store sales up by 1% year on year. After 111 store openings during the year, the number of stores worldwide totalled 1,841 at the year end, of which 488 were company-owned (2000: 437) and the remainder franchised.

Approximately 150 store openings are anticipated in the current year. Worldwide customer transactions were 4% lower than in the previous year at 77.4 million, with the average transaction value increasing by 11% to £8.94.

Operating performance

Group turnover for the year increased by 13% to £374.1 million, with 61% representing net sales through company-owned stores, mail order and The Body Shop Direct compared with 55% in the previous year. The balance of group turnover principally represents wholesale sales to franchisees.

Gross profit was 13% higher at £225.1 million (2000: £199.2 million), with gross margin broadly level year on year at 60.2% (2000: 60.3%). The margin benefit that was gained from the higher proportion of retail turnover was offset by the impact of the euro exchange rate on sales to the European region and lower margins on some newer products.

7.12 Impact of differing accounting practices on interpretation of performance

The differing accounting methods that can be adopted around the world have an affect on the apparent performance of companies and make global inter-company comparison difficult. Reconciliations between different versions of GAAP improve the comparability but real comparability will only be achieved if accounting treatments are unified.

The European Commission has set a deadline of 2005 for companies in Europe to prepare their consolidated accounts in accordance with IAS. It is interesting therefore to consider the impact on a company that has reconciled to IAS from national standards.

To illustrate the impact that different versions of GAAP can have on the performance interpretation of companies, key ratios based on the financial statements of the Incentive Group 1999 financial statements have been calculated using Danish GAAP and the restated position for IAS.

The extract from which the financial ratios are calculated is shown in Figure 7.15.

The alteration in the ratios shown in Figure 7.15 have been caused by the following accounting policy changes that were necessary to restate the financial statements from Danish GAAP to IAS.

- Goodwill: Under IAS goodwill is capitalised and amortised over its useful life which cannot exceed twenty years.

- Development costs: Development costs have been capitalised and amortised under IAS over a life not exceeding five years.

- Inventory measurement: Production overheads are included in the measurement of inventories and allocated on a pro rata basis to cost of goods sold.

- Deferred tax: Deferred tax assets related to tax loss carry-forwards are capitalised or set off against deferred tax liabilities provided that the losses are likely to be utilised in the future.

Figure 7.15 Incentive Group – changes in accounting policy to IAS

	Before change in accounting policies	Effect of change in accounting policies	After change in accounting policies
Effect on the consolidated income statement 1999 (DKKm)			
Net sales	3,451		3,451
Gross margin	1,357	(236)	1,121
Operating profit before amortisation of goodwill etc.	1	13	14
Operating income	17	(61)	(44)
Ordinary income before tax	(68)	(61)	(129)
Net income	**(98)**	**6**	**(92)**
Effect on the consolidated balance sheet 1999 (DKKm)			
Intangibles	7	1,486	1,493
Property, plant and equipment	676		676
Investments	147		147
Inventories etc.	624	34	658
Receivables	818	206	1,024
Cash and cash equivalents	220		220
Total asset	**2,492**	**1,726**	**4,218**
Stockholders' equity	(57)	1,659	1,602
Allowances	186	67	253
Long-term and short-term debt *	2,363		2,363
Total liabilities and shareholders' equity	**2,492**	**1,726**	**4,218**

Effect 1998–1999 for the group DKKm	1999	1998
Net income before change in accounting policies	**(98)**	**152**
- Production overheads	0	0
- Amortisation of goodwill	(74)	(43)
- Development costs	13	(2)
- Warranty and pension allowances	0	5
- Tax	67	(19)
Net effect of the change in accounting policies	**6**	**(69)**
Net income after change in accounting policies	**(92)**	**83**
Total assets before change in accounting policies	**2,492**	**2,248**
- Production overheads	34	31
- Goodwill	1,405	686
- Development costs	81	61
- Tax assets	206	92
Net effect of the change in accounting policies	**1,727**	**870**
Total assets after change in accounting policies	**4,218**	**3,118**

Figure 7.15 (*cont.*)

Total liabilities before change in accounting policies	2,492	2,248
Stockholders' equity before change	(57)	930
- Production overheads	34	31
- Goodwill	1,405	686
- Development costs	81	61
- Warranty and pension allowances	(28)	(28)
- Tax	167	(9)
Net effect on stockholders' equity	1,659	741
Allowances and debt before change	2,549	1,318
- Warranty and pension allowances	28	28
- Tax	39	101
Net effect on allowances and debt	67	129
Total liabilities after change in accounting policies	4,218	3,118

* The short- and long-term debt includes short-term debt of DKK1,227m and long-term debt of DKK1,136m.

Ratio	Danish GAAP	IAS GAAP
Return on capital employed		
Operating income/total assets less current liabilities	1.3	(1.5%)
Operating profit margin		
Operating profit/sales	0.5%	(1.3%)
Current ratio		
Current assets/current liabilities	1.35	1.55
Gearing		
Long-term debt/total assets less current liabilities	89.8%	38%
Earnings per share		
Net income/number of shares	DKK(18.1)	DKK(17)

Summary

The published accounts of a listed company are intended to provide a report to enable shareholders to assess current year stewardship and management performance and to predict future cash flows. In order to assess stewardship and management performance, there have been mandatory requirements for standardised presentation, using formats prescribed by statute and accounting standards. There have also been mandatory requirements for the disclosure of accounting policies, which allow shareholders to make comparisons between years. As regards future cash flows, these are normally perceived to be influenced by past profits, the asset base (as shown in the balance sheet) and any significant changes. In order to assist shareholders to predict future cash flows with an understanding of the risks involved, more information has been required by the ASB.

This has taken two forms:

- more quantitative information in the accounts, e.g. segmental analysis and the impact of changes on the operation, e.g. a breakdown of turnover, costs and profits for both new and discontinued operations; and

- more qualitative information, e.g. the operating and financial review, related party disclosures, effect of changes in accounting policy.

REVIEW QUESTIONS

1 Explain why two companies carrying out identical transactions could produce different gross profit figures.

2 Classify the following items into cost of sales, distribution costs, administrative expenses, other operating income or item to be disclosed after trading profit:

   (a) personnel department costs

   (b) computer department costs

   (c) profit on sale of fixed assets

   (d) bad debts

   (e) provision for warranty claims

   (f) loss on sale of fixed assets

   (g) interest on funds borrowed to finance an increase in working capital

   (h) interest on funds borrowed to finance the construction of fixed assets.

3 A Format 1 profit and loss account contains the following profit figures: gross profit; trading profit; profit on ordinary activities before tax; profit on ordinary activities after tax; and profit for the year.

   Explain how each is derived and when you would use each profit figure for analysis purposes, e.g. trading profit may be used to calculate the percentage return on capital employed.

4 Explain the changes proposed by FRED 22 and how your analysis of a set of accounts will be affected following the adoption of FRED 22 as an FRS.

5 'Companies should begin to move to greater disclosure of:

● Days training per year for categories of staff.

● Expenditure on training, both in total and differentiated between categories of employees. This could be supplemented with information regarding the spread of expenditure during the year. This is most likely to be best presented in diagrammatic form.

● Career and development policy, both vertically and horizontally. A short statement setting out the relevance of the approach to the future of the company and how management plan to deal with it should be provided and could, over time, be extended to include information on staff turnover rates, average length of service, costs of recruitment, voluntary payments on termination of employment and number of professionally qualified staff.'[30]

(a) Discuss the extent to which this information would assist the investor to:

(i) assess stewardship performance;

(ii) predict future cash flows.

(b) Discuss the extent to which the annual report should contain the information suggested in the CIMA publication and the reasons for its inclusion.

6 What are the fundamental objectives of corporate reports?[31]

7 'A single set of multi-purpose financial statements are unable to satisfy the needs of shareholders for both a stewardship report and a report to assist the prediction of future cash flows.' Discuss.

8 Discuss the relevance of the information in the statement of total recognised gains and losses to an investor. Explain the advantages and disadvantages of combining the profit and loss account and statement into a single report.

9 Describe the content of an OFR statement and discuss whether it should be made mandatory, more prescriptive and audited.

EXERCISES

An extract from the solution is provided in the appendix at the end of the text for exercises marked with an asterisk (*).

* Question 1

The following trial balance was extracted from the books of Old plc on 31 December 20X1.

	£000	£000
Sales		12,050
Returns outwards		313
Provision for depreciation		
plant		738
vehicles		375
Rent receivable		100
Trade creditors		738
Debentures		250
Issued share capital – ordinary £1 shares		3,125
– preference shares		625
Share premium		250
Profit and loss account balance		875
Stock	825	
Purchases	6,263	
Returns inwards	350	
Carriage inwards	13	
Carriage outwards	125	
Salesmen's salaries	800	
Administrative wages and salaries	738	
Plant (includes £362 acquired in 20X1)	1,562	
Motor vehicles	1,125	
Goodwill	1,062	
Distribution expenses	290	
Administrative expenses	286	
Directors' remuneration	375	
Trade debtors	3,875	
Cash at bank and in hand	1,750	
	19,439	19,439

Note of information not taken into the trial balance data:

(a) Provide for:
   (i) An audit fee of £38,000.
   (ii) Depreciation of plant at 20% straight-line.
   (iii) Depreciation of vehicles at 25% reducing balance.
   (iv) Amortise the goodwill over six years.
   (v) Corporation tax of £562,000.
   (vi) Debenture interest of £25,000.
   (vii) A preference dividend of 8%.

(viii) An ordinary dividend of 10p per share.

(b) Closing stock was valued at £1,125,000 at the lower of cost and net realisable value.

(c) Administrative expenses were prepaid by £12,000.

Required:
(a) **Prepare a profit and loss account for internal use for the year ended 31 December 20X1.**
(b) **Prepare a profit and loss account for the year ended 31 December 20X1 and a balance sheet as at that date in Format 1 style of presentation.**

* Question 2

UKAY plc has prepared its draft trial balance to 30 June 20X1, which is shown below.

The authorised share capital is 4,000,000 9% preference shares of £1 each and 18,000,000 ordinary shares of 50p each.

Trial balance at 30 June 20X1

	£000	£000
Freehold land	2,880	
Freehold buildings (cost £4,680)	4,126	
Plant and machinery (cost £3,096)	1,858	
Fixtures and fittings (cost £864)	691	
Goodwill	480	
Trade debtors	7,263	
Trade creditors		2,591
Stock	11,794	
Bank balance	11,561	
Income tax on loan interest	151	
Development grant received		85
Profit on sale of freehold land		536
Sales		381,600
Cost of sales	318,979	
Administration expenses	9,000	
Distribution costs	35,100	
Directors' emoluments	562	
Bad debts	157	
Auditors' remuneration	112	
Hire of plant and machinery	2,400	
Loan interest paid net	454	
Dividends paid during the year – preference	162	
– ordinary	426	
9% loan		7,200
Share capital – preference shares		3,600
– ordinary shares		5,400
Profit and loss account		6,364
Revaluation account		780
	408,156	408,156

The following information is available:

1 The depreciation policy of the company is to provide depreciation at the following rates:

Plant and machinery	20% on cost
Fixtures and fittings	10% on cost
Buildings	2% on cost

In addition, it has been decided to create a Reserve of 10% on the cost of plant and machinery to allow for the increased cost of replacement. (Depreciation for 20X1 has not been provided in the draft trial balance.) Charge all depreciation to cost of sales.

2 Acquisitions of fixed assets during the year were:

Plant	£173,000	Fixtures	£144,000

3 Government grants of £85,000 have been received in respect of plant purchased during the year and are shown in the trial balance.

4 During the year freehold land which cost £720,000 was sold for £2,036,000. It was valued in last year's balance sheet at £1,500,000. The revaluation surplus had been credited to revaluation reserve.

5 Stock shown in the trial balance (£11,794,000) consists of:

Raw materials	£1,872,000
Work-in-progress	£6,660,000
Finished goods	£3,262,000

6 Trade debtors and creditors are all payable and due within the next financial year. The loan is unsecured and repayable in ten years' time.

7 During the year a fire took place at one of the company's depots, involving losses of £200,000. These losses have been written off to cost of sales shown in the trial balance. Since the end of the financial year a settlement of £150,000 has been agreed with the company's insurers.

8 It is agreed that £500,000 of the finished goods stock is obsolete and should be written off. However, since the end of the financial year an offer has been received from another company to buy this stock for £300,000, subject to certain modifications being made at an estimated cost to UKAY plc of £50,000. This has now been agreed.

9 A contract has been entered into, with a building contractor, to extend the company's premises. The contract price is £5,000,000 and the work is scheduled to start in December 20X1.

10 A final ordinary dividend of 3p per share is proposed, together with the balance of the preference dividend.

11 The corporation tax charge in the profit and loss account is to be that based on the net profit for the year, at a rate of 35%.

12 Goodwill is to be amortised over 5 years.

Required:

(a) **Prepare the company's profit and loss account for the year to 30 June 20X1 and a balance sheet as at that date, complying with the Companies Act 1985 and relevant accounting standards in so far as the information given permits.**
(All calculations to nearest £000.)
(b) **Prepare the tangible fixed asset schedule for the notes to the accounts.**

Question 3

Basalt plc is a wholesaler. The following is its trial balance as at 31 December 20X0.

	£000	£000
Ordinary share capital: £1 shares		300
Share premium		20
General reserve		16
Profit and loss account as at 1 January 20X0		55
Stock as at 1 January 20X0	66	
Sales		962
Purchases	500	
Administrative expenses	10	
Distribution expenses	6	
Plant and machinery – cost	220	
Plant and machinery – provision for depreciation		49
Returns outwards		25
Returns inwards	27	
Carriage inwards	9	
Warehouse wages	101	
Salesmen's salaries	64	
Administrative wages and salaries	60	
Hire of motor vehicles	19	
Directors' remuneration	30	
Rent receivable		7
Trade debtors	326	
Cash at bank	62	
Trade creditors		66
	1,500	1,500

The following additional information is supplied:
 (i) Depreciate plant and machinery 20% on straight-line basis.
 (ii) Stock at 31 December 20X0 is £90,000.
 (iii) Accrue auditors' remuneration £2,000.
 (iv) Corporation tax for the year will be £58,000 payable October 20X1.
 (v) There is a proposed ordinary dividend of £75,000 for the year.
 (vi) It is estimated that 7/11 of the plant and machinery is used in connection with distribution, with the remainder for administration. The motor vehicle costs should be assigned to distribution.

Required:
(a) Prepare a profit and loss account and balance sheet in a form that complies with the Companies Act 1985. No notes to the accounts are required.
(b) Briefly explain what you would expect to find in the following sections of an annual report:
     (i) Directors' report.
     (ii) Chairman's report.
     (iii) Auditors' report.

Question 4

Fresno Group plc have prepared their financial statements for the year ended 31 January 20X4. However, the financial accountant of Fresno Group plc had difficulty in preparing the statements required by FRS 3 *Reporting Financial Performance* and approached you for help in preparing those statements. The accountant furnished you with the following information:

(i)

Fresno Group plc profit and loss account extract for year ended
31 January 20X4

	£m
Operating profit – continuing operations	290
Profit on sale of property in continuing operations	10
Profit on ordinary activities before taxation	300
Tax on ordinary activities	(90)
Profit after taxation	210
Dividends	(15)
Retained profit for year	195

The accountant did not provide for the loss on any discontinued operations in the profit and loss account. (However, you may assume that the taxation provision incorporated the effects of any provision for discontinued operations.)

(ii) The shareholders' funds at the beginning of the financial year were as follows:

	£m
Share capital – £1 ordinary shares	350
Share premium	55
Revaluation reserve	215
Profit and loss reserve	775
	1,395

(iii) Fresno Group plc regularly revalues its fixed assets, and at 31 January 20X4 a revaluation surplus of £375m had been credited to the revaluation reserve. During the financial year, a property had been sold on which a revaluation surplus of £54m had been credited to reserves. Further, if the company had charged depreciation on a historical cost basis rather than the revalued amounts, the depreciation charge in the profit and loss account for fixed assets would have been £7m. The current year's charge for depreciation was £16m.

(iv) The group has a policy of writing off goodwill on the acquisition of subsidiaries over ten years. The goodwill charge for the period amounted to £250m. In order to facilitate the purchase of subsidiaries, the company had issued £1 ordinary shares of nominal value £150m and share premium of £450m. All subsidiaries are currently 100% owned by the group.

(v) During the financial year to 31 January 20X4, the company had made a decision to close a 100% owned subsidiary, Reno plc. However, the closure did not take place until May 20X4. Fresno Group plc estimated that as at 31 January 20X4 the operating loss for the period 1 February 20X4 to 31 May 20X4 would be £30m and that in addition redundancy costs, stock and plant write-downs would amount to £15m. In the event, the operating loss for the period 1 February 20X4 to 31 May 20X4 was £65m, but the redundancy costs, stock and plant write downs amounted to only £12m.

(vi) The following information relates to Reno plc for the period 1 February 20X4 to 31 May 20X4.

	£m
Turnover	175
Cost of sales	(195)
Gross loss	(20)
Administrative expenses	(15)
Selling expenses	(30)
Operating loss before taxation	(65)

Required:

(a) Prepare the following statements in accordance with current statutory requirements and FRS 3 *Reporting Financial Performance* for Fresno Group plc for the year ending 31 January 20X4.
   (i) Statement of total recognised gains and losses.
   (ii) Reconciliation of movements in shareholders' funds.
   (iii) Analysis of movements on reserves.
   (iv) Note of historical cost profits and losses.

(b) Explain the reasons why the ASB required companies to produce the information in (i)–(iv) above.

(c) Appraise the information prepared in (a)(i)–(a)(iv) above.

(d) Explain to the accountant:
   (i) How the decision to close the subsidiary, Reno plc, affects the financial statements of Fresno Group plc for the year ended 31 January 20X4.
   (ii) How the subsidiary, Reno plc, should be dealt with in the financial statements of Fresno Group plc for the year ended 31 January 20X5.

Question 5

Phoenix plc trial balance at 30 June 20X7 was as follows:

	£000	£000
Freehold premises	2,400	
Plant and machinery	1,800	540
Furniture and fittings	620	360
Stock at 30 June 20X7	1,468	
Sales		6,465
Administrative expenses	1,126	
Ordinary shares of £1 each		4,500
Trade investments	365	
Revaluation reserve		600
Development cost	415	
Share premium		500
Personal ledger balances	947	566
Cost of goods sold	4,165	
Distribution costs	669	
Over-provision for tax		26
Dividend received		80
Interim dividend paid	200	
Profit and loss account		488
Disposal of warehouse		225
Cash and bank balances	175	

The following information is available:

1 Freehold premises acquired for £1.8 million were revalued in 20X4, recognising a gain of £600,000 These include a warehouse, which cost £120,000, was revalued at £150,000 and was sold in June 20X7 for £225,000. Phoenix does not depreciate freehold premises.

2 Phoenix wishes to report plant and machinery at open market value which is estimated to be £1,960,000 on 1 July 20X6.

3 Company policy is to depreciate its assets on the straight-line method at annual rates as follows:

Plant and machinery   10%
Furniture and fittings   5%

4 Until this year the company's policy has been to capitalise development costs, to the extent permitted by relevant accounting standard. The company has decided to write off all such expenses, including £124,000 incurred in the year.

5 During the year the company has issued one million shares of £1 at £1.20 each

6 Included within administrative expenses are the following:

Staff salary (including £125,000 to directors)   £468,000
Directors' fees   £96,000
Audit fees and expenses   £86,000

7 Corporation tax for the year is estimated at £122,000.

8 Directors propose a final dividend of 4p per share.

Required:
(a) In respect of the year ended 30 June 20X7:
the profit and loss account;
the statement of total recognised gains and losses;
the note on historical cost profit and loss;
the reconciliation of shareholders' funds.
(b) The balance sheet as at 30 June 20X7.
(c) The statement of movement of tangible fixed assets.

References

1 Companies Act 1985, Schedule 4, para. 8.
2 FRS 3, *Reporting Financial Performance*, ASB, October 1992.
3 *Ibid.*, paras 41–45.
4 *Ibid.*, Dissenting View.
5 *Ibid.*, para. 18.
6 *Ibid.*, para. 20.
7 *Ibid.*, para. 19.
8 FRED 22 *Revision of FRS 3 Reporting Financial Performance*, ASB, December 2000, paras 63–64.
9 *Ibid.*, para. 1.
10 IAS 8 *Net Profit or Loss for the Period, Fundamental Errors and Changes in Accounting Policies*, IASC, revised 1993, para. 14.
11 SSAP 25 *Segmental Reporting*, ASB, June 1990, paras 7–16.
12 FRS 3 *Reporting Financial Performance*, ASB, October 1992, para. 56.
13 FRED 22 *Revision of FRS 3 Reporting Financial Performance*, ASB, 2000, Appendix, 4 para. 26.
14 *Ibid.*, para. 1.
15 *Ibid.*, summary (m).
16 G4 + 1, *Reporting Financial Performance*, 1997.
17 FRED 22 *Revision of FRS 3 Reporting Financial Performance*, ASB, 2000, Appendix 4, para. 15.
18 *Ibid.*, Appendix 4, para. 16.
19 *Ibid.*, paras 93–95.
20 R. Paterson, 'A remarkable performance', *Accountancy*, February 2001, p. 94.
21 FRS 8 *Related Party Disclosures*, ASB, 1995, para. 1.
22 *Ibid.*, para. 2.5.
23 ACCA Rulebook, January 2001, para. 3.2.
24 Companies Act 1985, section 228.
25 K. Wild and A. Guida, *Touche Ross Manual of Financial Reporting and Accounting* (3rd edition), Butterworth, 1990, p. 433.
26 K. Wild and C. Goodhead, *Touche Ross Financial Reporting Manual* (4th edition), Butterworth, 1994, p. 5.
27 'Differing views on true and fair', *Certified Accountant*, October 1994, p. 12.
28 Companies Act 1985, section 235.
29 *Modern Company Law for a Competitive Economy – Final Report*, DTI, July 2001, para. 8.68.
30 CIMA, *Corporate Reporting – The Management Interface*, CIMA, 1990, p. 27.
31 V. Beatty and M. Jones, 'Company reporting: the US leads the way', *Certified Accountant*, March 1994, p. 50.

CHAPTER 8

Preparation of published accounts

8.1 Introduction

In this chapter we illustrate the preparation of a profit and loss account and balance sheet using Format 1 from trial balance to published accounts. We then take into account the effects of FRS 3. We follow a progressive stage approach to the problem.

Stage 1 is the preparation of the internal profit and loss account from the trial balance data. Stage 2 is the preparation of a profit and loss account in Format 1. Stage 3 is the preparation of a balance sheet in Format 1 style. The aim is that you should be able to prepare a set of accounts that conform to the prescribed formats and that you should also understand how a company arrives at the figures that appear in the published financial statements that it presents to its shareholders.

8.2 Stage 1: preparation of the internal profit and loss account from a trial balance

In this chapter we use Format 1, i.e. the vertical format, with costs analysed according to the type of operation.[1]

The data given in Figure 8.1 are available for Illustrious plc for the year ended 31 December 20X1. The following information has not yet been taken into account in the amounts shown in the trial balance.

- Stock at cost at 31 December 20X1 was £22,875,000. Stock at net realisable value at 31 December 20X1 was £3,000,000. The cost of this stock was £4,000,000. The reduction to net realisable value was necessitated because the customer who would normally have taken the products assembled from these stock items had gone into liquidation.

- Depreciation is to be provided as follows:

  2% on freehold buildings using the straight-line method;

  10% on equipment using the reducing balance method;

  25% on motor vehicles using reducing balance.

- £2,300,000 was prepaid for repairs and £5,175,000 has accrued for wages.

Figure 8.1 Trial balance of Illustrious plc as at 31 December 20X1

	£000	£000
Bank interest	1,150	
Bank overdraft		8,625
Cash in hand	4,600	
Debentures		63,250
Debtors	28,750	
Depreciation – equipment		3,450
– motor vehicles		9,200
Directors' remuneration	1,150	
Dividends	1,725	
Equipment	14,950	
Fees – audit	1,150	
Freehold land	57,500	
Freehold buildings	57,500	
Hire charges	300	
Interest on debentures	6,325	
Issued share capital		17,250
Lighting and power	920	
Miscellaneous expenses	275	
Motor expenses	9,200	
Motor vehicles	20,700	
Post, telephone, courier	1,840	
Profit and loss account		57,500
Provision for corporation tax		5,750
Purchases	258,750	
Rates and insurance	3,450	
Repairs and maintenance	2,760	
Salaries and wages	18,055	
Tax – corporation	5,750	
Sales		345,000
Stock at 1 Jan 20X1	43,125	
Trade creditors		29,900
	539,925	539,925

A profit and loss account prepared for internal purposes is set out in Figure 8.2. We have arranged the expenses in the profit and loss account in descending monetary value. This is not a prescribed method and companies may organise the items in a number of ways, such as alphabetical sequence or grouping by function, e.g. establishment, administration, selling, distribution and financial expenses.

Figure 8.2 Profit and loss account of Illustrious plc for the year ended 31 December 20X1

	£000	£000
Sales		345,000
Less:		
Opening stock	43,125	
Purchases	258,750	
	301,875	
Closing stock	25,875	
Cost of sales		276,000
Gross profit		69,000
Less: Expenses:		
Salaries and wages	23,230	
Motor expenses	9,200	
Debenture interest	6,325	
Depreciation	5,175	
Rates and insurance	3,450	
Post, telephone, courier	1,840	
Fees – audit	1,150	
Bank interest	1,150	
Directors' remuneration	1,150	
Lighting and power	920	
Repairs and maintenance	460	
Hire charges	300	
Miscellaneous expenses	275	
		54,625
Profit before tax		14,375
Tax		5,750
Profit after tax		8,625
Dividends		1,725
Amount transferred to reserves		6,900

8.3 Stage 2: preparation of the profit and loss account of Illustrious plc in Format 1 style

The information contained in the internal profit and loss account in Figure 8.2 needs to be redrafted into the format required by the Companies Act. In addition, specific information that would not necessarily appear within the format information needs to be disclosed. First we redraft using Format 1 with its vertical presentation and costs analysed according to type of operations, as set out in Figure 8.3.

Figure 8.3 Illustrious plc profit and loss account redrafted into Format I style

Profit and loss account of Illustrious plc
for the year ended 31 December 20X1

	£000
Turnover	345,000.00
Cost of sales	293,422.50
Gross profit	51,577.50
Distribution, selling and marketing costs	25,041.25
Administrative expenses	4,686.25
Operating profit	21,850.00
Interest payable	7,475.00
Profit on ordinary activities before tax	14,375.00
Tax	5,750.00
Profit on ordinary activities after tax	8,625.00
Dividends	1,725.00
Amount transferred to reserves	6,900.00

		£000	Cost of sales £000	Distribution costs £000	Administration expenses £000
Cost of sales		276,000	276,000		
Salaries and wages	NI	23,230	12,075	10,580	575
Motor expenses		9,200		9,200	
Depreciation	N2	5,175	1,150	3,450	575
Rates and insurance	N3	3,450	1,725	862.5	862.5
Post, telephone, courier	N3	1,840	920	460	460
Fees – audit		1,150			1,150
Directors' salaries	N4	1,150	575		575
Lighting and power	N3	920	460	230	230
Repairs and maintenance	N3	460	230	115	115
Hire charges	N3	300	150	75	75
Miscellaneous expenses	N3	275	137.5	68.75	68.75
		323,150	293,422.5	25,041.25	4,686.25

Interest will be disclosed after the trading profit:

	£000
Debenture interest	6,325
Bank interest	1,150
	7,475

8.3.1 How did we arrive at the figures for cost of sales, distribution costs and administrative expenses?

In order to analyse the costs, we need to consider each item in the detailed profit and loss account. Each item will be allocated to a classification or apportioned if it relates to more than one of the classifications. This requires the company to make a number of assumptions about the basis for allocating and apportioning. The process is illustrated in Figure 8.4.

From the assumptions that have been made, it is clear that the figures appearing under each of the cost classifications may be apportioned differently in different companies.

Figure 8.4 Assumptions made in analysing the costs

NI An analysis of salaries and wages

	£000	Cost of sales £000	Distribution costs £000	Administration expenses £000
Factory assembly staff	11,500	11,500		
Inspectors	575	575		
Warehouse staff	4,600		4,600	
Accounts department	575			575
Drivers	3,680		3,680	
Salespersons' salaries	2,300		2,300	
	23,230	12,075	10,580	575

N2 An analysis of depreciation

Freehold buildings	1,150	575	287.5	287.5
Equipment	1,150	575	287.5	287.5
Motor vehicles	2,875		2,875	
	5,175	1,150	3,450	575

N3 An apportionment of operating expenses

It is assumed that the following expenses can be apportioned on the basis of the space occupied by the activity, as follows:

	£000	£000	£000	£000
Rates and insurance	3,450	1,725	862.5	862.5
Post, telephone, courier	1,840	920	460	460
Lighting and power	920	460	230	230
Repairs and maintenance	460	230	115	115
Hire charges	300	150	75	75
Miscellaneous expenses	275	137.5	68.75	68.75

N4 An allocation of directors' salaries

It is assumed that the directors spend half their time on production and half on administration.

Figure 8.5 Illustrious plc disclosure note accompanying the profit and loss account

Profit on ordinary activities before tax is stated after charging:

	£000
Depreciation and amortisation	5,175
Auditors' remuneration	1,150
Hire of equipment	300
Exceptional loss on stock	1,000

8.3.2 What information would be disclosed by way of note to the profit and loss account?

We have mentioned that sensitive information is required to be disclosed in the notes to the profit and loss account. The usual practice is to have a note referenced to the profit on ordinary activities before tax. For Illustrious plc the note would read as in Figure 8.5, with additional information regarding the loss on the stock. This treatment – the inclusion of the expense in its cost type heading with more detail in the notes – complies with FRS 3, which does not allow for the highlighting of exceptional items. These should be disclosed separately either by way of note or on the face of the profit and loss account if that degree of prominence is necessary in order to give a true and fair view.[2]

8.4 Stage 3: preparation of the balance sheet in Format 1 style

The balance sheet in Figure 8.6 follows the headings set out in Chapter 7.

Figure 8.6 Illustrious plc balance sheet and disclosure notes

Disclosure notes to show make-up of balance sheet items

Note 1 Tangible fixed asset movements

Tangible fixed assets	Freehold property £000	Equipment £000	Motor vehicles £000	Total £000
Cost				
At 1 January 20X1	115,000	14,950	20,700	150,650
Additions				
Disposals				
At 31 December 20X1	115,000	14,950	20,700	150,650
Accumulated depreciation				
At 1 January 20X1		3,450	9,200	12,650
Charge for year	1,150	1,150	2,875	5,175
At 31 December 20X1	1,150	4,600	12,075	17,825
Net book value				
At 31 December 20X1	113,850	10,350	8,625	132,825
At 31 December 20X0	115,000	11,500	11,500	138,000

Figure 8.6 (cont.)

Balance sheet of Illustrious plc as at 31 December 20X1

	£000	£000
Fixed assets		
Tangible assets Note 1		132,825
Current assets		
Stocks	25,875	
Debtors	28,750	
Cash at bank and in hand	4,600	
Prepayments	2,300	
	61,525	
Creditors: amounts falling due within one year		
Creditors	29,900	
Provision for corporation tax	5,750	
Accrued charges	5,175	
Bank overdraft	8,625	
	49,450	
Net current assets		12,075
Total assets less current liabilities		144,900
Creditors: amounts falling due after more than one year		
Debentures		63,250
		81,650
Capital and reserves		
Share capital		17,250
Profit and loss account		64,400
		81,650

8.5 Preparation of accounts in Format 1 and FRS 3 format

By way of illustration, assume you are the chief accountant of Lewes Road Wines plc, a wholesale distributor currently operating from a single warehouse/office complex in Brighton. Until June 20X2 the company had a plant at Dover, where wine that was imported in bulk was bottled prior to its sale to retail outlets. The profitability of this activity had declined and the plant had closed.

One of your unqualified assistants has prepared the following draft for the published profit and loss account for the year to 31 December 20X2, which he has given to you together with his notes and workings in Figure 8.7.

Figure 8.7 Lewes Road Wines plc profit and loss account (1)

Profit and loss account for the year ended 31 December 20X2

		£000
Turnover (Note 1)		1,288
Cost of sales (Note 2)		744
Gross profit		544
Distribution costs (Note 3)	232	
Administration costs (Note 4)	142	
		374
Operating profit		170
Other operating income (Note 5)		286
Profit on ordinary activities before interest		456
Interest receivable		4
		460
Interest payable		33
Profit on ordinary activities before taxation		427
Tax on profit on ordinary activities (Note 6)		103
Profit on ordinary activities after taxation		324
Proposed dividend		45
Retained profit for the year		279
Retained profits brought forward		274
Retained profits carried forward		553

Notes and workings

1 Turnover includes £175,000 in respect of bottling plant revenue.

2 *Cost of sales*

Wine purchased (including duty and carriage in)	536
Labour	72
Bottles, etc	150
Stock variation (all wine)	(14)
	744

£72,000 (at cost) of wine had to be discarded during the year owing to contamination at source.

Labour costs included £10,000 for wages at the bottling plant and £30,000 in respect of redundancy payments to former employees at the Dover works.

3 *Distribution costs*

Carriage	120
Sales department salaries	51
Bad debts	61
	232

£55,000 represented the bad debt incurred following the collapse of a chain of cut price wine shops.

Figure 8.7 (cont.)

4 *Administrative expenses*	
Salaries (£10,000 in respect of Dover)	78
Premises costs (£1,000 in respect of Dover)	19
Other overheads (£2,000 in respect of Dover)	21
Cost relating to the closure of the Dover plant	24
	142
5 *Other operating income*	
Profit on revaluing Brighton premises	100
Profit on sale of Dover premises	212
Loss on sale of bottling equipment	(26)
	286
6 *Taxation*	
Corporation tax due on 20X2 operating profit	44
Corporation tax on the capital gain on sale of	
Dover premises	56
Under provision for taxation in 20X1	3
	103

There was an error on the previous year closing stock calculation resulting in an understatement of stock by £100,000.

You need now to redraft the profit and loss account so that it complies with the Companies Act 1985 and generally accepted accounting principles. Corporation tax is 30%. In approaching this task you need to consider the provisions of FRS 3 relating to the treatment of discontinued operations, exceptional items and prior period adjustments.

Discontinued operations

Applying the layered treatment of FRS 3, para. 14, which requires the results of continuing and discontinued operations to be disclosed separately, it is necessary to identify the turnover, cost of sales and expenses that relate to the discontinued bottling operation in arriving at the operating profit.

Exceptional items

Exceptional items that require disclosure on the face of the profit and loss account are set out in para. 20 of FRS 3. They include losses arising on termination of an operation and profit on sale of fixed assets.

Revaluation

The revaluation surplus, being unrealised, cannot appear in the profit and loss account. It should, however, appear in the statement of total recognised gains and losses.

Prior period adjustments

Paragraph 29 of FRS 3 requires prior period adjustments to be accounted for by restating the comparative figures and adjusting the opening balance of reserves for the cumulative effect. Note that this means that it is also necessary to take the tax effect into account.

The detailed workings and profit and loss account are given in Figure 8.8.

Figure 8.8 Lewes Road Wines plc profit and loss account (2)

Profit and loss account for the year ended 31 December 20X2

	Continuing operations £000	Discontinued operations £000	Total £000
Turnover	1,113	175	1,288
Cost of sales	654	160	814
Gross profit	459	15	474
Administrative costs	(105)	(13)	(118)
Distribution costs	(232)	—	(232)
Operating profit	122	2	124
Profit on property sale		212	212
Loss on disposal of discontinued activity		(80)	(80)
Profit on ordinary activities before interest	122	134	256
Interest receivable			4
			260
Interest payable			33
Profit on ordinary activities before taxation			227
Taxation			73
Profit on ordinary activities after taxation			154
Proposed dividend			45
Retained profit for the year			109
Retained profits b/f:			
As previously reported		274	
Prior year adjustment		100	
Tax thereon		(30)	344
Retained profits carried forward			453

Notes

Exceptional items

Cost of sales includes £72,000 in respect of wine that had to be discarded during the year owing to contamination at source.

Sales costs include £55,000 in respect of a bad debt incurred following the collapse of a chain of cut price wine shops.

Figure 8.8 (cont.)

Workings

Cost of sales	Bottling	Other	Total
Per draft – labour	40	32	72
bottles, etc.	150		150
stock		(14)	(14)
wine		536	536
Prior year item		100	100
Loss on sale	(30)		(30)
	160	654	814

Administration expenses			
Per draft – salaries	10	68	78
premises	1	18	19
other	2	19	21
closure	24		24
Loss on sale	(24)		(24)
	13	105	118

Loss on closure			
Administration	24		
Redundancy	30		
Bottling equipment			
	80		

Statement of total recognised gains and losses

Profit for the financial year	154	[Figure 8.8 Profit after tax]
Unrealised surplus on revaluation	100	[Figure 8.7 Note 5 premises revalued]
Total recognised gains	254	
Prior year adjustment	70	[Figure 8.8 adjusting profit brought
	324	forward]

8.6 Additional information value of FRS 3

8.6.1 Changes in the operation

The additional disclosure of the effect of discontinued or acquired operations is intended to assist the user to assess more readily the current performance and to predict future maintainable profits. However, care is required when comparing current performance with that of previous years. The provisions of FRS 3 are vague relating to the treatment of acquisitions and, although the contribution from an acquisition is included as part of continuing operations, FRS 3 indicates that it is shown as a separate item of that constituent part; in the second and subsequent years it will not be shown as a separate item.

The contribution from acquisitions, the making of comparisons and the usefulness of the information can be problematical depending on when an acquisition occurs. If it was made in the first week of an accounting year, virtually a whole year will be reported as a contribution from acquisitions. But if it was made in the last week of the previous accounting period, the second period will include the results as part of continuing operations and, as the amount of the contribution for the few days in the period of acquisition will not be material, it will never be reported as an acquisition. This could have a material effect on users' perception of current and future growth rates. This indicates the need always to look behind ratios and percentage changes.[3]

8.6.2 Effect on comparisons of different bases of accounting

Some companies, e.g. Coats Viyella, prepare accounts under the historical cost convention. The majority of companies, however, prepare their accounts under the historical cost convention but as modified by the revaluation of fixed assets.

In order to facilitate comparisons a note is required of the profit calculated on a historical cost basis, i.e. eliminating the effect of revaluations on the reported profit. A note would provide the following information:

	£
Reported profit on ordinary activities before tax	x
Realisation of fixed asset revaluation gains of previous years	y
Difference between depreciation charge based on historical cost and that based on revalued amounts	z
Historical cost profit on ordinary activities before tax	$x + y + z$
Historical cost retained after tax and dividends	$(x + y + z) - \text{tax} - \text{dividend}$

Where there has been a disposal of a previously revalued property there can be a significant difference in the profit before tax as shown in the extract from the Annual report and accounts of Associated British Ports Holdings plc:

Note of Group historical cost profits and losses for the year ended 31 December 2001

	£m	£m
Profit on ordinary activities before tax	129.5	138.9
Realisation of property revaluation surplus of previous years	0.7	19.3
Historical cost profit on ordinary activities before taxation	130.2	158.2
Taxation on profit on ordinary activities	(32.3)	(30.8)
Dividends	(45.4)	(43.1)
Historical cost profit for the year retained for the group and its share of associates	52.5	84.3

8.6.3 Changes in shareholders' funds

Shareholders' funds may be changed as a result of profit or loss from trading, revaluation of fixed assets, goodwill write-offs against reserves, and prior year adjustments to the opening shareholders' funds brought forward. FRS 3 requires a statement to explain to the shareholders how their funds have changed. A statement would be built up as follows:

Reconciliation of movements in shareholders' funds for the year ended 31.12.20X9

Step 1 – identify realised profits/losses that have been retained:

Profit for financial year	a
Dividends	b
Realised and retained	$a - b$

Step 2 – identify asset changes arising from unrealised revaluations:

Other recognised gains/losses [net unrealised gains less unrealised losses] c

Step 3 – identify share capital movements:

Add new share capital raised/deduct share capital repaid d

Step 4 – identify changes in goodwill other than by way of amortisation:

Deduct goodwill written off against reserves		(e)
Net additions to shareholders' funds		$(a - b) + c + d - e$
Opening shareholders' funds	f	
Less prior period adjustments	(g)	$f - g$
Closing shareholders' funds		$[(a - b) + c + d - e] + (f - g)]$

8.7 Summary financial statements

In this chapter we have explained how disclosure requirements have been increasing, e.g. FRS 3 additional information in order to assist informed users such as financial analysts. However, recognising that there was a the risk of the informed layperson being overwhelmed with detail and/or recognising the cost of sending out annual reports running to 60 or more pages, the Companies Act 1989 allowed listed companies to offer a summary financial statement to shareholders.

The Shell Transport and Trading Company plc Summary Financial Statements for 2000 are a typical example. These contain:

● Financial highlights, e.g. a bar chart of 5 years' earnings and dividends

● Chairman's review explaining how the company had achieved exceptional returns and how it proposed to realise its opportunities

● Summary financial statements – these are the the income statement, balance sheet and cash flow statement without the detailed notes that accompany a full set of accounts

● Summary operational and financial review

● Investors' information on earnings and dividends

● Financial calendar, e.g. dates of AGM and payment of dividends.

8.7.1 ICAEW review of summary financial statements[4]

This review by the ICAEW Working Party indicated that summary statements were not widely used but that companies that had used the format had received favourable shareholder response. The chairman of the Working Party commented in his own company's (BAT Industries plc) 1995 accounts that the various new accounting regulations made the full Report and Accounts even harder to understand than hitherto.[5]

However, just as the full Report and Accounts has become overloaded with more and more reports, e.g. corporate governance, operating and financial review, Remuneration Committee report, there is the risk that summary financial statements will go down the same route and become more complex.

The relatively low rate of adoption by companies of the summary format, the risk of the summary reports becoming more complex and the cost of supplying full reports to all shareholders have prompted the ASB to address the problem.

8.7.2 ASB response to need for clarity for lay user

The ASB has taken the view that the option allowed by the Companies Act for companies to offer summary financial statements should be given greater emphasis. It also recognises that, for some shareholders, even the summary financial statements might be too detailed and it issued a Discussion Paper[6] in which it proposed that companies should be allowed to offer such shareholders an even shorter and simpler narrative financial review.

The detailed content of summary financial statements has been incorporated in a Statutory Instrument[7] and there would need to be an amendment to company law. Any proposed amendment could be considered by the Company Law Review.

The ASB's chairman has commented that for many private shareholders, accounting has always been something of a mysterious black art and even the informed layperson may get lost in the welter of detail of a full Annual Report and Accounts.

There is a contrasting view[8] that the reduction of results and financial position of a highly complex organisation might encourage the misguided view that these can be encapsulated in simple headline measures such as EPS and gearing. One can understand this concern given that this has actually been the ASB's own stance when promoting the needs for greater transparency and explanation.

The reality is, of course, that many shareholders appear not to be interested in anything other than a general narrative and highlights.

8.7.3 Company law reform

The Company Law Review Steering Committee in its Final Report (para. 8.72) commented that it had considered that summary financial statements should be abolished but after consultation it recommends that they should be retained with the following recommended changes:

● a summary operational and financial review should be included (this is already good practice as we saw with the Shell extract);

● the power to determine the form and content should be devolved to the Standards Board; and

- the enforcement regime of the Financial Reporting Review Panel should apply as for full sets of accounts.

8.8 Related party transactions

Financial reports are presumed to record transactions carried out on an arm's-length basis between independent parties. This has two implications. The first is that the transfer of resources has been recorded at fair value; the second is that predictions can be made with confidence that any future transfer of resource will occur on the same basis. This presumption is not correct however when one of the parties has the ability to control or influence the financial and operating policies of the other, or the parties are subject to common control or influence.

8.8.1 Related party classifications

Doubtless great ingenuity will be shown by parties who wish to avoid related party disclosure. One approach will be to avoid classification as a related party. Consequently the ASB in FRS 8 *Related Party Transactions* set out a list of relationships that are related, while recognising that each situation will need to be assessed.

Parties are related when during the financial year:

- One party has direct or indirect control of the other party
- The parties are subject to common control
- One party has influence over the financial and operating polices of the other party to an extent that the other party might be inhibited from pursuing at all times its own separate interests
- The parties, in entering a transaction, are subject to influence from the same source to such an extent that one of the parties has subordinated its own separate interests

8.8.2 Relationship that is always related

Related parties of a company issuing a financial report include:

- parent, subsidiary and fellow subsidiary companies
- associates and joint ventures
  - Note that transactions between parent, subsidiary and associated companies within the same group are now a common feature of business. We will discuss the treatment on intragroup transactions in Chapters 11, 13 and 14.
- directors of the company and the parent company
  - Transactions between companies with common director pose a problem. Financial scandals in recent years have featured dominant, powerful chief executives who were also involved with a related party, e.g. Robert Maxwell, the MGN Group and Maxwell Communications.
- pension funds for the benefit of employees of the company or of any entity that is a related party of the reporting entity.

8.8.3 Relationships in which related party is presumed

There is a presumption, unless it can be demonstrated that neither party has influenced the financial and operating policies of the other in such a way as to inhibit the pursuit of separate interest, where one party is:

- in a senior position having authority or responsibility for directing or controlling the major activities and resources of the reporting entity, i.e. in a position of key management

- a person owning or able to exercise control over 20% or more of the voting rights of the reporting entity, whether directly or through nominees

- each person acting in concert in such a way as to be able to exercise control or influence over the reporting entity

- an entity managing or managed by the reporting entity under a management contract

- members of the close family of any person who is related party

The need to prepare such a list of actual and presumed related relationships indicates the problem that the ASB faced when related parties are determined to avoid disclosure. The ASB would prefer a broad approach setting out principles, but it is well aware that related parties who wish to avoid disclosure will look for loopholes. It therefore follows a legalistic approach to frustrate attempts to structure relationships to fall outside the definition of related party.

8.8.4 Related party transactions

Just as parties will attempt to avoid being classified as related parties, so they will structure transactions to avoid their classification as related transactions. FRS 8 therefore lists many examples, including purchase or sale of intangible and tangible assets; providing or receiving services; agency arrangements; leasing arrangements; licence agreements; loan and share financing; and contingent arrangements such as guarantees and provisions of collateral security.

8.8.5 Related party disclosures

Where there is a transaction between related parties it would be helpful to have the following information:

- The names of the parties
- A description of the relationship between them
- The amounts involved
- Any other information needed to make the effect of transaction understandable
- Amounts due at the balance sheet date
- Amounts written off in the period in respect of debts between the parties

8.8.6 Illustrations of related party disclosures

There is disclosure required where the transaction has not been on normal commercial terms. This is not to imply that it is detrimental to the company but expenses and liquidity in future periods could be affected if commercial terms became necessary. For example:

An extract from 1998 Annual Report and Accounts of Leicester City plc reported as follows:

The following loans from directors and their related parties, on which no interest was charged and for which there are no repayment terms, existed during the year:

	Balance at 24.10.97	Maximum amount outstanding during the year	Balance at 31.7.98
	£	£	£
J. M. Elsom (director)	10,000	10,000	10,000
Capital Construction (GB) Limited	250,000	250,000	250,000

R.W. Parker (a director of Leicester City plc) is a director of Capital Construction (GB) Ltd.

There is also disclosure required when terms are normal commercial terms. For example:
An extract from the 1998 Report and Accounts of Sheffield United plc reported as follows:

During the year the group received secretarial and associated services from Townsend Estate Management Limited totalling £7,000. Neither Mr I. Townsend or his wife are materially interested as either a director or shareholder in this company. These services have been provided on normal commercial terms.

Related party disclosure puts users on notice. In the introduction to FRED 8 *Related Party Disclosures*, David Tweedie, the ASB Chairman said:

in the nature of things, the requirement to disclose related party transactions can never be a complete safeguard against deliberate dishonesty.

Nevertheless the disclosure of all material related party transactions and the name of the party controlling the reporting entity will be a useful step forward. Users of accounts will be put on notice of the existence of transactions of this kind and given information about them.

8.8.7 FRED 25: Related party disclosure

FRED 25 proposes to replace FRS 8 *Related Party Disclosures* with the revised IAS 24. There are minor differences between the two standards, e.g. the name of the related party is required in FRS 8 and exemption is permitted if a subsidiary is 90% owned as opposed to the wholly owned requirement in IAS 24.

8.9 Definitions cannot remove uncertainty: SSAP 17 and FRS 12

We have seen that the ASB has issued standards to help determine the nature of a transaction, by defining assets and liabilities and requiring the substance of commercial transactions to be reflected in the accounts. However, there are times when the nature of the transaction is clear, but the events have not crystallised to the extent that the effect on the accounts is certain. There has to be an estimate and this requires the directors to exercise judgement.

The ASC had already issued standards in two areas: SSAP 17 *Accounting for Post Balance Sheet Events* and SSAP 18 *Accounting for Contingencies*, both issued in 1980. SSAP 18 has now been superseded by FRS 12.

8.9.1 SSAP 17 *Accounting for Post Balance Sheet Events*

SSAP 17 requires financial statements to reflect the conditions that existed at the balance sheet date. There is a period of perhaps two months after the year-end before the accounts are signed by the directors and auditors, and information that becomes available during that period should be appraised to determine whether the accounts need to be adjusted.

Adjusting events

If information becomes available during this period that gives further evidence of the conditions that existed **at the balance sheet date**, it is described as an **adjusting event** and, if it is **material**, will require changes in the amounts to be included in the financial statements. Examples are the subsequent determination of the purchase price or proceeds of sale of fixed assets sold before the year-end, and a valuation of property that provides evidence of a permanent diminution in value. The standard also deals with the valuation of stock in assessing its value at the balance sheet date. It states that there is a presumption that the sale proceeds of stock realised after the balance sheet date represent the realisable value at the balance sheet date, unless there is objective evidence that he decline occurred as a result of conditions which did not exist at the balance sheet date.

Non-adjusting events

Non-adjusting events are post balance sheet events which concern conditions that did not exist at the balance sheet date, but which are **so material** that non-disclosure would affect the ability of the users of financial statements to reach a proper understanding of the financial position. These events are required to be disclosed by way of note. The following is an extract from the 2001 Annual Report of Leicester City plc:

> **Post balance sheet events**
> On 1 October 2001, the Group announced that the contract of Football Manager, Peter Taylor, had been terminated. On 10 October 2001, the Group announced the appointment of Dave Bassett as the new Football Manager.
>   Since 31 July 2001 the Group has sold the registration of one player for a transfer fee receivable of £700,000.

Other examples given in SSAP 17, para. 31, include the purchase or sale of fixed assets, opening new trading activities and closing existing activities.

8.9.2 FRED 27: Events after the balance sheet date

The IASB is proposing limited improvements to its existing standard IAS 10 *Events after the balance sheet date*. FRED 27, issued in May 2002, recommends that SSAP 17 should be replaced by the revised IAS 10 which has a stricter definition of 'adjusting events' and would not allow dividends declared after the balance sheet date to be recognised as a liability in the balance sheet. The proposed dividend is treated as a non-adjusting item to be disclosed on the face of the balance sheet or as a note to the accounts.

8.9.3 FRS 12 *Provisions, Contingent Liabilities and Contingent Assets*[9]

The ASB published FRS 12 in September 1998. The FRS was based on FRED 14 *Provisions and Contingencies* and superseded SSAP 18 *Accounting for Contingencies*. The key objective of FRS 12 is to ensure that appropriate recognition criteria and measurement bases are applied and that sufficient information is disclosed in the notes to enable users to understand their nature, timing and amount.

The FRS sets out a useful **decision tree** for determining whether an event requires the creation of a provision, the disclosure of a contingent liability or no action, as shown in Figure 8.9.

Figure 8.9 Decision tree

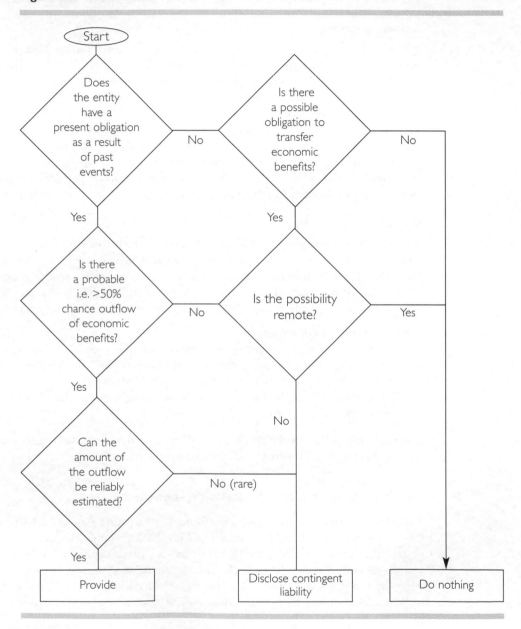

We will now consider provisions, contingent liabilities and contingent assets.

8.9.4 **Provisions**

The FRS is mainly concerned with provisions which it defines as 'Liabilities in respect of which the amount or timing of the expenditure that will be undertaken is uncertain'.

In particular it targets 'big bath' provisions that companies have been able to make. These are the type of provisions that it has been tempting for directors to make in order to smooth profits without any reasonable certainty that the provision would actually be required in subsequent periods. Sir David Tweedie has said:

> A main focus of FRED 14 is 'big-bath' provisions. Those who use them sometimes pray in aid the concept of prudence. All too often however the provision is wildly excessive and conveniently finds its way back to the profit and loss account in a later period. The misleading practice needs to be stopped and FRED 14 proposes that in future provisions should only be allowed when the company has an unavoidable obligation – an **intention** which may or may not be fulfilled will **not be enough**. Users of accounts can't be expected to be mind readers.

8.9.5 What are the general principles that FRS 12 applies to the *recognition* of a provision?

The general principles are that a provision should be recognised when:[10]

(a) an entity has a **present obligation** (legal or constructive) **as a result of past events**;
(b) it is **probable** that a transfer of **economic benefits will be required to settle the obligation;**
(c) **a reliable estimate** can be made of the amount of the obligation.

Provisions by their nature relate to the future. This means that there is a need for estimation and FRS 12 comments[11] that **the use of estimates is an essential part of the preparation of financial statements and does not undermine their reliability.**

The FRS addresses the uncertainties arising in respect of present obligation, past event, probable transfer of economic benefits and reliable estimates when deciding whether to recognise a provision.

Present obligation

The test to be applied is whether it is more likely than not i.e. more than a 50% chance of occurring. For example, if involved in a disputed lawsuit, the company is required to take account of all available evidence including that of experts and of post balance sheet events to decide if there is a greater than 50% chance that the lawsuit will be decided against the company.

Where it is more likely that no present obligation exists at the balance sheet date, the company discloses a contingent liability, unless the possibility of a transfer of economic resources is remote.

Past event[12]

A past event that leads to a present obligation is called an **obligating event**. This is a new term with which to become familiar. This means that the company has no realistic alternative to settling the obligation. The FRS defines no alternative as being only where the settlement of the obligation can be enforced by law or in the case of a constructive obligation, where the event creates valid expectations in other parties that the company will discharge the obligation.

The FRS stresses that it is only those obligations arising from past events existing independently of a company's future actions that are recognised as provisions, e.g. clean-up costs for unlawful environmental damage that has occurred require a provision; environmental damage that is not unlawful but is likely to become so and involve clean-up costs will not be provided for until legislation is virtually certain to be enacted as drafted.

Probable transfer of economic benefits[13]

The FRS defines probable as meaning that the event is more likely than not to occur. Where it is not probable the company discloses a contingent liability unless the possibility is remote.

8.9.6 What are the general principles that FRS 12 applies to the *measurement* of a provision?

FRS 12 states[14] that the amount recognised as a provision should the *best estimate* of the expenditure required to settle the present obligation at the balance sheet date.

Best estimate is defined as the amount that a company would rationally pay to settle the obligation or to transfer it to a third party. The estimates of outcome and financial effect are determined by the judgement of management supplemented by experience of similar transactions and reports from independent experts. Management deal with the uncertainties as to the amount to be provided in a number of ways:

- A class obligation exists
  - where the provision involves a large population of items such as a warranty provision statistical analysis of expected values should be used to determine the amount of the provision.
- A single obligation exists
  - where a single obligation is being measured the individual most likely outcome may be the best estimate;
  - however, there may be other outcomes that are significantly higher or lower indicating that expected values should be determined.

Management must avoid creation of excessive provisions based on a prudent view:

- Uncertainty does not justify the creation of excessive provisions[15]
  - if the projected costs of a particular adverse outcome are estimated on a prudent basis that outcome should not then be deliberately treated as more probable than is realistically the case.

The FRS states[16] that **where the effect of the time value of money is material, the amount of a provision should be the present value of the expenditures expected to be required to settle the obligation**.

Present value is arrived at by:

- using pre-tax cash flows and a discount rate that will, after deduction of tax, give the required post-tax rate of return;
- where the estimated cash flows required to meet the obligation have not been risk-adjusted, at a discount rate adjusted for the risks specific to the obligation;
- where the estimated future cash outflow has been risk-adjusted, a risk-free rate should be used;
- if the cash flows to be discounted are expressed in current prices, a real discount rate should be used;
- if the cash flows are in terms of expected future prices, a nominal discount rate should be used;
- as the settlement date approaches, the carrying value of the provision should be increased.

8.9.7 Application of criteria illustrated

Scenario 1

An offshore oil exploration company is required by its licence to remove the rig and restore the seabed. Management have estimated that 85% of the eventual cost will be incurred in removing the rig and 15% through the extraction of oil. The company's practice on similar projects has been to account for the decommissioning costs using the 'unit of production' method whereby the amount required for decommissioning was built up year by year, in line with production levels, to reach the amount of the expected costs by the time production ceased.

Decision process

1 Is there a present obligation as a result of a past event?
The construction of the rig has created a legal obligation under the licence to remove the rig and restore the seabed.

2 Is there a probable transfer of economic benefits?
This is probable.

3 Can the amount of the outflow be reasonably estimated?
A best estimate can be made by management based on past experience and expert advice.

4 Conclusion
A provision should be created of 85% of the eventual future costs of removal and restoration.
This provision should be discounted if the effect of the time value of money is material.
A provision for the 15% relating to restoration should be created when oil production commences.
The unit of production method is not acceptable in that the decommissioning costs relate to damage already done.

Scenario 2

A company has a private jet costing £24m. Air regulations required it to be overhauled every four years. An overhaul costs £1.6m. The company policy has been to create a provision for depreciation of £2m on a straight-line basis over 12 years and an annual provision of £400,000 to meet the cost of the required overhaul every four years.

Decision process

1 Is there a present obligation as a result of a past obligating event?
There is no present obligation. The company could avoid the cost of the overhaul by, for example, selling the aircraft.

2 Conclusion
No provision for cost of overhaul can be recognised. Instead of a provision being recognised, the depreciation of the aircraft takes account of the future incidence of maintenance costs, i.e. an amount equivalent to the expected maintenance costs is depreciated over four years.

8.9.8 **Disclosures**

Specific disclosures,[17] for each material class of provision, should be given as to the amount recognised at the year-end and about any movements in the year. For example:

- **Increases in provisions** – any new provisions; any increases to existing provisions; and, where provisions are carried at present value, any change in value arising from the passage of time or from any movement in the discount rate.

- **Reductions in provisions** – any amounts utilised during the period; management are required to review provisions at each balance sheet date and

    adjust to reflect the current best estimates; and

    – if it is no longer probable that a transfer of economic benefits will be required to settle the obligation, the provision should be reversed.

Disclosures need not be given in cases where to do so would be seriously prejudicial to the company's interests.

In practice, this would mean that:

- **A provision for future operating losses** should not be recognised (unless under a contractual obligation) **because there is no obligation at the date of the balance sheet**. However, where a contract becomes onerous i.e. where it becomes more costly to fulfil or avoid a contract than the associated revenues the company could derive from it and cannot be avoided, then a provision should be made.

    This can be contrasted to cases where a company supplies a product as a loss leader to gain a foothold in the market. In the latter case, the company may cease production at any time. Accordingly, no provision should be recognised as no obligation exists.

- **A provision for restructuring** should only be recognised when there is a commitment supported by
  (a) a detailed formal plan for the restructuring identifying at least:
      (i) the business or part of the business concerned;
      (ii) the principal locations affected;
      (iii) details of the approximate number of employees who will receive compensation payments;
      (iv) the expenditure that will be undertaken; and
      (v) when the plan will be implemented; and
  (b) has raised a valid expectation in those affected that it will carry out the restructuring by implementing its restructuring plans or announcing its main features to those affected by it.

- **A provision for restructuring should not be created merely on the intention to restructure**. For example, a management or board decision to restructure taken before the balance sheet date does not give rise to a constructive obligation at the balance sheet date unless the company has, before the balance sheet date:
    – started to implement the restructuring plan, e.g. dismantling plant or selling assets;
    – announced the main features of the plan with sufficient detail to raise the valid expectation of those affected that the restructuring will actually take place.

- **A provision for restructuring** should only include the direct expenditures arising from the restructuring which are necessarily entailed and not associated with the ongoing activities of the company. For example, the following costs which relate to the future conduct of the business are not included:
    – retraining costs; relocation costs; marketing costs; investment in new systems and distribution networks.

- **A provision for environmental liabilities** should be recognised at the time and to the extent that the entity becomes obliged, legally or constructively, to rectify environmental damage or to perform restorative work on the environment. This means that a provision should be set up only for the entity's costs to meet its *legal* obligations. It could be argued that any provision for any additional expenditure on environmental issues is a public relations decision and should be written off.

- **A provision for decommissioning costs** should be recognised to the extent that decommissioning costs relate to damage already done or goods and services already received.

The last point may require a change of accounting policy in the way in which companies provide for restoration costs. Gold Mines of Sardinia Ltd, an Australian company listed on the Alternative Issues Market in the UK, stated in its accounting policies in the 1997 accounts:

Restoration costs
Restoration costs that are expected to be incurred are provided for as a part of the exploration, evaluation, development, construction or production phases that give rise to the need for restoration. Accordingly, these costs are recognised gradually over the life of the facility as these phases occur. The costs include obligations relating to reclamation, waste site closure, plant closure, platform removal and other costs associated with the restoration of the site. These estimates of the restoration obligations are based on anticipated technology and **legal** requirements and future costs, which have been **discounted to their present value**.

It would appear that the company is applying the units of production method in respect of restoration costs.

8.9.9 The use of provisions

Only expenditures that relate to the original provision are to be set against it because to set expenditures against a provision that was originally recognised for another purpose would conceal the impact of two different events.

8.9.10 Tax treatment moves closer to accounting practice

The Inland Revenue now accepts that provisions made under FRS 12 are tax-deductible except where there remain specific tax rules to the contrary. The change has arisen because it is recognised that under FRS 12 provisions are only made where a business expects to pay out money in the future and has taken that *probable* expense into account when calculating its profits.

8.9.11 Contingent liabilities

FRS 12 deals with provisions and contingent liabilities within the same FRS because the ASB regards all provisions as contingent because they are uncertain in timing and amount. For the purposes of the accounts, it distinguishes between provisions and contingent liabilities in that:

- Provisions are a present obligation requiring a probable transfer of economic benefits that can be reliably estimated – a provision can therefore be recognised as a liability.

- Contingent liabilities fail to satisfy these criteria, e.g. lack of a reliable estimate of the amount; not probable that there will be a transfer of economic benefits; yet to be confirmed that there is actually an obligation – a contingent liability cannot therefore be recognised in the accounts but may be disclosed by way of note to the accounts or not disclosed if an outflow of economic benefits is remote.

Where the occurrence of a contingent liability becomes sufficiently probable, it falls within the criteria for recognition as a provision as detailed above and should be accounted for accordingly and recognised as a liability in the accounts.

Where the likelihood of a contingent liability is possible, but not probable and not remote, disclosure should be made, for each class of contingent liability, where practicable, of:

(a) an estimate of its financial effect, taking into account the inherent risks and uncertainties and, where material, the time value of money;

(b) an indication of the uncertainties relating to the amount or timing of any outflow; and

(c) the possibility of any reimbursement.

For example, an extract from the 2000 Annual Report of Unilever Group plc informs as follows:

> *Contingent liabilities*
> Contingent liabilities amounted to some €450 million (1999: €181 million) of which €210 million relates to guarantees. These guarantees are not expected to give rise to any material loss ... Other contingent liabilities arise in respect of litigation against companies in the Group, investigations by competition authorities and obligations under environmental legislation in various countries. These are not expected to give rise to any material loss.

8.9.12   Contingent asset

A contingent asset is a possible asset that arises from past events whose existence will be confirmed only by the occurrence of one or more uncertain future events not wholly within the entity's control.

Recognition as an asset is only allowed if the asset is *virtually certain,* i.e. and therefore by definition no longer contingent.

Disclosure by way of note is required if an inflow of economic benefits is *probable*. The disclosure would include a brief description of the nature of the contingent asset at the balance sheet date and, where practicable, an estimate of their financial effect taking into account the inherent risks and uncertainties and, where material, the time value of money.

No disclosure is required where the chance of occurrence is anything less than probable. For the purposes of FRS 12, probable is defined as more likely than not, i.e. more than a 50% chance.

Summary

A public company that is listed on the Stock Exchange is required to present an annual report and accounts to its shareholders.

The annual report consists of a number of statements. In Chapters 7 and 8 we have considered the following statements: the directors' report; the operating and financial review; the profit and loss account; the statement of total recognised gains and losses; the reconciliation to the historical cost profit; the balance sheet and the reconciliation of movements in shareholders' funds. We have seen the following:

- There is more than one format for presenting the profit and loss account and even companies operating in the same industry sector might choose a different format.
- Even where companies use the same format, they may classify costs into different cost categories.
- The additional information disclosed, e.g. staff costs, cannot necessarily be related to the categories of operations into which the company has classified its costs in its profit and loss account.
- FRS 8 *Related Party Disclosures* assists users to identify where there are related parties which could result in transactions not being at arm's length.
- There is no obvious, overriding rationale for the disclosure of information; it has grown in an *ad hoc* fashion with disclosure required:
  - for stewardship accounting, e.g. the disclosure of directors' remuneration;
  - for the shareholders as principal stakeholders, e.g. trading profit;
  - for interested stakeholders, e.g. an analysis of employees and details of staff costs;
  - on political grounds, e.g. the disclosure of political donations;
  - for the community as an interested stakeholder, e.g. company policy on the employment of disabled applicants.
- The balance sheet can be prepared under historical cost accounting rules **or** alternative accounting rules or a mixture of historical and alternative accounting rules.
- The Companies Act has not defined the costs to be used in the alternative accounting model.
- Excessive provisions which are fed back into later periods are no longer permitted.

Perhaps we have reached a stage where the purpose of the annual report needs to be reappraised and given a clearer focus.

REVIEW QUESTIONS

1 The directors of Ufool Ltd are aware that a sizeable number of shareholders, although still a minority, are extremely unhappy with current dividend levels and are agitating for larger distributions.

They have raised several points with the directors, who have turned to you as their trusty financial and accounting adviser for assistance. The points put forward by these shareholders are as follows:

(i) Although the annual accounts disclose that £150,000 profit was available for distribution, it is disclosed elsewhere in these accounts that £520,000 of the loan stock had been repaid. The shareholders assert that this repayment was an attempt to lower the true profit and that, if it were written back, more profit would be available for distribution.

(ii) Despite this year's relatively low profit, there is a very large balance of retained profits brought forward from preceding years. A significant proportion of these retained profits from preceding years should be used to pay a larger dividend this year.

(iii) It is unfair to have kept the dividend rate at 10% over the past few years when the average dividend yield on the Stock Exchange has risen from 12% to 18%. The company's dividend rate should follow this average.

(iv) The return on capital employed for the company is 20% and this high rate of profitability accurately reflects the ability of the company to pay far higher dividend levels.

(v) As profit figures can so easily be manipulated by the company's accountants, the £150,000 is more than likely to be a significant underestimate of the real profit, so more profit could be distributed if different accounting bases were used.

Comment on each of the above assertions to enable the board of directors to refute them convincingly.

2 It is said that Format 1 extends the management accounting concept of responsibility accounting to published financial statements. Explain what this means.

3 Under FRS 3 more disclosure is required than under the Companies Act. Explain the major additional disclosures and discuss how they can be justified.

4 When preparing accounts under Format 1, how would a bad debt that was materially larger than normal be disclosed?

5 Explain the conditions set out in FRS 3 for determining whether operations have been discontinued and the problems that might arise in applying them.

6 'Annual accounts have been put into such a straitjacket by the EU directives' overemphasis on uniform disclosure that there will be a growing pressure by national bodies to introduce changes unilaterally, e.g. the FRS 3 requirements, which will again lead to diversity in the quality of disclosure. This is both healthy and necessary.' Discuss.

7 Explain the relevance to the user of accounts if expenses are classified as 'administrative expenses' rather than as 'cost of sales'.

8 FRS 3 *Reporting Financial Performance* requires the publication of:

(i) the statement of total recognised gains and losses; (ii) the note of historical cost profit or loss; (iii) the reconciliation of movements in shareholders' funds.

Explain the need for the publishing of these statements, identifying the circumstances in which they have to be published, and identify the items you would include in each of the statements.

9 Mining, nuclear and oil companies have normally provided an amount each year over the life of an enterprise to provide for decommissioning costs. Explain why the ASB considered this to be an inappropriate treatment and how these companies would be affected by FRS 12 *Provisions, Contingent Liabilities and Contingent Assets*.

10 (a) The Manchester United plc Annual Report for the year ended 31 July 2001 contained the following note:

Post balance sheet events
On 28 August 2001 the playing registration of Jaap Stam was transferred to SS Lazio for a total consideration, net of associated costs, of £15.3 million.

Explain why this information is given as a note and not included as a disposal of a registration under intangible assets in the balance sheet.

(b) Discuss the problems of interpreting financial reports when there are post balance sheet events, and the extent to which you consider SSAP 17 should be amended. Illustrate your decisions with practical examples as appropriate.

EXERCISES

An extract from the solution is provided in the appendix at the end of the text for exercises marked with an asterisk (*).

* Question 1

Springtime Ltd is a trading company buying and selling as wholesalers fashionable summer clothes. The following balances have been extracted from the books as at 31 March 20X4:

	£000
Auditor's remuneration	30
Corporation tax based on the accounting profit:	
For the year to 31 March 20X4	3,200
Overprovision for the year to 31 March 20X3	200
Delivery expenses (including £300,000 overseas)	1,200
Dividends: final (proposed – to be paid 1 August 20X4)	200
interim (paid on 1 October 20X3)	100
Fixed assets at cost:	
Delivery vans	200
Office cars	40
Stores equipment	5,000
Franked investment income (amount received from listed companies)	1,200
Office expenses	800
Overseas' operations: closure costs of entire operations	350
Purchases	24,000
Sales (net of value added tax)	35,000
Stock at cost:	
At 1 April 20X3	5,000
At 31 March 20X4	6,000
Storeroom costs	1,000
Wages and salaries:	
Delivery staff	700
Directors' emoluments	400
Office staff	100
Storeroom staff	400

Notes:

1   Depreciation is provided at the following annual rates on a straight-line basis: delivery vans 20%; office cars 25%; stores 1%.
2   The following taxation rates may be assumed: corporation tax 35%; income tax 25%.
3   The franked investment income arises from investments held in fixed asset investments.
4   It has been decided to transfer an amount of £150,000 to the deferred taxation account.
5   The overseas operations consisted of exports. In 20X3/X4 these amounted to £5,000,000 (sales) with purchases of £4,000,000. Related costs included £100,000 in storeroom staff and £15,000 for office staff.
6   Directors' emoluments include:

Chairperson	100,000	
Managing director	125,000	
Finance director	75,000	
Sales director	75,000	
Export director	25,000	(resigned 31 December 20X3)
	£400,000	

Required:

(a) Produce a profit and loss account suitable for publication and complying as far as possible with company law and generally accepted accounting practice.

(b) Comment on how FRS 3 has improved the quality of information available to users of accounts.

(c) Give two reasons why information contained in the accounting policies notes is of importance to users of accounts.

* Question 2

Olive plc, incorporated with an authorised capital consisting of one million ordinary shares of £1 each, employs 646 persons, of whom 428 work at the factory and the rest at the head office. The trial balance extracted from its books as at 30 September 20X4 is as follows:

	£000	£000
Land and Building (cost £600,000)	520	—
Plant and machinery (cost £840,000)	680	—
Proceeds on disposal of plant and machinery	—	180
Fixtures and equipment (cost £120,000)	94	—
Sales	—	3,460
Carriage inwards	162	—
Share premium account	—	150
Advertising	112	—
Stock in trade on 1 Oct 20X3	211	—
Heating and lighting	80	—
Prepayments	115	—
Salaries	820	—
Trade Investments at cost	248	—
Dividend received (net) on 9 Sept 20X4	—	45
Directors' emoluments	180	—
Pension cost	100	—
Audit fees and expense	65	—
Profit and loss account balance b/f	—	601
Sales commission	92	—
Stationery	28	—
Development cost	425	—
Formation expenses	120	—
Debtors and creditors	584	296
Interim dividend paid on 4 Mar 20X4	60	—
12% Debentures issued on 1 Apr 20X4	—	500
Debenture interest paid on 1 Jul 20X4	15	—
Purchases	925	—
Corporation tax on year to 30 Sept 20X3	—	128
Other administration expenses	128	—
Bad debts	158	—
Cash and bank balance	38	—
Ordinary shares of £1 fully called	—	600
	5,960	5,960

You are informed as follows:

(a) As at 1 October 20X3 land and buildings were revalued at £900,000. A third of the cost as well as all the valuation is regarded as attributable to the land. Directors have decided to report this asset at valuation.

(b) New fixtures were acquired on 1 January 20X4 for £40,000; a machine acquired on 1 October 20X1 for £240,000 was disposed of on 1 July 20X4 for £180,000, being replaced on the same date by another acquired for £320,000.

(c) Depreciation for the year is to be calculated on the straight-line basis as follows:

Buildings: 2% p.a.
Plant and machinery: 10% p.a.
Fixtures and equipment: 10% p.a.

(d) Stock in trade, including raw materials and work-in-progress on 30 September 20X4, has been valued at cost at £364,000.

(e) Prepayments are made up as follows:

	£000
Amount paid in advance for a machine	60
Amount paid in advance for purchasing raw materials	40
Prepaid rent	15
	£115

(f) In March 20X3 a customer had filed legal action claiming damages at £240,000. When accounts for the year ended 30 September 20X3 were finalised, a provision of £90,000 was made in respect of this claim. This claim was settled out of court in April 20X4 at £150,000 and the amount of the under-provision adjusted against the profit balance brought forward from previous years.

(g) The following allocations have been agreed upon:

	Factory	Administration
Depreciation of building	60%	40%
Salaries other than to directors	55%	45%
Heating and lighting	80%	20%

(h) Pension cost of the company is calculated at 10% of the emoluments and salaries.

(i) Corporation tax on 20X3 profit has been agreed at £140,000 and that for 20X4 estimated at £185,000. Corporation tax rate is 35% and the basic rate of income tax 25%.

(j) Directors propose a final dividend of 20% and wish to write off the formation expenses as far as possible without reducing the amount of profits available for distribution.

Required:
Prepare for publication:

(a) The profit and loss account of the company for the year ended 30 September 20X4, and

(b) the balance sheet as at that date along with as many notes (other than the one on accounting policy) as can be provided on the basis of the information made available.

Question 3

Cryptic plc extracted its trial balance on 30 June 20X5 as follows:

	£000	£000
Land and building at cost	750	—
Plant and machinery at cost	480	—
Accumulated depreciation on plant and machinery at 30 Jun 20X5	—	400
Depreciation on machinery	80	—
Furniture, tools and equipment at cost	380	—
Accumulated depreciation on furniture, etc. at 30 Jun 20X4	—	95
Debtors and creditors	475	360
Stock of raw materials at 30 Jun 20X4	112	—
Work-in-progress at factory cost at 30 Jun 20X4	76	—
Finished goods at cost at 30 Jun 20X4	264	—
Sales including VAT	—	2,875
Purchases of raw materials including VAT	1,380	—
Share premium account	—	150
Advertising	65	—
Deferred taxation	—	185
Salaries	360	—
Rent	120	—
Profit and loss account balance at 30 Jun 20X4	—	226
Factory power	48	—
Trade investments at cost	240	—
Overprovision for tax for the year ended 30 Jun 20X4	—	21
Electricity	36	—
Stationery	12	—
Dividend received (net)	—	24
Interim dividend paid on 15 April 20X5	60	—
Other administration expenses	468	—
Disposal of furniture	—	64
Value added tax account	165	—
Ordinary shares of 50p each	—	1,000
12% Preference shares of £1 each	—	200
Cash and bank balance	29	—
	5,600	5,600

The following information is relevant:

(a) The company discontinued a major activity during the year and replaced it with another. All fixed assets involved in the discontinued activity were redeployed for the new one. The following expenses incurred in this respect, however, are included in 'Other administration expenses':

	£000
Cancellation of contracts re. terminated activity	165
Fundamental reorganisation arising as a result	145

(b) On 1 January 20X4 the company acquired new land and buildings for £150,000. The remainder of land and building, acquired 9 years earlier, have NOT been depreciated until this year. The company has decided to depreciate the building, on the straight-line method, assuming that one-third of the cost relates to land and that the buildings have an estimated economic life of 50 years.

(c) Plant and machinery, acquired on 1 July 20X0, have been depreciated at 10% per annum on the straight-line method. The estimate of useful economic life had to be revised this year when it was realised that if the market share is to be maintained at current levels, the company has to replace all its machinery by 1 July 20X6. The balance in the 'Accumulated provision for depreciation' account on 1 July 20X4 was amended to reflect the revised estimate of useful economic life and the impact of the revision adjusted against the profit and loss balance brought forward from prior years.

(d) Furniture acquired for £80,000 on 1 January 20X3 was disposed of for £64,000 on 1 April 20X5. Furniture, tools and equipment are depreciated at 5% p.a. on cost.

(e) Results of the stocktaking at year-end are as follows:

Stock of raw materials at cost including VAT	£197,800
Work-in-progress at factory cost	£54,000
Finished goods at cost	£364,000

(f) The company allocates its expenditure as follows:

	Production cost	Factory overhead	Distribution cost	Administrative expenses
Salaries and wages	65%	15%	5%	15%
Rent	—	60%	15%	25%
Electricity	—	10%	20%	70%
Depreciation of building	—	40%	10%	50%

(g) The directors wish to make a provision for audit fees of £18,000 and estimate the corporation tax for the year at £65,000. £11,000 should be transferred from the deferred tax account. The directors propose to pay the preference dividend and a final dividend of 3p per share for ordinary shares.

(h) The following analysis has been made:

	New activity	Discontinued activity
Sales excluding VAT	£165,000	£215,000
Cost of sales	£98,000	£155,000
Distribution cost	£16,500	£48,500
Administrative expenses	£22,500	£38,500

(i) Assume that VAT applicable to all purchases and sales is 15%, the basic rate of income tax is 25% and the corporation tax rate is 35%.

Required:
(a) Advise the company on the accounting treatment in respect of information stated in (b) above.
(b) In respect of the information stated in (c) above, state whether a company is permitted to revise its estimate of the useful economic life of a fixed asset and comment on the appropriateness of the accounting treatment adopted.
(c) Set out a statement of movement of tangible fixed assets in the year to 30 June 20X5.
(d) Set out for publication the profit and loss account for the year ended 30 June 20X5, the balance sheet as at that date and any notes other than that on accounting policy, in accordance with the Companies Act 1985 and relevant standards.

Question 4

The following is the draft trading and profit and loss account of Parnell Ltd for the year ending 31 December 1997:

	£m	£m
Turnover		563
Cost of sales		310
		253
Distribution costs	45	
Administrative expenses	78	
		123
Profit on ordinary activities before tax		130
Tax on profit on ordinary activities		45
Profit on ordinary activities after taxation – all retained		85
Profit brought forward at 1 January 1997		101
Profit carried forward at 31 December 1997		186

You are given the following additional information, which is reflected in the above trading and profit and loss account only to the extent stated:

1.   Distribution costs include a bad debt of £15 million which arose on the insolvency of a major customer. There is no prospect of recovering any of this debt. Bad debts have never been material in the past.

2.   The company has traditionally consisted of a manufacturing division and a distribution division. On 31 December 1997, the entire distribution division was sold for £50 million; its book value at the time of sale was £40 million. The surplus on disposal was credited to administrative expenses. (Ignore any related corporation tax.)

3.   During 1997, the distribution division made sales of £100 million and had a cost of sales of £30 million. There will be no reduction in stated distribution costs of administration expenses as a result of this disposal.

4.   The company owns offices which it purchased on 1 January 1995 for £500 million, comprising £200 million for land and £300 million for buildings. No depreciation was charged in 1995 or 1996, but the company now considers that such a charge should be introduced. The buildings were expected to have a life of 50 years at the date of purchase, and the company uses the straight-line basis for calculating depreciation, assuming a zero residual value. No taxation consequences result from this change.

5.   During 1997, part of the manufacturing division was restructured at a cost of £20 million to take advantage of modern production techniques. The restructuring was not fundamental and will **not** have a material effect on the nature and focus of the company's operations. This cost is included under administration expenses in the profit and loss account.

Required:

(a)   State the objective of FRS3 entitled 'Reporting Financial Performance'.

(b)   State how each of the items 1–5 above must be accounted for in order to comply with the requirements of FRS3.

(c) Redraft the trading and profit and loss account of Parnell Ltd for 1997, taking into account the additional information so as to comply, as far as possible, with relevant standard accounting practice. Show clearly any adjustments you make. Notes to the accounts are not required.

(The Chartered Institute of Bankers)

Question 5 Related party scenarios

(a) In 20X3 Arthur is a large loan creditor of X Ltd and receives interest at 20% p.a. on this loan. He also has a 24% shareholding in X Ltd. Until 20X1 he was a director of the company and left after a disagreement. The remaining 76% of the shares are held by the remaining directors. Is Arthur a related party to X Ltd?

(b) Brenda joined Y Ltd, an insurance broking company, on 1 January 20X0 on a low salary but high commission basis. She brought clients with her that generated 30% of the company's 20X0 turnover. Is Brenda a related party to Y Ltd?

(c) Carrie is a director and major shareholder of Z Ltd. Her husband, Donald, is employed in the company on administrative duties for which he is paid a salary of £25,000 p.a. Her daughter, Emma, is a business consultant running her own business. In 20X0 Emma carried out various consultancy exercises for the company for which she was paid £85,000. Are Donald or Emma related parties to Z Ltd?

(d) Fred is a director of V Ltd. V Ltd is a major customer of W Ltd. In 20X0 Fred also became a director of W Ltd. Are related party disclosures required in either V Ltd or W Ltd?

Required:
Discuss whether parties are related in the above situations.

Question 6

Maxpool plc, a listed company, owned 60% of the shares in Ching Ltd. Bay plc, a listed company, owned the remaining 40% of the £1 ordinary shares in Ching Ltd. The holdings of shares were acquired on 1 January 20X0.

On 30 November 20X0 Ching Ltd sold a factory outlet site to Bay plc at a price determined by an independent surveyor.

On 1 March 20X1 Maxpool plc purchased a further 30% of the £1 ordinary shares of Ching Ltd from Bay plc and purchased 25% of the ordinary shares of Bay plc.

On 30 June 20X1 Ching Ltd sold the whole of its fleet of vehicles to Bay plc at a price determined by a vehicle auctioneer.

Required:
Explain the implications of the above transactions for the determination of related party relationships and disclosure of such transactions in the financial statements of (a) Maxpool Group plc, (b) Ching Ltd and (c) Bay plc for the years ending 31 December 20X0 and 31 December 20X1.

(ACCA)

Question 7

(a) Post balance sheet events are those events, both favourable and unfavourable, which occur between the balance sheet date and the date on which the financial statements are approved by the board of directors.

Required:

Set out the treatment of post balance sheet events as laid down by SSAP 17. Explain why this treatment is required by that SSAP in order to ensure that financial statements show a true and fair view and give appropriate information to the shareholders and other legitimate users.

(b) You are the financial accountant of Tooting Engineering Ltd (a substantial private company). You are responsible for preparing the company's financial statements and are at present finalising those for the year ended 31 December 20X6 for presentation to the board. The following items are material:

 (i) You have recently discovered that during September and October 20X6, while you were away sick, the cashier took advantage of the weakened internal controls to defraud the company of £8,000.

 (ii) At a board meeting on 3 February 20X7 the directors agreed to purchase the business of Mr N. M. Patel (a small engineering business) for £45,000.

 (iii) On 18 January 20X7 the company made a 1 for 4 rights issue to existing ordinary shareholders. This involved the issue of 20,000 £1 ordinary shares for a consideration of £25,000.

 (iv) A customer, General Products Ltd, owed Tooting Engineering Ltd £16,000 on 31 December 20X6. This company had always been considered a good credit risk until on 15 February 20X7 it went into voluntary liquidation. Of the £16,000 debt, £12,000 is still outstanding and General Products Ltd is expected to pay approximately 25p in the £ on this £12,000.

Required:

Explain how you will treat items (i)–(iv) above in the financial statements and give a brief explanation of why you are adopting your proposed treatment.

References

1 Companies Act 1985, 4 Sch. Formats, 4A Sch. 17, 21.
2 FRS 3, para. 19.
3 M. Stead, *How to Use Company Accounts for Successful Investment Decisions*, Pitman, 1995, p. 155.
4 *Summary Financial Statements – The Way Forward*, ICAEW, 1996.
5 M. Davies, R. Paterson and A. Wilson, *UK GAAP* 5th Edition, Macmillan, p. 32.
6 Discussion Paper, *Year-end Financial Reports: Improving Communication*, ASB, 2000.
7 The Companies (Summary Financial Statement) Regulations 1995, SI 1995/2092.
8 M. Davies, R. Paterson and A. Wilson, *UK GAAP* 5th Edition, Macmillan, p. 33.
9 FRS 12, *Provisions, Contingent Liabilities and Contingent Assets*, ASB, 1998.
10 *Ibid.*, para. 14.
11 *Ibid.*, para. 25.
12 *Ibid.*, para. 17.
13 *Ibid.*, para. 23.
14 *Ibid.*, para. 36.
15 *Ibid.*, para. 43.
16 *Ibid.*, para. 45.
17 *Ibid.*, para. 89.

PART 3

Balance sheet – liability and asset measurement and disclosure

CHAPTER 9

Share capital, capital maintenance and distributable profits

9.1 Introduction

In this chapter, we consider the constituents of total shareholders' funds and the nature of distributable and non-distributable reserves. We then analyse the role of the capital maintenance concept in the protection of creditors, before discussing the effectiveness of the protection offered by the Companies Act 1985 in respect of both private and public companies.

9.2 Total shareholders' funds: an overview

Total shareholders' funds consist of the issued share capital stated at nominal value, non-distributable and distributable reserves. Here we comment briefly on the main constituents of total shareholders' funds. We go on to deal with them in greater detail in subsequent sections.

9.2.1 Right to issue shares

Companies incorporated under the Companies Act 1985 are able to raise capital by the issue of shares and debentures. There are two main categories of company: private limited companies and public limited companies. Public limited companies are designated by the letters **plc** and have the right to issue shares and debentures to the public. Private limited companies are often family companies; they are not allowed to seek share capital by invitations to the public. The shareholders of both categories have the benefit of limited personal indemnity, i.e. their liability to creditors is limited to the amount they agreed to pay the company for the shares they bought.

9.2.2 Types of share

Broadly, there are two types of share: ordinary and preference.

Ordinary shares

Ordinary shares, often referred to as equity shares, carry the main risk and are entitled to the residual profit after paying any fixed interest or fixed dividend to investors who have invested on the basis of a fixed return. Distributions from the residual profit are made in the form of dividends, which are normally expressed as pence per share.

Preference shares

Preference shares usually have a fixed rate of dividend, which is expressed as a percentage of the nominal value of the share. The dividend is paid before any distribution to the ordinary shareholders. The specific rights attaching to a preference share can vary widely.

9.2.3 Non-distributable reserves

There are two types of **statutory** non-distributable reserve: share premium and capital redemption reserve. These are considered in greater detail below. In addition to the statutory non-distributable reserves, a company might have restrictions on distribution within its memorandum and articles, stipulating that capital profits are non-distributable as dividends.

9.2.4 Distributable reserves

Distributable reserves are normally represented by the balance on the profit and loss account that appears in the balance sheet and belong to the ordinary shareholders. However, as we shall see, there may be circumstances where credits that have been made to the profit and loss account are not actually distributable, usually because they do not satisfy the **realisation** concept.

Although the balance sheet profit and loss account figure contains the cumulative residual distributable profits, it is the earnings per share (EPS), based on the post-tax earnings for the year as disclosed in the profit and loss account, that influences market valuation of the shares, applying the price/earnings ratio.

When deciding whether to issue shares, the directors will therefore probably consider the impact on the EPS figure. If the EPS increases, the share price can normally be expected also to increase.

9.3 Total shareholders' funds: more detailed explanation

9.3.1 Methods and reasons for issuing shares

Methods of issuing shares

Some of the common methods of issuing shares are: *offer for subscription* where the shares are offered directly to the public, *placings* where the shares are arranged (placed) to be bought by financial institutions and *rights issues* whereby the new shares are offered to the existing shareholders at a price below the market price of those shares. The rights issue might be priced significantly below the current market price but this may not mean that the shareholder is benefiting from cheap shares as the price of existing shares will be reduced, e.g. the British Telecommunications plc £5.9 billion rights issue announced in 2001 made UK corporate history in that no British company had attempted to raise so much cash from its shareholders. The offer was three BT shares for every ten held and to encourage take-up, the new shares were offered at a deeply discounted rate of £3 which was at a 47% discount to the share price on the day prior to the launch.

Reasons for issuing shares

● **For future investment** e.g. Watford Leisure plc (Watford Football Club) offered and placed 540,000,000 ordinary shares and expected to raise cash proceeds of about £4.7 million. The company is to be floated on the AIM.

- **As consideration on an acquisition** e.g. Microsoft Corp. acquired Great Plains Software Incorporated, a leading supplier of mid-market business applications. The acquisition was structured as a stock purchase and was valued at approximately $1.1 billion. Each share of Great Plains common stock was exchanged for 1.1 shares of Microsoft common stock.

- **To shareholders to avoid paying out cash from the company's funds** e.g. the BIDVest Group Ltd which decided in 2001 that in lieu of an interim dividend, a cash payment of 40 cents per share should be paid out of share premium, and a capitalisation issue of shares awarded in the ratio of 0.8631 new shares per 100 shares held, being equivalent to 41 cents per share. The total value awarded to shareholders in lieu of a dividend was 81 cents per share.

- **To directors and employees to avoid paying out cash in form of salary from company's funds** e.g. in the Psion 2000 Annual Report the note on directors' remuneration stated:

Name	As at 1/1/00	Exercised	As at 31.12.00	Option price	Market price
M.M. Wyatt	150,000	150,000	–	£0.73	£12.09

9.3.2 Types of preference shares

The following illustrate some of the ways in which specific rights can vary.

Cumulative preference shares
Dividends not paid in respect of any one year because of a lack of profits are accumulated for payment in some future year when distributable profits are sufficient.

Non-cumulative preference shares
Dividends not paid in any one year because of a lack of distributable profits are permanently forgone.

Participating preference shares
These shares carry the right to participate in a distribution of additional profits over and above the fixed rate of dividend after the ordinary shareholders have received an agreed percentage. The participation rights are based on a precise formula.

Redeemable preference shares
These shares may be redeemed by the company at an agreed future date and at an agreed price.

Convertible preference shares
These shares may be converted into ordinary shares at a future date on agreed terms. The conversion is usually at the preference shareholder's discretion.

There can be a mix of rights, e.g. Dixon plc in its 1994 accounts contained 5% dividend convertible cumulative redeemable preference shares with a note that stated 'Subject to certain conditions, preference shares are convertible at the shareholders' option into fully paid Ordinary shares of the Company on 31 October in any years 1994–2002 on the basis of 26.667 Ordinary shares for every 100 Preference shares. The Company will be entitled after 1 January 2003, and will be obliged on 31 December 2007, to redeem at 100p per share any outstanding.'

9.4 Accounting entries on issue of shares

9.4.1 Shares issued at nominal value

If shares are issued at nominal value, the company simply debits the cash account with the amount received and credits the ordinary share capital or preference share capital, as appropriate, with the **nominal value** of the shares.

9.4.2 Shares issued at a premium

The market price of the shares of a company, which is based on the prospects of that company, is invariably different from the par (nominal) value of those shares.

On receipt of consideration for the shares, the company again debits the cash account with the amount received and credits the ordinary share capital or preference share capital, as appropriate, with the **nominal value** of the shares.

Assuming that the market price exceeds the nominal value, a premium element will be credited to a share premium account. The share premium is classified as a **non-distributable reserve** to indicate that it is not repayable to the shareholders who have subscribed for their shares: it remains a part of the company's permanent capital.

The accounting treatment for recording the issue of shares is straightforward. For example, the journal entries to record the issue of 1,000 £1 ordinary shares at a market price of £2.50 per share payable in the following instalments:

on application	on 1 January 20X1	25p
on issue	on 31 January 20X1	£1.75 including the premium
on first call	on 31 January 20X2	25p
on final call	on 31 January 20X4	25p

would be as follows:

1 Jan 20X1	Dr £	Cr £
Cash account	250	
Application account		250

31 Jan 20X1	Dr £	Cr £
Cash account	1,750	
Issue account		1,750

31 Jan 20X1	Dr £	Cr £
Application account	250	
Issue account	1,750	
Share capital account		500
Share premium		1,500

The first and final call would be debited to cash account and credited to share capital account on receipt of the date of the calls.

The other **non-distributable reserve** is the **capital redemption reserve**, which may be created when a company redeems some of its shares without replacing them with new ones. There are detailed accounting rules regarding this, which will be considered in the next chapter.

9.5 Creditor protection: capital maintenance concept

We have seen in earlier chapters that the Companies Act 1985 contains detailed provisions to protect shareholders, e.g. legislation relating to the presentation and disclosure of information in financial statements. To protect **creditors**, the Act has rules relating to the use of the **total shareholders' funds** which determine how much is distributable.

As a general rule, the issued share capital is not repayable to the shareholders and the reserves are classified into two categories: distributable and non-distributable. The directors have discretion as to the amount of the distributable profits that they recommend for distribution as a dividend to shareholders. However, they have no discretion as to the treatment of the non-distributable funds. There is a statutory requirement for the company to retain within the company net assets equal to the non-distributable reserves. This requirement is to safeguard the interests of creditors and is known as **capital maintenance**.

9.6 Creditor protection: why capital maintenance rules are necessary

It is helpful at this point to review the position of unincorporated businesses in relation to capital maintenance.

9.6.1 Unincorporated business

An unincorporated business such as a sole trader or partnership is not required to maintain any specified amount of capital within the business to safeguard the interests of its creditors. The owners are free to decide whether to introduce or withdraw capital. However, they remain personally liable for the liabilities incurred by the business, and the creditors can have recourse to the personal assets of the owners if the business assets are inadequate to meet their claims in full.

When granting credit to an unincorporated business the creditors may well be influenced by the personal wealth and apparent standing of the owners and not merely by the assets of the business as disclosed in its financial statements. This is why in an unincorporated business there is no external reason for the capital and the profits to be kept separate.

In partnerships, there are frequently internal agreements that require each partner to maintain his or her capital at an agreed level. Such agreements are strictly a matter of contract between the owners and do not prejudice the rights of the business creditors.

Sometimes owners attempt to influence creditors unfairly, by maintaining a lifestyle in excess of what they can afford, or to frustrate their legal rights as creditors by putting their private assets beyond their reach, e.g. by transferring their property to relatives or trusts. These subterfuges become apparent only when the creditors seek to enforce their claim against the private asets. Banks are able to protect themselves by seeking adequate security, e.g. a charge on the owners' property.

9.6.2 Incorporated limited liability company

Because of limited liability, the rights of creditors against the private assets of the owners, i.e. the shareholders of the company, are restricted to any amount unpaid on their shares. Once the shareholders have paid the company for their shares, they are not personally liable for the company's debts. Creditors are restricted to making claims against the assets of the company.

Hence the legislature considered it necessary to ensure that the shareholders did not make such distributions to themselves so that the assets needed to meet creditors' claims were put beyond creditors' reach. This was achieved by setting out statutory rules.

9.7 Creditor protection: how to quantify the amounts available to meet creditors' claims

Creditors are exposed to two types of risk: the business risk that a company will operate unsuccessfully and will be unable to pay them; and the risk that a company will operate successfully, but will pay its shareholders rather than its creditors.

The legislature has never intended trade creditors to be protected against ordinary business risks, e.g. the risk of the debtor company incurring either trading losses or losses that might arise from a fall in the value of the assets following changes in market conditions.

The Companies Act 1985 requires the amount available to meet creditors' claims to be calculated by reference to the company's annual financial statements. There are two possible approaches:

- The **direct** approach which requires the **asset** side of the balance sheet to contain assets with a realisable value sufficient to cover all outstanding liabilities.

- The **indirect** approach which requires the **liability** side of the balance sheet to classify reserves into distributable and non-distributable reserves i.e. not available to the shareholders by way of dividend distributions.[1]

The Act follows the indirect approach by specifying capital maintenance in terms of the total shareholders' funds. It thus avoids the thorny problem of asset valuation, which would have led straight back to the arguments considered in Chapter 4 concerning the use of historic cost, realisable values and replacement costs.

However, this has not stopped certain creditors taking steps to protect themselves by following the direct approach, e.g. it is bank practice to obtain a mortgage debenture over the assets of the company. The effect of this is to disadvantage the trade creditors. The statutory restrictions preventing shareholders from reducing capital accounts on the liability side are weakened when management grants certain parties priority rights against some or all of the company's assets.

We will now consider total shareholders' funds and capital maintenance in more detail, starting with share capital. Two aspects of share capital are relevant to creditor protection: minimum capital requirements and reduction of capital. Reduction of capital is dealt with in the next chapter.

9.8 Issued share capital: minimum share capital

The creditors of public companies are protected by the requirements that there should be a minimum share capital and that capital should be reduced only under controlled conditions.

The minimum share capital requirement for a public company is currently set at £50,000, although this can be increased by the Secretary of State for Trade and Industry.[1] A company is not permitted to commence trading unless it has issued this amount.

However, given the size of many public companies, it is questionable whether this figure is adequate.

The minimum share capital requirement refers to the nominal value of the share capital. In the UK, the law requires each class of share to have a stated nominal value. This value is used for identification and also for capital maintenance. The law ensures that a company receives an amount that is at least equal to the nominal value of the shares issued, less a controlled level of commission, by prohibiting the issue of shares at a discount and by limiting any underwriting commissions on an issue. This is intended to avoid a material discount being granted in the guise of commission. However, the requirement is concerned more with safeguarding the relative rights of existing shareholders than with protecting creditors.

There is effectively no minimum capital requirement for private companies. We can see many instances of such companies having an issued and paid-up capital of only a few £1 shares, which cannot conceivably be regarded as adequate creditor protection. The lack of adequate protection for the creditors of private companies is considered again later in the chapter.

9.9 Distributable profits: general considerations

We have considered capital maintenance and undistributable reserves. However, it is not sufficient to attempt to maintain the permanent capital accounts of companies unless there are clear rules on the amount that they can distribute to their shareholders as profit. Without such rules, they may make distributions to their shareholders out of capital. The question of what can legitimately be distributed as profit is an integral part of the concept of capital maintenance in company accounts.

9.9.1 The position before 1980

Before the Companies Act 1980 – now part of the 1985 Act – the position of distributable profits rested largely on case law from the early 1900s. The judgments in those cases were sometimes contradictory and confusing, and often did not coincide with an accountant's view of what constituted distributable profits. This was due to the fact that until 1980 statutes stated only that dividends must not be paid out of capital, and Table A also mentioned that 'dividends must only be paid out of profits'. However, these requirements begged questions as to the nature of profit and capital, rather than providing any clear guidance.

Two questions of general importance should be addressed:

● Should distributable profits include only realised profits, or should they also include unrealised gains?

● Should distributions also include realised capital profits, e.g. arising from the sale of fixed assets?

Realised profits and unrealised gains

Historically, the accounting profession has considered that only realised profits should be distributed. This is because realisation implies the availability of liquid assets, i.e. cash, for distribution. Unrealised profits are not represented by any cash receipt and depend on the subjective views of valuers. This is a good practical view and is reflected in the preparation of profit and loss accounts today.

Legally, in the past, any accumulated realised losses of previous years could have been ignored in deciding the amount of distributable profits of the year in which a distribution was to be made.

Realised revenue profits and realised capital profits

Differentiation between these two is the result of accountant's classification of assets into fixed and current. The accountant's view is that normal trading activities create current assets of a revenue nature, whereas fixed assets are of a capital nature. Therefore, any proceeds from the sale of fixed assets are of a capital nature.

If only realised profits were to be distributed, it was not clear whether this meant only revenue profits, or whether capital profits should also be included. In some companies the latter were taken to a capital reserve, while in others they were taken to the profit and loss account. The now defunct SSAP 6 recommended that the profit and loss account should include all realised profits, which in turn influenced distribution policies. The legal situation was that realised capital profits could be distributed, provided there remained a surplus of assets over liabilities.

9.9.2 Present position

The issue of what constituted distributable profits was clarified by the Companies Act 1980. It is surprising that it took successive governments such a long time to clarify the situation. However, if the EC had not issued its Second Directive, it would probably have taken much longer. In the following sections we will describe the present rules for private and public companies.

9.10 Distributable profits: general rule for private companies

The definition of distributable profits under the Companies Act 1985 is:

Accumulated, realised profits, so far as not previously utilised by distribution or capitalisation, less its accumulated, realised losses, as far as not previously written off in a reduction or reorganisation of capital.

This means the following:

- Unrealised profits cannot be distributed.

- There is no difference between realised revenue and realised capital profits.

- All accumulated net realised profits (i.e. realised profits less realised losses) on the balance sheet date must be considered.

EXAMPLE ● An analysis of the shareholders' funds section of a company's balance sheet as at the end of its latest financial year is set out in Figure 9.1.

The distributable profit of this private company on the balance sheet date is simply its accumulated net realised profit, i.e. £1,600,000. No account need be taken of any accumulated net unrealised gains or losses. This means that there could be a reduction in the permanent capital of the company of £100,000 if the maximum amount is distributed. Its net assets after such a distribution are shown in Figure 9.2.

Figure 9.1 Shareholders' funds

	£000	£000
Share capital		2,000
Share premium		600
Capital redemption reserve		200
Permanent capital at beginning of year		2,800
Unrealised: gains	100	
: losses	(200)	
		(100)
Permanent capital at end of the year		2,700
Realised: current year's profits	500	
: current year's losses	(100)	
	400	
: previous year's b/f	1,200	
		1,600
Net assets of company		4,300

Figure 9.2 Net assets after distribution of profits

	£000	£000
Share capital		2,000
Share premium		600
Capital redemption reserve		200
Permanent capital at beginning of year		2,800
Unrealised: gains	100	
: losses	(200)	
		(100)
Permanent capital at end of the year – net assets		2,700

9.11 Distributable profits: general rule for public companies

According to the Companies Act, the undistributable reserves of a public company are its share capital, share premium, capital redemption reserve and also 'the excess of accumulated unrealised profits over accumulated unrealised losses at the time of the intended distribution and … any reserves not allowed to be distributed under the Act or by the company's own Memorandum or Articles of Association'.

This means that, when dealing with a public company, the distributable profits have to be reduced by any net unrealised loss. In our example above, the distributable profits would be £1,500,000 if the company were a public company. We arrive at this by applying the wording of the Act that its net assets will not be less than:

	£000
Share capital	2,000
Share premium	600
Capital redemption reserve	200
Excess of unrealised profits over unrealised losses	No excess
	2,800

The net accumulated unrealised loss figure of £100,000 in the above example would be unusual in practice, since any net deficiency on the revaluation of an asset would normally be taken to the profit and loss account and may be deemed to have implications for distribution policy.

9.11.1 Investment companies

The Act allows for the special nature of some businesses in the calculation of distributable profits. There are additional rules for investment companies in calculating their distributable profits. For a company to be classified as an investment company, it must invest its funds mainly in securities with the aim of spreading investment risk and giving its members the benefit of the results of managing its funds.

Such a company has the option of applying one of two rules in calculating its distributable profits. These are either:

● the rules that apply to public companies in general, but excluding any realised capital profits, e.g. from the disposal of investments; or

● the company's accumulated realised revenue less its accumulated realised and unrealised revenue losses, provided that its assets are at least one and a half times its liabilities both before and after such a distribution.

The reasoning behind these special rules seems to be to allow investment companies to pass the dividends they receive to their shareholders, irrespective of any changes in the values of their investments, which are subject to market fluctuations. However, the asset cover ratio of liabilities can easily be manipulated by the company simply paying creditors, whereby the ratio is improved, or borrowing, whereby it is reduced.

EXAMPLE ● Figure 9.3 provides an analysis of the shareholders' funds and liabilities of an investment company.

Distributable profits of the company are:

● Under the general rule:

	£000
Realised revenue profits	700
Less: Excess of unrealised losses over unrealised profits (£900,000 + £100,000 − £0)	(1,000)
Nil distributable	(300)

Figure 9.3 Shareholders' funds and liabilities of an investment company

	£000
Share capital	2,000
Capital profits (losses):	
Realised	400
Unrealised	(900)
Revenue profits (losses):	
Realised	700
Unrealised	(100)
Shareholders' funds, i.e. net assets	2,100
Liabilities	1,000
Total assets	3,100

or, applying the net asset maintenance rule:

	£000
Share capital	2,000
Excess of unrealised profits over unrealised losses	No excess
Other undistributable profits:	
Realised capital profit	400
	2,400

Under this option the company cannot distribute any profits unless net assets can be maintained at £2,400,000, whereas its net assets at the balance sheet date are £2,100,000.

● Under the second (investment company) rule:

	£000
Realised revenue profits	700
Less: Realised or unrealised revenue losses	(100)
Distributable profit	600

Subject to asset cover ratio of liabilities:

$$\text{Before distribution} \quad \frac{3,100,000}{1,000,000} \quad = 3.1 \text{ times}$$

$$\text{After distribution} \quad \frac{3,100,000 - 600,000}{1,000,000} \quad = 2.5 \text{ times}$$

In both cases the asset cover ratio of liabilities is more than 1.5 times and therefore the company can distribute £600,000 profit to its shareholders.

9.12 Distributable profits: how to arrive at the amount using relevant accounts

The Companies Act stipulates that distributable profits of a company must be based on **relevant accounts**. These would normally be the audited annual accounts, which have been prepared according to the requirements of the Act to give a true and fair view of the company's financial affairs. In the case of a qualified audit report, the auditor is required to prepare a written statement stating whether such a qualification is material in determining a company's distributable profit. Interim dividends are allowed to be paid provided they can be justified on the basis of the latest annual accounts, otherwise interim accounts will have to be prepared that would justify such a distribution.

9.13 Distributable profits: realisation principle applies

Realisation is central to the determination of profits which can be legally distributed to shareholders in either cash or non-cash form. The Companies Act provides that 'only profits realised at the balance sheet date shall be included in the profit and loss account'.

9.13.1 Retained profit figure may not consist only of realised profits

It is not always the case that the retained profit on a balance sheet consists only of realised profits and is therefore wholly distributable. The overriding requirement that accounts should give a true and fair view can lead to a mismatch between profits that are reported in order to present a true and fair view and profits that are distributable within the legal definition of the Companies Act.

An example is the calculation of the depreciation charge on revalued assets. The true and fair requirement as set out in FRS 15 is that the depreciation charge should be calculated on the carrying value of the asset in the balance sheet. If it were revalued from £100 to £200, the depreciation would be based on the £200. However, the legal requirement is that it should be based on the cost figure of £100.

In general, however, the retained balance may be regarded as realised and distributable.

9.13.2 Companies Act and the concept of realised profit

On the key question of whether a profit is realised or not, the Act simply says that realised profits or realised losses are:

> such profits or losses of the company as fall to be treated as realised in accordance with principles generally accepted, at the time when the accounts are prepared, with respect to the determination for accounting purposes of realised profits or losses. (Schedule 4, para. 91)

Hence the Act does not lay down detailed rules on what is and what is not a realised profit; indeed, it does not even refer specifically to 'accounting principles'. Nevertheless, it would seem reasonable for decisions on realisation to be based on **generally accepted accounting principles** at the time, subject to the court's decision in cases of dispute.

Generally, revenue is deemed to have been realised on receipt of cash or if the receipt of cash is reasonably certain. But the basis of realisation is viewed differently now, whereby realisation is associated with the occurrence of the critical (risky) event in the operating cycle of a business. The latest FRS 18, which supersedes SSAP 2, follows the recent recommendations of the ASB, whereby a gain is accepted to have realised if it is reasonably certain that it will occur and that it can be measured with sufficient reliability.

There seems to be a case for clarifying the basis and nature of costs and expenses, too, which can be deducted from realised revenue in calculating realised profit. One example covered by the Companies Act is the depreciation charge in the profit statement. According to FRS 15, the depreciation charge in the profit and loss account should be based on the carrying value of a fixed asset. However, the Companies Act only requires a deduction of depreciation based on the historic cost of a fixed asset, in calculating the distributable profit of a company. The Act regards any excess depreciation, over the historic cost based figure, as part of the realised profit.

Besides the question of depreciation, the Companies Act includes only a few specific provisions on the treatment of other events. We consider two such provisions: development costs and fixed asset valuations.

Development costs

The Act provides that (product) development costs can be treated as a **realised** loss unless directors can justify treating it differently by special circumstances. An ICAEW Technical Release (TECH 7/03)[2] states that, if the accounts have been prepared according to the requirements of the Companies Act and professional accounting and reporting standards, any consequent profit or loss is to be taken as realised unless a standard specifically states that an item is unrealised.

This seems to imply that, if the development costs have been accounted for in accordance with the requirements of SSAP 13, the amount taken to the profit and loss account is the realised part of the total cost.

Fixed asset revaluations

The Act provides that any diminution in the value of a fixed asset arising as a result of revaluations of **all** fixed assets (whether including goodwill or not) is an **unrealised** loss. This seems to imply that the revaluation of an **individual** asset would amount to a **realised** loss. In practice, the Act allows such a loss to be regarded as unrealised, provided directors can satisfy themselves (without an actual revaluation of all assets) that the aggregate value of assets is not less than their book value.

Summary

Creditors of companies are not expected to be protected against ordinary business risks as these are taken care of by financial markets, e.g. through the rates of interest charged on different capital instruments of different companies. However, the creditors are entitled to depend on the non-erosion of the permanent capital where the shareholders may pay themselves out of capital.

A major part of this protection is the regulation of distributions (e.g. dividends) to shareholders. Until the early 1980s the situation regarding this was confusing and unclear, but this has changed a great deal as a result of the Companies Act 1985.

> Nevertheless, the question of distributable profits carries the problem of the application of the generally accepted accounting principles in deciding on what constitutes as 'realised profit'. These accounting principles are subject to change over time.

REVIEW QUESTIONS

1 What is the relevance of dividend cover if dividends are paid out of distributable profits?

2 How do industries differ in the levels of distributable profits?

3 What is the significance of high distributable profits to an existing/potential investor/loan creditor/creditor?

4 Why is the distributable profits figure not apparent from the accounts?

5 Give four examples of reasons why the retained profit figure might not equal distributable profits.

6 Is there any relationship between non-distributable reserves and total assets?

7 How can distributable profits become non-distributable?

8 In what circumstances can non-distributable reserves become distributable?

9 The Companies Act requires capitalised development costs to be deducted from realised profits unless circumstances justify the policy of capitalisation. Discuss (a) why you think the Act contains this provision and (b) what you consider would provide adequate justification for deferring the charge to the current year's profit and loss account.

10 (a) The regional electricity companies and the National Grid argued strongly against the ASB proposal to require full provisioning for deferred tax on its revision of SSAP 15. Explain why these companies would have been so strongly opposed.

   (b) Full provisioning for deferred tax would result in increased tax charges on earnings and large deferred tax liabilities, neither of which are likely to materialise. Explain (i) why they are unlikely to materialise, and (ii) how to reduce the impact while still following the principle of full provisioning.

   (c) It has been stated that 'by reducing distributable reserves the proposals directly affect not only annual dividends but also the apparent gearing position and balance sheet strength of companies. These proposals would do serious damage to the strength of an important sector of the economy.'[3] Discuss whether the effect on distributable profit is an acceptable reason for not providing in full for deferred tax.

EXERCISES

An extract from the solution is provided in the appendix at the end of the text for exercises marked with an asterisk (*).

* Question I

(a) Define the term 'distribution', and state what items the Companies Act 1985 excludes from its definition of a distribution.

(b) Explain the need for the introduction of statutory rules concerning the distribution of a company's profits.

(c) State the Companies Act 1985 requirements regarding distributions by both public and private limited companies.

(d) State what other principal non-legal limitations the directors of a company would take into account when deciding on a distribution policy.

(e) You have draft balance sheets of two companies as follows:

	Company A £000	Company B £000
Fixed assets		
Property at valuation	90	90
Investment at cost	10	10
Net current assets (liabilities)	60	(20)
	160	80

	Company A £000	Company B £000
Share capital	10	10
Share premium	20	20
Revaluation reserve	40	50
Profit and loss account	90	—
	160	80

You also ascertain the following:

1 Additional depreciation charged to the profit and loss account to date as a result of revaluations is £5,000 for company A and £10,000 for company B.

2 The fixed asset investments of both company A and company B have subsequent to the year-end proved to be worthless.

3 A court case has commenced against company B for £20,000. The directors have not come to a conclusion on the accounting treatment of this case, but they believe the loss after tax would be £13,000.

4 Company B had sold a plot of land at its revalued amount. However, the net gain of £15,000 over the original cost was still shown in the revaluation reserve and not in the profit and loss account.

Required:
State with clear reasoning the maximum dividends that could be paid by companies A and B respectively:
(a) treating them as private companies;
(b) treating them as public limited companies.

Question 2

V.R. Confident Ltd
Profit and loss account for the year ended 30 November 20X2

	£000
Net profit for the year, before taxation	604
Corporation tax, at 33%	290
	314

Balance sheet as on 30 November 20X2

Ordinary share capital		800
6% preference share capital		300
Share premium		200
Capital redemption reserve		400
Asset revaluation reserve		250
General reserve		160
Profit and loss account:		
Balance brought forward	(288)	
Current year	314	26
		2,136

Notes

(a) One-half of the asset revaluation reserve represents an increase in the value of a freehold property which was sold during the year to 30 November 20X2 (at the revalued amount). This sale was not recorded in the accounts. A tax liability of £35,000 is expected in connection with the disposal.

(b) The £300,000 depreciation charge to the profit and loss account was based on revalued figures. This charge would have been £240,000 if it had been based on the original cost of fixed assets.

(c) Some of the stock-in-trade, which appeared on the draft balance sheet at cost, was later sold for £90,000 below this figure.

(d) The draft balance sheet of company includes £500,000 research and development expenditure under fixed assets.

(e) Since the preparation of the draft accounts, one of the debtors of the company has gone into liquidation and is not expected to pay more than 50p in the £1 to its creditors. This debtor owed £120,000 to V.R. Confident Ltd on 30 November 20X2.

Required:
(a) Explain briefly the provisions of Companies Act 1985 relating to profits that a company can distribute as dividends.
(b) Calculate the maximum amount of dividends that the directors of V.R. Confident Ltd may propose to pay to ordinary shareholders within the legal requirements and in conformity with the relevant Statements of Standard Accounting Practice. Also state whether your answer would be different if V.R. Confident Ltd were a public limited company (plc).

* Question 3

The following are details of three separate companies' summarised balance sheets at 31 March 20X7.

	Alpha plc £000	Beta plc £000	Gamma Ltd £000
Fixed assets	5,000	760	1,000
Current assets	1,800	360	600
Current liabilities	(1,400)	(320)	(400)
	5,400	800	1,200
Share capital	400	600	4,000
Reserves: revaluation	2,200	(400)	—
Realised capital profit	1,600	—	—
Brought forward realised revenue profit (loss)	800	1,000	(3,200)
Current year realised revenue profit (loss)	400	(400)	400
	5,400	800	1,200

Alpha's property, previously included in the financial statements at original cost of £1,800,000, was revalued on 1 April 20X6 at £4 million. The revalued amount is included in the figures above, subject to the full amount being written off equally over the next 50 years from 1 April 20X6. Prior to this date, no depreciation had been provided on property. At 31 March 20X7, no transfer had been made between revaluation reserve and realised revenue profit.

Required:
(a) Compare briefly the bases for calculating the maximum distribution under the provisions of the Companies Act 1985 in respect of public and private companies.
(b) Calculate the maximum distribution that Alpha, Beta and Gamma could each make under the Companies Act 1985.

References

1 Companies Act 1985.
2 Tech 7/03 *Guidance on the Determination of Realised Profits and Losses in the Context of Distributions under the Companies Act 1985*, ICAEW 2003.
3 *Revenue Recognition*, discussion paper by ASB, 2001.

CHAPTER 10

Reduction of share capital

10.1 Introduction

In this chapter, we consider restrictions on the reduction of share capital and the accounting treatment of the share premium and the capital redemption reserve. We outline the legal requirements under the Companies Act 1985 for the redemption of shares by public and private companies, and for fundamental changes in a company's capital structure.

10.2 Capital: restrictions on reduction of capital

Once the shares have been issued and paid up, the share capital account is credited with the nominal value of such shares and this value forms part of the capital to be maintained. The intention is that this amount should not be reduced. However, there might be commercially sound reasons for a company to reduce its capital. The Companies Act therefore has provision for share capital to be reduced, subject to the consent of the court, in three ways.

1 Writing off part of capital which has already been lost and is not represented by assets

This situation normally occurs when a company has accumulated trading losses which prevent it from making dividend payments under the rules relating to distributable profits. The general approach is to credit the profit and loss account in order to eliminate any debit balance, and to debit share capital and non-distributable reserves. This has the effect of eliminating current losses, thus making future profits distributable. The debit balance on profit and loss account is transferred to a capital reduction account, and this account is credited with amounts transferred from the share capital and reserves.

The consent of the creditors may be required by order of the court. The rules governing a reduction of capital are that no reduction can be made unless it is authorised by the articles of association of the company, is approved by a special resolution of the shareholders and secures the consent of the court. The rights of the creditors are thus protected directly or indirectly through the court.

2 Repayment of part of paid-up capital to shareholders or cancellation of unpaid share capital

This can occur when a company wishes to reduce its unwanted liquid resources. The accounting entries for the repayment are to credit cash and debit share capital. The consent of the creditors is required.

3 Redemption of shares

This is discussed in section 10.5 below.

10.3 Non-distributable reserves: share premium

Prior to the Companies Act 1948, if a company issued shares at a premium, the premium could be distributed to the shareholders. However, it came to be recognised that the premium represented a capital receipt and should be treated in the same way as the nominal value of the shares. Consequently, the Companies Act now requires any premium to be taken to a separate share premium account as a non-distributable reserve. For example, if a company issued 100 £1 shares (nominal value) at a premium of £2.50 per share, the capital receipt of £350 would be recorded as follows:

	£	£
Cash	350	
Share capital		100
Share premium		250

Although both the proceeds from the nominal value of the shares and the premium element are regarded as capital receipts, the company has more flexibility in using its shares premium account. For example, it can be used to:

1 issue fully paid bonus shares;

2 write off preliminary expenses (i.e. company formation costs);

3 write off any share or debenture issue expenses or any discounts on the issue of debentures;

4 write off any premiums (payable) on redemption or purchase of own shares, provided the shares being redeemed or purchased were themselves issued at a premium and that adequate funds exist in the share premium account.

Let us consider each of these uses in terms of their impact on creditor protection. The capitalisation of the reserve indicated by (1) maintains the creditors' protection, since the share premium is reclassified as share capital, i.e.:

	£	£
Share premium	250	
Share capital		250

However, uses (2)–(4) reduce their protection, even though no direct payment has been made to any of the shareholders. To illustrate this, let us assume that the company's balance sheet includes the following items:

	£
Share capital	100
Share premium	250
Permanent capital	350

Further, assume that the company issues one 10% debenture (nominal value £100) for £90 cash and decides, applying (3) above, to write off the discount against the share premium account. The entries in the company's books would be:

	£	£
Cash	90	
Debentures discount	10	
10% Debentures		100
Share premium	10	
Debenture discount		10

The balance sheet items following these transactions would be:

	£
Share capital	100
Share premium	240
Permanent capital	340
10% Debentures	100
	440

Because the rules permit the discount to be classified as a capital item, the permanent capital available for the protection of capital has been depleted to the extent of the discount. The same would apply to uses (2) and (4). This did not matter unduly when the amount of discount on debentures was immaterial, but we have seen many examples in recent years of financial instruments being issued at material discounts, e.g. deep discounting.

10.4 Non-distributable reserves: capital redemption reserve

Until the beginning of the twentieth century, companies were not allowed to buy back their own shares after they had been issued. Shareholders could convert their investment into cash only by selling their shares to a third party either privately or via the Stock Exchange. This meant that the share capital base of the company could not be depleted by a return of capital, so the level of protection afforded to the creditors was unchanged by share transfers between existing and new shareholders.

However, commercial considerations caused a relaxation in the rules to accommodate shareholders who wanted to be reasonably certain of recovering the capital amount that they originally invested. To attract their investment, companies were permitted to issue **redeemable preference shares**.

When redeemable preference shares were redeemed, the company was required either to replace them with other shares or to make a transfer from distributable reserves to non-distributable reserves in order to maintain the permanent capital. The non-distributable reserve was called a capital redemption reserve and there were restrictions on how it could be used.

The accounting entries were to credit cash and debit the redeemable preference share account on redemption, and to credit a capital redemption reserve and debit the profit and loss account with an equal amount.

This right to redeem preference shares was later extended by the Companies Act 1981 to permit companies to purchase their own ordinary shares.

10.4.1 Purchase of own shares

The Companies Act now permits a company to effect **market** or **off-market** purchases of its own ordinary shares. Market purchases are those shares purchased from a recognised Stock Exchange and off-market purchases are all other shares. Market purchases must be authorised by the articles of association and an **ordinary resolution** of the shareholders setting out terms such as the price to be paid and the timing of the purchase.

Off-market purchases offer a greater opportunity for abuse by the directors and there are accordingly more stringent legal requirements, such as the need for a **specific purchase contract** which requires a **special resolution** of the shareholders.

In this chapter we will not distinguish between redemption and purchase of own shares, since the same accounting considerations apply to both.

10.4.2 Buyback of own shares

There are a number of reasons for companies buying back shares. These include:

● to return excess cash for which the company is unable to find suitable investment opportunities

● to optimise the company's capital structure and debt ratio

● to increase earnings per share – this is achieved by reducing the number of shares; however, there is an opposite effect to be taken into account in that there may be lower interest income or higher interest expense which has an impact on the earnings figure

● to increase the share price over the long term by increasing continuing shareholders' future cash flow per share

● to make a distribution more tax efficient than the payment of a cash dividend

An example of a buyback is the Royal Dutch Petroleum Company (NV Koninklijke Nederlandsche Petroleum Maatschappij) which announced that on 27 September 2001 it had purchased 865,000 ordinary shares at a price of €51.97 per share. This meant that since the launch of the company's share buyback programmes on 8 February 2001 the Royal Dutch Petroleum Company had repurchased a total of 42,861,352 ordinary shares leaving 2,101,435,000 ordinary shares outstanding in the market.

10.4.3 Companies Act requirements

The Companies Act states that:

● No redemption can take place unless the shares are fully paid up. This is to protect creditors who regard any uncalled capital as part of the capital base of the company.

● No redemption can take place which would result in there being no shareholders. This would in effect be a winding-up or liquidation of the company and other rules would then apply.

● All redeemed shares are to be cancelled. This is to prevent the directors attempting to manipulate the market so as to create an artificial price for the shares.

Different rules apply to the redemption of shares by public companies and by private companies. We will consider each in turn.

10.5 Capital: redemption of shares by a public company

Although a public company is now permitted to redeem shares so that an individual shareholder can liquidate a shareholding, it is required to maintain the same overall level of permanent capital for the protection of the creditors. This can be achieved in two different ways.

Firstly, redemption can be made **out of the distributable profits** of a company. In this case the Act requires the transfer of an amount equal to the nominal value of the redeemed shares from distributable profits to a capital redemption reserve.

A capital redemption reserve may only be used for issuing fully paid bonus shares to the shareholders. In other words, it is like share capital in its permanence. Such a transfer from distributable profits is described as a capitalisation, which means that profits have been capitalised and the permanent capital has been maintained.

Furthermore, if the shares are redeemed at a premium, i.e. at a price above their nominal value, any such premium cannot be carried forward in the accounts, but must be written off against distributable profits.

For example, a company buys 50 of its own £1 shares at a premium of £2 each, i.e. it makes a capital repayment of £150. The accounting entries are shown in Figure 10.1.

Secondly, shares may be redeemed **out of the proceeds of a new share issue**. In practice, a redemption may be made partly out of profits and partly out of the proceeds of a new issue. The accounting requirements are as follows:

1 An amount equal to the excess of the nominal value of redeemed shares over the total proceeds of any new issue is to be transferred from distributable profits to capital redemption reserve, i.e. they become classified as an undistributable reserve.

2 Any premium on redemption may be written off against distributable profits. However, if the company wishes to reduce the impact on its distributable profits, it may set off the premium on redemption against the share premium account, i.e. an undistributable

Figure 10.1 Balance sheet before and after redemption

Balance sheet before redemption		Purchase	W/off premium	Transfer to CRR	Balance sheet
	£	£	£	£	£
Share capital	100	(50)			50
Capital redemption reserve (CRR)				50	50
Share premium	240				240
Permanent capital	340				340
P&L account	160		(100)	(50)	10
	500				350
Cash	200	(150)			50
Other assets	300				300
Premium on redemption		100	(100)		—
	500				350

reserve. However, this is subject to certain constraints. The amount of set-off is restricted to the lowest of:

(a) any share premium originally received on the issue of the shares that are now being redeemed; or
(b) the amount standing to the credit of the share premium account, including any premium received on the newly issued shares; or
(c) the total proceeds of the new issue.

EXAMPLE ● Ozer plc had issued class B shares at a premium of £1 each, i.e. at £2 per share in 20X1. In 20X4 the company issued 20 class A shares of £1 each at a premium of £1 each, receiving a total capital receipt of £40. It then redeemed 50 class B shares of £1 each at a premium of £3 for a total capital repayment of £200, i.e. there was a premium on redemption of £150.

Management would normally propose writing off the premium on redemption of £150 against the share premium account to avoid reducing the distributable profits. However, the outcomes of the above criteria are as follows:

● Share premium originally received on the issue of the class B shares which are now being redeemed: £50.

● Amount standing to the credit of the share premium account, including any premium received on the newly issued shares: £240 + £20 = £260.

● Total proceeds of the new issue: £40.

We can see that the maximum that can be written off the share premium is £40. The remaining £110 has to be written off the distributable profits.

It then remains to determine the amount required to be transferrred to the capital redemption reserve account. This is calculated as follows:

	£
Nominal value of shares redeemed	50
Less: Total proceeds of the new issue	(40)
Required transfer from distributable profits	10

The balance sheet items before and after the issue of the class A shares and the redemption of the class B shares are shown in Figure 10.2.

We can see from the revised balance sheet that, in spite of the legal requirements, the permanent capital of the company has not been maintained. It has actually been reduced by £40 from £340 to £300. This means that part of the redemption has been made out of capital. It could be maintained by the transfer to capital redemption reserve of £30, which is the difference in the nominal value of shares redeemed (£50) and issued (£20), and by the premium chargeable to share premium account not being more than the premium received from the new issue, i.e. £20. Nevertheless, as the law stands, on redemption the capital of a public company may be reduced or increased rather than being maintained. It is the reduction in capital that is important to the creditors.

Figure 10.2 Balance sheet before and after issue and redemption of shares

Balance sheet before redemption		New issue	Purchase	W/off premium	Transfer to CRR	Balance sheet
	£	£	£	£	£	£
Share capital:						
Class A	50	20				70
Class B	50		(50)			—
Capital redemption reserve					10	10
Share premium	240	20	___	(40)	___	220
Permanent capital	340					300
P&L account	160	___	___	(110)	(10)	40
	500					340
Cash	200	40	(200)			40
Other assets	300					300
Premium on redemption	___		150	(150)		___
	500					340

10.6 Capital: redemption of shares by a private company

The Companies Act explicitly accepts that private companies may reduce their permanent capital in order to keep control within the same family or group of people.

This can arise when a shareholder dies or decides to leave the company and the other shareholders are not in a position to buy the shares. In such cases, if the company buys the shares, the control remains with the remaining shareholders. However, the legislature recognised that a counterbalance was required to provide additional protection for the creditors. Consequently, the rights of the creditors are protected by requiring the directors to make a declaration of solvency.

The company must declare that it will still be able to pay its creditors after the redemption and that it will continue to be able to do so for a year after the date of the redemption. The declaration is also required to be agreed and reported upon by the company's auditors. Furthermore, the company must publicise the intended redemption in order to inform the creditors who may object to such a redemption through the courts.

It is perhaps ironic that private companies are required to make a declaration of solvency in relation to an intentional reduction of capital, whereas public companies are not required to do so, although a reduction might also have occurred in their case. The creditors of a private company may actually be in a stronger position than those of a public company.

The accounting requirements for private companies are that any reduction in their permanent capital should not exceed the **permissible capital payment** as defined by the Act. This payment is the excess of the total amount paid on redemption of shares over the distributable profits of a company and the proceeds of any new share issue specifically made for the purposes of redemption. The accounting entries needed to confine the reduction in permanent capital to the permissible capital payment are as follows:

● If the nominal value of shares redeemed exceeds the permissible capital payment, an amount equal to the excess must be transferred from distributable profits to the capital redemption reserve account.

● If the nominal value of shares redeemed is less than the permissible capital payment, an amount equal to this plus the proceeds of any new share issue may be used to reduce any undistributable reserves. Undistributable reserves for this purpose include any unrealised gain, share premium, capital redemption reserve and share capital.

The general effect is that, in limiting the reduction in permanent capital to the permissible amount, a private company first utilises its distributable profit before reducing any undistributable reserves. The following two examples show the nature of adjustments needed for this purpose.

EXAMPLE ● A private company redeems 50 of its shares of £1 each at a premium of £3 per share, i.e. for £200. It does not issue any new shares. Its balance sheet is shown in Figure 10.3.

Figure 10.3 Balance sheet before and after redemption at a premium

Balance sheet before redemption		Redemption of shares	Write-off redemption premium	Transfer to CRR	Balance sheet after redemption
	£	£	£	£	£
Share capital	100	(50)			50
Capital redemption reserve				10	10
Share premium	240				240
Permanent capital	340				300
P&L account	160		(150)	(10)	—
	500				300
Cash	260	(200)			60
Other assets	240				240
Premium on redemption	—	150	(150)		—
	500				300

Calculation of permissible capital payment:	£
Amount payable on redemption	200
Less: Distributable profits	(160)
Permissible capital payment	40
Transfer to capital redemption reserve:	
Nominal value of shares redeemed	50
Less: Permissible capital payment	(40)
Capital redemption reserve	10

In this case the nominal value of shares redeemed is more than the permissible capital payment. A transfer is made from distributable profits to the capital redemption reserve to limit the reduction to the permissible capital amount of £40.

EXAMPLE ● A private company redeems 50 of its class B shares of £1 each at a premium of £5 per share, i.e. for £300. It also issues 20 class A shares of £1 each at a premium of £2 per share, i.e. for £60, to help finance the redemption. Its balance sheet is shown in Figure 10.4.

In this case the nominal value of redeemed shares is less than the permissible capital payment and therefore the permanent capital (i.e. undistributable reserves) can be reduced by the difference. However, as the newly issued shares have already increased

Figure 10.4 Balance sheet before and after issue and redemption of shares at a premium

Balance sheet before redemption		Issue of A shares	Redemption of B shares	Transfer from P&L a/c	Transfer from permanent capital	Balance sheet
	£	£	£	£	£	£
Share capital:						
Class A	50	20				70
Class B	50		(50)			—
Share premium	240	40			(90)	190
Permanent capital	340					260
P&L account	160			(160)		—
	500					260
Cash	260	60	(300)			20
Other assets	240					240
Premium on						
redemption	—		250	(160)	(90)	—
	500					260

Calculation of permissible capital payment:

Amount payable on redemption		300
Less: Distributable profits	160	
Less: New issue proceeds	60	
		(220)
Permissible capital payment		80

Required transfer in the accounts:

Nominal value of shares redeemed	50
Less: Permissible capital payment	(80)
Allowed reduction in permanent capital:	(30)
Also: New issue proceeds because it has increased the permanent capital	(60)
Total allowed reduction in permanent capital	(90)

the permanent capital, the total reduction in undistributable reserves includes the new issue too. The result is a reduction of £80 in the original permanent capital, which is the permissible capital payment in this case.

10.7 Distributable profits: effect of accumulated trading losses

A company's distributable profits made in the current year are affected by its accumulated profit or loss position. We have seen that existing losses must be made good before a distribution can be made. However, a company might have experienced significant losses which require a fundamental change to its capital structure.

10.7.1 Elimination that affects only the ordinary shareholders

The Companies Act 1985, section 135, allows a company to reduce its capital where it has incurred losses and the share capital is no longer represented by available assets. This provides the statutory authority for a company that has suffered losses, but now believes that it has overcome the problems and will be profitable, to adjust its capital to reflect the current level of asset backing.

One of the results of doing this is that future profits become available for distribution rather than being required to be set off against the accumulated losses. It is a material change for the shareholders, who will be able to receive a dividend from future profits without losses being required to be made good first. Consequently, authority for the reduction must be contained in the articles of association, there must be a special resolution with a majority of at least 75% of the members voting in favour of the proposal and court approval must be obtained.

10.7.2 Accounting treatment for a capital reduction to eliminate accumulated trading losses

The accounting treatment is straightforward. A capital reduction account is opened. It is debited with the accumulated losses and credited with the amount written off the share capital.

For example, assume that the capital and reserves of Hopeful Ltd were as follows at 31 December 20X1:

	£
200,000 ordinary shares of £1 each	200,000
Profit and loss account	(180,000)

The directors estimate that the company will return to profitability in 20X2, achieving profits of £4,000 per annum thereafter. Without a capital reduction, the profits from 20X2 must be used to reduce the accumulated losses. This means that the company would be unable to pay a dividend for forty-five years if it continued at that level of profitability and ignoring tax. Perhaps even more importantly, it would not be attractive for shareholders to put additional capital into the company because they would not be able to obtain any dividend for some years.

The directors therefore obtained a special resolution and court approval to reduce the £1 ordinary shares to ordinary shares of 10p each. The accounting entries would be:

	Dr £	Cr £
Capital reduction account	180,000	
Profit and loss account:		180,000
Transfer of debit balance		
Share capital	180,000	
Capital reduction account:		180,000
Reduction of share capital		

10.7.3 Accounting treatment for a capital reduction to eliminate accumulated trading losses and loss of value on fixed assets

Companies often take the opportunity to revalue all of their assets at the same time as they eliminate the accumulated trading losses. Any loss on revaluation is then treated in the same way as the accumulated losses and transferred to the capital reduction account.

For example, assume that the capital and reserves and assets of Hopeful Ltd were as follows at 31 December 20X1:

	£	£
200,000 ordinary shares of £1 each		200,000
Profit and loss account		(180,000)
		20,000
Fixed assets		
Plant and machinery		15,000
Current assets		
Cash	17,000	
Current liabilities		
Creditors	12,000	
Net current assets		5,000
		20,000

The plant and machinery is revalued at £5,000 and it is resolved to reduce the share capital to ordinary shares of 5p each. The accounting entries would be:

	Dr £	Cr £
Capital reduction account	190,000	
Profit and loss account		180,000
Plant and machinery:		10,000
Transfer of accumulated losses and loss on revaluation		
Share capital	190,000	
Capital reduction account:		190,000
Reduction of share capital to 200,000 shares of 5p each		

The balance sheet after the capital reduction shows that the share capital fairly reflects the underlying asset values:

	£	£
200,000 ordinary shares of 5p each		10,000
		10,000
Fixed assets		
Plant and machinery		5,000
Current assets		
Cash	17,000	
Current liabilities		
Creditors	12,000	5,000
		10,000

An interesting illustration appears in the 1996 accounts of T&N plc. T&N plc is one of the world's leading suppliers of high technology automotive components and industrial materials. In 1996 the company achieved operating profits of £178m on a turnover of £2,038m. The company is amongst many defendants named in court actions brought in the United States relating to alleged asbestos-related diseases resulting from exposure to asbestos products. The company made a provision of £515m in respect of asbestos-related claims. This resulted in a debit balance on profit and loss account in the 1996 balance sheet of £259.6m and the company shareholders and court approved a reduction in the issued share capital by the cancellation of 60p per £1 ordinary share. The capital reduction was to take effect after 31 December 1996 and the accounts contain a proforma statement amended as follows:

	Called up share capital	Share premium	Special reserve (iii)	Revaluation reserves	Goodwill write off reserve	Associates reserves	P & L	Equity shareholders funds
As at 31.12.1996	532.2	0.2	—	21.6	(181.1)	5.0	(259.6)	118.3
Capital reduction (i)	(319.3)	—	319.3	—	—	—	—	—
Eliminate deficit on Holding company P&L Account (ii)	—	—	(262.5)	—	5.3	—	257.2	—
After capital reduction	212.9	0.2	56.8	21.6	(175.8)	5.0	(2.4)	118.3

(i) Reduction in the nominal value of each ordinary share from £1 to 40p.
(ii) Application of special reserve to eliminate the deficit on the holding company's profit and loss account, including goodwill previously written off.
(iii) The special reserve is not distributable.

Following a capital reduction there is a natural concern for shareholders as to the level of future dividends. T&N addressed any such concerns by the following note which indicated that the large asbestos-related provision in 1996 and the resulting capital reduction was to have no effect on the income shareholders could expect from their shares compared to previous years. It read:

As a result of the capital reduction the company is only able to declare dividends out of profits arising after January 1997. Accordingly, there will be no final dividend for the year ended 31 December 1996. Subject to there being sufficient profits available, however, the directors intend to declare a special first 1997 dividend of 3p per share in lieu of the final 1996 dividend with the result that the shareholders will receive the same dividend as in 1996.

Clearly the provision of £515m will have an impact on the rate of growth the company is able to achieve after 1996 but at least the dividends are being maintained.

10.7.4 Elimination that affects the ordinary shareholders and other stakeholders

In the Hopeful Ltd example, the ordinary shareholders alone bore the losses. The Companies Act, sections 425–427, provides a procedure for a reconstruction that involves a compromise between shareholders and creditors, with an amendment of the rights of the latter.

Such a reconstruction requires the support of 75% of each class of creditor whose rights are being compromised, 75% of each class of shareholder and the permission of the court. Once it has been approved by the court, it is binding on all parties. The court seeks to ensure that there is reasonable evidence of commercial viability and that anticipated profits are sufficient to service the proposed new capital structure.

Assuming in the Hopeful Ltd example that the creditors agree to bear £5,000 of the losses, the accounting entries would be as follows:

	£	£
Share capital	185,000	
Creditors	5,000	
Capital reduction account:		190,000
Reduction of share capital to 200,000 shares of 7.5p each		

Reconstruction schemes can be complex, but the underlying evaluation by each party will be the same. Each will assess the scheme to see how it affects their individual position.

Trade creditors

In their decision to accept £5,000 less than the book value of their debt, the trade creditors of Hopeful Ltd would be influenced by their prospects of receiving payment if Hopeful were to cease trading immediately, the effect on their results without Hopeful as a continuing customer, and the likelihood that they would continue to receive orders from Hopeful following reconstruction.

Loan creditors

Loan creditors would take into account the expected value of any security they possess and a comparison of the opportunities for investing any loan capital returned in the event of liquidation with the value of their capital and interest entitlement in the reconstructed company.

Preference shareholders

Preference shareholders would likewise compare prospects for capital and income following a liquidation of the company with prospects for income and capital from the company as a going concern following a reconstruction.

Relative effects of the scheme

In practice, the formulation of a scheme will involve more than just the accountant except in the case of very small companies. A merchant bank, major shareholders and major debenture holders will undoubtedly be concerned. Each vested interest will be asked for its opinion on specific proposals: unfavourable reactions will necessitate a rethink by the accountant. The process will continue until a consensus begins to emerge.

Each stakeholder's position needs to be considered separately. For example, any attempt to reduce the nominal value of all classes of shares and debentures on a proportionate basis would be unfair and unacceptable. This is because a reduction in the nominal values of preference shares or debentures has a different effect from a reduction in the nominal value of ordinary shares. In the former cases, the dividends and interest receivable will be reduced; in the latter case, the reduction in nominal value of the ordinary shares will have no effect on dividends as holders of ordinary shares are entitled to the residue of profit, whatever the nominal value of their shares.

Total support may well be unachievable. The objective is to maintain the company as a going concern. In attempting to achieve this, each party will continually be comparing its advantages under the scheme with its prospects in a liquidation.

Illustration of a capital reconstruction

XYZ plc has been making trading losses, which have resulted in a substantial debit balance on the profit and loss account. The balance sheet of XYZ plc as at 31 December 20X3 was as follows:

		£000
Ordinary share capital (1 shares)		1,000
Less: Accumulated losses	Note 1	(800)
		200
10% Debentures (£1)		600
Net assets at book value	Note 2	800

Notes:
1 The company is changing its product and markets and expects to make £150,000 profit before interest and tax every year from 1 January 20X4.
2 (a) The estimated break-up or liquidation value of the assets at 31 December 20X3 was £650,000.
   (b) The going concern value of assets at 31 December 19X3 was £700,000.

The directors are faced with a decision to liquidate or reconstruct. Having satisfied themselves that the company is returning to profitability, they propose the following reconstruction scheme:

● Write off losses and reduce asset values to £700,000.

● Cancel all existing ordinary shares and debentures.

● Issue 1,200,000 new ordinary shares of 25p each and 400,000 12.5% debentures of £1 each as follows:
   – the existing shareholders are to be issued with 800,000 ordinary 25p shares;
   – the existing debenture holders are to be issued with 400,000 ordinary 25p shares and the new debentures.

The stakeholders, i.e. the ordinary shareholders and debenture holders, have first to decide whether the company has a reasonable chance of achieving the estimated profit for 20X4. The company might carry out a sensitivity analysis to show the effect on dividends and interest over a range of profit levels.

Next, stakeholders must consider whether allowing the company to continue provides a better return than that available from the liquidation of the company. Assuming that it does, they assess the effect of allowing the company to continue without any reconstruction of capital and with a reconstruction of capital.

The accountant writes up the reconstruction accounts and produces a balance sheet after the reconstruction has been effected.

The accountant will produce the following information:

Effect of liquidating		*Debenture holders*	*Ordinary shareholders*
	£	£	£
Assets realised	650,000		
Less: Prior claim	(600,000)	600,000	
Less: Ordinary shareholders	(50,000)		50,000
	—	600,000	50,000

This shows that the ordinary shareholders would lose almost all of their capital, whereas the debenture holders would be in a much stronger position. This is important because it might influence the amount of inducement that the debenture holders require to accept any variation of their rights.

Company continues without reconstruction

		Debenture holders	*Ordinary shareholders*
	£	£	£
Expected annual income:			
Expected operating profit	150,000		
Debenture interest	(60,000)	60,000	
Less: Ordinary dividend	(90,000)		90,000
Annual income	—	60,000	90,000

However, as far as the ordinary shareholders are concerned, no dividend will be allowed to be paid until the debit balance of £800,000 has been eliminated, i.e. there will be no dividend for more than nine years (for simplicity the illustration ignores tax effects).

Company continues with a reconstruction

		Debenture holders	*Ordinary shareholders*
	£	£	£
Expected annual income:			
Expected operating profit	150,000		
Less: Debenture interest	(50,000)	50,000	
(12.5% on £400,000)			
Dividend on shares	(33,000)	33,000	
Less: Ordinary dividend	(67,000)		67,000
Annual income	—	83,000	67,000

How will debenture holders react to the scheme?

At first glance, debenture holders appear to be doing reasonably well: the £83,000 provides a return of 14% on the amount that they would have received in a liquidation (83,000/600,000 × 100), which exceeds the 10% currently available, and it is £23,000 more than the £60,000 currently received. However, their exposure to risk has increased because £33,000 is dependent upon the level of profits. They will consider their position in relation to the ordinary shareholders.

For the ordinary shareholders the return should be calculated on the amount that they would have received on liquidation, i.e. 130% (67,000/50,000 × 100). In addition to receiving a return of 130%, they would hold two-thirds of the share capital, which would give them control of the company.

A final consideration for the debenture holders would be their position if the company were to fail after a reconstruction. In such a case, the old debenture holders would be materially disadvantaged as their prior claim will have been reduced from £600,000 to £400,000.

Accounting for the reconstruction

The reconstruction account will record the changes in the book values as follows:

Reconstruction account			
	£000		£000
Profit and loss account	800	Ordinary share capital	1,000
Assets (losses written off)	100	10% Debentures (old debentures cancelled)	600
Ordinary share capital (25p shares)	300		
12.5% Debentures (new issue of debentures)	400		
	1,600		1,600

The post-reconstruction balance sheet will be as follows:

	£
Ordinary share capital (25p)	300,000
12.5% Debentures of £1	400,000
	700,000

10.8 Proposals for changes to company law

The Company Law Steering Group was appointed by the government to look into the question of any changes that may be needed to the company law 'for a competitive economy'. In October 1999, it published a number of consultation documents. One of these is on the formation of companies and the maintenance of their capital. The Review Group makes some important proposals for changes regarding the documents that the companies should produce (on their formation), and also regarding the question of their capital maintenance (for the protection of their creditors).

10.8.1 Company formation

Here it is proposed to replace the Memorandum of Association and Articles of Association with two different documents and to make it easier for companies to alter some of the contents of these. At present, the Memorandum acts as a declaration by a company to the outside world of its name, place, share capital, limitation of members' liability and its objects; whereas the Articles are the internal rules of a company, e.g. meetings etc. It is proposed to replace these with (a) the Registration Form, which will have roughly the same information as on the Memorandum, but it will be easier for companies to change some of its contents; and (b) the Company Constitution, which will, generally, resemble the Articles.

Two major changes proposed in relation to the contents of these new documents are that (a) the objects clauses (i.e. the nature of trade of a company), and (b) authorised share capital of companies should be abolished. Historically, object clauses of companies have created many problems and the legal requirement as to the contents of the objects clause was simplified in recent legislation. The present proposal of abolishing it completely will mean that companies will be able to undertake any lawful trade. The only problem here seems to be the Second Directive of the European Commission ('the Directive') which requires every public company to have an objects clause. So, unless the Directive can be changed, the proposal will only apply to private companies. The second proposal is to abolish the requirement for companies to have an authorised share capital. This will make it easier for companies to increase or reduce their intended capital.

Another proposal is to allow a company to be formed by one person. At present only private companies are allowed to have one member. This is to be extended to cover all types of companies, private as well as public ones.

10.8.2 Capital maintenance

A major proposal here is to allow companies to issue shares of no par value (NPV shares) i.e. shares without nominal values. This will affect the way a share issue is recorded and the permanent capital of a company is maintained.

Shares with no par value

At present any kind of shares issued by UK companies are required to have a nominal value. It seems difficult to defend this requirement today. There seem to be two main arguments for it, namely that (a) the total (nominal) value of share capital of a company can be known and therefore can be maintained, and (b) dividend by a company can be based on the (nominal) value of its shares. But the starting point of these arguments seems to be wrong. Nominal values of shares have no real financial meaning, as they are usually the result of an arbitrary value put on them in the past. What is more, in accounting, the net proceeds of a share issue are artificially divided between share capital and share premium accounts as a result of a legal requirement. This is so even though this receipt is the result of one single financial transaction (a capital receipt on sale of a stake in the company). This would not have mattered if share capital and share premium accounts were treated in the same way by the Companies Act, but they are not. So the amount (i.e. nominal value) in the share capital account can not be an appropriate base in measuring the capital to be maintained by a company. Secondly, basing any dividends on such unrealistic figures can only be misleading. Dividends can easily be based on 'per share'.

In 1952, a committee appointed by the government recommended the introduction of shares of no par value, but the then government failed to legislate for it. The current report by the Steering Group also states that creditors of a company attach more importance to other indicators (e.g. asset values and cash flows) than share capital. But today it is not possible for the UK government to allow all companies to issue NPV shares as the Directive requires public companies to have nominal values for their shares. So the proposal to allow such shares will only apply to private companies. This will lead to different rules of writing-up and maintaining the share capital accounts of private and public companies. The Review Group expresses its wish for the Directive to be changed so that all companies can be allowed to issue NPV shares. Until then it is proposed that the new Statute should retain the obligation to have shares with a par or nominal value.

Minimum capital and share issue

At present, there is no requirement for private companies to have a minimum amount of share capital and no change is proposed in this.

Public companies are at present required to have a minimum share capital of £50,000. Whether this amount is adequate for a public company has been questionable from its inception. The Steering Group does not make any proposal for this but seeks further consultation.

Accounting for the issue of shares by public companies will not change, as they have to have nominal values for their shares. Nominal values will continue to be credited to share capital account and any excess of net receipt over this value to share premium account.

At present, no company is allowed to give discounts or commissions on the issue of shares (except for underwriting or placing an issue) as this will amount to a reduction of share capital. It is proposed to maintain this requirement for public and private companies.

Share premium

Public companies will continue to have a share premium account which, at present, can be used for the following purposes:

(a) issue bonus shares;

(b) write off formation expenses;

(c) write off expenses, commissions and discounts on issue of shares or debentures;

(d) provide for premium on redemption of debentures.

It is proposed to:

(a) allow this as it does not reduce capital;

(b) disallow this as it reduces capital;

(c) allow only for the shares of the same class (which has created share premium);

(d) disallow as debentures are of different class.

Reduction of share capital

There are two major proposals here, namely to reduce the power of courts in these cases and to require a solvency declaration by all companies before a reduction can be affected.

At present a company can reduce its share capital for three purposes, namely to:

● eliminate or reduce the part which has not been called up;

● pay back part which is in excess of it needs;

● write off lost capital (i.e. accumulated losses).

Currently, in all these cases, the court's consent is required to protect the interests of creditors.

It is proposed to retain the purposes for which share capital can be reduced, but to eliminate the need for court approval for private companies completely and, in the case of public companies, to allow their creditors the right to challenge the intended reduction through the courts. It is also proposed that the directors of all companies, whether private or public, would issue a formal solvency statement stating that the company will be able to pay its debts during a year after the reduction or on winding up in that year. If the company has auditors, their opinion on the solvency statement would also be needed.

Redemption of shares

At present, a public company is allowed to buy back its own shares or redeem them out of the proceeds of a new share issue or out of its distributable profits. To the extent that this is not possible, there must be a transfer from distributable profits to an account called capital redemption reserve which becomes part of the permanent capital of the company and which can only be used to issue bonus shares. It is proposed to maintain this requirement for public companies.

Private companies are at present allowed to reduce their capital to the extent of their 'permissible capital payment'. It is proposed to drop the notion of permissible capital payment and to allow these companies to reduce their capital, provided any redemption is first met from a new share issue or distributable profits and that a solvency statement – as mentioned above – is issued by the directors. There will be no need for a capital redemption reserve account for them.

At the moment, all shares redeemed by any type of company are required to be cancelled on redemption. There are other current proposals by the Department of Trade to allow companies to retain (i.e. not to cancel) these shares but to hold them as part of their treasury activities to the extent that they do not exceed 10% of the issued capital. The Steering Group proposes that this should also be introduced into the new legislation.

When shares are redeemed at a premium, this premium is required to be written off against the distributable profits. But companies are also given the option to utilise their share premium account to the extent of the lower of: (a) premium received on the issue of shares now being redeemed, and (b) balance existing on the share premium account. It is argued by the Steering Group that this enables a company to avoid a situation whereby a redemption may cause its capital to increase, and therefore this option should be maintained for public companies. On the other hand, it can be demonstrated that this provision may cause a company's permanent capital to decrease. It is surprising that this possibility has been missed out by the Review Group after so many years.

This demonstrates how easy and straightforward the situation would have been if companies could also have NPV shares; any excess of the payment for a redemption over the net proceeds of a new issue would have caused an equivalent transfer from distributable profits to the subscribed capital (or to a redemption account) thereby maintaining the permanent capital exactly as it was.

10.8.3 Distributable profits

It is intended to maintain the substance of provisions relating to distributable profits.

The Steering Group concedes that there are problems relating to the definition of 'realised profits' and to the valuation of assets and liabilities for this purpose. It also states that there is a need to look at accounting standards in this context. As these are complex accounting matters, it will be interesting to see how they can be adequately covered by legislation.

10.8.4 Comments on the proposed changes

The proposed abolition of authorised capital and the elimination of the need to obtain court approval for a reduction in issued capital will make it less onerous and less expensive for all companies to increase or reduce their issued capital.

For creditors of private companies, the only protection will be a forecast (solvency declaration by directors) that the company will be able to pay its debts in the short term. Small family-run companies could always, effectively, reduce their capital through their remuneration. Creditors of these companies had to depend on the character and personal guarantees of their owners. The proposed changes should not materially alter the position of the creditors of these companies. But the position of creditors of large private companies will be less secure than that of creditors of public companies.

For creditors of public companies there will not be a material change, as these companies will still be required to maintain their permanent capital through transfers from distributable to undistributable reserves, on any capital reduction. But the problem of the flexibility of the use of share premium will remain, which may still lead to an erosion of capital.

10.8.5 Final Report

In June 2001, The Company Law Review Steering Group produced its Final Report which recommended changes to the Companies Act according to its earlier proposals (as summarised above), except for one important omission as regards the issue of no par value shares. The Steering Group was not prepared to recommend the issue of such shares because of the difficulties and anomalies that may arise as a result of private companies being able to issue them but not the public companies. Nevertheless the Final Report stated that the abolition of par values for shares of all companies should be the long-term objective of the law.

The Government published its response to the Company Law Review's major recommendations and set out its core proposals for reform in a White Paper 'Modernising Company Law' (Cm 5553) published on 16 July 2002. The consultation period for the receipt of views on the proposals concluded on 29 November 2002. The Act is now awaited.

Summary

The regulation of any reduction in share capital is part of the question of capital maintenance and creditor protection. The Act provides, in detail, the conditions under which capital can be reduced and shares can be bought back by companies. It lays down detailed rules to maintain the permanent capital of a company by the creation of a capital redemption reserve and utilisation of share premium account. But, contrary to the aim of the Act, the final result may not necessarily lead to the maintenance of permanent capital.

Also, the chapter covers the question of capital reconstructions and the need to consider the effect of any proposed reconstruction on the rights of different parties.

Finally, a view of the possible future shape of all these matters is given in a summary of the recommendations of the Company Law Review Steering Group.

REVIEW QUESTIONS

1 How can distributable profits become non-distributable?

2 In what circumstances can non-distributable become distributable?

3 Why do companies reorganise when they have accumulated realised losses?

4 What does the court consider in those circumstances?

5 The directors of Edac plc are considering purchasing some or all of the company's preference shares (nominal value £1 per share) on the open market during the year ending 30 June 20X1. Edac plc's share premium account balance at purchase date will be £320,000.

Three completely independent scenarios are under consideration.

Scenario A

- 80,000 of the shares are to be bought back at a premium of 40p per share. There will be no accompanying new share issue.
- Legally distributable profits at buyback date are estimated to be £376,000.
- The preference shares had originally been issued at par.

Scenario B

- 120,000 of the shares are to be bought back at a premium of 25p per share. There will be no accompanying new share issue.
- Legally distributable profits at buyback date are estimated to be £205,900.
- The preference shares had originally been issued at 115p per share.

Scenario C

- As Scenario B, except that partial financing is to be provided by an issue of 90,000 ordinary shares of £1 per share at 110p per share.

(a) For each scenario A, B and C, calculate and identify the amounts which Edac plc would appropriate from distributable profits in connection with the buyback. Assume that the share premium account would be utilised to the full extent permitted under the Companies Act 1985.

(b) Assume now that Edac plc is a private limited company (Edac Ltd) and that it has distributable profits which are estimated at £15,000 (not £205,000). Recalculate the figures for scenario C as follows:

(i) Show the permissible capital payment.

(ii) Compare the nominal value of bought-back shares with the aggregate of the new share proceeds and the permissible capital payment. Show the surplus or deficit which arises from this.

(c) Say how Edac Ltd would be most likely to deal with the balance in (b)(ii).

Your answers should show your calculations and contain a brief written explanation.

6 The Woolwich repurchased 1.79 million shares at a cost of around £221m.
Discuss possible reasons for the buyback of shares.

EXERCISES

An outline solution is provided in the appendix at the end of the text for exercises marked with an asterisk (*).

Question 1

(a) Company law defines 'share premium' and attempts to protect it from reduction.

(i) Define 'share premium'.

(ii) State the circumstances in which company law requires a company to place an amount in the share premium account.

(iii) State why and how company law seeks to protect any balance placed in the share premium account.

(b) State whether each of the following are realised or unrealised profits (or losses) for the purpose of calculating distributable profits:

(i) Depreciation charged on a revalued fixed asset.

(ii) Development expenditure in the profit and loss account which was previously capitalised in the balance sheet.

(iii) The share of profits from an associated company to an investing company which does not prepare consolidated financial statements.

(iv) The profit on the disposal of a fixed asset which had been revalued in a previous year.

(v) A provision for libel damages in a forthcoming court case.

(vi) Surpluses arising on revaluation of assets before sale.

(vii) A charge to the profit and loss account is a provision for bad debts.

Question 2

You are the auditor of Smith Family Ltd, which is a family owned private company. One of the members, Otto Smith Senior, who is also a director, wishes to retire from business and would like to dispose of his holding of 200,000 ordinary £1 shares. These had originally been purchased at a premium of 20 pence per share. Independent valuations of the company suggested that a reasonable price for his holding would be £300,000.

The remaining family members are happy with this proposal and are considering financing the purchase as follows:

either (i) from internal resources;

or (ii) partly from internal resources and partly by the issue of 50,000 ordinary £1 shares at a premium of £1 per share to Otto Smith Junior.

The summarised balance sheet of Smith Family Ltd at 31 July 20X7 (before the proposed buyback) shows:

Net assets	
Cash	400,000
Other sundry assets	850,000
	1,250,000
Financed by:	
Ordinary £1 shares	1,000,000
Share premium	100,000
Profit and loss account	150,000
	1,250,000

The directors have approached you for advice.

Required:
Draft a report to the directors of Smith Family Ltd which:

(a) outlines the power of a private limited company to purchase its own shares;

(b) explains the procedure which must be followed;

(c) describes the special rules allowing the purchase of the shares;

(d) includes for both financing options the necessary journal entries, the balance sheets after the purchase of the shares, and an explanation of the changes to the balance sheet.

(Chartered Institute of Public Finance and Accounting)

* Question 3

The draft balance sheet of Telin plc at 30 September 20X5 was as follows:

	£000		£000
Ordinary shares of £1 each, fully paid	12,000	Product development costs	1,400
12% Preference shares of £1 each, fully paid	8,000	Sundry assets	32,170
Share premium	4,000	Cash and bank	5,450
Retained (distributable) profits	4,600		
Creditors	10,420		
	39,020		39,020

Preference shares of the company were originally issued at a premium of 2p per share. The directors of the company decided to redeem these shares at the end of October 20X5 at a premium of 5p per share. They also decided to write off the balances on development costs and discount on debentures (see below).

All write-offs and other transactions are to be entered into the accounts according to the provisions of Companies Acts and in a manner financially advantageous to the company and to its shareholders.

The following transactions took place during October 20X5:

(a) On 4 October the company issued for cash 2,400,000 10% debentures of £1 each at a discount of $2\frac{1}{2}\%$.

(b) On 6 October the balances on development costs and discount of debentures were written off.

(c) On 12 October the company issued for cash 6,000,000 ordinary shares at a premium of 10p per share. This was a specific issue to help redeem preference shares.

(d) On 29 October the company redeemed the 12% preference shares at a premium of 5p per share and included in the payments to shareholders one month's dividend for October.

(e) On 30 October the company made a bonus issue, to all ordinary shareholders, of one fully paid ordinary share for every twenty shares held.

(f) During October the company made a net profit of £275,000 from its normal trading operations. This was reflected in the cash balance at the end of the month.

Required:
(a) Write up the ledger accounts of Telin plc to record the transactions for October 20X5.
(b) Prepare the company's balance sheet as at 31 October 20X5.
(c) Briefly explain accounting entries which arise as a result of redemption of preference shares.

Question 4

The following is the balance sheet of Alpha Ltd as on 30 June 20X8:

	£000	£000	£000
Fixed assets	Cost	Accumulated	
Tangible assets		depreciation	
Freehold property	46	5	41
Plant	85	6	79
	131	11	120
Investments			
Shares in subsidiary company		90	
Loans		40	130
Current assets			
Stock		132	
Debtors		106	
		238	
Creditors: amounts falling due within one year			
Trade creditors		282	
Bank overdraft		58	
		340	
Net current liabilities			(102)
Total assets *less* liabilities			148
Capital and reserves			
250,000 8½% Cumulative redeemable preference shares of £1 each fully paid			250
100,000 ordinary shares of £1 each 75p paid			75
			325
Profit and loss account			(177)
			148

The following information is relevant:

1 There are contingent liabilities in respect of (i) a guarantee given to bankers to cover a loan of £30,000 made to the subsidiary and (ii) uncalled capital of 10p per share on the holding of 100,000 shares of £1 each in the subsidiary.

2 The arrears of preference dividend amount to £106,250.

3 The following capital reconstruction scheme, to take effect as from 1 July 20X8, has been duly approved and authorised:

   (i)   the unpaid capital on the ordinary shares to be called up;

   (ii) the ordinary shares thereupon to be reduced to shares of 25p each fully paid up by cancelling 75p per share and then each fully paid share of 25p to be subdivided into five shares of 5p each fully paid;

   (iii) the holders to surrender three of such 5p shares out of every five held for reissue as set out below;

(iv) the 8½% cumulative preference shares together with all arrears of dividend to be surrendered and cancelled on the basis that the holder of every 50 preference shares will pay to Alpha a sum of £30 in cash, and will be issued with:

1 one £40 convertible 7¾% note of £40 each, and

2 60 fully paid ordinary shares of 5p each (being a redistribution of shares surrendered by the ordinary shareholders and referred to in (iii) above);

(v) the unpaid capital on the shares in the subsidiary to be called up and paid by the parent company whose guarantee to the bank should be cancelled;

(vi) the freehold property to be revalued at £55,000;

(vii) the adverse balance on profit and loss account to be written off, £55,000 to be written off the shares in the subsidiary and the sums made available by the scheme to be used to write down the plant.

Required:

(a) Prepare a capital reduction and reorganisation account.

(b) Prepare the balance sheet of the company as it would appear immediately after completion of the scheme.

* Question 5

A summary of the balance sheet of Doxin plc, as at 31 December 20X0, is given below:

	£000		£000
800,000 Ordinary shares of		Assets other than bank (at	
£1 each	800,000	book values)	1,500,000
300,000 6% preference shares			
£1 each	300,000	Bank	200,000
General reserves	200,000		
Creditors	400,000		
	1,700,000		1,700,000

During 20X1, the company:

(i) Issued 200,000 ordinary shares of £1 each at a premium of 10p per share (a specific issue to redeem preference shares).

(ii) Redeemed all preference shares at a premium of 5%. These were originally issued at 25% premium.

(iii) Issued 4,000 7% debentures of £100 each at '90'.

(iv) Used share premium, if any, to issue fully paid bonus shares to members.

(v) Made a net loss of £500,000 by end of year which affected the bank account.

Required:

(a) Show the effect of each of the above items in the form of a moving balance sheet (i.e. additions/deductions from original figures) and to draft the balance sheet of 31 December 20X1.

(b) Consider to what extent the interests of the creditors of the company are being protected.

Bibliography

Companies Act 1985.

Company Law Review Steering Group, *Company Formation and Capital Maintenance*, October 1999; *The Final Report*, June 2001.

Off-balance-sheet finance and capital instruments

11.1 Introduction

Accountants have traditionally followed an objective, transaction-based book-keeping system for recording financial data and an accrual, conservative-based system for classifying into income and capital and reporting to users and financial analysts.

However, since the 1950s there has been a growth in the use of off-balance-sheet finance and complex capital instruments. The financial analyst can no longer rely on the residual balances that appear in the traditional balance sheet when assessing risks and returns.

The traditional balance sheet is undergoing conceptual change. To understand this change we need to consider the evolving treatment in the primary financial statements of the various forms of loan capital and the changing needs of financial analysts. In this chapter we consider:

- Primary financial statements: their interrelationship
- Reasons that companies borrow
- Capital gearing and its implications
- Off-balance-sheet finance
- Substance over form
- FRS 5 *Reporting the Substance of Transactions*
- FRS 5 Application Notes
- FRS 4 *Capital Instruments*
- FRS 4 Application Notes
- Why companies take steps to strengthen their balance sheet.

11.2 Primary financial statements: their interrelationship

11.2.1 Profit and loss account

At a mechanistic level, the historical profit and loss account is an integral feature of the book-keeping system, in that receipts and payments of a revenue nature are transferred to this account.

At a conceptual level, it is an integral part of the financial reporting system, in that the matching, accruals and prudence concepts are applied to the receipts and payments transaction balances in order to arrive at the reported profit or loss for the period.

11.2.2 Balance sheet

At a mechanistic level, the historical cost balance sheet simply contains all those monetary balances remaining within the ledger after revenue and expenses have been transferred to the profit and loss account. It is a form of second trial balance representing the balances of residual data at the end of the financial year as liabilities or assets.

Liabilities are expenses incurred and expected as a consequence of activities not yet finalised by cash transaction with creditors and other third parties; assets constitute expenditure whose economic benefits have not been fully utilised.

These **residual** values are a direct result of the accruals, or matching, concept.

11.3 Primary financial statements: changes in their interrelationship

11.3.1 Importance of the profit and loss account

Although the profit and loss account and balance sheet were presented in tandem, the profit and loss account used to be considered more important than the balance sheet. It was seen as having a dynamic quality, in that it reported the change in wealth that had occurred during the year with details of costs, taxation, earnings and dividends.

In contrast, the balance sheet's static quality revealed only the left-over balances arising from the double entry book-keeping system.

11.3.2 Emerging importance of the balance sheet

This picture was irrevocably altered by the emergence of capital-hungry joint stock companies. Equity capital, which was the traditional source of finance, was unable to satisfy total demand and loan capital became important. Later, other financial institutions such as insurance companies, merchant banks and pension funds entered the field. The balance sheet came to be viewed in a new light.

Equity or ordinary shareholders were the risk carriers of the limited company. Risk-averse investors seeking greater security of investment income at the expense of capital growth were able to invest in preference shares.

Risk-averse investors seeking greater security of both investment income and investment capital became loan creditors; however, they demanded greater security, and evidence of such security, before parting with money.

While all investors looked to the profit and loss account as a means of assessing the borrower's ability to service the interest and dividend payments, the loan creditors, as a further precaution, looked to the balance sheet to determine the safety of the principal sum secured on the net assets available in the event of foreclosure or liquidation.

11.4 Reasons that companies borrow

Companies borrow money for many reasons:

- **Temporary cash flow problems.** Cash may be needed as a consequence of temporary cash flow problems, and early repayment might be foreseen.
- **Lower cost.** Prevailing interest rates may be attractively low.
- **Fiscal advantages.** Loan interest might attract tax relief for the borrower; such relief is not available for dividend payments.

- **Income gearing.** A fixed rate of loan interest may be less than the anticipated return obtainable by the company in employing the loan funds. The excess will benefit shareholders via earning per share and increased dividends and, perhaps, capital growth.

- **Timing.** When there is a lack of buoyancy in the capital market, a company might satisfy a medium-term capital requirement by borrowing with a view to redeeming the debt and making a share issue when market conditions are favourable.

- **Dilution of voting power.** Shareholders and management might be reluctant to issue shares if this would dilute the control of the existing shareholders. They might also consider that an increase in the number of shares would increase the risk of a take-over bid.

- **Earnings per share considerations.** The anticipated return on any proposed new share capital, although desirable in absolute terms, might be insufficient to prevent a fall in EPS. A resultant fall in the market value per share might be unacceptable.

In practice, capital gearing decisions will be influenced by a mixture of motives.

11.5 Capital gearing and its implications

Capital gearing is an attempt to measure the risk to the equity shareholders arising from a company's capital structure. It is the arithmetic relationship between borrowed capital and total capital employed. There is no single definition or standard description, but companies operating with a low proportion of borrowed capital as compared with equity capital are described as **low geared**.

The usual arithmetical model compares long-term debt with equity funds. However, it is customary to include within long-term debt any form of long-term capital demanding fixed servicing costs. Hence, preference shares are included because they receive a priority payment of fixed dividend before any distribution to the ordinary shareholders, thus increasing the risk that the latter will receive little or nothing.

The measurement usually takes the form of a ratio, which we illustrate using two definitions of gearing. The first definition excludes bank overdraft; the second includes it.

Overdraft excluded

Company Y:

$$\frac{\text{Debentures} + \text{Preference shares}}{\text{Debentures} + \text{Preference shares} + \text{Equity}}$$

Year 2	Year 1
£m	£m
$\dfrac{£10 + £20}{£10 + £20 + £50}$	$\dfrac{£5 + £20}{£5 + £20 + £30}$
37.5%	45.5%

Company Z:

$\dfrac{£2 + £6}{£2 + £6 + £80}$	$\dfrac{£0 + £10}{£10 + £72}$
9.1%	12.2%

Industry average: 25%   27%

Company Y is shown in year 2 to be more highly geared than the industry's average. However, a reduction has occurred in the gearing from 45.5% to 37.5% because the increase in borrowing of £5m has been more than offset by a growth in equity of £20m.

Company Z is shown in year 2 to be lower geared than the industry's average. It too has experienced a reduction in gearing due to a change in its capital structure. The change arises from the redemption of £4m preference shares, the issue of £2m debentures and an increase of £8m in equity shares. Notice the gearing of each company as a proportion of the industry average:

	Year 2	Year 1
Company Y	150%	168.5%
Company Z	36.4%	45.2%

In general, 'long-term debt' means borrowed funds (and preference shares) assumed to be repayable after one year. However, where companies make a habit of maintaining a bank overdraft, it can be argued that such funding is in effect long or medium term and should be treated as such when assessing risk.

Overdraft included

$$\frac{\text{Debentures} + \text{Preference shares} + \text{Overdraft}}{\text{Debentures} + \text{Preference shares} + \text{Overdraft} + \text{Equity}}$$

£000 (Year 2) £000 (Year 1)

Company Y: $\dfrac{£10 + £20 + £5}{£10 + £20 + £5 + £50}$ $\qquad$ $\dfrac{£5 + £20 + £7}{£5 + £20 + £7 + £30}$

41.2% $\qquad$ **51.6%**

Company Z: $\dfrac{£2 + £6 + £3}{£2 + £6 + £3 + £80}$ $\qquad$ $\dfrac{£0 + £10 + £4}{£10 + £4 + £72}$

12.1% $\qquad$ **16.3%**

Industry average: **31%** $\qquad$ **36%**

The measure of risk is increased for both entities:

	Year 2	Year 1
Company Y	132.9%	143.3%
Company Z	39.0%	45.3%

In comparison with the industry's average, the gearing of Y is higher for both years and the gearing of Z is lower.

11.5.1 Implication of gearing

The risk to the ordinary shareholders in the above example is higher with company Y than with company Z. The fixed dividend of preference shareholders and the fixed interest of loan creditors remains constant irrespective of the level of profits. This leads to fluctuations in the amount of profits attributable to equity. In times of high profits, the return will be generous; in periods of low profits, the return may be low or non-existent.

This volatility is a measure of the risk inherent in an equity shareholding arising from the level of loan finance; it influences dividend yield and the market price of the equity shares.

11.5.2 Interest cover

Interest cover is calculated from the profit and loss account. It indicates the extent to which profits before interest and tax cover the interest charges shown in the profit and loss account. It can be adapted to take account of fixed dividends on preference shares. An illustration for companies Y and Z shows:

$$\frac{\text{Profit before interest and tax}}{\text{Interest}}$$

Company Y	Company Z	Industry average	Company Y	Company Z	Industry average
$\dfrac{£27}{4}$	$\dfrac{£18}{3}$		$\dfrac{£21}{£5}$	$\dfrac{£14}{4}$	
6.75 times	6 times	4 times	4.2 times	3.5 times	4.5 times

The interest cover ratios suggest that, while Y is more highly geared than Z, it has a marginally greater safety factor (6.75 times compared with 6; 4.2 times compared with 3.5). It has a considerably greater cover than the industry. However, if profits suffered a severe decline, the relative interest cover ratios could change drastically.

An analysis of the capital structure indicates an entity's ability to discharge its obligations in respect of interest and principal on long-term borrowings. This information is of value to all types of provider of funds, e.g. bankers, debenture holders, preference and ordinary shareholders.

It is primarily the balance sheet that provides the capital structure information; it thus performs a key role in financial decision-making. But is its information adequate?

11.6 Off-balance-sheet finance

Off-balance-sheet finance is the descriptive phrase for all financing arrangements where strict recognition of the legal aspects of the individual contract results in the exclusion of liabilities and associated assets from the balance sheet.

The impact of such transactions is to understate resources (assets) and obligations (liabilities) to the detriment of the true and fair view.[1] The analyst cannot assess the value of capital employed or the real gearing ratio, and attempts to determine risk are nullified.

This can happen as an innocent side-effect of the transaction-based book-keeping system. For example, when a company undertakes the long-term hire of a machine by payment of annual rentals, the rental is recorded in the profit and loss account, but the machine, because it is not owned by the hirer, will not be shown in the hirer's balance sheet.

If the facility to hire did not exist, the asset could still be used and a similar cash outflow pattern incurred by purchasing it with the aid of a loan. A hiring agreement, if perceived in terms of its **accounting substance** rather than its **legal form**, has the same effect as entering into a loan agreement to acquire the machine.

The exclusion of a liability and its associated asset undermines the use of the balance sheet as a vehicle for assessing risk by means of the gearing ratio.

The true and fair view can also be compromised by deliberate design. The problem of off-balance-sheet finance became exacerbated by attempts to camouflage the substance of transactions by relying on a strictly legal distinction. For example, loan capital arrangements were concealed from shareholders and other creditors by a legal subterfuge to which management and lenders were party, and with which the auditors colluded.

11.7 Substance over form

SSAP 21 *Accounting for Leases and Hire Purchase Contracts*[2] was the first formal imposition of the principle of accounting for substance over legal form, aiming to ensure that the legal characteristics of a financial agreement did not obscure its commercial impact. In particular, it was intended to prevent the inherent gearing implications of the traditional balance sheet being circumvented and, consequently, the true and fair view being jeopardised.

The standard's aim has generally been achieved, but total elimination of leasing as a vehicle for generating off balance sheet finance has proved difficult. For instance, some companies have manipulated an escape from the '90% clause' of the standard, which distinguishes a finance lease from an operating lease.

The explosive growth of additional and complex forms of financial arrangements during the 1980s focused attention on the need to increase the disclosure and awareness of such arrangements and led to the issue of FRS 5 *Reporting the Substance of Transactions*.[3]

11.8 FRS 5 *Reporting the Substance of Transactions*

FRS 5 was formulated to ensure that financial statements reveal the substance of the transactions undertaken by an entity, rather than merely representing their legal aspects. The standard sets about its task by defining assets and liabilities as follows:

- **Assets**: rights or other access to future economic benefits controlled by an entity as a result of past transactions or events.
- **Liabilities**: an entity's obligations to transfer economic benefits as a result of past transactions or events.

The definitions emphasise **economic benefits controlled** (assets) and **economic benefits transferable** (liabilities). Thus the issues of legal ownership of, or title to, assets and the possession of legal responsibilities for liabilities are necessarily evaded in the quest for an identification of substance inherent within the individual transaction. The definitions are not new; they are the same as those proposed in the ASB's *Statement of Principles*.

11.8.1 Applying the definitions

This involves the consideration of key factors in analysing the commercial implications of an individual transaction. The standard specifies the following key factors:

1 **Substance** must first be identified by determining whether the transaction has given rise to new assets or liabilities for the reporting entity and whether it has changed the entity's existing assets and liabilities.

2 **Rights** or other access to benefits (i.e. possession of an asset) must be evidenced by the entity's exposure to risks inherent in the benefits, taking into account the likelihood of those risks having a commercial effect in practice.

3 **Obligations** to transfer benefits (i.e. acceptance of a liability) must be evidenced by the existence of some circumstance by which the entity is unable to avoid, legally or commercially, an outflow of benefits.

4 **Options, guarantees or conditional provisions** incorporated in a transaction should have their commercial effect assessed within the context of all the aspects and implications of the transaction in order to determine what assets and liabilities exist.[4]

11.8.2 Recognition in the balance sheet

Having applied the definition to determine the existence of an asset or liability, it is then necessary to decide whether to include the asset or liability in the balance sheet. This decision necessitates:

- sufficient evidence being extant of the item (including, where appropriate, evidence that a future inflow or outflow of benefit will occur); and
- that monetary evaluation of the item is measurable with sufficient reliability.[5]

11.8.3 Transactions in assets previously recorded

Transactions in assets previously recorded are also dealt with by FRS 5 because they may be affected by future transactions, perhaps deliberately so in order to avoid continued recognition. The standard mandates that the substance of the new transaction needs to be identified as specified in factor (1) above (section 11.8.1) to determine if:

- the asset should continue to be reported at its current amount;
- its value should be altered to take account of the change; or
- it should cease to be recognised and a disposal should be recorded.

Continued recognition should be maintained at the current carrying amount if the new transaction does not result in any significant change in either:

- the entity's rights or other access to benefits relating to that asset; or
- its exposure to the risks inherent in those benefits.[6]

Discontinued recognition should be effected where transfers to other parties involve:[7]

- all significant rights or other access to benefits relating to that asset, and
- all significant exposure to risks inherent in those benefits.

It is interesting to note that the *Conceptual Framework* is applied in the standard, since general principles are expounded to assist the determination of base characteristics and recognition of assets and liabilities. However, the standard also assists by including in its application notes specific kinds of off-balance-sheet finance.

11.9 FRS 5 application notes

The application notes illustrate the appropriate treatment for transactions such as consignment stocks, sale and repurchase agreements, and debt factoring.

11.9.1 Consignment stocks

Consignment stocks are a regular feature of some trades, whereby transfers from one party to another are arranged so that legal title is retained by the consignor, but the economic risks and benefits move to the consignee. Determining the absolute commercial impact of the transaction requires consideration of the rights of each party to have the stock returned to the consignor. The agreement may contain an absolute right of return of the stocks to the consignor, but in practice penalty provisions may effectively neutralise the right so that stocks are never returned.

EXAMPLE ● Producer P plc supplies leisure caravans to caravan dealer C Ltd on the following terms:

1 Each party has the option to have the caravans returned to the producer.
2 C Ltd pays a rental charge of 1% per month of the cost price of the caravan as consideration for exhibiting the caravan in its display compound.
3 Eventual sale of a caravan necessitates C Ltd remitting to P plc the lower of:
 (a) the ex-factory price of the caravan when first delivered to C Ltd, or
 (b) the current ex-factory price of the caravan, less all rentals paid to date.
4 If the caravans remain unsold for six months, C Ltd must pay for each unsold caravan on the terms specified above.

To some extent the risks and rewards of ownership are shared between both parties. However, in practice we must decide in favour of one party because it is not acceptable to show the caravans partly on each balance sheet.

The factors in favour of treating the consigned goods as stock of P plc are:

● P plc's right to demand the return of the vans.
● C Ltd's ability to return the vans to P plc.
● P plc is deriving a rental income per caravan for six months or until the time of sale, whichever occurs first.

The factors in favour of treating the goods as the stock of C Ltd are:

● C Ltd's obligation to pay for unsold vans at the end of six months.
● The payment of a monthly rental charge. This may be considered as interest on the amount outstanding.
● C Ltd's payment need not exceed the ex-works price existing at the time of supply.

However, if C Ltd has an **unrestricted** right to return the caravans before the six months have elapsed it can, in theory, avoid the promise to pay for the caravans. Indeed, providing the ex-works cost has not increased beyond the rental (i.e. 1% per month), the company can recover the sum of the rental.

On balance the factors seem to favour treating the transaction as a sale to C Ltd, so its balance sheet would carry the caravans as stock and P plc would carry them as a liability.

Consider also the option of return held by C Ltd. This may not be unrestricted. Disputes may develop if the exhibited caravans suffer wear and tear considered excessive by P plc; or other restrictions may be considered inherent in the various clauses. Thus substance over form is not always easy to identify or isolate. In practice, a decision may be delayed to observe how the terms actually operated, on the basis that what actually transpired constitutes the substance.

11.9.2 Sale and repurchase agreements

Sale and repurchase agreements appear in a variety of guises. The essential ingredient is that the original holder or purported vendor of the asset does not relinquish physical control: it retains access to the economic benefits and carries exposure to the commercial risks. In short, the characteristics of a normal sale are absent. FRS 5 deems that such a transaction be treated as non-sale, the asset in question remaining in the balance sheet of the purported vendor.

EXAMPLE ● A company specialising in building houses sells a proportion of its land-holding to a merchant bank for £750,000 on 25 March 20X5, agreeing to repurchase the land for £940,800 on 24 March 20X7. The land remains under the control and supervision of the vendor.

FRS 5 deems this contract to be a financing arrangement. The risks and rewards of ownership have not been transferred to the bank. Money has been borrowed on the security of the land. The bank is to receive a fixed sum of £190,800 at the end of a two-year term. This equates to 12% per annum compound interest. The balance sheet should retain the land as an asset, the cash inflow of £750,000 being displayed as a loan, redeemed two years later by its repayment at £750,000 plus accrued interest of £190,800.

In deciding whether it is a sale or a finance agreement, consider which party enjoys the benefits and suffers the risk between sale and repurchase. In the simplest version of this kind of contract, this will usually be indicated by the prices at which the two transactions are arranged. If the prices are market prices current at the date of each transaction, risks and rewards of ownership rest with the buyer for the period between the two transactions. But if the later price displays any arithmetic linking with the former, this suggests a relationship of principal and interest between the two dates. Thus benefits and risk reside with the original entity-seller, who is in effect a borrower; the original entity-buyer is in effect a lender.

11.9.3 Debt factoring

Factoring is a means of accelerating the cash inflow by selling debtors to a third party. Sales ledger administration and protection from bad debts may be involved. Is the transaction really a sale in substance, or merely a borrowing arrangement with collateral in the form of accounts receivable? Once again, identification of substance will necessitate consideration of the overall terms of the factoring contract as the factor may be supplying a variety of services. We may safely dispense with the benefits of ownership and concentrate on the risks: there is no likelihood of any improvement in benefit in relation to debtors, apart perhaps from a reduction in finance costs as a side-effect of earlier cash inflow.

FRS 5 specifies three accounting treatments for factored debts: derecognition, a linked presentation and a separate presentation.

Derecognition

This is the treatment whereby the carrying value of the transferred debtors is removed entirely from the balance sheet, i.e. the debts are derecognised. Proceeds received from the factor will be debited to cash account and credited to debtors, the imbalance on the latter being seen as a discount and transferred to the profit and loss account as a finance cost. Any other factoring costs should be identified separately and classified as administration charges.

Derecognition can be applied only if all the significant benefits and risks in respect of the debts are transferred to the factor. Three conditions must exist:

● The transaction is one of arm's-length price for an outright sale.

● The transaction is for a fixed amount and there is no recourse to the seller, implicit or explicit, in the event of loss caused by non-payment or slow payment.

● The seller derives no benefit and carries no risk if the debts outperform or underperform expectations.

Linked presentation

This is the treatment whereby the funds received from the factor are deducted from the debtor's gross carrying value, the gross, deduction and net figures all being shown in the balance sheet. For example, S assigns debts to F and receives 80% of the gross amount of debts assigned at any time. F charges interest of 15% p.a. on a daily basis. F provides protection from bad debts for a charge of 1% of the gross value of all debts factored. S continues to administer the sales ledger and to handle all aspects of debt collection. Any debt not recovered after 90 days becomes the responsibility of F. F pays for all debts assigned, less any advances and credit protection charges, 90 days after purchase.

The commercial effect of this factoring arrangement is that, although the debts have been legally transferred to F, S continues to carry significant benefits and risks; the risk of slow payment is carried by S at a cost of a daily rate of interest charged by F. Assuming a gross debt of £1,200 outstanding for 90 days and that each month is of 30 days, S's balance sheet would be:

	As at the end of month:		
	1	*2*	*3*
Current assets:			
Stock	x	x	x
Debts factored without recourse:			
Gross debts (after providing for credit protection fee and accrued interest)	1,176	1,164	1,152
Less: Non-returnable proceeds	960	960	960
	216	204	192

Linked protection is a novel but rather ambiguous accounting treatment. There are alternative treatments, but these have been rejected by FRS 5. Showing the non-returnable proceeds as a liability on the balance sheet would be nonsense because non-returnability means that the proceeds cannot be a liability. Showing net debts factored only – namely, 216, 204 and 192 – would not show that the entity retains significant benefits and risks associated with the asset because of the failure to reveal the gross figure.

The method was formulated by the ASB in response to representation from banks in relation to securitisation (see below), but the method is not confined to a particular type of asset. The standard does not envisage that situations requiring linked presentation will occur often, and it sets extremely strict criteria for its adoption. The conditions may be summarised as follows:

- The finance relates to a specific item (or group of similar items).
- If a loan is involved, it is secured on that item only.
- The provider of finance has no recourse to other assets.
- There is no obligation to repay the finance.
- The entity is not able to acquire the asset by repayment of the finance.
- If funds generated by the item are insufficient to repay the finance, this does not constitute default by the company.
- The provider of finance has given a written undertaking that repayment will be sought from the asset concerned only, without recourse to other assets.

Partial linked presentation may be adopted where a financing agreement meets the conditions only in part. This situation necessitates dividing the finance into two components: that component meeting all the conditions will be linked; the other component will be treated as a liability on the balance sheet.

11.9.4 Securitised assets

Securitising is a process of raising finance from external sources by offering security in the form of a specific block of assets. Domestic household mortgages have been the most commonly securitised assets in the UK. Other **receivables**, such as credit card balances, hire purchase loans and trade debts, are sometimes securitised, and non-monetary assets such as property and stocks.

Figure 11.1 illustrates the processing structure of a securitisation deal. The originating company (1) makes a loan to (2) a mortgage company and then sells the loan to (3) another company, which pays cash in return for the loan documents. This company usually has shareholders in the form of (4) a charitable trust. If it is not a charitable trust, it is likely to be a company friendly to the originating company (1). Company (3) is invariably thinly capitalised and, if its shares are issued to a third party, it often avoids classification as a subsidiary of the originating company (1). In addition, the major financial

Figure 11.1 Processing structure of a securitised loan

and operating policies of (3) the issuer are usually predetermined by agreements which constitute the securitisation, such that neither (4) the owner of its share capital nor (1) the originator has any significant discretion over its management. The issuer (3) issues loan notes to (5) the investment market in order to finance the loans. The loan notes will carry coupon rates related to the rate of interest receivable on the mortgage.

Entries in the originating company's balance sheet

Whether or not the mortgage appears as an asset and the sale proceeds as a liability depends upon two main issues:

- Has the sale of the mortgages involved the transfer of all significant benefits and risks to the issuing company? If not, the originator must show the mortgages as an asset and the sale proceeds as a loan received.
- Is the issuing company a subsidiary or quasi-subsidiary of the originating company? If it is, consolidating the issuing company's accounts with those of the originator will mean that transactions between the two companies are self-cancelling. Thus the assets and liabilities on the issuer's balance sheet will appear on the consolidated balance sheet of the originator, possibly as a linked presentation if the issuing company is a quasi-subsidiary.

The way the transaction is structured via a company issuing loan notes to the investment market is meant to remove the asset and loan from the originator's balance sheet. Success in achieving this depends on the transfer of benefit and risks associated with granting a securitised loan. The outcome of the benefit/risks analysis determines the accounting treatment, i.e. derecognition, linked presentation or separate presentation, whereby the gross value of the securitised asset is included with the assets in the balance sheet and the proceeds of the sale of loans with the creditors.

11.9.5 Loan transfers

A loan transfer occurs when one lender transfers an advance to a different lender. In addition to the balance sheet aspects of recognition and disclosure, there may be a profit or loss to be considered through the profit and loss account.

Loans are inherently applicable to the named parties in the individual contract. Consequently, such loans cannot be bought and sold in the same fashion as tangible assets. The whole process is a specialist area. Three types of arrangement may be identified: novation, assignment and subparticipation.

Novation

Novation means that a new contract with a new lender replaces the original contract, which is then cancelled. In effect, one creditor is substituted for another. The loan is removed from the balance sheet of the original lender and so are any residual obligations in favour of the borrower. Aspects of off-balance-sheet finance do not arise unless intervening side-arrangements have been contracted.

Assignment

Assignment means that rights to principal sum and interest, but not obligations, are transferred to a third party known as the assignee. There are two types of assignment:

- Statutory assignment may relate to the whole of the loan and must be given in writing to the borrower and other obligors (such as a guarantor).

- Equitable assignment may relate to only part of a loan and does not require notice being given to the borrower.

Under both types of assignment the borrower's rights under the original contract must not be prejudiced. Assignments may retain residual rights and obligations regarding other parties.

Subparticipation

Subparticipation means that rights and obligations are not transferred. The lender enters into a non-recourse, back-to-back agreement with a third party, the subparticipant. This subparticipant deposits a money amount, equal to the whole or a portion of the loan, with the lender in exchange for a share of the cash flows emanating from the borrower. The transaction raises the question of whether or not the deposit and the loan can be offset in the balance sheet to reveal only the net effect via a single asset caption.

What is the accounting treatment for loan transfers under FRS 5?

FRS 5 describes two critical tests to apply to determine the correct treatment for loan transfers:

1 Whether the original lender has access to significant benefits and exposure to risks regarding the loan or part transferred.

2 Whether the lender has a liability to repay the transfer.

If the original lender does not have access to the benefits in (1) and does not have a liability in (2), derecognition can be applied; otherwise linked presentation or separate presentation is appropriate.

The standard specifies the benefits and risks relating to loans and calls for specific disclosures when a linked presentation is adopted. Benefits are the future cash flows from payments of principal and interest. Risks include bad debts, slow payment and a change in the interest rate paid by the borrower which is not matched by a change in the rate paid to the transferee.

Disclosures where there is linked presentation are as follows:

- The main terms of the agreement.

- The gross amount of loans transferred and outstanding at the balance sheet date.

- The profit or loss recognised in the period, appropriately analysed.

- The directors of the entity must state explicitly in each set of financial statements using linked presentation that the entity is not obliged to support any losses, nor does it intend to do so.

- The provider of finance must give a written undertaking that repayment of the finance will be sought only to the extent that sufficient funds are generated by the specific item it has financed, and that it will not seek recourse otherwise.

11.10 FRS 4 *Capital Instruments*[8]

The introduction to FRS 4 draws attention to the rampant growth in the number, variety and complexity of capital instruments since the mid-1980s. A significant feature of such instruments has been the combination of equity and debt in a form of hybrid instrument, such as debt carrying the option of ultimate conversion into equity. This has led to an indistinct definition of shareholders' funds, which can confuse analysts and other users of the two primary financial statements. For example:

● Use of the gearing ratio to measure risk is jeopardised by the blurring of equity and debt.

● The proportion of total capital employed financed by shareholders becomes difficult to assess when debt is categorised with shares.

● Excluding the cost of servicing debt from the interest in the profit and loss account may mislead as to the cost of capital.

These factors may mean that the financial statements fail to give a true and fair view, and may cause a loss of confidence in the accountancy profession.

11.10.1 Aim of FRS 4

The prime aim of FRS 4 is to counter the growing confusion by standardising the definition of capital instruments and their presentation. Its stated threefold objective is to ensure the following:

● Financial statements provide a clear, coherent and consistent treatment of capital instruments, particularly in the classification of instruments as debt or equity.

● Costs associated with capital instruments are allocated to accounting periods on a fair basis over the period the instrument is in issue.

● Financial statements provide relevant information concerning the nature and amount of the entity's sources of finance and the associated costs, commitments and potential commitments.

11.10.2 Scope of FRS 4

The FRS is applicable to all reporting entities, irrespective of size or nature of ownership, which issue capital instruments and whose financial statements are intended to give a true and fair view.

It defines capital instruments as 'all instruments that are issued by reporting entities as a means of raising finance', and includes shares, debentures, loans and other debt instruments and options and warrants that give the holder the right to subscribe for or obtain capital instruments. It requires capital instruments to be categorised as shareholders' funds or liabilities. It provides that capital instruments are reportable as liabilities if they contain an obligation or contingent obligation to transfer economic benefits, and as shareholders' funds if they do not contain an obligation to transfer benefits.

11.10.3 Hybrid capital instruments and split accounting

The classification of capital instruments necessitates identification of the existence or non-existence of any **obligation to transfer economic benefits**. Instruments are described as hybrid when there is an element of equity, such as convertible debt. It could be argued that the instrument should be split into its component parts, but FRS 4, with certain exceptions, rejects this approach and insists that if obligation exists in any form then the instrument should be classified as debt. For example, convertible debt must be reported as a liability on the assumption that the debt will never be converted.

When is split accounting permissible?

Split accounting, such as the splitting of convertible debt into debt and the option to acquire shares, is permissible only if the constitutent parts of a hybrid instrument are able to be transferred, cancelled or redeemed independently of each other. Otherwise, the instrument must be classified as a single instrument.

11.10.4 Accounting treatment of debt instruments

There are two aspects to consider: the balance sheet treatment and the profit and loss account treatment.

The initial carrying value of the debt appearing in the balance sheet immediately following the issue should be the net proceeds, usually cash, received on issue less any issue costs attributable to the instrument. Such issue costs should be deferred and treated as a deduction from the carrying value of the debt. If the net proceeds received are not in cash form (being of non-monetary assets), an assessment of fair values of such assets will be necessary.

The carrying value of the debt appearing at subsequent accounting dates should be increased by finance costs attributable to the period less any portion of such costs remitted to the lender. Any accrued finance costs payable in the succeeding period may be excluded from the carrying value and treated as an accrued expense.

The finance costs will be debited in the profit and loss account. The finance cost of debt is the total payments to be incurred over the life-span of that debt less the initial carrying value. Such costs should be allocated to the profit and loss account over the life-term at a constant rate of interest based on the outstanding carrying value per period. If a debt is settled before maturity, any profit or loss should be reflected immediately in the profit and loss account – unless the substance of the settlement transaction fails to generate any change in liabilities and assets.

Illustration of the allocation of finance costs and the determination of carrying value

On 1 January 20X6 a company issued a debt instrument of £1,000,000 spanning a four-year term. It received from the lender £950,000, being the face value of the debt less a discount of £50,000. Interest was payable yearly in arrears at 8% per annum on the principal sum of £1,000,000. The principal sum was to be repaid on 31 December 20X9. The cost of issuing the instrument was £60,000.

To determine the yearly finance costs and year-end carrying value it is necessary to compute:

- the aggregate finance cost;
- the implicit rate of interest carried by the instrument;
- the finance charge per annum; and
- the carrying value at successive year-ends.

Figure 11.2 Allocation of finance costs and determination of carrying value

	(i) Cash flows £000		(ii) Finance charge to P&L a/c £000		(iii) Carrying value in balance sheet £000
At 1 Jan 20X6	(890)	(1,000 − 50 − 60)	—		890
At 31 Dec 20X6	80	(8% × 100)	103.2	(11.59% × 890)	913.2
At 31 Dec 20X7	80	(8% × 100)	105.8	(11.59% × 913.2)	939.2
At 31 Dec 20X8	80	(8% × 100)	108.8	(11.59% × 939)	967.8
At 31 Dec 20X9	1,080	(8% × 100)	112.2	(11.59% × 967.8)	—
Net cash flow	430		= Cost 430		

Aggregate finance cost

This is the difference between the total future payments of interest plus principal, less the net proceeds received less costs of the issue, i.e. £430,000 in column (i) of Figure 11.2.

Implicit rate of interest carried by the instrument

This can be computed by using the net present value (NPV) formula:

$$\sum_{t=1}^{t=n} \frac{At}{(1+r)^t} - I = 0$$

where A is forecast net cash flow in year A, t time (in years), n the life-span of the debt in years, r the company's annual rate of discount and I the initial net proceeds less the cost of issue. Note that the application of this formula can be quite time-consuming. A reasonable method of assessment is by interpolation of the interest rate.

The aggregate formula given above may be disaggregated for calculation purposes:

$$\sum_{t=1}^{t=n} \frac{A1}{(1+r)^1} + \frac{A2}{(1+r)^2} + \frac{A3}{(1+r)^3} + \frac{A4}{(1+r)^4} - I = 0$$

Using the data concerning the debt and assuming (allowing for discount and costs) an implicit constant rate of, say, 11%:

$$\Sigma = \frac{80,000}{(1.11)^1} + \frac{80,000}{(1.11)^2} + \frac{80,000}{(1.11)^3} + \frac{1,080,000}{(1.11)^4} - 890,000 = 0$$

$$= 72,072 + 64,930 + 58,495 + 711,429 - 890,000 = +16,926$$

The chosen implicit rate of 11% is too low. We now choose a higher rate, say 12%:

$$\Sigma = \frac{80,000}{(1.12)^1} + \frac{80,000}{(1.12)^2} + \frac{80,000}{(1.12)^3} + \frac{1,080,000}{(1.12)^4} - 890,000 = 0$$

$$= 71,429 + 63,776 + 56,942 + 686,360 - 890,000 = -11,493$$

This rate is too high, resulting in a negative net present value. Interpolation will enable us to arrive at an implicit rate:

$$11\% + \left[\frac{16,926}{16,926+11,493} \times 12\% - 11\% \right]$$

$$= 11\% + 0.59\% = 11.59\%$$

Figure 11.2 shows the entries for each year 20X6–20X9.

This is a trial and error method of determining the implicit interest rate. In this example the choice of rates, 11% and 12%, constituted a change of only 1%. It would be possible to choose, say, 11% and then 14%, generating a 3% gap within which to interpolate. This wider margin would result in a less accurate implicit rate and an aggregate interest charge at variance with the desired £430,000 of column (ii). The aim is to choose interest rates as close as possible to either side of the monetary zero, so that the exact implicit rate may be computed.

The object is to determine an NPV of zero monetary units, i.e. to identify the discount rate that will enable the aggregate future discounted net flows to equate to the initial net proceeds from the debt instrument. In the above illustration, a discount (interest) rate of 11.59% enables £430,000 to be charged to the profit and loss account after allowing for payment of all interest, costs and repayment of the face value of the instrument.

11.11 FRS 4 application notes

There are various capital instruments. Some are explained in FRS 4 and we consider them below.

Auction market preferred shares (AMPS)

These are shares whereby a fixed rate of annual dividend is determined by an auction process involving a panel of investors. The investor, invariably an investing institution, bidding to accept the lowest rate of dividend will succeed in obtaining the shares. If the auction process fails – perhaps owing to a lack of bids – the original anticipated dividend will be increased to a rate prescribed by formula. This increase is known as a default rate.

AMPS are shares in receipt of dividends payable from distributable profits. They can be redeemed only out of such profits or out of the proceeds of a fresh issue of shares. Thus because redemption rights and amounts are restricted, and dividend rights limited, there is no obligation to transfer economic benefits. These shares are non-equity shares reportable as shareholders' funds, the finance cost being the dividend rights accruing per period.

Participating preference shares

These are shares with preferential rights to dividend of a fixed amount but which, in addition, carry an entitlement to extra dividend based on a proportion of the dividends paid to equity shares. The shares' participation in profits is restricted and they carry priority rights against other classes of share: they are non-equity shares and must be classed as such in shareholders' funds.

The important aspect to appreciate in classifying AMPS and participating preference shares (and, indeed, other shares carrying preferential rights) is that:

● they must be classified as shareholders' funds in accordance with the Companies Act and FRS 4 rules; and

- within shareholders' funds, they must be subclassified as non-equity; they are obviously not debt, thus not liabilities.

However, when considering an entity's capital structure and computing the gearing ratio, both should be included with debt for comparison with equity in order to measure the element of risk carried by the equity shareholders.

Perpetual debt

This arises when the capital instrument conveys no right or obligation on the part of the issuer to repay the principal sum of the debt. Interest is often at a fixed rate or at a fixed margin above a benchmark, such as the banks' base rate. An example of perpetual debt is irredeemable debentures. Invariably such debt is a marketable commodity bought and sold on the international stock exchange, so that the individual investor is able to recoup the market value of the loan at will.

There is an argument that, because such debt is irredeemable, it need not be recorded on the balance sheet of the issuing company. However, this would make the gearing measure misleading.

The standard mandates the reporting of the debt on successive balance sheets. The annual servicing charge must be shown in the profit and loss account. Because such interest will not reduce the carrying amount of the debt, the debt should continue to be reported at the amount of the net proceeds received. The substance of the original transaction must continue to take precedence over its legal form.

Repackaged perpetual debt

This is debt that often carries an abnormally high rate of fixed interest for a set number of years. This interest then reduces to zero or to a nominal rate. The debt is irredeemable, but its value, after the expiry of the primary period of high interest, is negligible. In substance the high servicing cost has redeemed the loan. In practice, an arrangement ensues whereby the debt is transferred to a friendly third party, which arranges with the issuing entity to redeem the loan for a token amount.

EXAMPLE ● This example necessitates the use of the NPV formula, and the trial and error process, in computing the annual finance charge. As most practical versions of repackaged perpetual debt cover extensive periods of time (perhaps ten years or more), the example features an unusually short life-span and very high interest rate in order to reduce the arithmetic workload in computing the percentage finance charge. These unrealistic theoretical features do not dilute the validity of the exercise.

PPD Ltd borrowed £1,000 on 1 January 20X6. The debt is said to be irredeemable. An interest rate of 40% per annum (i.e. £400 per year) is payable for four years. The debt incurs no further interest after the lapse of the four-year span.

The finance charge to be shown in the profit and loss account, together with the carrying value of the debt instrument in successive balance sheets, are computed as follows.

Calculating using a 20% p.a. rate:

$$\sum_{t=1}^{t=n} \frac{At}{(1+r)^t} - I = 0$$

$$\Sigma = \frac{400}{(1.2)^1} + \frac{400}{(1.2)^2} + \frac{400}{(1.2)^3} + \frac{400}{(1.2)^4} - 1{,}000 = +35$$

Recalculating using 22% p.a.:

$$\Sigma = \frac{400}{(1.22)^1} + \frac{400}{(1.22)^2} + \frac{400}{(1.22)^3} + \frac{400}{(1.22)^4} - 100,000 = -2$$

For the amount of −£2 involved it hardly seems worth interpolating. For simplicity the illustration only deals in small figures, but in practice millions of pounds may be involved and interpolation would be essential.

Interpolation:

$$20\% + \left(\frac{35}{37} \times 2\%\right) = 21.89\%$$

Figure 11.3 shows the entries for each year.

Figure 11.3 Repackaged perpetual debt

	(i) Cash flows £	(ii) Finance charge to P&L a/c £	(iii) Carrying value in balance sheet £
At 1 Jan year 1	(1,000)		1,000
At 31 Dec year 1	400	219	819
At 31 Dec year 2	400	179	598
At 31 Dec year 3	400	131	329
At 31 Dec year 4	400	71[a]	—
Net cash flow	600 = Cost	600	

[a] Reduced by rounding error of £1.

FRS 4 provides that repackaged perpetual debt is a liability and must appear on the balance sheet until the zero or notional rate of interest emerges. Meanwhile, in the profit and loss account the finance charge is calculated at a constant rate on the amount outstanding.

Stepped interest bonds

Stepped interest bonds are bonds with a varying pattern of yearly interest, usually stepped upwards, so that low rates in the early years are compensated by high rates in the later years of the loan.

EXAMPLE ● SIB Ltd borrowed £1,000 on 1 January 20X5. It was arranged that interest of 7% in 20X5 would be stepped up by 2% over successive years, making 9%, 11%, 13% and 15% over years 20X6, 20X7, 20X8 and 20X9 respectively. The rates were to apply to the principal sum borrowed.

Solution using the NPV formula (variables as defined in section 11.11 above):

$$\sum_{t=1}^{t=n} \frac{A}{(1+r)^2} - \text{Investment} = 0$$

Trying first 10% then 11% produced the following:

At 10%: $\dfrac{70}{(1.1)^1} + \dfrac{90}{(1.1)^2} + \dfrac{110}{(1.1)^3} + \dfrac{130}{(1.1)^4} + \dfrac{1,150}{(1.1)^5} - 1,000$

NPV = +£24

At 11%: $\dfrac{70}{(1.11)^1} + \dfrac{90}{(1.11)^2} + \dfrac{110}{(1.11)^3} + \dfrac{130}{(1.11)^4} + \dfrac{1,150}{(1.11)^5} - 1,000$

NPV = −£16

By interpolation:

$$10\% + \left(\dfrac{24}{40} \text{ of } 1\%\right) = 10.6\%$$

Figure 11.4 shows the finance charge and carrying value per year throughout the time-span of the loan.

Figure 11.4 Stepped interest bonds

		(i) Cash flows £	(ii) Finance charge to P&L a/c £	(iii) Carrying value in balance sheet £
At 1 Jan 20X5	(1,000)			1,000
At 31 Dec 20X5	70	(7% × 1,000)	106 (10.6% × 1,000)	1,036
At 31 Dec 20X6	90	(9% × 1,000)	110 (10.6% × 1,036)	1,056
At 31 Dec 20X7	110	(11% × 1,000)	112 (10.8% × 1,056)	1,058
At 31 Dec 20X8	130	(13% × 1,000)	112 (10.6% × 1,058)	1,040
At 31 Dec 20X9	150	(15% × 1,000)	110 (+ cash 1,000)	—
Net cash flow	550	= Cost	550	

Deep discount bonds

Deep discount bonds are another version of variable rate capital instrument. They are usually issued at a discount against their face value and on redemption this face value sum is paid. In the meantime a low annual coupon rate of interest is payable on the bond. In some cases the instruments are free of annual interest and are often referred to as zero coupon bonds. The total cost to the borrower is that of discount on issue plus any yearly interest payment. In accordance with FRS 4, the costs should be spread by using constant rate on the carrying value of the bond. The discount must not be treated as an asset.

The illustration in Figure 11.4, showing the calculation of finance charges and carrying values, is identical to that of a deep discount bond.

Index-linked loans

These agreements may utilise a fixed formula for computing the servicing cost rather than carry a specific interest rate. A base rate may be part of the formula, such as LIBOR + 3%. Alternatively, index linking may be applied in conjunction with the annual interest rate to calculate the redemption principal sum.

A cardinal feature of index-linked borrowings is that finance costs contingent upon uncertain events, such as movements in a price index, should be adjusted to reflect those events only after they have occurred. The carrying value at each balance sheet date will need to be recomputed to reflect changes that have taken place during the accounting period concerned. The change between opening and closing carrying values will be treated as an increase or decrease in finance costs per period (FRS 4, para. 31).

EXAMPLE ● ILL Ltd issued an index-linked bond for £1,000 on 1 January 20X5. The bond was to bear interest at 5% p.a. for five years. At the end of the five-year term, the principal sum was to be repaid in accordance with a price index. The index movements measured at the end of years 1 to 5 were 108, 111, 117, 124 and 131 respectively. The index at 1 January 20X5 was 100.

We need to compute the finance charge chargeable to the profit and loss account, the carrying value in each successive year's balance sheet (see Figure 11.5) and the redemption principal payable at the end of 20X9.

Figure 11.5 Index-linked bonds

	(i) Cash flow £	Index	(ii) Finance charge in P&L a/c £	(iii) Carrying value in balance sheet £
At 1 Jan 20X5	(1,000)	100	(1,000)	
At 31 Dec 20X5	50 (5% × 1,000)	108	130 (1,080 – 1,000 + 50)	1,080
At 31 Dec 20X6	50 (5% × 1,000)	111	80 (1,110 – 1,080 + 50)	1,110
At 31 Dec 20X7	50 (5% × 1,000)	117	110 (1,170 – 1,110 + 50)	1,170
At 31 Dec 20X8	50 (5% × 1,000)	124	120 (1,240 – 1,170 + 50)	1,240
At 31 Dec 20X9	50 (5% × 1,000)	131	120 (1,310 – 1,240 + 50)	—
			Cost = 560	

The redemption principal at 31 December 20X9 will be:

$$1,000 \times \frac{131}{100} = £1,310$$

The total sum payable on that day will be £1,360 inclusive of £50 interest.

Subordinated debt

This is debt under which the lender's rights rank lower than the rights of other creditors of the issuing entity. This usually means that repayment of the subordinated debt is subject to specified conditions aimed at protecting other creditors. Such conditions vary considerably: they might embrace all other creditors, or just other loan creditors, or perhaps only one or two types of loan creditor. The aim is to ensure that repayment of the subordinated stock is subjected to prohibition until the priority creditors have been reimbursed.

The accounting treatment of FRS 4 demands that subordinated debt be classified as a liability, which of course it is, but that in addition the balance sheet should disclose by way of note the nature of the subordination.

Convertible loan stock

This is debt that carries the right of convertibility into shares at some specified future date. It can take many forms, e.g. it may carry a fixed interest rate, a stepped rate or a zero rate, and conversion may be optional or mandatory. Compensation to the lender lies in a compound of obligations by the issuer, e.g. in the interest rate, the conversion terms and the discount at issue (if any). The fundamental characteristic of such stock is its **convertibility into shares**, invariably ordinary shares, but sometimes preference shares. Because the stock carries a **shareholder content**, it is a hybrid instrument. It should not be split between shareholder funds and liabilities unless its constituent parts are able to be transferred independently of each other. In practice, most convertible instruments will be non–splitting. The payment of interest is an obligation and, as an obligation equates with liability, the instrument should be classified as a liability. Although the conversion is for the future and, if optional, may not occur, the obligation to pay interest exists.

EXAMPLE ● CLS Ltd issued £1,000 of 10% convertible loan stock on 1 January 20X5. The stock was convertible into ordinary shares on 31 December 20X5 at the rate of five £1 ordinary shares for every £10 of convertible loan stock. Alternatively the lender would receive cash to the nominal value of the loan stock held. The market price of the shares on 31 December 20X8 was £2.50 per share. All the stock was converted.

The finance charge and carrying value of the stock over each of the four years is shown in Figure 11.6. Note the following:

● The finance charge is identical to the fixed interest payable per annum because it is a constant rate on the amount of the loan outstanding. If stepped interest had been involved and/or a discount on issue, the finance charge would have necessitated use of the NPV formula.

Figure 11.6 Convertible loan stock

	(i) Cash flow	(ii) Finance charge P&L a/c	(iii) Balance sheet carrying value		
			Convertible liability	Issued capital nominal	Share premium
	£	£	£	£	£
At 1 Jan 20X5	(1,000)		1,000		
At 31 Dec 20X5	100	100	1,000		
At 31 Dec 20X6	100	100	1,000		
At 31 Dec 20X7	100	100	1,000		
At 31 Dec 20X8	100	100	—	500	500
		Cost 400			

- The proceeds of the shares issued on conversion are deemed to be the carrying value of the instrument at the date of conversion. Consequently, no gain or loss can arise in conversion. The market value is irrelevant in terms of accounting treatment, even though it is the motivating factor inducing conversion, i.e. shares worth an aggregate of £1,250 (500 × £2.50) as against a cash option on redemption of £1,000.

- The issue of 500 shares at a market value of £1,250 does not merit recognition of £250 loss because such loss was not incurred. The proceeds for the shares were, in effect, received in advance, i.e. on the issue date of the loan stock.

- Then again, such a loss could not be estimated throughout the life of the loan and spread (via the NPV formula) as part of the finance cost because convertibility was not certain. This lack of certainty is due to the volatility of share prices.

- If the share price had fallen to £2 or below, the conversion would probably not have taken place. Redemption would have been for cash of £1,000. At a price of £2.50 the lenders have gained £250 profit, but it is realisable only by selling the shares at the market price.

Illustration of convertible carrying zero interest and mandatory conversion

CLS plc issued £1,000 of convertible loan stock on 1 January 20X5. The instrument does not pay a coupon rate and is mandatorily convertible into ordinary shares at 31 December 20X9 at a rate of seven £1 ordinary shares for every £10 of loan stock.

Since no interest is payable, there is no obligation to transfer economic benefits. Hence the constituent element of conversion is the dominant characteristic – there is no liability element. **The lender is induced** to lend on the basis of compensatory conversion rights attached to the instrument, i.e. an attractive exchange of debt for shares compared with the share price at the time of the loan issue. The benefit to the company is that capital has been obtained by loan rather than shares, so that dilution of shareholders' interest has been postponed. The loan money is tantamount to the purchase of a fully paid warrant to acquire shares at a specified future date. In **substance** the transaction is one of shares in the **form** of debt.

Under FRS 4 this capital instrument should be classified as shareholders' funds, sub-analysed as equity interest. On 1 January 20X5 the equity interest should be recorded at an increase of £1,000, i.e. the net proceeds of the loan issue. FRS 4 is silent regarding which reserve in shareholders' funds should be credited with the proceeds. It might be considered prudent to include them in a separate capital reserve. Bearing in mind that conversion is mandatory, the equity interest concerned, £1,000, will be reclassified from capital reserve to:

	£
Ordinary shares of £1, at issue	+700
Share premium	+300

11.11.1 What other disclosures are required for capital instruments?

FRS 4 lays down a number of detailed requirements regarding disclosure, but its main concern is categorisation in the balance sheet. This consists of the threefold analysis of shareholders' funds, minority interests and liabilities. Within each category a sub-analysis is mandated as follows:

Category	Sub-analysed
Shareholders' funds	Equity interests
	Non-equity interests
Minority interests in subsidiaries	Equity interests in subsidiaries
	Non-equity interests in subsidiaries
Liabilities	Convertible liabilities
	Non-convertible liabilities

The object of the disclosure is to enable risk associated with gearing to be more readily assessed.

11.12 Balance sheet as valuation document

Another evolutionary feature of the modern balance sheet is its increasing tendency to be perceived as a valuation document. The traditional balance sheet was seen as a form of second trial balance, i.e. a statement listing economic benefits still to come, unused expenditures of earlier accounting periods, prepayments, obligations not yet discharged, unsettled accounts, and accruals.

The main motives for the change in perception are to report the financial strengths of an entity and to allow an assessment of risk by extracting appropriate ratios, such as gearing and net asset cover. We have already discussed the gearing ratio and will now discuss net asset cover.

11.12.1 Net asset cover

Net asset cover compares the current market price of a company's equity share with the value of underlying net assets attributable to that share as revealed by the entity's most recent published balance sheet.

EXAMPLE ● Each of NAC plc's 25p fully paid ordinary shares has a current middle market price of 80p on 31 January 20X7. Its summarised balance sheet as at 31 December 20X6 is shown in Figure 11.7.

Figure 11.7 Balance sheet to determine net asset cover

	£	£
Fixed assets		1,100
Current assets	300	
Less: Current liabilities	(100)	
Net current assets		200
Total assets *less* current liabilities		1,300
10% Debentures		200
		1,100
Capital and reserves:		
Ordinary shares of 25p fully paid		600
6% Preference shares of £1 fully paid		200
Reserves		300
		1,100

Two methods – the micro and macro – may be used to compute the net asset cover, but the formula is:

$$\frac{\text{Net assets per equity share}}{\text{Current market price per equity share}}$$

NAC plc's net assets attributable to the equity shares are £900. The computations of net asset cover are, then:

(i) Micro method: $\dfrac{£900/2400}{80p} = 47 : 1$ or   47%

(ii) Macro method: $\dfrac{£900}{80p \times 2400} = 47 : 1$ or   47%

What does the ratio reveal?

In NAC's case, the ratio reveals that the current market price per share of 80p is represented by assets of 37.5p, i.e. the price is covered by 47% in the form of net assets. Thus, it may be argued, if the company is forced into liquidation, the equity holders will receive some 47% of the current market price. It pretends to reveal the extent of the **safety net** underpinning the current share price by assuming the following:

● The net asset carrying value in the balance sheet is a current market price value and all assets in the balance sheet will be saleable, even in a piecemeal situation.

● The aggregate values will be received after allowing for liquidation expenses.

● The share price is inclined to be static.

In order to differentiate the quality or realisability of individual assets, assets such as goodwill, copyright and patents were often deducted in arriving at the net assets applicable to each ordinary share. In other words, the safety net was seen to consist only of tangible assets; but not all city analysts applied such rules.

Is the ratio any use?

Yes, as long as we appreciate that the inherent assumptions may be questionable and that it is a very rough measurement of risk in a capital market where share prices are volatile and where balance sheet data may not be representative of market values. Fundamentally, it is a basis for comparison between like companies in the same industry. It is subjective and considerable care must be applied in the assessment using this ratio.

In spite of its shortcomings, management perceives that the balance sheet is used as a risk measure. Management attention is therefore often given to strengthening the balance sheet. For example, assets may be revalued to improve the apparent asset cover.

11.13 Why companies take steps to strengthen their balance sheet

One of several reasons is management's belief that the gearing ratio is important, and that it can be improved by increasing equity reserves as a consequence of revaluing existing assets in the balance sheet. The revaluation can have an effect on the gearing ratio and earnings per share (EPS).

11.13.1 Gearing ratio improved

In addition to revaluing the book values of assets appearing in the balance sheet, companies may introduce assets into the balance sheet. For example, brand accounting is a system of asset creation designed to bolster the net worth of the entity, and was adopted by a number of major companies during the late 1980s. It caused major concern throughout the accountancy profession because it violated the transaction basis of traditional accountancy reporting; valuation was extremely subjective and it was thought that a brand was too ephemeral to be recorded as an asset.

11.13.2 EPS improved

Earnings per share may be improved by the method chosen to eliminate assets. For example, a company may wish to create reserves, perhaps for use in a capitalisation issue, but more often for the purpose of writing off rather than amortising goodwill. If amortisation can be avoided, profits will be higher than otherwise and EPS may avoid a decline; hence the share price might be maintained.

11.13.3 Commercial pressures to revalue

Pressure on management to strengthen the balance sheet is often associated with a perceived commercial benefit from doing so. Strengthening might be undertaken to frustrate a potential takeover, either real or anticipated. A company experiencing or expecting a hostile bid may revalue its assets to improve the interpretation of its balance sheet and so influence its equity share price. The management may feel that the current price is too low and consequently attractive to a would-be predator. Thus revaluation becomes part of an attempt to make shareholders believe that the current share price does not reflect the true worth of the entity; hence the bidder's offer price is not adequate.

Strengthening might also be undertaken to support a potential takeover bid. A predator might try to improve its own balance sheet to encourage shareholders of the target company to accept its offer. Such an offer invariably embraces an exchange of shares between target company shareholders and the bidder.

We saw in earlier chapters that there have been proposals to reflect current values in the balance sheet by implementing a coherent price-level model to adjust the historic carrying amounts. To date, these proposals have not been adopted and historic values, with some modification, still appear in the balance sheet.

Summary

Traditional book-keeping resulted in the production of a balance sheet that was simply a list of unused and unpaid balances on account at the close of the financial year. It was intrinsically a document confirming the veracity of the double entry system, but it revealed the capital structure of the reporting entity. Hence it became a document for measuring the risk encountered by the providers of capital.

Unfortunately the transaction-based nature of book-keeping created a balance sheet incapable of keeping pace with a developing financial market of highly sophisticated transactions. By operating within the legal niceties, management was able to keep future benefits and obligations off the balance sheet. It was also possible for capital instruments of one kind to masquerade as those of another – sometimes by accident, but often by design. This dilution in the effectiveness of the balance sheet had to be remedied.

The ASB has addressed the problem from first principles by requiring consideration to be given to the definitions of assets and liabilities; to the accounting substance of a transaction over its legal form; to the elimination of off-balance-sheet finance; and to the standardisation of accounting treatment in respect of items such as leases and capital instruments.

As a consequence, the former balance sheet paradigm has been changed beyond recognition. It is rapidly becoming the primary reporting vehicle. In so doing it is tending to be seen as a valuation document and as a definitive statement of assets used and liabilities incurred by the reporting entity.

This will create an ongoing pressure on the regulators and companies to produce a relevant valuation document. The process of change is unlikely to be painless and considerable controversy will doubtless arise about whether a transaction falls within the ASB definition of an asset or liability; whether it should be recognised; and how it should be disclosed. This will remain an important developing area of regulation and the ASB is to be congratulated on its approach, which requires accountants to exercise their professional judgement.

REVIEW QUESTIONS

1   Some members of the board of directors of a company deliberating over a possible source of new capital believe that irredeemable debentures carrying a fixed annual coupon rate would suffice. They also believe that the going concern concept of the balance sheet would obviate the need to include the debt thereon: the entity is a going concern and there is no intention to repay the debt; therefore disclosure is unwarranted. Discuss.

2   A company is obliged to reveal, in note form, a quantitative assessment of the dilution of future earnings per share on the assumption that convertible stock in issue will experience total conversion into ordinary shares at the earliest possible date. Why should this philosophy not apply to the balance sheet and thus enable such stock to be classified as equity? Discuss.

3   In 20X6 Alpha plc made the decision to close a loss-making department in 20X7. The company proposed to make a provision for the future costs of termination in the 20X6 profit and loss account. Its argument was that a liability existed in 20X6 which should be recognised in 20X6. The auditor objected to recognising a liability, but agreed to recognition if it could be shown that the management decision was irrevocable. Discuss whether a liability exists and should be recognised in the 20X6 balance sheet.

4   Explain the following terms and the circumstances in which each is appropriate: (a) derecognised, (b) partially derecognised, and (c) linked presentation.

5   As a sales incentive, a computer manufacturer offers to buy back its computers after three years at 25% of the original selling price, so providing the customer with a guaranteed residual value which would be exercised if he or she were unable to achieve a higher price in the second-hand market.

Discuss whether derecognition, partial recognition or linked presentation is the appropriate disclosure treatment.

6 A boat manufacturer, Swann plc, supplies its dealers on a consignment basis, which allows either Swann plc or a dealer to require a boat to be returned. Each dealer has to arrange insurance for the boats held on consignment.

When a boat is sold to a customer, the dealer pays Swann plc the lower of:

● the delivery price of the boat as at the date it was first supplied, or
● the current delivery price less the insurance premiums paid to date of sale.

If a boat is unsold after three months, the dealer has to pay on the same terms.

Discuss, with reasons, whether boats held by the dealers on consignment should appear as stock in the balance sheet of Swann plc or the dealer.

7 D plc has a balance on its debtors' account of £100,000. Previous experience would anticipate bad debts to a maximum of 3%. The company adopts a policy of factoring its debts. Explain how the transaction would be dealt with in the books of D plc under each of the following independent sets of circumstances:

(i) The factoring agreement involves a sole payment of £95,000 to complete the transaction. No further payments are to be made or received by either party to the agreement.

(ii) The debtors are transferred to the factoring entity on receipt of £93,000. The agreement provides for further payments, which will vary on the basis of timing and receipts from debtors. Interest is chargeable by the factor on a daily basis, based on the outstanding amount at the close of the day's transactions. The factor also has recourse to D plc for the first £10,000 of any loss.

EXERCISES

An extract from the solution is provided in the appendix at the end of the text for exercises marked with an asterisk (*).

* Question 1

On 1 April year 1, a deep discount bond was issued by DDB plc. It had a face value of £2.5 million covering a five-year term. The lenders were granted a discount of 5%. The coupon rate was 10% on the principal sum of £2.5 million, payable annually in arrears. The principal sum was repayable in cash on 31 March year 5. Issuing costs amounted to £150,000.

Required:
Compute the finance charge per annum and the carrying value of the loan to be reported in each year's profit and loss account and balance sheet respectively.

* Question 2

On 1 October year 1, RPS plc issued one million £1 5% redeemable preference shares. Issue costs of £50,000 were incurred. The anticipated date for dividend payments was 30 September every year. The company's share premium account amounted to £100,000 on 30 September year 1.

Required:
Show the accounting treatment of the total finance costs (i.e. issue costs and dividend) throughout the life-span of the capital instrument (take care: the instrument is non-equity shareholders' funds) and the balance sheet extracts.

Question 3

October 20X1, Little Raven plc issued 50,000 debentures, with a par value of £100 each, to investors at £80 each. The debentures are redeemable at par on 30 September 20X6 and have a coupon rate of 6%, which was significantly below the market rate of interest for such debentures issued at par. In accounting for these debentures to date, Little Raven plc has simply accounted for the cash flows involved, namely:

● On issue: Debenture 'liability' included in the balance sheet at £4,000,000.

● Profit and loss accounts: Interest charged in years ended 30 September 20X2, 20X3 and 20X4 (published accounts) and 30 September 20X5 (draft accounts) – £300,000 each year (being 6% on £5,000,000).

The new finance director, who sees the likelihood that further similar debenture issues will be made, considers that the accounting policy adopted to date is not appropriate. He has asked you to suggest a more appropriate treatment.

Little Raven plc intends to acquire subsidiaries in 20X6.

Profit and loss accounts for the years ended 30 September 20X4 and 20X5 are as follows:

	y/e 30 Sept 20X5 (Draft) £000	y/e 30 Sept 20X4 (Actual) £000
Turnover	6,700	6,300
Cost of sales	(3,025)	(2,900)
Gross profit	3,675	3,400
Overheads	(600)	(550)
Interest payable – debenture	(300)	(300)
– others	(75)	(50)
Profit for the financial year	2,700	2,500
Retained profits brought forward	4,300	1,800
Retained profit carried forward	7,000	4,300

Extracts from the balance sheet are:

	at 30 Sept 20X5 (Draft) £000	at 30 Sept 20X4 (Actual) £000
Share capital	2,250	2,250
Share premium	550	550
Profit and loss account	7,000	4,300
	9,800	7,100
6% Debentures	4,000	4,000
	13,800	11,100

Required:

(a) Outline the considerations involved in deciding how to account for the issue, the interest cost and the carrying value in respect of debenture issues such as that made by Little Raven plc. Consider the alternative treatments in respect of the profit and loss account and refer briefly to the appropriate balance sheet disclosures for the debentures. Conclude in terms of the requirements of FRS 4 (on accounting for capital instruments) in this regard.

(b) Detail an alternative set of entries in the books of Little Raven plc for the issue of the debentures and subsequently; under this alternative the discount on the issue should be dealt with under the requirements of FRS 4. The constant rate of interest for the allocation of interest cost is given to you as 11.476%. Draw up a revised profit and loss account for the year ended 30 September 20X5 – together with comparatives – taking account of the alternative accounting treatment.

(c) List the requirements of FRS 7 *Fair Values in Acquisition Accounting* in respect of determining the fair values of identifiable assets and liabilities acquired, and briefly discuss the need for an accounting standard in this regard.

References

1 K.V. Peasnell and R.A. Yaansah, *Off-Balance Sheet Financing*, ACCA, 1988.
2 SSAP 21, *Accounting for Leases and Hire Purchase Contracts*, ASC, 1984.
3 FRS 5, *Reporting the Substance of Transactions*, ASB, 1994.
4 *Ibid.*, paras 16–18.
5 *Ibid.*, para. 20.
6 *Ibid.*, para. 21.
7 *Ibid.*, para. 22.
8 FRS 4, *Capital Instruments*, ASB, 1993.

CHAPTER 12

Retirement benefits

12.1 Introduction

In this chapter we consider the application of FRS 17 *Retirement Benefits*.[1] FRS 17 is concerned with the determination of the cost of retirement benefits in the financial statements of **employers**[2] having retirement benefit plans (sometimes referred to as 'pension schemes', 'superannuation schemes' or 'retirement benefit schemes').

12.1.1 Employee interest in pensions has widened

The percentage of pensioners and public pension expenditure is increasing, as shown in Figure 12.1. This had led to gloomy projections that countries could even be bankrupted by the increasing demand for state pensions. In an attempt to avert what governments see as a national disaster, there have been increasing efforts to encourage private funding of pensions.

As people become more and more aware of the possible failure of governments to provide adequate basic state pensions, they recognise the advisability of making their own provision for their old age. This has raised their expectation that their employers should offer a pension scheme and other post-retirement benefits. These have increased, particularly in Ireland, the UK and the USA and what was a 'fringe benefit' for only certain categories of staff has been broadened across the workforce. This has been encouraged by various governments with favourable tax treatment of both employer's and employee's contributions to pension schemes.

Figure 12.1 Percentage of pensions and public pension expenditure

	% of population over 60		Public pension as % of GDP
	2000	2040	2040
	%	%	%
Germany	24	33	18
Italy	24	37	21
Japan	23	34	15
UK	21	30	5
USA	17	29	7

12.2 Financial reporting implications

The provision of pensions for employees as part of an overall remuneration package has led to the related costs being a material part of the accounts. The very nature of such arrangements means that the commitment is a long-term one that may well involve estimates. The way the related costs are allocated between accounting periods and are reported in the financial statements needs careful consideration to ensure that a fair view of the position is shown.

In recent years there has been a shift of view on the way that pension costs should be accounted for. The older view was that pension costs (as recommended by SSAP 24 *Accounting for Pension Costs* prior to its revision in 2000) should be matched against the period of the employee's service so as to create an even charge for pensions in the profit and loss account, although the balance sheet amount could have been misleading. The more recent approach is to make the balance sheet more sensible but this can result in greater volatility in the pension cost that appears in the performance statements which in turn impacts on the profit for the year figure. The ASB has attempted in FRS 17 to reduce the volatility of the earnings per share and profit for the year by putting some gains and losses through the statement of total realised gains and losses.

Before examining the detail of how FRS 17 requires pensions and other long-term benefits to be accounted for, we need to consider the types of pension scheme that are commonly used.

12.3 Types of scheme

12.3.1 Ex gratia arrangements

These are not schemes at all but are circumstances where an employer agrees to grant a pension to be paid for out of the resources of the firm. Consequently these are arrangements where pensions have not been funded but decisions are made on an *ad hoc* or case-by-case basis, sometimes arising out of custom or practice. No contractual obligation to grant or pay a pension exists. However, a constructive obligation may exist which would need to be provided for[3] in accordance with FRS 12 *Provisions, Contingent Liabilities and Contingent Assets*.

12.3.2 Defined contribution schemes

These are schemes in which the employer undertakes to make certain contributions each year, usually a stated percentage of salary. These contributions are usually supplemented by contributions from the employee. The money is then invested and, on retirement, the employee gains the pension benefits that can be purchased from the resulting funds.

Such schemes have uncertain future benefits but fixed, pre-determined costs. Schemes of this sort were very common among smaller employers but fell out of fashion for a time. In recent years, due to the fixed cost to the company and the resulting low risk to the employer for providing a pension, these schemes have been becoming increasingly popular. This type of scheme is also popular with employees who regularly change employers as the funds accrued within the schemes are relatively easy to transfer. The contributions may be paid into a wide variety of plans, e.g. government plans to ensure state pensions are supplemented (these may be optional or compulsory), schemes operated by insurance companies, or even schemes operated and run directly by the company.

The following is an extract from the 2000 Annual Report of Peter Black Holdings plc.

Pensions

The group operates pension schemes for most of its permanent employees, the majority of which are defined contribution (money purchase) arrangements. The assets of the schemes are held separately from those of the group in independently administered funds. The pension cost charge for the year equates to the contributions payable by the company to the schemes.

12.3.3 Defined benefit schemes

Under these schemes the employees will, on retirement, receive a pension based on the length of service and salary, usually final salary or an average of the last few (usually three) years' salary.

These schemes form the majority of company pension schemes. They are, however, becoming less popular when new schemes are formed because the cost to employers is uncertain and there are greater regulation requirements being introduced.

Whilst the benefits to the employee are not certain, they are more predictable than under a defined contribution scheme. The cost to the employer, however, is uncertain as the employer will need to vary the contributions to the scheme to ensure it is adequately funded to meet the pension liabilities when employees eventually retire.

The following is an extract from the accounting policies of Granada Media plc 2000 Annual Report, prepared for defined benefit pensions schemes accounted for under SSAP 24.

The expected cost to the Group of pensions in respect of its participation in Granada Group PLC's defined benefit pension schemes is charged to the profit and loss account so as to spread the cost of pensions over the service lives of employees in the schemes. Variations from the regular cost are spread over the remaining service lives of current employees in the schemes. The pension cost is assessed in accordance with the advice of qualified actuaries and accounted for as explained in note 5.

However, the Group registered a deficit in 2001 when it adopted FRS 17 instead of the surplus reported under the old rules.

12.3.4 Equity compensation plans

FRS 17 does not specify recognition or measurement requirements for equity compensation plans such as shares, or share options issued to employees at less than fair value.

The following is an extract from the accounting policies in the 2000 Annual Report of the Nestlé Group.

Equity compensation plans

Members of the Group's Management

Members of the Group's Management are entitled to participate each year in a share option plan without payment. The benefit consists of the rights to buy Nestlé shares at predetermined fixed prices.

As from 1st January 1999, this plan has a rolling seven year duration and the rights are vested after three years (previously five years and two years respectively).

In order to hedge the related exposure, the Group buys the number of shares necessary to satisfy all potential outstanding obligations under the plan when the benefit is awarded and holds them until the maturity of the plan or the exercise of the rights. No additional shares are issued as a result of the equity compensation plan. The Group is not exposed to any additional cost and there is no dilution of the rights of the shareholders.

12.4 Defined contribution pension schemes

Defined contribution schemes (otherwise known as money purchase schemes) have not presented any major accounting problems. The cost of providing the pension, usually a percentage of salary, is recorded as a remuneration expense in the profit and loss account in the period in which it is due. Balance sheet assets or liabilities may exist for the pension contributions if the company has not paid the amount due for the period. No significant changes were made to the accounting for defined contribution schemes when FRS 17 replaced SSAP 24.

Disclosure is required of the pension contribution charged to the profit and loss account for the period.

EXAMPLE ● Andrew Ltd has payroll costs of £2.7m for the year ended 30 June 2000. Andrew Ltd pays pension contributions of 5% of salary, but for convenience paid £10,000 per month standard contribution with any shortfall to be made up in the July 2000 contribution.

Profit and loss account charge
The pension cost is £2,700,000 × 5% = £135,000

Balance sheet
The amount paid over the period is £120,000 and therefore an accrual of £15,000 will be made in the balance sheet at 30 June 2000.

12.5 Defined benefit pension schemes

12.5.1 Position under SSAP 24

To consider the accounting requirements for defined benefit pension schemes, it is useful to look at the differences between SSAP 24 and FRS 17. By looking at SSAP 24 it is possible to see why a revision was necessary and what the revision to the standard is trying to achieve.

Profit and loss account

Under SSAP 24 both the costs and the fund value were computed on an actuarial basis. The valuation needed to give an estimate of the costs of providing the benefits over the remaining service lives of the relevant employees. This was normally done in such as way as to produce a pension cost that was a level percentage of both the current and future pensionable payroll. Both the accounting standard and the actuarial professional bodies gave guidance on the assumptions and methods to be employed in the valuation and required that those guidelines were followed.

Treatment of variations from regular costs

If a valuation gave rise to a variation in the regular costs, it would normally be allocated over the remaining service lives of the employees. If, however, a variation arose out of a surplus or deficit arising from a significant reduction in pensionable employees, it was recognised when it arose unless such treatment was not prudent and involved anticipating income.

Balance sheet

This was a much simpler approach and was based purely on the accruals principle for defined benefit pension schemes. The difference between cumulative pension costs charged in the profit and loss account and the money paid either as pensions or contributions to a scheme or fund was shown as either a prepayment or an accrual. In effect the balance sheet value was a balancing figure representing the difference between the amounts charged against the profit and loss account and the amounts paid into the fund.

EXAMPLE ● Hart plc operates a defined benefit pension scheme on behalf of its employees. At an actuarial valuation in early 2000 the following details were calculated:

Regular service costs (per annum)	£10,000
Estimated remaining average service lives of staff	10 years
Surplus on scheme at 31 December 1999	£30,000

Hart plc has been advised to eliminate the surplus on the scheme by taking a three-year contribution holiday, and then returning to regular service cost contributions.

The amounts shown in financial statements over the remaining service lives of the employees are shown in Figure 12.2. The profit and loss account charge is the total contributions paid over the period (£70,000) divided by the average remaining service lives of ten years. The effect of this is to spread the surplus evenly over the remaining service lives in the profit and loss account with the balance sheet figure varying from £0 to £21,000.

Figure 12.2 Amounts shown in financial statements

Year	Contribution	Profit and loss charge	Balance sheet liability
	£	£	£
2000	Nil	7,000	7,000
2001	Nil	7,000	14,000
2002	Nil	7,000	21,000
2003	10,000	7,000	18,000
2004	10,000	7,000	15,000
2005	10,000	7,000	12,000
2006	10,000	7,000	9,000
2007	10,000	7,000	6,000
2008	10,000	7,000	3,000
2009	10,000	7,000	–
	70,000		

12.5.2 Problems of SSAP 24

SSAP 24 gave a number of problems in its approach which needed to be addressed by the revised standard.

A misleading balance sheet position

Making the balance sheet accrual or prepayment a balancing figure based on the comparison of the amount paid and charged to date could be very misleading. In the above illustration it can be seen that the balance sheet shows a liability even though there is a surplus on the fund. A user of the financial statements who was unaware of the method used to account for the pension scheme could be quite misled into believing that contributions were owed to the pension fund, e.g. £7,000 owing at the end of 2000. In addition, the item appearing as a liability in the balance sheet did not satisfy the ASB's definition of a liability.

Current emphasis is on getting the balance sheet to report assets and liabilities more accurately

There is an issue regarding the consistency of the presentation of the pension asset or liability with other assets and liabilities. Accounting is moving towards ensuring that the balance sheet shows a sensible position with the profit and loss account recording the change in the balance sheet position. We can see that accounting for pension schemes under SSAP 24 does not do this.

SSAP 24 was also inconsistent with the way that US GAAP and IAS 19 (revised 1998) would require pensions to be accounted for.

Valuation basis

SSAP 24 required the use of an actuarial valuation basis for both assets and liabilities of the fund in deciding what level of contribution was required and whether any surplus or deficit had arisen. In addition the liabilities of the fund (i.e. the obligation to pay future pensions) were discounted at the expected rate of return on the assets. However, there is no evidence that a scheme's liabilities are matched by equity investments which meant that the liability needed to be measured on a basis independent of equity funding.[4] The approaches to valuation are difficult to justify and could give rise to unrealistic pension provision being made.

12.6 FRS 17 *Retirement Benefits*

After a relatively long discussion and exposure period FRS 17 was issued in 2000 and it redefined how all employee benefits were to be accounted for. FRS 17 has chosen to follow a 'balance sheet' approach to accounting for the pension scheme contributions by the employer and, therefore, it defines how the balance sheet asset or liability should be built up. The change in the asset or liability is recognised in the profit and loss account or the statement of total recognised gains and losses, depending on the reason for the change.[5] The pension fund must be valued at least every three years, and updated according to actuarial assumptions in intervening years. The valuation would normally be done by a qualified actuary[6] and is based on actuarial assumptions.

12.7 The liability for pension and other post-retirement costs

The liability for pension costs is made up from the following amounts:

- the present value of the defined benefit obligation at the balance sheet date;
- minus any past service cost not yet recognised;
- minus the fair value at the balance sheet date of plan assets (if any) out of which the obligations are to be settled directly.

If this calculation produces a negative amount the company should recognise a pension asset in the balance sheet. The asset can only be recognised[7] to the extent that it will be recovered through future refunds or reduced contributions to the scheme.

The asset or liability is presented[8] in the balance sheet as a separate item below net assets. The balance sheet would therefore show:

	£
Net assets excluding pension liability	X
Pension liability	(X)
Net assets including pension liability	X

Any deferred tax that arises on the pension fund asset or liability should be adjusted for against the pension asset or liability and not presented as part of the deferred tax asset or liability of the company.

Each of the elements making up the balance sheet position can now be considered.

12.7.1 Obligations of the fund

The pension fund obligation must be calculated[9] using the 'projected unit credit method'. This method of allocating pension costs builds up the pension liability each year for an extra year of service and a reversal of discounting. Discounting of the liability is done using the market yields on high quality corporate bonds with similar currency and duration.

The Grado plc illustration below shows how the obligation to pay pension accumulates over the working life of an employee.

EXAMPLE ● For employees of Grado plc, a lump sum benefit is payable on termination of service equal to 1% of final salary for each year of service. The salary in year 1 is £10,000 and is assumed to increase at 7% (compound) each year. The discount rate used is 10%. Figure 12.3 shows how an obligation (in £) builds up for an employee who is expected to leave at the end of year 5. For simplicity, this example ignores the additional adjustment needed to reflect the probability that the employee may leave service at an earlier or later date.

12.7.2 Past service costs

Past service costs are costs that arise for a pension scheme as a result of improving the scheme or when a business introduces a plan. They are the extra liability in respect of previous years' service by employees. Do note, however, that past service costs can only arise if actuarial assumptions did not take into account the reason why they occurred. Typically they would include:

Figure 12.3 Obligation (in £) for an employee who is expected to leave at the end of year 5

Year	1	2	3	4	5
Benefit attributed to prior years	0	131	262	393	524
Benefit attributed to current year (1% of final salary)*	131	131	131	131	131
Benefit attributed to current and prior years	131	262	393	524	655
Opening obligation (present value of benefit attributed to prior years)	—	89	196	324	476
Interest at 10%	—	9	20	33	48
Current service cost (present value of benefit attributed to current year)	89	98	108	119	131
Closing obligation (present value of benefit attributed to current and prior years)†	89	196	324	476	655

* Final salary is £10,000 × $(1.07)^4$ = £13,100.

† Discounting the benefit attributable to current and prior years at 10% e.g. at the end of year 1
   89 = $131/(1.1)^4$

- estimates of benefit improvements as a result of actuarial gains (if the company proposes to give the gains to the employees); or
- the effect of plan amendments that increase or reduce benefits for past service.

Accounting treatment

The past service cost should be recognised on a straight-line basis[10] over the period to which the benefits become vested. If already vested the cost should be recognised immediately in the profit and loss account. A benefit becomes vested[11] when an employee becomes unconditionally entitled to pension benefits. For example, if a company offered a scheme whereby an employee would only be entitled to pension if they worked for at least five years, the benefits would be vested as soon as they started their sixth year of employment. The company will still have to make provision for pensions for the first five years of employment (and past service costs could arise in this period), as these will be pensionable service years provided the employee works for more than five years.

12.7.3 Fair value of plan assets

This is usually the market value[12] of the assets of the plan (or the estimated value if no immediate market value exists). The use of market values to value the plan assets is supported by the fact that they are more objective than actuarial values and more easily understood. As mentioned above, the ASB had to consider how best to report the variations that could occur in market values from one year to the next and chose to use the statement of total recognised gains and losses to avoid reporting volatile profit figures which were not indicative of the operating performance of the enterprise or its capacity to cover dividends.

12.8 The profit and loss account

The profit and loss account charge for a period should be made up[13] of the following parts:

- current service cost;
- interest cost;
- the expected return on any plan assets;
- past service cost, to the extent that it is recognised;
- the effect of any curtailments or settlements.

The items making up the profit and loss account charge are most of the items that cause a movement in the balance sheet position. Actuarial gains and losses (see below) are the only thing that changes the balance sheet position that are not recognised in the profit and loss account, because these are recognised in the statement of total recognised gains and losses.[14]

The charge to the profit and loss account should be presented as either an operating cost or a financing cost (adjacent to interest).

Operating costs are:

- current service cost;
- past service cost;
- effect of curtailments and settlements (see 12.11 below).

Financing costs are:

- interest cost;
- expected return on plan assets.

12.9 The statement of total recognised gains and losses

Actuarial gains and losses that arise in a period are recognised in the statement of total recognised gains and losses.

Actuarial gains and losses are defined[15] as:

Changes in actuarial deficits or surpluses [net pension asset or liability] that arise because:

(a) events have not coincided with actuarial assumptions made for the last valuation (experience gains or losses) or

(b) the actuarial assumptions have changed.

Actuaries perform valuations of the pension funds at least every three years and base their valuations on assumptions. The assumptions would include things such as expected return on assets of the fund, average remaining working lives of employees, discount rates for liabilities for example, and these assumptions will not always coincide with actual events. Any differences with actual events or changes to these assumptions cause the actuarial gains and losses.

This treatment of actuarial gains and losses is the main difference between UK and international practice in accounting for defined benefit pension schemes. IAS 19 (revised 1998) requires[16] that material actuarial gains and losses are recognised in the income statement (profit and loss account) recognised over the average remaining service lives of employees, or a shorter period.

12.10 Comprehensive illustration

The following comprehensive illustration demonstrates how a pension liability and income statement charge is calculated. The example does not include the effect of curtailments or settlements.

The following information is given about a funded defined benefit plan. To keep the computations simple, all transactions are assumed to occur at the year-end. The present value of the obligation and the market value of the plan assets were both 1,000 at 1 January 2000.

	2000	2001	2002
Discount rate at start of year	10%	9%	8%
Expected rate of return on plan assets at start of year	12%	11%	10%
Current service cost	130	140	150
Benefits paid	150	180	190
Contributions paid	90	100	110
Present value of obligations at 31 December	1,100	1,380	1,455
Market value of plan assets at 31 December	1,190	1,372	1,188

In 2002 the plan was amended to provide additional benefits with effect from 1 January 2002. The present value as at 1 January 2002 of additional benefits for employee service before 1 January 2002 was 50, all for vested benefits. All surpluses on the pension fund are expected to be recovered by future reductions on contributions.

We will now show how the pension scheme would be shown in the accounts for 2000, 2001 and 2002.

Step 1: Change in the obligation. The changes in the present value of the obligation must be calculated and used to determine what, if any, actuarial gains and losses have arisen. This calculation can be done by comparing the expected obligations at the end of each period with the actual obligations as follows:

	2000	2001	2002
Present value of obligation, 1 January	1,000	1,100	1,380
Interest cost	100	99	110
Current service cost	130	140	150
Past service cost − vested benefits	–	50	–
Benefits paid	(150)	(180)	(190)
Actuarial (gain) loss on obligation (balancing figure)	*20*	*171*	*5*
Present value of obligation, 31 December	1,100	1,380	1,455

Step 2: Change in the assets. The changes in the fair value of the assets of the fund must be calculated and used to determine what, if any, actuarial gains and losses have arisen. This calculation can be done by comparing the asset values at the end of each period with the actual asset values. The changes in the assets are as follows:

	2000	2001	2002
Fair value of plan assets, 1 January	1,000	1,190	1,372
Expected return on plan assets	120	131	137
Contributions	90	100	110
Benefits paid	(150)	(180)	(190)
Actuarial gain (loss) on plan assets (balancing figure)	*130*	*131*	*(241)*
Fair value of plan assets, 31 December	1,190	1,372	1,188

Step 3: The financial statements can now be prepared for each period. The balance sheet shows the net pension asset or liability at the end of each period. This is calculated as the market value of the assets less the present value of the obligations, as follows:

	2000	2001	2002
Market value of the assets	1,190	1,372	1,188
Present value of the obligations	(1,100)	(1,380)	(1,455)
Pension asset (liability)	**90**	**(8)**	**(267)**

The profit and loss account shows the pension charge for the period presented as operating cost and financing cost. The analysis of the make up of the operating cost and financing cost is shown in the notes to the accounts, as follows:

Operating cost:

	2000	2001	2002
Current service cost	(130)	(140)	(150)
Past service cost		(50)	
Operating cost	**(130)**	**(190)**	**(150)**

	2000	2001	2002
Financing cost			
Interest on pension scheme liabilities	(100)	(99)	(110)
Expected return on assets	120	131	137
Net return	**20**	**32**	**27**

The statement of total recognised gains and losses (STRGL) shows the actuarial gains and losses that have been recognised in the period. The actuarial gains and losses are the total of both gains and losses arising on the assets, and gains and losses arising on the obligations. The following shows how the charge or credit to the STRGL would be disclosed in the notes to the accounts:

	2000	2001	2002
Actual return less expected return on plan assets	130	131	(241)
Experience gains and losses arising on scheme liabilities	(20)	(171)	(5)
Actuarial gain (loss) recognised in STRGL	**110**	**(40)**	**(246)**

12.11 Plan curtailments and settlements[17]

A curtailment of a pension scheme occurs when a company is committed to make a material reduction in the number of employees of a scheme or when the employees will receive no benefit for a substantial part of their future service. A settlement occurs when an enterprise enters into a transaction that eliminates any further liability from arising under the fund.

The accounting for a settlement or curtailment is that a gain or loss is recognised when the settlement or curtailment occurs. The gain or loss on a curtailment or settlement should comprise:

● any resulting change in the present value of the defined benefit obligation;

● any resulting change in the fair value of the plan assets;

● any related actuarial gain/loss and past service cost that had not previously been recognised.

Before determining the effect of the curtailment the enterprise must re-measure the obligations and the liability to get it to the up-to-date value.

12.12 Eliminating surpluses and deficits on pension funds

The above analysis has concentrated on the amounts to be included in the financial statements for a company following FRS 17, but it is also useful to consider how a company might eliminate surpluses or deficits, and what the effect of this would be in the financial statements.

If a pension fund has a surplus, as indicated by the assets of the fund exceeding the obligations of the fund, a company has options on how to eliminate this surplus. One of the most common ways to eliminate a surplus is to take a contribution holiday, which means to stop paying into the pension fund for a period as advised by actuaries. This will have the effect of reducing the rate at which the assets of the fund grow, and therefore reducing the surplus over time. An alternative to a contribution holiday would be to reduce contributions for a period advised by the actuaries.

Less common ways of eliminating a surplus could be taking a refund from the scheme or perhaps increasing the benefits to the employees. If either of these methods is to be used, again the actuaries will advise on the amounts of refunds for the potential extra benefits that should be provided.

In the case of a deficit (the obligations exceeding the assets of the fund) the company has an obligation to ensure that there are sufficient funds to pay future pensions and therefore they may need to take action to reduce the deficit. Possibilities to reduce the deficit include a one-off contribution to the pension fund, or increased payments into the pension fund over a number of years. As with a surplus, the actuaries will advise the company of the amounts required.

A further theoretical way to reduce a deficit is to alter the terms of the scheme and effectively reduce the benefits to current or future employees. This may be difficult to do, and certainly the legal position of the company and its employees will need to be considered, but it is an option being explored by some companies facing large deficits.

12.12.1 Impact on the financial statements

Assuming that the method of eliminating the surplus or deficit involves a variation in contributions, the impact of using different methods should mainly be on the balance sheet and not the performance statements.

If, for example, a company had a deficit on its fund and chose to eliminate the deficit by means of a one-off payment, the value of the assets of the fund would increase immediately and reduce the balance sheet liability. There is no reason that the expected return on opening net assets should change, or that the interest cost and current service cost would change and therefore the profit and loss account would keep the same figures.

It is possible that some changes would occur to the profit and loss account in future years as a variation in the market value of the assets at the end of a period (due to different contributions) would have an impact on the expected return on plan assets in future years. These variations would usually be small unless a very major surplus or deficit existed on the pension fund.

If the surplus or deficit is removed by altering the terms of the scheme then the actuaries would need to re-perform the calculations for the pension fund and all items in the balance sheet, profit and loss account and statement of total recognised gains and losses would change.

The impact of the eliminating surpluses or deficits under SSAP 24 would also only have a major impact on the balance sheet of the company. The surplus or deficit would still be spread out over the remaining working lives of the employees in the profit and loss account, and the balance sheet would still take the difference in the profit and loss account charge and the contributions paid. Differing cash flows would therefore only alter the balance sheet position.

12.13 Disclosures

The disclosure requirements of FRS 17 are quite extensive and are designed to give full information to the users of the financial statements about the status of the pension schemes. The disclosures required together with examples from FRS 17 are given below.

12.13.1 Defined contribution schemes

For a defined contribution scheme the disclosures are brief:

- the nature of the scheme (i.e. a defined contribution scheme);
- the cost for the period;
- any outstanding or prepaid contributions at the balance sheet date.

12.13.2 Defined benefit schemes

For a defined benefit scheme the disclosures are much more extensive. The main disclosures are as shown below.

Details of the scheme

These disclosures should include:

- the nature of the scheme;

● the date of the most recent full actuarial valuation, and that the actuary is an officer or employee of the reporting entity (or its group) if this is the case;

● the contribution for the current period, and any agreed contribution for future periods;

● for closed schemes, or ones with rapidly increasing age profile of members, the fact that under the projected unit credit method the current service cost will increase as the members approach retirement.

Assumptions

The main financial assumptions used in the pension scheme valuation should be disclosed. The main assumptions include:

● the inflation assumption;

● the rate of increase in salaries;

● the rate of increase for pensions in payment and deferred pensions; and

● the rate used to discount scheme liabilities.

EXAMPLE[18] ● The group operates a defined benefit scheme in the UK. A full actuarial valuation was carried out at 31 December 20X1 and updated to 31 December 20X2 by a qualified independent actuary. The major assumptions used by the actuary were as follows:

	31 Dec. 20X2	31 Dec. 20X1	31 Dec. 20X0
Rate of increase in salaries	4.0%	5.5%	6.5%
Rate of increase in pensions in payment	2.0%	3.0%	3.5%
Discount rate	4.5%	7.0%	8.5%
Inflation assumption	2.5%	4.0%	5.0%

Fair value and expected return on assets

The fair value of the assets held by the pension scheme at the beginning and end of the period should be analysed into the following classes and disclosed together with the expected rate of return assumed for each class for the period and the subsequent period:

● equities;

● bonds; and

● other.

EXAMPLE ● The disclosure of the assets in the scheme and the expected rate of return would be as follows:

	Long-term rate of return expected at 31 Dec. 20X2	Value at 31 Dec. 20X2 £m	Long-term rate of return expected at 31 Dec. 20X1	Value at 31 Dec. 20X1 £m	Long-term rate of return expected at 31 Dec. 20X0	Value at 31 Dec. 20X0 £m
Equities	7.3%	1,116	8.0%	721	9.3%	570
Bonds	5.5%	298	6.0%	192	8.0%	152
Property	6.0%	74	6.1%	49	7.9%	38

Total market value of assets	1,488	962	760
Present value of scheme liabilities	(1,009)	(758)	
Surplus in the scheme	479	204	
Related deferred tax liability	(144)	(61)	
Net pension asset	335	143	

History of amounts recognised in the statement of total recognised gains and losses

For the current and previous four periods the financial statements should disclose:

- the difference between the expected and actual return on assets expressed in (a) an amount, and (b) a percentage of scheme assets at the balance sheet date;
- the experience gains and losses arising on scheme liabilities expressed as a percentage of scheme liabilities at the balance sheet date;
- the total actuarial gain or loss expressed as above.

EXAMPLE ● The disclosure in the STRGL would be as follows:

	20X2	20X1	20X0	20W9	20W8
Difference between the expected and actual return on scheme assets					
Amount (£m)	480	130	(6)	94	(73)
Percentage of scheme assets	32%	14%	(1%)	16%	(26%)
Experience gains and losses on scheme liabilities					
Amount (£m)	(58)	(6)	34	25	(23)
Percentage of the present value of scheme liabilities	(6%)	(1%)	5%	2%	(2%)
Total amount recognised in statement of total recognised gains and losses					
Amount (£m)	276	91	1	66	(158)
Percentage of present value of scheme liabilities	27%	12%	0.5%	5%	(14%)

Movement in the surplus or deficit during the year

An analysis of the movement in the surplus or deficit during the year should be disclosed.

EXAMPLE ● The disclosure would be as follows:

	20X2 £m	20X1 £m
Surplus in scheme at beginning of year	204	92
Movement in year:		
Current service cost	(34)	(25)
Contributions	25	35
Past service costs	(12)	–
Other finance income	20	11
Actuarial gain	276	91
Surplus in scheme at end of year	479	204

Reserves note

The analysis of reserves in a note to the accounts should distinguish the amount relating to the defined benefit asset or liability net of the related deferred tax.

EXAMPLE ● The disclosure would be as follows:

Reserves note

	20X2 £m	20X1 £m
Profit and loss reserve excluding pension asset	400	350
Pension reserve	335	143
Profit and loss reserve	735	493

12.14 Introduction to the standard

FRS 17 is a very complex standard with significant disclosure requirements, and its introduction will have a major effect on financial statement presentation. Due to this the ASB have decided to implement the standard in stages. The dates by which the various parts of the standard are to be introduced are as follows:

	Periods ending on or after		
	22 Jun. 2001	22 Jun. 2002	22 Jun. 2003
Disclosures:			
Details of the scheme	✔	✔	✔
Assumptions	✔	✔	✔
Fair value of scheme assets	✔	✔	✔
History of actuarial gains and losses		✔	✔
Movement in the surplus	✔	✔	✔
Reserves note		✔	
Presentation in the primary statements			✔

12.15 Experience of the application of FRS 17

12.15.1 Fair value measurement and treatment of actuarial gains and losses

Fair value measurement at the balance sheet date has now been adopted by FRS 17, and internationally, with the intention of reflecting the consensus of market participants on the current value of the assets and to quantify the present value of the liability on the same basis.[19] However, actuarial gains and losses are treated differently in that, under FRS 17, these are taken to the statement of total recognised gains and losses, whereas under IAS 19 these may be deferred and amortised.

12.15.2 Shortfalls in pension funds

Shortfalls have arisen in many companies beginning to implement FRS 17 in 2002 due to:

- Changes in economic environment: assets have fallen in value with falls in world stock markets.
- Changes in the basis of valuation:
  - the liability forecast has increased with the application of the more conservative method required by FRS 17 whereby the forecast is based on the yields on corporate bonds rather than on historic equity market yields;
  - asset fair values will normally be market values with mid-market for quoted securities, open market for property and best estimates for unquoted securities. This is the major change from an actuarial valuation approach that SSAP 24 employed.
- Changes in tax regulations: the abolition of the dividend tax credit reduced income going into pension funds by removing the right to reclaim imputed tax on dividend income.

The combination of lower asset values, higher estimated liabilities and the abolition of the dividend tax credit has created a shortfall in company pension funds affecting a number of FTSE 100 companies, such as BAE Systems (£776 million), AstraZeneca (£463 million) and Marks & Spencer (£134 million). In overall terms, it has been estimated that the total shortfall in leading British companies could exceed £10 billion.

The potential risk of volatility can be high, e.g. in some companies, such as British Airways, the final salary pension scheme might exceed the market capitalisation of the company behind it.

12.15.3 Implications for the balance sheet and profit and loss account

Balance sheets will present a more volatile net asset picture when there are movements in the prices of shares held by the pension fund. Income statements will record the actuarial gains and losses although they will have no effect on cash flows, key financial measures that use pre-tax profits and earnings per share. However, profit and loss accounts in future periods may see a higher pension charge, e.g. George Wimpey said that there was a £57 million net liability under FRS 17 and conceded in 2001 that it would force the group to increase its pension charge to the profit and loss account from £4 million to £13 million in subsequent years.[20]

12.15.4 Implications for shareholders

There is also the possible adverse effect on shareholders:

- They might become uneasy about the overall quality of the company's accounting, as in the case of Rolls Royce with the shortfall of £325 million in its pension fund[21]
- Statutory solvency requirements might affect a company's ability to distribute dividends, e.g. the engineering company Eliza Tinsley blamed a dividend cut on FRS 17 rules[22]
- Immediate funding of any deficit could threaten a company's solvency.[23]

12.15.5 Implications for existing employees

Some companies with deficits have taken the view that the funding position is temporary and would have no direct effect on pension fund members. Others, however, have decided to close their schemes and move to money purchase schemes where the employee carries the investment risk, as follows:

- some companies have ended final salary pension schemes for new employees, e.g. BT
- some companies have ended final salary pension schemes to existing employees moving them to a money purchase scheme, e.g. Ernst & Young
- some companies offering money purchase schemes have reduced the percentage that the company contributes[24] so that the employee carries the investment risk
- some companies making good the deficit might decide to remove the inflation indexing of pensions[25]
- some companies might no longer make discretionary top-ups to existing pensioners.

12.15.6 Conflicting responses to FRS 17

FRS 17 has had the effect of making transparent fluctuations in the values of pension schemes and requiring these to be included on the face of the balance sheet rather than merely being disclosed by way of a note to the accounts. Where the fluctuation reduces net assets there have been perceived adverse economic consequences such as the closure of final salary schemes.

Although there have been representations to the ASB for it to change FRS 17 to reduce the impact of fluctuations on the balance sheet even at a political level,[26] the ASB is committed to the view that the FRS has brought transparency to an area that has traditionally been opaque and that it reveals rather than causes the underlying economic position.

12.15.7 ASB defer full implementation of FRS 17

The ASB in December 2002 issued an amendment to FRS 17 which deferred the full adoption of its requirements until IAS 19 has been revised by the IASB to avoid mandating two changes in quick succession. However, the ASB is confident that the FRS 17 approach will be preferred and it encourages early adoption of all its requirements.

Summary

Accounting for post-retirement employee benefits has always been a difficult problem with different views as to the appropriate method. The different types of scheme and the risks associated with the schemes add to the difficulties in terms of accounting. The accounting treatment for these benefits has recently changed with the current view that the balance sheet position takes priority over the profit and loss account.

In order to prevent significant volatility in the pension cost in the profit and loss account, FRS 17 has chosen to record actuarial gains and losses directly into the statement of total recognised gains and losses. It is possible that the international community will consider moving towards this approach in the future. In IAS 19 (revised) it states:

the [IASC] Board found the immediate recognition approach attractive. However the Board believes that it is not feasible to use this approach for actuarial gains and losses until the Board resolves substantial issues about performance reporting. When the Board makes further progress with those issues, it may decide to revisit the treatment of actuarial gains and losses.

In FRS 17 the UK has introduced an accounting treatment that has met the objectives of a sensible balance sheet position and a reasonable consistent profit and loss account charge, and it may set international treatments for pensions in the future.

REVIEW QUESTIONS

1 Outline the differences between a defined benefit and a defined contribution pension scheme.

2 If a defined contribution pension scheme provided a pension that was 6% of salary each year, the company had a payroll cost of £5m, and the company paid £200,000 in the year, what would be the profit and loss account charge and the balance sheet liability at the year end?

3 The approach taken in SSAP 24 before its revision was to match an even pension cost against the period the employees provided service. This follows the accruals principle and is therefore fundamentally correct. Discuss.

4 What measures were introduced by FRS 17 to ensure that the items reported in the balance sheet satisfied the ASB *Statement of Principles* definition of an asset and a liability?

5 Why did the ASB consider it necessary to use the statement of total realised gains and losses in reporting gains and losses? Discuss.

6 Under FRS 17, what amount of actuarial gains and losses should be recognised in the profit and loss account?

7 Past service costs are recognised under FRS 17 immediately if the benefit is 'vested'. In what circumstances would the benefits not be vested?

8 Explain curtailment and its required accounting treatment in defined benefit pension scheme.

9 Explain why a company needs to use a discount rate to value the obligations of a pension fund.

10 'FRS 17 is being used as a scapegoat for companies anxious to reduce their costs.'[27] Discuss.

11 The National Association of Pension Funds responded to the ASB exposure draft that the approach proposed in FRS 17 would have a considerable negative effect on the willingness of company boards to continue to provide defined benefit pension schemes for their employees.[28] Discuss the reasons for the NAPF's concern.

EXERCISES

* Question 1

Hardiste plc has a defined benefit plan.

For the sake of simplicity and clarity, all transactions are assumed to occur at the year end. The following data apply to the post-employment defined benefits compensation scheme of Hardiste plc.

Expected return on plan assets:	12% p.a.
Discount rate:	10% p.a.
Present value of obligation at start of 20X2:	£1m
Market value of plan assets at start of 20X2:	£1m

The following figures are relevant.

	20X2 £000	20X3 £000	20X4 £000
Current service cost	140	150	150
Benefits paid out	120	140	150
Contributions paid by enterprise	110	120	120
Present value of obligation at year end	1,200	1,600	1,700
Market value of plan assets at year end	1,250	1,450	1,610

Any pension scheme asset will be recovered through reduced contributions in the future.

Required:
Show how Hardiste plc should account for this defined benefit plan in years 20X2, 20X3 and 20X4.

Question 2

The Accounting Standards Board recently revised their standard on pensions and changed the way that the accounting for defined benefit pension schemes is done. The standard now requires companies to value the liability in the balance sheet based upon:

Present value of the defined benefit obligation	X
Less: Past service cost not yet recognised	(X)
Less: Market value of the plan assets	(X)
Defined benefit liability (asset)	X(X)

Required:
(a) Briefly explain the terms:
  (i)   present value of the defined benefit obligation;
  (ii) actuarial gains and losses;
  (iii) past service costs.
(b) Show the extracts from the balance sheet and the income statement for 20X1, 20X2 and 20X3 based on the following information.

	20X1	20X2	20X3
Discount rate at start of year	10%	9%	8%
Expected rate of return on plan assets	12%	11%	10%
Current service cost	260	280	300
Benefits paid	300	360	380
Contributions paid	180	200	220
PV of obligation at 31 December	2,282	2,394	2,590
FV of plan assets at 31 December	2,184	2,218	2,058

The present value (PV) of the obligation and the fair value (FV) of the assets at the start of 20X1 was £2,000. Any pension scheme assets are recoverable by reduced contributions in future years.

Question 3

You are Mr F. Smith, the financial controller of PQR plc, a medium-sized UK listed company.

Mrs J. Jones, the financial director of PQR plc, has just read an article in *The Financial Times* on FRS 17 and its implications for companies. She has asked you to prepare a brief report on the implications of FRS 17 for PQR plc, and the possible courses of action the company could take if the fund is in deficit.

PQR plc has prided itself on its retirement benefit provision to staff and all staff are members of the company's defined benefit pension scheme. The last actuarial valuation of the pension fund was in June 1999, and the fund had neither a surplus nor a deficit. The actuaries had recommended that the company paid 6% of salaries into the fund and the company hoped that this level of contribution would continue.

An actuarial valuation is to be done at 30 June 2002, and the investment managers' indications are that the fund will be in deficit. The poor stock market performance has hit the assets of the fund badly.

Required:
Prepare the report as required by Mrs Jones.

References

1 FRS 17, *Retirement Benefits*, ASB, 2000.
2 *Ibid.*, para. 1.
3 FRS 12, *Provisions, Contingent Liabilities and Contingent Assets*, ASB, 1998.
4 A. McGeachen, 'A Transparent Solution', *Accountancy*, January 2001, p. 88.
5 FRS 17, *Retirement Benefits*, ASB, 2000, Summary f.
6 *Ibid.*, para. 35.
7 *Ibid.*, Summary g.
8 *Ibid.*, Appendix 1.
9 *Ibid.*, para. 20.
10 *Ibid.*, para. 60.
11 *Ibid.*, para. 2.
12 *Ibid.*, para. 14.
13 *Ibid.*, para. 50.
14 *Ibid.*, para. 57.
15 *Ibid.*, para. 2.
16 IAS 19, *Employee Benefits* (revised 1998), IASC, paras 92–95.
17 FRS 17, *Retirement Benefits*, ASB, 2000, para. 2.
18 *Ibid.*, Appendix 1.
19 *Inside Track*, ASB, January 2002.
20 J. Kipphoff, 'Wimpey acts on liability for pensions', *Financial Times*, 28 February 2002.
21 M. Odell, 'Rolls-Royce to reveal pension fund deficit', *Financial Times*, 2 March 2002.
22 P. Jenkins and M. Peel, 'Little name, enormous impact', *Financial Times*, 2 March 2002.
23 J. Plender, 'Zulu bean count', *Financial Times*, 4 March 2002.
24 A. Jolliffe, 'Money purchase switch amounts to a pay cut for many of us', *Financial Times*, 16 February 2002.
25 P. Jenkins, 'Actuaries warn of FRS 17 blow to pensions', *Financial Times*, 2 March 2002.
26 M. Peel and N. Timmins, 'Head of Treasury review calls for change to FRS 17', *Financial Times*, 5 March 2002.
27 J. Morley, 'FRS 17: A statement for the defence', *Accountancy Age*, 6 March 2002.
28 P. Thompson, 'Dangers of snapshot accounting', *Accountancy Age*, 7 March 2002.

CHAPTER 13

Taxation in company accounts

13.1 Introduction

Limited companies, and indeed all corporate bodies, are treated for tax purposes as legally separate from their proprietors. Thus, a limited company is itself liable to pay tax on its profits. This tax is known as **corporation tax**. The shareholders are only accountable for tax on the income they receive by way of any dividends distributed by the company. If the shareholder is an individual, then **income tax** will become due on the dividend received.

This is in contrast to the position in a partnership, where each partner is then individually liable for the tax on that share of the pre-tax profit that has been allocated. Note that it is different from the treatment of an employee who is charged tax on the amount of salary paid. A partner is taxed on the profit and not simply on drawings.

In this chapter we consider the different types of company taxation and their accounting treatment. In addition, we consider the major changes to the UK corporation tax system that took place in April 1999.

13.2 Corporation tax

Corporation tax is calculated under rules set by Parliament each year in the Finance Act. The Finance Act may alter the existing rules; it also sets the rate of tax payable. Because of this annual review of the rules, circumstances may change year by year, which makes comparability difficult and forecasting uncertain.

A further complication is that although the tax payable is **based** on the accounting profits as disclosed in the profit and loss account, the tax rules may differ from the accounting rules which apply prudence to income recognition. For example, the tax rules do not accept that all the expenses which are recognised by the accountant under the FRS 18 accrual concept are deductible when arriving at the taxable profit.

The accounting profit may therefore be lower or higher than the taxable profit. For example, the Companies Acts require that the formation expenses of a company, which are the costs of establishing it on incorporation, must be written off in its first accounting period; the rules of corporation tax, however, state that it is a capital expense and cannot be deducted from the profit for tax purposes. Another example of this might be a royalty expense under a licence agreement which is charged in arrears but is deducted from accounting profit on a time apportionment basis under FRS 18. The expense is only allowed in calculating taxable profit on a cash basis of when it is paid in order to ensure that one taxpayer does not reduce his potential tax liability before another becomes liable to tax on the income received. The expenses may therefore reduce the reported accounting profit but the taxable profit will be higher. This means that more tax will be assessed as payable than one would assume from an inspection of the published profit and loss account.

Similarly, although most businesses would consider that entertaining suppliers and other business associates was a normal commercial trading expense, it is not allowed as a deduction for tax purposes.

A more complicated situation arises in the case of depreciation. Because the directors have the choice of method of depreciation to use, the legislators have decided to require all companies to use the same method when calculating taxable profits. If one thinks about this, then it would seem to be the equitable practice. Each company is allowed to deduct a uniform percentage from its profits in respect of the depreciation that has arisen from the wear and tear and diminution in value of fixed assets. The substituted depreciation that the tax rules allow is known as a **capital allowance**. The capital allowance is calculated in the same way as depreciation; the only difference is that the rates are those set out in the Finance Acts. At the time of writing, most commercial fixed assets (excluding land and buildings) qualify for a capital allowance of 25% calculated on the reducing balance method. There are restricted allowances, called industrial buildings allowances, for certain categories of buildings used in manufacturing.

Just as the depreciation that is charged by the company under accrual accounting concepts is substituted by a capital allowance, profits or losses arising on the sale of fixed assets are not used for tax purposes.

Thus, the calculation of the corporate tax liability of a company (known as the tax computation) may appear as in Figure 13.1. These are only examples of the adjustments that may be made to the accounting profit for tax purposes. They are intended to demonstrate solely the principles involved. The tax liability of £21,124.77, rounded to £21,125 (disclosed in the accounts as shown in Figure 13.2) will be payable to the Inland Revenue nine months after the end of the accounting period in January 2004. It must, therefore, appear on the balance sheet at 31 March 2003 as a current liability under the heading 'Other creditors including taxation and social security'.

Mithras was a simple company with trading income only. Had it had a more complex income structure it might have more items comprising its tax charge which would have to be disclosed either on the face of the profit and loss account or in the notes to that account.

Figure 13.1 Mithras plc

Corporation tax computation for the year to 31 March 2003		£
Net profit on ordinary activities before tax		110,000
ADD BACK to the accounting profit:	£	
Formation expenses	1,200	
Entertaining	4,983	
Depreciation expense	35,000	
		41,183
		151,183
DEDUCT Substitute amounts allowed by the tax rules:		
Capital allowances		40,000
		111,183
Corporation tax at 19% as set by the Finance Act		21,125

Figure 13.2 Tax charge on profit and loss account

	£
Profit on ordinary activities before tax	110,000
Tax on profit on ordinary activities	21,125
Profit on ordinary activities after tax	88,875

Figure 13.3 European Colours plc note on taxation

6 Taxation

	2001 £m	2000 £m
UK corporation tax for the current year on ordinary activities at 30% (2000: 30%)	1,118	1,312
Overprovision in previous years	(89)	(226)
UK current taxation change	1,029	1,086

Other items could include, for example, foreign taxes paid on overseas earnings and tax suffered on investment income.

Accountants have guidance on how to disclose tax information in the published accounts. Accounting for taxation in the accounts of an entity subject to corporation tax is governed by FRS 16 *Current Tax*. The intention is that the user of the accounts should be able to see the significance of tax when predicting the future performance of the company.

There is guidance on the information that must be shown by way of note. For example, the note to the accounts must show an analysis of the charge to taxation shown in the profit and loss account. This may be illustrated by the following extract from the accounts of European Colours plc, set out in Figure 13.3.

You will observe that the note shows the breakdown of the charge against profits between corporation tax on the trading income and an adjustment in respect of the preceding year. It is usual to have an adjustment because it is rare for a company to be able to state its ultimate tax liability accurately when the accounts are prepared. It still has to agree with the Inland Revenue on exactly which expenses are allowable.

13.3 Corporation tax systems

The distinguished tax theoretician Professor G.S.A. Wheatcroft described '…writing a … book on tax is like painting a picture of the sunset; as fast as a chapter is in draft the law has changed'. Fortunately this only applies to one chapter of this book.

There are three possible systems of company taxation (classical, imputation and split rate).[1] **These systems differ solely in their tax treatment of the relationship between the limited company and those investors who have invested in it.** In the classical system, a company pays tax on its profits, and then the shareholders suffer a second tax liability when their share of the profits is distributed to them. In effect, the dividend income of the shareholder is regarded as a second and separate source of income from that of the profits of the company. The payment of a dividend creates an additional tax liability which falls directly on the shareholders. It could be argued that this double taxation is inequitable when compared to the taxation system on unincorporated bodies (such as partnerships) where the rate of taxation suffered overall is unaltered if profits are withdrawn from the business or not. It is suggested that the classical system discourages the distribution of profits to shareholders since the second tranche of taxation (the tax on dividend income of the shareholders) only becomes payable on payment of the dividend, although some argue that the effect of the burden of double taxation on the economy is less serious than it might seem.[2] The UK had a classical system until 1971, as Austria, Belgium, Denmark, Holland and Sweden have today.

In an imputation system, the dividend is regarded merely as a flow of the profits on each sale to the individual shareholders, this being considered to be merely one source of income which could either be retained in the company or distributed to the shareholders. It is certainly correct that the payment of a dividend results from the flow of monies into the company from trading profits, and that the choice between retaining profits to fund future growth and the payment of a dividend to investing shareholders is merely a strategic choice unrelated to a view as to the nature of taxable profits. In an imputation system the total sum of tax payable is unaffected by the payment of dividends, and the payment of tax by the company is treated as if it were also a payment of the individual shareholders' liabilities on dividends received. It is this principle of the flow of net profits from particular sales to individual shareholders that is used to justify no further taxation charge being levied upon a company in receipt of a dividend from another company. **The UK has an imputation system, as does France and Germany.**

In a partial imputation system only part of the underlying corporation tax paid is treated as a tax credit. All three systems are based on the taxation of profits earned as shown under the same basic principles used in the preparation of financial accounts.

13.3.1 Advance corporation tax – the system until 5 April 1999

As stated previously, under this system a company pays corporation tax on its income. When that company pays a dividend to its shareholders it is distributing some of its taxed income among the proprietors. In this system the tax paid by the company is 'imputed' to the shareholders who therefore receive a dividend which has already been taxed.

This means that, from the paying company's point of view, the concept of gross dividends does not exist. From the paying company's point of view, the amount of dividends paid and proposed shown in the profit and loss account will equal the cash that the company will have paid or will pay to the shareholders in the case of proposed dividends.

However, from the shareholder's point of view, the cash received from the company is treated as a net payment after deduction of tax. The shareholders will have received, with the cash dividend, a note of a tax credit, which is regarded as equal to basic rate income tax on the total of the dividend plus the tax credit. For example:

	£
Dividend being the cash paid by the company and disclosed in the company's profit and loss account	400
Tax credit calculated assuming a basic rate of income tax of 20% applied to the 'gross' dividend of £500 (being the rate until 5 April 1999)	100
Gross dividend	500

The ACT calculation (as shown above) has been based on a basic tax rate of 20% for dividends paid, being the basic rate of income tax on investment income until 5 April 1999. The concession of a lower rate of basic income tax on dividends was introduced as from 1 April 1993 as a signal of the then governmental intent to reduce the basic rate of income tax down from the rate at that time of 25% to 20% in due course.

This meant that an individual shareholder, who only paid basic rate income tax, had no further liability in that the assumption is that the basic rate tax has been paid by the company. A non-taxpayer could have claimed back the tax credit of £100 from the Inland Revenue (except for pension funds in respect of dividends paid on or after 2 July 1997).

This last point about the reclaim of the tax credit had a strong influence on the introduction of the second stage of imputation tax. The position was that while shareholders were able to recover tax credits immediately on receipt of the dividend, the companies paying the dividend would not have had to pay their corporation tax until nine months after the end of the accounting period. As you may imagine, the result of this lack of synchronisation between the recovery of the tax and the payment of the tax would have an adverse effect on the government's cash flow. The government consequently introduced measures to counter this by the introduction of **advance corporation tax** (ACT). Statute required that when a company paid a dividend it was required to make a payment to the Inland Revenue equal to the total tax credit associated with that dividend. This payment was called 'advance corporation tax' because it was a payment on account of the corporation's tax liability that would be paid on the profits of the accounting period. When the company eventually made its payment of the corporation tax liability, it was allowed to reduce the amount paid by the amount paid as ACT. The net amount of corporation tax that was paid after offsetting the ACT is known as **mainstream corporation tax**. The total amount of corporation tax is no greater than that assessed on the taxable profits of the company; there is merely a change in the timing of the amount of tax paid by paying it in two parts – the ACT element and the mainstream corporation tax element.

ACT was accounted for quarterly and paid to the Inland Revenue on the 14th of the month following the end of the calendar quarter. Thus if a dividend was paid during the three months to 31 March, the ACT payable on that dividend had to be paid to the Inland Revenue on 14 April. The date of the payment of the dividend was the crucial factor for ACT purposes, not the date the dividend was declared. This was because the shareholder was only able to claim a refund after payment of the dividend. This meant that the declaration of a proposed dividend gave rise to a potential liability for ACT which did not actually crystallise until after the dividend was actually paid.

As mentioned above, the ACT paid by the company was recovered by deducting the amount paid from the corporation tax liability. This could be illustrated by looking at the Mithras example above (although treating the example as if the accounts were for the year ended 31 March 1999 rather than 31 March 2003):

	£
Profit after taxation	88,875
Dividends paid	40,000
Retained profits for the period	48,875

The dividend of £40,000 that was paid in cash would have given rise to an ACT payment by the company of £10,000. This would have been offset against the £21,125 of corporation tax giving a net current liability (the mainstream corporation tax) of £11,125.

What would be the position if the company had declared a dividend but had not paid it out to the shareholders by the date of the balance sheet? In this case the offset would not have been possible because the £10,000 of ACT could only be offset against the corporation tax in the accounting period during which the tax was actually paid.

The offset of ACT against corporation tax is effectively restricted to the ACT rate multiplied by the company's profits chargeable to corporation tax. A further refinement was that for offset purposes the ACT rate was multiplied by the UK profit – this does not include profits generated overseas. In the case of Mithras, for example, the offset was limited to the chargeable profits of £111,183 multiplied by 19%, i.e. £21,125. Should a distribution have exceeded the chargeable profits for that period, then the ACT could not be recovered immediately. Under tax law, such unrelieved ACT can be carried back against corporation tax payments in the preceding six years or forward against future liabilities indefinitely. In this example, say that only £40,000 of Mithras's total profits represented UK income. This would reduce the offset limit to £8,000 (£40,000 multiplied by 20%) and result in unrelieved ACT of £2,000. Therefore, the mix of UK versus overseas income had potential implications on the level of unrelieved ACT.

Unrecovered ACT would appear in the balance sheet as an asset. At this point the accountant must have considered the prudence concept. In order for it to have remained as such on the balance sheet it must have been reasonably certain and foreseeable that it would be recoverable at a future date. If the ACT could be reasonably seen as recoverable then it should have been shown on the balance sheet as a deferred asset. If, for any reason, it seemed improbable that there would be sufficient future tax liabilities to 'cover' the ACT, then it must have been written off as irrecoverable.

13.3.2 Corporation tax – the system from 6 April 1999

The system altered radically as from 6 April 1999, although a company continues to pay corporation tax on its income and when that company pays a dividend to its shareholders it is still considered to be distributing some of its taxed income among the proprietors. In this revised system the tax payable by the company is 'imputed' to the shareholders who therefore receive a dividend which has already been taxed. This means that, from the paying company's point of view, the concept of 'gross' dividends continues not to exist. From the paying company's point of view, the amount of dividends paid and proposed shown in the profit and loss account will equal the cash that the company will have paid or will pay to the shareholders in the case of proposed dividends.

However, from the shareholder's point of view, the cash received from the company is treated as a net payment after deduction of tax. The shareholders will receive, with the cash dividend, a note of a tax credit, which is regarded as equal to basic rate income tax on the total of the dividend plus the tax credit. For example:

	£
Dividend being the cash paid by the company and disclosed in the company's profit and loss account	400.00
Imputed tax credit of 1/9 of dividend paid (being the rate from 6 April 1999)	44.44
Gross dividend	444.44

The imputed tax credit calculation (as shown above) has been based on a basic tax rate of 10% for dividends paid, being the basic rate of income tax on investment income from 6 April 1999. This means that an individual shareholder, who only pays basic rate income tax, has no further liability in that the assumption is that the basic rate tax has been paid by the company. A non-taxpayer can no longer obtain a repayment of tax.

The essential difference from the previous system up to 5 April 1999 is that the dividend paying company makes absolutely no deduction from the dividend **nor is any payment made by the company to the Inland Revenue**. The addition of 1/9 of the dividend paid as an imputed tax credit is purely nominal. A tax credit of 1/9 of the dividend will be deemed to be attached to that dividend (in effect an income tax rate of 10%). That credit is notional in that no payment of the 10% will be paid to the Inland Revenue.[3]

Large companies (those with taxable profits of £1,500,000) started paying a proportion of their corporation tax liability in quarterly instalments starting within the year of account rather than paying their mainstream corporation tax liability nine months thereafter. Previously only those companies that paid dividends would have been required to hand over any corporation tax until nine months after the year end. The payment of taxation is no longer associated with dividends. Smaller companies will continue to pay their corporation tax nine months after the year end.

As there have no longer been payments of advance corporation tax (ACT) from 6 April 1999, there will no longer be unrecovered ACT arising that cannot be offset against the balance of the corporation tax that had been due nine months after the year end under the old system (described in 13.3.1). Such unrelieved ACT which was still an asset in April 1999 will be carried forward against future taxation liabilities indefinitely (in a system known as 'Shadow ACT').

The payment of taxation is no longer associated with dividends.

It has been argued by the Treasury that the imputation system encouraged the payment of dividends, and consequently discourages firms from reinvesting earnings. Since 1985, both investment and the ratio of dividend payments to GDP have soared in Britain relative to the USA, but it is not obvious that such trends are largely attributable to tax policy.[4] It was suggested that the then newly proposed changes in the corporation tax system from 5 April 1999 would tend to discourage companies from paying 'excessive' dividends because the major pressure for dividends has come from the pension fund investors who could reclaim the tax paid, and that the decrease in cash flow to the company caused by the start of quarterly corporation tax payments might tend to assist company directors in resisting dividend increases to compensate for this loss.

13.4 Investment income

It is recognised under the Companies Act format for the presentation of the profit and loss account that dividends received as investment income are disclosed as a constituent part of the profits. When a company receives a dividend from another UK company it carries with it a tax credit. Under the imputation system there is no further tax liability; such dividends are not subject to corporation tax in the receiving company. Until 6 April 1999 the amounts of dividends received was 'grossed up' in the accounts by adding back the tax credit to the cash received and the tax charge disclosed in the profit and loss account was then increased by the amount of the imputed tax credit. For example, if a company had received the dividend of £400 in Figure 13.4, the entries in the profit and loss account would have been as set out for the year to 5 April 1999.

FRS 16 provides that from 6 April 1999 dividends received from other UK companies are not 'grossed up' with the imputed tax credit (of 1/9 of the dividend) on the grounds that the imputed tax credit can no longer be reclaimed under changes in the legislation (even if losses are made in the receiving company).

Figure 13.4 Profit and loss account entries for investment income

Profit and loss account for investment income

	To 5 April 1999		From 6 April 1999	
	£	£	£	£
Profits on ordinary activities before tax, say		1,000		1,000
Tax:				
On profits on ordinary activities	210		200	
		210		200
		790		800
Profit and loss account after receipt of the dividend				
Profit on ordinary activities before tax – say		1,000		1,000
Investment income		500		400
Profit before tax		1,500		1,400
Tax				
On profits on ordinary activities	210		200	
Tax credit on investment income	100		—	
		310		200
		1,190		1,200

13.5 Investment income other than dividends from shares

Certain forms of income are subject to the deduction of income tax at source. An example of these is debenture interest from debentures held by the company. Tax suffered by being deducted from such income before being paid to the company is treated as a payment on account of corporation tax and relieved in that way.

Just as with income, certain forms of expense are also subject to the deduction of income tax at source. Examples of these are debenture interest paid by the company on debentures issued by the company and royalties on licences granted to the company. This income tax is accounted for to the Inland Revenue quarterly. Tax deducted from payments must be treated as part of the related expense and passed over to the Inland Revenue.

As far as the published accounts are concerned, all items of income and expenditure which are subject to the **deduction of tax at source** should appear gross (i.e. before deduction of tax) in the profit and loss account.

13.6 Deferred tax

The profit on which tax is paid may differ from that shown in the published profit and loss account. This is caused by two separate factors.

One factor that we looked at above is that certain items of expenditure may not be legitimate deductions from profit for tax purposes. For example, we saw that formation expenses and entertainment expenses were not allowable as a deduction for tax purposes and were required to be added back to the accounting profit. These differences are referred to as **permanent** differences because they will not be allowed at a different time and will be permanently disallowed, even in future accounting periods.

The other factor is that there are some other expenses that are legitimate deductions in arriving at the taxable profit but are allowed as a deduction for tax purposes at a later date. These are simply differences of **timing** in that tax relief and charges to profit and loss account occur in different accounting periods. The accounting profit is prepared on an accruals basis but the taxable profit requires certain of the items to be dealt with on a cash basis. An example of this could be accrued royalty payments, properly included in the profit and loss account under the accruals concept but not eligible for tax relief until actually paid, thus giving tax relief in a later period.

The most significant timing difference, however, is in the treatment of depreciation for it is believed that the consequent deferral of taxation liabilities serves as an incentive to capital investment (this incentive is not forbidden by European Union law or the OECD rules). The depreciation charge made in the profit and loss account must be added back in the tax computation and replaced by capital allowances. The substituted capital allowance calculated in accordance with the tax rules is rarely the same amount as the depreciation charge computed in accordance with FRS 15 *Tangible Fixed Assets*.

The classic effect of this is for corporation tax to be payable on a lower figure than the accounting profit in the earlier years of an asset's life because the capital allowances usually exceed depreciation in the earlier years of an asset's life. In later accounting periods, the capital allowances will be lower than the depreciation charges and the taxable profit will then be higher than the accounting profit that appears in the published profit and loss account.

The process whereby the company pays tax on a profit that is lower than the reported profit in the early years and on a profit that is higher than reported profit in later years is known as **reversal**. Given the knowledge that, ultimately, these timing differences will reverse, the accruals concept requires that consideration be given to making provision for the future liability in those early years in which the tax payable is calculated on a lower figure. The provision that is made is known as a **deferred tax provision**.

There has been a history of disagreement within the accounting profession over the method to use to calculate the provision. There have been, historically, two methods of calculating the provision for this future liability – the **deferral** method and the **liability** method.

The deferral method, which had been traditionally favoured in the USA, involves the calculation each year of the tax effects of the timing differences that have arisen in that year. The tax effect is then debited or credited to the profit and loss account as part of the tax charge; the double entry is effected by making an entry to the deferred tax account. This deferral method of calculating the tax effect ignores the effect of changing tax rates on the timing differences that arose in earlier periods. This means that the total provision may consist of differences calculated at the rate of tax in force in the year when the entry was made to the provision.

The liability method requires the calculation of the total amount of potential liability each year at current rates of tax, increasing or reducing the provision accordingly. This means that the company keeps a record of the timing differences and then recalculates at the end of each new accounting period using the rate of corporation tax in force as at the date of the current balance sheet.

To illustrate the two methods we will take the example of a single asset, costing £10,000, depreciated at 10% straight line, but subject to capital allowances of 25% on the reducing balance method, and show the workings in Figure 13.5. This shows that,

Figure 13.5 Timing differences

		ACCOUNTS (depreciation) £	TAX (allowances) £	DIFFERENCE (timing) £	TAX rate
1.1.1996	Cost of asset	10,000	10,000	—	
31.12.1996	Depreciation/capital allowances	1,000	2,500	1,500	25%
		9,000	7,500	1,500	
31.12.1997	Depreciation/capital allowances	1,000	1,875	875	25%
		8,000	5,625	2,375	
31.12.1998	Depreciation/capital allowances	1,000	1,406	406	25%
		7,000	4,219	2,781	
31.12.1999	Depreciation/capital allowances	1,000	1,055	55	24%
		6,000	3,164	2,836	
31.12.2000	Depreciation/capital allowances	1,000	791	(209)	24%
		5,000	2,373	2,627	

if there were no other adjustments, for the first four years the profits subject to tax would be lower than those shown in the accounts, but afterwards the situation would reverse.

The deferral method would charge to the profit and loss account each year the variation multiplied by the current tax rate, i.e. 1996 at 25% on £1,500 giving £375.00, and 1999 at 24% on £55 giving £13.20. This is in accordance with the accrual concept which matches the tax expense against the income that gave rise to it. Under this method the deferred tax provision will be credited with £375 in 1996 and this amount will not be altered in 1999 when the tax rate changes to 24%.

For example, the calculation for the five years would be as in Figure 13.6. The liability method would make a charge so that the total balance on deferred tax equalled the cumulative variation multiplied by the current tax rate. The intention is that the balance sheet liability should be stated at a figure which represents the tax effect as at the end of each new accounting period. This means that there would be an adjustment made in 1999 to recalculate the tax effect of the timing difference that was provided for in earlier years. For example, the provision for 1996 would be recalculated at 24%, giving a figure of £360 instead of the £375 that was calculated and charged in 1996. The decrease in the expected liability will be reflected in the amount charged against the profit and loss account in 1999. The £15 will in effect be credited to the 1999 profit and loss account.

The effect on the charge to the 1999 profit and loss account (Figures 13.6 and 13.7) is that there will be a charge of £13.20 using the deferral method and a **credit** of £14.61 using the liability method. The £14.61 is the reduction in the amount provided from £695.25 at the end of 1998 to the £680.64 that is required at the end of 1999.

Figure 13.6 Deferred tax provision using deferral method

Year ended	Timing difference £	Basic rate %	Deferred tax charge in year £	Deferred tax provision Deferral method £
31.12.1996	1,500	25%	375.00	375.00
31.12.1997	875	25%	218.75	593.75
31.12.1998	406	25%	101.50	695.25
31.12.1999	55	24%	13.20	708.45
31.12.2000	(209)	24%	(50.16)	658.29

Figure 13.7 Deferred tax provision using liability method

Year ended	Timing difference £	Basic rate %	Deferred tax charge in year £	Deferred tax provision Deferral method £	Rate in 1999	Deferred tax charge Liability method £
31.12.1996	1,500	25%	375.00	375.00	24%	360.00
31.12.1997	875	25%	218.75	593.75	24%	210.00
31.12.1998	406	25%	101.50	695.25	24%	97.44
31.12.1999	55	24%	13.20	708.45	24%	13.20
				708.45		680.64

The deferral method places the **emphasis on the profit and loss account** because the tax, as it is calculated, is not truly a calculation of a liability, but is better characterised as deferred income or expenditure. The liability method places the **emphasis on the balance sheet**, as the sum is recalculated to take account of changes in the rate of tax charged.

13.7 History of the development of deferred tax accounting

The history of the accounting standards for deferred taxation has been a mixed and somewhat controversial one and is worth examining.

Accounting for deferred tax in the UK predates the issue of accounting standards. Prior to the issue of standards, companies applied an accounting practice known as 'tax equalisation accounting', whereby they recognised that accounting periods should each be allocated an amount of income tax expense that bears a 'normal relationship to the income shown in the income statement', and to let reported income taxes follow reported income has been the objective of accounting for income taxes ever since.[5] There is also an economic consequence that flows from the practice of tax equalisation in that the trend of reported after-tax income is smoothed, and there is less likelihood of pressure for a cash dividend distribution based on the crediting of the tax benefit of capital investment expenditure to the early years of the fixed assets.

In tax equalisation accounting practice, it was usual to follow the liability method. However, when, in 1973, ED 11 was issued there was an increasing trend among UK companies to have their shares quoted on the US stock exchanges, coupled with a desire for international harmonisation of accounting standards, and the ASC, in the exposure draft, chose the deferral method and required full provision.

Because the deferral method was not widely used in the UK, there was a considerable debate which reflected the lack of agreement with the deferral method. As one might expect, given the lack of consensus, the standard-setting bodies followed a course of allowing both methods. Therefore, when SSAP 11 was issued, companies were given the choice of the liability or the deferral method.

There followed a period of very high rates of capital allowances and, with a naive belief that this situation would continue and allow permanent deferral, companies complained that to provide full provision was unrealistic and so in 1977 ED 19 introduced the concept of **partial provision** in which deferred tax is only provided in respect of timing differences that are likely to be reversed. This means that, in the preceding example, there would only be an additional tax charge of £375 in 1996 and a credit to a deferred tax provision if it could be seen with reasonable certainty that the situation would arise as in 2000 where the depreciation charge would exceed the capital allowances for the year. The argument was that if the company continued with the replacement of fixed assets, and if the capital allowances were reasonably certain to exceed the depreciation in the foreseeable future, it was unrealistic to make charges against the profit and create provisions that would not crystallise. This would merely lead to the appearance of an ever-increasing provision on the balance sheet.

The position for accounting periods ending on or before 22 January 2002 under SSAP 15 *Accounting for Deferred Tax* (which superseded SSAP 11) may be summarised as follows.

- Provision for deferred tax should be computed under the **liability method** in which the potential liability is computed at the corporation tax rate at which it is estimated that the tax will be paid. This is normally the rate ruling at the balance sheet date applied to all items within the provision.

- Tax deferred or accelerated should only be accounted for **to the extent that a liability or asset will crystallise**. Thus a liability might be considered permanently deferred by virtue of the company's plans for continued investment in fixed assets. It ceases to be a timing difference for all practical purposes and becomes reclassified as a notional permanent difference.

- The decisions as to whether or not to provide must be based on **reasoned assumptions** each time accounts are prepared; a prudent view should be taken.

- Debit balances of deferred tax should only be carried forward if their recovery without replacement can be foreseen.

- Recoverable ACT may be offset against the deferred tax provisions.

- The total amount of unprovided deferred tax should be disclosed by way of a note so that the shareholder can see the potential liability if the assumptions were to be ill-founded.

Under the liability method the focus is on the balance sheet (the objective being to compute the deferred tax liabilities), whereas the deferral method places the focus on the profit and loss account (the objective being to show the annual effect that has arisen in the year of account).[6] Such an emphasis on the balance sheet, at the possible expense of the profit and loss account, is the trend that the ASB has adopted in its *Draft Statement of Principles* (as modified in March 1999).[7]

It is clear that under the full provision method, provision is made for the tax consequences of all gains and losses that have been recognised in the published accounts at the balance sheet date and that are expected to enter into the determination of taxable profit at some stage. The ASB discussion paper of March 1995 *Accounting for Taxation* proposed that the liability method of accounting for deferred tax continued to be used but that the method should revert to the making of the full provision, i.e. no more partial provision should be permitted. The Board argued that making provision for deferred tax without taking account of when it will be paid overstates the liability to tax and proposed for discussion a method of discounting the deferred tax (which would also mitigate the effects of future transactions such as the replacement of fixed assets as referred to above). The discussion paper, in recommending the liability method, follows the change in the USA to this method in SFAS 96. **The Board stated its belief that, in principle, deferred tax should be discounted but took the view that, in the interest of comparison between reporting entities, discounting should be either required or prohibited** but not merely permitted so as to give a choice to the preparer of the accounts. Before the ASB managed to come to a conclusion on the matter of deferred taxation, the IASC modified IAS 12 in October 1996 with effect for accounting periods beginning on or after 1 January 1998. The modified IAS 12 bans the deferral method and provides that full provision should be made for deferred taxation without any discounting. Research has indicated that European Union harmonisation for deferred tax has been inadequate.[8]

Before proceeding further, it would be appropriate to illustrate the three methods for accounting for deferred tax referred to in the ASB discussion paper of March 1995 *Accounting for Taxation* which discusses three methods in the first stage of its project to replace SSAP 15 with a new FRS. The three methods are: flow-through, under which no provision is made for deferred tax; full provision, under which deferred tax is provided in full; and partial provision, under which deferred tax is only provided to the extent that it is likely to crystallise taking into account the tax effects of future transactions.

A comparative illustration of the flow-through, full provision and partial provision methods are given below based on the following data (assuming a 33% tax rate):

	Profit before tax and depreciation £000	*Depreciation* £000	*Capital allowances* £000
19X5	800	25	125
19X6	900	50	25
19X7	950	75	25
19X8	1,050	50	175

Tax charge:	*19X5*	*19X6*	*19X7*	*19X8*
	£000	£000	£000	£000
Accounting profit	800	900	950	1,050
Capital allowances	125	25	25	175
Taxable profit	675	875	925	875
Tax payable @ 33%	**223**	**289**	**305**	**289**

Flow-through method – assuming nil provision for deferred tax and deducting tax payable

Entries in the profit and loss account are as follows:

	19X5 £000	19X6 £000	19X7 £000	19X8 £000
Accounting profit	775	850	875	1,000
Tax	**223**	**289**	**305**	**289**
Deferred tax	—	—	—	—
Profit after tax	552	561	570	711

Full provision method

Calculation of deferred tax on difference between capital allowances and depreciation:

Year	Capital allowances	Depreciation	Difference	Tax on difference in profit & loss a/c	Provision in balance sheet
	£000	£000	£000	£000	£000
19X5	125	25	100	33	33
19X6	25	50	(25)	(8)	25
19X7	25	75	(50)	(16)	9
19X8	175	50	125	41	50

Entries in profit and loss account and balance sheet:

	19X5 £000	19X6 £000	19X7 £000	19X8 £000
Accounting profit	775	850	875	1,000
Tax payable	223	289	305	289
Deferred tax	**33**	**(8)**	**(16)**	**41**
Total tax @ 33%	256	281	289	330
Profit after tax	519	569	586	670
Provision in balance sheet	**33**	**25**	**9**	**50**

If the £50,000 provision is not expected to reverse because the company proposes to maintain its capital investment spending programme indefinitely, the liability could be discounted to reduce the amount that appears in the balance sheet as a provision. The reason for discounting is that the liability would not crystallise with the current capital investment plan.

Partial provision method

Calculation to ensure that the provision in the balance sheet is the expected tax liability:

The approach is to estimate in 19X5 the amount of the provision of £33,000 that is likely to crystallise into a liability. This is assumed to happen when the depreciation charge in succeeding years exceeds the capital allowances (known as *reversing timing differences*) for those years. This may be presented in tabular form as follows:

Capital allowance > depreciation *(Originating)* £000	Depreciation > capital allowances *(Reversing)* £000	Cumulative *(Cumulative reversing differences)* £000
100	—	—
	25	25
	50	**75**
125	—	—

From this it can be seen that, although a full provision in 19X5 would be £33,000, only £24,000 is estimated to become a liability, i.e. 33% of the cumulative amount of £75,000.

Entries in profit and loss account and balance sheet:

	19X5 £000	19X6 £000	19X7 £000	19X8 £000
Accounting profit	775	850	875	1,000
Tax payable	223	289	305	289
Deferred tax	**24**	(8)	(16)	—
Total tax in P & L A/c @ 33%	247	281	289	289
Profit after tax	528	569	586	711
Provision in balance sheet	**24**	**16**	—	—

This assumes that the effect of the capital expenditure in 19X8 will not reverse.

The foreword to *Accounting Standards* published in June 1993 by the ASB states that 'FRSs are formulated with due regard to international developments ... the Board supports the IASC in its aim to harmonise ... where the requirements of an accounting standard and an IAS differ, the accounting standard should be followed.'

Professor Andrew Lennard, Assistant Technical Director of the ASB, confirmed during a lecture on 17 March 1999 that this was a matter where there was a divergence of view between the ASB and international regulators, where the ASB was unhappy to account in full for deferred tax where there was no discounting for long delays until the anticipated payment; indeed he expressed his exasperation with the topic in stating that he 'wished deferred tax accounting would go away'.[9]

Applying the full provision method is more consistent with both international practice and the ASB's *Draft Statement of Principles* (as modified in March 1999). However, a criticism of the full provision method in the past was that it could, if the company had a continuous capital expenditure programme, lead to a build-up of large liabilities that may fall due only far into the future, if at all. The ASB produced the long delayed FRED 19 in August 1999. It was noted that most respondents to the Discussion Paper supported continuation of the partial provision method, but accepted that the partial provision method would become less well understood as more companies adopted the International Standard IAS 12. The ASB noted that deferred tax is not one of the areas where a good case can be made for taking a stand against the direction of international opinion.

The Board pointed out that a feature of the UK tax system is that there can be a significant delay between the recognition of certain items in tax computations and their recognition in the accounts, and that a problem of the full provision method is that it fails to take account of when the deferred tax liability will actually be paid. It has been suggested, FRED 19 states, that discounting of the delayed tax liability could remedy the problem (of these timing differences) but there was a divergence of views as to whether there was a conceptual justification for discounting and whether the benefits of the complicated discounting calculations outweigh the costs. The majority of the Board supported discounting, but the Board decided that they would invite views on discounting before coming to a conclusion. However, although discounting appears an attractive method for allowing for the delay in payment of the liability, it has been pointed out that in some cases where capital expenditure is uneven, an unexpected effect of discounting both the initial and final cash flow effects could be to turn an eventual liability into an initial asset. It will be interesting to see how the ASB deals with such an unexpected result.[10]

13.8 Deferred tax accounting under FRS 19 (from 23 January 2002)

The ASB eventually issued FRS 19 in December 2000, a gap of thirteen months since the consultation period ended in November 1999. The Standard is in force for accounting periods ending on or after 23 January 2002, although earlier adoption is encouraged. As an example BG Group plc (formerly known as British Gas) adopted FRS 19 from 1 January 2001.[11]

The **liability method** of accounting for deferred tax is to be continued to be used **but practice should revert to the making of the full provision**, i.e. no more partial provision is be permitted. The most significant change from the original ASB discussion paper of March 1995 *Accounting for Taxation* is that **discounting is made optional**. In the discussion paper the Board had stated its belief that, in principle, deferred tax should be discounted but took the view that, in the interest of comparison between reporting entities, discounting should be either required or prohibited but not merely permitted so as to give a choice to the preparer of the accounts. The Board stated that providing that discounting was applied consistently from one period to the next, and the impact of discounting was highlighted clearly, there would not be a serious loss of comparability if not all entities discounted deferred tax. Because of the complexities involved it is suggested that only companies with significant capital investments where material sums of tax had been deferred and not provided for previously (on the view that a liability might be considered permanently deferred by virtue of the company's plans for continued investment in fixed assets) are likely to consider discounting.

There is a general requirement that a deferred tax charge **should not be recognised on revaluation gains** on non-monetary assets which are revalued to fair values on the acquisition of a business.

The question remains as to the long-term viability of FRS 19 as a core national accounting standard that is different to the international norm set out in IAS 12. In 1995, the IASC reached an agreement with the International Organisation of Securities Commissions that, provided the IASC could complete a core set of upgraded standards to their satisfaction by 1999, they would consider recommending that its members accept financial statements prepared on the basis of the resulting standards in documents used for cross-border securities issues and listings. This core set of upgraded standards has been completed. Consideration is also being given to changes in European Union law to force companies that are quoted on stock exchanges to follow International Accounting Standards, but there is at present no international system to assist companies in deciding on conflicting national and international standards. The ASB is aware of the problem. Indeed it is suggested that the ASB developed and implemented FRS 19 with a view that it would 'encourage the International Accounting Standards Committee to think again' about IAS 12.[12]

13.9 A critique of deferred taxation

It could be argued that deferred tax is not a legal liability until it accrues. The consequence of this argument would be that deferred tax should not appear in the financial statements and financial statements should:

- present the tax expense for the year equal to the amount of income taxes that has been levied based on the income tax return for the year;

- accrue as a receivable any tax refunds that are due from taxing authorities or as a payable any unpaid current or past income taxes;

- disclose in the notes to the financial statements differences between the income tax bases of assets and liabilities and the amounts at which they appear in the balance sheet. The significance for investors in British companies of a move to full provision for deferred taxation should not be underestimated.

The argument is that the process of accounting for deferred tax is confusing what **did** happen to a company, i.e. the agreed tax payable for the year, and what **did not** happen to the company, which is the tax that would have been payable if the adjustments required by the tax law for timing differences had not occurred. It is argued that the investor should be provided with details of the tax charge levied on the profits for the year and an explanation of factors that might lead to a different rate of tax charge appearing in future financial statements. The argument against adjusting the tax charge for deferred tax and the creation of a deferred tax provision holds that shareholders are accustomed to giving consideration to many other imponderables concerning the amount, timing and uncertainty of future cash receipts and payments, and the treatment of tax should be considered in the same way. This view has received support from others,[13] who have held that tax attaches to taxable income and not to the reported accounting income and that there is no legal requirement for the tax to bear any relationship to the reported accounting income. Indeed it has been argued that 'deferred tax means income smoothing'[14] – although it could be argued just as validly that deferred tax means the fullest possible use of accrual accounting.

However, this legal argument runs counter to the substance over form criteria that gives weight to the economic aspects of the event rather than the strict legal aspects. It is a fact that substance over form has achieved a growing importance since the 1980s and the legal arguments are receiving less recognition.

Before discussing the arguments it is appropriate to consider the economic reality of deferred taxation. Those industries which are capital intensive tend to have benefited from the benefits of tax deferral by way of accelerated tax depreciation on plant investment, and it could be suggested that their accounts do not truly reflect the economic reality without provision for deferred taxation. Studies in the UK certainly support this view.

As Nick Ellis, the retiring financial director of BAA pointed out in his financial review for the year ended 31 March 1995, a move to a full provision would increase the normal rate of taxation from 23.9% to around 35% and reduce reserves by between £300 million and £600 million.

An example of the importance of the topic of deferred tax can be shown during the period from 13 March 1984 to 31 March 1986 when the capital allowances on plant were dropped in stages from 100% to 25%. British banks had assumed that the high levels of capital allowances would continue and had made inadequate provision for deferred tax in line with SSAP 15. As the banks were unable to increase their capital expenditure fourfold to compensate, there were a series of rights issues to fund the resulting depletion in capital.

Terry Smith pointed out in Table 17.2 of his *Accounting for Growth* (2nd edition)[15] that according to the companies' own figures their estimated EPS would fall as follows if full provision for deferred tax were made:

British Airways	36.4%
Severn Trent	25.3%
British Gas	20.5% (Based on CCA earnings of 15.1p per share adjusted to exclude restructuring costs)
TI Group	13.8%

In his Table 17.3 Smith lists companies which expected an EPS fall of over 10% and more than 10% of shareholders' funds in unprovided deferred tax:

	Estimated impact on historic gearing of full provision	
	From	*To*
	%	%
British Airways	148	214
BP	67	78
British Gas	56	68

He points out in his Table 17.4 that the five companies he lists without any exposure to an increase in deferred tax charge include some of the UK's most successful and, in financial terms, conservative large companies:

	Tax Rate – %
General Electric	32
Marks & Spencer	32
Reuters	32
GUS	33
Wolesey	33

In the light of such economic facts, it is possible to understand why business managers might oppose deferred tax accounting, for it would lower their company stock valuation, whereas investment advisors might support deferred tax accounting as enabling them to form a better view of future prospects. It is suggested that the arguments for and against deferred taxation accounting should be based solely on the theory underpinning accounting, and should be unaffected by commercial considerations.

It is also suggested that the above arguments against the use of deferred tax accounting are unconvincing if one considers the conceptual framework to accounting. The International Accounting Standards Committee's (IASC's) *Framework for the Preparation and Presentation of Financial Statements* makes the following underlying assumption about accrual accounting:

In order to meet their objectives, financial statements are prepared on the accrual basis of accounting. ... Financial statements prepared on the accrual basis inform users not only of past transactions involving the payment and receipt of cash but also of obligations to pay cash in the future and of resources that represent cash to be received in the future.[16]

Although similar words are not used in the ASB's *Statement Of Principles For Financial Reporting*, the following appears in Appendix II:

The IASC Framework describes the accruals basis and the going concern assumption as underlying assumptions. Although the Statement does not give them such a title, their role and the way in which they are described are, to all intents and purposes, the same.[17]

This underlying assumption set out in the Framework confirms that deferred tax accounting makes the fullest possible use of accrual accounting. The fact is that accounting practice has moved definitively towards making such a provision for deferred taxation.

The legal argument that deferred tax is not a legal liability until it accrues runs counter to the substance over form criteria that gives weight to the economic aspects of the event rather than the strict legal aspects:

Substance over form
If information is to represent faithfully the transactions and other events that it purports to represent, it is necessary that they are accounted for and presented in accordance with their substance and economic reality and not merely their legal form. The substance of transactions or other events is not always consistent with that which is apparent from their legal or contrived form.[18]

This argument is followed in Chapter 3 of the ASB's *Statement Of Principles* as follows:

A transaction or other event is faithfully represented in the financial statements if the way in which it is recognised, measured and presented in those statements corresponds closely to the effect of that transaction or event.[19]
    The substance of a transaction or other event is not always consistent with that suggested by its legal form: although the effects of the legal characteristics of a transaction or other event are themselves a part of its substance and commercial effect, they have to be construed in the context of the transaction as a whole, including any related transactions.[20]

It is a fact that substance over form has achieved a growing importance since the 1980s and the legal arguments are receiving less recognition. Investments are made on economic criteria, investors make their choices on the basis of anticipated cash flows, and such flows would be subject to the effects of deferred taxation. Thus one can theoretically justify deferred tax provisions on the basis of both the ASB and IASC conceptual frameworks.

We can now turn to an examination of the two significant differences between UK (FRS 19) and international practice (IAS 12). The first significant difference is that IAS 12 provides for a deferred tax provision on revaluation gains on non-monetary assets which are revalued to fair values on the acquisition of a business, whereas FRS 19 does not do so.

The IASC's *Framework for the Preparation and Presentation of Financial Statements* states:

The future economic benefit embodied in an asset is the potential to contribute, directly or indirectly, to the flow of cash and cash equivalents to the enterprise.[21]

If a balance sheet includes current market valuations based on this view of an asset, it is difficult to argue logically that the implicit taxation arising on this future economic benefit should not be provided for at the same time.

Thus the IASC justifies a deferred tax provision for current market valuations. On the other hand the ASB's *Statement of Principles* states:

Both the IASC Framework and the (ASB) Statement approach the initial recognition process by asking whether a new asset or liability has been created (or an existing one has been added to), then applying recognition criteria to that new (or increased) asset or liability to determine whether it should be recognised. Both documents also adopt similar recognition criteria, although they are described in slightly different terms in that, while the (ASB) Statement's criteria require, *inter alia*, that sufficient evidence should exist that the new asset or liability has been created or that there has been an addition to an existing asset or liability, the IASC Framework refers to it needing to be probable that any future economic benefit associated with the item will flow to or from the enterprise. The Board believes that this difference reflects a development in accounting thought since the publication of the IASC Framework.[22]

Thus the ASB could be seen to be justifying the argument against a deferred tax liability on fair values in that there may not be sufficient evidence of the future liability.

The second significant difference is that IAS 12 does not permit discounting of the deferred tax provision, whereas FRS 19 does do so. The IASC does not preclude discounting on theoretical grounds (although it is non-directive in merely describing four means of valuation including present value):

A number of different measurement bases are employed to different degrees and in varying combinations in financial statements. They include the following: ...
(d) Present value. Assets are carried at the present discounted value of the future net cash inflows that the item is expected to generate in the normal course of business. Liabilities are carried at the present discounted value of the future net cash outflows that are expected to be required to settle the liabilities in the normal course of business.[23]

IAS 12 justifies the prohibition against discounting purely on practical grounds:

The reliable determination of deferred tax assets and liabilities on a discounted basis requires detailed scheduling of the timing of the reversal of each temporary difference. In many cases such scheduling is impracticable or highly complex. Therefore, it is inappropriate to require discounting of deferred tax assets and liabilities. To permit, but not to require, discounting would result in deferred tax assets and liabilities which would not be comparable between enterprises. Therefore, this Standard does not require or permit the discounting of deferred tax assets and liabilities.[24]

The ASB justifies the discounting of deferred taxation liabilities on theoretical grounds:

Most transactions take place at fair value. Rational buyers and sellers will ensure that this fair value reflects the time value of money and the risk associated with the future expected cash flows, which means that market prices generally will reflect such factors.[25]
    To be consistent, these factors need also to be reflected in the other measures that can be used to determine the carrying amount of assets (in other words, value in use and net realisable value) and the carrying amount of any liabilities measured by reference to expected future cash flows. It follows that, when basing carrying amounts on future cash flows, those cash flows will need to be discounted.[26]

Utilising such a strong argument of the theoretical need for discounting results is a stronger argument for risking a degree of unreliability in discounting than would be justifiable under the IASC criteria.

13.10 Disclosure of the accounting policy for deferred tax

Under FRS 18 (and formerly SSAP 2) the accounting policy for depreciation and deferred tax has to be disclosed. For illustration the accounting policy of EMI Group plc is set out as follows:

Accounting policies

Deferred taxation is calculated using the liability method in respect of timing differences arising primarily from the difference between the accounting and tax treatments of depreciation. Provision is made, or recovery anticipated, where timing differences are expected to reverse without replacement in the foreseeable future.

The company discloses the deferred tax provision in the notes to the accounts, as follows:

Note 22. Deferred taxation

	31.3.2001 £m	31.3.2000 £m
Excess of accumulated taxation allowances over depreciation provided against tangible fixed assets	13.0	13.0
Other timing differences	14.6	14.7
	27.6	27.7

In this example, the other timing differences relate to items where tax is payable on a receipts and payments basis, e.g. the receipt or payment of interest on a loan, whereas the accounts are prepared on an accrual basis.

The ASB Discussion Paper of March 1995 *Accounting for Taxation* stated that disclosures relating to tax should aim to give the reader more insight into the tax affairs of the reporting entity than at present. In particular, a simple reconciliation between the actual tax and expected tax (the profit before tax multiplied by the UK tax rate) should be provided.

FRS 19 also provides that company reports should disclose a reconciliation of the current tax charge for the period to a standard rate of tax (as included in IAS 12).

13.11 Interpretation

The pre-tax profit is frequently the figure used when calculating ratios to assess the management performance, e.g. return on capital employed. However, the post-tax profit is an important figure when assessing the ability of a company to make dividend distributions.

The accounting profession has attempted to develop a system for allocating tax that achieves a greater degree of uniformity and explains the differences between the taxable income and the reported income.

The policy chosen by EMI plc is a common one – it is a company with a significant capital expenditure. It can therefore assume with reasonable confidence that capital allowances will exceed depreciation for the foreseeable future. Consequently, the tax relief will continue without the company being called upon to pay the Revenue authorities.

If, however, one was looking at the accounts of a weaker company, one might well consider that such a policy might be less than prudent and, were one to be doubtful that the entity was a going concern, then it would be important to remember that on liquidation a liability will, in all probability, crystallise.

It is necessary to remember that although the deferred tax is included in the balance sheet, there is still some uncertainty over its ultimate value because the tax rates that will be in force in the future are unknown and the level of earnings that the firms will experience in future years is unknown.

13.12 Value added tax

VAT is one other tax that affects most companies and for which there is an accounting standard (SSAP 5 *Accounting for Value Added Tax*). This standard was issued in 1974 when the introduction of value added tax was imminent and there was considerable worry within the business community on its accounting treatment. We can now look back, having lived with VAT for well over two decades, and wonder, perhaps, why an SSAP was needed. VAT is essentially a tax on consumers collected by traders and is accounted for in a similar way to PAYE income tax, which is a tax on employees collected by employers.

13.12.1 The effects of the standard

These vary depending on the status of the accounting entity under the VAT legislation. The term 'trader' appears in the legislation and is the terminology for a business entity. The 'traders' or companies, as we would normally refer to them, are classified under the following headings.

(a) Registered trader

Accounts should only include figures net of VAT.

This means that the VAT on the sales will be deducted from the invoice amount. The VAT will be payable to the government and the net amount of the sales invoice will appear in the profit and loss account in arriving at the sales turnover figure. The VAT on purchases will be deducted from the purchase invoice. The VAT will then be reclaimed from the government and the net amount of the purchases invoice will appear in the profit and loss account in arriving at the purchases figure.

The only exception to the use of net of VAT amounts is when the input tax is not recoverable, e.g. on entertaining and on 'private' motor cars.

(b) Non-registered or exempt trader

For a company that is classified as non-registered or exempt, the VAT that it has to pay on its purchases and expenses is not reclaimable from the government. Because the company cannot recover the VAT, it means that the expense that appears in the profit and loss account must be inclusive of VAT. It is treated as part of each item of expenditure and the costs treated accordingly. It will be included, where relevant, with each item of expense (including capital expenditure) rather than being shown as a separate item.

(c) Partially exempt trader

This entity can only recover a proportion of input VAT, and the proportion of non-recoverable VAT should be treated as part of the costs on the same lines as the exempt trader. The VAT rules are complex but, for the purpose of understanding the figures that appear in published accounts of public companies, treatment as a registered trader would normally apply.

Summary

The major change that will have an impact on reported post-tax profits will be the decision in FRS 19 to change from the partial provisioning approach applying in the UK in 2000 to the full provisioning method which is favoured by the IASC.

This will have varying effects on the trend of reported profits. Those companies that have heavy investment programmes are likely to take advantage of the possibility of discounting the deferred tax charged to the profit and loss account for the timing delay to anticipated payment although the charge will still be heavier than under the partial provision method. There may be some increase in the deferred tax charge and the earnings per share correspondingly reduced for those companies with smaller investment programmes who do not take advantage of discounting.

From April 1999, the UK corporation tax system changed radically. Advance Corporation Tax (ACT) is no longer paid to the Inland Revenue when a company pays a dividend. Also, all but smaller companies pay their corporation tax liability in quarterly instalments starting within the year of account rather than paying their mainstream corporation tax liability nine months after the year end.

REVIEW QUESTIONS

1   Why doesn't the charge to taxation in a company's accounts equal the profit multiplied by the current rate of corporation tax?

2   (a) Explain clearly how advance corporation tax arose and its effect on the profit and loss account and the year-end balance sheet figures. (Use a simple example to illustrate.)
    (b) Explain how the corporation tax system changed as from April 1999.
    (c) Deferred tax accounting is an income-smoothing device and distorts the true and fair view. Explain the impact of deferred tax on reported income and justify its continued use.

3   How are the dividends received and paid shown in the accounts?

4   Distinguish between the treatment for taxation of dividends received and debenture interest received.

5   Distinguish between (a) the deferral and the liability methods of company deferred tax; and (b) the flow-through and full provision methods.

6   Explain the criteria a deferred tax provision needs to satisfy under SSAP 15 *Accounting for Deferred Tax* in order to be accepted as a liability in the balance sheet and how FRS 19 has changed the position.

7   Explain the effect of SSAP 5 *Accounting for Value Added Tax*.

EXERCISES

An extract from the solution is provided in the appendix at the end of the text for exercises marked with an asterisk (*).

Question 1

In your capacity as chief assistant to the financial controller, your managing director has asked you to consider the following letter received from a substantial shareholder who holds 4% of the company's voting shares:

I note that whilst the current rate of corporation tax for last year was at 33% for companies making profits in excess of £1,500,000, your company is showing a tax charge for the year (on profits of £3,621,000) of only 24%. I asked a friend with a knowledge of these matters if he could explain this apparent discrepancy to me, but he was unable to do so. He informed me that the usual reason for such a discrepancy lay in the deferral of a tax liability because of significant capital expenditure, but that there was no reference to deferred taxation in the accounts. I would be obliged if you could explain this to me in a letter before the Annual General Meeting.

You are aware that the reason for the low rate of taxation is indeed because of the significant excess of capital allowances for corporation tax over depreciation in the accounts, and that your financial controller convinced the auditors that it was reasonable to make no provision for deferred tax because of the plans for significant capital expenditure over the next ten years.

Required:
The managing director has asked that you write a report to him, in which:
(a) You explain the reason for any discrepancy to him and justify to him the use of a methodology in the preparation of the accounts which caused the above apparent discrepancy (which justification will not be shown to any shareholders);
(b) You draft a reply to the shareholder for him, which letter should explain and justify the reason for any discrepancy in the most general of terms.

* Question 2

A fixed asset (a machine) was purchased by Adjourn plc on 1 July 1996 at a cost of £25,000.

The company prepares its annual accounts to 31 March in each year. The policy of the company is to depreciate such assets at the rate of 15% straight line (with depreciation being charged *pro rata* on a time apportionment basis in the year of purchase). The company was granted capital allowances at 25% per annum on the reducing balance method (such capital allowances are apportioned *pro rata* on a time apportionment basis in the year of purchase).

The rate of corporation tax has been as follows:

Year ended	31 Mar	1997	26%
	31 Mar	1998	25%
	31 Mar	1999	25%
	31 Mar	2000	24%
	31 Mar	2001	24%

Required:
(a) Calculate the deferred tax provision using both the deferral method and the liability method.

(b) Explain why the liability method is considered by commentators to place the emphasis on the balance sheet, whereas the deferral method is considered to place the emphasis on the profit and loss account.

References

1 OECD, *Theoretical and Empirical Aspects of Corporate Taxation*, Paris, 1974: van den Temple, *Corporation Tax and Individual Income Tax in the EEC*, EEC Commission, Brussels, 1974.

2 G.H. Partington and R.H. Chenhall, *Dividends, Distortion and Double Taxation*, Abacus, June 1983.

3 R. Altshul, 'Act now', *Accountancy Age*, 5 February 1998, p. 19.

4 William Gale, 'What can America Learn from the British Tax System?' *Fiscal Studies*, Vol. 18, No. 4, November 1997.

5 P. Rosenfield and W.C. Dent, 'Deferred income taxes', in R. Bloom and P.T. Elgers (eds) *Accounting Theory and Practice*, Harcourt Brace Jovanovich, 1987, p. 545.

6 J.T. Parkes, 'A Guide to FASB's Overhaul of Income Tax Accounting', *Journal of Accounting*, Vol. 165, April 1988.

7 Ron Paterson, 'Accountancy column: In support of the profit and loss account', *The Financial Times*, 16 September 1993.

8 L.G. Van der Tas, 'Evidence of EC Financial Reporting Harmonisation: the case of deferred taxation', *European Accounting Review*, 1992, p. 213.

9 Andrew C. Lennard during a guest lecture at Sunderland Business School.

10 M. Metcalf, 'Alchemical accounting', *Accountancy*, November 1999, p. 100.

11 Accounts of BG Group plc for the year ended 31 December 2000, Note 1.

12 J. Brown, 'A step closer to harmony', *Accountancy*, January 2001, p. 90.

13 R. J. Chambers, *Tax Allocation and Financial Reporting*, Abacus, 1968.

14 Prof. D. R. Middleton, Letters to the Editor, *The Financial Times*, 29 September 1994.

15 T. Smith, *Accounting for Growth: stripping the camouflage from Company Accounts*, 2nd edn, Random House, 1996.

16 *Framework for the Preparation and Presentation of Financial Statements*, IASC, para. 22.

17 *Statement Of Principles For Financial Reporting*, ASB, Appendix II, para. 9(b).

18 *Framework for the Preparation and Presentation of Financial Statements*, IASC, para. 35.

19 *Statement Of Principles For Financial Reporting*, ASB, para. 3.10.

20 *Ibid.*, para. 3.13.

21 *Framework for the Preparation and Presentation of Financial Statements*, IASC, para. 53.

22 *Statement Of Principles For Financial Reporting*, ASB, Appendix II, para. 11.

23 *Framework for the Preparation and Presentation of Financial Statements*, IASC, para. 100.

24 *IAS 12*, IASC, para. 54.

25 *Statement Of Principles For Financial Reporting*, ASB, para. 6.31.

26 *Ibid.*, para. 6.33.

CHAPTER 14

Tangible fixed assets and depreciation

14.1 Introduction

In this chapter we consider tangible fixed assets. It is helpful to consider the importance of fixed assets relative to intangible fixed assets, stocks and debtors. This will, of course, vary with the nature of the industry as shown if we consider the pharmaceutical and brewing industries.

The relative importance of the different categories of asset within the two industries based on average industry profile has been compiled from *IPA UK Industrial Performance Analysis 1996/97* (ICC Business Publications Ltd 1996 – ISSN 0262 3684) based on 83 pharmaceutical manufacturers and developers and 55 brewers and appears in Figure 14.1.

For fixed tangible assets the accounting treatment is based on the accruals or matching concepts, under which expenditure is capitalised until it is charged as depreciation against revenue in the period in which benefit is gained from its use. Thus, if an item is purchased that has an economic life of two years, so that it will be used over two accounting periods to help earn profit for the enterprise, then the cost of that asset should be apportioned in some way between the two accounting periods.

Figure 14.1 Ratio of assets to total assets for 1994/95 for 83 pharmaceutical manufacturers and developers and 55 brewers

1994/95 Averages (£000)
Pharmaceutical manufacturers and developers (83 companies)

	Tangible fixed assets	Intangible fixed assets	Stock	Trade debtors	Total assets
Average (£000)	82,375	31,246	23,471	35,452	243,667
% of total assets	33.8%	12.8%	9.6%	14.5%	

1994/95 Averages (£000)
Brewers (55 companies)

	Tangible fixed assets	Intangible fixed assets	Stock	Trade debtors	Total assets
Average (£000)	202,284	123	8,410	11,525	258,256
% of total assets	78.3%	0%	3.3%	4.5%	

However, this does not take into account the problems surrounding fixed asset accounting and depreciation, which have so far given rise to four statements of standard accounting practice. We will consider these problems in this chapter covering:

- FRS 11 – What is a fixed asset?
- FRS 15 – What is depreciation and the constituents in the depreciation formula?
- Determining the cost and valuation of fixed assets
- How is the economic life of an asset determined?
- Residual value
- Calculation of depreciation
- Disclosure requirements
- SSAP 4 – Government grants
- SSAP 19 – Investment properties
- Effect of depreciation on the interpretation of accounts.

14.2 What is a fixed asset?

There are two definitions, one in the Companies Act 1985 which is supplemented by that in FRS 11 *Impairment of Fixed Assets and Goodwill*.

The Companies Act defines fixed assets as those which are intended for use on a continuing basis in the company's activities and any assets which are not intended for such use are taken to be current assets.[1]

FRS 11 supplements this by defining tangible fixed assets as 'assets that have a physical substance and are held for use in the production or supply of goods or services, for rental to others, or for administrative purposes on a continuing basis in the reporting entity's activities'.[2]

Certain assets fall very clearly into these definitions, e.g. production plant and machinery, equipment owned by a plant hire company, the building that houses the accounts department, a computer used by that department.

14.2.1 Problems that may arise

Problems may arise in relation to the interpretation of the definition and in relation to the application of the materiality concept.

The definitions give rise to some areas of practical difficulty. For example, an asset that has previously been employed in the business but whose use has now ceased should no longer be treated as a fixed asset, even if it still has a value and the enterprise is endeavouring to sell it. Under both definitions the asset should not be treated as fixed.

Differing accounting treatments arise if there are different assessments of materiality. This may result in the same expenditure being reported as an asset in the balance sheet of one company and as an expense in the profit and loss account of another company. In the accounts of a self-employed carpenter, a kit of handtools that, with careful maintenance, will last many years will, quite rightly, be shown as a fixed asset. Similar assets used by the maintenance department in a large factory will, in all probability, be treated as 'loose tools' and written off as acquired.

Many enterprises have *de minimis* policies, whereby only items exceeding a certain value are treated as fixed assets; items below the cut-off amount will be expensed through the profit and loss account.

14.3 What is depreciation?

FRS 15 defines depreciation as:

> the measure of the cost or revalued amount of the economic benefits of the tangible asset that have been consumed during the period. Consumption includes the wearing out, using up or other reduction in the useful economic life of a tangible fixed asset whether arising from use, effluxion of time or obsolescence through either changes in technology or demand for the goods and services produced by the asset.[3]

Note that this definition places an emphasis on the consumption in a particular accounting period rather than an average over the asset's life. We will consider two aspects of the definition: the measure of wearing out; and the useful economic life.

14.3.1 Measure of wearing out

Depreciation is a measure of wearing out that is calculated annually and charged as an expense against profits. Under the 'matching concept', the cost of the asset is allocated over its productive life.

It is important to make clear what depreciation is **not**:

- It is not 'saving up for a new one'; it is not setting funds aside for the replacement of the existing asset at the end of its life; it is the matching of cost to revenue. The effect is to reduce the profit available for distribution, but this is not accompanied by the setting aside of cash of an equal amount to ensure that liquid funds are available at the end of the asset's life.

- It is not 'a way of showing the real value of assets on the balance sheet' by reducing the cost figure to realisable value.

We emphasise what depreciation is not because both of these ideas are commonly held by non-accountant users of accounts; it is as well to realise this possible misconception when interpreting accounts for non-accountants.

Depreciation is currently conceived as a charge for funds **already expended**, and thus it cannot be considered as the setting aside of funds to meet future expenditure. If we consider it in terms of capital maintenance, then we can see that it results in the maintenance of the initial invested monetary capital of the company. It is concerned with the allocation of that expenditure over a period of time, without having regard for the **value** of the asset at any intermediate period of its life.

Where an asset has been revalued the depreciation is, however, based on the revalued amount. This ensures that capital maintenance continues in monetary terms.

14.3.2 Useful economic life

FRS 15 para. 2 defines this as: 'The period over which the entity expects to derive economic benefits from the asset. In estimating useful economic life regard should be had to reasonably expected technological changes that will have an effect on the asset's life.'

The FRED definition is based on the premise that almost all assets have a finite useful economic life. This may be true in principle, but it is incredibly difficult in real life to arrive at an average economic life that can be applied to even a single class of assets, e.g. plant. This is evidenced by the accounting policy in the ICI 1999 accounts which states:

Depreciation – The Group's policy is to write-off the book value of each tangible fixed asset to its residual value evenly over its estimated remaining life. Reviews are made annually of the estimated remaining lives of individual productive assets, taking account of commercial and technological obsolescence as well as normal wear and tear. Under this policy it becomes impractical to calculate average asset lives exactly; however, the total lives approximate to 33 years for buildings and 16 years for plant and equipment. Depreciation of assets qualifying for grant is calculated on their full cost.

In addition to the practical difficulty of estimating economic lives, there are also exceptions where nil depreciation is charged. Two common exceptions found in the accounts of UK companies relate to freehold land and certain types of property.

14.3.3 Freehold land

Freehold land (but not the buildings thereon) is considered to have an infinite life unless it is held simply for the extraction of minerals, etc. Thus land held for the purpose of, say, mining coal or quarrying gravel will be dealt with for accounting purposes as a coal or gravel deposit. Consequently, although the land may have an infinite life, the deposits will have an economic life only as long as they can be profitably extracted. If the cost of extraction exceeds the potential profit from extraction and sale, the economic life of the quarry has ended. When assessing depreciation for a commercial company, we are concerned only with these private costs and benefits, and not with public costs and benefits which might lead to the quarry being kept open.

An example of the reporting of mineral deposits appears in the 1996 accounts of Redland plc, where the accounting policies contain the following statement:

Depreciation is provided on mineral bearing land to reflect the diminution in economic values as a result of mineral extraction. As a result no provision is made where the remaining life is judged to be in excess of 20 years since the amount is not material. No depreciation is provided on other freehold land.

14.3.4 Certain types of property

Prior to FRS 15, it was relatively common for companies not to charge depreciation on certain types of property. This was particularly true of companies in the brewing industry and others with a large property portfolio. The reason frequently cited was that the values of the property were maintained through refurbishment and repairs.[4]

An example is provided by this extract from the accounts of Whitbread plc for the year ended 1 March 1997. An extract from the accounting policy reads:

While it is the group's policy to depreciate fixed assets, the nature of the retail trade requires that, in order to protect that trade, retail premises are maintained to such a state of repair that their residual value is at least equal to their book amounts based on prices prevailing at the date of acquisition or subsequent valuation.

Depreciation charges are omitted as being immaterial in such cases but the companies are still required to conduct regular impairment reviews.

FRS 15 recognises[5] that there has been a growing trend towards the non-depreciation of certain tangible fixed assets, particularly property where it has been argued by companies that maintenance is carried out regularly, thereby extending the economic life or maintaining the residual value. The ASB response has been to state their belief that the estimate of a tangible fixed asset's useful economic life cannot be extended limitlessly through maintenance, refurbishment, overhaul or replacement of components of the asset because the physical life cannot be indefinite.

The Board view[6] is that the only grounds for not charging depreciation are that the depreciation charge and related accumulated depreciation are not material owing to a long estimated remaining useful life or high residual value.

This would appear to allow companies to continue not to provide for depreciation on grounds of immateriality or to adopt a long economic life of more than 50 years. There is, however, a sting in FRS 15's tail for companies that follow that path – it requires them to carry out an annual impairment review. This can be onerous and expensive. Consequently, companies will probably follow the example of PizzaExpress plc in its 1999 Annual Report, where it states its accounting policy as follows:

Tangible fixed assets
Until 1 July 1998 no amortisation was provided on freehold and long leasehold properties because they were kept in a continual state of sound repair and the directors considered their lives and residual values were such that the amortisation would be insignificant. In accordance with FRS 15 *Tangible fixed assets*, it is now the Group's policy to amortise prospectively the cost of freehold and long leasehold properties over the lesser of 50 years or the outstanding term of the lease.

14.4 What are the constituents in the depreciation formula?

In order to calculate depreciation it is necessary to determine three factors:

- Cost (or revalued amount if the company is following a revaluation policy).
- Economic life.
- Residual value.

A simple example is the calculation of the depreciation charge for a company that has acquired an asset on 1 January 20X1 for £1,000 with an estimated economic life of four years and an estimated residual value of £200. Applying a straight-line depreciation policy, the charge would be £200 per year using the formula

$$\frac{\text{Cost} - \text{Estimated residual value}}{\text{Estimated economic life}} = \frac{£1,000 - £200}{4} = £200 \text{ per annum}$$

We can see that the charge of £200 is influenced in all cases by the definition of cost; the estimate of the residual value; the estimate of the economic life; and the management decision on depreciation policy.

In addition, if the cost were to be revalued at the end of the second year to £900, then the depreciation for 20X3 and 20X4 would be recalculated using the revised valuation figure. Assuming that the residual value remained unchanged, the depreciation for 20X3 would be:

$$\frac{\text{Revalued asset} - \text{Estimated residual value}}{\text{Estimated economic life}} = \frac{£900 - £200}{2} = £350 \text{ per annum}$$

14.5 Determination of the cost of fixed assets

The Companies Act 1985 states that, subject to any provisions for depreciation or diminution in value, all fixed assets shall be included at their purchase price or production cost.[7] Guidance is available on the definition of production cost in both the Companies Act and FRS 15 para. 6.

14.5.1 Guidance in the Companies Act

Production cost is defined as including:

> the price of the raw materials and consumables used and the costs incurred by the company which are directly attributable to the production cost of that asset. In addition, the production cost may include the following to the extent that they relate to the period of production:
>
> (a) a reasonable proportion of the costs incurred by the company indirectly attributable to the production of the asset; and
>
> (b) interest on the capital borrowed to finance the production of that asset.[8]

The Act also defines purchase price as 'the actual price paid and any expenses incidental to the acquisition'.

14.5.2 Guidance in FRS 15 *Tangible Fixed Assets*

FRS 15 provides additional guidance to cover items that may be included in production cost. An asset that is purchased and simply installed in, say, a factory presents little problem. There the cost will include, *inter alia*:

● the invoice price of the asset;

● any delivery costs (including, for imported assets, duty, etc.); and

● installation or erection costs, including site preparation.

Difficulty arises when major projects to build fixed assets are undertaken, particularly if the company's own labour or resources are employed in actual construction or project management. In these circumstances, the FRS provides that only costs attributable to bringing the asset into working condition for its intended use should be included.

Directly attributable costs are defined as:

(a) the direct labour costs of own employees (e.g. site workers, in-house architects)

(b) incremental costs that would have been avoided if the tangible fixed asset were not acquired, i.e. administration and general overheads would be excluded.

Examples of directly attributable costs include cost of site preparation and clearance, initial delivery and handling costs, installation costs, professional fees, estimated cost of dismantling and removing the asset and restoring the site, to the extent that it is recognised under FRS 12 *Provisions, Contingent Liabilities and Contingent Assets*.

There are restrictions on the time over which costs may be capitalised, namely:

● The capitalisation of costs should not begin until there is reasonable probability that the project will be undertaken, or has been undertaken, and is expected to be successfully completed.

- When the construction of a fixed asset is completed in parts and each part is capable of being used commercially while construction continues on the other parts, capitalisation of costs on each part should cease when it is completed.

- When costs are incurred in commissioning a fixed asset, capitalisation of costs should cease when the fixed asset is substantially complete and ready for use even if it has not yet been brought into use.

In addition to the rules relating to the commencement and cessation of expenditure capitalisation, there are a number of other considerations. We deal briefly with three of these: how to treat cost over-runs; how to treat assets that are purchased from another member of a group; and how to treat borrowing costs incurred in connection with the fixed asset construction.

14.5.3 Treatment of cost over-runs

The material factor is the reason for the over-run. If the over-run arose from circumstances outside the planning or control of the company, such as a nationally agreed pay rise, then the expenditure is capitalised. If, however, the costs arose from inefficiencies, such as failure to ensure that materials were on site at the planned date, then these should not be included in the production cost of a fixed asset; they should be expensed through the profit and loss account of the period in which the inefficiency occurred.

14.5.4 Treatment of intragroup sales

In consolidated financial statements, the cost of a fixed asset should not include any intragroup profit or loss. This is intended to prevent a group creating unrealised profits in the consolidated profit and loss account. In selling and buying between subsidiary companies, the assets will be recorded in their individual company accounts at whatever transfer price they agree between themselves. It is only at group level that the price is adjusted to the net book value as at the date of the transfer.

14.5.5 Treatment of borrowing costs

The capitalisation of borrowing costs is addressed by an international standard. This standard does not insist on capitalisation of borrowing costs; rather it requires the company that has incurred borrowing costs to adopt, and consistently apply, a policy of capitalisation or non-capitalisation, to establish criteria if it decides on a capitalisation policy, and to disclose the amount of borrowing costs that have been capitalised during the current accounting period.

Views differ on the appropriate accounting treatment. Some regard borrowing costs as part of the cost of the asset; others regard them as costs that are charged to income regardless of how borrowing is applied. The significant borrowing costs incurred by companies make their accounting treatment an important consideration in the preparation of financial statements.[9]

The arguments in favour of capitalisation are based on the reality that, when a major project is undertaken which takes a substantial time to complete, borrowing will occur and will form a real part of the overall cost of the asset; if such costs are not capitalised, the earnings will be distorted during the production period. Problems will also occur if accounts are compared with companies that have acquired similar assets 'ready-made', where the supplier will have undoubtedly taken into account financing costs when determining the selling price.

However, it can be argued that capitalising financing costs during construction and then treating the continuing financing costs as a normal trading expense is illogical, and that the allocation of total borrowing costs between 'trading' and 'project' may be arbitrary. These arguments can be closely debated.

This is recognised by FRS 15, which proposes that the practice be allowed, but only if the reporting entity employs a consistent policy. There are specific requirements if it is company policy to capitalise borrowing costs; FRS 15 para. 19 states 'Where an entity adopts a policy of capitalising finance costs, finance costs that are directly attributable to the construction of tangible fixed assets should be capitalised as part of the cost of those assets. The total amount of finance costs capitalised during a period should not exceed the total amount of finance costs incurred during that period.' However, comparability is frustrated by allowing companies to choose whether or not to capitalise borrowing costs.

14.5.6 No unique cost

There is not a unique, correct cost. The determination of cost is influenced by a number of factors, such as the time when expenditures are to commence and cease being capitalised; the reason for the costs arising; and the company policy on the capitalisation of borrowing costs. Management decisions in each of these areas will have a direct impact on the asset figure that appears in the balance sheet and the profit for the year.

14.6 Determination of the valuation on the revaluation of fixed assets

It has become commonplace for accounts, otherwise prepared under the historical cost convention, to include some assets (usually interests in land and buildings) at valuation. This could provide useful information for the users of the accounts, in terms of both the current replacement cost of the fixed assets and the current replacement cost of at least the fixed asset content of the balance sheet when calculating the capital employed. However, in practice the information is not as useful as it could be because:

● the same balance sheet may contain a mixture of two accounting conventions at the expense of the integrity of both;

● it has also been possible for a company to revalue individual assets at will.

This is shown by the following extracts from the 2001 accounts of Galliford Try plc:

Accounting policy

The financial statements are prepared under the historical cost convention, as modified by the revaluation of certain freehold properties, and in accordance with applicable accounting standards.

Extract from note 12 of the 2001 accounts

Note 12 Land and buildings

	£000
Cost or valuation at 1 July 2000	9,592
Disposals	(370)
Additions	1,203
	10,425

Comprising:

Cost	4,177
As valued 1978	548
As valued 1990	5,700
	10,425
Depreciation	1,589
Net book value at 30 June 2001	8,836

There is a mix of costs and valuations and the valuations are selective and at different dates. The company does however provide information of the position if historical cost convention had not been modified:

Land and buildings would have been included at the following amounts, but for certain revaluations in 1978 and 1990:

Cost	6,270
Aggregate depreciation	(1,365)
	4,905

FRS 15 proposes that the practice of revaluation should be allowed to continue, but with some restrictions:

● The accounting policy of whether or not to carry assets at valuation rather than cost must be applied consistently by class of asset.

● The valuation should be prepared by a qualified valuer (usually an external valuer) on an existing use basis although investment properties should be on an open market valuation.

● When the valuation is carried out by an officer or employee of the company, the basis of the valuation should be reviewed externally.

● Where an asset is revalued, all assets of the same class should be revalued.

● Depreciation provisions should be based on the revalued amount, so that the profit and loss account and balance sheet articulate. This avoids the process known as split depreciation, whereby the charge to the profit and loss account is based on a figure other than the carrying amount of the asset in the balance sheet.

14.6.1 Accounting for a revaluation

When an asset is revalued the following is required:

● the cost of the asset is restated to the revaluation figure – this appears in balance sheets prepared at that and subsequent dates until the disposal of the asset;

● the depreciation provision that exists at the date of the valuation is no longer required – the accumulated depreciation does not therefore appear in balance sheets prepared at that and subsequent dates; and

● the difference between the cost and revaluation figure together with the accumulated depreciation are transferred to a revaluation reserve.

The exact entries will depend on whether the revalued amount is higher or lower than the original cost.

● If the revalued amount is higher than the original cost, the asset account will be increased with a debit to the account.

● If the revalued amount is lower than the original cost, the asset account will be decreased with a credit to the asset account.

Example where revaluation is higher than cost

A machine tool acquired on 1 January 2000 for £5,000 and depreciated over 5 years using the straight-line method and assuming no residual value was revalued on 1 January 2003 at £6,500.

The accounting entries would be:

	Dr	Cr
Provision for depreciation (accumulated depreciation)	£3,000	
Fixed asset – machine tool (increased by difference)	£1,500	
Revaluation reserve		£4,500

Example where revaluation is lower than cost

A machine tool acquired on 1 January 2000 for £5,000 and depreciated over 5 years using the straight-line method and assuming no residual value was revalued on 1 January 2003 at £4,500.

The accounting entries would be:

	Dr	Cr
Provision for depreciation	£3,000	
Fixed asset (machine tool)		£500
Revaluation reserve		£2,500

Accounting entries in subsequent years

Assuming that the machine tool has been revalued at £6,500 and economic life is unchanged at 5 years, the accounting entries at 31 December 2003 would be based on the new carrying value as follows:

Profit for year charged with proportion of carrying value used:

	Dr	Cr
Profit and loss account (£6,500/2 years remaining life)	£3,250	
Provision for depreciation		£3,250

Effect on distributable profits

Distributable profits are based on historical cost depreciation. To achieve this, a proportionate amount is transferred from revaluation reserve to profit and loss reserve to indicate that it is realised and available for distribution as follows:

	Dr	Cr
Revaluation reserve (realised over remaining economic life)	£2,250	
Profit and loss reserve (excess depreciation added back)		£2,250

14.6.2 Reporting gains and losses on revaluation

Revaluation gains should be recognised in the statement of total recognised gains and losses unless they represent the reversal of losses previously recognised in the profit and loss account. Revaluation losses that are due to the consumption of economic benefits should be recognised in the profit and loss account. An example of this could be the revaluation of mineral deposits in a mine following a geological survey or when an asset is physically damaged.

Gains or losses on disposal should be similarly treated. Thus a gain or loss, which is fundamentally a final adjustment to depreciation, will pass through the profit and loss account whilst a gain resulting from holding an asset will simply appear in the Statement of total recognised gains and losses.

A number of companies already strictly apply the historical cost convention in their accounts, e.g. The Body Shop International, and, following the increased regulation of revaluation, it could well be that companies will follow the example of the BOC Group and revert to accounting for land and buildings on a historical cost basis – in which case the net book value of assets previously revalued is regarded as the historical cost. Companies will need to balance the effect of revaluation, e.g. valuation fees and, higher depreciation charges, in the profit and loss account and lower return on capital employed ratio against the increased relevance of information based on current values. Decisions will be influenced by a board assessment of relative importance, for example, if a company is likely to be the subject of a takeover or to need to raise additional finance, there could be merit in revaluing its assets.

14.6.3 How objective are valuations?

Company management may be tempted to put pressure on a valuer to give a high figure e.g. when seeking a loan secured on the property being valued or when seeking to strengthen the balance sheet. The valuer's objectivity may be perceived to be affected by the size of the valuation fee and the provision of non-valuation services. It is important, therefore, that there should be transparency in the valuation process so that users are able to assess the degree of objectivity of the valuer.

The RICS addressed this through a Working Party[10] chaired by Sir Bryan Carsberg which recommended that the proportion of the client fees to total fees should be disclosed in bands, e.g. 5–10% and the amount on non-valuation fees should be disclosed – this is similar to the requirement on auditors to disclose non-audit fees. The Working Party considered that there could be advantages for a company in receiving a mix of valuation and non-valuation services and did not recommend that this should be prohibited.

14.6.4 FRED 29: Property, plant and equipment; Borrowing costs

FRED 29 issued in May 2002 includes the text of a revised IAS 16 *Property, plant and equipment* and IAS 23 *Borrowing costs*. There are many similarities with FRS 15 but also some differences which the ASB raised with the IASB in October 2002 such as:

● the proposal that residual values used in the calculation of depreciable amount should be reviewed at each balance sheet date and revised to reflect current estimates whilst FRS 15 requires prices at the date of acquisition or latest valuation to be used so that depreciation expense on a historical cost basis is not reduced by inflation in residual values;

● the ASB view that existing use value is the appropriate measurement base for fixed assets.

14.7 How is the useful economic life of an asset determined?

FRS 15 defines useful economic life as 'the period over which the entity expects to derive economic benefits from that asset'. This is not necessarily the total life expectancy of the asset. Most assets become less economically and technologically efficient as they grow older. For this reason, assets may well cease to have an economic life long before their working life is over. It is the responsibility of the preparers of accounts to estimate the economic life of all assets.

It is conventional for enterprises to consider the economic lives of assets by class or category, e.g. buildings; plant; office equipment; or motor vehicles. However, this is not necessarily appropriate, since the level of activity demanded by different users may differ. For example, compare two motor cars owned by a business: one is used by the national sales manager, covering 100,000 miles per annum visiting clients; the other is used by the accountant to drive from home to work and occasionally the bank, covering perhaps one-tenth of the mileage.

FRS 15 takes this argument a stage further by stating that it might be appropriate to break down certain assets into their component parts. It gives the example of an aircraft where the engines may well have a shorter life-span than their airframe, which will continue flying (with the aid of replacement engines) long after the original engines have reached the end of their useful lives.

In practice, the useful economic life would be determined by reference to factors such as repair costs, the cost and availability of replacements, and the comparative cash flows of existing and alternative assets. The problem of optimal replacement lives is a normal financial management problem; its significance in financial reporting is that the assumptions used within the financial management decision may provide evidence of the expected economic life.

14.7.1 Other factors affecting the economic life figure

We can see that there are technical factors affecting the estimated economic life figure. In addition, other factors have prompted companies to set estimated lives that have no relationship to the active productive life of the asset. One such factor is the wish of management to take into account the effect of inflation.[11] This led some companies to reduce the estimated economic life, so that a higher charge was made against profits during the early period of the asset's life to compensate for the inflationary effect on the cost of replacement. The total charge will be the same, but the timing is advanced. This does not result in the retention of funds necessary to replace; but it does reflect the fact that there is at present no coherent policy for dealing with inflation in the published accounts – consequently, companies resort to *ad hoc* measures that frustrate efforts to make accounts uniform and comparable. *Ad hoc* measures such as these have prompted changes in the standards.

14.8 Residual value

FRS 15 defines residual value as:

> the net realisable value of an asset at the end of its useful economic life. Residual values are based on prices prevailing at the date of acquisition (or revaluation), and do not take account of expected future price changes.

This definition is not without its critics. While most would accept that it is proper when preparing accounts under the historical cost convention to ignore the potential effects of future inflation, it has been suggested that basing residual values on current prices without considering expected changes in technology or in the position of supply and demand will lead to inaccuracies in the regular charges to profit and loss. This highlights a weakness in the FRS, which requires economic lives to be reviewed regularly, but does not require similar reviews of residual values.

Besides inflation, residual values can be affected by changes in technology and market conditions. For example, during the period 1980–90 the cost of small business computers fell dramatically in both real and monetary terms, with a considerable impact on the residual (or second-hand) value of existing equipment.

14.9 Calculation of depreciation

Having determined the key factors in the computation, we are left with the problem of how to allocate that cost between accounting periods. For example, with an asset having an economic life of five years:

Asset cost	£11,000
Residual value	£ 1,000
Depreciable amount	£10,000

How should the depreciable amount be charged to the profit and loss account over the five years? FRS 15 tells us that it should be allocated on a systematic basis and the depreciation method used should reflect as fairly as possible the pattern in which the asset's economic benefits are consumed. The two most popular methods are **straight-line**, in which the depreciation is charged evenly over the useful life, and **reducing balance**, where depreciation is calculated annually on the net written-down amount. In the case above, the calculations would be as in Figure 14.2.

Note that, although the reducing balance is generally expressed in terms of a percentage, this percentage is arrived at by inserting the economic life into the formula as n; the 38% reflects the expected economic life of five years. As we change the life, so we change the percentage that is applied. The normal rate applied to vehicles is 25% reducing bal-

Figure 14.2 Effect of different depreciation methods

	Straight-line (£2,000) £	Reducing balance (38%) £	Difference £
Cost	11,000	11,000	
Depreciation for year 1	2,000	4,180	2,180
Net book value (NBV)	9,000	6,820	
Depreciation for year 2	2,000	2,592	592
NBV	7,000	4,228	
Depreciation for year 3	2,000	1,606	(394)
NBV	5,000	2,622	
Depreciation for year 4	2,000	996	(1,004)
NBV	3,000	1,626	
Depreciation for year 5	2,000	618	(1,382)
Residual value	1,000	1,008	

The reducing balance formula was $1 - \sqrt[n]{(\text{Residual value/Cost})}$

ance; if we apply that to the cost and residual value in our example, we can see that we would be assuming an economic life of eight years. It is a useful test when using reducing balance percentages to refer back to the underlying assumptions.

We can see that the end result is the same. Thus, £10,000 has been charged against profits, but with a dramatically different pattern of profit and loss charges. The charge for straight-line depreciation in the first year is less than half that for reducing balance.

14.9.1 Arguments in favour of the straight-line method

The method is simple to calculate. However, in these days of calculators and computers this seems a particularly facile argument, particularly when one considers the materiality of the figures.

14.9.2 Arguments in favour of the reducing balance method

First, the charge reflects the efficiency and maintenance costs of the asset. When new, an asset is operating at its maximum efficiency, which falls as it nears the end of its life. This may be countered by the comment that in year 1 there may be 'teething troubles' with new equipment, which, while probably covered by a supplier's guarantee, will hamper efficiency.

Second, the pattern of reducing balance depreciation gives a net book amount that approximates to second-hand values. For example, with motor cars the initial fall in value is very high.

14.9.3 Other methods of depreciating

Besides straight-line and reducing balance, there are a number of other methods of depreciating, such as sum of the digits, the machine-hour and the annuity method. We will consider these briefly.

Sum of the digits method

A compromise between straight-line and reducing balance that is popular in the USA is the sum of the digits method. The calculation based on the information in Figure 14.2 is now shown in Figure 14.3. This has the advantage that, unlike reducing balance, it is simple to obtain the exact residual amount (zero if appropriate), while giving the pattern of high initial charge shown by the reducing balance approach.

Machine-hour method

The machine-hour system is based on an estimate of the asset's service potential. The economic life is measured not in accounting periods but in working hours, and the depreciation is allocated in the proportion of the actual hours worked to the potential total hours available. This method is commonly employed in aviation, where aircraft are depreciated on the basis of flying hours.

Annuity method

Although rarely employed, the annuity method is theoretically most attractive.[12] The asset, or rather the amount of capital representing the asset, is regarded as being capable of earn-

Figure 14.3 Sum of the digits method

		£
Cost		11,000
Depreciation for year 1	£10,000 × 5/15	3,333
Net book value (NBV)		7,667
Depreciation for year 2	£10,000 × 4/15	2,667
NBV		5,000
Depreciation for year 3	£10,000 × 3/15	2,000
NBV		3,000
Depreciation for year 4	£10,000 × 2/15	1,333
NBV		1,667
Depreciation for year 5	£10,000 × 1/15	667
Residual value		1,000

ing a fixed rate of interest. The sacrifice incurred in using the asset within the business is therefore twofold: the loss arising from the exhaustion of the service potential of the asset; and the interest forgone by using the funds invested in the business to purchase the fixed asset. With the help of annuity tables, a calculation shows what equal amounts of depreciation, written off over the estimated life of the asset, will reduce the book value to nil, after debiting interest to the asset account on the diminishing amount of funds that are assumed to be invested in the business at that time, represented by the value of the asset.

Figure 14.4 contains an illustration based on the treatment of a five-year lease which cost the company a premium of £10,000 on 1 January 20X1.

An extract from the annuity tables to obtain the factor for year 5 and assuming a rate of interest of 10% would show:

Year	Annuity $A_{\overline{n}|}^{-1}$
1	1.1000
2	0.5762
3	0.4021
4	0.3155
5	0.2638

The interest debited to the asset account is credited to the interest account, whence it is subsequently transferred to the credit of the profit and loss account; the depreciation is credited to the asset account, and debited to the depreciation account, which account is transferred to the debit of the profit and loss account each year.

The charge for depreciation increases each year, while the credit for interest gradually falls as the book value of the asset decreases; the result on profits is seen to be an increasing net charge in respect of the asset. However, when the interest earned by the assets, representing the preceding amounts written off, is taken into consideration, this method tends to give an equal real charge each year.

Figure 14.4 Annuity method

Year	Cost/WDV b/f £	Interest credited £	Depreciation charged £	WDV c/f £	Net P&L £
1	10,000	1,000	2,638	8,632	1,638
2	8,362	836	2,638	6,560	1,802
3	6,560	656	2,638	4,578	1,982
4	4,578	458	2,638	2,398	2,180
5	2,398	240	2,638	—	2,398
		3,190	13,190		10,000

A variation on this system involves the investment of a sum equal to the net charge in fixed interest securities or an endowment policy, so as to build up a fund that will generate cash to replace the asset at the end of its life.

This last system has significant weaknesses. It is based on the misconception that depreciation is 'saving up for a new one', whereas in reality depreciation is charging against profits funds already expended. It is also dangerous in a time of inflation, since it may lead management not to maintain the capital of the enterprise adequately, so that it is able to replace the assets at their new (inflated) prices.

The annuity method, with its increasing net charge to profit and loss, does tend to take inflationary factors into account, but it must be noted that the *total* net profit and loss charge only adds up to the cost of the asset.

14.9.4 Which method should be used?

The answer to this seemingly simple question is 'it depends'. On the matter of depreciation FRS 15 is designed primarily to force a fair charge for the use of assets into the profit and loss account each year, so that the earnings reflect a true and fair view. It is regarded as defective by a number of companies, which consider the charge inadequate in times of inflation. We have seen that some companies reduced the economic life in order to generate a higher earlier charge; other companies, such as GEC,[13] adopted a practice of charging supplementary depreciation on assets without changing the balance sheet carrying value. This practice was disallowed by the ASC, which required the company either to revalue the assets so that the profit and loss account and balance sheet articulated after the charge, or to treat the supplementary charge as an appropriation rather than an expense. Treating the supplementary charge as an appropriation has an impact on the EPS figure and the return on capital figure.

Straight-line is most suitable for assets such as leases which have a definite fixed life. It is also considered most appropriate for assets with a short working life, although with motor cars the reducing balance method is usually employed to match second-hand values. Extraction industries (mining, oil wells, quarries, etc.) usually employ a variation on the machine-hour system, where depreciation is based on the amount extracted as a proportion of the estimated reserves.

14.9.5 **What are substitute methods of depreciation?**

The accounting policy of Scottish Power in its 1999 accounts states:

Tangible fixed assets – Infrastructure accounting
The depreciation charge for water infrastructure assets is the estimated level of annualised expenditure required to maintain the operating capability of the network and is based on the asset management plan agreed with the water industry regulator as part of the price regulation process… The method of accounting for water infrastructure renewals has been revised following the introduction of FRS 12 'Provisions, contingent liabilities and contingent assets' and the infrastructure renewals accounting basis as set out in FRS 15 'Tangible fixed assets'. … The change of accounting policy has no effect on the profit and loss account other than to reclassify the renewals charge as depreciation.

FRS 15 accepts this approach under what it terms *Renewals Accounting*. It considers that *Renewals Accounting* is a substitute method of calculating the depreciation of infrastructure assets and proposes that the annual level of expenditure required to maintain the operating capacity of the infrastructure assets is treated as a depreciation provision and deducted from the carrying value of the asset; when the actual expenditure takes place it is capitalised.

14.9.6 **Impairment of fixed assets**

FRS 11 *Impairment of Fixed Assets and Goodwill*[14] was issued by the ASB in July 1998 based on FRED 15 issued in June 1997. FRS 11 deals with the problems of the measurement, recognition and presentation of material reductions in value of fixed assets both tangible and intangible.

Fixed assets will be required to be reviewed for impairment only if there is some indication that impairment has occurred, e.g. slump in property market or expected future losses.

The ASB's aim is to ensure that fixed assets are recorded **at no more than recoverable amount**. This is defined as being the higher of net realisable value and value in use. Value in use is defined as the **present value** of future cash flows obtainable from the asset's continued use using a **discount rate** that is equivalent to the rate of return that the market would expect on an equally risky investment.

There could be a temptation to assume high growth rates when estimating future cash flows. FRS 11 adopts the FRED 15 approach which provided (para. 51) that:

In the periods following an impairment review, the cash flows achieved should be compared with those forecast. If the actual cash flows are so much less than those forecast that use of the actual cash flows could have required recognition of an impairment in previous periods, the original impairment calculation should be re-performed using the actual cash flows. Any impairment identified should be recognised in the current period unless the impairment has reversed.

14.9.7 **ASB Paper,** *Discounting in Financial Reporting*, 1997[15]

Discounting has been already been used for leases, pensions and capital instruments. Although there has been concern that discounting is being introduced piecemeal into financial statements, the view of the ASB appears to be to apply discounting on a case by case basis. In general, discounting is not required for current assets and current liabilities because the period of the cash flows is unlikely to see a material change in amounts realised. For long-term assets and liabilities however the effect of discounting can be significant.

The ASB view is that discounting should take account of the risk attaching to the cash flows by adjusting the cash flows or by adjusting the discount rate. For the impairment of fixed assets test, it favours the use of risk-adjusted discount rates from the market.

14.10 FRS 11 – *Impairment of Tangible Fixed Assets*

14.10.1 FRS 11 approach

FRS 11 sets out the principles and methodology for accounting for impairments of fixed assets and goodwill. Where possible, individual fixed assets should be tested for impairment. However, where cash flows do not arise from the use of a single fixed asset, impairment is measured for the smallest group of assets which generates income that is largely independent of the company's other income streams. This smallest group is referred to as an Income-Generating Unit (IGU).

Impairment of a fixed asset, or IGU (if fixed assets are grouped), occurs when:

- the carrying amount of a fixed asset or IGU is greater than its recoverable amount; where
  - carrying amount is the depreciated historical cost (or depreciated revalued amount);
  - recoverable amount is the higher of net realisable value and value in use; where
    - net realisable value is the amount at which an asset could be disposed of, less any direct selling costs, and
    - value in use is the present value of the future cash flows obtainable as a result of an asset's continued use, including those resulting from its ultimate disposal.

When impairment occurs a **revised carrying amount** is calculated for the balance sheet as follows:

Note that it is only necessary to calculate value in use if:

Depreciated historical cost > Value in use > Net realisable value.

The revised carrying amount is based on the measurement principles set out in Chapter 6 of the *Statement of Principles* discussed previously in para. 6.9.

The revised carrying amount is then depreciated over the remaining useful economic life.

14.10.2 Dividing activities into IGUs

In order to carry out an impairment review it is necessary to decide how to divide activities into IGUs. There is no single answer to this – it is extremely judgmental, e.g. if the company has multi-retail sites, the cost of preparing detailed cash flow forecasts for each site could favour grouping.

The risk of grouping is that poor performing operations might be concealed within an IGU and it would be necessary to consider if there were any commercial reasons for breaking an IGU into smaller constituents, e.g. if a location was experiencing its own unique difficulties such as local competition or inability to obtain planning permission to expand to a more profitable size.

14.10.3 Indications of impairment

A review for impairment is required when there is an indication that an impairment has actually occurred. The following are indicators of impairment:

- External indicators
  - a fall in the market value of the asset
  - material adverse changes in regulatory environment
  - material adverse changes in markets
  - material long-term increases in market rates of return used for discounting.

- Internal indicators
  - material changes in operations
  - major reorganisation
  - loss of key personnel
  - loss or net cash outflow from operating activities if this is expected to continue or is a continuation of a loss-making situation.

If there is such an indication, it is necessary to determine the depreciated historical cost if a single fixed asset or the net assets employed if an IGU and compare this with the net realisable value and value in use.

14.10.4 Value in use calculation

Value in use is arrived at by estimating and discounting the income stream. In some cases a detailed calculation of value in use will not be necessary if a simple estimate is sufficient to demonstrate that either value in use is higher than carrying value, in which case there is no impairment, or value in use is lower than net realisable value, in which case impairment is measured by reference to net realisable value.

The **income streams**:

- are likely to follow the way in which management monitors and makes decisions about continuing or closing the different lines of business;

- may often be identified by reference to major products or services (FRS 11 para. 29);

- should be based on reasonable and supportable assumptions;

- should be consistent with the most up-to-date budgets and plans that have been formally approved by management:
  - if for a period beyond that covered by formal budgets and plans should, unless

there are exceptional circumstances, assume a steady or declining growth rate (FRS 11 para. 36);

● should be projected cash flows unadjusted for risk, discounted at a rate of return expected from a similarly risky investment or should be projected risk-adjusted pre-tax cash flows discounted at a risk-free rate.

The **discount rate** should be:

● calculated on a pre-tax basis;

● an estimate of the rate that the market would expect on an equally risky investment excluding the effects of any risk for which the cash flows have been adjusted (FRS 11 para. 41):
  – increased to reflect higher risk if the cash flow forecasts assume a rate of growth that exceeds the long-term average growth rate for more than five years (FRS 11 para. 43);
  – reduced to a risk-free rate if the cash flows have been adjusted for risk (FRS 11 para. 45).

14.10.5 Treatment of impairment losses

If the depreciated historical cost (or net assets employed) exceeds the higher of net realisable value and value in use, then an impairment loss has occurred. The accounting treatment of such a loss is as follows:

Asset not previously revalued

An impairment loss should be recognised in the profit and loss account in the year in which the impairment arises.

Asset previously revalued

The reason for the impairment is important. If the impairment loss arises from damage, or other deterioration, the fall in value is similar to depreciation and must be charged to the profit as an operating cost. If however the impairment loss arises from a general change in prices, e.g. a fall in property prices, this would be reflected in the statement of total recognised gains and losses up to the amount of any previously recognised gain on revaluation. Any excess impairment (below depreciated historical cost) would be charged to the profit and loss account.

Allocation of impairment losses

Where an impairment loss arises the loss should be set against the specific fixed asset to which it relates. Where the loss cannot be identified as relating to a specific fixed asset, it should be apportioned within the IGU to reduce the most subjective values first, as follows:

● first, to reduce any goodwill within the IGU;

● second, to reduce any identifiable intangibles, but not below their readily ascertainable market values; and

● finally to the unit's tangible assets, allocated on suitable basis, but likewise not below their readily ascertainable market values.

Restoration of past impairment losses

Past impairment losses in respect of a tangible fixed asset may be restored where the recoverable amount increases due to an improvement in economic conditions or a change in use of the asset. Such a restoration should be reflected in the profit and loss account to the extent of the original impairment previously charged to the profit and loss account, adjusting for depreciation which would have been charged otherwise in the intervening period.

14.10.6 Illustration of data required for an impairment review

Pronto plc has a product line producing wooden models of athletes for export. The carrying amount of the net assets employed on the line as at 31 December 1999 was £96,500 comprising net assets of £94,500 directly attributable to the line and net assets of £2,000 apportioned from Head Office assets. The scrap value of the net assets at 31 December 2002 is estimated to be £5,000.

There is an indication that the export market will be adversely affected in 2002 by competition from plastic toy manufacturers. This means that the net assets employed to produce this product might have been impaired.

The finance director estimated the net realisable value of the net assets at 31 December 1999 to be £70,000. The value in use is now calculated to check if it is higher or lower than £70,000. If it is higher it will become the revised carrying amount; if lower the net realisable value will be the revised carrying amount.

Pronto plc has prepared budgets for the years ended 31 December 2000, 2001 and 2002. The assumptions underlying the budgets are as follows:

Unit costs and revenue:

	£
Selling price	10.00
Buying in cost	(4.00)
Production cost: material, labour, overhead	(0.75)
Head office overheads apportioned	(0.25)
Cash inflow per model	5.00

Estimated sales volumes:

	1999	2000	2001	2002
Estimated at 31 December 1998	6,000	8,000	11,000	14,000
Revised estimate at 31 December 1999	—	8,000	11,000	4,000

Determining the discount rate to be used:

	2000	2001	2002
The rate obtainable elsewhere at the same level of risk is	10%	10%	10%
The expected rates of inflation are estimated to be	10%	8%	6%

The real cost of capital to be applied to the income streams is as follows:

	Money cost of capital		Inflation rate			Real cost of capital		%
2000	(1.10)	×	(1.10)	−1	=	0.21	i.e.	21.0
2001	(1.10)	×	(1.08)	−1	=	0.188	i.e.	18.8
2002	(1.10)	×	(1.06)	−1	=	0.166	i.e.	16.6

The discount factors to be applied to each year are then re-calculated using real cost of capital discount rates as follows:

2000 $1/1.21 = 0.826$
2001 $(1/1.21)(1/1.188) = 0.696$
2002 $(1/1.21)(1/1.188)(1/1.166) = 0.597$

Alternatively, cash flows could be adjusted to reflect the rates of inflation expected for each type of income and expense, e.g. a different rate would be applied to material imported from a country with a weakening currency and local labour rates.

14.10.7 Illustrating calculation of value in use

Before calculating value in use, it is necessary to ensure that the assumptions underlying the budgets are reasonable, e.g. is the selling price likely to be affected by competition in 2002 in addition to loss of market? Is the selling price in 2001 likely to be affected? Is the estimate of scrap value reasonably accurate? How sensitive is value in use to the scrap value? Is it valid to assume that the cash flows will occur at year ends? How accurate is the real cost of capital? How reasonable are the inflation rate estimates? Will components making up the income stream, e.g. sales, materials, labour, be subject to different rates of inflation?

Assuming that no adjustment is required to be budgeted figures provided above, the estimated income streams are discounted using normal DCF approach as follows:

	2000	*2001*	*2002*
Sales (models)	8,000	11,000	4,000
Income per model	£5	£5	£5
Income stream (£)	40,000	55,000	20,000
Estimated scrap proceeds			5,000
Cash flows to be discounted	40,000	55,000	25,000
Discounted (using real cost of capital factors)	0.826	0.696	0.597
Present value	33,040	38,280	14,925

Value in use = £86,245

14.10.8 Illustration determining the *revised* carrying amount

If the carrying amount at the balance sheet date exceeds net realisable value and value in use, it is revised to an amount which is the higher of net realisable value and value in use. For Pronto plc:

	£
Carrying amount as at 31 December 1999	96,500
Net realisable value	70,000
Value in use	86,245
Revised carrying amount	86,245

14.11 Disclosure requirements

14.11.1 Mandatory disclosure requirements

FRS 18 *Accounting Policies*[16] requires the accounting policy for fixed assets and depreciation to be disclosed. This should enable readers to compare policies of different companies and attempt to make any necessary adjustments for comparison purposes. The relevant notes in the 2002 Annual Report and Accounts of ICI plc appear as follows:

Fixed assets

The financial statements are prepared under the historical cost convention.

Depreciation

The Group's policy is to write off the book value of each tangible asset excluding land to its residual value evenly over its estimated remaining life. Reviews are made annually of the estimated remaining lives of individual productive assets, taking account of commercial and technological obsolescence as well as normal wear and tear. Under this policy it becomes impracticable to calculate average asset lives exactly; however, the total lives approximate to 35 years for buildings and 14 years for plant and equipment. Depreciation of assets qualifying for grants is calculated on their full cost. No depreciation has been provided on land.

14.11.2 Statutory disclosure requirements

The Companies Act 1985 requires that movements on fixed assets be disclosed by way of a note to the balance sheet. The style employed by British Sky Broadcasting Group plc in its 2001 accounts is almost universally employed for this:

Tangible fixed assets
The movements in the year were as follows:

	Freehold land and buildings	Leasehold improvements	Equipment, fixtures and fittings	Total
	£m	£m	£m	£m
Group				
Cost				
Beginning of year	26.9	75.6	335.3	437.8
Subsidiaries acquired	1.7	0.1	28.7	30.5
Additions	1.3	4.9	126.8	133.0
Disposals	—	(0.1)	(2.3)	(2.4)
End of year	29.9	80.5	488.5	598.9
Depreciation				
Beginning of year	4.0	36.1	172.8	212.9
Charge	1.0	3.7	66.4	71.1
Disposals	—	(0.1)	(0.4)	(0.5)
End of year	5.0	39.7	238.8	283.5
Net book value				
Beginning of year	22.9	39.5	162.5	224.9
End of year	24.9	40.8	249.7	315.4

Additionally, the net book amount of interests in land and buildings must be split between freehold, long and short leasehold interests.

In the directors' report there is a requirement that significant movements in fixed assets be reported and that directors express an opinion on whether or not the value of interests in land and buildings varies materially from the net book amount.

14.12 Government grants towards the cost of fixed assets

The accounting treatment of government grants is covered by SSAP 4, which, while primarily concerned with grants made by government (both central and local, encompassing EU agencies and a wide range of so-called quangos) to enterprise, should also be followed in the case of grants received from other sources.[17]

The basis of the standard is the accruals concept, which requires the matching of cost and revenue so as to recognise both in the profit and loss accounts of the periods to which they relate. This should, of course, be tempered with the prudence concept, which requires that revenue is not anticipated. Therefore, in the light of the complex conditions usually attached to grants, credit should not be taken until receipt is assured.

Similarly, there may be a right to recover the grant wholly or partially in the event of a breach of conditions, and on that basis these conditions should be regularly reviewed and, if necessary, provision made.

Should the tax treatment of a grant differ from the accounting treatment, then the effect of this would be accounted for in accordance with SSAP 15 *Accounting for Deferred Taxation*.

SSAP 4

Government grants should be recognised in the profit and loss account so as to match the expenditure towards which they are intended to contribute. If this is retrospective, they should be recognised in the period in which they became receivable.

Grants in respect of fixed assets should be recognised over the useful economic lives of those assets, thus matching the depreciation or amortisation.

On the balance sheet, any portion of a grant that has been deferred (e.g. a grant in respect of a fixed asset where economic life has not yet ended) should be shown as deferred income.

Any potential liability to repay grants should be disclosed in accordance with FRS 12 *Provisions, Contingent Liabilities and Contingent Assets*. This could arise if the company failed to satisfy any conditions attaching to the grant, e.g. to create more employment opportunities.

The revision to the standard dropped an alternative approach of deducting the value of any grant received from the cost of the asset. The reason for withdrawing this previously popular, simpler approach was that it seemed to contravene the Companies Act 1985.

14.13 Investment properties

While FRS 15 requires all fixed assets to be subjected to a systematic depreciation charge, this was considered inappropriate for properties held as fixed assets but not employed in the normal activities of the enterprise, rather being held as investments. For such properties a more relevant treatment is to take account of the current market value of the property. The accounting treatment is set out in SSAP 19 *Accounting for Investment Properties*.[18]

Such properties may be held either as a main activity (e.g. by a property investment company) or by a company whose main activity is not the holding of such properties. In each case the accounting treatment is similar.

Definition of an investment property

For the purposes of the statement, an investment property is an interest in land or buildings:

- in respect of which construction work and development have been completed;
- which is held for its investment potential, any rental income being negotiated at arm's length.

The following are exceptions to the definition:

- A property owned and occupied by a company for its own purposes is not an investment property.
- A property let to and occupied by another group company is not an investment property for the purposes of its own accounts or the group accounts.

Additionally, the standard does not apply to charities.

SSAP 19

Under SSAP 19 *Accounting for Investment Properties*:

- Unless the property is a lease with an unexpired term of twenty years or less, no depreciation should be charged.
- Instead, investment properties should be shown in the balance sheet at their open market value.
- Changes in value should be reflected in an investment revaluation reserve rather than through the profit and loss account.

Valuation

The following should be disclosed:

- The names or qualifications of the valuers.
- Whether or not they are employees of the company or group.
- The basis of valuation adopted.

While the standard does not insist on the valuation being carried out by independent, qualified valuers, it states in the explanatory note that where investment properties represent a substantial proportion of the total assets of a major enterprise, then the valuation should be carried out:

- annually by persons holding a recognised professional qualification and having recent post-qualification experience in the location and category of the properties concerned; and
- at least every five years by an external valuer.

14.14 Effect of depreciation on the interpretation of the accounts

A number of difficulties exist when attempting to carry out inter-firm comparisons using the external information that is available to a shareholder.

14.14.1 Effect of inflation on the carrying value of the asset

The most serious difficulty is the effect of inflation, which makes the charges based on historical cost inadequate. Companies have followed various practices to take account of inflation; these have ranged from revaluation to reducing the estimated economic life to increasing the charge in the profit and loss account by making a supplementary charge. None of these is an acceptable surrogate for index adjustment using specific asset indices on a systematic annual basis: this is the only way to ensure uniformity and comparability of the cost/valuation figure upon which the depreciation charge is based.

The method that is currently acceptable under FRS 15 is to revalue the assets. This is a partial answer, but it results in lack of comparability of ratios such as gearing.

14.14.2 Effect of revaluation on ratios

The rules of double entry require that when an asset is revalued the 'profit' (or, exceptionally, 'loss') must be credited somewhere. As it is not a 'realised' profit, it would not be appropriate to credit the profit and loss account, so a 'revaluation reserve' must be created. As the asset is depreciated, this reserve may be realised to profit and loss; similarly, when an asset is ultimately disposed of, any residue relevant to that asset may be taken into profit.

One significant by-product of revaluing assets is the effect on gearing. The revaluation reserve, while not distributable, forms part of the shareholders' funds and thus improves the debt/equity ratio. Care must therefore be taken in looking at the revaluation policies and reserves when comparing the gearing of companies.

The problem is compounded because the carrying value may be amended at random periods and on a selective category of asset.

14.14.3 Choice of depreciation method

There are a number of acceptable depreciation methods that may give rise to very different patterns of debits against the profits of individual years.

14.14.4 Inherent imprecision in estimating economic life

One of the greatest difficulties with depreciation is that it is inherently imprecise. The amount of depreciation depends on the estimate of the economic life of assets, which is affected not only by the durability and workload of the asset, but also by external factors beyond the control of management. Such factors may be technological, commercial or economic. Here are some examples:

- The production by a competitor of a new product rendering yours obsolete, e.g. watches with battery-powered movements replacing those with mechanical movements.
- The production by a competitor of a product at a price lower than your production costs, e.g. imported goods from countries where costs are lower.
- Changes in the economic climate which reduce demand for your product.

This means that the interpreter of accounts must pay particular attention to depreciation policies, looking closely at the market where the enterprise's business operates.

However, this understanding is not helped by the lack of requirement to disclose specific rates of depreciation and the basis of computation of residual values. Without such information the potential effects of differences between policies adopted by competing enterprises cannot be accurately assessed.

14.14.5 Mixed values in the balance sheet

The effect of depreciation on the balance sheet is also some cause for concern. The net book amount shown for fixed assets is the result of deducting accumulated depreciation from cost (or valuation); it is not intended to be (although many non-accountants assume it is) an estimate of the value of the underlying assets. The valuation of a business based on the balance sheet is extremely difficult. The valuer may be faced with a mixture of **cost** and **valuation**.

14.14.6 Different policies may be applied within the same sector

Intercompany comparisons are even more difficult. Two enterprises following the historical cost convention may own identical assets, which, as they were purchased at different times, may well appear as dramatically different figures in the accounts. This is particularly true of interests in land and buildings.

14.14.7 Effect on the return on capital employed

There is an effect not only on the net asset value, but also on the return on capital employed. To make a fair assessment of return on capital it is necessary to know the current replacement cost of the underlying assets, but under present conventions, up-to-date valuations are required only for investment properties.

14.14.8 Effect on EPS

FRS 15 is concerned to ensure that the earnings of an enterprise reflect a fair charge for the use of the assets by the enterprise. This should ensure an accurate calculation of earnings per share. But there is a weakness here. If assets have increased in value without revaluations, then depreciation will be based on the historical cost.

Summary

Before FRS 11 and FRS 15 there were significant problems in relation to the accounting treatment of tangible fixed assets such as the determination of a cost figure and the adjustment for inflation; companies providing nil depreciation on certain types of asset; revaluations being made selectively and not maintained current.

With FRS 11 and FRS 15 the ASB has made the accounts more consistent and comparable. These FRSs have resolved some of these problems, principally requiring companies to provide for depreciation and if they have a policy of revaluation to keep such valuations reasonably current and applied to all assets within a class, i.e. removing the ability to cherry pick which assets to revalue.

However, certain difficulties remain for the user of the accounts in that different management policies on the method of depreciation, which can have a major impact on the profit for the year; there are subjective assessments of economic life that may be reviewed each year with an impact on profits; and inconsistencies such as the presence of modified historical costs and historical costs in the same balance sheet. In addition, with pure historical cost accounting, where fixed asset carrying values are based on original cost, no pretence is made that fixed asset net book amounts have any relevance to today's values. The investor is expected to know that the depreciation charge is arithmetical in character and will not wholly provide the finance for tomorrow's assets or ensure maintenance of the business's operational base. To give recognition to these factors requires the investor to grapple with the effects of lost purchasing power through inflation; the effect of changes in supply and demand on replacement prices; technological change and its implication for the company's competitiveness; and external factors such as exchange rates. To calculate the effect of these variables necessitates not only considerable mental agility, but also far more information than is contained in a set of accounts.[19] This is an area that needs to be revisited by the standard-setters.

REVIEW QUESTIONS

1 Define a 'fixed asset' and explain how materiality affects the concept of 'fixed assets'.

2 Define depreciation. Explain what assets need not be depreciated and list the main methods of calculating depreciation.

3 What is meant by the phrases 'useful economic life' and 'residual value'?

4 Define 'cost' in connection with fixed assets.

5 What effect does revaluing assets have on gearing?

6 How should grants received towards expenditure on fixed assets be treated?

7 Define an investment property and explain what investment properties must be depreciated.

8 'Split depreciation should have been encouraged instead of prohibited.' Discuss.

9 'Depreciation should mean that a company has sufficient resources to replace assets at the end of their economic lives.' Discuss.

10 Explain why there are different treatments for gains and losses in the following tangible fixed asset accounting policy extract from John Laing plc 2000 Financial Statements:

> Revaluation gains are recognised in the profit and loss account only to the extent that they reverse losses on the same assets that were previously recognised in the profit and loss account. All other revaluation gains are recognised in the revaluation account. Revaluation losses caused by a consumption of economic benefits are recognised in the profit and loss account. Other revaluation losses are taken to the revaluation reserve until the carrying amount equates to the depreciated historic cost. Thereafter, revaluation losses are recognised in the profit and loss account.

11 The following is an extract form the Unilever 2000 Annual Report and Accounts:

Tangible fixed assets	2000	1999
	€m	€m
At cost less depreciation	9,839	8,820
Approximate current replacement cost net of accumulated current cost depreciation	10,982	10,237
On a current replacement cost basis the depreciation charge to the profit and loss account would have been	(264)	(258)
Commitments for capital expenditure at 31 December 2000	392	248

Discuss the usefulness of the current cost data.

12 The following is an extract from the ICI Plc 2002 Annual Report:

	Land and buildings £m	Plant and equipment £m	Payments on account assets in course of construction £m
Transfers to assets in use	16	14	(30)

Explain the costs that would be included in this transfer.

EXERCISES

An extract from the solution is provided in the appendix at the end of the text for exercises marked with an asterisk (*).

Question 1

(a) Discuss why SSAP 19 Accounting for Investment Properties was produced.

(b) Universal Entrepreneurs plc has the following items on its fixed asset list:

(i) £1,000,000 – the right to extract sandstone from a particular quarry. Geologists predict that extraction at the present rate may be continued for ten years.

(ii) £5,000,000 – a freehold property, let to a subsidiary on a full repairing lease negotiated on arm's-length terms for fifteen years. The building is a new one, erected on a green field site at a cost of £4,000,000.

(iii) A fleet of motor cars used by company employees. These have been purchased under a contract which provides a guaranteed part exchange value of 60% cost after two years' use.

(iv) A company helicopter with an estimated life of 150,000 flying hours.

(v) A nineteen-year lease on a property let out at arm's-length rent to another company.

Required:
Advise the company on the depreciation policy it ought to adopt for each of the above assets.

(c) The company is considering revaluing its interests in land and buildings, which comprise freehold and leasehold properties, all used by the company or its subsidiaries.

Required:
Discuss the consequences of this on the depreciation policy of the company and any special instructions that need to be given to the valuer.

Question 2

You have been given the task, by one of the partners of the firm of accountants for which you work, of assisting in the preparation of a trend statement for a client.

Mercury has been in existence for four years. Figures for the three preceding years are known but those for the fourth year need to be calculated. Unfortunately, the supporting workings for the preceding years' figures cannot be found and the client's own ledger accounts and workings are not available.

One item in particular, plant, is causing difficulty and the following figures have been given to you:

12 months ended 31 March	20X6 £	20X7 £	20X8 £	20X9 £
(A) Plant at cost	80,000	80,000	90,000	?
(B) Accumulated depreciation	(16,000)	(28,800)	(28,080)	?
(C) Net (written down value)	64,000	51,200	61,920	?

The only other information available is that disposals have taken place at the beginning of the financial years concerned:

	Date of		Original	Sales
	Disposal	Original acquisition	cost	proceeds
	12 months ended 31 March		£	£
First disposal	20X8	20X6	15,000	8,000
Second disposal	20X8	20X6	30,000	21,000

Plant sold was replaced on the same day by new plant. The cost of the plant which replaced the first disposal is not known but the replacement for the second disposal is known to have cost £50,000.

Required:
(a) Identify the method of providing for depreciation on plant employed by the client, stating how you have arrived at your conclusion.
(b) Reconstruct a working schedule to support the figures shown at line (B) for each of the years ended 31 March 20X6, 20X7 and 20X8. Extend your workings to cover year ended 31 March 20X9.
(c) Produce the figures that should be included in the blank spaces on the trend statement at lines (A), (B) and (C) for year ended 31 March 20X9.
(d) Calculate the profit or loss arising on each of the two disposals.

* **Question 3**

In the year to 31 December 20X9, Amy bought a new fixed asset and made the following payments in relation to it:

	£	£
Cost as per suppliers list	12,000	
Less: Agreed discount	1,000	11,000
Delivery charge		100
Erection charge		200
Maintenance charge		300
Additional component to increase capacity		400
Replacement parts		250

Required:
(a) State and justify the cost figure which should be used as the basis for depreciation.
(b) What does depreciation do, and why is it necessary?
(c) Briefly explain, without numerical illustration, how the straight-line and reducing balance methods of depreciation work. What different assumptions does each method make?
(d) Explain the term 'objectivity' as used by accountants. To what extent is depreciation objective?
(e) It is common practice in published accounts in Germany to use the reducing balance method for a fixed asset in the early years of its life, and then to change to the straight-line method as soon as this would give a higher annual charge. What do you think of this practice? Refer to relevant accounting conventions in your answer.

(ACCA)

* Question 4

The finance director of the Small Machine Parts Ltd company is considering the acquisition of a lease of a small workshop in a warehouse complex that is being redeveloped by City Redevelopers Ltd at a steady rate over a number of years. City Redevelopers are granting such leases for five years on payment of a premium of £20,000.

The accountant has obtained estimates of the likely maintenance costs and disposal value of the lease during its five-year life. He has produced the following table and suggested to the finance director that the annual average cost should be used in the financial accounts to represent the depreciation charge in the profit and loss account.

Table prepared to calculate the annual average cost

Years of life	1	2	3	4	5
	£	£	£	£	£
Purchase price	20,000	20,000	20,000	20,000	20,000
Maintenance/repairs					
Year 2		1,000	1,000	1,000	1,000
3			1,500	1,500	1,500
4				1,850	1,850
5					2,000
	20,000	21,000	22,500	24,350	26,350
Resale value	11,500	10,000	8,010	5,350	350
Net cost	8,500	11,000	14,490	19,000	26,000
Annual average cost	8,500	5,500	4,830	4,750	5,200

The finance director, however, was considering whether to calculate the depreciation chargeable using the annuity method with interest at 15%.

Required:
(a) Calculate the entries that would appear in the profit and loss account of Small Machine Parts Ltd for each of the five years of the life of the lease for the amortisation charge, the interest element in the depreciation charge and the income from secondary assets using the ANNUITY METHOD. Calculate the net profit for each of the five years assuming that the operating cash flow is estimated to be £25,000 per year.
(b) Discuss briefly which of the two methods you would recommend.
   The present value at 15% of £1 per annum for five years is £3.35214.
   The present value at 15% of £1 received at the end of year 5 is £0.49717.
   Ignore taxation.

(ACCA)

Question 5

(a) The following are extracts from the accounting policies' section of two different sets of accounts:

Greene King plc

Depreciation
Freehold and leasehold properties with 25 years or more to run (other than production premises) are repaired and refurbished such that their values are not impaired by the passage of time. In the opinion of the directors any depreciation would accordingly be immaterial and none has therefore been provided. Leasehold properties with fewer than 25 years to run are depreciated over the remainder of their lease.

The BOC Group plc 1999 Report and Accounts

Tangible fixed assets

No depreciation is charged on freehold land … Depreciation is charged on all other fixed assets on the straight-line basis over the effective lives except for certain tonnage plants where depreciation is calculated on an annuity basis over the life of the contract.

Required:

(i) Compare the two accounting policies quoted above, especially the treatment of buildings. Comment on the different methods of depreciation used. How applicable are they in each set of circumstances?

(ii) Discuss the purpose(s) of the depreciation charge in the profit and loss account.

(b) Simple Ltd has just purchased a roasting/salting machine to produce roasted walnuts. The finance director asks for your advice on how the company should calculate the depreciation on this machine. Details are as follows:

Cost of machine	£800,000
Residual value	£104,000
Estimated life	4 years
Annual profits	£2,000,000
Annual turnover from machine	£850,000

Required:

(a) Calculate the annual depreciation charge using the straight-line method and the reducing balance method. Assume that an annual rate of 40% is applicable for the reducing balance method.

(b) Comment upon the validity of each method, taking into account the type of business and the effect each method has on annual profits. Are there any other methods which would be more applicable?

References

1 Companies Act 1985 Sec. 262 (1).
2 FRS 11, *Impairment of Fixed Assets and Goodwill*, ASB, 1998, para. 2.
3 FRS 15, *Tangible Fixed Assets*, ASB, 1999, para. 2.
4 N.C.L. MacDonald, *Depreciation and Revaluations of Fixed Assets Financial Reporting*, ICAEW, 1986–7, p. 25.
5 FRS 15, *Tangible Fixed Assets*, ASB, 1999, Appendix 4, para 4.8.
6 *Ibid.*, Appendix 4, para. 52.
7 Companies Act 1985, Schedule 4, para. 17.
8 *Ibid.*, para. 26.
9 FRS 15, *Tangible Fixed Assets*, ASB, 1999, paras 6–14.
10 Carsberg Report, RICS, January 2003 see: www.rics.org/downloads/carsberg_valuation_report.pdf
11 P.R. Kirkman, *Accounting under Inflationary Conditions*, Prentice Hall, 1978, chapter 5.
12 W.T. Baxter, *Depreciation*, Sweet & Maxwell, 1978.
13 *Certified Accountant*, June 1986, p. 37.
14 FRS 11, *Impairment of Fixed Assets and Goodwill*, ASB, 1998.
15 *Discounting in Financial Reporting*, ASB, 1997.
16 FRS 18 *Accounting Policies*, ASB, 2000.
17 SSAP 4, *Accounting for Government Grants*, ASC, July 1990.
18 SSAP 19, *Accounting for Investment Properties*, ASC, November 1981.
19 N.C.L. MacDonald, *op. cit.*, pp. 3–4.

CHAPTER 15

Fixed tangible assets (not owned) – lessee

15.1 Introduction

This chapter introduces the accounting principles and policies that apply to lease agreements from the viewpoint of the lessee. We are interested in developing a wider understanding of leasing and leasing-related issues, so that you can understand how they should be represented in the financial statements and why a company might favour a particular type of lease agreement.

In this chapter we consider the following:

● Leasing – an introduction
● SSAP 21 (and its international equivalents) – the controversy
● SSAP 21 – classification of a lease
● SSAP 21 – accounting for leases by lessees
● Leasing – a form of off-balance-sheet financing
● Materiality in relation to SSAP 21
● FRS 5 – *Reporting the Substance of Transactions*
● FRS 5 – The Private Finance Initiative

We must understand not only what a lease is and the mechanical adjustments required to account for any given leasing agreement in the financial statements, but also the economic consequences of the accounting treatment that is applied and the impact of these economic consequences on company behaviour.

15.2 Leasing – an introduction

In this section we consider the nature of the lease; historical developments in leasing; reasons for its popularity; and why it was necessary to introduce SSAP 21.

15.2.1 What is a lease?

SSAP 21 *Accounting for Leases and Hire Purchase Contracts* provides the following two definitions:

> A **lease** is a contract between a lessor and a lessee for the hire of a specific asset. The lessor retains ownership of the asset but conveys the right to use of the asset to the lessee for an agreed period of time in return for the payment of specific rentals.

In practice, there might well be more than two parties involved in a lease. For example, on leasing a car the parties involved are the motor dealer, the finance company and the company using the car.

A hire purchase contract is a contract for the hire of an asset which contains a provision giving the hirer an option to acquire legal title to the asset upon the fulfilment of certain conditions stated in the contract.

As with leasing, there would probably be three parties involved.

The main difference between a lease and a hire purchase contract (also known as a lease purchase) can be expressed in terms of the legal ownership and eventual possession of the asset. In the case of a lease, the legal ownership of the asset remains with the lessor throughout the agreement, and possession of the asset returns to the lessor after the lease is completed. In a hire purchase contract, the legal ownership eventually lies with the hirer and possession continues once all the agreed payments have been made.

15.2.2 Historical developments in leasing

The growth in the leasing industry until the advent of SSAP 21, and indeed after its introduction, was staggering.[1] Statistics produced by the Finance and Leasing Association, whose members account for 80% of all leasing in the UK, show that the cost of assets acquired for leasing each year rose from £288m in 1973 to £2,894m in 1983 to £10,200m in 1991 (after the introduction of SSAP 21).[2] In fact, it was estimated that in 1985 the value of leased equipment represented over 20% of capital expenditure in the UK.[3]

15.2.3 Why did leasing become popular?

There were two major reasons: the tax advantage to the lessor; and the commercial advantage to the lessee.

Tax advantage

The government is responsible for the initial stimulus to the leasing industry. In 1972, first-year allowances (FYA) on equipment were increased to 100%. These allowances could be offset against taxable profits, which reduced a company's tax bill.

Companies, especially in the manufacturing sector, which had sustained tax losses in preceding years could not utilise the tax benefits of FYAs. This resulted in lessors claiming the FYAs and then leasing out equipment to these other companies at a reduced rental, thus enabling both lessors and lessees to benefit from a leasing agreement.

The leasing industry flourished even more in times of high interest rates. In these periods, lessors can achieve even greater cash flow benefits by deferring tax payments. Consequently, lessors are even more committed to leasing.

Many of these tax advantages were removed by the Finance Act 1984. This implemented a gradual reduction in the corporation tax rate and a gradual removal of FYAs.

Commercial advantage

Despite the Finance Act 1984, there are still a number of advantages associated with leases. These are attributable in part to the ability to spread cash payments over the lease period instead of making a one-off lump sum payment. They include the following:

- **Cash flow management**. If cash is used to purchase fixed assets, it is not available for the normal operating activities of a company.

- **Conservation of capital**. Lines of credit are kept open and may be used for purposes where finance might not be available easily (e.g. financing working capital).

- **Continuity**. The lease agreement is itself a line of credit that cannot easily be withdrawn or terminated due to external factors, in contrast to an overdraft that can be called in by the lender.

- **Flexibility of the asset base**. The asset base can be more easily expanded and contracted. In addition, the lease payments can be structured to match the income pattern of the lessee.

- **Off-balance-sheet financing**. Leasing provides the lessee with the possibility of off-balance-sheet financing,[4,5] whereby a company has the use of an economic resource that does not appear in the balance sheet, with the corresponding omission of the liability.

15.2.4 Why was SSAP 21 necessary?

As with many of the standards, action was required because there was no uniformity in the treatment and disclosure of leasing transactions. The need became urgent following the massive growth in the leasing industry and the growth in off-balance-sheet financing. In the former case, leasing had become a material economic resource; in the latter case, the accounting treatment of the lease transaction was seen to distort the financial reports of a company so that they did not represent a true and fair view of its commercial activities.

However, for the first time attention was paid to the economic consequences of introducing a standard, the ASC expressing a concern that the standard might have undesirable economic consequences.[6] The inclusion of the lease obligation might affect the lessee company's gearing adversely and, indeed, cause it to exceed its legal borrowing powers under the memorandum and articles. The memorandum and articles might, for example, have a stipulation that the total borrowings should not exceed the total shareholders' funds. In the event, the commercial reasons for leasing and the capacity of the leasing industry to structure lease agreements to circumvent the standard have prevented a reduction in lease activity. Evidence of lessors varying the term of the lease agreements is supported by Cranfield[7] and Abdel-Khalik *et al*.[8]

Macdonald[9] made the point that most transactions will be undertaken with a commercial purpose; some may be undertaken, or undertaken in a particular form, so as to change materially the accounting message communicated by the accounts; even those commercially motivated may be accounted for in one way rather than another so as to improve the accounting message. Macdonald also observed that, while it might be thought that the overriding requirement of the true and fair view could cope with such pressures, this was prevented by the lack of auditor independence, the inadequacy of qualified reports as opposed to revised accounts, and the absence of a codified conceptual framework with which to constrain auditor judgement.

A standard was necessary to ensure uniform reporting and to prevent the accounting message being manipulated.

15.3 SSAP 21 (and its international equivalent) – the controversy

This section considers the development of SSAP 21, its main thrust and why it was so controversial. It also discusses how the accounting and legal professions differ in their approach to the reporting of lease transactions.

15.3.1 Development of SSAP 21

SSAP 21 proved to be an extremely controversial accounting standard. The extent of the controversy is demonstrated by the amount of time that elapsed before it was issued.

SSAP 21 was issued in August 1984 to supersede ED 29 *Accounting for Leases and Hire Purchase Contracts*, which was issued in October 1981. ED 29 itself was the result of about five years' discussion and debate.[10]

Despite the controversy associated with legislating for leasing, accounting standards and pronouncements similar to SSAP 21 were appearing all over the world. For example, in the USA there was Financial Accounting Standard 13 (SFAS 13),[11] which was effective for leases entered into on or after 1 January 1977, and internationally we saw International Accounting Standard 17 (IAS 17),[12] issued in September 1982 and effective for accounting periods beginning on or after 1 January 1984 and subsequently revised in November 1997.

15.3.2 What is the main thrust of SSAP 21?

First, SSAP 21 distinguishes between two types of lease – finance and operating – and recommends different accounting treatment for each. In brief, the definitions were as follows:

- **Finance lease**. A lease that transfers substantially all the risks and rewards of ownership of an asset to the lessee.
- **Operating lease**. A lease similar to a short-term hire of an asset, with no suggestion of transferral of risks and rewards of ownership to the lessee.

The accounting treatment and definition of each lease will be explored in greater depth in sections 15.4 and 15.5

Second, the standard requires finance leases to be capitalised in the lessee's accounts. This means that the leased item should be recorded as an asset in the balance sheet, and the obligation for future payments should be recorded as a liability in the balance sheet. It is not permissible for the leased asset and lease obligation to be left out of the balance sheet. In the case of operating leases, the lessee is required only to expense the annual payments as a rental through the profit and loss account.

The Accounting Standards Committee's concern about off-balance-sheet financing and the need for capitalisation is emphasised in the foreword to SSAP 21:

> Why is a capitalisation requirement necessary? When a company is leasing a substantial amount of assets instead of buying them, the effect is that, unless the leased assets and obligations are capitalised, potentially large liabilities build up off balance sheet; equally, the leased assets employed are not reflected on the balance sheet. These omissions may mislead users of a company's accounts – both external users and the company's own management.

It went on to make another interesting point:

> Capitalisation of assets held under finance leases results in a company's assets and obligations being more readily apparent than if leased assets and obligations are not recognised.[13]

The implication of this is that a disclosure by way of note is not sufficient. Hence the need to record the asset and obligation in the balance sheet.

15.3.3 Why was SSAP 21 so controversial?

The proposal to classify leases into finance and operating leases, and to capitalise those which are classified as finance leases, appears to be a feasible solution to the accounting problems that surround leasing agreements. So, why did the ASC encounter so much controversy in its attempt to stop the practice of charging all lease payments to the profit and loss account?

The whole debate centres on one accounting policy: **substance over form**. Although this is not cited as a fundamental accounting concept in SSAP 2 *Disclosure of Accounting Policies*, it is defined in IAS 1.[14] Paragraph 9 states that in:

> the selection and application by management of the appropriate accounting policies and the preparation of financial statements … transactions and other events should be accounted for and presented in accordance with their substance and financial reality and not merely with their legal form.

The real sticking point was that SSAP 21[15] (and ED 29[16] before it) invoked a substance over form approach to accounting treatment that was completely different to the traditional approach, which has strict regard to legal ownership. The ASC argued that in reality there were two separate transactions taking place. In one transaction, the company was borrowing funds to be repaid over a period. In the other, it was making a payment to the supplier for the use of an asset.

The correct accounting treatment for the borrowing transaction, based on its substance, was to include in the lessee's balance sheet a liability representing the obligation to meet the lease payments, and the correct accounting treatment for the asset acquisition transaction, based on its substance, was to include an asset representing the asset supplied under the lease.

Although SSAP 21 does not mention substance over form explicitly, it does state in the foreword that:

> It is sometimes argued that leased assets should not be recognised on a company's balance sheet as the company does not have legal title to the asset … SSAP 21 … recognises that whether an asset is owned, leased or held under a hire purchase contract, it represents an economic source which is needed in the business and which the accounts ought to reflect in a consistent manner.

In addition, IAS 17, para. 5 states categorically that 'whether a lease is a finance lease or not depends on the substance of the transaction rather than the form of the contract'.

15.3.4 How do the accounting and legal professions differ in their approach to the reporting of lease transactions?

The accounting profession sees itself as a service industry that prepares financial reports in a dynamic environment, in which the user is looking for reports that reflect commercial reality. Consequently, the profession needs to be sensitive and responsive to changes in commercial practice. This is demonstrated in a technical release (TR 603) issued by the ICAEW in December 1985, which advised members to consider the economic substance of a transaction and not just the legal form.

There was still some opposition within the accounting profession to the inclusion of a finance lease in the balance sheet as an 'asset'. The opposition rested on the fact that the item that was the subject of the lease agreement did not satisfy the existing criterion for classification as an asset because it was not 'owned' by the lessee. To accommodate this, the definition of an asset has been modified from 'ownership' to 'the right to use the item for substantially the whole of its useful economic life'.

The legal profession, on the other hand, concentrates on the strict legal interpretation of a transaction. The whole concept of substance over form is contrary to their normal practice.

It is interesting to reflect that, whereas an equity investor might prefer the economic resources to be included in the balance sheet under the substance over form principle, this is not necessarily true for a loan creditor. The equity shareholder is interested in resources available for creating earnings; the lender is interested in the assets available as security.

15.4 SSAP 21 – classification of a lease

As discussed earlier in the chapter, SSAP 21 provides definitions for classifying leases as finance or operating leases, then prescribes the accounting and disclosure requirements applicable to the lessor and the lessee for each type of lease.

The crucial decision in accounting for leases is whether a transaction represents a finance or an operating lease. We have already offered brief definitions of each type of lease, but SSAP 21 gives a fuller definition:

> A **finance lease** is a lease that transfers substantially all the risk and rewards of ownership of an asset to the lessee. It should be presumed that such a transfer of risks and rewards occurs if at the inception of the lease the present value of the minimum lease payments, including any initial payments, amounts to substantially all (normally 90% or more) of the fair value of the asset. The present value should be calculated by using the interest rate implicit in the lease. If the fair value of the asset is not determinable, an estimate thereof should be used.
>
> An **operating lease** is a lease other than a finance lease.

Welcome to one of the biggest problems in the application of lease accounting – determining how to categorise a lease transaction on the basis of these definitions![17]

The two ways to determine lease type are by applying either a financial terms test or a contractual terms test. In the financial terms test, a calculation is made of the present value of all lease payments to see if the 90% barrier is passed. In the contractual terms test, the terms and conditions applicable to the leasing agreement are considered. Typical terms and conditions that suggest a finance lease include the lessee bearing any losses associated with cancellation, the lessee having an option to renew a lease on completion, and the lessee receiving a residual value based on market value.

More specifically, note that there are three possible elements to the minimum lease payment:

I   the minimum payments over the remaining part of the lease period;

II   any residual amount guaranteed by the lessee (or related party);

III any residual amount guaranteed by any other party.

The normal treatment is for any amount guaranteed by the lessee to be included in the minimum lease calculation for the purpose of the 90% criteria test. Guaranteed amounts are dealt with extensively in SSAP 21 but we will deal briefly with the **classification** aspect (i.e. whether or not a lease is a finance lease). Briefly, lessees use elements I and II for the purposes of the 90% test.

TimCross plc enters into a lease agreement for which the implicit rate is computed and then the lease is classified using the 90% test:

- Fair value of leased asset   =   £20,000
- Term of lease   =   5 years
- Annual lease payments   =   £4,000
- Estimated residual value   =   £6,000
- Guaranteed final amount (by lessee)   =   £4,000

Step 1

The implicit rate is computed so that the DCF value of the five annual payments (of £4000) and the estimated residual amount (of £6,000) equals the fair value of the leased asset (£20,000). If the fair value is not known then an estimate should be used.

Step 2

To classify the lease, we need to consider the relationship between the estimated residual value and the guaranteed final amount carefully because it affects the 90% test. To classify the lease we need to calculate the present value (using the implicit rate calculated in step 1) of the five annual payments (of £4,000) and the guaranteed final amount (£4,000) rather than the residual value. In this example the present value of the minimum lease payments is £18,810, which exceeds 90% of the fair value (£20,000).

IAS 17 includes a helpful flow chart, prepared by the IAS secretariat, which represents examples of some possible positions that would normally be classified as a finance lease (Figure 15.1).

Figure 15.1 IAS 17 aid to categorising operating and finance leases

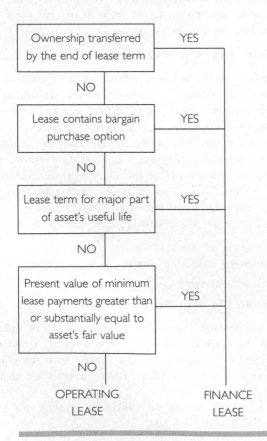

15.5 SSAP 21 – accounting for leases by lessees

15.5.1 Accounting requirements for operating leases

The treatment of operating leases conforms to the legal interpretation and corresponds to the lease accounting practice that existed pre-SSAP 21. No asset or obligation is shown in the balance sheet; the operating lease rentals payable are charged to the profit and loss account on a straight-line basis.

15.5.2 Disclosure requirements for operating leases

SSAP 21 requires that the total of operating lease rentals charged as an expense in the profit and loss account should be disclosed, and these rentals should be broken down in respect of hire of plant and machinery and other operating leases. Disclosure is required of the payments that a lessee is committed to make during the next year, in the second to fifth years inclusive, and over five years.

EXAMPLE ● OPERATING LEASE Clifford plc is a manufacturing company. It negotiates a lease to begin on 1 January 20X1 with the following terms:

Term of lease	4 years
Estimated useful life of machine	9 years
Age of machine on inception of lease	4 years
Purchase price of new machine	£75,000
Annual payments	£8,000

This is an operating lease as it applies only to a part of the asset's useful life, and the present value of the lease payments does not constitute 90% of the fair value.

The amount of the annual rental paid – £8,000 p.a. – will be charged to the profit and loss account and disclosed with hire of plant and machinery. There will also be a disclosure of the ongoing commitment with a note that £8,000 is payable within 1 year and £24,000 within 2 to 5 years.

15.5.3 Accounting requirements for finance leases

We follow a step approach to illustrate the accounting entries in both the balance sheet and the profit and loss account.

When a lessee begins a finance lease, both the leased asset and the related lease obligations need to be shown in the balance sheet.

Balance sheet steps for a finance lease

Step 1 The leased asset should be capitalised in the fixed asset account (and recorded separately) at the present value of lease payments or its fair value.

Step 2 The annual depreciation charge for the leased asset should be calculated by depreciating over the shorter of the estimated useful life of the asset or the lease period.

Step 3 The net book value of the leased asset should be reduced by the annual depreciation charge.

Step 4 The finance lease obligation is a liability which should be recorded in the borrowings element of creditors. At the inception of a lease agreement, the value of the leased asset and the leased liability will be the same.

Step 5 (a) The finance charge for the finance lease should be calculated as the difference between the total of the minimum lease payments and the fair value of the asset (or the present value of these lease payments if fair value is unknown), i.e. it represents the charge made by the lessor for the credit that is being extended to the lessee.

(b) The finance charge should be allocated to the accounting periods over the term of the lease. Three methods for allocating finance charges are used in practice:

- **Actuarial method.** This applies a constant periodic rate of charge to the balance of the leasing obligation. The rate of return applicable can be calculated by applying present value tables to annual lease payments.
- **Sum of digits method.** This method ('Rule of 78') is much easier to apply than the actuarial method. The finance charge is apportioned to accounting periods on a reducing scale.
- **Straight-line method.** This spreads the finance charge equally over the period of the lease.

Step 6 The finance lease obligation should be reduced by the difference between the lease payment and the finance charge. This means that first the lease payment is used to repay the finance charge, and then the balance of the lease payment is used to reduce the book value of the obligation.

Profit and loss account steps for a finance lease

Step 1 The annual depreciation charge should be recorded.

Step 2 The finance charge allocated to the current period should be recorded.

EXAMPLE ● FINANCE LEASE Clifford plc negotiates another lease to commence on 1 January 20X1 with the following terms:

Term of lease	3 years
Purchase price of new machine	£16,500
Annual payments (payable in advance)	£6,000
Clifford plc's borrowing rate	15%

Finance charges are allocated using the sum of digits method.

Categorise the transaction

First we need to decide whether the lease is an operating or a finance lease. We do this by applying the test to the financial terms as follows:

- Calculate the fair value:
  Fair value of asset = £16,500
- Calculate the present value of minimum lease payments:
  $$£6,000 + \frac{£6,000}{1.15} + \frac{£6,000}{(1.15)^2} = £15,754$$
- Compare the fair value and the present value. It is a finance lease because PV of the lease payments account is approximately 95% of the fair value of the asset, which passes SSAP 21's 90% rule.

Balance sheet steps for a finance lease

Step 1 Capitalise lease at fair value:

Asset value = £16,500

Step 2 Calculate depreciation (using straight-line method):

£16,500/3 = £5,500

Step 3 Reduce the asset:

Balance sheet (extract) as at		31 Dec 20X1	31 Dec 20X2	31 Dec 20X3
ASSET	Opening value	16,500	11,000	5,500
(Right to	Depreciation	5,500	5,500	5,500
use asset)	Closing value	11,000	5,500	—

Or if we keep the asset at cost as in published accounts:

ASSET	Cost	16,500	16,500	16,500
(Right to	Depreciation	5,000	11,000	16,500
use asset)	Net book value	11,000	5,500	—

Step 4 Obligation on inception of finance lease:

Liability = £16,500

Step 5 Finance charge:

Total payments	3 × £6,000	= £18,000
Asset value		= £16,500
		£1,500

Finance charge
Allocated using sum of digits:

Year 1 = 2/(1 + 2) × £1,500 = (£1,000)
Year 2 = 1/(1 + 2) × £1,500 = (£500)

Note that the allocation is only over two periods because the instalments are being made in advance. If the instalments were being made in arrears, the liability would continue over three years and the allocation would be over three years.

Step 6 Reduce the obligation:

Balance sheet (extract) as at		31 Dec 20X1	31 Dec 20X2	31 Dec 20X3
Liability	Opening value	16,500	11,500	6,000
(Obligation	Lease payment	6,000	6,000	6,000
under finance		10,500	5,500	—
lease)	Finance charge	1,000	500	—
	Closing value	11,500	6,000	—

Note that the closing balance on the asset represents unexpired service potential and the closing balance on the liability represents the capital amount outstanding at the balance sheet date.

Profit and loss account steps for a finance lease

Step 1 A depreciation charge is made on the basis of use. The charge would be calculated in accordance with existing company policy relating to the depreciation of that type of asset.

Step 2 A finance charge is levied on the basis of the amount of financing outstanding.

Both then appear in the profit and loss account as expenses of the period:

	P&L account (extract) for year ending		
	31 Dec 20X1	*31 Dec 20X2*	*31 Dec 20X3*
Depreciation	5,500	5,500	5,500
Finance charge	1,000	500	—
Total	6,500	6,000	5,500

In the Clifford example, we used the sum of the digits method to allocate the finance charge over the period of the repayment. In the following example, we will illustrate the actuarial method of allocating the finance charge.

EXAMPLE 3 – FINANCE LEASE Witts plc negotiates a four-year lease for a fixed asset with a cost price of £35,000. The annual lease payments are £10,000 payable in advance. The cost of borrowing for Witts plc is 15%.

First we need to determine whether this is a finance lease. Then we need to calculate the implicit interest rate and allocate the total finance charge over the period of the repayments using the actuarial method.

● Categorise the transaction to determine whether it is a finance lease.

Fair value of asset   = £35,000
PV of future lease payments:
£10,000 + (10,000 × $a_{\overline{3}|15}$)
£10,000 + (10,000 × 2.283)   = £32,830

The PV of the minimum lease payments amounts to 93.8% of the fair value of the asset. It is therefore categorised as a finance lease.

● Calculate the 'interest rate implicit in the lease'.

Fair value = Lease payments discounted at the implicit interest rate
£35,000   = £10,000 + (10,000 × $a_{\overline{3}|i}$)
$a_{\overline{3}|i}$ = £25,000/10,000 = 2.5
i = 9.7%

● Allocate the finance charge using the actuarial method.

Figure 15.2 shows that the finance charge is levied on the obligation during the period at 9.7%, which is the implicit rate calculated above.

Figure 15.2 Finance charge allocation using actuarial method

Period	Obligation (start) £	Rentals paid £	Obligation (during) £	Finance 9.7% £	Obligation (end) £
Year 1	35,000	10,000	25,000	2,425	27,425
Year 2	27,425	10,000	17,425	1,690	19,115
Year 3	19,115	10,000	9,115	885	10,000
Year 4	10,000	10,000	—	—	—

15.5.4 Disclosure requirements for finance leases

SSAP 21 requires that assets subject to finance leases should be identified separately and stated in terms of gross amount and accumulated depreciation. This can be achieved either by separate entries in the fixed asset schedule or by integrating owned and leased assets in this schedule and disclosing the breakdown in the notes to the accounts.

The obligations relating to finance leases can also be treated in two different ways. The leasing obligation should be shown either separately from other liabilities in the balance sheet or integrated into 'creditors due within one year' and 'creditors due after one year' and disclosed separately in the notes to the accounts.

The notes to the accounts should also analyse the leasing obligations in terms of the timing of the payments. The analysis of the amounts payable should be broken down into those obligations falling due within one year, two to five years, and more than five years.

Note that Figure 15.2 also provides the information required for the balance sheet. For example, at the end of year 1 the table shows, in the final column, a total obligation of £27,425. This can be further subdivided into its non-current and current components by using the next item in the final column, which represents the amount outstanding at the end of year 2. This amount of £19,115 represents the non-current element, and the difference of £8,310 represents the current liability element at the end of year 1.

This method of calculating the current liability from the table produces a different current figure each year. For example, the current liability at the end of year 2 is £9,115, being £19,115 – £10,000. This has been discussed in *External Financial Reporting*, where the point was made that the current liability should be the present value of the payment that is to be made at the end of the next period, i.e. £10,000 discounted at 9.7%, which gives a present value for the current liability of £9,115 for inclusion in the balance sheet each year until the liability is discharged.[18] We use the conventional approach in working illustrations and exercises, but you should bear this point in mind.

EXAMPLE ● DISCLOSURE REQUIREMENTS IN THE LESSEE'S ACCOUNTS It is interesting to refer to the disclosures found in published accounts as illustrated by the Greenalls Group accounts here:

Extract from the Greenalls Group plc – Annual Report and Accounts 1999

Accounting Policies

Leasing
Assets which are subject to finance leases are capitalised and the related depreciation charged to the profit and loss account. Lease payments are treated as consisting of interest and capital, interest being charged to the profit and loss account over the term of the lease on an actuarial basis. Rental payments in respect of operating leases are charged to the profit and loss account on a straight-line basis.

Notes to the Accounts

2 *Costs of sales and other operating expenses*

	1999 £000	1998 £000
Costs and expenses include the following:		
Depreciation of leased tangible assets	1,611	1,720
Operating leases – plant and machinery	4,101	4,268
– land and buildings	14,832	9,040

6 *Interest payable*

	1999 £000	1998 £000
Finance lease charges	3,461	3,527

10 *Tangible fixed assets*

The net book value of tangible fixed assets includes an amount of £54,028,000 (1998 – £54,857,000) in respect of assets held under finance leases of which £50,920,000 (1998 – £51,749,000) relates to hotels.

14 *Creditors: amounts falling due within one year (extract)*

	1999 £000	1998 £000
Net obligations under finance leases	933	1,564

15 *Creditors: amounts falling due after more than one year (extract)*

	1999 £000	1998 £000
Hotel finance lease obligations	48,010	44,952
Other finance lease	1,251	3,222

(The repayment schedule of the total borrowings is then disaggregated.)

21 *Commitments under Operating Lease for the next financial year (extract)*

	Group 1999 £000	1998 £000
Other operating lease ending:		
Within one year	1,050	559
Between one and five years	2,279	2,813
After five years	632	83
	3,961	3,455

15.6 Leasing – a form of off-balance-sheet financing

Prior to SSAP 21, one of the major attractions of leasing agreements for the lessee was the off-balance-sheet nature of the transaction. However, the introduction of SSAP 21 required the capitalisation of finance leases and removed part of the benefit of off-balance-sheet financing.

The capitalisation of finance leases effectively means that all such transactions will affect the lessee's gearing, return on assets and return on investment. Consequently, SSAP 21 substantially alters some of the key accounting ratios which are used to analyse a set of financial statements.

Operating leases, on the other hand, are not required to be capitalised. This means that operating leases still act as a form of off-balance-sheet financing.[19] Hence they are extremely attractive to many lessees. Indeed, leasing agreements are increasingly being structured specifically to be classified as operating leases, even though they appear to be more financial in nature.[20,21]

An important conclusion is that some of the key ratios used in financial analysis become distorted and unreliable in instances where operating leases form a major part of a company's financing.[22]

To illustrate the effect of leasing on the financial structure of a company, we present a buy versus leasing example.

EXAMPLE ● RATIO ANALYSIS OF BUY VERSUS LEASE DECISION Kallend Tiepins plc requires one extra machine for the production of tiepins. The MD of Kallend Tiepins plc is aware that the gearing ratio and the return on capital employed ratio will change depending on whether the company buys or leases (operating lease) this machinery. The relevant information is as follows.

The machinery costs £100,000, but it will improve the operating profit by 10% p.a. The current position, the position if the machinery is bought and the position if the machinery is leased are as follows:

It is clear that the impact of a leasing decision on the financial ratios of a company can be substantial.[23] Although this is a very simple illustration, it does show that the buy versus lease decision has far-reaching consequences in the financial analysis of a company.

	Current £	Buy £	Lease £
Operating profit	40,000	44,000	44,000
Equity capital	200,000	200,000	200,000
Long-term debt	100,000	200,000	100,000
Total capital employed	300,000	400,000	300,000
Gearing ratio	0.5:1	1:1	0.5:1
ROCE	13.33%	11%	14.66%

15.7 Materiality in relation to SSAP 21

The guidance notes on SSAP 21 state that 'the standard need not be applied to immaterial items', where the relevant criterion 'is the size of the lease in the context of the size of the lessee or lessor'. More specifically, the guidance notes also state:

> In deciding whether or not a lease is material, regard should be had to the effect which treating the lease according to the main requirements of the standard (e.g. capitalising it) would have on the financial statements as a whole. Thus, it may be necessary to consider the whole effect of (in this example) capitalisation on (a) total fixed assets, (b) total borrowings and obligations, (c) the gearing ratio and (d) the profit or loss for the year (as a result of the difference between charging the total of depreciation plus financial charge). If capitalisation of the lease would not have a material effect on any of these items, the lease need not be capitalised.

15.8 FRS 5 – *Reporting the Substance of Transactions*[24]

The main principle underlying FRS 5[25] is that transactions should be accounted for on the basis of their economic substance rather than their legal form. In relation to leases, FRS 5 states that 'the general principles of the FRS will also be relevant in ensuring that leases are classified as finance or operating leases in accordance with their substance'. However, to reduce the conflict between FRS 5 and existing standards, the standard with the more specific provisions should be applied. Consequently SSAP 21 remains the relevant accounting standard for dealing with straightforward leases but FRS 5 is the relevant accounting standard for dealing with more complex leases or for leases which form part of a series of transactions.

One particular instance in which FRS 5 tends to be more specific than SSAP 21 is for sale and leaseback arrangements in which the original owner sells an asset but continues to use it by leasing it back. The main issue with sale and leaseback transactions is whether the 'lessee' can derecognise the asset, show any profit or loss on the sale in the P&L account, and treat the lease as an operating lease. The classification will depend on whether substantially all the risks and rewards of asset ownership have, in reality, passed to the buyer. To determine the nature of the transaction, one must consider a series of qualitative tests. Was the sale at market price and are the lease rentals at a market rate? What happens if the value of the leased asset changes? Is the lease term equivalent to the useful economic life of the asset? Does the lessor lease assets as a normal part of business?

The main difference between the requirements of FRS 5 and SSAP 21 is that FRS 5 is much stricter concerning the required accounting treatment of the leased asset. In particular, economic substance requires that the leased asset should remain on the lessee's balance sheet.

One example of this treatment is evident in Associated Nursing Services plc 1997 Annual Report (as a result of adverse comment by the Financial Reporting Review Panel):

> In accordance with SSAP 21 and FRS 5 the assets subject to these sale and leaseback transactions have been retained on the Group's balance sheet and the proceeds of sale are included within creditors as liabilities under sale and leaseback arrangements. The rent payable by the Group throughout the term of the lease is apportioned first as a partial repayment of the related liabilities, and, secondly, as interest charged to profits.

There are a number of other examples of companies applying FRS 5 to classify leases. Vaux Group increased its 1994 balance sheet debt by £26.1m and fixed assets by £24m when it applied FRS 5 to sale and leaseback agreements for two hotels (with an option to repurchase).[26] First Choice Holidays reclassified operating leases on two aircraft and one engine as finance leases, increasing the group's assets by £55.2m.[27]

15.9 FRS 5 – The Private Finance Initiative

An exposure draft proposes an amendment to FRS 5 to take account of transactions subject to the evolving Private Finance Initiative (PFI).[28] The fundamental accounting issue is whether a party to a PFI contract has an asset of the property used to fulfil the contract. The exposure draft sets out the main features of a PFI contract, considers whether SSAP 21 or FRS 5 should be applied to the contract, and explains how the relevant standard should be applied.

Definition (para. F1)

Under a PFI contract, the private sector is responsible for supplying services that traditionally have been provided by the public sector. It is integral to most PFI contracts that the operator designs, builds, finances and operates a property in order to provide the contracted service. Examples of such properties are roads, bridges, hospitals, prisons, information technology systems and educational establishments.

The main features of a PFI contract in brief are (para. F2):

- A contract to provide services is awarded by the purchaser (a public sector entity) to the operator (a private sector entity).
- A property, which is legally owned by the purchaser or leased to the operator, will usually be necessary to perform the contract.
- The PFI contract will specify arrangements for the property at the end of the contract term.
- As a public sector body, the purchaser is required to demonstrate both that the involvement of the private sector offers value for money when compared with alternative ways of providing the services and that there has been a transfer of risk from the public to the private sector.

The exposure draft uses a flow chart to determine whether FRS 5 or SSAP 21 should be used to determine the accounting treatment of the relevant asset. The determination is as follows:

- SSAP 21 should be applied if (a) the contract **can** be separated into property and service elements, and (b) the payments for the property **do not** vary with factors such as usage or the operator's costs.
- FRS 5 should be applied in either of the following cases:
  - the contract **cannot** be separated into property and service elements;
  - (a) the contract **can** be separated into property and service elements, and (b) the payments for the property **do** vary with factors such as usage or the operator's costs.

If FRS 5 should be applied, the benefits and risks of the property and any non-separable services attributable to each party needs to be assessed. This assessment will determine whether the purchaser or the operator recognises the asset of property. The key aspect is that the ASB is insistent that someone recognises the obligation.

15.10 Accounting for leases – a new approach

As discussed earlier in this chapter, SSAP 21 makes a distinction between finance leases and operating leases. However, an international group has questioned this distinction. Standard setters from the UK, Australia, Canada, New Zealand, the USA and the IASC (an extension of the G4 + 1 group) issued a Special Report[29] which concluded that non-cancellable operating leases should be treated in the same way as finance leases. The similar treatment is based on the premise that the rights and obligations created under a lease contract meet the definitions of an asset and liability of a conceptual framework. This approach is consistent with the ASB's draft *Statement of Principles*. The G4 + 1 group issued a discussion paper in 1999.

W. McGregor[30] explained that:

A lease contract conveys a right to a lessee to use the leased property; in the language of the conceptual frameworks, the lessee controls the future economic benefits embodied in the leased property for the period of the lease term. Similarly, the lease contract establishes an obligation on the lessee to sacrifice future economic benefits to an external party in payment for the use of the leased property.

This approach addresses one of the main problems with the current accounting treatment, namely, the potential for framing a finance lease as an operating lease and not having to capitalise the lease contract on the lessee's balance sheet.

The ASB published a Discussion Paper[31] presenting the Position Paper developed by the G4 + 1 standard setters. The main thrust of the paper is that operating leases which are not currently included in the balance sheet would give rise to assets and liabilities reported at the fair value of the rights and obligations conveyed in the lease, e.g. where a lease is only for a small part of an asset's economic life, only that part would be reflected in the lessee's balance sheet. The ASB has said that a persuasive factor in adopting the main principles of the paper is the common and growing practice of analysts recasting financial statements by capitalising operating leases.

In principle it is an attractive idea that all leased assets and liabilities should be treated in the same way to avoid the manipulation we have seen with lease agreements drawn up so that finance leases in substance are classified as operating leases. However, there is a problem that needs to be resolved which is how to measure the asset and liability that is reported in the balance sheet. When treated as an operating lease there was no asset or liability recorded on the face of the balance sheet. Under new proposals the decision has to be made as to whether to include the leased item as an asset at full value in which case the liability would be the present value of the minimum payments plus the obligation to return the asset at the end of the rental period, or at another value such as simply the present value of the minimum payments.

Summary

The initial upturn in leasing activity in the 1970s was attributable to the economy and tax requirements rather than the popularity of lease transactions *per se*. High interest rates, a high inflation rate, 100% first-year tax allowances and a sequence of annual losses in the manufacturing industry made leasing transactions extremely attractive to both the lessors and the lessees.

Once the leasing industry was firmly established, the amount of leasing activity continued to increase, even when many of the original benefits were no longer applicable. The Finance Act 1984 had removed the major tax advantages of leases, but by then many other benefits of leasing as a form of finance had been discovered.

Off-balance-sheet financing was considered a particular advantage of lease financing. SSAP 21 recognised this and attempted to introduce stricter accounting policies and requirements. However, although SSAP 21 introduced the concept of 'substance over form', the hazy distinction between finance and operating leases still allows companies to structure lease agreements to achieve either type of lease. This is important because, while stricter accounting requirements apply to finance leases, operating leases can still be used as a form of off-balance-sheet accounting.

We do not know the real extent to which SSAP 21 is either observed or ignored. However, it is true to say that creative accountants and finance companies are able to circumvent SSAP 21 by using structured leases. FRS 5 should reduce the scope for this practice. Also the IASC have revised IAS 17[32] to require enhanced disclosures by lessees, including disclosure of rental expenses, sublease rentals, and a description of leasing arrangements.

REVIEW QUESTIONS

1 Can the legal position on leases be ignored now that substance over form is used for financial reporting? Discuss.

2 Look at the extract from the Greenalls Group plc at the end of section 15.5. Consider this information in conjunction with the following information:

	1999	1998
	£000	£000
Operating profit	133,382	209,104
Fixed assets	1,665,921	1,892,883
Current assets	158,024	183,134

(a) Consider the effects of both operating leases and finance leases on the 'return on capital employed'.

(b) Consider the importance of the categorisation of lease transactions into operating lease or finance lease decisions when carrying out financial ratio analysis in general. What ratios might be affected?

(c) Discuss the effects of renegotiating/reclassifying all operating leases into finance leases. What effect might it have for Greenalls? For which industries might this classification have a significant impact on the financial ratios?

3 Explain the major provisions of SSAP 21 *Accounting for Leases*.

4 The favourite off-balance-sheet financing trick used to be leasing. Using any illustrative numerical examples you may wish to:

(a) Define the term 'off-balance-sheet financing' and state why it is popular with companies.

(b) Illustrate what is meant by the above quotation in the context of leases and discuss the accounting treatments and disclosures required by SSAP 21 which have limited the usefulness of leasing as an off-balance-sheet financing technique.

(c) Suggest two other off-balance-sheet financing techniques and discuss the effect that each technique has on balance sheet assets and liabilities, and on the profit and loss account.

5 What effect will FRS 5 have on accounting for leases?

6 Private Finance Initiative contracts were discussed in 15.9. Using the Exposure Draft[33] described in that section (and any subsequent accounting releases) find out more details on the following:

(a) In what situations will the contract have separable service elements?

(b) What are the indications that the property is either an asset of the purchaser or the operator?

7 The BOC Group 2001 Accounting Policies state:

Where finance leases have been entered into, the obligations to the lessor are shown as part of borrowings and the rights in the corresponding assets are treated in the same way as owned fixed assets.

(a) Explain the terms 'obligations to the lessor' and 'rights in corresponding assets'.

(b) Explain how these amounts would be quantified in the balance sheet.

(c) Describe the entries that would appear in the profit and loss account.

8 The Body Shop International 2001 Annual Report included the following accounting policy:

Leased assets

Assets held under finance leases are capitalised at amounts approximating to the present value of the minimum lease payments payable over the term of the lease ... Leasing payments are analysed between capital and interest components so that the interest element is charged to the profit and loss account over the period of the lease and approximates to a constant proportion of the balances of capital repayments outstanding.

(a) Explain the terms 'minimym lease payments' and 'approximates to a constant proportion of the balances of capital repayments outstanding.'

(b) Explain why it is necessary to use present values and approximate to a constant proportion.

EXERCISES

An extract from the solution is provided in the appendix at the end of the text for exercises marked with an asterisk (*).

* Question 1

On 1 January 20X8, Grabbit plc entered into an agreement to lease a widgeting machine for general use in the business. The agreement, which may not be terminated by either party to it, runs for six years and provides for Grabbit to make an annual rental payment of £92,500 on 31 December each year. The cost of the machine to the lessor was £350,000, and it has no residual value. The machine has a useful economic life of eight years and Grabbit depreciates its fixed assets using the straight-line method.

Required:

(a) Show how Grabbit plc will account for the above transaction in its balance sheet at 31 December 20X8, and in its profit and loss account for the year then ended, if it capitalises the leased asset in accordance with the principles laid down in SSAP 21.

(b) Explain why the standard setters considered accounting for leases to be an area in need of standardisation and discuss the rationale behind the approach adopted in the standard.

(c) The lessor has suggested that the lease could be drawn up with a minimum payment period of one year and an option to renew. Discuss why this might be attractive to the lessee.

* Question 2

(a) When accounting for hire purchase transactions and finance leases, accountants prefer to overlook legal form in favour of commercial substance.

Required:

Discuss the above statement in the light of the requirements of SSAP 21 *Accounting for Leases and Hire Purchase Contracts*.

(b) State briefly how you would distinguish between a finance lease and an operating lease.

(c) Smarty plc finalises its accounts annually on 31 March. It depreciates its machinery at 20% per annum on cost and adopts the 'Rule of 78' for allocating finance charges among different accounting periods. On 1 August 2007 it acquired machinery on a finance lease on the following agreement:

(i) a lease rent of £500 per month is payable for 36 months commencing from the date of acquisition;

(ii) cost of repairs and insurance are to be met by the lessee;

(iii) on completion of the primary period the lease may be extended for a further period of three years, at the lessee's option, for a peppercorn rent.

The cash price of the machine is £15,000.

Required:

(1) Set out how all ledger accounts reflecting these transactions will appear in each of the four accounting periods 2007/8, 2008/9, 2009/10 and 2010/11.

(2) Show the profit and loss account entries for the year ended 31 March 2008 and balance sheet extracts as at that date.

Question 3

The Mission Company Ltd, whose year end is 31 December, has acquired two items of machinery on leases, the conditions of which are as follows:

Item Y: Ten annual instalments of £20,000 each, the first payable on 1 January 20X0. The machine was completely installed and first operated on 1 January 20X0 and its purchase price on that date was £160,000. The machine has an estimated useful life of ten years, at the end of which it will be of no value.

Item Z: Ten annual instalments of £30,000 each, the first payable on 1 January 20X2. The machine was completely installed and first operated on 1 January 20X2 and its purchase price on that date was £234,000. The machine has an estimated useful life of twelve years, at the end of which it will be of no value.

The Mission Company Ltd accounts for finance charges on finance leases by allocating them over the period of the lease on the sum of the digits method.

Depreciation is charged on a straight-line basis. Ignore taxation.

Required:

(a) Calculate and state the charges to the profit and loss account for 20X6 and 20X7 if the leases were treated as operating leases.

(b) Calculate and state the charge to the profit and loss account for 20X6 and 20X7 if the leases were treated as financial leases and capitalised using the sum of the digits method for the finance charges.

(c) Show how items Y and Z should be incorporated in the balance sheet, and notes thereto, at 31 December 20X7, if capitalised.

Question 4

X Ltd entered into a lease agreement on the following terms:

Cost of leased asset	£100,000
Lease term	5 years
Rentals six-monthly in advance	£12,000
Anticipated residual on disposal of the assets at end of lease term	£10,000
Lessee's interest in residual value	97%
Economic life	8 years
Inception date	1 January 20X4
Lessee's financial year-end	31 December
Implicit rate of interest is applied half-yearly	4.3535%

Required:

(a) Show the profit and loss account entries for the year ended 31 December 20X4 and balance sheet extracts as at that date.

(b) Show the profit and loss account entries for the year ended 31 December 20X7 and balance sheet extracts as at that date.

References

1 C. Drury and S. Braund, 'A survey of UK leasing practice', *Management Accounting*, April 1989, pp. 40–43.

2 N. Cope, 'Big ticket to ride out the recession', *Accountancy*, December 1992, pp. 55–57.

3 R. Perera, 'To buy or not to buy – how to decide', *Certified Accountant*, December 1986.

4 G. Allum *et al.*, 'Fleet focus: to lease or not to lease', *Australian Accountant*, September 1989, pp. 31–58.

5 R.L. Benke and C.P. Baril, 'The lease vs. purchase decision', *Management Accounting*, March 1990, pp. 42–46.

6 B. Underdown and P. Taylor, *Accounting Theory and Policy Making*, Heinemann, 1985, p. 273.

7 Cranfield School of Management, *Financial Leasing Report*, Bedford, 1979.

8 Abdel-Khalik *et al.*, 'The Economic Effects on Lessees of FASB Statement No. 13', *Accounting for Leases*, FASB, 1981.

9 G. Macdonald, in J. Freedman and M. Power (eds), *Law and Accountancy*, Paul Chapman Publishing, 1992, p. 76.

10 R. Owens, 'Why SSAP 21 isn't the answer', *Accountancy*, January 1984, pp. 49–51.

11 SFAS 13, *Accounting for Leases*, FASB, November 1976.

12 IAS 17, *Accounting for Leases*, IASC, September 1982.

13 J.H. Davison, Chairman, Accounting Standards Committee, foreword, SSAP 21, *Accounting for Leases and Hire Purchase Contracts*, 1984.

14 IAS 1, *Disclosure of Accounting Policies*, IASC, 1984.

15 N. Hyndman and R. Kirk, 'The latest accounting standards', *Management Accounting*, December 1989, pp. 20–22.

16 R. Speyer, 'What ED 29 means to the lessee', *Accountancy*, January 1982, pp. 112–115.

17 G. Macmillan, 'Lease accounting update', *Australian Accountant*, March 1986, pp. 36–39.

18 R. Main, *External Financial Reporting*, B. Carsberg and S. Dev (eds), Prentice Hall, 1984.

19 R.H. Gamble, 'Off-balance-sheet diet: greens on the side', *Corporate Cashflow*, August 1990, pp. 28–32.

20 R.L. Benke and C.P. Baril, 'The lease vs. purchase decision', *Management Accounting*, March 1990, pp. 42–46.

21 N. Woodhams and P. Fletcher, 'Operating leases to take bigger market share with changing standards', *Rydge's (Australia)*, September 1985, pp. 100–110.

22 C.H. Volk, 'The risks of operating leases', *Journal of Commercial Bank Lending*, May 1988, pp. 47–52.

23 Chee-Seong Tah, 'Lease or buy?' *Accountancy*, December 1992, pp. 58–59.

24 FRS 5, *Reporting the Substance of Transactions*, ASB, March 1995.

25 I. Sharp, 'A question of substance', *Accountancy*, December 1994, p. 138.

26 'Brewer applies FRS5 just in case', *Accountancy*, March 1995, p. 104.

27 'Leased assets reach balance sheet', *Accountancy*, March 1995, p. 104.

28 Amendment to FRS 5 *Reporting the Substance of Transactions*, 'The Private Finance Initiative' (exposure draft), ASB, December 1997.

29 'G4+1', *'Accounting for Leases – A New Approach'*, July 1996.

30 W. McGregor, 'Lease accounting: righting the wrongs', *Accountancy*, September 1996, p. 96.

31 *Leases: Implementation of a New Approach*, Discussion Paper, ASB, December 1999.

32 IAS 17 (revised), *Accounting for Leases*, IASC, November 1997.

33 Amendment to FRS 5 *Reporting the Substance of Transactions*, 'The Private Finance Initiative' (exposure draft), ASB, December 1997.

CHAPTER 16

R&D; goodwill and intangible assets; brands

16.1 Introduction

In this chapter we consider the accounting treatments of the following:

- Research and development
- Goodwill and intangible assets
- Brands
- Intellectual property.

16.2 Accounting treatment for research and development

In the UK, the accounting treatment for R&D may differ depending on whether the expenditure relates to research expenditure or development expenditure. Broadly speaking, the research expenditure must always be charged to the profit and loss account, and the option to capitalise development expenditure is available only if a strict set of criteria are met. In this section, we will consider why there is pressure to write off research and development expenditure, the accounting requirements for R&D, and how development costs are defined.

16.2.1 Why is there a pressure to write off R&D expenditure?

The Companies Act refers in the balance sheet to costs, rather than to projects or investment in research. However, many readers will think of research and development (R&D) as an investment rather than as a cost. They may well perceive it as a strategic investment that is essential if we are to be competitive in world markets. This applies particularly to an advanced technical industry such as chemicals, where a sustained high level of R&D investment is required.

The 'R&D Scoreboard' is prepared for the DTI by Company Reporting and the *Financial Times*[1] analysed the results for figures published in annual reports up to 31 May 1999. It was reported that the UK has the next to lowest ratio of R&D to sales of any large industrialised country. According to the figures, average R&D-to-sales figures for individual countries were (figures for 2000 have been extracted from the R&D Scoreboard):

	1998	1999	2000
Sweden	7.4%	7.2%	6.5%
Switzerland	6.3%	6.4%	5.7%
Japan	4.8%	4.7%	4.2%

Germany	4.3%	4.2%	4.0%
USA	4.9%	5.7%	4.8%
France	4.0%	4.0%	3.2%
UK	2.5%	2.9%	2.6%
Italy	2.0%	1.8%	2.2%

In the table of 'Top 50 International Companies by R&D Expenditure', only two UK companies feature. An extract, which includes a comparison with each of the top US, German and Japanese companies, is shown below:

Position	Company	Country	1998/9 R&D expenditure (£000)	R&D-to-sales (%)
1	Ford Motor	USA	4,552,149	4.0
3	Daimler/Chrysler	Germany	3,982,779	3.9
6	Matsushita	Japan	3,080,783	7.2
18	Glaxo Wellcome	UK	2,526,000	14.0
25	Astra-Zeneca	UK	1,936,672	16.0

The R&D as a % of sales data is based on overall company position and segmental information would be helpful where companies have diversified and there are different divisional research intensities.

One publication mentioned that the recognition of R&D as an asset had appeared in a report from the House of Lords Select Committee on Science and Technology, stating that 'R&D has to be regarded as an investment which leads to growth, not a cost'.[2,3] Unfortunately, two constraints militate against companies incurring high levels of expenditure. First, there is a commercial constraint: it is felt that a company which pursues a commitment to R&D is vulnerable to takeover bids. It is perhaps an irony that the threat comes from companies that have not had such a commitment. There is presumably an attraction for the company with the lower R&D commitment to mount a takeover with the prospect of a short-term increase in its earnings per share merely by reducing R&D by, say, 25%. That would show an immediate increase in disclosed trading profit.

So why do companies write off all of their research and development costs to the profit and loss account in the year in which the cost arises? As far as the company is concerned, one may hypothesise that directors have been pleased to take the expense in a year when they know its impact rather than carry it forward. They are aware of profit levels in the year in which the R&D arises and could find it embarrassing to take the loss in a subsequent year when profits were lower or the company even reported a trading loss.

This brings us to our second constraint: the difficulty of being reasonably certain that the intended economic benefits of R&D activities will flow to the enterprise. Because of this uncertainty, the accounting profession has traditionally considered it more prudent to write off the investment in research as a cost rather than report it as an asset in the balance sheet.

ED 14, the initial exposure draft issued in 1975, was influenced by the prudence concept, and required companies to write off all R&D expenditure in the year in which it arose. This was changed in the following year by the proposal in ED 17 that companies should be required to capitalise development costs.

The standard that eventually appeared was different again. A compromise was arrived at in SSAP 13, which permitted, rather than required, a company to capitalise development costs, provided stringent conditions were met. Companies were permitted the choice of treatment provided there was disclosure in the notes to the accounts. The Companies Act also permitted capitalisation, but only in special circumstances.

Directors wanted the capacity to choose the accounting treatment on a variety of grounds. Some felt that it would give their competitors an advantage if the build-up of a large development cost flagged the fact that a new product was about to be launched. Others rated a strong balance sheet higher than commercial secrecy and wanted to be able to include the asset on the balance sheet. Neither of these reasons has any basis in accounting principles, but the accounting profession was subject to the constraints of consensus standard-setting.

In its *Statement of Intent: Comparability of Financial Statements*, the IASC is moving away from these constraints.[4] It is proposing that the choice should be removed and that, if development costs meet the conditions for capitalisation, they must be capitalised and depreciated. This is the approach that has since been adopted by IAS 9[5] and IAS 38.[6]

There has been some research on both analysts'[7] and accountants'[8] reactions to R&D expenditure. Nixon[9] found that 'Two important dimensions of the corporate reporting accountants' perspective emerge: first, disclosure is seen as more important than the accounting treatment of R&D expenditure and, second, the financial statements are not viewed as the primary channel of communication for information on R&D'.

16.2.2 How are development costs defined?

SSAP 13 has given a definition of development costs and also sets out the conditions that need to be met in order to capitalise.

Development costs are defined in SSAP 13 as costs relating to the development of the company's use of knowledge acquired through research to produce new or substantially improved materials, devices, products, processes, systems or services before commercial production begins.

Examples of activities that are typically development are the evaluation of product or process alternatives; the design, construction and testing of preproduction prototypes and models; the design of tools, jigs, moulds and dies involving new technology; and the design, construction and operation of a pilot plant that is not of an economically feasible scale for commercial production.

The types of cost that are included within this classification are those incurred in R&D activities relating to salaries and wages; the costs of materials and services consumed; the depreciation of property, plant and equipment to the extent that they are used for R&D activities; overhead costs related to R&D activities: and other related costs such as the amortisation of patents and licences.

The standard also defines pure and applied research. Pure research is experimental or theoretical work undertaken primarily to acquire new scientific or technical knowledge for its own sake, rather than directed towards any specific aim or application. Applied research is original or critical investigation undertaken in order to gain new scientific or technical knowledge and directed towards a specific practical aim or objective.

Neither pure nor applied research may be capitalised under existing standards and legislation. This conflicts with the view put forward by the select committee that research is an investment.

Activities that are related to research and to development but are not classified as either include engineering follow-through in an early phase of commercial production; quality control during commercial production, including routine testing of products; troubleshooting in connection with breakdowns during commercial production; routine efforts to refine, enrich or otherwise improve on the qualities of an existing product;

adaptation of an existing capability to a particular requirement or customer's need as part of a continuing commercial activity; seasonal or other periodic design changes to existing products; routine design of tools, jigs, moulds and dies; and activities, including design and construction engineering, related to the construction, relocation, rearrangement or start-up of facilities or equipment other than facilities whose sole use is for a particular R&D development project.

The conditions that SSAP 13 requires to be met for development costs to be capitalised are as follows:

- There is a clearly defined project. Without this it would be difficult to ensure appropriate matching of revenue and expense. There would be a temptation in a poor year for a company to decide that costs should be classified as development and inappropriately carried forward.

- The expenditure on the project is separately identifiable. This relates to the first point. The amount carried forward needs to be verifiable.

- The outcome of the project has been assessed with reasonable certainty as to its technical feasibility and commercial viability. This requires a level of confidence that the future benefits and costs are not so uncertain that it is impossible to assess whether the project will be commercially successful.

- Revenue will exceed costs. This requires that there should be a matching of revenues and expenses and the recognition of a causal relationship between the development costs and the increased future benefits arising from subsequent sales.

- Adequate resources can reasonably be expected to be available to allow the project to be completed, including any consequential increases in working capital. This is an assessment of the financial structure of the company. It looks at solvency, liquidity and financing capability.

Alternative treatment of development costs

SSAP 13 states that development expenditure *may* be deferred if the above conditions are met (although many companies have an accounting policy of writing off immediately) and that fixed assets should be depreciated, e.g. Severn Trent plc 2000 annual report accounting policy states:

> Research and development
> Research and development expenditure is charged to the profit and loss account in the year in which it is incurred. Expenditure on fixed assets relating to research and development projects is written off over the expected useful life of those assets.

Where a company reports under IAS 38 *Intangible Assets* the reason for writing off rather than deferring is stated, e.g. Serona SA, which is Europe's largest biotech company, states in its 2000 annual report accounting policy:

> Research and development
> Research and development costs are generally expensed as incurred. In the opinion of management, due to the regulatory and other uncertainties inherent in the development of the company's new products, the criteria for development costs to be recognised as an asset, as prescribed by IAS 38 (Intangible Assets) are not met until the product has received regulatory approval...

Where the development costs, together with any further development costs, related production costs and selling and administrative costs directly incurred in marketing the product, are not probably recoverable from related future revenues, then the part that is not recovered should be written off as an expense in the profit and loss account.

To illustrate partial deferral, the R&D policy of Racal (now part of the Thales Group) and the amount charged to the profit and loss account is included below:

Racal Electronics plc Annual Reports and Accounts 1999

Accounting policies
Research and Development – Private venture research and development expenditure is written off in the year in which it is incurred. Uninvoiced research and development fully funded by customers is carried forward as work in progress.

Operating profit arrived at after:

	1999 £m
Research and development:	
Continuing operations	44.0
Discontinued operations	5.9

16.3 Introduction to goodwill and intangible assets

The discussion of goodwill and intangibles proceeds as follows:

- the current position is considered briefly;
- historical developments are considered;
- goodwill and intangibles are introduced along with an illustration of their accounting treatment;
- the economic consequences of accounting for goodwill are discussed;
- the amortisation of goodwill is discussed;
- the main requirements of FRS 10 are set out and evaluated.

16.4 Introduction to the current position

The question of what is the appropriate accounting treatment for both goodwill and intangible assets has posed problems for the accounting standard-setting bodies for many years. In particular, accounting for goodwill has been continually under discussion for about twenty-five years. A number of exposure drafts and standards have been issued to address the problems associated with it. Each successive attempt to tackle goodwill received criticism from the profession, management or academic accountants. The latest accounting standard to deal with goodwill (FRS 10[9]) has tackled the associated problem of accounting for other intangibles within the same standard.

The stated objective of FRS 10 is to ensure that:

(a) capitalised goodwill and intangible assets are charged in the profit and loss account in the periods in which they are depleted; and

(b) sufficient information is disclosed in the financial statements to enable users to determine the impact of goodwill and intangible assets on the financial position and performance of the reporting entity. (para. 1)

In the summary to FRS 10, it states that:

> Purchased goodwill and intangible assets should be capitalised as assets. Internally generated goodwill should not be capitalised and internally developed intangible assets should be capitalised only where they have a readily ascertainable market value (para. d).

In addition, capitalised assets are subject to amortisation and/or impairment review. These requirements are explained in more detail later in the chapter.

However, as with its predecessors, FRS 10 has not received unanimous support. Although FRS 10 has been greeted by some as the ultimate solution, Paterson[10] contests this view:

> The publication of FRS 10 … was hailed as the culmination of a long debate within the accounting profession. However, I find it hard to regard this standard as having brought the debate to a real conclusion. I have little doubt that it will in due course be replaced by a further standard, and indeed FRS 10's own useful life may be found to be quite limited.

Although FRS 10 applies to both goodwill and intangible assets, they are differentiated and the requirements are stated separately within the accounting standard. Although some of the required accounting treatments apply to both goodwill and intangible assets, Paterson[10] argues that the attempt to cater for both in a single standard has some severe drawbacks:

> I am also concerned that this issue [goodwill] has dominated the ASB's thinking, with the result that both negative goodwill and the wider issue of intangibles have received less attention than they deserve.

16.5 Historical developments

The accounting treatment of goodwill has been under consideration since the early 1970s. Since then the standard-setters have produced a series of discussion papers, exposure drafts and accounting standards, culminating in FRS 10. Some of the key publications include:

- ED 30[11]
- EC Seventh Directive[12]
- SSAP 22[13]
- ED 44[14]
- SSAP 22 revised[15]
- ED 47[16]
- Corfield Report[17]
- ASB Discussion Paper[18]
- ASB Working Paper[19]
- FRED 12[20]
- FRS 10[19]

In 1993 the ASB issued a discussion paper *Goodwill and Intangible Assets*, in which it suggested a restrictive approach to reporting intangible assets and in which it set out six possible treatments for goodwill.

It stated that internally generated intangibles should not be recognised in the balance sheet; intangibles acquired on the acquisition of another business should be subsumed within the goodwill arising on acquisition. This was far too general a treatment to provide either a true and fair view or the commercial substance of the transaction. The reasoning was no doubt the ASB's concern that companies would use the availability of separating intangibles from goodwill in order to change materially the accounting message communicated to the shareholders by a process of arbitrage.

The ASB did not recommend any single treatment in its discussion paper concerning goodwill, but, as a way of focusing the debate, the Board indicated support for capitalisation and predetermined life amortisation and separate write-off reserve.

In 1995 the ASB issued a working paper *Goodwill and Intangible Assets*, in which it stated that the approach to intangibles had been reconsidered. The revised proposal was that **internally generated** intangibles may be recognised, but only when there is a specific accounting standard, e.g. SSAP 13 *Accounting for Research and Development*,[21] allowing their recognition or when they have a **reliable market value** obtainable from frequent transactions in a **homogeneous population** of identical assets.[22] Also the ASB agreed that where goodwill has an indefinitely long life, this longevity should be mirrored in the accounting treatment.

Following these publications, the ASB released FRED 12 and then FRS 10. FRS 10 broadly follows FRED 12.[23,24] In the next two sections we introduce intangible assets followed by goodwill.

16.6 Intangible assets

16.6.1 Introduction to intangible assets

FRS 10 defines **intangible assets** and describes some categories of intangible assets:

- 'Non-financial fixed assets that do not have physical substance but are identifiable and controlled by the legal entity through custody or legal rights' (para. 2). Therefore, they fall within the definition of an asset when the reporting entity controls the access to the future economic benefits that it represents.

- 'Licences, quotas, patents, copyrights, franchises and trade marks are examples of categories that may be treated as separate classes of intangible assets' (para. 2).

The real debate concerning intangibles begins with the issue of initial recognition – can an intangible asset be separately identified? Then, even if it can be separately identified, how should it be measured? There are a number of principal methods which have been used to value intangibles,[25] but opponents argue that in general these valuations are not sufficiently reliable to allow their inclusion in the financial statements.

Once an intangible asset has been recognised in the financial statements, further difficulties arise. How should this asset be amortised (depreciated)? What is the useful economic life of the asset? Is the useful life infinite? How should any reductions in value be measured and/or treated in the accounts?

16.6.2 Impact of FRS 10 on accounting policies

Prior to FRS 10 companies applied a range of different accounting policies ranging from attaching no value to intangible assets (with no accompanying note explaining this treatment) to capitalising with no annual amortisation on grounds there was no permanent diminution to capitalising with annual amortisation.

Following FRS 10 companies have amended their accounting policies, as with EMI Group for music publishing copyrights and Charterhouse Communications plc for publishing rights.

The EMI Group in its 1997 accounting policies stated:

Music Publishing Copyrights purchased prior to 1 April 1989 were written off against shareholders' funds on acquisition. Copyrights acquired as a result of the acquisition of a business, on or after 1 April 1989, are treated as intangible assets in the Group balance sheet. The capitalised amount of such copyrights, being their purchase cost, is subject to amortisation only to the extent that the royalty income generated by the total music publishing portfolio is insufficient to support its book value. All costs attributable to copyrights obtained in the normal course of trade, and not as a result of the acquisition of a business, are written off as incurred.

In its 1999 Annual Report (and subsequent years), EMI has changed its accounting policy due to the FRS 10 rigorous impairment review requirement. Its Accounting Policy reads as follows:

Music copyrights

Music publishing copyrights purchased prior to 1 April 1989 were written off against shareholders' funds on acquisition. Copyrights acquired as a result of acquisitions on or after 1 April 1989 have previously been capitalised as intangible assets in the Group balance sheet, but amortised only to the extent that royalty income generated by the total music publishing copyrights portfolio was insufficient to support its book value.

On adoption of FRS 10, our accounting policy for copyrights had to change because we could not perform the detailed annual impairment review required by FRS 10 to support an indefinite useful economic life. Consequently, copyrights are now amortised by equal annual amounts over up to 20 years, other than in exceptional circumstances when sufficient ongoing impairment tests can be performed to support a useful economic life of over 20 years. Where a useful economic life of up to 20 years has been adopted, copyrights are reviewed for impairment at the end of the first full financial year following acquisition and in other periods if events or changes in circumstances indicate that the carrying value may not be recoverable.

Charterhouse Communications includes newly acquired publishing rights in its financial statements. Note that the intangible assets dwarf the tangible assets. In its annual reports and accounts 1998 it stated:

Accounting policies

Intangible Fixed Assets – Publishing rights and titles are stated at cost in these financial statements. On an annual basis, the directors consider the fair value of these assets on the basis of cash flow projections. Amortisation is not provided as there has been no permanent diminution in their value.

Balance Sheet at 31 May 1998

Fixed assets	£000
Intangible assets	6,501
Tangible assets	92
Investments	—
	6,593

In its 2001 accounting policy this has been changed to state:

Amortisation is calculated to write down the cost of goodwill and intangible assets through the Group's profit and loss account over their expected useful economic lives subject to a maximum period of 20 years, in accordance with FRS 10 'Goodwill and Intangible Assets'.

16.7 Goodwill

16.7.1 Introduction to goodwill

FRS 10 defines purchased goodwill as 'the difference between the cost of an acquired entity and the aggregate of the fair values of an entity's identifiable assets and liabilities'. Fair values (according to FRS 6 and 7) have been explained in an earlier chapter and their effect on goodwill is considered in section 18.10.

16.7.2 Goowill may be positive or negative

Goodwill is positive if the agreed value of the business based on future cash flows is greater than the aggregate of the fair value of the identifiable assets and liabilities. It is negative if the agreed value of the business based on future cash flows is lower than the aggregate of the fair value of the identifiable assets and liabilities.

16.7.3 Goodwill may also be realised or unrealised

Goodwill is realised if it is arrived at as a result of an actual transfer of the business for consideration. It is unrealised if an actual transfer of the business has not occurred, but the directors have estimated a value for the business as a whole and the separable net assets. If there has been an actual transfer, the difference is referred to as **purchased** goodwill. If there has not been an actual transfer, the estimated difference is referred to as non-purchased or **inherent** goodwill.

Purchased goodwill is based on a transaction with a third party at arm's length; the difference is objective and verifiable. Non-purchased goodwill has not arisen from a transaction with a third party at arm's length; the difference is subjective.

For financial reporting purposes, it is normal accounting practice that only purchased goodwill should be recognised in the accounts.

We illustrate the calculation of goodwill using the CW Group.

EXAMPLE ● Assume that on 31 December 20X1 Cooper Woosnam plc (CW plc) purchases all of the assets and liabilities of Worthington Windsurfers plc (WW plc) for £300,000. (Note CW is *not* acquiring the shares in WW plc.) The separate balance sheets as at 31 December 20X1 immediately prior to the purchase are shown below:

	CW plc £000	WW plc £000	Fair value estimate £000
Fixed assets			
Goodwill			
Plant and machinery	1,000	110	150
Net current assets	1,050	90	90
	2,050	200	240
Long-term creditors	450	40	40
	1,600	160	200
Capital and reserves			
Share capital	900	150	150
Share premium account	300	—	—
Profit and loss account	400	10	10
Revaluation reserve			40
	1,600	160	200

A revaluation reserve will arise only if the fair values are actually incorporated into the books of WW plc. It will not appear in the books of CW plc.

The purchased goodwill is calculated as:

Valuable consideration paid – Fair value (estimate) of identifiable assets and liabilities

= £300,000 – £200,000
= £100,000

The goodwill will appear as an intangible asset in the accounts of CW plc as follows:

	CW plc £000	
Fixed assets		
Goodwill	100	
Plant and machinery	1,150	
Net current assets	840	(1,050 – 300 + 90)
	2,090	
Long-term creditors	(490)	
	1,600	
Capital and reserves		
Share capital	900	
Share premium account	300	
Profit and loss account	400	
	1,600	

Note that the £300,000 is an arm's-length payment and is verifiable. However, even though goodwill arises as a result of an arm's-length transaction, the fair values attached to the separable assets are subjective. In this example, an increase of £40,000 is made to the plant; it is an estimate made by the directors of CW plc. The result of the increase in the fair value over the book value is that a lower goodwill figure is calculated than would have appeared using book values. This means that there is scope for the directors of CW plc to adjust the purchased goodwill figure by revising the fair value estimates.

We often meet goodwill in the context of a takeover of one company by another. We illustrate this using the same data for both companies, but now assuming that CW plc acquires all of the issued shares of WW plc instead of the individual assets and liabilities.

EXAMPLE ● Assume that on 31 December 20X1 Cooper Woosnam plc (CW plc) purchases all the equity shares in Worthington Windsurfers plc (WW plc) for £300,000 for a cash consideration. The separate balance sheets as at 31 December 20X1 immediately after the acquisition of the shares are shown below:

The purchased goodwill is calculated exactly as in the preceding example:

Valuable consideration paid − Fair value (estimate) of identifiable assets and liabilities

= £300,000 − £200,000 = £100,000

	CW plc £000	WW plc £000	Fair value estimate £000
Fixed assets			
Plant and machinery	1,000	110	150
Investment in WW plc	300		
Net current assets	750	90	90
	2,050	200	240
Long-term creditors	450	40	40
	1,600	160	200
Capital and reserves			
Share capital	900	150	150
Share premium account	300	—	—
Profit and loss account	400	10	10
Revaluation reserve	—	—	40
	1,600	160	200

We have discussed the possibility for directors to make goodwill larger or smaller by adjusting the fair value of the assets and liabilities. In the past it has also been possible for the directors to increase the goodwill figure by providing for reorganisation costs that might arise on integrating the new subsidiary into the group.

If CW plc acquires the shares of WW plc, the goodwill appears in the consolidated accounts and not in the balance sheet of CW plc. The consolidated balance sheet immediately after the acquisition of the shares would be as follows:

CW consolidated balance sheet
£000

Fixed assets

Goodwill	100
Plant and machinery	1,150
Investment in WW plc	—
Net current assets	840
	2,090
Long-term creditors	490
	1,600

Capital and reserves

Share capital	900
Share premium account	300
Profit and loss account	400
	1,600

This meant that there was scope for the directors of CW plc to adjust the purchased goodwill figure, e.g. by revising the fair value estimates as in Example 1 or by making a provision for reorganisation costs. However FRS 7 was introduced to prevent abuse by overprovisioning.

The following illustration is from the 2001 Annual Report of Galliford Try plc on its acquisition of Burton Communications Ltd and Gerald Wood Homes Ltd:

	Burton book value £000	Gerald Wood book value £000	Total book value £000	Fair value adjustment £000	Assets acquired £000
Fixed assets	3	–	3	–	3
Land and work in progress	–	2,366	2,366	447	2,813
Bank and cash balances	14	–	14	–	14
Bank loans	–	(1,474)	(1,474)	–	(1,474)
Net current assets/(liabilities)	7	(620)	(613)	–	(613)
Deferred tax	–	–	–	(134)	(134)
	24	272	296	313	609
Total consideration					1,344
Goodwill					735

16.7.4 Implication of FRS 7 *Fair Values in Acquisition Accounting*

On making an acquisition it became customary for the acquiring company to reduce the apparent value of the net assets that were being acquired by creating provisions as at the date of the acquisition. These were described as provisions for future losses and provisions for the cost of reorganising a company following acquisition. As a result the goodwill figure was increased. We have already seen that there was no requirement for the goodwill amount to be amortised through the profit and loss account of future years. This is illustrated in the following example.

EXAMPLE ● Pushy plc, which was making a consistent profit of £50m per year, acquired all of the shares in Slow plc, which was making a consistent profit of £8m per year. The acquisition was made for a cash consideration of £40m on 1 January 20X7. The balance sheets of the two companies as at 1 January 20X7 were as follows:

	Pushy plc £m	Slow plc book values £m	Slow plc fair values £m
Fixed assets	100	20	18
Net current assets	80	15	14
	180	35	32
Share capital	50	20	
Reserves	130	15	
	180	35	

The initial calculation of the goodwill figure was as follows:

	£m
Cost of shares in Slow plc	40
Less: Fair value of net assets	(32)
Goodwill	8

At this point, the creative genius of the directors came into play. If the company estimated that the costs of reorganisation were going to be £12m, the position would change:

	£m	£m
Cost of shares in Slow plc		40
Less: Fair value of net assets	32	
Less: Provision for cost of reorganisation	(12)	(20)
Goodwill		20

In any of the years following the acquisition, the provision could be used to soak up expenses, and the profits of the combined group would be inflated as follows:

Pre FRS 7 and FRS 10

	Normal profits £m	Reorganisation costs incurred £m	Reorganisation provision released £m	Profits reported £m
20X7	50 + 8	(10)	10	58
20X8	50 + 8	(10)	10	58

The reported profit would be increased above normal profit of £58m if the fair value provision made exceeded the reorganisation costs incurred.

Post FRS 7 and FRS 10

There are two differences:

● Reorganisation provisions are not allowed
● Goodwill is required to be amortised (now left unchanged at £8m)

	Normal profits	Reorganisation costs incurred	Re-organisation provision released (no provision created)	Goodwill amortised assume 20 years	Profits reported
	£m	£m	£m	£m	£m
20X7	50 + 8	(10)		(0.4)	47.6
20X8	50 + 8	(10)		(0.4)	47.6

The effect of this was to charge expenses incurred in the period following the acquisition to the goodwill account, i.e. capitalise the expenses. Some will argue that this is entirely appropriate because the reorganisation costs are actually in the nature of capital outlay. The finance director of Reed-Elsevier and chairman of the 100 Group of UK Finance Directors took this view when he stated that there needed to be a distinction between revenue and capital items; that while provisioning against future losses should not be permissible, restructuring costs were a capital item and should be treated as such.

However, the investment community believed that companies were abusing the opportunity to create provisions by overprovisioning at the time of an acquisition to bolster subsequent years' accounts. The ASB took a similar view and issued FRS 7 *Fair Values in Acquisition*, which stated that the identifiable assets and liabilities to be recognised in the fair value/goodwill calculation should be those of the acquired entity that **existed** at the date of the acquisition. Provisions for reorganisation costs **expected** to be incurred as a result of the acquisition are not permitted because they were not liabilities of the acquired company at the date of acquisition.

In other words, the ASB considers management intent an insufficient basis for recognising changes to an entity's assets and liabilities. This is a different approach from that taken in the USA and in international accounting standards. No doubt, in taking this strong line, the ASB was influenced less by the niceties of theory than by the need to counteract the abuses that were occurring unchecked prior to FRS 7. Companies have only themselves to blame.

16.7.5 Accounting for purchased goodwill

The source of most disagreement in the goodwill debate has centred on which of two accounting treatments should be used to account for purchased goodwill. The two methods are:

● Goodwill should be treated as an asset and written off over its expected useful life through the profit and loss account.
● Goodwill should not be treated as an asset, but should be written off against reserves in the year of acquisition.

Prior to the publication of FRS 10, SSAP 22 allowed a choice of the two different methods with the preferred method being immediate write-off. **Under FRS 10 this choice has been removed and the purchased goodwill should be capitalised as an asset and amortised over its useful life and/or subject to an impairment review.**

We can illustrate the two treatments with the CW Group, whose balance sheets as at 31 December 20X1, the date of acquisition, are shown in Figure 16.1.

As can be seen from the figure, if the policy of immediate write-off against reserve is followed, the reserve (in this case the profit and loss balance) is reduced by the value of the purchased goodwill. This means that the original value of £400,000 is reduced by £100,000 to a value of £300,000.

If the policy is to capitalise and amortise, goodwill is held as an intangible asset of £100,000 in the balance sheet and amortised through the profit and loss account over its useful economic life. Assuming that the directors of CW plc decide to amortise the goodwill over twenty years, the goodwill diminishes by £5,000 each year.

Following these accounting policies, at 31 December 20X2 the balance sheet will record goodwill at £95,000 (£100,000 – £5,000), and 'other income and expenses' of £5,000 will be charged to the profit and loss account. Note that this method has an impact on the earnings and therefore on the EPS in the twenty years following the acquisition.

Each of these methods attracts a degree of criticism. The most important explanation, then, for the general criticism of capitalisation and amortisation of purchased goodwill is the effect it has on reported earnings and EPS. An annual amortisation charge to the profit and loss account will naturally lower the reported earnings and the resultant EPS figure.

Immediate write-off is criticised because it results in the understatement of balance sheet totals. But, given the choice, past practice has shown that UK companies prefer a weakened balance sheet to the threat of a reduction in the all-important EPS.

The potential effect of the amortisation versus immediate write-off decision on financial statements was demonstrated by WPP's 1998 report and accounts. In the notes to the accounts, WPP adjusted its UK financial statements to take account of US accounting practices.

Figure 16.1 Comparison of immediate write-off with amortisation of goodwill

	CW plc £000	WW plc £000	Fair value £000	Write off immediately £000	Amortise over life £000
		Consolidated CW Group			
Fixed assets					
Goodwill				—	100
Plant and machinery	1,000	110	150	1,150	1,150
Investment in WW plc	300				
Net current assets	750	90	90	840	840
	2,050	200	240	1,990	2,090
Long-term creditors	(450)	(40)	(40)	(490)	(490)
	1,600	160	200	1,500	1,600
Capital and reserves					
Share capital	900	150	150	900	900
Share premium account	300	—	—	300	300
Profit and loss account	400	10	10	300	400
Revaluation reserve			40		
	1,600	160	200	1,500	1,600

	1998
	£m
Net income before dividends under UK GAAP	140.3
US GAAP adjustments:	
Amortisation of goodwill and other intangibles	(38.2)
Executive compensation	(2.6)
Net income as adjusted for US GAAP	99.5

The WPP accounts demonstrate that the adjustment for US GAAP (notably the capitalisation and amortisation of goodwill) has decreased the earnings per share from 19.1p to 13.5p. This is clearly a significant change – a reduction of almost 30%.

16.8 Economic consequences of each method

We have seen that amortisation has an effect on future EPS, while immediate write-off has an effect on the balance sheet structure. Writing off goodwill against reserves acts to distort some of the primary ratios, since it reduces the shareholders' reserves and therefore the capital employed as well. This has important effects on inter-firm comparison. As an example, let us compare WPP's UK accounts with its US-adjusted accounts. If we concentrate purely on the goodwill adjustments, what is the effect on the return on capital employed (ROCE) ratio as per the above? In brief, the profit in the US is decreased by the annual amortisation charge and the capital employed is increased by the capitalised value of goodwill (which had been written off in the UK). This will reduce the US ROCE. For comparability, the accounts need to be adjusted so that they use exactly the same goodwill policy.

Gearing ratios are also affected by writing off goodwill against reserves. These ratios include:

$$\text{Gearing ratio} = \frac{\text{Total liability} - \text{Current liability}}{\text{Capital employed}}$$

The gearing ratio measures the proportion of capital employed which has been raised by fixed interest debt. A highly geared company has a high proportion of borrowings, while a company with low gearing relies more on shareholders' funds and equity. The gearing ratio is interpreted in different ways by different users: shareholders might seek higher ratios because this will increase the EPS; creditors might prefer lower ratios as this means that there are fewer secured claims against the company's assets.

16.9 FRS 10

16.9.1 Summary of FRS 10

In 1997, the ASB published FRS 10, which superseded SSAP 22. We consider some of its requirements here. In addition some responses to a working paper concerning specific aspects of goodwill and intangibles are included in this section.[26]

Goodwill

● After purchase should be capitalised and classified as an asset on the balance sheet.

● Internally generated goodwill should not be capitalised.

Intangible assets

- Separately purchased intangibles should be capitalised as an asset on the balance sheet.
- If the value of an intangible asset acquired as part of the acquisition of a business can be measured reliably on initial recognition then it should be capitalised separately from goodwill.
- Internally developed intangibles may be capitalised if they have a readily ascertainable market value.

Cadbury Scwheppes support this separation of goodwill and other intangibles:

> We strongly believe that any attempt to subsume all intangibles in goodwill is nothing less than a cop out. The modern business environment is very different from that which existed twenty or thirty years ago and it is clear that accounting, like many other activities, must move with the times. Many intangibles are far more significant to certain types of business than tangible assets (e.g. a drinks franchise business) and not to recognise them is to present an incomplete picture.[27]

Their view is understandable given the significance of intangible assets in their 1999 accounts:

	£m
Intangible assets	1,656
Goodwill	69
	1,725
Shareholders' funds	2,240

Recent standards by the IASC include IAS 38[28] and IAS 22 (revised).[29] On initial inspection it appears that the IASC have expanded the potential for capitalising internally generated intangible assets. Capitalisation is permitted whenever costs can be measured reliably rather than when the assets are traded on an active market. However, IAS 38 specifically excludes the cost of generating brands, mastheads and similar assets.

Amortisation

- Purchased goodwill and intangible assets with a limited useful economic life should be amortised on a systematic basis over that period. The rebuttable assumption is that this period is twenty years or less. These intangible assets should only be subject to an impairment review in the year following acquisition and if specific circumstances indicate that the carrying value may not be recoverable.

Kalamazoo questions capitalisation and amortisation with regard to intellectual property rights (IPR) of software products:

> This practice could potentially result in a discrepancy in the treatment of IPR in computer software companies, with acquired software products being capitalised as assets but internal R&D written off ... in fact the estimated useful life of a software product is notoriously difficult to predict and it is regarded as prudent by the industry to write off such expenditure in the year in which it is incurred. If this logic were consistently applied to acquired software products the buyer would be expected to write off the entire value of IPR acquired to the P&L account in the year of acquisition.[30]

It is interesting to note that in its 2001 Annual Report, Invensys plc, a leading global provider of automation and controls, changed its accounting policy as follows:

On 7 September 2000 Invensys plc announced that it had reviewed its software development capitalisation policy ... and decided to discontinue the policy of capitalising such costs.

The company then proceeded to write off the book value of existing software development costs against the profit and loss reserve.

Impairment

- FRS 11[31] provides that intangible assets with an indefinite useful economic life should not be amortised but should be subject to impairment review at the end of each reporting period. The procedures for carrying out an impairment review were originally published in an exposure draft (FRED 15).

Although there has been an accounting standard on impairment in the USA since 1995, impairment reviews have received mixed reactions in the UK over recent years. Unilever's comments were:

We continue to believe that it [impairment testing] will be a costly and impractical exercise in many cases, and will inevitably involve a considerable element of subjective judgement.[32]

Guinness responded:

Having been involved in the field testing for the new impairment review procedures we are pleased to have been able to conclude that they:
(a) required relatively limited expertise and effort;
(b) were straightforward to apply and required only data that is readily at head office;
(c) gave credible results that corresponded with management expectations;
(d) called for no more subjective judgement than that necessary when evaluating an acquisition or producing the Group's Financial and Strategic Plan.[33]

16.9.2 The impairment review

According to Sir David Tweedie, ASB Chairman on introducing FRS 11:

There has been a need for more consistency in the way in which companies recognise and measure impairment losses. FRS 11 will improve comparability and transparency and it will introduce a welcome note of reality in the valuation of fixed assets. It will no longer be possible to pretend that long-standing losses with no realistic hope of recovery are temporary. FRS 11 also completes the package of requirements for goodwill and intangible assets. Companies with goodwill and assets with indefinite lives now have the equipment they need to perform impairment reviews instead of charging arbitrary amounts of depreciation against the profit and loss account.[34]

The ASB argues that FRS 11 'puts forward a coherent and consistent approach for measuring and recognising impairments of fixed assets and goodwill'.[34] The main aspects of the proposals are:

- In general, an impairment review only needs to be carried out if there is an indication that impairment has taken place. Examples include expected future losses; a significant adverse change in either the business or its market (e.g. entry of a competing product); physical damage; a significant adverse change in the legal or other regulatory environment; a significant decrease in market value; a forthcoming reorganisation; or, loss of key employees.

● Although it is preferable to test individual assets for impairment, it might be possible only to test groups of assets. In this case, the impairment should be carried out on the smallest group of assets (income generating unit) which produce a largely independent income stream.

● Impairment is measured by comparing the carrying value of the assets with the recoverable amount. The recoverable amount is the higher of the selling price (net realisable value) and the value in use.

● 'Value in use' is computed by discounting the asset or income-generating unit's expected cash flows at a rate of return that the market would expect from an equally risky asset. This rate of return is a post-tax interest rate which might equate to the implicit rate implicit in market transactions of similar assets or the weighted average cost of capital (WACC) of a listed company (with similar risk profile).

● The rules for restoring past impairment losses for intangible assets and goodwill are strict. It is possible to recognise reversals if both the initial impairment and the subsequent reversal were due to external factors. However, the restrictions do not allow the recognition of internally generated goodwill.

Although these proposals do provide some guidance for tackling impairment, it is unclear whether they will deliver the 'coherent and consistent approach' suggested by the ASB. For instance, the 'value in use' depends on how the income generating units are determined, the assumptions underlying the expected cash flows, and the discount rate selected.

16.9.3 Negative goodwill

Negative goodwill should be recognised in the profit and loss account over the period in which non-monetary assets are depreciated or sold. Any negative goodwill in excess of non-monetary assets acquired should be recognised in the profit and loss account in the periods expected to be benefited. The amount of the release should be separately disclosed in the profit and loss account.

The following is an extract from the 2001 Annual Report of Babcock International Group plc:

> Where the fair value of the separable net assets exceeds the fair value of the consideration for an acquired undertaking the difference is treated as negative goodwill and is capitalised and amortised through the profit and loss account in the period in which the non-monetary assets acquired are recovered. In the case of fixed assets this is the period over which they are depreciated, and in the case of current assets, the period over which they are sold or otherwise realised.

16.9.4 What happens to goodwill previously written off to reserves?

Perhaps one of the biggest difficulties both users and preparers will face is the accounting treatment of goodwill previously written off to reserves. Although FRS 10 states that ideally this goodwill should be reinstated, it recognises that 'this will not always be practicable in all circumstances, and therefore does not require reinstatement' (para. 68). In other words, FRS 10 allows flexibility and choice in the treatment of goodwill associated with 'old' acquisitions. This means that balance sheets in the future might consist of some capitalised purchased goodwill and some purchased goodwill written off to reserves.

It remains to be seen quite how the transitional arrangements are applied in practice. The arrangements for both goodwill and other intangibles are summarised as follows:

● Goodwill previously written off to reserves can remain eliminated. However, it must be offset against the profit and loss account or another appropriate reserve, not shown as a separate goodwill reserve. Also, it must be taken into account if the related business is disposed of.

● Goodwill previously written off to reserves can be reinstated as an asset. It can be reinstated in totality or excluding either pre-FRS 7 goodwill or pre-1989 goodwill where there is insufficient information.

● Any capitalised internally developed intangible assets which do not meet the new recognition criteria should be written off by making a prior year adjustment.

● Any impairment losses on capitalised goodwill or intangible assets that are due to the initial implementation of the new standard should be reported as a current year loss.

For example, consider the impact of restatement of goodwill previously written off to reserves on a company such as The GGT Group. At 1996 the goodwill reserve was −£242,957,000 and the earnings were £4,691,000. If the total goodwill was reinstated as an asset and amortised over twenty years there would be an annual amortisation charge of over £12m. Earnings would need to increase by 250% and be maintained at that level for the next 20 years to break even.

The rate of growth in earnings is therefore an important factor. The WPP Group, for example, had £1,160m negative goodwill reserve in 1997 and profit after tax of £116m indicating that it would take 50% of the annual profit if goodwill were amortised over 20 years. However, WPP Group profits had increased by over 70% in 3 years.

16.10 Brand accounting

Brand accounting refers to the practice of representing a specific type of intangible asset – brand names – as a fixed asset in the balance sheet and typically not amortising them but subjecting them to regular review.

Prior to FRS 10, brand accounting emerged for two main reasons.

● For acquisitive companies it could be attributed to the accounting treatment required for measuring and reporting goodwill. The London Business School carried out research into the 'brands phenomenon' and found that 'a major aim of brand valuation has been to repair or pre-empt equity depletion caused by UK goodwill accounting rules'.[35, 36]

● Non-acquisitive companies do not incur costs for acquiring goodwill, so their reserves are not eroded by writing off purchased goodwill. However, these companies may have incurred promotional costs in creating home-grown brands and it would strengthen the balance sheet if they were permitted to include a valuation of these brands.[37]

Justifications for brand accounting

We now consider some other justifications that have been put forward for the inclusion of brands as a separate asset in the balance sheet.

Effect on shareholders' funds

Immediate goodwill write-off results in a fall in net tangible assets as disclosed by the balance sheet, even though the market capitalisation of a company increases. One way to maintain the asset base and avoid such a depletion of companies' reserves is to divide the purchased goodwill into two parts: the amount attributable to brands and the remaining amount attributable to pure goodwill.[38] For instance, WPP have capitalised two corporate brand names (J.Walter Thompson; Hill and Knowlton) which were originally valued in 1988 at £350m (and remain at that amount in the balance sheet). Without this capitalisation, the share owners' funds of £187.7m in the 1998 accounts would have been reduced by £350m to a negative figure of (£162.3m).

Effect on borrowing powers

The borrowing powers of public companies may be expressed in terms of multiples of net assets. In its articles of association there may be strict rules regarding the multiple that the company must not exceed. In addition, borrowing agreements and Stock Exchange listing agreements are generally dependent on net assets.

Effect on ratios

Immediate goodwill write-off distorts the gearing ratios, but the inclusion of brands as intangible assets minimised this distortion by providing a more realistic value for shareholders' funds. Guinness plc provided information on its gearing ratio in its five-year financial summary:

| | 31 December | | | | |
Gearing ratio	1992	1993	1994	1995	1996
including cost of acquired brands	56%	49%	35%	28%	34%
excluding cost of acquired brands	140%	111%	63%	49%	58%

Effect on management decisions

It is claimed that including brands on the balance sheet leads to more informed and improved management decision-making. The quality of internal decisions is related to the quality of information available to management.[39] As brands represent one of the most important assets of a company, management should be aware of the success or failure of each individual brand. Knowledge about the performance of brands ensures that management reacts accordingly to maintain or improve competitive advantage.

There is also evidence[40] that companies with valuable brand names are not including these in their balance sheets and are not, therefore, taking account of the assets for insurance purposes.

16.11 Intellectual property

According to the World Intellectual Property Organisation (WIPO), intellectual property refers to creations of the mind: inventions, literary and artistic works and symbols, names, images and designs used in commerce. Intellectual property is divided into two categories, namely:

● **Industrial property** which includes inventions (patents) trademarks, industrial designs and geographic indications of source.

- **Copyright** which includes literary and artistic works such as novels, poems, plays, films, musical works, artistic works such as drawings, paintings, photographs and sculptures, and architectural designs. Rights related to copyright include those of performing artistes in their performances and those of broadcasters in their radio and television programmes.

WIPO[41] is an international organisation dedicated to promoting the use and protection of works of the human spirit. These works – intellectual property – are expanding the bounds of science and technology and enriching the world of arts. Through its work, WIPO plays an important part in enhancing the quality and enjoyment of life as well as creating real wealth for nations. With headquarters in Geneva, Switzerland, WIPO is one of the 16 specialised agencies of the UN system of organisations. It administers 21 international treaties dealing with different aspects of intellectual property protection. The organisation counts 175 nations as member states. Its importance is recognised in the following comment by Peter Drucker:

> Knowledge has become the 'key resource' of the world economy. The traditional factors of production – land, labour, capital – are becoming restraints rather than driving forces

and in the UK, the 1998 White Paper placed 'know how' at the heart of our competitiveness.[42]

> Our competitiveness depends on making the most of our distinctive and valuable assets which competitors find hard to imitate. In a modern economy those distinctive assets are increasingly knowledge, skills and creativity rather than traditional factors.

In looking at the relative importance of asset values in businesses, in the 1980s 70% was attributed to tangible assets and 30% to intangible assets. In the mid 1990s, the situation has reversed and 30% is tangible assets and 70% intangible assets. More recently 95% has been attributed to intangible assets and 5% to physical and financial assets.

16.11.1 The rise of the new economy

This has been principally driven by information and knowledge. It has been identified by The Organisation for Economic Co-operation and Development (OECD) as explaining the increased prominence of intellectual capital as a business and research topic.[43]

Through a brief examination of the period since the Industrial Revolution, the following chain of events is observable:[44, 45]

- Capital and labour were brought together and the factors of production became localised and accessible.
- Firms pushed to increase volumes of production to meet the demands of growing markets.
- Firms began to build intangibles like brand equity and reputation (goodwill) in order to create a competitive advantage in markets where new entrants limited the profit-making potential of a strategy of mass production.
- Firms invested heavily in information technology to increase the quality of products and improve the speed with which those products could be brought to market.
- Firms realised the value of information and worked at managing information and transforming it into the intellectual capital needed to drive the organisation.

At each state of this corporate evolution fixed assets became less important in relative terms, compared with intangible assets in determining a company's success. Accounting and financial reporting practices, however, have remained largely unchanged.

Guthrie, while arguing[46] that accountants must find a way to incorporate accurate measures and values of intellectual capital in formal company reports or they will become irrelevant, suggests that the importance of intellectual capital is specifically emphasised in:

- the revolution in information technology and the information society;
- the rising importance of knowledge and the knowledge-based economy;
- the changing patterns of interpersonal activities and the network society; and
- the emergence of innovation and creativity as the principal determinant of competitiveness.

In a world of dot.com companies, virtual corporations and a flourishing service industry, book values correlate poorly with market capitalisation.

The OECD definition

The OECD describes intellectual capital[47] as

the economic value of two categories of intangible assets of a company:

(a) organisational ('structural') capital and
(b) human capital.

Structural capital refers to things like proprietary software systems, distribution networks, and supply chains. Human capital includes human resources within the organisation (i.e. staff resources) and resources external to the organisation (namely, customers and suppliers). The term intellectual capital has often been treated as being synonymous with intangible assets. The definition by the OECD makes a distinction by identifying intellectual capital as a subset of, rather than the same as, the intangible assets base of a business.

Traditionally accounting reports have been prepared on the basis of historical cost. This does not provide for the identification and measurement of intangibles in organisations – especially knowledge-based organisations. The limitations of the existing financial reporting systems have resulted in a move towards finding new ways to measure and report on a company's intellectual capital.

The legal view

Gallafent, Eastaway and Dauppe suggest[48] that the principal characteristic of all forms of intellectual property is the so called 'incorporeal' nature of that property. It is an abstraction, intangible and as such more difficult to protect than other less nebulous forms of property. To be eligible for legal protection, the author's or inventor's work must have been rendered into some tangible form. The term intellectual property denotes the rights over a tangible object of the person whose mental efforts created it. The high speed development in communications initially left the practical application of copyright law in disarray, as in the recent example of the Napster case. The new technology of genetic engineering and the genome project leaves this wide open.

The bankers' view

From about 1945 until 1975, bankers traditionally thought of intangibles as worthless and deducted them from net worth to arrive at tangible net worth. Liquidation analysis assumes that a loan will be repaid solely from the proceeds of sale of assets at forced sale prices. It stressed the value of the collateral as the main reason for lending.

By the early 1980s credit analysts from US banks in London began to input some value to some intangible assets, at first on a case-by-case judgement. The major change in the attitude to intangibles arose from the wave of acquisitions and particularly leverage acquisitions. Donaldson suggests[49] the following principles:

- An asset which generates cash in ways that can be understood and forecast has value to its owner.

- Where the asset and cash flow can be sold, a market price higher than the valuation of actual cash flow suggests that the owner is failing to extract the maximum value from the asset. The cash flow valuation may underestimate the real value.

- The cost to replace an asset provides a useful check on other methods of value.

- Given that valuation techniques are likely to remain underdeveloped for some time it will often be possible to give a range rather than pinpoint value.

- Value is the critical element not cost. Where money is spent creating an asset it is well spent only if the asset has value, i.e. it is the value of the asset rather than the cost reflected in the balance sheet.

- Once established an asset should be depreciated in ways to reflect the facts of each case.

- A tendency to lose value in liquidation is one factor to consider in assessing overall value. The ability to generate cash which helps to avoid liquidation remains important at all times.

16.11.2 Financial reporting models

Principal among the new reporting models are:

- The intangible asset monitor[50, 51]
- The balanced scorecard[52, 53]
- The Skandia value scheme[54, 55]
- The intellectual capital accounts[56, 57]

At the OECD symposium referred to above, the focus of reported issues was on four issues:

- assessing what motivates firms to want to measure their intellectual capital;

- examining who within an organisation is best positioned to measure and manage intellectual capital;

- determining the potential effects that the reporting of intellectual capital is expected to have; and

- improved methods of measuring intellectual capital.

The findings of almost 20 national research studies cover some common ground as follows:

- Organisations are motivated to:
  - measure their intellectual capital to assist with competitive benchmarking exercises;
  - create a consciousness within the organisation that intellectual capital and human resources in particular do matter; and
  - provide structured information to the capital and labour markets that may enhance perceptions of the company.

- There was agreement that everyone in an organisation needs to be committed to the task of measuring and managing intellectual capital if a company is to do so successfully.

- The effects of reporting intellectual capital included improved employee morale, lower staff turnover, increased investment in developing intellectual capital, a higher value being attributed to a company's intellectual capital by senior corporate officers than previously and an improved understanding of what specific factors are crucial to continued growth and development.

Techniques commonly used by public and private sector organisations to measure their intellectual capital included Kaplan and Norton's balanced scorecard[52, 53] and Karl-Erik Sveiby's intangible asset monitor.[50]

Two innovative approaches are those followed by Celemi and Skandia which are described below.

Celemi experience

Celemi is a Swedish-based company specialising in facilitating a learning process within other organisations. It was one of the first to open its eyes to the wisdom of measuring the value of its intellectual capital. Celemi published in 1995 what has been described as the world's first audit of its intangible assets as part of the company annual report. Celemi uses the Sveiby framework to classify its intangibles into three groups: individual competence, external structure and internal structure. Celemi's reports provide answers to two questions asked by stakeholders: first, the overall size of the balance sheet (what type of assets does Celemi have?) and, second, are intangibles increasing or decreasing and are they being utilised efficiently?

As regards individual competence, Celemi views its employees and their competencies (its knowledge base) as its most important strength in business. Celemi uses non-financial metrics to assess the value represented by its employees. The idea is to report the same metrics each year to facilitate benchmarking over time. This reveals whether the human capital is improving or declining.

Skandia experience

Skandia started work on developing a system for reporting the value of its knowledge capital in 1991. While early reports by Skandia adopted the same format as Celemi, it has more recently developed a management and reporting model called the Skandia Navigator. This creates a balance between the past (financial focus), the present (customer focus, process focus and human focus) and future (renewal and development focus).

The measurement of the past, financial focus includes performance ratios and balance sheet and profit and loss account. The customer focus is assessed in terms of market penetration. The human focus deals with levels of employee training, leadership training and teaming. The process focus looks at operational methods used and the levels of information technology support. The renewal and development focus measures the extent to which resources are being directed towards the work of teams and methods of the future. A unique aspect of the model is the measure of the extent to which human capital is converted to structural capital, i.e. retained to provide corporate value.

16.11.3 Knowledge management

Another term that is currently being used is knowledge management (KM). It has been described as developing business practices and processes that ensure that a business creates, accesses and embeds the knowledge that it needs. Binney[58] sees different elements of the knowledge management spectrum, namely:

● transactional knowledge management;

● analytical knowledge management;

● asset knowledge management;

● process knowledge management;

● innovation/creation based knowledge management; and

● developmental knowledge management.

In transactional KM, the use of knowledge is embedded in the system. Knowledge is presented to the user of a system in the course of completing a transaction or a unit of work such as entering an order or handling an inquiry from a customer.

In analytical KM, large amounts of data or information are used to derive trends and patterns, making apparent that which is hidden due to the vastness of source material – turning data into information which if acted upon can become knowledge.

In asset KM the focus is on processes associated with the management of knowledge assets. The treatment of knowledge is either the management of explicit knowledge assets which have been codified in some way or the management of intellectual property and the processes surrounding its identification, exploitation and protection.

Process KM as its name implies is concerned with the codification and improvement of process. This is usually related to other disciplines such as TQM or BPR. The knowledge assets produced are known as engineered assets as they involve third parties.

Innovation/creation based KM focuses on providing an environment in which knowledge workers often from different disciplines can come together in collaboration to create new knowledge resulting in new products or company capabilities.

Developmental KM focuses on either the transfer of explicit knowledge via training or education or the conscious development of tacit knowledge through developments such as experiential assignments aimed at increasing companies' human capital.

As far as financial reporting is concerned the key requirement is that the intellectual property should be capable of meeting the criteria established in the *Statement of Principles* for classification as an asset if it is to be reported in the balance sheet.

16.12 Future developments

16.12.1 The US approach to goodwill

In the USA the view has been taken that goodwill and intangibles are not wasting assets to be amortised over a predetermined period but assets that may have an indefinite life and be subject to impairment on an irregular basis. SFAS 142 *Goodwill and Intangible Assets* was issued with effect from 1 January 2002 whereby goodwill and certain intangible assets are reported in the balance sheet and only reduced if there is an impairment following the annual review.

The FASB has justified this approach on the grounds that it improves financial reporting because the financial statements of entities that acquire goodwill and other intangible assets will better reflect the underlying economics of those assets. The profit may become more volatile but users will be better able to understand the investments made in those assets and their subsequent performance. It should in theory highlight those cases where an acquirer has overpaid, e.g. if future performance is below expectation there will be a double impact with lower profits reduced even further by the impairment charge.

16.12.2 Impact on UK/US reconciliations

UK Companies preparing UK/US reconciliation statements which had written off pre-1998 goodwill against reserves would, pre-SFAS 142, have made an amortisation adjustment; the adjustment post-SFAS 142 will only be required if there has been an impairment charge.

16.12.3 The proposed IASB approach to goodwill

An Exposure Draft of Amendments to IAS 38 *Intangible Assets* follows the US approach in that it would no longer require or permit the amortisation of goodwill or intangible assets with indefinite useful lives. Instead, any goodwill or intangible assets would be tested for impairment annually, or more frequently if events or changes in circumstances indicate a possible impairment. There is opposition to the impairment-only approach on the grounds that it does not achieve an acceptable balance between 'representational faithfulness' and practicality with most smaller companies adversely affected with the cost outweighing any possible benefit.

The IASB approach to intangible assets

The IASB proposes to adopt the practice of SFAS 141 *Business Combinations* which attached an illustrative list of intangible assets categorised under five headings as follows:

- Marketing-related
  trademarks; trade dress; newspaper mastheads; internet domain names; non-competition agreements
- Customer-related
  customer lists; order or production backlog; customer contracts
- Artistic-related
  plays, operas, ballets; books, magazines, newspapers; other literary works; musical

works such as compositions, song lyrics, advertising jingles; pictures, photographs; video and audiovisual material, including motion pictures, music videos, television programmes.

- Contract-based
  licensing, royalty; advertising, construction, management, service or supply contracts; lease agreements; franchise agreements; operating and broadcast rights; use rights such as drilling, water, air, mineral, timber cutting, and route authorities; servicing contracts; employment contracts.

- Technology-based
  patented technology; computer software; unpatented technology; databases; trade secrets, such as secret formulas, processes, recipes

This should make it easier to estimate useful economic lives and reduce reliance on impairment reviews.

Summary

As business has become more complex and industrial processes more sophisticated, the amount paid to develop or acquire an intangible asset has become significant in comparison to the fixed asset base of some companies. Under FRS 10 internally generated intangible assets may be capitalised if they have a readily ascertainable market value. Under FRS 10 purchased goodwill and intangibles should be capitalised in the balance sheet. Once capitalised, FRS 10 requires that these assets either be amortised or subject to a regular impairment review, depending on their useful economic life.

REVIEW QUESTIONS

1 In connection with SSAP 13 *Accounting for Research and Development*:

   (a) Define 'applied research' and 'development'.

   (b) Why is it considered necessary to distinguish between applied research and development expenditure, and how does this distinction affect the accounting treatment?

   (c) State whether the following are included within the SSAP 13 definition of research and development, and give your reasons:

   (i) Market research.

   (ii) Testing of preproduction prototypes.

   (iii) Operational research.

   (iv) Testing in search of process alternatives.

2 Discuss the suggestion that the requirement for companies to write off research investment rather than showing it as an asset exposes companies to short-term pressure from acquisitive companies that are damaging to the country's interest.

3 The immediate expense of R&D depresses reported earnings and book values, despite the fact that future cash flows and share prices are generally enhanced by such activities.

Discuss the suggestion that this is an unacceptable source of bias in financial statements.

4 Describe the problems encountered when accounting for:

(a) tangible fixed assets;

(b) leasing (in lessees' accounts);

(c) research and development;

and outline the recommended accounting treatment given in the relevant Statements of Standard Accounting Practice (SSAPs) or Financial Reporting Standards (FRSs). How effective are the SSAPs/FRSs in limiting the use of different accounting treatments of the above areas?

5 Discuss the advantages and disadvantages of the proposal that there should be a separate category of asset in the balance sheet clearly identified as 'research investment – outcome uncertain'.

6 The Chloride 2001 Annual Report included the following accounting policy for goodwill:

Goodwill is subject to review at the end of the year of acquisition and at any other time when the directors believe that impairment may have occurred. Any impairment would be charged to the profit and loss account in the period in which the loss occurs.

(a) Explain the indications that a review for impairment is required.

(b) Once there are indications of impairment, how is impairment measured?

7 How is 'value in use' calculated for an impairment review? What are the areas of subjectivity?

8 Critically evaluate the basis of the following assertion:

I am sceptical that it [the impairment test] will work reliably in practice, given the complexity and subjectivity that lie within the calculation. (Paterson[10])

9 Here is an extract from the Reckitt Benckiser 2000 Annual Report:

	2000	1999
	£m	£m
Fixed assets		
Intangible assets		
Brands	1,584	1,489
Goodwill	54	48
Tangible assets	535	514
	2,173	2,051
Total shareholders' funds	1,116	1,056

The accounting policy states:

Acquired brands are only recognised on the balance sheet as intangible assets where title is clear, brand earnings are separately identifiable, the brand could be sold separately from the rest of the business and where the brand achieves earnings in excess of those achieved by unbranded products. The value of an acquired brand is determined by allocating the purchase consideration of an acquired business between the underlying fair values of the tangible assets, goodwil and brands acquired.

Brands are not amortised, as it is considered that their useful economic lives are not limited. Their carrying values are reviewed annually by the Directors to determine whether there has been any permanent impairment in value and any such reductions in their values are taken to the profit and loss account.

A note to the accounts states:

> A brand is only recognised where it is supported by a registered trademark, is established in the market place and holds significant market share.

Given the materiality of the brands (these include products such as Dettol, Air Wick, Calgonit-2-in-1, Lysol, Dettox, Finish, Vanish, Harpic) in relation to the total shareholders' funds, discuss the information that you consider appropriate to be disclosed in the annual report in order to assess the level and nature of risk to an investor.

10 The Nestlé 2000 Annual Report included goodwill of 3,395 CHF million arising on the acquisition of various companies such as PowerBar Inc., the US leader in the emerging energy bar category, and 188 CHF million on payment for intellectual property rights, operating rights and data processing software.

Discuss reasons for not including in the balance sheet brand valuations for such brands as Nestlé, Nescafé, Nestea, Maggi, Buitoni and Friskies which contribute about 70% of the group's total sales.

EXERCISES

An extract from the solution is provided in the appendix at the end of the text for exercises marked with an asterisk (*).

Question 1

Environmental Engineering plc is engaged in the development of an environmentally friendly personal transport vehicle. This will run on an electric motor powered by solar cells, supplemented by passenger effort in the form of pedal assistance.

At the end of the current accounting period, the following costs have been attributed to the project:

(a) A grant of £500,000 to the Polytechnic of the South Coast Faculty of Solar Engineering to encourage their research.

(b) Costs of £1,200,000 expended on the development of the necessary solar cells prior to the decision to incorporate them in a vehicle.

(c) Costs of £5,000,000 expended on designing the vehicle and its motors, and the planned promotional and advertising campaign for its launch on the market in twelve months' time.

Required:
  (i) Explain, with reasons, which of the above items could be considered for treatment as deferred revenue expenditure, quoting any relevant Statements of Standard Accounting Practice.
 (ii) Set out the criteria under which any items can be so treated.
(iii) Advise on the accounting treatment that will be afforded to any such items after the product has been launched.

Question 2

As chief accountant at Italin plc, you have been given the following information by the director of research:

Project Luca	
	£000
Costs to date (pure research 25%, applied research 75%)	200
Costs to develop product (to be incurred in the year to 30 September 20X1)	300
Expected future sales per annum for 20X2–X7	1,000
Fixed assets purchased in 20X1 for the project:	
Cost	2,500
Estimated useful life	7 years
Residual value	400
(These assets will be disposed of at their residual value at the end of their estimated useful lives.)	

The board of directors considers that this project is similar to the other projects that the company undertakes, and is confident of a successful outcome. The company has enough finances to complete the development and enough capacity to produce the new product.

Required:
Prepare a report for the board, outlining the principles involved in accounting for research and development, and showing what accounting entries will be made in the company's accounts for each of the years ending 30 September 20X1–20X7 inclusive.
Indicate what factors need to be taken into account when assessing each research and development project for accounting purposes, and what disclosure is needed for research and development in the company's published accounts.

* Question 3

Oxlag plc, a manufacturer of pharmaceutical products, has the following research and development projects on hand at 31 January 20X2:

(a) A general survey into the long-term effects of its sleeping pill Chalcedon upon human resistance to infections. At the year-end the research is still at a basic stage and no worthwhile results with any particular applications have been obtained.

(b) A development for Meebach plc in which the company will produce market research data relating to Meebach's range of drugs.

(c) An enhancement of an existing drug, Euboia, which will enable additional uses to be made of the drug and which will consequently boost sales. This project was completed successfully on 30 April 20X2, with the expectation that all future sales of the enhanced drug would greatly exceed the costs of the new development.

(d) A scientific enquiry with the aim of identifying new strains of antibiotics for future use. Several possible substances have been identified, but research is not sufficiently advanced to permit patents and copyrights to be obtained at the present time.

The following costs have been brought forward at 1 February 20X1:

Project	A	B	C	D
			£000	
Specialised laboratory				
Cost	—	—	500	—
Depreciation	—	—	25	—
Specialised equipment				
Cost	—	—	75	50
Depreciation	—	—	15	10
Capitalised development costs	—	—	200	—
Market research costs	—	250	—	—

The following costs were incurred during the year:

Project	A	B	C	D
			£000	
Research costs	25	—	265	78
Market research costs	—	75	—	—
Specialised equipment cost	50	—	—	50

Depreciation on specialised laboratories and special equipment is provided by the straight-line method and the assets have an estimated useful life of 25 and 5 years respectively. A full year's depreciation is provided on assets purchased during the year.

Required:
  (i) Write up the research and development, fixed asset and market research accounts to reflect the above transactions in the year ended 31 January 20X2.
 (ii) Calculate the amount to be charged as research costs in the profit and loss account of Oxlag plc for the year ended 31 January 20X2.
(iii) State on what basis the company should amortise any capitalised development costs and what disclosures the company should make in respect of amounts written off in the year to 31 January 20X3.
 (iv) Calculate the amounts to be disclosed in the balance sheet in respect of fixed assets, deferred development costs and work-in-progress.
  (v) State what disclosures you would make in the accounts for the year ended 31 January 20X2 in respect of the new improved drug developed under project C, assuming sales begin on 1 May 20X2, and show strong growth to the date of signing the accounts, 14 July 20X2, with the expectation that the new drug will provide 25% of the company's pre-tax profits in the year to 31 January 20X3.

Question 4

(a) Briefly examine the case for and against treating goodwill in accounts differently from other assets.

(b) The consolidated balance sheet, as at 31 December 20X8, of Selma plc and its subsidiaries, reports the value of goodwill as £400,000, arrived at as follows:

	Notes	Balance 31 Dec 20X7	Cost in 20X8	Expenses in 20X8	Balance 31 Dec 20X8
Ora Nectar	(i)	—	£150,000	£50,000	£100,000
Wilma Ltd	(ii)	£200,000	£160,000	£60,000	£300,000

Notes:

(i) A canned orange juice, named Ora Nectar, launched in 20X8, was distributed free to schoolchildren during their short breaks. The cost incurred in the process is estimated to benefit Selma plc's sales during the next three years.

(ii) Selma plc acquired a 100% stake in Wilma Ltd on 1 January 20X6, paying £1,200,000. Aggregate fair value of separable net assets of Wilma Ltd on that date was valued at £900,000. The group adopted a policy of amortising the goodwill over an estimated useful life of six years. During 20X8, Selma plc incurred £160,000 on a campaign calculated to revamp the image of Wilma Ltd and it is estimated that as a direct result of this campaign the economic life of goodwill in Wilma Ltd was prolonged by a further two years.

£110,000 written-off goodwill in 20X8 was charged against the capital reserve arising from consolidation that resulted from the acquisition of another subsidiary.

Required:
Critically comment on Selma plc's accounting for goodwill.

Question 5

Financial Reporting Standard FRS 10 addresses the accounting for goodwill and intangible assets. Accounting for goodwill has been a contentious issue in the UK for several years and FRS 10 *Goodwill and Intangible Assets* attempts to eliminate the problems associated with SSAP 22 *Accounting for Goodwill*.

Required:
(a) **Describe the requirements of FRS 10 regarding the initial recognition and measurement of goodwill and intangible assets.**
(b) **Explain the proposed approach set out by FRS 10 for the amortisation of positive goodwill and intangible assets.**
(c) **Territory plc acquired 80% of the ordinary share capital of Yukon plc on 31 May 20X6. The balance sheet of Yukon plc at 31 May 20X6 was:**

Yukon plc – Balance sheet at 31 May 20X6	£000
Fixed assets	
Intangible assets	6,020
Tangible assets	38,300
	44,320
Current assets	
Stocks	21,600
Debtors	23,200
Cash	8,800
	53,600
Creditors: amounts falling due within one year	24,000
Net current assets	29,600
Total assets less current liabilities	73,920
Creditors: amounts falling due after more than one year	12,100
Provision for liabilities and charges	886
Accruals and deferred income	
Deferred government grants	2,700
	58,234

	£000
Fixed assets	
Capital reserves	
Called up share capital (ordinary shares of £1)	10,000
Share premium account	5,570
Profit and loss account	42,664
	58,234

Additional information relating to the above balance sheet

(i) The intangible assets of Yukon plc were brand names currently utilised by the company. The directors felt that they were worth £7 million but there was no readily ascertainable market value at the balance sheet date, nor any information to verify the directors' estimated value.

(ii) The provisional market value of the land and buildings was £20 million at 31 May 20X6. This valuation had again been determined by the directors. A valuers' report received on 31 November 20X6 stated the market value of land and buildings to be £23 million as at 31 May 20X6. The depreciated replacement cost of the remainder of the tangible fixed assets was £18 million at 31 May 20X6, net of government grants.

(iii) The replacement cost of stocks was estimated at £25 million and its net realisable value was deemed to be £20 million. Debtors and creditors due within one year are stated at the amounts expected to be received and paid.

(iv) 'Creditors amounts falling due after more than one year' was a long-term loan with a bank. The initial loan on 1 June 20X5 was £11 million at a fixed interest rate of 10% per annum. The total amount of the interest is to be paid at the end of the loan period on 31 May 20X9. The current bank lending rate is 7% per annum.

(v) The provision for liabilities and charges relates to costs of reorganisation of Yukon plc. This provision had been set up by the directors of Yukon plc prior to the offer by Territory plc and the reorganisation would have taken place even if Territory plc had not purchased the shares of Yukon plc. Additionally Territory plc wishes to set up a provision for future losses of £10 million which it feels will be incurred by rationalising the group.

(vi) The offer made to all of the shareholders of Yukon plc was 2.5 £1 ordinary shares of Territory plc at the market price of £2.25 per share plus £1 cash, per Yukon plc ordinary share.

(vii) Goodwill is to be dealt with in accordance with FRS 10. The estimated useful economic life is deemed to be 10 years. The directors of Yukon plc informed Territory plc that as at 31 May 20X7, the brand names were worthless as the products to which they related had recently been withdrawn from sale because they were deemed to be a health hazard.

(viii) A full year's charge for amortisation of goodwill is included in the group profit and loss account of Territory plc in the year of purchase.

Required:

Calculate the amortisation of goodwill in the group profit and loss account of Territory plc for accounting periods ending on 31 May 20X6 and 31 May 20X7.

Question 6

The brands debate

Prior to FRS 10, the depletion of equity reserves caused by the accounting treatment for purchased goodwill resulted in some companies capitalising brands on their balance sheets. This practice was started by Rank Hovis McDougall (RHM) – a company which has since been taken over. Martin Moorhouse, the group chief accountant at RHM, claimed that:

> … putting brands on the balance sheet forced a company to look to their value as well as to profits. It served as a reminder to management of the value of the assets for which they were responsible and that at the end of the day those companies which were prepared to recognise brands on the balance sheet could be better and stronger for it.[59]

There were many opponents to the capitalisation of brands. A London Business School research study found that brand accounting involves too many risks and uncertainties and too much subjective judgement. In short, the conclusion was that 'the present flexible position, far from being neutral, is potentially corrosive to the whole basis of financial reporting and that to allow brands – whether acquired or home-grown – to continue to be included in the balance sheet would be highly unwise'.[60]

Required:
Consider the arguments for and against brand accounting. In particular, consider the issues of brand valuation; the separability of brands; purchased vs home-grown brands; and the maintenance/substitution argument.[61–65]

References

1 'The R&D Scoreboard', *Financial Times*, 25 June 1999.
2 B. Nixon and A. Lonie, 'Accounting for R&D: the need for change', *Accountancy*, February 1990, p. 91.
3 B. Nixon, 'R&D disclosure: SSAP 13 and after', *Accountancy*, February 1991, pp. 72–73.
4 *Statement of Intent: Comparability of Financial Statements*, IASC, 1990.
5 IAS 9 (revised), *Research and Development Costs*, IASC, December 1993.
6 IAS 39 *Intangible Assets*, IASC, September 1998.
7 A. Goodacre and J. McGrath, 'An experimental study of analysts' reactions to corporate R&D expenditure', *British Accounting Review*, 1997, 29, 155–179.
8 B. Nixon, 'The accounting treatment of research and development expenditure: Views of UK company accountants', *European Accounting Review*, vol. 6, no. 2, 265–277.
9 FRS 10, *Goodwill and Intangible Assets*, ASB, December 1997.
10 R. Paterson, 'Will FRS 10 hit the target?' *Accountancy*, February 1998, 74–75.
11 ED 30, *Accounting for Goodwill*, ASC, October 1982.
12 EC Seventh Directive, 1983.
13 SSAP 22, *Accounting for Goodwill*, ASC, December 1984.
14 ED 44, *Accounting for Goodwill*, ASC, September 1988.
15 SSAP 22, *Accounting for Goodwill (Revised)*, ASC, July 1989.
16 ED 47, *Accounting for Goodwill*, ASC, February 1990.
17 Sir Kenneth Corfield, *Intangible Assets: Their Value and How to Report It*, Coopers and Lybrand, Deloitte, 1990.
18 *Goodwill and Intangible Assets*, ASB Discussion Paper, 1993.
19 *Goodwill and Intangible Assets*, ASB Working Paper, 1995.
20 FRED 12, *Goodwill and Intangible Assets*, ASB, June 1996.
21 SSAP 13 (revised), *Accounting for Research and Development*, ASC, January 1989.
22 *Ibid.*, para. 2.1.1.

23 J. Brown, 'Accounting for goodwill and intangible assets', *Accountancy*, July 1996, p. 97.

24 S. Kennedy, 'Intangible aspects of goodwill', *Accountancy*, August 1996, p. 122.

25 M. Mullen, 'How to value intangibles', *Accountancy*, November 1993, p. 92.

26 *Responses to Working Paper 'Goodwill and Intangible Assets'*, ASB, London 1995.

27 Cadbury Schweppes, Extracts from *Responses to Working Paper 'Goodwill and Intangible Assets'*, ASB, London 1995, p. 36.

28 IAS 38, *Intangible Assets*, IASC, September 1998.

29 IAS 22 (revised), *Business Combinations*, IASC, September 1998.

30 Kalamazoo, Extracts from *Responses to Working Paper 'Goodwill and Intangible Assets'*, ASB, London 1995, pp. 208–209.

31 FRS 11, *Impairment of Fixed Assets and Goodwill*, ASB, July 1998.

32 Unilever, Extracts from *Responses to Working Paper 'Goodwill and Intangible Assets'*, ASB, London 1995, pp. 348–349.

33 Guinness plc, Extracts from *Responses to Working Paper 'Goodwill and Intangible Assets'*, ASB, London 1995, pp. 164–167.

34 Sir D Tweedie, FRS 11, *Impairment of Fixed Assets and Goodwill*, ASB, 1998.

35 P. Barwise, C. Higson, A. Likierman and P. Marsh, *Accounting for Brands*, ICAEW, June 1989.

36 M. Cooper and A. Carey, 'Brand valuation in the balance', *Accountancy*, June 1989.

37 A. Pizzey, 'Healing the rift', *Certified Accountant*, October 1990.

38 'Finance directors say yes to brand valuation', *Accountancy*, January 1990, p. 12.

39 M. Moorhouse, 'Brands debate: wake up to the real world', *Accountancy*, July 1990, p. 30.

40 M. Gerry, 'Companies ignore value of brands', *Accountancy Age*, March 2000, p. 4.

41 http://www.wipo.org

42 *Our Competitive Future: Building the Knowledge Driven Economy*, HMSO, London, 1998 White Paper.

43 Organisation for Economic Co-operation and Development (OECD), *Measuring and Reporting Intellectual Capital: Experience, Issues and Prospects*, OECD, Paris 2000, final report.

44 J. Guthrie, and R. Petty, 'Knowledge management: the information revolution has created the need for a codified system of gathering and controlling knowledge', *Company Secretary*, January 1999, vol. 9, no. 1, pp. 38–41.

45 R. Tissen, *et al.*, *Value Based Knowledge Management*, Longman Nederland BV, 1998, Chapter 2, pp. 25–44.

46 'Measuring up to change', *Financial Management*, December 2000, CIMA London, p. 11.

47 Organisation for Economic Co-operation and Development (OECD) *Guidelines and Instructions for OECD Symposium* on *Measuring and reporting Intellectual capital: Experiences, Issues and Prospects*, OECD, Paris, 1999.

48 R. J. Gallafent, N. A. Eastaway and V. A. Dauppe, *Intellectual Property Law and Taxation*, Longman, London, 1992.

49 T. H. Donaldson, *The Treatment of Intangibles, A Bankers' View*, St Martins Press, New York, 1992.

50 K.-E. Sveiby, *The New Annual Report*, Stockholm, 1988 (in Swedish); see www.sveiby.com.au for English translation.

51 Celemi, *Growing a knowledge company*, Celemi, 1999, www.celemi.com. Site includes Celemi intangible assets monitor: http://www.celemi.se/sbc/sbc2.html

52 R. S. Kaplan and Norton, 'The balanced scorecard – measures that drives performance', *Harvard Business Review*, 1992, Jan–Feb.

53 R. S. Kaplan and Norton, 'Using the balanced scorecard as a strategic management system', *Harvard Business Review*, 1996, Jan–Feb.

54 L. Edvinsson and M. Malone, *Intellectual Capital: Realising Your company's True Value By Finding its Hidden Power*, HarperCollins, New York, 1997.

55 L. Edvinsson, 'Developing intellectual capital at Skandia', *Long Range Planning*, vol. 30, no. 3, pp. 266–373.

56 Danish Agency for Trade and Industry (DATI), *Intellectual Capital Accounts: New Tool for Companies*, DATI Council, Copenhagen, 1998 (English version).

57 Danish Agency for Trade and Industry *Developing Intellectual Capital Accounts, Experiences from 19 companies*, Ministry of Business and Industry, Copenhagen, 1999.

58 D. Binney, 'The knowledge management spectrum – a technique for optimising knowledge management strategies', *Journal of Intellectual Capital*, to be published.

59 M. Moorhouse, *op. cit.*

60 P. Barwise, *et al.*, *op. cit.*

61 D. Tonkin and B. Robertson, 'Brand names in a conceptual framework', *Accountancy*, March 1991, p. 28.

62 'Finance directors say yes to brand valuation', *op. cit.*

63 I. Cameron-Smith and F. Mattiussi, 'Intangible valuations – the expert view', *Accountancy*, March 1989, pp. 25–26.

64 S. Srikanthan *et al.*, 'Marketing: the unrecognised asset', *Management Accounting*, May 1987, pp. 38–42.

65 T. Arnold and M. Sherer, 'Valuation of brands: the RHM approach', *The Accountants' Magazine*, March 1989, p. 43.

CHAPTER 17

Stocks and work-in-progress

17.1 Introduction

This chapter explains the accounting principles involved in the valuation of stocks and work-in-progress, and how this impacts not only on balance sheet valuation, but also on the computation of annual profit.

We attempt to combine mechanics with a theoretical understanding of the accounting principles and illustrate this with practical examples showing how the interpretation of financial statements can be affected by differing treatments. In this chapter we consider:

- Stock defined and the controversy
- SSAP 9 and legal requirements
- Stock and work-in-progress valuation
- Stock control
- Creative accounting
- Audit of year-end physical stocktake
- Published accounts

17.2 Stock defined

SSAP 9 (Revised) *Stocks and Long-term Contracts* provides the following definition of stocks:[1]

Stocks comprise the following categories:

(a) goods or other assets purchased for resale;
(b) consumable stores;
(c) raw materials and components purchased for incorporation into products for sale;
(d) products and services in intermediate stages of completion;
(e) finished goods.

The valuation of stocks involves:[2]

(a) the establishment of physical existence and ownership;
(b) the determination of unit costs;
(c) the calculation of provisions to reduce cost to net realisable value, if necessary.

The resulting evaluation is then disclosed in the published accounts in accordance with legal requirements.

These definitions appear to be very precise. We shall see, however, that although SSAP 9 was introduced to bring some uniformity into financial statements, there are many areas where professional judgement must be exercised. Sometimes this may distort the financial statements to such an extent that we must question whether they do represent a 'true and fair' view.

17.3 The controversy

The valuation of stocks and work-in-progress has been a controversial issue in accounting for many years. The stock value is a crucial element not only in the computation of profit, but also in the valuation of assets for balance sheet purposes.

Figure 17.1 presents information relating to Coats Viyella plc. It shows that the stock is material in relation to total assets and pre-tax profits. In relation to the profits we can see that an error of 4% in the 2001 interim report stocks value would potentially cause the profits for the group to change from a pre-tax profit to a pre-tax loss. As stock is usually a multiple rather than a fraction of profit, stock errors may have a disproportionate effect on the accounts. It is therefore crucial in determining earnings per share, net asset backing for shares and the current ratio. Consequently, the basis of valuation should be consistent, so as to avoid manipulation of profits between accounting periods, and comply with generally accepted accounting principles, so that profits are comparable between different companies.

Unfortunately, there are many examples of manipulation of stock values in order to create a more favourable impression. By increasing the value of stock at the year end, profit and current assets are automatically increased (and vice versa). Of course, closing stock of one year becomes opening stock of the next, so profit is thereby reduced. But such manipulation provides opportunities for profit-smoothing and may be advantageous in certain circumstances, e.g. if the company is under threat of takeover.

Figure 17.2 illustrates the point. Simply by increasing the value of stock in year 1 by £10,000, profit (and current assets) is increased by a similar amount. Even if the two values are identical in year 2, such manipulation allows profit to be 'smoothed' and £10,000 profit switched from year 2 to year 1.

According to normal accrual accounting principles, profit is determined by matching costs with related revenues. If it is unlikely that the revenue will in fact be received, prudence dictates that the irrecoverable amount should be written off immediately against current revenue.

It follows that stock should be valued at cost less any irrecoverable amount. But what is cost? Companies have used a variety of methods of determining costs, and these are explored later in the chapter. There have been a number of disputes relating to the valuation of stocks which affected profits (e.g. the AEI/GEC merger of 1967).[3] Naturally,

Figure 17.1 Coats Viyella plc

	2000	2001 (Half year)
Pre-tax profits losses (£m)	(29.9)	9.9
Stock (£m)	304.2	320.2
Total assets (£m)	1,321.8	1,310.4

Figure 17.2 Stock values manipulated to smooth income

		Year 1		Year 1 With stock inflated
Sales		100,000		100,000
Opening stock	—		—	
Purchases	65,000		65,000	
Less: Closing stock	5,000		15,000	
COST OF SALES		60,000		50,000
		40,000		50,000
		Year 2		Year 2 With stock inflated
Sales		150,000		150,000
Opening stock	5,000		15,000	
Purchases	100,000		100,000	
	105,000		115,000	
Less: Closing stock	15,000		15,000	
COST OF SALES		90,000		100,000
PROFIT		60,000		50,000

such circumstances tend to come to light with a change of management, but it was considered important that a definitive statement of accounting practice be issued in an attempt to standardise treatment.

17.4 SSAP 9 and legal requirements

The first attempt by the profession to achieve uniformity came in 1972 with the issue of ED 6. Its purpose was to set out a defined practice of accounting for stocks and work-in-progress, provide rules for valuation and set out precise definitions of cost.

After the appropriate discussion period, SSAP 9 (original) *Stocks and Work in Progress* was issued in May 1975. Its introduction stated:

No area of accounting has produced wider differences in practice than the computation of the amount at which stocks and work in progress are stated in financial accounts. This Statement of Standard Accounting Practice seeks to define the practices, to narrow the differences and variations in those practices and to ensure adequate disclosure in the accounts.

SSAP 9 has been added to since 1975, and was revised in September 1988. Although the main substance of the original standard remained, the major revision concerned the accounting provisions relating to long-term contracts (dealt with in Section 17.11).

The revised standard, now renamed SSAP 9 *Stocks and Long-term Contracts*, provides that the amount at which stocks are stated in periodic financial statements should be the total of the lower of cost and net realisable value of the separate items of stock or of groups of similar items. This is emphasised in the Companies Act 1985 (Schedule 4, para. 22), which requires that under the historical cost rules 'the amount to be included in respect of any current asset shall be its purchase price or production cost' or net realisable value if lower (para. 23(1)). The standard also emphasises the need to match costs against revenue, and it aims, like other standards, to achieve greater uniformity in the measurement of income as well as improving the disclosure of stock valuation methods. It includes an appendix for general guidance on practical considerations, although in the end it relies on management to choose the most appropriate method of stock valuation for the production processes used and the company's environment. Legal requirements in the Companies Act 1985 allow various methods of valuation, including FIFO, LIFO and weighted average or any similar method (see below). In selecting the most suitable method, management 'must exercise judgement to ensure that the methods chosen provide the fairest practical approximation to cost'.[4]

SSAP 9 does not recommend the use of base stock or LIFO because they often result in stocks being stated in the balance sheet at amounts that bear little relation to recent cost levels. This is one of several areas of conflict between SSAP 9 and the Companies Act 1985. In practice, companies exercise the wider choice available under the Companies Act.

Clearly, therefore, even though there are legal requirements and an SSAP in existence, the valuation of stocks and work-in-progress can provide areas of subjectivity and choice to management, and no definitive method is legally enforced. We will return to this theme many times in the following sections of this chapter.

17.5 Stock valuation

The valuation rule outlined in SSAP 9 is difficult to apply because of uncertainties about what is meant by cost and what is meant by net realisable value.

17.5.1 What is meant by cost?

There are a variety of methods of arriving at a 'cost' figure. Some are approved by SSAP 9, others are most certainly not, and this has caused controversy since SSAP 9 was first issued.

Methods acceptable under SSAP 9

The acceptable methods of stock valuation include FIFO, AVCO and standard cost.

First-in-first-out (FIFO)
Stock is valued at the most recent 'cost', since the cost of oldest stock is charged out first, whether or not this accords with the actual physical flow (Figure 17.3).

Average cost (AVCO)
Stock is valued at a 'weighted average cost', i.e. the unit cost is weighted by the number of items carried at each 'cost'. This is popular in manufacturing and in organisations holding a large volume of stock at fluctuating 'costs'. The practical problem of actually

Figure 17.3 First-in-first-out method (FIFO)

Date	Receipts Quantity	Rate	£	Issues Quantity	Rate	£	Balance Quantity	Rate	£
January	10	15	150				10		150
February				8	15	120	2		30
March	10	17	170				12		200
April	20	20	400				32		600
May				2	15	30			
				10	17	170			
				12	20	240			
				Cost of goods sold		560			
				Stock			8	20	160

recording and calculating the weighted average cost has been overcome by the use of sophisticated computer software (Figure 17.4).

Standard cost
In many cases this is the only way to value manufactured goods in a high-volume/turnover environment. However, the standard is acceptable only if it approximates to actual cost. This means that variances need to be reviewed to see if they affect the standard cost and for stock evaluation.

SSAP 9 recognises that an acceptable method of arriving at cost is the use of selling price, less an estimated profit margin. This method is only acceptable if it can be demonstrated that the method gives a reasonable approximation of the actual cost. It is the method employed by major retailers, e.g. Tesco 1999 accounts state in accounting policies:

> Stocks comprise goods held for resale and development properties and are valued at the lower of cost and net realisable value. Stocks in stores are calculated at retail price and reduced by appropriate margins to the lower of cost and net realisable value.

Figure 17.4 Average cost method (AVCO)

Date	Receipts Quantity	Rate	£	Issues Quantity	Rate	£	Balance Quantity	Rate	£
January	10	15	150				10		150
February				8	15	120	2		30
March	10	17	170				12		200
April	20	20	400				32		600
May				24	18.75	450			600
				Cost of goods sold		570			
				Stock			8	18.75	150

And Somerfield 1997 accounting policy states:

> Stock is valued at the lower of cost or net realisable value. Cost represents invoiced cost or selling price less the relevant profit margin to reduce it to estimated cost, including an appropriate element of overheads. Stock at warehouses is valued at weighted average cost and stock at stores on a first-in-first-out basis.

SSAP 9 does not recommend any specific method. This is a decision for each organisation based upon sound professional advice and the organisation's unique operating conditions.

Methods rejected by SSAP 9

These include LIFO, base stock and replacement cost.

Last-in-first-out (LIFO)

The cost of the stock most recently received is charged out first at the most recent 'cost'. The practical upshot is that the stock value is based upon an 'old cost', which may bear little relationship to the current 'cost' (Figure 17.5).

US companies commonly use the LIFO method as in the following extract from the Eastman Kodak Company Annual Report 2000:

> Inventories are valued at cost, which is not in excess of market. The cost of most inventories in the US is determined by the 'last-in, first-out' (LIFO) method. The cost of other inventories is determined by the 'first-in, first-out' (FIFO) or average cost method, which approximates current cost. The Company provides inventory reserves for excess, obsolete or slow-moving inventory based on changes in customer demand, technology developments or other economic factors

Where LIFO is used the effect of using FIFO is quantified as in the Wal Mart Stores Inc. Annual Report:

	2001 $m	2000 $m
Inventories at replacement cost	21,644	20,171
Less LIFO reserve	202	378
Inventories at LIFO cost	21,442	19,793

Figure 17.5 Last-in-first-out method (LIFO)

Date	Receipts Quantity	Rate	£	Issues Quantity	Rate	£	Balance Quantity	Rate	£
January	10	15	150				10		150
February				8	15	120	2		30
March	10	17	170				12		200
April	20	20	400				32		600
May				20	20	400			
				4	17	68			
			Cost of goods sold			588			
			Stock				8		132

May closing balance = $[(2 \times 15) + (6 \times 17)]$

The company's summary of significant accounting policies states that the company uses the retail last-in-first-out (LIFO) method. The LIFO reserve shows the cumulative, pre-tax effect on income between the results obtained using LIFO and the results obtained using a more current cost inventory valuation method (e.g. FIFO) – this gives an indication of how much higher profits would be if FIFO were used.

Base stock

The stock is valued at some predetermined value based upon the 'cost' at a specified time (Figure 17.6). This is an attractive idea for commodities which rapidly change cost owing to seasonal factors (e.g. fresh food), market forces (e.g. gold, oil, steel) or the influence of either on supply (coffee, tea, cocoa). The main difficulty is the choice of the 'base point', which leaves great scope for subjective manipulation and may not give a 'reliable' profit calculation for the purposes of performance evaluation.

An example was provided in the accounts of the Cookson Group for 1990, whose accounting policy is stated as follows:

> Certain stocks of the Group's metals and minerals companies are valued in the profit and loss account on the base stock or, for certain overseas companies, the last in first out (LIFO) method. As market prices of the materials involved can fluctuate widely over a period, and because these companies are processors and not traders, the effects of such variations in stock values are not operating profits or losses. The use of the base stock and LIFO methods, together with covering arrangements for quantities in excess of base stock levels, **causes the profit and loss account to be charged with the current cost of the materials consumed**. The directors believe that this method of accounting is more appropriate for these stocks than that required by SSAP 9. All stocks are stated in the balance sheet at the lower of cost over net realisable value on the FIFO method. The difference between the base stock or LIFO valuations, where these methods are used, and the FIFO valuation is included in reserves.

The 1996 accounts indicate a different treatment. The note to the accounts states:

> The Group's precious metal fabrication operations utilise significant amounts of precious metals, primarily gold, held on consignment terms. The terms provide, inter alia, that the consignor retains title to the metal and both parties have the right of return over the metal without penalty.

Figure 17.6 Base stock method

Stocks	1990	1989
Included in current assets at the lower of cost and net realisable value		
Raw materials	95.9	123.5
Work-in-progress	32.6	38.1
Finished goods	91.1	116.0
Valuation for the balance sheet	219.6	277.6
Included in reserves and minorities		
Amount required to reduce £54.1m (1989 £71.1m) of stocks to their base and LIFO value	(7.5)	(18.3)
Valuation for the profit and loss	212.1	259.3

The accounting policy in the 1999 Accounts addresses FRS 5 *Substance of Transactions* and states:

> Stocks held under consignment are reviewed regularly in order to assess whether the substance of the arrangements is such that those stocks constitute assets which should be reflected in the Group balance sheet.

The effect of the consignment arrangement is the same as in 1990, i.e. it **causes the profit and loss account to be charged with the current cost of the materials consumed** without a stockholding to be dealt with under SSAP 9.

Replacement cost

The stock is valued at the current cost of the individual item rather than the actual cost (i.e. the cost to the organisation of replacing the item rather than the actual cost at the time of manufacture or purchase). This is an attractive idea since the 'value' of stock could be seen as the cost at which a similar item could be currently acquired. The problem again is in arriving at a 'reliable' profit figure for the purposes of performance evaluation. Wild fluctuation of profit could occur simply because of such factors as the time of the year, the vagaries of the world weather system or the manipulation of market forces. Let us take three examples, involving coffee, oil and silver.

Coffee. Wholesale prices collapsed over three years (1999–2002) from nearly $2.40 per lb to just under 50 cents. This was the lowest level in thirty years and, allowing for the effects of inflation, coffee became uneconomic to sell and farmers resorted to burning their crop for fuel. The implication for financial reporting was that the objective was to increase the stock unit cost by 100% by forcing the price back above $1 per lb. What value should be attached to the coffee stock? 50 cents or the replacement cost of $1 which would create a profit equal to the existing stock value?

Oil. When the Gulf Crisis of 1990 began, the cost of oil moved from around $13 per barrel to a high of around $29 per barrel in a short time. If oil companies had used replacement cost, this would have created huge fictitious profits. This might have resulted in higher tax payments and shareholders demanding dividends from a profit that existed only on paper. When the Gulf Crisis settled down to a quiet period (before the 1991 military action), the market price of oil dropped almost as dramatically as it had risen. This might have led to fictitious losses for companies in the following financial year with an ensuing loss of business confidence.

This scenario was not unique to the Gulf Crisis and we see the same situation arising with fluctuations in the price of Arab Light which moved from $8.74 per barrel on 31 December 1998 to $24.55 per barrel on 31 December 1999 and down to $17.10 on 31 December 2001 (www.eia.doe.gov).

Silver. In the early 1980s a Texan millionaire named Bunker Hunt attempted to make a 'killing' on the silver market by buying silver to force up the price and then selling at the high price to make a substantial profit. This led to remarkable scenes in the UK, with long lines of people outside jewellers wanting to sell items at much higher prices than their 'real' cost. Companies using silver as a raw material (e.g. jewellers, mirror manufacturers and electronics companies, which use silver as a conductive element) would have been badly affected had they used replacement cost in a similar way to the preceding two cases. The 'price' of silver in effect doubled in a short time, but the Federal Authorities in the USA stepped in and the plan was defeated.

Although LIFO, base stock and replacement cost do not have SSAP 9 approval, they are still used in practice. For example, LIFO is commonly used by UK companies with US subsidiaries, since LIFO is the main method of stock valuation in the USA.

Procedure to ascertain cost

Having decided upon the accounting policy of the company, there remains the problem of ascertaining the cost. In a retail environment, the 'cost' is the price the organisation had to pay to acquire the goods, and it is readily established by reference to the purchase invoice from the supplier. However, in a manufacturing organisation the concept of cost is not as simple. Should we use prime cost, or production cost, or total cost? SSAP 9 attempts to help by defining cost as the expenditure 'incurred in the normal course of business in bringing the product or service to its present location and condition'.

In a manufacturing organisation each expenditure is taken to include three constituents: direct materials, direct labour and appropriate overhead.

Direct materials

These include not only the costs of raw materials and component parts, but also the costs of insurance, handling (special packaging) and any import duties. An additional problem is waste and scrap. For instance, if a process inputs 100 tonnes at £45 per tonne, yet outputs only 90 tonnes, the output's stock value **must** be £4,500 (£45 × 100) and not £4,050 (90 × £45). (This assumes the 10 tonnes loss is a normal, regular part of the process.) An adjustment may be made for the residual value of the scrap/waste material, if any. The treatment of component parts will be the same, provided they form part of the finished product.

Direct labour

This is the cost of the actual production in the form of gross pay and those incidental costs of employing the direct workers (employer's national insurance contributions, additional pension contributions, etc.). The labour costs will be spread over the goods' production.

Appropriate overhead

It is here that the major difficulties arise in calculating the true cost of the product for stock valuation purposes. Normal practice is to classify overheads into five types and decide whether to include them in stock. The five types are as follows:

● Direct overheads – subcontract work, royalties.

● Indirect overheads – the cost of running the factory and supporting the direct workers; and the depreciation of capital items used in production.

● Administration overheads – the office costs and salaries of senior management.

● Selling and distribution overheads – advertising, delivery costs, packaging, salaries of sales personnel and depreciation of capital items used in the sales function.

● Finance overheads – the cost of borrowing and servicing debt.

We will look at each of these in turn, to demonstrate the difficulties that the accountant experiences.

Direct overheads. These should normally be included as part of 'cost'. But imagine a situation where some subcontract work has been carried out on *some* of our products because of a capacity problem (i.e. the factory could normally do the work, but due to a short-term problem some of the work has been subcontracted at a higher price/cost). In theory, those items subject to the subcontract work should have a higher stock value than 'normal' items. However, in practice, the difficulty of identifying such 'subcontracted' items is so great that many companies do not include such non-routine subcontract work in the stock value as a direct overhead. For example, if a factory produces 1,000,000 drills per month and 1,000 of them have to be sent out because of a machine breakdown, since all the drills are identical it would be very costly and time consuming to treat the 1,000 drills differently from the other 999,000. Hence the subcontract work would *not* form part of the overhead for stock valuation purposes (in such an organisation, the standard cost approach would be used when valuing stock). On the other hand, in a customised car firm producing 20 vehicles per month, special subcontract work would form part of the stock value because it is readily identifiable to individual units of stock.

To summarise, any regular, routine direct overhead will be included in the stock valuation, but a non-routine cost could present difficulties, especially in a high-volume/turnover organisation.

Indirect overheads. These always form part of the stock valuation, as such expenses are incurred in support of production. They include factory rent and rates, factory power and depreciation of plant and machinery; in fact, any indirect factory-related cost, including the warehouse costs of storing completed goods, will be included in the value of stock.

Administration overheads. This overhead is in respect of the whole business, so only that portion easily identifiable to production should form part of the stock valuation. For instance, the costs of the personnel or wages department could be apportioned to production on a head-count basis and that element would be included in the stock valuation. Any production-specific administration costs (welfare costs, canteen costs, etc.) would also be included in the stock valuation. If the expense cannot be identified as forming part of the production function, it will not form part of the stock valuation.

Selling and distribution overheads. These costs will not normally be included in the stock valuation as they are incurred after production has taken place. However, if the goods are on a 'sale or return' basis and are on the premises of the customer but remain the supplier's property, the delivery and packing costs will be included in the stock value of goods held on a customer's premises.

An additional difficulty concerns the modern technique of 'just-in-time' (JIT) stocking. Here, the customer does not keep large stocks, but simply 'calls off' stock from the supplier and is invoiced for the items delivered. There is an argument for the stock still in the hands of the supplier to bear more of this overhead within its valuation, since the only selling and distribution overhead to be charged/incurred is delivery. The goods have in fact been sold, but ownership has not yet changed hands. As JIT becomes more popular, this problem may give accountants and auditors much scope for debate.

Finance overheads. Normally these overheads would never be included within the stock valuation because they are not normally identifiable with production. In a job-costing context, however, it might be possible to use some of this overhead in stock valuation. Let us take the case of an engineering firm being requested to produce a turbine engine, which requires parts/components to be imported. It is logical for the financial charges for these imports (e.g. exchange fees or fees for letters of credit) to be included in the stock valuation.

Thus it can be seen that the identification of the overheads to be included in stock valuation is far from straightforward. In many cases it depends upon the judgement of the accountant and the unique operating conditions of the organisation.

In addition to the problem of deciding **whether** the five types of overhead should be included, there is the problem of deciding **how much** of the total overhead to include in the stock valuation at the year-end. SSAP 9 stipulates the use of 'normal activity' when making this decision on overheads. The vast majority of overheads are 'fixed', i.e. do not vary with activity, and it is customary to share these out over a normal or expected output. If this expected output is not reached, it is not acceptable to allow the actual production to bear the full overhead for stock purposes. A numerical example will illustrate this:

Overhead for the year	£200,000
Planned activity	10,000 units
Closing stock	3,000 units
Direct costs	£2 per unit
Actual activity	6,000 units

Stock value based on actual activity

Direct costs	$3,000 \times £2$	£6,000
Overhead	$\dfrac{3,000}{6,000} \times £200,000$	£100,000
Closing stock value		£106,000

Stock value based on planned or normal activity

Direct cost	$3,000 \times £2$	£6,000
Overhead	$\dfrac{3,000}{10,000} \times £200,000$	£60,000
Closing stock value		£66,000

Comparing the value of stock based upon actual activity with the value based upon planned or normal activity, we have a £40,000 difference. This could be regarded as increasing the current year's profit by carrying forward expenditure of £40,000 to set against the following year's profit.

The problem occurs because of the organisation's failure to meet expected output level (6,000 actual versus 10,000 planned). By adopting the **actual activity basis**, the organisation makes a profit out of failure. This cannot be an acceptable position when evaluating performance. Therefore, SSAP 9 stipulates **the planned or normal activity model** for stock valuation. The failure to meet planned output could be due to a variety of sources (e.g. strikes, poor weather, industrial conditions); the cause, however, is classed as abnormal or non-routine, and all such costs should be excluded from the valuation of stocks.

17.5.2 What is meant by net realisable value?

Section 17.5.1 attempted to identify the problems of arriving at the **true** meaning of cost for the purpose of stock valuation. Net realisable value is an alternative method of stock valuation if 'cost' does not reflect the true value of the stock. Prudence dictates that net realisable value will be used if it is lower than the 'cost' of the stock (however that may be calculated). These occasions will vary among organisations, but can be summarised as follows:

● There is a permanent fall in the market price of stock. Short-term fluctuations should not cause net realisable value to be implemented.

● The organisation is attempting to dispose of high stock levels or excessively priced stock to improve its liquidity position (quick ratio/acid test ratio) or reduce its stock holding costs. Such high stock volumes or values are primarily a result of poor management decision-making.

● The stock is physically deteriorating or is of an age where the market is reluctant to accept it. This is a common feature of the food industry, especially with the use of 'sell by' dates in the retail environment.

● Stock suffers obsolescence through some unplanned development. (Good management should never be surprised by obsolescence.) This development could be technical in nature, or due to the development of different marketing concepts within the organisation or a change in market needs.

● The management could decide to sell the goods at 'below cost' for sound marketing reasons. The concept of a 'loss leader' is well known in supermarkets, but organisations also sell below cost when trying to penetrate a new market or as a defence mechanism when attacked.

Such decisions are important and the change to net realisable value should not be undertaken without considerable forethought and planning. Obsolescence should be a decision based upon sound market intelligence and not a managerial 'whim'. The auditors of companies always examine such decisions to ensure they were made for sound business reasons. The opportunities for fraud in such 'price cutting' operations validate this level of external control.

Realisable value is, of course, the price the organisation receives for its stock from the market. However, getting this stock to market may involve additional expense and effort in repackaging, advertising, delivery and even repairing of damaged stock. This additional cost must be deducted from the realisable value to arrive at the net realisable value.

A numerical example will demonstrate this concept:

Item	Cost value	Net realisable value	Stock value
1 No. 876	£7,000	£9,000	£7,000
2 No. 997	£12,000	£12,500	£12,000
3 No. 1822	£8,000	£4,000	£4,000
4 No. 2076	£14,000	£8,000	£8,000
5 No. 4732	£27,000	£33,000	£27,000
	(a) £68,000	(b) £66,500	(c) £58,000

The stock value chosen for the accounts is (c) £58,000, although each item is assessed individually.

17.6 Work-in-progress

Stock classified as work-in-progress (WIP) is mainly found in manufacturing organisations and is simply the production that has not been completed by the end of the accounting period.

The valuation of WIP must follow the same SSAP 9 rules and be the lower of cost or net realisable value. We again face the difficulty of deciding what to include in cost. The three basic classes of cost – direct materials, direct labour and appropriate overhead – will still form the basis of ascertaining cost.

17.6.1 Direct materials

It is necessary to decide what proportion of the total materials have been used in WIP. The proportion will vary with different types of organisation, as the following two examples illustrate:

● If the item is complex or materially significant (e.g. a custom-made car or a piece of specialised machinery), the WIP calculation will be based on actual recorded materials and components used to date.

● If, however, we are dealing with mass production, it may not be possible to identify each individual item within WIP. In such cases, the accountant will make a judgement and define the WIP as being $x\%$ complete in regard to raw materials and components. For example, a drill manufacturer with 1 million tools per week in WIP may decide that in respect of raw materials they are 100% complete; WIP then gets the full materials cost of 1 million tools.

In both cases **consistency** is vital so that, however WIP is valued, the same method will always be used.

17.6.2 Direct labour

Again, it is necessary to decide how much direct labour the items in WIP have actually used. As with direct materials, there are two broad approaches:

● Where the item of WIP is complex or materially significant, the actual time 'booked' or recorded will form part of the WIP valuation.

● In a mass production situation, such precision may not be possible and an accounting judgement may have to be made as to the average percentage completion in respect of direct labour. In the example of the drill manufacturer, it could be that, on average, WIP is 80% complete in respect of direct labour.

17.6.3 Appropriate overhead

The same two approaches as for direct labour can be adopted:

● With a complex or materially significant item, it should be possible to allocate the overhead actually incurred. This could be an actual charge (e.g. subcontract work) or an application of the appropriate overhead recovery rate (ORR). For example, if we use a direct labour hour recovery rate and we have an ORR of £10/direct labour hour and the recorded labour time on the WIP item is twelve hours, then the overhead charge for WIP purposes is £120.

● With mass production items, the accountant must either use an overhead recovery rate approach or simply decide that, in respect of overheads, WIP is $y\%$ complete.

The above approaches must always be sanctioned by the firm's auditors to ensure that a true and fair view is achieved. The approach must also be consistent provided the basic product does not vary.

EXAMPLE I ● A company produces drills. The costs of a completed drill are:

	£
Direct materials	2.00
Direct labour	6.00
Appropriate overhead	10.00
Total cost	18.00 (for finished goods stock value purposes)

The company accountant takes the view that for WIP purposes the following applies:

Direct material	100% complete
Direct labour	80% complete
Appropriate overhead	30% complete

Therefore, for one WIP drill:

Direct material	£2.00 × 100% =	£2.00
Direct labour	£6.00 × 80% =	£4.80
Appropriate overhead	£10.00 × 30% =	£3.00
WIP value		£9.80

If the company has 100,000 drills in WIP, the value is:

100,000 × £9.80 = £980,000

This is a very simplistic view, but the principle can be adapted to cover more complex issues. For instance, there could be 200 different types of drill, but the same calculation can be done on each. Of course, sophisticated software makes the accountant's job mechanically easier.

This technique is particularly useful in processing industries, such as petroleum, brewing, dairy products or paint manufacture, where it might be impossible to identify WIP items precisely. The role of the auditor in validating such practices is paramount.

EXAMPLE 2 ● A custom-car company making sports cars has the following costs in respect of No. 821/C, an unfinished car, at the end of the month:

Materials charged to job 821/C	£2,100
Labour 120 hours @ £4	£480
Overhead £22/DLH × 120 hours	£2,640
WIP value of 821/C	£5,220

This is an accurate WIP value provided *all* the costs have been accurately recorded and charged. The amount of work involved is not great as the information is required by a normal job cost system. An added advantage is that the figure can be formally audited and proven. Work-in-progress valuation has its difficulties, but they are not insurmountable, given the skill of an accountant and a good working knowledge of the production process.

17.7 Stock control

The way in which stocks are physically controlled should not be overlooked. Discrepancies are generally of two types: disappearance through theft and improper accounting.[5] Management will, of course, be responsible for adequate systems of internal control, but losses may still occur through theft or lack of proper controls and recording.

Figure 17.7 Adjusted stock figure

	£
Stock on 7 January 20X1	XXX
Less: Purchases	(XXX)
Add: Sales	XXX
Stock at 31 December 20X0	XXX

Inadequate systems of accounting may also cause discrepancies between the physical and book stocks, with consequent correcting adjustments at the year-end.

Many companies are developing in-house computer systems or using bought-in packages to account for their stocks. Such systems are generally adequate for normal recording purposes, but they are still vulnerable to year-end discrepancies arising from errors in establishing the physical stock on hand at the year-end, and problems connected with the paperwork and the physical movement of stocks.

A major cause of discrepancy between physical and book stock is the 'cut-off' date. In matching sales with cost of sales, it may be difficult to identify exactly into which period of account certain stock movements should be placed, especially when the annual stocktake lasts many days or occurs at a date other than the last day of the financial year. It is customary to make an adjustment to the stock figure, as shown in Figure 17.7. This depends on an accurate record of movements between the stocktake date and the financial year-end.

Auditors have a special responsibility in relation to stock control. They should look carefully at the stocktaking procedures and satisfy themselves that the accounting arrangements are satisfactory. For example, in September 1987 Harris Queensway announced a stock reduction of some £15m in projected profit caused by write-downs in its furniture division. It blamed this on the inadequacy of control systems to 'identify ranges that were selling and ensure their replacement'. Interestingly, at the preceding AGM, no hint of the overvaluation was given and the auditors insisted that 'the company had no problem from the accounting point of view'.[6]

In many cases the auditor will be present at the stocktake. Even with this apparent safeguard, however, it is widely accepted that sometimes an accurate physical stocktake is almost impossible. The value of stocks should nevertheless be based on the best information available; and the resulting disclosed figure should be acceptable and provide a true and fair view on a going concern basis.

In practice, errors may continue unidentified for a number of years,[7] particularly if there is a paper-based system in operation. This was evident when T. J. Hughes reduced its profit for the year ended January 2001 by £2.5–3m from a forecast £8m.

17.8 Creative accounting

No area of accounting provides more opportunities for subjectivity and creative accounting than the valuation of stocks and work-in-progress. This section summarises the major methods employed.

17.8.1 Year-end manipulations

There are a number of stratagems companies have followed to reduce the cost of goods sold by inflating the stock figure. These include:

Manipulating cut-off procedures

Goods are taken into stock but the purchase invoices are not recorded.

Fictitious transfers

Year-end stock is inflated by recording fictitious transfers of non-existent stock e.g. it was alleged in the Miniscribe Corporation[8] that the company increased its year-end stock by recording fictitious transfers of non-existent stock from a Colorado location to overseas locations where physical stocktaking would be more difficult for the auditors to verify or the goods are described as being 'in-transit'.

Including obsolete stock at cost

In Miniscribe it was alleged that the company repackaged scrap and obsolete stock and treated as stock instead of expensing.

Inaccurate stock records

Where stock records are maintained it has been possible for senior management to fail to record material shrinkage due to loss and theft as in the Rite Aid Corporation.[9]

Journal adjustments

In addition to suppressing purchase invoices, making fictitious transfers, failing to write off obsolete stock or recognise stock losses, the senior management may simply reduce the cost of goods sold by adjusting journal entries, e.g. when preparing quarterly reports by crediting cost of goods and debiting accounts payable.[9]

17.8.2 Net realisable value (NRV)

Although the determination of net realisable value is dealt with extensively in the appendix to SSAP 9, the extent to which provisions can be made to reduce cost to NRV is highly subjective and open to manipulation. A provision is an effective smoothing device and allows overcautious write-downs to be made in profitable years and consequent write-backs in unprofitable ones.

17.8.3 Overheads

The treatment of overheads has been dealt with extensively in section 17.5.1 and is probably the area that gives the greatest scope for manipulation. Including overhead in the stock valuation has the effect of deferring the overhead's impact and so boosting profits. The Companies Act 1985 allows expenses incidental to the acquisition or production cost of an asset to be included in its cost. We have seen that this includes not only directly attributable production overheads, but also those which are indirectly attributable to production and interest on borrowed capital. SSAP 9 provides guidelines on the classification of overheads to achieve an appropriate allocation, but in practice it is difficult to make these distinctions and auditors will find it difficult to challenge management on such matters.

The statement suggests that the allocation of overheads included in the valuation needs to be based on the company's normal level of activity. The cost of unused capacity should be written off in the current year. The auditor will insist that allocation should be based on normal activity levels, but if the company underproduces, the overhead per unit increases and can therefore lead to higher year-end values. The creative accountant will be looking for ways to manipulate these year-end values, so that in bad times costs are carried forward to more profitable accounting periods.

17.8.4 Other methods of creative accounting

A simple manipulation is to show more or less stock than actually exists. If the commodity is messy and indistinguishable, the auditor may not have either the expertise or the will to verify measurements taken by the client's own employees. This lack of auditor measuring knowledge and involvement allowed one of the biggest frauds ever to take place, which became known as 'the great salad oil swindle'.[10]

Another obvious ploy is to include, in the stock valuation, obsolete or 'dead' stock. Of course, such stock should be written off. However, management may be 'optimistic' that it can be sold, particularly in times of economic recession. In high-tech industries, unrealistic values may be placed on stocks that in times of rapid development become obsolete quickly.

This can be highly significant, as in the case of Cal Micro[11] On 6 February 1995, Cal Micro restated its financial results for fiscal year 1994. The bulk of the adjustments to Cal Micro's financial statements – all highly material – occurred in the areas of accounts inventory, accounts receivable and property and, from an originally reported net income of approximately $5.1 million for the year ended 30 June 1994, the restated allowance for additional inventory obsolescence decreased net income by approximately $9.3 million.

This is a problem that investors need to be constantly aware of, particularly when a company experiences a downturn in demand but a pressure to maintain the semblance of growth. An example is provided by Lexmark[12] which was alleged to have made highly positive statements regarding strong sales and growth for its printers although there was intense competition in the industry – the company reporting quarter after quarter of strong financial growth whereas the actual position appeared to be very different with unmarketable inventory in excess of $25 million to be written down in the fourth quarter of fiscal year 2001. The share price of a company that conceals this type of information is maintained and allows insiders to offload their shareholding on an unsuspecting investing public.

17.9 Audit of the year-end physical stocktake

The problems of accounting for stock and work-in-progress are highlighted at the company's year-end. This is when the closing stock figure to be shown in both the profit and loss account and balance sheet is calculated. In practice, the company will assess the final stock figure by physically counting all stock held by the company for trade. The year-end stocktake is therefore an important accounting procedure, one in which the auditors are especially interested.

The auditor generally attends the stocktake to verify both the physical quantities and the procedure of collating those quantities. At the stocktake, values are rarely assigned to stock items, so the problems facing the auditor relate to: the identification of stock items; their ownership; and their physical condition.

17.9.1 Identification of stock items

The auditor will visit many companies in the course of a year and will spend a considerable time looking at accounting records. However, it is important for the auditor also to become familiar with each company's products by visiting the shopfloor or production facilities during the audit. This makes identification of individual stock items easier at the year-end. Distinguishing between two similar items can be crucial where there are large differences in value. For example, steel-coated brass rods look identical to steel rods, but their value to the company will be very different. It is important that they are not confused at stocktake because, once recorded on the stock sheets, values are assigned, production carries on, and the error cannot be traced.

17.9.2 Ownership of stock items

The year-end cut-off point is important to the final stock figure, but the business activities continue regardless of the year-end, and some account has to be taken of this. Hence the auditor must be aware that the recording of accounting transactions may not coincide with the physical flow of stock. Stock may be in one of two locations: included as part of stock; or in the loading bay area awaiting dispatch or receipt. Its treatment will depend on several factors (Figure 17.8). The auditor must be aware of all these possibilities and must be able to trace a sample of each stock entry through to the accounting records, so that:

● if purchase is recorded, but not sale, the item must be in stock;

● if sale is recorded, purchase must also be recorded and the item should not be in stock.

17.9.3 Physical condition of stock items

Stock in premium condition has a higher value than damaged stock. The auditor must ensure that the condition of stock is recorded at stocktake, so that the correct value is assigned to it. Items that are damaged or have been in stock for a long period will be written down to their net realisable value (which may be nil) as long as adequate details are given by the stocktaker. Once again, this is a problem of identification, so the auditor must be able to distinguish between, for instance, rolls of first quality and faulty fabric. Similarly, items that have been in stock for several stocktakes may have little value, and further enquiries about their status should be made at the time of stocktake.

Figure 17.8 Treatment of stock items

Sales	In stock	Loading bay
If invoiced to customer	Delete from stock	Stock not counted
If credited (i.e. returned)	Include	Include
If not invoiced/credited	Include unless accounting entry falls into this year	Include
Purchases		
If invoiced to company	Include in stock	Include in stock
If credited (i.e. to be returned)	Delete stock	Delete stock
If invoiced/credited	Include unless accounting entry falls into next year	Include

17.10 Published accounts

Disclosure requirements in the Companies Act 1985 and SSAP 9 have already been indicated. The standard requires the accounting policies that have been applied to be stated and applied consistently from year to year. Stocks should be subclassified in the balance sheet or in the notes to the financial statements so as to indicate the amounts held in each of the main categories in the standard balance sheet formats. Extensive disclosure requirements are required for long-term contracts. But will the ultimate user of those financial statements be confident that the information disclosed is reliable, relevant and useful? We have already indicated many areas of subjectivity and creative accounting, but are such possibilities material?

In 1982 Westwick and Shaw examined the accounts of 125 companies with respect to stock valuation and its likely impact on reported profit.[13] The results showed that the effect on profit before tax of a 1% error in closing stock valuation ranged from a low of 0.18% to a high of 25.9% (in one case) with a median of 2.26%. The industries most vulnerable to such errors were household goods, textiles, mechanical engineering, contracting and construction.

Clearly, the existence of such variations has repercussions for such measures as ROCE, EPS and the current ratio. The research also showed that, in a sample of audit managers, 85% were of the opinion that the difference between a pessimistic and an optimistic valuation of the same stock could be more than 6%.

Figure 17.9 Impact of a 5% change in closing stock

Company:	1	2	3	4	5	6	7	8
	£m	£m	£m	£m	£m	£m	£m	£m
Actual stock	390.0	428.0	1,154.0	509.0	509.0	280.0	360.0	232.0
Actual pre-tax profit	80.1	105.6	479.0	252.5	358.4	186.3	518.2	436.2
Change in pre-tax profit	19.5	21.4	57.7	25.2	25.5	14.0	18.0	11.6
Impact of a 5% Change in Closing Stock (%)								
(i) Pre-tax profit	24.0	20.0	12.0	10.0	7.0	7.5	3.5	2.7
(ii) Post-tax profit	22.0	27.0	12.0	8.8	6.8	6.3	3.4	2.5
(iii) Current assets	2.6	2.3	2.8	3.1	2.8	1.8	2.9	1.4
(iv) Current assets								
Less: Current liabilities	4.9	4.6	14.1	14.0	48.8	8.2	2.2	3.8
(v) Earnings per share	27.0	25.0	12.0	9.3	8.4	6.9	3.4	3.4

KEY COMPANIES:
1 Electrical retailer
2 Textile, etc., manufacturer
3 Brewing, public houses, etc.
4 Retailer – diversified
5 Pharmaceutical and retail chemist
6 Industrial paints and fibres
7 Food retailer
8 Food retailer

SSAP 9 has since been strengthened and these results may not be so indicative of the present situation. However, using the same principle, let us take a random selection of eight companies' recent annual accounts, apply a 5% increase in the closing stock valuation and calculate the effect on EPS (taxation is simply taken at 35% on the change in stock).

Figure 17.9 shows that, in absolute terms, the difference in pre-tax profits could be as much as £57.7m and the percentage change ranges from 2.7% to 24%. Of particular note is the change in EPS, which tends to be the major stock market indicator of performance. In the case of the electrical retailer (company 1), a 5% error in stock valuation could affect EPS by as much as 27%. The stocks of such a company could well be vulnerable to such factors as changes in fashion, technology and economic recession.

17.11 Long-term contracts

There is a wide selection of contract types in order to provide the flexibility needed to recognise the degree and timing of the responsibility assumed by the contractor for the costs of performance and the amount and nature of the profit offered to the contractor as an incentive to achieve targets such as an agreed date for completion.

There are two main categories of contract, namely:

(a) fixed-price contracts in which the contractor has full responsibility for the performance costs and resulting profit (or loss) – these are appropriate where the contractor has experience which allows it to assess the feasibility of completing the project within a predetermined cost; and

(b) cost-plus contracts in which the contractor has minimal responsibility for the performance costs and the negotiated fee (profit) is a fixed amount or percentage – these are appropriate for complex research and development projects where there are performance uncertainties and the possibility of changes being made to the specification.

Major projects may well require a range of subcontracts with perhaps the initial research stage being on a cost-plus percentage basis, the development stage being on a cost-plus fixed fee basis and the construction stage being on a fixed-price basis. If the project extends over a relatively long time there might also be economic price adjustment terms.

17.11.1 Financial accounting implications

Auditors require adequate internal accounting procedures to be in place where a company enters into a fixed-price contract in order to be able to confirm the amount of profit recognised at the balance sheet date.

Contracting officers placing the contract require similar internal accounting procedures to be in place for cost-plus contracts in order to be confident that the contractor will be able to supply appropriate cost data to support their invoices.

17.11.2 Financial reporting implications

SSAP 9 (revised) defines a long-term contract as:

> A contract entered into for the design, manufacture or construction of a single substantial asset or the provision of a service where the time taken to substantially complete the contract is such that the contract activity falls into different accounting periods. A contract that is accounted for as long-term will usually extend for a period exceeding one year...[14]

The important and controversial areas in the treatment of contracts concern the fact that the activity normally falls into different accounting periods and is expected to 'extend for a period exceeding one year'. Given this, how should we deal with the determination and timing of profit in accordance with the matching concept and 'value' long-term contracts in the balance sheet?

The justification for recognising profit as the contract progresses is contained in the explanatory note preceding SSAP (revised):

> Owing to the length of time taken to complete such contracts, to defer recording turnover and taking profit into account until completion may result in the profit and loss account reflecting not so much a fair view of the results of the activity of the company during the year but rather the results relating to contracts that have been completed in the year. It is therefore appropriate to take credit for ascertainable turnover and profit while contracts are in progress.[15]

Ever since the Companies Act 1981 stipulated that only 'realised' profits were to be included in profit for the year, the profession has been concerned about the legality of taking profit in accordance with SSAP 9. In addition, the Companies Act 1985 states that the amount to be included in the current assets (including uncompleted long-term contracts) is the lower of purchase price or production cost and net realisable value. In these circumstances, there was much debate centred on the legal position of SSAP 9 and the accounting procedures necessary for presenting and disclosing relevant and reliable information to users.

17.12 Recognition of profit

Turning to the first problem: recognition of profit. Legally, the profit and loss account should give a 'true and fair view' of the profit or loss for the financial year (section 228(2) Companies Act 1985). In the application of the matching principle it has always been generally accepted that a prudently calculated 'attributable profit' be included in the profit and loss account for the period under review. The objective, as always, was to give a 'true and fair' view of the results of activities during the period. SSAP 9 states that this attributable profit should be calculated on a prudent basis and, as a prerequisite, that the outcome of the contract can be assessed with reasonable certainty. Only then should profit be taken. Extensive guidelines are given in the appendix to SSAP 9 but the overriding principle is that no profit should be taken until the outcome of the contract can reasonably be foreseen. The profit to be recognised should prudently reflect the amount of work performed to date, and the method used to calculate such profit should be consistently applied. Inevitably, the recognition of attributable profit leaves much scope for the exercise of professional judgement, but there are generally accepted methods, e.g. the following:

(a) Attributable profit

$$= \frac{\text{Value of work certified to date}}{\text{Total contract price}} \times \text{Total estimated contract profit}$$

(b) **or**

$$= \frac{\text{Cost of work completed}}{\text{Estimated total costs}} \times \text{Total estimated contract profit}$$

(c) **or** (more prudently)

$$= \frac{\text{Cash received}}{\text{Total contract price}} \times \text{Total estimated contract profit}$$

SSAP 9 states that attributable profit is

> that part of the total profit currently estimated to arise over the duration of the contract ... that fairly reflects the profit attributable to that part of the work performed at the accounting date.[16]

This definition appears to favour approach (b) above, but it is emphasised that there are a number of ways of calculating 'attributable profit', all theoretically acceptable and not inconsistent with SSAP 9. If we accept that attributable profit is calculated, how then should this be reflected in the financial statements? Prior to 1988, there was a process of 'accumulating costs'. An account would be opened for each contract and into this account would be charged all costs (not only direct but also attributable overheads) **plus the attributable profit**. The resulting balance would then appear in the balance sheet as work-in-progress (net of any foreseeable losses and progress payments received or receivable). The accounting treatment resulted in attributable profit being introduced directly into the profit and loss account and likewise included in the work-in-progress valuation. This practice appeared to conflict with legal requirements in the Companies Act 1985. The usual way out of the dilemma was to include a statement in the notes to the accounts.

This situation was clearly unacceptable and after several years of debate the ASC developed the revised SSAP 9 to deal with this and at the same time bring UK accounting practice into line with international standards (IAS 2 and IAS 11).

17.13 Integrated approach

In general terms, the accounting requirements of SSAP 9 (revised) provide that the value of work completed by the year end should be included in turnover, against which the cost incurred in achieving that turnover should be charged as 'cost of sales'. This integrated approach radically changed the way in which long-term contracts were reported. The effect is that all attributable profit is removed from the balance sheet figure by treating all amounts recoverable on contracts as turnover and contract costs as cost of sales.

An example of the accounting entries at this point may help understanding:

(a) Contract price	1,600,000
(b) Costs to date	796,000
(c) Estimated costs to complete the contract	484,000
(d) Value of work satisfactorily completed	800,000
(e) Amount taken as cost of sales	760,000
(f) Cash received	752,000

Tabular format

	£000	
Recorded as turnover (being value of work done)	800	(A)
Cumulative payments on account	752	(B)
Classified as amounts recoverable	48	(C)
Total costs incurred	796	(D)
Transferred to cost of sales	760	(E)
Classified as long-term contract balances	36	(F)
Gross profit	40	(A–E)

Ledger account format

Contract account

(D) Costs incurred	796	(E) Cost of sales	760
		(F) Balance c/f	36
	796		796

Sales account

| (A) Value of work completed – P/L a/c | 800 | (A) Debtor | 800 |

Debtor account (contractee)

(A) Sales value of work	800	(B) Cash	752
		(C) Balance c/f	48
	800		800

Profit and loss account (extract)

	£000
Turnover	800
Cost of sales	760
Gross profit	40

Notes:

1 A provision for foreseeable losses is unnecessary since estimated costs to complete (£484) plus actual cost to date (£796) is substantially less than the contract price (£1,600).

2 An alternative approach would be to calculate the 'attributable profit' on one of the bases previously outlined, viz:

$$\frac{\text{Work certified}}{\text{Contract price}} \times \text{Total estimated contracted profit}$$

$$= \frac{800}{1,600} \times £320$$

$$= \underline{£160,000}$$

This calculation assumes that future costs are guaranteed as predicted and no unforeseen events will take place. This increase in reported profit, £120,000, may of course influence such areas as tax liabilities, dividend potential, EPS and other performance measures. The profit declared, £160,000 may prove to be overoptimistic if we take into account such matters as cost increases and the vagaries of long-term operations. Prudence dictates, therefore, that the lower profit figure, £40,000, be used for reporting purposes at the intermediate stage of the project. This approach defers profit taking to the later stages when contract profitability is more certain and may be vital when the contract is of a fixed price nature, e.g. governmental contracts. The more prudent practice also complies with the realisation concept whereby profits should only be taken when truly realised. (Consider the difficulties involved in calculating profits in respect of the Channel Tunnel project and the potential dangers of using the 'profit' for dividend payments.)

In addition to the general accounting principles involved in long-term contracts the example shown in Figure 17.10 is given in Appendix 3 of SSAP 9 to illustrate the financial statement presentation in a variety of circumstances. The following list refers to Figure 17.10.

Figure 17.10 Example as given in SSAP 9

	1	2	3	4	5	Balance sheet total	Profit and loss account
		Project number				*Balance*	*Profit and loss account*
Recorded as turnover – being value of work done	145	520	380	200	55		1,300
Cumulative payments on account	(100)	(600)	(400)	(150)	(80)		
Classified as amounts recoverable on contracts	45			50		95DR	
Balance (excess) of payments on account		(80)	(20)		(25)		
Applied as an offset against long-term contract balances – see below		60	20		15		
Residue classified as payments on account		(20)	—		(10)	(30)CR	
Total costs incurred	110	510	450	250	100		
Transferred to cost of sales	(110)	(450)	(350)	(250)	(55)		(1,215)
	—	60	100	—	45		
Provision/accrual for foreseeable losses				(40)	(30)		(70)
charged to cost of sales		60	100		15		
Classified as provision/accrual for losses				(40)		(40)CR	
Balance (excess) of payments on account applied as offset against long-term contract balances		(60)	(20)		(15)		
Classified as long-term contract balances		—	80		—	80DR	
Gross profit on long-term contracts	35	70	30	(90)	(30)		15

Project

1 If turnover exceeds payments on account the 'amount recoverable on contracts' (45) is disclosed separately within debtors.

2 If payments on account are greater than turnover to date, the excess (80) is first offset against any debit balance on the contract included in stocks (60) and then any residual (20) is classified as payments on account – creditors.

3 Again, there are excess payments on account (20) which are offset against the debit balance on the contract (100). The residual amount (80) is classified as long-term contract balances.

4 Turnover exceeds payments on account and the excess (50) will be shown as 'amounts recoverable on contracts'. Turnover will be shown as 200, while against this will be recorded cost of sales (250) and a provision for a foreseeable loss (40) leaving a loss on this contract (90). The provision will appear in the balance sheet within 'creditors' or 'provisions for liabilities and charges' as appropriate.

5 The provision for the foreseeable loss (30) is deducted from the contract balance (45), so reducing it to net realisable value (15). The excess of payments on account (25) is first offset against the balance on the contract balance (now 15) and the residual (10) is classified as payment on account – creditors.

The effect of these various transactions on the profit and loss account and balance sheet can be summarised as follows:

Profit and loss account		£
Turnover		1300
Cost of sales	1215	
(provision for losses)	70	1285
Gross profit		15

Balance sheet	
Provision for foreseeable losses	40
Creditors – payments on account	30
Debtors – amounts recoverable on contracts	95
Long-term contract balances	80

The objective of this revised approach for recording and presenting the accounting information is to give an integrated presentation of long-term contract activity in the financial statements. The conflict with the Companies Act 1985 is also eliminated. There are of course still areas which involve the exercise of professional judgement. The John Laing plc 1999 accounts stated the following accounting policy for long-term contracts:

Profits on long-term contracts are calculated in accordance with standard accounting practice and do not therefore relate directly to turnover. Profit on current contracts is only taken at a stage near enough to completion for that profit to be reasonably certain. Provision is made for all losses incurred to the accounting date together with any further losses that are foreseen in bringing contracts to completion.

Amounts recoverable on contracts which are included in debtors are stated at cost, plus attributable profit to the extent that this is reasonably certain after making provision for contingencies, less any losses incurred or foreseen in bringing contracts to completion, and less amounts received as progress payments. Cost for this purpose includes valuations of all work done by subcontractors, whether certified or not, and all overheads other than those relating to the general administration of the relevant companies. For any contracts where receipts exceed the book value of work done, the excess is included in creditors as payments on account.

However, overall, the aim is to give a true and fair view of the profit or loss for the accounting period and of the financial position at the end of the accounting period.

Summary

Examples of differences in stock valuation are not uncommon.[17] For example, in 1984, Fidelity, the electronic equipment manufacturer, was purchased for £13.4m.[18] This price was largely based on the 1983/4 profit figure of £400,000. Subsequently, it was maintained that this 'profit' should actually be a loss of £1.3m – a difference of £1.7m. Much of this difference was attributable to stock discrepancies. The claim was contested, but it does illustrate that a disparity can occur when important figures are left to 'professional judgement'.

Another case involved the selling of British Wheelset by British Steel, just before privatisation in 1988, at a price of £16.9m.[19] It was claimed that the accounts 'were not drawn up on a consistent basis in accordance with generally accepted accounting practice'. If certain stock provisions had been made, these would have resulted in a £5m (30%) difference in the purchase price.

Other areas that cause difficulties to the user of published information are the capitalisation of interest and the reporting of write-downs on acquisition. Post-acquisition profits can be influenced by excessive write-downs of stocks on acquisition, which has the effect of increasing goodwill. These written-down stocks can eventually be sold at higher prices, thus improving post-acquisition profits.

Although legal requirements and SSAP 9 have improved the reporting requirements, many areas of subjective judgement can have substantial effects on the reporting of financial information.

REVIEW QUESTIONS

1 Discuss why some form of theoretical pricing model is required for stock valuation purposes.

2 Discuss the acceptability of the following methods of stock valuation: LIFO; base stock; replacement cost.

3 Discuss the application of individual judgement in stock valuation, e.g. changing the basis of overhead absorption.

4 Explain the criteria to be applied when selecting the method to be used for allocating costs.

5 Discuss the effect on work-in-progress and finished good valuation if the net realisable value of the raw material is lower than cost at the balance sheet date.

6 Discuss the point in a contract's life when it becomes appropriate to recognise profit and the feasibility of specifying a common point, e.g. when contract is 25% complete.

7 'Profit on a contract is not realised until completion of the contract.' Discuss.

8 'There should be one specified method for calculating attributable profit.' Discuss.

EXERCISES

An extract from the solution is provided in the appendix at the end of the text for exercises marked with an asterisk (*).

Question 1

Sunhats Ltd manufactures patent hats. It carries stocks of these and sells to wholesalers and retailers via a number of salespeople. The following expenses are charged in the profit and loss account:

Wages of: Storemen and factory foremen

Salaries of: Production manager, personnel officer, buyer, salespeople, sales manager, accountant, company secretary

Other: Directors' fees, rent and rates, electric power, repairs, depreciation, carriage outwards, advertising, bad debts, interest on bank overdraft, development expenditure for new type of hat.

Required:
Which of these expenses can reasonably be included in the valuation of stock?

* Question 2

Purchases of a certain product during July were:

July		
1	100 units @	10.00
12	100 units @	9.80
15	50 units @	9.60
20	100 units @	9.40

Units sold during the month were:

July	
10	80 units
14	100 units
30	90 units

Required: Assuming no opening inventories,
  (i) Determine the cost of goods sold for July under three different valuation methods.
 (ii) Discuss the advantages and/or disadvantages of each of these methods.
(iii) A physical stocktake revealed a shortage of five units. Show how you would bring this into account.

* Question 3

Alpha Ltd makes one standard article. You have been given the following information:

1 The stock sheets at the year-end show the following items:

Raw materials:
100 tons of steel:
Cost £140 per ton
Present price £130 per ton

40 semi-finished units
Cost of materials £50 per unit
Labour cost to date £100 per unit
Selling price £500 per unit (completed)

Finished goods:
100 finished units:
Cost of materials £50 per unit
Labour cost £150 per unit
Selling price £500 per unit

10 damaged finished units:
Cost to rectify the damage £200 per unit
Selling price £500 per unit (when rectified)

2 Manufacturing overheads are 100% of labour cost.

Selling and distribution expenses are £60 per unit (mainly salespeople's commission and freight charges).

Required:
From the information in notes 1 and 2, state the amounts to be included in the balance sheet of Alpha Ltd in respect of stock. State also the principles you have applied.

Question 4

Beta Ltd commenced business on 1 January and is making up its first year's accounts. The company uses standard costs. The company stocks a variety of raw materials and components for use in its manufacturing business. The accounting records show the following:

	Standard cost of purchases £	Price variance £	Adverse (favourable) variances Usage variance £
July	10,000	800	(400)
August	12,000	1,100	100
September	9,000	700	(300)
October	8,000	900	200
November	12,000	1,000	300
December	10,000	800	(200)
Cumulative figures for whole year	110,000	8,700	(600)

Raw materials control account balance at year-end is £30,000 (at standard cost).

Required:

The company's draft balance sheet includes 'Stocks, at the lower of cost and net realisable value £80,000'. This includes raw materials £30,000: do you consider this to be acceptable? If so, why? If not, state what you consider to be an acceptable figure.

(Note: for the purpose of this exercise, you may assume that the raw materials will realise more than cost.)

Question 5

MACTAR have a series of contracts to resurface sections of motorways in England and Wales. The scale of the contract means several years' work and each motorway section is regarded as a separate contract.

M1	£m
Contract	3.0
Costs to date	2.1
Estimated cost to complete	0.3
Certified value of work completed to date	1.8
Payments applied for to date	1.75
Payment received to date	1.5

M6	£m
Contract sum	2.0
Costs to date	0.3
Estimated cost to complete	1.1
Certified value of materials delivered	0.1
Payments applied for to date	0.1
Payments received to date	—

M62	£m
Contract sum	2.5
Costs to date	2.3
Estimated costs to complete	0.8
Certified value of work completed to date	1.3
Payments applied for to date	1.0
Payments received to date	0.75

This contract has had **major** difficulties due to difficult terrain, and the contract only allows for a 10% increase in contract sum for such events.

Required:
From the information above, calculate for each contract the amount of profit (or loss) you would show for the year and show how these contracts would appear in the balance sheet with all appropriate notes.

* Question 6

At 31 October 20X0, Lytax Ltd was engaged in various contracts including five long-term contracts, details of which are given below:

	1 £000	2 £000	3 £000	4 £000	5 £000
Contract price	1,100	950	1,400	1,300	1,200
At 31 October					
Cumulative costs incurred	664	535	810	640	1,070
Estimated further costs to completion	106	75	680	800	165
Estimated cost of post-completion guarantee rectification work	30	10	45	20	5
Cumulative costs incurred transferred to cost of sales	580	470	646	525	900
Progress payments:					
Cumulative receipts	615	680	615	385	722
Invoiced					
– awaiting receipt	60	40	25	200	34
– retained by contractee	75	80	60	65	84

It is not expected that any contractees will default on their payments.

Up to 31 October 20X9, the following amounts have been included in the turnover and cost of sales figures:

	1 £000	2 £000	3 £000	4 £000	5 £000
Cumulative turnover	560	340	517	400	610
Cumulative costs incurred transferred to cost of sales	460	245	517	400	610
Foreseeable loss transferred to cost of sales	—	—	—	70	—

It is the accounting policy of Lytax Ltd to arrive at contract turnover by adjusting contract cost of sales (including foreseeable losses) by the amount of contract profit or loss to be regarded as recognised, separately for each contract.

Required:
Show how these items will appear in the balance sheet of Lytax Ltd with all appropriate notes. Show all workings in tabular form.

* Question 7

During its financial year ended 30 June 20X7 Beavers Ltd, an engineering company, has worked on several contracts. Information relating to one of them is given below:

Contract X201

Date commenced	1 July 20X6
Original estimate of completion date	30 September 20X7
Contract price	£240,000
Proportion of work certified as satisfactorily completed (and invoiced) up to 30 June 20X7	£180,000
Progress payments from Dam Ltd	£150,000

Costs up to 30 June 20X7

Wages	£91,000
Materials sent to site	£36,000
Other contract costs	£18,000
Proportion of Head Office costs	£6,000
Plant and equipment transferred to the site (at book value on 1 July 20X6)	£9,000

The plant and equipment is expected to have a book value of about £1,000 when the contract is completed.

Stock of materials at site 30 June 20X7	£3,000
Expected additional costs to complete the contract:	
Wages	£10,000
Materials (including stock at 30 June 20X7)	£12,000
Other (including Head Office costs)	£8,000

At 30 June 20X7 it is estimated that work to a cost value of £19,000 has been completed, but not included in the certifications.

If the contract is completed one month earlier than originally scheduled, an extra £10,000 will be paid to the contractors. At the end of June 20X7 there seemed to be a 'good chance' that this would happen.

Required:
(a) Show the account for the contract in the books of Beavers Ltd, up to 30 June 20X7 (including any transfer to the profit and loss account which you think is appropriate).
(b) Show the balance sheet entries.
(c) Circulate the profit (or loss) to be recognised in the 20X6–X7 accounts.

References

1 SSAP 9 (Revised) *Stocks and Long-term Contracts*, ASC, September 1988.
2 'A guide to accounting standards – valuation of stocks and work-in-progress', *Accountants Digest*, Summer 1984.
3 M. Jones, 'Cooking the accounts', *Certified Accountant*, July 1988, p. 39.

4 SSAP 9, Appendix 1, para. 12.

5 T.S. Dudick, 'How to avoid the common pitfalls in accounting for inventory', *The Practical Accountant*, January/February 1975, p. 65.

6 *Certified Accountant*, October 1987, p. 7.

7 M. Perry, 'Valuation problems force FD to quit', *Accountancy Age*, 15 March 2001, p. 2.

8 www.sec.gov/litigation/admin/34-41729.htm

9 www.sec.gov/litigation/admin/34-41729.htm

10 E. Woolf, 'Auditing the stocks – part II', *Accountancy*, May 1976, pp. 108–110.

11 www.sec.gov/litigation/admin/34-41720.htm

12 http://securities.stanford.edu/1022/LXK01-01/

13 C. Westwick and D. Shaw, 'Subjectivity and reported profit', *Accountancy*, June 1982, pp. 129–131.

14 SSAP 9, *Stocks and Long-term Contracts*, ASC, 1988, para. 22.

15 SSAP 9, ASC, 1988, para. 7.

16 SSAP 9, ACS, 1988, para. 23.

17 E. Woolf, *op. cit.*, parts I and II.

18 K. Bhattacharya, 'More or less true, quite fair', *Accountancy*, December 1988, p. 126.

19 R. Northedge, 'Steel attacked over wheelset valuation', *Daily Telegraph*, 2 January 1991, p. 19.

PART **4**

Consolidated accounts

CHAPTER **18**

Accounting for groups at the date of acquisition – acquired for cash

18.1 Introduction

A group is a business combination that exists when there are two or more companies that act as an economic entity controlled by a single management. This definition does not extend to companies established by the same individuals, e.g. a husband and wife who own two or more companies. The creation of a business combination is variously referred to as a takeover, an acquisition or a merger. We include within the term 'business combination' all types of merger, including vertical, horizontal and conglomerate.

In this chapter we will be considering:

- Business combinations: reasons for and financial reporting requirements
  - reasons for business combinations
  - defining a group
  - when a parent is exempt or permitted to omit a subsidiary from group accounts
- Acquiring shares for cash at book values
  - accounting for an investment in a subsidiary in parent company accounts – no goodwill
  - preparing consolidated accounts at date of acquisition – no goodwill
  - accounting for an investment in a subsidiary in parent company accounts – with goodwill
  - preparing consolidated accounts at date of acquisition – with goodwill
- Acquiring shares for cash where fair values of assets and liabilities differ from book values
  - FRS 7 *Fair Values in Acquisition Accounting* definition of fair values
  - preparing consolidated accounts incorporating fair values
  - applying FRS 7 to specific assets and liabilities
- Minority interests
  - FRS 2 *Accounting for Subsidiary Undertakings* treatment
  - proportional consolidation
  - proprietary and entity goodwill

18.2 Business combinations: why they occur

In simple terms, the ownership of the shares of the acquired company allows the new owner to control the net assets of that company. Why should one company wish to gain ownership and control of the net assets of another company?

18.2.1 Motives for business combinations

Many studies have looked at the reasons for business combinations. Figure 18.1 lists some of the motives that have been identified from a number of different sources.[1-4]

Figure 18.1 Motives for business combinations

Production-based motives

- Synergies, e.g. economies of scale
- Accelerate growth or reduce risks and costs, e.g. acquiring a research department or new technology
- Acquire expanded capacity at a lower cost than buying new

Commercial-based motives for horizontal combinations between firms with similar products operating in the same or different markets

- Gain market share in the same industry, i.e. horizontal combinations
- Eliminate competition
- Acquire brands

Commercial-based motives for vertical combinations between firms in which a buyer/seller relationship could exist

- Acquire new sources of supply
- Acquire broader customer base

Financial-based motives for horizontal and vertical combinations

- Obtaining high profile image in the eyes of bankers, investors and suppliers, i.e. credit becomes cheaper

Financial-based motives for conglomerate combinations between two firms that have no buyer/seller relationship, no technical and distributional relationship and do not deal in similar products

- Acquire complementary resources to smooth earnings and balance cyclicality

Financial-based motives for any combination

- Utilise financial strengths of acquired company, e.g. tax credits, borrowing capacity
- Undervalued assets of the acquired company can be disposed of at a profit, i.e. asset stripping
- Underperforming parts of the acquired company can be disposed of and the proceeds used to defray the cost of the acquisition

Political-based motives

- Avoid being taken over, i.e. a defensive measure
- Avoid cultural problems associated with cross-border trade
- Enhance management salaries from the increased size of the combined business
- Ego, fashion and other 'irrational' reasons

Foster[5] cites an interesting survey carried out by Baker, Miller and Rampsberger,[6] which illustrates that merger motives depend on the type of merger. Chief executives of a sample of companies involved in merger activity were asked to rank motives for horizontal mergers (in which the two companies have identical products) and conglomerate mergers (in which the two companies have no buyer/seller relationship, no products in common, and no other relationship). The ranking is shown in Figure 18.2.

Although researchers agree on the list of motives for mergers, there is no general agreement about the importance of each motive.

On the merger of Guinness plc with Grand Metropolitan to form Diageo the directors gave their reasons for the merger in the circular to Guinness shareholders as follows:

> The directors of both Guinness and GrandMet believe that the Merger represents a significant opportunity to create a major new force in branded food and drinks which will operate on a truly international scale. Guinness will gain an increased interest in North America, the world's largest consumer market, through Pilsbury and Burger King. GrandMet will benefit from Guinness's successful spirits business in emerging markets. Both groups will benefit from the complementary nature of their respective spirits operations and the scope for cost savings as a result of the Merger.

They also told the shareholders that the step change in scale would provide the Merged Group with five valuable benefits which, together, would establish a platform for sustained future growth. The valuable benefits were:

- A complementary and broad product range from combined spirits and wines business allowing the Group to offer an expanded product range.
- Greater geographic breadth with the critical mass to exploit the opportunities for growth.
- Enhanced marketing capability from shared use of high calibre and experienced management team, translating into superior brand management, innovative new product and brand development and world class marketing.
- Greater cost efficiency generating operating cost savings of some £175m per annum by the third year.
- Financial capacity to develop the businesses both organically and by acquisition.

However, whether a merger achieves its objectives is another issue (within months there were rumours that Diageo would sell the Burger King operation as a management

Figure 18.2 Ranking motives for business combinations

Horizontal combinations	Conglomerate combinations
1 To effect more rapid growth	1 To effect more rapid growth
2 To gain economies of sale	2 To spread risk through diversification
3 To increase market share	3 To increase market value of stock
4 To expand geographical mix	4 To expand/improve the profit
5 To increase market value of seasonal sales	5 To counter cycle of stock
6 To expand/improve product mix	6 To enhance power/prestige of firm

buyout) and beyond the scope of this text. We will concentrate on the financial reporting requirements when a combination exists.

18.3 Business combinations: financial reporting requirements

The Companies Act 1985 (as amended by the Companies Act 1989) provides that accounts, known as **consolidated accounts** or **group accounts**, are to be prepared by the management of the acquiring company and presented to the shareholders of the acquiring company. Such consolidated accounts are required to present a **true and fair view** of the **combined profit (loss) of the entity and of the combined assets and liabilities** at the end of the year.[7]

There are also professional regulations emanating from the standard-setting authority. These are the Financial Reporting Standards issued by the ASB, e.g. FRS 2.

18.3.1 Why is it necessary to define when a group exists?

Groups are required to consolidate the results of members of the group to produce group accounts. It is therefore necessary to define when a company is to be regarded as a member of the group.

18.3.2 Why is an exact definition important?

If each of the member companies has a healthy profit and a strong balance sheet, the controlling company will have little incentive to avoid consolidation. However, if a member of the group makes losses or has a weak balance sheet, e.g. an excessive level of gearing, there is an obvious attraction in omitting the loss or weak asset/liability position of that member from the consolidation.

To prevent groups being able to manipulate the consolidated picture by including or excluding the results of a company, regulations have been introduced to define when a group relationship exists.

Definition of a group

A group exists if a dominant company, known as the **parent** undertaking or holding company, **controls** another company known as the **subsidiary** undertaking. For example, if Strong plc controls Weak plc, then Strong plc is the parent undertaking, Weak plc is the subsidiary undertaking, and together they comprise the Strong Group. FRS 2 *Accounting for Subsidiary Undertakings* defines control (para. 6) as 'the ability of an undertaking to direct the financial and operating policies of another undertaking with a view to gaining economic benefits from its activities'.

How is the existence of control determined?

The Companies Act 1985 stipulates that control exists in the following circumstances:[8]

1 Strong plc has **direct voting control** arising from its ownership of more than 50% of the voting shares.

2 Strong plc holds less than 50% of the voting shares but has organised affairs to achieve **indirect voting control**, e.g. by virtue of an agreement with the other shareholders or by virtue of the right to appoint the majority of the directors.

3 Strong plc holds no voting shares but has organised affairs so that it has the **right to**

exercise **dominant influence** over the operating and financial policies of Weak plc, e.g. by a clause to this effect in the memorandum or articles of association or by a contract entered into by Weak plc granting this influence.

4 Strong plc **actually exercises dominant influence** over the operating and financial policies of Weak plc, by virtue of arrangements mentioned in (3) above, and it has an **equity interest that exceeds 20%** of the voting power but is less than 50%.

5 Strong plc has more than 20% of the equity shares in Weak plc and both companies are **managed on a unified basis**, e.g. when the management of Strong plc treat the two companies as a single entity.

18.4 Business combinations: criteria for not consolidating

We will now look at when a parent or holding company is exempt from preparing consolidated accounts; may omit; or must omit the results of a subsidiary from the consolidated accounts.

18.4.1 FRS 2 exempts a parent in some circumstances from preparing consolidated accounts

This exemption applies, for example, if:

● the company is small or medium-size;

● the parent is a wholly-owned subsidiary whose immediate parent is incorporated in a European Community country;

● the parent is a majority-owned subsidiary and a request has not been made by 5% of the total shares or more than 50% of the total minority holdings. This recognises that it is unlikely that the minority shareholders would normally be interested in consolidated accounts;

● all the subsidiaries are permitted or required to be excluded from the consolidation. This would be a highly unusual position.

18.4.2 Subsidiaries in fact but not in name

Managements have been able to avoid including the results of subsidiaries by technically arranging the legal form of the investment so that the investee company fell outside the definition of a subsidiary.

The Companies Act 1989 removed some of the ways in which one company could control another but avoid consolidating the results. For example, prior to the Companies Act 1989, the definition of a group was that Strong plc should hold more than 50% of the **ordinary** shares. This meant that Strong plc could control Weak plc by issuing voting shares that were not ordinary shares but gave effective control. The change from holding more than 50% of the ordinary shares to holding more than 50% of the voting power has removed this possibility.

18.4.3 Subsidiaries in name but not included in the group accounts

Another form of manipulation was for the holding company to accept that the investee was a subsidiary, but then find grounds for excluding it anyway.

There may be good reasons why the consolidation of the two sets of accounts would not give a true and fair view of the group and so there are still statutory grounds for requiring or allowing the exclusion of a subsidiary from the consolidated accounts. The grounds are set out in the Companies Act 1985 as follows.[9]

When a subsidiary must be excluded

The Companies Act provides that a subsidiary must be excluded where the activities of the subsidiary are so different that consolidated accounts would not give a true and fair view.

The ASB were unhappy with this as a ground for exclusion and have effectively prevented it from being used in practice by making it a condition that exclusion is only permitted where to include the subsidiary would result in the failure of the consolidated accounts to give a true and fair view. It also expressed the view that it could not envisage any situations where this condition could be satisfied.

It could be argued that by making this condition the ASB are usurping the role of the legislature in that the Companies Act exclusion is for all practical purposes overridden.

However, the ASB approach could be justified on the grounds that, with the issue of SSAP 25 *Segmental Reporting*, it is now possible for the parent to provide explanatory segmental information dealing with the subsidiary whose activities were different.

When a subsidiary may be excluded under the Companies Act

There is a permissive statutory right to omit the subsidiary in the following circumstances:

- The results of the subsidiary cannot be obtained without **disproportionate expense or undue delay**.

- There is a **severe, long-term restriction** that substantially hinders the exercise of the rights of the parent company over the assets or management of the subsidiary.

- The investment in the subsidiary is held exclusively with a **view to resale** and the results have not previously been consolidated. The latter condition is to prevent a parent company omitting a subsidiary that has started to make a loss in the year the loss arises by deciding to dispose of its shares in the subsidiary.

- The results of the subsidiary are **immaterial** in the context of the group. The requirement to view the position in the context of the group is to dissuade parent companies from setting up a series of subsidiaries that are immaterial when taken singly but material when taken together. The right only exists if the combined totals are immaterial.

What view did the ASB take of these permissive statutory rights?

- FRS 2 *Accounting for Subsidiary Undertakings*, issued by the ASB in 1992, does not permit subsidiaries to be excluded merely because the results of the subsidiary cannot be obtained without **disproportionate expense or undue delay**. The reason for restricting this permissive right is that the two reasons are subjective and it is too easy for a company to raise the excuse of **disproportionate expense or undue delay** if it did not wish to include the subsidiary, e.g. because its results were poor.

- FRS 2 went further than the Companies Act by requiring, rather than permitting, the exclusion in the case of **severe long-term restrictions**. Where excluded, such subsidiaries are required to be treated as **fixed asset** investments and carried at a fixed amount. The fixed amount is to be calculated using the equity method and frozen at the amount calculated at the date the severe restrictions came into effect. If however the parent still exercises significant influence over it then this amount will be revised each year to bring into account its proportion of any profits or losses.

- FRS 2 also requires exclusion when the group's interest is held **exclusively with a view to a subsequent resale** and stipulates that such subsidiaries should be treated as **current assets** and carried at the lower of cost and net realisable value.

- FRS 2 and the Companies Act have the same approach to exclusion on grounds of **immateriality**.

18.5 Parent company: treatment of investment in a subsidiary acquired for cash and no goodwill

How is the investment in a subsidiary dealt with when all the shares are acquired for cash, or when the parent company issues shares equal to the net asset value of the subsidiary? We consider the parent company first and then the subsidiary company.

18.5.1 Accounting in the parent company

When a company acquires shares in another company, an immediate asset is recorded and there is a right to receive future dividends.

The asset

At the date of the acquisition, a non–current asset is created in the books of the investing company; this will give rise to a reduction in the **net current assets** if the consideration is in cash, or an increase in the share capital if the consideration is in shares.

Future dividends

The investing company effectively owns the earnings generated by the subsidiary. These earnings might be passed through to the holding company as dividends. The proportion of the earnings passed through will depend on the financial position of the subsidiary and the nature of the industry. For example, a subsidiary in the pharmaceutical industry might plough back a high proportion of its earnings; a subsidiary in the property industry, collecting rentals on properties, might pass all its earnings through to the holding company as a dividend.

Although the holding company can require the subsidiary to declare a dividend that would distribute all of the earnings, it has to have regard to the normal commercial facts, e.g. the need to replace and support development in the subsidiary.

Balance sheet entry for the investment when acquired for cash

Assume that Strong plc, the parent company, acquires shares in Weak plc, the subsidiary, which has a total issued capital of 5,000 £1 shares, for cash at a cost of £1.50 per share on 1 January 20X1 from existing shareholders. Figure 18.3 shows the balance sheet effect of acquiring different numbers of shares:

- The shares are reported as an investment in shares in the subsidiary and classified as a fixed asset valued at cost in the balance sheet of Strong plc.

- The net current assets of Strong plc are reduced by the payment made to the shareholders of Weak plc.

Figure 18.3 Balance sheet entries of Strong plc as at the date of acquisition if Strong plc acquires various percentages of the 5,000 shares in Weak plc for cash

	Before buying shares £	After buying 5% of Weak £	After buying 20% of Weak £	After buying 60% of Weak £	After buying 100% of Weak £
Fixed assets	12,250	12,250	12,250	12,250	12,250
Investment in Weak plc		375	1,500	4,500	7,500
Net current assets/(liabilities)	2,750	2,375	1,250	(1,750)	(4,750)
Net assets	15,000	15,000	15,000	15,000	15,000
Ordinary share capital	8,750	8,750	8,750	8,750	8,750
Profit and loss balance	6,250	6,250	6,250	6,250	6,250
Net capital employed	15,000	15,000	15,000	15,000	15,000

● The accounting for the transaction is not dependent on the number of shares acquired. Regardless of the number of shares acquired, there will be a new fixed asset entitled 'Investment in subsidiary' and a reduction in the net current assets.

In practice, the price of a share might differ according to the number of shares acquired, e.g. a 5% interest would be valued on a dividend basis, while a 60% interest would be valued on an earnings basis: the price has been kept constant for illustration only, on the basis that the shares were acquired in the open market at the quoted market price.

Will any of the balance sheet ratios for Strong plc be different after recording the investment?

Any ratio that uses the **net current asset** figure or the **current asset** figure will be different, e.g. the current ratio, the working capital turnover ratio. Any ratio that uses total assets or net assets of Strong plc will be unaffected by the acquisition of shares in Weak plc.

18.5.2 Accounting in the subsidiary company

There is often uncertainty about whether a takeover affects the accounts of the company that has been taken over. It depends on who sold the shares to the holding company and who received the consideration.

Assuming that Strong acquired shares in Weak for cash, (a) by purchasing the shares in the market from Big and Tiny who hold all the issued shares in Weak and (b) by acquiring new shares from Weak to give it more than 50% of the total shares in issue, i.e. Strong holds more shares than those held by Big and Tiny combined, the effect is as follows:

(a) Purchase in market

No effect on Weak

(b) New issue by Weak

Effect on Weak

Note that if Strong purchases all the Weak shares from the two existing shareholders then Weak becomes a wholly owned subsidiary of Strong. If, however, it acquires a new issue of shares from Weak then Big and Tiny remain as shareholders of Weak and Big and Tiny will appear as a minority interest in the Strong Group accounts.

If Strong plc acquired the shares directly from Weak plc by way of a new issue, Weak plc will receive the payment of cash and increase its issued share capital. If Strong plc acquired the shares on the stock market from an existing shareholder, the shareholder will receive the cash and no transaction will be recorded in the financial records of Weak plc.

Assuming that the shares acquired by Strong plc were obtained from existing shareholders of Weak plc, the balance sheet of Weak plc would appear as in Figure 18.4. The transfer of shares from one shareholder to another has no effect on the assets, liabilities and capital of the company that originally issued the shares. Weak plc will merely amend its register of members to record that the shares have been transferred to Strong plc.

What does a comparison of the amount paid by Strong plc and the Weak plc balance sheet show us?

Assuming that Strong plc acquired all of the shares in Weak plc, a comparison of the amount that Strong plc paid for the shares and the balance sheet of Weak plc at the date

Figure 18.4 Balance sheet entries of Weak plc after the acquisition by Strong plc of various percentages of the shares held by existing Weak plc shareholders

	Before buying shares £	After buying 5% of Weak £	After buying 20% of Weak £	After buying 60% of Weak £	After buying 100% of Weak £
Fixed assets	5,500	5,500	5,500	5,500	5,500
Net current assets	2,000	2,000	2,000	2,000	2,000
	7,500	7,500	7,500	7,500	7,500
Ordinary share capital	5,000	5,000	5,000	5,000	5,000
Profit and loss balance	2,500	2,500	2,500	2,500	2,500
	7,500	7,500	7,500	7,500	7,500

of acquisition reveals the following:

- Strong plc paid £7,500 for the 5,000 shares in Weak plc.
- The 5,000 shares in Weak plc are entitled to its reserves of £2,500.
- The shares and reserves of Weak plc are represented by net assets with a book value of £7,500 (consisting of fixed assets of £5,500 and net current assets of £2,000).
- The £7,500 investment in Weak plc on the Strong plc balance sheet is represented by the £7,500 net assets on the Weak plc balance sheet.

18.6 Consolidated accounts: acquisition accounting

We will now explain the preparation of consolidated accounts for Strong plc and its wholly owned subsidiary, Weak plc, as at the date of acquisition.

By 'wholly owned', we mean that the parent company holds 100% of the voting shares of the subsidiary. Let us assume that Strong plc acquired all of the issued share capital of Weak plc on 1 January 20X1, paying £1.50 in cash for each £1 share, i.e. it is paying the net asset value for the shares. The balance sheets of Strong plc and Weak plc immediately after the acquisition are shown in Figure 18.5.

18.6.1 Step 1 in the consolidation process: aggregate all balances

Figure 18.6 shows the position after aggregating all of the assets and liabilities of the two companies that make up the Strong Group.

The aggregation seems to indicate that the Group has combined total net assets of £22,500. This cannot be true because the combined fixed assets of £17,750 and negative net current assets of (£2,750) only total £15,000. The difference is the investment in Weak plc that appears in the balance sheet of Strong plc. We saw above that the investment is represented by the net assets in Weak plc, which are in turn represented by the shares and reserves in Weak plc. If we aggregate the amount paid for the shares in Weak plc *and* those same net assets, we are clearly double counting.

Figure 18.5 Balance sheets of Strong and Weak immediately after acquisition

	Strong plc £	Weak plc £
Fixed assets	12,250	5,500
Investment in Weak plc	7,500	
Net current assets/(liabilities)	(4,750)	2,000
	15,000	7,500
Ordinary share capital	8,750	5,000
Profit and loss balance	6,250	2,500
	15,000	7,500

Figure 18.6 Aggregate the assets and liabilities as at 1 January 20X1

	Strong plc £	Weak plc £	Aggregate the two £
Fixed assets	12,250	5,500	17,750
Investment in Weak plc	7,500		7,500
Net current assets/(liabilities)	(4,750)	2,000	(2,750)
Total net assets	15,000	7,500	22,500
Ordinary share capital	8,750	5,000	13,750
Profit and loss balance	6,250	2,500	8,750
	15,000	7,500	22,500

18.6.2 Step 2 in the consolidation process: eliminate shareholders' funds of the subsidiary

On consolidation, therefore, it is necessary to set the cost of the shares in the books of Strong plc (made to acquire the net assets of Weak plc) against the shares and reserves in the books of Weak plc (which represent the net assets of Weak plc); this is referred to as **elimination on consolidation**.

No entries are made in the books of the individual companies. The elimination will only appear in the consolidation working papers, as shown in Figure 18.7. Note that the reserves and the issued share capital of Weak plc have been eliminated on consolidation. This will always occur on consolidation, so that whenever one looks at a set of consolidated accounts, only the issued share capital and reserves of the parent company appear.

The consolidated balance sheet of the Strong Group as at 1 January 20X1 is shown in Figure 18.8. Note again that the share capital and reserves are those of the parent company only.

Figure 18.7 Elimination entries in the consolidated working papers as at 1 January 20X1

	Strong plc £	Weak plc £	Aggregate £	Eliminate Dr/(Cr) £	Group £
Fixed assets	12,250	5,500	17,750		17,750
Investment in Weak plc	7,500		7,500	(7,500)	—
Net current assets/(liabilities)	(4,750)	2,000	(2,750)		(2,750)
	15,000	7,500	22,500		15,000
Ordinary share capital	8,750	5,000	13,750	5,000	8,750
Profit and loss balance	6,250	2,500	8,750	2,500	6,250
	15,000	7,500	22,500	0	15,000

Figure 18.7 (cont.)

Supporting the consolidation working papers by ledger accounts:

Investment in Weak plc

	£			£
1 Jan 20X1 Bank	7,500	1 Jan 20X1 Share capital of Weak plc		5,000
			Reserves of Weak plc	2,500
	7,500			7,500

Share capital of Weak plc

	£			£
1 Jan 20X1 Investment in		1 Jan 20X1 Balance		5,000
Weak plc	5,000			
	5,000			5,000

Reserves of Weak plc

	£			£
1 Jan 20X1 Investment in		1 Jan 20X1 Balance		2,500
Weak plc	2,500			
	2,500			2,500

Consolidated reserves in consolidated balance sheet

	£			£
		1 Jan 20X1 Strong plc		6,250

Alternatively, the balances on the investment in Weak, share capital of Weak and reserves of Weak could be transferred to a cost of control account:

Cost of control account

	£			£
1 Jan 20X1 Investment in		1 Jan 20X1 Share capital of Weak plc		5,000
Weak plc	7,500		Reserves of Weak plc	2,500
	7,500			7,500

Figure 18.8 Consolidated balance sheet of Strong Group as at 1 January 20X1

	£	Explanatory Notes
Fixed assets	17,750	Includes both parent and subsidiary
Net current assets	(2,750)	Includes both parent and subsidiary
	15,000	
Ordinary share capital	8,750	Parent shares only
Profit and loss balance	6,250	Parent reserves only
	15,000	

18.7 Parent company: treatment of positive and negative goodwill

How is the investment in a subsidiary dealt with when the shares are acquired for a cash consideration that is more or less than the net asset value of the shares?

The acquiring company is often prepared to pay a **premium** to obtain control of the other company. The amount of the premium will, of course, be influenced by the motive for the acquisition. This premium is **positive goodwill**.

For example, Galen Holdings plc, which is an integrated pharmaceutical company manufacturing and supplying ethical pharmaceutical products, reported two acquisitions, Bartholomew Rhodes Ltd and ICTI Inc., in the note to the Cash Flow Statement in their 1999 Annual Report and Accounts. This showed:

	£000
Net assets acquired	318
Goodwill	35,543
Consideration	35,861
Consideration satisfied by:	
Cash	23,433
Related costs of acquisition	276
Deferred consideration (payable January 2000)	1,823
Contingent consideration	10,329
	35,861

The commercial reason for the goodwill of £35,543,000 was explained as follows:

> The major therapeutic categories of prescription medicines we sell are analgesics, gastrointestinal, respiratory, cardiovascular and antibiotics and good progress has been made in all categories. The Bartholomew Rhodes acquisition has provided products in the analgesic, respiratory and cardiovascular categories and will further strengthen our business in the future.

The rationale for the acquisition of ICTI Inc. was also spelt out.

Sometimes the shares of the acquiree company do not achieve their net asset value. Perhaps the trading record is unattractive or the assets are specialist and not easily realised separately. There is then a **discount** on acquisition, or **negative goodwill**.

Let us assume that Strong plc has acquired all of the issued share capital of Weak plc on 1 January 20X1, paying £2.00 in cash for each £1 share. The effect on the balance sheets of Strong plc and Weak plc as at 1 January 20X1 would then be as in Figure 18.9.

For the holding company, the only change occurs in the carrying value of the investment and the net current assets arising from the payment of a price of £2 per share on 5,000 shares rather than £1.50. There is no accounting effect for the subsidiary.

18.8 Consolidated accounts: treatment of positive goodwill

We will now explain the preparation of consolidated accounts for Strong plc and its wholly owned subsidiary, Weak plc, as at the date of acquisition, where the cash consideration is more than the net asset value of the subsidiary.

（

Figure 18.9 Balance sheets as at 1 January 20X1

	Strong plc £1.50 per £1 share £	Strong plc £2.00 per £1 share £	Weak plc at both prices £
Fixed assets	12,250	12,250	5,500
Investment in Weak plc	7,500	10,000	
Net current assets/(liabilities)	(4,750)	(7,250)	2,000
	15,000	15,000	7,500
Ordinary share capital	8,750	8,750	5,000
Profit and loss balance	6,250	6,250	2,500
	15,000	15,000	7,500

Figure 18.10 Elimination entries in the consolidated working papers where a premium has been paid on acquisition

	Strong plc £	Weak plc £	Aggregate £	Eliminate Dr/(Cr) £	Group £
Fixed assets	12,250	5,500	17,750		17,750
Investment in Weak plc	10,000		10,000	(7,500)	2,500
Net current assets/(liabilities)	(7,250)	2,000	(5,250)		(5,250)
	15,000	7,500	22,500		15,000
Ordinary share capital	8,750	5,000	13,750	5,000	8,750
Profit and loss balance	6,250	2,500	8,750	2,500	6,250
	15,000	7,500	22,500	0	15,000

Supporting the consolidation workings papers by ledger accounts:

Investment in Weak plc

	£		£
1 Jan 20X1 Bank	10,000	1 Jan 20X1 Share capital of Weak plc	5,000
		Reserves of Weak plc	2,500
		Balance c/d	**2,500**
	10,000		10,000
1 Jan 20X1 Balance b/d	2,500		

Share capital of Weak plc

	£		£
1 Jan 20X1 Investment in Weak plc	5,000	1 Jan 20X1 Balance	5,000
	5,000		5,000

Figure 18.10 (*cont.*)

Reserves of Weak plc

	£			£
1 Jan 20X1 Investment in		1 Jan 20X1 Balance		2,500
Weak plc	2,500			
	2,500			2,500

Alternatively, using a cost of control account:

Cost of control account/goodwill account

	£			£
1 Jan 20X1 Investment in		1 Jan 20X1 Share capital of Weak plc		5,000
Weak plc	10,000	Reserves of Weak plc		2,500
		Balance c/d		**2,500**
	10,000			10,000
Balance b/d	**2,500**			

Consolidated reserves in consolidated balance sheet

	£		£
		1 Jan 20X1 Strong plc	6,250

We still need to eliminate the share capital and reserves of the subsidiary against the amount of £10,000 paid to acquire them. However, the amount paid exceeded the net asset value of £7,500. The difference is classified as an intangible asset called **goodwill**. The elimination appears in the consolidation working papers as shown in Figure 18.10.

The consolidated balance sheet will have an additional debit balance of £2,500. This debit balance is variously described as **premium on acquisition** or **cost of control** or **goodwill**. The consolidated balance sheet is shown in Figure 18.11.

The accounting treatment of goodwill is covered in FRS 10 *Goodwill and Intangible Assets* which makes the presumption that the useful economic life of goodwill will not exceed 20 years, i.e. that goodwill will be amortised over a period not exceeding 20 years. This is considered in more detail in Chapter 16.

Figure 18.11 Consolidated balance sheet of Strong Group as at 1 January 20X1

	£	*Explanatory notes*
Fixed assets		
Intangible – goodwill	**2,500**	Excess of payment over net assets acquired
Tangible	17,750	
Net current assets/(liabilities)	(5,250)	Increased by payment for cost of control
	15,000	
Ordinary share capital	8,750	
Profit and loss balance	6,250	
	15,000	

18.9 Implications of fair values

Fair values are incorporated into the consolidated accounts when the fair values of assets and liabilities in the subsidiary differ from book values.

18.9.1 Consolidated accounts: effects of fair values

If the fair value of the net assets of the parent company and subsidiary differ from their book values at the date of acquisition, it might be expected that the net assets of the holding company and subsidiary would be dealt with in a similar fashion when preparing a set of consolidated accounts. This is not so.

Parent company net asset values

The values that appear in the books of the parent company will continue to be the values that are included in the consolidated working papers and consolidated accounts, i.e. they will be included at their **existing net book values**.

Subsidiary company net asset values.

In the acquiring company's consolidated accounts, the separable net tangible and net intangible assets acquired are recorded at fair value, as at the date of acquisition. Any difference between the fair value and the book value will be reflected in the goodwill calculation.

18.9.2 What do we mean by fair value?

The fair value is the value that willing parties would agree to if the transaction were at arm's length. The FRS gives more detailed guidance in relation to individual items.[10] The valuations for particular types of asset and liability are as follows:

- **Tangible fixed assets**. Fair value should be based on **market value**, if assets similar in type and condition are bought and sold on the open market; or depreciated replacement cost, reflecting the acquired business's normal buying process and the sources of supply and prices available to it. The fair value should **not exceed the recoverable amount** of the asset, which is defined as the greater of the net realisable value and, where appropriate, the value in use.

- **Intangible assets**. Where an intangible asset is recognised, its fair value should be based on its **replacement cost**, which is normally its estimated market value.

- **Stocks and work-in-progress**. Stocks and work-in-progress should be valued at the **lower** of net realisable value and replacement cost, which is the current cost of bringing the stocks to their present location and condition.

- **Quoted investments**. These should be valued at **market price** adjusted if necessary for unusual price fluctuations or for the size of the holding.

- **Monetary assets and liabilities**. Fair value should take into account the amounts expected to be received or paid and their **timing**. Fair value should be determined by reference to market prices, where available, by reference to the current price at which the business could acquire similar assets or enter into similar obligations, or by **discounting to present value**.

- **Contingencies**. These should be measured at fair values where these can be determined. For this purpose, reasonable **estimates of the expected outcome** may be made.

The following example from the 1999 Annual Report and Accounts of Galen Holdings plc, note 27, illustrates the re-statement of book values to fair values:

	Book value	Fair value adjustment	Fair value	ICTI Inc.	Other	Total
	£000	£000	£000	£000	£000	£000
Tangible fixed assets	—	—		170	11	181
Stock	604	(300)	304	—	—	304
Debtors	1,191	—	1,191	399	23	1,613
Cash	(218)	—	(218)	209	3	(6)
Creditors	(1,802)	—	(1,802)	(211)	(13)	(2,026)
Taxation	301	—	301	—	—	301
Lease obligations	—	—	—	(49)	—	(49)
Net assets acquired	76	(300)	(224)	518	24	318
Goodwill						35,543
Consideration						35,861

The fair value adjustment to stock reflects a write-down to estimated realisable value.

18.9.3 What is the effect on the fair values if the acquirer intends to incur additional liabilities after the date of the acquisition?

In determining fair values, the ASB has adopted an overriding principle that events occurring after the acquisition that resulted in the recognition of additional liabilities or the impairment of existing assets do not affect the fair values as at the date of acquisition. The effect of such adjustment to the liabilities or assets should be reflected in the accounts of the acquirer of that period and not treated as pre-acquisition. This means that identifiable liabilities are limited to obligations of the acquired entity that **existed at the date of acquisition**.

Note that there is a difference between additional liabilities which the acquirer might wish to enter into after acquisition and establishing a higher figure for liabilities as more information becomes available about the position **as at the date of acquisition**.

In practice, it may not always be possible for the acquirer to establish absolutely accurate fair values for the individual assets and liabilities as at the date of the acquisition e.g. the provision for bad debts is an estimate and debtors might realise a materially different figure in the period following the acquisition. If the fair value of the assets acquired is amended downwards then this means that the goodwill figure should be amended upwards. FRS 7 allows for this by providing that, if it has not been possible to complete the investigation for determining fair values by the date on which the first post-acquisition financial statements are approved, provisional valuations should be made and that these should be amended, if necessary, in the next financial statements **with a corresponding adjustment to goodwill**.

18.10 Preparing consolidated accounts where fair value differs from book values of subsidiary's net assets

Let us assume that the fair value of Weak plc's fixed assets is £5,750 and that the fair value of the net current assets is the same as the book value of £2,000. Let us further assume that all of the Weak plc shares were acquired for a cash payment of £2.00 per share.

The fair value of the fixed assets is £250 more than the book value and the amount paid for the goodwill is going to be reduced by this amount of £250, as shown in Figure 18.12, where the goodwill of £2,500 arising from the use of book values is reduced to £2,250 on the introduction of the fair value for the subsidiary's assets.

The consolidated balance sheet and the Weak plc balance sheet are shown in Figure 18.13. Note particularly that the consolidated balance sheet has a mixture of valuations, as follows:

- The parent company's net assets are brought in at their **net book value**.
- The subsidiary's net assets are brought in at their **fair value**.

Figure 18.12 Elimination entries in the consolidated working papers where a premium has been paid on acquisition and the subsidiary's assets adjusted to fair values

	Strong plc	Weak plc	Aggregate	Eliminate Dr/(Cr)	Group
	£	£	£	£	£
Fixed assets	12,250	5,500	17,750	250	18,000
Investment in Weak plc	10,000		10,000	(7,750)	2,250
Net current assets/(liabilities)	(7,250)	2,000	(5,250)		(5,250)
	15,000	7,500	22,500		15,000
Ordinary share capital	8,750	5,000	13,750	5,000	8,750
Profit and loss balance	6,250	2,500	8,750	2,500	6,250
	15,000	7,500	22,500	0	15,000

Supporting the consolidation workings papers by ledger accounts:

Fixed assets of Weak plc

	£			£
I Jan 20X1 Balance	5,500	I Jan 20X1 **Balance c/d**		**5,750**
I Jan 20X1 Investment in				
Weak plc	250			
	5,750			5,750

Investment in Weak plc

	£			£
I Jan 20X1 Bank	10,000	I Jan 20X1 Share capital of Weak plc		5,000
		I Jan 20X1 Reserves of Weak plc		2,500
		I Jan 20X1 Fixed assets of Weak plc		250
		Balance c/d		**2,250**
	10,000			10,000
I Jan 20X1 Balance b/d	2,250			

Figure 18.12 (*cont.*)

Share capital of Weak plc

	£		£
I Jan 20XI Investment in		I Jan 20XI Balance	5,000
Weak plc	5,000		
	5,000		5,000

Reserves of Weak plc

	£		£
I Jan 20XI Investment in		I Jan 20XI Balance	2,500
Weak plc	2,500		
	2,500		2,500

Alternatively, using a cost of control account:

Cost of control account

	£		£
I Jan 20XI Investment in		I Jan 20XI Share capital of Weak plc	5,000
Weak plc	10,000	Reserves of Weak plc	2,500
		Fixed assets	250
		Balance c/d	**2,250**
	10,000		10,000
Balance b/d	**2,250**		

Consolidated reserves in consolidated balance sheet

	£		£
		I Jan 20XI Strong plc	6,250

Figure 18.13 Consolidated balance sheet of Strong Group as at 1 January 20XI

	Based on book value £	Based on fair value £	Weak plc before and after the consolidation £
Fixed assets			
Intangible – goodwill	**2,500**	**2,250**	
Tangible	17,750	**18,000**	5,500
Net current assets/(liabilities)	(5,250)	(5,250)	2,000
	15,000	15,000	7,500
Ordinary share capital	8,750	8,750	5,000
Profit and loss balance	6,250	6,250	2,500
	15,000	15,000	7,500

The Weak plc balance sheet has been reproduced to emphasise that the book value in the company-only accounts of Weak plc does not need to be changed to reflect the fair value used in the consolidated accounts. This needs to be watched for carefully when preparing the consolidated accounts: if the subsidiary does not change the book value in its own accounts, it will be necessary to make an adjustment each year in the consolidated working papers, not only to change the carrying value of the asset, but also to change any **depreciation charge** that has been calculated in the subsidiary. This means that for consolidation purposes the profit in the subsidiary will be overstated by the difference in depreciation charge using book value rather than fair value, assuming that the fair value exceeds the book value. It might be group policy for the subsidiary company to revise its assets and liabilities to fair values, which reduces the risk of errors on consolidating.

18.11 Applying FRS 7 to specific situations

The approach taken by FRS is that the identifiable assets and liabilities to be **recognised** should be those of the acquired entity that **existed** at the date of acquisition, **measured** at fair values that reflect the **conditions at the date of acquisition**.

Tangible fixed assets

It is important not to be influenced by the intention of the acquirer. For example, assume that National Kennels plc acquired all the issued shares in Brighton Kennel Ltd on 1 January 20X0; that they sold certain of the Brighton Kennel Ltd equipment (which duplicated their existing equipment) on 2 January 20X0 for £69,000 and calculated a goodwill figure of £100,000 with the equipment included in the calculation at its net realisable value of £69,000.

Although the directors were proposing to treat the figure of £69,000 as the fair value of the equipment for the purpose of calculating the goodwill, this would not satisfy the FRS 7 criteria. The following additional information was provided by the directors:

Net book value	£216,000
Depreciated replacement cost	£270,000
Net realisable value	£69,000
Value in use:	
Present value of the future cash flows (assuming the equipment had not been sold)	£200,000

Although the initial thought would be to use the figure of £69,000, the correct fair value is the deprival value i.e. the lower of the depreciated replacement cost and the recoverable amount (being the higher of net realisable value and the value in use). The fair value using the deprival value approach is £200,000. The effect on the accounts for the year ended 31 December 20X0 would be:

Goodwill reduced by £131,000 to a negative figure of (£31,000).
Equipment increased by £131,000.
Negative goodwill to be released immediately to the statement of total recognised gains and losses (FRS 10 para. 49) on the sale of the equipment.
A loss on sale of equipment charged to the profit and loss account of £131,000.

In many acquisition situations it is the practice to identify assets that are regarded as surplus to requirements by the acquirer, e.g. assets that do not fit into the core business of the acquirer or where the production needs are already being adequately serviced. It would not be acceptable under FRS 7 to value these at net realisable value and a deprival value approach would need to be taken.

Contingencies

Contingent assets and liabilities are different in that under normal reporting practices they may not be recognised in the balance sheet. For the fair value exercise they will need to be estimated and included.

It could also be argued that as no provision would be allowed under FRS 12 because the contingency was not probable, i.e. less than 50% likely, then it should not be included in the fair value exercise. The reasoning is that if it crystallised in the post-acquisition period this would have been due to a change of circumstances after the date of acquisition which changed the status from possible to probable.

However, it needs to be recognised that companies will not be neutral in their treatment of contingent items. This arises because of the FRS 7 para. 25 rule restricting the period within which fair values may be revised after the date of acquisition:

> Any necessary adjustments to provisional fair values and the corresponding adjustment to purchased goodwill should be incorporated in the financial statements for the first full financial year following the acquisition. Thereafter, any adjustments, except for the correction of fundamental errors, which should be accounted for as prior period adjustments, should be recognised as profits or losses when they are identified.

Assume that there is a negligence claim for £200,000 and the assessment is that it is possible but not probable to crystallise. As it is not probable, it will not have been provided for in the acquiree company's accounts. It would therefore seem to be prudent to include an estimate. In the fair value exercise this is achieved by increasing the goodwill with accounting entries as follows:

Dr Goodwill	£200,000
Cr Contingent Liability	£200,000

However, if the contingent liability does not crystallise in two years' time, after the date when Goodwill is required to be revised, the contingent liability is recognised as a profit and credited to the profit and loss account. The net result, assuming that goodwill is being amortised over 20 years, will be an annual charge to the P&L account in the year of acquisition and the following two years of £10,000, i.e. a total charge of £30,000 but a credit of £200,000 in the third year – a highly attractive outcome for any finance director!

18.12 Treatment of minority interests in consolidated accounts

We have prepared the consolidated balance sheet so far on the basis that Weak plc is a wholly owned subsidiary of Strong plc. We have included all of the assets and liabilities of the subsidiary company in the consolidated balance sheet because they were **all owned** by the holding company. But what happens if the holding company acquires less than 100% of the issued shares and therefore owns less than 100% of the net assets?

18.12.1 Conventional practice where the parent company owns less than 100% of the net assets of the subsidiary

The conventional consolidation practice is to **include all resources that are under the control** of the directors of the holding company, i.e. include all net assets just as we did when they were all owned by the holding company. The shares and reserves that have been acquired by the parent company are still eliminated against the investment. The shares and reserves that have not been acquired need to be transferred to a separate liability heading to indicate the amount that does not belong to the holding company. This separate liability is called **minority interest**.

Let us assume that Strong plc acquired 60% of the voting shares at a price of £2 per share. The balance sheet of Strong plc immediately after the acquisition is shown in Figure 18.14.

Step 1 in the consolidation process

Aggregate all balances as in Figure 18.15.

Figure 18.14 Balance sheet of Strong plc as at the date of acquisition of 60% of the shares in Weak plc for cash

	£
Fixed assets	12,250
Investment in subsidiary	6,000
Net current assets/(liabilities)	(3,250)
	15,000
Ordinary share capital	8,750
Profit and loss balance	6,250
	15,000

Figure 18.15 Aggregated assets and liabilities as at 1 January 20X1

	Strong plc £	Weak plc £	Aggregate £
Fixed assets	12,250	5,500	17,750
Investment in Weak plc	6,000		6,000
Net current assets/(liabilities)	(3,250)	2,000	(1,250)
Total net assets	15,000	7,500	22,500
Ordinary share capital	8,750	5,000	13,750
Profit and loss balance	6,250	2,500	8,750
	15,000	7,500	22,500

Step 2 in the consolidation process

Eliminate shareholders' funds of the subsidiary against the investment in subsidiary, as in Figure 18.16. The net assets are correctly stated at £18,000, but the share capital and reserves need to be adjusted to show the minority interest of 40% under a separate heading.

Step 3 in the consolidation process

Eliminate shareholders' funds of the subsidiary that belong to the minority shareholders. This is simply a transfer from the share capital and reserves of Weak plc to a separate account known as **minority interest**. The consolidation worksheet would be as in Figure 18.17. The minority shareholders are entitled to 40% of the net assets of £7,500, which is the £3,000 calculated in Figure 18.17. The consolidated balance sheet will be as in Figure 18.18.

Figure 18.16 Entries in the consolidated working papers eliminating the investment

	Strong plc	Weak plc	Aggregate	Eliminate Dr/(Cr)	Group
	£	£	£	£	£
Fixed assets	12,250	5,500	17,750		17,750
Investment in Weak plc	6,000		6,000	(4,500)	**1,500**
Net current assets	(3,250)	2,000	(1,250)		(1,250)
	15,000	7,500	22,500		18,000
Ordinary share capital	8,750	5,000	13,750	3,000	10,750
Profit and loss balance	6,250	2,500	8,750	1,500	7,250
	15,000	7,500	22,500	0	18,000

Supporting the consolidation workings papers by ledger accounts:

Investment in Weak plc

	£			£
1 Jan 20X1 Bank	6,000	1 Jan 20X1	Share capital of Weak plc	3,000
			Reserves of Weak plc	1,500
			Balance c/d	**1,500**
	6,000			6,000
1 Jan 20X1 Balance b/d	1,500			

Share capital of Weak plc

	£			£
1 Jan 20X1 Investment in Weak plc	3,000	1 Jan 20X1	Balance	5,000

Reserves of Weak plc

	£			£
1 Jan 20X1 Investment in Weak plc	1,500	1 Jan 20X1	Balance	2,500

Figure 18.17 Entries in the consolidated working papers recording the minority interest

	Strong plc £	Weak plc £	Aggregate £	Eliminate Dr/(Cr) £	Group £
Fixed assets	12,250	5,500	17,750		17,750
Investment in Weak plc	6,000		6,000	(4,500)	1,500
Net current assets	(3,250)	2,000	(1,250)		(1,250)
	15,000	7,500	22,500		18,000
Ordinary share capital	8,750	5,000	13,750	3,000	
				2,000	8,750
Profit and loss balance	6,250	2,500	8,750	1,500	
				1,000	6,250
Minority interest				(3,000)	**3,000**
	15,000	7,500	22,500	0	18,000

Supporting the consolidation workings papers by ledger accounts:

Investment in Weak plc

		£			£
1 Jan 20X1	Bank	6,000	1 Jan 20X1	Share capital of Weak plc	3,000
				Reserves of Weak plc	1,500
				Balance c/d	**1,500**
		6,000			6,000
1 Jan 20X1	Balance b/d	1,500			

Share capital of Weak plc

		£			£
1 Jan 20X1	Investment in Weak plc	3,000	1 Jan 20X1	Balance	5,000
1 Jan 20X1	**Minority interest**	**2,000**			
		5,000			5,000

Reserves of Weak plc

		£			£
1 Jan 20X1	Investment in Weak plc	1,500	1 Jan 20X1	Balance	2,500
1 Jan 20X1	**Minority interest**	**1,000**			
		2,500			2,500

Figure 18.17 (*cont.*)

Alternatively, using a cost of control account:

Cost of control account

		£			£
1 Jan 20X1	Investment in		1 Jan 20X1	Share capital of Weak plc	3,000
	Weak plc	6,000		Reserves of Weak plc	1,500
				Balance c/d	**1,500**
		6,000			6,000
	Balance b/d	1,500			

Minority interest

		£			£
1 Jan 20X1	Balance c/d	3,000	1 Jan 20X1	Share capital	2,000
			1 Jan 20X1	Reserves	1,000
		3,000			3,000
			1 Jan 20X1	Balance b/d	3,000

Consolidated reserves in consolidated balance sheet

	£			£
		1 Jan 20X1	Strong plc	6,250

Figure 18.18 Consolidated balance sheet of Strong Group as at 1 January 20X1 including goodwill

	£
Fixed assets	
Intangible – goodwill	**1,500**
Tangible	17,750
Net current assets/(liabilities)	(1,250)
	18,000
Ordinary share capital	8,750
Profit and loss balance	6,250
Minority interest	**3,000**
	18,000

How are fair value adjustments treated when there is a minority interest?

The **control concept** requires all of the net assets of the subsidiary to be revalued to fair value and the minority interest to be stated as a percentage of this fair value. The minority shareholders are regarded as internal to the group and are stated at fair value.

The alternative would be to include mixed values in the consolidated balance sheet, i.e. the subsidiary's net assets being included as a mix of parent % of fair value and minority % of book value. The control concept forbids this treatment.

18.12.2 Alternative consolidation treatment of minority shareholders where the holding company owns less than 100% of the issued shares of the subsidiary

An alternative consolidation practice that is not used in the UK for controlled subsidiaries is **proportional consolidation**. This involves deducting from all the balances appearing in the accounts of the subsidiary the proportion that does not belong to the holding company. In the Strong example, this would involve deducting 40% from each of the items in the Weak plc balance sheet. This is illustrated in Figure 18.19.

The proportional consolidation technique was rejected in the EC Seventh Directive on the grounds that including, for example, 60% of the value of a factory and 60% of its sales gives an incomplete and possibly misleading picture of the resources available to the group and the performance achieved.[11] However, the technique has been used in the oil and gas and construction industries where joint ventures are often entered into for specific projects.[12] It is also used when consolidating partnership interests into a set of consolidated accounts. FRS 9 *Associates and Joint Ventures* issued in 1997 proposed that joint ventures, whether corporate or non-corporate, be accounted for under the expanded equity method as for associates and should not be proportionately consolidated.[13]

The assets and liabilities in the illustration in Figure 18.19 do not show proportional consolidation to its best effect. Where there are significant minority holdings it could be argued that a proportional presentation is useful when presented in addition to the full consolidation because it shows the specific items in which the minority has an interest and their relative size, e.g. the following extract from the 1998 Annual Report of Rodamco N.V.

Figure 18.19 Elimination entries in the consolidated working papers following proportional consolidation process

	Strong plc £	Weak plc 100% £	Weak plc 60% £	Aggregate £	Eliminate Dr/(Cr) £	Group £
Fixed assets	12,250	5,500	3,300	15,550		15,550
Investment in Weak plc	6,000			6,000	(4,500)	1,500
Net current assets	(3,250)	2,000	1,200	(2,050)		(2,050)
	15,000	7,500	4,500	19,500		15,000
Ordinary shares	8,750	5,000	3,000	11,750	3,000	8,750
Profit and loss	6,250	2,500	1,500	7,750	1,500	6,250
	15,000	7,500	4,500	19,500	0	15,000

Consolidated balance sheet (fl.x million)

	28.2.1998 Proportionally consolidated	28.2.1998 Fully consolidated	28.2.1997 Proportionally consolidated
Assets			
Land and buildings			
Property	8,791	11,731	8,675
Renovation projects	872	1,002	430
Financial investments			
Shares in property companies	362	460	286
Participating interest in property companies	197	253	—
Mortgage notes receivable	210	272	190
Investments in group companies and participating interests			
Participating interest in loans to group Companies	60	60	12
Total investments	10,492	13,778	9,593
Accounts receivable	372	454	439
Other assets			
Liquid funds	689	966	923
Total assets	11,553	15,198	10,955
Liabilities			
Provisions	214	266	200
Long term debts			
Loans	1,021	1,021	951
Mortgages	945	1,190	652
Accounts payable	404	499	322
Total liabilities	2,584	2,976	2,125
Minority interest		3,253	
Shareholders' equity	8,969	8,969	8,830

This shows that more than 75% of the assets, all the loans and more than 90% of the mortgages appear in the subsidiaries' accounts.

18.12.3 Conventional consolidation measurement of the proprietary goodwill arising on consolidation when a minority interest exists

Whereas the net assets were treated applying the **control concept**, the goodwill is treated applying the **ownership concept**. Dealings in the shares of the subsidiary are regarded as external to the group with the goodwill figure of £1,500 in Figure 18.18 and represents the premium that Strong plc paid in order to **gain a controlling** *ownership* **interest** in Weak plc. It does not represent the goodwill of the whole entity but the 60% held by Strong plc.

Consolidated accounts prepared to provide information to the parent company shareholders are applying the **proprietary** or **parent** method. The minority interest is regarded as a type of liability as far as the parent company shareholders are concerned.

18.12.4 Alternative consolidation measurement of the entity goodwill arising on consolidation

Proprietary goodwill is the figure that you will actually find in published accounts, i.e. the cost of control. However, there is an argument that if the goodwill is introduced into the balance sheet, it should be stated at the **entity value** of 100% representing the goodwill attaching to the **economic unit** as a whole and not the 60% that attaches to the interest of the controlling shareholders' interest.

If the entity value were to be used it would be arrived at by grossing up the 60% value of £1,500 to its 100% value of £2,500. This would increase the assets in the consolidated balance sheet by £1,000 representing the amount of goodwill assumed to be attaching to the minority shareholders' interest; the minority interest would need to be correspondingly increased to give them credit for their interest in the total goodwill of £2,500.

However, the entity approach is not followed in practice and FRS 2, para. 38, specifically states that no goodwill should be attributed to the minority interest.

The argument against using £2,500 as the goodwill value in the balance sheet is that, while Strong plc might be prepared to pay a premium of £1,500 in order to **control** Weak plc, there is no certainty that it would increase this figure *pro rata* in relation to the number of additional shares acquired, i.e. it is a payment to gain control over the assets of the company and not to purchase a separately identifiable asset.

Summary

When one company acquires a controlling interest in another and the combination is treated as an acquisition, the investment in the subsidiary is recorded in the acquirer's balance sheet at the fair value of the net assets acquired and the consideration is shown at this fair value.

On consolidation, the fair value of the net assets of the subsidiary is included in the consolidated balance sheet and any difference between the fair value of the net assets and consideration is treated as positive or negative goodwill and dealt with in accordance with FRS 10 *Goodwill and Intangible Assets*.

Companies used to be able to deflate the fair value of net assets taken over by creating a provision for costs that might be incurred in the future to improve the performance of the subsidiary or restructure it. This had two adverse effects, namely, goodwill was increased and written off against reserves and so bypassed the profit and loss account of future periods, and restructuring costs were charged against the provision created on acquisition and also bypassed the profit and loss account.

The first adverse effect has been eliminated by the defining of fair values under FRS 7 *Fair Values in Acquisition Accounting* and requiring goodwill to be capitalised and amortised under FRS 10 *Goodwill and Intangible Assets*. The second adverse effect has been eliminated by the issue of FRS 6 *Acquisitions and Mergers*, making the practice of creating provisions for restructuring costs unacceptable.

REVIEW QUESTIONS

1 'The Seventh Directive basically requires consolidated accounts to be prepared using the technique of acquisition accounting on a fair value basis.'[14]

(a) Explain the terms 'acquisition accounting' and 'on a fair value basis'.

(b) Explain why a fair value basis is required.

2 'The amounts recorded by each subsidiary against the individual headings for assets and liabilities must be incorporated in full in the consolidated accounts … even if the parent does not own all of the capital of the subsidiary and is not therefore entitled to all of its assets.'[15]

(a) Explain why assets that are not owned by a parent company are included in the consolidated balance sheet.

(b) Discuss how the subsidiary balances could be consolidated if it were wished to include only the amount of the assets that were owned by the parent.

3 How would you describe 'the difference between the cost of the investment to the parent and the value of the subsidiary's net assets at the time the investment is purchased'[16] if:

(a) the difference is positive;

(b) the difference is negative.

4 (a) Explain the major differences in the consolidated balance sheet between consolidations prepared using the proprietary acquisition method and the entity acquisition method.

(b) Explain why conventional consolidation follows the proprietary acquisition method.

5 When a company becomes a subsidiary there is no required change to the book values of assets and liabilities in its books, even though the book values will be restated to fair values in the consolidated accounts. This means that there may be two different values for the same asset: one in the subsidiary's own balance sheet and the other in the consolidated accounts. Discuss how it is possible to have two different values for the same asset and for both to be true and fair.

6 Discuss arguments for and against each of the following consolidation models:

Treatment of items on consolidation under the three models

	Proprietary	Entity	Parent
Net assets of holding company	100%	100%	100%
Net assets of subsidiary	% owned	100%	100%
Goodwill on consolidation	% owned	100%	% owned
Post-acquisition subsidiary profits	% owned	100%	100%
Minority interest	None	% net assets plus % goodwill	% net assets

7 Explain why in conventional acquisition accounting the pre-acquisition reserves of the subsidiary are eliminated on consolidation and not combined with the reserves of the acquiring company.

EXERCISES

An extract from the solution is provided in the appendix at the end of the text for exercises marked with an asterisk (*).

Questions 1–5

Required:

Prepare the balance sheets of Parent Ltd and the consolidated balance sheet as at 1 January 20X1 after each transaction, using for each question the balance sheets of Parent Ltd and Daughter Ltd as at 1 January 20X1 which were as follows:

	Parent Ltd £	Daughter Ltd £
Ordinary shares of £1 each	40,500	9,000
Retained profits	4,500	1,800
	45,000	10,800
Cash	20,000	2,000
Other net assets	25,000	8,800
	45,000	10,800

* Question 1

On 1 January 20X1 Parent Ltd acquired all the ordinary shares in Daughter Ltd for £10,800 cash. The fair value of the net assets in Daughter Ltd was their book value.

* Question 2

On 1 January 20X1 Parent Ltd acquired all the ordinary shares in Daughter Ltd for £16,200 cash. The fair value of the net assets in Daughter Ltd was their book value.

Question 3

On 1 January 20X1 Parent Ltd acquired all the ordinary shares in Daughter Ltd for £16,200 cash. The fair value of the net assets in Daughter Ltd was £12,000.

Question 4

On 1 January 20X1 Parent Ltd acquired all the ordinary shares in Daughter Ltd for £6,000 cash. The fair value of the net assets in Daughter Ltd was their book value.

Question 5

On 1 January 20X1 Parent Ltd acquired 75% of the ordinary shares in Daughter Ltd. for £9,000 cash. The fair value of the net assets in Daughter Ltd was their book value.

Question 6

Smile plc acquired 90% of the equity capital of Grimace plc on 1 January 20X2. The consideration was satisfied by cash payment of £400,000.

The balance sheets as at the date of acquisition were as follows:

	Smile plc £000	Grimace plc £000
Fixed assets	200	250
Net Current assets	600	50
	800	300
Ordinary share capital	400	100
Share premium	100	–
Profit and loss account	300	200
	800	300

As at the date of acquisition the fair value of Grimace plc's fixed assets exceeded book value by £50,000.

Required:
Prepare the consolidated balance sheet for the Smile Group after the acquisition.

Question 7

The following accounts are the consolidated balance sheet and parent company balance sheet for Alpha Ltd as at 30 June 20X2.

	Consolidated balance sheet £	Parent company £
Ordinary shares	140,000	140,000
Capital reserve	92,400	92,400
Profit and loss account	79,884	35,280
Minority interest	12,320	—
	324,604	267,680
Fixed assets		
Freehold premises	127,400	84,000
Plant and machinery	62,720	50,400
Goodwill	85,680	—

Investment in subsidiary (50,400 shares)			151,200
Current assets			
Stock	121,604		71,120
Debtors	70,420		46,760
Dividend receivable	—		5,040
Cash at bank	24,360		—
	216,384		122,920
Current liabilities			
Creditors	128,660		69,720
Corporation tax	27,160		20,720
Bank overdraft	—		39,200
Proposed dividend	11,760		11,200
	167,580		140,840
Working capital		48,804	(17,920)
		£324,604	£267,680

Notes:

(i) There was only one subsidiary company called Beta Ltd.

(ii) There were no capital reserves in the subsidiary.

(iii) Alpha produced stock for sale to the subsidiary at a cost of £3,360 in May 20X2. The stock was invoiced to the subsidiary at £4,200 and was still on hand at the subsidiary's warehouse on 30 June 20X2. The invoice had not been settled at 30 June 20X2.

(iv) The profit and loss of the subsidiary had a credit balance of £16,800 at the date of acquisition.

(v) There was a right of set-off between overdrafts and bank balances.

Required:

(a) **Prepare the balance sheet as at 30 June 20X2 of the subsidiary company from the information given above.**

(b) **Discuss briefly the main reasons for the publication of consolidated accounts.**

Question 8 Browncoats Ltd

Greycoats plc acquired all of the shares in Browncoats Ltd on 1 April 20X0 for a cash consideration.

The following items have yet to have fair values attributed to them:

(a) There was a bank loan of £100,000 outstanding on which interest was payable at 15% per annum. It was due to be repaid by Browncoats Ltd at the end of four years. The current interest rate on similar loans is 8%.

(b) There were trade debts of £200,000 representing retention on a contract which would not be released for three years. The current interest rate is 7%.

(c) There was a contingent claim of £75,000 against a supplier for the supply of defective stock. The likeliest outcome was that Browncoats would recover the full amount of the claim.

Required:

(a) State any additional information that you would require in order to determine fair values.

(b) Calculate the fair values for each item.

(c) Calculate the effect of each fair value adjustment on the profit and loss account and balance sheet in financial periods following the acquisition for items (a) and (b). Assume that goodwill is amortised over a 20-year period.

References

1 D.J. Ravenscraft, 'An industrial organisation perspective', in L.E. Browne and E.S. Rosengren (eds), *The Merger Room*, Proceedings of a conference sponsored by Federal Reserve Bank of Boston, October 1987.

2 M. Foley and J. Chesworth, 'The fundamentals of a sound acquisition strategy', *Acquisitions Monthly*, September 1991.

3 F. Trautwein, 'Merger motives and merger prescriptions', *Strategic Management Journal*, vol. 11, 1990, pp. 283–295.

4 G.A. Walter and J.B. Barney, 'Research notes and communications management objectives in mergers and acquisitions', *Strategic Management Journal*, vol. 11, 1990, pp. 79–86.

5 G. Foster, *Financial Statement Analysis*, Prentice Hall, 1990.

6 H.K. Baker, T.O. Miller and B.J. Rampsberger, 'A typology of merger motives', *Akron Business and Economic Review*, Winter 1981.

7 Companies Act 1985, section 227.

8 *Ibid.*, section 258.

9 *Ibid.*, section 229.

10 FRS 7, *Fair Values in Acquisition Accounting*, ASB, 1994, paras 9–15.

11 S.M. McKinnon, *The Seventh Directive Consolidated Accounts in the EEC*, Kluwer, 1984, p. 76.

12 K. Wild and A. Guida, *Touche Ross Manual of Financial Reporting and Accounting* (3rd edition), Butterworth, 1990, p. 209.

13 FRS 9, *Associates and Joint Ventures*, ASB, 1997, para. 26.

14 S.M. McKinnon, *op. cit.*, p. 321.

15 *Ibid.*, p. 76.

16 *Ibid.*, p. 65.

CHAPTER 19

Accounting for groups at the date of acquisition – acquired by issue of shares

19.1 Introduction

Companies generally prefer to make an acquisition by issuing their own shares. They may either issue new shares on an exchange basis to the existing shareholders of the company being acquired or issue new shares to the public in order to obtain the necessary funds to make a cash acquisition. In both cases they naturally attempt to choose a moment when their share price is high.

Companies using share exchange for an acquisition may range from relatively small acquisitions to very large ones. For example, in 2000 the European Commission conditionally approved the merger of UK mobile phone giant Vodafone Airtouch and Mannesmann of Germany – this £112 billion all-share deal was the largest corporate merger in history.

In making a decision, companies consider implications such as the availability of cash, the possibility of raising loans, the impact on debt ratios, the potential dilution of existing shareholders' interests and impact on the earnings per share figure. Many companies are now making strategic investments that do not necessarily give them control and in these cases similar considerations apply.

An interesting example of this is seen with NTT DoCoMo's acquisition in 2001 of 16 percent of AT&T Wireless which, at US$9.8 billion, was the single largest equity investment by a Japanese company in the USA aimed at creating a strategic partnership to enable business and technological co-operation between the two companies. DoCoMo had a strong balance sheet and could have raised loans to fund the acquisition but instead it issued new shares in order to avoid increasing its debt equity ratio.

Another consideration that has become increasingly important since the collapse of Enron is a company's credit rating. For example, prior to the AT&T acquisition Standard & Poor's (S&P) had lowered DoCoMo's and its parent, NTT's, long-term ratings to AA from AA+, citing concerns with its aggressive overseas acquisitions and, following the acquisition, S&P affirmed DoCoMo's and NTT's ratings, but warned the ratings' outlooks could be lowered if the NTT group engaged in expansion plans that significantly departed from those indicated by its existing growth strategy.

In this chapter we consider the accounting for:

● Investment acquired by the issue of shares:
  ● Accounting in the parent company's balance sheet
  ● Accounting in parent company's balance sheet where merger relief is available
  ● Preparing consolidated accounts where the consideration is in shares
● Merger accounting:
  ● Companies Act criteria for merger accounting:

- FRS 6 *Acquisitions and Mergers* criteria for merger accounting
- Preparing merger accounts

19.2 Parent company share-for-share exchange

When a company takes over another company it can satisfy the consideration in a number of ways. It can offer payment in full in cash; it can offer ordinary shares in the parent company in exchange for the shares in the subsidiary; or it can offer a complex package consisting of a mixture of cash, ordinary shares and other financial instruments such as debentures, convertible bonds and deferred shares.

We consider the position where the parent company issues ordinary shares in the holding company as consideration for all of the issued ordinary shares of the subsidiary.

19.2.1 How many shares will the holding company issue?

First, we need to know the value of a Strong plc share and the agreed value of a Weak plc share. Let us assume that a Strong plc share is valued at £2 per share and a Weak plc share at its net asset value of £1.50 per share. This means that the consideration of £7,500 would be satisfied by the issue of 3,750 shares in Strong plc with a par value of £3,750 and a share premium of £3,750.

19.2.2 Balance sheet entry for the investment when acquired with a share-for-share exchange

The transaction will appear in the balance sheet as at the date of purchase as in Figure 19.1. We can see the following:

Figure 19.1 Balance sheet entries of Strong plc as at the date of acquisition if Strong plc acquires 100% of the shares in Weak plc with a share-for-share exchange

	Strong plc		Weak plc
	Before buying shares	After buying 100% of shares of Weak	Before and after
	£	£	£
Fixed assets	12,250	12,250	5,500
Investment in Weak plc		7,500	
Net current assets	2,750	2,750	2,000
	15,000	22,500	7,500
Ordinary share capital	8,750	8,750	5,000
New shares		**3,750**	
Share premium		**3,750**	
Profit and loss balance	6,250	6,250	2,500
	15,000	22,500	7,500

- The investment is shown as a fixed asset valued at cost with cost defined as the fair value of the consideration given.
- The net assets of Strong plc are **not reduced** as a result of the takeover of Weak plc.
- The share capital and share premium are increased; the purchase of the shares is still recorded as an investment in shares at cost in the balance sheet of Strong plc; and the accounting for the investment is not dependent on the number of shares acquired.
- The balance sheet of the subsidiary is unaffected by the exchange of shares.

19.2.3 Which ratio will be different after recording the investment?

Any ratio that uses the total or net asset figure will be different, e.g. return on capital employed or capital turnover, and any ratio that uses total shareholder funds will be different, e.g. the balance sheet gearing ratio.

19.3 Consolidated accounts: acquisition accounting method after share exchange

We will explain the preparation of consolidated accounts for Strong plc and its wholly-owned subsidiary, Weak plc, as at the date of acquisition.

Assuming that the consideration was £1.50 per share, the consolidated working papers would be as in Figure 19.2 and the consolidated balance sheet as in Figure 19.3. Supporting the consolidation working papers by ledger accounts is virtually as illustrated in Figure 18.7. Note that after the issue of shares:

- The net assets of the two companies remain unchanged. The fixed assets and net current assets of Strong remain at £12,250 and £2,750 and the fixed assets and net current assets of Weak remain at £5,500 and £2,000. When the fixed assets and net current assets are

Figure 19.2 Elimination entries in the consolidated working papers where this is a share-for-share exchange

	Strong plc £	Weak plc £	Aggregate £	Eliminate Dr/(Cr) £	Group £
Fixed assets	12,250	5,500	17,750		17,750
Investment in Weak plc	7,500		7,500	(7,500)	—
Net current assets	2,750	2,000	4,750		4,750
	22,500	7,500	30,000		22,500
Ordinary share capital	8,750	5,000	13,750	5,000	8,750
New shares	3,750		3,750		3,750
Share premium	3,750		3,750		3,750
Profit and loss balance	6,250	2,500	8,750	2,500	6,250
	22,500	7,500	30,000	0	22,500

Figure 19.3 Consolidated balance sheet of Strong Group as at 1 January 20X1

	£	Explanatory notes
Fixed assets		
Tangible	17,750	Assets of parent and subsidiary
Net current assets	4,750	Assets of parent and subsidiary
	22,500	
Ordinary share capital	12,500	Old and new shares of parent
Share premium	3,750	Premium on new shares
Profit and loss balance	6,250	Parent only
	22,500	

combined as a group the total fixed assets are the combined total of £17,750 and the net current assets the combined total of £4,750.

● There is a share premium account of £3,750 in the Strong balance sheet.

● The profit and loss balance of the group is only £6,250 not £6,250 + £2,500.

This means that, whereas before the acquisition Strong could have paid out a dividend of £6,250 and Weak a dividend of £2,500, after the acquisition Strong is still only able to pay a total dividend of £6,250.

19.4 Parent company treatment of share-for-share exchange with merger relief

It is illogical for dividends to be restricted because of the acquisition when no assets have left the group, e.g. in Figure 19.2 above the fixed assets and net current assets still remained at a total of £22,500. The Companies Act 1985 therefore allowed the use of **merger relief**.

Merger relief is available under section 131 Companies Act 1985 where an issuing company has, by an arrangement which includes the exchange of shares, acquired at least a 90% equity holding in another company.

Merger relief relates **not** to the consolidated accounts, but to the company-only accounts of the parent company. It allows the parent company to value the investment in its balance sheet at the fair value of the shares issued but to record any premium on the shares issued in a merger reserve account rather than a share premium account.

It would perhaps be better to describe the relief as a share premium relief rather than merger relief in that it is relieving the parent from opening a share premium account.

The example used in Figure 19.1 is amended to show, in Figure 19.4, the investment in Strong plc's balance sheet on the assumption that merger relief is available. Note that the investment is carried in the balance sheet at the **fair value of the shares issued** (to comply with FRS 4 *Capital Instruments*) and there is no share premium account.

Figure 19.4 Balance sheet entries of Strong plc as at the date of acquisition if Strong plc acquires 100% of the shares in Weak plc with a share-for-share exchange

	Before buying shares £	Acquisition accounting no merger relief	Acquisition accounting with merger relief
Fixed assets	12,250	12,250	12,250
Investment in Weak		7,500	7,500
Net current assets	2,750	2,750	2,750
	15,000	22,500	22,500
Ordinary share capital	8,750	8,750	8,750
New shares		3,750	3,750
Share premium account		3,750	—
Merger reserve		—	3,750
Profit and loss balance	6,250	6,250	6,250
	15,000	22,500	22,500

Why is it important for the premium to be called merger reserve rather than share premium account?

The reason is that a share premium account is a capital reserve and may not be distributed as a dividend.

How is Strong able to use the merger reserve to make a distribution of a dividend to Strong shareholders?

The merger reserve is initially classified as unrealised profits and may not be used by Strong to make dividend payments until reclassified as realised profits. The reserve will become realised as dividends are paid by Weak to Strong out of the £2,500 pre-acquisition dividends that existed in Weak as at the date of the acquisition.

The accounting entries in Strong following a dividend payment from Weak to Strong, assuming that the whole amount of £2,500 is passed up as a dividend, would be:

	£	£
Dr Cash		2,500
Cr Profit and loss account		2,500

The payment of cash from Weak to Strong means that the investment of £7,500 has been impaired and it should be written down by £2,500 in recognition of the fact that the net assets backing the investment have been reduced by £2,500. The journal entry to record this is:

	£	£
Dr Profit and loss account	2,500	
Cr Investment in Weak		2,500

But then, the attraction of the merger relief takes effect – for every £1 written off the investment £1 can be transferred from the merger reserve to the profit and loss account. This means that the £2,500 has been reclassified as realised profit and has been made available to Strong to distribute as a dividend to the Strong shareholders.

In practice, it is more likely that the Weak pre-acquisition reserves of £2,500 would be distributed over a period and the reclassification from unrealised to realised would occur progressively as dividends were passed up to the parent.

19.5 Explanation of the merger accounting method

The method that we have used so far in this chapter to produce the consolidated balance sheet as at the date of acquisition is known as **acquisition accounting**. It assumes that the holding company has depleted its net assets to acquire the net assets represented by the share capital and reserves of the subsidiary as at the date of acquisition.

We have seen that merger relief is available in the accounts of the **parent** company when the consideration has been satisfied by the issue of shares in the parent so that the net assets of the parent have not been depleted.

There is an alternative method, known as **merger accounting**, which is available when the shares of a subsidiary are acquired by a share-for-share exchange and no assets leave the group.

There are a number of advantages to the parent from using merger accounting, two of which are:

● The full year's profit of the acquired company are brought into the consolidated profit and loss account although the acquisition might not have actually taken place until the last day of the accounting period. This allows a company to achieve apparent earnings growth in the current financial year by acquiring the shares in a profitable company and merging the profits at the year end.

● The pre-acquisition profits of the subsidiary are not capitalised and remain available for distribution as a dividend to the Strong shareholders. The effect is the same as that achieved by applying the merger relief provisions described above.

Given these advantages, it would clearly be to the benefit of Strong to treat every acquisition as a merger accounted for using merger accounting. To avoid companies doing this the Companies Act and later the ASB have set down criteria that must be satisfied before merger accounting can be applied.

19.5.1 Companies Act criteria

We have been assuming so far that a dominant, acquiring company wins control of another company. If it pays cash to gain control, the net current assets of the parent company are depleted.

However, there may be a mutual agreement between two companies to merge or pool their resources as equal partners, with a view to trading as a combined group. This might be accompanied by an agreement to exchange shares, so that the resources of the combined group are the aggregate of the individual company's resources, i.e. no assets will have left the group.

Criteria have been established by the Companies Act and professional standards to regulate when merger accounting may be used. The criteria set out in the Companies Act are as follows:[1]

- At least 90% in nominal value of the equity shares of the subsidiary are held by the parent or its subsidiaries.
- The shares were obtained as a result of an arrangement involving the issue of equity by the parent or its subsidiaries.
- The fair value of non-equity consideration given by the parent and its subsidiaries did not exceed 10% of the nominal value of the equity shares issued.

It is important to note that, because the last criterion uses 10% of the **nominal** value of the equity shares rather than 10% of the **fair** value of the equity shares when there is a mixture of equity and non-equity consideration, it is a difficult criterion to satisfy whenever there is a mixture.

19.5.2 FRS 6 *Acquisitions and Mergers* criteria

The ASB has defined a merger in FRS 6 *Acquisitions and Mergers* as:

A business combination that results in the creation of a new reporting entity formed from the combining parties, in which the shareholders of the combining parties come together in a partnership for the mutual sharing of the risks and benefits of the combined entity, and in which no party to the combination in substance obtains control over any other, or is otherwise seen to be dominant, whether by virtue of the proportion of its shareholders' rights in the combined entity, the influence of its directors or otherwise.[2]

It has also set out in FRS 6 the following additional points:[3]

- No party to the combination is portrayed as either acquirer or acquired, either by its own board or management or by that of another party to the combination.
- All parties to the combination, as represented by the boards of directors or their appointees, participate in establishing the management structure for the combined entity and in selecting the management personnel, and such decisions are made on the basis of a consensus between the parties to the combination rather than purely by exercise of voting rights.
- The relative sizes of the combining entities are not so disparate that one party dominates the combined entity by virtue of its relative size.

  (It is interesting to consider this criterion in more detail. There would be a presumption that one party was dominant if it was more than 50% larger than the other party. The test for being 50% larger is to look at the shareholdings. If, for example, there were two shareholders, Arnold and Bennett, in the parent company and two shareholders, Edward and Rutherford, in the subsidiary then the test would be to look at their respective holdings in the parent company after the combination. If Arnold and Bennett jointly held 240 shares in the parent, then Edward and Rutherford would need to jointly own more than 160 shares to satisfy this relative size criteria.

  If the group could produce evidence that the parties were working collaboratively then the presumption of a dominant party could be avoided.)
- Under the terms of the combination or related arrangements, the consideration received by equity shareholders of each party to the combination, in relation to their equity shareholding, comprises primarily equity shares in the combined entity.
- No equity shareholders of any of the combined entities retain any material interest in the future performance of only part of the combined entity.

19.6 Consolidated accounts: merger accounting method

We will now explain the preparation of consolidated accounts for Strong plc and its wholly-owned subsidiary, Weak plc, as at the date of acquisition using merger accounting.

The aim of merger accounting is to present the group accounts as if the companies that have combined have always been operating as a single group. The meaning of this is as follows:

- The shares issued by Strong plc would be issued at their nominal value and no share premium would be taken into account in the company-only accounts or in the consolidated accounts, assuming that merger relief is available.

- The investment in Weak plc would be carried in the Strong plc balance sheet at the nominal value of the shares issued, which means that there will be no goodwill on consolidation using the merger accounting method.

- The book values of the assets and liabilities of the subsidiary are included in the consolidation, even though the fair values might be different.

- There is an aggregation of the book values of net assets.

- The reserves of Weak plc are not treated as being pre-acquisition, but are aggregated with those of Strong plc in the consolidated balance sheet.

- Adjustments are kept to a minimum and would include only adjustments required to adopt uniform accounting policies within the group.

The example used in Figure 19.2 is reworked using the merger accounting method, as shown in Figures 19.5 and 19.6. Note the following:

- The tangible assets are at the same figure because the acquisition example had assumed that the book value and fair value of the subsidiary were the same; if the fair value of the subsidiary's fixed assets were to be £5,750, then the acquisition accounting balance sheet would have tangible assets of £18,000 whereas the merger accounting balance sheet would remain at £17,750.

- There is no share premium in the merger accounting method.

- The difference between the nominal value of the shares issued and the nominal value of the shares acquired is treated as:

  - a **capital reserve** if the issued nominal value is lower than the acquired nominal value; and

  - a reduction in one of the consolidated reserves if the issued nominal value is higher than the acquired nominal value. Normal practice is to apply it first against the most restricted categories of reserve.

- The available reserves in the merger accounting method are the total of the reserves of both companies. The pre-acquisition profits of the subsidiary are not capitalised as in the acquisition method.

19.6.1 Which method is preferred by management?

Management has generally favoured the merger accounting method because it results in:

(a) a better balance sheet in that the reserves of both companies are maintained and there is no intangible asset created

Figure 19.5 Elimination entries in the consolidated working papers where there is a share-for-share exchange

	Strong plc	Weak plc	Aggregate	Eliminate Dr/(Cr)	Group
	£	£	£	£	£
Fixed assets	12,250	5,500	17,750		17,750
Investment in Weak plc	3,750		3,750	(3,750)	
Net current assets	2,750	2,000	4,750		4,750
	18,750	7,500	26,250		22,500
Ordinary share capital	12,500	5,000	17,500	3,750	12,500
Capital reserve				(a)	1,250
Profit and loss balance	6,250	2,500	8,750		8,750
	18,750	7,500	26,250	0	22,500

Supporting the consolidation working papers by ledger accounts:

Investment in Weak plc

	£		£
1 Jan 20X1 Share capital	3,750	1 Jan 20X1 Share capital of Weak plc	3,750
	3,750		3,750

Share Capital of Weak plc

	£		£
1 Jan 20X1 Investment in Weak plc	3,750	1 Jan 20X1 Balance	5,000
1 Jan 20X1 Capital reserve	1,250 (a)		
	5,000		5,000

Reserves of Weak plc

	£		£
1 Jan 20X1 Consolidated reserves	2,500	1 Jan 20X1 Balance	2,500
	2,500		2,500

Capital reserve

	£		£
		1 Jan 20X1 Share capital of Weak plc	1,250

Consolidated reserves in consolidated balance sheet

	£		£
1 Jan 20X1 Balance c/d	8,750	1 Jan 20X1 Strong plc	6,250
		1 Jan 20X1 Weak plc	2,500
	8,750		8,750

Figure 19.6 Consolidated balance sheet of Strong Group as at 1 January 20X1

	Consolidated balance sheet of Strong Group as at 1 January 20X1 using acquisition accounting		Consolidated balance sheet of Strong Group as at 1 January 20X1 using merger accounting	
		£		£
Fixed assets			Fixed assets	
Tangible	17,750		Tangible	17,750
Net current assets	4,750		Net current assets	4,750
		22,500		22,500
Ordinary share capital	12,500		Ordinary shares	12,500
Share premium	3,750			
			Capital reserve	1,250
Profit and loss a/c	6,250		**Profit and loss a/c**	**8,750**
		22,500		22,500

(b) a better profit and loss account in that the depreciation charge for both companies is based on book values at the date of combination rather than on fair values for the acquired company and there is no amortisation charge for goodwill.

The income effects could be of particular importance to managers if their remuneration package contains a performance related element based on profit performance, e.g. rate of growth in the earnings per share – this will be higher if merger accounting is adopted with the lower depreciation and amortisation charges. However, the adverse effect arising from acquisition accounting could be avoided if the performance measure were to be based on earnings before depreciation and amortisation or the EBITDA figure (earnings before interest, tax, depreciation and amortisation) that many companies now report.

19.6.2 Which method would benefit the shareholders?

An interesting research study by PriceWaterhouseCoopers[4] indicates that, although the merger accounting treatment results in a stronger balance sheet and profit and loss account, companies using the merger method did not perform as well as those using the acquisition method despite the reported accounting benefits. It is suggested that this may be because the accounting benefits are outweighed by the economic consequences. The economic consequences include the possibility of:

(a) overpayment since the purchase price is relatively invisible;

(b) removing the incentive for management to cover costs in that goodwill is not required to be recognised and amortised

(c) removing the immediate possibility of restructuring, e.g. by disposing of non-core or underperforming assets.

The economic effects of acquisition accounting are more transparent and therefore of more benefit to shareholders seeking increased value from a combination.

In the UK the FRS 6 provisions are so stringent that most business combinations that have been accounted for as mergers would not meet the criteria laid down by FRS 6. It is therefore likely that merger accounting will be a rare occurrence as most business combinations will have to be regarded as acquisitions.[5]

19.6.3 Which method is used by other countries?

There is a need for international convergence on the method for accounting for business combinations.[6] At present, countries with more permissive regulations for treating business combinations as a merger are perceived as having an unfair advantage when they compete in making takeover bids. The perception is that their profits are overstated comparatively because there is no goodwill to amortise and pre-acquisition profits of acquired companies have not been required to be capitalised.

US practice

National standards vary. In the USA, for example, the Financial Accounting Standards Board issued in July 2001 Statement No. 141, *Business Combinations*, which requires all business combinations initiated after June 2001 to be accounted for under a single method – the purchase (acquisition) method and the pooling-of-interests (merger) method is no longer permitted. One effect of this is that a goodwill account may arise (this does not arise under the merger method) which would normally require an amortisation charge to be made to the profit and loss account. The FASB has attempted to avoid the need for such an amortisation charge by issuing Statement No. 142, *Goodwill and Other Intangible Assets*. This Statement requires that, instead of being amortised, goodwill should be reviewed for impairment. It is argued in support of this treatment that it provides investors with greater transparency regarding the economic value of goodwill and its impact on earnings, although the driving force was probably to avoid the amortisation charge that would have hit the profit and loss accounts following the issue of Statement 141. Canada had been collaborating with the USA for a number of years and issued similar standards effective from the same date supporting the new approach by taking the view that there would be a level playing field for all combinations, i.e. acquisition accounting rules would apply to all.

The existence of different standards for accounting for business combinations has become of increasing importance because cross-border deals account for more than 25% of business combinations. There is a need for convergence at a simultaneous moment to avoid individual countries feeling that they are losing competitive advantage.

IASB approach

The IASB is strongly influenced by the approach already taken in the USA and certain existing ASB requirements. This is reflected in the Consultation Paper on Business Combinations issued by the ASB in December 2002 which proposes, as in the USA, that merger accounting should be forbidden and goodwill arising on an acquisition should not be amortised but reviewed for impairment and, as in the UK, restructuring provisions recognisable on an acquisition should be subject to strict criteria.

A further Consultation Paper deals with acquisition accounting relating to joint ventures and where an acquirer is not readily identifiable following proposals developed jointly by the IASB and the US Financial Accounting Standards Board.

Conceptual acceptability

There is a view that all combinations should be treated as acquisitions and that it is conceptually deficient to retain the cost basis of the subsidiary when assets and liabilities are combined and the resulting merged accounts are not decision-useful. Whilst this may be true for listed companies it may not be material for private companies, many of which use merger accounting for its convenience and cost-effectiveness in that:

● there is no requirement to apply FRS 7 *Fair Values in Acquisition Accounting* and incurring the cost of determining fair values for each of the assets and liabilities;

● as assets are combined at book values and shares at nominal value, there is no goodwill and hence no requirement to apply FRS 10 *Goodwill and Intangible Assets* or to carry out impairment tests that may arise under FRS 11 *Impairment of Fixed Assets and Goodwill*.

Summary

When one company acquires a controlling interest in another and the combination is treated as a merger, the investment in the subsidiary is recorded in the acquirer's balance sheet at the nominal value of the shares issued and the consideration is shown at this nominal value.

On consolidation, the book value of the net assets of the subsidiary is included in the consolidated balance sheet and any difference between the nominal value of shares issued and acquired is treated as a reserve. No goodwill arises.

In the UK an attempt has been made by the ASB in FRS 6 to set stringent criteria to force companies to account for the substance of the combination. In practice, however, it is relatively simple for a company to satisfy the majority of the criteria, e.g. to demonstrate that no party is portrayed as either acquirer or acquired.

The ASB measures have made it a little more difficult for companies to enjoy the benefits of merger accounting for combinations that are to all intents and purposes acquisitions, and more difficult to deflate artificially the net assets acquired in order to avoid charges being made to profit and loss accounts of future years. The two FRSs (FRS 6 and FRS 7) have gone a long way to removing the capacity of companies to achieve earnings growth by technical compliance that failed to reflect the commercial reality of a combination.

REVIEW QUESTIONS

I A merger exists if 'the shareholders must achieve a continuing mutual sharing in the risks and benefits of the combining undertakings'.[7] Discuss the extent to which the criteria set out in the Companies Act follows this statement.

2 'An implicit assumption is that the consolidated accounts represent merely a change in the scope of the accounts, showing the combined results of the companies, as if separate streams were put side by side and taken together, nothing added and nothing taken away.'[8] Explain the method of consolidation that is being described.

3 Merger accounting results in a stronger balance sheet. Discuss.

4 Explain why managers may prefer the merger accounting method.

5 There are proposals by the IASB that
   (i) merger accounting should be prohibited and an acquirer for each business combination should be identified;
   (ii) goodwill should not be amortised; instead it should be carried on the balance sheet indefinitely subject to an impairment test; and
   (iii) 'negative goodwill' should be reported as a gain in income when it arises.

   (a) Discuss circumstances in which (i) might not fairly reflect the substance of the combination.
   (b) Discuss the rationale for assuming that goodwill should not be amortised to make an annual charge against the year's profits.
   (c) Discuss how the benefit from negative goodwill differs from a revaluation gain.

EXERCISES

An extract from the solution is provided in the appendix at the end of the text for exercises marked with an asterisk (*).

Questions 1–5

Use for each question the balance sheets of Parent Ltd and Daughter Ltd as at 1 January 20X1 which were as follows:

	Parent Ltd	Daughter Ltd
	£	£
Ordinary shares of £1 each	40,500	9,000
Retained profits	4,500	1,800
	45,000	10,800
Net assets	45,000	10,800

* Question 1

On 1 January 20X1 Parent Ltd acquired all the ordinary shares in Daughter Ltd. The purchase consideration was satisfied by the issue of 5,400 new ordinary shares in Parent Ltd. The fair value of a £1 ordinary share in Parent Ltd was £2. The fair value of the net assets in Daughter Ltd was their book value.

Required:
Prepare the balance sheet of Parent Ltd and the consolidated balance sheet as at 1 January 20X1, after the transaction.

* Question 2

On 1 January 20X1 Parent Ltd acquired all the ordinary shares in Daughter Ltd. The purchase consideration was satisfied by the issue of 5,400 new ordinary shares in Parent Ltd. The fair value of a £1 ordinary share in Parent Ltd was £3. The fair value of the net assets in Daughter Ltd was their book value.

Required:
Prepare the balance sheet of Parent Ltd and the consolidated balance sheet as at 1 January 20X1, after the transaction.

* Question 3

On 1 January 20X1 Parent Ltd acquired all the ordinary shares in Daughter Ltd. The purchase consideration was satisfied by the issue of 5,400 new ordinary shares in Parent Ltd. The fair value of a £1 ordinary share in Parent Ltd was £3. The fair value of the net assets in Daughter Ltd was £12,000.

Required:
Prepare the balance sheet of Parent Ltd and the consolidated balance sheet as at 1 January 20X1, after the transaction.

* Question 4

On 1 January 20X1 Parent Ltd acquired all the ordinary shares in Daughter Ltd for £6,000 cash. The fair value of the net assets in Daughter Ltd was their book value.

Required:
Prepare the balance sheet of Parent Ltd and the consolidated balance sheet as at 1 January 20X1, after the transaction.

Question 5

On 1 January 20X1 Parent Ltd acquired 75% of the ordinary shares in Daughter Ltd. The purchase consideration was satisfied by the issue of 4,500 new ordinary shares in Parent Ltd. The fair value of a £1 ordinary share in Parent Ltd was £2 and the fair value of the net assets in Daughter Ltd was their book value.

Required:
Prepare the balance sheet of Parent Ltd and the consolidated balance sheet as at 1 January 20X1, after the transaction.

* Question 6

The directors and shareholders of Y Ltd have agreed to accept an offer by B plc for the whole of Y Ltd's ordinary share capital. The offer comprises two newly issued ordinary shares (nominal value £0.20) of B plc for every five ordinary shares (nominal value £0.50) of Y Ltd. At the offer date the ordinary shares of B plc each had a stock market value of £3.00.

The summarised balance sheets of both companies immediately prior to the offer being effected on 1 January 20X5 are given below:

Balance sheets as at 1 January 20X5

	B plc		Y Ltd	
	£m	£m	£m	£m
Fixed assets		74.8		14.6
Current assets	29.7		12.3	
Current liabilities	19.5		9.9	
		10.2		2.4
Net assets		85.0		17.0
Retained profits		65.0		7.0
Ordinary share capital		20.0		10.0
		85.0		17.0

The book value of Y Ltd's assets at 1 January 20X5 approximated to their fair value. Y Ltd is a major supplier of B plc. On 1 January 20X5, B plc had £4.8 million of stock purchased from Y Ltd. This stock had cost Y Ltd £4.3 million to produce. In addition, at 1 January 20X5, B plc owed Y Ltd £3.2 million for goods supplied. (The 3.2 million is included in the current liabilities of B Ltd and the current assets of Y Ltd and must be eliminated from both on consolidation.)

Required:
Prepare, on an acquisition accounting basis, the opening balance sheet of the new group as at 1 January 20X5.

* Question 7

Use the information in Question 6.

Required:
(a) Prepare, on a merger accounting basis, the opening balance sheet of the new group as at 1 January 20X5.
(b) Outline in general terms, without reference to the above example, the factors that would influence a management decision on whether to use the merger or the acquisition basis for the consolidation of a new subsidiary.

Question 8

You are the finance director of X plc. At a recent board meeting it was decided to open negotiations with Z plc with a view to combining the two companies. The balance sheets of the two companies are set out below:

	X plc	Z plc
	£m	£m
Fixed assets	15	30
Net current assets	18	9
	33	39
10% Debentures	4	6
	29	33

Ordinary shares of 50p each	10	
Ordinary shares of £1 each		8
Share premium	4	5
Profit and loss account	15	20
	29	33

It is agreed that the fair value of the fixed assets of Z plc is £36m. The terms of the proposed merger are that X plc would issue 15m new ordinary shares in exchange for the whole of the share capital of Z plc. The current market prices of the shares of the two companies for the purpose of the combination are: X plc = £3 per share; Z plc = £5 per share.

Required:

Your managing director has asked you to prepare for the next board meeting:

(a) two consolidated balance sheets showing the effect of the combination using:
   (i) acquisition accounting;
   (ii) merger accounting;

(b) a brief report explaining for the board of directors:
   (i) Acquisition and merger accounting and the differences between them;
   (ii) The conditions to be satisfied if merger accounting is to be used;
   (iii) Whether the companies may choose either method, assuming the conditions in (ii) are satisfied.

(c) recommend to the board which method to use.   (CIPFA)

References

1 Companies Act 1989, Schedule 2, para. 10.
2 FRS 6, *Acquisitions and Mergers*, ASB, 1994, para. 2.
3 FRS 6, *Acquisitions and Mergers*, ASB, 1994, paras 6–12.
4 R. Beier and R. Stewart, *How Pooling-of-Interests Accounting Affects Value*, PriceWaterhouseCoopers Transaction Service, www.pwcglobal.com.
5 Ernst & Young, *UK GAAP*, Macmillan (4th edition), 1994, p. 254.
6 T. Johnson, 'Levelling the playing field', *Accountancy*, February 1999, p. 82.
7 S.M. McKinnon, *The Seventh Directive Consolidated Accounts in the EEC*, Kluwer, 1984, p. 76.
8 P.A. Taylor, *Consolidated Financial Reporting*, Paul Chapman Publishing, 1996, p. 38.

CHAPTER 20

Accounting for groups after acquisition

20.1 Introduction

An investment may be classified as either a fixed asset or a current asset. In this chapter we will consider the accounting treatment for fixed asset investments in both the investing company accounts and the consolidated accounts if the investment is in a subsidiary or an associate. This will include both the historical cost convention and the alternative accounting rules. We will also deal with questions relating to share capital, dividends and reserves.

20.2 Accounting treatment of the investment in the books of the investing company at the date of acquisition

We will continue with the Strong plc example from Chapters 18 and 19, but we will assume that on 1 January 20X1 Strong plc has undertaken four investments for cash by acquiring shares on the Stock Exchange in four identical companies. The companies are Five plc, Twenty plc, Sixty plc and Hundred plc, and Strong plc acquired a holding of 5%, 20%, 60% and 100%, respectively, as set out in Figure 20.1. Note that each of the investments appears **at cost** in the books of the investing company.

There are **no accounting entries** in the books of the investee companies arising from the transaction between Strong plc and the shareholders of the investee company. The balance sheets of the investee companies as at 1 January 20X1 are set out in Figure 20.2 to show the position before and after Strong plc has acquired its shareholdings.

20.3 Categories of fixed asset investments

Fixed asset investments are categorised according to the degree of **influence** that the investor is able to exercise over the investee company, as shown in Figure 20.3.

The ability to pass resolutions is one of the important factors in assessing the nature of the control that is exercisable. The size of the shareholding has a bearing on the type of resolution that can be passed. There are three types of resolution: ordinary, extraordinary and special.

Figure 20.1 Balance sheet of Strong plc as at 1 January 20X1, the date of acquisition by Strong plc at a market price of £2 per share

	Before buying shares	After buying 5% of Five plc	After buying 20% of Twenty plc	After buying 60% of Sixty plc	After buying 100% of Hundred plc
		£	£	£	£
Fixed assets	12,250	12,250	12,250	12,250	12,250
Investment in:					
Five plc		500	500	500	500
Twenty plc			2,000	2,000	2,000
Sixty plc				6,000	6,000
Hundred plc					10,000
Net current assets	2,750	2,250	250	(5,750)	(15,750)
	15,000	15,000	15,000	15,000	15,000
Share capital	8,750	8,750	8,750	8,750	8,750
Profit and loss account	6,250	6,250	6,250	6,250	6,250
Shareholders' funds	15,000	15,000	15,000	15,000	15,000

20.3.1 Ordinary resolutions

An ordinary resolution is passed by a simple majority of votes cast on the resolution. It is required to adopt the accounts that are put before the annual general meeting, approve the dividends that have been recommended by the directors and appoint a director.

Figure 20.2 Balance sheet of each of the investee companies as at 1 January 20X1 after the acquisition by Strong plc of various percentages of shares held by existing shareholders

	Each company before share transfer	Five plc after Strong buys 5%	Twenty plc after Strong buys 20%	Sixty plc after Strong buys 60%	Hundred plc after Strong buys 100%
	£	£	£	£	£
Fixed assets	5,500	5,500	5,500	5,500	5,500
Net current assets	2,000	2,000	2,000	2,000	2,000
Net assets	7,500	7,500	7,500	7,500	7,500
Ordinary share capital	5,000	5,000	5,000	5,000	5,000
Profit and loss balance	2,500	2,500	2,500	2,500	2,500
	7,500	7,500	7,500	7,500	7,500

Figure 20.3 Categorise the investments

Nature of influence exercised by the investing company	Accounting category given to the investment	Shareholding in investee
1 Complete control with ability to pass ordinary, extraordinary and special resolutions	1 Investment in subsidiary	More than 75%
2 Control with ability to pass ordinary resolutions	2 Investment in subsidiary	More than 50% up to 74%
3 Significant influence exercised over operating and financial policy	3 Investment in associate	20% or more up to 50%
4 Interest held on a long-term basis for the purpose of securing a contribution to its activities by the exercise of control or influence[a]	4 Participating interest	20% or more up to 50%
5 An undertaking jointly managed by the parent and undertakings that are not consolidated provided the undertaking is unincorporated	5 Joint venture proportionally consolidated	Not stated
6 No influence but a material interest based on shareholding %	6 Significant investment	10% or more up to 20%
7 No influence but a material interest based on relative size of investment to total assets of the investor company, i.e. more than 10%	7 Significant investment	
8 No influence and not material	8 Other investments	Under 10%

[a]Companies Act 1985, section 260.

20.3.2 Extraordinary and special resolutions

An **extraordinary resolution** is passed by a majority of not less than three-quarters of such members as are entitled to vote. It is required to:

- wind up a company voluntarily when, because of its liabilities, it cannot continue trading;[1]
- vary class rights.[2]

A **special resolution** is passed by a majority of not less than three-quarters of such members as are entitled to vote at a meeting of which twenty-one days' notice has been given. It is required in a number of circumstances, such as:

- to change the objects of a company;[3]
- to allow a private company to re-register as a public company;[4]
- to reduce share capital if so authorised by the company's articles;[5]
- to resolve that the company be wound up by the court;[6]
- to resolve that the company be voluntarily wound up.[7]

20.4 Carrying value of investments at the end of the financial year in the books of the investing company under the historical cost convention

Fixed assets are included at their purchase price, which will normally only include relatively minor dealing costs and stamp duty, but in the context of a contested takeover of a public company, the incidental costs may be very significant.[8] This applies to each accounting category of investment mentioned in Figure 20.3.

Just as for tangible fixed assets, provision **must** be made for any impairment under FRS 11 *Impairment of Fixed Assets and Goodwill*, para. 6. If the value subsequently increases, the provision must be written back.

The accounts of Strong plc and the four investee companies are set out in Figures 20.4 and 20.5. They are prepared using the historical cost convention and assuming that the investee companies have paid no dividends. Note that, in the balance sheet of the investing company (Strong plc), the investments are carried at cost and the only increase in shareholders' funds recorded is the £360 transferred from its profit and loss account in Figure 20.4.

No accounting entries are made in the profit and loss account of Strong plc in respect of the profits of the investee companies because the investee companies have not distributed any of their profits to Strong plc through dividends.

You will recall that at the date of acquisition the carrying value of the investment was equal to the net assets of the investee plus the premium paid as the cost of control. The carrying value is shown in Figure 20.6. However, after a year's trading, this will no longer be the case because the net assets of the investee company will have changed. They will have increased if the investee has made a profit, and a proportion will belong to the investing company.

If the investor company continues to carry the investment as its cost as at 1 January 20X1, it will not reflect the increase of £1,080 that has occurred during 20X1. However, under the historic cost convention, the realisation concept prevents the investor company from increasing the investment to reflect the profit made by the investee until there has been a dividend distribution by the investee company, i.e. until funds are transferred.

Figure 20.4 Profit and loss accounts assuming that each investee company has identical results

Profit and loss accounts of Strong plc, Five plc, Twenty plc, Sixty plc and Hundred plc for the year ended 31 December 20X1

	Strong plc £	Each investee £
Turnover	9,000	4,500
Cost of sales	4,500	2,250
Gross profit	4,500	2,250
Distribution costs	(900)	(450)
Administrative expenses	(720)	(360)
Trading profit	2,880	1,440
Investment income from:		
Subsidiaries		
Associates		

	Strong plc £	Each investee £
Other investments		
Profit before tax	2,880	1,440
Tax	720	360
Profit after tax	2,160	1,080
Extraordinary items	0	0
Profit for the year	2,160	1,080
Dividends	1,800	—
Transferred to reserves	360	1,080

Figure 20.5 Balance sheets assuming that each investee company has an identical position

Balance sheets of Strong plc, Five plc, Twenty plc, Sixty plc, and Hundred plc as at 31 December 20X1

	Strong plc		Investee companies	
	As at 1 Jan 20X1 Date shares were acquired £	As at 31 Dec 20X1 One year after shares were bought £	As at 1 Jan 20X1 £	As at 31 Dec 20X1 £
Fixed assets (net book value)	12,250	11,025	5,500	4,950
Investment in:				
Five plc	500	500		
Twenty plc	2,000	2,000		
Sixty plc	6,000	6,000		

Figure 20.5 *(cont.)*

Hundred plc	10,000	10,000		
Net current assets/(liabilities)	(15,750)	(14,165)	2,000	3,630
Net assets	15,000	15,360	7,500	8,580
Share capital	8,750	8,750	5,000	5,000
Profit and loss account	6,250	6,610	2,500 (+1,080)	3,580
Shareholders' funds	15,000	15,360	7,500	8,580

Figure 20.6 Carrying value at 1 January 20X1

	£	£
Cost of 5,000 shares at £2 per share		10,000
Represented by:		
Net assets of investee company		
as represented by: shares	5,000	
reserves	2,500	
		7,500
Cost of control		2,500
		10,000

20.5 Carrying value of investments at the end of the financial year in the books of the investing company under the alternative accounting rules

The Companies Act 1985 permits a company to apply alternative accounting rules. If these alternative accounting rules were to be applied, the carrying figure would be determined not by its cost, but by a market valuation.

20.5.1 How to value fixed asset investments under the alternative accounting rules

Under the alternative accounting rules, fixed asset investments may be included either at a market value determined as at the date of their last valuation or at a value determined on any basis which appears to the directors to be appropriate in the circumstances of the company, provided details are given of the basis and reasons for adopting it.[9]

20.5.2 Valuing a wholly owned subsidiary under the alternative accounting rules

One method is to value investments in subsidiaries and investments in associates at the amounts of the net assets shown in the historic cost balance sheets of the subsidiaries and associates. This maintains the reserves in the parent company at the same amount as the reserves in the subsidiary and associate.[10]

If this were applied to the investment in Hundred plc, the effect on the balance sheet

Figure 20.7 Alternative accounting valuation of shares in Hundred plc, which is a wholly owned subsidiary

	£	£
Cost of 5,000 shares at £2 per share at 1 Jan 20X1		10,000
Add: Increase in net assets during 20X1		1,080
		11,080
Represented by:		
Net assets of investee company at 31 Dec 20X1		
which are presented by: shares	5,000	
: reserves	3,580	
		8,580
Cost of control remains at the initial figure		2,500
		11,080

of Strong plc would be to increase the investment to £11,080, which reflects the net assets of Hundred plc as at 31 December 20X1 and the cost of control as at 1 January 20X1, as shown in Figure 20.7. The increase in the investment is an **unrealised gain** and may not be taken to the profit and loss account. Instead, an amount equal to the £1,080 that has been debited to the investment account is credited to a **revaluation reserve**.

20.5.3 Valuing a partly owned subsidiary and associated undertaking under the alternative accounting rules

The investments in Sixty plc and Twenty plc could be dealt with similarly. The investment in Sixty plc, the partly owned subsidiary, would be increased by £648, which is 60% of the increase of £1,080 in its net assets; the investment in Twenty plc, the associated company, would be increased by £216, which is 20% of the increase in its net assets.

The revaluation reserve would be credited in total with £1,944, consisting of the increases in the net assets of the two subsidiary companies and the associated company, i.e. £1,080 in Hundred plc; £648 in Sixty plc and £216 in Twenty plc.

The investment in Five plc would be maintained at cost or market value. We are assuming that the market value has remained at the amount paid by Strong plc on 1 January 20X1.

20.5.4 Balance sheet entries under the alternative accounting rules

The balance sheet of Strong plc would be as set out in Figure 20.8. We can see that using the alternative accounting rules enables the balance sheet values of the investments to be **amended** to continue to reflect the underlying net asset value of the investment.

The underlying net assets are allocated to the shares held so that the investment equals the value of the net assets that are **owned by** Strong plc in the two subsidiary companies and the associated company.

The alternative accounting rules do not mean that the investments show the value of the net assets that are **controlled by** Strong plc in these companies. In order to disclose this value as at 31 December 20X1, it is necessary to prepare a consolidated balance sheet.

Figure 20.8 Balance sheets under alternative accounting rules

Balance sheet of Strong plc as at 31 December 20X1

	Historical cost convention		Alternative accounting rules
	As at 1 Jan 20X1	As at 31 Dec 20X1	As at 31 Dec 20X1
	£	£	£
Fixed assets	12,250	11,025	11,025
Investment in:			
Five plc	500	500	500
Twenty plc	2,000	2,000	2,216
Sixty plc	6,000	6,000	6,648
Hundred plc	10,000	10,000	11,080
Net current assets/(liabilities)	(15,750)	(14,165)	(14,165)
Net assets	15,000	15,360	17,304
Share capital	8,750	8,750	8,750
Profit and loss account	6,250	6,610	6,610
Revaluation reserve			**1,944**
Shareholders' funds	15,000	15,360	17,304

20.6 Preparation of a consolidated balance sheet at the end of the financial year to account for an investment in a subsidiary

A consolidated balance sheet will incorporate all of the assets and liabilities of the subsidiaries, i.e. it will show the net assets **controlled** by Strong plc. In order to complete the consolidated balance sheet it will be necessary to calculate:

- the **cost of control** that was paid for the investment in Sixty plc and the investment in Hundred plc;
- the **minority interest** in Sixty plc;
- the **consolidated reserves**.

20.6.1 Cost of control

The cost of control over the two subsidiaries is £4,000, as set out in Figure 20.9. In both cases the cost of control will be the figure computed as at the date of acquisition on 1 January 20X1.

The ledger account will not appear in the nominal ledger of any of the individual companies. It is purely a memorandum record to support the entries in the consolidated accounts. This memorandum record is normally referred to as the **consolidation working papers**. The ledger accounts for the minority interest and consolidated reserves will likewise be a memorandum.

Figure 20.9 Cost of control at 1 January 20X1

On investment in Hundred plc:	£	£	£
Cost of 5,000 shares at £2 per share		10,000	
Less: Net assets of investee company			
represented by: shares	5,000		
: reserves	2,500		
		7,500	
Cost of control			2,500
On investment in Sixty plc:			
Cost of 3,000 shares at £2 per share		6,000	
Less: Net assets of investee company			
represented by: shares	3,000		
: reserves	1,500		
		4,500	
Cost of control			1,500
Total cost of control over Hundred plc and Sixty plc			4,000

If a ledger account format is used to record the consolidation adjustments in the consolidation working papers, the ledger account would be as follows:

Cost of control account

	£		£
1 Jan 20X1 Investment in Hundred	10,000	1 Jan 20X1 Shares in Hundred	5,000
		1 Jan 20X1 Reserves in Hundred	2,500
1 Jan 20X1 Investment in Sixty	6,000	1 Jan 20X1 Shares in Sixty	3,000
		1 Jan 20X1 Reserves in Sixty	1,500
		1 Jan 20X1 Balance c/d	4,000
	16,000		16,000

20.6.2 Minority interest

The minority interest is calculated in Figure 20.10 as £3,432. Alternatively, we can approach it from the net assets that belong to the minority shareholders. This would, of course, be the same amount, i.e. 40% of the net assets of £8,580 shown in Figure 20.5. Note that the cost of control is calculated as at the date of acquisition, i.e. 1 January 20X1, but the minority interest is calculated as at the date of the balance sheet, i.e. 31 December 20X1.

20.6.3 Consolidated reserves

The consolidated reserves will consist of the reserves of the parent company plus the parent company's proportion of the profits of the subsidiaries that have arisen **since the date the parent company acquired control**. The calculation is set out in Figure 20.11.

Figure 20.10 Minority interest in Sixty plc

	£
Shares at 31 December 20X1 40% of 5,000 shares	2,000
Reserves at 31 December 20X1 40% of £3,580	1,432
	3,432

Minority Interest				
	£			£
31 Dec 20X1 Balance c/d	3,432	31 Dec 20X1 Shares in Sixty plc		2,000
		31 Dec 20X1 Reserves in Sixty plc		1,432
	3,432			3,432

Figure 20.11 Consolidated reserves calculated as at 31 December 20X1

		£	£
Reserves of Strong plc as at 31 Dec 20X1			6,610
Reserves of Hundred plc as at 31 Dec 20X1	(Figure 20.5)	3,580	
Less: Reserves at 1 Jan 20X1 (pre-acquisition)		2,500	
Profits accrued since control was acquired		1,080	
Strong plc has a 100% interest of this amount			1,080
Reserves of Sixty plc as at 31 Dec 20X1	(Figure 20.5)	3,580	
Less: Reserves at 1 Jan 20X1 (pre-acquisition)		2,500	
Profits accrued since control was acquired		1,080	
Strong plc has a 60% interest of this amount			648
Consolidated reserves			8,338

The ledger account format would be as follows:

Consolidated reserves			
	£		£
31 Dec 20X1 Balance c/d	8,338	31 Dec 20X1 Strong plc reserves	6,610
		31 Dec 20X1 Hundred plc reserves	1,080
		31 Dec 20X1 Sixty plc reserves	648
	8,338		8,338

A consolidation worksheet (Figure 20.12) will be prepared to eliminate the investments and substitute the assets and liabilities of the two subsidiary companies. The illustration is based on the investments being carried at historical cost. Note that the consolidated balance sheet will include:

Figure 20.12 Consolidated worksheet as at 31 December 20X1

	Strong plc £	Sixty plc £	Hundred plc £	Aggregate £	Adjust Dr/(Cr)	Consolidated balance sheet £
Fixed assets	11,025	4,950	4,950	20,925		20,925
Investment in:						
Five plc	500			500		500
Twenty plc	2,000			2,000		2,000
Sixty plc	6,000			6,000	(4,500)[a]	1,500
Hundred plc	10,000			10,000	(7,500)[b]	2,500
Net current assets	(14,165)	3,630	3,630	(6,905)		(6,905)
Net assets	15,360	8,580	8,580	32,520		20,520
Share capital	8,750	5,000	5,000	18,750	3,000[a] 5,000[b] 2,000[c]	8,750
Profit and loss account	6,610	3,580	3,580	13,770	1,500[a] 2,500[b] 1,432[c]	8,338
Minority interest					(2,000)[c] (1,432)[c]	3,432
	15,360	8,580	8,580	32,520	0	20,520

Notes cross-referenced to the worksheet and Figure 20.5:

[a] £3,000 is 60% of the issued share capital of Sixty plc
£1,500 is 60% of the reserves of Sixty plc as at 1 Jan 20X1

[b] £5,000 is 100% of the issued share capital of Hundred plc
£2,500 is 100% of the reserves of Hundred plc as at 1 Jan 20X1

[c] £2,000 is 40% of the issued share capital of Sixty plc
£1,432 is 40% of the reserves of Sixty plc as at 31 Dec 20X1

- **all** of the fixed assets and net current assets of Hundred plc that are **100% owned**;
- **all** of the fixed assets and net current assets of Sixty plc that are only **60% owned** but are **controlled** by the directors of Strong plc via the 60% shareholding, which gives it the ability to pass ordinary resolutions.

In the consolidated balance sheet, the fixed assets and net current assets of Sixty plc that are not owned by Strong plc are represented by the **minority interest**.

20.7 Preparation of a consolidated balance sheet at the end of the financial year to account for an investment in an associate

As we have seen, subsidiaries are dealt with by aggregating their assets and liabilities with those of the parent company on the basis that the parent has control over them. Associates are dealt with differently. They are dealt with by **equity accounting** because the investing company has significant influence, but it does not have control over the operating and financial policy.

The intention is that shareholders in the investing company should be able to see the net assets that underlie the investment in the associate. To provide them with this information in the consolidated balance sheet, equity accounting follows the procedure that we described above for valuing an investment under the alternative accounting rules in the company-only accounts of the investing company.

The investment in associate is therefore adjusted in proportion to the shares held for the increase in the net assets of the associate that has occurred during the year. The rationale is ownership and not control.

Equity accounting is sometimes referred to as **one line consolidation** because the only change is to the investment in associate, which is adjusted to reflect the net asset backing. The individual assets and liabilities underlying the investment in the books of the investee company are not themselves aggregated with those of the holding company and subsidiaries.

The balance sheet valuation at 31 December 20X1 is set out in Figure 20.13. The £216 will be added to the consolidated reserves of £8,338. The consolidated balance sheet will be as in Figure 20.14. Note the use of the term 'stakeholders'. The net assets represent the investment by stakeholders rather than just the shareholders of the holding company because the minority shareholders' interest is also included.

Figure 20.13 Investment in associate accounted for using the equity method for the consolidated balance sheet (in accordance with FRS 9[11])

	£
Group share of net assets at 1 Jan 20X1 20% of £7,500	1,500
Premium paid on acquisition	500
Cost at 1 Jan 20X1	2,000
Increase in net assets during 20X1 20% of £1,080	216
Carrying value as at 31 Dec 20X1	2,216

There will be an increase of £216 in the assets and in the reserves

FRS 9[12] requires goodwill arising on the investor's acquisition, less any amortisation or write-down, to be separately disclosed.

Figure 20.14 Consolidated balance sheet as at 31 December 20X1

	£	Explanatory notes
Fixed assets		
Intangible	4,000	Cost of control of Hundred and Sixty
Tangible	20,925	Assets of Strong, Hundred and Sixty
Investment in:		
Five plc	500	At cost as at 1 Jan 20X1
Twenty plc	2,216	Valued using the equity method, i.e. cost as at 1 Jan 20X1 plus proportion of net asset increase in 20X1
Net current assets (liabilities)	(6,905)	Net current assets of Strong, Hundred, Sixty plc
Net assets	20,736	
Share capital	8,750	Share capital of Strong plc
Profit and loss account	8,554	(a) Reserves of Strong plc
		(b) Strong's proportion of the post-acquisition reserves of: Hundred and Sixty and Twenty
Minority interest	3,432	Interest in Sixty plc
Stakeholders' funds	20,736	

There is an argument that the consolidated accounts should include only the net assets that are owned by the holding company, not all the assets under its control. If this argument were accepted, the consolidated accounts would be prepared on a **proportional** basis. Only the proportion of assets and liabilities relating to the shares held would be included. The effect on Figure 20.12 would be to reduce the fixed assets in Sixty plc to £2,970 (60% of £4,950) and the net current assets to £2,178 (60% of £3,630). The difference of £3,432 (40% of £4,950 + 40% of £3,630) would eliminate the minority interest. The net assets appearing in the consolidated balance sheet would be owned by the holding company shareholders; the assets belonging to the minority shareholders would be excluded; and the consolidated balance sheet would be prepared to show the **proprietors'** interest rather than the stakeholders' interest.

There is no uniquely correct choice. The two statements are prepared under different definitions and the choice would be determined by assessing which definition produced the more decision-useful information. The normal procedure would be for the ASB to obtain views from interested parties in response to a discussion document or exposure draft on the topic. As a result of such consultation, the ASB, in the summary to FRS 2 *Accounting for Subsidiary Undertakings*, provides that minority interests should be reported separately in the consolidated balance sheet.

The traditional consolidated balance sheet is entity based, in that it includes all net assets of all stakeholders; the proportional consolidated balance sheet is proprietor based, in that it includes only the net assets of the proprietors of the group, i.e. the parent company shareholders.

20.8 How are shareholders' funds measured?

20.8.1 Parent company accounts under the historical cost convention

In the balance sheet of Strong plc, using the historical cost convention, we have seen in Figure 20.5 that the shareholders' funds at 31 December 20X1 are represented by **net assets of £15,360**. This includes the investments that are carried at cost and the profit of £360 realised by the holding company.

20.8.2 Parent company accounts under the alternative accounting rules

In the balance sheet of Strong plc, using the alternative accounting rules, we saw in Figure 20.8 that the shareholders' funds were represented by **net assets of £17,304**. The investments that appeared in the balance sheet were revalued under those rules. They were carried at cost if there was no influence, e.g. Five plc, and at cost plus the increase in the net assets applicable to the shares owned by the investing company if there was influence, e.g. Twenty, Sixty and Hundred plcs.

20.8.3 Consolidated accounts

In the consolidated balance sheet we saw in Figure 20.14 that the **net assets are stated at £20,736**. The investments in subsidiaries have been replaced by the assets and liabilities of the subsidiaries. In the consolidated balance sheet, the net assets of £3,432 that belong to the minority are also included – they are added to the assets of £17,304 that are owned by the shareholders of Strong plc to produce £20,736. They represent the **net assets that are controlled by Strong plc and owned by the stakeholders**.

20.9 How does a dividend distribution by a subsidiary affect the balance sheet of the investing company, the investee company and the group?

Simple logic tells us that if one company distributes a dividend to another company, the net current assets and the profit and loss balances in both companies will change. For example, a dividend paid by Sixty plc of £1,000 at 31 December 20X1 will be as shown in Figure 20.15 in the company-only accounts of Strong and Sixty.

We would expect the consolidated balance sheet to be £400 lower because that is the amount of the dividend that has gone outside the group, i.e. the net assets should fall from £20,736 to £20,336. We can confirm this when we prepare the consolidated balance sheet as in Figure 20.16. The consolidated reserve remains **unchanged** at £8,554 because it has merely moved from the net current assets of the investee to the net current assets of the investor. This indicates that intragroup dividends have no effect on the **group consolidated reserves** and that dividends **distributed outside** the group will reduce the net capital employed by the group. Of course, the reserves of the individual companies will change, as shown in Figure 20.15.

Figure 20.15 Balance sheets of Strong plc and Sixty plc as at 31 December 20X1

	Strong £	£	Strong after dividend £	Sixty £	£	Sixty after dividend £
Fixed assets	11,025		11,025	4,950		4,950
Investment in:						
Five plc	500		500			
Twenty plc	2,000		2,000			
Sixty plc	6,000		6,000			
Hundred plc	10,000		10,000			
Net current assets/ (liabilities)	(14,165)	600	(13,565)	3,630	(1,000)	2,630
Net assets	15,360		15,960	8,580		7,580
Share capital	8,750		8,750	5,000		5,000
Profit and loss account	6,610	600	7,210	3,580	(1,000)	2,580
Shareholders' funds	15,360		15,960	8,580		7,580

Figure 20.16 Consolidated balance sheet as at 31 December 20X1

	£	Explanatory notes
Fixed assets		
Intangible	4,000	Cost of control of Hundred and Sixty
Tangible	20,925	Assets of Strong, Hundred and Sixty
Investment in:		
Five plc	500	At cost as at 1 Jan 20X1
Twenty plc	2,216	Valued using the equity method, i.e. cost as at 1 Jan 20X1 plus proportion of net asset increase in 20X1
Net current assets (liabilities)	(7,305)	**Net current liabilities of Strong, Hundred and Sixty plc. The £400 paid outside the group increases (£6,905) in Figure 20.14**
Net assets	20,336	
Share capital	8,750	Share capital of Strong plc
Profit and loss account	8,554	(a) Reserves of Strong plc
		(b) Strong's proportion of the post-acquisition reserves of: Hundred and Sixty and Twenty
Minority interest	**3,032**	**Interest in Sixty plc reduced by the £400 received as a dividend**
Stakeholders' funds	20,336	

20.10 In what circumstances will the consolidated reserves be adjusted in respect of intragroup transactions?

We have seen that the consolidated reserves are not adjusted by the payment of a dividend by a subsidiary. This is because the profits **realised** by the group have not been reduced or increased. However, certain intragroup transactions do require adjustment because they give rise to **unrealised** profits as far as the group is concerned. An example is the sale of stock from one member of the group to another member.

20.10.1 Intragroup sales

If goods sold by one member of the group to another member are sold to a third party outside the group by the end of the accounting period, any profit added on the intragroup sale will have been realised.

For example, assume that on 1 January 20X1 Strong plc sold goods for which it had paid £200 to Hundred plc for £250 and that the stock was sold for £375 to a customer of Hundred plc before 31 December 20X1.

The intragroup profit made by Strong plc is £50 and the profit made by Hundred plc is £125. The group will have realised a profit of £175, being the difference between the cost to Strong plc of £200 and the selling price to Hundred's customer of £375.

However, if the stock remains in the possession of the group member, the profit on sale is **unrealised** as far as the group is concerned. The profit recorded in the company-only accounts of the selling member of the group needs to be eliminated from the **consolidated reserves**. If it were not eliminated, it would be a simple matter for the group to increase its reported consolidated profits merely by selling stock internally.

For example, assume that on 1 January 20X1 Strong plc sold goods for which it had paid £200 to Hundred plc for £250 and that the stock is still held by Hundred plc as at 31 December 20X1. No adjustments are required to the company-only accounts of either Strong plc or Hundred plc. The sale will be reported in the profit and loss account of Strong plc, the profit of £50 will appear in its profits for the year and the stock will appear in the balance sheet of Hundred plc at £250.

The consolidated balance sheet will, however, need to be adjusted, as shown in Figure 20.17.

If the sale had been made **by** a partly owned subsidiary, FRS 2 provides that:

to the extent that they are reflected in the book value of assets to be included in the consolidation, profits or losses on any intragroup transactions should be eliminated in full. The elimination of profits or losses relating to intragroup transactions should be set against the interests held by the group and minority interest in respective proportion to their holdings in the undertaking whose individual financial statements recorded the eliminated profit or loss.[13]

For example, if Sixty plc had sold goods costing £200 to Strong plc for £250 on 1 January 20X1 and the goods were still held by Strong plc at 31 December 20X1, then the stock would be reduced by £50, the consolidated reserves by £30 and the **minority interest by £20**.

In requiring the whole of the unrealised profit to be eliminated FRS 2 is following the **control concept** and regarding the transaction with the minority as being internal to the group and therefore to be fully eliminated. The **ownership concept** would have required only the parent % of the unrealised profit to be eliminated.

Figure 20.17 Consolidated balance sheet adjusted for unrealised profit

Consolidated balance sheet as at 31 December 20X1

Adjusted for unrealised profit on intragroup sales

	£	Explanatory notes
Fixed assets		
Intangible	4,000	Cost of control of Hundred and Sixty
Tangible	20,925	Assets of Strong, Hundred and Sixty
Investment in:		
Five plc	500	At cost as at 1 Jan 20X1
Twenty plc	2,216	Valued using the equity method, i.e. cost as at 1 Jan 20X1 plus proportion of net asset increase in 20X1
Net current assets (liabilities) (£7,305 + £50)	(7,355)	Net current assets of Strong, Hundred, Sixty plc **less unrealised profit of £50 in stock**
Net capital employed	20,286	
Share capital	8,750	Share capital of Strong plc
Profit and loss account (£8,554 – £50)	**8,504**	(a) Reserves of Strong plc (b) Strong's proportion of the post-acquisition reserves of: Hundred and Sixty and Twenty **less £50 unrealised profit on intragroup sales**
Minority interest	3,032	Interest in Sixty plc
Stakeholders' funds	20,286	

20.11 Why have the consolidated reserves increased during the year since acquisition?

The consolidated reserves as at 1 January 20X1 were £6,250, as shown in Figure 20.8. The consolidated reserves as at 31 December 20X1 were £8,504, as shown in Figure 20.17. In order to explain the change we need to prepare a consolidated profit and loss account. This is covered in the next chapter in Figure 21.5.

Summary

We have considered the accounting treatment for investments in associates and subsidiaries using the historical cost convention and the alternative accounting rules allowed under the Companies Act. Under the alternative accounting rules, we have seen that the carrying value of the investment in the investee company's balance sheet is adjusted to reflect the underlying net assets as disclosed in the subsidiary or associated company's own accounts.

On consolidation, the investments in associates are valued at their proportion of the net assets of the subsidiary plus any goodwill. In the next chapter we consider further the ASB proposals to amend the disclosure requirements for associates.

On consolidation, the net assets of subsidiaries are substituted for the investment accounts and any difference is treated as positive or negative goodwill and dealt with in accordance with group accounting policy; a minority interest is created for that proportion of the net assets that is not owned by the investee; and only post-acquisition reserves are included within the consolidated profit and loss account.

REVIEW QUESTIONS

1 On 1 January 20X1 Investor plc acquired 75% of the ordinary shares of Investee plc. When asked to explain what the company received for the outlay on this investment, the directors said that they had received '75% of the goodwill and 75% of the net assets of Investee plc valued at fair value'.

(a) State how the investment would be described in the balance sheet of Investor plc as at the date of acquisition, i.e. at cost under the historical cost convention or at valuation under the alternative accounting rules.

(b) If a consolidated balance sheet were to be prepared as at 1 January 20X1, state the consolidation process that would result in the consolidated accounts containing '75% of the goodwill and 75% of the net assets of Investee plc valued at fair value'.

(c) If a consolidated balance sheet were to be prepared as at 1 January 20X1, state the consolidation process that would result in the consolidated accounts containing '75% of the goodwill and 100% of the net assets of Investee plc valued at fair value'.

(d) If a consolidated balance sheet were to be prepared as at 1 January 20X1, state the consolidation process that would result in the consolidated accounts containing '100% of the goodwill and 100% of the net assets of Investee plc valued at fair value'.

(e) If a consolidated balance sheet were to be prepared as at 1 January 20X1, state the consolidation process that would result in the consolidated accounts containing '0% of the goodwill and 100% of the net assets of Investee plc valued at book value'.

2 Decide whether the following are true or false:

(a) '75% of the goodwill and 75% of the net assets of Investee plc valued at fair value at the date of acquisition' = 75% of the share capital and reserves of Investee plc as disclosed by its balance sheet at the date of acquisition.

(b) '0% of the goodwill and 100% of the net assets of Investee plc valued at book value at the date of acquisition' = the share capital and reserves of Investee plc as disclosed by its balance sheet at the date of acquisition.

(c) A minority interest will appear in each of the consolidated balance sheets prepared in question 1 above.

3 On 1 January 20X1 Hopeful plc acquired 25% of the ordinary shares of Hopeless plc. On 31 December 20X1 Hopeful plc was deciding whether to include its investment in the consolidated accounts at either:

(i) '25% of the goodwill and 25% of the net assets of Hopeless plc at fair valuation as at 1 January 20X1'; or

    (ii) '25% of the goodwill and 25% of the net assets of Hopeless plc at fair valuation as at 1 January 20X1' + '25% of the change in net assets of Hopeless from 1 January 20X1 to 31 December 20X1'.

Explain:

(a) the circumstances in which Hopeful plc would use (i);

(b) why choice (ii) is available.

4 Investments are treated in the consolidated balance sheet according to the percentage of voting rights acquired by the shareholding, e.g:

Shareholding	In the consolidating balance sheet
Less than 20%	At cost
More than 20% less than 50%	At cost + % of change in net assets
More than 50%	Investment replaced with net assets

(a) Explain the circumstances in which the investing company might wish to manipulate the treatment in the consolidated balance sheet by adjusting its shareholding, e.g. reducing its holding from 20% to 19.5%.

(b) Explain the qualitative criterion that controls the choice of accounting treatment for shareholdings of less than 50%.

5 In the text we illustrated the elimination of unrealised profit on sale where the sale was made by a holding company to a wholly owned subsidiary by eliminating 100% of the unrealised profit (cost to Strong plc was £200; sale to Hundred plc was £250; unrealised profit eliminated was £50). This is standard UK practice for all intragroup unrealised profits, whether from a holding company to a subsidiary or vice versa.

However, alternative treatments may be academically justifiable[13] in the following situations:

(a) Sale was made by Strong plc to Sixty plc, a 60% owned subsidiary.

(b) Sale was made by Sixty plc to Strong plc.

(c) Sale was made by Hundred plc to Sixty plc.

(d) Sale was made by Sixty plc to Hundred plc.

Discuss possible alternative treatments of the £50 intragroup profit in each of these situations.

EXERCISES

An extract from the solution is provided in the appendix at the end of the text for exercises marked with an asterisk (*).

Question 1

The accountancy profession has developed a range of techniques to measure and present the effects of one company owning shares in another company.

Required:
Briefly describe each of these techniques and how the resulting information might best be presented.

Question 2

(a) What criteria should you use when determining whether to include an investment under fixed or current assets in a balance sheet?

(b) What information does the Companies Act 1985 require to be disclosed for each subheading under the main heading 'Investments'? Explain why this information might be relevant to a reader of the accounts.

(c) What information must be disclosed where the investment exceeds 10%, but is less than 20% of the allotted share capital of the investee? Explain why this information might be relevant to a reader of the accounts.

* Question 3

The following are the balance sheets of Parent Ltd and its subsidiary Son Ltd.

	Parent Ltd £	Son Ltd £
Ordinary share capital	160,000	80,000
Reserves	12,000	11,000
Profit and loss	15,000	14,000
Creditors	30,000	16,000
Bills payable to Parent Ltd	—	16,000
	217,000	137,000
Plant	60,000	54,000
Fixtures		10,000
Investment in Son Ltd (60,000 shares at cost)	80,000	
Current assets		
Debtors: Son Ltd	4,000	—
Others	20,000	36,000
Bills receivable from Son Ltd	8,000	
Stock	24,000	28,000
Cash at bank	21,000	9,000
	217,000	137,000

1 On 1 January 20X5 Parent Ltd acquired the shares in Son Ltd. At that date the balances on Son Ltd general reserve was £7,000 and the balance on the profit and loss account was £6,000.

2 The stock held by Son Ltd includes stock purchased from Parent Ltd for £7,200. Parent Ltd had made a profit of 50% on cost.

3 At the date of acquisition the plant in Son Ltd, which had a book value of £60,000, was valued at £70,000. Depreciation is 10% straight line. The fixtures were valued at book value.

Required:
(a) Prepare a consolidated balance sheet as at 31 December 20X5.
(b) Explain any adjustments you may have made to fixed assets, current assets and current liabilities.

Question 4

The balance sheets of Tay plc and Avon plc as at 31 December 20X6 contained the following information:

	Tay £m	Avon £m
Fixed assets at book value	12.6	3.8
Net current assets	7.9	1.2
	20.5	5.0
Financed by:		
Share capital (£1 ordinary shares)	10.0	2.0
Retained profit at 1 January 20X6	8.3	2.5
Profit for 20X6	2.2	0.5
	20.5	5.0

The following additional information is provided:

1 Tay purchased 1.6 million shares in Avon on 1 January 20X6. The purchase consideration consisted of 1.2 million shares in Tay which were valued at £6.50 each at the acquisition date. This transaction has not yet been entered in the books of Tay and is not reflected in the above balance sheet.

2 The fair value of Avon's fixed assets at 1 January 20X6 was £4.8 million. Avon neither purchased nor sold any fixed assets during 20X6 and depreciation is to be ignored. There were no material differences between the book value and fair value of Avon's net current assets at the date of acquisition.

3 The directors of Tay estimated, at the date of acquisition, that costs of £0.7 million will need to be incurred in 20X7 to re-organise the activities of Avon so as to maximise the benefits arising from the amalgamation. The directors are of the opinion that that these re-organisations costs should be treated as part of the purchase price.

4 The policy of Tay is to write off goodwill over ten years.

Required:

(a) State the objective of FRS 7, entitled *Fair Value Accounting*. Advise the management of Tay plc concerning the appropriate accounting treatment of fixed asset values at the acquisition date, and planned future re-organisation costs, in order to comply with this objective.

(b) The consolidated balance sheet of Tay plc and its subsidiary at 31 December 20X6 in accordance with company policy and standard accounting practice.

(Chartered Institute of Bankers)

Question 5

The first topic covered by an accounting standard was how best to present in the investor company's financial statements the economic effects of an investment in another company that was less than that required for normal consolidation procedures.

Combination Ltd operates a hotel marina. Expansion Ltd, a manufacturing company, holds 30% of the ordinary shares of Combination Ltd.

The separate summarised accounts for the year to 31 October 20X8 of Combination Ltd and Expansion Ltd are:

	Combination Ltd £000	Expansion Ltd £000
Balance sheet at 31 October 20X8		
Issued share capital, ordinary shares of £1	1,000	2,000
Reserves and unappropriated profits	2,000	1,500
Long-term debt	8,700	2,000
Current liabilities	300	2,500
	12,000	8,000
Fixed assets	11,200	4,000
Investment in Combination Ltd	—	900
Current assets	800	3,100
	12,000	8,000
Profit and loss account		
Profit for the year after tax	3,000	950
Share of profits of Combination Ltd	—	900
Dividends paid	(2,000)	(1,500)
Retained earnings	1,000	350

Required:
Prepare alternative presentations for the annual accounts of Expansion Ltd based upon:
(i) a consolidation procedure bringing in the proportionate share of the assets, liabilities and profits of Combination Ltd;
(ii) an expanded equity method whereby the proportionate share of total assets, liabilities and profits is shown on the face of the accounts but not aggregated;
(iii) an expanded equity method whereby the proportionate share of assets, liabilities and profits is shown separately but also aggregated with the appropriate items from the investor accounts.

Question 6

Carr plc has invested in a number of companies. The directors usually acquire the entire share capital of a company in which Carr invests, but this did not prove possible in the case of an investment in Saunders Ltd. The directors are uncertain concerning the appropriate accounting treatment of Saunders Ltd and the following information is made available as at 31 December 20X6:

	Carr Group (excluding Saunders) £000	Saunders £000
Assets		
4 million shares in Saunders Ltd	23,500	—
Sundry net assets	126,500	20,000
	150,000	20,000

Financed by:

Share capital (ordinary shares of £1 each)	40,000	5,000
Retained profit at 1 January 20X5	100,000	11,000
Profit for 20X5	6,400	2,000
Profit for 20X6	3,600	3,000
Less: proposed dividend for 20X6	—	(1,000)
	150,000	20,000

Carr plc purchased the shares in Saunders Ltd on 1 January 20X5. No credit has been taken in the accounts of Carr for the dividend proposed by Saunders Ltd in respect of 20X6.

Required:

(a) Three separate balance sheets of the Carr Group at 31 December 20X6, incorporating the results of Saunders Ltd, on the assumption that Saunders Ltd is accounted for:

   (i) As a pure investment.

   (ii) As an associated company, using equity accounting.

   (iii) As a subsidiary, using acquisition basis.

(b) State the circumstances in which each of the three methods should be used. Advise the directors which of the above methods appears to be appropriate, based on the information provided, to comply with standard accounting practice.   *(Chartered Institute of Bankers)*

References

1 Insolvency Act 1986, section 84.
2 Companies Act 1985, section 125.
3 *Ibid.*, section 4.
4 *Ibid.*, section 43.
5 *Ibid.*, section 135.
6 Insolvency Act 1986, section 22.
7 *Ibid.*, section 84.
8 Ernst & Young, *UK GAAP* (5th edition), Longman, 1997, p. 720.
9 Companies Act 1985, Schedule 4, para. 31.
10 K. Wild and A. Guida, *Touche Ross Manual of Financial Reporting and Accounting* (3rd edition), Butterworth, 1990, p. 161.
11 FRS 9, *Associates and Joint Ventures*, ASB, 1997, para. 26.
12 *Ibid.*, para. 27.
13 FRS 2, *Accounting for Subsidiary Undertakings*, ASB, 1992, para. 39.

CHAPTER 21

Consolidated profit and loss account

21.1 Introduction

The profit and loss account of the parent company in its company-only accounts is subject to the realisation concept. Entries are made in the profit and loss account in respect of investments only if there is a gain evidenced by a cash flow, such as the receipt of a dividend, or if there is a loss evidenced by a permanent diminution in the investment's value which is recognised under the prudence concept.

A shareholder of the parent company is made aware of unrealised changes in the value of the net assets **owned by the parent** only if it chooses to value its investments in subsidiaries and associates using the alternative accounting rules described in the preceding chapter. Under either the historical cost convention or the alternative accounting rules, however, it would be unable to ascertain the level of profits achieved by the subsidiaries and associates from an inspection of the parent's company-only accounts.

The role of the consolidated profit and loss account is to show the shareholders of the parent company the full amount of profits achieved by the parent; the full amount of the profits achieved by the subsidiaries; and the parent's proportion of the profits achieved by the associates.

If there have been any intragroup transactions, such as sales by the parent to a subsidiary, these will need to be eliminated. Although each company can report profits made from other group companies in its company-only accounts, they must be cancelled on consolidation if they have not been realised as far as the group is concerned. In this chapter we consider the following:

- Format of the consolidated profit and loss account
- A step approach to preparing a consolidated profit and loss account for wholly and partly owned subsidiaries
- Subconsolidation stages where there is more than one subsidiary and an associate
- FRS 9 *Associates and Joint Ventures*.

21.2 Format of the consolidated profit and loss account

The format of the company consolidated profit and loss account is set out in Figure 21.1 in a sectional format that highlights the structure of the statement and the nature of the information it contains.

Figure 21.1 Sectional (FRS 9) format of a consolidated profit and loss account

First section
Trading activities of whole group

Group turnover	[Parent + subsidiary – intragroup sales]
Cost of sales	[Parent + subsidiary – intragroup purchases]
Gross profit	[Parent + subsidiary – intragroup]
Distribution costs	[Parent + subsidiary]
Administrative expenses	[Parent + subsidiary]
Other operating income	[Parent + subsidiary]
Group operating profit	[Parent + subsidiary]

Share of operating profit in
    Joint ventures   [Proportion of Joint Venture]
    Associates   [Proportion of Associate]

Interest:
    Interest receivable   [Parent + subsidiary]
                           [+ Proportion of Associate]
    Interest payable   [Parent + subsidiary]
    Interest payable   [Proportion of Associate]

Profit on ordinary
activities before tax   [Parent + subsidiary + proportion of associate and joint venture]
Tax on profits on ordinary
activities   [Parent + subsidiary + proportion of associate and joint venture]
Profit on ordinary
activities after tax   [Parent + subsidiary + proportion of associate and joint venture]

Second section
**Amount of profit in the subsidiaries that does not belong to the shareholders
of the parent company**

Minority interest in partly-owned subsidiaries   [Minority interest]

Third section
**Extraordinary items that are attributable to the shareholders
of the parent company**

Extraordinary items [under the provision of   [Parent + subsidiary – minority +
FRS 3 it is extremely unlikely that there will   proportion of associate]
be an entry under this heading]

Fourth section
**Profit that has been realised and is available to the shareholders
of the parent company**

Profit for the year. This is the parent company's profit plus the profit of wholly owned subsidiaries plus the parent company's share of the profits of partly owned subsidiaries plus the parent company's share of the profit of associated companies.

Fifth section
Amount of dividends declared by the parent company only

This section includes the interim and final dividends declared by the parent company for the financial year. The dividends include both proposed and paid dividends.

Sixth section
Amount retained out of the profit for the year for reinvestment

Amount transferred to reserves is the amount of the profit for the year that is not to be distributed as dividend by the parent. It is ploughed back into the business.

21.3 A step approach to preparing a consolidated profit and loss account for wholly and partly owned subsidiaries

The consolidated profit and loss account can be prepared in a series of steps. For a group with subsidiaries we follow the five steps shown in Figure 21.2. If there are also associates, then there are three additional steps, as shown in Figure 21.3.

21.4 Subconsolidation stages where there is more than one subsidiary and an associate

Where there is more than one subsidiary and an associate, the consolidation is built up by aggregating one company at a time. The steps explained in Figure 21.3 will be applied to each company as it is aggregated.

We will now prepare the consolidated accounts for Strong plc using subconsolidating stages:

Figure 21.2 Five steps to consolidate subsidiary companies

Steps 1 and 2 to arrive at profit on ordinary activities after tax

Aggregate the profit and loss accounts of the parent company and the subsidiary companies on a line-by-line basis.

Eliminate intragroup transactions such as intragroup sales; unrealised profit on intragroup sales; dividends paid by subsidiary companies to parent company.

Step 3 to arrive at the profit before extraordinary items

Deduct the minority interest for partly owned subsidiaries.

Step 4 to arrive at the profit for the financial year

Calculate the extraordinary profits and losses of the parent company plus the extraordinary profits and losses of wholly owned subsidiaries plus the parent company's share of the extraordinary gains and losses of partly owned subsidiaries.

Step 5 to arrive at the retained profit for the year

Disclose the dividends declared by the parent company.

Figure 21.3 Additional three steps to consolidate associated companies

Step 6 to arrive at the profit on ordinary activities before tax figure

Add the parent company's share of operating profit of associates and joint ventures.

Step 7 to arrive at the profit on ordinary activities after tax figure

Add the parent company's share of the tax on the profit on ordinary activities of associates and joint ventures.

Step 8 to arrive at the profit for the financial year

Add the parent company's share of the extraordinary gains and losses of the associates and joint ventures to the figure already calculated in Step 4.

- Stage 1: consolidate the wholly owned subsidiary.
- Stage 2: consolidate the partly owned subsidiary.
- Stage 3: consolidate the associate.

We take the profit and loss information from Figure 20.4 and assume that:

- Strong plc has sold goods that cost £200 to Hundred plc for £250 and the goods are still in stock at 31 December 20X1.
- Hundred plc paid a dividend of £1,000 to Strong plc on 31 December 20X1.

The subconsolidation worksheet for stage 1 is set out in Figure 21.4. The amount transferred to reserves in the consolidated profit and loss account is £1,390 because the unrealised profit has been deducted from the aggregate total.

Figure 21.4 Stage 1: subconsolidating the wholly owned subsidiary

Profit and loss accounts of Strong plc and Hundred plc
for the year ended 31 December 20X1 – subconsolidation worksheet

	Strong plc £	Hundred plc £	Aggregate £	Eliminate Dr/(Cr) £	Group P&L account £
Turnover	9,000	4,500	13,500	250 [a]	13,250
Cost of sales	4,500	2,250	6,750	(250) [a]	
				50 [b]	6,550
Gross profit	4,500	2,250	6,750		6,700
Distribution costs	(900)	(450)	(1,350)		(1,350)
Administrative expenses	(720)	(360)	(1,080)		(1,080)
Operating profit	2,880	1,440	4,320		4,270
Investment income from:					
Subsidiaries	1,000		1,000	1,000 [c]	
Associates					
Other investments					
Profit before tax	3,880	1,440	5,320		4,270
Tax	720	360	1,080		1,080
Profit after tax	3,160	1,080	4,240		3,190
Extraordinary items	0	0	0		0
Profit for the year	3,160	1,080	4,240		3,190
Dividends	1,800	1,000	2,800	(1,000) [c]	1,800
Transferred to reserves	1,360	80	1,440		1,390
Consolidated balance sheet entry to stock				(50) [b]	
				0	

Figure 21.4 (*cont.*)

Notes cross-referenced to the worksheet:
[a] The intragroup sales are eliminated.
[b] The unrealised profit on sale is eliminated from the profit and loss account. The corresponding credit entry will be to stock in the balance sheet so that the closing stock is reduced by £50.
[c] The dividend paid by the subsidiary to the holding company is cancelled against the income from subsidiary companies.

The subconsolidation worksheet for stage 2 is set out in Figure 21.5, and that for stage 3 in Figure 21.6.

Figure 21.5 Stage 2: subconsolidating the partly owned subsidiary

*Profit and loss accounts of Strong/Hundred and Sixty plc
for the year ended 31 December 20X1 – subconsolidation worksheet*

	Strong/ Hundred plc £	Sixty plc £	Aggregate £	Eliminate Dr/(Cr) £	Group P&L account £
Turnover	13,250	4,500	17,750		17,750
Cost of sales	6,550	2,250	8,800		8,800
Gross profit	6,700	2,250	8,950		8,950
Distribution costs	(1,350)	(450)	(1,800)		(1,800)
Administrative expenses	(1,080)	(360)	(1,440)		(1,440)
Operating profit	4,270	1,440	5,710		5,710
Investment income from:					
Subsidiaries					
Associates					
Other investments					
Profit before tax	4,270	1,440	5,710		5,710
Tax	1,080	360	1,440		1,440
Profit after tax	3,190	1,080	4,270		4,270
Minority interest				432 [d]	432
Profit before extraordinary items					3,838
Extraordinary items	0	0	0	0	0
Profit for the year	3,190	1,080	4,270		3,838
Dividends	1,800	—	1,800		1,800
Transferred to reserves	1,390	1,080	2,470		2,038
Consolidated balance sheet entry					
Minority interest				(432)[d]	
				0	

Figure 21.5 (*cont.*)

Notes cross-referenced to the worksheet in Figure 21.5:

[d]The minority shareholders are entitled to 40% of the profit of Sixty plc, i.e. 40% of £1,080. This is transferred to the minority interest in the consolidated balance sheet.

Figure 21.6 Stage 3: subconsolidating the associate

Profit and loss accounts of Strong/Hundred/Sixty and Twenty plc
for the year ended 31 December 20X1 – subconsolidation worksheet

	Strong/ Hundred/ Sixty £	Twenty plc adjustments	Group P&L account £
Group turnover	17,750		17,750
Cost of sales	8,800		8,800
Gross profit	8,950		8,950
Distribution costs	(1,800)		(1,800)
Administrative expenses	(1,440)		(1,440)
Group operating profit	5,710		5,710
Share of operating profit in:			
Associate company		20% of £1,440	288
			5,998
Tax on profit[*]	1,440		
Associate company tax		20% of £360	(1,512)
Profit after tax	4,270		4,486
Minority interest	432		432
Profit before extraordinary items	3,838		4,054
Extraordinary items	0	20% of £0	0
Profit for the year	3,838		4,054
Dividends	1,800		1,800
Transferred to reserves	2,038		2,254
[*]Tax relates to the following:	Parent and subsidiaries		1,440
	Associates		72

The consolidated profit and loss account of the Strong Group is now complete. We have aggregated Hundred plc and Sixty plc and accounted on an equity accounting basis for Twenty plc. The consolidated profit and loss account in Format 1 Companies Act 1985 style is set out in Figure 21.7.

Figure 21.7 Consolidated profit and loss account of the Strong Group for the year ended 31 December 20X1

	£
Turnover	17,750
Cost of sales	8,800
Gross profit	8,950
Distribution costs	(1,800)
Administrative expenses	(1,440)
Operating profit	5,710
Share of operating profits in associated company	288
Profit on ordinary activities before tax	5,998
Tax	(1,512)
Profit on ordinary activities after tax	4,486
Minority interest	432
Profit before extraordinary items	4,054
Extraordinary items	0
Profit for the year	4,054
Dividends	1,800
Transferred to reserves	2,254

21.5 ASB review of accounting for associates

The mechanics that we have illustrated in Figure 21.6 to account for the results of an associate were first used by the Royal Dutch Shell group in 1964. Prior to that the only entry in the profit and loss account would have been any dividend receivable from the associate.

In 1971 the ASC issued SSAP 1 *Accounting for Associated Companies*, which required all companies with investments that gave them significant influence to apply the same approach, provided their intention was to retain the investment for the long term. It would have been inappropriate for a company to acquire short-term investments and include a share of the profits in their profit and loss account; in such a case, dividend receivable should be brought into the accounts.

The treatment we have illustrated in Chapters 18–20 is a modified form of consolidation. It does not aggregate each of the assets, liabilities, income and expenses of the associate in the same way as subsidiaries are treated. Instead, it uses **equity accounting**, under which the investing company incorporates the investing company's share of the pre-tax profits, tax and post-tax profits of the associate in the consolidated profit and loss account, and adjusts the carrying value of the investment in the consolidated balance sheet by the investing company's proportion of undistributed retained profit. However, it was not until the Companies Act 1989 that there was a statutory requirement to equity account for associates.

21.5.1 Why is it important to establish whether an investee is an associate?

Associate status is established by the existence of the ability to exercise significant influence. This is important because, although an investing company is happy to recognise associate status as long as the associate is profitable, if the investee becomes unprofitable, there is a natural eagerness to cease recognising it as an associate in order to avoid the investing company's share of any losses being brought into the profit and loss account.

21.5.2 Accounting for associates under FRS 9 *Associates and Joint Ventures*[1]

SSAP 1 *Accounting for Associated Companies* set out various relationships that could indicate the ability to exercise significant influence.[2] These ranged from quantitative, such as the existence of a 20% holding, to qualitative, such as participation in the financial, operating and dividend policy decisions of the investee. FRED 11 *Associates and Joint Ventures*, issued by the ASB in 1996[3], broadly followed the basis set out in SSAP 1. SSAP 1 was replaced (for listed companies) by the issue of FRS 9 in 1997.

Definition of an associate

Companies legislation provides that an entity holding 20% or more of the voting rights should be presumed to exercise significant influence. The Companies Act does not define significant influence. FRS 9 gives more detailed guidance and definitions. It is not a mechanistic test under FRS 9 and the presumption is rebutted if the investor does not satisfy the FRS 9 criteria. A significant influence is normally exercised by the investor having a director on the board of the investee, but the key aspect is that there is a formal or informal understanding which allows the investor to participate in policy decisions. We will comment briefly on the FRS 9 definitions.

An associate is an entity (other than a subsidiary) in which another entity holds a **participating interest** and over whose operating and financial policies the investor exercises a **significant influence**.

A participating interest is a beneficial interest in shares held on a **long-term**, continuing basis to secure a benefit for the investor by the exercise of **control** or **influence** arising from holding those shares.

A significant influence exists when:

- there is **active involvement** by the investor in strategic decisions of the investee, such as changes in markets and product, changes in scale of the business, and dividend policy; and
- the investor's strategic interest determines the policies implemented by the investee.

To account for associates FRS 9 requires that:

- in consolidated financial statements an investor should use the equity method; and
- in the investor's individual accounts investments in joint ventures should be treated as fixed asset investments and shown either at cost, less any amounts written off, or at valuation.

21.5.3 Accounting for joint ventures under FRS 9 *Associates and Joint Ventures*

Definition of a joint venture

FRS 9 defines a joint venture as an entity that, as a result of a contractual relationship, is jointly controlled by the reporting entity and other venturers, i.e. none of the venturers individually controls it. This means that decisions on financial and operating policy essential to the activities, economic performance and financial position of that venture require each venturer's consent.

To account for joint ventures FRS 9 requires that:

- in consolidated financial statements an investor should use the **gross equity method**; and

- in the investor's individual accounts investments in joint ventures should be treated as fixed asset investments and shown either at cost, less any amounts written off, or at valuation.

Gross equity method

This is a new method which is a form of equity method under which the investor's share of the aggregate gross assets and liabilities underlying the net amount included for the investment is shown on the face of the balance sheet and, in the profit and loss account, **the investor's share of the investee's turnover is noted.**

The requirement to note the **turnover** was to respond to the objections of companies that equity accounting understated their turnover and companies such as British Aerospace had already adopted the practice of disclosing 'Sales, including share of joint venture sales' and deducting the 'Share of joint venture sales' to arrive at the statutory turnover figure.

The following are extracts from the 2000 Annual Report of United Utilities plc:

Consolidated profit and loss account for the year ended 31 March 2000 extract

	£m
Turnover: group and share of joint ventures	*2,425.9*
Less: share of joint venture turnover	*(69.6)*
Group turnover	2,356.3
Net operating costs	(1,694.9)
Group operating profit	661.4
Share of operating profit of joint ventures	*4.0*
Profit on ordinary activities before interest	665.4
Net interest payable and similar charges:	
Group	(196.1)
Joint venture	*(9.9)*
Profit on ordinary activities before tax	459.4

Consolidated balance sheet extract

Fixed assets	
Investments in joint ventures:	
share of gross assets	*297.1*
share of gross liabilities	*(231.1)*
	66.0

Note 13 Fixed asset investments – showing make-up of the £66m:

	Unlisted	Loans	Total
Cost:			
At 1 April 1999	57.3	9.1	66.4
Additions	7.2	4.5	11.7
Share of losses	(7.7)	–	(7.7)
Loan repayment	–	(4.1)	(4.1)
Exchange adjustments	(0.2)	(0.1)	(0.3)
At 31 March 2000	*56.6*	*9.4*	*66.0*

When is it considered appropriate by the ASB to use proportional consolidation?

Prior to FRS 9 companies such as construction companies set up unincorporated partnerships when carrying out certain joint ventures, e.g. assume that on 1 January 19X6 two construction companies, Tarcam plc and Liang plc, enter into a partnership to tender for the construction by 31 December 19X9 of a new bridge over the River Thames. When they prepared their prepare their accounts at 31 December 19X6 each company would account for the contract on a proportional consolidation basis.

However, because FRS 9 has defined a joint venture as 'an entity that, as a result of a contractual relationship, is jointly controlled' and defined an entity as 'a body corporate, partnership, **or unincorporated association**' such partnership arrangements as that between Tarcam plc and Liang plc now fall within the FRS and Companies Act requirements. The Companies Act does not permit proportional consolidation and the ASB has therefore accommodated the pre FRS 9 proportional consolidation treatment by creating a new animal, the Joint Arrangement that is Not an Entity (a JANE).

It defines a JANE as 'A contractual arrangement under which the participants engage in joint activities that do not create an entity **because it would not be carrying on a trade or business of its own**'.

FRS 9 para. 8 gives the following additional information, namely, that 'For a joint arrangement to amount to an entity, it must carry on a trade or business, meaning a trade or business **of its own and not just part of its participants' trades or businesses**'.

This means that if the arrangement falls within the definition of an entity, it will be accounted for as a joint venture by equity accounting. If it does not fall within the definition of an entity, i.e. it is a JANE it will be accounted for by proportional consolidation.

An illustration of approach to deciding if a joint arrangement is a joint venture or a JANE

Proportional consolidation would be appropriate for joint arrangements such as cost-sharing arrangements or one-off construction projects when each participant would include in their individual and consolidated accounts its share of the assets, liabilities and cash flows arising from the arrangement.

However, it can be difficult at first to understand how the decision is made to classify as a joint venture or JANE. The following illustration with Tarcam plc (a construction company) and Stagebus plc (a coach operator) explains the conceptual approach to classifying a joint arrangement:

● Assume that Tarcam plc entered into a contract with Stagebus plc to build **and operate** a toll bridge over the River Thames.

- The test is whether this arrangement falls within the definition of **an entity**.
- This means determining whether the joint arrangement is carrying on a **different trade of its own**.
- The joint arrangement is to trade as a toll bridge operator.
- This is different from the participants' trades of construction and coach operator.
- The joint arrangement is an entity.
- It is therefore a joint venture and accounted for using equity accounting.

21.5.4 **FRS 9 Disclosure requirement**

Under SSAP 1 there had been disclosure of the net tangible assets underlying the investment in the consolidated balance sheet and the investor's proportion of the associate pre-tax profits, tax and post-tax profits. FRS 9 *Associates and Joint Ventures* proposes additional disclosures. Where the investor's interest is substantial, i.e. where it exceeds 15% of the investor's gross assets, gross liabilities, turnover or results, then the following information should be disclosed for an associate (for a joint venture turnover is not required):

- turnover for the associates;
- fixed assets;
- current assets;
- liabilities due within one year;
- liabilities due after more than one year.

Where the interest exceeds 25%, there is additional disclosure. A note should name the associate or joint venture and give its share of profit before tax, taxation and profit after tax.

The likely effect of FRS 9

The significant influence test may be more difficult to satisfy than the 20% rule
It will probably be more difficult for investors to establish associate status for an investment. It will prevent investors who have failed to achieve a takeover from bringing in a proportion of the investee profits under the guise of accounting for an associate. There will be greater confidence that any profits brought into the consolidated accounts from associates will be accessible as cash flows, at least in the long term, and there will be greater transparency with regard to the implication for the investor of loans and liabilities incurred by the associate; after all, if an investor is unable to have a say in determining whether a dividend is paid or not, what justification could there be for including a share of the profit?

Failing the significant influence test may lead to re-classification of investments
The ASB in FRS 9 do not regard the 20% presumption as sufficient and companies should go back and review investments that had been classified as an associate pre-FRS 9 by testing for significant influence, e.g. checking if there is investor Board representation on the investee's Board.

Users will be more able to assess associate position and performance
The requirement to disclose the share of associates' operating profit and interest payable rather than simply share of profit before tax means that it will be possible to identify aspects such as interest cover, e.g. a pre-tax share of profits of £1,000 in an associate where there is a 25% holding might have arisen from an associate with £4,000 operating profit,

i.e. with no gearing, or from an associate with operating profits of £10m less interest payable of £9.999m, i.e. a dangerously highly geared company. This means a user is more able to assess the risk attached to an investment in an associate.

However, it will be easier for companies to argue that they should not equity account for an investment that becomes loss-making on the grounds of lack of significant influence.[4]

Summary

The profit and loss accounts of individual companies are subject to the realisation concept. Investment income is recognised only when it is declared by the investee company and reasonably certain to be realised in the form of cash.

Where subsidiaries do not pass all of their profit up as a dividend, the shareholders of the parent company are unable to form a view of management performance. They are unable to ascertain from the parent company accounts the profits that are attributable to investments in companies over which their directors have influence or control.

The consolidated profit and loss account provides them with the means to see the overall performance of the group.

The balance sheets of individual companies are constrained by the asset recognition criteria that assets must belong to the company. The shareholders of the parent company are unable to form a view from the accounts of the parent company of the net assets that are controlled by the management of the parent company. The alternative accounting rules allow the company to increase the investment value to reflect the underlying net asset values of the shares owned. But they do not allow the company to include all of the net assets of investee companies unless they have a 100% shareholding.

The consolidated balance sheet provides them with the means to see all assets and liabilities **controlled** by the parent company, even though they might not satisfy the strict ownership criteria applied to the individual company balance sheet.

The ASB has issued FRS 9 to improve the information given about associates and joint ventures, particularly where they are significant, by following a layered approach applying the 15% and 25% thresholds that satisfies user needs and recognises cost implication for preparers.

REVIEW QUESTIONS

1 If instead of selling stock intragroup, Strong plc had sold a fixed asset which it held at £200 book value to Hundred plc for £250 on 1 January 20X1, what additional matters would need to be considered and adjusted for at 31 December 20X1 in:

(a) the consolidated profit and loss account; and

(b) the consolidated balance sheet?

Illustrate the numerical effect, making any assumptions you consider necessary.

2 Some items in a consolidated profit and loss account relate to the combined entities and some items relate to the shareholders of the parent company. The consolidated profit and loss account has therefore been described as two-tiered.[5]

(a) Explain why it is constructed with this two-tier approach.

(b) How would you describe the consolidation process that produced a consolidated profit and loss account in which all items relate to the shareholders of the parent company?

(c) How would you describe the consolidation process that produced a consolidated profit and loss account in which all items relate to the combined entities?

3 The Shortfall Group has been discussing the question of security for loans and overdraft with the group's bankers. The bankers have suggested the following types of security:

(a) Guarantees from the directors.

(b) A guarantee from the parent company to secure a loan to a subsidiary.

(c) A guarantee from each of the companies in the group for a loan to one of the other companies.

(d) A guarantee from each company in the group for loans to all other companies in the group.

(e) A guarantee from each company in the group for loans to all other companies in the group with a debenture from each company.

Explain the rights of the bank against the assets shown in the consolidated balance sheet in each of the above arrangements.

4 In the early days of group accounting (up until about 1929), the consolidation and equity methods were regarded as alternative accounting treatments for investments in subsidiaries and for the profits/losses generated by them. Since then the consolidation method has prevailed in this field.

(a) Outline the similarities, and differences, between the two methods.

(b) Explain the conventional present-day uses of the two methods.

(c) Argue for or against the general use of the equity method, in accounting for investments in subsidiaries.

5 'Equity accounting should only be allowed if the investor is certain to obtain access to his share of the investee's cash flows within a period of time set by the ASB, e.g. within five years.' Discuss.

6 'Proportional consolidation would be a more informative form of presentation for associates than equity accounting supported by summarised financial statements.' Discuss and explain why the ASB has not permitted this treatment.

7 'Equity accounting is a confused concept. It is not consistent with the requirement that consolidated accounts should only contain assets and liabilities that are under the **control** of the management of the investor.' Discuss with particular consideration of the justification for revising the investment in associates in the consolidated accounts to reflect underlying net asset backing.

8 It has been stated by Allan Cook, ASB Technical Director, in the preface to the Exposure Draft *Associates and Joint Ventures* that 'Companies are increasingly seeking alliances to pool their resources as a means of sharing risk and gaining access to new markets. It is therefore important for users of financial statements to have clear information about such alliances and their effect on the company's financial position and performance.' Explain (a) how FRS 9 provides such information; and (b) likely effects on financial position and performance of associate and joint venture alliances.

9 'Return on capital employed based on a comparison of the consolidated operating profit with the net capital employed disclosed in the consolidated balance sheet is a meaningless figure because it is only the asset values of the subsidiaries that have been restated at fair values as at the date of acquisition.' Discuss and explain how the position could be improved.

10 The following is an extract from the Psion Annual Report and Accounts 1999:

> *Accounting policies*
> Joint ventures are accounted for using the gross equity method, which is a form of equity method under which the share of the gross assets and liabilities underlying the net amount included for the investment is shown on the face of the balance sheet and in the profit and loss account, the share of turnover is noted.

Discuss (a) the relevance to investors of the additional gross information disclosed in the balance sheet and the share of turnover noted in the profit and loss account; and (b) the advantages and disadvantages of presenting the joint venture information on a proportional consolidation basis.

EXERCISES

An extract from the solution is provided in the appendix at the end of the text for exercises marked with an asterisk (*).

Question 1

The profit and loss accounts of Try plc and Hard plc for the year ended 31 December 20X5 are as follows:

	Try plc £	Hard plc £
Profit before tax	80,000	56,000
Tax	42,000	28,600
	38,000	27,400
Proposed dividend	20,000	
	18,000	27,400

Try plc acquired 75% of the equity shares of Hard plc on 1 January 20X3.

Required:
Prepare a consolidated profit and loss account for the year ended 31 December 20X5.

Questions 2–5

The following profit and loss accounts and balance sheets of Mother plc and Daughter plc as at 31 December 20X6 are to be used for questions 2 to 5:

	Mother plc £000	Daughter plc £000
Profit before tax	300	100
(includes dividends received from Daughter plc)		
Tax	(120)	(30)
Profit after tax	180	70
Transfer to general reserves	(30)	(20)
Dividends	(50)	(20)
Retained	100	30
Balance brought forward at 1 Jan 20X6	50	10
	150	40
Balance sheets		
Fixed assets	300	150
Investment in Daughter plc	200	
Net current assets	280	110
	780	260
Share capital	500	200
General reserve	130	20
Profit and loss account	150	40
	780	260

* Question 2

Required:
(a) Prepare a consolidated profit and loss account and consolidated balance sheet as at 31 December 20X6 on the assumption that Mother plc acquired all of the shares in Daughter plc on its incorporation on 1 January 20X2.
(b) Explain accounting treatment.

* Question 3

Required:
(a) Prepare a consolidated profit and loss account and consolidated balance sheet as at 31 December 20X6 on the assumption that Mother plc acquired 80% of the shares in Daughter plc on its incorporation on 1 January 20X2.
(b) Explain accounting treatment.

* Question 4

Required:

(a) Prepare a consolidated profit and loss account and consolidated balance sheet as at 31 December 20X6 on the assumption that Mother plc acquired all of the shares in Daughter plc on 1 January 20X4, at which date the Daughter plc accounts showed credit balances on the general reserve of £15,000 and on the profit and loss account of £5,000, and corresponding net assets of £220,000.

(b) Explain accounting treatment.

* Question 5

Required:

(a) Prepare a consolidated profit and loss account and consolidated balance sheet as at 31 December 20X6 on the assumption that Mother plc acquired 80% of the shares in Daughter plc on 1 January 20X4, at which date the Daughter plc accounts showed credit balances on the general reserve of £15,000 and on the profit and loss account of £5,000, and corresponding net assets of £220,000.

(b) Explain accounting treatment.

Question 6

Dolphin plc owns 33.33% of the share capital of Bears Ltd. The shares (200,000) were purchased five years ago for £300,000. At that time, the balance sheet of Bears Ltd was as follows:

Net assets (at fair value)	£750,000
Represented by:	
Share capital (ordinary £1 shares)	600,000
Reserves	150,000
	£750,000

The current balance sheets of the two companies as at 31 December 20X7 are as follows:

	Dolphin plc £	Bears Ltd £
Net assets	1,000,000	1,500,000
Investment in Bears Ltd	300,000	—
	1,300,000	1,500,000
Represented by:		
Share capital (ordinary £1 shares)	900,000	600,000
Reserves	400,000	900,000
	1,300,000	1,500,000

Profit and loss accounts for the year ended 31 December 20X7 are:

	Dolphin plc £	Bears Ltd £
Operating profit	120,000	180,000
Dividend received from Bears Ltd	10,000	—
	130,000	180,000
Dividend paid	60,000	30,000
Retained profit, added to reserves	70,000	150,000

Required:

Prepare a consolidated profit and loss account and balance sheet as at 31 December 20X7.

Question 7

On 1 January 20X5 Tinker Ltd bought 6,300 of the shares of Tailor Ltd. The total issued share capital of Tailor was then, and remains, 7,000 fully paid shares of £1 nominal value.

Tinker's summarised accounts for 20X5 are as follows:

	Tinker Ltd and its subsidiary Tailor Ltd				
	Parent company's accounts £			Consolidated group accounts £	
Profit and loss account:					
Trading profit		8,400			10,200
Dividend from subsidiary		900			—
		9,300			10,200
Dividend on share capital		4,000			4,000
		5,300			6,200
Brought forward		22,700			22,700
Carried forward		28,000			28,900
Balance sheet:					
Plant and equipment (cost)		184,900			207,900
Depreciation		32,000			44,000
		152,900			163,900
Investment in subsidiary (cost)		9,100			—
Stock (cost) – Note 1	63,000			70,000	
Debtors	23,000			25,000	
Southern Bank	16,000			16,000	
	102,000			111,000	
Eastern Bank	—		6,000		
Creditors	56,000		58,000		
		46,000	64,000		47,000
		208,000			210,900
Ordinary share capital					
(£1 shares fully paid)		180,000			180,000
Reserves – Note 2		28,000			29,700
Minority interest		—			1,200
		208,000			210,900

Notes:

1   It is known that at 31 December 20X5 Tinker had in stock goods invoiced to it by Tailor during 20X5 for £1,200, the cost of which to Tailor was £900. An appropriate adjustment has been made for this (so far as it affects the parent company) in the group accounts.

2   The group reserves at 31 December 20X5 were as follows:

	£
Profit retained	28,900
Capital reserve on consolidation attributable to interest of parent company	800
	29,700

Required:
Prepare summarised accounts for Tailor Ltd for 20X5 in the same form.

Question 8

H Ltd has one subsidiary, S Ltd. The company has held a controlling interest for several years. The latest financial statements for the two companies and the consolidated financial statements for the H Group are as shown below:

Profit and loss accounts for the year ended 30 September 20X4

	H Ltd £000	S Ltd £000	H Group £000
Turnover	4,000	2,200	5,700
Cost of sales	(1,100)	(960)	(1,605)
	2,900	1,240	4,095
Administration	(420)	(130)	(550)
Distribution	(170)	(95)	(265)
Dividends receivable	180	—	—
Profit before tax	2,490	1,015	3,280
Corporation tax	(620)	(335)	(955)
Profit after tax	1,870	680	2,325
Minority interest	—	—	(170)
	1,870	680	2,155
Dividends	(250)	(240)	(250)
	1,620	440	1,905
Balance brought forward	2,700	1,020	2,335
Balance carried forward	4,320	1,460	4,240

	Balance sheets at 30 September 20X4					
	H Ltd		S Ltd		H Group	
	£000	£000	£000	£000	£000	£000
Fixed assets:						
Tangible	7,053		2,196		9,249	
Investment in S Ltd	1,700	8,753	—	2,196	—	9,249
Current assets:						
Stocks	410		420		785	
Debtors	400		220		595	
Dividend receivable	135		—		—	
Bank	27	972	19	659	46	1,426
Current liabilities						
Creditors	(100)		(80)		(155)	
Proposed dividend	(200)		(180)		(200)	
Dividend to minority	—		—		(45)	
Taxation	(605)	(905)	(375)	(635)	(980)	(1,380)
		8,820		2,220		9,295

	H Ltd	S Ltd	H Group
	£000	£000	£000
Share capital	4,500	760	4,500
Profit and loss	4,320	1,460	4,240
	8,820	2,220	8,740
Minority interest	—	—	555
	8,820	2,220	9,295

Goodwill of £410,000 was written off at the date of acquisition.

Required:

(a) Calculate the percentage of S Ltd which is owned by H Ltd.

(b) Calculate the value of sales made between the two companies during the year.

(c) Calculate the amount of unrealised profit which had been included in the stock figure as a result of intercompany trading and which had to be cancelled on consolidation.

(d) Calculate the value of intercompany debtors and creditors cancelled on consolidation.

(e) Calculate the balance on S Ltd's profit and loss account when H Ltd acquired its stake in the company.

(CIMA)

References

1 FRS 9, *Associates and Joint Ventures*, ASB, 1997.

2 SSAP 1, *Accounting for Associated Companies*, ASC, 1982, para. 13.

3 FRED 11, *Associates and Joint Ventures*, ASB, 1996.

4 Ernst & Young, *UK GAAP* (4th edition), Macmillan, 1994, p. 389.

5 P.A. Taylor, *Consolidated Financial Reporting*, Paul Chapman Publishing, 1996, p. 181.

CHAPTER 22

Foreign currency translation

22.1 The problem

A basic concept of traditional historical cost accounting is that transactions are recorded at cost. It would seem, therefore, that recording transactions that have been entered into in a foreign currency is quite straightforward, namely, convert the foreign currency into its local counterpart such as French francs to £ sterling and record the sterling equivalent in the books. Thus the purchase of goods from a French supplier costing 2,000 francs when the exchange rate was, say, 10 francs to the pound would reveal a cost of £200.

However, in practice, a period of credit is invariably involved so that by the time the debt is settled the exchange rate may have changed, causing the notion of cost to be perceived differently. For example, the debt of 2,000 francs may be discharged at a later date when the rate of exchange had changed to 8 francs to the pound. Consequently an invoice cost of 2,000 francs formerly converted to £200 would result in expenditure of £250 (2,000/8), an additional cost on settlement of £50 representing a loss caused by a changing exchange rate.

22.2 The background

For some twenty years following the 1939–1945 conflict fixed exchange rates between countries dominated international trade so that the problem outlined above was not of critical concern because changes in the fixed exchange rates were rare. But since the late 1960s there have been significant changes. There has been a massive growth in international trade, transnational conglomerates have developed and floating exchange rates have been substituted for fixed exchange rates. Changes now occur on a daily basis so that fluctuations in cost between contract date and settlement date are usual rather than exceptional. For example, companies making up accounts as at 31 March each year would translate at end of year rates. Rates for the three year-ends 1999–2001 for the US$, euro and Japanese yen show that the rate of exchange of £1 sterling weakened against the US$ and fluctuated against both the euro and the yen as follows:

Date	US dollar	% change	euro	% change	Yen	% change
31.3.1999	1.61		1.50		191	
31.3.2000	1.59	–1%	1.67	+11%	168	–12%
31.3.2001	1.42	–11%	1.61	–4%	178	+6%

These end of year figures might not, of course, indicate a uniform trend, and in addition, there has been substantial foreign equity investment over a broad geographical spread, e.g. the BOC Group listed in their 2001 accounts over 80 subsidiaries in over 50 countries.

22.3 The need for standardisation

The growth of foreign trade and foreign equity investment and the significant effect that exchange differences can potentially have on results necessitates the standardisation of the accounting treatment of foreign exchange conversion and translation. For example, the 1996 accounts of Kalon plc reported a profit for the year of £11.2m in its profit and loss account whereas the statement of total gains and losses showed:

	£000
Profit for year	11,171
Currency translation differences on the net investment in foreign subsidiaries	(21,354)
Total gains and losses recognised since last annual report	(10,183)

We will consider accounting treatment in both individual companies and consolidated accounts.

22.4 Accounting treatment in the individual company

We will illustrate the accounting treatment for exchange gains and losses for:

(i) the purchase of goods;

(ii) the purchase of fixed assets;

(iii) long-term loans;

(iv) obtaining a foreign loan to finance foreign company investment.

22.4.1 Treatment of exchange gains or losses arising on the purchase of goods

There are three critical events that may typically occur in the purchase/payment cycle. These are the receipt and recording of the purchase invoice, the payment and recording of cash paid in part or full settlement and the extraction of creditor balances at the balance sheet date if the invoice has not already been settled in full.

We will illustrate the decisions required at each of these critical events for the following transaction between UK Ltd and HK Ltd.

Assume HK Ltd manufactures an electric car which is imported by UK Ltd at a unit cost of HK$200,000 and sold for £25,000. UK Ltd plans to import and sell 100 cars per year and budgets for the years ended 30 June 20X0 and 20X1, assuming a rate of exchange of HK$10 to the £, for a unit gross profit of £5,000 and a total gross profit of £500,000. The contract is denominated in HK$, which means that from the UK Ltd's point of view it is a foreign currency transaction with the risk of a loss or a gain if the exchange rate should vary from HK$10 to the £. If the contract had specified payment in £ sterling it would have been a foreign currency transaction from the HK supplier's point of view and HK Ltd would have been exposed to the risk of exchange rate movements.

We will now consider the treatment of the purchase of one car on 30 April 20X0 to determine the effect of changes in the exchange rate on the financial year ended 30 June 20X0 and 20X1.

The invoice for HK$200,000 was received and recorded on 30 April 20X0. Payment was required in two equal instalments on 31 May and 31 August 20X0. Creditor balances were extracted at the financial year-end which was 30 June and 31 July for UK Ltd and HK Ltd respectively.

Calculate the necessary accounting data in the books of each company at each of these three critical events.

Exchange rates were as follows:

	HK$ to the £			HK$ to the £
30 April	10		31 July	13.5
31 May	12		31 August	11
30 June	12.5			

The entries would be as follows:

In the books of UK Ltd

At purchase/invoice date:

Purchases		Trade creditor		Memo			Sales		Trade debtor	
	£			HK$ (a)	£			HK$		HK$
30 April	20,000	30 April Purchases	200,000		20,000 (b)	30 April	200,000	30 April	200,000

At date of 1st instalment:

Trade creditor					Trade debtor	
31 May Cash	(100,000)	(8,333) (c)		31 May Cash	(100,000)
Exchange gain		(1,667) (d)			
31 May Balance	100,000	10,000		31 May Bal	100,000

In the books of HK Ltd

(a) Memorandum record: UK Ltd will keep a memorandum record of the liability in HK dollars e.g. HK$200,000 and an accounting creditors ledger entry in sterling e.g. £20,000 in the UK Ltd books.

(b) Purchases: HK$200,000/10 = £20,000

(c) Cash payment: HK$100,000/12 = £8,333

(d) Exchange difference: There is an exchange gain of £1,667 (£10,000 − £8,333). This is **realised** as a result of the **conversion** of HK$ into £ sterling. It will therefore be posted to a Gains/Losses on Exchange Account and transferred to the Profit and Loss Account at 30 June 20X0.

At UK Ltd balance sheet date:

Purchases		Trade creditor		Memo			Sales		Trade debtor	
	£			HK$ (a)	£			HK$		HK$
30 June		30 June								
Transfer to		Deduct								
trading	(20,000) (e)	exchange gain			(2,000) (g)					
account										
30 June		30 June					30 June		30 June	
Balance	nil	Balance	100,000		8,000 (f)		Balance	200,000	Balance	100,000

(e) Trading Account: purchases account balance is transferred to the trading account at the year-end.

(f) Balance sheet creditor figure: The HK$ balance is translated at closing rate (HK$100,000/12.5) = £8,000

(g) Exchange gain: This is the difference in the Creditor balance from £10,000 at 31 May to £8,000 at 30 June.

Accruals principle

The application of the accruals principle means that the company should recognise the change in value that has occurred during the current period and not wait until the foreign monetary liability has been turned into cash before recognising the change in value.[1] The closing rate is an objective measure set by the market. It is the exchange rate for spot trans-actions at the balance sheet date, being the mean between the buying and selling rates at the close of business on that day.[2] It could be argued, in theory, that the appropriate rate to use is that expected at the date of the contractual payment on 31 August. However, in practice, the rate current at the balance sheet date is regarded as an acceptable surrogate.

The exchange gain of £2,000 is classified as **realised** as a result of the **translation** of the debtor balance from francs to £ sterling. It is transferred to the profit and loss account, together with the **conversion** exchange gain of £1,667, as a total of £3,667 for the year. It has arisen from the strengthening of sterling since the date of entering into the contract.

Prudence principle

The effect of applying the accruals principle on reported profits can be significant. For UK Ltd the budgeted gross profit of £5,000 per car has been increased by £3,667, i.e. a 73% increase! This would, of course, have been a 73% decrease if sterling had weak-ened to the same extent during this period.

Assume HK Ltd manufactures an electric car which is imported by UK Ltd at a unit cost of HK$200,000 and sold for £25,000. UK Ltd plans to import and sell 100 cars per year and budgets for the years ended 30 June 20X0 and 20X1, assuming a rate of exchange of HK$10 to the £, for a unit gross profit of £5,000 and a total gross profit of £500,000. The contract is denominated in HK$ which means that from the UK Ltd's point of view it is a foreign currency transaction with the risk of a loss or a gain if the exchange rate should vary from HK$10 to the £. If the contract had specified payment in £ sterling it would have been a foreign currency transaction from the HK supplier's point of view and HK Ltd would have been exposed to the risk of exchange rate movements.

We will now consider the treatment of the purchase of 1 car on 30 April 20X0 to deter-mine the effect of changes in the exchange rate on the financial year ended 30 June 20X0 and 20X1.

The invoice for HK$200,000 was received and recorded on 30 April 20X0. Payment was required in two equal instalments on 31 May and 31 August 20X0. Creditor balances were extracted at the financial year-end which was 30 June and 31 July for UK Ltd and HK Ltd respectively.

Calculate the necessary accounting data in the books of each company at each of these three critical events.

Exchange rates were as follows:

	HK$ to the £		HK$ to the £
30 April	10	31 July	13.5
31 May	12	31 August	11
30 June	12.5		

It could be argued that, as any change in the rate of exchange could reverse as in section 22.2 above with the fluctuation of the Japanese yen to the £ in 1997, any gain arising from a reduction in the foreign liability should not be recognised in the current period on the grounds that the amount of the eventual sterling payment cannot be assessed with reasonable certainty. It has been suggested[3] that the best solution is a compromise that takes something from both methods e.g. value the monetary assets and liabilities at closing rate, but defer the transfer of any gain to the profit and loss account which is the approach taken in HK:

At HK Ltd balance sheet date:

Purchases £	Trade creditor	Memo HK$ (a)	£	Sales HK$	Trade debtor HK$
31 July	31 July			31 July	31 July
				Transfer to Trading A/c (200,000)	
Balance nil	Balance	100,000	8,000 (i)	Balance nil	Balance 100,000 (j)

(i) It is not necessary to re-calculate a balance in the books of UK Ltd because 31 July is neither a payment or a year-end date for UK Ltd.

(j) A balance is required in the books of HK Ltd for the purposes of its balance sheet.

At date of 2nd instalment:

Purchases £	Trade creditor	Memo HK$ (a)	£	Sales HK$	Trade debtor HK$
	31 August Cash	100,000	(9,091) (k)		31 August Cash (100,000)
	Exchange loss		1,091 (l)		
	31 August Balance		nil		31 August Balance nil

(k) Cash payment: HK$100,000/11 = £9,091

(l) Exchange loss: The difference between balance in books at 31 July and amount paid on 31 August (£9,091 − £8,000) = £1,091. This loss is **realised** and will therefore be posted to a gains/losses on exchange account and transferred to the Profit and Loss Account at 30 June 20X1. The gross profit of £5,000 per car is reduced by £1,091 i.e. a difference of 22%.

It can be seen from this illustration that the balances maintained in the foreign company's books do not entail gains or losses on exchange because the company, HK Ltd, receives in total HK$200,000 irrespective of the changes in the exchange rate. The gains or losses in UK Ltd are a consequence of the contract being denominated in HK$. If the contract had provided for payment in £ sterling, the supplier, HK Ltd, would have borne the gains and losses and UK Ltd would have only recorded the sterling liability of £20,000 and two payments of £10,000 on 31 May and 31 August.

Accounting policies

A typical example of a foreign currency accounting policy appears in European Colour plc 2001 accounts which state

> Transactions during the year and amounts receivable and payable at the year end denominated in foreign currencies are translated into sterling at the rates of exchange applicable at the date of the transaction and at the year end respectively. Resulting exchange differences are charged or credited to the profit and loss account.

22.4.2 How can fluctuations in reported profits arising from fluctuations in exchange rates be prevented?

Companies are able to enter into forward contracts to obtain the currency they require in the future at a specified rate.[4] This is known as hedging the transaction. For example, UK Ltd would enter into a contract to purchase HK$100,000 on 31 May and 31 August 20X0 at a rate specified at the invoice date on 30 April 20X0. Assuming that the market expects sterling to strengthen against the HK$, the forward rate will be at a higher rate of, say, HK$10.5 to the £.

● Calculate the necessary accounting data in the books of each company.
 The simplest method is to translate the invoice at the forward rate i.e. HK$200,000 @ 10.5 produces an invoice figure for the accounts of **£19,048**. The effect is that no exchange gain or loss would be recognised on the forward contract in either year. The risk of either an exchange gain or loss has been removed **at a cost of £952** per car representing a forward rate which has been quoted at a discount of HK$0.5 to the £ on the spot rate.
● Require payment in a stable currency.
 The problem is exacerbated when one currency is hard and the other soft. This implies that the exchange rate will be unstable. Companies might decide therefore to request payment in a third currency that is regarded as more stable, e.g. the contract with HK Ltd could be denominated in US$. This can also arise when there is international recognition of an international commodity being traded in an international hard currency, e.g. oil is generally contracted in US$ irrespective of the domicile of the contracting parties.

22.4.3 Treatment of exchange gains or losses arising on the purchase of fixed assets

The creditor account has the same entries as for the purchase of goods above. The main difference is that a fixed asset account is debited instead of the purchases account. Just as with the goods, the fixed asset is recorded at £20,000 and the gains and losses on exchange dealt with as **realised** through the profit and loss account. The depreciation charge is based on the £20,000, e.g. assuming a life of eight years with £4,000 residual value, there would be an annual charge of £2,000. The depreciation charge is not affected by exchange gains and losses.

It is important to note the following two points relating to:

(a) the realisation of exchange gains and losses; and

(b) the amounts attributable to purchases and fixed assets.

(a) Realisation of exchange gains and losses

Gains or losses arising from **conversion** at the date of payment, i.e. £1,667, are clearly realised and dealt with in the profit and loss account. The gains or losses arising from **translation** of creditors at the balance sheet date, i.e. £2,000, are also regarded as realised. At 30 June 20X0 it is not known that there will be an exchange loss on conversion in August causing a loss of £1,091 to appear in the year ended 30 June 20X1. It is normal practice to assume that the rate current at the balance sheet date on 30 June 20X0 is a reasonable estimate of the rate that will be applicable at the date of conversion on 31 August 20X0, i.e. the accruals principle applies.

Should gains or losses on translation be accepted as realised?

Such gains have not been realised in the form of cash, so what is the justification? Three justifications that could be made are:

- *The short-term nature* of the items concerned. This meant that there was a belief that the gain of £2,000 would be realised within 60 days of the year-end. It is, of course, true that exchange rates can vary and that the assumed gain may not be achieved or may even become negative. However, an estimate of foreign currency debt in terms of the reporting country currency must be determined for balance sheet purposes in order to assess total moneys due to creditors and the best objective evidence available on which to base a valuation of that debt at 30 June 20X0 is the rate current at that date. SSAP 17 *Accounting for Post Balance Sheet Events* specifies (para. 31 (item g)) that changes in rates of foreign exchange is an example of a non-adjusting event. This means that even though the exchange rate on 31 July shows a loss the balance sheet as at 30 June 20X0 does not require retrospective adjustment.

- *Symmetry of treatment* requires the translation difference to be treated the same way as the conversion difference. If, for example, there had been a translation loss at the balance sheet date, prudence would have required its recognition as realised. Symmetry requires that 'unrealised' translation gains and losses receive the same accounting treatment.

- SSAP 2 *Disclosure of Accounting Policies* lends support to this treatment of translation differences[5] stating that realisation is assumed when 'in the form of either cash or of other assets ... whether the amount is known with certainty or is a best estimate in the light of information available'.

(b) Carrying value of assets and recorded amounts for expenses

The rate of exchange used for making the entry into the books is the rate current at the date the contract was entered into. Exchange rate changes after the contract date do not affect the amount of either the expense or the asset.

(c) Preventing fluctuations

Just as in section 22.4.1 above, where we discussed how to prevent fluctuations by hedging, the transaction can be hedged **at a cost of £952** and the fixed asset brought into the books at **£19,048**.

22.4.4 Treatment of long-term loans

The two previous examples dealt with the treatment of conversion and translation gains and losses on exchange arising from transactions with short-term trade creditors.

Long-term loans are also **monetary items** within the meaning of SSAP 20 and gains and losses on translating long-term debt must therefore be dealt with in the same symmetrical fashion, i.e. by transfer to the profit and loss account, thus impacting on earnings and earnings per share. However, because of the long-term characteristic of the debt an increased risk is inherent in the assessment of any exchange difference and SSAP 20 *Foreign Currency Translation* brings such risks to our attention in two respects:

Prudence

This requires that where a gain is involved 'it is necessary to consider on the grounds of prudence whether the amount of the gain ... to be recognised in the profit and loss account should be restricted in the exceptional cases where there are doubts as to the convertibility or marketability of the currency in question'.[6]

Realised profits

Under the Companies Act 1985 all gains taken through the profit and loss account are regarded as having been realised and this includes all exchange gains. However, where para. 50 of SSAP 20 has been applied, this 'may result in unrealised exchange gains on unsettled long-term monetary items being taken to the profit and loss account'. This situation may appear to be in conflict with the requirement of the Companies Act 1985 but 'the need to show a true and fair view of results ... is considered to constitute a special reason for departure from the principle' (under para. 51 Sch. 4 Companies Act 1985).[7] Where this SSAP 20 'special circumstances' true and fair view overrider of the Companies Act is applied, additional disclosures are required. These involve a fourfold statement explaining:

- the normal requirements of the Companies Act;
- a description of the treatment adopted;
- reasons for the adoption of such treatment; and
- the effect of that treatment and, if necessary, an explanation why that effect cannot be quantified.[8]

Another point to consider in respect of realised profits is the distribution, via dividends, of such profits. If such a distribution requires gains arising on unsettled long-term monetary items to be included to cover the distribution, extra consideration of that dividend is vital. This would include a review of the possible legal implications of pursuing such a dividend policy.

Illustration

On 1 September 20X8 Sandwell Ltd purchased machinery from a Chinese company for 3,000,000 yuan, funded by a loan of this amount in yuans from a Chinese bank. The following information is available:

(a) The terms of the loan were:

(i) Repayments of principal were to be remitted in equal instalments of 600,000 yuans on 31 August each year commencing on 31 August Year 2.

(ii) Interest of 12% per annum is payable in arrears on 31 August each year.

(b) The depreciation charge was based on an estimated economic life of ten years and no residual value. Sandwell depreciation policy was to use the straight-line method.

(c) Sandwell Ltd makes up its accounts to 31 March each year.

(d) Spot rates for the yuan were:

	yuan to £
1 September Year 1	12.0
31 March Year 2	10.5
31 August Year 2	9.0
31 March Year 3	9.3
31 August Year 3	9.5
Average for year to 31 August Year 2	10.10
Average for year to 31 August Year 3	9.90

Requirements:

Show loan, interest, asset, depreciation and profit and loss account entries for the financial years ended 31 August Years 2 and 3.

Loan account		£	Interest account		£
1 Sept Year 1	Cash [3m/12]	250,000			
31 Mar Year 2	P & L A/c		31 Mar Year 2	P & L A/c charge	
	Loss on translation	35,714 (a)		Interest accrued c/f	20,000 (b)
		285,714			20,000

(a) Loss on translation: [(3m/10.5) − £250,000]

(b) Interest:[12% of (3m/10.5) × (7/12)] = £20,000

Loan account		£	Interest account		£
1 Apr Year 2	Balance	285,714	1 Apr Year 2	Balance b/f	20,000
31 Aug Year 2	Cash 1st instalment	(66,667) (c)	31 Aug Year 2	Cash interest	(40,000) (d)
31 Mar Year 3		219,047	31 Mar Year 3	Balance for P & L	20,000
	P & L A/c			Interest accrued c/f	18,065 (f)
	Loss on translation	39,018 (e)		P & L A/c charge is	38,065
		258,065			
1 Apr Year 3	Balance	258,065	1 Apr Year 3	Balance b/f	18,065

(c) Cash: (600,000/9) = £66,667

(e) The loss on translation is calculated as [(2.4m/9.3) − £219,047]

(d) Interest: 12% of (3m/9) = £40,000

(f) The interest accrued is calculated as [12% of (2.4m/9.3) × (7/12 months)]

Asset account		£	Depreciation account		£
1 Sep Year 1	Cash [3m/12]	250,000 (g)	31 Mar Year 2	P & L A/c	14,583 (h)
			31 Mar Year 3	P & L A/c	25,000 (i)
			31 Mar Year 3	Accumulated balance	39,583

(g) Cash: (3m/12) = £250,000

(h) Depreciation: (10% of £250,000) × (7/12) = £14,583

(i) Depreciation: (10% of £250,000) = £25,000

Profit and loss account – year ended 31 March Year 2	£	Profit and loss account – year ended 31 March Year 3	£
Depreciation	14,583	Depreciation	25,000
Interest on loan	20,000	Interest on loan	38,065
Loss on translation	35,714	Loss on translation	39,018

Illustration where transaction is hedged with a forward contract

We will show the loan and interest accounts for Sandwell Ltd as at 31 August Year 2 on the assumption that on 28 February Year 2 Sandwell entered into a forward contract with its local bank for the purchase of yuan at 10.8 yuan to the £ in order to meet its loan and interest payments due on 31 August Year 2.

The effect of the hedge is that the asset and initial entry in the loan account remain unaffected but, because the hedging agreement was entered into before 31 March Year 2, the translation balance is affected in respect of the instalment now hedged by a forward rate of 10.8 yuan. Similarly, the interest account is affected by the forward rate at the accrual stage. The entries are as follows:

	Loan account	£		Interest	£
1 Sept Year 1	Cash [3m/12]	250,000			
31 Mar Year 2	P & L A/c		31 Mar Year 2	P & L A/c charge	
	Loss on translation	34,127		Interest accrued c/f	19,444
		284,127			19,444

The loss on translation is calculated as
(2.4m/10.5) = 228,571
(0.6m/10.8) = 55,556
284,127 − 250,000 = 34,127

The interest accrued is calculated as
[12% of (3m/10.8) × (7/12 months)]

	Loan account	£		Interest	£
1 Apr Year 2	Balance b/f	284,127	1 Apr Year 2	Balance b/f	19,444
31 Aug Year 2	Cash 1st instalment		31 Aug Year 2	Cash	
	[600,000/10.8]	55,556		[12% of (3m/10.8)]	(33,333)
31 Aug Year 2	Balance c/f	228,571	31 Aug Year 2	Balance c/f	13,889

A comparison of position with and without hedging shows:

Profit and loss account without hedge   *Profit and loss account with hedge*
- for year ended 31 March Year 2

	£		£
Depreciation	14,583	Depreciation	14,583
Interest on loan	20,000	Interest on loan	19,444
Loss on translation	35,714	Loss on translation	34,127

Accounting policies where there are matched forward contracts

The following is an extract from the Reckitt Benckiser 2000 Annual Report:

Transactions denominated in foreign currencies are translated at the rate of exchange on the day the transaction occurs or at the contracted rate if the transaction is covered by a forward exchange contract. Assets and liabilities denominated in a foreign currency are translated at the exchange rate ruling on the balance sheet date or, if appropriate, at a forward contract rate. Exchange differences arising in the accounts of individual undertakings are included in the profit and loss account...

22.4.5 Foreign equity investments financed by foreign loans

An investment in foreign equity will usually be deemed to be a fixed asset, i.e. a non-monetary item. Non-monetary items, as seen above in the treatment of fixed assets, are not normally re-translated at the year-end and as a consequence no exchange difference arises. However, where a foreign investment is financed by a foreign loan, it would seem foolhardy to permit the profit and loss to bear an exchange loss arising from re-translating the loan when that loss is countered by an exchange gain in the equity investment concerned. The exchange risk, the liability, is in that case being hedged by the investment, the asset.

To facilitate the offsetting of a loss on a loan with a gain on an investment and vice-versa, it is necessary to breach the general rule that non-monetary items should not be amended by subsequent exchange rate movements. It is SSAP 20 which authorises this adjustment but it, and the offsetting process, are **not compulsory**.

SSAP 20 provides[9] that where a company has used foreign currency borrowings to finance, or provide a hedge against, its foreign equity investments and the conditions set out in this paragraph apply, the equity investments **may** be denominated in the appropriate foreign currencies and the carrying amounts translated at the end of each accounting period at closing rates for inclusion in the investing company's financial statements. Where investments are treated in this way, any exchange differences arising should be taken to reserves and the exchange gains or losses on the foreign currency borrowings should be off-set, as a reserve movement, against these exchange differences. The conditions which **must** apply are as follows:

(a) in any accounting period, exchange gains or losses arising on the borrowings may be off-set only to the extent of exchange differences arising on the equity investments;

(b) the foreign currency borrowings, whose exchange gains or losses are used in the offset process, should not exceed, in the aggregate, the total amount of cash that the investments are expected to be able to generate, whether from profits or otherwise; and

(c) the accounting treatment adopted should be applied consistently from period to period.

Illustration of foreign equity investments financed by foreign loans

On 1 July 20X8 Severn plc acquired a loan from a Norwegian company of 6,000,000 kroner and, on the same day, invested 4,000,000 kroner in the equity of a Norwegian company. Severn plc's year-end was 31 December 20X8. The exchange rates were:

	kroner to £
31 July	10
31 December	8

The changes in the loan, investment, reserves and profit and loss account are considered applying two assumptions:

(a) that Severn plc chose to offset exchange losses arising on translating the loan against the gain on the investment; and

(b) that Severn plc chose not to offset any loss on the loan against the gain on the investment.

(a) Applying offset					(b) Not applying offset	
	Loan account				*Loan account*	
		Kroner	Rate	£		£
31 July	Cash borrowed	6,000,000	10	600,000		600,000
	Loss to reserves			100,000		
	Loss to P & L A/C			50,000	Loss to profit and loss account	150,000
31 Dec.	Balance	6,000,000	8	750,000		750,000
	Investment account				*Investment account*	
31 July	Cash invested	4,000,000	10	400,000		400,000
	Gain			100,000		—
31 Dec.	Balance			500,000		400,000
	Reserves:				*Reserves:*	
31 Dec.	Increase from investment			100,000		—
	Decrease from loan			(100,000)		—
	Balance			nil		

Note that the transfer of the loss to reserves cannot exceed the change in the investment account.

	Profit and loss account:		*Profit and loss account:*	
31 Dec.	Loss on loan	50,000	Loss on loan	150,000

Accounting policies where borrowings hedge a foreign equity investment

The following is an extract from the Reckitt Benckiser 2000 Annual Report:

> ...where foreign currency borrowing has been used to finance equity investments in foreign currencies, exchange differences arising on the borrowing are dealt with through reserves to the extent that they are covered by exchange differences arising on net assets represented by equity investments.

22.4.6 Summary

The accounting treatment known as the temporal method is in harmony with the historical cost concept, namely:

- the cost of a non-monetary asset is established at the date of acquisition by translating the foreign currency amount on the invoice into local currency by adopting the spot exchange rate (or the forward rate if hedged) applicable at that date;
- the associated monetary liability is established using the same rate;
- the carrying value of non-monetary items remains unchanged by subsequent fluctuations in the exchange rates;
- the carrying value of the liability is dealt with differently in that it is changed for exchange differences arising from actual conversion of local currency or translation of local currency into the currency denominated under the contract.

22.5 The group situation

Here we are concerned with the impact and treatment of foreign exchange transactions on the consolidated accounts as distinct from the accounts of the individual company. Although individual group companies will employ the temporal method, it is not applicable to group accounts where there are independent foreign subsidiaries or branches. The result could be misleading and could, indeed, destroy the true and fair view relationships of the data. This is because the individual foreign subsidiary has acquired and financed its assets by using its own local currency, i.e. its own functional or operating currency. This means that:

- the historical cost in its own accounts will be recorded in its own currency;
- there will be no intention or need to translate, in its own books, into the currency of the parent;
- the assets concerned will remain with the subsidiary;
- the liabilities will be settled in local currency;
- no loss or gain will be suffered by the parent on settlement;
- there are no cash flow implications for the group as a consequence of any exchange differences arising on translating the accounts of a foreign subsidiary for consolidation purposes;
- the parent company's major interest is in the annual dividend received from the subsidiary;
- any exchange differences are not generally of a cash flow nature and, consequently, are not realisable, which prevents them being charged or credited to the consolidated profit and loss account.

The parent company is interested in the net worth of the subsidiary rather than the individual assets and liabilities. SSAP 20 *Foreign Currency Translation* has, therefore, stipulated that the closing rate method, rather than the temporal method, should be used when consolidating independent foreign subsidiaries. Because the closing rate is applied to the net worth, it must also be applied to the elements of the balance sheet if it is to balance.[10] The closing rate method provides that:

- the foreign assets and the foreign liabilities should be translated into the parent's currency using the exchange rate operating at the balance sheet date (hence the term 'closing rate' definition SSAP 20).[11] Amounts in the foreign subsidiaries' profit and loss accounts are also translatable at the closing rate but, although SSAP 20[12] makes a strong case for the adoption of the closing rate, it does permit the alternative of using the average rate for the profit and loss account if its use 'reflects more fairly the profits and losses and cash flows as they arise to the group';
- exchange differences are transferred to reserves including, where the average is applied to the profit and loss account, any differences between use of that average and the use of the closing rate.

This achieves the prime objective of SSAP 20 in using the closing rate, namely, the retention on translation of the relationships between revenue, expenses, individual assets and individual liabilities that exist in the foreign entity's local currency financial statements. The temporal method would apply different rates to different assets and liabilities and distort the relationships and ratios.

22.5.1 Illustrating the rationale for use of closing rate method for group accounts

Assume that a UK based company acquired a fixed asset from a HK supplier for HK$260,000 on 31 May, settlement was due on 31 July and the UK company's financial year ended on 30 June. Depreciation is charged commencing with the year following acquisition. For the purpose of the illustration we will only deal with the asset and associated liability in the profit and loss account and balance sheet extracts.

Exchange rate movements were:

	HK$ to £		HK$ to £		HK$ to £
31 May	10:1	30 June	9:1	31 July	8:1

In the UK company's books the following accounts and balance sheet would occur using the temporal method:

Year ended 30 June 20X1

Fixed asset account   *Balance sheet extract as at 30 June 20X1*

		£		£
31 May X1	Creditor [HK$260,000/10]	26,000	Fixed asset	26,000
			less depreciation	—
				26,000

Creditor account   Represented by:

			Capital	—
31 May X1	Fixed asset [HK$260,000/10]	26,000		
			Profit and loss account	(2,889)
30 June X1	Loss on exchange HK$260,000/9 =	2,889	Creditor	28,889
		28,889		26,000

Profit and loss account for year ended 30 June 20X1

	£
Loss on exchange	2,889
Depreciation	—
Loss for year	2,889

Year ended 30 June 20X2

Provision for depreciation   *Profit and loss account for year ended 30 June 20X2*

		£		£
30 June X2	Profit and loss account [(HK$260,000/10)/10]	2,600	Loss on exchange	3,611
			Depreciation	2,600
			Loss for year	6,211
			Balance b/f	2,889
			Balance c/f	9,100

Fixed asset account   *Balance sheet extract as at 30 June 20X2*

		£		£
1 July X1	Balance [HK$260,000/10]	26,000	Fixed asset	26,000
			less depreciation	2,600
				23,400

Creditor account

		£	Represented by:	
			Capital	—
1 July X1	Balance [HK$260,000/9]	28,889		
31 July X1	Loss on exchange [HK$260,000/8 − 28,889]	3,611	Profit and loss account	(9,100)
		32,500		
31 July X1	Cash [HK$260,000/8]	(32,500)	Bank overdraft	32,500
				23,400

The position would be quite different if the HK subsidiary were to acquire an identical asset. The accounts and balance sheet entries would be as follows:

Year ended 30 June 20X1

Profit and loss account for year ended 30 June 20X1

	HK$
Loss on exchange – not relevant	
Depreciation	—
Loss/profit for year	—

Fixed asset account			*Balance sheet extract as at 30 June 20X1*	
		HK$		HK$
31 May X1	Creditor	260,000	Fixed asset	260,000
30 June X1	Balance c/d	260,000	less depreciation	—
				260,000
			Represented by:	
			Capital	—
Creditor account			Profit and loss account	—
30 June X1	Fixed asset	260,000	Creditor	260,000
30 June X1	Balance c/d	260,000		260,000

Year ended 30 June 20X2

Provision for depreciation			*Profit and loss account for year ended 30 June 20X2*	
		HK$		HK$
30 June X2	Profit and loss account	26,000	Loss on exchange – not relevant	
			Depreciation	26,000
			Loss/profit for year	(26,000)

Fixed asset account			*Balance sheet extract as at 30 June 20X2*	
		HK$		HK$
1 July X1	Creditor	260,000	Fixed asset	260,000
30 June X2	Balance c/d	260,000	less depreciation	26,000
				234,000
			Represented by:	
			Capital	—
Creditor account			Profit and loss account	—
1 July X1	Fixed asset	260,000	Creditor	260,000
30 June X2	Balance c/d	260,000		234,000
31 July X2	Less cash	(260,000)		

Observe that when the UK company is involved in buying the asset, the result is:

- a foreign exchange transaction materialises with a flow of sterling from the UK to the HK supplier;
- this is reflected in the accounts at 30 June **20X1 when a potential loss of £2,889 is classified as realised** and charged to the profit and loss account because the loss is anticipated on the basis of the spot rate on 30 June;
- the spot rate is the best indication existing at the balance sheet date of the amount that will become payable to the creditor;
- the fixed asset is shown in the balance sheet at 30 June 20X1 at its historical cost of £26,000 applying the historical cost concept;
- the fixed asset is still shown in the balance sheet at 30 June 20X2 at its historical cost of £26,000, applying the historical cost concept subject to the depreciation provision, giving a net book value of £23,400;
- but that during the interim, between the balance sheet dates, the creditor's account has been settled with **the UK company incurring a loss of £3,611** due to the weakening of sterling against the HK$;
- **the total loss on exchange of £6,500** over the two years occurred as a consequence of the changes in spot rates between contract date and settlement date;
- **the total cash paid to the HK supplier in settlement of the invoice for £26,000 was £32,500**.

Now contrast this with the circumstances where a HK subsidiary buys the fixed asset from a HK supplier, the asset concerned to be retained and used by the HK subsidiary. The result is:

- a transaction which is not of a foreign nature;
- it is, therefore, without foreign exchange gain or loss exposure;
- it deals with the transaction in its own books using its own domestic currency of francs;
- it still adopts the historical cost concept but based on HK$.

Then consider the problem when the HK subsidiary's accounts are to be consolidated with the UK parent. This means that:

- subsidiary's financial data must be aggregated with that of the parent;
- this will require the translation of HK$ into £ sterling.

If the temporal method were applied, the result would be to treat the transactions of the HK subsidiary as if they had been carried out by the UK company. This would create a loss on exchange of £6,500. However, **the group is not exposed to exchange gains or losses of £6,500 because in reality there will be no flow of funds between parent and subsidiary**.

In order to avoid this unrealistic assumption, the closing rate method is adopted when translating the subsidiary's HK$ accounts into £ sterling. There is an additional benefit in that, after translation, all amounts will retain their same inter-relationships, e.g. all ratios will be unchanged.

22.5.2 Foreign consolidation illustrated – excluding treatment of capital and reserves

Continuing with the abbreviated example above, the items in the balance sheet and profit and loss account are translated at the closing rate, as follows:

Year ended 30 June 20X1

HK subsidiary accounts:		Group accounts:	
Balance sheet as at 30 June 19X1		Rate of	
	HK$	exchange	£
Fixed assets @ cost	260,000	9	28,889
Represented by:			
Capital	—		
Profit and loss account	—		
Creditor	260,000	9	28,889
	260,000		28,889

Year ended 30 June 20X2

HK subsidiary accounts:		Group accounts:	
		Rate of	
	HK$	exchange	£
Profit and loss account extract			
Depreciation	26,000	8	3,250
Loss for year	26,000	8	3,250
Balance b/f	—		—
	26,000		3,250

Balance sheet as at 30 June 19X2			
	HK$		£
Fixed assets @ cost	260,000	8	32,500
Less Depreciation	26,000	8	(3,250)
	234,000		29,250
Represented by:			
Capital	—		
Profit and loss account	(26,000)	8	(3,250)
Balance b/f	—		
	(26,000)		
Creditor	260,000	8	32,500
	234,000		29,250

Note that:

● the closing rate method maintains in the consolidated accounts the arithmetical relationship that existed in the foreign subsidiary's accounts;

● there is no difference on exchange as a consequence of the foreign subsidiary's transactions occurring within its own currency realm.

Will there be any differences if closing rate is used?

Invariably, yes. They have not appeared in the illustration above because the illustration specifically excluded the treatment of capital and reserves in order to emphasise that the closing rate (a) retains data relationships and (b) the lack of exchange differences involving cash flows.

How will differences arise when the closing rate is used?

Capital and reserves represents the net assets or net worth. The net assets value in sterling will have been calculated by using the exchange rate at the end of the year, e.g. HK\$9:£1 at the end of year 1. In the following year, these net assets will normally still be part of the balance sheet – however, they will be restated using the closing rate applicable at the end of year 2, e.g. HK\$8:£1. This means that the 'opening balance' net assets will require amendment unless the rate of exchange at the end of year 2 is the same as the rate at the end of year 1. The difference transpires as a consequence of translation purely for the purpose of consolidating the HK results with the parent's. The difference does not involve cash flows and it is, consequently, unrealised. It must therefore be transferred to consolidated reserves, as a credit if a gain and a debit if a loss, and not taken to the profit and loss account.

22.5.3 Illustration of use of average rate in translating the profit and loss account items

SSAP 20 permits a company to translate using the average rate.[13] Before discussing the rationale for this, we will illustrate the impact on the accounts taking year 2 above as an example. Assume that the average exchange spot rate for year 2 was HK\$12 to the £. The resulting consolidated statements are:

Year ended 30 June 20X2

HK subsidiary accounts:		*Group accounts:*	
	HK\$	Rate of exchange	**£**
Profit and loss account extract			
Depreciation	26,000	12	2,167
Loss for year	26,000		2,167
Balance b/f	—		—
	26,000		2,167

Balance sheet as at 30 June 20X2			
	HK\$	Rate of exchange	**£**
Fixed assets @ cost	260,000	8	32,500
Less Depreciation	26,000	8	3,250
	234,000		29,250
Represented by:			
Capital	—		—
Reserves		[(HK\$26,000/8) – (HK\$26,000/12)]	(1,083)
Profit and loss account	(26,000)	12	(2,167)
Balance b/f	—		—
	(26,000)		(3,250)
Creditor	260,000	8	32,500
	234,000		29,250

Treatment of exchange difference when the average rate is used to translate the profit and loss account

Note that the total loss of £3,250 is the same as when the closing rate is used to translate the profit and loss account. However, by using the average rate, the company has separated the total into a realised loss of £2,167 which appears in the profit and loss account and an unrealised loss of £1,083 that is a reserve movement in the consolidated balance sheet.

When is the average rate appropriate for translating the profit and loss account?

Standard accounting practice favours the use of the closing rate because it retains the underlying financial relationships. However, the average rate is permitted where the pattern of trade in the foreign subsidiary (e.g. it may be seasonal) justifies using average rather than closing rate to achieve greater fairness in representation. It also has the advantage that interim accounts do not have to be restated in that the annual profit will be equal to the total of the profits reported in the interim accounts.

How is the average rate calculated?

This can cause problems. A definitive definition of an average does not exist but its calculation is likely to involve some form of weighting. The quality of the average will also be influenced by the level of detail available from the foreign subsidiary's management accounting records. Because the average is related to each subsidiary's own individual trading patterns, it is possible for fellow subsidiaries operating in the same foreign currency and country to calculate and apply different average rates.

The consistency concept requires that, if the average rate method is chosen, it must be consistently applied from year to year. This is to avoid companies using average when it results in a realised gain and closing rate when the average rate would result in a realised loss, i.e. to prevent manipulation of data.

22.5.4 Foreign consolidation illustrated – *including* treatment of capital and reserves

In the above example we have assumed that the primary intention of SSAP 20 has been for the translated amounts included within the consolidated accounts to be the same as in the foreign currency accounts. This is appropriate when the foreign subsidiary is independent of the parent. The rationale where the foreign subsidiary is independent is that the investment by the parent is in the net worth – this is described as the net investment approach.

Net investment approach

SSAP 20 explains that the application of the closing rate recognises that:

- the investment of a holding company is in the net worth of its foreign subsidiary rather than a direct investment in the individual assets and liabilities of that enterprise;
- this enterprise will normally have net current assets and fixed assets which may be financed partly by local currency borrowings;
- its day to day operations will not normally be dependent on the reporting currency of the investing company;
- the net investment will remain extant until the foreign subsidiary is liquidated or the investment otherwise disposed of, although it may well look forward to a stream of dividends from realised profits.

The net investment is the net worth or net asset value – this is represented by the capital and reserves in the foreign subsidiary. At the end of each year the parent translates the net investment at the spot rate prevailing at the balance sheet date. If the spot rate is different from that at the beginning of the year there will be an exchange difference. This exchange difference is unrealised and will be taken to reserves.

Treatment as a net investment translated at the closing rate is dependent upon the foreign subsidiary being independent. SSAP 20 states[14] that 'in the UK and Ireland foreign operations are normally carried out through foreign enterprises which operate as separate or quasi-separate entities rather than as a direct extension of the trade of the investing company'. The presumption is that the foreign enterprise is independent. If it were not independent, the temporal method would be used to translate the foreign financial statements rather than the closing rate.

How can we establish that the foreign subsidiary is not independent?

This can only be determined by an analysis of the operating affairs of the foreign entity. If the analysis reveals a close interlinking between the two companies to the extent that the results of the foreign enterprise may be regarded as being more dependent on the economic environment of the investing company than on its own reporting currency, then the foreign statements should be included in the consolidated accounts as if all of its transactions had been entered into by the investing company itself in its own domestic currency. This means that the trading operations of the foreign entity are deemed to constitute a *de facto* direct extension of the trade of the investing company and the temporal method is the appropriate means of translation.

Key factors need to be analysed in reaching a decision.

What are the key factors in determining lack of independence?

The key factors stated in SSAP 20 are:[15]

- the extent to which the cash flows of the enterprise have a direct impact upon those of the investing company;
- the extent to which the functioning of the enterprise is dependent directly upon the investing company;
- the currency in which the majority of the trading transactions are denominated;
- the major currency to which the operation is exposed in its financing structure.

Examples of dependency are where the foreign enterprise:

- acts as a selling agency receiving stocks of goods from the investing company and remitting the proceeds back to the investing company;
- produces a raw material or manufactures parts or sub-assemblies which are then shipped to the investing company for inclusion in its own products;
- is located overseas for tax, exchange control or similar reasons to act as a means of raising finance for other companies in the group.

However, in practice, the directors of the parent company may find it difficult to assess where there is a degree of marginal dominance.

22.5.5 Illustration of consolidation using closing rate method – Dec Cruises plc

Dec Cruises plc is preparing its consolidated accounts for the year ended 30 June Year 6. Dec Cruises plc acquired 75% of the ordinary shares in Ferries Ltd in Year 1 for £12,000,000 when the issued share capital of Ferries Ltd was HK$100,000,000 and there was a credit balance on its profit and loss account of HK$16,000,000.

Exchange rates were as follows:

	HK$: £
Spot rates	
At date investment was acquired	8 : 1
At dates fixed assets were acquired:	
HK$223,700,000 purchased in Year 3/4	8.5 : 1

HK$27,000,000 purchased in Year 5/6	11.3 : 1
At 30 June Year 5	11.0 : 1
At 30 June Year 6	11.5 : 1
Average for year 5/6	11.2 : 1
At date of payment of interim dividend by Ferries Ltd in Year 5/6	11.1 : 1

We will follow a step approach to the net investment/closing rate method:

Step 1: Calculate the goodwill

			£000
Cost of investment by Dec Cruises plc			12,000
Less value of net assets in Ferries Ltd attributable to parent			
at date of acquisition		£000	
HK$100,000,000 @ HK$8 : £1		12,500	
HK$16,000,000 @ HK$8 : £1		2,000	
75% of		14,500	
			10,875
Goodwill			*1,125*

The value of goodwill is calculated as at date of acquisition and this value will not vary even though exchange rates change in subsequent years. Pre-FRS 10, most companies would have written off the £1,125,000 against reserves. Post-FRS 10, goodwill is to be amortised over its economic life. We are assuming for this illustration that the goodwill has been re-instated at 30 June Year 6 as an intangible asset on the balance sheet.

Step 2: Translate the foreign subsidiary's net assets in its balance sheet

	Dec Cruises	Ferries	Translation rate	Translated	Consolidated balance sheet
	(1)	(2)	(3)	(4)	(5)
	£000	HK$000	HK$: £	£000	£000
Fixed asset at cost	189,500	250,700	CR 11.5	21,800	211,300
Less depreciation at cost	74,930	40,700	CR 11.5	3,539	78,469
	114,570	210,000		18,261	132,831
Investment in Ferries Ltd	12,000				*1,125* [from Step 1]
Current assets					
Stocks at cost	25,470	33,000	CR 11.5	2,869	28,339
Trade debtors	7,810	18,700	CR 11.5	1,626	9,436
Dividend receivable	1,304				
Bank	316	4,350	CR 11.5	378	694
	34,900	56,050		4,873	38,469
Current liabilities					
Trade creditors	(7,470)	(30,170)	CR 11.5	(2,623)	(10,093)
Dividend proposed	(8,000)	(20,000)	CR 11.5	(1,739)	(8,000)
Minority interest dividend					
[25% of £1,739,000]					(435)
	(15,470)	(50,170)		(4,362)	(18,528)
Net current assets	19,430	5,880		511	19,941
	146,000	215,880		18,772	153,897
Long-term loans	(14,000)	(25,880)	CR 11.5	(2,250)	(16,250)
Net assets	132,000	190,000		16,522	137,647

Step 3: Calculate the minority interest

The minority shareholders are entitled to 25% of the net assets shown in the Ferries Ltd sterling balance sheet in Step 2 above, namely, 25% of £16,522,000 = **£4,131,000**.

Step 4: Translate the share capital and pre-acquisition reserves (Col 2 below) in Ferries Ltd balance sheet

The appropriate rate is the rate as at date of acquisition – the result will, of course, be the same as for the calculation of goodwill in Step 1.

	Dec Cruises (1)	*Currency Balance sheet* (2)	*Translation rate* (3)	*Translated balance sheet* (4)	*Consolidated balance sheet* (5)
	£000	HK$000	HK$: £	£000	£000
Ordinary shares £1	80,000				80,000
Ordinary shares HK$10		100,000	@ 8.0	12,500	
Profit and loss pre-acquisition		16,000	@ 8.0	2,000	

Step 5: Calculate the balancing figure in Column 4

Profit and loss account	52,000				
Profit and loss post-acquisition		74,000	**as a balancing figure 2,022**		
					53,516
Minority interest (Step 2)	—	—		—	4,131
	132,000	190,000		16,522	137,647

Step 6: Calculate the consolidated post-acquisition reserves in Column 5

These will be the parent reserves of **£52,000,000** plus the parent's 75% interest in the subsidiary's post-acquisition reserves of **£2,022,000** i.e. £1,516,000 giving a total of **£53,516,000**.

Step 7: Prepare consolidated profit and loss account

	Dec Cruises	*Ferries*	*Translation rate*	*Translated*	*Consolidated profit & loss account*
	£000	HK$000	HK$: £	£000	£000
Operating profit before tax	64,730	82,700	CR 11.5	7,191	71,921
Dividends received	676				cancelled out
Dividends receivable	1,304				cancelled out
Profit before tax	66,710	82,700	CR 11.5	7,191	71,921
Tax	13,710	31,700	CR 11.5	2,756	16,466
Profit after tax	53,000	51,000	CR 11.5	4,435	55,455
Less minority interest				25% of 4,435	1,109
					54,346
Dividend paid	4,000	10,000	CR 11.1	901	4,000
Dividend proposed	8,000	20,000	CR 11.5	1,739	8,000
Retained for year	41,000	21,000		1,795	42,346

Step 8: Reconciliation of residual balance in subsidiary's translated balance sheet

The sterling reserves figure of £1,516,000 of Ferries Ltd calculated in Step 6 above can be reconciled as follows under the following four headings:

1 Effect of changes in rate on net assets at beginning of year:

	£000
Net assets of subsidiary at 30 June Year 5	
[HK\$190m – Retained profit of HK\$21m]	
= HK\$169m @ HK\$11 to £1	15,363
Net assets of Ferries Ltd as at date of acquisition	
[HK\$116m @ closing rate on that date HK\$8 to £1]	14,500
Gains since acquisition to 30 June Year 5	
– this automatically includes retained profits	863

Note that the assets have increased by HK\$74m since acquisition but this has been largely offset by the weakening of the HK\$ against the £ from 8 to 11. Next adjust for any gain or loss through holding the net assets of HK\$169m during the year ended 30 June Year 6. This is calculated by restating the HK\$169m @ HK\$11.5 to £1, the weaker rate at 30 June Year 6:

Net assets at 1 July Year 5	15,363	
HK\$169m @ HK\$11.5 to £1	14,696	
Loss on exchange through holding these assets		(667)
Effect of changes in rate is a gain of		196

2 Profit for current year

Retained profit for year ended 30 June Year 6 from Step 7 above	1,795

3 Restate remittances not already translated at the closing rate

Adjustment in respect of remittance as the profit and loss has been translated at closing rate of HK\$11.5 except for interim dividend when the actual rate was used

HK\$10m @ HK\$11.1 to £1	901	
HK\$10m @ HK\$11.5 to £1	870	
		31

4 Restate profit and loss items at closing rate if already at average rate

In this example we have used the closing rate to translate the profit and loss account. If we had used the average rate, the reconciliation statement would have included the difference between translating at average and translating at closing rate as an additional item.

Residual balance in balance sheet of Ferries Ltd	2,022
Less: Minority interest 25% is included in total minority interest in Step 3	506
Dec Cruises plc 75% interest to appear in the consolidated balance sheet	1,516

22.5.6 Illustration of consolidation using temporal method – Dec Cruises plc

Step 1: Calculate the goodwill

The goodwill is calculated at £1,125,000 as for the net investment/closing rate method:

	£000
Cost of investment by Dec Cruises plc	12,000

Less value of net assets in Ferries Ltd attributable to parent
at date of acquisition

	£000	
HK$100,000,000 @ HK$8 : £1	12,500	
HK$16,000,000 @ HK$8 : £1	2,000	
75% of	14,500	
		10,875
Goodwill		1,125

Step 2: Translate the foreign subsidiary's net assets in its balance sheet

The main difference between the net investment/closing rate method and temporal method is that the fixed assets and depreciation provisions are translated at the rates (AR) applying at the date of acquisition:

	Dec Cruises	Ferries	Translation rate	Translated	Consolidated balance sheet
	(1)	(2)	(3)	(4)	(5)
	£000	HK$000	HK$: £	£000	£000
Fixed asset at cost	189,500	223,700	AR 8.5	26,318	
		27,000	AR 11.3	2,389	218,207
Less depreciation at cost	74,930	38,000	AR 8.5	(4,471)	—
		2,700	AR 11.3	(239)	(79,640)
Net Book Value – temporal	114,570	210,000		23,997	138,567
Less: Net Book Value – closing rate	114,570			18,261	132,831
Increase in fixed assets	—			5,736	5,736
Net assets per closing rate were (Step 2)				16,522	137,647
Net assets per temporal method increased to				22,258	143,383

Step 3: Calculate the Minority Interest

The minority shareholders are entitled to 25% of the net assets shown in the Ferries Ltd sterling balance sheet. This will be increased from the 25% of £16,522,000 = £4,131,000 in Step 3 of the closing rate method to 25% of (£16,522,000 + £5,736,000) = £5,565,000.

Step 4: Translate the share capital and pre-acquisition reserves in Ferries Ltd balance sheet

Just as for the net investment/closing rate method, the appropriate rate is that at date of acquisition

	Dec Cruises	Currency balance sheet	Translation rate	Translated balance sheet	Consolidated balance sheet
	£000	HK$000	HK$: £	£000	£000
Ordinary shares £1	80,000				80,000
Ordinary shares HK$10		100,000	@ 8.0	12,500	
Profit and loss pre-acquisition		16,000	@ 8.0	2,000	

Step 5: Calculate the balancing figure in the Ferries £000 column

Profit and loss account	52,000				
Profit and loss post-acquisition		74,000	as a balancing figure 7,758		
					57,818
Minority interest	—	—		—	5,565
Net assets (see Step 2 above)	132,000	190,000		22,258	143,383

Step 6: Calculate the consolidated post-acquisition reserves

These will be the parent reserves of £52,000 plus the parent's 75% interest in the subsidiary's post-acquisition reserves of £7,758,000 i.e. £5,818,000 giving a total of £57,818,000.

Step 7: Prepare consolidated profit and loss account

A necessary task in the practical application of the temporal method is the need to keep a formal record of the spot rates applicable to the various transactions. Some companies maintain a daily record of the spot rates of all the foreign subsidiaries within the group.

In the Dec Cruises illustration, we need to deal with depreciation separately in the profit and loss account because we need to translate at the historical spot rate, i.e. the acquisition rate (AR).

	Dec Cruises	Ferries	Translation rate	Translated	Consolidated profit & loss account
	£000	HK$000	HK$: £	£000	£000
Operating profit before deprn.	83,680	107,770	AR 11.2	9,622	93,302
Depreciation	(18,950)	(22,370)	AR 8.5	(2,632)	
	—	(2,700)	AR 11.3	(239)	(21,821)
Profit before tax	64,730	82,700		6,751	71,481
Dividends received	676				cancelled out
Dividends receivable	1,304				cancelled out
Profit before tax	66,710	82,700		6,751	71,481
Tax	13,710	31,700	AR 11.2	2,830	16,540
Profit after tax	53,000	51,000		3,921	54,941
Less minority interest				25% of 3,921	980
				25% of £51	13 See Step 8
					53,948
Dividend paid	4,000	10,000	AR 11.1	901	4,000
Dividend proposed	8,000	20,000	AR 11.5	1,739	8,000
Retained for year	41,000	21,000		*1,281*	41,948

Step 8: Reconciliation of residual balance in subsidiary's translated balance sheet

Under the temporal method the difference on exchange should be treated as part of reported operating profits. Under the closing rate method it would be transferred to reserves. The difference on exchange is calculated as follows:

	HK$000	Rate	£000
Net assets of subsidiary at 30 June Year 5:			
Fixed assets			
At 30 June Year 6	250,700		
Less purchases year ended 30 June Year 6	27,000		
	223,700	8.5	26,318
Depreciation			
At 30 June Year 6	40,700		
Less depreciation year ended 30 June Year 6	25,070		
	15,630	8.5	(1,839)
	208,070		24,479
Stock at 30 June Year 5			
Assuming same level as at 30 June Year 6	33,000	11.0	3,000
	241,070		27,479
Net monetary liabilities			
Balancing figure	(72,070)	11.0	(6,552)
Net assets [HK$190m – HK$21m retained profit] =	169,000		*20,927*
Equity interest at 30 June Year 6 per translated balance sheet see Step 2 above (rounded)			22,259
Net assets at 30 June Year 5 as above			*20,927*
Growth in net assets during year ended 30 June Year 6			1,332
Less profit for year ended 30 June Year 6 (see Step 7 above)			1,281
Exchange difference assuming no new capital movements during year			51

22.6 The hyperinflationary economy

A foreign subsidiary operating within a hyperinflationary economy may have such a material impact on the consolidated financial statements that the quality of the true and fair view may be jeopardised. Here are two of the factors of paramount influence in this situation:

(i) the foreign currency carrying amounts of assets and liabilities and the day-to-day transaction values of expenses and revenue may reflect increases that are considerably higher than those experienced in previous financial periods, thus destroying meaningful comparison;

(ii) the exchange spot rate of the foreign local currency is very likely to depreciate against the harder currency of the parent entity country as it reflects the different inflation rates between the two countries. Under the net investment/closing rate method the exchange losses will be taken to reserves and so by-pass the consolidated profit and loss account.

SSAP 20 suggests[16] that the local currency financial statements should be adjusted where possible to reflect current price levels before the translation process is undertaken. However, the standard omits to give guidance as to just how this should be done. The problem has been addressed by the Urgent Issues Task Force[17] which accepts two methods of eliminating or, perhaps, only alleviating financial distortions. These methods are:

(i) adjustment of the local currency accounting statements to reflect the domestic current price levels before proceeding with the translation – any gain or loss on the holding of net monetary assets or liabilities taken to the profit and loss account; or

(ii) designating a relatively stable currency as the functional currency into which the foreign subsidiary's accounts should be translated, using the temporal method, before translating into the monetary unit of the parent company – exchange differences to be passed through the consolidated profit and loss account. This requires two decisions: (a) a decision to pre-translate and (b) the choice of a functional currency.

(a) When to pre-translate?

The UITF suggest that pre-translation is considered necessary to businesses operating within economies suffering a cumulative inflation rate, over a three-year span, approaching or exceeding 100%. This might actually be taken as a definition of hyperinflation – although some might regard this as being a modest level of inflation.

(b) How is a functional currency selected?

The functional currency will depend on the prevailing circumstances, e.g. the hard currency of the US$ may suit some operational environments, such as South America or, indeed, the oil producing areas where the US$ already operates.

REVIEW QUESTIONS

1 Explain the difference between conversion and translation exchange differences.

2 Summarise the procedures when translating foreign currency transactions at the individual company stage for both trade purchase and fixed asset purchase.

3 Explain how forward contracts affect the amount and accounting treatment of exchange gains and losses.

4 Explain how and why foreign currency loans may be used to hedge equity investments.

5 The Wiggins Group plc Annual Report 2001 includes the following accounting policy relating to foreign currencies:

> Assets and liabilities in foreign currencies are translated into sterling at the financial year end exchange rates. Profits and losses of overseas subsidiaries are translated into sterling at average rates of exchange. Gains and losses arising on the translation of the net assets of overseas subsidiaries are taken to reserves. Other exchange differences are taken to the profit and loss account.

> (a) Explain why gains and losses arising on the translation of the net assets are taken to reserves.

> (b) Explain what may be included in other exchange differences and why these are taken to the profit and loss account and not to the reserves.

6 Explain how it can be established that the foreign subsidiary is not independent and why this is relevant for financial reporting.

7 It has been argued that the use of the closing rate method of translating subsidiary financial statements produces accounting statements that give the impression that exchange rates are stable. Explain the basis for this view, discuss the validity of the argument and present an acceptable alternative method of translation.

8 Explain how a foreign subsidiary operating within a hyperinflationary economy may have such a material impact on the consolidated financial statements that the quality of the true and fair view may be jeopardised.

9 Discuss, in relation to financial statements, the ASB view of **costs**, the **consequences with accounting implications** and the **issues** arising on the introduction of the euro.

10 Explain the reason for the italicised policy from the Accounting Policies of Holiday Chemical Holdings 1996 accounts:

> In the accounts of individual undertakings, transactions denominated in foreign currencies are recorded at *actual exchange rates as at the date of the transaction.*

> Monetary assets and liabilities denominated in foreign currencies at the year end are reported *at the rates of exchange prevailing at the balance sheet date* or, where appropriate, *at the rate of exchange of a matched forward contract.* Any gain or loss arising from a change in the exchange rates subsequent to the date of the transaction *is included in the profit and loss account.*

> For the purposes of balance sheet consolidation *the closing rate method is used* under which translation gains or losses are shown as a movement on reserves.

> Profit and loss accounts of overseas subsidiary undertakings are translated *at the average exchange rate.*

> Exchange differences on foreign currency investment loans, to the extent that they offset exchange differences on related investments in overseas operations, are also *taken to reserves* and separately reported with *any excess being charged or credited to the profit and loss account* as appropriate.

> Gains or losses on forward exchange contracts in existence at the year end not matched against monetary assets or liabilities are accounted *for on the date of maturity of the contract.*

EXERCISES

An extract from the solution is provided in the appendix at the end of the text for exercises marked with an asterisk (*).

Question 1

The directors of Pragmatic Ltd have sought your advice on the following issues which relate to events that took place in the accounting year ended 31 December 20X5.

(i) During the year ended 31 December 20X5, the company made a bulk purchase of raw materials from a Moroccan supplier on credit terms. The transaction took place on 1 October 20X5 and was worth 1,000,000 Moroccan Dirham. Payment was to be made in MAD in two equal instalments on 1 December 20X5 and 1 February 20X6.

(ii) On 1 June 20X5, Pragmatic Ltd purchased a 10% equity interest in a Danish company for 1,335,000 Danish kroner. As a hedge against future exchange rate fluctuations, it financed the cost of this investment by taking out a Singapore dollar denominated loan on the same date for 345,000 Singapore dollars.

You also obtained the following information relating to exchange rates against the pound:

	Moroccan Dirham	Danish krone	Singapore dollar
1 January 20X5	16.0	9.0	2.31
1 June 20X5	16.2	8.9	2.30
1 October 20X5	16.0	8.9	2.30
1 December 20X5	16.3	9.0	2.28
31 December 20X5	16.2	8.8	2.29
Average for Year	16.3	8.9	2.30

Required:

Prepare a report to the board of directors, explaining, in accordance with best accounting practice as embodied in the Companies Acts and Accounting Standards, how the transactions numbered (i) and (ii) should be treated in the financial statements for the year ended 31 December 20X5. Your report should include the relevant figures to be included in the accounts as well as an explanation and justification of the accounting treatment.

(CIPFA 1996 amended)

* Question 2

The draft financial statements of Smith Ltd for 20X3 below incorporated the transactions listed in the Notes below at rates of exchange on the dates of the transactions.

Profit and Loss Account for year ended 31 December 20X3

		£000
Turnover		3,000
Cost of goods sold		2,076
Gross profit		924
Distribution costs	366	
Administration expenses	118	484
		440
Less interest payable and similar charges		20
		420
Taxation on profit on ordinary activities		184
		236
Dividends		200
Retained profit for year		36

Balance sheet as at 31 December 20X3

Fixed assets		£000
Land and buildings		800
Plant and machinery		1200
Current assets		
Stock	700	
Debtors	818	
Bank balance	190	
	1,708	
Creditors: due within 1 year:		
Trade creditors	330	
Other creditors	360	
Tax and dividends	385	
	1,075	
Net current assets		633
		2,633
Creditors: due after more than 1 year		
Debenture loans		1,134
		1,499
Capital reserves		
Share capital		1,000
Profit and loss account		499
		1,499

Notes:

1 Plant and machinery includes a machine purchased from a Swiss company for SFR1,008,000 in October 20X3 when the exchange rate was £1 = SFR 2.8. At 31.12.20X3 the rate was £1 = SFR 3.0. The amount due is included in other creditors.

2 Sales and debtors figures include:

(a) amount in respect of goods sold to an Argentinian company for 31,200 pesos in November 20X3 when the rate was £1 = 4.0 pesos. At 31 December 20X3 the exchange rate was £1 = 3.9 pesos;

(b) amount receivable from a Swedish company for sales in September 20X3 for Kr68,400 at the rate £1 = Kr9.5. A forward rate of £1 = Kr10 has been agreed. At 31 December 20X3 the rate was £1 = Kr9.0.

3 Cost of sales, creditors and stock figures include an amount relating to the purchase of material for $20,240 from a US company in November 20X3 when the exchange rate was £1 = $2.3. At 31 December 20X3 the rate was £1 = $2.2.

4 Smith Ltd raised finance in the form of a five-year loan from an Indian Bank in December 20X3 (denominated in rupees) for 69,210,600 rupees at 10% interest when the rate of exchange was £1 = 61 rupees. The full amount was outstanding at 31 December 20X3 when the rate was £1 = 62 rupees.

Required:

(a) A re-drafted profit and loss account and balance sheet as at 31 December 20X3 to incorporate provisions of SSAP 20.

(b) A summary of SSAP 20 provisions applied and a brief comment on their effect in the case of Smith Ltd.

* Question 3

Kish plc is a manufacturing company specializing in ballet shoes. The directors reviewed their strategy and consequently acquired a 100% interest in a Malaysian company, Johannsen-Lisa. The Malaysian company manufactures tap dancing shoes.

Kish plc acquired its 100% interest on 1 January 20X1 for £1,000,000, at which time the reserves of Johannsen-Lisa were 3,487,500 ringgit.

The balance sheet of Johannsen-Lisa as at 31 December 20X1 was as follows:

	ringgit 000	ringgit 000
Fixed assets		
Plant at cost		12,400
Depreciation		5,232
		7,168
Current assets		
Stock	5,715	
Debtors	7,944	
	13,659	
Creditors: amounts falling due within one year		
Creditors	7,459	
Net current assets		6,200
		13,368

Capital and reserves

7,750,000 shares of 1 ringgit each	7,750
Reserves	5,618
	13,368

The rates of exchange have been as follows:

ringgit to £

4.75	1 January 20X1
4.25	Average for 20X1
4.00	31 December 20X1

Required:

Translate the balance sheet of Johannsen-Lisa as at 31 December 20X1 using the closing rate. Translate the profit and loss account reserves for the year ended 31 December 20X1 using the average rate, and calculate the exchange difference between the opening equity and the closing balance sheet equity.

Question 4

Set out below is the balance sheet for Cuchulain, at 31 December 20X5. Cuchulain is a subsidiary of Conchubar plc, a UK company with numerous overseas operations and subsidiaries. Cuchulain operates in Inguba where the currency is the Emer.

	20X5
	Emer 000s
Fixed assets – cost	6,400
– depreciation	(2,700)
	3,700
Stock (cost)	2,950
Debtors	4,100
Creditors (including overdraft)	(3,350)
Proposed dividend	(500)
	6,900
Share capital	
4,000,000 shares at 1 Emer	4,000
Retained profits	2,900
	6,900

The following Information is also available:

1 Conchubar acquired an 80% interest in Cuchulain on 31 December 20X4, at which time the retained earnings of Cuchulain were 1,800,000. The cost of the acquisition was £550,000.

2 Rates of exchange have been as follows:

Date	Exchange rate £1 = Emers
1 January 20X4	12
Average 20X4	10.5
31 December 20X4	10
Average 20X5	8.5
31 December 20X5	8

Required:

Translate the balance sheet into sterling using the closing rate method (with the average rate for profit and loss account) and outline, with supporting calculations, the effect that consolidation of Cuchulain would have on the group accounts of Conchubar plc.

* Question 5

Set out below are the transactions of April Inc, a subsidiary company of June Ltd, during 20X7. April was incorporated at the beginning of 20X7 to operate in Peruvia. The exchange rates ruling during 20X7 between sterling and the Peruian sol are also given.

Date of transaction	Exchange rate	Transactions	000s
1 January 20X7	3 : £1	Initial share capital issued	4,000
		Bank loan raised	1,000
		Fixed assets purchased	3,000
		Stock purchased	1,000
		Cash at bank	1,000
Average during 20X7	4 : £1	Sales/Purchases/Other transactions	
31 October 20X7	4.5 : £1	Stock purchased	2,000
31 December 20X7	5 : £1	Interest on loan paid*	100

Profit and loss account of April Inc. for the year ended 31 December 20X7

	000s	000s
Sales		12,000
Opening stock	1,000	
Purchases	8,000	
Closing stock	(2,000)	
Cost of sales		7,000
Depreciation		300
Other expenses		1,600
Interest		100
Total expenses		9,000
Profit before tax		3,000
Tax		1,500
Net profit		1,500

Balance sheet as at 31 December 20X7

Fixed assets	3,000	
Less depreciation	(300)	2,700
Current assets		
Stock	2,000	
Debtors	3,000	
Bank	1,300	6,300
Current liabilities		
Creditors	1,000	
Tax	1,500	(2,500)

Long term loan	(1,000)
Net assets	5,500
Share capital	4,000
Profit and loss account	1,500
	5,500

Required:

(a) Translate the accounts for April for 20X7 into sterling, using:
    (i) the temporal method and
    (ii) the closing rate method.

(b) Analyse the exchange gain or loss that arises in part (a).

References

1 C. Nobes and R. Parker, *Comparative International Accounting*, (4th edition), Prentice Hall, 1995, p. 353.
2 SSAP 20, *Foreign Currency Translation*, ASC, 1983, para. 41.
3 C. Nobes and R. Parker, *op. cit.*, p. 353.
4 SSAP 20, para. 42.
5 SSAP 2, *Disclosure of Accounting Policies*, ASC, 1971, para. 14(d).
6 SSAP 20, paras 50 and 11.
7 SSAP 20, paras 65 and 10.
8 UITF Abstract 7, *True and fair view override disclosures*, ASB, 1992.
9 SSAP 20, para. 51.
10 C. Nobes and R. Parker, *op. cit.*, p. 367.
11 SSAP 20, para. 41.
12 SSAP 20, paras 2 and 17.
13 SSAP 20, para. 17.
14 SSAP 20, para. 21.
15 SSAP 20, para. 23.
16 SSAP 20, para. 20.
17 UITF Abstract 9, *Accounting for Operations in Hyper-inflationary Economies*, ASB, June 1993.

PART 5

Interpretation

CHAPTER 23

Earnings per share

23.1 Introduction

In this chapter we consider

- why the earnings per share figure is important
- how it is used by shareholders
- FRS 3 calculation of basic earnings per share (BEPS)
- BEPS when there has been a bonus issue, share split, new issue and buyback of shares
- BEPS when there has been a rights issue
- Calculation of diluted EPS
- FRS 14 procedure where there are several potential dilutions, e.g. conversion rights and options
- EPS when conversion rights are exercised
- Institute of Investment Management and Research (IIMR) definition of an alternative EPS.

23.2 Why is the earnings per share figure important?

One of the most widely publicised ratios for a public company is the price/earnings or PE ratio. The PE ratio is significant because, by combining it with a forecast of company earnings, analysts can decide whether the shares are currently over- or undervalued.[1]

The ratio is published daily in the financial press and is widely employed by those making investment decisions. The following is a typical extract from the *Risk Measurement Service:*[2]

Breweries, Pubs and Restaurants

Company	Price 31/3/98	PE ratio
Greenalls Group	453	12.6
J D Wetherspoon	340	39.3
Whitbread	1,125	19.6

The PE ratio is calculated by dividing the market price of a share by the earnings that the company generated for that share. Alternatively, the PE figure may be seen as a multiple of the earnings per share, where the multiple represents the number of years' earnings required to recoup the price paid for the share. For example, it would take a shareholder in J D Wetherspoon just under forty years to recoup her outlay if all earnings were to be distributed, whereas it would take a shareholder in Greenalls Group just over twelve years to recoup his outlay, and one in Whitbread just under twenty years.

23.2.1 What factors affect the PE ratio?

The PE ratio for a company will reflect investors' confidence and hopes about the international scene, the national economy and the industry sector, as well as about the current year's performance of the company as disclosed in its financial report. It is difficult to interpret a PE ratio in isolation without a certain amount of information about the company, its competitors and the industry within which it operates.

For example, a **high PE ratio** might reflect investor confidence in the existing management team: people are willing to pay a high multiple for expected earnings because of the underlying strength of the company. Conversely, it might also reflect lack of investor confidence in the existing management, but an anticipation of a takeover bid which will result in transfer of the company assets to another company with better prospects of achieving growth in earnings than has the existing team.

A **low PE ratio** might indicate a lack of confidence in the current management or a feeling that even a new management might find problems that are not easily surmounted. For example, there might be extremely high gearing, with little prospect of organic growth in earnings or new capital inputs from rights issues to reduce it.

These reasons for a difference in the PE ratios of companies, even though they are in the same industry, are market-based and not simply a function of earnings. However, the current earnings per share figure and the individual shareholder's expectation of future growth relative to that of other companies also have an impact on the share price.

23.2.2 How is the EPS figure calculated?

Because of the importance attached to the PE ratio, it is essential that there is a consistent approach to the calculation of the EPS figure. FRS 14 *Earnings per Share* was issued for this purpose.

The EPS figure is of major interest to shareholders not only because of its use in the PE ratio calculation, but also because it is used in the earnings yield percentage calculation. It is a more acceptable basis for comparing performance than figures such as dividend yield percentage because it is not affected by the distribution policy of the directors. The formula is:

$$\text{EPS} = \frac{\text{Earnings}}{\text{Number of ordinary shares}}$$

The standard defines two EPS figures for disclosure, namely,

- **basic** EPS based on ordinary shares currently in issue; and
- **diluted** EPS based on ordinary shares currently in issue *plus* potential ordinary shares.

Basic EPS is defined in FRS 14 as follows:

- Basic earnings per share is a measure of past performance, calculated by dividing the net profit or loss attributable to ordinary shareholders by the weighted average number of ordinary shares outstanding during the period.
  - The net profit or loss attributable to ordinary shares should be the net profit or loss for the period after deducting dividends and other appropriations in respect of non-equity shares.[3]

– The weighted average number of ordinary shares should be adjusted for events, other than the conversion of potential ordinary shares, *that have changed the number of ordinary shares outstanding, without a corresponding change in resources.*[4]

Diluted EPS is defined as follows:

● For the purpose of calculating diluted earnings per share, the net profit attributable to ordinary shareholders and the weighted average number of shares outstanding should be *adjusted for the effects of all dilutive potential ordinary shares.*[5]

This means that **both** the earnings and the number of shares used *may* need to be adjusted from the amounts that appear in the profit and loss account and balance sheet.

23.3 The use to shareholders of the EPS

Shareholders use the reported EPS to estimate future growth which will affect the future share price. It is an important measure of growth over time. There are, however, limitations in its use as a performance measure and for inter-company comparison.

23.3.1 How does a shareholder estimate future growth in the EPS?

The current EPS figure allows a shareholder to assess the wealth-creating abilities of a company. It recognises that the effect of earnings is to add to the individual wealth of shareholders in two ways: first, by the payment of a dividend which transfers cash from the company's control to the shareholder; and, second, by retaining earnings in the company for reinvestment, so that there may be increased earnings in the future.

The important thing when attempting to arrive at an estimate is to review the profit and loss account of the current period and identify the earnings that can reasonably be expected to continue. In accounting terminology, you should identify the **maintainable post-tax earnings** that arise in the **ordinary course of business**.

Companies are required to make this easy for the shareholder by disclosing separately, by way of note, any exceptional items and by analysing the profit and loss on trading between discontinued, continuing and acquired activities.[6]

Shareholders can use this information to estimate for themselves the maintainable post-tax earnings, assuming that there is no change in the company's trading activities. This is in line with the ASB's view that companies should provide an information set from which each user can make an individual estimate or appraisal.

Clearly, in a dynamic business environment it is extremely unlikely that there will be no change in the current business activities. The shareholder needs to refer to any information on capital commitments which appear as a note to the accounts and also to the chairman's statement and any coverage in the financial press. This additional information is used to adjust the existing maintainable earnings figure.

23.3.2 Limitations of EPS as a performance measure

EPS is thought to have a significant impact on the market share price. However, there are limitations to its use as a performance measure.

The limitations affecting the use of EPS as an inter-period performance measure include:

● It is based on historical earnings. Management might have made decisions in the past to encourage current earnings growth at the expense of future growth, e.g. by reducing the amount spent on capital investment and research and development. Growth in the EPS cannot be relied on as a predictor of the rate of growth in the future.

- EPS does not take inflation into account. Real growth might be materially different from the apparent growth.

The limitations affecting inter-company comparisons include:

- The earnings are affected by management's choice of accounting policies, e.g. the choice of the depreciation method
- EPS is affected by the capital structure, e.g. changes in number of shares by making bonus issues.

However, the **rate of growth** of EPS may be compared between different companies and over time within the same company.

23.4 Illustration of the basic EPS calculation

Assume that Watts plc had post-tax profits for 20X1 of £1,250,000 and an issued share capital of £1,500,000 comprising 1,000,000 ordinary shares of 50p each and 1,000,000 £1 10% preference shares. The basic EPS (BEPS) for 20X1 is calculated at 115p as follows:

	£000
Profit on ordinary activities after tax	1,250
Less preference dividend	(100)
Profit for the period attributable to ordinary shareholders	1,150

$$\text{BEPS} = £1,150,000/1,000,000 \text{ shares} = £1.15$$

Note that it is the *number* of issued shares that is used in the calculation and *not the nominal value* of the shares. The market value of a share is not required for the BEPS calculation.

23.5 Adjusting the number of shares used in the basic EPS calculation

The earnings per share is frequently used by shareholders and directors to demonstrate the growth in a company's performance over time. Care is required to ensure that the number of shares is stated consistently to avoid distortions arising from changes in the capital structure that have changed the number of shares outstanding without a corresponding change in resources during the whole or part of a year. Such changes occur with (a) bonus issues and share splits; (b) new issues and buybacks at full market price during the year and (c) bonus element of a rights issue

We will consider the appropriate treatment for each of these capital structure changes in order to ensure that EPS is comparable between accounting periods.

23.5.1 Bonus issues

A bonus issue, or capitalisation issue as it is also called, arises when a company capitalises reserves to give existing shareholders more shares. In effect, a simple transfer is made from reserves to issued share capital. In real terms, neither the shareholder nor the company is giving or receiving any immediate financial benefit. The process indicates that the reserves will not be available for distribution, but will remain invested in the physical assets of the company. There are, however, more shares.

Treatment in current year

In the Watts plc example, assume that the company increased its shares in issue in 20X1 by the issue of another 1 million shares and achieved identical earnings in 20X1 as in 20X0. The EPS reported for 20X1 would be immediately halved from 115p to 57.5p. Clearly, this does not provide a useful comparison of performance between the two years.

Restatement of previous year's BEPS

The solution is to restate the EPS for 20X0 that appears in the 20X1 accounts, using the number of shares in issue at 31.12.20X1, i.e. £1,150,000/2,000,000 shares = BEPS of 57.5p.

23.5.2 Share splits

When the market value of a share becomes high some companies decide to increase the number of shares held by each shareholder by changing the nominal value of each share. The effect is to reduce the market price per share but for each shareholder to hold the same total value. A share split would be treated in the same way as a bonus issue.

For example, if Watts plc split the 1,000,000 shares of 50p each into 2,000,000 shares of 25p each, the 20X1 BEPS would be calculated using 2,000,000 shares. It would seem that the BEPS had halved in 20X1. This is misleading and the 20X0 BEPS is therefore restated using 2,000,000 shares. The total market capitalisation of Watts plc would remain unchanged, e.g. if, prior to the split, each share had a market value of £4 and the company had a total market capitalisation of £4,000,000, after the split each share would have a market price of £2 and the company market capitalisation would remain unchanged at £4,000,000.

23.5.3 New issue at full market value

Selling more shares to raise additional capital should generate additional earnings. In this situation we have a real change in the company's capital and there is no need to adjust any comparative figures. However, a problem arises in the year in which the issue took place. Unless the issue occurred on the first day of the financial year, the new funds would have been *available to generate profits* for only a part of the year. It would therefore be misleading to calculate the EPS figure by dividing the earnings generated during the year by the number of shares in issue at the end of the year. The method adopted to counter this is to use a time-weighted average for the number of shares.

For example, let us assume in the Watts example that the following information is available:

	No. of shares
Shares (50p nominal value) in issue at 1 January 20X1	1,000,000
Shares issued for cash at market price on 30 September 20X1	500,000

The time-weighted number of shares for EPS calculation at 31 December 20X1 will be:

		No. of shares
Shares in issue for 9 months to date of issue		
	$(1,000,000) \times (9/12 \text{ months})$	750,000
Shares in issue for 3 months from date of issue		
	$(1,500,000) \times (3/12 \text{ months})$	375,000
Time-weighted shares for use in BEPS calculation		1,125,000

BEPS for 20X1 will be £1,150,000/1,125,000 shares = **£1.02**

23.5.4 Buybacks at market value

Companies are prompted to buy back their own shares when there is a fall in the stock market. The main arguments that companies advance for purchasing their own shares are:

● To reduce the cost of capital when equity costs more than debt.
● The shares are undervalued.
● To return surplus cash to shareholders.
● To increase the apparent rate of growth in BEPS.

Examples are found amongst the FTSE 100 companies, e.g. in 1998 NatWest Bank purchased 175,000; Rio Tinto 2.965m; BTR 700,020 ordinary shares.[7]

The shares bought back by the company are included in the basic EPS calculation time apportioned from the beginning of the year to the date of buyback.

For example, let us assume in the Watts example that the following information is available:

	No. of shares
Shares (50p nominal value) in issue at 1 January 20X1	1,000,000
Shares bought back on 31 May 20X1	240,000
Profit attributable to ordinary shares	£1,150,000

The time-weighted number of shares for EPS calculation at 31 December 20X1 will be:

1.1.20X1	Shares in issue for 5 months to date of buyback		
		$1,000,000 \times 5/12$	416,667
31.5.20X1	Number of shares bought back by company	(240,000)	
31.12.20X1	Opening capital less shares bought back	$760,000 \times 7/12$	443,333
	Time-weighted shares for use in BEPS calculation		860,000

BEPS for 20X1 will be £1,150,000/860,000 shares = **£1.34**

Note that the effect of this buyback has been to increase the BEPS for 20X1 from £1.15 as calculated in para 11.4 above. This is a mechanism for management to lift the BEPS and achieve EPS growth.

23.6 Rights issues

A rights issue involves giving existing shareholders 'the right' to buy a set number of additional shares at a price below the fair value which is normally the current market price. A rights issue has two characteristics being both an issue for cash and, because the price is below fair value, a bonus issue. Consequently the rules for *both* a cash issue *and* a bonus issue need to be applied in calculating the weighted average number of shares for the basic EPS calculation.

The following four steps are required:

Step 1: Calculate the average price of shares before and after a rights issue to identify the amount of the bonus the company has granted.

Step 2: The weighted average number of shares is calculated for current year.

Step 3: The BEPS for current year is calculated.

Step 4: The previous year BEPS is adjusted for the bonus element of the rights issue.

Step 1: Calculate the average price of shares before and after a rights issue to identify the amount of the bonus the company has granted

Assume that Mr Radmand purchased two 50p shares at a market price of £4 each in Watts plc on 1 January 20X1 and that on 2 January 20X1 the company offered a 1:2 rights issue (i.e. one new share for every two shares held) at £3.25 per share.

If Mr Radmand had bought at the market price, the position would simply have been:

		£
2 shares at market price of £4 each on 1 January 20X1	=	8.00
1 share at market price of £4.00 per share on 2 January	=	4.00
Total cost of 3 shares as at 2 January		12.00
Average cost per share unchanged at		4.00

However, this did not happen. Mr Radmand only paid £3.25 for the new share. This meant that the total cost of 3 shares to him was:

		£
2 shares at market price of £4 each on 1 January 20X1	=	8.00
1 share at discounted price of £3.25 on 2 January 20X1	=	3.25
Total cost of 3 shares	=	11.25
Average cost per share (£11.25/3 shares)	=	3.75

The rights issue has had the effect of reducing the cost per share of each of the three shares held by Mr Radmand on 2 January 20X1 by (£4.00 − £3.75) **£0.25 per share**.

The accounting terms applied are:

● Average cost per share after the rights issue (£3.75) is: *the theoretical ex-rights value.*

● Amount by which the average cost of each share is reduced (£0.25) is: *the bonus element.*

In accounting terminology Step 1 is described as follows:

Step 1: The bonus element is ascertained by calculating the theoretical ex-rights value, i.e. the £0.25 is ascertained by calculating the £3.75 and deducting it from £4 pre-rights market price

Step 1: Theoretical ex-rights calculation

In accounting terminology, this means that existing shareholders get an element of bonus per share (£0.25) at the same time as the company receives additional capital (£3.25 per new share). The bonus element may be quantified by the calculation of a **theoretical ex-rights price (£3.75)**, which is compared with the last market price (£4.00) prior to the issue; the difference is a bonus. The theoretical ex-rights price is calculated as follows:

		£
2 shares at fair value of £4 each prior to rights issue	=	8.00
1 share at discounted rights issue price of £3.25 each	=	3.25
3 shares at fair value after issue (i.e. ex-rights)	=	11.25
The theoretical ex-rights price is £11.25/3 shares	=	3.75
The bonus element is fair value £4 less £3.75	=	0.25

Note that for the calculation of the number of shares and time-weighted number of shares for a bonus issue, share split and issue at full market price per share the market price per share is not relevant. The position for a rights issue is different and the market price becomes a relevant factor in calculating the number of bonus shares.

Step 2: The weighted average number of shares is calculated for current year

There is a formulaic approach illustrated in Figure 23.1 which can be applied when calculating BEPS following a rights issue. However, it is helpful to understand the underlying rationale which is explained as follows.

Figure 23.1 Formula approach to calculating weighted average number of shares

				No. of shares
Shares to date of rights issue:				
No. of shares	× Increase by bonus fraction	× Time adjustment		
1,000,000		× 9/12	=	750,000
Bonus:	((1,000,000 × 4/3.75) −1,000,000)	× 9/12	=	50,000
Shares from date of issue:				
1,500,000	×	× 3/12	=	375,000
Weighted average number of shares				1,175,000

Assume that Watts plc made a rights issue of 1 share for every 2 shares held on 1 January 20X1.

There would be no need to calculate a weighted average number of shares. The total used in the BEPS calculation would be as follows:

		No. of shares
Shares to date of rights issue:		
1,000,000 shares held for a full year	=	1,000,000
Shares from date of issue:		
500,000 shares held for full year	=	500,000
Total shares for BEPS calculation		1,500,000

However, if a rights issue is made part way through the year, a time apportionment is required. For example, if we assume that a rights issue is made on 30 September 20X1, the time-weighted number of shares is calculated as follows:

		No. of shares
Shares to date of rights issue:		
1,000,000 shares held for a full year	=	1,000,000
Shares from date of issue:		
500,000 shares held for 3 months (500,000 × 3/12)	=	125,000
Weighted average number of shares		1,125,000

Note, however, that the 1,125,000 has not taken account of the fact that the new shares had been issued at less than market price and that the company had effectively granted the existing shareholders a bonus. We saw above that when there has been a bonus issue the number of shares used in the BEPS is increased. We need, therefore, to calculate the number of bonus shares that would have been issued to achieve the reduction in market price from £4.00 to £3.75 per share. This is calculated as follows:

Total market capitalisation was 1,000,000 shares @ £4.00 per share	=	£4,000,000
Number of shares that would reduce the market price to £3.75	=	£4,000,000/£3.75
	=	1,066,667 shares
Number of shares prior to issue	=	1,000,000
Bonus shares deemed to be issued to existing shareholders	=	66,667
Bonus share for period of 9 months to date of issue (66,667/12 × 9)	=	**50,000**

The bonus shares for the 9 months are added to the existing shares and the time apportioned new shares as follows:

		No. of shares
Shares to date of rights issue: 1,000,000 shares held for a full year	=	1,000,000
Shares from date of issue: 500,000 shares held for 3 months (500,000 × 3/12)	=	125,000
Weighted average number of shares		1,125,000
Bonus share: 66,667 shares held for 9 months (66,667/12 × 9)	=	50,000
		1,175,000

The same figure of 1,175,000 can be derived from the following approach using the relationship between the market price of £4.00 and the theoretical ex-rights price of £3.75 to calculate the number of bonus shares as in Figure 23.1.

Step 3: Calculate BEPS for current year

BEPS for 20X1 is then calculated as £1,150,000 / 1,175,000 shares = **97.9p**

Step 4: Adjusting the previous year's BEPS for the bonus element of a rights issue

The 20X0 BEPS of £1.15 needs to be restated i.e. reduced to ensure comparability with 20X1.

In Step 2 above we calculated that the company had made a bonus issue of 66,667 shares to existing shareholders. In re-calculating the BEPS for 20X0 the shares should be increased by 66,667 to 1,066,667. The restated BEPS for 20X0 is as follows:

Earnings	/ restated number of shares		
£1,150,000	/ 1,066,667	=	£1.078125

Assuming that the earnings for 20X0 and 20X1 were £1,150,000 in each year the 20X0 BEPS figures will be reported as follows:

As reported in the 20X0 accounts as at 31.12.20X0 =
£1,150,000/1,000,000   =   £1.15
As restated in the 20X1 accounts as at 31.12.20X1 =
£1,150,000/1,066,667   =   £1.08

The same result is obtained using the bonus element approach by reducing the 20X0 BEPS as follows by multiplying it by:

$$\frac{\text{Theoretical ex-rights fair value per share}}{\text{Fair value per share immediately before the exercise of rights}} = \frac{£3.75}{£4.00}$$

As restated in the 20X1 accounts as at 31.12.20X1 = £1.15 x (3.75/4.00)   =   £1.08

23.6.1 Would BEPS for current and previous year be the same if the company had made a separate full market price issue and a separate bonus issue?

This section is included to demonstrate that the BEPS is the same, i.e. £1.078125, if we approach the calculation on the assumption that there was a full price issue followed by a bonus issue. This will demonstrate that the BEPS is the same as that calculated using theoretical ex-rights. There are five steps as follows:

Step 1: Calculate the number of full value and bonus shares in the company's share capital

	No. of shares
Shares in issue *before* bonus	1,000,000
Rights issue at full market price	
(500,000 shares × £3.25 issue price / full market price of £4)	406,250
	1,406,250
Total number of bonus shares	93,750
Total shares	1,500,000

Step 2: Allocate the total bonus shares to the 1,000,000 original shares

(Note that the previous year will be restated using the proportion of original shares: original shares + bonus shares allocated to these original 1,000,000 shares)

Shares in issue before bonus		1,000,000
Bonus issue applicable to pre-rights:		
93,750 bonus shares × (1,000,000/1,406,250) =		
66,667 shares × 9/12months	= 50,000	
Bonus issue applicable to post-rights		
93,750 bonus shares × (1,000,000/1,406,250) =		
66,667 shares × 3/12months	= 16,667	
Total bonus shares allocated to existing 1,000,000 shares		66,667
Total original holding plus bonus shares allocated to that holding		1,066,667

Step 3: Time weight the rights issue and allocate bonus shares to rights shares

Rights issue at full market price
500,000 shares × (£3.25 issue price / full market price of £4)

= 406,250 × 3/12 months	101,563
Bonus issue applicable to rights issue:	
93,750 bonus shares × (406,250/1,406,250) = 27,083 shares × 3/12 months	6,770
Weighted average ordinary shares (includes shares from Steps 2 and 3)	1,175,000

Step 4: BEPS calculation for 20X1

Calculate the BEPS using the post-tax profit and weighted average ordinary shares, as follows:

$$20\text{X1 BEPS} = \frac{£1{,}150{,}000}{1{,}175{,}000} = 97.9\text{p}$$

Step 5: BEPS restated for 20X0

There were 93,750 bonus shares issued in 20X1. The 20X0 BEPS needs to be reduced, therefore, by:

the same proportion as applied to the 1,000,000 ordinary shares in 20X1 i.e. 1,000,000:1,066,667
20X0 BEPS = 20X0 BEPS × Bonus adjustment = Restated 20X0 BEPS
i.e. 20X0 = £1.15 × (1,000,000/1,066,667) = £1.078125

This approach illustrates the rationale for the time-weighted average and the restatement of the previous year's BEPS. The adjustment using the theoretical ex-rights approach produces the same result and is simpler to apply but the rationale is not obvious.

23.7 Adjusting the earnings and number of shares used in the diluted EPS calculation

We will consider briefly what dilution means and the circumstances which require the weighted average number of shares and the net profit attributable to ordinary shareholders used to calculate basic EPS to be adjusted.

23.7.1 What is dilution?

In a modern corporate structure, a number of classes of person such as the holders of convertible bonds, the holders of convertible preference shares, members of share option schemes and share warrant holders may be entitled as at the date of the balance sheet to become equity shareholders at a future date.

If these people exercise their entitlements at a future date, the EPS would be reduced. In accounting terminology, the EPS will have been diluted. The effect on future share price could be significant. Assuming that the share price is a multiple of the EPS figure, any reduction in the figure could have serious implications for the existing shareholders; they need to be aware of the potential effect on the EPS figure of any changes in the way the capital of the company is or will be constituted. This is shown by calculating and disclosing both the basic and 'fully diluted EPS' figures.

FRS 14 therefore requires a diluted EPS figure to be reported using as the denominator potential ordinary shares that are dilutive, i.e. would decrease net profit per share or increase net loss from continuing operations.[8]

23.7.2 Circumstances in which the number of shares used for basic EPS is increased

The holders of convertible bonds, the holders of convertible preference shares, members of share option schemes and the holders of share warrant will each be entitled to receive ordinary shares from the company at some future date. Such additional shares, referred to as potential ordinary shares, *may* need to be added to the basic weighted average number *if they are dilutive*. It is important to note that if a company has potential ordinary shares they are not automatically included in the fully diluted EPS calculation. There is a test to apply to see if such shares actually are dilutive – this is discussed further in section 23.8 below.

23.7.3 Circumstances in which the earnings used for basic EPS is increased

The earnings are increased to take account of the post-tax effects of amounts recognised in the period relating to dilutive potential ordinary shares that will no longer be incurred on their conversion to ordinary shares, e.g. the loan interest payable on convertible loans will no longer be a charge after conversion and earnings will be increased by the post-tax amount of such interest.

23.7.4 Procedure where there are share warrants and options

Where options, warrants or other arrangements exist which involve the issue of shares below their fair value, i.e at a price lower than the average for the period, then the impact is calculated by notionally splitting the potential issue into shares issued at fair value and shares issued at no value for no consideration.[9] Since shares issued at fair value are not dilutive that number is ignored but the number of shares at no value is employed to calculate the dilution. The calculation is illustrated for Watts plc:

Assume that Watts plc had at 31 December 20X1:

- an issued capital of 1,000,000 ordinary shares of 50p each nominal value;
- post-tax earnings for the year of £1,150,000;
- an average market price per share of £4; and
- share options in existence 500,000 shares issuable in 20X2 at £3.25 per share.

The computation of basic and diluted EPS is as follows:

	Per share	Earnings	Shares
Net profit for 20X1		£1,150,000	
Weighted average shares during 20X1			1,000,000
Basic EPS (£1,150,000/1,000,000)	*1.15*		
Number of shares under option			500,000
Number that would have been issued			
At fair value (500,000 × £3.25)/£4			(406,250)
Diluted EPS	*1.05*	*£1,150,000*	*1,093,750*

23.7.5 Procedure where there are convertible bonds or convertible preference shares

The post-tax profit should be adjusted[10] for

- any dividends on dilutive potential ordinary shares that have been deducted in arriving at the net profit attributable to ordinary shareholders;
- interest recognised in the period for the dilutive potential ordinary shares; and
- any other changes in income or expense that would result from the conversion of the dilutive potential ordinary shares, e.g. the reduction of interest expense related to convertible bonds results in a higher post-tax profit.

23.7.6 Convertible preference shares calculation is illustrated for Watts plc

Assume that Watts plc had at 31 December 20X1:

- an issued capital of 1,000,000 ordinary shares of 50p each nominal value;
- post-tax earnings for the year of £1,150,000;
- convertible 8% preference shares of £1 each totalling £1,000,000;
- convertible at one ordinary share for every five convertible preference shares.

The computation of basic and diluted EPS for convertible bonds is as follows:

	Per share	Earnings	Shares
Post-tax net profit for 20X1 (after interest)		£1,150,000	
Weighted average shares during 20X1			1,000,000
Basic EPS (£1,150,000/1,000,000)	*£1.15*		
Number of shares resulting from conversion			200,000
Add back the preference dividend paid in 20X1		80,000	
Adjusted earnings and number of shares		1,230,000	1,200,000
Diluted EPS (£1,230,000/1,200,000)	*£1.025*		

23.7.7 Convertible bonds calculation is illustrated for Watts plc

Assume that Watts plc had at 31 December 20X1:

- an issued capital of 1,000,000 ordinary shares of 50p each nominal value;
- post-tax earnings after interest for the year of £1,150,000;
- convertible 10% loan of £1,000,000;
- an average market price per share of £4; and
- convertible loan is convertible into 250,000 ordinary shares of 50p each.

The computation of basic and diluted EPS for convertible bonds is as follows:

	Per share	Earnings	Shares
Post-tax net profit for 20X1 (after interest)		£1,150,000	
Weighted average shares during 20X1			1,000,000
Basic EPS (£1,150,000/1,000,000)	*£1.15*		
Number of shares resulting from conversion			250,000

Interest expense on convertible loan	100,000	
Deferred tax liability relating to interest expense –		
Assuming the firm's marginal tax rate is 40%	(40,000)	
Adjusted earnings and number of shares	1,210,000	1,250,000
Diluted EPS (£1,210,000/ 1,250,000)	*£0.97*	

23.8 Procedure where there are several potential dilutions

Where there are several potential dilutions the calculation must be done in progressive stages starting with the most dilutive and ending with the least.[11] Any potential 'anti-dilutive' (i.e. potential issues that would increase earnings per share) are ignored.

Assume that Watts plc had at 31 December 20X1:

- an issued capital of 1,000,000 ordinary shares of 50p each nominal value;
- post-tax earnings after interest for the year of £1,150,000;
- an average market price per share of £4; and
- share options in existence for 500,000 shares
  – exercisable in year 20X2 at £3.25 per share
- convertible 10% loan of £1,000,000
  – convertible in year 20X2 into 250,000 ordinary shares of 50p each.
- convertible 8% preference shares of £1 each totalling £1,000,000
  – convertible in year 20X4 at 1 ordinary share for every **40** preference shares.

There are two steps in arriving at the diluted EPS, namely:

Step 1: Determine the increase in earnings attributable to ordinary shareholders on conversion of potential ordinary shares;

Step 2: Determine the potential ordinary shares to include in the diluted earnings per share.

Step 1: Determine the increase in earnings attributable to ordinary shareholders on conversion of potential ordinary shares

	Increase in earnings	*Increase in number of ordinary shares*	*Earnings per incremental share*
Options			
Increase in earnings			
Incremental shares issued			
for no consideration			
500,000 × (£4–3.25)/£4	nil	93,750	nil
Convertible preference shares			
Increase in net profit			
8% of £1,000,000	80,000		
Incremental shares			
1,000,000/40		25,000	3.20

10% convertible bond
Increase in net profit
£1,000,000 × 0.10 × (60%)   60,000
(assumes a marginal tax rate of 40%)
Incremental shares
1,000,000/4   250,000   0.24

Step 2: Determine the potential ordinary shares to include in the computation of diluted earnings per share

	Net profit attributable to continuing operations	Ordinary shares	Per share
As reported for BEPS	1,150,000	1,000,000	1.15
Options	—	93,750	
	1,150,000	1,093,750	1.05 dilutive
10% convertible bonds	60,000	250,000	
	1,210,000	1,343,750	0.90 dilutive
Convertible preference shares	80,000	25,000	
	1,290,000	1,368,750	0.94 antidilutive

Since the diluted earnings per share is increased when taking the convertible preference shares into account (from 94p to 90p), the convertible preference shares are antidilutive and are ignored in the calculation of diluted earnings per share. The lowest figure is selected and the diluted EPS will, therefore, be disclosed as 90p. The following illustration is from the 1998 Accounts of the Sony Corporation.

Reconciliation of the differences between basic and diluted net income per share (EPS) for the year ended 31 March 1998:

	Yen (million) income	Shares (000s) weighted average	Yen	Dollars
			\multicolumn{2}{c}{EPS}	
Basic EPS				
Net income available to common stockholders	222,068	398,181	557.7	4.23
Effect of dilutive securities				
Warrants		51		
Convertible bonds	2,271	65,890		
Diluted EPS				
Net income for computation	224,339	464,122	Y483.4	$3.66

This shows that warrants currently carry no interest expense cost and will increase the shares when issued; that convertible bonds currently incur an interest expense of 2,271m yen that will no longer be paid on conversion and that both are dilutive.

23.9 Exercise of conversion rights during financial year

Shares actually issued will be in accordance with the terms of conversion and will be included in the basic EPS calculation on a time apportioned basis from the date of conversion to the end of the financial year.

23.9.1 Calculation of basic EPS assuming that convertible loan has been converted and options exercised during the financial year

This is illustrated for the calculation for the year 20X2 accounts of Watts plc as follows. Assume that Watts plc had at 31 December 20X2:

- an issued capital of 1,000,000 ordinary shares of 50p each as at 1 January 20X2;
- convertible 10% loan of £1,000,000 **converted** on 1 April 20X2 into 250,000 ordinary shares of 50p each;
- share options for 500,000 ordinary shares of 50p each **exercised** on 1 August 20X2.

The weighted average number of shares for basic EPS is calculated as follows:

1.1.20X2	Ordinary shares in issue	1,000,000 × 3/12	250,000
1.4.20X2	Issued on conversion of the 10% Loan	250,000	
		1,250,000 × 4/12	416,667
1.8.20X2	Issued on exercise of options	500,000	
		1,750,000 × 5/12	729,167
31.12.20X2	**Weighted average number of shares**		**1,395,834**

23.10 Disclosure requirements of FRS 14

The standard[12] requires the following disclosures:

- All listed companies should disclose the basic and diluted EPS figures, whether positive or negative, on the face of the profit and loss account for each class of ordinary share that has a different right to share in the profit for the period.
- The amounts used as the numerators in calculating basic and diluted earnings per share, and a reconciliation of those amounts to the net profit or loss for the period.
- The weighted average number of shares used as the denominator in calculating the basic and diluted earnings per share and a reconciliation of these denominators to each other.

23.10.1 FRED 26: *Earnings per share*

FRED 26, issued in May 2002, proposes that the replacement for FRS 14 should be based on revised IAS 33 *Earnings per Share*. Changes in disclosures e.g. basic and diluted EPS to be disclosed on the face of the profit and loss account for both net profit or loss for the period and additional per share amounts are to be disclosed by note only.

23.11 Critique

The strategy of many companies is directed towards ensuring that the EPS figure is maintained or increased, with the financial markets applauding companies that achieve a growth in their EPS.

Management is aware of this concentrated focus and endeavour to produce a stable or growing EPS figure. This can be achieved in a number of ways, ranging from operational activities, such as increasing output or reducing costs, to accounting distortions such as bootstrapping, whereby companies with high PE ratios acquire companies with lower PE ratios.[13]

Until 1992 management had the flexibility to manipulate the earnings figure used in the BEPS calculation by the way in which it classified items in the profit and loss account, e.g. omitting expenses and losses selectively from the earnings figure used.[14] The practice may be seen as unacceptable or as a rational response.[15] The ASB stamped this practice out by the issue of FRS 3 in 1992 which prescribed how the earnings figure should be calculated, i.e. it took away from management their ability to choose which losses and gains to include. This avoids the element of subjectivity that remained after the revision of SSAP 6 in 1986.[16]

The issue of FRS 14 has been prompted by the different approach taken by the IASC to the calculation of diluted EPS. The ASB approach illustrated in 23.7 above reflects IASC practice.

23.11.1 The future of EPS

Confidence in the use of EPS to assess performance has been shaken by financial failures such as Polly Peck, where profits of £161m were reported shortly before the company collapsed, and by profit restatements such as Daimler Benz, which reported a high profit in Germany in 1993 but a loss when the accounts were restated to comply with US GAAP following its admission to the New York Stock Exchange.

The ASB has a twofold approach. On the one hand, it is persuading users to treat the accounts as an information set and *not to rely on a single figure*;[17] and on the other, it is attempting to limit management capacity to manipulate the figures.

The response of investment advisers is to look for an alternative to EPS, such as future cash flows. However, although cash flows are an important factor in assessing share values, managers still perceive EPS as an important measure for comparing company performance with competitors.

23.12 Analysts' approach to calculating an alternative EPS figure

In 1993 the Institute of Investment Management and Research (IIMR)[18] published *Statement of Investment Practice No. 1*, entitled *The Definition of Headline Earnings*, in which it identified two purposes for producing an EPS figure:

- As a measure of the company's **maintainable earnings** capacity, suitable in particular for forecasts and for inter-year comparisons, and for use on a per share basis in the calculation of the price/earnings ratio.
- As a factual headline figure for historical earnings, which can be a benchmark figure for the **trading outcome for the year**.

The Institute recognised that the maintainable earnings figure required exceptional or non-continuing items to be eliminated, which meant that, in view of the judgement involved in adjusting the historic figures, the calculation of maintainable earnings figures could not be put on a standardised basis. It took the view that there was a need for an earnings figure, calculated on a standard basis, which could be used as an unambiguous reference point among users. The Institute accordingly defined a **headline earnings** figure for that purpose.

The ASB position is that it is not possible to distil the performance of a complex organisation into a single measure.[19] The Institute acknowledges that the headline figure is inferior to maintainable earnings as a basis for forecasts, and to the use of maintainable earnings in the calculation of PE ratios, but takes the view that the headline figure is justified by its practical usefulness. It believes it to be a reliable figure and therefore suitable for publication in objective contexts such as newspapers and statistical services.

23.12.1 Definition of IIMR headline figure

The Institute criteria for the headline figure are that it should be:

1 **A measure of the trading performance**, which means that it will:
  (a) *exclude* capital items such as profits/losses arising on the sale or revaluation of fixed assets; profits/losses arising on the sale or termination of a discontinued operation and amortisation charges for goodwill, because these are likely to have a different volatility from trading outcomes;
  (b) *exclude* provisions created for capital items such as profits/losses arising on the sale of fixed assets or on the sale or termination of a discontinued operation; and
  (c) *include* abnormal items with a clear note and profits/losses arising on operations discontinued during the year.

2 **Robust**, in that the result could be arrived at by anyone using the financial report produced in accordance with FRS 3.

3 **Factual**, in that it will not have been adjusted on the basis of subjective opinions as to whether a cost is likely to continue in the future.

The strength of the Institute's approach is that, by defining a headline figure, it is producing a core definition. Additional earnings, earnings per share and price/earnings ratio figures can be produced by individual analysts, refining the headline figure in the light of their own evaluation of the quality of earnings.

In accordance with FRS 3, para. 25, if an additional EPS is calculated at any other level than that set out on FRS 14, it should be presented on a consistent basis over time and reconciled to the amount required by the FRS.

An illustration of a reconciliation is set out in Statement of Investment Practice No. 1, appendix C, shown in Figure 23.2.

23.12.2 How are companies reacting to the ASB's permission to include an alternative EPS figure?

In 1994 Coopers & Lybrand surveyed the treatment of exceptional items and EPS based on the published accounts of 100 top UK companies.[20] The results showed the following frequency of reporting:

● Exceptional items credited or charged most frequently in arriving at the operating profit were:

Item	No. of companies
Reorganisation costs, e.g. redundancy	9
Restructuring costs	9
Provision for permanent diminution in value of property	6
Provision for business rationalisation	4

Figure 23.2 IIMR headline earnings: adjustments for 1993

	Notes	Profits on ordinary activities £m	Tax £m	Minority interests £m	Profit £m
Per accounts	(i)	45	(14)	(2)	29
Adjustments					
Less: 1992 provision	(ii)	(10)	3	—	(7)
Exceptional items:					
Loss on disposal of discontinued operations	(iii)	17	(5)	—	12
Less: 1992 provision	(iv)	(20)	6	—	(14)
Provision for loss on operations to be discontinued	(v)	1	—	—	1
Profit on sale of properties	(vi)	(12)	3	1	(8)
Goodwill amortisation	(vii)	2	—	—	2
Total adjustments					
(per share 19p)	(viii)				(14)
IIMR headline earnings	(ix)	23	(7)	(1)	£15
IIMR headline earnings per share					20p

Notes:

(i) Figures as shown in the published profit and loss account as 'profit on ordinary activities'.

(ii) This adjustment is in respect of the provision made in the 1992 accounts in respect of loss on operations to be discontinued and relates only to the operating losses of the operations in the 1993 financial year up to the date of termination/sale (and not the direct costs of termination/sale).

(iii) As shown in the published profit and loss account.

(iv) This adjustment is similar to that described in note (ii) above: in this case it relates to a provision made in the 1992 accounts in respect of the loss on disposal of operations discontinued in 1993.

(v) This adjustment relates to the provision made in the 1993 financial year in respect of loss on an operation to be discontinued in the next financial year – 1994. This provision, when released in 1994, will be adjusted for in arriving at 1994 IIMR headline earnings.

(vi) As shown in the published profit and loss account.

(vii) It is assumed that this charge to the profit and loss account is disclosed in the notes to the accounts.

(viii) It is assumed that both the associated tax credit or charge and the minority charge in respect of each adjustment are disclosed in the notes to the accounts as required by FRS 3.

(ix) It is assumed that the review of the remaining exceptional items (i.e. those other than those disclosed on the face of the profit and loss account) does not necessitate any further adjustment to the headline earnings figure.

● Exceptional items credited or charged most frequently below the operating profit were:

Item	No. of companies
Profits or losses on sale or termination of an operation	59
Profits or losses on the disposal of fixed assets	46
Costs of fundamental reorganisation or restructuring	18

The survey then considered additional EPS figures. It found that 54 companies reported additional EPS figures, which varied from 62% lower to 278% higher than the reported FRS 3 figure. The basis of the most frequently used additional EPS figures was as follows:

Basis of additional EPS	No. of companies
IIMR headline EPS	16
Adjusted for exceptional items reported below operating profit	16
Adjusted for all exceptional items above and below operating profit	13

A number of other bases were used. Commenting on the choice of basis, the authors stated:

> This may result in stability for an individual company, but they certainly do not give rise to comparability across companies. To our surprise, only 16 of the 54 companies used the IIMR headline figures as their EPS. The remainder evidently preferred to tell their own story despite the analysts' announcement of the basis on which they will perform their analysis.

It was a widely held view that, prior to FRS 3, companies would disclose gains as exceptional and losses as extraordinary in order to show the highest EPS figure possible. The survey, therefore, also tested the hypothesis that companies would produce an alternative EPS figure where the alternative exceeded the FRS 3 figure. The outcome suggested that companies show additional EPS figures primarily to stabilise their earnings figures and not merely to enhance their reported performance.

Summary

While most analysts have welcomed the greater detail disclosed as a result of FRS 3, the new definition has been more controversial. The Association of Investment Analysts has expressed the view that EPS should be calculated to show the future maintainable earnings and has arrived at a formula designed to exclude the effects of unusual events and of activities discontinued during the period.

FRS 3 permits the inclusion of an EPS figure calculated in a different way, provided that there is a reconciliation of the two figures. The ASB's view remains that only the employment of the all-inclusive principle can produce an EPS figure capable of showing a true and fair view.

For many years the EPS figure was regarded as *the* key figure. It was widely believed that management performance could be assessed by the comparative rate of growth in this figure. This meant that the earnings available for distribution, which was the base for calculating the EPS, became significant. Management action was directed towards increasing this figure: sometimes by healthy organic growth; sometimes by buying-in earnings by acquisition; sometimes by cosmetic manipulation, e.g.

structuring transactions so that all or part of the cost by-passed the profit and loss account; and other times by the selective exercise of judgement, e.g. under-estimating provisions.

The regulators intervened to control management practice by defining as extraordinary the gains and losses that should be excluded from the earnings available for distribution. However, the definition proved impossible to enforce and companies were able to classify gains as exceptional, and so within the earnings available for distribution figure, and losses as extraordinary, and so outside that figure.

The ASB has tried to reduce the emphasis given to the EPS figure by presenting the financial statements as an information set for individual shareholder evaluation. It removed the distinction between exceptional and extraordinary items and required all realised gains and losses to being reflected in the EPS figure. It also required disclosure of the reasons for the exceptional items, so that shareholders could make their own assessment of the implication for future cash flows.

Shareholders are still perceived to be interested in an EPS figure based on maintainable earnings. The IIMR, in recognition of this, has produced a definition that shareholders might find more meaningful than the ASB figure. The ASB approach has accepted the publication of alternative figures, provided the ASB-defined figure is also produced and there is a clear reconciliation of the two figures.

The increasing globalisation of stock market transactions places an increasing level of importance on international comparison and, in consequence, is pushing the work of the International Accounting Standards Committee into greater prominence. EPS is considered a key indicator by analysts throughout the world and it thus becomes important to follow an international basis for its calculation. It is, perhaps, this consideration that led the ASB to adopt in FRS 14 virtually all of the IASC's proposals which also now coincide with US GAAP.

REVIEW QUESTIONS

1 Explain: (i) basic earnings per share; (ii) fully diluted earnings per share; (iii) potential ordinary shares; and (iv) limitation of EPS as a performance measure.

2 Why are issues at full market value treated differently from rights issues?

3 Directors are permitted to show their own EPS figure in addition to that calculated in accordance with FRS 14. In the 1999 Annual Report and Accounts of Associated British Ports Holdings plc, the directors report earnings per share – basic and underlying – as follows:

	Underlying	Goodwill Amortisation	Exceptional items	Total 1999	1998
	£m	£m	£m	£m	£m
Profit on ordinary activities after tax attributable to shareholders	86.3	(3.8)	(76.9)	5.6	84.1
Dividends	(39.4)	—	—	(39.4)	(37.2)
Retained profit/(loss)	46.9	(3.8)	(76.9)	(33.8)	46.9
Earnings per share – basic	24.6	(1.1)	(21.9)	**1.6p**	22.4p
Earnings per share – underlying				**24.6p**	22.4p

Note 11 reconciliation of profit used for calculating the basic and underlying earnings per share:

	1999 £m	1998 £m
Profit for year attributable to shareholders for calculating basic earnings per share	**5.6**	84.1
Amortisation of goodwill	3.8	2.0
Impairment of goodwill	60.6	—
Impairment of fixed assets	19.6	—
Profit on sale of fixed assets	(3.3)	(1.2)
Withdrawal from a discontinued business	—	(1.2)
Attributable tax	—	0.3
Profit for year attributable to shareholders for calculating the underlying earnings per share	**86.3**	84.0

The directors state that the underlying basis is a more appropriate basis for comparing performance between periods.

Discuss the relevance of the basic figure of 1.6p reported for 1999.

4 When disclosing EPS, how should a company deal with the issue of a separate class of equity shares which do not rank for any dividend in the current accounting period, but will do so in the future?

5 The following note appeared in the 1997 Accounts of Mercer International Inc.

The EPS data is summarised as follows:

Income (loss)	1997	1996
Income (loss) from continuing operations	(32,623)	15,557
Effect of dilutive securities, interest on convertible debentures	—	11
	(32,623)	15,568

Shares	1997	1996
BEPS, weighted number of shares outstanding	14,994,826	13,829,056
Effect of dilutive securities:		
Convertible debentures	—	21,756
Warrants	—	33,900
Options	—	72,393
	14,994,826	13,957,105

For the year ended 31 December 1997 convertible debentures, warrants and options were not included in the computation of diluted EPS because they were antidilutive. Options to acquire 192,500 were outstanding at 31 December 1996, but were not included in the computation of diluted shares because the options' exercise price was greater than the average market price of the shares.

Explain

(a) why interest of 11 was added in 1996;

(b) why the BEPS shares were weighted;

(c) what is meant by antidilutive;

(d) why the difference in exercise price and market price meant that options were not included in 1996.

6 Would the following items justify the calculation of a separate EPS figure under FRS 3?

(a) A charge of £1,500m that appeared in the 1989 accounts of Lloyds Bank plc, described as additional provisions relating to exposure to countries experiencing payment difficulties.

(b) Costs of £14m that appeared in the 1990 accounts of Johnson Matthey plc, described as redundancy and other non-recurring costs.

(c) Costs of £62.1m that appeared in the 1990 accounts of Johnson Matthey plc, described as cost of rationalisation and withdrawal from business activities.

(d) The following items that appeared in the 1989 accounts of Grand Metropolitan plc:
   (i) Profit on sale of property   £80m
   (ii) Reorganisation costs   £35m
   (iii) Disposal and discontinuance of hotels   £659m

7 Income smoothing describes the management practice of maintaining a steady profit figure.

(a) Explain why managers might wish to smooth the earnings figure. Give three examples of how they might achieve this.

(b) It has been suggested that debt creditors are most at risk from income smoothing by the managers. Discuss why this should be so.

8 In connection with FRS 14 *Earnings per Share*:

(a) Define the profit used to calculate basic and diluted EPS.

(b) Explain the relationship between EPS and the price/earnings (P/E) ratio. Why may the P/E ratio be considered important as a stock market indicator?

EXERCISES

An outline solution is provided in the appendix at the end of the text for exercises marked with an asterisk (*).

* Question 1

Alpha plc had an issued share capital of 2,000,000 ordinary shares at 1 January 20X1. The nominal value was 25p and the market value £1 per share. On 31 March 20X1 the company made a rights issue of 1 for 4 at a price of 80p per share. The post-tax earnings were £4.5m and £5m for 20X0 and 20X1 respectively.

Required:
(i) Calculate the basic earnings per share for 20X1
(ii) Restate the basic earnings per share for 20X0

* Question 2

Beta plc had the following changes during 20X1:

1 January	1,000,000 shares of 50p each
31 March	500,000 shares of 50p each issued at full market price of £5 per share
30 April	Bonus issue made of 1 for 2
31 August	1,000,000 shares of 50p each issued at full market price of £5.50 per share
31 October	Rights issue of 1 for 3. Rights price was £2.40 and Market value was £5.60 per share

Required:
Calculate the time-weighted average number of shares for the basic earnings per share

denominator. Note that adjustments will be required for time, the bonus issue and the bonus element of the rights issue.

* Question 3

The computation and publication of earnings per share (EPS) figures by listed companies are governed by FRS 14 *Earnings per Share* and FRS 3 *Reporting Financial Performance*.

Nottingham Industries plc
Profit and loss account for the year ended 31 March 20X6
(extract from draft unaudited accounts)

		£000
Profit on ordinary activities before taxation	(Note 2)	1,000
Tax on profit on ordinary activities	(Note 3)	(420)
Profit on ordinary activities after taxation		580
Dividends		(479)
Amount added to reserves for the financial year		101

Notes:

1 Called-up share capital of Nottingham Industries plc:

In issue at 1 April 20X5:

   16,000,000 ordinary shares of 25p each
   1,000,000 10% cumulative preference shares of £1 each

   1 July 20X5: Bonus issue of ordinary shares, 1 for 5.
   1 October 20X5: Market purchase of 500,000 of own ordinary shares at a price of £1.00 per share.

2 In the draft accounts for the year ended 31 March 20X6, 'profit on ordinary activities before taxation' is arrived at after charging or crediting the following items:
   (i) accelerated depreciation on fixed assets, £80,000;
   (ii) book gain on disposal of a major operation, £120,000.

3 Profit after tax included a write-back of deferred taxation (accounted for by the liability method) in consequence of a reduction in the rate of corporation tax from 45% in the financial year 20X4 to 40% in the financial year 20X5.

4 The following were charged:
   (i) Provision for bad debts arising on the failure of a major customer, £150,000. Other bad debts have been written off or provided for in the ordinary way.
   (ii) Provision for loss through expropriation of the business of an overseas subsidiary by a foreign government, £400,000.

5 In the published accounts for the year ended 31 March 20X5, Basic EPS was shown as 2.2p; Fully diluted EPS was the same figure.

Required:

(a) On the basis of the facts given, compute the basic EPS figures for 20X6 and restate the basic EPS figure for 20X5, stating your reasons for your treatment of items that may affect the amount of EPS in the current year.

(b) Compute the fully diluted earnings per share for 20X6 assuming that on 1 January 20X6 Executives of Nottingham Industries plc were granted options to take up a total of 200,000 unissued ordinary shares at a price of £1.00 per share: no options had been exercised at 31 March 20X6. The average fair value of the shares during the year was £1.10.

(c) Give your opinion as to the usefulness (to the user of financial statements) of the EPS figures that you have computed.

* Question 4

The following information relates to Simrin plc for the year ended 31 December 20X0:

	£
Turnover	700,000
Operating costs	476,000
Trading profit	224,000
Net interest payable	2,000
	222,000
Exceptional charges	77,000
	145,000
Tax on ordinary activities	66,000
Profit after tax	79,000
Dividends – ordinary	(15,000)
– preference	(9,000)
Profit retained for the year	55,000

Simrin plc had 100,000 ordinary shares of £1 each in issue throughout the year. Simrin plc has in issue warrants entitling the holders to subscribe for a total of 50,000 shares in the company. The warrants may be exercised after 31 December 20X5 at a price of £1.28 per share. The average fair value of shares was £1.1.

Required:

(a) Calculate the basic EPS for Simrin plc for the year ended 31 December 20X0, in accordance with best accounting practice.

(b) Calculate the fully diluted EPS figure, to be disclosed in the statutory accounts of Simrin plc in respect of the year ended 31 December 20X0.

(c) Briefly comment on the need to disclose a fully diluted EPS figure and on the relevance of this figure to the shareholders.

(d) In the past, the single most important indicator of financial performance has been earnings per share. In what way has the profession attempted to destroy any reliance on a single figure to measure and predict a company's earnings, and how successful has this attempt been?

* Question 5

Gamma plc had an issued share capital at 1 April 20X0 of:

● £200,000 made up of 20p shares.

● 50,000 £1 convertible preference shares receiving a dividend of £2.50 per share
   – these shares were convertible in 20X6 on the basis of 1 ordinary share for 1 preference share.

There was also loan capital of:

- £250,000 10% convertible loans
  - the loan was convertible in 20X9 on basis of 500 shares for each £1,000 of loan;
  - the tax rate was 40%.

Earnings for the year ended 31 March 20X1 were £5,000,000 after tax.

Required:
(a) Calculate the fully diluted EPS for 20X1.
(b) Calculate the fully diluted EPS assuming that the convertible preference shares were receiving a dividend of £6 per share instead of £2.50.

Question 6

Delta plc has share capital of £1m in shares of 25p each. At 31 May 20X9 shares had a market value of £1 each. On 1 June 20X9 the company makes a rights issue of 1 share for every 4 held at 60p per share. Its profits were £500,000 in 20X9 and £440,000 in 20X8. The year end is 30 November.

Required:
Calculate
(a) the theoretical ex-rights price
(b) the bonus issue factor
(c) the basic EPS for 20X8
(d) the basic EPS for 20X9.

Question 7

The following information is available for X plc for the year ended 31 May 20X1:

Net profit after tax and minority interest	£18,160,000
Ordinary shares of £1 (fully paid)	£40,000,000
Average fair value for year of ordinary shares	£1.50

1 Share options have been granted to directors giving them the right to subscribe for ordinary share between 20X1 and 20X3 at £1.20 per share. The options outstanding at 31 May 20X1 were 2,000,000 in number.

2 The company has £20 million of 6% convertible loan stock in issue. The terms of conversion of the loan stock per £200 nominal value of loan stock at the date of issue were

Conversion date	No. of shares
31 May 20X0	24
31 May 20X1	23
31 May 20X2	22

No loan stock has as yet been converted. The loan stock had been issued at a discount of 1%.

3 There are 1,600,000 convertible preference shares in issue. The cumulative dividend is 10p per share and each preference share can convert into two ordinary shares. The preference shares can be converted in 20X2.

4 Assume a corporation tax rate of 33% when calculating the effect on income of converting the convertible loan stock.

Required:

(a) Calculate the diluted EPS according to FRS 14.

(b) Discuss why there is a need to disclose diluted earnings per share.

References

1 J. Day, 'The use of annual reports by UK investment analysts', *Accounting Business Research*, Autumn 1986, pp. 295–307.

2 *Risk Measurement Service*, London Business School, April–June 1998.

3 FRS 14, *Earnings per Share*, ASB, 1998 para. 10.

4 *Ibid.*, para. 21.

5 *Ibid.*, para. 27.

6 FRS 3, ASB, 1992, paras 13–17.

7 *Accountancy*, November 1998, p. 73.

8 FRS 14, *Earnings per Share*, ASB, 1998 para. 56.

9 *Ibid.*, para. 35.

10 *Ibid.*, para. 53.

11 *Ibid.*, para. 61.

12 *Ibid.*, para. 71.

13 B. Rees, *Financial Analysis*, Prentice Hall, 1990, pp 356–357.

14 A. Barnea, J. Ronen and S. Sadan, 'Classifactory smoothing of income with extraordinary items', *The Accounting Review*, 1976, vol. 51, pp. 110–122.

15 P. Lambert, 'Income smoothing as rational equilibrium behaviour', *Accounting Review*, 1984, vol. 59(4), pp. 604–618.

16 M. Greener, 'The accountant's extraordinary predicament', *Accountancy*, June 1988, pp. 95–96.

17 *The Structure of Financial Statements – Reporting of Financial Performance*, ASB, December 1991, FRED 1, preface para. iv.

18 Statement of Investment Practice No. 1, *The Definition of Headline Earnings*, IIMR, 1993.

19 FRS 3, *Reporting Financial Performance*, ASB, 1992, para. 52.

20 Coopers & Lybrand, *EPS and Exceptional Items*, 1994.

CHAPTER 24

Cash flow statements

24.1 Introduction

In this chapter we consider why funds flow statements came to be replaced by cash flow statements in recent years. We analyse the application of FRS 1 and the extent to which it gives users of financial statements more information about the solvency and liquidity of companies, and enables them to make comparisons between firms.

24.2 Development of cash flow statements

In 1975 SSAP 10 was issued, requiring companies to publish a funds flow statement with the annual accounts.[1] The funds flow statement explained the changes between the opening and closing balance sheet by classifying the changes in fixed assets and long-term capital under two headings:

- **source of funds**, comprising funds from operating and other sources such as sale of fixed assets and issue of shares and loans; and
- **application of funds**, comprising tax paid, dividends paid, fixed asset acquisitions and long-term capital repayments.

The difference between source of funds and application of funds represented the net change in working capital.

In 1987 SFAS 95 *Statement of Cash Flows* was published in the USA.[2] It concluded that a cash flow statement should replace the funds flow statement, concentrating on **changes in cash** rather than **changes in working capital**. The cash flow statement should represent all of a company's cash receipts and cash payments during a period. There was also widespread support in the UK, e.g. Macdonald in 1988,[3] for the belief that **cash flow statements were more decision-useful** and that they should replace the funds flow statement.

In 1990 the ASC issued ED 54, which appeared to be based on SFAS 95.[4] It proposed that cash flow statements should replace funds flow statements in financial reporting. Guidelines were given about reporting cash flows, appropriate formats and minimum disclosure.

A report by the Institute Research Board, entitled *The Future Shape of Financial Reports*, recommended a number of reporting reforms.[5] One of the main areas for improvement was reporting a company's cash position. Professor Arnold wrote:

> little attention is paid to the reporting entity's cash or liquidity position. Cash is the lifeblood of every business entity. The report ... advocates that companies should provide a cash flow statement ... preferably using the direct method.[6]

An important issue is the relationship of cash flows to the existing financial statements.

As the following quotation illustrates, cash flows are not a substitute for the profit and loss account:

> The emphasis on cash flows, and the emergence of the statement of cash flows as an important financial report, does not mean that operating cash flows are a substitute for, or are more important than, net income. In order to analyse financial statements correctly we need to consider **both** operating cash flows and net income.[7]

The overwhelming reason for replacing a funds flow statement with a cash flow statement was that the latter provides more relevant and useful information to users of financial statements. When used in conjunction with the accrual-adjusted data included in the profit and loss account and the balance sheet, cash flow information helps to assess liquidity, viability and financial flexibility. This view is held by Henderson and Maness, who stress the need to integrate different types of analysis to achieve an overall assessment of an organisation's financial health: 'cash flow analysis should be used in conjunction with traditional ratio analysis to get a clear picture of the financial position of a firm'.[8]

The financial viability and survival prospects of any organisation rest on the ability to generate net positive cash flows. Cash flows help to reduce an organisation's dependency on external funding, service existing debts and obligations, finance investments, and reward the investors with an acceptable dividend policy. The end-result is that, independent of reported profits, if an organisation is unable to generate sufficient cash, it will eventually fail.

Cash flow statements can also be used to evaluate any economic decisions related to the financial performance of an organisation. Decisions made on the basis of expected cash flows can be monitored and reviewed whenever additional cash flow information becomes available.

Finally, the quality of information contained in cash flow statements should be better than that contained in funds flow statements because it is more consistent and neutral. Cash flows can be reliably traced to when a transaction occurred, while funds flows are distorted by the accounting judgements inherent in accrual-adjusted data.[9]

The following extract from Heath and Rosenfield's article on solvency is a useful conclusion to our analysis of the benefits of cash flow statements:

> Solvency is a money or cash phenomenon. A solvent company is one with adequate cash to pay its debts; an insolvent company is one with inadequate cash … Any information that provides insight into the amounts, timings and certainty of a company's future cash receipts and payments is useful in evaluating solvency. Statements of past cash receipts and payments are useful for the same basic reason that income statements are useful in evaluating profitability: both provide a basis for predicting future performance.[10]

24.3 Applying FRS 1 *Cash Flow Statements*

24.3.1 FRS 1 issued

FRS 1 was the first standard issued by the ASB. Its objective was to require companies to report on a standardised basis their cash generation and cash absorption for a period. Its principal feature was the analysis of cash flows under **five** standard headings of 'operating activities', 'returns on investments and servicing of finance', 'taxation', 'investing activities' and 'financing'.

The chairman of the ASB, David Tweedie, said: 'It is right that cash flow should be the subject of the Board's first standard. Recent experience has demonstrated all too clearly that adequate information on cash is an essential element of a company's financial statements.'[11] The ASB issued the following statement on publishing FRS 1 in 1991:

> The ASB's view is that a cash flow statement forms an essential element of the information required for accounts to give a true and fair view of the state of affairs of **large** companies at the end of the financial year, and of the profit or loss for the year. Accordingly, non-compliance with the standard may be ... taken into account by the Financial Reporting Review Panel or the court in any consideration of whether or not the accounts comply with the Companies Act.

24.3.2 FRS I reviewed and revised by ASB

In 1994 the ASB decided to review FRS 1 following the criticisms that had been made since its issue in 1991. Such a review of the standard after being in force for three years was in line with the ASB view that standards should be amended regularly in the light of experience in their operation and changes in circumstances.

We will consider briefly how three of the criticisms have been dealt with in the FRS 1 (Revised) issued in October 1996, namely, **method of presenting cash flows from operating activities, cash equivalents and reconciling operating profit in FRS 3 format to operating cash flows**.

Method of presenting cash flows from operating activities

FRS 1 permitted either the direct or indirect method of presentation to be used.

● The **direct** method reports cash inflows and outflows directly, starting with the major categories of gross cash receipts and payments. This means that cash flows such as receipts from customers and payments to suppliers are stated separately within the operating activities.

● The **indirect** method starts with the operating profit (before tax and extraordinary items) and then adjusts this figure for non-cash items such as depreciation and changes in working capital.

The two methods provide different types of information to the users. The indirect method applies changes in working capital to net income and FRS 1 para. 70 states:

> The principal advantage of the indirect method is that it highlights the differences between operating profit and net cash flow from operating activities. Many users of financial statements believe that such a reconciliation is essential to give an indication of the quality of the reporting entity's earnings. Some investors and creditors assess future cash flows by estimating future income and then allowing for accruals adjustments; thus information about past accruals adjustments may be useful to help estimate future adjustments.

The direct method demonstrates more of the qualities of a true cash flow statement because it provides more information about the sources and uses of cash. This information is not available elsewhere and helps in the estimation of future cash flows.

FRS 1 para. 70 states:

The principal advantage of the direct method is that it shows operating cash receipts and payments. Knowledge of the specific sources of cash receipts and the purposes for which cash payments were made in past periods may be useful in assessing future cash flows. However, the Board does not believe at present that in all cases the benefits to users of this information outweigh the costs of providing it and has not, therefore, required the information to be given. Nevertheless, in those circumstances **where the benefits to users ... outweigh the costs of providing it the Board encourages reporting entities to provide the relevant information.**

When are benefits to users likely to outweigh costs?

One such time is when the user is attempting to predict bankruptcy or future liquidation of the company. A research study looking at the cash flow differences between failed and non-failed companies[12] established that seven cash flow variables and suggested ratios captured statistically significant differences between failed and non-failed firms as much as five years prior to failure. The study further showed that the research findings supported the use of a direct cash flow statement and the authors commented that:

An indirect cash flow statement will not provide a number of the cash flow variables for which we found significant differences between bankrupt and non-bankrupt companies. Thus, using an indirect cash flow statement could lead to ignoring important information about creditworthiness.

The major deficiency therefore with the ASB approach is that few, if any, companies would elect to use the direct method if it was more likely than the indirect method to indicate that the company was at risk of failing!

Although the Gahlon research supports the direct method and, also, the Board proposal was criticised during the exposure draft stage on the basis that the availability of a choice between the direct and indirect methods made inter-company comparisons misleading and allowed companies to select the less informative indirect method, FRS 1 Revised continues to permit the choice on cost grounds and there is no guidance offered on 'when benefits to users are likely to outweigh costs'.

Cash equivalents

FRS 1 recognised that companies' cash management practices vary in the range of short- to medium-term deposits and instruments in their cash and near-cash portfolio. In 1991 it standardised the treatment of near-cash items by applying the following definition when determining whether items should be aggregated with cash in the cash flow statement. The definition stated 'Cash equivalents are short-term, highly liquid investments which are readily convertible into known amounts of cash without notice and which are within three months of maturity when acquired'. Near-cash items falling outside this definition were reported under the 'Investment' heading.

There was criticism that this definition was not always appropriate. It is not, for example, commercially appropriate to deal with deposits over three months under the heading of 'investments' rather than as cash. The effect was to split the activities of corporate treasury operations between investing activities and increases/decreases in cash. If cash was put on deposit for more than three months it was shown as a cash outflow under 'Investing'; if it was put on deposit for less than three months it was not shown as actually being a cash outflow. This made the evaluation of the movements on cash misleading.

FRS 1 Revised has taken account of this criticism by adding a new classification within the cash flow statement headed *Management of liquid resources*. FRS 1 Revised defines liquid resources as 'Current asset investments held as readily disposable stores of value. A readily disposable investment is one that:

(a) is disposable by the reporting entity without curtailing or disrupting its business; and is either:

(b) (i) readily convertible into known amounts of cash at or close to its carrying amount; or

(ii) traded in an active market.'

Reconciling operating profit in FRS 3 format to operating cash flows

FRS 1 Revised takes account of the FRS 3 format in Example 2 of Appendix 1 with details of operating profits arising under Continuing and Discontinued operations as follows:

Reconciliation of operating profit to operating cash flows:

	£000	Continuing £000	Discontinued £000	Total £000
Operating profit		20,249	(1,616)	18,633
Depreciation charges		3,108	380	3,488
Share of profit of associate	(1,420)			
Dividend from associate	350			
		(1,070)		(1,070)
Cash flow relating to previous years' restructuring provision			(560)	(560)
Increase in stock		(11,193)	(87)	(11,280)
Increase in debtors		(3,754)	(20)	(3,774)
Increase in creditors		9,672	913	10,585
Net cash flow from continuing operations		17,012		
Net cash flow in respect of discontinued activities			(990)	
Net cash flow from operating activities				16,022

24.4 FRS 1 Revised format of cash flow statements

An illustration is provided below, Tyro Bruce, of the application of the FRS 1 Revised format.

24.4.1 The FRS 1 Revised format is classified under 9 headings as follows:

1 Reconciliation of operating profit to cash flows from operating activities

- Operating profit before interest and tax
  - **Adjust for non-cash charges:**
    + Depreciation charges for tangible assets and Amortisation charges for intangible assets
    + Loss on sale of fixed assets
    − Profit on sale of fixed assets

- Adjust for changes in current assets and current liabilities:
  - Stock increase
  - Debtor and prepayment increases
  - Creditor and accrual decreases (excluding tax and dividends which are dealt with separately)
  - + Stock decrease
  - + Debtor and prepayment decreases
  - + Creditor and accrual increases (excluding tax and dividends which are dealt with separately)

The subtotal of these two adjustments gives net cash inflow/(outflow) from operating activities.

2 Returns on investments and servicing of finance

- Interest received/paid
- Interest element of finance lease rentals payments
- Preference dividends paid

3 Taxation

- Tax paid

4 Capital expenditure and financial investments

- Purchase of intangible assets, tangible assets and trade investments
- Proceeds from sale of intangible assets, tangible fixed assets and trade investments

5 Acquisitions and disposals

- This section is relevant for group accounts

6 Equity dividends paid

- Cash paid to ordinary shareholders

7 Management of liquid resources

- Purchase of government securities, corporate bonds or placing of funds on short-term deposit
- Proceeds from sale of government securities, corporate bonds or cash withdrawn from short-term deposits

8 Financing

- Proceeds from issue of shares, short-term and long-term debt
- Payments to redeem shares, short-term and long-term debt
- Capital element of finance lease rental payments

9 Increase/(Decrease) in cash

Thus is the sum of sections 1 to 8

24.4.2 Tyro Bruce accounts

The profit and loss account for the year ended 31 March 20X2 and balance sheets as at 31 March 20X1 and 20X2 (including the fixed asset schedule) for Tyro Bruce with explanatory notes to explain how each item is classified in the cash flow statement are as follows:

Profit and loss account of Tyro Bruce for the year ended 31 March 20X2

How treated in cash flow statement

	£000		
Sales	6,000		
Cost of sales	4,000		
Gross profit	2,000		
Net operating expenses	(986)		
Operating profit before interest and tax	1,014		
Profit on sale of land	80		
Loss on sale of plant	(54)		
Profit before interest and tax	**1,040**	(1) **Reconciliation statement starts here**	**(+1,040)**
Interest payable	(40)	(2) Returns on investment and servicing of finance	(−40)
Profit before tax	1,000		
Tax	(400)	(3) Tax	(−400)
Profit after tax	600		

Balance sheets for 20X1 and 20X2   *How treated in cash flow statement*

	20X2 £000	20X1 £000	Change £000		
Intangible fixed assets					
R & D written off	360	840	480	(1) Reconciliation of operating profit	
Tangible fixed assets	4,596	4,136	460	(4) The figure of 460 is not used. Refer to fixed asset schedule for **Additions**	
Stock	2,400	1,600	800	(1) Reconciliation of operating profit	(−800)
Debtors	1,800	1,360	440	(1) Reconciliation of operating profit	(−440)
Government securities	30	—	30	(7) Management of liquid resources	(+30)
Cash	30	20	10	(9) Cash increase	(10)
Creditors	1,360	1,080	280	(1) Reconciliation of operating profit	(+280)
Taxation	340	380	40	(3) Taxation	(−40)
Dividends	—	140	140	(6) Equity dividends paid	(−140)
Overdraft	1,116	1,356	240	(9) Cash increase	(240)
	6,400	5,000			
Ordinary shares	2,000	1,600	400	(8) Financing	(+400)
7% Preference shares	2,000	2,000			no change
Share premium account	400	100	300	(8) Financing	(+300)
Revaluation reserve	400	200			non cash movement
Retained profits at 31.3.20X1	700	700			no change
Retained profit for year	600	—		(1) Reconciliation of profit uses profit before interest and tax	
10% Debentures 20X0 – 04	300	400	100	(8) Financing	(−100)
	6,400	5,000			

The non-cash items required for the Reconciliation are calculated as follows:

- Depreciation is given in Schedule of Fixed Assets
- R&D amortised obtained from Change in Balance Sheets: £840,000 − £360,000 = £480,000

- Profit on sale of land is an FRS 3 exceptional item in the profit and loss account: £80,000
- Loss on sale of plant is an FRS 3 exceptional item in the profit and loss account: £54,000

The fixed asset schedule for Tyro Bruce as at 31 March 20X2 is as follows:

	Land £000	*Buildings* £000	*Plant* £000	*Vehicles* £000	*Total* £000	*How treated in cash flow statement*
At cost 31.3.20X1	3,200	800	840	200	5,040	
Additions	800	200	120		1,120	(4) Capital expenditure
Revaluations	200				200	non-cash movement
	4,200	1,000	960	200	6,360	
Disposals	600	—	240	—	840	(4) Used to calculate proceeds
At cost/valuation 31.3.20X2	3,600	1,000	720	200	5,520	
Depreciation						
At 31.3.20X1		384	400	120	904	
P & L charge		20	144	40	204	(1) Reconciliation of operating
		404	544	160	1,108	profit
Disposals		—	184	—	184	(4) Used to calculate proceeds
At 31.3.20X2	3,600	404	360	160	924	
Net book value 20X1	3,200	416	440	80	4,136	
Net book value 20X2	3,600	596	360	40	4,596	

The sales proceeds from the sale of land and plant are calculated for the capital expenditure section as follows:

- Cost £600,000 in fixed asset schedule + profit on disposal £80,000 = £680,000 proceeds
- Cost £240,000 – £184,000 depreciation – loss on disposal £54,000 = £2,000 proceeds

Reconciliation of operating profit to operating cash flows

A note is required when companies use the indirect method to support the £738,000 net cash flow from operating activities appearing in the cash flow statement. It is calculated as follows:

	£000
Profit before interest and tax	**1,040**
Add back non-cash charges:	
Depreciation	204
R & D amortisation charge	480
Loss on sale of plant	54
Less non-cash creditors:	
Profit on sale of land	(80)
Changes in current assets:	
Less current asset increases	
Stock	(800)
Debtors	(440)
Add current liability increases	
Creditors	280
Net cash flow from operating activities	**738**

One criticism of FRS 1 was that it did not standardise on the use of the direct method. The 'operating activities' of the cash flow statement are presented differently under the direct method. Actual cash flows from customers and to suppliers are disclosed as follows:

	£000
Cash received from customers (Working 1)	5,560
Cash payments to suppliers (Working 2)	4,822
Net cash inflow from operations	738

Working 1: Sales £6,000,000 – Debtors increase £440,000

Working 2: Cost of sales £4,000,000 – Creditors increase £280,000 + Stock increase £800,000 – Depreciation £204,000 – R & D £480,000 – Loss on sale of plant £54,000 + Profit on sale of land £80,000 + Selling and distribution expenses £600,000 + Administration costs £360,000

24.4.3 Tyro Bruce cash flow statement

The cash flow statement can now be prepared for Tyro Bruce for the year ended 31.3.20X2 (using indirect method)

		£000
1 Net cash inflow from operating activities (detail required as a Note)		738
2 Returns on investments and servicing of finance		
Interest *[40 (P & L) there are no accruals in 20X1 or 20X2]*		(40)
3 Taxation		
Tax paid *[380 (20X1 accrual) + 400 (P & L) – 340 (20X2 accrual)]*		(440)
4 Capital expenditure		
Fixed asset purchase	(1,120)	
Proceeds from sale of land and plant	682	
		(438)
5 Acquisitions and disposals		—
6 Equity dividends *[140 (P & L) there are no accruals in 20X1 or 20X2]*		(140)
		(320)
7 Management of liquid resources		
Government securities		(30)
8 Financing		
Issue of shares	700	
Repayment of debentures	(100)	600
9 Increase in cash		250

24.4.4 Additional notes required by FRS 1 Revised

A general criticism of FRS 1 was that it did not help to assess the solvency and liquidity of a company, as it did not show the changes in the company's **net debt** position. It was argued that it was necessary to consider changes not only in its cash flow position, but also in its debt position.

FRS 1 Revised requires a statement reconciling net cash flow to movement in net debt. This statement should include all cash flows in the main cash flow statement which affect the net debt position, with a note reconciling net debt at the beginning of the period to net debt at the end of the period. Hence it should include the changes in cash, debt and liquid resources, and also any changes in finance leases and translation differences. The notes for Tyro Bruce are as follows:

Note 2: Analyses of changes in net debt

	At 1.4.20X1	Cash flows	Other changes	At 31.3.20X2
	£000	£000	£000	£000
Cash	20	10	—	30
Overdraft	(1,356)	240	—	(1,116)
Debts due after 1 year	(400)	100	—	(300)
Also Finance lease (if appropriate)				
Current asset investment	—	30	—	30
Total	(1,736)	380	—	(1,356)

Note 3: Reconciliation of net cash flow to movements in net debt

	£000
Increase in cash in period	250
Cash repurchase debentures	100
Cash used to increase liquid resources	30
Change in net debt	380
Net debt at 1 April 20X1	(1,736)
Net debt at 31 March 20X2	1,356

The reconciliation statement and note will help to assess the company's liquidity and financial adaptability.

24.5 Consolidated cash flow statements

A consolidated cash flow statement differs from that for a single company in two respects, namely, there are additional items and adjustments may be required to the actual amounts.

24.5.1 Additional items

Additional items appear in Sections 1, 2 and 5 of the statement, as follows:

1 Cash flows from operating activities

- Operating profit before interest and tax
  Adjust for non-cash charges:
  Adjust for changes in current assets and current liabilities:
  Adjust for additional items if a consolidated cash flow statement:
  – Share of associate profit less dividend received by investor

2 Returns on investments and servicing of finance

● Interest paid and payable

Minority interest – dividends paid

[calculated as minority interest in opening consolidated balance sheet plus minority interest in consolidated profit and loss account less minority interest in closing consolidated balance sheet]

3 Acquisitions and disposals

● *Purchase of subsidiary, interest in associated/joint venture undertaking or of a business*

● *Proceeds from sale of subsidiary, interest in associated/joint venture undertaking or of a business*

24.5.2 Adjustments to amounts

Adjustments are required if the closing balance sheet items have been increased or reduced as a result of **non-cash movements**. Such movements occur (a) if there has been a purchase of a subsidiary to reflect the fact that the asset and liabilities from the new subsidiary have not necessarily resulted from cash flows; and (b) if there are exchange differences arising on consolidating foreign subsidiaries.

(a) Subsidiary acquired during year

For example, if in Tyro Bruce a subsidiary had been acquired at 31 March 20X2 on the following terms:

In consolidated cash flow the effect will be:

Net assets acquired:

	£000	
Working capital:		
Stock	10	**(1)** Reduce stock difference
Creditors	(12)	**(1)** Reduce creditor difference
Capital expenditure:		
Vehicles	20	**(4)** Reduces capital expenditure
Cash/Bank:		
Cash	5	**(5)** Inflow in Acquisitions section
Net assets acquired	23	
Consideration from Tyro Bruce:		
Shares	10	**(8)** Reduce share cash inflow
Premium	10	**(8)** Reduce share cash inflow
Cash	3	**(5)** Outflow in Acquisition section
	23	

The cash flow statement can now be prepared for Tyro Bruce for the year ended 31.3.20X2 using indirect method

			£000
1 Net cash inflow from operating activities **Note 1**			736
2 Returns on investments and servicing of finance interest			(40)
3 Taxation			
Tax paid			(440)
4 Capital expenditure			
Fixed asset purchase		(1,120)	
Less Vehicles brought in on acquisition		*20*	
		(1,100)	
Proceeds from sale of land and plant		682	
			(418)
5 Acquisitions and disposals			—
Cash flow arising from acquisition			
[Cash flow in £5,000 less cash flow out £3,000]			2
6 Equity dividends			(140)
			(300)
7 Management of liquid resources			
Government securities			(30)
8 Financing			
Issue of shares		700	
Less shares issued on acquisition not for cash		(20)	
		680	
Repayment of debentures		(100)	580
9 Increase in cash			250

Note 1: Reconciliation of operating profit to operating cash flows

			£000
Profit before interest and tax			1,040
Add back non-cash charges:			
Depreciation			204
R & D amortisation charge			480
Loss on sale of plant			54
Less non-cash credits:			
Profit on sale of land			(80)
Changes in current assets:			
Less current asset increases			
Stock	*(800)*		
Less stock brought in on acquisition	*10*		
	(790)		
		(790)	
Debtors		(440)	
Add current liability increases			
Creditors	*280*		
Less creditors brought in on acquisition	*12*		
	268		
		268	
Net cash flow from operating activities			736

If there had been a disposal of a subsidiary, the same adjustments would have been required except that they would have been in the opposite direction, e.g. capital expenditure on vehicles would have been increased from £1,120,000 to £1,140,000.

(b) Exchange differences arising on consolidation

If the subsidiary's accounts have been translated using the net investment method whereby the closing rate has been used and the exchange differences taken to reserves, then the asset and liabilities in the consolidated balance sheet will contain **non-cash movements**. Let us assume that the non-cash differences that arose from exchange rate translation were the same amounts as those that arose on an acquisition of a subsidiary, namely:

Working capital:	£000	*Cash flow treatment*
Stock	10	(1) Reduce stock difference
Creditors	(12)	(1) Reduce creditor difference
Fixed assets:		
Vehicles	20	(4) Reduces capital expenditure
Cash/ Bank:		
Cash	5	(9) Reduces cash
Exchange gain	23	

Section 1 Cash flow from operations would be the same as for the subsidiary acquired during the year, i.e. £736,000 (£738,000 – Creditor increase of £12,000 + Stock decrease of £10,000).

Section 4 Capital expenditure would be the same as for subsidiary acquired during the year, i.e. £418,000 (£438,000 – Fixed asset decrease of £20,000).

Section 9 Cash balance would be reduced by the exchange difference of £5,000, i.e. £245,000 (£250,000 – £5,000).

Note: The exchange gain of £23,000 would have been credited to reserves in Tyro Bruce.

24.6 Analysing a cash flow statement

The cash flow statement provides additional information on interest cover, working capital and fixed asset investment and financing cash flows.

24.6.1 Interest cover

Interest cover is normally defined as the number of times the profit before interest and tax covers the interest charge: in the Tyro Bruce example, £1,040,000/£40,000 = 26.1 times.

The position as disclosed in the cash flow statement is weaker. It is the number of times the net cash flow from operating activities covers the payment, i.e. £738,000/£40,000 = 18.45 times.

This does not allow us to assess the financing policy of the company, e.g. whether the capital was raised the optimum way. Nor does it allow us to assess whether the company would have done better to provide finance by improved control over its assets, e.g. working capital reduction.[13]

24.6.2 Impact of working capital movements on cash flows

From the Reconciliation on page 651 we can see that there has been an increase in working capital of £960,000. This is made up of:

	£000
Stock increase	800
Debtor increase	440
Creditor increase	(280)
	960

Using the information in the Reconciliation, we are able to calculate how much of the funds from operations are reinvested into working capital. This shows that the working capital increase is taking 56% of the funds flow from operations, i.e. £960,000/£1,698,000 × 100:

	£000
Profit before interest and tax	1,040
Non-cash items:	
Depreciation charged	204
Loss on sale of plant	54
R & D written off	480
Profit on sale of land	(80)
	1,698

We can see the cash implication, but not the reason for the working capital change or the likelihood of the cash flow movements recurring in future years.

To assess the underlying reasons for the change, we would need to extract additional ratios such as stock turnover. If the increase in the investment in stock is related to turnover, a similar increase could recur if the turnover is forecast to continue increasing. If it is due to poor stock control, it is less likely that the increase will recur: in fact, the opposite.

The same comments could be made in relation to the debtors and creditors. The cash flow statement indicates the cash extent of the change: additional ratios are required to allow us to evaluate the change.

24.6.3 Evaluating the investing activities cash flows

It is useful to consider how much of the expenditure is to replace existing fixed assets. One way is to relate the cash expenditure to the depreciation charge; this indicates that the cash expenditure is 549% greater than the depreciation charge calculated as follows: [(£1,120,000/£204,000) × 100]. This seems to indicate a possible increase in productive capacity. However, the cash flow does not itemise the expenditure and referring to the fixed asset schedule reveals that only £120,000 of the total of £1,120,000 was spent on plant.

There has been a criticism that it is not possible to assess how much of the investing activities cash outflow related to simply maintaining operations by replacing fixed assets that were worn out rather than related to increasing existing capacity with a potential for an increase in turnover and profits. The solution proposed was that investment that merely maintained should be shown as an operating cash flow and that the investing cash flow should be restricted to increasing capacity. The ASB doubted the reliability of such a distinction but there is a view[13] that such an analysis provides additional information, provided the breakdown between the two types of expenditure can be reliably ascertained.

24.6.4 Evaluating the financing cash flows

A comparison of the net cash outflow before financing with the cash inflow from financing indicates the extent to which the cash flow after investing has been utilised or financed, e.g. financing has contributed over 100% [(£600,000/£320,000) × 100] and there has been no reduction in cash.

Arranging cash flows into specific classes provides users with relevant and decision-useful information. This specific categorisation into operating, investing and financing activities allows users to draw conclusions about future cash flows. It would be difficult to make these conjectures using traditional accrual-based techniques.[14]

24.7 Critique of cash flow accounting

In this section we look at cash flow accounting from the viewpoint of users. We discuss the conflicting objectives of flexibility and uniformity, and comment on the two methods available under FRS 1.

24.7.1 Users

One of the main measures for evaluating the effectiveness of cash flow statements is the extent to which user needs are satisfied. Initial questions surrounding the replacement of funds flow statements with cash flow statements involved consideration of the following:

● For which user groups was the original SSAP 10 designed?

● Which user groups actually used funds flow statements and found the resultant information useful?

● Which user groups were consulted during the formulation of FRS 1?

● For which user groups was FRS 1 designed?

During this chapter we have identified the strengths and weaknesses of funds flow statements and cash flow statements. Funds flow statements did provide some useful information and were perceived as useful by users. Different user groups were able to extract different information from the statement; for instance:

● **Shareholders** could assess the stability of the company's dividend distribution policy by determining what proportion of net profit was accounted for by tax and dividends.

● **Creditors** could assess the company's ability to meet long-term obligations and maintain the working capital investment.

● **Lenders** could assess the company's reliance on either borrowings or share capital for financing investment and expansion projects.

Unfortunately, even though the funds flow statement satisfied some user needs, many areas could not be evaluated using it. Solomons explains this aspect of user needs:

> If ... the main concerns of the primary groups of users of general purpose financial reports are with the profitability and the viability of the enterprises in which they have an interest, that points to the need for financial statements that at least disclose:
> (a) the enterprise's capacity to generate income for its owners, employees, and lenders who are entitled to interest on their loans;
> (b) its present and probable future solvency.[15]

Solomons states that the link between profitability and viability is expressed by an enterprise's cash flows. The disclosure of this information is one of the arguments in favour of producing a cash flow statement.

24.7.2 Flexibility versus uniformity

One premise for the replacement of funds flow statements with cash flow statements is that SSAP 10 allowed too much flexibility in the presentation of funds flow information. This led to an increase in the variety of formats and a decrease in comparability between companies.

There appears to be an assumption that management, left to its own devices, will choose an accounting format for purely self-satisfying motives that will mislead the user. But perhaps the format of funds flow statements was properly left to the discretion of management. This discretion allowed management to decide which user groups the statement was aimed at, so that management could then select the most appropriate format to disclose and highlight the relevant information about recent activities. This might be more helpful than having the figures arrayed in a standard, uniform fashion.

On the assumption that too much flexibility was undesirable, FRS 1 applied stricter requirements to the format and presentation of cash flow statements. However, it still allowed companies to choose between the direct and indirect methods, and hence it could be argued that it failed to rectify the problem of lack of comparability between statements.

An important point is that, in its search for improved comparability, FRS 1 reduced the scope for innovation. It might be argued that standard-setters should not be reducing innovation, but that there should be a concerted effort to increase innovation and improve the information available to user groups. The acceptability of innovation is a fundamental issue in a climate that is becoming increasingly prescriptive under the influence of Europe.

24.7.3 Cash flows or funds flows

Our final consideration is the option of direct or indirect methods allowed in FRS 1. The direct method appears to be a genuine format for a cash flow statement, whereas the indirect method is a cross between a cash flow statement and a funds flow statement. Is it appropriate to continue to offer this hybrid format in FRS 1 Revised as a replacement for a funds flow statement?

Summary

The funds flow statements produced in accordance with SSAP 10 from 1975 to 1991 were criticised for not highlighting potential financial problems and for allowing too much choice to companies in how items were disclosed. FRS 1 defines more tightly the format and treatment of individual items within the cash flow statement. This leads to uniformity and greater comparability between companies.

In response to several criticisms, FRS 1 Revised has made a number of changes. These are based on the need to:

- Separate discretionary and non-discretionary cash flows. Dividends are discretionary payments and should be treated separately from items such as interest. FRS 1 Revised shows dividends as a separate heading after non-discretionary payments.

- Separate cash flows for expansion from cash flows for capital maintenance. FRS 1 did not differentiate and it was not always easy in practice to make such a separation. FRS 1 Revised shows cash flows arising from acquisitions and disposals of shares and from acquisitions and disposals of a business separately from fixed asset expenditure.

- Separate cash from near cash. FRS 1 Revised defines cash as cash in hand, cash at bank (receivable on demand) less bank overdraft (repayable on demand). It requires current asset investments that are readily disposable in an active market without significant effect on prices and without disrupting a company's business to be disclosed separately under a heading 'Management of liquid resources'. This category will include cash flows from the sale or purchase of liquid resources such as government securities, equities, debts and other instruments, which will help the user to understand the treasury activities of a company.

REVIEW QUESTIONS

1   The management of any enterprise may put considerable emphasis on the cash flow effects of its decisions and actions, monitoring these with the internal reporting system. Cash flow information is also relevant to those with external interests in the enterprise. Discuss the importance of cash flow information for both internal and external decisions. What internal and external user needs does cash flow reporting satisfy? Is the current cash flow information adequate for these purposes?

2   FRS 1 *Cash Flow Statements* preferred the direct method, but did not require it. Discuss possible reasons for allowing choice and the effectiveness of the ASB's encouragement to companies to use the direct method.

3   Explain the information that a user can obtain from a cash flow statement that cannot be obtained from the current or comparative balance sheets.

4   Explain the reasons for FRS 1 Revised increasing the number of sections in the cash flow statement.

5 'The traditional profit and loss statement in published accounts should be replaced (or at least supplemented) by a cash flow statement.'

   (a) Explain what you understand by such a cash flow statement.

   (b) Explain the basis on which the above view can be justified, and state any drawbacks of disclosing cash flow information.

6 Explain why the fixed assets acquired on the acquisition of a subsidiary during the year have the same effect on the consolidated cash flow statement as an exchange gain of equal amount resulting from the translation at closing rate.

EXERCISES

An extract from the solution is provided in the appendix at the end of the text for exercises marked with an asterisk (*).

* Question 1

The draft balance sheets of Example plc as at 31 March 20X0 and 31 March 20X1 are as follows:

			20X1			20X0	
(£000)		Cost	Depn	NBV	Cost	Depn	NBV
Fixed assets		2,760	462	2,298	2,520	452	2,068
Current assets							
Stock			1,200			800	
Debtors			900			640	
Government securities			20			—	
Cash			10			80	
			2,130			1,520	
Current liabilities							
Creditors			500			540	
Taxation			170			190	
Dividends			—			—	
Overdraft			478			8	
			1,148			738	
Net current assets				982			782
				3,280			2,850
Ordinary share capital				1,400			1,300
Share premium account				400			200
Retained profits at 31 Mar 20X0				1,150			1,150
Profit for year				180			—
10% Debentures repayable 20X0–X4				150			200
				3,280			2,850

The profit and loss account of Example plc for the year ended 31 March 20X1 is as follows:

	£000	£000
Sales		3,000
Cost of sales		2,000
Gross profit		1,000
Selling and distribution expenses	300	
Administrative expenses	180	(480)
		520
Interest payable		(20)
Profit before tax		500
Tax		(200)
Profit after tax		300
Dividend		(120)
		180

Notes:

1 Fixed assets having a cost of £320,000 on which £92,000 of depreciation had been provided were sold during the year at a profit of £13,000.

2 The fixed asset schedule included the following:

Cost	£000	Depreciation	£000	Net book value	£000
At cost 31 Mar 20X0	2,520	At 31 Mar 20X0	452	At 31 Mar 20X0	2,068
Additions	560	P & L charge	102		
	3,080		554		
Disposals	320	Disposal	92		
At 31 Mar 20X1	2,760		462	At 31 Mar 20X1	2,298

Required:
A statement using the format of FRS 1 Revised on the Example plc data.

* Question 2

Shown below are the summarised final accounts of Martel plc for the last two financial years:

Balance sheet as at 31 December

	20X1 £000	20X1 £000	20X0 £000	20X0 £000
Fixed assets				
Tangible				
Land and buildings	1,464		1,098	
Plant and machinery	520		194	
Motor vehicles	140		62	
		2,124		1,354
Current assets				
Stocks	504		330	
Trade debtors	264		132	
Government securities	40		—	
Bank	—		22	
	808		484	

	20X1		20X0	
	£000	£000	£000	£000
Creditors – less than one year				
Trade creditors	266		220	
Taxation	120		50	
Proposed dividend	72		40	
Bank overdraft	184		—	
	642		310	
Net current assets		166		174
Total assets less current liabilities		2,290		1,528
Creditors – more than one year				
9% Debentures		(432)		(350)
		1,858		1,178
Capital and reserves				
Ordinary shares of 50p each fully paid		900		800
Share premium account	120		70	
Revaluation reserve	360		—	
Gerneral reserve	100		50	
Retained profit	378		258	
		958		378
		1,858		1,178

---

*Summarised profit and loss account for the
year ending 31 December*

	20X1	20X0
	£000	£000
Operating profit	479	215
Interest paid	52	30
Profit before taxation	427	185
Corporation tax	149	65
Profit after taxation	278	120
Less: Dividends – interim	36	30
– proposed	72	40
	170	50
Less: Transfer to general reserve	50	—
Retained profit	120	50

Additional information:

1 The movement in fixed assets during the year ended 31 December 20X1 was as follows:

	Land and buildings £000	Plant, etc. £000	Motor vehicles £000
Cost at 1 January 20X1	3,309	470	231
Revaluation	360	—	—
Additions	81	470	163
Disposals	—	(60)	—
Cost at 31 December 20X1	3,750	880	394
Depreciation at 1 January 20X1	2,211	276	169
Disposals	—	(48)	—
Added for year	75	132	85
Depreciation at 31 December 20X1	2,286	360	254

The plant and machinery disposed of during the year was sold for £20,000.

2 During 20X1, a rights issue was made of one new ordinary share for every eight held at a price of £1.50.

Required:
(a) Prepare a cash flow statement for the year ended 31 December 20X1, in accordance with FRS 1.
(b) Prepare a report on the liquidity position of Martel plc for a shareholder who is concerned about the lack of liquid resources in the company.

Question 3

The following financial statements relate to Blue Ting plc for the year ended 31 May 20X5.

Profit and loss account for the year ended 31 May 20X5

	£m	£m
Turnover		335
Cost of sales		(177)
Gross profit		158
Distribution costs	(31)	
Administrative expenses	(27)	(58)
Operating profit		100
Interest payable	(7)	
Interest receivable	3	(4)
Profit before tax		96
Taxation		(22)
Profit for the financial year		74
Dividends		(12)
Retained profit for financial year		62

Balance sheets at 31 May

	20X5		20X4	
	£m	£m	£m	£m
Tangible fixed assets		272		196
Intangible fixed assets				
(development expenditure)		3		4
		275		200
Current assets				
Stock	140		155	
Debtors	130		110	
Cash and liquid resources	102		23	
	372		288	
Creditors: Amounts falling due				
within one year	(249)		(172)	
Net current assets		123		116
Total assets less current liabilities		398		316
Creditors: Amounts falling due				
after more than one year		(80)		(90)
		318		226
Capital and reserves				
Ordinary share capital		120		100
Share premium account		45		35
Capital redemption reserve		12		—
Profit and loss account		141		91
		318		226

The following information relates to the financial statements of Blue Ting plc

(1) Ordinary share capital

	£m
£1 Shares fully paid at 1.6.X4	100
Issued during year	10
Purchase of own shares	(12)
Shares converted	22
	120

(2) Reserves

	Share premium account	Capital redemption reserve	Profit and loss account
	£m	£m	£m
At 1.6.X4	35		91
Premium on issue			
(net of issue costs of £1m)	3		
Premium on conversion of debentures	7		
Transfer to CRR		12	(12)
Profit for period			62
	45	12	141

(3) Creditors: Amounts falling due after more than one year

	20X5 £m	20X4 £m
Obligations under finance leases	49	30
6% Debentures 20X5–2011	31	60
	80	90

£29m of 6% Debentures 20X5–20Y1 were converted into £22m of ordinary shares during the year and interest paid in the year amounted to £2m.

(4) Creditors: Amounts falling due within one year

	20X5 £m	20X4 £m
Bank overdraft	8	20
Obligations under finance leases	5	3
Trade creditors	220	131
Taxation	16	10
Dividends	—	8
	249	172

(5) Tangible fixed assets

	£m
Carrying value at 1.6.X4	196
Additions – finance leases	28
– purchases at cost	104
Disposals at carrying value	(19)
Depreciation for the year	(37)
Carrying value at 31.5.X5	272

The fixed assets disposed of realised £21m.

(6) Cash and liquid resources

	20X5 £m	20X4 £m
Treasury Stock 8.5% 20X9	60	—
Treasury Stock 12.75% 20X9 (June)	20	20
Loan notes repayable on demand	15	—
Cash at bank and in hand	7	3
	102	23

(Notes that all of the interest due on the Treasury Stock for the year ending 31.5.X5 has been received and there was no interest due on 31.5.X4.)

(7) Interest payable

	20X5 £m
Bank overdraft	2
Finance charges payable under finance leases	3
Debentures not wholly repayable within five years	2
	7

(8) Obligations under finance leases

	20X5	20X4
	£m	£m
Amounts payable within one year	6	4
Within two to five years	55	33
	61	37
Less finance charges allocated to future periods	(7)	(4)
	54	33

Interest paid on finance leases in the year to 31 May 20X5 amounted to £3m.

Required:

(a) **Prepare a cash flow statement for Blue Ting plc for the year ended 31 May 20X5 in compliance with FRS 1 (Revised)** *Cash Flow Statements.* **Students should show as a note to the cash flow statement a reconciliation of operating profit to net cash inflow from operating activities.**

(b) **Discuss the principal advantages and disadvantages of publishing forecast cash flow statements for the next accounting period.**

(ACCA)

Question 4

Carver plc is a listed company incorporated in 1958 to produce models carved from wood. In 1975 it acquired a 100% interest in a wood importing company, Olio Ltd; in 1989 it acquired a 40% interest in a competitor, Multi-products Ltd; and on 1 October 1993 it acquired a 75% interest in Good Display Ltd. It is planning to make a number of additional acquisitions during the next three years.

The draft consolidated accounts for the Carver Group are as follows:

Draft consolidated profit and loss account for the year ended 30 September 1994

	£000	£000
Operating profit		1,485
Share of profit of associated undertakings		495
Income from fixed asset investment		200
Interest payable		(150)
Profit on ordinary activities before taxation		2,030
Tax on profit on ordinary activities		
Corporation tax	391	
Deferred taxation	104	
Taxation attributable to income of associated undertakings	145	
Tax attributable to franked investment income	45	
		(685)
Profit on ordinary activities after taxation		1,345
Minority interests		(100)
Profit for the financial year		1,245
Dividends paid and proposed		(400)
Retained profit for the year		845

Draft consolidated balance sheet as at 30 September

	1993		1994	
	£000	£000	£000	£000
Fixed assets				
Tangible assets				
Buildings at net book value		2,200		2,075
Machinery				
Cost	1,400		3,000	
Aggregate depreciation	(1,100)		(1,200)	
Net book value		300		1,800
		2,500		3,875
Investments in associated undertaking		1,000		1,100
Fixed asset investments		410		410
Current assets				
Stocks		1,000		1,975
Trade debtors		1,275		1,850
Cash		1,820		4,515
		4,095		8,340
Creditors: Amounts falling due within one year				
Trade creditors		280		500
Obligations under finance leases		200		240
Corporation tax		217		462
Dividends		200		300
Accrued interest and finance charges		30		40
		927		1,542
Net current assets		3,168		6,798
Total assets less current liabilities		7,078		12,183
Creditors: Amounts falling due after more than one year				
Obligations under finance leases		170		710
Loans		500		1,460
Provisions for liabilities				
Deferred taxation		13		30
Net assets		6,395		9,983
Capital and reserves				
Called up share capital in 25p shares		2,000		3,940
Share premium account		2,095		2,883
Profit and loss account		2,300		3,045
Total shareholders' equity		6,395		9,868
Minority interest		—		115
Net assets		6,395		9,983

Note 1: There had been no acquisitions or disposals of buildings during the year. Machinery costing £500,000 was sold for £500,000 resulting in a profit of £100,000. New machinery was acquired in 1994 including additions of £850,000 acquired under finance leases.

Note 2: Information relating to the acquisition of Good Display Ltd.

	£000
Machinery	165
Stocks	32
Trade debtors	28
Cash	112
Less: Trade creditors	(68)
Corporation tax	(17)
	252
Less: Minority interest	(63)
	189
Goodwill	100
	289

	£000
880,000 shares issued as part consideration	275
Balance of consideration paid in cash	14
	289

It is group policy to write off goodwill to reserves.

Note 3: Loans were issued at a discount in 1994 and the carrying amount of the loans at 30 September 1994 included £40,000 representing the finance cost attributable to the discount and allocated in respect of the current reporting period.

Required:
Prepare a consolidated cash flow statement for the Carver Group for the year ended 30 September 1994.

(ACCA)

References

1 SSAP 10, *Statements of Source and Application of Funds*, July 1975.
2 SFAS 95, *Statement of Cash Flows*, FASB, November 1987.
3 N. MacDonald, 'Funds flow reporting', in L.C.L. Skerrat and D.J. Tonkin (eds), *Financial Reporting 1987–88: A Survey of UK Reporting Practice*, ICAEW, 1988.
4 ED 54, *Cash Flow Statements*, ASC, July 1990.
5 J. Arnold *et al.*, *The Future Shape of Financial Reports*, ICAEW and ICAS, 1991.
6 J. Arnold, 'The future shape of financial reports', *Accountancy*, May 1991, p. 26.
7 G.H. Sorter, M.J. Ingberman and H.M. Maximon, *Financial Accounting: An Events and Cash Flow Approach*, McGraw-Hill, 1990.
8 J.W. Henderson and T.S. Maness, *The Financial Analyst's Deskbook*, Van Nostrand Reinhold, 1989, p. 12.
9 J. Crichton, 'Cash flow statements – what are the choices?' *Accountancy*, October 1990, p. 30.
10 L.J. Heath and P. Rosenfield, 'Solvency: the forgotten half of financial reporting', in R. Bloom and P.T. Elgers (eds), *Accounting Theory and Practice*, Harcourt Brace Jovanovich, 1987, p. 586.
11 ASB Press Notice 6, 26 September 1991.

12 J.M. Gahlon and R.L. Vigeland, 'Early warning signs of bankruptcy using cash flow analysis', *Journal of Commercial Lending*, December 1988, pp. 4–15.

13 G. Holmes and A. Sugden, *Interpreting Company Reports and Accounts* (5th edition), Woodhead Faulkner, 1995, p. 134.

14 J.W. Henderson and T.S. Maness, *op. cit.*, p. 72.

15 D. Solomons, *Guidelines for Financial Reporting Standards*, ICAEW, 1989.

CHAPTER 25

Review of financial ratio analysis

25.1 Introduction

In this chapter we consider the following:

- Accounting ratios and ratio analysis
- Six key ratios
- Pyramid of ratios
- Other important ratios
- Application of pyramid of ratios to J D Wetherspoon
- Segmental analysis
- Interfirm comparisons and industry averages
- Interfirm comparisons: J D Wetherspoon and the independent public houses and bars sector
- World Wide Web (WWW) pages
- Non-financial ratios
- Interpretation problems when using consolidated financial statements

This chapter reviews the use of financial ratio analysis for the interpretation of a company's financial statements. The techniques that we discuss are fundamental to user appraisal of financial statements and should be used in conjunction with any alternative interpretative techniques available.

The key to understanding and interpreting financial statements is an extremely inquisitive and enquiring frame of mind. When examining a set of accounts, we should try to understand exactly what the figures mean.

Some issues will be evident from a cursory look at the accounts. For example, an initial glance might reveal a company that has made losses in the past two years; that has a declining sales turnover, a large overdraft and a greatly increased creditor figure. This would clearly raise questions about, for example, the increase in creditors. The initial look is a prelude to a more systematic review and is helpful in quickly putting the accounts into context.

Following the overview, financial ratios become important. One of the main strengths of financial ratios is that they help to direct the user's focus of attention. They identify and highlight areas of good and bad performance, and areas of significant change. In each instance, the user should attempt to explain exactly why the accounts reveal this behaviour.

Before we embark on a full investigation of financial ratios, a word of warning. Ian Griffiths has written a book on creative accounting which questions the reliability of financial statements: 'Every company in the country is fiddling its profits. Every set of published accounts is based on books which have been gently cooked or completely roasted … it is the biggest con trick since the Trojan Horse.'[1]

We should take heed of these reservations when we undertake any analytical interpretations. They should make us even more open-minded and investigative when confronted by a set of financial statements:

> Whether the differences in accounting treatment and presentation are real or imagined, it is clear that there is scope for tremendous variation in reported figures … perhaps the best safeguard is to look upon the annual accounts with a more cynical and jaundiced eye. The myth that the financial statements are an irrefutable and accurate reflection of the company's trading performance for the year must be exploded once and for all. The accounts are little more than an indication of the broad trend.

25.2 Accounting ratios and ratio analysis

Accounting ratios identify irregularities, anomalies and surprises that require further investigation to ascertain the current and future financial standing of a company. This sounds very useful, but what are ratios and how can we use them?

25.2.1 What are ratios?

Ratios describe the relationship between different items in the financial statements. Obviously, we could calculate hundreds of ratios from a set of financial statements; the expertise lies in knowing which ratios provide useful information. The relative usefulness of each ratio depends on what aspects of a company's business affairs are being investigated. Some of the most important and frequently used ratios are outlined in section 25.3.

25.2.2 How can we use ratios?

An important lesson about ratios is that, if they are applied incorrectly, they may be completely useless or, perhaps even worse, misleading. Alternatively, if they are used correctly, they are a powerful tool for understanding and interpreting company accounts. Some basic rules for financial ratio analysis are as follows.

Compare like with like

The relative performance of a company can be gauged in a number of different terms by comparing that company's financial ratios with:

- financial ratios for a preceding period;
- budgeted financial ratios for the current period;
- financial ratios for other profit centres within the company;
- financial ratios for other companies within the same industrial sector.

In each case, comparison is possible only if an identical basis of compilation is employed. There must be conformity and uniformity in the preparation of accounts to ensure a comparison of like with like. In addition, if one is comparing companies in different countries, one needs to be aware of any differences in international accounting policies (see Chapter 28).

Clear definition of the financial ratio

A full understanding of the precise implications of a given ratio is possible only if it is accompanied by a clear definition of its constituent parts. The user must be able to judge the accuracy and reliability of the underlying business operations before the reliability of the ratio can be assessed. In addition, the definitions of ratios may vary from source to source as concepts and terminology are not universally defined.[2]

Awareness of underlying trends

As a ratio compares two values, changes in either of these underlying values over time may be obscured in the final ratio figure. Let us take the example of Radmand plc:

	Net profit £	*Capital employed* £	*Return on capital employed*
20X1	100,000	1,000,000	10%
20X2	150,000	1,500,000	10%
20X3	225,000	2,250,000	10%

Although the return on capital employed (ROCE) remains a constant 10% over the years 20X1–20X3, no assumptions can be made about the underlying figures. As we can see, the net profit increased by 50% in both 20X2 and 20X3, and this trend is not ascertainable in the ROCE ratio. The user should be aware that a ratio is not saying anything about the trends of its individual components – only about the combined effect of both components.

25.3 Six key ratios

In our analysis we identify six key ratios and a number of subsidiary ratios. The key ratios are presented as a pyramid in Figure 25.1. The pyramid illustrates how the constituent parts of each ratio relate to a set of financial statements.

The six key ratios are divided into three categories, as follows:

Primary investment level ratios

1 Primary investment ratio (**operating return on equity**)

$$\frac{\text{Net profit before interest and tax}}{\text{Shareholders' funds}}$$

2 Primary financing ratio (**financial leverage multiplier**)

$$\frac{\text{Capital employed}}{\text{Shareholders' funds}}$$

Primary operative level ratios

3 Primary operating ratio (**return on capital employed**)

$$\frac{\text{Net profit before interest and tax}}{\text{Capital employed}}$$

Figure 25.1 Pyramid of key ratios

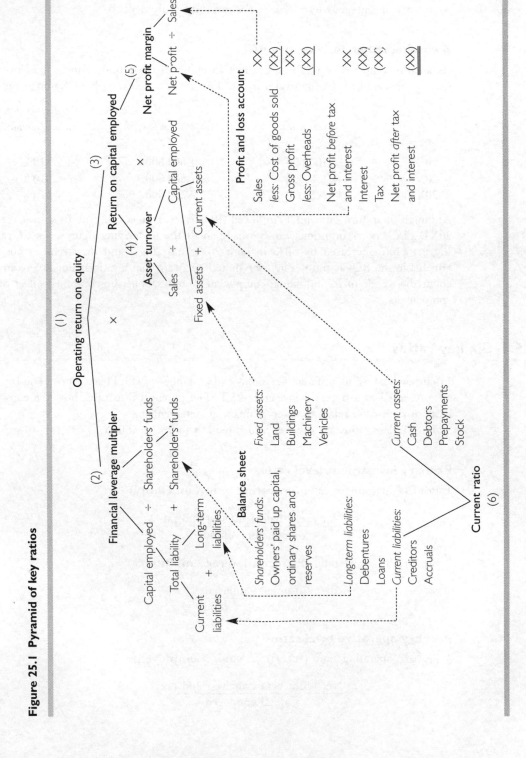

4 Primary utilisation ratio (**asset turnover**)

$$\frac{\text{Sales}}{\text{Capital employed}}$$

5 Primary efficiency ratio (**net profit margin**)

$$\frac{\text{Net profit before interest and tax}}{\text{Sales}}$$

Primary liquidity level ratios

6 Primary liquidity ratio (**current ratio**)

$$\frac{\text{Current assets}}{\text{Current liabilities}}$$

25.4 Description of the six key ratios

25.4.1 Primary investment level ratios

1 Primary investment ratio (operating return on equity)

The operating return on equity represents the net profit of a company as a percentage of the shareholders' funds (i.e. the total investment by the owners). This ratio is at the apex of the ratio pyramid, and it is the product of the financial leverage multiplier and the ROCE. Note that our 'operating return on equity' is defined differently to a more traditional 'return on equity' (Earnings/Shareholders' funds).

2 Primary financing ratio (financial leverage multiplier)

The financial leverage multiplier expresses how many times bigger the capital employed is than the shareholders' funds. This multiplier implies that assets funded by sources other than the owners will increase the profit or loss of the company relative to shareholders' funds.

25.4.2 Primary operative level ratios

3 Primary operating ratio (return on capital employed)

The ROCE is a fundamental measure of the profitability of a company. It is a popular indicator of management efficiency because it contrasts the net profit generated by the company with the total value of fixed and current assets, which are presumed to be under management control. Therefore, the ROCE demonstrates how well the management has utilised total assets.

ROCE is the product of the remaining two primary operative level ratios:

$$\text{ROCE} = \text{Asset turnover} \times \text{Net profit margin}$$

Many different factors impact on the ROCE figure, including asset valuation policies, depreciation policies, revaluation policies, pricing policies, the treatment of goodwill and the treatment of expenses. In particular, the accounting treatment of goodwill (prior to FRS 10) resulted in the vast majority of companies writing off goodwill against their reserves. For some acquisitive companies, the goodwill write-off was so substantial that their shareholders' funds became negative. For instance, in The GGT Group's 1997 annual report their shareholders' funds were −£98,688,000. This makes interpretation and comparisons more difficult.

ROCE is also used by companies as part of their strategic planning, e.g. the following extract from the 1998 Annual Report of VIAG AG states:

> VIAG made excellent progress in 1998 towards reaching its stated profitability goal. Return on capital employed increased significantly from 6.5% in 1997 to 7.0% in 1998. ...The goal is to increase the Group's return on capital employed to at least 10% by the year 2003. The target figures we have adopted are based on our own experience and on the results of our leading competitors.

Care needs to be taken with ROCE as there is no single definition. For example, VIAG explain how their ROCE might be affected by their definition:

> Capital employed is defined on the basis of very restrictive criteria, as evidenced by the fact that Bayernwerk's accruals for decommissioning are included in the capital employed totalling DM59.5 billion. We are legally obliged to establish these accruals for decommissioning expenses, which account for 20% of capital employed. Consequently, VIAG's return on equity and capital costs tend to be lower than those of other industrial corporations.

4 Primary utilisation ratio (asset turnover)

The asset turnover is a measure of how much sales are generated by the capital asset base of a company. Although this ratio can act as a good guide to company performance, it can also be misleading. Its magnitude should therefore be evaluated in terms of its constituent parts.

If asset turnover increases, either the total value of sales is increasing, or the capital asset base is decreasing, or both. If it is because sales are increasing, this might signify improved performance. However, if it is because the capital asset base is reduced, this needs further investigation. For example, it could be caused by failure to maintain fixed assets, or a massive drop in stock levels.

5 Primary efficiency ratio (net profit margin)

Net profit margin is another widely used ratio in the assessment of company performance and in comparisons with other companies.

Profit margin depends on the type of industry a company is operating within (e.g. high-volume/low-margin), the company pricing policies, the sales volumes and cost handling. A higher margin generally suggests good performance, but the profit margin should not be taken at face value. When analysing profit margin we should ask questions such as: why is the profit margin higher than average; or why it is lower than it was last year; or is the company management setting profit margin strategically?

25.4.3 Primary liquidity level ratios

6 Primary liquidity ratio (current ratio)

The current ratio is a short-term measure of a company's liquidity position. This ratio (which should be appraised in conjunction with the acid test ratio) compares current assets with current liabilities. In cases where the value is greater than unity, the current asset value exceeds the value of current liabilities. It is often claimed that the current ratio should be greater than 2, but the recommended current ratio depends (as always) on the industry sector and each individual company's experience. This can be assessed by referring to the times series summaries, e.g. an extract from the 2000 Annual Report of Barloworld, a South African conglomerate:

	2000	1999	1998	1997	1996	1995	1994
Current ratio	1.6	1.7	1.2	1.3	1.5	1.5	1.5

This indicates that the company's current ratio for 2000 is within its own normal range.

The sector norms become relevant if a prospective acquirer is considering a takeover and subsequently revising the existing financial structure.

What if the current ratio increases beyond the normal range?

This may arise for a number of reasons, some beneficial, others unwelcome.

Beneficial reasons

- A build up of stock in order to support a recent advertising campaign or increasing popular demand as for, say, a PlayStation. Management action will be to establish from a cash budget that the company will not experience liquidity problems from holding such stock, e.g. a short-term loan, extended credit or bank overdraft may be appropriate.

- A permanent expansion of the business which will require continuing higher levels of stock. Management action will be to arrange additional finance, e.g. equity or long-term borrowings to finance the increased working capital.

Unwelcome reasons

- Operating losses may have eroded the working capital base. Management action will vary according to the underlying problem, e.g. implementing a cost reduction programme, disposing of under-performing segments, arranging a sale of assets or inviting a takeover.

- Inefficient control over working capital, e.g. poor stock or debtor control.

- Adverse litigation, e.g. liability to employees for asbestosis.

- Adverse trading conditions, e.g. stock becoming obsolete or introduction of new models by competitors.

Moreover, the current ratio should be analysed in terms of its constituent parts to test the quality of the value. We should ask: what part of current assets is cash, debtors or stock; what is the likelihood of debtors defaulting; what is the condition of the stock; and what are the timings of all the current liabilities?

25.5 Description of subsidiary ratios

25.5.1 Gearing ratios

$$\text{Gearing ratio} = \frac{\text{Total liability} - \text{Current liability}}{\text{Capital employed}}$$

The gearing ratio represents the proportion of capital employed which is accounted for by long-term fixed interest debt. The gearing structure of a company refers to the amount of borrowings compared with the amount of shareholders' funds. A company with high gearing is predominantly financed by debt, whereas a company with low gearing relies on equity finance. Different user groups prefer different gearing structures. Creditors and shareholders will be influenced by gearing as it affects factors such as annual interest payments and earnings per share.

This particular definition of gearing concentrates on long-term debt financing. An alternative measure might be total liabilities/capital employed, which includes short-term financing as well as long-term financing. This might be more pertinent because some companies rely on high levels of overdraft. As a further refinement one might disaggregate current liabilities into interest-bearing finance (overdrafts; short-term loans) and more indirect finance (trade creditors; tax payable; dividends payable).

$$\text{Shareholders' ratio} = \frac{\text{Shareholders' funds}}{\text{Capital employed}}$$

This represents the proportion of capital employed that is made up by shareholders' funds.

$$\text{Interest cover} = \frac{\text{Net profit before interest and tax}}{\text{Interest}}$$

Most companies are committed to paying a certain amount of interest charges. This ratio describes how many times greater the profit is than the interest charges. It gives creditors an indication of how secure these repayments are. An alternative measure is to compare the actual cash flow (rather than profit) to interest payments to give an indication of the availability of cash to cover interest charges.

The earnings before interest and tax (EBIT) might move in the same way as the earnings before interest, tax, depreciation and amortisation (EBITDA). However, if they differ significantly, as in periods of unusual growth, it may be more useful to calculate the cash flow interest cover. Even so, attention should also be given to free cash flow, e.g. the following is an extract from the 1999 Annual Report of Sauer Inc.:

> While EBITDA should not be construed as a substitute for operating income or a better indicator of liquidity than cash flow from operating activities, which is determined in accordance with generally accepted accounting principles, it is included herein to provide additional information with respect to the ability of Sauer to meet its future debt service, capital expenditure and working capital requirements. EBITDA is not necessarily a measure of Sauer's ability to fund its cash needs, and its discretionary use of EBITDA will be subject to Sauer's future cash needs relating to its capital expenditures, working capital requirements, future debt service requirements and dividend payments.

25.5.2 Liquidity ratios

$$\text{Acid test ratio} = \frac{\text{Current assets} - \text{Stock}}{\text{Current liabilities}}$$

The acid test or quick ratio indicates the company's ability to repay immediate commitments using cash or near-cash. It excludes the value of stock in order to show the immediate solvency of the company.

The following is an extract from the 2000 Annual Report of Barloworld:

	2000	1999	1998	1997	1996	1995	1994
Quick ratio	0.9	1.1	0.7	0.8	0.9	0.9	1.0

This indicates that the company's quick (or acid test) ratio is within its own normal range.

25.5.3 Asset utilisation ratios

The asset turnover ratio can be subdivided into more specific component parts, so that each element of fixed and current assets can be analysed separately. The asset turnover ratio measures the amount of sales generated by the capital employed as a whole, whereas individual asset utilisation ratios compare total sales with the selected asset under management control. The breakdown of the asset turnover ratio is illustrated in Figure 25.2.

The fixed asset, tangible, property and plant utilisation ratios are measures of efficiency. They all indicate the sales volume produced by the available fixed assets. Although an improvement in these ratios will also improve the ROCE, it must be remembered that the depreciation policies and historical cost valuation of fixed assets will cause a distortion.

Three utilisation (or turnover) ratios that are particularly informative for understanding and interpreting financial statements are stock turnover, debtor turnover and creditor turnover. Stock turnover can be calculated as:

$$\text{Stock turnover} = \frac{\text{Sales}}{\text{Stock}} \quad \text{or} \quad \frac{\text{Cost of sales}}{\text{Average stock}} \quad \text{or more usually} \quad \frac{\text{Cost of sales}}{\text{Closing stock}}$$

Stock control involves careful planning and management. A company must avoid tying up too much capital in stock, yet the stock levels must always be sufficient to meet customer demand and maintain continuous production. Any changes in this ratio must be investigated to determine exactly why stock turnover is fluctuating – it could be due to changing sales volumes; different stock valuation policies; or obsolete stock. The average stock holding period (in days) can be calculated as:

$$\frac{\text{Closing stock}}{\text{Cost of sales}} \times 365$$

The company's management report may be helpful in assessing changes in inventory levels. The following is an extract from the 1999 Annual Report of Schering AG:

Good balance-sheet ratios maintained
The balance-sheet ratios demonstrate the healthy financial state of the Schering Group.

Figure 25.2 Asset turnover ratio

Inventories and receivable rose to 41% of the balance-sheet total. Among other things, this was due to a build-up of stocks to keep the market supplied during implementation of our European Production Concept and to cater for any problems that might have arisen in connection with Y2K.

The debtor ratio (usually trade debtors) is usually expressed in terms of the debtor collection period (in days):

$$\frac{\text{Debtors}}{\text{Sales}} \times 365$$

This ratio can be used to evaluate credit control and how quickly the company receives cash. Changes in the debtor collection period might be misleading, so the root cause must be ascertained. A falling debt collection period might mean that the company is successfully reducing bad debts and eliminating poor risks; or the liquidity position might be so poor that the company is extending discounts and incentives to customers who pay early (or on time). An increasing debt collection period might mean that the company has poor credit control and is besieged with bad debts; or that it has a strategy for attracting new customers.

The creditors turnover ratio (usually trade creditors) is calculated as:

$$\text{Creditors turnover} = \frac{\text{Sales}}{\text{Creditors}} \text{ or more usually } \frac{\text{Cost of sales}}{\text{Creditors}}$$

It is usually expressed in terms of the creditor payment period (in days):

$$\frac{\text{Creditors}}{\text{Sales}} \times 365 \text{ or more usually } \frac{\text{Creditors}}{\text{Cost of Sales}} \times 365$$

This ratio indicates the credit facilities extended to a company by its suppliers. Any changes in the payment period might be due to suppliers altering credit terms (either more or less generous), the company trying to gain maximum credit facilities, or the company utilising early payment incentives.

25.5.4 Investment ratios

Investment ratios such as earnings per share (EPS), price/earnings ratio (PE ratio) and dividend cover are of great interest to investors.

Earnings per share

EPS indicates the amount of profit after tax, interest and dividends to preference shares has been earned for each ordinary share. Its importance is recognised by some management who use the EPS as part of their strategic planning; e.g. the 1999 Annual Report of Gamma Holding N.V. states:

Gamma Holding aims to maximise shareholder value, taking into account the interests of the employees and other stakeholders in the company. In doing so, Gamma Holding strives to offer its shareholders an attractive return based on continuous growth of earnings per share of an average 10% over a number of years whilst maintaining healthy balance sheet ratios and generating positive cash flows. Furthermore, the company aims to achieve an average return on capital employed (including goodwill) of 15%.

PE ratio

The ratio is calculated using the current share price and current earnings. It is a measure of market confidence in the shares of a company. However, the market price also takes into account anticipated changes in the earnings arising from their assessment of macro events such as political factors, e.g. imposition of trade embargos and sanctions, economic factors, e.g. the down-turn in manufacturing activity, and company related events, e.g. possibility of organic or acquired growth and the implication of financial indicators on future cash flow estimates. These financial indicators may be identified from the balance sheet, income statement and trade sources, as follows:

- Balance sheet
  - change in debt/equity ratio in relation to prior periods;
  - new borrowings to finance expansion;
  - debt restructuring following inability to meet current repayment terms;
  - adequacy of working capital;
  - low acid test (quick) ratio in relation to prior periods indicating liquidity difficulties;
  - change in current ratio in relation to prior periods i.e. higher indicating a build up of slow moving stock and lower possible stock outs;
  - contingent liabilities that could be damaging if they crystallise;
  - fixed assets being increased or not being replaced.
- Income statement:
  - change in sales trend;
  - limited product range, products moving out of patent protection period;
  - expanding product range;
  - changes in technology beneficial or otherwise to company;
  - high or low capital expenditure/depreciation ratio indicating that productive capacity is not being maintained;
  - loss of key suppliers/customers e.g. loss of long standing Marks & Spencer contracts;
  - change in ratio of R&D to sales.
- Trade sources:
  - suppliers applying more/less stringent credit terms;
  - loss/gain of key staff.

Earnings yield expresses earnings as a percentage of the share price.

Dividend cover

Dividend cover is ascertained by comparing EPS to dividend per share. It indicates the cushion that exists to meet dividends in the future if earnings were to deteriorate. The cover is expressed as number of times or, in some annual reports, as a payout ratio. Dividend yield expresses dividend as a percentage of the share price.

25.5.5 Profitability ratios

Profitability ratios allow a more specific analysis of profit margin, e.g. expressing individual expenses as a proportion of sales or cost of sales. These ratios will identify any irregularities or changes in specific expenses from year to year.

A list of the subsidiary ratios is set out in Figure 25.3.

Figure 25.3 Subsidiary ratios

Gearing ratios

$$\text{Gearing ratio} = \frac{\text{Total liability} - \text{Current liability}}{\text{Capital employed}}$$

$$\text{Shareholders' ratio} = \frac{\text{Shareholders' funds}}{\text{Capital employed}}$$

$$\text{Interest cover} = \frac{\text{Net profit before interest and tax}}{\text{Interest}}$$

Liquidity ratios

$$(6)\ \text{Current ratio} = \frac{\text{Current assets}}{\text{Current liabilities}}$$

$$\text{Acid test ratio} = \frac{\text{Current assets} - \text{Stock}}{\text{Current liabilities}}$$

Investment ratios

Earnings per share =

$$\frac{\text{Net profit after tax} - \text{Preference dividends}}{\text{Number of ordinary shares}}$$

$$\text{Price/earnings ratio} = \frac{\text{Share price}}{\text{Earnings per share}}$$

Dividend cover (ordinary shares) =

$$\frac{\text{Net profit after tax} - \text{Preference dividends}}{\text{Dividends on ordinary shares}}$$

$$\text{Dividend yield} = \frac{\text{Dividend on ordinary shares}}{\text{Market value of ordinary shares}}$$

Asset utilisation ratios (turnover ratios)

$$\frac{\text{Sales}}{\text{Fixed assets}}$$

$$\frac{\text{Sales}}{\text{Current assets}}$$

$$\frac{\text{Sales}}{\text{Working capital}}$$

$$\frac{\text{Cost of sales}}{\text{Stock}}$$

$$\frac{\text{Sales}}{\text{Debtors}}$$

$$\frac{\text{Cost of sales}[a]}{\text{Trade creditors}}$$

[a]Ideally cost of materials used should be used.

Profitability ratios

$$\frac{\text{Gross profit}}{\text{Sales}}$$

$$\frac{\text{Cost of sales}}{\text{Sales}}$$

$$\frac{\text{Total overheads}}{\text{Sales}}$$

$$\frac{\text{Cost of materials}}{\text{Cost of sales}}$$

$$\frac{\text{Cost of labour}}{\text{Cost of sales}}$$

25.6 Application of pyramid of ratios to J D Wetherspoon plc

To illustrate financial ratio analysis and trend analysis we are using the accounts of J D Wetherspoon plc.[3] The company's principal activities are the development and management of public houses.[4] J D Wetherspoon's profit and loss account and balance sheet are reproduced in Figure 25.4. The 1998 and 1999 Accounts for J D Wetherspoon are set out in Question 10 (see also http://www.wetherspoon.co.uk for 2001 accounts).

Figure 25.4 Wetherspoon (JD) Consolidated profit and loss account for the year ended 31 July 1997

	1997 £000	1996 £000
Turnover from continuing operations	139,444	100,480
Cost of sales	(106,972)	(76,001)
Gross profit	32,472	24,479
Administrative expenses	(9,533)	(7,476)
Operating profit	22,939	17,003
Net interest payable	(5,373)	(3,898)
Profit on ordinary activities before tax	17,566	13,105
Tax on profit on ordinary activities	(770)	(564)
Profit on ordinary activities after tax	16,796	12,541
Dividends	(3,894)	(3,417)
Retained profit for the year	12,902	9,124

Wetherspoon (JD)
Group balance sheet at 31 July 1997

	1997 £000	1996 £000
Fixed assets		
Tangible assets	244,513	182,123
	244,513	182,123
Current assets		
Stocks	2,215	1,167
Debtors	3,026	1,544
Cash	7,196	14,801
	12,437	17,512
Creditors due within one year	(34,998)	(24,450)
Net current liabilities	(22,561)	(6,938)
Total assets less current liabilities	221,952	175,185
Creditors due after one year	(97,289)	(67,077)
	124,663	108,108
Capital and reserves		
Called up share capital	3,898	3,866
Share premium account	59,676	57,728
Revaluation reserve	22,023	20,350
Profit and loss account	39,066	26,164
Equity shareholders' funds	124,663	108,108

Calculation of the six key ratios

1 **Operating return on equity**

$$1997 \quad \frac{22,939}{124,663} = 18.40\% \qquad 1996 \quad \frac{17,003}{108,108} = 15.73\%$$

2 Financial leverage multiplier

1997 $\dfrac{256{,}950}{124{,}663}$ = 2.06 times   1996 $\dfrac{199{,}635}{108{,}108}$ = 1.85 times

3 Return on capital employed

1997 $\dfrac{22{,}939}{256{,}950}$ = 8.93%   1996 $\dfrac{17{,}003}{199{,}635}$ = 8.52%

4 Asset turnover

1997 $\dfrac{139{,}444}{256{,}950}$ = 0.54 times   1996 $\dfrac{100{,}480}{199{,}635}$ = 0.50 times

5 Net profit margin

1997 $\dfrac{22{,}939}{139{,}444}$ = 16.45%   1996 $\dfrac{17{,}003}{100{,}480}$ = 16.92%

6 Current ratio

1997 $\dfrac{12{,}437}{34{,}998}$ = 0.36 : 1   1996 $\dfrac{17{,}512}{24{,}450}$ = 0.72 : 1

Five of these key ratios are shown in the pyramid structure of Figure 25.5 (allowing for rounding).

Figure 25.5 Pyramid of ratios

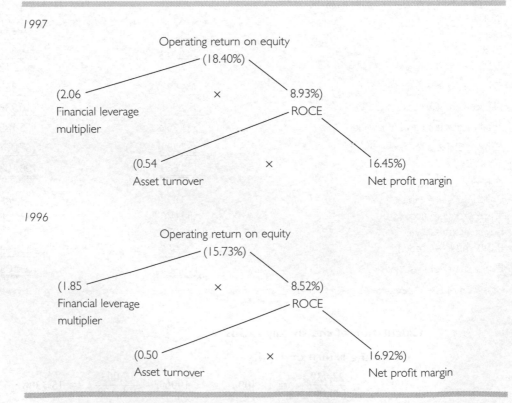

25.6.1 Interpretation of J D Wetherspoon plc's accounts

Using the pyramid structure to analyse JD Wetherspoon in 1997 and 1996 we can identify a number of areas of the business in which further investigations should be carried out. To begin with, the operating return on equity has improved from 15.73% to 18.40%. Disaggregating this ratio we can see that the improvement is due to both an increase in the financial leverage multiplier (1.85 to 2.06) and an increase in the ROCE (8.52% to 8.93%).

The increase in the financial leverage multiplier means that there has been an increased proportion of total liabilities within the capital employed figure. Looking at the balance sheet, it is evident that long-term loans have risen by nearly £30 million (from £67,077,000 to £97,289,000). For interest, the cash flow statement (not reproduced here) shows that the company has received £30 million of 'advances under secured bank loans' (in the Financing section) primarily to finance the 'investment in new pubs and pub extensions' of £63,010,000 (in the Capital expenditure section).

The increase in the ROCE is driven by an improved asset turnover (from 0.5 to 0.54), despite a drop in the net margin (16.92% to 16.45%). The improved asset turnover means that each £ of capital employed (or total assets) produces a higher level of sales. If the decline in net margin is investigated further it is evident that the main cause has been a decline in the gross margin (gross profit/sales) from 24.36% to 23.29%. The declining gross margin might be due to a decline in sales prices or higher cost of sales (which, according to the Wetherspoon annual report, include distribution costs and all pub operating costs).

Some other considerations become apparent when evaluating the accounts in general. First of all, consider the profit and loss account:

- The tax charge in both years is extremely low. For instance, in 1997 the tax is 4.4% of profit before tax. The explanation for this is that the company has utilised unused tax allowances brought forward and high capital allowances generated in the year.

- The company distributed only 23.2% of the after-tax profits in the form of dividends. The explanation for this, in the Finance Director's report, is that the company 'wishes to preserve cash for future expansion'.

- There are no exceptional items to consider.

  Second, consider the balance sheet:

- The cash balance has fallen by over £7 million. The cash flow statement shows that this has been used to part-finance expansion.

- The current liabilities are much higher than the current assets, generating a net current liability. This is illustrated by the current ratio (0.36 in 1997 and 0.72 in 1996). One would need to compare this with the industry average (note that the current ratio for brewers is quite low) and determine whether this drop in current ratio is deliberate policy or needs attention. The notes to the accounts (not reproduced here) show that trade creditors have doubled from £9.4m to £18.4m.

- There is a revaluation reserve of £22,023,000 (17.7% of shareholders' funds). One would need to consider the impact of this figure on some of the ratios, especially when comparing with other brewers.

25.7 Segmental analysis

In this section we review the reasons for and importance of segmental accounting in the analysis of financial statements.

Reasons for segmental accounting

Segmental information is provided on a consistent basis that allows it to be comparable over time so as to assist the users to:

● appreciate more thoroughly the results and financial position by permitting a better understanding of past performance and thus a better assessment of future prospects;

● be aware of the impact that changes in significant components of a business may have on the business as a whole.

Importance of segmental accounting

Segmental information makes the user aware of the balance between the different operations and thus able to assess:

● the quality of the company's reported earnings;

● the specific risks to which the company is subject;

● the areas where long-term growth may be expected.

Constraints on comparison between companies

Segmental analysis is intrinsically subjective. This means that there are likely to be major differences in the way segments are determined, and because costs, for example, may be allocated differently by companies in the same industry it is difficult to make inter-company comparisons at the segment level and the user still has to take a great deal of responsibility for the interpretation of that information.[5]

Management reservations

Standard setters have not been totally prescriptive recognising that management's attitude to segmental reporting is coloured by their fear that they will suffer some competitive disadvantage, e.g. host countries or competitors becoming aware of profit margins. They may also fear that they may not have reciprocal access to sensitive information if their own reporting jurisdiction, e.g. in the UK, requires a higher level of disclosure than that required of their international competitors, e.g. in Switzerland.

However, empirical evidence[6] indicates that such disadvantage arising from disclosure is limited and restricted to geographic segmental disclosure, particularly for smaller companies where such a segment might relate to a single contract.

We also consider the rules applicable to segmental accounting, provide an extract from a set of accounts to illustrate what information might be disclosed, and evaluate the information provided in Bass plc accounts (see 25.7.2).

25.7.1 Segmental accounting

Although the Companies Act 1967 introduced some requirements for the disclosure of segmental information, an accounting standard on the topic was not issued until June 1990.[7] The objective of segmental reporting is to assist users of accounts in evaluating the different business segments and geographical regions of a group and how they affect its overall results.[8] SSAP 25 *Segmental Reporting* sets out how these different segments should be defined and the information that should be disclosed.

SSAP 25 gives guidance on the factors that directors should take into account when defining segments, e.g. the nature of the products or services, and how the group's activities are organised. These factors help to determine whether a segment is distinguishable. However, it must also be a significant segment to require disclosure: a significance test will measure if any of the turnover, results (profit or loss) or net assets accounts for more than 10% of the group's total. SSAP 25 also states that turnover, results (profit or loss before tax, minority interests and extraordinary items) and net assets (not defined in the standard) should be disclosed for both business and geographic segments.

Despite the existence of SSAP 25, there are many concerns about the extent of segmental disclosure and its limitations must be recognised.[9] A great deal of discretion is imparted to the directors concerning the **definition of each segment**. However, 'the factors which provide guidance in determining an industry segment are often the factors which lead a company's management to organise its enterprise into divisions, branches or subsidiaries'.[10] There is discretion concerning the **allocation of common costs** to segments on a reasonable basis. There is flexibility in the **definition of some of the items** to be disclosed (particularly net assets). Finally, there is a get-out clause. Where the directors consider the disclosure of information to be seriously prejudicial to the interests of their group, they do not have to disclose it (as long as the accounts report this non-disclosure).

The revised version of IAS 14[11] requires a much greater disclosure of information than both the original IAS 14[12] and SSAP 25. In particular, separate disclosure of both segment assets and segment liabilities are required (as opposed to net assets for SSAP 25) and the basis of inter-segment pricing. In the UK, ED 45[13] proposed that the basis of inter-segment pricing (transfer pricing[14]) should be disclosed, but this particular proposal was not implemented in SSAP 25.

25.7.2 Segmental accounting – extract from a set of accounts

Where a segment can be distinguished, it is significant and the 'seriously prejudicial' clause is not invoked, one would expect to see disclosure of turnover, results and net assets for both business segments and geographical segments. However, a business may have only one business segment or operate in only one geographical region. Also, not all groups disclose net asset information, e.g. Leicester City plc state in the 1999 Accounts: 'In the opinion of the Directors, it is not possible to analyse the assets between the businesses due to the shared nature of many of the assets'.

The following extract shows a summarised segmental report from the Bass plc 1999 Accounts of their Business Segment and Geographical Segment (turnover by origin):

	External turnover £m	Operating profit £m	Non-operating exceptionals £m	Profit on ordinary activities before int £m
Bass Hotels & Resorts	1,162	321	(107)	214
Bass Leisure Retail	1,428	298	—	298
Bass Brewers	1,576	160	(7)	153
Britvic Drinks	507	44	—	44
Other activities	13	1	2	3
	4,686	824	(112)	712
United Kingdom	3,564	556	3	559
Rest of Europe, Middle East and Africa	496	71	(6)	65
United States	482	170	(110)	60
Rest of Americas	86	17	1	18
Asia Pacific	58	10	—	10
	4,686	824	(112)	712

Assets	£m
UK	5,328
Rest of Europe, Middle East and Africa	1,076
United States	1,144
Rest of Americas	85
Asia Pacific	107
	7,740

The segmental information provides a rough idea about how a group is performing in its main business segments and geographical regions. Bearing in mind the initial discussions on segmental accounting, a number of general observations can be made. Bass has significant interests in hotels, leisure retailing and branded drinks. Although most of Bass business is UK-based, there are high levels of sales in the United States and the Rest of Europe, the Middle East and Africa.

To get a feel for the profitability of the different business segments and markets, it is possible to calculate profit margins (based on operating profit/external sales as disclosed in the above note). For instance the profit margin for the hotel segment is 27.6% compared to 10.2% for Bass Brewers. In addition, the profit margin for the UK is 15.6% compared to 35.3% for the US. This illustrates just how important it is to understand what different business segments are part of a group and which different markets the company is operating in. Furthermore, is the group changing its direction from one year to the next? The profit margin on the hotel segment might indicate that the company would make acquisitions to strengthen this area. The 1998 Accounts showed that this happened with the acquisition of Inter-Continental Hotels for £1,765 million. Is the group a conglomerate operating in numerous different business segments? What are the group's core competencies? Have there been any acquisitions during the year? Have there been any divestments? In relation to Bass, the 1998 Operating and Financial Review stated that there had been a switch in its focus from one of maximising Group benefits through operating tied beer outlets to one of being a leisure retailer.

The 1999 Review stated that the Group made significant progress during 1999, capitalising on the strategic activity undertaken in 1998 which saw the acquisition of the Inter-Continental Hotel (ICH) business, the disposal of the leased pub operation and the leisure businesses and the return of over £800m of capital to shareholders.

With regard to the Bass Hotels & Resorts segment of the business, the OFR states: 'As an indicator of future expansion, at 30 September 1999, BHR had approved franchise applications for 571 hotels (1998 – 575) with approximately 58,000 rooms, though the hotels had yet to enter the system…'

The refocusing was completed in December 2000 when Bass, the UK's third largest brewer, sold off its brewing division to Belgium's Interbrew – this has resulted in more than 50% of UK brewing being owned by non-UK owners (refer to www.bass.com).

Implication of segment reporting for share valuation

There may be different risks attaching to the cash flows from the individual segments. This should be taken into account when assessing the overall value of the company, e.g. an extract from the Lex Column of the *Financial Times*, 17 November 2000, reads:

Bayer

As other old-style chemical giants have broken themselves up to focus on pharmaceuticals, the inventor of aspirin has stuck to its unloved conglomerate formula. So when results on its healthcare business – on which it is increasing its focus – undershoot expectations, the market punishes its shares.

In fact the slippage in healthcare margins came mainly from one-offs ... The pharmaceuticals business is in reasonable shape ... The 20% operating profit margin for healthcare by 2002 is not unrealistic ... So Bayer should be valued more highly. Put healthcare on an earnings multiple of, say, 20% below the sector average, and it would be worth close to the group's €49.20 share price on its own. Adding on chemicals and polymers on an average sector multiple suggests a value closer to €75 ... Achieving its margin targets should provoke a rerating. Otherwise, counterparts such as Novartis or even Roche – with hostile takeovers no longer taboo in Germany – might sniff a bargain.

25.7.3 Identifying segment trends and management strategy

Segmental reports are helpful in assessing current and future performance of companies which operate across a number of business or geographical segments. These may report year on year overall improvements in total operating revenues and operating profits whereas the underlying performance of individual segments may be deteriorating. In such cases, the directors' explanation of the reasons and their proposals for dealing with the situation are important. For example, the following are extracts from the 1999 Annual Report of Royal Ten Cate NV:

In millions of euros	1999	1998	1997
Revenues	655.9	627.7	629.7
Operating result	40.9	34.5	36.9
Return on capital employed	13.5%	11.5%	11.3%

The segmental information is:

	High grade textiles sector			Plastics sector			Rubber sector		
	1999	1998	1997	1999	1998	1997	1999	1998	1997
Revenues	329.1	303.1	278.0	237.7	221.0	222.4	97.4	107.0	117.2
Operating result	24.5	17.6	13.5	10.1	14.6	7.7	9.1	3.6	5.8
Return on capital employed %	15.0	12.2	10.3	9.5	16.8	20.6	17.6	7.0	11.3

With regard to the rubber sector, management action was taken in 1998 to reverse the deterioration:

The result improved sharply, thanks to fundamental cost reductions, the introduction of the production of cell structure and increased volume. As a result of the above-mentioned cost reductions, efficiency improvements and changes to product design, substantial sales price reductions were implemented. This restored the confidence of major customers and generated higher volumes. However, the volume growth was unable to offset the effects of the price reductions and sales fell in net terms by 9%.

Management also indicated medium-term and longer-term thinking:

> In the medium term part of the production will be transferred from Europe and the United States to eastern Europe and central America respectively ... In the longer term it will be necessary to examine the strategic position of Ten Cate Enbi in the sector, partly in the light of the increasing importance of assembly plants.

With regard to the plastics sector, management action was implemented in the latter half of 1999:

> 1999 was an extremely difficult year, partly because customers experienced a decline in sales. A negative result was recorded in net terms. This led to a reorganisation, which was implemented in the second half of the year. Management changes were made and led to the loss of over 70 jobs in three countries. The French operation was converted from a supplier of technical injection-moulded products to a producer specialising in caps. In America a small production unit was started in the Chicago area ... thereby adding a further geographical area.

25.8 Interfirm comparisons and industry averages

Financial ratios are a convenient way of assessing the current financial health and performance of a company relative to similar companies in the same industrial sector. This enables a company to be judged directly against its competitors, rather than merely against its own previous performance. Provided that each company uses exactly the same bases in calculation ratios, interfirm comparisons provide a more controlled and objective means of evaluation. Every company is subject to identical economic and market conditions in the given review period, allowing a much truer comparison than a single company's fluctuating results over several years.

Interfirm comparisons are ideal for identifying the strengths and weaknesses of a company relative to its industrial sector. These comparisons can be analysed by both internal users (management can take the necessary actions to maintain strengths and rectify weaknesses) and external users (lenders, creditors, investors, etc.). There are numerous sources of interfirm information, but the organisations providing it can be divided into those which gather their data from external published accounts and those which collect the data directly from the surveyed companies on a strictly confidential basis.

25.8.1 Data collected from external published accounts

Organisations that prepare interfirm comparisons from external published accounts face all the limitations associated with company accounts. These limitations include the following:

● The comparative ratios that can be included in an interfirm comparison are limited to the information content of a set of published accounts. The inadequacies of compulsory disclosure restrict the amount of useful information and make it impossible to prepare every desirable ratio.

● There is insufficient standardisation in the preparation of published accounts. This is particularly relevant to ratio analysis because comparisons are meaningful only if the ratios are calculated from financial data that have been prepared on the same basis.

● The timeliness of any interfirm comparison is dependent on the timeliness of published accounts. As published accounts are not usually available immediately after a financial year-end, there will be a time lag in the publication of interfirm comparison information.

Although these drawbacks affect the reliability and completeness of survey results, such agencies have several advantages:

● The scope of an interfirm comparison is extremely wide as it can include an analysis of any firm that produces published accounts.

● The quality of ratio analysis is improved because survey organisations attempt to standardise the bases of every ratio in the survey. This increases the uniformity and comparability of the ratio information.

● The survey information is easy to access and available at a relatively low cost.

What organisations provide interfirm comparisons prepared from external published accounts?

Useful sources for interfirm ratio comparisons include *Company REFS*,[15] *Handbook of Market Leaders*,[16] Dun & Bradstreet's *Key Business Ratios: The Guide to British Business Performance*,[17] *'The Company Guide'*[18] and the online and CD-ROM computer services, including Datastream, Company Analysis, OneSource,[19] Fame and Extel Financial Workstation. In addition, the World Wide Web (WWW) provides an excellent source for corporate information.

25.8.2 Data collected direct from member companies of the private interfirm comparison scheme

These interfirm comparisons are prepared on a confidential basis and the analysed information is usually available only to the participating companies.

The advantages of private schemes are that interfirm comparisons consist of a comprehensive analysis of every firm in the scheme, and a higher degree of reliability can be attached to their findings than if external published accounts alone were used.

The drawbacks of private schemes are as follows:

● There are onerous requirements concerning the quality of information that companies contribute to private schemes. All information must comply with strict uniformity requirements.

● The cost of these schemes is relatively high.

The advantages of private schemes are that interfirm comparisons consist of a comprehensive analysis of every firm in the scheme, and a higher degree of reliability can be attached to their findings than if external published accounts alone were used.

What organisations provide private schemes?

Numerous organisations coordinate private interfirm comparison schemes for the majority of different trade groups and industrial sectors. One of the best known is the Centre for Interfirm Comparison, which was founded by the British Institute of Management.

25.9 Interfirm comparisons: JD Wetherspoon and the brewing industry

The necessity for comparing like with like has been stressed throughout this chapter. For true comparisons, we must ensure not only that the bases of ratios are identical, but that one company is compared only with companies in the same industrial sector. If it is compared with a company in a different industrial sector, the results might be interesting, but they might not be suitable for any decision-useful analysis.

25.9.1 Brewing industry results – FAME (Financial Analysis Made Easy)

FAME (November 1999) provides the following information on the top 10 public house chains in the UK by turnover. The 10 companies listed below are selected on the basis of an industry code (SIC Code 5540 – primary description 'bars'). The list illustrates the number of employees, turnover (£000) and profit margin. In addition, the lower quartile, median and upper quartile values of each of these measures are shown. We can see that J D Wetherspoon has a turnover of £188,515,000 in 1998 making it the fifth highest, although the top four groups are substantially larger. However, its profit margin, 10.7%, is broadly in line with the median of the top 10 companies.

Top 10 Public House Chains in the UK
Selected by SIC code and ranked by turnover

Company name	Trade description	Primary SIC 92 Code	Primary SIC 92 Code description	Latest number of employees	Turnover £000	Profit margin (%) last year
Allied Domecq (Holdings) Plc	The production, marketing and sale of spirits and wine, the operation of public houses and franchising.	5540	Bars	49,709	4,308,000	10.56
Punch Retail Limited	Retailing of beers and other drink and food through licensed and off-licensed premises.	5540	Bars	36,571	1,599,000	7.65
Bass Taverns Limited	Leisure retailing through the ownership and management of public houses.	5540	Bars	45,755	1,294,000	10.12
The Greenalls Group Plc	The operation of public houses, hotels, restaurants and off-licences.	5540	Bars	14,153	983,432	16.09
J D Wetherspoon Plc	The develpment and management of public houses.	5540	Bars	5,538	188,315	10.7
John Marston's Taverners Limited	Licensed retailer.	5540	Bars	59	88,541	10.97
Mansfield Inns Limited	The principal activities of the company during the period have been food and drinks retailing.	5540	Bars	3,894	84,551	12.96
Punch Taverns Limited	The management and operation of public houses.	5540	Bars	119	66,076	8.84
Old English Inns Plc	The ownership and management of character freehouses.	5540	Bars	2,117	63,252	11.5
Pubmaster Limited	Management of public houses.	5540	Bars	165	58,430	9.73
	Lower quartile			653	70,695	9.8
	Median			4,716	138,528	10.6
	Upper quartile			30,967	1,216,358	11.4

Source: FAME November 1999

Of course, when using any published inter-company comparison data, it is essential to understand how the ratios are calculated. Each publication defines key terms, how ratios are computed and the methodologies used. The principal activities of the companies are similar, e.g. Bass Taverns Ltd: leisure retailing through the ownership and management of public houses; J D Wetherspoon: development and management of public houses. However, Allied Domecq is slightly wider, with 'the production, marketing and sale of spirits and wine, the operation of public houses and franchising'.

As stressed before, ratio definitions are not 'set in stone'. Different publications and inter-company comparison schemes will use different definitions of seemingly identical ratios. For instance, when using FAME's profit margin, we would need to ascertain what measure of profit is used (e.g. is other income and/or interest received included?).

25.9.2 Independent public houses and bars – OneSource

OneSource is a service available on the WWW. It provides plenty of useful industry information including a 'Peer Listing – 9 closest companies by sales anywhere in the UK in the same primary SIC code' and an analysis of selected ratios for 55402 – Independent public houses and bars. The extracts included in this section for J D Wetherspoon's are from their 1999 Accounts. However, its profit margin is in line with Allied Domecq and Bass.

Peer Listing Extract – 9 closest companies by sales anywhere in the UK in the same primary SIC code:

Company	Sales (£000)	Pre-tax profit (£000)	Number of employees	Total assets (£000)
Greene King plc	292,600	46,700	6,536	550,000
Wolverhampton & Dudley Breweries (Trading) Ltd	285,710	9,187	10,369	174,848
Wolverhampton & Dudley Breweries Public Co Ltd	285,700	44,200	10,369	620,900
Greene King Brewing & Retailing Ltd	282,945	21,921	6,431	275,660
Wetherspoon, JD plc	269,699	48,002	8,314	453,884
Marston Thompson & Evershed Ltd	212,400	30,300	6,624	400,500
Mansfield Brewery plc	175,890	18,438	4,450	321,976
Yates Bros Wine Lodges plc	120,281	14,126	3,253	175,907
Yates Wine Lodges Ltd	95,746	8,011	2,752	22,704
Mansfield Inns Ltd	84,551	10,959	3,894	19,675

55402 – Independent public houses and bars extract

	Wetherspoon	25th percentile	50th percentile	75th percentile	90th percentile	Number of companies
Turnover (£000)	269,699	1,811	4,328	16,888	63,252	148
Pre-tax profit	48,002	0	187	1,957	8,011	154
Pre-tax profit margin	17.80	0.00	6.17	12.71	20.23	146

25.10 World Wide Web (WWW) pages for company information[20, 21]

The WWW offers enormous opportunities to access company information and selected accounting information. A number of sources include:

CORPORATE REPORTS	http://www.corpreports.co.uk/
Companies' annual reports on line	http://www.carol.co.uk
BIZ/ED	http://bized.ac.uk
COMPANY REFS (demo)	http://www.companyrefs.com
Hemmington Scott	http://www.hemscott.com
Financial Reporting Council	http://www.frc.org.uk
Accounting Standards Board	http://www.asb.org.uk
The Financial Reporting Review Panel	http://www.frrp.org.uk

Some good link pages (for other accounting sites) include:

ICAEW	http://www.icaew.co.uk
IASC	http://www.iasc.org.uk
British Accounting Association	http://www.shef.ac.uk/~baa
European Accounting Association	http://www.bham.ac.uk/EAA/

Accounting Firms:	
Deloitte & Touche	http://www.deloitte.co.uk
Ernst & Young	http://www.ernsty.co.uk
KPMG	http://www.kpmg.com
PriceWaterhouseCoopers	http://www.pwcglobal.com

25.11 Non-financial ratios

As well as some of the more traditional financial statistics, each industry will have important operational statistics which provide some clues to the direction a company is moving and its performance in its area of expertise. For instance, BT provides information which charts the changes in technology (from the BT Annual Report and Accounts 2001):

BT Cellnet	1997	1998	1999	2000	2001
Digital GSM ('000)	1,125	2,303	4,163	7,249	11,162
Analogue ('000)	1,573	774	359	155	–
% growth over previous year	12.9	14.0	47.0	63.7	50.8

Optical fibre					
Kilometres in the network ('000)	1997	1998	1999	2000	2001
Fibre	3,302	3,591	4,058	4,555	5,100

25.12 Interpretation of problems when using consolidated financial statements

Certain limitations need to be recognised when analysing a consolidated balance sheet, making inter-company comparisons and forming a judgement on distributable profits based on the consolidated profit and loss account. These are as follows:

- The consolidated balance sheet aggregates the assets and liabilities of the parent company and its subsidiaries. The current and liquidity ratios that are extracted to indicate to creditors the security of their credit and the likelihood of the debt being settled will be valid only if all creditors have equal rights to claim against the aggregated assets. This may be the case if there are cross-guarantees from each company, but it is more likely that the creditors will need to seek payment from the individual group company to which it allowed the credit. One needs to be aware that the consolidated accounts are prepared for the shareholders of the parent company and that they may be irrelevant to the needs of creditors. This is not a criticism of consolidation, merely a recognition of the purpose for which they are relevant.

- Inter-company comparisons may be invalidated if groups follow different accounting policies in relation to the choice of consolidation process. For example, one group might organise a combination to fall within the criteria for treatment as a merger, without goodwill and using book values for the aggregation; another group might organise the combination to be treated as an acquisition, with goodwill arising on consolidation and fair values used for the aggregation.

- The consolidated profit and loss account does not give a true picture of the profits immediately available for distribution by the holding company to its shareholders. It shows the group profit that could become available for distribution if the holding company were to exercise its influence and control, and require all its subsidiary companies and associated companies to declare a dividend of 100% of their profits for the year. Legally, it is possible for the company to exercise its voting power to achieve the passing up to it of the subsidiary companies' profits – although commercially this is highly unlikely. The position of the associated companies is less clear: the holding company only has influence and does not have the voting power to guarantee that the profit disclosed in the consolidated profit and loss account is translated into dividends for the holding company shareholders.

Summary

Financial ratio analysis is integral to the assessment and improvement of company performance. Financial ratios help to direct attention to the areas of the business that need additional analysis. In particular, they provide some measure of the profitability and cash position of a company.

Financial ratios can be compared against preceding period's ratios, budgeted ratios for the current period, ratios of other companies in the same industry and the industry sector averages. This comparison is meaningful and decision-useful only when like is compared with like. Users of financial ratios must ensure that the composition of ratios is clearly defined and agreed.

Unfortunately, many of the problems that arise are not simply problems of different definitions for ratios, but far more fundamental. They result from the lack of uniformity and comparability of published financial statements.

Ratios are useful only if they are used properly. They are a starting point for further investigations and should be used in conjunction with other sources of information and other analytical techniques. Financial reports are only one of many sources of information available about an enterprise; others include international, national and industrial statistics and projections, trade association reports, market and consumer surveys, and reports prepared by professional analysts.

In Chapter 26 we consider some additional techniques that complement the pyramid approach to ratio analysis.

REVIEW QUESTIONS

1 Explain how the reader of an annual report prepared for a group might become aware if any subsidiary or associated company was experiencing:

(a) solvency problems;

(b) profitability problems.[22]

2 Using the segmental analysis from the Bass plc 1999 accounts in section 25.7.2, discuss the following:

(a) Explain the value of the segmental analysis to an existing shareholder, a potential shareholder and a creditor of the company.

(b) Which is the most profitable business segment?

(c) What further segmental information would it be useful for a shareholder to receive in the Operating and Financial Review?

(d) How subjective are the figures for turnover and profit?

(e) How useful do you consider the separate disclosure of business and geographic segment information?

3 'The problems of using ratio analysis on a set of published accounts exceed the benefits to be gained.' Discuss.

4 (a) Explain the uses and limitations of ratio analysis when used to interpret the published financial accounts of a company.

(b) State and express two ratios that can be used to analyse each of the following:

(i) profitability;
(ii) liquidity;
(iii) management control.

(c) Explain briefly points which are important when using ratios to interpret accounts under each of the headings in (b) above.

5 (a) Describe the current requirements for the disclosure of segmental information in the annual report.

(b) Discuss the advantages and disadvantages to the users and preparers of annual reports of disclosing segmental data classified by (i) industry groupings, (ii) legal entities within the group structure.

(c) Discuss the importance of the disclosure of exceptional items to the users of the annual report in addition to the operating profit.

6 'Unregulated segmental reporting is commercially dangerous to companies making disclosures.'[23] Discuss.

EXERCISES

An outline solution is provided in the appendix at the end of the text for exercises marked with an asterisk (*).

Question 1

Saddam Ltd is considering the possibility of diversifying its operations and has identified three firms in the same industrial sector as potential takeover targets. The following information in respect of the companies has been extracted from their most recent financial statements.

	Ali Ltd	Baba Ltd	Camel Ltd
ROCE before tax %	22.1	23.7	25.0
Net profit %	12.0	12.5	3.75
Asset turnover ratio	1.45	1.16	3.73
Gross profit %	20.0	25.0	10.0
Sales/fixed assets	4.8	2.2	11.6
Sales/current assets	2.1	5.2	5.5
Current ratio	3.75	1.4	1.5
Acid test ratio	2.25	0.4	0.9
Average number of weeks debtors outstanding	5.6	6.0	4.8
Average number of weeks' stock held	12.0	19.2	4.0
Ordinary dividend %	10.0	15.0	30.0
Dividend cover	4.3	5.0	1.0

Required:
(a) **Prepare a report for the directors of Saddam Ltd, assessing the performance of the three companies from the information provided and identifying areas which you consider require further investigation before a final decision is made.**
(b) **Discuss briefly why a firm's balance sheet is unlikely to show the true market value of the business.**

* Question 2

The major shareholder/director of Esrever Ltd has obtained average data for the industry as a whole. He wishes to see what the forecast results and position of Esrever Ltd would be if in the ensuing year its performance were to coincide with the industry averages.

At 1 July 20X0, actual figures for Esrever Ltd included:

	£
Land and buildings (at written-down value)	132,000
Fixtures, fittings and equipment (at written-down value)	96,750
Stock	22,040
12% loan (repayable in 20X5)	50,000
Ordinary share capital (50p shares)	100,000

For the year ended 30 June 20X1 the following forecast information is available:

1 Depreciation of fixed assets (on reducing balance)

Land and buildings	2%
Fixtures, fittings and equipment	20%

2 Net current assets will be financed by a bank overdraft to the extent necessary.

3 At 30 June 20X0 total assets minus current liabilities will be £231,808.

4 Profit after tax for the year will be 23.32% of gross profit and 11.16% of total assets minus all external liabilities, both long-term and short-term.

5 Corporation tax will be an effective rate of 20% of profit before tax.

6 Cost of sales will be 68% of turnover (excluding VAT).

7 Closing stock will represent 61.9 days' average cost of sales (excluding VAT).

8 Any difference between total expenses and the aggregate of expenses ascertained from this given information will represent credit purchases and other credit expenses, in each case excluding VAT input tax.

9 A dividend of 2.5p per share will be proposed.

10 The collection period for the VAT-exclusive amount of trade debtors will be an average of 42.6 days of the annual turnover. All the company's supplies are subject to VAT output tax at 15%.

11 The payment period for the VAT-exclusive amount of trade creditors (purchases and other credit expenses) will be an average of 29.7 days. All these items are subject to (reclaimable) VAT input tax at 15%.

12 Creditors, other than trade creditors, will comprise corporation tax due, proposed dividends and VAT payable equal to one-quarter of the net amount due for the year.

13 Calculations are based on a year of 365 days.

Required:
Construct a forecast profit and loss account for Esrever Ltd for the year ended 30 June 20X1 and a forecast balance sheet at that date in as much detail as possible. (All calculations should be made to the nearest £1.)

* Question 3

Amalgamated Engineering plc makes specialised machinery for several industries. In recent years, the company has faced severe competition from overseas businesses, and its sales volume has hardly changed. The company has recently applied for an increase in its bank overdraft limit from £750,000 to £1,500,000. The bank manager has asked you, as the bank's credit analyst, to look at the company's application.

You have the following information:

(i) Balance sheets as at 31 December 20X5 and 20X6:

	20X5		20X6	
	£000	£000	£000	£000
Tangible fixed assets				
Freehold land and buildings, at cost		1,800		1,800
Plant and equipment, at net value		3,150		3,300
		4,950		5,100
Current assets				
Stock and work in progress	1,125		1,500	
Trade debtors	825		1,125	
Short-term investments	300		—	
	2,250		2,625	
Current liabilities				
Bank overdraft	225		675	
Trade creditors	300		375	
Taxation payable	375		300	
Dividends payable	225		225	
	1,125		1,575	
Net current assets		1,125		1,050
		6,075		6,150
Long-term liability				
8% Debentures, 20X9		1,500		1,500
		4,575		4,650
Capital and reserves				
Ordinary shares of £1 each		2,250		2,250
Share premium account		750		750
Profit and loss account		1,575		1,650
		4,575		4,650

(ii) Profit and loss accounts for the years ended 31 December 20X5 and 20X6:

	20X5		20X6	
	£000	£000	£000	£000
Turnover		6,300		6,600
Cost of sales: materials	1,500		1,575	
: labour	2,160		2,280	
: production				
: overheads	750		825	
		4,410		4,680
		1,890		1,920
Administrative expenses		1,020		1,125
Operating profit		870		795
Investment income		15		—
		885		795

	20X5		20X6	
	£000	£000	£000	£000
Interest payable: debentures	120		120	
: bank overdraft	15		75	
		135		195
Profit before taxation		750		600
Taxation		375		300
Profit attributable to shareholders		375		300
Dividends		225		225
Retained earnings for year		150		75

You are also provided with the following information:

(iii) The general price level rose on average by 10% between 20X5 and 20X6. Average wages also rose by 10% during this period.

(iv) The debenture stock is secured by a fixed charge over the freehold land and buildings, which have recently been valued at £3,000,000. The bank overdraft is unsecured.

(v) Additions to plant and equipment in 20X6 amounted to £450,000: depreciation provided in that year was £300,000.

Required:
(a) Prepare a cash flow statement for the year ended 31 December 20X6.
(b) Calculate appropriate ratios to use as a basis for a report to the bank manager.
(c) Draft the outline of a report for the bank manager, highlighting key areas you feel should be the subject of further investigation. Mention any additional information you need, and where appropriate refer to the limitations of conventional historical cost accounts.
(d) On receiving the draft report the bank manager advised that he also required the following three cash-based ratios:
    (i) Debt service coverage ratio defined as EBITDA/annual debt repayments and interest.
    (ii) Cash flow from operations to current liabilities.
    (iii) Cash recovery rate defined as ((cash flow from operations + proceeds from sale of fixed assets)/average gross assets)×100
    The director has asked you to explain why the bank manager has requested this additional information given that he has already been supplied with profit-based ratios.

Question 4

Sally Gorden seeks your assistance to decide whether she should invest in Ruby plc or Sapphire plc. Both companies are quoted on the London Stock Exchange. Their shares were listed on 20 June 20X4 as Ruby 475p and Sapphire 480p.

The performance of these two companies during the year ended 30 June 20X4 is summarised as follows:

	Ruby plc £000	Sapphire plc £000
Operating profit	588	445
Interest and similar charges	(144)	(60)
	444	385
Taxation	(164)	(145)
Profit after taxation	280	240
Interim dividend paid	(30)	(40)
Preference dividend proposed	(90)	—
Ordinary dividend proposed	(60)	(120)
Retained profit for the year	100	80

The companies have been financed on 30 June 20X4 as follows:

	Ruby plc £000	Sapphire plc £000
Ordinary shares of 50p each	1,000	1,500
15% Preference shares of £1 each	600	—
Share premium account	60	—
Profit and loss account balance	250	450
17% Debentures	800	—
12% Debentures	—	500
	2,710	2,450

On 1 October 20X3 Ruby plc issued 500,000 ordinary shares of 50p each at a premium of 20%. On 1 April 20X4 Sapphire plc made a 1 for 2 bonus issue. Apart from these, there has been no change in the issued capital of either company during the year.

Required:
(a) Calculate the earnings per share (EPS) of each company.
(b) Determine the price/earnings ratio (PE) of each company.
(c) Based on the PE ratio alone, which company's shares would you recommend to Sally?
(d) On the basis of appropriate accounting ratios (which should be calculated), identify three other matters Sally should take account of before she makes her choice.
(e) Describe the advantages and disadvantages of gearing.

Question 5

Segmental Reporting

Briefly state:
(i) the case for segmental reporting;
(ii) the case against segmental reporting.

Question 6

Filios Products plc brews beers, owns and manages pubs and hotels, manufactures and supplies alcoholic and soft drinks, and is a supplier and operator of amusement machines and other leisure facilities.

The accounts for 1997 contain the following information:

Balance Sheet of Filios Products

	£m
Fixed assets at book value	1,663
Current assets	
Stocks and debtors	381
Bank balance	128
	509
Less: Creditors falling due within one year	193
Net current assets	316
Total assets less current liabilities	1,979
Less: 10% debentures	140
	1,839
Capital and reserves	
Share capital	800
Retained profit	1,039
	1,839

Profit and Loss Account of Filios Products

	£m	£m
Turnover		1,028
Less: Cost of sales	684	
Administration expenses	110	
Distribution costs	101	
Interest charged	14	909
Net profit		119

The following breakdown is provided of the company's results into three divisions and head office:

	Beer and pub operations	Hotel business	Other drinks & leisure	Head office
	£m	£m	£m	£m
Turnover	508	152	368	—
Cost of sales	316	81	287	—
Administration expenses	43	14	38	15
Distribution costs	64	12	25	—
Interest charged	10	—	—	4
Fixed assets at book value	890	332	364	77
Stocks and debtors	230	84	67	—

Bank balance	73	15	28	12
Creditors	66	40	56	31
10% debentures	100	—	—	40

The following information is obtained for competitor companies: Dean, which brews beer and manages pubs; and Clarke, which is in the hotel business:

	Dean	Clarke
	£m	£m
Turnover	600	150
Operating profit	80	60
Net assets	1,300	300

Required:

(a) Outline the nature of segmental reports and explain the reason for presenting such information in the published accounts.

(b) Prepare a segmental statement for Filios Products plc for 1997 complying, so far as the information permits, with the provisions of SSAP 25 entitled 'Segmental Reporting', so as to show for each segment and the business as a whole:
   – turnover;
   – profit;
   – net assets.

(c) (i) Examine the relative performance of the operating divisions of Filios Products; and
   (ii) Compare the performance of the operating divisions of Filios Products, where appropriate, with that of the competitor companies.

   The examination and comparison should be based on the following accounting ratios:
   – operating profit percentage;
   – net asset turnover;
   – return on net assets.

(The Chartered Institute of Bankers)

Question 7

The Housing Department of Chaldon District Council has invited tenders for re-roofing 80 houses on an estate. Chaldon Direct Services (CDS) is one of the Council's direct services organisations and it has submitted a tender for this contract, as have several contractors from the private sector.

The Council has been able to narrow the choice of contractor to the four tenderers who have submitted the lowest bids, as follows:

	£
Nutfield & Sons	398,600
Chaldon Direct Services	401,850
Tandridge Tilers Ltd	402,300
Redhill Roofing Contractors plc	406,500

The tender evaluation process requires that the three private tenderers be appraised on the basis of financial soundness and quality of work. These tenderers were required to provide their latest final accounts (year ended 31 March 20X4) for this appraisal; details are as follows:

	Nutfield & Sons	Tandridge Tilers Ltd	Redhill Roofing Contractors plc
Profit and loss account for year ended 31 March 20X4			
	£	£	£
Turnover	611,600	1,741,200	3,080,400
Direct costs	(410,000)	(1,190,600)	(1,734,800)
Other operating costs	(165,000)	(211,800)	(811,200)
Interest	—	(85,000)	(96,000)
Net profit before taxation	36,600	253,800	438,400
Balance sheet as at 31 March 20X4			
	£	£	£
Fixed assets (net book value)	55,400	1,542,400	2,906,800
Stocks and work in progress	26,700	149,000	449,200
Debtors	69,300	130,800	240,600
Bank	(11,000)	10,400	(6,200)
Creditors	(92,600)	(140,600)	(279,600)
Proposed dividend	—	(91,800)	(70,000)
Loan	—	(800,000)	(1,200,000)
	47,800	800,200	2,040,800
Capital	47,800	—	—
Ordinary shares @ £1 each	—	250,000	1,000,000
Reserves	—	550,200	1,040,800
	47,800	800,200	2,040,800

Nutfield and Sons employ a workforce of six operatives and have been used by the Council for four small maintenance contracts worth between £60,000 and £75,000 which they have completed to an appropriate standard. Tandridge Tilers Ltd have been employed by the Council on a contract for the replacement of flat roofs on block of flats, but there have been numerous complaints about the standard of the work. Redhill Roofing Contractors plc is a company which has not been employed by the Council in the past and, as much of its work has been carried out elsewhere, its quality of work is not known.

CDS has been suffering from the effects of increasing competition in recent years and achieved a return on capital employed of only 3.5% in the previous financial year. CDS's manager has successfully renegotiated more beneficial service level agreements with the Council's central support departments with effect from 1 April 20X4. CDS has also reviewed its fixed asset base which has resulted in the disposal of a depot which was surplus to requirements and in the rationalisation of vehicles and plant. The consequence of this is that CDS's average capital employed for 20X4/X5 is likely to be some 15% lower than in 20X3/X4.

A further analysis of the tender bids is provided below:

	Nutfield & Sons £	Chaldon Direct Services £	Tandridge Tilers Ltd £	Redhill Roofing Contractors plc £
Labour	234,000	251,400	303,600	230,400
Materials	140,000	100,000	80,000	140,000
Overheads (including profit)	24,600	50,450	18,700	36,100

The Council's Client Services Committee can reject tenders on financial and/or quality grounds. However, each tender has to be appraised on these criteria and reasons for acceptance or rejection must be justified in the appraisal process.

Required:

In your capacity as accountant responsible for reporting to the Client Services Committee, draft a report to the Committee evaluating the tender bids and recommending to whom the contract should be awarded.

(CIPFA)

Question 8

Chelsea plc has embarked on a programme of growth through acquisitions and has identified Kensington Ltd and Wimbledon Ltd as companies in the same industrial sector, as potential targets. Using recent financial statements of both Kensington and Wimbledon and further information obtained from a trade association, Chelsea plc has managed to build up the following comparability table:

	Kensington	Wimbledon	Industrial average
Profitability ratios			
ROCE before tax %	22	28	20
Return on Equity %	18	22	15
Net profit margin %	11	5	7
Gross profit ratio %	25	12	20
Activity ratios			
Total assets turnover = times	1.5	4.0	2.5
Fixed asset turnover = times	2.3	12.0	5.1
Debtor collection period in weeks	8.0	5.1	6.5
Stockholding period in weeks	21.0	4.0	13.0
Liquidity ratios			
Current ratio	1.8	1.7	2.8
Acid test	0.5	0.9	1.3
Debt/Equity ratio %	80.0	20.0	65.0

Required:

(a) Prepare a performance report for the two companies for consideration by the directors of Chelsea plc indicating which of the two companies you consider to be a better acquisition.

(b) Indicate what further information is needed before a final decision can be made.

Question 9

'The consolidation of financial statements hides rather than provides information.'

Required:

Discuss the above statement.

Question 10

Required:

Analyse the 1999 Accounts of J D Wetherspoon below:

JD Wetherspoon consolidated profit and loss account for the year ended 1 August 1999

	1999 Before exceptional items £000	1999 exceptional items £000	1999 After exceptional items £000	1998 Before exceptional items £000	1998 exceptional items £000	1998 After exceptional items £000
Turnover from continuing operations	269,699		269,699	188,515		188,515
Cost of sales	−219,035	0	−219,035	−149,317	0	−149,317
Gross profit	50,664	0	50,664	39,198	0	39,198
Administrative expenses	−14,438	−837	−15,275	−10,831	0	−10,831
Operating profit	36,226	−837	35,389	28,367	0	28,367
Profit on disposal of tangible fixed assets	0	22,625	22,625	0	14,968	14,968
Net interest payable	−10,012	0	−10,012	−8,202	0	−8,202
Profit on ordinary activities before tax	26,214	21,788	48,002	20,165	14,968	35,133
Tax on profit on ordinary activities	−751	0	−751	−726	0	−726
Profit on ordinary activities after tax	25,463	21,788	47,251	19,439	14,968	34,407
Dividends	−4,809	0	−4,809	−4,321	0	−4,321
Retained profit for the year	20,654	21,788	42,442	15,118	14,968	30,086

JD Weatherspoon balance sheet as at 1 August 1999

	1999 £000	1998 £000
Fixed assets		
Tangible assets	370,148	334,695
	370,148	334,695
Current assets		
Investments	253	286
Stock	3,845	3,195
Debtors due within 1 year	11,472	11,385
Debtors due after more than 1 year	5,588	0
Cash	62,578	12,750
	83,736	27,616
Creditors due within 1 year	−67,296	−62,564
Net current assets/(liabilities)	16,440	−34,948
Total assets less current liabilities	386,588	299,747
Creditors due after 1 year	−180,592	−140,555
Total net assets	205,996	159,192
Capital and reserves		
Called-up share capital	3,962	3,931
Share premium account	65,463	62,000
Revaluation reserve	25,166	22,843
Profit and loss account	111,405	70,418
Equity shareholders' funds	205,996	159,192

References

1 I. Griffiths, *Creative Accounting*, Sidgwick & Jackson, 1986.
2 M. Stead, *How to Use Company Accounts for Successful Investment Decisions*, FT Pitman Publishing, 1995, pp. 134–136.
3 'Brought to account: Richard Pennycook, Finance Director, J D Wetherspoon', *Accountancy*, July 1996, p. 58.
4 N. Cope, 'Bitter battles in the beer business', *Accountancy*, May 1993, p. 32.
5 D. Chopping, R. Carroll and R. Skerratt, *Applying GAAP*, ICAEW, 1999/2000, p. 100.
6 Neil Garrod, *Competitive Disadvantage and Segmental Disclosure*, Working Paper 2000/5, University of Glasgow.
7 SSAP 25, *Segmental Reporting*, ASC, June 1990.
8 S. Hussain, 'What do segmental definitions tell us?' *Accountancy*, June 1996, p. 103.
9 C. Emmanuel and N. Garrod, 'Segmental reporting in the UK – how does SSAP 25 stand up to international comparison?' *European Accounting Review*, vol. 3, no. 3, 1994, pp. 547–562.
10 M. Davies, R. Patterson and A. Wilson, *UK GAAP*, Ernst & Young (5th edition), 1997, p. 1079.
11 IAS 14 (revised), *Reporting Financial Information by Segment*, IASC, July 1997.
12 IAS 14, *Reporting Financial Information by Segment*, IASC, 1981.
13 ED 45, *Segmental Reporting*, ASC, November 1988.
14 C.R. Emmanuel and M. Mehafdi, *Transfer Pricing*, The Chartered Institute of Management Accountants and Academic Press, London, 1994.
15 *Company REFS – Really Essential Statistics*: Tables Volume devised by Jim Slater, Hemmington Scott Publication.
16 *Handbook of Market Leaders*, Extel Financial Ltd.
17 *Key Business Ratios: The Guide to British Business Performance*, Dun & Bradstreet Ltd.
18 *The Company Guide*, Hemmington Scott Publishing.
19 http://www.onesource.co.uk.
20 L. Meall and T. Reardon, 'Surfing for Beginners', *Accountancy*, January 1998, pp. 63–67.
21 A.M. Lymer, A. Sangster and A.A. Baldwin, 'Using the World Wide Web in accounting research: a huge step forward or a new constraint?' *British Accounting Review*, 29, pp. 395–407.
22 P. Anderson, 'Are you ready for ratio analysis?' *Accountancy*, September 1996, p. 92.
23 G.J. Kelly, 'Unregulated segment reporting: Australian evidence', *British Accounting Review*, 26(3), 1994, p. 217.

CHAPTER 26

Trend analysis and multivariate analysis

26.1 Introduction

In the preceding chapter we introduced ratio analysis as a means for interpreting financial statements. In this chapter we present further techniques that can be used in conjunction with ratio analysis. The main similarity between these techniques is their purpose: each technique acts as a focus for more detailed investigation. By various means, they can be applied to a set of financial statements to identify areas of interest and concern. If the initial investigation throws up unexpected and unexplained results, the root cause should then be ascertained by more rigorous investigation.

In this chapter we consider the following:

- Horizontal analysis between two periods
- Trend analysis over a series of periods
- Historical summaries
- Vertical analysis – common size statements
- Multivariate analysis – Z-scores
- A-scores
- H-scores
- Balanced scorecards
- Valuing shares of an unquoted company – quantitative process
- Valuing shares of an unquoted company – qualitative process
- Shareholder value analysis
- Financial reporting and risk

We will illustrate the techniques using the accounts of J D Wetherspoon plc, which were used in the preceding chapter to demonstrate ratio analysis.

26.2 Horizontal analysis between two periods

The mechanics of horizontal analysis between two periods are very simple. The percentage change (positive or negative) for each item in the financial statements between two periods needs to be calculated. Usually, the percentage changes are calculated for all balance sheet items and profit and loss items over two successive years.

Although the calculations are straightforward, the skill rests with their interpretation. What do the percentages mean? Which changes are significant and warrant detailed analysis? Which changes require an explanation so that we can determine whether or not we need to implement rectifying measures?

The percentage changes between J D Wetherspoon plc's 1996 and 1997 consolidated profit and loss accounts are calculated below.

	% change	1997 £000	1996 £000
Turnover from continuing operations	38.8%	139,444	100,480
Cost of sales	40.8%	(106,972)	(76,001)
Gross profit	32.7%	32,472	24,479
Administrative expenses	27.5%	(9,533)	(7,476)
Operating profit	34.9%	22,939	17,003
Net interest payable	37.8%	(5,373)	(3,898)
Profit on ordinary activities before tax	34.0%	17,566	13,105
Tax on profit on ordinary activities	36.5%	(770)	(564)
Profit on ordinary activities after tax	33.9%	16,796	12,541
Dividends	14.0%	(3,894)	(3,417)
Retained profit for the year	41.4%	12,902	9,124

The profile of the profit and loss accounts for both years is very similar. The turnover has increased by 38.8%, but most of the other items have also increased by around 30–40%. The obvious exception to this is the low growth in dividends (14%), which is consistent with the company's expansion plans, and the subsequent increase in retained profit (41.4%).

26.3 Trend analysis over a series of periods

Trend analysis is used to analyse company accounts over a series of years. It is usually applied to five-year or ten-year summaries supplied in company accounts. The main advantage of this technique is that it gives a very quick rough guide to specific trends in individual items in the financial statements. The main disadvantage is that the figures may ignore the effects of inflation and not represent company performance in real terms. An easy way to take some account of inflation is to use the retail price index (RPI) as a proxy for inflation and adjust calculated trends for the trend in RPI.

The two forms of trend analysis considered here are percentage changes and index numbers.

Percentage changes illustrate the change each year and show the exact trend in percentage changes. For instance, Jacklin Cripes plc records the following profits in the five-year record:

	20X1 £000	20X2 £000	20X3 £000	20X4 £000	20X5 £000
Net profit	150	195	249	309	375
% change		+30.0%	+27.7%	+24.1%	+21.4%

The percentage changes show that the net profit for Jacklin Cripes plc has increased every year between 20X1 and 20X5. However, the rate of increase in net profit has decreased. The increase is 30% in 20X2, but only 21.4% in 20X5.

Index numbers give a good indication of how the results over a series of years compare with each other, and the general direction of the trend. To calculate index numbers, year 1 in the series is set to 100 and the other years are scaled down to correspond to the index number. To demonstrate this, consider Jacklin Cripes plc:

	20X1 £000	20X2 £000	20X3 £000	20X4 £000	20X5 £000
Net profit	150	195	249	309	375
Index number	100	130	166	206	250

where index (20X2) = 195/150 × 100 = 130
where index (20X3) = 249/150 × 100 = 166
where index (20X4) = 309/150 × 100 = 206
where index (20X5) = 375/150 × 100 = 250

The index numbers show that net profit increases every year over this period.

Now consider the trends in the five-year record for J D Wetherspoon plc (Figure 26.1). Both the percentage changes and the index numbers show that J D Wetherspoon's turnover, operating profit and retained profit have increased significantly each year from 1993 to 1997.

26.4 Historical summaries

The Companies Act 1985 does not require a company to include a historical summary in its annual report. However, following a comment by the chairman of the Stock Exchange, the practice has arisen for companies to include a five-year historical summary.

Figure 26.1 J D Wetherspoon's five-year record

	1993 £000	1994 £000	1995 £000	1996 £000	1997 £000
Turnover	30,800	46,600	68,536	100,480	139,444
Operating profit	6,115	8,787	12,232	17,003	22,939
Retained profit	2,176	3,680	6,031	9,124	12,902
a) *Percentage changes*	*1993*	*1994*	*1995*	*1996*	*1997*
Turnover		+51.3%	+47.1%	+46.6%	+38.8%
Operating profit		+43.7%	+39.2%	+39.0%	+34.9%
Retained profit		+69.1%	+63.9%	+51.3%	+41.4%
b) *Index number*	*1993*	*1994*	*1995*	*1996*	*1997*
Turnover	100	151	222	326	452
Operating profit	100	144	200	278	375
Retained profit	100	169	277	419	593

There is no accounting standard relating to such summaries, but there may well be circumstances where the reported figures need to be adjusted to make the series comparable: for example, a change in accounting policy; a change in the composition of the group; bonus issues, rights issues and share splits. In the ASC handbook *Accounting for the Effects of Changing Prices*, it was recommended that companies which publish historical summaries should restate certain figures such as turnover, earnings and dividends in units of current purchasing power.[1]

The following extract from the 2000 Annual Report of a South African company, Barloworld, considers inflation in relation to earnings and dividends per share:

Inflation adjusted information

	2000	1999
South African consumer price index (base 1994 = 100)	145.6	138.2
Deflation factor	*68.7*	*72.4*
Earnings per share (cents)	380.4	285.8
EPS deflated	*261.3*	*206.8*
Dividends per share (cents)	180.0	141.0
Dividend deflated	*123.7*	*102.0*
Total assets	16550	14951
Total assets deflated	*11369*	*10820*

Historical summaries should assist shareholders to answer such questions as: Is growth being achieved in excess of the rate of inflation? Is the growth in all segments of the business? What is the dividend cover over the past five years? Is the change in turnover and profitability constant or fluctuating?

Given the usefulness of the historical summaries, this is an area that requires a standard approach of the kind provided by SSAP 25 for segmental reporting. Without such a standard, the information may be unavailable or partially presented, e.g. it may disclose profit and loss data, but no balance sheet data to assess the rate of change in assets and rates of return.

26.5 Vertical analysis – common size statements

Vertical analysis concentrates solely on one year's financial statements, rather than comparing a number of years. Common size statements express all items in each financial statement as a percentage of a selected figure. For instance, all items in the profit and loss account can be expressed in terms of turnover; and all items in the balance sheet can be expressed in terms of capital employed or total shareholders' funds.

The advantages of vertical analysis are as follows:

● Common size statements allow comparisons between companies of different sizes. However, like ratio analysis, particular care should be taken to ensure the comparison of like companies with like.

● The balance sheet will identify changes in financial structure relative to the total capital employed or total shareholders' funds. The profit and loss account will identify changes in expenses relative to turnover.

● As all figures are expressed as annual percentages, this will redress many of the distortions of inflation. However, different financial statement items might be affected by different specific rates of inflation.

The disadvantages are as follows:

- Accounting policies might distort changes in financial structure and expenditure.
- Common size statements eliminate the concept of different-sized companies so that comparison is possible. However, the actual size of a company determines the specific risks to which the company is subject.

To illustrate common size statements, the 1997 balance sheet and profit and loss accounts for J D Wetherspoon plc are analysed below. The balance sheet expresses all items in terms of shareholders' funds, while the profit and loss account expresses all items in terms of turnover.

Wetherspoon (JD)
Consolidated profit and loss account for the year ended 31 July 1997

	1997 £000	Calculations	%
Turnover from continuing operations	139,444	139,444/139,444	100
Cost of sales	(106,972)	(106,972)/139,444	(76.7)
Gross profit	32,472	32,472/139,444	23.3
Administrative expenses	(9,533)	(9,533)/139,444	(6.8)
Operating profit	22,939	22,939/139,444	16.5
Net interest payable	(5,373)	(5,373)/139,444	(3.9)
Profit on ordinary activities before tax	17,566	17,566/139,444	12.6
Tax on profit on ordinary activities	(770)	(770)/139,444	(0.6)
Profit on ordinary activities after tax	16,796	16,796/139,444	12.0
Dividends	(3,894)	(3,894)/139,444	(2.8)
Retained profit for the year	12,902	12,902/139,444	9.2

Balance sheet at 31 July 1997

	1997 £000	Calculations	%
Fixed assets			
Tangible assets	244,513	244,513/124,663	196.1
	244,513	244,513/124,663	196.1
Current assets			
Stocks	2,215	2,215/124,663	1.8
Debtors	3,026	3,026/124,663	2.4
Cash	7,196	7,196/124,663	5.8
	12,437	12,437/124,663	10.0
Creditors due within one year	(34,998)	(34,998)/124,663	(28.1)
Net current liabilities	(22,561)	(22,561)/124,663	(18.1)
Total assets less current liabilities	221,952	221,952/124,663	178.0
Creditors due after one year	(97,289)	(97,289)/124,663	(78.0)
	124,663	124,663/124,663	100

Capital and reserves			
Called up share capital	3,898	3,898/124,663	3.1
Share premium account	59,676	59,676/124,663	47.9
Revaluation reserve	22,023	22,023/124,663	17.7
Profit and loss account	39,066	39,066/124,663	31.3
Equity shareholders' funds	124,663	124,663/124,663	100

Another strength of common size statements is to identify their trends over time. In effect, this applies horizontal analysis to vertical analysis, analysing the changes in financial structure and cost structure over time. To examine the technique, we compare the 1996 and 1997 common size statements for J D Wetherspoon's profit and loss account.

	1997 %	1996 %
Turnover from continuing operations	100	100
Cost of sales	(76.7)	(75.6)
Gross profit	23.3	24.4
Administrative expenses	(6.8)	(7.4)
Operating profit	16.5	16.9
Net interest payable	(3.9)	(3.9)
Profit on ordinary activities before tax	12.6	13.0
Tax on profit on ordinary activities	(0.6)	(0.5)
Profit on ordinary activities after tax	12.0	12.5
Dividends	(2.8)	(3.4)
Retained profit for the year	9.2	9.1

What are the main questions which arise from these two common size statements? Some of the issues were identified also in the previous chapter using other analytical methods. All the ratios are expressed as a proportion of sales:

- The gross profit and operating profit in 1997 have decreased. However, the administrative expenses have improved from 7.4% to 6.8%.
- The dividend distribution has decreased.
- The retained profit is very similar for 1996 and 1997.

26.6 Multivariate analysis – Z-scores

In the preceding chapter we extolled the virtues of ratio analysis for the interpretation of financial statements. However, ratio analysis is an excellent indicator only when applied properly. Unfortunately, a number of limitations impede its proper application. How do we know which ratios to select for the analysis of company accounts? Which ratios can be combined to produce an informative end-result? How should individual ratios be ranked to give the user an overall picture of company performance? How reliable are all the ratios – can users place more reliance on some ratios than others?

Z-score analysis can be employed to overcome some of the limitations of traditional ratio analysis. It evaluates corporate stability and, more importantly, predicts potential instances of corporate failure. All the forecasts and predictions are based on publicly available financial statements.[2] The aim is to identify potential failures so that 'the appropriate action to reverse the process [of failure] can be taken before it is too late'.[3]

26.6.1 What are Z-scores?

Inman describes what Z-scores are designed for:

> Z-scores attempt to replace various independent and often unreliable and misleading historical ratios and subjective rule-of-thumb tests with scientifically analysed ratios which can reliably predict future events by identifying bench marks above which 'all's well' and below which there is imminent danger.[4]

Z-scores provide a single-value score to describe the combination of a number of key characteristics of a company. Some of the most important predictive ratios are weighted according to perceived importance and then summed to give the single Z-score. This is then evaluated against the identified benchmark.

The two best known Z-scores are: Altman's Z-score and Taffler's Z-score.

Altman's Z-score

The original Z-score equation was devised by Professor Altman in 1968 and developed further in 1977.[5] The original equation is:

$$Z = 0.012X_1 + 0.014X_2 + 0.033X_3 + 0.006X_4 + 0.999X_5$$

where

X_1 = Working capital/Total assets
X_2 = Retained earnings/Total assets
X_3 = Earnings before interest and tax/Total assets
X_4 = Market capitalisation/Book value of debt
X_5 = Sales/Total assets

Altman identified two benchmarks. Companies scoring over 3.0 are unlikely to fail and should be considered safe, while companies scoring under 1.8 are very likely to fail. The value of 3.0 has since been revised down to 2.7.[6] Z-scores between 2.7 and 1.8 fall into the grey area. The 1968 work is claimed to be able to distinguish between successes and failures up to two or three years before the event. The 1977 work claims an improved prediction period of up to five years before the event.

Taffler's Z-score

The exact definition of Taffler's Z-score[7,8] is unpublished, but the following components form the equation:

$$Z = c_0 + c_1X_1 + c_2X_2 + c_3X_3 + c_4X_4$$

where

X_1 = Profit before tax/Current assets (53%)
X_2 = Current assets/Current liabilities (13%)
X_3 = Current liabilities/Total assets (18%)
X_4 = No credit interval = Length of time which the company can continue to finance its operations using its own assets with no revenue inflow (16%)

c_0 to c_4 are the coefficients, and the percentages in brackets represent the ratios' contributions to the power of the model.

The benchmark used to detect success or failure is 0.2.[9] Companies scoring above 0.2 are unlikely to fail, while companies scoring less than 0.2 demonstrate the same symptoms as companies that have failed in the past.

PAS-score: performance analysis score

Taffler adapted the Z-score technique to develop the PAS-score. The PAS-score evaluates company performance relative to other companies in the industry and incorporates changes in the economy.

The PAS-score ranks all company Z-scores in percentile terms, measuring relative performance on a scale of 0 to 100. A PAS-score of X means that $100 - X\%$ of the companies have scored higher Z-scores. So, a PAS-score of 80 means that only 20% of the companies in the comparison have achieved higher Z-scores.

The PAS-score details the relative performance trend of a company over time. Any downward trends should be investigated immediately and the management should take appropriate action. For other danger signals see Holmes and Dunham.[10]

26.7 H-scores

An H-score is produced by Company Watch to determine overall financial health. The H-score is an enhancement of the Z-score technique in giving more emphasis to the strength of the balance sheet. The Company Watch system calculates a score ranging from 0 to 100 with below 25 being in the danger zone. It takes into account profit management, asset management and funding management using seven factors – these are profit from the profit and loss account, three factors from the asset side of the balance sheet, namely, current asset cover, stock and debtor management and liquidity and three factors from the liability side of the balance sheet, namely, equity base, debt dependence and current funding.

The factors are taken from published financial statements which makes the approach taken by the ASB to bring off-balance-sheet transactions on to the balance sheet particularly important.

A strength of the H-score is that it can be applied to all sectors (other than the financial sector) and there is clear evidence that it can predict possible failures, e.g. the model indicated that Hollas plc was at risk in 1994 and it eventually failed in 1998.

The ability to chart each factor against the sector average and to twenty-five level criteria over a five-year period means that it is valuable for a range of user needs from trade creditors considering extending or continuing to allow credit to potential lenders and equity investors and in reviewing audit risk. It appears to be a robust, useful and exciting new tool for all user groups. Further information appears on the company's website at www.companywatch.net which includes additional examples.

26.8 A-scores

A-scores concentrate on non-financial signs of failure.[11] This method sets out to quantify different judgmental factors. The whole basis of the analysis is that financial difficulties are the direct result of management defects and errors which have existed in the company for many years.

A-scores assume that many company failures can be explained by similar factors. Company failure can be broken down into a three-stage sequence of events:

1 **Defects**. Specific defects exist in company top management. Typically, these defects centre on management structure; decision-making and ability; accounting systems; and failure to respond to change.

2 **Mistakes**. Management will make mistakes that can be attributed to the company defects. The three mistakes that lead to company failure are very high leverage; overtrading; and the failure of the company's main project.

3 **Symptoms**. Finally, symptoms of failure will start to arise. These are directly attributable to preceding management mistakes. Typical symptoms are financial signs (e.g. poor ratios, poor Z-scores); creative accounting (management might attempt to 'disguise' signs of failure in the accounts); non-financial signs (e.g. investment decisions delayed; market share drops); and terminal signs (when the financial collapse of the company is imminent).

To calculate a company A-score, different scores are allocated to each defect, mistake and symptom according to their importance. Then this score is compared with the benchmark values. If companies achieve an overall score of over 25, or a defect score of over 10, or a mistakes score of over 15, then the company is demonstrating typical signs leading up to failure. Generally, companies not at risk will score below 18, and companies which are at risk will score well over 25.

The scoring system attaches a weight to individual items within defects, mistakes and symptoms. By way of illustration we set out the weights applied within defects which are as follows:

Defects in management:

	Weight
The chief executive is an autocrat	8
The chief executive is also the chairman	4
There is a passive board	2
The board is unbalanced, e.g. too many accountants	2
There is poor management depth	1

Defects in accountancy:

There are not budgets for budgetary control	3
There are no current cash flow plans	3
There is no costing system or product costs	3
There is a poor response to change, e.g. out of date plant, old-fashioned products, poor marketing	15

Consider our A-score assessment of DNB Computer Systems plc:

Defects:		
	Weak finance director	2
	Poor management depth	1
	No budgeting control	3
	No current updated cash flows	3
	No costing system	3

12

Mistakes:	Main project failure	15	
			15
Symptoms:	Financial signs – adverse Z-scores	4	
	Creative accounting – unduly low debtor provisions	4	
	High staff turnover	3	
			11
Total A-score:			38

According to our benchmarks, DNB Computer Systems plc is at risk of failure because the mistakes score is 15 and the overall A-score is 38. Therefore, there is some cause for concern, e.g. Why did the main project fail? To which of the symptoms was it due?

26.9 Accounting policies

Auditors are required to assess whether a company has any going concern problems which would indicate that it might not be able to continue trading for a further financial year. This typically requires an assessment of solvency and future cash flows. The following is an extract from the accounting policies in the 1999 Annual Report of Scoot.com plc:

Going concern

The Group incurred a loss of approximately £206m during the year ended 30 September 1999 and had net liabilities at that date of approximately £12m. The losses during that financial year were principally funded by the issue of convertible debt, in total amounting to approximately £24m, raised in various tranches as detailed in note 16.

As at 30 September 1999, the Group had net cash of approximately £12.4m. Subsequent to the year end, the Group has raised approximately £13m (before costs) from the placement of 15 million shares with Vivendi at 70p (approximately £10.5m) and the issue of further convertible debentures...

The directors have prepared projections for the foreseeable future to assess working capital requirements of the Group and, after taking into account the additional funding to be received, the directors consider it appropriate to adopt the going concern basis in preparing the financial statements.

The auditors do not refer to going concern in their audit report which indicates that they are satisfied with the company's accounting policy as stated above.

26.10 Balanced scorecards

Move away from a single performance measure

We saw in Chapter 23 that the ASB wished to move away from the EPS figure as *the* single performance measure. It did this through the FRS 3 *Reporting Financial Performance* disclosures and the *Operating and Financial Review* (OFR) document. Similarly, business is moving away from relying simply on traditional financial measures, such as the return on capital and earnings per share. These can encourage companies to achieve short-term financial results, while damaging employee morale and customer service to the extent of causing long-term damage to the organisation's profitability.[12]

Move towards different perspectives

Four perspectives are seen to affect the long-term economic value of a company.

1 **Financial perspective**. This includes consideration of factors such as the return on capital employed, cash flows, project profitability and the setting of realistic targets. For example, was the company aiming to maximise its return on capital employed or maintain a steady rate of improvement?

2 **Customer perspective**. This requires the company to set specific goals, besides price, that are important to the customer, e.g. quality, performance and service. For example, was the customer interested in the lowest price or in obtaining a regular, guaranteed supply at a reasonable price?

3 **Internal business perspective**. This includes consideration of factors such as tender success rate. For example, was the presentation and preparation effective?

4 **Innovation and learning perspective**. This includes the generation of new business from innovation, and staff attitudes and morale.

The balanced scorecard approach requires a company to focus both on hard financial targets and on important soft or non-financial factors that affect long-term profitability, and to understand the links between the different perspectives. For example, reducing staff numbers might produce an immediate improvement in the short-term financial performance as measured by ROCE and EPS, but could so adversely affect customer satisfaction and staff morale that it has a long-term adverse effect.

According to Kaplan and Norton,[13] the balanced scorecard allows managers to look at the business from four important perspectives. It provides answers to four basic questions:

● How do customers see us? (customer perspective)

● What must we excel at? (internal perspective)

● Can we continue to improve and create value? (innovation and learning perspective)

● How do we look to shareholders? (financial perspective).

There is nothing particularly new in the perspectives. Customers and staff are invariably referred to by the chairman in the annual report as important contributors to the company's success. The difference that the balanced scorecard approach makes is to raise awareness that the perspectives are interdependent and that management performance can be appraised on more than just the bottom line. Of course, the bottom line needs to be healthy for a company to be successful, but it does not exist in isolation; other important factors affect long-term health.

26.11 Valuing shares of an unquoted company – quantitative process

The valuation of shares brings together a number of different financial accounting procedures that we have covered in previous chapters. The assumptions may be highly subjective, but there is a standard approach. This involves the following:

● Estimate the maintainable income flow based on earnings defined in accordance with the IIMR Guidelines, as described in Chapter 23. Normally the profits of the past five years are used, adjusted for any known or expected future changes.

- Estimate an appropriate dividend yield, as described in Chapter 25, if valuing a minority holding; or an appropriate earnings yield if valuing a majority holding.

- Make a decision on any adjustment to the required yields. For example, the shares in the unquoted company might not be as marketable as those in the comparative quoted companies and the required yield would therefore be increased to reflect this lack of marketability; or the balance sheet might not be as strong with lower current/acid test ratios or higher gearing, which would also lead to an increase in the required yield.

- Calculate the economic capital value, as described in Chapter 3, by applying the required yield to the income flow.

- Compare the resulting value with the net realisable value (NRV), as described in Chapter 4, when deciding what action to take based on the economic value.

EXAMPLE ● The Doughnut Ltd is an unlisted company engaged in the baking of doughnuts. The balance sheet of The Doughnut Ltd as at 31 December 20X4 showed:

	£000	£000
Freehold land		100
Fixed assets at cost	240	
Accumulated depreciation	40	
		200
Current assets	80	
Current liabilities	(60)	
		20
		320
Share capital in £1 shares		300
Profit and loss account		20
		320
Estimated net realisable values:		
Freehold land		310
Fixed assets		160
Current assets		70

It achieved the following profit after tax (adjusted to reflect maintainable earnings) for the past five years ended 31 December:

	20X0	20X1	20X2	20X3	20X4
Maintainable earnings (£000)	36	40	46	38	42
Dividend payout history: Dividends	10%	10%	12%	12%	12%

Current yields for comparative quoted companies as at 31 December 20X4:

	Earnings yield %	Dividend yield %
Ace Bakers plc	14	8
Busi-Bake plc	10	8
Hard-to-beat plc	13	8

You are required to value a holding of 250,000 shares for a shareholder, Mr Quick, who makes a practice of buying shares for sale within three years.

Now, the 250,000 shares represent an 83% holding. This is a majority holding and the steps to value it are as follows:

1 Calculate average maintainable earnings (in £000):

$$\frac{36,000 + 40,000 + 46,000 + 38,000 + 42,000}{5} = £40,000$$

2 Estimate an appropriate earnings yield:

$$\frac{14\% + 10\% + 13\%}{3} = 12.3\%$$

3 Adjust the rate for lack of marketability by, say, 3% and for the lower current ratio by, say, 2%. Both these adjustments are subjective and would be a matter of negotiation between the parties.

		%
Require yield	=	12.3
Lack of marketability weighting	=	3
Balance sheet weakness	=	2
Required earnings yield		17.3

The adjustments depend on the actual circumstances. For instance, if Mr Quick were intending to hold the shares as a long-term investment, there might be no need to increase the required return for lack of marketability.

4 Calculate share value:

$$(£40,000 \times 100/17.3)/300,000 = 77\text{p}$$

5 Compare with the net realisable values on the basis that the company were to be liquidated:

		£
Net realisable values = 70,000 + 160,000 + 310,000	=	540,000
Less: Current liabilities		60,000
		480,000
Net asset value per share = £480,000/300,000	=	£1.60

The comparison indicates that, on the information we have been given, Mr Quick should acquire the shares and dispose of the assets and liquidate the company to make an immediate capital gain of 83p per share.

Let us extend our illustration by assuming that it is intended to replace the fixed assets at a cost of £20,000 per year out of retained earnings, if Mr Quick acquires the shares. Advise Mr Small, who has £10,000 to invest, how many shares he would be able to acquire in The Doughnut Ltd.

There are two significant changes: the cash available for distribution as dividends will be reduced by £20,000 per year, which is used to replace fixed assets; and Mr Small is acquiring only a minority holding, which means that the appropriate valuation method is the **dividend yield** rather than the **earnings yield**.

The share value will be calculated as follows:

1 Estimate income flow:

	£
Maintainable earnings	40,000
Less: Fixed asset investment	20,000
Cash available for distribution	20,000

Note that we are here calculating not distributable profits, but the available cash flow.

2 Required dividend yield:

	%
Average dividend yield	8
Lack of negotiability, say	2
Financial risk, say	1.5
	11.5

3 Share value:

$$\frac{£20,000}{300,000} \times \frac{100}{11.5} = 58p$$

At this price it would be possible for Mr Small to acquire ($£10,000/58p$) = 17,241 shares.

26.12 Valuing shares of an unquoted company – qualitative process

In the section above we illustrated how to value shares using the capitalisation of earnings and capitalisation of dividends methods. However, share valuation is an extremely subjective exercise: for example, when Rhône-Poulenc Rorer made a bid for Fisons in 1995 the share price moved from 193p per share to 265p, with the analysts expecting the final bid price to be between 270p and 300p. The values we have calculated for The Doughnut Ltd shares could therefore be subject to material revision in the light of other relevant factors.

A company's future cash flows may be affected by a number of factors. These may occur as a result of action within the company (e.g. management change, revenue investment) or as a result of external events (e.g. change in the rate of inflation, change in competitive pressures).

● **Management change** often heralds a significant change in a company's share price. For example, the new chief executive of Fisons made significant changes to Fisons in 1994/5 by reducing the business to its valuable core, which then saw the share price move from 103p to 193p.

● **Revenue investment** refers to discretionary revenue expenditure, such as charges to the profit and loss account for research and development, training, advertising and major maintenance and refurbishment. The ASB in its exposure draft for FRS 3 *Reporting Financial Performance* had proposed to disclose this information in the profit and loss account. The proposal did not find support at the exposure stage and it is suggested that such information should instead be disclosed in the operating and financial review, which was discussed in Section 5.9.

- **Changes in the rate of inflation** can affect the required yield. If, for example, it is expected that inflation will fall, this might mean that past percentage yields will be higher than the percentage yield that is likely to be available in the future.

- **Change in competitive pressures** can affect future sales. For example, increased foreign competition could mean that past maintainable earnings are not achievable in the future and the historic average level might need to be reduced.

These are a few of the internal and external factors that can affect the valuation of a share. The factors that are relevant to a particular company may be industry-wide (e.g. change in rate of inflation), sector-wide (e.g. change in competitive pressure) or company-specific (e.g. loss of key managers or employees). They may not be immediately apparent from an appraisal of financial statements alone: for example, the application and success of the balanced scorecard approach might not be immediately apparent without discussions with all of the stakeholders. The valuer will need to carry out detailed enquiries in order both to identify which factors are relevant and to evaluate their impact on the share price.

If the company supports the acquisition of the shares, the valuer will be able to gain access to relevant internal information. For example, details of research and development expenditure may be available analysed by type of technology involved, by product line, by project and by location, and distinguishing internal from externally acquired R&D.

If the acquisition is being considered without the company's knowledge or support, the valuer will rely more heavily on information gained from public sources: for example, statutory disclosures such as the annual accounts, voluntary disclosures such as the OFR, and industry information such as trade journals. Information on areas such as R&D may be provided in the OFR, but probably in an aggregated form, constrained by management concerns about use by potential competitors.[14]

26.13 Shareholder value analysis (SVA)

Rappaport[15] identified a number of reasons why there has been a growing interest in shareholder value analysis:

- a belief that takeovers are based on undervalued assets;
- a belief that accounting measures (e.g. EPS) are unrelated to share value;
- wider reporting of returns to shareholders;
- wider adoption and endorsement;
- the linkage of executive rewards to shareholders' returns.

Copeland *et al*.[16] argued that 'managers at both business-unit and corporate levels need to broaden their conceptions of strategy; they need to manage value'. Mills[17, 18] explained that 'the pursuit of such an approach involves moving the focus of attention away from simply looking at short-term profits to a longer-term view of value creation'.

Essentially, SVA discounts forecasted cash flows, factors in a terminal value for the period beyond the forecast period, and adjusts for the value of debt. Rappaport proposed a seven value-driver approach (which was adopted by Mills et al.[19]) based on:

- Sales growth
- Operating margin
- Fixed capital investment
- Working capital investment
- Cash taxes
- Planning period
- Cost of capital

There are several other variations for determining wealth. Two of these measures[20] are:

Market Value Added (MVA) – the difference between total market value and invested capital (i.e. the difference between what investors can take out of a business and what they put in).

Economic Value Added (EVA) – this is the wealth a company creates each year as measured by net income from operations less the cost of capital needed to generate that income. Essentially, MVA is the valuation of all future annual EVAs.

The strength of the MVA/EVA framework is that it 'improves a company's focus on the maximisation of shareholder value ... discourages new investments that are likely to earn inadequate rates of return while encouraging periodic culling of existing assets'.[21]

26.14 Measuring and reporting values in the annual report

26.14.1 Shareholder value (SV)

It has been a long standing practice for analysts to arrive at shareholder value of a share by calculating the internal rate of return (IRR%) on an investment from the dividend stream and realisable value of the investment at date of disposal, i.e. taking account of dividends received and capital gains. However, it is not a generic measure in that the calculation is specific to each shareholder. The reason for this is that the dividends received will depend on the length of period the shares are held and the capital gain achieved will depend on the share price at the date of disposal – and, as we know, the share price can move significantly even over a week.

For example, consider the SV for each of the following three shareholders, Miss Rapid, Mr Medium and Miss Undecided, who each invested £10,000 on 1 January 20X1 in Spacemobile Ltd which pays a dividend of £500 on these shares on 31 December each year. Miss Rapid sold her shares on 31 December 20X2. Mr Medium sold his on 31 December 20X4, whereas Miss Undecided could not decide what to do with her shares. The SV for each shareholder is as follows:

Shareholder	Date acquired	Investment at cost	Dividends amount (total)	Date of disposal	Sale proceeds	IRR%
Miss Rapid	1.1.20X1	10,000	1,000	31.12.20X2	11,050	10%*
Mr Medium	1.1.20X1	10,000	2,000	31.12.20X4	15,000	15%
Miss Undecided	1.1.20X1	10,000	2,000	undecided		

*(500 × .9091) + (11,500 × .8265)

We can see that Miss Rapid achieved a shareholder value of 10% on her shares and Mr Medium, by holding until 31.12.20X4, achieved an increased capital gain raising the SV to 15%. We do not have the information as to how Miss Rapid invested her £11,050 for the 2 years from 1.1.20X3 and so we cannot evaluate her decision – it depends on the subsequent investment and the economic value added by that new company.

26.14.2 Total shareholder return

Miss Undecided has a *notional SV* at 31.12.20X4 of 15% as calculated for Mr Medium. However, this has not been realised and, if the share price changed the following day, the SV would be different. The notional 15% calculated for Miss Undecided is referred to as the total shareholder return (TSR) – it is dependent, however, on the assumption made about the length of the period the shares are held.

Some companies now report TSR, e.g. the following extract from the 2000 Annual Report of South African Breweries Ltd:

Shareholder value
Shareholder value is best measured by the total return to shareholders, being the appreciation in share price, plus dividends over the long-term. From its listing in London to 31 March 2000, SAB delivered a respectable return of 5.3% which compares favourably with its peer group. Independent research shows that we ended the year in fourth position in a survey of 18 of our peers.

The TSR is also used by Unilever which has set itself a TSR target in the top third of a reference group of 21 international consumer goods companies. Unilever calculates the TSR over a three-year rolling period which it considers 'sensitive enough to reflect changes but long enough to smooth out short-term volatility'. Since 1995 the company has improved its position relative to the peer group and reached the top third in 1998 – although the company stated in its 1999 Annual Report that if TSR were measured over a single year it would not have achieved its benchmark due to the focus by investors on high technology and internet stocks.

26.14.3 Economic value added

Need to generate above average returns

Companies are increasingly becoming aware that investors need to be confident that the company can deliver above average rates of return i.e. achieve growth and that communication is the key. This is why companies are using the annual report to provide shareholders and potential shareholders with a measure of the company's performance that will give them confidence to maintain or make an investment in the company. The directors of the Belgian company, Coil SA, make this explicit in the company's 2000 Annual Report:

A larger company, particularly a public company, competes for financial resources in the market. In order to induce investors to invest in the Company, management must show that it has the expectation to earn more than companies with the equivalent risk profile taking into account the size of the company, the risk of the industry, the capital structure of the company measured as a premium to the 'risk-free' rate, equivalent to the highest quality debt obligations issued by sovereign issuers.

If the Company cannot convince investors of its ability to deliver above average rates of return, more investors will sell shares than will buy shares and the share price will fall. Financial communication is key to the process of convincing investors.

If the Company's rate of return is in excess of that of the market average, the Company creates additional value for the shareholder. If it is less than the market average, the investor earns less than he could have done by investing in another company with the same risk profile. This loss is a destruction of value for the investor.

Formula for calculating economic value added

The formula applied is explained by Geveke nv Amsterdam in their 1999 Annual Report:

EVA measures economic value achieved over a specific period. It is equal to net operating profit after tax (NOPAT), corrected for the cost of capital employed (the sum of interest bearing liabilities and shareholders' equity). The cost of capital employed is the required yield R times capital employed (CE).

In the form of a formula: $NOPAT - (R \times CE) = EVA$

A positive EVA indicates that over a specific period economic value has been created. Net operating profit after tax is then greater than the cost of finance (i.e. the company's weighted average cost of capital). Research has shown that a substantial part of the long-term movement in share price is explained by the development of EVA. The concept of EVA can be a very good method of performance measurement and monitoring of decisions.

We will illustrate the formula for Alpha nv, which has the following data (in euros):

	31 March 20X1	31 March 20X2	31 March 20X3
NOPAT	10m	11m	13m
Weighted average cost of capital (WACC)	12%	11.5%	11%
Capital employed	70m	77m	96m

The EVA is:

		% change
31 March 20X1	EVA = 10m − (12% of 70m) = 1.6m	–
31 March 20X2	EVA = 11m − (11.5% of 77m) = 2.145m	34%
31 March 20X3	EVA = 12.5m − (11% of 96m) = 1.94m	(9%)

The formula allows weight to be given to the capital employed to generate operating profit. The percentage change is an important management tool in that the annual increase is seen as the created value rather than the absolute level, i.e. the 34% is the key figure rather than the 2.145m. Further enquiry is necessary to assess how well Alpha nv will employ the increase in capital employed in future periods.

It is useful to calculate rate of change over time. However, as for all inter-company comparisons of ratios, it is necessary to identify how the NOPAT and capital employed have been defined. This may vary from company to company, e.g.

- Geveke defines capital employed as total assets (excluding goodwill) less non-interest-bearing liabilities; whereas

- Koninklijke Wessanen nv defines capital invested as net assets plus historic goodwill, although it states that internally 'we use the goodwill on a market basis rather than the historically paid goodwill'.

Making EVA operational within a company

The directors of Coil SA state in their 1999 Annual Report:

> Increasingly companies are applying this type of business measurement model in detail to their business. It is a complex process, because the capital employed in the business must be allocated to the various activities of the business. Only then can all the various processes, which are carried out, be measured to see which activities satisfy the return hurdles of the company. Activities which do not pass the return hurdle are being outsourced to third parties who can consolidate these ancillary activities with those of other companies and achieve economies of scale and know-how to create, in turn, a business which creates value.

For a company to apply this type of business measurement in detail it is necessary to involve and motivate line managers. This is recognised by Geveke nv Amsterdam which stated in its 1999 Annual report:

> However, successful implementation stands or falls with its acceptance by line management and its successful anchoring in day-to-day practice. A great deal of attention will again be paid to this in the year ahead. An indispensable element in this context is therefore the linking of value creation at operating company level to the variable level of remuneration. A substantial part of the variable remuneration of Geveke's operating company management therefore depends on the return on capital employed and the resulting value creation.

Achieving increases in EVA

EVA can be improved in three ways by increasing NOPAT, reducing WACC and/or improving the utilisation of capital employed.

- Increasing NOPAT: this is achieved by optimising strategic choices by comparing the cash flows arising from different strategic opportunities, e.g. appraising geographic and product segmental information, cost reduction programmes, appraising acquisitions and divestments.
- Reducing WACC: This is achieved by reviewing the manner in which a company is financed, e.g. determining a favourable gearing ratio and reducing the perceived risk factor by a favourable spread of products and markets.
- Improving the utilisation of capital employed: This is achieved by consideration of activity ratios, e.g. fixed asset turnover, working capital ratio.

26.15 Financial reporting of risk

The ICAEW has proposed that listed companies should be at the forefront of improved risk reporting in financial statements. In a recent discussion paper,[22] the ICAEW attempt to encourage the inclusion of better quality information on business risks so that users of accounts have a better understanding of the risks underlying a business's activity. With specific reference to ratio analysis, the discussion paper argues that 'the preparation of a statement of business risk should help preparers and users to focus on the ratios that are most relevant to the particular business risks that are most relevant to individual companies' (para. 6.16).

The summary of the main thrust of the discussion paper is as follows:

Why increase risk reporting in annual reports?

'Enhanced information about what companies do to assess and manage key business risks of all types will:

- provide practical forward-looking information;
- reduce the cost of capital;
- encourage better risk management;
- help ensure the equal treatment of all investors; and
- improve accountability for stewardship, investor protection and the usefulness of financial reporting.'

What should a statement of business risk include?

- Identification: a company should identify and prioritise its key risks;
- Risk management: a company should describe the actions it has taken to manage each of the identified risks;
- Measurement: the company should identify how each risk is measured.

What should preparers consider when preparing the statement of business risk?

Preparers need to ensure that the information satisfies a range of qualitative characteristics (e.g. relevant, reliable); is forward-looking; is suitable for users; is clear with respect to time-scales; and is not too commercially sensitive.

At present, there are a number of accounting standards which ensure that a certain element of risk-related information is reported in the financial statements. These standards include:

SSAP 25	*Segmental Reporting*
FRS 4	*Capital Instruments*
FRS 5	*Reporting the Substance of Transactions*
FRS 8	*Related Party Disclosures*
FRS 12	*Provisions, Contingent Liabilities and Contingent Assets*
FRS 13	*Derivatives and other Financial Instruments: Disclosure*

Derivatives and financial instruments is the area of financial reporting for business risk which we concentrate on in this chapter.

26.16 Professional risk assessors

Credit agencies such as Standard & Poor and Moody's Investor Services assist investors, lenders and trade creditors by providing a credit rating service. Companies are given a rating that can range from AAA for companies with a strong capacity to meet their financial commitments down to D for companies that have been unable to make contractual payments or have filed for bankruptcy with more than 10 ratings in between e.g. BBB for companies that have adequate capacity but which are vulnerable to internal or external economic changes.

26.16.1 How are ratings set?

The credit agencies take a broad range of internal company and external factors into account.

Internal company factors may include:

- An appraisal of the financial reports to determine:
  - trading performance, e.g. specific financial targets such as return on equity and return on assets; earnings volatility; past and projected performance; how well a company has coped with business cycles
  - cash flow adequacy, e.g. EBITDA interest cover; EBIT interest cover; free operating cash flow
  - capital structure, e.g. gearing ratio; debt structure; implications of off-balance-sheet financing
  - a consideration of the notes to the accounts to determine possible adverse implications, e.g. contingent liabilities, heavy capital investment commitments which may impact on future profitability, liquidity and funding requirements
- Meetings and discussions with management
- Monitoring expectation, e.g. against quarterly reports, company press releases, profit warnings
- Monitoring changes in company strategy, e.g. changes to funding structure with company buy back of shares, new divestment or acquisition plans and implication for any debt covenants.

However, experience with companies such as Enron makes it clear that off-balance-sheet transactions can make appraisal difficult even for professional agencies if companies continue to avoid transparency in their reporting.

External factors may include:

- Growth prospects, e.g. trends in industry sector; technology possible changes; peer comparison
- Capital requirements, e.g. whether company is fixed capital or working capital intensive; future tangible fixed asset requirements; R&D spending requirements
- Competitors, e.g. the major domestic and foreign competitors; product differentiation; what barriers there are to entry
- Keeping a watching brief on macro-economic factors, e.g. environmental statutory levies, tax changes, political changes such as restrictions on the supply of oil, foreign currency risks
- Monitoring changes in company strategy, e.g. implication of a company embarking on a heavy overseas acquisition programme which changes the risk profile, e.g. difficulty in management control and in achieving synergies, increased foreign exchange exposure.

16.16.2 What impact does a rating have on a company?

The rating is a risk measure and influences decisions as to whether to grant credit and also as to the terms of such credit, e.g. if a company's rating is downgraded then lenders may refuse credit or impose a higher interest rate or set additional debt covenants.

16.16.3 What are debt covenants?

Lenders may require borrowers to do certain things by affirmative covenants or refrain from doing certain things by negative covenants.

Affirmative covenants may, for example, include requiring the borrower to:

● Provide quarterly and annual financial statements

● Remain within certain ratios whilst ensuring that each agreed ratio is not so restrictive that it impairs normal operations:
  ● maintain a current ratio of not less than an agreed ratio – say 1.6 to 1
  ● maintain a ratio of total liabilities to tangible net worth at an agreed rate – say no greater than 2.5 to 1.
  ● maintain tangible net worth in excess of an agreed amount – say £1m

● Maintain adequate insurance.

Negative covenants may, for example, include requiring the borrower **not** to:

● Grant any other charges over the company's assets

● Repay loans from related parties without prior approval

● Change the group structure by acquisitions, mergers or divestment without prior agreement.

16.16.4 What happens if a company is in breach of its debt covenants?

Borrowers will normally have prepared forecasts to assure themselves and the lenders that compliance is reasonably feasible – such forecasts will also normally include the worse case scenario, e.g. taking account of seasonal fluctuations that may trigger temporary violations with higher borrowing required to cover higher levels of stock and debtors.

If any violation has occurred, the lender has a range of options, such as:

● amending the covenant, e.g. accepting a lower current ratio, or

● granting a waiver period when the terms of the covenant are not applied, or

● granting a waiver but requiring the loans to be restructured, or

● requiring the terms to be met within a stipulated period of grace, or, as a last resort,

● declaring that the borrower is in default and demanding repayment of the loan.

16.16.5 Audit implications when there is a breach of a debt covenant

Auditors are required to bring a healthy scepticism to their work. This applies particularly at times such as when there is a potential debt covenant breach. There may then well be a temptation to manipulate to avoid reporting a breach. This will depend on the specific covenant, e.g. if the current ratio is below the agreed figure, management might be more optimistic in setting stock obsolescence and debtor provisions and have a lower expectation of the likelihood of contingent liabilities crystallising.

Summary

This chapter has introduced a number of additional analytical techniques to complement ratio analysis. These techniques include horizontal analysis, vertical analysis, Z-scores, H-scores, A-scores and balanced scorecards. In addition, this chapter has described how to value unquoted shares and introduced the concept of shareholder value analysis. Finally, the ICAEW has published a discussion paper on the financial reporting of risk. Business risk reporting is an area which will become increasingly important and prominent.

The prime purpose of each analytical method in the first half of the chapter is to identify potential financial problem areas. Once these have been identified, thorough investigations should be carried out to determine the cause of each irregularity. Management should then take the necessary actions to correct these irregularities and deficiencies.

All users of financial statements (both internal and external users) should be prepared to utilise any or all of the interpretative techniques suggested in this chapter and the preceding one. These techniques help to evaluate the financial health and performance of a company. Users should approach these financial indicators with real curiosity – any unexplained or unanswered questions arising from this analysis should form the basis of a more detailed examination of the company accounts.

REVIEW QUESTIONS

1 As well as the balance sheet, profit and loss account and cash flow statement, a company's annual report and accounts contain other useful information.

Discuss the interpretative importance of the report of the directors, the chairman's statement, group structure information, employee statistics, geographical and activity breakdowns, and other supplementary information.

How useful and reliable is this additional information in the assessment of financial performance and the interpretation of financial statements?

2 Discuss Z-score analysis with particular reference to Altman's Z-score and Taffler's Z-score. In particular:

(i) What are the benefits of Z-score analysis?

(ii) What criticisms can be levelled at Z-score analysis?

3 Robertson identifies four main elements which cause changes in the financial health of a company: trading stability; declining profits; declining working capital; increase in borrowings.[23]

Robertson's Z-score is represented by:

$$Z = 3.0X_1 + 3.0X_2 + 0.6X_3 + 0.3X_4 + 0.3X_5$$

where

X_1 = (Sales – Total assets)/Sales
X_2 = Profit before tax/Total assets
X_3 = (Current assets – Total debt)/Current liabilities
X_4 = (Equity – Total borrowing)/Total debt
X_5 = (Liquid assets – Bank overdraft)/Creditors

Interpretation of the Z-score concentrates on rate of change from one period to the next. If the score falls by 40% or more in any one year, immediate investigations must be made to identify and rectify the cause of the decrease in Z-score. If the score falls by 40% or more for two years running, the company is unlikely to survive.

Compare and contrast Robertson's Z-score with:

(i) Altman's Z-score;

(ii) Taffler's Z-score and PAS-score.

4 The Datastream Multivariate Model uses a classification model developed by Marais[24] based on a sample of 100 UK companies consisting of 50 failed and 50 non-failed companies and using four variables:

X_1 measures profitability
X_2 measures liquidity
X_3 measures gearing
X_4 measures stock turnover

The Altman model is described in the text (section 26.6.1). Research by Letza[25] looked at the accuracy of these two models, with the following results:

| | *Ex-ante classification accuracy* | | | |
| | *Altman* | | *Datastream* | |
Years prior to event	1	3	1	3
Correct classification				
Survivor	108	109	112	113
Failure	2	3	2	2
Incorrect classification				
Wrongly predicting failure	29	28	25	24
Wrongly predicting survival	1	0	1	1
Total	140	140	140	140

Discuss the effectiveness of these two predictive models for financial analysts and consider what other variables could be incorporated into each of the models that might make the predictions more accurate.

5 The details given below are a summary of the balance sheets of six public companies engaged in different industries:

| | A | B | C | D | E | F |
	%	%	%	%	%	%
Land and buildings	10	2	26	24	57	5
Other fixed assets	17	1	34		13	73
Stocks and work in progress	44		22	55	16	1
Trade debtors	6	77	15	4	1	13
Other debtors	11			8	2	5
Cash and investments	12	20	3	9	11	3
	100	100	100	100	100	100

	A	B	C	D	E	F
Capital and reserves	37	5	62	58	55	50
Creditors: over one year	12	5	4	13	6	25
Creditors: under one year						
Trade	32	85	34	14	24	6
Other	16	5		14	15	11
Bank overdraft	3			1		8
Total capital employed	100	100	100	100	100	100

The activities of each company are as follows:

1 Operator of a chain of retail supermarkets.

2 Sea ferry operator.

3 Property investor and house builder. Apart from supplying managers, including site management, for the house building side of its operations, this company completely subcontracts all building work.

4 A vertically integrated company in the food industry which owns farms, flour mills, bakeries and retail outlets.

5 Commercial bank with a network of branches.

6 Contractor in the civil engineering industry.

Note: No company employs off-balance-sheet financing such as leasing.

(a) State which of the above activities relate to which set of balance sheet details, giving a brief summary of your reasoning in each case.

(b) What do you consider to be the major limitations of ratio analysis as a means of interpreting accounting information?

6 It has been suggested that 'growth in profits which occurred in the 1960s was the result of accounting sleight of hand rather than genuine economic growth'. Consider how 'accounting sleight of hand' can be used to report increased profits and discuss what measures can be taken to mitigate against the possibility of this happening.

7 Discuss the main features/perspectives of the 'Balanced Scorecard'.

8 The Unilever 1999 Annual Review stated:

Total Shareholder Return (TSR) is a concept used to compare the performance of different companies' stocks and shares over time. It combines share price appreciation and dividends paid to show the total return to the shareholder. The absolute size of the TSR will vary with stock markets, but the relative position is a reflection of the market perception of overall performance. The Company calculates the TSR over a three year rolling period…. Unilever has set itself a TSR target in the top third of a reference group of 21 … companies.

Discuss (a) why a three year rolling period has been chosen, and (b) the criteria you consider appropriate for selecting the reference group of companies.

EXERCISES

An extract from the solution is provided in the appendix at the end of the text for exercises marked with an asterisk (*).

Question 1

The following five-year summary relates to Wandafood Products plc and is based on financial statements prepared under the historical cost convention:

Financial ratios			20X9	20X8	20X7	20X6	20X5
Profitability							
Margin	$\dfrac{\text{Trading profit}}{\text{Sales}}$ %		7.8	7.5	7.0	7.2	7.3
Return on assets	$\dfrac{\text{Trading profit}}{\text{Net operating assets}}$ %		16.3	17.6	16.2	18.2	18.3
Interest and dividend cover							
Interest cover	$\dfrac{\text{Trading profit}}{\text{Net finance charges}}$ times		2.9	4.8	5.1	6.5	3.6
Dividend cover	$\dfrac{\text{Earnings per ordinary share}}{\text{Dividend per ordinary share}}$ times		2.7	2.6	2.1	25	3.1
Debt to equity ratios							
	$\dfrac{\text{Net borrowings}}{\text{Shareholders' funds}}$ %		65.9	61.3	48.3	10.8	36.5
	$\dfrac{\text{Net borrowings}}{\text{Shareholders' funds plus minority interests}}$ %		59.3	55.5	44.0	10.1	33.9
Liquidity ratios							
Quick ratio	$\dfrac{\text{Current assets less stock}}{\text{Current liabilities}}$ %		74.3	73.3	78.8	113.8	93.4
Current ratio	$\dfrac{\text{Current assets}}{\text{Current liabilities}}$ %		133.6	130.3	142.2	178.9	174.7
Asset ratios							
Operating asset turnover	$\dfrac{\text{Sales}}{\text{Net operating assets}}$ times		2.1	2.4	2.3	2.5	2.5
Working capital turnover	$\dfrac{\text{Sales}}{\text{Working capital}}$ times		8.6	8.0	7.0	7.4	6.2

Per share

Earnings per	– pre-tax basis	p	23.62	21.25	17.96	17.72	15.06
share	– net basis	p	15.65	13.60	10.98	11.32	12.18
Dividends per							
share		p	5.90	5.40	4.90	4.60	4.10
Net assets per							
share		p	102.1	89.22	85.95	85.79	78.11

Net operating assets include tangible fixed assets, stock, debtors and creditors. They exclude borrowings, taxation and dividends.

Required:

Prepare a report on the company, clearly interpreting and evaluating the information given. Include comments on possible effects of price changes which may limit the quality of the report.

(ACCA, June 1990)

Question 2

The following are the accounts of Bouncy plc, a company that manufactures playground equipment, for the year ended 30 November 20X6

Profit and loss accounts for years ended 30 November

	20X6	20X5
	£000	£000
Profit before interest and tax	2,200	1,570
Interest expense	170	150
Profit before tax	2,030	1,420
Taxation	730	520
Profit after tax	1,300	900
Dividends paid	250	250
Retained profit	1,050	650

Balance sheets as at 30 November 20X6

	20X6	20X5
	£000	£000
Fixed assets (written down value)	6,350	5,600
Current assets		
Stock	2,100	2,070
Debtors	1,710	1,540
	10,160	9,210
Creditors: amounts due within one year		
Trade creditors	1,040	1,130
Taxation	550	450
Bank overdraft	370	480
Total assets less current liabilities	8,200	7,150
Creditors: amounts due after more than one year		
10% Debentures 20X7/20X8	1,500	1,500
	6,700	5,650

Capital and reserves		
Share capital: Ordinary shares of 50p fully paid up	3,000	3,000
Share premium	750	750
Profit and loss account	2,950	1,900
	6,700	5,650

The directors are considering two schemes to raise £6,000,000 in order to repay the debentures and finance expansion estimated to increase profit before interest and tax by £900,000. It is proposed to make a dividend of 6p per share whether funds are raised by equity or loan. The two schemes are:
(1) an issue of 13% Debentures redeemable in 30 years
(2) a rights issue at £1.50 per share. The current market price is £1.80 per share (20X5:£1.50; 20X4 £1.20).

Required:
(a) Calculate the return on equity and any three investment ratios of interest to a potential investor.
(b) Calculate three ratios of interest to a potential long-term lender.
(c) Report briefly on the performance and state of the business from the viewpoint of a potential shareholder and lender using the ratios calculated above and explain any weaknesses in these ratios.
(d) Advise management which scheme they should adopt on the basis of your analysis above and explain what other information may need to be considered when making the decision.

* Question 3

Liz Collier runs a small delicatessen. Her profits in recent years have remained steady at around £21,000 per annum. This type of business generally earns a uniform rate of net profit on sales of 20%.

Recently, Liz has found that this level of profitability is insufficient to enable her to maintain her desired lifestyle. She is considering three options to improve her profitability.

Option 1 Liz will borrow £10,000 from her bank at an interest rate of 10% per annum, payable at the end of each financial year. The whole capital sum will be repaid to the bank at the end of the second year. The money will be used to hire the services of a marketing agency for two years. It is anticipated that turnover will increase by 40% as a result of the additional advertising.

Option 2 Liz will form a partnership with Joan Mercer, who also runs a local delicatessen. Joan's net profits have remained at £12,000 per annum since she started in business five years ago. The sales of each shop in the combined business are expected to increase by 20% in the first year and then remain steady. The costs of the amalgamation will amount to £6,870, which will be written off in the first year. The partnership agreement will allow each partner a partnership salary of 2% of the revised turnover of their own shop. Remaining profits will be shared in the ratio of Liz 3/5, Joan 2/5.

Option 3 Liz will reduce her present sales by 80% and take up a franchise to sell Nickson's Munchy Sausage. The franchise will cost £80,000. This amount will be borrowed from her bank. The annual interest rate will be 10% flat rate based on the amount borrowed. Sales of Munchy Sausage yield a net profit to sales percentage of 30%. Sales are expected to be £50,000 in the first year, but should increase annually at a rate of 15% for the following three years then remain constant.

Required:
(a) Prepare a financial statement for Liz comparing the results of each option for each of the next two years.

(b) Advise Liz which option may be the best to choose.

(c) Discuss any other factors that Liz should consider under each of the options.

Question 4

Background information

The directors of Chekani plc, a large listed company, are engaged in a policy of expansion. Accordingly, they have approached the directors of Meela Ltd, an unlisted company of substantial size, in connection with a proposed purchase of Meela Ltd.

The directors of Meela Ltd have indicated that the shareholders of Meela Ltd would prefer the form of consideration for the purchase of their shares to be in cash and you are informed that this is acceptable to the prospective purchasing company, Chekani plc.

The directors of Meela Ltd have now been asked to state the price at which the shareholders of Meela Ltd would be prepared to sell their shares to Chekani plc. As a member of a firm of independent accountants, you have been engaged as a consultant to advise the directors of Meela Ltd in this regard.

In order that you may be able to do so, the following details, extracted from the most recent financial statements of Meela, have been made available to you.

Meela Ltd accounts for year ended 30 June 20X4

Balance sheet extracts as at 30 June 20X4:

	£000
Purchased goodwill unamortised	15,000
Freehold property	30,000
Plant and machinery	60,000
Investments	15,000
Net current assets	12,000
10% Debentures 20X9	(30,000)
Ordinary shares of £1 each, (cumulative)	(40,000)
7% preference shares of £1 each, (cumulative)	(12,000)
Share premium account	(20,000)
Profit and loss account	(30,000)

Meela Ltd disclosed a contingent liability of £3.0m in the notes to the Balance Sheet.

(Amounts in brackets indicate credit balances)

Profit and loss account extracts for the year ended 30 June 20X4:

		£000
Profit before interest payments and taxation and exceptional items		21,000
Exceptional items		1,500
Interest		(3,000)
Taxation		(6,000)
Dividends paid	– Preference	(840)
	– Ordinary	(3,000)
Retained profit for the year		9,660

(Amounts in brackets indicate a charge or appropriation to profits)

The following information is also supplied:

(i) Profit before interest and tax for the year ended 30 June 20X3 was £24.2m and for the year ended 30 June 20X2 it was £30.3m.

(ii) Assume Corporation Tax at 30%.

(iii) Exceptional items in 20X4 relate to the profit on disposal of an investment in a related company. The related company contributed to profit before interest as follows:

To 30 June 20X4	£0
To 30 June 20X3	£200,000
To 30 June 20X2	£300,000

(iv) The preference share capital can be sold independently, and a buyer has already been found. The agreed purchase price is 90 pence per share.

(v) Chekani plc has agreed to purchase the debentures of Meela Ltd at a price of £110 for each £100 debenture.

(vi) The current rental value of the freehold property is £4.5m per annum and a buyer is available on the basis of achieving an 8% return on their investment.

(vii) The investments of Meela Ltd have a current market value of £22.5m.

(viii) Meela Ltd is engaged in operations substantially different from those of Chekani plc. The most recent financial data relating to two listed companies that are engaged in operations similar to those of Meela Ltd are:

	NV per share	Market price per share	P/E	Net dividend per share	Cover	Yield
Ranpar plc	£1	£3.06	11.3	12 pence	2.6	4.9
Menner plc	50p	£1.22	8.2	4 pence	3.8	4.1

Required:

Write a report, of approximately 2000 words, to the directors of Meela Ltd, covering the following:

(a) Advise them of the alternative methods used for valuing unquoted shares and explain some of the issues involved in the choice of method.

(b) Explain the alternative valuations that could be placed on the ordinary shares of Meela Ltd.

(c) Recommend an appropriate strategy for the Board of Meela Ltd to adopt in their negotiations with Chekani plc.

Include, as appendices to your report, supporting schedules showing how the valuations were calculated.

Question 5

R. Johnson inherited 810,000 £1 ordinary shares in Johnson Products Ltd on the death of his uncle in 20X5. His uncle had been the founder of the company and managing director until his death. The remainder of the issued shares were held in small lots by employees and friends, with no one holding more than 4%.

R. Johnson is planning to emigrate and is considering disposing of his shareholding. He has had approaches from three parties, who are:

1 A competitor – Sonar Products Ltd. Sonar Products Ltd considers that Johnson Products Ltd would complement their own business and they are interested in acquiring all of the 810,000 shares. Sonar Products Ltd currently achieve a post-tax return of 12.5% on capital employed.

2 Senior employees. Twenty employees are interested in making a management buy-out with each acquiring 40,500 shares from R. Johnson. They have obtained financial backing, in principle, from the company's bankers.

3 A financial conglomerate – Divest plc. Divest plc is a company that has extensive experience of acquiring control of a company and breaking it up to show a profit on the transaction. It is their policy to seek a pre-tax return of 20% from such an exercise.

The company has prepared draft accounts for the year ended 30 April 20X9. The following information is available.

(a) Past earnings and distributions:

Year ended 30 April	Profit/(Loss) after tax	Gross dividends declared
£	%	
20X5	79,400	6
20X6	(27,600)	—
20X7	56,500	4
20X8	88,300	5
20X9	97,200	6

(b) Balance sheet of Johnson Products Ltd as at 30 April 20X9:

	£000	£000
Fixed assets		
Land at cost		376
Premises at cost	724	
Aggregate depreciation	216	
		508
Equipment at cost	649	
Aggregate depreciation	353	
		296
Current assets		
Stock	141	
Debtors	278	
Cash at bank	70	
	489	
Creditors due within one year	(335)	
Net current assets		154
Non-current liabilities		(158)
		1,176
Represented by:		
£1 Ordinary shares		1,080
Profit and loss account		96
		1,176

(c) Information on the nearest comparable listed companies in the same industry:

Company	Profit after tax for 20X9 £000	Retention %	Gross dividend yield %
Eastron plc	280	25	15
Westron plc	168	16	10.5
Northron plc	243	20	13.4

Profit after tax in each of the companies has been growing by approximately 8% per annum for the past five years.

(d) The following is an estimate of the net realisable values of Johnson Products Ltd's assets as at 30 April 20X9:

	£000
Land	480
Premises	630
Equipment	150
Debtors	168
Stock	98

Required:

(a) As accountant for R. Johnson, advise him of the amount that could be offered for his shareholding with a reasonable chance of being acceptable to the seller, based on the information given in the question, by each of the following:

   (i) Sonar Products Ltd;

   (ii) the 20 employees;

   (iii) Divest plc.

(b) As accountant for Sonar Products Ltd, estimate the maximum amount that could be offered by Sonar Products Ltd for the shares held by R. Johnson.

(c) As accountant for Sonar Products Ltd, state the principal matters you would consider in determining the future maintainable earnings of Johnson Products Ltd and explain their relevance.

(ACCA)

Question 6

Discuss the following issues with regard to financial reporting for risk:

(a) How can a company identify and prioritise its key risks?

(b) What actions can a company take to manage the risks identified in (a)?

(c) How can a company measure risk?

References

1 *Accounting for the Effects of Changing Prices: A Handbook*, ASC, 1986.

2 C. Pratten, *Company Failure*, Financial Reporting and Auditing Group, ICAEW, 1991, pp. 43–45.

3 R.J. Taffler, 'Forecasting company failure in the UK using discriminant analysis and financial ratio data', *Journal of the Royal Statistical Society*, Series A, vol. 145, part 3, 1982, pp. 342–358.

4 M.L. Inman, 'Altman's Z-formula prediction', *Management Accounting*, November 1982, pp. 37–39.

5 E.I. Altman, 'Financial ratios, discriminant analysis and the prediction of corporate bankruptcy', *Journal of Finance*, vol. 23(4), 1968, pp. 589–609.

6 M.L. Inman, 'Z-scores and the going concern review', *ACCA Students' Newsletter*, August 1991, pp. 8–13.

7 R.J. Taffler, *op. cit.*

8 R.J. Taffler, 'Z-scores: an approach to the recession', *Accountancy*, July 1991, pp. 95–97.

9 M.L. Inman, 1991, *op. cit.*

10 G. Holmes and R. Dunham, *Beyond the Balance Sheet*, Woodhead Faulkner, 1994.

11 J. Argenti, 'Predicting corporate failure', *Accountants Digest*, no. 138, Summer 1983, pp. 18–21.

12 R. Newing, 'Benefits of a balanced scorecard', *Accountancy*, November 1994, pp. 52–53.

13 R.S. Kaplan and D.P. Norton, 'The balanced scorecard – measures that drive performance', *Harvard Business Review*, January–February 1992, pp. 71–79.

14 W.A. Nixon and C.J. McNair, 'A measure of R&D', *Accountancy*, October 1994, p. 138.

15 A. Rappaport, *Creating Shareholder Value: The new standard for business performance*, The Free Press, 1986.

16 T. Copeland, T. Koller and J. Murrin, *Valuation: Measuring and Managing the Value of Companies*, John Wiley and Sons, New York, 1990.

17 R.W. Mills, 'Shareholder value analysis', *Management Accounting*, February 1998, pp. 39–40.

18 R.W. Mills *et al.*, *The Use of Shareholder Value Analysis in Acquisition and Divestment Decisions by Large UK Companies*, CIMA, 1997.

19 R.W. Mills, J. Robertson and T. Ward, 'Strategic value analysis: Trying to run before you can walk', *Management Accounting*, November 1992, pp. 48–49.

20 'America's best wealth creators', *Forbes*, 28 November 1994, pp. 77–91.

21 J. Stern, 'Management: its mission and its measure', *Director*, October 1994, pp. 42–44.

22 ICAEW, *Financial Reporting of Risk*, Discussion Paper, 1998.

23 J. Robertson, 'Company failure – measuring changes in financial health through ratio analysis', *Management Accounting*, November 1983.

24 D.A. Marais, *A Method of Quantifying Companies' Relative Financial Strength*, Bank of England Discussion Paper No. 4, 1979.

25 S.R. Letza, 'Issues in assessing MDA models of corporate failure: a supporting research note', *British Accounting Review*, vol. 26(3), 1994, p. 281.

CHAPTER 27

Financial instruments

27.1 Introduction

In July 1993, an international association of bankers and former government officials published a document which called for improved disclosure in financial statements of transactions involving derivatives and other financial instruments[1]. However, it took three years for the ASB to issue a discussion paper on financial instruments in July 1996[2] and a further two years to issue FRS 13, the standard on disclosure[3]. At the time of the Discussion Paper's release, Sandra Thompson, a project director at the ASB, summed up the importance of financial instruments:

> Derivatives: The word can strike fear into finance directors, auditors and shareholders alike. Companies increasingly use derivatives and financial instruments to manage risk. But, improperly used, such instruments can turn into dangerous gambles, giving rise to spectacular losses. While much has been written about the use of financial instruments, there is relatively little guidance on their accounting.[4]

The main problem is that for a relatively small outlay financial instruments can transform the risk profile of a company. In particular some organisations which have been exposed to huge risks have suffered the consequences of their dealings in financial instruments. These well-publicised losses highlighted the fact that existing accounting practice did not provide an adequate framework for reporting the risk associated with financial instruments. For instance, some derivatives cost nothing and their book value is nil under a historical cost system. Similarly, the gains or losses on a derivative might not be realised, and hence reported, until it is sold. Consequently, how can shareholders assess the riskiness of an investment if they are unaware of the existence and/or the implications of an organisation's transactions involving financial instruments?

27.2 FRS 13 Definitions

FRS 13 defines a financial instrument as 'any contract that gives rise to both a financial asset of one entity and a financial liability or equity instrument of another entity'.

A financial asset is defined as any asset that is:

- Cash, or
- A **contractual** right to receive cash or another financial asset from another entity, e.g. a trade debtor, or
- A **contractual** right to exchange financial instruments with another entity under conditions that are potentially favourable (in other words, a derivative – see later), or
- An equity instrument of another entity (in other words an equity investment).

A financial liability is defined as a **contractual** obligation:

- To deliver cash or another financial asset to another entity, e.g. a trade creditor, or
- A **contractual** right to exchange financial instruments with another entity under conditions that are potentially unfavourable (in other words, a derivative – see later).

In Chapter 11 we discussed FRS 4 *Capital Instruments*. However, it is clear that the scope of FRS 13 is wider than the scope of FRS 4 which deals with financial instruments from the perspective of the issuer only and calls them 'capital instruments'. FRS 13 deals with financial instruments both from the perspective of the issuer and from the perspective of the investor.

27.3 The underlying financial reporting issue

There are three aspects to consider, namely, the identification of business risk, the impact of derivative financial instruments on business risk and the need for the development of financial reporting in this area.

27.3.1 Identification of business risks

A key objective of FRS 13 is that users should be able to receive relevant and reliable information about the extent to which financial instruments contribute to business risk. Appendix I to FRS 13 identifies four components of risk arising from financial instruments:

- **Credit risk** – the possibility that a loss may occur from the failure of another party to perform according to the terms of a contract.
- **Liquidity risk** – the risk that an entity will have difficulty in raising the cash that is required to meet commitments associated with its financial instruments.
- **Cash flow risk** – the risk that future cash flows generated by a monetary financial instrument will fluctuate in amount, for example the interest available on a floating rate deposit.
- **Market price risk** – the possibility that future changes in market prices may change the value, or the burden, of a financial instrument.

It is the contention of the ASB that a reasonable amount of information is already available in financial statements to enable the user to appreciate the credit and liquidity risks the entity is running.

Credit risk

This is a familiar risk and it is already possible for a user to ascertain the nature of an entity's business and the level of its debtors and creditors which makes it possible to make some reasonable judgment on the level of credit risk. Reference can also be made to credit agencies for ratios such as H-scores and detailed credit reports.

Liquidity risk

This is again a familiar risk and there is already information provided from balance sheet based ratios, e.g. gearing, cash-based ratios (e.g. cash flow from operations to current liabilities and the cash recovery rate) and details in the notes to the accounts on borrowings and future capital commitments, which can give the user some feel for the liquidity risk.

Cash flow and market price risks

The particular risks to which an entity is exposed will depend on the characteristics of its financial instruments. For example, if an entity has taken out a fixed rate loan then the entity is not subject to cash flow risk when the rate of interest changes. However, that same entity **may** be subject to market price risk since the market value of a fixed interest security is vulnerable to changes in general interest rates. The reverse applies if the loan is variable rate. If the loan that is taken out is denominated in a foreign currency then the entity is potentially vulnerable to both cash flow and market price risk when the rate of exchange changes.

What does a user need to know to assess the risks?

It should hopefully be obvious from the previous paragraph that, in order to appreciate the risk profile of an entity, a user needs information on such things as:

● Whether its financing is at fixed or variable rates of interest.

● Whether the currency of repayment is £ sterling or some other currency.

27.3.2 The impact of derivative financial instruments on business risk

A derivative financial instrument includes such examples as forward contracts, futures and options. It derives its value from the price or rate of some underlying item. 'Underlying items' include:

● equities
● bonds
● commodities
● interest rates
● exchange rates.

How can derivative financial instruments alter the risk profile of a company?

Let us take an example, Newport plc, to demonstrate how derivative financial instruments can radically alter the risk profile of an entity:

On 30th September 20X0 Newport plc, a UK company, signs a contract for $1,000,000 to take delivery of a large quantity of raw material from a US supplier on 31 March 20X1. The US supplier would expect payment two months later on 31 May 20X1. On the date the contract is signed the £/$ rate is $1.66 to £1. Newport plc is concerned that the $ will strengthen against the £ and so covers the position with a forward contract to buy $1,000,000 on 31 May 20X1 for £615,385 (an effective rate of $1.625 = £1). The effect of this is that Newport plc has completely eliminated its exchange risk on the transaction by locking in on the rate of $1.625 = £1.

Whether this proves to be financially the best option will depend on the spot rate of exchange on the date the $ are required – 31 May 20X1 in this case. If the spot rate at 31 May 20X1 was $1.60 = £1 then $1,000,000 would have cost £625,000 on the spot market and the decision to purchase forward would have been financially beneficial.

If, however, the rate on 31 May 20X1 had slipped only marginally to $1.65 = £1 then $1,000,000 would have cost £606,061 on the spot market. With the benefit of hindsight the decision would not have been the correct one. However, the company can use a forward exchange contract to completely remove the exchange risk.

In this example we have assumed that the company has used a derivative financial instrument to **eliminate** financial risk. It is quite possible that some organisations may wish to do just the opposite – in other words to make money by speculating on the future behaviour of exchange rates.

27.3.3 The need for development of financial reporting in this area

A key feature of many financial instruments is that cost-based concepts are not an adequate basis for recognition and measurement. This is because businesses can enter into financial transactions that substantially alter their business risk without incurring any up front cost. However, if underlying price movements change in a particular way the business may well have generated a substantial potential gain or loss as we can see from the Newport example above.

Approach to measurement

Recognising that cost based accounting is not relevant, many countries are seeking to develop a form of fair value accounting for financial instruments. The former International Accounting Standards Committee (IASC) has published an accounting standard IAS 39[5] dealing with recognition and measurement. The UK Accounting Standards Board (ASB) is somewhat behind the IASC in this respect. The ASB certainly intends to publish a recognition and measurement standard in the future but, as its name suggests, FRS 13 deals merely with the **disclosure** of various issues regarding the financial instruments of an entity.

27.4 FRS 13 An outline of the standard

The standard applies to most financial assets and liabilities and to non-equity shares issued by the reporting entity although short-term debtors and creditors can be exempted from the disclosures.

The disclosures required by FRS 13 fall into two major categories:

- Narrative disclosures – which may either be included in the financial statements themselves or within the operating and financial review, with reference in this latter case being made in the financial statements themselves.
- Numerical disclosures – which must be included in the notes to the accounts. The numerical disclosures differ depending on whether or not the entity is a financial institution. Not surprisingly, the numerical disclosures are more detailed for financial than for non-financial institutions. If the financial institution is a bank then the numerical disclosures are more detailed still.

27.4.1 Narrative disclosures

The purpose of the narrative disclosures is to inform the user of the objectives, policies and strategies of the entity in using financial instruments. The idea is to put the numerical disclosures that are required into some sort of context. The primary focus of the disclosures is to identify in broad terms the risks that arise in connection with financial instruments and how they have been managed. Therefore, the narrative disclosures might reasonably include:

- An explanation of financial instruments in creating or changing the risks that an entity faces in its activities.

- A description of the financial risk management and treasury policies agreed by the board of directors. This description would include matters such as the extent to which borrowings are at fixed rate or floating rate and the extent to which foreign currency net assets are hedged to the functional currency of the entity – almost certainly £ for a UK entity.

- An explanation of how the year-end figures reflect the agreed objectives. This is particularly important if the year-end figures are unrepresentative of the position during the year for whatever reason.

- An explanation of how financial instruments (particularly derivative financial instruments) are (or are not) recognised in the financial statements. It is highly likely that a 'recognition FRS' will be published in the foreseeable future.

27.4.2 Numerical disclosures

The main numerical disclosures required by FRS 13 fall under four headings:

- interest rate risk disclosures
- currency risk disclosures
- liquidity disclosures
- fair value disclosures.

There are also further numerical disclosures for particular types of financial instruments – for example hedges.

Interest risk disclosure

The required disclosures relate to **interest rate risk** on all significant financial assets and all financial liabilities. What is required is an analysis of the carrying amount by principal currency, further subdivided between:

- those at fixed interest rates
- those at floating interest rates
- those on which no interest is paid.

The above analysis should be after taking account of any risk management that the entity has undertaken using derivatives. For example, if the entity has taken out a currency swap in respect of US$ borrowings that effectively converts the liability into £ then in the 'interest risk' analysis the borrowing should be treated as a £ liability.

Currency risk disclosure

FRS 13 requires an analysis of the net monetary assets and liabilities at the balance sheet date by reference to the principal functional **currency of operations**. The purpose of this analysis is to explain the currency exposures that give rise to exchange gains or losses.

As with the interest risk disclosures these should be after taking account of any risk management that the entity has undertaken using derivatives. This means that if a UK company has hedged a US$ receivable using a forward exchange contract then the receivable would be treated as a £ asset for the purpose of the analysis.

Liquidity disclosures

Liquidity disclosures focus on the maturity profile of the financial instruments. The FRS requires disclosure of the maturity profile in the following bands:

- in one year or less, or on demand
- in more than one year, but not more than two years
- in more than two years, but not more than five years
- in more than five years.

In addition to requiring disclosure of the maturity profile of financial instruments FRS 13 also requires a similar analysis of any committed but un-drawn borrowing facilities. The required analysis is of facilities expiring:

- in one year or less
- in more than one year, but not more than two years
- in more than two years.

Fair value disclosure

The basic requirement of the **fair value disclosures** is that an entity should divide its financial assets and liabilities into appropriate categories and to disclose either:

- The aggregate fair value at the balance sheet date compared to the aggregate book value; or
- The aggregate fair value of those financial instruments at the balance sheet date with a positive fair value (i.e. in excess of book value) and, separately, those with a negative fair value.

Market price risk

FRS 13 encourages, but does not require, the disclosure of overall market price risk. This involves attempting to predict the overall effect on an entity of changes in key indicators such as interest rates and exchange rates. This is a relatively complex matter and it is sufficient for you to be aware of the fact that it is in the process of development.

27.4.3 Accounting treatment in practice

Appendix III of FRS 13 provides illustrations of the required disclosures and Appendix IV gives guidance on procedures for estimating fair values. In this section, we include an extract from the finance and treasury review of the BOC Group 2001 Report and Accounts on the way in which financial instruments are accounted for:

Management of financial risks

The board of directors sets the treasury policies and objectives of the Group which include controls over the procedures used to manage currency, interest rate and credit risk. The approach to managing risk is set out below. This approach is expected to continue during the next financial year. On a day-to-day basis, Group treasury carries out these policies, with regular review meetings with the Group finance director. Specific and significant activities need approval from the finance committee, which includes any two directors of the company.

Currency risk The Group faces currency risk principally on its net assets, most of which are in currencies other than sterling. Currency movements can therefore have a significant effect on the Group's balance sheet when translating these foreign currency assets into sterling. In order to reduce this effect the Group manages its borrowings, where practicable and cost effective, to hedge foreign currency assets...

The balance sheets of overseas operations are translated into sterling at the closing rates of exchange for the year and any exchange difference is dealt with as a movement on reserves. The profit and loss accounts of overseas businesses are translated at average rates of exchange and this translation impact directly affects the profit and loss account of the Group.

The Group manages its currency flows to minimise currency transaction exchange risk and forward contracts are used as appropriate to hedge net currency flows and selected individual transactions... The aggregate principal amount of forward cover outstanding at 30 September 2001 amounted to £245.0 million (2000: £435.1 million).

Interest rate risk At 30 September 2001, the Groups' net debt position after interest rate hedging activity included a net exposure of £379.4 million (2000: £627.4 million) to floating rates. Based on the Group's 2001 year end level and composition of net debt, an increase in average interest rates of 1 per cent per annum would result in a decrease in future earnings, before tax, of £3.8 million per annum (2000: £6.3 million).

In order to manage interest rate risk the Group maintains both floating rate and fixed rate debt. At 30 September 2001, there is a 30:70 ratio (2000: 48:52) between floating and fixed rate net debt. Underlying borrowings are arranged on both a fixed rate and a floating rate basis and, where appropriate, the Group uses interest rate swaps to vary its mix and to manage the Group's interest rate exposure.

Foreign exchange risk At 30 September 2001, the Group had outstanding forward exchange contracts totalling £245.0 million (2000: £435.1 million) in respect of its actual and forecast transaction exposure. The fair value of these contracts at 30 September 2001 amounted to a loss of £9.1 million (2000: a loss of £12.2 million). A ten per cent appreciation of sterling would increase the fair value of these contracts by £19.2 million (2000: £36.9 million).

The above extract is a statement of policies and details of the financial amounts are set out in the notes to the accounts.

27.5 Likely future developments

27.5.1 Measurement

We said earlier in the chapter that one of the problems regarding measurement of many financial instruments is that cost-based concepts often do not work. Consider once again the example we looked at in section 27.3.2. Contracts to buy foreign currency (to name but one of many examples of derivative financial instruments) do not have a meaningful 'cost' that can be used as a basis for recognition in the financial statements.

27.5.2 **Recognition of gains and losses**

A further problem concerns the recognition of any gain or loss associated with financial instruments. If a company enters into a contract to buy $ at a fixed rate (see earlier example) then as soon as the spot rate starts moving the company is potentially in a more or less favourable position. When should this be recognised? Is it necessary to wait until the contract has been completed or is appropriate recognition possible before that date? SSAP20 *Foreign Currency Translation* says that where a trading transaction is covered by a forward contract then the forward rate **may** be used to translate the foreign currency asset or liability into £. It is silent on forward contracts that are entered into for speculative purposes.

27.5.3 **Hedge accounting**

The use of the exchange rate inherent in a hedging instrument to translate a foreign currency asset or liability is an example of **hedge accounting**. We will see later in this section that such practice may well be prohibited by a future accounting standard on measurement of financial instruments.

27.5.4 **Discussion Paper *Derivatives and other Financial Instruments***

The ASB first explored concerns about accounting for financial instruments in a Discussion Paper, *Derivatives and other Financial Instruments*, published in 1996. That Paper focused in particular on disclosure, measurement and hedge accounting. As we have already seen, FRS 13 *Derivatives and other Financial Instruments: Disclosure* was issued in 1998.

On measurement, the Paper concluded that present measurement practices were no longer adequate for financial instruments. Instead, greater use needed to be made of current value. The Paper explained that, for these purposes, 'current value' meant the amount at which an instrument could be exchanged in an arm's length transaction between informed and willing parties, other than in a forced or liquidation sale.

27.5.5 **Joint Working Group**

The ASB also made it clear in its Discussion Paper that, before taking a decision to develop an accounting standard requiring all financial instruments to be measured at fair value, it would first be necessary to explore further the full fair value model. In order to ensure that the implications of the full fair value model were explored fully at the earliest opportunity, in 1997 a number of standard-setters joined together in setting up the Joint Working Group (JWG) and asking it to develop proposals for a credible, comprehensive and internationally harmonised accounting standard on financial instruments.

The JWG has now completed its work, and has prepared a paper setting out its proposals on the recognition (and de-recognition), measurement, presentation and disclosure of financial instruments. The paper has been issued in the UK as an ASB consultation paper *Financial Instruments and Similar Items* (December 2000).

The main proposals of the consultation paper are that:

- Virtually all financial instruments should be measured at fair value.

- Virtually all gains and losses arising from changes in those fair values should be recognised immediately in the profit and loss account.

- There should be no special accounting (i.e. hedge accounting) for financial instruments that are hedged or are used as a hedging instrument.

- There should be changes to the way in which gains and losses on financial instruments are presented in the profit and loss account, and changes in the way that financial instruments are presented in the balance sheet (a key issue here is the distinction between debt and shares).

- There should be some refinement of the note disclosures on financial instruments, particularly those dealing with the financial risks arising from them.

27.5.6 Volatility arising from use of fair values

The view has been put forward by the Association of Corporate Treasurers[6] that there is disappointment that the Joint Working Group did not consult this body, which is the professional body for those responsible for their companies' management of financial instruments, before proposals were published. There is a concern that if a company is hedging currency exposures a year or more away, the fair value of these hedges could be quite material and could result in high volatility which financial reporting would portray as high risk whereas the economic effect was to reduce risk. This concern seems to be supported by a survey[6] indicating that many companies reporting under IAS 39 have implemented strategies to ensure minimum accounting volatility which may, however, from a group-wide point of view increase risk.

Summary

The disclosure provisions of FRS 13 are now a regular feature of financial reports.

With regard to measurement, the ASB will decide how to proceed with this project when it has considered the JWG's proposals and the comments received in response to them. However, it has already made it clear that it is concerned about existing accounting practice for financial instruments and that it believes that significant changes in practice are necessary. Furthermore, it regards the development of an accounting standard on financial instruments as a priority for standard-setters throughout the world. In developing its own standard it intends to make every effort to develop requirements that achieve the same accounting in the UK and the Republic of Ireland as is achieved by the standards issued in other jurisdictions participating in the JWG. The concern that companies will implement sub-optimal policies in order to reduce the accounting volatility will also need to be addressed.

REVIEW QUESTIONS

1 As a company's credit standing declines, the fair value of its debt is reduced.
   Explain why this happens and the effect it might have on a gearing covenant.

2 Measurement of financial instruments at fair value and recognition of gains and losses on remeasurement in the performance statements would result in a gain for a company when the

market value of its debt reduces (see Question 1 above). This is counter-intuitive if the gain is caused by a decline in the company's credit rating. Discuss.

3 Disclosure of the fair values of financial instruments (as required by FRS 13) is better than measuring them at fair values in the financial statements (as is often required by IAS 39) because measurement at fair value would introduce unwanted volatility to the reported earnings. Discuss.

4 Measurement of financial instruments at fair values is consistent with the concepts underlying the ASB *Statement of Principles for Financial Reporting*. Explain why this statement is true and identify key concepts in the *Statement of Principles* that might be relevant to this issue.

5 It would be better for the ASB to adopt the internationally accepted solution to the issue of accounting for financial instruments rather than developing a recognition and measurement standard of its own. Discuss.

EXERCISES

Question 1

On 1 January 20X0 XYZ Ltd issued debt of £10 million, repayable at par on 31 December 20X2. The fixed interest rate payable on the debt was 8% per annum, payable in arrears. General interest rates stayed relatively constant each year but changed at the end of each year as follows:

31 December 20X0   7%

31 December 20X1   6%

31 December 20X2   5%

The market value of the debt as at 31 December 20X0 and 20X1 is based on the present value of the future expected cash outflows relating to the debt.

The company wishes to comply with the provisions of FRS13 and is wondering about the effect of actually reflecting the debt at market value in the financial statements. The directors have asked for your advice on this matter.

Required:
(a) Compute the fair value of the debt at 31 December 20X0 and 20X1.
(b) Outline the disclosures that would be required in respect of the debt under the provisions of FRS 13.
(c) Indicate why mere disclosure of information regarding the fair value of debt may not be sufficient to meet the needs of users.
(d) Reconcile the movements on the market value of the debt instrument for each of the three years ending 31 December 20X0, 20X1 and 20X2 and indicate where each element of the reconciliation would be presented in the financial statements.

References

1 Group of Thirty (G30), *Derivatives:Practice and Principles*, July 1993, Washington.
2 Discussion Paper, *Derivatives and other Financial Instruments*, ASB, July 1996.
3 FRS 13, *Derivatives and Other Financial Instruments: Disclosure*, ASB, September 1998.
4 S.Thompson, 'Playing a different tune on financial instruments', *Accountancy*, November 1997, p. 85.
5 IAS 39, *Financial Instruments: Recognition and Measurement*, February 1999.
6 C. Bradley, 'Fair Values, wrong answers', *Accountancy*, September 2001, p. 102.

CHAPTER **28**

International reporting and interpretation

28.1 Introduction

There has been a globalisation of world capital markets. This has provided an additional opportunity for lucrative investment across national boundaries. For example, the all share indices in the following markets rose as follows:[1]

	Stockmarket index 12 January 2000	*% change on 31 December 1998 in local currency*
UK (FTSE 100)	6,532.8	+11.7%
US (DJIA)	11,551.0	+25.8%
France (SBF 250)	3,608.7	+44.3%
Germany (Xetra DAX)	6,912.8	+38.1%
Sweden (Affärsvärlden Gen)	5,443.3	+64.2%
China	1,528.4	+25.3%
Greece	5,187.3	+89.5%
Russia	189.2	+328.4%
Japan (Nikkei 250)	18,677.4	+34.9%

Private investors may therefore seek to benefit from variations in growth rates by simply buying shares listed on the overseas stock exchanges.

Corporate investors have an additional strategy open to them in that they can set up trading branches or subsidiaries abroad and carry on business in the other countries. Such investment opportunities have increased with the changes that we have seen in political regimes that have resulted in the emerging markets of Eastern Europe, Asia and the Far East. At the same time actual management of the branches and subsidiaries has been made easier by the improvements in world travel and communications.

Financial reports are required from the foreign investees by both the private and corporate investors in order to assess performance and make buy, hold and sell decisions. However, just as there are national cultural differences, there are also financial reporting differences within countries. In order to assist the reader to understand some of the issues pertinent to interpreting international financial statements, in this chapter we consider the following:

● National differences generate different accounting systems

● Reasons for differences in financial reporting

● Classification of national accounting systems

- Attempts to reduce national differences
- International analysis of financial statements
- Country studies

28.2 National differences generate different accounting systems

We are all familiar with national differences that have become almost stereotypes. Consider the French, for example, who are described as:

> ... proud, patriotic, sardonic people driven by a clear sense of their own greatness ... social interactions are profoundly affected by social stereotypes ... status depends to a great degree on family origins ... outward signs of social status are the individual's level of education, a tasteful house or flat, and knowledge of literature and fine arts. But the all important structure within which the system operates depends on each individual's family origins.[2]

It is natural that such strongly felt influences such as family origin should be reflected in the way business is structured. This can be seen in the extent of family firms in France with a large proportion of all businesses family owned, run, or dominated through major shareholdings and in the strongly autocratic style of management.

On the other hand, it is pointed out that:

> maximising profitability is not always the German's first priority. As in the case of many other Europeans, Germans often feel that the firm has a responsibility to society and the environment.[3]

28.2.1 How do national differences affect financial reporting?

The French business structure indicates that the owners are also frequently the managers. This is different from the UK where there is separation of ownership and management. Consequently, in France, there is far less need for regulations to ensure that financial reports present a true and fair view; the emphasis is not so much on attempting to compensate for potential conflicts of interest between owners and managers as ensuring that the financial reports are accurate.

However, this is only one aspect. There are many other differences in economic and cultural conditions, which have led to an array of different financial reporting practices around the world. An understanding of this improves the awareness of potential misinterpretation when appraising financial statements prepared in non-UK countries. It is useful to appreciate the reasons for these variations in order to improve understanding of the business activities represented by the accounts.

28.3 Reasons for differences in financial reporting

A number of attempts have been made to identify reasons for differences in financial reporting.[4] The issue is far from clear but most writers agree that the following are among the main factors influencing the development of financial reporting:

- the character of the national legal system;
- the way in which industry is financed;

- the relationship of the tax and reporting systems;
- the influence and status of the accounting profession;
- the extent to which accounting theory is developed;
- accidents of history;
- language.

We will consider the effect of each of these.

28.3.1 The character of the national legal system

There are two major legal systems namely, that based on common law and that based on Roman law. It is important to recognise this because the legal systems influence the way in which behaviour in a country, including accounting and financial reporting, is regulated.

Countries with a legal system based on common law include England and Wales, Ireland, United States, Australia, Canada and New Zealand. These countries rely on the application of equity to specific cases rather than a set of detailed rules to be applied in all cases. The effect in the UK, as far as financial reporting was concerned, was that there was limited legislation regulating the form and content of financial statements until the government was required to implement the EC Fourth Directive. The Directive was implemented in the UK by the passing of the Companies Act 1981 and this can be seen as a watershed because it was the first time that the layout of company accounts had been prescribed by statute in England and Wales.

English common law heritage was accommodated within the legislation by the provision that the detailed regulations of the Act need not be applied if, in the judgement of the directors, strict adherence to the Act would result in financial statements that did not present a true and fair view.

Countries with a legal system based on Roman law include France, Germany and Japan. These countries rely on the codification of detailed rules, which are often included within their companies act legislation. The result is that there is less flexibility in the preparation of financial reports in those countries. They are less inclined to look to fine distinctions to justify different reporting treatments which are inherent in the common law approach.

However, it is not just that common law countries have fewer codified laws than Roman law countries. There is a fundamental difference in the way in which the reporting of commercial transactions is approached. In the common law countries there is an established practice of creative compliance. By this we mean that the spirit of the law is elusive[5] and management is more inclined to act with creative compliance in order to escape effective legal control. By creative compliance we mean that management complies with the form of the regulation but in a way that might be against its spirit, e.g. structuring leasing agreements in the most acceptable way for financial reporting purposes.

28.3.2 The way in which industry is financed

Accountancy is the art of communicating relevant financial information about a business entity to users. One of the considerations to take into account when deciding what is relevant is the way in which the business has been financed, e.g. the information needs of equity investors will be different from those of loan creditors. This is one factor responsible for international financial reporting differences because the predominant provider of capital is different in different countries.[6] Figure 28.1 makes a simple comparison between

**Figure 28.1 Domestic equity market
capitalisation/gross domestic product**

	Market capitalisation/GDP (%)	
	1994	1998
Germany	22	49
France	33	65
UK	116	170
Sweden	64	125
USA	73	158

domestic equity market capitalisation and gross domestic product (GDP).[7] The higher the ratio, the greater the importance of the equity market compared with loan finance.

We see that in the UK, the US and Sweden, companies rely more heavily on individual investors to provide finance than in France or Germany. An active stock exchange has developed to allow shareholders to liquidate their investments and a system of financial reporting has evolved to satisfy a stewardship need where prudence and conservatism predominate and a capital market need for fair information[8] which allows interested parties to deal on an equal footing where the accruals concept and the doctrine of substance over form predominate. It is important to note that equity has gained importance in all the countries in Figure 28.1. This can be an important factor in the development of accounting.

In Germany, as well as equity investment having a lower profile, there is also a significant difference in the way in which shares are registered and transferred. In the UK individual shareholders are entered onto the company's Register of Members. In Germany many shares are bearer shares which means that they are not registered in the individual investor's name but are deposited with a bank that has the authority to exercise a proxy. It could perhaps appear at first glance that the banks have undue influence but they state that, in the case of proxy votes, shareholders are at liberty to cast their votes as they see fit and not to follow the recommendations of the bank.[9] In addition to their control over proxy votes, the big three German banks, The Deutsche Bank, the Dresdner Bank and the Commerzbank, also have significant direct equity holdings, e.g. in 1992 the Deutsche Bank had a direct holding of 28% in Daimler-Benz.[10]

There was an investigation carried out in the 1970s by the Gessler Commission into the ties between the Big Three and large West German manufacturing companies. The Commission established that the banks' power lay in the combination of the proxy votes, the tradition of the house bank which kept a company linked to one principal lender, the size of the banks' direct equity holdings and their representation on company supervisory boards.[11]

In practice, therefore, the banks are effectively both principal lenders and shareholders in Germany. As principal lenders they receive internal information such as cash flow forecasts which, as a result, is also available to them in their role as nominee shareholders. We are not concerned here with questions such as conflict of interest and criticisms that the banks are able to exert undue influence. Our interest is purely in the financial reporting implications which are that the banks have sufficient power to obtain all of the information they require without reliance on the annual accounts. Published disclosures are far less relevant than in the UK.

During the 1990s there has been a growth in the UK and US of institutional investors such as pension funds which form an ever increasing proportion of registered shareholders. In theory, the information needs of these institutional investors should be the same as of individual investors. However, in practice, they might be in a position to obtain information by direct access to management and the directors. One effect of this might be that they will become less interested in seeking disclosures in the financial statements – they will have already picked up the significant information at an informal level.

28.3.3 The relationship of the tax and reporting systems

In the UK separate rules have evolved for computing profit for tax and computing profit for financial reporting purposes. The legislation for tax purposes tends to be more prescriptive, e.g. there is a defined rate for capital allowances on fixed assets which means that the reduction in value of fixed assets for tax purposes is decided by the government. The financial reporting environment is less prescriptive but this is compensated for by requiring greater disclosure. For example, there is no defined rate for depreciating fixed assets but there is a requirement for companies to state their depreciation accounting policy. Similar systems have evolved in the US and the Netherlands.

However, certain countries give primacy to taxation rules and will only allow expenditure for tax purposes if it is given the same treatment in the financial accounts. In France and Germany the tax rules effectively become the accounting rules.

This can lead to difficulties of interpretation, particularly when capital allowances, i.e. depreciation for tax purposes, are changed to secure public policy objectives such as encouraging investment in fixed assets by permitting accelerated write-off when assessing taxable profits. In fact, the depreciation charge against profit would be said by a UK accountant not to be fair, even though it could certainly be legal or correct.[12]

Depreciation has been discussed to illustrate the possibility of misinterpretation because of the different status and effect of tax rules on annual accounts. Other items that require careful consideration include stock valuations, bad debt provisions, development expenditure and revaluation of fixed assets. There might also be public policy arrangements that are unique to a single country, e.g. the availability of transfers to reserves to reduce taxable profit as occurs in Sweden.[13]

28.3.4 The influence and status of the accounting profession

The development of a capital market in the UK for dealing in shares created a need for reliable, relevant and timely financial information. Legislation was introduced requiring companies to prepare annual accounts and have them audited. This resulted in the growth of an established and respected accounting profession able to produce relevant reports and attest to their reliability by performing an audit.

In turn, the existence of a strong profession had an impact on the development of UK accounting regulations. It is the profession that has been responsible for the promulgation of accounting standards and recommendations. This pattern is seen in other countries, e.g. US, Australia, Canada, Netherlands.

In countries where there has not been the same need to provide market sensitive information, e.g. in Eastern Europe in the 1980s, accountants have been seen purely as bookkeepers and have been accorded a low status. This explains the lack of expertise among financial accountants. There was also a lack of demand for financial management skills because production targets were set centrally without the emphasis for maximising the use of scarce resources at the business entity level. The attributes that are valued in a market economy such as the exercise of judgement and the determination of relevant information were not required. This position is rapidly changing and there will be a growth in the training, professionalism and contribution for both financial and management accountants as these economies become market economies.

28.3.5 The extent to which accounting theory is developed

Accounting theory can influence accounting practice. Theory can be developed at both an academic and professional level but for it to take root it must be accepted by the profession. For example, we saw in Chapter 4 the attempts in the UK to introduce a form of current value accounting. In the UK, theories such as current purchasing power and current cost accounting first surfaced in the academic world and there were many practising accountants who regarded them then, and still regard them now, as academic.

In the Netherlands, professional accountants receive an academic accountancy training as well as the vocational accountancy training which is typical in the UK. Perhaps as a result of that there is less reluctance on the part of the profession to view academics as isolated from the real world. This might go some way to explaining why it was in the Netherlands that we saw general acceptance by the profession for the idea that for information to be relevant it needed to be based on current value accounting. Largely as a result of pressure from the Netherlands, the Fourth Directive contained provisions which allowed member states to introduce inflation accounting systems.[14]

In Chapter 6, we discussed the search for a conceptual framework for financial reporting. Attempts have been made to formulate a conceptual framework in countries such as the UK, USA, Canada and Australia[15] and the International Standards Committee has also contributed to this field. One of the results has been the closer collaboration between the regulatory bodies which might assist in reducing differences in the longer term.

28.3.6 Accidents of history

The development of accounting systems is often allied to the political history of a country. Scandals surrounding company failures, notably in the US in the 1920s and 1930s and in the UK in the 1960s and 1980s had a marked impact on financial reporting in those countries. In the US the Securities and Exchange Commission was established to control listed companies, with responsibility to ensure adequate disclosure in annual accounts. Ever increasing control over the form and content of financial statements through improvements in the accounting standard setting process has evolved from the difficulties in the UK.

International boundaries have also been crossed in the evolution of accounting. In some instances it has been a question of pooling of resources to avoid repeating work already carried out elsewhere, e.g. the Norwegians studied the report of the Dearing Committee in the UK before setting up their new accounting standard setting system.[16] Other changes in nations' accounting practices have been a result of external pressure, e.g. Spain's membership of the European Community led to radical changes in accounting,[17] while the Germans influenced accounting in the countries they occupied during the Second World War.[18] Such accidents of history have changed the course of accounting and reduced the clarity of distinctions between countries.

28.3.7 Language

Language has often played an important role in the development of different methods of accounting for similar items. Certain nationalities are notorious for speaking only their own language, which has prevented them from benefiting from the wisdom of other nations. There is also the difficulty of translating concepts as well as phrases, where one country has influenced another.

28.4 Classification of national accounting systems

A number of attempts have been made to classify national accounting systems in much the same way that biologists attempt to classify flora and fauna.[19] However, as can be seen from the reasons for different systems described above, national differences are far from straightforward. Any classifications need to be constantly updated as accounting is such a dynamic activity. There are constant changes as a result of events taking place both within and beyond the accounting profession. Such classifications are therefore useful in gaining a greater understanding of particular features of accounting in a country, but do need to be treated with a degree of caution.

28.5 Attempts to reduce national differences

Given the increasing numbers of transnational users of accounts, many attempts have been made to reduce the differences between reports prepared in different countries. There are, in essence, two approaches: standardisation and harmonisation.[20] These terms have become technical terms in the study of international accounting. Standardisation advocates the setting out of rules for accounting for similar items in all countries. Harmonisation is less radical in that it allows for some different national approaches but provides a common framework so that major issues will be dealt with in similar ways across national borders. Gradually, as efforts to improve comparability of financial statements have increased, these two approaches have come closer together.

Attempts have been made to standardise or at least harmonise financial reporting to satisfy the needs of a number of different groups. The main emphasis of this chapter is on users of accounts who are seeking to assess a company's past or potential investment performance. However, government agencies, such as tax and customs authorities also have an interest in greater compatibility of information between countries. International accountancy firms deal with large numbers of multi-national clients, whose accounts frequently need to be adjusted to common accounting principles before consolidations can be prepared. A reduction in national accounting differences would reduce the training costs of these firms and increase staff mobility (however, it would ultimately limit the fees they could charge!). Companies seeking capital through cross-border listings may currently need to prepare financial statements under more than one set of regulations to meet the needs of different stock exchanges. This is both costly and time consuming.

A number of international bodies are involved in the processes of harmonisation or standardisation. These have included organisations, which may not immediately be associated with accounting, such as the United Nations and the Organisation for Economic Co-operation and Development (OECD). However, the most influential have probably been the International Accounting Standards Committee and the European Community. Their contribution is summarised in Section 28.7.

28.6 Arguments in support of standards

In preparation for considering the work of the international bodies, it is worth spending some time considering the needs for accounting standards. In most countries there is at least some legislation governing financial reporting, so why is there a need for further regulation? Four important arguments in support of standards are set out below and are based on matters of comparability, credibility, influence and discipline.

28.6.1 Comparability

Financial statements should allow a user to make predictions of future cash flows, make comparisons with other companies[21] and evaluate the management's performance. For comparisons of performance, progress and trends to be valid, investment decision-makers should be supplied with relevant and reliable data that have been standardised. Such comparisons would be distorted and valueless if companies were permitted to select accounting policies at random, or, even worse, with the intention of disguising changes in performance and trends. Much accounting legislation merely provides a framework, giving general principles rather than detailed regulations. To ensure there is comparability of items that are not covered in detail in legislation, accounting standards can be helpful by providing further guidance.

28.6.2 Credibility

The accountancy profession would lose all credibility if it permitted companies experiencing similar events to produce financial reports that disclosed markedly different results simply because they could select different accounting policies. Uniformity of subjective treatment (or sufficient explanation of variations in treatment) is essential if financial reports are to present events fairly. However, the existence of accounting standards is no substitute for judgement. For example, in the UK or Sweden, an accountant might occasionally depart from the detailed provisions of a particular accounting standard to ensure the accounts give a 'true and fair view' or reflect 'good accounting practice'.

28.6.3 Influence

The process of formulating standards has encouraged a constructive appraisal of the policies being proposed for individual reporting problems and has often stimulated the development of a conceptual framework. This can then provide a coherent theoretical underpinning for the development of standards to ensure consistency of approach between different financial statement items. Most national bodies that are responsible for setting accounting standards draw on the expertise of a range of preparers and users of financial statements in their drafting process and allow a period of 'exposure' of standards for public comment. This ensures that all issues are fully considered and that no interest group would be disadvantaged by the proposed standard.

28.6.4 Discipline

Companies left to their own devices without the need to observe standards will eventually be disciplined by the financial market. However, in the short term, investors in such entities may suffer loss. Mandatory standards will impose systematic ongoing regulation, which should prevent serious loss to the entity and those who rely on the annual accounts when making credit, loan and investment decisions. The existence of standards provides a benchmark for accountants and auditors to use to determine whether the proposed treatment is acceptable. Standards can be made mandatory in a number of ways. In the UK, standards were given legal backing by the Companies Act 1989, which requires large companies to state that they have followed the standards or to explain why they have not. In Denmark, stock exchange regulations require financial statements to be prepared in accordance with good accounting practice and hence accounting standards. Perhaps the strongest authority given to non-legislative pronouncements is that given to Generally Accepted Accounting Principles (GAAP) in the US. Compliance with GAAP is specifically mentioned in the audit report.

Bodies such as the UK's Urgent Issues Task Force and the US's Emerging Issues Task Force ensure standards are not being abused and identify areas where new regulations (and possibly new standards or amendments to existing standards) are required.

There is a tension between the desire that standards should not be a comprehensive code of rigid rules and the desire to regulate accounting practices that are imaginatively devised by directors and their financial advisors to create a picture that they might consider true and fair – but which others may not. Directors are under pressure to maintain and improve the market valuation of their securities; they will attempt to influence any financial statistic that has an impact on the market valuation, e.g. the trend in the EPS figure, the net asset backing for the shares or the gearing ratios. The UK's Financial Reporting Council has proved to be an effective way of ensuring companies follow accounting standards.

28.6.5 Non-mandatory recommendations

Another approach to avoiding an excessive burden of standards is to increase the volume of non-mandatory 'requirements'. These may be prepared by professional accounting bodies, stock exchanges or investor groups to improve the usefulness of financial reports. The UK's operating and financial review (OFR) is an example of how such non-mandatory recommendations can take effect.

28.7 The work of international bodies in harmonising and standardising financial reporting

The major international bodies have accelerated their programmes of work and have sought greater co-operation in recent years. This section sets out something of their histories and structures before relating the latest developments in their strategies and the effect this is likely to have on the annual reports of companies.

28.7.1 The International Accounting Standards Committee

The International Accounting Standards Committee (IASC) was established in 1973 by the professional accounting bodies of Australia, Canada, France, Germany, Japan, Mexico, the Netherlands, the UK and Ireland and the USA.

The membership now comprises all professional accounting bodies that are members of the International Federation of Accountants (IFAC). The objectives of the IASC are:

(a) to develop, in the public interest, a single set of high quality, understandable and enforceable global accounting standards that require high quality, transparent and comparable information in financial statements and other financial reporting to help participants in the world's capital markets and other users make economic decisions;

(b) to promote the use and rigorous application of those standards; and

(c) to bring about convergence of national accounting standards and International Accounting Standards to high quality solutions.[22]

The IASC was restructured, following a review between 1998 and 2000, to give an improved balance between geographical representation, technical competence and independence.[23] The nineteen trustees of the IASC will represent a range of geographical and professional interests and are responsible for raising the organisation's funds and appointing the members of the Board and the Standing Interpretations Committee (SIC). The International Accounting Standards Board (IASB) has responsibility for all technical matters including the preparation and implementation of International Accounting Standards (IASs). In future, the standards issued by the IASB will be known as International Financial Reporting Standards (IFRSs).[24]

The process of producing a new IFRS is similar to the processes of some national accounting standard setters. Once a need for a new (or revised) standard has been identified, a steering committee is set up to identify the relevant issues and draft the standard. Drafts are produced at varying stages and are exposed to public scrutiny. Subsequent drafts take account of comments obtained during the exposure period. The final standard is approved by the Board and an effective date agreed. International Accounting Standards currently in effect are shown in Figure 28.2. The IASC has also issued a *Framework for the Preparation and Presentation of Financial Statements*.[25] This will assist in the development of future accounting standards and improve harmonisation by providing

Figure 28.2 International Accounting Standards

International Accounting Standards (effective date)	Corresponding UK Standards	Principal requirements of IAS where different from UK Standard
IAS 1 Presentation of Financial Statements (1/7/98 replaces IAS 1 Disclosure of Accounting Policies)	FRS 3, FRS 18	
IAS 2 Inventories (1/1/76, revised in 1993)	SSAP 9	
IAS 7 Cash Flow Statements (1/1/79 revised in 1992)	FRS 1	Concentrates on 'cash and cash equivalents' rather than cash. Does not require a reconciliation to movement in net debt. Permits direct and indirect methods and does not require reconciliation to operating profit. No separate headings for returns on investments and servicing of finance, taxation, capital expenditure and financial investments, acquisitions and disposals and equity dividends paid.

Figure 28.2 (*cont.*)

International Accounting Standards (effective date)	Corresponding UK Standards	Principal requirements of IAS where different from UK Standard
IAS 8 Net Profit or Loss for the Period, Fundamental Errors and Changes in Accounting Policies (1/1/79 revised in 1993; paragraphs 19–22 superseded by IAS 35)	FRS 3	Definition of extraordinary items is less rigorous, but they will arise only on rare occasions.
IAS 10 Contingencies and Events Occurring After the Balance Sheet Date (1/1/80, revised 1999; IAS 37 supersedes those parts of IAS 10 that deal with contingencies, effective 1/7/1999)	SSAP 17, FRS 11	Disclosure of tax implications of contingencies not required.
IAS 11 Construction Contracts (1/1/80 revised in 1993)	SSAP 9	
IAS 12 Income Taxes (1/1/98 replaces IAS 12 Accounting for Taxes on Income)	FRS 16	Separate presentation of current tax on face of balance sheet. Disclosure of tax expense relating to discontinued operations.
IAS 14 Segment Reporting (1/7/98 replaces Reporting Financial Information by Segment)	SSAP 25	No exemption from disclosure on grounds that it would be damaging to the company. Requires segmental capital expenditure, depreciation, details of associates and assets and liabilities in addition to that required by SSAP 25.
IAS 15 Information Reflecting the Effects of Changing Prices (1/1/83)		Standard is not mandatory, but requires: – depreciation adjustment; – cost of sales adjustment; – monetary items adjustment; – overall effects of above and other adjustments.
IAS 16 Property, Plant and Equipment (1/1/83, revised in 1993 and by IAS 36 in 1998)	FRS 15	Where revaluations are used, this must be to 'fair value' which is broader than FRS 15's 'value to the business model'. Revaluation gains and losses may be recognised through the statement of total recognised gains and losses. Additional disclosures required regarding pledges of assets, assets under construction, commitments to acquire assets, measurement bases and revaluation surpluses (these are mostly required under the Companies Act 1985 in the UK but are not specifically mentioned in FRS 15).

Figure 28.2 (*cont.*)

International Accounting Standards (effective date)	Corresponding UK Standards	Principal requirements of IAS where different from UK Standard
IAS 17 Accounting for Leases (1/1/84 revised 1997 effective 1/1/99)	SSAP 21, FRS 5	
IAS 18 Revenue (1/1/84 revised in 1993)	Statement of Principles	Greater disclosure of revenue recognition policies and amounts.
IAS 19 Employee Benefits (1/1/85 revised in 1993 and 1998 effective 1/1/99)	FRS 17	Actuarial gains and losses may be taken to P&L immediately or amortised over a period up to the average remaining work life of employees
IAS 20 Accounting for Government Grants and Disclosure of Government Assistance (1/1/84)	SSAP 4	Deduction of grant is permitted in arriving at carrying amount of the asset.
IAS 21 The Effects of Changes in Foreign Exchange Rates (1/1/85 revised in 1993)	SSAP 20, FRS 3	Income and expenses of foreign enterprises are to be translated at the rate ruling on the date of the transaction (or an average rate). Disclosure required of amount of exchange differences taken to P&L. Disclosure required of impact of changes from/to temporal and closing rate methods and vice versa.
IAS 22 Business Combinations (1/1/85 revised in 1993 and 1996 and by IAS 36 in 1998)	FRS 6, FRS 7, FRS 10	Positive goodwill is to be capitalised and is normally amortised over a maximum period of five years unless a longer period (which cannot exceed twenty years) can be justified. Requirements relating to contingent consideration less prescriptive than FRS 7. Disclosures for mergers not as onerous as FRS 6.
IAS 23 Borrowing Costs (1/1/86 revised in 1993)	FRS 15	Capitalisation is an allowed alternative treatment similar to the strict application of the Companies Act 1985.
IAS 24 Related Party Disclosures (1/1/86)	FRS 8	Disclosures generally less rigorous than FRS 8, e.g. do not need to give names of related parties or amounts of transactions.
IAS 25 Accounting for Investments (1/1/87, portions relating to investments in financial assets are superseded by IAS 39)	SSAP 19	Investment properties must be depreciated in accordance with IAS 16. Long-term investments may be revalued or stated at cost.

Figure 28.2 (*cont.*)

International Accounting Standards (effective date)	Corresponding UK Standards	Principal requirements of IAS where different from UK Standard
IAS 26 Accounting and Reporting by Retirement Benefit Plans (1/1/88)		
IAS 27 Consolidated Financial Statements and Accounting for Investments in Subsidiaries (1/1/90 amended by IAS 39)	FRS 2	
IAS 28 Accounting for Investments in Associates (1/1/90)	FRS 9	Emphasis in definition of associate in IAS 28 requires investor to have the potential to participate in the financial and operating policy decisions, whereas FRS 9 definition requires investor to participate and exert significant influence. When investments are shown at cost, dividends made from post-acquisition projects are treated as a reduction in the cost of the investment in the associate. In the entity accounts, the associate can be accounted for using equity method, cost or revalued amounts.
IAS 29 Financial Reporting in Hyperinflationary Economies (1/1/90)		Hyperinflation is where (amongst other things) cumulative inflation over three years exceeds 100%. Financial statements must be presented in a measuring unit current at the balance sheet date.
IAS 30 Disclosures in the Financial Statements of Banks and Similar Financial Institutions (1/1/91 amended by IAS 39)		
IAS 31 Financial Reporting of Interests in Joint Ventures (1/1/92 amended by IAS 36 and IAS 39 in 1998)	FRS 9	Broader definition of types of operation which may be joint venture. Proportional consolidation is the preferred method, with equity accounting a permitted alternative.
IAS 32 Financial Instruments: Disclosure and Presentation (1/1/96 revised by IAS 39)	FRS 13 FRS 4 FRS 5	'Split accounting' required for hybrid instruments, e.g. proceeds of issue of convertible bond must be split between the financial liability and equity instrument. Additional specific disclosures about credit risk and hedging.

Figure 28.2 (*cont.*)

International Accounting Standards (effective date)	Corresponding UK Standards	Principal requirements of IAS where different from UK Standard
IAS 33 Earnings per Share (1/1/98)	FRS 14	IAS provides less specific guidance than FRS 14.
IAS 34 Interim Financial Reporting (1/1/99)	–	Minimum content: condensed balance sheet, income statement, cash flow statement, statement of changes in equity and notes. Accounting policies should be the same as for year-end financial statements.
IAS 35 Discontinuing Operations (1/1/99)	FRS 3	FRED 22 proposing to use discontinuing terminology.
IAS 36 Impairment of Assets (1/7/99)	FRS 11	Impairment caused by consumption of economic benefits need only be recognised in the profit and loss account to the extent that the loss exceeds the balance on the revaluation reserve relating to the assets in question.
IAS 37 Provisions, Contingent Liabilities and Contingent Assets (1/7/99)	FRS 12	–
IAS 38 Intangible Assets (1/7/99)	FRS 10	Internally generated intangible assets should be capitalised if certain strict criteria are met.
IAS 39 Financial Instruments: Recognition and Measurement (1/1/2001)	FRS 13	
IAS 40 Investment Property (1/1/2001)	SSAP 19	Under IAS 40 a company may use fair values.
IAS 41 Agriculture (1/1/2003)	–	

a basis for reducing the number of accounting treatments permitted by IASs. Professional accountancy bodies have prepared and published translations of IASs, making them available to a wide audience and the IASC itself has set up a mechanism to issue interpretation of the standards.

International Accounting Standards (IASs) may be applied in one of the following ways:

● An IAS may be adopted as a national accounting standard. This can be useful where there are limited resources and an 'off the peg' solution is required. This is the practice in countries such as Botswana, Cyprus and Zimbabwe. The disadvantage is that the standard may not meet specific local needs, due to the influence of the larger industrialised nations on the IASC.

● An IAS may be used as a national requirement but adapted for local purposes. This approach is used in Fiji and Kuwait for example.

● National requirements may be derived independently, but adapted to conform with

IASs. This is currently the procedure in the UK, although recently the programmes of the IASC and ASB have converged. Indeed, IAS 37 and FRS 12 were developed jointly.

It is important to note that if a company wishes to describe its financial statements as complying with IASs, IAS 1 requires the financial statements to comply with all the requirements of each applicable standard and each applicable interpretation of the SIC. This clearly outlaws the practice of 'IAS-lite' reporting, where companies claimed compliance with IASs while neglecting some of their more onerous requirements.

The large number of members of the IASC has meant that it has been difficult to achieve a consensus on many of the issues that the Committee has addressed. Consequently, many IASs initially permitted a range of treatments. Whilst this was an improvement on not having a standard at all, it was still far from ideal. In response to this criticism, the IASC began its comparability/improvements project in 1987, which resulted in the revision of ten standards.

28.7.2 The European Union[26]

The Treaty of Rome was signed in 1957 to establish a European Economic Community. The objectives of the Community were set out in article 2 of the Treaty:

> The Community shall have as its task, by establishing a common market and progressively approximating the economic policies of member states, to promote throughout the Community a harmonious development of economic activities, a continuous and balanced expansion, an increase in stability, an accelerated raising of the standard of living and closer relations between the States belonging to it.

In order to achieve these objectives, the Treaty set out specific provisions for the free movement of goods, services, people and capital. The single European currency (the euro) in operation in 12 European countries (and some of their trading partners) since January 2000 (with notes and coins in circulation from January 2002) has removed yet another barrier to trade and will link the economies of members more closely.

It was envisaged that the Treaty would be supported by action in other spheres developing common legislation where necessary. The harmonisation of company law across the Community has been part of this process. To date, the most important EC Directives adopted in respect of financial reporting are the Fourth (company accounts), Seventh (consolidated accounts) and Eighth (auditing). The Fifth Directive (corporate governance) is yet to be adopted by member states and the draft Tenth Directive (international mergers) is still under debate.

Member states are required to incorporate these Directives into their national legislations within an agreed time scale. This has succeeded in achieving greater comparability between financial statements prepared in different member states, although a number of cultural differences remain. The Directives have also had an impact on financial reporting in countries seeking membership or involved in trade with existing members of the EU (e.g. Norway has implemented the Directives as a condition of membership of the European Economic Area and Latvia has based its new accounting legislation on the Danish implementation of the Directives).

Although they have had a major impact on accounting in some countries, e.g. Greece and Spain, the Directives still only provide a framework for financial reporting and provide a range of options. This has to be supported by national legislation or accounting standards to provide the detailed regulation that leads to comparability within countries. Consequently, these national practices can then counteract the harmonisation efforts. One solution would be to have a European Accounting Standards Board. However, the practicalities of setting up such an organisation and reaching agreement on accounting issues within a reasonable time have meant that such a board has not been established. At the end of 1995, it was decided that the European Union could play a more active role in the IASC with a view to using IASs to support the Directives. As a first step, the Contact Committee on the Accounting Directives prepared a report entitled *An examination of the conformity between the international accounting standards and the European accounting Directives* in 1996. This established that there were few major differences between the IASs and the Directives.

28.7.3 IASC and the International Organisation of Securities Commissions (IOSCO)

The IASC and IOSCO have been co-operating on the accounting problems of multinational companies involved in foreign listings since 1987.[27] In July 1995 it was agreed that if the IASC were to produce a set of core standards that were acceptable to the technical committee of IOSCO, any company would be able to use IAS financial statements to obtain listings of its securities on any foreign stock exchange. This would be particularly useful for companies seeking listing on the US stock exchange, which currently requires companies to present financial statements in accordance with US GAAP or reconcile domestic accounts to US GAAP. The ramifications of this for preparers and users of financial statements of multinational companies are tremendous: considerable time and effort would be saved. The IASC completed its core standards in December 1998. In May 2000, IOSCO recommended that its members permit the use of IASs by multinational issuers for cross-border offerings and listings, supplemented where necessary to address outstanding substantive issues at a national or regional level. This is clearly a major step towards the acceptance of IASs and the elimination of the necessity for multiple reporting. Nevertheless, there could still be extensive demands on preparers to provide supplementary information. The US Securities and Exchange Commission (SEC) is seen as being a potential stumbling block. This is perhaps unsurprising given the remaining differences between IASs and US GAAP[28] and the SEC's requirement for strict application of US GAAP. Nevertheless, the SEC took a constructive approach to the issue in seeking further information on the use and quality of IASs in its *Concept Release on International Accounting Standards* in February 2000.

28.7.4 EU and IAS

In a communication from the Commission of the European Communities to the Council and the European Parliament (*EU Financial Reporting Strategy: the way forward*) in June 2000, it was proposed that all listed companies be required to prepare their consolidated financial statements in accordance with IASs from 2005 onwards. In February 2001 the European Commission published a proposal for a regulation on the application of international accounting standards in the EU which aimed to harmonise financial reporting in the EU on the basis of globally agreed accounting standards by 2005 and to enhance EU companies' access to international capital markets. This proposal became a regulation in June 2002.[29] Member states are allowed to extend the application of IASs to unlisted companies and to individual accounts. In the UK the Government will conduct a consultation on these issues. This will clearly be helpful for the increasing numbers of companies that have juggled to meet the requirements of international investors without falling foul of national regulations. The proposals followed changes in legislation in a number of member states to permit certain companies to use international standards. This could be seen as having led to a reduction in comparability as companies take different approaches. For example, in 1999 reports in Finland, Stora Enso (listed in Helsinki and Stockholm) and Nokia (listed in Helsinki, Stockholm, London, Frankfurt and New York) used IASs, but UPM Kymmene (listed in Helsinki and New York) used Finnish accounting practice. The proposals also reflect companies' perceptions of market demands. For example, a Danish company, Berendsen, changed its accounting policies on goodwill and restructuring provisions in 1999. The annual report explains that the changes were made 'in order to come more into line with international accounting standards, thus making comparisons with foreign company accounts easier'.

However, it is important to note that the EU has not simply handed over its powers to the IASC. There is to be an endorsement mechanism in the EU, which is to ensure IASs meet the needs of EU listed companies. This may limit the number of options available to EU companies or require additional disclosures.

28.7.5 Current convergence and improvement projects

In 2001 the IASB announced a project to improve 12 IASB standards.[30] The objective of this project is to improve the quality of financial reporting under IASs by converging on best practice around the world and reducing choice in the application of the standards. The project deals with standards that are not the subject of separate projects and, therefore, changes to individual standards could be considered to be relatively minor. The IASB is responding to suggestions from IOSCO, the EU, national standard setters, accounting firms and the SIC. The date for compliance with IASs by EU listed companies of 2005 has given added impetus to this project.

Examples of where the improvements project will converge with the requirements of some of the national standard setters include:

- Removal of the distinction between fundamental errors and errors (IAS 8)
- Clarification that when classifying a lease of both land and buildings that the lease shall be split into two elements: a lease of land and a lease of buildings (IAS17)
- Introducing and explaining the notion of functional currency (IAS21)
- Requiring amounts, not just proportions, to be disclosed for related party transactions and balances (IAS 24)
- Including 'joint venture' and 'post-employment benefit plans' in the definition of related parties (IAS 24)
- Aligning guidance for the calculation of earnings per share with that of other standard-setters (IAS 33).

A number of options are to be removed from certain standards. This will have the effect of both reducing choice (and hence increasing comparability) and converging with most of the national standards in countries where the IASB has a liaison member. The proposals include eliminating the following treatments:

- LIFO (IAS 2)
- Inclusion of correction of fundamental errors and adjustments arising from voluntary changes in accounting policies in the income statement (opening retained earnings will be adjusted instead) (IAS 8)
- Separate expensing of lessor's initial direct costs in negotiating a lease or allocation of them against income over the lease term (to be capitalised and allocated over the lease term) (IAS 17)

- Recognition of foreign exchange losses on the acquisition of an asset as part of the cost of the asset (to be recognised in the income statement in the period of acquisition) (IAS 21)

- Translation of goodwill and fair value adjustments to assets and liabilities arising on acquisition of a foreign entity at historical rate (closing rate to be used) (IAS 21)

- Measurement of investments in subsidiaries, associates and jointly controlled entities in an investor's separate financial statements using the equity method (cost or IAS 39 treatment to be used) (IAS 28)

- Measurement of investments in associates when the investor does not prepare consolidated financial statements because it has no subsidiaries using cost or IAS 30 method (equity method to be used) (IAS 28).

Other improvements involve clarification of key terms (such as 'present fairly'), removing duplication of regulations between standards, and transferring material between standards to make them easier to follow.

Convergence is a two-way process. At the same time as the IASB is making changes to bring its standards in line with global best practice national standard setters are working to align their standards with IASs. In the UK, the ASB's FREDs 24–30 are part of its 'convergence project'. The UK and international regulations involved are summarised below.[31] The ASB is taking account of any changes to the IASs expected as a result of the IASB's improvements project.

FRED	UK regulations to be replaced	IAS(s) on which new UK regulations will be based
FRED 24 The effects of changes in foreign exchange rates; financial reporting in hyperinflationary economies	SSAP 20 Foreign currency translation UITF Abstract 9 Accounting for operations in hyperinflationary economies	IAS 21 The effects of changes in foreign exchange rates IAS 29 Financial reporting in hyperinflationary economies
FRED 25 Related party disclosures	FRS 8 Related party disclosures	IAS 24 Related party disclosures
FRED 26 Earnings per share	FRS 14 Earnings per share	IAS 33 Earnings per share
FRED 27 Events after the balance sheet date	SSAP 17 Accounting for post-balance sheet events	IAS 10 Events after the balance sheet date
FRED 28 Inventories; construction and service contracts	SSAP 9 Stocks and long-term contracts	IAS 2 Inventories IAS 11 Construction contracts IAS 18 Revenue (limited text)

(*continued*)

FRED	UK regulations to be replaced	IAS(s) on which new UK regulations will be based
FRED 29 Property, plant and equipment; borrowing costs	FRS 15	IAS 16 Property, plant and equipment IAS 23 Borrowing costs
FRED 30 Financial instruments: disclosure and presentation; recognition and measurement	FRS 4 Capital instruments UITF 11 Capital instruments: issuer call options UITF 33 Obligations in capital instruments FRS 13 Derivatives and other financial instruments: disclosures	IAS 32 Financial instruments: disclosure and measurement IAS 39 Financial instruments: recognition and measurement

28.7.6 The future

Financial reporting is clearly about to enter a period of transition. When the US energy giant Enron collapsed in 2001, a number of important issues were raised regarding the conduct of directors and auditors. More importantly, in the context of this chapter, it highlighted a number of deficiencies in financial reporting. The application of US GAAP had led to a lack of transparency regarding matters including revenue recognition, valuation of intangible assets, so-called special purpose entities and off-balance-sheet finance, and derivatives. This has demonstrated that, in spite of (or perhaps because of) its detailed regulations, US GAAP is not without its faults. The broader debate has been opened as to whether detailed regulations or broader regulations based on principles (as applied by the UK's ASB and the IASB) are a more appropriate way forward. The US Senate Committee investigating the Enron collapse has heard evidence from Sir David Tweedie, chairman of the International Accounting Standards Board.

The use of IASs will become more widespread in the European Union and it seems set to become the standard for cross-border listings on a global basis. The new structure of the IASC has been designed to ensure the IASB will continue to produce high quality standards to provide comparable information to users. However, before true comparability can be achieved, a more effective mechanism is necessary to ensure consistent interpretation and application of IASs. Surveys of companies purporting to follow IASs[32] have demonstrated that many companies disclose exceptions from full compliance. While IAS 1 (revised) bans this practice (i.e. companies are required to follow all IASs if they wish to claim their financial statements comply with IASs), it is difficult to see how it can be enforced without a more rigid enforcement structure. The work of the International Financial Reporting Interpretations Committee will contribute to ensuring consistent interpretations of IASs. Increased interest in IASs has led to an increase in the number of textbooks referring to their use. As auditors and regulatory bodies become more familiar with IASs it is likely that they will be enforced more rigorously.

The increase in the use of IASs will be significant for the largest companies, but what will happen to financial reporting in non-listed companies? These companies will continue to use national accounting standards, but eventually it seems likely that national requirements will move closer to IASs, thus reducing differences further. This will be necessary to allow an easier transition to listed status. The European Commission communication on financial reporting strategy[33] set out the commission's plan for achieving common internationally agreed accounting standards by 2005 for listed companies in the EU. This may see the position of IASs clarified in the Directives and may lead to further dispensations for the smallest companies.

The move towards IASs will also be significant for national standard-setters. In the short to medium term they will still be needed to provide accounting standards for unlisted companies and to provide the expertise to support the IASC. In the 2002 report of the UK's Accounting Standards Board, Sir Bryan Carsberg pointed out that the ASB needed to have an effective voice in the development of international standards. This would involve building on its own ideas to lead the debate and keeping in touch with its UK constituency. The ASB will continue to work with the IASB and the European Financial Reporting Advisory Group. Its quarterly newsletter, *Inside Track*, provides useful comparisons of current UK and international financial reporting standards.

In the longer term, it is difficult to imagine that it will be possible to justify accounting standard-setters operating independently in each country.

28.7.7 Economic consequences of accounting differences

While the debate continues about the future regulatory framework, businesses and employees are facing the economic consequences of different accounting practices. Following the acquisition of British car maker Rover in 1994 by German company BMW, performance was measured in accordance with the generally more conservative German accounting principles. This information was used for making management decisions. The publication of the £620m loss for 1998 led to a wave of speculation about possible closure of production plants with consequent redundancies. However, it has been pointed out that results under UK accounting rules (which were published later) would not have been quite so dramatic. Figure 28.3 shows a comparison of the company's results under British and German rules.

Nevertheless, the danger of making assumptions about a particular country's measurement rules was highlighted in 1993 when Daimler Benz became the first German company to be listed on the New York Stock Exchange. Figure 28.4 summarises the company's results under German and US rules. In the year of listing (1993) there was a

Figure 28.3 Rover results under UK and German rules[34]

	Rover results using UK rules £m	Rover results using German rules £m
1994	279	unpublished
1995	(51)	(163)
1996	(100)	(109)
1997	19	(91)
1998	(571)	(620)

Figure 28.4 Daimler Benz results under US and German rules[35]

	Daimler Benz results using German rules DM m	Daimler Benz results using US rules DM m
1990	1,795	884
1991	1,942	1,886
1992	1,451	1,350
1993	615	(1,839)
1994	895	1,052
1995	(5,734)	(5,729)

large difference between the two sets of figures, which created the impression that US and German accounting principles were very different and that US rules were more prudent. With hindsight, it is easy to see that 1993 was atypical and most of the differences could be attributed to permitted treatments of provisions which vary between the two countries. However, the financial markets did not have the benefit of hindsight and responded to the information available at the time.

28.8 International analysis of financial statements

From the examples in 28.7.6 it can be seen that, in spite of the best efforts of the bodies described in 28.7, there are still a number of difficulties which the financial analyst faces when approaching the accounts of multinational enterprises or enterprises based in another country. Analysts tend to concentrate on the primary financial statements,[36] but do they provide sufficient background information for adequate understanding? Areas where particular caution should be exercised when dealing with international financial statements are set out below.

28.8.1 Language

Language may present a difficulty for the analysis of accounts. Differences in language may be apparent when, for example, an Italian is using accounts prepared in Canada, as there is clearly a different language. However, there may also be difficulties for an English user of US financial statements, because usage of the language may be different (e.g. in the US 'notes' are what would be called 'bills' in the UK and vice versa). Translations of accounting terms create difficulties because not only the words but their meanings must be conveyed. The requirement of the EC Fourth Directive for annual accounts to give a 'true and fair view' has generated a wealth of research into the degree of success with which this Anglo-Saxon concept has been translated into the other language versions of the Directive and the corresponding national legislations.[37] Briefly, the understanding of the 'true and fair' term has been described as being virtually synonymous with Generally Accepted Accounting Practice (GAAP). It is therefore heavily influenced by prior accounting traditions, so countries with a history of applying accounting plans will consider accounts prepared in accordance with the rules give a true and fair view.

However, this is to ignore the English understanding of the term as some kind of higher ideal, which can be appealed to in order to devise an appropriate accounting treatment for new situations.

Certain companies operating in countries with a minority language but with significant overseas investors have taken to publishing English language versions of their annual accounts. This is particularly common in Scandinavia, but an increasing number of German and Japanese companies are adopting this practice.

28.8.2 Format and extent of disclosure

Information may be presented in an unfamiliar format. UK users have become accustomed to standard formats for the presentation of financial statements. However, these formats are not as prescriptive as those applied in countries dominated by accounting plans, such as France and Spain. The application of judgement in presenting information has been important in Anglo-Saxon countries, whereas continental Europeans are more concerned with the application of rules. Balance sheets in the US present assets and liabilities in a different order from the UK, but there is consistent presentation. Developing countries may have very little standardisation of formats, so it may be quite difficult to locate a particular item in a set of Chinese accounts for example.

28.8.3 Currency

Financial statements usually use the currency of the country of domicile. Dealing with financial statements denominated in an unfamiliar currency can make it difficult to assess the true size of the entity or the volume of transactions. Some companies have responded to this by publishing 'convenience' accounts, showing amounts in, for example, US Dollars. Since The Companies Act 1985 (Accounts of Small and Medium-Sized Enterprises and Publication of Accounts in ECUs) Regulations 1992, UK companies have been permitted to file their annual financial statements in European Currency Units. Increased use of the euro for financial reporting (and trading) purposes in Europe should reduce these difficulties for preparers and users of financial statements.

The second pitfall associated with currency is the translation of transactions within a company denominated in a variety of currencies. Further complications arise in consolidating companies whose accounts have been prepared using more than one currency. IAS 21 sets out the way in which transactions and balances in foreign currencies should be recorded, but there is more than one permitted treatment for some items. Consequently comparability is not guaranteed, even among companies using the same accounting standard.

When a parent acquires a foreign subsidiary it is necessary to translate the items in the subsidiary company's accounts, i.e. convert the foreign currency into sterling, in order to aggregate the parent and subsidiary figures. The actual conversion is a purely mechanical exercise, e.g. if the item is stated at €1,600 and the exchange rate is €1.6 to the pound then clearly the sterling equivalent is £1,000. However, there are differences of opinion as to the choice of the appropriate date in selecting the rate to be used.

The appropriate date might be considered to be either:

(a) the date upon which the transaction was recorded in the foreign currency; or

(b) the accounting reference date.

If the date upon which the transaction was recorded in the foreign currency is chosen and applied to all items in the balance sheet, we describe this as the temporal method.

If the accounting reference date is chosen and applied to all items in the balance sheet, we describe this as the closing rate method. This has been explained more fully in Chapter 22 'Foreign currency translation'.

However, there have been other approaches under which items in the same balance sheet have been treated differently, i.e. some translated using the rate applicable to the date of the transaction and some using the rate applicable at the end of the current financial year. The two major methods have been the Current/Non-current (CNC) method and the Monetary/Non-monetary (MNM) method.

The application of the four methods is illustrated in Figures 28.5 and 28.6:[38]

Figure 28.5 Translation rates for balance sheet items under historical cost

	Closing rate	CNC	MNM	Temporal
Fixed assets and long-term investments: cost	C	H	H	H
Stocks and short-term investments: cost	C	C	H	H
Stocks and short-term investments: market	C	C	H*	C
Debtors	C	C	C	C
Cash	C	C	C	C
Long-term debt	C	H	C	C
Current liabilities	C	C	C	C

C = closing rate

H = historical rate

*Some variants of MNM translate current items held at NRV using the closing rate

Figure 28.6 Example of translation

Foreign HC balances in Picos	Balances	Closing rate £	CNC £	MNM £	Temporal £
10,000	Fixed assets	5,000	2,500	2,500	2,500
3,000	Stock (cost)	1,500	1,500	1,000	1,000
2,000	Stock (NRV)	1,000	1,000	667	1,000
3,000	Debtors	1,500	1,500	1,500	1,500
1,000	Cash	500	500	500	500
19,000	Total assets	9,500	7,000	6,167	6,500
12,000	Equity	6,000	4,500	2,667	3,000
4,000	Loans	2,000	1,000	2,000	2,000
3,000	Creditors	1,500	1,500	1,500	1,500
19,000	Total capital	9,500	7,000	6,167	6,500

Historical rate for fixed assets and loans: 4 picos = £1

Historical rates for stocks: 3 picos = £1

Closing rate: 2 picos = £1

28.8.4 Valuation and profit measurement

The value at which items appear in financial statements will vary, depending on the regime under which they are reported. An example of this would be fixed assets, which may be shown at current market value in the UK. They may be revalued at certain dates according to official indices in France and they must always be shown at historical cost in Japan. It is possible to make some generalisations about approaches to valuation, so the Japanese seem to be more conservative than the British. However, there are still surprises: the US is seen to be extremely prudent, yet accounts do not include an accrual for proposed dividends.

There is some interest in using a form of current cost accounting (CCA) in countries where there is high inflation, such as in South America, which can necessitate adjustments by outside users. A full understanding of measurement rules is therefore required before jumping to conclusions about apparently unsatisfactory performance indicators.

Gray[39] identified that there was a tendency to be more pessimistic in measuring profit in certain countries. At the time of his study, he concluded that financial statements prepared in the UK were more optimistic than those prepared in France or Germany. The results of his study are summarised in Figure 28.7.

28.8.5 Taxation

The development of taxation rules and their effect on financial statements have been mentioned above. Caution should therefore be exercised when considering the treatment of fixed assets, stock and bad debts. The presentation of tax itself is also an area of variation, particularly provisions (full or partial) for deferred tax.

28.8.6 Groups

The company law harmonisation programme in Europe has improved the comparability of group accounts within the EU, but there are many variations across the world. These may derive simply from consolidation or non-consolidation of a 'subsidiary', because the definition of a subsidiary varies. Where figures are consolidated, there are potential variations in the choice of method, e.g. acquisition, equity or merger method, and in the application of the selected method, for example, the treatment of goodwill in acquisition accounting can range from capitalisation with impairment reviews to amortisation over forty years. There may also be different accounting policies applied in the group accounts from in the individual accounts, e.g. in France. Once again, a detailed study of the notes to the accounts will be necessary to ensure accurate interpretation.

Figure 28.7 A comparative analysis of profit measurement behaviour (percentage of companies falling into classes I, II and III)

	France %	West Germany %	UK %
I Pessimistic	77	75	14
II Neutral	8	8	28
III Optimistic	15	17	58

The treatment of investments in subsidiaries and associates in the holding company's accounts may also vary. In some countries, e.g. the UK, the investment is shown at cost, while in others, e.g. Norway, the equity method is used.

28.8.7 Transfer pricing

Multinational enterprises take advantage of the different tax systems of the countries in which they operate. Careful organisation of production and selling divisions and the prices charged between the divisions can ensure that most profits are earned in the country with the lowest effective rate of tax. This can lead to somewhat misleading information if the accounts of a single division are considered in isolation. It is therefore important to ensure that any analysis is based on the financial statements of the enterprise as a whole.

28.8.8 Extraordinary items

The issue of extraordinary items in the UK has been 'resolved' relatively recently by their virtual abolition with FRS 3. However, accountants world wide have made efforts to focus analysts' attention on 'the good news'. This is another area where international users must ensure that any decisions are based on full information, that may be published in an imaginative form, if at all.

28.8.9 Financial instruments

The variety of financial instruments that are available to companies has added greater complexity to the presentation of financial statements. It would seem that some of these instruments have been designed to obscure the source of finance. While national and international accounting standard-setters are doing their best to keep pace with the financial markets, this is an area that is causing some significant national differences.

28.8.10 Surveys of accounting practice

The variety of accounting treatments that are possible in the areas described above may seem confusing to a potential analyst. However, it is possible to quickly ascertain the most likely policies in particular countries by reference to published surveys of accounting practice. Some surveys may concentrate on a particular country (e.g. the annual ICAEW surveys in the UK) while others may be international (e.g. those produced periodically by PriceWaterhouseCoopers). They may provide details on areas which are topical (e.g. *Fédération des Experts Comptables Européens* published a survey in 1993 on Seventh Directive options and their implementation) or may attempt to be more comprehensive (e.g. PriceWaterhouseCoopers). The surveys do provide useful background information, but do have limitations insofar as they have been prepared for a specific purpose (which may not match the analyst's) and they may contain data that could be misleading or even incorrect. There is therefore no substitute for performing your own analysis that satisfies your objectives.

28.9 Country studies

Given that it will take some time for the harmonisation and standardisation efforts described in section 28.7 to take effect, it is important to be aware of the structures that determine financial reporting in other countries, to have an awareness of areas of potential difference in the recognition or measurement of financial statement items and areas where practice might change in future. The differences and similarities between financial statements prepared in different countries are now investigated more closely by looking at some countries in greater detail.

28.9.1 United States

Given the historical links between the UK and the US, it is unsurprising that the two systems of financial reporting have much in common. However, there are more rules in the US than in the UK (or perhaps even than anywhere in the world) which has resulted in greater standardisation and disclosure of information.

Legal

There is no direct equivalent of the UK Companies Acts in the US. The main federal regulation of trade in shares comprises the Securities Act 1933 and the Securities Exchange Act 1934. Neither of these includes any detailed provisions for the form and content of financial statements. The Securities and Exchange Commission (SEC) was born out of this legislation. This body is responsible for requiring the publication of financial information for the benefit of shareholders. It has the power to dictate the form and content of these reports. The largest companies whose shares are listed must register with the SEC and comply with its regulations. However, the majority of companies fall outside of its jurisdiction, although shareholders or lenders may require publication of equivalent information and a full audit. Individual states have the power to introduce their own legislation to control businesses and even set taxes. They are also responsible for conferring the right to practise as a public accountant.

Standard-setting body

The Financial Accounting Standards Board (FASB) is responsible for setting accounting standards in the US. Its independence is ensured by limiting the voluntary contributions to its funding from the various public accounting firms, industry and other interested parties. FASB issues the following documents:

- Statements of Financial Accounting Standards – deal with specific issues
- Statements of Concepts – give general information
- Interpretations – clarify existing standards

A subcommittee of FASB is the Emerging Issues Task Force which provided the inspiration for the UK Urgent Issues Task Force. The SEC recognises the authority of FASB's pronouncements, thus ensuring compliance by the largest companies.

Financial statements

The main financial statements are:

- Balance sheet
- Income statement
- Statement of cash flows

Treatment of specific items

Historical cost accounting predominates and transactions are not recognised in the financial statements until an arm's-length transaction has taken place. All fixed assets are therefore disclosed at historical cost and are depreciated over their anticipated useful life (there are no exceptions for investment properties). The straight-line method of depreciation is the most common although other methods are permitted. Leasing of assets is well established in the USA and leases are accounted for in a similar manner to in the UK.

Stocks (known as 'inventories') are valued at the lower of cost and market value (usually replacement cost). The most noticeable difference between the US and the UK is that the LIFO method of stock valuation is permitted in the US. This can be confusing when dealing with the accounts of long established companies as the balance sheet stock figure could be based on very old prices. However, it is argued that the income statement is more realistic as the cost of sales figure reflects the most recent prices.

Research and development expenditure must be written off as soon as it is incurred, unless a tangible asset is created. This is more conservative than SSAP 13, which allows certain expenditure to be carried forward. However, the cost of developing computer software products in the US may be capitalised at the lower of cost and net realisable value.

Both acquisition and merger methods of accounting for business combinations were permitted historically, with restriction of merger accounting to circumstances involving a pooling of interests in exchange for equity shares. Any goodwill on acquisition may be capitalised and used to be written off over a period not exceeding forty years. This meant that in practice, most groups amortised goodwill over forty years. FASB reduced the amortisation period for goodwill from forty to twenty years and discontinued the pooling of interests method from 1 January 2000.[40]

Audit

All companies are required to have an annual audit if they are registered with the SEC or shareholders or lenders require it. The report of the independent auditor explains the basis of his opinion before expressing an opinion on whether the financial statements present fairly the results and changes in financial position in conformity with generally accepted accounting principles. This emphasises the importance of regulations over subjective application of broader concepts.

Effect of differences between UK and US accounting principles

As international, US and other national standards converge, the effect on net income and shareholders' equity should be apparent. However, at present there can be significant differences in the reported results and financial position. For example, the BT 2001 Annual Report and Accounts disclosed the following:

	2001 £m	2000 £m	1999 £m
Net income (loss) – UK GAAP	(1,810)	2,055	2,983
Adjustments to conform with US GAAP	(543)	(662)	(394)
Net income (loss) – US GAAP	(2,357)	1,393	2,589
Shareholders' equity – UK GAAP	14,069	15,795	
Adjustments to conform with US GAAP	3,838	2,161	
Shareholders' equity – US GAAP	10,231	13,634	

28.9.2 Sweden

Accounting in Sweden has some peculiarly Scandinavian traits. The relatively high proportion of multi-national corporations compared with its population in Sweden[41] has led to greater consideration of outsiders as potential users of financial reports. This has resulted in extensive disclosure to explain the basis of preparation of accounts and differences from other accounting conventions.

Legal

There is a long history of regulations governing book-keeping and financial reporting in Sweden and there were attempts to harmonise accounting legislation with the other Nordic countries (Denmark, Finland, Iceland and Norway) as early as the 1930s. Tangible evidence of this harmonisation effort came in similar companies acts which were implemented in each of the five countries in the 1970s. Sweden joined the European Union in 1995 following a referendum with a marginal 52% of voters in favour of membership. The accounting Directives were implemented in the Financial Statements Act 1995 (*Årsredovisningslag, ÅRL*) which supports the 1976 Accounting Act (*Bokföringslag*). Sweden has decided that the true and fair view cannot override the law, although it has been suggested that the principle could be used to justify departures from standards and guidelines.[42] Sweden has also retained its requirement that financial statements should be prepared in accordance with 'Good Accounting Practice' (*god redovisningssed*).

Standard-setting bodies

Sweden has a plethora of bodies which have provided and, in some cases, continue to provide guidance on accounting and financial reporting matters. The output of these bodies is generally referred to as 'standards' although direct translation of the Swedish would be 'guidelines' or 'recommendations'. The governmental body, *Bokföringsnämnden* (BFN) deals with accounting (as opposed to reporting) issues, dealing with documentation and providing specific answers to more limited accounting issues and has a general overview. The professional body, *Föreningen Auktoriserade Revisorer* (FAR) issued pronouncements until the end of the 1980s. The Accounting Council (*Redovisningsrådet*, RR) took over standard-setting in 1991 and is gradually replacing FAR's standards. A body equivalent to the UK's Urgent Issues Task Force was set up in 1995 to deal with matters requiring prompt actions or interpretations.

Financial statements

The financial statements comprise:

- Balance sheet
- Profit and loss account
- Cash flow statement
- Notes
- Management Report.

Swedish companies must use the horizontal format balance sheet and the vertical profit and loss account (although expenditure may be shown by nature or by function) from the 4th Directive's formats. A special feature of Swedish financial statements is the inclusion of an additional category, 'untaxed reserves' in the balance sheet, between equity and provisions. As in Germany, there is a close relationship between the financial accounts and the tax accounts. The disclosure of untaxed reserves is intended to help users understand items such as undervaluation of fixed assets or stocks which have been made to achieve tax benefits. Untaxed reserves are partly equity and partly deferred tax.[43]

With a view to informing investors, the group accounts (which are not affected by tax considerations) may use principles that are different from the entity's accounts. This is permitted by law. In the 1990s some Swedish companies were keen to point out compliance with IASs. It was quite common to include a sentence along the lines of 'the financial statements comply with IASs in all material respects'. However, this is somewhat misleading, as Swedish companies did not comply with IAS 1 and follow all relevant IASs. Standards with onerous disclosure requirements, e.g. employee benefits, or those that would not comply with the Directives, were not followed.

Treatment of specific items

Fixed assets are generally shown at historical cost less depreciation, but revaluation is permitted where the difference is permanent and material. Most leases were treated as operating leases but the RR's standard, which was effective from 1 January 1997, requires capitalisation of finance leases with provision for the leasing liability.

Stocks are valued at the lower of cost and net realisable value and LIFO is expressly prohibited. Tax deductible obsolescence provisions are permitted. Long-term work in progress is usually valued using the completed contract method, although percentage completion may be used.

Research and development can be capitalised and written off over a period that does not normally exceed five years. This is a provision of the ÅRL and does not include the detailed conditions of the UK standard, although there is further guidance in the Swedish accounting standards.

Group accounts must be prepared in accordance with the seventh Directive. Merger accounting is extremely rare. Goodwill should be capitalised and written off over up to five years, unless a longer period can be justified (but this cannot be more than 20 years).

As indicated above, different principles may be applied in the group accounts, which are independent of tax, so this leads to provisions for deferred tax in certain consolidated financial statements.

Audit

All companies are required to have their financial statements audited, but smaller companies may use the services of an auditor registered with a second tier body. In addition to expressing an opinion on compliance with statute, the audit report must indicate whether the directors have discharged their responsibilities and provide guidance on the board's suggestion on the use of profit.

28.10 Reconciliations and supplementary statements

To assist users, or to comply with the requirements of foreign stock exchanges, some companies present financial statements in more than one currency, in more than one format or in accordance with more than one accounting convention. Some examples of this are shown in Figure 28.8 for Eybl International AG (Austria's largest textile company) and Glaxo Wellcome plc (UK pharmaceuticals company, now part of GlaxoSmithKline).

Restating figures in another currency may present information so that it is more familiar, but, of course, there is no effect on financial ratios, as all figures have been adjusted by the same factor. This can be seen from the Eybl accounts presented in Austrian

Figure 28.8 Examples of multiple reporting in financial statements for the year ended 31 December 1998

Company	Eybl	Eybl	Eybl	Glaxo Wellcome	Glaxo Wellcome
Accounting convention	Austrian	Austrian	IAS	UK	US
Currency	ATSm	€m	ATSm	£m	£m
Shareholders' equity	631	46	628	2,702	8,112
Income attributable to ordinary shareholders	128	9	119	1,836	1,015
Return on shareholders' equity	20%	20%	19%	68%	13%
Earnings per share	ATS54	€4	ATS50	51.1p	28.2p

schillings and euros. The difficulty of finding information presented in a different format was addressed by Glaxo Wellcome, which also presented its UK financial statements in the US format. This has not been reproduced in Figure 28.8, as there are no amendments to individual figures.

Presenting financial statements in accordance with another accounting convention will result in amendments to figures. The differences between Eybl's financial statements prepared in accordance with Austrian regulations and IASs are not substantial. This is perhaps unsurprising given that Austrian regulations have implemented the European Directives and IASs are generally in line with the European Directives. In the 1999 report, Eybl only published financial statements prepared under IASs, taking advantage of dispensations under the Austrian commercial code. The main differences between IASs and the Austrian commercial code led to the publication of a cash flow statement and illustration of the development of equity.

The differences between Glaxo Wellcome's financial statements prepared in accordance with UK and US practice are far more significant. The financial statements provide a full reconciliation of the profit under UK GAAP to net income under US GAAP and between shareholders' equity under each convention. The largest reconciling items related to goodwill, intangible fixed assets and deferred tax. By the 1999 financial statements, the company had changed its accounting policy with respect to goodwill to follow FRS 10 'such that no material difference will exist between UK and US GAAP'. While some differences remain in respect of prior years' goodwill, practice in the two countries is clearly converging.

Summary

The expansion in the number of multinational enterprises and transnational investments has led to a demand for a greater understanding of financial statements prepared in a range of countries. The study of international accounting has developed from being purely descriptive to being more analytical. In spite of a number of attempts to improve comparability of accounts, there remain a number of international differences. The way forward for analysts would seem to be continued pressure for harmonisation along with increased education. A full interpretation of financial statements can only be made in the context of the financial and cultural environment in which a business operates. This chapter has given an indication of the diversity of accounting around the world and opportunities for further study.

REVIEW QUESTIONS

1 How does the regulatory framework for financial reporting in the UK differ from that in the USA? Which is better for particular interest groups and why?

2 'Standardisation is the only way forward for European financial reporting.' Discuss this statement in the light of efforts which have already been made in the harmonisation of company law and the forthcoming requirement for listed companies to follow IASs.

3 Suggest criteria which could be used to classify systems of financial reporting employed in different countries. What difficulties are there in performing an exercise of this nature?

4 Identify the main problems which an analyst would face when dealing with financial statements prepared in another country.

5 Consider the role of scandal in the development of accounting regulation.
Compare the reaction to the Enron financial statements in the early part of the 21st century with the reaction to the financial statements of AEI and Pergamon Press in the 1960s. (We discussed these UK scandals in Chapter 5.)

6 The current differences between IAS and UK GAAP are extensive and the recent pairing of the US Financial Accounting Standards Board and IASB to align IAS and US GAAP will probably result in IAS moving further from current UK GAAP.[44]

Discuss the implication of this on any decision that non-listed UK companies should comply with IASs rather than UK GAAP after 2005.

EXERCISES

Question 1

Compare the treatment of tangible and intangible fixed assets in accounts prepared in North America and Europe. You may wish to focus your answer on specific countries in these continents.

Question 2

Discuss the degree of conservatism apparent in financial statements prepared in North America and Europe. How does this manifest itself in the treatment of research and development expenditure?

Question 3

Consider the effect of taxation on the interpretation of published financial statements in three countries. Discuss the advantages and disadvantages of congruence between tax and commercial accounts from the point of view of:
(a) the preparers of the financial statements
(b) the users of the financial statements
(c) those responsible for collecting the taxes.

Question 4

Comment on the following audit report issued to shareholders of Credicorp Ltd (a Peruvian company) in the 2000 Annual Report. Discuss the similarities and differences between it and a standard UK or US audit report. Evaluate the impact that these similarities and differences have for users of the accounts of multinational enterprises.

Report of Independent Auditors   9 February 2001

To the Board of Directors and Shareholders – Credicorp Ltd

We have audited the accompanying consolidated balance sheet of Credicorp Ltd (a Bermuda limited liability company) and subsidiaries as at 31 December 2000 and 1999, and the related consolidated statements of income, of changes in shareholders' equity and of cash flows for the three years in the period ended 31 December 2000. These financial statements are the responsibility of the management of Credicorp Ltd; our responsibility is to express an opinion on these financial statements.

We conducted our audits in accordance with International Auditing Standards. Those standards require that we plan and perform the audit to obtain reasonable assurance about whether the financial statements are free of material misstatement. An audit includes examining, on a test basis, evidence supporting the amounts and disclosures in the financial statements. An audit also includes assessing the accounting principles used and significant estimates made by Credicorp Ltd's management, as well as evaluating the overall financial statement presentation. We believe that our audits provide a reasonable basis for our opinion.

In our opinion, the consolidated statements audited by us present fairly, in all material respects, the financial position of Credicorp Ltd and subsidiaries at 31 December 2000 and 1999, and the results of their operations and cash flows for the three years in the period ended 31 December 2000, in conformity with International Accounting Standards.

References

1 *The Economist*, 15 January 2000, pp. 123–124.
2 R.T. Moran, *Cultural Guide to doing Business in Europe* (2nd edition), Butterworth-Heinemann Ltd, 1992, p. 51.
3 *Ibid.*, p. 60.
4 C. Nobes and R. Parker, *Comparative International Accounting* (6th edition), Pearson Education, 2000, pp. 16–44.
5 J. Freedman, and M. Power, *Law and Accountancy – Conflict and Cooperation in the 1990s*, Paul Chapman Publishing Ltd, 1992, p. 105.
6 For more detailed discussion see C. Nobes, 'Corporate financing and its effects on European accounting differences,' Reading University discussion paper, 1996.
7 Sources: GDP: International Monetary Fund, *International Financial Statistics Yearbook 1999*, IMF, 1999; Market capitalisation: International Finance Corporation, *Emerging Stock Markets Factbook 1999*, (13th Edition), IFC, 1999.
8 C. Nobes, *Towards 1992*, Butterworths, 1989, p. 15.
9 C. Randlesome, *Business Cultures in Europe* (2nd edition), Heinemann Professional Publishing, 1993, p. 28.
10 J.D. Daniels and L.H. Radebaugh, *International Business* (8th edition), Addison-Wesley, 1998, p. 818.
11 C. Randlesome, *op cit.*, p. 25.
12 C. Nobes, *Towards 1992*, Butterworths, 1989, p. 8.
13 T. Cooke, *An Empirical Study of Financial Disclosure by Swedish Companies*, Garland, 1989, pp. 112–113.
14 C. Nobes and R. Parker, *op cit.*, p. 66.

15 S.P. Agrawal, P.H. Jensen, A.L. Meader and K. Sellers, 'An international comparison of conceptual frameworks of accounting', *The International Journal of Accounting*, Vol. 24, 1989, pp. 237–249.

16 *Accountancy*, June 1989, p. 10.

17 See, for example, B. Chauveau, 'The Spanish *Plan General de Contabilidad*: Agent of development and innovation?' *European Accounting Review*, Vol. 4, no. 1, 1995, pp. 125–138.

18 See, for example, P.E.M. Standish, 'Origins of the *Plan Comptable Général*: a study in cultural intrusion and reaction', *Accounting and Business Research*, Vol. 20, no. 80, 1990, pp. 337–351.

19 C. Nobes and R. Parker, *op cit.*, pp. 46–62.

20 *Ibid.*, p. 66.

21 *Framework for the Presentation and Preparation of Financial Statements*, IASC, 1989, para. 40.

22 International Accounting Standards Committee, *International Accounting Standards*, Burgess Science Press, 1994, p. 7.

23 For further details, see *Accountancy*, International Edition, December 1999, p. 5.

24 For up-to-date information about the constitution of the IASC, see its website www.iasb.org.uk.

25 International Accounting Standards Committee, *IASC Constitution*, IASC, amended 5 March 2002, www.iasb.org.uk.

26 The European Economic Community established by the Treaty of Rome in 1957 became known as the European Community in 1985 and the European Union in November 1993 following the Maastricht Treaty.

27 For further details see D. Cairns (1997) 'The future of the IASC and the implications for UK companies' in ICAEW, *Financial reporting today – current and emerging issues*, Accountancy Books, 1998, pp. 115–152.

28 A comprehensive analysis of these differences is provided in C. Bloomer (ed.) *The IASC-US Comparison Project: A Report on the Similarities and Differences between IASC Standards and US GAAP* (2nd edition), Financial Accounting Standards Board, 1999.

29 EU (2002) Regulation of the European Parliament and of the Council on the application of international accounting standards, Brussels.

30 The following summary is based on IASB (2002) *Improvements to International Accounting Standards*, project summary posted on the IASB web site (www.iasb.org.uk)

31 Up to date summaries of the position on this project are available from the ASB web site www.asb.org.uk

32 For example, D. Cairns, *Financial Times International Accounting Standards Survey 1999*, FT Business. 1999.

33 Commission of the European Communities, *The EU's Financial Reporting Strategy: The Way Forward*, COM(2000), 359 final.

34 C. Quick and D. Wild, 'Rover trouble was avoidable', *Accountancy Age*, 18 February 1999, p. 7.

35 Source: Daimler Benz, Form 20-F 1995; L.H. Radebaugh, G. Gebhardt and S.J. Gray, 'Foreign stock exchange listings: A case study of Daimler Benz', *Journal of International Financial Management and Accounting*, 1995, 6(2), pp. 158–92.

36 See L.S. Chang, K.S. Most and C.W. Brian, 'The utility of annual reports: an international study', *Journal of International Business Studies*, Spring/Summer 1983, pp. 63–84.

37 See for example *The European Accounting Review*, Vol. 2, No. 1, May 1993, which devoted a whole section to the issue.

38 C. W. Nobes, 'A review of the translation debate' in S.J. Gray (ed.), *International Accounting and Transnational Decision*, Butterworths, 1983, p. 216.

39 S.J. Gray, 'The impact of international accounting differences from a security analysis perspective', *Journal of Accounting Research*, Spring 1980, pp. 64–76.

40 For further discussion, see *Accountancy*, International Edition, July 1999, p. 62.

41 T.E. Cooke, 'Disclosure in the corporate annual reports of Swedish companies', *Accounting and Business Research*, 19: 74, 1989, pp. 113–124.

42 KPMG, *Accounting Principles: Significant Differences Between Sweden And The US*, KPMG, 1997, p. 1.

43 For a more detailed explanation of untaxed reserves, see K. Artsberg (1998) in P. Walton, A. Haller and B. Raffournier, *International Accounting*, Thompson Business Press, 1998, pp. 288–290.

44 Y. Dinwoodie and P. Holgate, Singing from the same songsheet?, *Accountancy*, May 2003, pp. 94–95.

PART **6**

Accountability

CHAPTER 29

Corporate governance

29.1 Introduction

In this chapter we consider:

Corporate governance – directors

- The need for corporate governance guidelines
- Corporate governance in different countries
- Corporate governance requirements
- UK Voluntary Code
- Directors' remuneration – illustration from the annual report of Diageo plc
- Influence of institutional investors

Corporate governance – auditors

- Auditor's report to shareholders
- Competence of the auditor – educational requirements
- Independence of the auditor
- Assessing quality of management performance

29.2 The need for corporate governance guidelines

Where shares are widely held, and management of the company is delegated to directors who are not major shareholders of the company, there is a need for corporate governance guidelines.

The 'theory' of listed companies is that the shareholders own the company. However, there are too many shareholders to run the company, and they may not have the expertise or desire to run the company. So, the task of running the company is delegated to the directors. The 'duty' of the directors is to run the company in a way which maximises the long-term return to the shareholders (i.e. maximises the company's profit and cash flow).

Corporate governance guidelines are developed so that it can be seen whether the directors are maximising returns to shareholders, that business risk is set at a reasonable level, that a director or the board of directors do not become dominant to the detriment of the shareholders and the remuneration of the directors is reasonable.

Disclosure of this information is made in the company's annual financial statements. To ensure the reliability of this information, it must be checked by an independent auditor. The national accounting bodies and the International Federation of Accountants provide ethical rules and auditing standards which aim to ensure that auditors are competent to perform their work and have the appropriate independence from the audit client.

29.3 Corporate governance in different countries

There are four interesting correlations when considering the development of corporate governance requirements in different countries. These are:

(a) the ratio of the value of listed companies to the country's gross domestic product (GDP). The higher this ratio, the more developed are the corporate governance requirements;

(b) how widely the shares of listed companies are held. If a large number of financial institutions and individuals hold shares in listed companies, there is a greater need for corporate governance requirements;

(c) cultural considerations. The USA and the UK and its colonies tend to have much more developed corporate governance requirements than other countries;

(d) the different levels of management in the organisation structures of companies.

We will consider each of these correlations below.

29.3.1 The ratio of the value of listed companies to the country's GDP (gross domestic product)

Figure 29.1 shows, for a variety of countries, the value of listed companies as a percentage of GDP in 1993. The UK percentage of over 130% is an indication that the pressure for greater transparency came from the investors.

Equity investment in other countries has grown significantly since that date, as seen

Figure 29.1 Domestic listed companies by country and their total market value in 1993

Country	€m	% of GDP
Austria	25,178	16.3
Belgium	69,526	38.6
Denmark	35,504	30.6
Finland	20,922	29.7
France	404,926	37.9
Germany (East)	10,738	17.1
Germany (West)	409,610	25.1
Ireland	15,259	38.9
Italy	128,056	15.1
Japan	2,672,638	73.8
Luxembourg	17,170	195.1
Netherlands	162,356	61.5
Norway	24,332	27.8
Portugal	10,432	16.3
Spain	105,675	25.9
Sweden	95,095	59.7
Switzerland	240,812	113.9
UK	1,065,515	132.4
USA – NY SE	3,752,446	70.3

in the following market capitalisation data which has brought a greater international pressure for transparency and good corporate governance:

		000,000
Copenhagen	DKK	710,955.0
Deutsche Borse	EUR	1,203,681.0
Euronext	EUR	2,070,467.0
Helsinki	EUR	213,900.9
Italy	EUR	592,398.5
London	GBP	1,487,376.5
Oslo	NOK	622,871.0
Stockholm	SEK	2,480,965.0

29.3.2 How widely the shares in listed companies are held

The second factor influencing corporate governance requirements is how widely the shares in listed companies are held. In the USA and the UK, a large number of financial institutions and individuals hold shares in listed companies, so there is a greater need for corporate governance requirements. In Japan and most European countries (except the UK) shares in listed companies tend to be held by a small number of banks, financial institutions and individuals. Where there are few shareholders in a company, they can question the directors directly, so there is less need for corporate governance requirements.

A further related factor is that US and UK companies tend to have a low gearing, so most of the finance is provided by shareholders. However, in other countries the gearing of companies is much higher, which indicates that most finance for companies comes from banks. If the majority of the finance is provided by shareholders, then there is a greater need for corporate governance requirements than if finance is in the form of loans where the lenders are able to stipulate conditions and loan covenants, e.g. the maximum level of gearing and action available to them if interest payments or capital repayments are missed.

29.3.3 Cultural

The third factor is cultural. It is apparent that the most detailed corporate governance requirements come from the USA, the UK and former UK Colonies (Australia, Canada, Singapore, Malaysia, Hong Kong and South Africa).

29.3.4 Organisational structures

In the UK system there is just one level of management represented by a board of directors who may delegate to members of the board such functions as remuneration committee and audit committee membership. Corporate governance is achieved by the financial regulatory authorities requiring compliance with a voluntary code of conduct from the directors of listed companies

Other countries have a two tier system of management with a management (or executive) board responsible for the operational management of the company, and a supervisory board which acts on an *ad hoc* basis, e.g. approving an important business transaction, and at the year-end when it receives the audit report, management report on the activities and dividend proposed by the management board and approves the financial statements and dividend distribution. This two-tier structure might be seen as providing a greater degree of control than the single tier system and so there is less need for an imposed code of conduct.

29.3.5 Future developments

Corporate governance requirements are less developed in the European Union countries (except the UK) and Japan. What about the future? Developments in the European Union, Japan, China, Russia and other Eastern Bloc (former communist) countries are leading to a model of much wider ownership of shares (i.e. like the USA and the UK).

In the European Union restrictions on who may hold shares in major companies are inconsistent with the Union's desire for 'free movement of goods and capital', so there will be a trend for a greater proportion of companies' shares being listed on a stock exchange.

In Japan, major losses by some large companies have led to 'negative equity' and those companies being purchased in part or whole by companies in the USA and other countries. In China, Russia and the former communist countries in Eastern Europe, the economies are being changed from state controlled businesses to privately owned companies. The 'model' of these companies is similar to those in the USA and UK. So, the trend is towards the US and UK model of companies' shares being listed on their national stock exchange. This trend to wider share ownership will doubtless encourage the development of corporate governance criteria similar to those in the USA and the UK.

29.4 Corporate governance requirements

Figure 29.2 summarises the main corporate governance requirements for listed companies in OECD[2] recommendations, the Commonwealth,[3] USA, and UK

Figure 29.2 Corporate governance guidelines in different countries

Country	Australia	Canada	Hong Kong	India	Malaysia
1 Disclosure of Compliance	Yes	Yes	Yes	Yes	Yes
2 Board responsible to	Share-holders	Share-holders	n/c	n/c	Share-holders
3 Separation of Chairman & CEO	Yes	Yes	n/c	n/c	Yes
4 Non-executive directors	Majority	Majority	n/c	Majority	at least a third
5 Audit committee	Yes all NED	Yes all NED	Yes majority NED	Yes all NED	Yes majority NED
6 Governance committee	n/c	Yes	n/c	n/c	n/c
7 Nomination committee	Yes majority NED	Yes all NED	n/c	n/c	Yes all NED

Figure 29.2 (*cont.*)

Country	Australia	Canada	Hong Kong	India	Malaysia
8 Remuneration Committee	Yes majority NED	Yes	n/c	n/c	Yes majority NED
9 Director re-election	n/c	n/c	n/c	n/c	3 years
10 One share, one vote	Yes	n/c	n/c	n/c	n/c
11 Shareholder approval of remuneration	n/c	n/c	n/c	n/c	No

Country	OECD	Singapore	UK	USA
1 Disclosure of Compliance	Yes	Yes	Yes	n/c
2 Board responsible to	n/c	Shareholders	Shareholders	Shareholders
3 Separation of Chairman & CEO	Encouraged	n/c	Yes	No firm recommendation
4 Non-executive directors	Majority	n/c	Yes	Majority
5 Audit committee	Yes majority NED	Yes majority NED	Yes majority NED	Yes only NED
6 Governance committee	n/c	n/c	n/c	Yes only NED
7 Nomination committee	Yes only NED	n/c	Yes majority NED	Yes only NED
8 Remuneration Committee	Yes only NED	n/c	Yes only NED	Yes only NED
9 Director re-election	n/c	3 years (CEO 5 years)	3 years	n/c
10 One share, one vote	n/c	n/c	n/c	n/c
11 Shareholder approval of remuneration	n/c	n/c	only long term incentive schemes	n/c

Abbreviations:

NED Non-executive directors (or independent directors) not involved in the day-to-day running of the company; n/c not covered; OECD Organization for Economic Co-operation and Development.

Note also that OECD requirements might be implemented differently in different countries.

Corporate governance requirements for other countries are either undeveloped or far less developed.

29.4.1 Status of corporate governance requirements

The above list of points are **recommendations** and not requirements. Thus, they are not as strong as statutory requirements or even accounting standards. However, stock exchanges will expect listed companies to comply with the recommendations, and failure to comply with some of them may have an adverse effect on the company's share price.

Generally, the recommendations have been drawn up by committees comprising directors and representatives of listed companies, their auditors and financial institutions which invest in the shares. There is little, if any, representation of 'ordinary' shareholders on these committees. So, the recommendations may be biased. Many companies and their directors would prefer not to have to comply with corporate governance requirements, as this will limit their independence, and there will be additional cost in setting up and monitoring corporate governance systems within the company. However, pressures from governments, the general public, shareholders and financial institutions will mean the directors have to accept some corporate governance requirements. The agreed corporate governance requirements will be a compromise between the pressures of the directors of the listed companies (who would have few, if any, requirements) and those of the government, shareholders and financial institutions (who would prefer to have detailed corporate governance requirements).

29.4.2 Setting directors' remuneration

Consideration of requirements to disclose directors' remuneration illustrates these pressures and the final compromise which is reached. In the UK there has been considerable concern at:

(a) the high salaries paid to listed company directors;

(b) the high annual increase in these salaries, often at least twice the annual increase of other employees;

(c) the salaries continuing to remain high, even when the company is performing badly.

Although the general public may believe that directors' salaries are set by the shareholders, this does not happen, as it is not a requirement of the Companies Acts. With no statutory control over directors' setting their salaries, there has been a rapid increase in their salaries. So, one would expect corporate governance requirements to require some controls over the levels of directors' salaries, probably by their salaries being approved by the shareholders at the annual general meeting. However, the corporate governance requirements of the countries in the tables above, show there is no requirement for approval of directors' salaries by the shareholders, and the only specific requirement is in the UK where it is suggested that the shareholders should approve long term incentive schemes for directors. However, evidence suggests that few, if any, listed companies in the UK allow shareholders to approve long-term incentive schemes.

29.4.3 Role of Remuneration Committees

The other requirement suggested in a number of countries is that the company should have a remuneration committee, comprising wholly or mainly non-executive directors, who consider the performance and remuneration of the executive directors. The corporate governance requirements do not suggest shareholders or other more independent people should be members of the remuneration committee. As directors will want to maximise their earnings, it appears that remuneration committees will have little effect in limiting the increase in salaries of executive directors. Nevertheless, they should hopefully help to link directors' remuneration more closely to the financial performance of the company.

In the UK, it has been reported[4] that the 'sole instance where a majority of companies fail to comply with the code (on corporate governance) is in having a board Remuneration Committee composed entirely of non-executive directors'. The article goes on to say, 'Indeed, they [i.e. investors] may think that having colleagues and chums deciding executive pay may have a great deal to do with pay rises that regularly outdo rises for non-board managers or employees, and with over-generous packages that reward success, mediocrity and failure with equal munificence.' It then says, 'But the remorseless upward pay ratchet should be less highly geared in their hands' (i.e. when the remuneration is decided by the non-executive directors).

Although not part of the Companies Act, listed companies now include a resolution for shareholders to approve the Directors' remuneration report. However, a vote 'for' or 'against' (or abstention) does not allow shareholders to criticise aspects of directors' remuneration (e.g. individual director's remuneration, calculation of bonuses or pension, and the disclosure of how their bonuses are calculated).

29.5 UK Voluntary Code – The Cadbury Report[5]

The Cadbury Committee was set up by the Financial Reporting Council, the London Stock Exchange and the accountancy profession in 1991 under the chairmanship of Sir Adrian Cadbury. The London Stock Exchange adopted as part of its Listing Rules a statement in the annual report as to whether the company had complied with the Code or not.

The Cadbury Report produced a *voluntary* Code of Best Practice. The points it made were as follows:

The board

1.1 The board should meet regularly, retain full and effective control over the company and monitor the executive management.

1.2 There should be a clearly accepted division of responsibilities at the head of a company, which will ensure a balance of power and authority, such that no one individual has unfettered powers of decision. Where the chairman is also the chief executive, it is essential that there should be a strong and independent element on the board, with a recognised senior member.

1.3 The board should include non-executive directors of sufficient calibre and number for their views to carry significant weight in the board's decisions.

1.4 The board should have a formal schedule of matters specifically reserved to it for decision to ensure that the direction and control of the company is firmly in its hands.

1.5 There should be an agreed procedure for directors in the furtherance of their duties to take independent professional advice if necessary, at the company's expense.

1.6 All directors should have access to the advice and services of the company secretary, who is responsible to the board for ensuring that board procedures are followed and that applicable rules and regulations are complied with. Any question of the removal of the company secretary should be a matter for the board as a whole.

Non-executive directors

2.1 Non-executive directors should bring an independent judgement to bear on issues of strategy, performance and resources, including key appointments and standards of conduct.

2.2 The majority should be independent of management and free from any business or other relationship that could materially interfere with the exercise of their independent judgement, apart from their fees and shareholdings. Their fees should reflect the time which they commit to the company.

2.3 Non-executive directors should be appointed for specified terms and reappointment should not be automatic.

2.4 Non-executive directors should be selected through a formal process and both the process and their appointment should be a matter for the board as a whole.

Executive directors

3.1 Directors' service contracts should not exceed three years without shareholders' approval.

3.2 There should be full and clear disclosure of directors' total emoluments and those of the chairman and the highest-paid UK director, including pension contributions and stock options. Separate figures should be given for salary and performance related elements and the basis on which performance is measured should be explained.

3.3 Executive directors' pay should be subject to the recommendations of a remuneration committee made up wholly or mainly of non-executive directors.

Reporting and controls

4.1 It is the board's duty to present a balanced and understandable assessment of the company.

4.2 The board should ensure that an objective and professional relationship is maintained with the auditors.

4.3 The board should establish an audit committee of at least three non-executive directors with written terms of reference which deal clearly with its authority and duties.

4.4 The directors should explain their responsibility for preparing the accounts next to a statement by the auditors about their reporting responsibilities.

4.5 The directors should report on the effectiveness of the company's system of internal control.

29.6 The Greenbury Report[6]

In July 1995 the Greenbury Committee issued a four-part code on directors' remuneration and covering good practice in relation to the following:

- **The remuneration committee**. The board should set up remuneration committees of non-executive directors to determine the company's policy on executive remuneration and specific remuneration packages for each of the executive directors, including pension rights and compensation payments.

- **Disclosure**. The remuneration committee should report to the shareholders each year the company's policy on executive directors' remuneration, including levels, comparative groups of companies, individual components (e.g. basic salary, benefits in kind, annual bonuses and long-term incentive schemes including share options), performance criteria and measurement, pension provision, contracts of service and compensation commitments on early termination.

- **Remuneration policy.** Remuneration committees must provide the packages needed to attract, retain and motivate directors of the quality required, but avoiding paying more than is necessary.

- **Service contracts.** Remuneration committees should consider what compensation commitments their directors' contracts of service would entail in the event of early termination, particularly for unsatisfactory performance, with a strong case for setting contract periods at one year or less.

Two of the most controversial recommendations – issuing options at discounts and pension entitlements – were initially resisted by a number of companies maintaining that they were unable to value these benefits. However, the existence of the code was yet another step exerting pressure on companies to give more information to the shareholders. The Greenbury Report was followed by the *Committee on Corporate Governance: Final Report (Hampel Committee Report)*.

29.7 The Hampel Report[7]

In January 1998 the Hampel Report was produced which was defined by the chairman as a 'fine tuning exercise' of the Cadbury and Greenbury Reports. The main provisions are:

- Chairman and chief executive should be separate roles. This was stronger than the Cadbury recommendation that where the chairman is also the chief executive, it is essential that there should be a strong and independent element on the board, with a recognised senior member.

- Directors should be on contracts lasting one year or less. This was more restrictive than the Cadbury recommendation that directors' service contracts should not exceed three years without shareholders' approval.

- Remuneration committee should be made up of independent non-executive directors. This was more restrictive than the Cadbury recommendation that executive directors' pay should be subject to the recommendations of a remuneration committee made up wholly **or mainly of non-executive directors**.

- Non-executive directors may be paid in company shares although this is not recommended. This view is more restrictive than the existing Cadbury recommendation that accepts non-executive directors **holding shares** but is **against** them **holding share options** that means they are tied to the company performance. The Hampel view appeared more logical. It was difficult to see why independence was not compromised by holding shares whilst it was by holding share options – if anything the pressure on the non-executive director was even greater if he or she actually had an existing shareholding to protect rather than a speculative gain.

- A senior non-executive director should be nominated to deal with shareholders' concerns. Hampel has expressed the view that, if directors pay themselves too much or do not invest enough in the company, it was the power wielded by the shareholders rather than books of corporate governance rules that really counted. However, it is difficult to see how a busy non-executive director, often with extensive commitments elsewhere, will be in a position to respond to other than limited requests for information or action.

- Directors should be trained.

The Hampel Report was followed by the *Combined Code*.

29.8 The Higgs Report[8]

The Higgs Report on a 'Review of the role and effectiveness of non-executive directors' (NEDs) was published in January 2003. The main recommendations are:

29.8.1 Board operation

- The company's annual report should state the number of meetings of the board and its main committees, and the attendance of each director. There should be a description of how the board operates.
- At least half the members of the board, excluding the chairman, should be independent NEDs.
- The performance of the Board, its committees and its members should be evaluated at least once a year.
- A nomination committee of the board should conduct the process of board appointments and make recommendations. It should consist of a majority of independent NEDs.

Comment on possible success of the proposal that at least 50% of the directors of listed companies should be NEDs:

- It is beneficial when executive directors and NEDs work together, valuing each other's experience and contribution. The NEDs can provide an independent check on the executives' plans and decisions, and their experience will be different from the executive which should lead to better decision making.
- However, there can be 'splits' between the executives and NEDs. The executives may propose a future plan, but (some or all of) the NEDs may disagree. This can lead to distrust between the executives and NEDs, which will adversely affect the running of the company. Because of these problems, the executives may 'hide' certain decisions and information from the NEDs. The executives are likely to feel the NEDs are 'interfering' – they will see the NEDs as less valuable than themselves, as the NEDs will be paid substantially less than the executives, and the NEDs will spend only a small part of their time on the company's affairs while the executives will be working full time.
- Boards try to keep 'splits' (i.e. disagreements) between directors secret until the matter is resolved. If this information becomes public, it can have a very adverse effect on the company's share price, and it could precipitate the collapse of the company. For instance, the Board may be considering dismissing the Chief Executive (e.g. the company is performing poorly), but it will not make an announcement until it has been agreed by a majority of the members of the Board. There may be a further delay while termination payments of the Chief Executive are being agreed.

- There may be situations when the NEDs' approach to running the business is too cautious. The executives may make a proposal which the NEDs reject. However, the executives will understand the market better than the NEDs, and the executives proposal would have been very profitable. The decision by the NEDs will have led to a reduction in future profitability and expansion of the business.

- Even with a board of at least 50% NEDs, it is questionable whether they will have the courage and power to over-ride the proposals of the executives. For instance, would the NEDs of Marconi have prevented the executives from buying companies for cash and increasing the company's borrowings by many billions of pounds? However, some years ago the NEDs were effective when British Airways (BA) produced unjustified publicity against Virgin. Virgin took legal action against BA, and the NEDs replaced the directors involved in this unjustified publicity.

Comment on proposal for nominations:

- Appointments to the Board has often been seen as the Chairman's prerogative and the proposal may well be opposed by Chairmen.

29.8.2 Chairman

- The role of the chairman and chief executive should be separated, with their responsibilities set out in writing and approved by the board.
- A chief executive should not become chairman of the same company.

Comment:
There are still companies that consider it is more efficient for the roles to be combined.

29.8.3 NEDs – appointment

- Before appointment, NEDs should satisfy themselves that they have the knowledge, skills, experience and time to make a positive contribution to the board.
- The board should set out to shareholders why they propose a new NED and how they meet the requirements.
- There should be an induction programme for new NEDs, which is the responsibility of the chairman and company secretary.
- NEDs should be expected to serve two three-year terms.

29.8.4 NEDs – independence

- NEDs should meet at least once a year without the chairman or executive directors present.
- NEDs may hold shares in the company but should not be awarded share options.
- NEDs should inform the chairman of their reasons for resignation.

29.8.5 NEDs – effectiveness

- A full-time executive director should not have more than one non-executive directorship and should not become chairman of a major company.

- The remuneration committee should comprise at least three members, all of whom should be NEDs. It should have delegated responsibility for setting the remuneration of all the executive directors and the chairman.

29.8.6 Senior NED

- There should be a senior independent NED, who should be available to shareholders for concerns that have not been resolved by the chairman or chief executive.
- The senior NED should attend meetings of management with a range of major shareholders.

Comment:
There have been objections to the proposal for a Senior NED on the grounds that it reduces the power of the Chairman and the Unitary Board principle.

29.9 The Smith Report[9]

The Smith Report on 'Audit Committees – Combined Code Guidance', was set up by the Financial Reporting Council, and was designed as a 'junior companion' to Higgs' wider brief on non-executive directors. The committee was chaired by Sir Robert Smith, Chairman of the Weir Group.

The recommendations on audit committees include:

- At least three members, all independent NEDs.
- At least one member should have significant, recent and relevant financial experience.

The audit committee should:

- Monitor the integrity of the financial statements.
- Review the company's internal financial control system and monitor the effectiveness of internal audit.
- Recommend the appointment of the external auditor, and approve the remuneration and terms of engagement.
- Monitor the external auditor's independence, objectivity and effectiveness.
- Develop and implement a policy on the external auditor supplying non-audit services.
- The directors' report should describe the role of the audit committee and the action it has taken. The chairman of the audit committee should be present at the AGM.

29.9.1 What impact will the Higgs and Smith Reports have on UK corporate governance?

Greater transparency

Future annual reports should reflect the emphasis for greater transparency. An example of this is requirement for disclosure by the Board of the NEDs considered to be independent and, where circumstances might imply otherwise, the reasons why they are so considered, e.g. where the NED represents a major shareholder.

Audit Committee's responsibilities more explicit

The Committee will have a more proactive role and broader overview rather than the previous rather reactive role of keeping the scope and results of the audit under review, e.g. a requirement to monitor the integrity of the financial statements and review significant financial reporting issues and judgements. There is a possibility that misunderstandings may arise:

- For the NEDs who have a conflict of roles with the Committee acting as Board members with the executive management to achieve strategic objectives and as Committee members, overseeing the executive management to protect shareholders' long-term interests.

- For the other Board members who may believe that they have been relieved of responsibility for the work carried out by the Audit Committee.

What will the impact be in practice?

There are two aspects that may affect the impact:

- The degree to which the NEDs achieve constructive informal relationships beyond the formal meetings.
- The extent to which Boards exercise discretion with disclosure.[10]

29.10 The Combined Code[11]

The *Combined Code* is described in the Preamble to the Code as 'a consolidation of the work of the three committees, not a new departure'.

It made clear that companies should be ready to explain their governance policies, including any circumstances, justifying departure from best practice and that those concerned with the evaluation of governance should do so with common sense and with due regard to companies individual circumstances.

The Code proposes principles and code provisions under five headings:

(a) directors
(b) directors' remuneration
(c) relations with shareholders
(d) accountability and audit
(e) institutional shareholders

We considered directors in Chapter 5. We will now consider headings (b), (c) and (e).

29.11 Directors' remuneration

The proposals are as in previous reports, i.e.

- companies should establish a formal and transparent procedure for developing policy;
- companies should pay enough to attract suitable directors;
- companies should pay no more than enough;
- part of the remuneration should be linked to individual and corporate performance;
- policy and remuneration of each director should be disclosed in the Annual Report.

29.11.1 Where do accountants feature in setting directors' remuneration?

The equity of the remuneration is not normally seen as an accounting matter, but accountants should ensure transparent disclosure of the performance criteria and of the payments.

29.11.2 Performance criteria

Directors are expected to produce increases in the share price and dividends. Traditional measures have been largely based on growth in earnings per share (EPS), which has encouraged companies to seek to increase short-term earnings at the expense of long-term earnings, e.g. by cutting back capital programmes. Even worse, concentrating on growth in earnings per share can result in a reduction in shareholder value, e.g. by companies borrowing and investing in projects that produce a return in excess of the interest charge, but less than the return expected by equity investors.

29.11.3 What alternatives are there?

It is interesting to identify the suggested criteria because they could have an impact on the financial information that has to be disclosed in the annual accounts. Suggested criteria include the following:

- **Relative share price increase**, i.e. using market comparisons. Grand Met has revised its scheme so that, before executives gain any benefit from their share options, Grand Met's share price must outperform the FT All-Share Index over a three-year period, i.e. the scheme focuses management on value creation.[12] If this policy is adopted, it would be helpful for the annual accounts to contain details of share price and index movements. Comparative share price schemes should also, in the opinion of the Association of British Insurers, be conditional on a secondary performance criterion, validating sustained and significant improvement in underlying financial performance over the same period.

- **Indicators related to business drivers**, i.e. using internal data. Schemes would need to identify business drivers appropriate to each company, such as customer satisfaction or process times. If this policy is adopted, it would be helpful for the annual accounts to contain details in the business review section of the nature of the drivers and how well they have been achieved. The 1997 Allied Colloids Annual Report explains the company's Remuneration Policy as:

  (i) Basic salary
  Basic salaries and benefits are determined after an annual review of performance. The Remuneration Committee also takes into account external information on remuneration for similar positions in comparable companies. Any increases reflect both individual and business performance.

  (ii) Performance related bonuses
  Senior management participate in a performance related bonus scheme which can pay up to 40% of salary as an annual bonus. The amount of the bonus is determined by achievement of performance targets set by the Committee, in respect of growth in sales, gross profit, profit before interest and tax, cash flow and return on shareholders' funds. The targets set are demanding and are intended to reward substantial improvements in performance. The scheme will pay a bonus of 9% in respect of the year ended 31 March 1997.

The problem for the shareholder is 'How is this to be interpreted?' It could be argued that the directors only achieved 23% of the improvement that was being sought – in which case, why is there any bonus being paid?

● **Indicators based on factors such as size and complexity.** Schemes would need to take account of factors such as market capitalisation, turnover, number of employees, breadth of product and markets, risk, regulatory and competitive environment, and rates of change experienced by the organisation. This information could again be disclosed in the business review section of the annual report.

The indications are that there will be a growth in the number of firms offering schemes. However, regulators will need to keep a close eye on the position to avoid schemes creeping in that avoid the existing disclosure requirements. For example, there has been a growth in long-term incentive plans, under which free shares are offered in the future if the executive remains with the company and achieves a certain performance level. This is a perfectly healthy development that retains staff, but such schemes fall outside the definition of a share option plan and allow companies to avoid disclosure.

One of the problems is the innovative nature of the remuneration packages that companies might adopt and the fact that there is no uniquely correct scheme. The Association of British Insurers, in its publication *Share Option and Profit Sharing Incentive Schemes* (February 1995), commented on this very point:

> There is growing acceptance that the benefit arising from the exercise of options should be linked to the underlying financial performance of the company.
>
> Initially, attention focused on performance criteria showing real growth in normalised earnings; however, a number of other criteria have subsequently emerged. The circumstances of each individual company will vary and there is a reluctance, therefore, on the part of institutional investors to indicate a general preference for any particular measurement. On the other hand, a considerable number of companies have stated that they welcome indications of the sort of formulae that are considered to be acceptable ... It is felt that remuneration committees should have discretion to select the formula which is felt to be most appropriate to the circumstances of the company in question. Nevertheless ... it is important that whatever criterion is chosen ... the formula should be supported by, or give clear evidence of, sustained improvement in the underlying financial performance of the group in question.[13]

29.11.4 Requiring adequate disclosure

There is a need for greater disclosure because, in addition to their salaries, directors have been rewarded with bonuses and share options which were not disclosed in the annual accounts in a form that was readily understandable.

In the UK, this prompted the ASB[14] in 1994 to issue a UITF Abstract *Disclosure of Directors' Share Options*, recommending disclosure of information about option prices and market prices. In the USA, the SEC had already addressed the issue by requiring a precise description of salary, bonuses and share options for the five most highly paid executives, identified by name; and requiring the options to be valued and the information to be presented in a standardised format.

29.11.5 Why should disclosure be required?

In the USA, the disclosure approach has indicated that the very fact of disclosure exerted a moderating influence on the levels of executive reward.[15] It might be argued that financial reporting should not concern itself with the level of an individual executive's remuneration. However, there is a statutory duty to report on directors' remuneration and, under the *Statement of Principles*, a requirement that the information should be reliable. This is an excellent example of where the *Statement of Principles* can assist the financial reporting process. Details about the remuneration package need to be relevant and reliable.

29.11.6 Relevance implication

For information to be relevant, it needs to be predictive. Given that the major purpose of the motivational aspects of the package is to guide the directors towards maximising a defined attribute, e.g. EPS, it is vital to be aware of this when assessing the future performance of the company. If the scheme succeeds, the defined attributes will be the ones that the directors concentrate on. The financial statements should make the shareholder aware of the aim and in subsequent periods provide confirmation as to the level of achievement.

29.11.7 Reliability implication

The *Statement of Principles* states that for information to be reliable it needs to be a valid description and measure, to be complete and to convey the substance of the transaction in an understandable fashion with due regard for the user's abilities. This has not yet been achieved with directors' remuneration and the ASB approach of substance over form could well be followed.

29.11.8 Evaluation of current practice

Following the Greenbury Committee in 1995, remuneration committees now make their own reports to shareholders. The accounts have clearer messages concerning basic salary, constituents of the bonus calculation (although no information that allows the shareholder to assess targets or achievement of targets), long-term incentive plans, share options and pension contributions.

This would seem to indicate that all is well. However, this is certainly not the view presented in an article in *Management Today*.[16] This makes positive reference to the effect of Cadbury, Greenbury and Hampel in forcing companies to adopt long-term incentive plans linked to future performance over a three- to five-year period which, on the surface, appears to be a far more effective way of aligning the interests of executives with those of their investors and their workers; it also recognises that some companies are introducing more stringent performance criteria, e.g. the Whitbread requirement that, unless over a three-year period it improves its minimum total shareholder ranking from 75th to 60th out of the FTSE 100, executives participating in the scheme will not be entitled to any shares. There is a note of caution, however, in that 40% of FTSE 100 companies are still paying above average rewards for poor performing executives and more challenging objectives should be found that support shareholder value creation.

The search to tailor remuneration packages will continue and may see a move away from measures such as share price movements which are often a reflection of market movements rather than executive performance. An interesting suggestion was made by Robert Heller in *Management Today*, July 1997,[17] that, if the true top task is to provide successful medium and long-term strategic direction, and to ensure its implementation, then this should loom largest in determining rewards, and never mind the short-term price of shares. This could be implemented by the use of techniques such as the balanced scorecard with its combination of financial measures and non-financial measures.

The Code itself sets out provisions to act as warnings to the remuneration committee, e.g. 'comparisons with other companies should be used with caution, in view of the risk that they can result in an upward ratchet of remuneration levels with no corresponding improvement in performance' and 'avoid paying more than is necessary' and 'options should not be exercisable in under three years' and 'total rewards potentially available should not be excessive' and 'incentive schemes should be subject to challenging performance criteria'.

However, in the *Combined Code* there is recognition that the achievement of a fair remuneration policy has not been completed and it states in its preamble: 'We wish to make it clear in our report that it is still too soon to assess definitively the results of the Cadbury and, more especially, the Greenbury codes'.

29.11.9 How well do executives' rewards correlate with performance?

A comparison[18] of the top FTSE 100 performers with those at the bottom showed that the presence or otherwise of long-term incentive plans (LTIPs) made very little difference to an executive's performance. The comparison showed the following information for the chief executive officers (CEOs):

Footsie leaders

Company	Salary (£)	Bonus (£)	LTIP (£)	Total (£)
Misys	285,717	329,287	193,228	808,232
Stagecoach	372,000	250,000	80,069	630,069
Legal & General	440,000	400,000	361,215	1,201,215
Vodafone	587,000	0	3,246,985	3,833,985
Lloyds TSB	475,000	199,000	940,797	1,614,797

Footsie laggards

Company	Salary (£)	Bonus (£)	LTIP (£)	Total (£)
Hanson	310,000	155,000	544,223	1,009,223
Rio Tinto	669,000	144,000	1,179,548	1,992,548
EMI Group	543,300	105,500	361,600	1,010,400
Allied Domecq	460,000	165,000	732,065	1,357,065
Reuters	522,000	255,000	815,938	1,592,938

29.12 Directors' remuneration – illustration from the annual report of Diageo plc[19]

One would imagine that the remuneration which is paid to directors is a simple subject. A director's salary should comprise a basic salary and a bonus based on the profits of the company. However, looking at the financial statements of listed companies, it can be seen that directors' remuneration includes:

(a) basic salary;
(b) benefits in kind;
(c) bonus;

(d) pension entitlements;

(e) share options.

Each of these elements of remuneration are considered below. An example of disclosure of directors' remuneration is taken from the financial statements of Diageo plc, a UK listed company. These disclosures are long and very detailed. However, careful consideration of them reveals a number of unclear matters and unanswered questions.

29.12.1 Remuneration committee

As shown in the table of corporate governance requirements, it is suggested that listed companies should have a remuneration committee. Diageo has a remuneration committee; its financial statements say: 'The Remuneration Committee is responsible for making recommendations to the board on remuneration policy as applied to Diageo's executive directors. It consists wholly of independent non-executive directors'. (The names of the directors are given, including the Chairman).

Remuneration Committees are common in US and UK listed companies, but it is far from clear that remuneration is based on the financial performance of the companies. In the UK, the evidence suggests that the larger the company, the larger is the remuneration of the directors, and there is little correlation between remuneration and profitability of the company.

The weakness of the remuneration committee is that it comprises non-executive directors of the company, rather than individuals independent of the company. The initial appointment of the non-executive directors will have been by the executive directors and existing non-executive directors of the company. Also, it is not uncommon for a non-executive director of company A to be an executive director of company B, and a non-executive director of company B is an executive director of company A – an incestuous circle in which executive directors of A approve the remuneration of the executive directors of B and vice versa. However, the existence of a remuneration committee should discourage excessive remuneration being paid to executive directors, particularly where the financial performance of the company is poor. Note that Diageo's Remuneration Committee includes the Chairman – Higgs' proposals (2003) prohibit this.

29.12.2 Basic salary

The Diageo financial statements say 'Basic salaries are determined according to the competitive market for senior executives, taking into account their experience, contribution and performance.' As expected, this is more a qualitative statement than a quantitative one. One could not determine the basic salary of any director from this statement.

29.12.3 Benefits in kind

The notes to the financial statements of Diageo plc say benefits include: 'Company cars, private use of chauffeur, fuel, product allowance, financial counselling, spouse travel, medical insurance and life insurance premiums.' Once again, these vary significantly from 6% to 77% of the basic salary. Some explanation is given of the larger sums, such as £279,000 in payment for relocation of a director to the United Kingdom.

A recent example of excessive 'benefits in kind' by a director is Greg Hutchings, chief executive of Tomkins plc. The 'benefits' paid by the company include providing two flats in London, a Rolls-Royce, four jet aircraft, a helicopter, paying his wife and housekeeper, and paying for his son's flight on Concorde. An earlier non-executive Chairman of

Tomkins had resigned over being unable to quantify and control Mr Hutchings' 'benefits'. A new non-executive chairman, David Newlands, investigated the extent of his benefits in kind. This led to Mr Hutchings' resignation from the board of Tomkins plc in October 2000.

It can be very difficult to determine the extent of a director's benefits in kind, particularly when the director is in a dominant position and unwilling to disclose these benefits. The financial director, chief accountant and company secretary may be aware of the chief executive's benefits in kind, but a dominant chief executive may prevent them from disclosing the benefits to the non-executive directors and the auditors. However, the Tomkins plc example shows how strong non-executive directors (including the chairman) can act as a control on the actions of executive directors.

29.12.4 Director's bonus

Diageo's financial statements say:

> Bonus payments are based on improvement in the economic profit (EP) of Diageo and its businesses for the year in question. The targets for EP and for the level of bonus are determined by the remuneration committee at the commencement of each year. EP is calculated as net trading profit after tax, less a capital charge which takes into account returns expected by lenders and shareholders. However, for the financial years commencing 1 July 2002, the primary performance measure for the annual performance bonus will be trading profit before exceptional items. This reflects Diageo's objectives of driving organic growth.

Note that:

(i) Trading profit is **before** charging or crediting losses or profits on sale of fixed assets and sale of businesses and interest payments. The profit before taxation is **after** charging/crediting these items. So, for instance, the bonus could be increased by reducing the depreciation charge, so increasing the trading profit. Any losses on sale of fixed assets would be after the trading profit, so they would have no effect on the bonus.

(ii) EP is defined as the **improvement** in economic profit. Would any improvement in EP lead to a bonus? How is 'improvement' calculated? Is it the 'improvement' over last year, or from a basic target or from a long-term trend?

(iii) There is no explanation of how the **capital charge** is determined.

(iv) There is no statement about how much of the 'improvement' in EP is paid to the directors.

(v) There is no explanation why the bonus as a percentage of the basic salary varies so much. The monetary amount of the bonus of directors varies in the ratio 3:1.

From 1 July 2002 the calculation of the bonus is even less detailed and less clear, and it could be much more generous. There is no mention of deducting a 'capital charge', so is a bonus paid as long as there is a profit before exceptional items? There should be a 'normal profit' below which no bonus should be paid (i.e. the intention of the previous capital charge). Using the 'profit before exceptional items' is more generous than using the 'profit after exceptional items', as almost all 'exceptional items' are deductions from profit. The 'real' profit of a business is the profit *after* exceptional items, as such exceptional items as closure, redundancy and reorganisation costs are 'real' costs to a business.

It can be seen that the note on the bonus raises more questions than it answers!

Considering bonuses generally, most bonuses are based on the current year's profit, rather than the trend in profits. The bonus cannot be based on future profits, as they are unknown. Basing the bonus on the current year's profit could lead directors to maximise this year's profit by:

(a) the way in which they exercise their judgement in relation to asset vales in the balance sheet, e.g.
  ● valuing stock and debtors at the highest possible value by having low provisions for stock obsolescence and bad debts;
  ● reducing the depreciation on fixed assets;
  ● capitalizing development costs;

(b) making decisions that affect the timing of cash flows, e.g.
  ● delaying capital expenditure;
  ● delaying routine commitments such as the maintenance programme;
  ● delaying decisions on staff benefits;
  ● holding back on developing new products.

Developing new products is expensive, and will adversely affect the current year's profit. Some of the costs of developing new products will have to be charged against the current year's profits, as not all these costs can be included in capitalised development expenditure. Also, few companies capitalise development expenditure, and it may not be possible to capitalise development expenditure (particularly in the early stages) as it may not be possible to guarantee there will be sufficient profits from the new product to cover the development costs. So, basing directors' bonuses on the current year's profits could encourage directors to delay (or cancel) development of new products.

If no new products are developed, the company will probably fail in the long term. Thus, providing a bonus based on the current year's profit tends to encourage 'short-termism', which is not in the best interests of the shareholders. The allocation of share options to directors will tend to encourage directors to consider longer term profitability, which is in the interests of the shareholders. 'Share options' are considered in section 29.10.6 below.

A further problem with paying directors on the basis of the company's profits is that no one would want to be a director in a loss-making company. In many ways, it can be much more difficult to be a director of a company which is in trouble and making losses (in terms of skills required, hours worked and stress) than a successful and profitable company. Normally, a company makes losses because of a change in market conditions and has not been able to keep up with the changes. Implementing changes in the company is very difficult and time consuming. The directors have to decide the new direction of the company. This is very risky, and taking the wrong direction may result in failure of the company. This requires very skilled directors, working very long hours and making difficult decisions. Some decisions, such as making employees redundant, will increase losses (or reduce profits). So, a directors' bonus scheme based on the profitability of the company would be inappropriate. In this situation a remuneration committee would be very valuable. The members of the remuneration committee will be able to see the contributions of each director towards 'turning around' the company. So, they will be good at deciding the appropriate remuneration of each of the directors. The shareholders would be less effective at this task, as they would not have the necessary detailed understanding of the contribution of each director.

From the above discussion, it can be seen that the remuneration committee can be an effective way of determining the remuneration of the individual directors.

29.12.5 Pension entitlements

The disclosure of this item in Diageo's financial statements states the director's annual pension at retirement, and the increase in the pension over inflation since last year. However, this disclosure does not give the pension cost to the company this year, which is the amount the company would have to pay into a pension scheme this year to provide a fund sufficient to pay the director's pension on retirement.

How this pension cost can be calculated is shown by the following example. In the 2001 accounts, a director's pension on retirement was £468,000, and in the 2002 accounts this pension had increased to £509,000. The computation of this cost is performed by actuaries. The following additional information is used in the calculation:

(i) the director would retire in 2005;

(ii) the director's planned pension in 2001 was £468,000 and in 2002 it is £509,000;

(iii) a return on investments of 6% is assumed;

(iv) no inflation or increase is assumed in the director's pension after retirement;

(v) it is assumed the director receives a pension for 15 years, starting in 2005.

The pension fund required in 2005 to pay a pension of £468,000 for 15 years
= £468,000 × (1 + annuity for 14 years)
= £468,000 × (1 + 9.2950)   = £4,816,000

The pension fund required in 2001 to pay a pension of £468,000 for 15 years
= £4,816,000 × discount factor for 4 years
= £4,816,000 × 0.792094   = £3,815,000

By 2002 this pension fund will have grown to
= £3,815,000 × 1.06   = £4,044,000

Considering the year 2002 pension of £509,000:
The pension fund required in 2005 to pay a pension of £509,000 for 15 years
= £509,000 × (1 + annuity for 14 years)
= £509,000 × (1 + 9.2950)   = £5,240,000

The pension fund required in 2002 to pay a pension of £468,000 for 15 years
= £5,240,000 × discount factor for 3 years
= £5,240,000 × 0.839619   = £4,400,000

So, the company's contribution to the pension fund in 2002
= pension fund required in 2002 – pension fund accrued by 2002
= £4,400,000 – £4,044,000   = £356,000

These figures illustrate how the calculation would be performed. In practice, the following factors would be included:

(i) the real increase in the pension fund investments from 2001 to 2002;

(ii) the assumed increase in the director's salary each year to retirement;

(iii) the increase in the director's pension in retirement (frequently, pensions are increased by the retail price index).

29.12.6 Share options

As indicated earlier, share options are believed to be an effective way of paying directors and of avoiding 'short-termism', as the value of a share should be a reflection of the long-term profitability of the company. Until recently, there has been no charge to the income statement for share options, so the shareholders are not aware of the value of the options granted to the directors. However, share options can be very valuable to directors. Excluding the cost of share options from the financial statements understates the directors' remuneration.

An illustration of how share options work

A company granted a share option on 1 January 2003 (the **grant date**) to its chief executive officer (CEO) for 100,000 shares at the current market price of 350c. The option required the director to meet profit targets for the three years to 31 December 2005 (the **vesting date**). If these profit targets are met, the director will be able to purchase the shares at the **exercise date** of 30 June 2004 at the option price of 350c a share.

Normally, the option is granted at the market price of the shares at the grant date (i.e. 350c a share). If the value of the shares is less than 350c on 30 June 2006, the director will not purchase the shares (as they would make a loss), so the director's gain on the option will be zero. If the value of the shares is 410c on 30 June 2006, the director will buy the shares for $350,000 and immediately sell them in the market for $410,000, making a gain of $60,000.

Interestingly, most directors of listed companies in the UK buy and sell the shares at the **exercise date** (30 June 2006 in this case). Only a small minority of directors buy the shares at the option price and continue to hold them.

The 'theory' of share options is that the share price on 30 June 2006 will be based on the company's long-term profitability, so if the company is doing well, the share price will be higher and the director's profit on buying the shares (and subsequently selling them) will be higher. So the director's gain on selling the shares will reflect the director's success in increasing the profits and hence the share price of the company. To a certain extent, this 'theory' is correct in that the share price tends to increase if the company's profitability increases. However, share price movements also depend on other factors, such as the general price movement of other shares and investors' views about the future profitability and growth in the particular type of trade the company is in. For instance, in late 1999 and early 2000 there was an enormous increase in the value of telecom and dot.com shares, yet many of these companies had never made a profit. Thus, the increase in the share price did not depend on the profitability of the companies, and it could be argued that the share prices of these shares increased because this was a fashionable sector of the market in which to invest.

At the same time as the increase in value of telecom and dot com shares there was a substantial fall in the value of other shares, including well known retailers. In some of these cases the share prices were falling, despite the fact that the companies' profits were increasing. So, it can be seen that the increase in the share price of a company may be more related to market conditions than the long term profitability of the company. Thus, awarding options on shares may not be a very effective way of paying directors, as the change in the share price may have little to do with profitability of the company and the directors' contribution to increasing those profits.

29.12.7 Accounting for share options

As has been discussed earlier, share options have become an important way of paying directors, motivating them to ensure the long term profitability of the company. There has been disclosure of these options in the financial statements of companies for a number of years, but no cost of the share options has been included in the income statement. However, as explained below, there is a cost to the company of awarding these options.

The problems are:

(i) when should the cost of the options be charged in the financial statements?

(ii) how much should be charged in the financial statements?

Taking the example above, we will provide some definitions. First, the dates:

- The **grant date** (i.e. 1 January 2003) is the date when the employee and employer enter into an agreement that will entitle the employee to receive an option on a future date, provided certain conditions are met.
- The **service date** (1 January 2003 to 31 December 2005) is the date or dates on which the employee performs the services necessary to become unconditionally entitled to the option.
- The **vesting date** (31 December 2005) is the date when the employee, having satisfied all the conditions, becomes unconditionally entitled to the option.
- The **exercise date** (30 June 2006) is when the option is exercised.

Using the figures in our example, we will show how these affect the charge to the income statement for three methods:

(a) The UK Accounting Standards Board, which proposes that the vesting date should be used to measure and date the charge for the option made in the financial statements;

(b) The US Financial Accounting Standards Board in FAS 123 *Accounting for stock-based compensation*, which uses the grant date as when the charge should be made to the income statement;

(c) A proposal based on the International Accounting Standards Board IAS 37 *Provisions, Contingent Liabilities and Contingent Assets*.[20]

Grant date

At this date, it may appear the value of the option is zero, as the option is granted at the current market price of the shares. This argument has been used to justify not charging directors' share options in the income statement. However, the value of the option is not zero, as the director will make either a nil profit or a gain on exercising the share option on 30 June 2006. So, the value of the option is the market price of an option to purchase the company's shares at 350c on 30 June 2006 – we will take the value of this option at 1 January 2003 as 30c a share. But the director may not be eligible to take the option as the profitability target may not be met. The probability of the CEO meeting the target is 60%.

US treatment

Then, at the grant date, the value of the option

$$= 100,000 \times 0.30 \times 60\% = \$18,000$$

So, at the grant date (of 1 January 2003), a charge would be made in the financial statements of $18,000 for this option, and an equal provision included in the balance sheet. This is the amount charged using the US FAS 123 method.

UK treatment

There would be no charge at this stage under the UK ASB proposals, as the charge does not arise until the vesting date.

IAS treatment[20]

Under IAS 37, the $18,000 is a **provision**, as it is a 'present obligation and it is probable that an outflow of resources embodying economic benefits will be required to settle the obligation' (IAS 37, para. 13(a)). Under IAS 37 (para. 37) the provision should be the 'best estimate of the expenditure required to settle the present obligation, which is the amount the enterprise would rationally pay to settle the obligation at the balance sheet date'. The value of the provision is the $18,000 we have calculated, as it is the value of an option to purchase the shares at 350c on 30 June 2006 (30c a share × 100,000 shares) multiplied by the probability of the option being exercised (60%).

Service date

IAS treatment

At each year end during the service date, under IAS 37, the provision at the year end will be calculated as: 100,000 × value of option × probability of option being granted. The year's charge to the income statement for the option will then be the difference between this year's provision and last year's provision.

In this example, for the IAS 37 treatment, the value of the provision at each year end has been taken as providing an equal charge to the income statement for each year between the **Grant Date** and the **Vesting Date**.

Vesting date

At the Vesting Date (31 December 2005), we will assume the value of an option to purchase shares at $3.50 on 30 June 2006 is 55c a share. Assuming the director has achieved the target, the value of this option at 31 December 2005 will be: 100,000 × 0.55 = $55,000

- US – Under FAS 123 there would be no additional charge, as this is after the grant date.
- UK – Under the UK ASB method, the charge of $55,000 will be made to the income statement on 31 December 2005.
- IAS – Under IAS 37, the charge to the income statement for the year ended 31 December 2005 will be the difference between the provision at 31 December 2003 and 31 December 2004.

Exercise date

At the exercise date, the value of the company's shares is $4.10. By buying the shares from the company and immediately selling them, the director's profit will be: 100,000 × (4.10 − 3.50) = $60,000. Thus, under IAS 37, the value of the options will be:

(a) at 1 January 2003, the grant date   = $18,000

(b) at 31 December 2005, the vesting date = $55,000

(c) at 30 June 2006, the exercise date   = $60,000

The US FAS 123 would include the figure of $18,000 on 1 January 2003, and no subsequent charge to the income statement. The UK ASB would include the figure of $55,000 on 31 December 2005, and no prior or subsequent charge to the income statement.

Summarising the discussion, the annual charge and the total charge for the CEO's options using the three methods is shown in Figure 29.3.

With the IAS 37 method, the annual charge is spread equally between the years 2003 to 2005. The ultimate cost to the company is the difference in the amount it would receive on 30 June 2006 from selling the shares in the market and the amount it receives

Figure 29.3 Comparison of income statement charge for different accounting methods

Year ended	IAS 37 method	US FAS 123	UK ASB
31 Dec 2003	18,000 + 12,333 = 30,333	18,000	0
31 Dec 2004	12,333	0	0
31 Dec 2005	12,334	0	55,000
31 Dec 2006	5,000	0	0
Total charge	**60,000**	**18,000**	**55,000**

by selling the shares to the director at 350c each (i.e. 60c a share). This method treats the provision at each year end as the amount the company would have to pay in the market to discharge itself of the provision. This is consistent with a financial management view of the problem.

So, the IAS 37 method complies with IAS 37 *Provisions, Contingent Liabilities and Contingent Assets* and with financial management principles. However, the US FAS 123 and UK ASB proposals are not consistent with IAS 37. Both the US FAS123 and the UK ASB proposals produce a lower charge to the income statement for the director's options. Why is this happening?

It appears the IAS 37 method is not acceptable to the US or UK accounting standards committees. As has been indicated earlier, accounting standards are often an acceptable compromise between the views of the representatives of the listed companies and those of the financial institutions represented on the accounting standards committees. The US proposal has met with hostility from the listed companies, as it makes them charge the cost of the options in the financial statements, and in many cases the costs are very high. The directors of the listed companies would prefer there to be no charge for the cost of the options, as had previously been the case. The hostility of the listed companies to the FAS123 proposals probably set a line beyond which they would not go, so the FAS123 proposal is set at valuing the option at the grant date. In our example, this gives a charge of $18,000.

The UK ASB's proposal of using the vesting date gives a charge which is much closer to the actual cost to the company. However, its weakness is that this charge is made at a relatively late date, and it would be preferable if this charge was made over the period when the CEO earned the right to the options.

In conclusion, it can be seen that the US FAS123's and the UK ASB's proposals give a lower charge to the income statement for the share options than the IAS 37 method, which is, however, the correct method to use as it is consistent with IAS 37 on *Provisions, Contingent Liabilities and Contingent Assets* and with financial management principles.

29.13 Directors' remuneration – conclusion

From the above discussion on directors' remuneration, it can be seen that current disclosure of the costs to the company of employing directors is incomplete, and the disclosed cost is understated. In particular:

(a) the current year's cost of providing directors' pensions is not disclosed. Only directors' annual pensions on retirement are disclosed;

(b) the cost of providing directors' share options is either understated (under US FAS123 or UK ASB proposals) or taken as zero. A method which is consistent with IAS 37 *Provisions, Contingent Liabilities and Contingent Assets* should be used to determine the annual cost of these options to the company.

In the example of Diageo plc taken in this chapter, the disclosure of directors' remuneration and benefits is probably close to the best available for listed companies. For most other listed companies in the UK and other countries, the disclosure of directors remuneration is probably less detailed and less helpful than for Diageo. This shows how much further listed companies need to go to provide a complete disclosure of directors' remuneration in the annual financial statements.

29.14 Relations with shareholders

There is simply a proposal that companies enter into dialogue with institutional shareholders and for chairmen of the remuneration, audit and nomination committees to be available to answer questions at the AGM.

29.15 Institutional investors

There are three principles, namely that institutional shareholders:

- have a responsibility to make considered use of their votes,
- should be ready to enter into dialogue with companies,
- should give due weight to all factors drawn to their attention when evaluating companies' governance arrangements.

For greater detail, we need to refer to the governance documents produced by the various institutional investor organisations, e.g. the Association of British Insurers and National Association of Pension Funds.

29.15.1 Association of British Insurers (ABI)

The ABI[21] has published a Statement of Voting Policy and Corporate Governance Good which sets out that ABI members' overall objective is, and must be, to achieve on behalf of those for whom they act a competitive return on the funds invested and that the exercise of their voting policy will be in support of the proper management of companies and directed towards the enhancement of long-term shareholder value and the wider economic benefits which this should engender.

The Statement includes the following points:

- ABI members fully support the principles of the Cadbury, Greenbury and Hampel committees.
- The exercise of voting rights is inseparable from the investment management function and the objective of maximisation of long-term shareholder value.
- It is considered important to support boards by a positive use of their voting rights unless they have good reason for doing otherwise so that it would be a matter of concern for the board if that support was not forthcoming.
- If considering voting against a proposal it is important to make representations to the board in time for consultation and satisfactory resolution.

- Voting decisions by ABI members will reflect the Association's guidance notes, e.g. on share incentive schemes and policy statements, e.g. roles of chairman and chief executive should not normally be combined.

- Structured dialogue is encouraged to better understand management's objectives, the problems confronting management and the quality of management whilst at the same time making clear the expectations and requirements of shareholders.

- Institutional investors will not wish to receive price sensitive information and, if they do, there would be a requirement that they suspend their ability to deal in the shares.

- They are concerned to ensure the appointment of a core of non-executives of sufficient number and of appropriate calibre, experience and independence to identify where there may be undue concentrations of decision-making power not formally constrained by appropriate checks and balances.

- On directors' remuneration, institutional investors support the key recommendations of the Greenbury Committee.

29.16 The Myners Report

Developing a Winning Partnership is a report of a joint City/industry working group established under the chairmanship of Paul Myners. The report considered how companies and institutional investors are working together.

The report recognises that there has been a perceived antagonism between companies and institutional investors. Institutional investors have been accused of short-termism which has discouraged investment. Companies need supportive long-term shareholders to encourage them to invest for the future. There is an urgent need for a long-term working relationship to be developed.

What is meant by short-termism?

Short-termism of investors has been blamed for the UK's lack of investment. It is evidenced by the churning of shares, driven in part by the buy and sell recommendations of stockbrokers' analysts, the ready acceptance of hostile take-overs, and unreasonable demands for early earnings growth and increasing dividends. However, the National Association of Pension Funds has estimated that the average holding period for a share in a pension fund portfolio is over eight years.

There is also, of course, the short-termism of management evidenced by excessive management remuneration and share option schemes which are not in the best interest of the shareholders.

The Combined Code refers to 'dialogue'. This implies a two-way commitment from both the institutional investors and the company managers.

Institutional investors

Institutional investors want company managers to articulate more clearly their long-term corporate objectives and financial policies, of which dividend policy is an important part, and to emphasise in the discussion their vision for the company and the corporate values. They want managers to be consistent in their communication with investors and the press, and to be open about bad news as well as good.

Company managers

Whilst many companies are spending more time and effort in investor relations the report comments:

> They recognise the benefit of more constructive dialogue with their shareholders, which leads to better understanding. What company managers want now is greater value from the time and effort they are putting in to investor relations. They want more openness from investors, candour about objectives and expectations, and a professional approach to the relationship. They justifiably expect better shareholder preparation for meetings, better sector and industry knowledge and better use of time in meetings.

Constraints on dialogue

The report identified that as regards the companies:

- Many company managers are not confident that their messages will be listened to and fear that information given to investors beyond the minimum required will be used against them.
- Many companies are reluctant to give details of investment plans fearing that:
  - explicit forecasting is a hostage to fortune;
  - investors will use the plans against them;
  - plans were too commercially sensitive.

The report identified that as regards the investors:

- Most fund managers are ambivalent about the responsibilities of ownership where these have been delegated by beneficial owners.
- There is a difficulty in determining the boundaries of legitimate involvement.

How will constraints on dialogue be removed?

The report comments that there was frequently a lack of confidence between company managers and investors but that open and informed dialogue can overcome this lack of trust. It is important also to see the company manager/institutional investor relationship in the context of the growing pressure for more transparency as seen with the corporate governance developments discussed above and the social and environmental reporting and business ethics discussed in the following two chapters.

29.17 Corporate governance – summary

On directors' remuneration, it is apparent that Corporate Governance in the UK is not working. On the 'beneficial' side:

- Directors' service contracts have been limited to a year, thus limiting the termination payments when directors are dismissed.
- Higgs' proposals that an individual should be chairman of only one listed company and executive directors should be non-executive directors of only one listed company are welcome proposals (i.e. executive directors should devote most of their time to their company, rather than being distracted by being non-executive directors of other companies).

- Although not part of the Companies Act, listed companies now include a resolution for shareholders to approve the Directors' remuneration report. However, a vote 'for' or 'against' does not allow shareholders to criticise or obtain further details of directors' remuneration.

However, there are many 'adverse' signs:

- Directors' remuneration is increasing at a much greater rate than employees' wages, and often it appears not to be related to the performance of the company. Directors' remuneration is increasing at a much faster rate than the increase in companies' profits (e.g. in Rolls-Royce plc, the 2001 profits increased by 15.7% over 2000, but the Chairman's remuneration increased by 42% and the Chief Executive's by 38.2%).

Directors are still deciding their own remuneration (even though the decision is by non-executives for the executive directors). When companies make many millions of pounds profit, it seems hardly surprising that directors decide to take an increasingly large proportion of this profit, as there is little or no control over their actions.

- The full remuneration of directors is not being disclosed in accounts (the disclosed remuneration is significantly less than the 'actual' remuneration). In particular, it has not been possible to quantify the value of share options. Pension entitlements are disclosed (i.e. the pension the director will receive on retirement) but the cost to the company of providing a fund for these pensions is not disclosed.

- Large payments are made to directors who are dismissed, even if this is for incompetence or following disastrous strategies. For instance, the chairman and chief executive of Marconi who may be seen as effectively overseeing the destruction of the company through its strategy of buying for cash internet/telecoms companies at the top of the market. The result was enormous borrowings for which interest could not be paid, as the companies made little or no profits. On dismissal, these directors were paid substantial termination payments (over £1 million in total). However, the loss to the company and its shareholders were millions of pounds and seems inappropriate when related to shareholders' losses.

In conclusion, the proposals of Corporate Governance are 'a step in the right direction', but there is a long way to go before a satisfactory conclusion is reached.

29.18 Auditors

The purpose of an audit is summarised by the audit report on the financial statements of the company being audited. The international body which gives guidance to auditors is the International Federation of Accountants (IFAC). This body has published International Standards on Auditing (ISAs), and ethical and educational matters relating to auditors. National bodies of accountants have published their own auditing standards and ethical and educational rules. These national standards are generally very similar to the equivalent IFAC's pronouncement. For instance, in the UK, the Statements of Auditing Standard (SASs) were published soon after the IFAC's Standards on Auditing, and it is apparent they are based on the IFAC's ISAs with only minor differences. The ethical and educational requirements of the UK's Association of Chartered Certified Accountants (ACCA) and the Institute of Chartered Accountants in England and Wales (ICAEW) are very similar, but slightly more restrictive than the IFAC's requirements.

Returning to the Audit Report, ISA 700 *The Auditor's Report on Financial Statements*,[22] proposes (para. 28) the following unqualified audit report:

Report to the Shareholders of ABC

We have audited the accompanying balance sheet of ABC company as of December 31 20X1, and the related statements of income, and cash flows for the year then ended. These financial statements are the responsibility of the Company's management. Our responsibility is to express an opinion on these financial statements based on our audit.

We conducted our audit in accordance with International Standards on Auditing. These Standards require that we plan and perform the audit to obtain reasonable assurance about whether the financial statements are free of material misstatement. An audit includes examining, on a test basis, evidence supporting the amounts and disclosures in the financial statements. An audit also includes assessing the accounting principles used and significant estimates made by management, as well as evaluating the overall financial statement presentation. We believe that our audit provides a reasonable basis for our opinion.

In our opinion, the financial statements give a true and fair view of the financial position of the Company as of December 31 20X1, and of the results of its operations and its cash flows for the year then ended in accordance with the Companies Act (date).

Auditor's name .... Date .... Address ....

The principal statement in the audit report is in the last paragraph when it says 'the financial statements give a true and fair view'. This means that the auditor is saying the financial statements do not contain any significant errors. For the word 'significant', auditors use the word 'material'. The auditor is not saying the financial statements are exactly correct. There may be small errors in the financial statements, but these errors will not create a 'material' error in the financial statements.

Many items in the balance sheet cannot be determined exactly. These include depreciation rates on fixed assets, stock value and bad debts which cannot be determined exactly at the time of the audit. It may be many years after the date of the audit when fixed assets are sold, all stock is sold and all debts from customers are repaid. So, depreciation, bad debts and estimating the net realisable value of stock have to be best estimates at the time of the audit, so their value in the financial statements must be a best estimate.

Materiality is a complex subject, but the principal measure is profit before tax, and errors in the financial statements which are 5% or less of profit before tax are not material, and errors which are greater than 10% of profit before tax are material. Between 5% and 10% of profit before tax, the error may be material – the auditor has to apply judgement to determine whether the error is material. If there are material errors or uncertainties in the financial statements, the auditor will give a 'qualified audit report', in which the auditor will explain why the financial statements 'do not show a true and fair view'. The subject of qualified audit reports is covered in detail in ISA 700 *The Auditor's Report on Financial Statements*.

29.18.1 Principal qualities of an auditor

The ethical[23] and educational[24] requirements of the IFAC are very detailed, but they can be summarised under three headings:

(a) Competence of the auditor;

(b) Independence of the auditor;

(c) Other ethical/professional matters.

29.18.2 Competence of the auditor

This can be summarised as:

(a) the basic educational requirements to become a member of a professional body and auditor;

(b) the continued education required of auditors to keep them up to date; and

(c) the practical experience of the auditor.

Basic educational requirements

The IFAC (para. 19) says 'The core of knowledge to which all accountants should be exposed should cover:

Core subjects:

Financial Accounting	Management Accounting	Information Technology
Auditing	Taxation	Business Finance

Supportive Subjects:

Economics	Law	Mathematics and Statistics
Behavioural Science	Management	

The IFAC places considerable emphasis on information technology, and includes a separate section on 'Information technology in the accounting curriculum'. Accounting systems are information systems, and most information systems are computerised, hence the importance of information technology in the work of the accountant. Thus, the accountant is interested both in ensuring the information system is reliable, and ensuring the information produced by the system is relevant and easily understood.

Continued professional education

The newly qualified accountant should have the required technical knowledge when he/she has passed the professional examinations. However, accountants may be in practice for up to forty years after they have qualified. Thus, their knowledge will have become out of date only a few years after they qualified, because of changes in legislation (particularly tax law and practice), accounting and auditing Standards. There is therefore a need for accountancy bodies to show that their members are keeping their knowledge up to date.

This is achieved by means of continued professional education (CPE). Section 2 of the IFAC's section on education covers this topic in detail. The IFAC says the minimum CPE should be 30 hours a year (or 90 hours in a 3 year period) of structured learning activity, supplemented by regular unstructured learning. Essentially, 'structured learning' comprises attending lectures or conferences, or taking correspondence courses. Being a lecturer or leader in a conference also comprises 'structured learning'. Unstructured learning will usually comprise reading technical, professional, financial or business literature. Many accountancy bodies provide or approve courses with 'approved CPE hours'. If the accountancy body requires CPE to be mandatory, they will have to provide and monitor a system for members to record their CPE activities and hours.

In conclusion, it is apparent that accountancy bodies must have a system of compulsory CPE to ensure their members keep up to date with changes in legislation (including accounting and auditing standards). Also, there will be a need for members to increase the depth of their knowledge in the specialised areas they work in, over and above the basic knowledge they learnt when taking the exams of their professional body.

Practical experience

The IFAC says (para. 54) that this should be at least three years' duration. Also, they suggest professional bodies should have a system for approving employers who are suitable for providing the appropriate experience to students (para. 56). These 'approved employers' should be checked periodically by the professional body. The employer is responsible for designing and implementing a programme which meets the practical experience requirements of the student and the needs of the employer. The employer is responsible for recording the actual experience provided for each student.

29.18.3 Independence of auditors

Part B of the IFAC's *Code on Professional Ethics* considers matters applicable to professional accountants in public practice. The principal points made in this section include:

1. **Independence**. Professional accountants in public practice when undertaking a reporting assignment should be and appear to be free of any interest which might be regarded, whatever its actual effect, as being incompatible with integrity, objectivity and independence.

2. The following paragraphs indicate some of those situations which, because of the actual or apparent lack of independence, would give a reasonable observer grounds for doubting the independence of a professional accountant in public practice.

3. **Financial involvement with or in the affairs of clients**. Financial involvement with a client affects independence and may lead a reasonable observer to conclude that it has been impaired. Such involvement can arise in a number of ways, such as:

   (a) by direct financial interest in a client;

   (b) by indirect material financial interest in a client, e.g., by being a trustee of any trust or executor or administrator of any estate if such a trust or estate has a financial interest in a client company;

   (c) by loans to or from the client or any officer, director or principal shareholder of a client company;

   (d) by holding a financial interest in a joint venture with a client or employee of a client;

   (e) by having a financial interest in a nonclient that has an investor or investee relationship with the client.

4. **Appointments in companies**. When professional accountants in public practice are or were, within the period under current review or immediately preceding an assignment:

   (a) a member of the board, an officer or employee of a company; or

   (b) a partner of, in the employment of, a member of the board or an officer or employee of a company

   they would be regarded as having an interest which could detract from independence when reporting on that company.

5. **Provision of other services to audit clients**. When a professional accountant in public practice, in addition to carrying out an audit or other reporting function, provides other services to a client, care should be taken not to perform management functions or make management decisions, responsibility for which remains with the board of directors and management.

6. **Personal and family relationships**. Personal and family relationships can affect independence. There is a particular need to ensure that an independent approach to any assignment is not endangered as a consequence of any personal or family relationship.

7. **Fees**. When the receipt of recurrent fees from a client or group of connected clients represents a large proportion of the total gross fees of a professional accountant in public practice or of the practice as a whole, the dependence on that client or group of clients should inevitably come under scrutiny and could raise doubts as to independence.

8. **Contingency fees**. Professional services should not be offered or rendered to a client under an arrangement whereby no fee will be charged unless a specified finding or result is obtained or when the fee is otherwise contingent upon the findings or results of such services.

9. **Goods and services**. Acceptance of goods and services from a client may be a threat to independence. Acceptance of undue hospitality poses a similar threat.

10. **Ownership of the capital**. Ideally, the capital of a practice should be owned entirely by professional accountants in public practice. However, ownership of capital by others may be permitted provided that the majority of both the ownership of the capital and the voting rights lies only with the professional accountants in public practice.

11. **Former partners**. A partner in a practice may leave the practice by resignation, termination, retirement, or sale of the practice. Such a partner may accept an appointment with a client in practice, of which he or she is a former partner when an audit or other reporting function is being performed by that practice of which he or she is a former partner.

12. **Actual or threatened litigation**. Litigation involving the professional accountant in public practice and a client may cause concern that the normal relationship with the client is affected to the extent that the professional accountant's independence and objectivity may be impaired.

13. **Long association of senior personnel with audit clients**. The use of the same senior personnel on an audit engagement over a prolonged period of time may pose a threat to independence. The professional accountant in public practice should take steps to ensure that objectivity and independence are maintained on the engagement.

29.18.4 Current position on auditor providing consultancy services

Pre Enron

In 2000, the chairman of the US Securities and Exchange Commission (SEC), Arthur Levitt, proposed that other services provided by audit firms to their audit clients should be severely restricted, probably solely to audit and tax work.[25] The provision of any other service to audit clients would be prohibited.

Whilst the profession was opposed to the blanket approach appearing to be taken by the SEC there was also support for a selective approach to restricting particular types of work, e.g. that external auditors should not provide internal audit services for client companies.[26]

Post Enron

Enron filed for bankruptcy in early December 2001 by which time the share price had fallen from a 2000 figure of about $83 a share to less than $1 a share. The bankruptcy was unexpected by those investors who might have based their investment decisions on the historical financial statements on the mistaken assumption that these were accurate.

Equity shareholders are rewarded for taking risks and understand that no company in which they invest is immune to the risk of failure. However, in the case of Enron there appear to have been three major problems.

The first problem was that the US financial reporting standards were not as robust in dealing with off-balance-sheet transactions such as special purpose entities (SPE) as FRS 5 *Reporting the Substance of Transactions* which has been effective in the UK since 1995.

What is an SPE?

An SPE might be set up for a variety of purposes ranging from those that are commercially acceptable (e.g. to finance fixed assets) to those that are unacceptable (e.g. to conceal from investors who rely on the company's financial statements presenting an accurate or true and fair view of material items such as the existence of liabilities or losses or the payment of fees to directors of the sponsor company). In the case of Enron it is reported that there was concealment of all three such material items.

How does SPE operate?

Typically there are four parties involved, namely,

- the sponsor (a company such as Enron that wishes to acquire a fixed asset but wants to keep the asset and liability off the balance sheet);
- the SPE (this is the entity that will borrow the funds to acquire the fixed asset);
- the lender (a bank or institution prepared to advance funds to the SPE to acquire the fixed asset); and
- the independent investor (who puts in at least 3% of the cost of the fixed asset and who technically controls the SPE).

As far as the sponsor is concerned, both the asset and liability are off the balance sheet and the sponsor enters into a lease arrangement with the SPE to make lease payments to cover the loan repayments. If required by the lender, the sponsor might also arrange for a guarantee to be provided using its own share price strength or through another party. As we recognised in the UK prior to the introduction of FRS 5, by keeping debt off the balance sheet a company's creditworthiness is improved.

The second problem was that investors were unable to rely on advice from analysts. It is reported that analysts failed to follow sound financial analysis principles, being under pressure to hype the shares e.g. to keep the share price up particularly where their employers, such as investment banks, were making significant advisory fees.[27]

The third problem was that investors were not alerted by the auditors to the fact that such liabilities, losses and the payment of fees existed. It could be that the auditors were convinced that the financial statements complied with the requirements of US GAAP and that the SPEs did not therefore need to be consolidated. If that were the case, it could be argued that the auditor was acting professionally in reporting that the financial statements complied with US GAAP.

29.18.5 Future developments on auditor providing consultancy services

SEC testimony concerning legislative solutions to problems raised by events relating to Enron Corporation

It is interesting to review the testimony made by Harvey L. Pitt, Chairman, US Securities and Exchange Commission before the Subcommittee on Capital Markets,

Insurance and Government Sponsored Enterprises, United States House of Representatives.[28]

Within the testimony the Chairman makes the following points:

- Accounting standard-setting should reflect business realities – observing that for too many years the FASB has failed to set standards for accounting for special purpose entities. In the wake of Enron, it must act and act quickly to give guidance.

- A system that ensures that those entrusted with the important public responsibility of performing audits of public companies are single-minded in their devotion to the public interest, and are not subject to conficts that might confuse or divert them from their efforts – observing that those who perform audits must be truly independent and in particular must not be subject to the conflict of increasing their own compensation at the risk of jeopardising the public's protection.

US Senate investigation

We need to recognise that the auditors could well be actively involved in designing schemes such as SPEs and representation was made by Lynn Turner on 24 January 2002 to the Committee of Governmental Affairs of the United States Senate[29] that auditors should be prohibited from designing and structuring transactions, such as SPEs, that result in less, rather than more, transparency for those they are reporting to.

The fact that the auditors become actively involved in designing such schemes could well be seen as evidence that they are moving into consultancy which gives rise to a conflict of interest. This move deprives investors, creditors, employees and pension scheme members of an independent audit.

UK accountancy press

There is a view[30] that audit failures are made in the boardrooms of accountancy firms where, in pursuit of money, low-balling is rife and audits are used as stalls to sell other wares. The same writer takes a similar view to the SEC, namely, that auditors should act exclusively as auditors.

EU recommendations

In May 2002 the European Commission issued Recommenditions.[31] There is an over-riding recommendation that a statutory auditor should not carry out an audit if there are any financial, business, employment or other relationships that a reasonable and informed third party would conclude could compromise the auditor's independence and detailed recommendations such as the requirement for the audit fee to be sufficient to cover the necessary audit work i.e. effectively prohibiting low-balling. The Recommendations do not however prohibit auditors accepting consultancy work.

UK Government initiatives

Following the collapse of Enron the Secretary of State, Patricia Hewitt, announced in early 2002 the creation of a Co-ordinating Group on Audit and Accounting Issues with a remit to ensure that the effectiveness of the UK systems of financial reporting and audit regulation is carefully reviewed. Issues that have been raised include:[32]

- the adequacy of existing ethical standards of the professional audit bodies in ensuring the independence of auditors particularly as to whether they provide sufficient protection where auditors also provide non-audit services to clients;
- the possible requirement for the mandatory rotation of auditors or re-tendering for company audits;

- the need for more detailed disclosure in company accounts of the fees paid to the auditors for audit and non-audit services.

The above references are a sample of the steps now being taken following the collapse of Enron. It will be interesting to see the extent to which confidence in financial reporting and auditing is restored during the next few years.

Summary

Corporate governance requirements are being developed in many countries. Most of the proposals have come from the USA, the UK and its former Colonies where shares are widely held. In this situation there needs to be some controls and monitoring of the directors. Developments in other countries are leading to wider ownership of shares of companies, and this will lead to the extension of corporate governance requirements in those countries.

The disclosure of the remuneration of directors was studied. It showed the many ways directors are remunerated, and highlighted current weaknesses in disclosing pension costs and the cost of issuing share options. Different methods of accounting for share options were examined and criticised.

The other side of corporate governance concerns controls over auditors. The educational and practical experience requirements were considered as were the independence requirements of the IFAC and the provision of consultancy services to audit clients.

REVIEW QUESTIONS

1 The Association of British Insurers held the view that options should be exercised only if the company's earnings per share growth exceeded that of the retail price index. The National Association of Pension Funds preferred the criterion to be a company's outperformance of the FTA All-Share Index.

   (a) Discuss the reasons for the differences in approach.

   (b) Discuss the implication of each approach to the financial reporting regulators and the auditors.

2 'Management will become accountable only when shareholders receive information on corporate strategy, future-based plans and budgets, and actual results with explanations of variances.' Discuss.

3 (i) Discuss the extent to which directors should be accountable to: (a) shareholders; (b) employees; (c) suppliers; (d) customers; (e) the government; (f) the public.

   (ii) Research[33] suggests that companies whose managers own a significant proportion of the voting share capital tend to violate the Cadbury recommendations on board composition far more frequently than other companies. Discuss the advantages and disadvantages of enforcing greater compliance.

4 'Companies should be forced by law to follow Italian experience, where there is compulsory competitive tendering and auditors are rotated every nine years.' Discuss (refer to current reviews that are being undertaken by the DTI and the Review Board).

5 There has been much criticism of the effectiveness of non-executive directors following failures such as Enron. Some consider that their interests are too close to those of the executive directors and they have neither the time nor professional support to allow them to be effective monitors of the executive directors. Draft a job specification and personal criteria that you think would allay these criticisms.

6 The Chartered Institute of Management Accountants (CIMA) has warned that linking directors' pay to EPS or return on assets is open to abuse, since these are not the objective measures they might appear.

(a) Can shareholders rely on the ASB to prevent abuse? Discuss.

(b) Identify five ways in which the directors might manipulate the EPS and return on assets without breaching existing standards.

7 It has been suggested that 'changes in market capitalisation from period to period should be the subject of comment [and] it would be sensible for investors to be guided on the nature of the market capitalisation figure and to be given an indication of share price trends'.[34] Discuss the advantages and disadvantages of such disclosure in relation to corporate governance.

8 (a) The Companies Act 1985 (Disclosure of Remuneration for Non-audit Work) Regulations SI No 1991/2181 requires companies[35] to disclose all payments made to their auditors. Discuss the additional information that would be required in order to make the disclosure of the non-audit fees meaningful.

(b) The *Combined Code* provides that the audit committee should keep the nature and extent of non-audit services provided by the auditor under review, seeking to balance the maintenance of objectivity and value for money. Discuss criteria that could be applied in seeking to establish this balance.

9 In the modern commercial world, auditors provide numerous other services to complement their audit work. These services include the following:

(a) Accountancy and book-keeping assistance, e.g. in the maintenance of ledgers and in the preparation of monthly and annual accounts.

(b) Secretarial help, e.g. ensuring that the company has complied with the Companies Act in the maintenance of shareholder registers and in the completion of annual returns to Companies House.

(c) Consultancy services, e.g. advice on the design of information systems and organisational structures, advice on the choice of computer equipment and software packages, and advice on the recruitment of new executives.

(d) Investigation work, e.g. appraisals of companies that might be taken over.

(e) Receivership work, e.g. when the firm assumes the role of receiver or liquidator on behalf of an audit client.

(f) Taxation work, e.g. tax planning advice and preparation of tax returns to the Inland Revenue for both the company and the company's senior management.

Discuss:

(i) Whether any of these activities is unacceptable as a separate activity because it might weaken an auditor's independence.

(ii) The advantages and disadvantages to the shareholders of the audit firm providing this range of service.

10 The audit fee disclosed for Cable & Wireless plc was £1.7 million in its 1997 accounts.

(a) Discuss how many man-days of audit time you think would be reasonable to audit an industrial company where:

(i) the sales were £7,002 million;

(ii) the fixed assets were £6,442 million;

(iii) the current assets were £3,225 million; and

(iv) there were 37,448 staff in Hong Kong, the UK, continental Europe, North America, Caribbean and the rest of the world.

(b) Discuss the suggestion that audit fees are inadequate.

EXERCISES

Question 1

The financial statements of AB, a listed company, disclose the following information on the Chairman's pension entitlements:

(a) for the year ended 31 December 20X0 the pension fund is sufficient to pay the director a pension of $200,000 a year from his retirement date of 1 January 20X4;

(b) for the year ended 31 December 20X1 the pension fund is sufficient to pay the director a pension of $250,000 a year from his retirement date of 1 January 20X4.

It is expected that the pension fund will pay the director's pension for 12 years, and the expected return on investments is 8% per annum.

Required:
Calculate the cost of the director's pension entitlements for the year ended 31 December 20X1.

Note: The value of an annuity for 11 years at 8% is 7.139
The present value of $1 at 8% for 2 years is 0.85734; and for 3 years is 0.79383

Question 2

On 31 December 20X0, the Chief Executive of BC, a listed company, was awarded the option to purchase 1,000,000 shares in the company at $4.50 a share on 30 June 20X4. This option was subject to her achieving specified performance targets for the three years ending on 31 December 20X3. The following information has been provided:

Date	Option price (c)	Probability of achieving option (%)
31.12.X0	5c	60%
31.12.X1	10c	70%
31.12.X2	15c	85%
31.12.X3	30c	100%
30 .6.X4	35c	100%

Required:
(a) Calculate the charge for the share option to be included in the financial statements for the years ended 31 December 20X0, 20X1, 20X2, 20X3 and 20X4 using the IAS 37 method;
(b) Calculate the total cost of the share option using:
  (i) the IAS 37 method;
  (ii) the US FAS 123 method;
  (iii) the UK recommendation.
(c) Discuss the different answers you have calculated in part (b).

Question 3

The financial statements of Rolls-Royce plc (aero engine manufacturer) for the year ended 31 December 1999 disclose the following matters in relation to the directors:

(a) Remuneration committee

The remuneration committee, which operates within agreed terms of reference, has responsibility for making recommendations to the board on the Group's general policy towards executive remuneration. The committee also determines, on the board's behalf, the specific remuneration packages of the executive directors and a number of senior executives.

The membership of the committee consists exclusively of independent non-executive directors (*the financial statements disclose the names of these directors*). The committee meets regularly and has access to professional advice from inside and outside the Company.

The Chairman of the Company (*a part-time executive director*) and the Chief Executive (*an executive director*) generally attend meetings but are not present during any discussion of their own emoluments.

(b) Base salary

The committee believes that in order to attract and retain executive directors of the right calibre and to provide them with adequate incentives to deliver the Group's objectives, the Group should pursue a policy of offering median-level base salaries for its executive directors, and through the performance-related schemes, the opportunity of upper quartile earnings for upper quartile performance.

(c) Annual performance award scheme

The scheme enables a maximum performance award of up to 60% of salary to be paid to executive directors for exceptional performance against pre-determined targets based upon return on capital employed with a tapered and reducing scale of maximum percentages for senior employees. The targets are set by the committee based upon the Group's annual operating plans, Such payments do not form part of pensionable earnings. One-third of total awards made are paid in Rolls-Royce shares which are held in trust for two years, with release normally being conditional on the individual remaining in the Group's employment until the end of the period. The required shares are purchased on the open market. This arrangement provides a strong link between performance and remuneration and provides a culture of share ownership amongst the Group's senior management.

(d) Long-term incentive plan

The LTIP involves the grant of awards of shares in the Company, which can be realized in the form of shares and cash if demanding performance targets are met. The maximum value of the awards is 60% of salary for executive directors, with a tapered and reducing scale of maximum percentages for senior executives. The required shares for the LTIP are purchased on the open market.

The percentage of the award, and therefore the value which can be realised, depends upon the Company's total shareholder return (TSR) over a three-year performance measurement period, compared to that achieved over the same period by a group of 19 comparator companies comprising other leading engineering and industrial companies. No award is realised unless the average growth in the Group's EPS over the three-year period is at least 2% per annum greater than the average increase in the UK retail price index over the same period.

Under the rules of the LTIP, the percentage of shares comprised in the award which can be realised is determined by the Company's TSR ranking against the comparator group. 100% of the award is secured for a first, second or third ranking with a uniform sliding scale of percentages then being applied to each ranking down to, and including, ninth place which earns 40% of the share award. No award is made if the Company's TSR ranking is tenth or below. If an award is realised, the participant receives one-half of its value at the release date in the form of shares and the other half in cash. He or she is required to retain at least half of the shares for a maximum of two years.

The performance period for the 1997 LTIP grant ended on 31 December, 1999 and no award was realised.

(e) Service contracts

In the light of the Combined Code (*which recommends rolling contracts of no more than one year*), the committee has reviewed its previous policy of offering UK executive directors two-year rolling contracts. It has concluded that new appointees to the board will be offered notice periods of one year. The committee recognises that in the case of appointments to the board from outside the Company, it may be necessary to offer a longer initial notice period, which would be subsequently reduced to twelve months after that initial period. Five executive directors (*which the report names*) all have two-year rolling contracts, which provide for 24 months' notice in the event of termination of employment by the company. These contracts were entered into before the change in policy described above.

(f) Compensation and mitigation

The committee has a defined policy on compensation and mitigation to be applied in the event of a director's contract being permanently terminated. In these circumstances, steps are taken to ensure that poor performance is not rewarded. When calculating termination payments, the committee takes into account a range of factors such as age, years of service and the director's obligation to mitigate his own loss.

A director (*named in the accounts*) retired early from the Company on 31 December 1999 and received a termination payment of £530,000 and a payment of £20,298 in lieu of benefits. The committee considered this compensation in the light of its policy on mitigation and in line with that policy concluded that it would not be appropriate to apply mitigation.

The accounts disclose the retiring director's base salary for the year ended 31 December 1999 was £240,000.

For the retiring director, there was no disclosure of:

 (i) his age at 31 December 1999

(ii) his executive position in the company, and

(iii) the reasons why he took early retirement.

The financial statements did disclose the executive position and age of the other directors at 31 December 1999.

There were no exceptional points included in the financial statements about directors' pensions. Items included in *italics* in the text above are comments or additional information provided by the author.

Required:
Comment on the notes to the financial statements included above.

Question 4

A rational auditor would stop audit work when the total cost is a minimum. However, it is apparent that auditors are 'risk averse' and they perform more work than is necessary to minimise their total costs. Explain why auditors perform more work than is necessary.

Question 5

(a) Describe the value to the audit client of the audit firm providing consultancy services.

(b) Why is it undesirable for audit firms to provide consultancy services to audit clients?

(c) Why do audit firms want to continue to provide consultancy services to audit clients?

Question 6

How is the relationship between the audit firm and the audit client different for:

(a) the provision of statutory audit when the auditor reports to the shareholders

(b) the provision of consultancy services by audit firms.

Question 7

Why is there a prohibition of auditors owning shares in client companies. Is this prohibition reasonable? Discuss.

References

1 www.world-exchanges.org.
2 'Corporate Governance in Europe', Report of Centre for European Policy Studies Working Party, June 1995.
3 'Principles for Corporate Governance in the Commonwealth', Commonwealth Association for Corporate Governance Guidelines, November 1999.
4 *The Times*, Tuesday October 10, 2000, p. 29.
5 *Report of the Committee on the Financial Aspects of Corporate Governance, (Cadbury Committee Report)*, December 1992, Gee Publishing.
6 *Directors' Remuneration: Report of a Study Group Chaired by Sir Richard Greenbury (Greenbury Committee Report)*, July 1995, Gee Publishing.
7 *Committee on Corporate Governance: Final Report (Hampel Committee Report)*, January 1998, Gee Publishing.
8 www.dti.gov.uk/cld/non_exec_review
9 www.frc.org.uk
10 S. Turley and M. Zaman, Higgs and Smith: what difference will they really make?, *Accounting & Business*, April 2003, pp 40–42
11 *Committee on Corporate Governance: The Combined Code*, June 1998, Gee Publishing.
12 *Accountancy*, September 1995.
13 ABI, *Share Option and Profit Sharing Incentive Schemes*, February 1995.
14 UITF Abstract, *Disclosure of Directors' Share Options*, ASB, 1994.
15 *The Times*, 30 March 1995.
16 M. Pagano, *Management Today*, January 1998, pp. 70–72.
17 Robert Heller, *Management Today*, July 1997.
18 'What is the incentive?' *Management Today*, July 1999, p. 46.
19 '2000 Annual Report and Accounts', Diageo plc, September 2000, pp. 10–16.
20 IAS 37, *Provisions, Contingent Liabilities and Contingent Assets*, IASC, July 1998.
21 ABI, *Statement of Voting Policy and Corporate Governance Good*, 1998.
22 ISA 700, *The Auditor's Report on Financial Statements*, IFAC, 1996, pp. 223–224.
23 *Code of Ethics for Professional Accountants*, IFAC, 1996, pp. 451–504.
24 *Guidelines on Education*, IFAC, 1996, pp. 505–637.
25 'PwC and E&Y in favour of rules to restrict services', *Accountancy*, October 2000, p. 7.
26 I.H. Davison, 'Non-audit fees and auditor independence', *Accountancy*, November 2000, p. 1.
27 B. Singleton-Green, 'Enron – how the fraud worked', *Accountancy*, May 2002, pp. 20–21.
28 http://www.sec.gov/news/testimony/020402tshlp.htm.
29 www.senate.gov.
30 A. Mitchell, 'Reform or nemesis', *Accountancy*, May 2002, p. 10.
31 European Commission, *Statutory Auditors' Independence in the EU: A Set of Fundamental Principles*, see http://www.europa.eu.int/comm/internal_market/en/company/audit/official/6D42–01/6942-01_en.pdf.
32 http://www.dti.gov.uk/cld/post_enron.html.
33 K. Peasnell, P. Pope and S. Young, *Accountancy*, July 1998, p. 115.
34 ICAS, *Making Corporate Reports Valuable*, p. 103.
35 The Companies Act 1985 (Disclosure of Remuneration for Non-audit Work) Regulations SI No 1991/2181.

CHAPTER 30

Environmental and social reporting

30.1 Introduction

In this chapter we consider the following:

- Accountants' role in a capitalist society
- Sustainability
- Background to companies' reporting practices
- EC Recommendations for annual report disclosures
- Evolution of stand-alone environmental reports
- International charters and guidelines
- Economic consequences of environmental reporting
- Summary on environmental reporting
- Environmental auditing international initiatives
- The activities involved in an environmental audit
- Concept of social accounting
- Background to social accounting
- Corporate social responsibility
- Need for comparative data
- International initiatives towards triple bottom line reporting
- Summary

30.2 Accountants' role in a capitalist industrial society

In a capitalist, industrial society, production requires the raising and efficient use of capital largely through joint stock companies. These operate within a legal framework which grants them limited liability subject to certain obligations. The obligations include **capital maintenance provisions** to protect creditors, e.g. restriction on distributable profits, and **disclosure provisions** to protect shareholders, e.g. the publication of annual reports.

The state issues statutes to ensure there is effective control of the capital market; the degree of intervention depends on the party in power. Accountants issue standards to ensure there is reliable information to the owners to support an orderly capital market. Both the state and the accountancy profession have directed their major efforts towards servicing the needs of capital. This has influenced the nature of the legislation, e.g. removing obligations that are perceived to make a company uncompetitive, and the nature of the accounting standards, e.g. concentrating on earnings and monetary values.

However, production and distribution involve complex social relationships between private ownership of property and wage labour[1] and other stakeholders. This raises the question of the role of accountants. Should their primary concern be to serve the interests of the shareholders, or the interests of management, or to focus on equity issues and social welfare?[2]

Prior to the ASB, the profession identified with management and, willingly or unwillingly, it appeared to allow information to be reported to suit management. If management was unhappy with a standard, e.g. SSAP 11 and SSAP 16, it was able to frustrate its implementation. Often, reported results bore little resemblance to the commercial substance of the underlying transactions.

The ASB has concentrated on making reports congruent with commercial reality; it sees financial information as being an economic commodity in its own right. It has developed a conceptual framework for financial reporting to underpin its reporting standards; assets, liabilities, income and expense have been defined with criteria for their recognition which include the ability to state them in monetary terms.

The ASB has not produced mandatory requirements for narrative or qualitative disclosures – the *Operating and Financial Review* (OFR) is voluntary. However, the proposal for the publication of an OFR was an important shift: it was recognition that there was a need for narrative disclosure, even where this was not capable of audit verification.

Why is the qualitative information voluntary?

It is voluntary in recognition of the fact that market and political pressures exist; that each company balances the perceived costs, e.g. competitive disadvantage, and the perceived benefits of voluntary disclosure,[3] e.g. improved investor appeal in determining the extent of its voluntary disclosures.

Companies have traditionally been ranked according to various criteria, e.g. their ability to maximise their shareholders' wealth or return on capital employed or EPS growth rates. However, there is a philosophical view that holds that a company:

possesses a role in society because society finds it useful that it should do so ... cannot expect to find itself fully acceptable to society if it single-mindedly pursues its major objective without regard for the range of consequences of its actions.[4]

This means that a company is permitted to seek its private objectives subject to legal, social and ethical boundaries. This takes accounting beyond the traditional framework of reporting monetary transactions that are of interest primarily to the shareholders. It takes it into a realm where there is, at present, no obvious paymaster.

30.3 Sustainability

There has been a growing concern since the early 1990s that insufficient attention has been given to the impact of current commercial activities on future generations. This has lead to the need for sustainable development which meets the needs of the present without compromising the ability of future generations to meet their own needs.

Why have companies become sensitive to the environmental concerns of stakeholders other than their shareholders? This has been a reaction to pressure from a variety of stakeholders ranging from the government to local communities and environmental groups to individual consumers and individual investors.

30.3.1 Environmental information in the annual accounts

Much of the environmental information falls outside the expertise of the accountant, so why was it included in the annual report? The annual report had already become the accepted vehicle for providing shareholders with information on matters of social interest such as charitable donations and this extended to present qualitative information such as a statement of company policy.

However, in addition to recognising the concerns of other stakeholders companies also began to realise that there could be adverse financial implications for their companies on capacity to raise funds.

Potential individual investors

The government in *This Common Inheritance*[5] indicated that shareholders could seek information about environmental practices from companies that they invest in and make their views known.

Potential corporate investors

Acquisitive companies needed to be aware of contingent liabilities[6] which can be enormous e.g. in the USA the potential cost of clearing up past industrially hazardous sites has been estimated at $675 billion. Even in relation to individual companies the scale of the contingency can be large, as in the Love Canal case. In this case a housing project was built at Love Canal in Upper New York State on a site that until the 1950s had been used by the Hooker Chemicals Corporation for dumping a chemical waste containing dioxin. Occidental, which had acquired Hooker Chemicals, was judged liable for the costs of clean-up of more than $260 million.[7] Existing shareholders and the share price would also be affected by these increased costs.

There is recognition that there is a wider interest than short-term profits.

30.4 Background to companies' reporting practices

During the past decade some companies have independently instituted comprehensive environmental management systems but most have not. There was been a tendency initially for companies to target the area that it considered to be the most sensitive and to treat it rather as a PR exercise or damage limitation. There was a concern that resources devoted to achieve environmental benefits would merely increase costs and companies made a point of referring to cost benefits to justify their outlay as in the following extract from the Scottish Power 1994 Annual Report:

> The company is committed to meeting or bettering increasingly stringent
> environmental controls for electricity generation and is developing new technologies
> and plant which can achieve significant benefits at realistic cost. At Longannet Power
> Station, more than £24 million is being invested in low Nox burners, which produce
> fewer nitrous oxides, and in renewing equipment to reduce dust from flue gases...
> This process is expected to be environmentally superior and lower in costs than
> alternative technologies.

This was quite understandable as it had been estimated that the enforcement of stringent environmental controls to reduce pollution could have substantial cost implications estimated at £15 billion for Britain in 1991.[8]

Companies were reactive and concentrated on satisfying statutory obligations or explaining their treatment of what they perceived to be the major environmental concern affecting their company. For example, in the case of Pearson, a major publishing company, a major concern was the use for printing of renewable resources and their 1993 Annual Report included the following:

> One aspect of our company's environmental responsibilities is to keep their purchasing policies under review. Pearson's most significant purchase is paper. Our publishing companies between them buy some 180,000 tonnes of paper a year... Pearson makes certain that it buys paper only from responsibly managed forests and avoids paper bleached with chlorinated organic compounds where possible...

Although this was an *ad hoc* approach to environmental reporting it did not mean that significant benefits were not achieved e.g. the following extract from 2001 Annual Report of The Body Shop indicates the level of benefit:

> At the Body Shop, we have made a significant commitment to reducing our CO_2 impact by switching electricity supply at both our Littlehampton sites and all UK company-owned shops to a renewable source. This initiative, together with our 15% investment in Bryn Titli wind farm, means that we offset an estimated 48% of electricity, gas and road freight used for all our UK operations including company-owned shops in the last financial year.

In some jurisdictions there have been mandatory requirements as in the USA where the Securities and Exchange Commission requires quoted companies to disclose some environmental information such as the following extract from the Schering AG Group 2000 Annual Report:

Outlay on safety and environmental protection in 2000

		€m
1.	Safety, clean-up, miscellaneous	16
2.	Environmental protection departments	6
3.	Recycling, processing and disposal	40
	Operating expenses	62
4.	Environmental protection investment	4

30.5 European Commission recommendations for disclosures in annual accounts[9]

In May 2001 the Commission issued a *Recommendation on the recognition, measurement and disclosure of environmental issues in the annual accounts and annual reports of companies.*

The Commission view was that there were two problems. The first was that there was a lack of explicit rules which meant that any one or all of the different stakeholder groups, e.g. investors, regulatory authorities, financial analysts and the public in general, could feel that the disclosures were insufficient or unreliable; the second was that there was a low level of voluntary disclosure, even in sectors where there was significant impact on the environment.

30.5.1 Lack of explicit rules

The lack of harmonised guidelines has meant that investors have been unable to compare companies or to adequately assess environmental risks affecting the financial position of the company. Whilst recognising that there are existing financial reporting standards on the disclosure of provisions and contingent liabilities and that companies in environmentally sensitive sectors are producing stand alone environmental reports, the Commission was of the opinion that there is a justified need to facilitate further harmonisation on what to disclose in the annual accounts.

As mentioned above, the cost of collecting and reporting are frequently perceived to be a deterrent and the *Recommendation* intends to avoid unjustified burdensome obligations. It also proposes that Recommendations should be within existing European Directives, e.g. Fourth and Seventh Directives.

30.5.2 Stakeholder groups' information needs

All groups require relevant disclosures that are consistent and comparable – particularly disclosure in the notes to the accounts relating to environmental expenditures either charged to the profit and loss account or capitalised including fines and penalties for non-compliance and compensation payments.

30.5.3 Key points relating to recognition, measurement and disclosure

The approach to recognition and measurement is a restatement of current financial reporting requirements with some additional illustrations and explanations. The disclosures are fuller than currently met within annual accounts.

Recognition and measurement

For the recognition of environmental liabilities the criteria is the same as for FRS 12 *Provisions, Contingent Liabilities and Contingent Assets* (Section 8.9.3), e.g. requirement for probable outflow of resources, reliable estimate of costs and recognition of liability at the date operations commence if relating to site restoration.

For the capitalisation of environmental expenditure the criteria to recognise as an asset apply, e.g. it produces future economic benefits. There are also detailed proposals relating to environmental expenditure which improves the future benefits from another asset and to asset impairment.

Disclosures

Disclosure is recommended if the issues are material to either the financial performance or financial position. Detailed proposals in relation to environmental protection are for the disclosure of:

● The policies that have been adopted and reference to any certification such as EMAS (see below)

● The improvements made in key areas with physical data if possible, e.g. on emissions

● Progress implementing mandatory requirements

● Environmental performance measures, e.g. trends for percentage of recycled packaging

● Reference to any separate environmental report produced.

There are, in addition, detailed cross-references to the requirements of the Fourth and Seventh Directives, e.g. description of valuation methods applied and additional disclosures, e.g. if there are long-term dismantling costs, the accounting policy and, if the company gradually builds up a provision, the amount of the full provision required.

30.6 Evolution of stand-alone environmental reports

There is a steady growth in the rate at which environmental reports are being produced. As one would perhaps expect, they are more prevalent in sectors where there is high risk such as forestry, pulp and paper, chemicals, oil and gas and pharmaceuticals.

This has been response to consumer pressure and also in response to the PR value of obtaining an award from one of the award schemes.

30.6.1 The effect of award schemes

Companies were encouraged to develop their environmental reporting by entering for various award schemes in which companies are invited to submit their report for scrutiny by a panel of judges.

Several such schemes have been established in Europe and North America, such as the competitions organised in Europe and the UK each year for the European Environmental Reporting Awards and the ACCA UK Environmental Reporting Awards. These last two schemes are discussed briefly below.

The European Environmental Reporting Awards

At the Europe-wide level, there are the European Environmental Reporting Awards (EERA) which commenced in1997, in which entries are selected from the winners of 12 national schemes organised by EU member states.

In 2000, the four winners in the EERA scheme, picked from a field of 24 entries, were as follows:

- Overall winner: Shell International (UK)
- Best first-time reporter: Acquedotto Pugliese (Italy)
- Best SME reporter: Obermurtaler Brauereigenossenschaft (Austria)
- Best sustainability report: Novo Nordisk (Denmark)

It is interesting to refer to the judges' comments on the strengths of each of the winners. For example, in respect of the best SME reporter some of the strengths listed included:

- its comprehensive reporting on corporate performance including 5-year trend data for various indicators and quantified targets;
- an analysis of the environmental impact arising from the product development activity;
- detailed description of supplier audits;
- disclosure of internal audit procedures and results; and
- evidence of environmental interest including obtaining EMAS registration (the first site to do this in Austria).

ACCA UK Environmental Reporting Awards

In 2000 the ACCA commemorated ten years of progress in environmental reporting. After these ten years the ACCA established in 2002 a new structure for the UK awards to reflect the ever-increasing public awareness of the environmental, social and economic impacts of business. The ACCA Award scheme was restructured in 2001 under the title 'The ACCA Awards for Sustainability Reporting'. There are three different award categories: the ACCA UK Environmental Reporting Awards, the ACCA Social Reporting Awards and a new category, the ACCA Sustainability Reporting Awards.

These schemes have given environmental reporting a high profile and contributed greatly to the present quality of reports.

30.7 International charters and guidelines

There have been a number of international and national summits, charters and recommendations issued. In some jurisdictions such as Denmark, The Netherlands, Norway and Sweden there is now legislation requiring environmental statements from environmentally sensitive industries either in their financial statements or in a stand-alone report, in other countries voluntary disclosures are proposed. The following is a brief description of just some of the voluntary disclosures proposed by the United Nations, Europe, the USA and self-regulating schemes in which companies can elect to participate.

30.7.1 United Nations

At the United Nations we can see the United Nations Environmental Programme (UNEP)[10] has made major impacts, e.g. it was the driving force behind the 1987 Montreal Protocol on Substances that Deplete the Ozone Layer whereby industrialised countries ceased production and consumption of a significant proportion of all ozone depleting substances in 1996. It is estimated that 1.5 million cases of melanoma skin cancer due to the sun's UV-B radiation will be averted by the year 2060 as a result of the Protocol. It has had similar success as the leading force for the global sound management of hazardous chemicals, the protection of the world's biological diversity by forging the Convention on Biological Diversity. It is innovative in its approach, e.g. entering into a partnership agreement with the International Olympic Committee (IOC) in 1995 as a result of which the environment now figures as the third pillar of Olympism, along with sport and culture in the IOC's Charter. UNEP has initiated the development of environmental guidelines for sports federations and countries bidding for the Olympic Games.

30.7.2 Europe

In Europe[11] the Eco-Management and Audit Scheme, (EMAS), was adopted by the European Council on 29 June 1993, allowing voluntary participation in an environmental management scheme. Its aim is to promote continuous environmental performance improvements of activities by committing organisations to evaluate and improve their own environmental performance.

The main elements of the current EMAS regulations include:

● making environmental statements more transparent;

● the involvement of employees in the implementation of EMAS; and

● a more thorough consideration of indirect effects including capital investments, administrative and planning decisions and procurement procedures.

Companies that participate in the scheme are required to adopt an environmental policy containing the following key commitments:

● compliance with all relevant environmental legislation;

● prevention of pollution; and

● achieving continuous improvements in environmental performance.

The procedure is for an initial environmental review to be undertaken and an environmental programme and environmental management system established for the organisation.

Verification is seen as an important element and environmental audits, covering all activities at the organisation concerned, must be conducted within an audit cycle of no longer than three years. On completion of the initial environmental review and subsequent audits or audit cycles a public environmental statement is produced.

An organisation's environmental statement will include the following key elements:

● a clear description of the organisation, and its activities, products and services;

● the organisation's environmental policy and a brief description of the environmental management system;

● a description of all the significant direct and indirect environmental aspects of the organisation and an explanation of the nature of the impacts as related to these aspects;

● a description of the environmental objectives and targets in relation to the significant environmental aspects and impacts;

● a summary of the organisation's year-by-year environmental performance data which may include pollution emissions, waste generation, consumption of raw materials, energy, water and noise;

● other factors regarding environmental performance including performance against legal provisions; and,

● the name and accreditation number of the environmental verifier, the date of validation and deadline for submission of the next statement.

The following extract from the Schering 2000 Annual Report indicates the persuasive influence of schemes such as EMAS:

> We aim at achieving the ISO 14001 certification or the Eco Management and Audit Scheme (EMAS) validation for all production sites. We have begun to integrate the existing management systems for quality, safety and environmental protection, and to organise throughout the Group. This Integrated Management System (IMS) is based on International Standard ISO 9000 (for quality) as well as ISO 14001 and EMAS (for environmental protection).

30.7.3 The USA

In the USA the Environmental Accounting Project began in 1992 to encourage companies to adopt environmental accounting techniques which would make environmental costs more apparent to managers and, therefore, make them more controllable. It was thought that this could result in three positive outcomes namely, the significant reduction of environmental costs, the gaining of competitive advantage and the improvement of environmental performance with the initial concern being to reduce pollution.

30.7.4 Self-regulation schemes

There are a number of examples of self-regulatory codes of conduct from institutions, e.g. The International Chamber of Commerce (ICC),[12] The International Organization for Standardization (ISO), and bodies representing particular industries, e.g. the European Chemical Industry Council CEFIC.[13] We will describe briefly the ICC Charter and ISO standards.

The International Chamber of Commerce (ICC)

The ICC launched The Business Charter for Sustainable Development in 1991 to help business around the world improve its environmental performance relating to health, safety and product stewardship. The Charter set out sixteen Principles which include:

- *Policy statements* – such as giving environmental management high corporate priority; aiming to integrate environmental policies and practices as an essential element of management; continuing to improve corporate policies performance; advising customers, distributors and the public in the safe use, transportation, storage and disposal of products provided; promoting the adoption of these principles by contractors acting on behalf of the enterprise; developing products that have no undue environmental impact and are efficient in their consumption of energy and natural resources, and that can be recycled, reused, or disposed of safely; fostering openness and dialogue with employees and the public, anticipating and responding to their concerns about the potential hazards and impacts of operations, products, wastes or services; and measuring environmental performance.

- *Financially quantifiable practices* – such as employee education; assessment of environmental impacts before starting a new activity or decommissioning; conduct or support of research on the environmental impacts of raw materials, products, processes, emissions and wastes associated with the enterprise and on the means of minimising such adverse impacts; modification of the manufacture, marketing or use of products or services to prevent serious or irreversible environmental degradation.

The following extract from the Nestlé 2000 Environment Progress Report is a good example of a company that has applied the ICC approach and is proactive in seeking improvements:

Message from CEO

I am pleased about the clear progress in a number of key areas, including a significant decline in the amounts of water and energy used to bring each kilo of Nestlé product into your home, and a similar reduction in factors which potentially affect global warming. However, we are never completely satisfied with our current performance, and are committed to further environmental improvements.

We try to remain sensitive to the environmental concerns of our consumers and the public as a whole. ... we have pledged our allegiance to *The Business Charter for Sustainable Development* of the International Chamber of Commerce, and we are committed to being a leader in environmental performance.

The Report then proceeded to deal in detail with three key areas on which the company focus, namely,

- An integrated approach throughout the supply chain, quantifying:
  - The average annual investment reporting, for example, that 'From 1997 to 1999, Nestlé invested an average of CHF 100 million per year for the protection of the environment. This included readily-identifiable environmental investments, and amounted to more than 3% of total capital expenditure'.
  - Environmental performance indicators for greenhouse gases, air acidification potential, ozone depleting substances and energy consumption. As an example of the level of detail, it reported for energy: 'Energy consumption is the sum of all energy purchased or obtained – less any energy which, in rare cases, is sold. This includes electricity, steam, fuels such as oil and natural gas, and by-products such as spent coffee grounds. Through different approaches, global energy consumption per tonne of product was reduced and, thus, energy use efficiency was improved by

20%. Even with the significant increase in manufacturing production, the total energy use company-wide has remained stable'.

- Water as a key priority, quantifying:
  - Environmental performance indicators for water consumption, water waste management and by-products/water generation.
- Systematic management of environmental performance, committing itself to:
  - compatability with international standards, e.g. ISO 14001 and EMAS of the European Union
  - focus on performance and improvements in all aspects of sutainability.

The International Organisation for Standards (ISO)

ISO is a non-governmental organisation established in 1947, and comprises a worldwide federation of national standards with the aim of establishing international standards to reduce barriers to international trade. Its standards, including environmental standards, are voluntary and companies may elect to join in order to obtain ISO certification.

One group of standards, the ISO 14000 series, is intended to encourage organisations to systematically assess the environmental impacts of their activities through a common approach to environmental management systems. Within the group, the ISO 14001 standard states the requirements for establishing an EMS and companies must satisfy its requirements in order to qualify for ISO certification.

What benefits arise from implementation of ISO 14001?

Those who support the ISO approach consider that there are a number of positive advantages, such as:

- **Top-level management become involved** – they are required to define an overall policy and, in addition, they recognise significant financial considerations from certification, e.g. customers might in the future prefer to deal with ISO compliant companies, insurance premiums might be lower and there is the potential reduce costs by greater production efficiency.

- **Environmental management** – ISO 14001 establishes a framework for a systematic approach to environmental management which can identify inefficiencies that were not apparent beforehand resulting in operational cost savings and reduced environmental liabilities. We have seen above, for example, that Nestlé reduced its energy consumption by 20%.

- **A framework for continual improvements is established** – there is a requirement for continual improvement of the management system.

What criticisms are there of a compliance approach?

Compliance approaches which set out criteria such a commitment to minimise environmental impact can allow companies to set low objectives for improvement and report these as achievements with little confidence that there has been significant environmental benefit.

30.8 Economic consequences of environmental reporting[14]

There can be internal and external favourable economic consequences for companies in the form of internal cost reductions and external share price whose value can be influenced by activities which affect a company's reputation.

30.8.1 Cost reductions

It has been reported that the discipline of measuring these risks can yield valuable management information with DuPont, for example, reporting that since it began measuring and reporting on the environmental impact of its activities, its annual environmental costs dropped from a high of US$1 billion in 1993 to $560 million in 1999.

30.8.2 Investment

Investors are gradually beginning to require information on a company's policy and programmes for environmental compliance and performance in order to assess the risk to earnings and balance sheet risks. One would expect that the more transparent these are the less volatile the share prices will be which could be beneficial for both the investor and the company. This will be a fruitful field for research as environmental reporting evolves with more consistent, comparable, relevant and reliable numbers and narrative disclosures.

This has also given rise to Socially Responsible Investing (SRI) which considers both the investor's financial needs **and** the investee company's impact on society to an extent that in 1999 over US$2,000 billion in assets were invested in 'ethical' investment funds. In the UK there is pressure from bodies such as the Association of British Insurers for institutional investors to take SRI principles into account.

30.9 Summary on environmental reporting

Environmental reporting is in a state of evolution ranging from *ad hoc* comments in the annual report to a more systematic approach again in the annual report to stand-alone environment reports.

Environmental investment is no longer seen as an additional cost but as an essential part of being a good corporate citizen and environmental reports are seen as necessary in communicating with stakeholders to address their environmental concerns.

Companies are realising that it is their corporate responsibility to achieve sustainable development whereby they meet the needs of the present without compromising the ability of future generations to meet their own needs. Economic growth is important for both shareholders and other stakeholders alike in that it provides the conditions in which protection of the environment can best be achieved, and environmental protection, in balance with other human goals, is necessary to achieve growth that is sustainable.

However, there is still a long way to go and the EU's Sixth Action Programme 'Environment 2010: Our Future, Our Choice' recognises[15] that effective steps have not been taken by all member states to implement EC environmental directives and there is weak ownership of environmental objectives by stakeholders. The programme focuses on four major areas for action climate change, health and the environment, nature and biodiversity and natural resource management and emphasises how important it is that all stakeholders should be involved to achieve more environmentally friendly forms of production and consumption as well as integration into all aspects of our life such as as transport, energy and agriculture.

As with the other environmental reporting initiatives discussed above and the corporate governance approach we have seen with the Hampel Report and the OFR, the programme concentrates on setting general objectives rather than quantified targets apart from the targets relating to climate change where there is the Community's 8% emission reduction target for 2008–2012 under the Kyoto Protocol. This is a sensible way to progress with an opportunity for best practice to evolve.

30.10 Environmental auditing international initiatives

The need for environmental auditors has grown side by side with the growth of environmental reporting. This is prompted by the need for investors to be confident that the information is reliable and relevant. There have been various initiatives around the world and we will briefly refer to three as examples from Canada, USA and Europe.

Canada

The Canadian Environmental Auditing Association (CEAA) was founded in 1991 to encourage the development of environmental auditing and the improvement of environmental management through environmental auditor certification and the application of environmental auditing ethics, principles and standards. It is a multidisciplinary organisation whose international membership base now includes environmental managers, ISO 14001 registration auditors, EMS consultants, corporate environmental auditors, engineers, chemists, government employees, accountants and lawyers. The CEAA is now accredited by the Standards Council of Canada as a certifying body for EMS Auditors.[16]

USA[17]

The Registrar Accreditation Board (RAB) was established in 1989 by the American Society for Quality to provide accreditation services for ISO 9000 Quality Management Systems (QMS) registrars.

In 1991, the American National Standards Institute (ANSI) and RAB joined forces to establish the American National Accreditation Program for Registrars of Quality Systems.

In 1996, with the release of new ISO 14000 Environmental Management Systems (EMS) standards, the ANSI-RAB National Accreditation Program (NAP) was formed covering the accreditation of QMS and EMS registrars as well as accreditation of course providers offering QMS and EMS auditor training courses. Certification programmes for both EMS and QMS auditors are now operated solely by RAB.

RAB exists to serve the conformity assessment needs of business and industry, registrars, course providers and individual auditors.

Europe[18]

Since 1999 the European Federation of Accountants (FEE) Sustainability Working Party (formerly Environmental) has been active in the Providing Assurance on Environmental Reports and is actively participating with other organisations and collaborating on projects such as GRI Sustainability Guidelines which are discussed further below.

30.11 The activities involved in an environmental audit

There are many activities commonly seen in practice. These can be grouped into those assessing the *current position* and those evaluating decisions affecting the *future*.

30.11.1 Assessing the current position

The assessment embraces physical, systems and staff appraisal.

- Physical appraisal is carried out by means of:
  - **site inspections;**
  - **scientific testing** to sample and test substances including air samples;
  - **off-site testing and inspections** to examine the organisation's impact on its immediate surroundings; after all, the company's responsibility does not stop at the boundary fence.
- Systems appraisal is carried out by means of:
  - **systems inspections** to review the stated systems of management and control in respect of environmental issues;
  - **operational reviews** to review actual practices when compared to the stated systems.
  - **compliance audits for certification schemes.**
- Staff appraisal is carried out by means of:
  - **awareness tests for staff** to test, by questionnaire, the basic knowledge of all levels of staff of the systems and practices currently used by the organisation. This will highlight any areas of weakness.

20.11.2 Assessing the future

The assessment embraces planning and design processes and preparedness for emergencies.

- Planning and design appraisal is carried out by means of:
  - **review of planning procedures** to ensure that environmental factors are considered in the planning processes adopted by the organisation;
  - **design reviews** to examine the basic design processes of the organisation (if applicable) to ensure that environmental issues are addressed at the design stage so the organisation can avoid problems rather than have to solve them when they happen.
- Preparedness for emergencies is appraised by means of:
  - **review of emergency procedures** to assess the organisation's preparedness for specific, predictable emergencies;
  - **review of crisis plans** to review the organisation's general approach to crisis management with the audit covering such topics as the formation of **crisis management teams** and resource availability.

30.11.3 The environmental audit report

We can see from the above than an environmental audit may be wide-ranging in its scope and time consuming, particularly when auditing a major organisation. A typical report could include:

- Current practice
  - a comprehensive review and comment on current operational practices.
- List of action required
  - areas of **immediate concern** which the organisation needs to address as a matter of urgency;
  - areas for improvement over a set period of time.

- Qualitative assessment
  - a **statement of risk** as seen by the audit team based on an overview of the whole situation with a qualitative assessment of the level of environmental risk being faced by the organisation.
- An action plan
  - a **schedule of improvement** may also be produced which gives a timetable and series of stages for the organisation to follow in improving its environmental performance.
- Encouraging good practice
  - a positive statement of 'good practice' may be included. This has a dual value in that it is a motivational tool for management and an educational tool to foster staff awareness of what constitutes 'good practice'.

30.11.4 What is the status of an environmental audit report?

Legal position

There is no legal obligation to carry out an environmental audit or to inform outside parties of any critical findings when such an audit is carried out. The reports are usually regarded as 'confidential' even when carried out by external auditors who provide the service as an 'optional extra' which is offered to the organisation for an additional fee.

Public interest

There is a strong case for requiring both environmental audits and the publication of the resultant reports. Requiring reports to be put into the public domain would encourage transparency in the process and avoid accusations of secrecy. However, this 'public interest' argument has been heard before in accounting and has met with some resistance in the guise of commercial sensitivity.

Mandatory position

The lack of legal obligation could be regarded as a crucial weakness of the environmental audit process as there could be a major danger to the environment which remains 'secret' until after the crisis when it is then too late. The responsible organisation will of course inform all appropriate parties of any revealed risk but it would be foolhardy to assume that all organisations are responsible. The ASB has become involved with potential liability for the company in its consideration of *Provisions*. Whilst this is only viewing it from the viewpoint of the shareholder, it may well be the only pragmatic way forward at present.

30.11.5 Experience in the USA

The increasing importance of environmental accounting can be seen in the USA by the work of the United States Environmental Protection Agency (EPA) and its Environmental Accounting Project (EAP) which has been operating since 1992.

In this large project the EPA attempts to identify the currently 'hidden' societal costs faced by organisations. These costs are those which an organisation incurs in its interaction with the environment and which in theory are totally avoidable. By identifying these costs, the organisation is motivated to address them and by implication make every attempt to reduce them, thus improving the environment.

The EPA has a very impressive website, which can be found at the following address: *http://www.epa.gov/opptinr/acctg/eaproject.htm*. Here the basic ideas and concepts governing the EPA's study of environmental accounting are set out.

The work of the EPA has also been of a more practical nature in helping organisations address environmental issues from an environmental viewpoint. A brief review of three such cases may help explain the proactive approach to environmental accounting, which goes beyond traditional reporting.

A. The Chrysler Corporation (a major vehicle manufacturer) was faced with a problem with the use of mercury switches in its electrical systems on vehicles. Mercury is dangerous to use and is very dangerous as a waste product when the vehicle is scrapped. The company had always resisted the use of non-mercury switches on pure cost terms.

However, during the EPA project, by looking at the environmental cost it was seen that non-mercury switches actually made an $0.11 per unit saving. The company on an annual basis would make an $18,000 annual saving on one plant alone by this component change.

B. Amoco Corporation (a major oil company) needed to identify the cost of complying with environmental protection regulations and used one of its refineries in Yorktown, Virginia, as an experimental site. From an analysis of the financial accounts it was found that environmental costs represented 21.9% of the non-crude cost of the product (crude oil being the major cost).

This figure was six times the level previously assumed to be the environmental cost of production. The realisation of the scale of the cost led to changes in managerial policies and practices.

C. Majestic Metals Inc. of Denver, Colorado, had a problem with pollution caused by its paint spraying machinery and practices. Through an environmental accounting exercise, the company decided to use high-volume, low-pressure (HVLP) sprayers and this reduced the cost of environmental damage (as shown by fines and rectification costs) by $40,000 per year. From a capital investment appraisal viewpoint the project gave a positive NPV over 8 years of $140,000, an internal rate of return (IRR) of 906% and a discounted payback of 0.12 years – an impressive range of results in any terms.

The EPA's website has many more cases showing the impact of an environmental accounting approach.

30.12 Concept of social accounting

This is a difficult place to start because there are so many definitions of social accounting[19] – the main points are that it includes non-financial as well as financial information and addresses the needs of stakeholders other than the shareholders. Stakeholders can be broken down into three categories:

- **internal stakeholders** – managers and workers;
- **external stakeholders** – shareholders, creditors, banks and debtors;
- **related stakeholders** – society as represented by national and local government and the increasing role of pressure groups such as Amnesty International and Greenpeace.

30.12.1 Reporting at corporate level

Prior to 1975, social accounting was viewed as being in the domain of the **economist** and concerned with national income and related issues. In 1975, *The Corporate Report* gave a different definition:

the reporting of those costs and benefits, which may or may not be quantifiable in money terms, arising from economic activities and subsequently borne or received by the community at large or particular groups not holding a direct relationship with the reporting entity.[20]

This is probably the best working definition of the topic and it establishes the first element of the social accounting concept, namely **reporting at a corporate level** and interpreting corporate in its widest sense as including all organisations of economic significance regardless of the type of organisation or the nature of ownership.

30.12.2 Accountability

The effect of the redefinition by *The Corporate Report* was to introduce the second element of our social accounting concept: accountability. The national income view was only of interest to economists and could not be related to individual company performance – *The Corporate Report* changed that. Social accounting moved into the accountants' domain and it should be the aim of accountants to learn how accountability might be achieved and to define a model against which to judge their own efforts and the efforts of others.[21]

30.12.3 Comprehensive coverage

The annual report is concerned mainly with monetary amounts or clarifying monetary issues. Despite the ASB identifying employees and the public within the user groups,[22] no standards have been issued that deal specifically with reporting to employees or the public.

Instead, the ASB prefers to assume that financial statements that meet the needs of investors will meet most of the needs of other users.[23] For all practical purposes, it disassociates itself from the needs of non-investor users by assuming that there will be more specific information that they may obtain in their dealings with the enterprise.[24]

The information needs of different categories, e.g. employees and the public, need not be identical. The provision of information of particular interest to the public has been referred to as **public interest accounting**,[25] but there is a danger that, whilst valid as an approach, it could act as a constraint on matters that might be of legitimate interest to the employee user group. For example, safety issues at a particular location might be of little interest to the public at large but of immense concern to an employee exposed to work-related radiation or asbestos. The term 'social accounting' as defined by *The Corporate Report* is seen as embracing all interests, even those of a small group.

Equally, the information needs within a category, say employees, can differ according to the level of the employees. One study identified that different levels of employee ranked the information provided about the employer differently, e.g. lower-level employees rated safety information highest, whereas higher-level employees rated organisation information highest.[26] There were also differences in opinion about the need for additional information, with the majority of lower-level but minority of higher-level employees agreeing that the social report should also contain information on corporate environmental effects.[27]

The need for social accounting to cope with both intergroup and intragroup differences was also identified in a Swedish study.[28]

30.12.4 Independent review

The degree of credibility accorded a particular piece of information is influenced by factors such as whether it is historical data or deals with the future; whether appropriate techniques exist for obtaining it; whether its source causes particular concern about deliberate or unintentional bias towards a company view; whether past experience has been that the information was reasonably complete and balanced; and, finally, the extent of independent verification.[29]

Given that social accounting is complex, technically underdeveloped, dealing with subjective areas or future events, reported on a selective basis within a report prepared by the management, it is understandable that its credibility will be called into question. Questions will be raised as to why particular items were included or omitted – after all, it is not that unusual for companies to want to hide unfavourable developments.

30.13 Background to social accounting

A brief consideration of the history of social accounting in the UK could be helpful in putting the subject into context. *The Corporate Report* (1975) was the starting point for the whole issue. This was at a time when there was the general dissatisfaction with the quality of financial reporting which had resulted in the creation of a standard-setting regulatory body (Accounting Standards Steering Committee – ASSC) and additional statutory provisions, e.g. Companies Act provisions relating to directors.

The Corporate Report was a discussion paper issued by the ASSC which represented the first UK conceptual framework. Its approach was to identify users and their information needs. It identified seven groups of user, which included employees and the public, and their information needs. However, although it identified that there were common areas of interest among the seven groups, such as assessing liquidity and evaluating management performance, it concluded that a single set of general-purpose accounts would not satisfy each group – a different conclusion from that stated by the ASB in 1991, as discussed above.[30] The conclusions reached in *The Corporate Report* were influenced by the findings of a survey of the chairmen of the 300 largest UK listed companies. They indicated a trend towards acceptance of multiple responsibilities towards groups affected by corporate decision-making and their interest as stakeholders.[31]

The Corporate Report proposed that there should be additional reports to satisfy the needs of the other stakeholders. These included a statement of corporate objectives, a statement of future prospects, an employment report and a value added statement.

Statement of corporate objectives

Would this be the place for social accounting to start? Would this be the place for vested interests to be represented so that agreed objectives take account of the views of all stakeholders and not merely the management and, indirectly, the shareholders? At present, social accounting appears as a series of add-ons, e.g. a little on charity donations, a little on disabled recruitment policy. Corporate objectives or the mission statement are often seen as something to be handed down; could they assume a different role?

The employment report

The need for an employment report was founded on the belief that there is a trust relationship between employers and employees and an economic relationship between employment prospects and the welfare of the community. The intention was that such a report should contain statistical information relating to such matters as numbers, reasons for change, training time and costs, age and sex distribution, and health and safety.

Statement of future prospects

There has always been resistance to publishing information focusing on the future. The arguments raised against it have included competitive disadvantage and the possibility of misinterpretation because the data relate to the future and are therefore uncertain.

The report nevertheless considered it appropriate to publish information of future employment and capital investment levels that could have a direct impact on employees and the local community.

Value added reports

A value added report was intended to give a different focus from the profit and loss account with its emphasis on the bottom line earnings figure. It was intended to demonstrate the interdependence of profits and payments to employees, shareholders, the government and the company via inward investment. It reflected the mood picked up from the survey of chairmen that distributable profit could no longer be regarded as the sole or prime indicator of company performance.[32]

The value added statement became a well-known reporting mechanism to measure how effectively an organisation utilised its resources and added value to its raw materials to turn them into saleable goods. Figure 30.1 is an example of a value added statement.

Figure 30.1 Barloworld Limited value added statement for year ended 30 September 2000

	Rm	Rm	%	Rm	Rm	%
Revenue		21,969			19,337	
Paid to suppliers for materials and sevices		15,521			13,214	
Value added		6,448			6,123	
Income from investments		179			210	
Total wealth created		6,627			6,333	
Wealth distribution						
Salaries, wages and other benefits		3,746	57		3,443	54
Providers of capital		510	8		510	8
Interest paid on borrowings	128			146		
Dividends paid to Barlow Ltd shareholders	334			277		
Dividends paid to outside shareholders in subsidiaries	48			87		
Government taxes and duties		423	6		307	5
Reinvested in group to maintain and develop operations		1,948	29		2,073	33
Depreciation	876			855		
Retained profit – normal	1,058			1,187		
Deferred taxation	14			31		
		6,627	100		6,333	100
Value added ratios						
Number of employees (30 September)		21,966			22,148	
Turnover per employee (Rand)		996,010			774,223	
Wealth created per employee (Rand)		300,449			253,563	

Several advantages have been claimed for these reports, including improving employee attitudes by reflecting a broader view of companies' objectives and responsibilities.[33,34]

There have also been criticisms, e.g. they are merely a restatement of information that appears in the annual report; they only report data capable of being reported in monetary terms; and the individual elements of societal benefit are limited to the traditional ones of shareholders, employees and the government, with others such as society and the consumers ignored.

There was also criticism that there was no standard so that expenditures could be aggregated or calculated to disclose a misleading picture, e.g. the inclusion of PAYE tax and welfare payments made to the government in the employee classification so that wages were shown gross whereas distributions to shareholders were shown net of tax. The effect of both was to overstate the apparent employee share and understate the government and shareholders' share.[35]

In the years immediately following the report, companies published value added statements on a voluntary basis but their importance has declined. There was a move away from industrial democracy and the standard-setting regulators did not make it mandatory.

30.13.1 Why *The Corporate Report* was not implemented

The Corporate Report's proposals for additional reports have not been implemented. There are a number of views as to why this was so. There is a view that the business community, despite the results of the chairmen survey, were concerned about the possibility of their reporting responsibility being extended through the report's concept of public accountability and welcomed the release of the Sandilands Report on inflation accounting which overshadowed *The Corporate Report*. There is a view that *The Corporate Report* fell short of making a significant contribution 'by virtue of its failure to select the accounting models appropriate to the informational needs of the individual user groups which it had identified'.[36]

However, the most likely reason for it not being fully implemented was the change of government. The Labour government produced a Green Paper in 1976, *Aims and Scope of Company Reports*, which endorsed much of *The Corporate Report* concept. The reaction from the business community and the Stock Exchange was hostile to any move away from the traditional stewardship concept with its obligations only to shareholders. The CBI view was that other users could ask for information, but that was no reason for companies to be required to provide it.[37] In the event, there was a change of government and the Green Paper sank without trace.

The new government supported the view of Friedman, who wrote in 1962 that 'few trends could so ... undermine the very foundations of our free society as the acceptance by corporate officials of a social responsibility other than to make as much money ... as possible'.

Many responsible members of the business community pressed for change,[38] but the mid 1980s saw a decline in the commercial support for social accounting, as profit, dividends and growth superseded all other social goals in business. The movement continued but advocates were regarded at best as well-meaning radicals and at worst as dangerous politicised activists devoted to the destruction of the capitalist system.

By the early 1990s, interest was appearing in the commercial sector but from a free market rather than regulatory viewpoint. The thought was that socially responsible policies need not mean lower profits – in fact, quite the opposite. Given this change in perception, companies began to embrace social accounting concepts – suddenly accountants were able to make a contribution, e.g. evaluating the profit implication of providing crêche facilities for working mothers by the employer rather than the state. There was also a growth within society in general of a socially responsible point of view which even extended to share investment decisions with the marketing of ethically sound investments.

30.14 Corporate social responsibility

Companies are increasingly recognising the importance of adopting a social, ethical and environmentally responsible approach to business activity and entering into dialogue with all groups of stakeholders. We have discussed the environmental responsible approach above – the socially responsible approach includes a wide range of activities including the companies' dealings in the marketplace, the workplace, the community and in the field of human rights.

Reporting is slowly evolving from simply reporting the amount of charitable donations in the annual report to including additional activities which the company considers to be of key interest. The reporting might be brief but gives an attractive picture of a company's social responsibility. For example, the 2001 Kingfisher Annual Report has a brief two-page section for social responsibility in which it gives information on:

- environmental issues, e.g. a commitment to sustainable forestry, winning the Business in the Environment award for energy saving; and

- social issues, e.g. from training young unemployed people to recycling electrical goods; making charitable donations that supported the Woolworth Kids First, You Can Do It and Green Grants schemes; and winning a Business in the Community award for Innovation relating to its work forming partnerships with local disability organisations.

We can see from this that community involvement can take many forms, e.g. charitable donations, gifts in kind, employee volunteering initiatives, staff secondments, and sustainable and mutually beneficial partnerships with community and voluntary organisations active in a variety of fields including education, training, regeneration, employment and homelessness.

30.15 Need for comparative data

There is evidence[39] that environmental performance could be given a higher priority when analysts assess a company if there were comparable data by sector on a company's level of corporate responsibility.

We will consider two approaches that have taken place to satisfy this need for comparable data: benckmarking and comprehensive guidelines.

30.15.1 Benchmarking

There are a number of benchmarking schemes and we will consider two by way of illustration – these are the London Benchmarking Group, established in 1994, and the Impact on Society established December 2001.

The London Benchmarking Group[40]

The Group started in 1994 and consists of companies who join in order to measure and report their involvement in the community which is a key part of any corporate social responsibility programme and who have a tool to assist them effectively assess and target their community programmes. Organisations such as Deloitte & Touche, British Airways and Lloyds TSB are members.

The scheme is concerned with corporate community involvement. It identifies three categories into which different forms of community involvement can be classified, namely, charity donations, social or community investment and commercial initiatives and includes only contributions made over and above those that result from the basic business operations.

It uses an input/output model, putting a monetary value on the 'input' costs which include contributions made in cash, time or in kind, together with full cost of staff involved; and collecting 'output' data on the community benefit, e.g. number who benefitted, leveraged resources and benefit accruing to the business.

Impact on Society[41]

This is a new website created in 2001 which provides free access to corporate social responsibility information from leading companies. It is the first time a common set of indicators against which companies can be measured has been provided, offering insight into areas such as the environment, the workplace, the community in which the company operates, the marketplace and human rights. The information ranges from relatively easy-to-measure numeric data, such as water usage, through to more complex, often perception-based information, for example from employee surveys. The information is then summarised into clear company profiles and can be compared and contrasted according to a range of parameters, such as specific indicators or industry sectors.

The site provides **qualitative** information for each company with key indicators as shown in Figure 30.2. It also provides quantitative information as a percentage, absolute cash value or physical volume.

An illustration of the scheme for Marks & Spencer for human rights and the environment are as follows:

Human rights
Particularly applicable to countries with operations or suppliers in developing countries.

The issues measured under human rights largely apply to companies who operate in, or buy from suppliers in, developing countries. What does or does not constitute a human right is always under some debate. However, the Universal Declaration of Human Rights is a main reference point. Before they can report that they definitely fall outside the scope of this section, companies need to answer a 'gatekeeper' question. Unless they can answer that they are definitely not exposed to human rights issues, they need to do more research and report against this indicator area.

The human rights indicators are being developed further: in consultation with non-governmental organisations and businesses engaged in human rights issues. While some companies have chosen to report, others await more fully developed indicators in this area.

Environment
Use of recycled material
% of material used from recycled sources
Non-weight bearing food product cardboard packaging

	Recycled cardboard
2000	60%
1999	50%
1998	25%

Figure 30.2 Impact on society key indicators

Indicator area	Indicators reported against
Marketplace	Advertising complaints upheld; upheld cases of anti-competitive behaviour; customer satisfaction levels; average time to pay bills to suppliers; customer retention; customer complaints about products and services, provision for customers with special needs.
Environment	Overall energy consumption; water usage; quantity of waste produced by weight; upheld cases of prosecution for environmental offences; CO_2/greenhouse gas emissions; percentage of waste recycled; environmental impact; benefits or costs of company's core products and services; environmental impact over the supply chain.
Workplace	Workforce profile by race-gender, race-age; number of legal non-compliances with health and safety and equal opportunities legislation; upheld cases of corrupt or unprofessional behaviour; staff turnover, value of staff training, perception measures of the company by its employees; absenteeism rates; pay and conditions compared to local equivalent average; work profile compared to local community profile.
Community	Cash value of support as % of pre-tax profits; estimated combined value of staff company time; gifts in kind and management time; leverage of other resources; perception measure of company as a good neighbour.
Human rights	Existence of confidential grievance procedures for staff; proportion of suppliers or partners screened for human rights compliance; proportion of suppliers or partners meeting company's own standards on human rights; perception by staff and local community of company's performance on human rights; wage rates.

Many types of packaging use recycled materials as a matter of course, glass bottles, tin cans and transport boxes. Where we believe that the use of recycled materials is the best environmental option and that we are able to achieve improvements we set targets. We have been working to increase our use of recycled cardboard (made from at least 50% post-consumer waste) for all our non-weight bearing food product packaging.

30.16 International initiatives towards triple bottom line reporting

There are no mandatory standards for sustainability reporting but there are Sustainability Reporting Guidelines which were issued in 2000 by the Global Reporting Initiative Steering Committee on which a number of international organisations are represented including the ACCA, the Institute of Social and Ethical Accountability, the New Economics Foundation and SustainAbility Ltd from the UK.

30.16.1 The Global Reporting Initiative (GRI)

The GRI has a mission to develop global sustainability reporting guidelines for voluntary use by organisations reporting on the three linked elements of sustainability, namely, the economic, environmental and social dimensions of their activities, products and services.

Economic dimension

This includes financial and non-financial information on R&D expenditure, investment in the workforce, current staff expenditure and outputs in terms of labour productivity.

Environmental dimension

This includes any adverse impact on air, water, land, biodiversity and human health by an organisation's production processes, products and services.

Social dimension

This includes information on health and safety and recognition of rights, e.g. human rights for both employees and outsourced employees.

30.16.2 How will the guidelines assist organisations?

The aim is to assist organisations to report information that complements existing reporting standards and is consistent, comparable and easy to understand so that:

● Parties contemplating a relationship such as an institutional investor assessing risk, obtaining goods or services or entering into any other commercial partnership arrangement will have available to them a clear picture of the human and ecological impact of the business so that they can make an informed decision.

● Management have the means to develop information systems to provide the basis for monitoring performance, making inter-company comparisons and reporting to stakeholders.

30.16.3 What information should appear in an ideal GRI report?

There are six parts to the ideal GRI report:

1. CEO statement – describing key elements of the report.

2. A profile – providing an overview of the organisation and the scope of the report (it could for example be dealing only with environmental information) which sets the context for the next four parts:

3. Executive summary and key indicators – to assist stakeholders to assess trends and make inter-company comparisons.

4. Vision and strategy – a statement of the vision for the future and how that integrates economic, environmental and social performance.

5. Policies, organisation and systems – an overview of the governance and management systems to implement this vision with a discussion of how stakeholders have been engaged. This reflects the GRI view that the report should not be made in isolation but there should have been appropriate inputs from stakeholders.

6. Performance review.

30.16.4 How are GRI reports to be verified?

Whilst it is preferable that there should be independent verification, the GRI recognises that sustainability reporting is at an early stage and evolving and that there could be other ways of verification such as internal auditing and a compliance statement from the board of directors.

30.16.5 Will there be any impact on matters that are currently disclosed?

There may be an overlap with existing disclosures in the OFR and there is also a pressure for additional information to permit a greater understanding of future risks, e.g. the GRI acknowledges that in financial reporting terms a going concern is one that is considered to be financially viable for at least the next financial year but seeks additional information such as:

● The extent to which significant internal and external operational, financial, compliance, and other risks are identified and assessed on an ongoing basis. Significant risks may, for example, include those related to market, credit, liquidity, technological, legal, health, safety, environmental and reputation issues.

● The likely impact of prospective legislation, e.g. product, environmental, fiscal or employee-related.

30.16.6 The nature of the accountant's involvement

There will be inputs from accountants in each of the three elements with a greater degree of quantification at present for the economic and environmental dimensions. For example:
The economic dimension may require economic indicators such as:

● Profit: segmental gross margin, net profit, EBIT, return on average capital employed
● Intangible assets: ratio of market valuation to book value
● Investments: human capital, R&D, debt/equity ratio
● Wages and benefits: totals by country
● Labour productivity: levels and changes by job category
● Community development: jobs by type and country showing absolute figures and net change
● Suppliers: value of goods and services outsourced, performance in meeting credit terms.

The environmental dimension may require environmental indicators such as:

● Products and services: major issues, e.g. disposal of waste, packaging practices, percentage of product reclaimed after use
● Suppliers: supplier issues identified through stakeholder consultation, e.g. forest stewardship
● Travel: objectives and targets, e.g. product distribution, fleet operation, quantitaive estimates of miles travelled by transport type.

Social dimensions may require social indicators such as:

● Quality of management: employee retention rates, ratio of jobs offered to jobs accepted, ranking as an employer in surveys
● Health and safety: reportable cases, lost days, absentee rate, investment per worker in injury prevention
● Wages and benefits: ratio of lowest wage to local cost of living, health and pension benefits provided
● Training and education: ratio of training budget to annual operating cost, programmes to encourage worker participation in decision making
● Freedom of association: grievance procedures in place, number and types of legal action concerning anti-union practices.

Summary

As environmental and social reporting evolves there are proposals being made to harmonise the content and disclosure and to set up benchmark schemes which will allow stakeholders to compare corporate social reports and evaluate an individual company's performance. The management systems that are being developed within companies should result in data that are consistent and reliable and capable of external verification. The benchmarking systems should assist in both identifying best practice and establishing the performance indicators that are relevant.

Corporate social reporting has been relatively ignored by commercial organisations until the mid-1990s but, with the recognition that a company's reputation can have favourable and unfavourable economic consequences, it is now receiving serious attention from companies.

REVIEW QUESTIONS

1 Discuss the relevance of corporate social reports to an existing and potential investor.

2 Obtain a copy of the environmental report of a company that has taken part in the ACCA Awards for Sustainability Reporting and critically discuss from an investor's and public interest viewpoint.

3 Charters and guidelines help make reports reliable but inhibit innovation and reduce their relevance. Discuss.

4 Discuss the implications of the Global Reporting Initiative for the accountancy profession.

5 Discuss *The Corporate Report*'s relevance to modern business, identify changes that would improve current reporting practice and the conditions necessary for such changes to become mandatory.

6 (a) Explain the term 'stakeholders' in a corporate context.

   (b) Social accounting recognises all *Corporate Report* users as stakeholders. Discuss.

7 Discuss the value added concept, giving examples, and ways to improve the statement.

8 Outline the arguments for and against a greater role for the audit function in corporate social reporting.

9 (a) Human assets are incapable of being valued. Discuss.

   (b) Football clubs have followed various policies in the way in which they include players within their accounts. For example, some clubs capitalise players, as shown by a 1992 Touche Ross survey:[42]

Club	Value £m	Basis	Which players
Tottenham Hotspur	9.8	Cost	Those purchased
Sheffield United	8.7	Manager's valuation	Whole squad
Portsmouth	7.0	Directors' valuation	Whole squad
Derby County	6.5	Cost	Those purchased

Other clubs disclose squad value in notes to the accounts or in the directors' report:

Manchester United	24.0	Independent valuation
Charlton Athletic	4.1	Directors' valuation
Millwall	11.0	Manager's valuation

Discuss arguments for and against capitalising players as assets. Explain the effect on the profit and loss account if players are not capitalised.

10 (a) Examine the recent financial press to identify examples of a failure to meet information needs in respect of an area of public interest.

(b) Obtain a set of accounts from a public listed company and assess the success in meeting the needs of the traditional users. Repeat the process for non-traditional users and discuss how you could improve the situation (a) marginally, (b) significantly.

11 Discuss the impact of the following groups on the accounting profession:

(a) Environmental groups;

(b) Customers;

(c) Workforce;

(d) Ethical investors.

12 Nissan, the Japanese car company, decided that 'any environmentalism should pay for itself and for every penny you spend you must save a penny. You can spend as many pennies as you like as long as other environmental actions save an equal number.'[43] Discuss the significance of this for each of the stakeholders.

13 (a) Accounting should contribute to the protection of the environment. Discuss whether this is a proper role for accounting and outline ways in which it could.

(b) Outline, with reasons, your ideas for an environmental report for a company of your choice.

(c) Discuss the arguments against the adoption of environmental accounting.

14 (a) Obtain the annual reports of companies that claim to be environmentally aware and assess if these reports and accounts reflect the claim. The various oil, chemical and pharmaceutical companies are useful for this.

(b) Look at your own organisation/institution, outline the possible environmental issues and discuss how these could or should be disclosed in the annual report.

The following references have been helpful for students carrying out assignments in the developing areas of environmental and social reporting:

Accounting Advisory Forum, *Environmental Issues in Financial Reporting*, 1995, Accounting Advisory Forum (Brussels).

C. A. Adams, W. -Y. Hill and C. B. Roberts, 'Corporate social reporting practices in Western Europe: legitimating corporate behaviour?' *British Accounting Review*, 1998, Vol. 30(1), pp. 1–22.

C. C. Adams, A. Coutts and G. Harte, 'Corporate equal opportunities (non-) disclosure', *British Accounting Review*, 1995, Vol. 27(2), pp. 87–108.

F. K. Birkin, 'Environmental Management Accounting', *Management Accounting*, 1996, pp. 34–37.

F. Birkin and D. Woodward, 'Management accounting for sustainable development', *Management Accounting*, June 1997, pp. 24–26.

J. H. Blokdijk and F. Drieenhuizen, 'The environment and the audit profession – a Dutch research study', *The European Accounting Review*, December 1992, pp. 437–443.

R. L. Burritt and G. Lehman, 'The Body Shop wind farm – an analysis of accountability and ethics', *British Accounting Review*, 1995, Vol. 27(3), pp. 167–186.

J. Colllier, *The Corporate Environment*, Prentice Hall, 1995.

D. Dodds, J. A. Lesser and R. O. Zerbe, *Environmental Economics and Policy*, Addison Wesley, 1997.

R. Gray, J. Bebbington, D. Walters and M. Houldin (eds), *Accounting for the Environment*, Paul Chapman Publishing, 1993.

R. Gray, D. Owen and C. Adams, *Accounting and Accountability – Changes and Challenges in Corporate Social and Environmental Reporting*, Prentice Hall, 1996.

M. J. Jones, 'Accounting for Biodiversity', *British Accounting Review*, 1996, Vol. 28(4), pp. 281–304.

L. Lewis, C. Humphrey and D. Owen, 'Accounting and the Social: A Pedagogic Perspective', *British Accounting Review*, 1992, Vol. 24(3), pp. 219–234.

M. Lynn, 'A Note on Corporate Social Disclosure in Hong Kong', *British Accounting Review*, 1992, Vol. 24, No. 2, pp. 105–110.

M. Matthews and M. H. B. Perera, *Accounting Theory and Development* (3rd edition), Thompson Business Press, 1996.

T. Mouck, 'Financial reporting, democracy and environmentalism: a critique of the commodification of information', *Critical Perspectives on Accounting*, 1995, Vol. 6(6), pp. 535–553.

M. K. Neimark, *The Hidden Dimensions of Annual Reports – Sixty Years of Social Conflict at General Motors*, Paul Chapman Publishing, 1993.

D. Owen (ed.), *Green Reporting – Accounting and the Challenge of the Nineties*, Thompson Business Press, 1992.

R. Roslender and J. R. Dyson, 'Accounting for the worth of employees: a new look at an old problem', *British Accounting Review*, 1992, Vol. 24(4), pp. 311–330.

D. Rubenstein, *Environmental Accounting for the Sustainable Corporation*, Westport, Quorum Books, 1994.

S. Schaltegger, K. Muller and H. Hindrichsen, *Corporate Environmental Reporting*, Wiley, 1996.

C. A. Tilt, 'Environmental policies of major companies: Australian evidence', *British Accounting Review*, 1997, Vol. 29(4), pp. 367–394.

T. Tinker and T. Puxy, *Policing Accounting Knowledge – The Market for Excuses Affair*, Paul Chapman Publishing, 1995.

G. Tower, 'A public accountability model of the accounting profession', *British Accounting Review*, 1992, Vol. 25(1), pp. 61–86.

EXERCISES

An extract from the solution is provided in the appendix at the end of the text for exercises marked with an asterisk (*).

* Question I

The following information relates to the Plus Factors Group plc for the years to 30 September 20X8 and 20X9:

	Notes	20X9 £000	20X8 £000
Associated company share of profit		10.9	10.7
Auditors' remuneration		12.2	11.9
Creditors for materials			
At beginning of year		1,109.1	987.2
At end of year		1,244.2	1,109.1
Debtors			
At beginning of year		1,422.0	1,305.0
At end of year		1,601.0	1,422.0
11% Debentures	1	500.0	600.0
Depreciation		113.7	98.4
Employee benefits paid		109.9	68.4
Hire of plant, machinery and vehicles	2	66.5	367.3
Materials paid for in year		3,622.9	2,971.4
Minority interest in profit of the year		167.2	144.1
Other overheads incurred		1,012.4	738.3
Pensions and pension contributions paid		319.8	222.2
Profit before taxation		1,437.4	1,156.4
Provision for corporation tax		464.7	527.9
Salaries and wages		1,763.8	1,863.0
Sales	3	9,905.6	8,694.1
Shares at nominal value			
Ordinary at 25p each fully paid	4	2,500.0	2,000.0
7% Preference at £1 each fully paid	4	500.0	200.0
Stocks of materials			
Beginning of year		804.1	689.7
End of year		837.8	804.1

Ordinary dividends were declared as follows:

> Interim   1.12 pence per share (20X8, 1.67p)
> Final   3.57 pence per share (20X8, 2.61p)
> Average number of employees was 196 (20X8, 201)

Notes:

1 £300,000 of debentures were redeemed at par on 31 March 20X9 and £200,000 new debentures at the same rate of interest were issued at £98 for each £100 nominal value on the same date. The new debentures are due to be redeemed in 5 years time.

2 This is the amount for inclusion in the profit and loss account in accordance with SSAP 21.

3 All the groups' sales are subject to value added tax at 15% and the figures given include such tax. All other figures are exclusive of value added tax.

4 All shares have been in issue throughout the year.

The statement of value added is available for 20X8 and the 20X9 statement needs to be completed.

	Workings	£000	
Turnover	1	7,560.1	
Less: Bought-in materials and services	2	4,096.4	
Value added by group		3,463.7	
Share of profits of Associated company		10.7	
		3,474.4	
Applied in the following ways			
To pay employees	3	2,153.6	62.0%
To pay providers of capital	4	566.5	16.3%
To pay government		527.9	15.2%
To provide for maintenance and expansion of assets	5	226.4	6.50%
		3,174.4	100.0%

Workings

1 *Turnover*

Sales inclusive of VAT	8,694.1
VAT at 15%	1,134.0
	7,560.1

2 *Bought-in materials and services*
Cost of materials

Creditors at end of year	1,109.1
Add: Payments in year	2,971.4
	4,080.5
Less: Creditors at beginning of year	987.2
Materials purchased in year	3,093.3
Add: Opening stock	689.7
Less: Closing stock	(804.1)
Materials used	2,978.9
Add: Cost of bought-in services	
Auditors' remuneration	11.9
Hire of plant, machinery and vehicles	367.3
Other overheads	738.3
	4,096.4

3 *To pay employees*

Benefits paid	68.4
Pensions and pension contributions	222.2
Salaries and wages	1,863.0
	2,153.6

4 *To pay providers of capital*
Debenture interest

11% of £600,000	66.0
Dividends	
Preference 20X8 7% of £200,000	14.0
Ordinary 20X8 8 million shares at 4.28p	342.4
Minority interest	144.1
	566.5

5 *To provide for maintenance and expansion of assets*

Profit before tax	1,156.4
Less: tax	(527.9)
: minority interest	(144.1)
: dividends	(356.4)
Retained profits	128.0
Depreciation	98.4
	226.4

Required:

(a) Prepare a statement of value added for the year to 30 September 20X9. Include a percentage breakdown of the distribution of value added.
(b) Produce ratios related to employees' interests based on the statement in (a) and explain how they might be of use.
(c) Explain briefly what the difficulties are of measuring and reporting financial information in the form of a statement of value added.

Question 2

David Mark is a sole trader who owns and operates supermarkets in each of three villages near Ousby. He has drafted his own accounts for the year ended 31 May 20X4 for each of the branches. They are as follows:

	Arton £	Arton £	Blendale £	Blendale £	Clifearn £	Clifearn £
Sales		910,800		673,200		382,800
Cost of sales		633,100		504,900		287,100
Gross profit		277,700		168,300		95,700
Less: Expenses:						
David Mark's salary	10,560		10,560		10,560	
Other salaries and wages	143,220		97,020		78,540	
Rent			19,800			
Rates	8,920		5,780		2,865	
Advertising	2,640		2,640		2,640	
Delivery van expenses	5,280		5,280		5,280	
General expenses	11,220		3,300		1,188	
Telephone	2,640		1,980		1,584	
Wrapping materials	7,920		3,960		2,640	
Depreciation:						
Fixtures	8,220		4,260		2,940	
Vehicle	3,000	203,620	3,000	157,580	3,000	111,237
Net profit/(loss)		74,080		10,720		(15,537)

The figures for the year ended 31 May 20X4 follow the pattern of recent years. Because of this, David Mark is proposing to close the Clifearn supermarket immediately.

David Mark employs twelve full-time and twenty part-time staff. His recruitment policy is based on employing one extra part-time assistant for every £30,000 increase in branch sales. His staff deployment at the moment is as follows:

	Arton	Blendale	Clifearn
Full-time staff (including managers)	6	4	2
Part-time staff	8	6	6

Peter Gaskin, the manager of the Clifearn supermarket, asks David to give him another year to make the supermarket profitable. Peter has calculated that he must cover £125,500 expenses out of his gross profit in the year ended 31 May 20X5 in order to move into profitability. His calculations include extra staff costs and all other extra costs.

Additional information:

1 General advertising for the business as a whole is controlled by David Mark. This costs £3,960 per annum. Each manager spends a further £1,320 advertising his own supermarket locally.

2 The delivery vehicle is used for deliveries from the Arton supermarket only.

3 David Mark has a central telephone switchboard which costs £1,584 rental per annum. Each supermarket is charged for all calls actually made. For the year ended 31 May 20X4 these amounted to:

Arton	£2,112
Blendale	£1,452
Clifearn	£1,056

Required:

(a) A report addressed to David Mark advising him whether to close Clifearn supermarket. Your report should include a detailed financial statement based on the results for the year ended 31 May 20X4 relating to the Clifearn branch.

(b) Calculate the increased turnover and extra staff needed if Peter's suggestion is implemented.

(c) Comment on the social implications for the residents of Clifearn if (1) David Mark closes the supermarket, (2) Peter Gaskin's recommendation is undertaken.

* Question 3

(a) You are required to prepare a value added statement to be included in the corporate report of Hythe plc for the year ended 31 December 20X6, including the comparatives for 20X5, using the information given below:

	20X6 £000	20X5 £000
Fixed assets (net book value)	3,725	3,594
Debtors	870	769
Creditors	530	448
14% Debentures	1,200	1,080
6% Preference shares	400	400
Ordinary shares (£1 each)	3,200	3,200
Sales	5,124	4,604
Materials consumed	2,934	2,482
Wages	607	598

Depreciation	155	144
Fuel consumed	290	242
Hire of plant and machinery	41	38
Salaries	203	198
Auditors' remuneration	10	8
Corporation tax provision	402	393
Ordinary share dividend	9p	8p
Number of employees	40	42

(b) Although value added statements were recommended by *The Corporate Report*, as yet there is no accounting standard related to them. Explain what a value added statement is and provide reasons as to why you think it has not yet become mandatory to produce such a statement as a component of current financial statements either through a Financial Reporting Standard or company law.

Question 4

Gettry Doffit plc is an international company with worldwide turnover of £26 million. The activities of the company include the breaking down and disposal of noxious chemicals at a specialised plant in the remote Scottish countryside. During the preparation of the financial statements for the year ended 31 March 20X5, it was discovered that:

1 Quantities of chemicals for disposals on site at the year-end included:
(A) Axylotl peroxide   40,000 gallons
(B) Pterodactyl chlorate   35 tons

Chemical A is disposed of for a South Korean company, which was invoiced for 170 million won on 30 January 20X5, for payment in 120 days. It is estimated that the costs of disposal will not exceed £75,000. £60,000 of costs have been incurred at the year-end.

Chemical B is disposed of for a British company on a standard contract for 'cost of disposal plus 35%', one month after processing. At the year-end the chemical has been broken down into harmless by-products at a cost of £77,000. The by-products, which belong to Gettry Doffit plc, are worth £2,500.

2 To cover against exchange risks, the company entered into two forward contracts on 30 January 20X5:

No. 03067   Sell 170 million won at 1,950 won = £1: 31 May 20X5
No. 03068   Buy $70,000 at $1.60   = £1: 31 May 20X5

Actual sterling exchange rates were:

	won	$
30 January 20X5	1,900	1.70
31 March 20X5	2,000	1.38
30 April 20X5 (today)	2,100	1.80

The company often purchases a standard chemical used in processing from a North American company, and the dollars will be applied towards this purpose.

3 The company entered into a contract to import a specialised chemical used in the breaking down of magnesium perambulate from a Nigerian company which demanded the raising of an irrevocable letter of credit for £65,000 to cover 130 tons of the chemical. By 31 March 20X5 bills of lading for 60 tons had been received and paid for under the letter of credit. It now appears that the total needed for the requirements of Gettry Doffit plc for the foreseeable future is only 90 tons.

4 On 16 October 20X4 Gettry Doffit plc entered into a joint venture as partners with Dumpet Andrunn plc to process perfidious recalcitrant (PR) at the Gettry Doffit plc site using Dumpet Andrunn plc's technology. Unfortunately, a spillage at the site on 15 April 20X5 has led to claims being filed against the two companies for £12 million. A public inquiry has been set up, to assess the cause of the accident and to determine liability, which the finance director of Gettry Doffit plc fears will be, at the very least, £3 million.

Required:

Discuss how these matters should be reflected in the financial statements of Gettry Doffit plc as on and for the year ended 31 March 20X5.

Question 5

Examine the EPA's website and prepare one of the cases as a presentation to the group showing clearly how environmental accounting was used and the results of the exercise.
[http://www.epa.gov/opptintr/acctg/earesources.htm]

References

1 C. Lehman, *Accounting's Changing Roles in Social Conflict*, Markus Weiner Publishing, 1992, p. 64.
2 *Ibid.*, p. 17.
3 S.J. Gray and C.B. Roberts, *Voluntary Information Disclosure and the British Multinationals: Corporate Perceptions of Costs and Benefits, International Pressures for Accounting Change*, Prentice Hall, 1989, p. 117.
4 AICPA, *The Measurement of Corporate Social Performance*, 1977, p. 4.
5 *This Common Inheritance*, Government White Paper, 1990.
6 KPMG Peat Marwick McLintock, *Environmental Considerations in Acquiring*, Corporate Finance Briefing, 17 May 1991.
7 M. Jones, 'The cost of cleaning up', *Certified Accountant*, May 1995, p. 47.
8 M. Campanale, 'Cost or opportunity', *Certified Accountant*, November 1991, p. 32.
9 see www.europa.eu.int/
10 see www.unep.org
11 see http://europa.eu.int/comm/environment/emas/
12 see www.iccwbo.org
13 see http://www.cefic.be/
14 see http://www.pwcglobal.com/
15 see http://europa.eu.int/
16 see http://www.ceaa-acve.ca/aboutus.htm
17 see http://www.rabnet.com/
18 see http://www.fee.be/issues/other.htm#Sustainability
19 M.R. Matthews and M.H.B. Perera, *Accounting Theory and Development*, Chapman and Hall, 1991, p. 350.
20 *The Corporate Report*, ASSC, 1975.
21 R. Gray, D. Owen and K. Maunders, *Corporate Social Reporting*, Prentice Hall, 1987, p. 75.
22 *Statement of Principles: The Objective of Financial Statements*, ASB, 1991, para. 9.
23 *Ibid.*, para. 10.
24 *Ibid.*, para. 11.
25 F. Okcabol and A. Tinker, 'The market for positive theory: deconstructing the theory for excuses', *Advances in Public Interest Accounting*, 1990, Vol. 3.
26 H. Sebreuder, 'Employees and the corporate social report: the Dutch case', in S.J. Gray (ed.), *International Accounting and Transnational Decisions*, Butterworth, 1983, p. 287.
27 *Ibid.*, p. 289.

28 *Ibid.*, p. 287.
29 AICPA, *op. cit.*, p. 243.
30 *Statement of Principles, op cit.*
31 R. Gray, D. Owen and K. Maunders, *op. cit.*, p. 44.
32 *Ibid.*
33 S.J. Gray and K.T. Maunders, *Value Added Reporting: Uses and Measurement*, ACCA, 1980.
34 B. Underwood and P.J. Taylor, *Accounting Theory and Policy Making*, Heinemann, 1985, p. 298.
35 *Ibid.*, p. 174.
36 M. Davies, R. Patterson and A. Wilson, *UK GAAP* (4th edition), Ernst & Young, 1994, p. 71.
37 R. Gray, D. Owen and K. Maunders, *op. cit.*, p. 48.
38 R.W. Perks and R.H. Gray, 'Corporate social reporting – an analysis of objectives', *British Accounting Review*, 1978, Vol. 10(2), pp. 43–59.
39 *Investing in the Future*, BiE, May 2001.
40 see http://www.lbg-online.net/
41 see www.iosreporting.org
42 R. Bruce, *The Independent*, 25 October 1993, p. 29.
43 M. Brown, 'Greening the bottom line', *Management Today*, July 1995, p. 73.

CHAPTER 31

Ethics for accountants

31.1 Introduction

In this chapter we consider the following:

- The nature of business ethics
- The ethical code of business
- The background to business ethics
- The role of ethics in modern business
- The role of professional accounting ethics
- The role of the accountant as a guardian of business ethics

The issue of ethics is at the very centre of all societies. Every society, such as a nation, must operate according to some ethical guidelines, however idiosyncratic or singular they may seem to outsiders – without such guidelines the society would lapse into anarchy and eventual collapse. This also applies to sub-societies, e.g. a family, a group of friends or even a business organisation and in this chapter we introduce the student of accounting to the basics of ethics as they could be applied to business.

What do we mean by 'ethics'?

In any study a good starting point is the production of a working definition of the issue under consideration. The *Oxford English Dictionary* has one of the more accessible definitions of ethics, it states four possible views of ethics:

> Ethics can be defined as (i) the science of morals; (ii) moral principles; (iii) a philosophy **or (iv) a code.**

In this chapter we will adopt the fourth definition of ethics as **an ethical code**, i.e. we will concentrate on the bureaucratic view of how to operate ethics in practice. The other three views are more properly the domain of philosophers as they are really concerned with what ethics should be.

31.2 The nature of business ethics

Business ethics refers to the relationship of a business to three significant 'environments' or 'levels'. Each business seeks for a harmonisation (or even a compromise) between the three levels of ethics which are traditionally viewed as follows:

1 The macro level

The macro ethical guidelines applied to a business in the national and international context are usually the result of political, cultural, legal and religious pressures.

2 The organisational level

The organisational ethical guidelines are the ethics specific to an organisation. In many texts they are referred to as 'corporate social responsibility'. The guidelines may be of long duration, e.g. the ethics of the original founders of the organisation (such as the Co-Operative Wholesale movement or the John Lewis Partnership) or short duration, e.g. the ethical beliefs of the current senior managers of the business and of the current trading partners in the industrial sector within which the organisation operates.

3 The individual level

Individual ethical guidelines or personal ethics refers to the ethics of each individual in the organisation. These are naturally the result of a much more varied set of influences or pressures. As an individual each of us 'enjoys' a series of ethical pressures or influences including the following:

- parents – the first and, according to many authors, the most crucial influence on our ethical guidelines;
- family – the *extended* family which is common in Eastern societies (aunts, uncles, grandparents and so on) can have a significant impact on personal ethics; the *nuclear* family which is more common in Western societies (just parent(s) and siblings) can be equally as important but more narrowly focused;
- social group – the ethics of our 'class' (either actual or aspirational) can be a major influence;
- peer group – the ethics of our 'equals' (again actual or aspirational) can be another major influence;
- religion – ethics based in religion are more important in some cultures, e.g. Islamic societies have some detailed ethics demanded of believers as well as major guidelines for business ethics. However, even in supposedly secular cultures, individuals are influenced by religious ethics;
- culture – this is also a very effective formulator of an individual's ethics;
- professional – when an individual becomes part of a professional body then s/he is subject to the ethics of the professional body.

How do professional ethics differ from those arising from parents and peers?

The essential difference is that the ethics handbook which governs the behaviour of all staff in an organisation are more likely to be formally codified. A code of behaviour may be written as a formal Statement of Professional Ethics or subsumed within the staff. The fact that the Code is formally specified means that it is capable of being policed with information systems in place to assist monitoring and enforcement.

Harmonisation

We have seen above that 'business' has a complex 'web' of relationships with various parties each operating with their own ethics guidelines. The task of the business is therefore to ensure effective operations whilst meeting the various ethical demands of all interested parties.

31.3 The ethical code of a business

There are two approaches to defining an ethical code, namely, the positive and normative approaches.

The rationale for the positivist approach

This places emphasis on the preparation of a formal, written ethical code for the guidance of all employees within an organisation. Such an approach is to be expected as, in all control models, it is considered to be essential to have a fixed, rigid standard against which to measure performance. Any ambiguities of performance measurement can lead to disputes and confusion. This is especially true with ethics as the term has a variety of meanings and constructs within the mind of each individual. It is, therefore, hardly surprising that a business tries to produce a 'hard copy' of ethics for the use of all interested parties.

There are many examples of ethical codes in practice and for further study reference can be made to the codes of the following organisations:

- Trusthouse Forte plc – with its 'Company Philosophy' document.
- British Gas plc – with its 'Code of Conduct'.
- Royal Dutch Shell Group of Companies – with its 'Statement of General Business Principles'.
- BICC plc – with its 'Statement of Company Principles'.
- The Body Shop – which publish a considerable amount of information showing their belief in classic business ethics.

The limitations of the positivist approach

Key arguments against the positivist approach of written codes can be summarised as follows:

- **Status of the source**: the source, or who writes the code of ethics, can be a crucial question with the risk that ethical codes could be imposed on a business against the 'natural' beliefs of its employees. This is always a key danger in multinational companies where the management in the parent country may impose ethical beliefs on subsidiaries in other counties which are contrary to the cultural or religious beliefs of the host country.

- **Flexibility**: it is a well known axiom that rules once in place do tend to have an existence well beyond their appointed time and this could cause serious ethical problems. It is important that there are procedures in place determining how written codes may be changed to meet changing beliefs and customs.

- **Comprehensiveness**: it is questionable whether one written code can cover all the possible issues raised under ethics. It is a weakness of all codified rules that they tend to apply only to known or, at least, anticipated situations. As discussed under flexibility, procedures are required to cope with totally new and unexpected situations – ethical issues often fall into this category and new situations and potential conflicts are always arising which limits the effectiveness of a written code.

The rationale for the normative approach

The alternative approach is to adopt a more 'normative' ethical stance where a philosophy is developed for the business following a theoretical, religious or pragmatic approach as follows:

The theoretical approach

A business may take any one of the many theoretical stances on ethics. It is not the purpose of the chapter to go into detail but typically the business could adopt any philosophy including:

- **Utilitarianism**, as propounded by Jeremy Bentham (1748–1832) or John Stuart Mill (1806–1873), where individual happiness is balanced against the needs of society.

- **Deontological philosophy**, as propounded by Immanuel Kant (1724–1804), revised by David Hare (b. 1919), which is a philosophy based upon perceived absolutes of 'right', 'wrong' and 'duty'.

- **Marxism and post-Marxism**, based on the ideas of Karl Marx (1818–1883) and the post-marxists such as Herbert Marcuse (1898–1979), Roland Barthes (1915–1980) and Michel Foucault (1926–1984). Their views are of importance in multi-national situations and look at the imposition of ethics based upon economic power.

- **Postmodernism**, put forward by those such as A.J. Ayer (1910–1989), Jean Francois Lyotard (b. 1924) and Jacques Derrida (b. 1930), has a particular resonance for business by offering an almost 'free market' approach to ethics.

- **Social philosophy**, with the work of John Rawls (b. 1921) and Alasdair MacIntyr (b. 1929), who adopt a more community centred approach.

There are many theorists whose views can be explored for a deeper understanding of the approach.

The religious approach

This approach is applied when business ethics are formulated on some basic religious foundation, e.g. Judeo-Christian or Islamic or Hindu or Buddhist or Jainist.

The pragmatic approach

This is the approach where a business simply addresses each ethical problem as it arises and solves such problems by committee – the establishment of ethical committees is commonplace in many large organisations.

There are, however, difficulties with the approach which can be summarised as:

- Inefficiency: this is a very time-consuming process and some issues are urgent and need a swift solution.

- Inconsistency: the approach can, over time, lead to inconsistencies and apparent changes of approach which can be embarrassing and confusing.

- Theoretical underpinning: there is the question of who is qualified to sit on such committees, which can be a major question for a business. In some hospitals in the USA philosophers are employed by hospitals to help medical staff address key ethical issues on a case-by-case basis. These philosophers, however, will operate from one of the theoretical standpoints highlighted above.

Thus the 'normative' approach, whilst being sound in concept, does raise enormous practical difficulties for business. This explains the reliance on a written code, which despite its drawbacks is at least accessible and in many ways 'reliable'.

31.4 The background to business ethics

A brief survey of the recent history of business ethics may prove useful at this point in our study.

The separatist view

In classical economic theory the business has only one purpose, as typified by the following précis of the ideas of Milton Friedman:

> Managers should single-mindedly pursue only one goal: the maximisation of profit for the benefit of shareholders. The invisible hand of the market then guarantees their actions contribute to social welfare in the best possible way.
>
> (Jeurissen 1995)

This view of ethics is often referred to as the 'separatist view' and assumes that the business will conform to some ethical standard because of the combined influence of the law (via governmental pressure) and the (almost magical) powers of 'market forces'. Thus it assumes that businesses will behave ethically because it makes sound business sense to do so!

The integration view

The alternative view proposed by Jeurissen in his Sankt Gallen lecture is known as the 'integration view'. This view recognises the impact of law and market forces but also gives the organisation a duty or responsibility to respond and reflect the views of the moral community within which it operates. In other words the business may well have a wider social responsibility with objectives broader than simply profit maximisation.

Thus society allows the business the freedom to operate on 'market lines' provided that the 'public' can rely upon the integrity of the management to operate for the wider benefit of society in the long term. It is the conditional nature of the freedom that makes business ethics important.

Promotion of business ethics

At an institute level, the Chair of the Institute of Business Ethics, Neville Cooper put the issue with remarkable clarity in 1987 when he said:

> Our conviction is that, essentially, industry and commerce are highly ethical undertakings. The ethical demands on us ... are to run them supremely efficiently, responsibly and with clear moral standards.[1]

At a corporate level, the Chairman of a major UK food company in referring to his company's code of ethics said:

> ... business ethics are not negotiable – a well founded reputation for scrupulous dealing is itself a priceless company asset and the most important single factor in our success is faithful adherence to our beliefs.

Management commitment to business ethics

This view of business ethics has its spiritual home in the development of codes of behaviour formulated in the United States since the 1960s and imported into Britain in the 1980s. Research carried out by the Institute of Business Ethics in 1987 in respect of the 300 largest UK companies did support this view, where the replies received did show ethics being taken seriously by senior management. Many ethical statements were shown to be published in the Annual Accounts and Report documents produced by these companies. This research supported other surveys especially that carried out by the journal *International Management* in 1982.

Well known failures to follow acceptable ethical practices

The importance of business ethics is also, sadly, reinforced by a series of high profile scandals caused by an obvious lack of business ethics. There are many examples including BCCI and the activities of the late Robert Maxwell with the Mirror Group of companies.

The issue of public confidence in business integrity is at the key of the continued acceptance of the freedom to operate within a market economy. It was as a result of such scandals that the Institute of Business Ethics was formed in 1987 to:

> ... clarify ethical issues in business, to propose positive solutions to problems and to establish common ground with people of goodwill of all faiths.

This, voluntary, organisation has been attempting to spread the issue of ethics and ethical behaviour across all business enterprises both nationally and internationally.

UK commitment to self-regulation

The self-regulation approach is a feature of the business culture of the UK. The work of the Cadbury Committee (1991, updated in 1992) helped the issue of corporate governance and managerial behaviour and the Greenbury Report (1995), which looked in detail at the issue of directors' remuneration packages, included an ethical view of such, again reflecting the usual UK approach. The Hampel Report (1998) reinforced the voluntary, self-regulatory nature of such views of business ethics.

Thus the issue of business ethics is seen to be a key feature of business success but ethics are (in the view of business) best 'enforced' on a voluntary basis.

31.5 The role of ethics in modern business

When considering the issues raised under business ethics a useful starting point is to examine the areas covered by the Ethical Codes published by the various organisations which indicate the key areas of concern.

1 Conflicts of interest

These are always issues of concern as management must be concerned with the benefit of the organisation and they must not put personal gain ahead of the gain for the organisation. Where there is a possibility of conflict, the usual practice is for the manager (including directors) to declare an interest to their fellow managers who can then assess the actions of the manager in such a light. Ideally the manager should withdraw from taking decisions where s/he may gain personally, but this may not always be practical. The awarding of contracts, employment of relatives and share dealings are all areas of concern here.

Public perceptions

The manager needs to not only be behaving ethically but also to be **seen** to be behaving ethically. Recent issues in Parliament have highlighted the dangers of conflicts of interest and how even innocent conflicts can be seen to have a more sinister, ulterior motive. The whole issue of **insider dealing** has recently caused problems in respect of share options for directors and their actions in taking up the options at advantageous times.

2 Gifts

The practice of giving and receiving gifts in business has always been a very fine ethical question. Ideally gifts should not be seen as an inducement to promote business in a manner which is less than open and honest. However, gifts are often intended as a sign of goodwill and respect and have no other motive than this. The issue becomes even more cloudy when we consider corporate hospitality, e.g. are tickets for the Football World Cup given to potential customers a legitimate gift? An apparently innocent social event could be seen to have sinister overtones in the 'cold light of day'.

There is a normal, human need to show respect and the giving and receiving of gifts is a key part of this. Japan for example is an illustration of cultural ethical differences where gifts are commonplace in business. In most businesses the key factor is scale. Small, low value gifts are not perceived as a threat to ethical behaviour (diaries, low cost pens etc.) but high value gifts are not acceptable.

The issue also applies to the payment of 'bribes' to encourage business, totally unacceptable in the eyes of most managers but common practice in many countries and industries (e.g. the defence industry). Thus, ethically no bribes (however named) should be paid or received.

There is a growing concern over the use of gifts of cash, goods or services in relation to governmental officials. Such officials, by the very nature of their work, must be above reproach in respect of ethical behaviour. Unfortunately these officials are often very poorly paid and thus the temptation is great.

Commercial organisations must have very precise codes for dealing with governmental officials. This code must also cover the relationship with the official before, during and after the main business has been carried out. This is to prevent the temptation of payment paid later, even after the official has left government service, since the suspicion will always remain of unfair treatment.

3 Confidentiality

The business has secrets which could have commercial value if revealed, so the manager is required to maintain confidentiality. This does however raise itself a keen ethical point: what should the manager do if the organisation is carrying out an illegal or immoral act? In most codes of practice, published by organisations and professional bodies, secrecy must be maintained but there is, surely, a wider social element of the individuals duty to society? It is here that the concept of **whistle-blowing** starts to be a possible course of action. This involves the employee in informing an outside agency of the organisation's unacceptable behaviour. Most organisations would regard this as 'gross misconduct' and would dismiss the employee even though the employee was acting with the highest of motives.

Governments have seen the danger to individuals of this and have taken steps to prevent the victimisation of employees who whistle-blow. The UK and USA governments are taking a lead in this approach. In the USA many organisations have **whistle-blowing hotlines** where employees can tell about unethical behaviour in confidence; in the UK there are professional organisations who provide this service to their members. An interesting approach to whistle-blowing can be seen in the work of the charity Public Concern at Work. They outline the process and protection offered to whistle-blowers on their website: *http://www.pcaw.demon.co.uk*.

4 Products and processes

It is becoming a recognised fact of business that society expects certain standards in respect of processes of production and products, and businesses could face severe censure if these standards are broken.

Processes

The environment is a major topic of concern so businesses have to be 'green' in their products and processes; this is very apparent in the oil industry.

Products

The product can also be an issue; for instance tobacco products cause major issues of concern for much of society. An additional example was the sale of 'alco-pops', the alcoholic drink in an apparent 'soft drink' form.

Selling practices

Selling practices can also cause concern as instanced by the concern voiced over the sale of baby milk substitute products in the Third World. Changes in marketing practices were demanded and were forthcoming because of ethical concerns.

5 Employment practices

The treatment of employees is also a major ethical concern for business; they need to be seen to be fair to their workers. This means looking, for example, at the status of women, ethnic minorities, older employees and disabled people within the workplace.

It also covers the employment of children, a very sensitive issue as evidenced by the recent court case of a major high street retailer taking legal action against a TV programme for suggesting they **knowingly** bought products from manufacturers overseas who employed child labour. Thus the ethics of an organisation in this area is a matter of interest to society.

Most business organisations of any size will take action to address these very real areas of societal concern within their formal, written, ethical code. It is here that the main ethical effort in business is concentrated.

31.6 The role of professional accounting ethics

Within the UK the various professional accounting bodies do provide their members with very detailed ethical guidelines. Accountants both in practice and in businesses are required to follow these guidelines in their normal patterns of work and can be punished individually for breaches of these professional codes of ethics. There are, however, two distinct approaches to ethics, one for the accountant in practice and another for those within business.

Accountants in practice

The accountant in practice has a considerable body of ethical support to work from, particularly if s/he is a member of one of the various Chartered Accountancy bodies.

These bodies (for England and Wales, Scotland and Ireland) publish guidelines covering key areas of accounting work and behaviour such as:

- their relationship with the client;
- the type of work they can do for the client;
- the way to safeguard independence;

- the standards of behaviour expected of accountants;
- the manner of dealing with conflicts of interest;
- the way in which they will behave in given situations such as takeovers, insolvencies and so on;
- the nature and type of advice they can give clients.

In 2002 following the recommendations of the Co-ordinating Group on Audit and Accounting Issues, the Accountancy Foundation, which had been set up in 1999 as a self-regulatory body, was replaced by extending the powers of the Financial Reporting Council. The new structure is as follows:

Financial Reporting Council

| Accounting Standards Board (ASB) | Auditing Practices Board (APB) | Financial Reporting Review Panel (FRRP) | Investigation and Discipline Board | Professional Oversight Board |

The ASB will continue to be responsible for accounting standards; the APB will be responsible for standards for audit integrity, independence and objectivity previously set by the professional bodies; the FRRP will become more proactive in investigating possible departures from standards; the Investigation and Discipline Board provides an independent hearing for those disciplinary cases where there is a public interest; the Professional Oversight Board will oversee ethical standards.

The intention has been to put in place a regime (supplemented by the Higgs and Smith Reports) that will maintain public confidence that there is sound corporate governance, that the financial reports are true and fair and the audit process is effective to avoid the prospect of the large-scale accounting frauds that have occurred in the USA.

Accountants in business

The accountant working within business has a different set of problems due to the dual position as an employee and a professional accountant. There is a potential clash of issues where the interests of the business could be at odds with professional standards.

The various professional bodies approach things in different ways. For example, the ICAEW established the Industrial Members Advisory Committee on Ethics (IMACE) in the late 1970s to give specific advice to members with ethical problems in business. This is supported by a strong local support network as well as a national helpline for the guidance of accountants. At the moment IMACE is dealing with 200 to 300 problems per year but this is more a reflection of the numbers of chartered accountants in business than a reflection on the lack of ethical problems. A survey[2] carried out by the Board of Chartered Accountants in Business indicated that 11% of members had put their jobs on the line over ethical issues.

Type of ethical problems

The type of problem raised is a good indication of the ethical issues raised for accountants in business. They include:

- requests by employers to manipulate tax returns;
- requests to produce figures to mislead shareholders;
- requests to conceal information;

- requests to manipulate overhead absorption rates to extort more income from customers (an occurrence in the defence industries);
- requests to authorise and conceal bribes to buyers and agents, a common request in some exporting businesses;
- requests to produce misleading projected figures to obtain additional finance;
- requests to conceal improper expense claims put in by senior managers;
- requests to over- or undervalue assets;
- requests to misreport figures in respect of government grants;
- requests for information, which could lead to charges of 'insider dealing';
- requests to redefine bad debts as 'good' or vice versa.

These issues are also reflected by the other professional bodies, the Chartered Association of Certified Accountants (ACCA), the Chartered Institute of Management Accountants (CIMA) and the Chartered Institute of Public Finance and Accountancy (CIPFA). The last of these organisations has added problems in that there is an overt political dimension to many decisions taken as its members are working in Local Government and the concept of 'value for money' is becoming a key feature of their work. Cases in respect of local councils in Westminster and Doncaster have demonstrated the ethical difficulties encountered by CIPFA members in carrying out their duties within their very singular environment.

The accountant in business has this problem of dual ethical structures; they are professionals but they are also employees and on a surprising number of occasions there is a conflict between the two roles on ethical issues. The solution of this conflict causes many problems for the accountant who is left with only three possible solutions, namely:

1 Take some action by either informing a superior (letting them take some action) or by whistle-blowing to an outside agency such as the professional body, the police, the media or whatever. This may well cause the accountant some personal problems and is difficult if the superior is the 'guilty party'.

2 Resign on principle and leave the organisation with personal and professional ethics intact but with a possibly damaged career.

3 Ignore the action and hope someone else notices the unethical behaviour and takes the appropriate action.

Each accountant has to face these choices at some time during their career and it is a test of character which choice is made. The choice itself may well be a function of the individual's own ethical background influenced by the factors mentioned earlier.

National and international regulation

It is likely that there will be an increase in formal regulation as the search for greater transparency and ethical business behaviour continues.

National regulation

Money laundering – overview

There are various estimates of the scale of money laundering ranging up to over 2% of global gross domestic product. Certain businesses are identified as being more prone to money laundering, e.g. import/export companies and cash businesses such as antiques, art dealers, auction houses, casinos and garages. However, the avenues are becoming more and more sophisticated with methods varying between countries, e.g. in the UK there is the increasing use of smaller non-bank institutions whereas in Spain it includes cross-border carrying of cash, money-changing at bureaux de change and investment in real estate.

Money laundering – implications for accountants

In 1997 the APB in the UK issued Practice Note 12 Money Laundering which required auditors to take the possibility of money laundering into account when carrying out their audit and to report to the appropriate authority if they become aware of suspected laundering.

In 1999 there was also guidance from the professional accounting bodies e.g. Money Laundering: Guidance Notes for Chartered Accountants issued by the Institute of Chartered Accountants which deal with the statute law, regulations and professional requirements in relation to the avoidance, recognition and reporting of money laundering.

Since that date, there has been an intensification of efforts to control it in the EU and the UK prompted by terrorist implications and the determination to target criminal activities. For example:

- In 2001 the EU Parliament approved a New Money Laundering Directive (effective from June 2003) which stipulated that accountants are included in existing legislation requiring suspicious activities to be reported.

- In 2002 the UK Parliament passed the Proceeds of Crime Act under which the Assets Recovery Agency (http://www.assetsrecovery.gov.uk/) began operations in February 2003 with opportunities for accountants to be employed as Financial Investigators to follow often complex financial arrangements in order to link the proceeds of crime to extant assets.

Whistleblowing – defined

Some disclosures which may be embarrassing to senior management may also be a statutory obligation, e.g. in the UK an accountant or internal auditor has the same legal duty to report to external authorities suspicions of terrorism or money laundering as any other employee. This means that there is an implicit authorisation by management. By whistleblowing, we mean the unauthorised disclosure, in good faith, of serious information relating to questionable practices, where disclosure is perceived to be in the public interest. Such information can be extremely varied from a financial accountant reporting the managing director of a subsidiary company for materially padding his expenses to an internal auditor disclosing audit findings.

Whistleblowing – proportionate response

Because every whistleblowing situation is different there is no right answer and any response needs to be proportionate. What is proportionate will of course reflect the potential whistleblower's own value system, e.g. deciding what he ought to do if there was a dangerous product defect which management considered too expensive to rectify and were concealing or a theft of funds or over-optimistic projections.

Whistleblowing – protection

In the UK the Public Interest Disclosure Act came into force in 1999 protecting whistleblowers who raised genuine concerns about malpractice from dismissal and victimisation in order to promote the public interest. The scope of malpractice is wide-ranging including, for example, the covering up of a suspected crime, a civil offence such as negligence, a miscarriage of justice and health and safety or environmental risks.

Whistleblowing – policies

Companies should have in place a policy which gives clear guidance to employees on the appropriate internal procedures to follow if there is a suspected malpractice.

Employees, including accountants and internal auditors, are expected to follow these procedures as well as acting professionally and in accordance with their own professional code.

However, although the whistleblowing policies might have followed and the accountant protected by the provisions of the Public Interest Disclosure Act, it could result in a breakdown of trust making their position untenable; this means that a whistleblower might be well advised to have an alternative position in mind.

Breach of confidentiality

Auditors are protected from the risk of liability for breach of confidence provided that:

(a) disclosure is made in the public interest

(b) disclosure is made to a proper authority

(c) there is no malice motivating the disclosure.

International regulation

The OECD drew up a new anti-bribery convention making it a criminal offence for business executives to bribe foreign officials. The implication for accountants is that companies will have to ensure financial statements do not omit or falsify cases involving bribery and prohibit the establishment of off-the-books accounts for the purpose of bribing foreign public officials or of hiding the bribery. The convention has been ratified by major trading nations including the UK, USA, Japan and Germany. The pressure for the OECD convention came initially from the USA where there were already anti-bribery legislation and then from multinational companies who were finding that some government officials were demanding not 1% but up to 30% of contract prices to award contracts; this not only made it far more difficult to conceal but was seen to be hitting the bottom line too hard. The convention had commercial support and has been ratified by major trading nations including the UK, USA, Japan and Germany. In the UK, the Anti-Terrorism, Crime and Security Act 2001 has extended the common law relating to bribery of UK officials to include the bribery of foreign officials.

Events with the European Commission have highlighted the potential for ethical issues and the inevitability of whistleblowing as being a logical step in the absence of an effective internal process for dealing with ethical issues. In this case, the whole Commission resigned due to the ethical malpractice of a few, brought to light by the public revelation of a whistleblower in the accounting function.

31.7 The role of the accountant as guardian of business ethics

There is therefore an established need for business ethics but the question arises who can police the organisation for ethical breaches? This is a crucial question as any set of rules is only as effective as its enforcement mechanism allows it to be.

There needs to be some sort of 'ethical guardian' who can police the code of ethics within an organisation to bring out any unethical practices and ensure that corrective action is taken as appropriate.

There are 'ethics committees' in some organisations which act as a court to judge ethical breaches, but in themselves they are only part of the guardian function.

It is therefore a possible function of an accountant's role to be the guardian of ethics within a business because the following attributes are possessed by the accountant:

- skill – the accountant is trained in the establishment and management of control systems and ethics is simply another layer of control;
- stewardship – the accountant already acts as the steward of the shareholders' interests and the function is similar when discussing ethics;
- rule orientation – the accountant is a trained follower of rules and is accomplished at ensuring others obey stated rules and regulations;
- judgement – ethics requires the application of fine judgement, an attribute common in many accountants;
- professionalism – the accountant is one of the main professionals working within businesses and the attributes of a professional are essential to make judgements on ethical breaches.

The role of the accountant in practice

This could well prove to be a new area of responsibility for accountants in both practice and business and it is not without precedent. The work, for example, of the Audit Commission in the public sector is perhaps an indication of the future role of accountants in practice. The Commission does make judgements on the traditional accounting areas but it is also looking at other more subjective measures of performance within public sector organisations and perhaps this is a growth area, especially as the demand by society for more accountability in business becomes more powerful and politically impossible to ignore.

The role of the accountant in business

The accountant within business could also be seeing a growth in the ethical policing role as internal auditors take on the role of assessing the performance of managers as to their adherence to the ethical code of the organisation. This is already partially happening as conflicts of interest are often highlighted by internal audits and comments raised on managerial practices. This is after all a traditional role for accountants, ensuring that the various codes of practice of the organisation are followed. The level of adherence to an ethical code is but another assessment for the accountant to undertake.

Implications for training

If, as is likely, the accountant has a role in the future as 'ethical guardian', additional training will be necessary. This should be done at a very early stage, as in the USA, where accountants wishing to be Certified Public Accountants (CPAs) are required to pass formal exams on ethical practices and procedures before they are allowed the privilege of working in practice. Failure in these exams prevents the prospective accountant from practising in the business environment.

31.8 Growth of voluntary standards

Social, environmental and ethical reporting is at an early stage but it is receiving increasing attention from industry and commerce with the growing recognition that long-term shareholder value cannot be achieved without acknowledging responsibility to wider stakeholder groups.[3] There has already been stakeholder pressure for management to balance the interests of investors, employees, suppliers, customers and the public. Finally, industry, commerce and stakeholders are moving towards a common goal which is to provide innovative reports. However, this requires a commitment from the directors who are the ones who control the information and an acceptance of the fact that it is not appropriate to produce only favourable comments. This has now been recognised by some of our major companies, e.g. BT's 1999 Social Report.

The Institute of Social and Ethical Accountability was founded in 1996 as an international membership organisation, based in the UK. In November 1999 the institute launched a world first international processing standard, AA1000, enabling organisations to build quality into their existing and developing social and ethical management systems. The standard defines how companies should report on issues such as pollution and labour issues. Its objective is to encourage a collaborative approach, with inputs from stakeholders including interest and pressure groups. Two major concerns that have been voiced are:

● Companies should not see consultation with a wide range of stakeholders as an excuse to avoid their responsibility for dealing with adverse social and environmental effects.

● Credibility will only be achieved if there is an independent audit and there could be a risk of ineffectual auditing.

AA1000 addresses the latter point by setting out criteria for the social and ethical auditor, namely:

● Integrity

● Objectivity and independence

● Professional competence

● Professional behaviour exercising rigour, judgement and clear communication

● Confidentiality

● Due care to stakeholders.[4]

AA1000 will provide a consistent measure of performance and a uniform basis for reporting but the institute recognises that this is a dynamic field and plans to keep the standard under constant review. In this it resembles the ASB policy of revisiting FRSs when there has been experience and feedback from stakeholders and management.

Summary

In this chapter we have attempted to explain how business ethics has adopted the definition of ethics as **an ethical code** in order to have a mechanism that (a) makes the ethical expectations of the business clear to staff and other stakeholders and (b) allows performance to be monitored. Although ethics are often perceived as a qualitative or philosophical matter, there is a public expectation and demand for quantitative measures – after all, we live in the age of performance criteria and league tables!

Accountability requires that a report should be made to relevant parties if the monitoring provides evidence that there has been a breach of the code. The relevant party would depend on the nature of the breach, e.g. petty dishonesty by junior staff might be reported to the immediate line manager, fraud by senior managers reported to the audit committee and material misrepresentation of the profit reported to the shareholders.

The accountant is heavily involved with ethical issues as a member of society, as a member of a professional body with a formal code of ethics and as a member/employee of a business. The prevalence of the self-regulation ethos in the UK also supports directors delegating to the accountant responsibility for ethical policing.

Accountants' expertise in designing systems and measuring compliance leaves them in a strong position to undertake the monitoring of the ethical code and, as with all control systems, there will be a continuing need to balance costs and benefits. It would, for example, be uneconomic to require all staff to take a truth test to support every expense claim that was lodged!

It is interesting to note that the Auditing Practices Board is actively considering an approach to the government to provide auditors with greater powers in relation to fraud. Given that companies might be reluctant to increase the fees paid to auditors, there might well be a case for state funding for monitoring that is a form of ethical policing. One attraction of this might be that there would be pressure from the government to formulate an ethical code. It is a strength of the self-regulatory ethos that best practice trickles down but it can trickle mighty slowly!

REVIEW QUESTIONS

1 Outline **three** areas where ethics and ethical behaviour are of importance to business.

2 Discuss the role of the accounting profession in the issue of ethics.

3 How might a company develop a code of ethics for its own use?

4 Outline the advantages and disadvantages of a written code of ethics.

5 (a) Obtain an ethical statement from:
    (i) a commercial organisation;
    (ii) a charitable organisation.

  (b) Review each statement for content and style.

  (c) Compare each of the two statements and highlight any areas of difference which, in your view, reflect the different nature of the two organisations.

6 In each of the following scenarios outline the ethical problem and suggest ways in which the organisation may solve the problem and prevent its reoccurrence.

  (a) The use by a director's wife of his company car for shopping.

  (b) The inclusion of groceries bought for personal use on a director's company credit card.

  (c) The director is sent overseas on business with a business air ticket but he converts it to two economy class tickets and takes his wife with him.

  (d) A director negotiates a contract for management consultancy services but it is later revealed that her husband is a director of the management consultancy company.

(e) The director of a company hires her son for some holiday work within the company but does not mention the fact to her fellow directors.

(f) You are the accountant to a small engineering company and you have been approached by the Chairman to authorise the payment of a fee to an overseas government employee in the hope that a large contract will be awarded.

(g) Your company has had some production problems which have resulted in some electrical goods being faulty (possibly dangerous) but all production is being despatched to customers regardless of condition.

(h) Your company is about to sign a contract with a repressive regime in South America for equipment which **could** have a military use. Your own government has given you no advice on this matter.

(i) Your company is in financial difficulties and a large contract has just been gained in partnership with an overseas supplier who employs children as young as seven years old on their production line. The children are the only wage earners for their families and there is no welfare available in the country where they live.

(j) You are the accountant in a large manufacturing company and you have been approached by the manufacturing director to prepare a capital investment proposal for a new production line. After your calculations the project meets **none** of the criteria necessary to allow the project to proceed but the director instructs you to change the financial forecast figures to ensure the proposal is approved.

(k) Review the last week's newspapers and select **three** examples of failures of business ethics and justify your choice of examples.

(l) At the year-end goods are despatched although not tested in order to improve the current year's sales figures. The management fully expect returns to be made but not within the period prior to the auditor signing the accounts.

7 Select one philosophical viewpoint of ethics and prepare a single A4 piece of paper with a set of notes summarising the viewpoint.

8 With your researches produced for question 7 discuss how this viewpoint may be applied to a **named** business of your choice to help develop appropriate ethics for this business.

9 The management of a listed company has a fiduciary duty to act in the best interest of the shareholders and it would be unethical for them to act in the interest of other shareholders if this did not maximise the existing earnings per share. Discuss.

10 The Financial Director of a listed company makes many decisions which are informed by statute, e.g. the Companies Act, the Public Interest Disclosure Act and mandatory pronouncements, e.g. the ASB, APB and his professional accounting body. What guidance is available when there is a need for an ethical decision which does not contravene statutory or mandatory demands – how can there be confidence that the decision is right?

11 An approach has been made to the Board to support a takeover bid where the offer price exceeds the current market capitalisation.

(a) Discuss situations where you consider it (i) ethical to recommend the offer to shareholders and (ii) unethical; and

(b) Discuss whether an aggrieved shareholder should be able to obtain relief from the Court if the decision was unethical.

12 The Finance Director has been carrying out some sensitivity analysis and produced figures that show the return on capital employed could be improved if the company were to downsize, make existing staff redundant and replace them with lower paid temporary staff. The current return on capital employed and PE ratio exceed the industry average but the change of policy would take the company into the top quartile with a favourable impact on the Directors' performance targets and bonuses. This is a common commercial practice. Discuss if there is an ethical problem in (a) the company pursuing such a policy; (b) the Finance Director submitting such a proposal; and (c) the Finance Director failing to submit such a proposal.

13 Discuss the following:

(a) Why an accountant should be involved with designing or monitoring ethical codes.

(b) What additional training this would require.

(b) How an accountant could become an effective 'guardian of business ethics'.

14 Confidentiality means that an accountant in business has a loyalty to the business which employs him/her which is greater than any commitment to a professional code of ethics. Discuss.

15 Lord Borrie QC has said[5] of the Public Interest Disclosure Bill that came into force in July 1999 that the new law would encourage people to recognise and identify with the wider public interest, not just their own private position and it will reassure them that if they act reasonably to protect the legitimate interest of others, the law will not stand idly by should they be vilified or victimised. Confidentiality should only be breached, however, if there is a statutory obligation to do so. Discuss.

References

1 Simon Webley, *Company Philosophies and Codes of Business Ethics*, Institute of Business Ethics (1988).
2 Dispute Resolution, *Accountancy*, May 1998, p. 99.
3 Andrew Bolger, *Financial Times*, 2 July 1998, p. 10.
4 John Plender, *Financial Times*, 15 July 1999.
5 W. Raven, 'Social auditing', *Internal Auditor*, February 2000, p. 8.

Bibliography

Tom Burke and Julie Hill, *Ethics Environment and the Company*, Institute of Business Ethics, 1990.
T. Cannon, *Corporate Responsibilty. A Textbook on Business Ethics, Governance, Environment: Roles and Responsiblities*, Pitman, 1994.
Neville Cooper, *What's All This About Business Ethics*, Institute of Business Ethics, 1989.
J. Donaldson, *Key Issues in Business Ethics*, Academic Press, 1989.
Trevor Gambling and Rifaat Ahmed Abdel Karim, *Business and Accounting Ethics in Islam*, Mansell, 1991.
R.M. Green, *The Ethical Manager: A New Method for Business Ethics*, Macmillan, 1994.
B. Harvey (ed.), *Business Ethics: A European Approach*, Prentice Hall, 1994.
V. Henderson, *What's Ethical in Business?* McGraw Hill, 1992.
ICAEW, *Guide to Professional Ethics*, ICAEW Members Handbook, Vol. 1, 1996.
Institute of Business Ethics, *Take-overs – What Ethical Considerations Should Apply?* Institute of Business Ethics, 1990.
Institute of Applied Professional Ethics – http://www.cats.ohiou.edu/ethics.
International Business Ethics Institute – http://www.business-ethics.org.
H. van Luijk, *Business Ethics: The Field and its Importance*, Prentice Hall, 1994.

Jack Maurice, *Accounting Ethics*, Pitman Publishing, 1996.

Peter Pratley, *The Essence of Business Ethics*, Prentice Hall, 1995.

M. Velasquez, *Business Ethics, Concepts and Cases*, Prentice Hall, 1992.

Marcia P. Miceli and Janet P. Near, *Blowing the Whistle: The Organizational & Legal Implications for Companies and Employee*, Lexington Books, 1992.

William Shaw and Vincent Barry. *Moral Issues in Business*, Seventh Edition, Wadsworth, 1998.

Simon Webley, *Business Ethics and Company Codes*, Institute of Business Ethics, 1992.

Simon Webley, *Codes of Business Ethics*, Institute of Business Ethics, 1993.

Simon Webley, *Apply Codes of Business Ethics*, Institute of Business Ethics, 1995.

Simon Webley, *Codes of Ethics and International Business*, Institute of Business Ethics, 1997.

Outline solutions to selected exercises

Chapter 1

Question 1

(a) (i) (£000)	Jan	Feb	Mar	Apr	May	Jun
Cash balance c/f	17.55	(17.85)	(70.05)	(51.75)	(55.95)	(47.25)

(ii) Operating cash flow at 30 June 20X1   (143.55)

Question 2

(b)(£000)	Jan	Feb	Mar	Apr	May	Jun
Cash balance c/f	(28.80)	(26.40)	(18.10)	(12.10)	(7.70)	(0.80)

(c) Operating cash flow at 30 June 20X8   £29.20

Chapter 2

Question 1

(a)(£000)	Jan	Feb	Mar	Apr	May	Jun
Cash balance c/f	17.25	(17.25)	(69.75)	(74.25)	(63.75)	(4.65)

(b) Net profit   £47.90
Net capital employed   £263.90

Question 2

(b)(£000)	Jan	Feb	Mar	Apr	May	Jun
Cash balance c/f	85.90	67.50	87.15	104.95	119.55	142.30

(c) Net profit   £34.87
Net capital employed   £184.87

Chapter 3

Question 2

Economic income: $Y_1 = £153$, $Y_2 = £168$, $Y_3 = £185$

Question 3

(a) (i)   Accounting income = £36,700; (ii) Realisable income = £26,200; (iii) Economic income *ex ante* = £27,894; (iv) Economic income *ex post* = £35,000

Chapter 4

Question 1 Income statements and balance sheets show:

(i) Historical profit = £3,800; Total assets £13,800

(ii) *CPP*: Monetary gains = £11,200; Monetary losses = £(6,000); Net income = £10,720; Total assets £23,520

(iii) *Replacement cost*: Realised holding gains = £3,200 (Fixed assets £1,200 + Stock £2,000); Unrealised holding gains = £6,900 (Fixed assets £4,800 + Stock £2,100); Net income = £10,700; Total assets £20,700

(iv) *Continuous contemporary accounting*: Operating income = £5,000; Price variation adjustments = (£1,900); Capital maintenance (£2,800); Net income = £300; Total assets £13,100

Question 3

(a) MWCA = £6,190

Question 4 (£000)

(a) (i) Cost of goods sold = £39,162; (ii) Stock = £11,735; (iii) Depreciation charge = £10,083 or £10,614; (iv) Equipment = £49,822

Question 6

		£
GPP net profit before loss on monetary items	=	263,859
Loss on monetary items	=	(142,003)
GPP net profit		121,856
RCA profit	=	236,083
NRV operating gain	=	241,800
Holding gain	=	18,188
		259,988

Chapter 6

Question 1

(a) Turnover = £200; Charge for goods sold = £64; Wealth created by operations = £97

(b) Realisable increase in net assets = £157

Chapter 7

Question 1 (£000)

(a) Gross profit = £5,724; Profit before tax = £2,795; Profit for year = £2,233; Retained profit = £1,871

(b) Trading profit = £2,820; Profit on ordinary activities before tax = £2,795; Amount to reserves = £1,871

Question 2 (£000)

(a) Profit before tax = £14,243; Profit for year = £9,059; Retained profit = £7,985

Chapter 8

Question 1 (£000)

(a) Gross profit = £12,000; Operating profit – continuing operations = £6,710, discontinued operations = £210; Profit after tax = £4,970

Question 2 (£000)

(a) Gross profit = £1,902.9; Profit after tax = £447

(b) Net capital employed = £1,938; Net current assets = £285

Chapter 9

Question 1

(a) Distributable profit for private company A = £95,000

(b) Distributable profit for public company A = £95,000

Question 3

(b) Alpha plc maximum distribution = £2,844,000; Beta plc = £200,000; Gamma plc = (£2,800,000)

Chapter 10

Question 3

(ii) Sundry assets = £32,170,000; Cash = £6,185,000; Share capital = £18,900,000; CRR = £500,000; Share premium = £4,380,000; Retained profits = £1,755,000; Debentures = £2,400,000; Creditors = £10,420,000

Question 5

(a) *Balance sheet as at 31 Dec 20X1*: Ordinary shares = £1,005,000; CRR = £80,000; Reserves = (£380,000); Debentures = £400,000; Creditors = £400,000

Chapter 11

Question 1

Finance charge for year 1 = £284,375; Carrying value in balance sheet = £2,309,375

Question 2

Finance charge for year 1 = £58,900; Balance sheet = £958,900

Chapter 12

Question 1

Present value of obligation

	20X2	20X3	20X4
	£000	£000	£000
PV of obligation at end of year	1,200	1,600	1,700

Market value of plan assets

	20X2	20X3	20X4
MV of plan assets at year end	1,250	1,450	1,610

Balance sheet

	20X2	20X3	20X4
Pension asset/(liability)	50	(150)	(90)

Profit and loss account
Operating cost

	20X2	20X3	20X4
Current service cost	(140)	(150)	(150)

Financing cost

	20X2	20X3	20X4
Interest cost	(100)	(120)	(160)
Expected return on plan assets	120	150	174
Net return	20	30	14

Statement total recognised gains and losses

	20X2	20X3	20X4
	£000	£000	£000
Actuarial gain (loss) recognised in STRGL	60	(200)	76

Chapter 13

Question 2

(a) (i) Deferred tax provision – *deferral method*
    31/3/97 = £487.50; 31/3/98 = £819.53; 31/3/99 = £833.59; 31/3/00 = £619.14;
    31/3/01 = £233.30

   (ii) Deferred tax provision – *liability method*
    31/3/97 = £487.50; 31/3/98 = £800.78; 31/3/99 = £782.81; 31/3/00 = £586.36;
    31/3/01 = £182.52

Chapter 14

Question 3

(a) £11,700

Question 4

The solution for Years 1 and 2:

(a) Year 1 Depreciation = £5,914.43; Income from secondary assets = £0; Interest = £3,000;
    Net profit = £22,085.57

   Year 2 Income from secondary assets = £437.16; Interest = £2,562.84

Chapter 15

Question 1

(a) Fixed asset = £306,250; Liability = £310,000; Interest = £52,500; Depreciation = £43,750

Question 2

(e) Depreciation 2008 = £2,000; Finance charges 2008 = £1,200; Liability 31 Mar 2008 = £12,200

Chapter 16

Question 3

(i) *Balance c/f*: R&D costs account = £500,000; Laboratory account cost = £500,000; Depreciation = £45,000; Equipment cost = £225,000; Depreciation = £70,000

Chapter 17

Question 2

(i) *Cost of goods sold*: FIFO = £2,648, LIFO = £2,626, Weighted average = £2,638

Question 3

Raw materials = £14,000; Finished units = £35,000; Semi-finished units = £10,000

Question 6

Long-term contracts = £214,000. Amounts recoverable on long-term contracts = £108,000; Payments on account = £165,000; Provision for foreseeable losses = £45,000

Question 7

(b) Stock = £3,000; Long-term contracts = £14,900; Amount recoverable on long-term contract £30,000

Chapter 18

Question 1

Parent company investment in subsidiary £10,800

Question 2

Group accounts: Capital and reserves £45,000

Chapter 19

Question 1

Parent company accounts: Investment in subsidiary = £10,800

Question 2

Group accounts: Capital and reserves = £61,200

Question 3

Parent company accounts: Investment in subsidiary = £16,200; Group accounts: Capital and reserves = £61,200

Question 4

Group accounts: Negative goodwill = (£4,800)

Question 6

Share capital = £21.6m; Retained profit = £65.0m; Share premium = £22.4m; Fixed assets = £89.4m; Current assets = £38.8m; Current liabilities = £26.2m; Goodwill = £7.0m

Question 7

Share capital = 21.6m; Retained profit = £72.0m; Capital reserve = £8.4m; Fixed assets = £89.4m; Current assets = £38.8m; Current liabilities = £26.2m

Chapter 20

Question 3

Capital and reserves = £192,600; Minority interest = £28,750; Total capital employed = £271,350

Chapter 21

Question 2

(a) Profit after tax = £230,000; Retained profit = £130,000; Share capital and reserves = £840,000

Question 3

(a) Profit after tax = £234,000; Retained profit = £124,000; Share capital and reserves = £880,000

Question 4

(a) Retained profit = £130,000; Balance c/f = £185,000; Capital reserve = £20,000

Question 5

(a) Retained profit = £124,000; Balance c/f = £178,000; Goodwill = £24,000

Chapter 22

Question 2

Exchange gains: Creditors = £24,000; Debtors = £200 gain on pesos; Loan = £18,300; Exchange losses: Debtors = £360 on KR; Cost of sales = £400

Question 3

Exchange gains = £474,916

Question 5

(b) Exchange losses: Temporal method = £45,000; Closing rate method = £608,000

Chapter 23

Question 1

(a) (i)   BEPS for 20X1 = £2.29
              BEPS for 20X0 = £2.16 (restated)

Question 2

(a) 2,885,416 shares

Question 3

(a) Basic EPS for 20X6 = 2.53p; Basic EPS for 20X5 = 1.83p; (b) Fully diluted EPS = 2.53p

Question 4

(a) Basic EPS = 70p (b) Diluted EPS = 66.15p

Question 5

(a) Diluted EPS = £4.37
(b) Diluted EPS = £4.48

Chapter 24

Question 1

Net cash flow from operations = (£91,000); Returns on investments = (£20,000); Tax = (£220,000); Capital expenditure = (£319,000); Equity dividends = (£120,000); Management of liquid resources = (£20,000); Financing = £250,000

Question 2

(a) Net cash flow from operations = £503,000; Returns on investment = (£52,000); Tax = (£79,000); Capital expenditure = (£694,000); Equity dividends = (£76,000); Management of liquid resources = (£40,000); Financing = £232,000

Chapter 25

Question 2

Turnover = £271,897; Cost of goods sold = £184,890; Profit before tax = £25,362; Retained profit = £15,290; Fixed assets = £206,760; Net current assets = £25,048; Net capital employed = £181,808

Question 3

(a) Net cash flow from operating = £495,000; Servicing finance = £195,000; Taxation = £375,000; Capital expenditure = (£150,000); Dividend paid = £225,000

Chapter 26

Question 3

(a) Option 1: Profit Year 1 = £28,400; Year 2 = £28,400; Option 2: Profit Year 1 = £19,782; Profit Year 2 = £23,904; Option 3: Profit Year 1 = £23,800; Profit Year 2 = £26,050

Chapter 30

Question 1

(a)

	20X9
	£000
Employees	2,193.5
Providers of capital	735.7
Government	464.7
Asset maintenance	415.2

Question 3

(a)

	20X5
	£000
Employees	796
Providers of capital	431
Government	393
Asset maintenance	214

Index